SUMMARY OF AMERICAN LAW

(WITH LAW QUIZZER)

by

GEORGE L. CLARK

AUTHOR OF PRINCIPLES OF EQUITY
THE LAW OF TORTS, COMMON LAW PLEADING

Former member of law faculties of Stanford, Illinois, Michigan, Missouri, and New York Universities

WITH INTRODUCTION

by

ROSCOE POUND

Dean Emeritus Harvard Law School
University Professor, Harvard

THE LAWYERS CO-OPERATIVE PUBLISHING COMPANY
ROCHESTER 3, NEW YORK

1956 Reprint

INTRODUCTION

By Roscoe Pound

Dean Emeritus Harvard Law School
University Professor Harvard University

Dr. Clark has set himself a task which has recurred from time to time in legal history. Using the term "law" in the sense of the body of authoritative grounds of or guides to judicial and administrative determinations, there come to be times when the field covered by the law has so broadened, the interests to be secured have so multiplied, the number of precepts has become so great, and the details on any subject so minute, as to impair the effective teaching on which the law depends. New starts for application of law become needful and new methods are sought for to make the law (to use Bentham's word) more cognoscible. When a body of law has reached this stage of development, there is more involved than a question of pedagogy. Whatever affects the teaching of law affects the law itself, whether we think of law as the body of authoritative materials to which courts are expected to and do resort for the basis of their determinations, or think of it rather as the judicial and administrative processes which are expected to and, on the whole, do go on upon the basis of those materials. For a system of law, such as the civil or modern Roman law or the common law or Anglo-American law, is a taught tradition of ideals, methods, doctrines, and principles, continuous so long as the course of teaching remains unbroken. In the common law we have a tradition of taught law, continuous in England from the establishment of an organized teaching in the Inns of Court to the decay of that teaching in the sixteenth and seventeenth centuries and then as remade in the age of Coke continuous in the several lands of the English-speaking world from the seventeenth century.

Indeed, law, as we understand it in the modern world, has been a taught tradition into which teachers have fitted legislation and the results of judicial and professional empiricism and thus have developed experience by reason, as the judges and practitioners in turn have tested reason by experience. This compound of reason and experience organized by teaching and handed down as a taught tradition has had that character at least from the time when at Rome the first plebian Pontifex Maximus began to give consultations in public so that students could attend and take notes. Out of this beginning of teaching grew the traditional teaching of the schools of jurists in the earlier empire. Out of that in turn grew the teaching of the ecumenical doctors in the Eastern empire in the fifth century. From this there is a link with law teaching at Ravenna in the earlier Middle Ages, and thence with the teaching at Bologna in the twelfth century. From the latter there is a continuous tradition of teaching to the present wherever throughout the world the modern Roman law prevails. In the same way, a tradition of teaching from the pleaders of the beginnings of English law in the King's courts, attested by the name apprentice, which belonged to the junior bar down to the age of Coke, became a tradition of teaching in the Inns of Court, and, when that decayed, a tradition of teaching by lawyers who had pupils in their chambers. Thence in America it was carried on by lawyers trained in the Inns of Court, by their pupils in independent America as lawyers training pupils in their offices, by schools which grew out of expanded law offices, and finally by academic law schools which gradually replaced those of the apprentice type.

Note the general lines of such a development through teaching. With the rise of professional lawyers distinctions come to be drawn between the often oracularly expressed rules of primitive codes in the endeavor to give each rule more precise definition. Then cases begin to be distinguished as to those coming within and those without particular rules. Presently principles come to be put behind the distinctions and for convenience of teaching and learning are put in the form of maxims. Soon these principles become the basis of further distinctions and thus become starting points for legal reasoning. At this point teaching begins to make itself felt in the working out of broad doctrines to unify the principles, and the teacher's ideal of a body of logically interdependent precepts, born of the exigencies of instruction, begins to organize the received precepts in order to make them teachable, and so begins to make them more easy to find and to apply. Thus a tradition of organization of the law through principles and doctrines arises and makes for certainty of application, taking care of the need for stability, as the professional and judicial application to concrete cases makes for a continual unsettling of the details of the teacher's logical organization and overhauling of the doctrines and so takes care of the need for change. As the two correct each other a system of law grows up and achieves and maintains a balance between the general security, which calls for stability, and the individual life, which demands change. So long as the balance between the teacher and the practitioner is preserved, the taught system, into which legislation and new institutions and adaptations from without and novel adjudications are carefully fitted, becomes a powerful instrument for making a body of legal precepts effective for its purposes.

But teaching the law as a body of authoritative precepts and organizing it so as to make it teachable and readily applicable also require a balance. When it has to be or is taught as single unconnected rules and those rules become greatly multiplied and overlaid with glosses of interpretation and application teaching becomes impracticable. An organizing and systematizing activity follows which results in better teaching but has often resulted in an overdevelopment of logical technique making logical interdependence of legal precepts and precise fitting of cases to a logical plan an end instead of a means. In consequence, there is a counterreaction in which system is scouted and the basis thought of in terms of independent rather than interdependent propositions.

An example from the history of the modern Roman law will bring this out. When the study of Roman law was revived in the Italian universities in the twelfth century, the Corpus Juris was thought of as a body of legislation and each text of the Digest was held a *lex*—as we should say, a statute. The medieval jurists, therefore, confined themselves to analysis of the text and wrote elaborate glosses or commentaries, in which they dissected the contents of the several sections and sought to develop all their consequences. There was no synthetical element in their work. As a consequence, knowledge of the law was split up into an enormous mass of detail, devoid of logical connection, which made teaching of law difficult and unsatisfactory. Legal learning had become so diffuse that only a small fraction of the whole could be brought within the term of a reasonable course of instruction. A teacher could take up only a few texts at a term, expounding them or the glosses upon them and showing the technique of analysis and application, and leaving the rest to private study by the student. The inevitable reaction led to working out of a system of the modern Roman law and establishment of a synthetical method postulating that the law was a body of logically interdependent precepts. This system culminated in the writings of the Pandectists in the maturity of the law in the nineteenth century. But the balance was lost once more. The system was thought of as existing for its own sake. A jurisprudence of conceptions, as Jhering called it, grew up as a result of which the law in its application was out of accord with life and a gulf arose once more between teaching and practice. In the present century, there has been a reaction in Roman-law lands from the synthetical work of the Pandectists.

A like story can be told for Anglo-American law. The method of Coke's Institutes or of Serjeant Williams's notes to Saunders' Reports is that of the Glossators. Blackstone's great institutional book in the latter part of the eighteenth century followed a systematic plan. But the interconnection of legal precepts was achieved (so far as it was achieved) by developing them in relation to common-law actions in which they could be enforced. The textbook writing of nineteenth-century America dealt with subjects, not with law as a whole, and applied an analytical method to the precepts derived from the course of judicial decision. Thus we have a situation like that in the modern Roman law when systematic exposition of the law as a whole superseded analytical commentary on the sections or titles of the Digest.

Law in the sense of the body of authoritative grounds of or guides to decision is made up of authoritative precepts (rules, principles, precepts defining legal conceptions, and precepts establishing legal standards), an authoritative technique, and received ideals. It is not possible to teach all the precepts in detail even if it were worth while. What can be taught is the outstanding starting points for legal reasoning in the more important subjects and the precepts which must be borne in mind as the basis of finding and applying the law as to those subjects. What can be taught most effectively and what, as things are, it is most profitable to have taught is the technique of the common-law lawyer. The case method in the American law school of today does this thoroughly. It is that that the law school can do best and it is doing it well.

But the different subjects of the law are interrelated. One cannot know any one of them completely without knowledge of many others. As a teacher masters some one of them he cannot fail to be struck with the general lack of appreciation of its possibilities both in its own field and in its relation to other fields which prevails among even the best-read practitioners trained as they must be today. There is manifest need of a system of Anglo-American law. There is need of an institutional book, which we cannot expect until we have developed a system. The books on "elementary law" in the last century and the perennial attempts at new editions of Blackstone failed because they purported to set forth a system in a subject in which there was no system to expound.

In the modern Roman law the Glossators put system into the sections of the Digest. The Commentators put system in the titles. After the fifteenth century the jurists increasingly put system into the law as a whole. In our law, teaching for a long time expounded the law around the common-law actions. Blackstone expounds the named torts under the actions of trespass and case. From the last quarter of the nineteenth century teachers have more and more systematized particular branches of the law, and much has been done for a number of important subjects by the American Law Institute. But until this putting of system into particular subjects or branches has been carried out to substantial completeness, we shall not be able to put system effectively into our law as a whole. Hence even if system in each subject is nearing completion so that we need to be thinking of a system of the whole, we must for a long time to come be thinking of how to make the best of the present condition of our law with the materials and methods we have at hand. It is not likely that system of our law as a whole will come at once by the fiat of some juristic genius. Nor can our law borrow system from the modern Roman law, although we can learn much if we apply ourselves wisely to study of system from the work of the nineteenth-century Pandectists. All this is, however, in a future that is by no means immediately impending. What is immediately before American law teachers is a condition which cannot wait for the ideal system of Anglo-American law or for the ideal institutional book. For thorough understanding of any particular subject there is no substitute for study of the cases. A few subjects studied in this way are worth many studied by reading about the cases instead of by reading the cases themselves. But in the term of a reasonable studentship thorough reading of a good selection of decisions on every branch of the law is not possible.

Instead of a premature institutional book or an encyclopaedic book to supersede the case books which enable teaching of the technique of application of our law and give a grasp of its principles in leading departments such as no abstract statements in texts can give, Dr. Clark proposes to supplement the work done with case books by a text covering the subjects of which the student should have real knowledge. Thus the parts of important subjects which are not treated in the case books or cannot be taken up by the instructor for lack of time, and other subjects for which there is no room in the crowded curricula, study of which is nonetheless highly desirable, are made available in convenient form.

Sir William Holdsworth believed that the characteristic presentation of our law by subjects in alphabetical order was better suited to the common law than the systematic presentation according to a logical plan, regarding each part as in logical connection with the whole, which obtains in the world of the civil law. It is, at any rate, all that we are prepared for at present. But the appearance of independence of the several departments of the law which our traditional teaching and exposition by subjects gives rise to requires mitigation. Dr. Clark has this in view also.

In the readjustments and modifications which legal education is undergoing at present, Dr. Clark's plan deserves thoughtful consideration. It is the result of many years of experience of law teaching and observation of and reflection upon the needs of students of our law.

ROSCOE POUND

PREFACE

Before Blackstone published, in 1765, his Commentaries on English Law, law students in England received most of their law training as apprentices. They attended court, took notes of proceedings, copied pleadings, deeds and other legal documents. There were only a few textbooks and they were difficult to read.

The Commentaries, the first readable synthesis of English law, supplemented the English law student's training. Not only that; it was so understandable that it was read with great interest by a large number of laymen. In this country, with courts few in number and not easily accessible, the Commentaries had greater utility and influence than in England; it became the chief basis for preparation for the bar, so that as late as 1880 "reading Blackstone" and "reading law" were synonymous.

Kent's Commentaries on American Law appeared in 1825 and were much read by law students, but not so much by laymen because the style was not as popular as Blackstone's. Later, training for the bar was further aided by the publication of such outstanding texts as Greenleaf on Evidence, Story on Bailments, Cooley's Constitutional Limitations and Minor's Institutes.

Then in 1870 the new president of Harvard, Charles W. Eliot, recalled that when he was a student at Harvard College there was a law student who insisted that the proper way to study law was to read and study and analyze the decisions of courts of last resort. This former law student—Christopher Columbus Langdell—was practicing law in New York. President Eliot persuaded him to become a professor and later the dean of the Harvard Law School, where he inaugurated the "case method." It was some twenty years before any other law school adopted it but President Eliot never faltered in his support and by 1920 the case method was used in most of the law schools of the country.

In its early days the new method was ridiculed even at Harvard where the students who elected to take Langdell's courses were referred to contemptuously as "Kit's freshmen" or "Langdell's chickens." And it was criticized not only by other law schools but by members of the bar who insisted that the case method would make its students "case lawyers"—that is, lawyers who would be unable to argue a legal question on its merits but would merely try to find a case "on all fours" with their own.

The old lecture and textbook system which was displaced laid emphasis upon giving the student a general view of the law; analysis and discussion of cases were incidental. Yet in the hands of such gifted teachers as Story and Greenleaf of Harvard, Dwight of Columbia, Cooley of Michigan and Minor of Virginia, excellent results were obtained. Under the case method the emphasis shifted from synthesis to analysis—from the use of the telescope to the use of the microscope—and the older textbooks, having been written from the synthetic viewpoint, became less and less useful. Whatever synthesis was done was the product of the individual law teacher who, in the pioneer days of the case method, was the *deus ex machina* whose pronouncements were likely to be accepted as final by the student. Much was said, in those days, of the case method being an inductive method; the student, without help of any sort—at least, theoretically—read the assigned cases before attending class and came to his own conclusions concerning them, the conclusions to be corrected, if necessary, by the discussion in class.

Those were the golden days of the case method. Later it came about that the student was likely to have considerable help before attending class—printed notes, "canned briefs," law review articles and notes and texts written from the new analytical viewpoint.

In its emphasis upon the application of legal rules to concrete cases the case method has made a valuable permanent contribution to legal education. But within recent years some law teachers have begun to have doubts about the efficacy of the case method by itself under modern conditions, and have begun to realize that the law should be taught as a system and not as a series of mutually exclusive subjects each in its own air-tight compartment. That there is now a considerable interest in trying to give the student a general view of the law is shown by experiments with comprehensive examinations and by the preparation and use of case books with large amounts of informational material either as part of the body of the book or in the footnotes.

The problem of giving the student a general view of the law has been rendered more difficult and more worth solving by the tremendous increase, during the last half century, of the number of decided cases and by the addition to the law school curriculum of several new subjects, such as Administrative Law, Labor Law and Taxation. The result is that even if the student is fortunate enough to get a bird's-eye view of each subject which he studies in the law school there is a large number of subjects—about a third—which he does not take at all. This is in striking contrast with the curricula of medical, dental and engineering schools where the student is required, in his undergraduate course, to study every subject a knowledge of which is deemed important to him in his particular profession.

In the present volume there are thirty subjects; a knowledge of each one of these subjects is highly desirable for every law graduate. And now such knowledge will be available to such students as will read at least a part of a case book on the subjects which he does not take in his law school course, and then read carefully the text treatment of it in the present volume. Such a student, with the background of his case book training in the law school can, with the aid of the present volume, covering as it does practically the entire legal field, acquire an even more effective general view of the law than was generally achieved before the days of the case method.

And the law schools can make his obtaining such a bird's-eye view easier and even more effective by using a small part—say, one fifth—of the law school time for the giving of lectures on those subjects which the student does not take in the usual way, the lectures being supplemented by assigned readings of cases, text and law review articles. With such a general view of the law he will later be able to pigeonhole promptly any legal question that may be presented to him, to argue it through on its merits, and thus to become a more efficient and capable lawyer.

NATURE AND SOURCES OF LAW

SEC. 1. *What is law?*

The word "law" has various meanings. When we speak of a law of nature such as the law of gravity or the phenomenon that water at sea level always boils at a certain temperature what we mean is that certain facts regularly follow or accompany certain other facts—so regularly that we think of such natural laws as inherent in the physical universe which surrounds us.

"Things equal to the same thing are equal to each other" is said to be a law or rule of logic. Such a law is inherent in human reasoning; we cannot conceive of any alternative. When we speak of the laws of art or architecture or of the drama we mean that as to certain matters there is such a general agreement among people who are familiar with these fields that they must correspond to something inherent in the artistic mind.

When we say that one should treat others as he wishes to be treated by others we are speaking of a rule of morals or ethics which has been the product of so many centuries of moral and ethical development that we are accustomed to regard it as inherent in the ethical consciousness of the race; there is no compulsion behind it except that of public opinion and the conscience of the individual.

When we say that men buy in the cheapest market and sell in the dearest market we are stating what is usually called an economic law. It is not, however, inherent either in the physical universe or in the human mind; men ordinarily act thus merely because it is usually to their interest to do so.

The word "law" as used in this book means something different from any of these. When we say, for example, that an employer is liable for the acts of his employee within the apparent scope of his employment we are stating a rule of human conduct that—in the Anglo-American system of law—is enforced by the state through its courts. This is the meaning of law as used in the following pages. The rule just stated, as well as other rules of law, may or may not have behind it inherent reasonableness but in the long run rules of law do not usually survive unless they are in substantial accord with the community's concepts of justice.

SEC. 2. *Sources of law.*

The law of any one state consists of the United States Constitution, the public acts of Congress, its own state constitution, the public acts of its own legislature, the decisions of the United States Supreme Court on constitutional questions and the decisions of its own higher courts. In spite of the large amount of legislation in recent years the bulk of our law is found in the reported decisions of our higher courts which are used as precedents for future decisions. Where a question of law comes before any court in the state of New York the court will feel itself bound to follow the decisions of the higher courts of New York and especially of its highest court, the Court of Appeals. By "bound" we mean merely that it is bound by the tradition of the legal profession. If there is no decision in the New York reports on the particular point the court will consult the decisions in other states or in any other country, such as England, Canada or Australia, having the common-law system. Even where statutes have been passed the courts must usually interpret them; this interpretation is done from the standpoint of the common law, and the decisions interpreting the statutes become precedents to be followed in future cases raising the same question of interpretation.

SEC. 3. *The common law.*

The term common law is used in decisions and legal textbooks with a variety of meanings, but the particular meaning is usually apparent from the context. In its widest sense the term is used to contrast the entire system of Anglo-American law with the civil-law system which prevails in most of the non-English speaking countries and which has descended from the Roman law. The civil-law system is based upon statutes, very little attention being paid to precedents. The common-law system originated in England, the word "common" dating from the time when the customs from which the English law later developed became common to all parts of England.

In a narrower sense the term "common law" is used to distinguish the rules which have originated with the courts—sometimes called "unwritten law"—from those which have originated with legislative bodies—i.e., with written or statute law. In a still narrower sense the term "common law" is used to distinguish the rules which have originated in courts of common law from those which have originated in courts of equity.

SEC. 4. *Equity.*

Before the Norman conquest of England in 1066 justice was administered in England chiefly in people's courts and the law enforced was in the strictest sense unwritten; that is, it was handed down by oral tradition. After the conquest the king gradually established a system of royal or king's courts which eventually all but crowded out the Anglo-Saxon courts. The theory of the king's courts was that the king was the fountainhead of justice and judges acted as his agents. This was not only theory but fact, and it was not till several centuries later that the independence of the English judiciary became established.

Purely traditionary law, being administered by the people themselves, does not need to be justified to the people; but the law as administered by judges who are set over the people must be thus justified. The judge must give his reason or basis for his decision. In the Roman law there had been statutes—the Twelve Tables—upon which to rest decisions, but in English law, there being no such early statutes, the habit grew up of deciding according to the decisions of previous cases and, in the absence of such precedents, according to a process of judicial reasoning which itself became traditional. This habit of adhering to precedent became so firmly fixed that when it became necessary to relieve against this formal and rigid system in order to meet the demands of a later and more complex civilization, the common-law judges were not equal to the task and the work fell into other hands.

The English king was in theory and fact the fountain of justice. If justice could not be procured in the common-law courts the disappointed party might be able to get justice by appealing directly to the king who, not skilled in the law, would naturally turn to one of his advisers who was. The adviser to whom were entrusted these appeals for justice outside the common-law courts was the king's secretary or chancellor. These early chancellors were clergymen, not learned in the common law but in the Roman and canon or church law. Hence it was quite natural that in giving relief he should do it on ethical grounds. Gradually the task of relieving from inadequacies of the common law became so heavy that the chancellor came to have a separate court of his own which became known as the court of chancery or equity. In a few states the terms "chancery" and "chancellor" are still used.

As contrasted with the common law, equity was flexible instead of rigid, the chancellor often being able, in reaching his decision, to take into consideration all the circumstances of a case instead of laying down a hard and fast rule; he could give a command to a defendant instead of merely to the sheriff; he could exercise a preventive jurisdiction by issuing injunctions against a threatened wrong instead of waiting till after the wrong had been committed; and he could deal not merely with a two-sided case but with a case having any number of sides, settling the rights of all the parties against each other.

In some states equity is still administered in a separate court, as it was formerly in England; in other states law and equity are administered by the same court but the procedure is kept distinct. In the rest of the states, following the lead of New York, codes of procedure have been adopted which purport to abolish the distinction between common-law and equity procedure, but it has been generally held that under these codes the essential distinctions between legal and equitable rights and remedies still exist.

SEC. 5. *Importance of forms of action.*

Even in states which have adopted some form of code pleading, a knowledge of common-law pleading and especially of forms of action is still important for the following reasons:

(1) Most of our substantive law has grown up around the various forms of action, and the attempt, by statute, to abolish them did not put an end to substantive law distinctions which have either come into existence because of them or were closely entwined with them. It is therefore necessary to have a knowledge of forms of action in order to understand thoroughly the substantive law.

(2) Even in a code pleading state a knowledge of the scope of and essential allegations of the declarations in the various common-law actions is likely to be of considerable assistance to a lawyer in drawing his petition or complaint.

(3) A knowledge of the proceedings subsequent to the declaration is highly desirable because it was in the light of those proceedings that many provisions of the various codes of civil procedure were adopted.

The subject of forms of action has been placed at the beginning of the book before the various substantive law subjects because of the importance of understanding those forms in order to understand thoroughly the substantive law.

TITLES IN

SUMMARY OF AMERICAN LAW

PART I—ELEMENTARY

PART II—EQUITY AND COMMERCIAL

PART III—PUBLIC LAW

PART IV—PROCEDURE

SUMMARY OF AMERICAN LAW

PART I. ELEMENTARY SUBJECTS

FORMS OF ACTION *

* The rest of the subject of Criminal Law and Procedure is discussed later, see p. 116.

CHAPTER I

TRESPASS

A. Trespass to the Person

§ 1. Battery—scope.[1] The action of trespass lies for a direct violation of personal security or of the possession of property. If the trespass consists of contact with the plaintiff's person it is called a battery. One's person has been held to include the clothes he is wearing, the horse he is riding or the carriage in which he is driving. It is not necessary that the defendant act intentionally; it is enough that he act negligently or that he act accidentally if the trespass was committed while attempting to commit an unlawful battery on a third person. It is not necessary that the plaintiff be damaged by the battery; the mere touching is enough.

§ 2. Assault—scope.[2] If the trespass consists of an attempted battery which does not quite succeed but comes so close to success as to imperil the plaintiff's security from unlawful contact; or if it consists of an apparent attempt to commit a battery which puts the plaintiff in reasonable apprehension of a battery it is called an assault. There must be either the actual or the apparent attempt; an assault cannot be committed either negligently or accidentally but wanton negligence may suffice. If the defendant negligently puts the plaintiff in reasonable apprehension of a battery, the remedy, if any, is an action on the case.

1 4 **Am Jur**, Assault and Battery, §§ 2, 3, 5. 52 **Am Jur**, Trespass, § 9.
Civil action for assault upon female person. 6 **ALR** 985–1031.

2 4 **Am Jur**, Assault and Battery, §§ 2, 3, 5, 52 **Am Jur**, Trespass, § 9.

A mere threat or mere preparation to commit a battery is not enough; there must be some physical act which looks toward the commission of a battery and an apparent present ability to commit a battery. It is not necessary that plaintiff be damaged.

§ 3. Imprisonment—scope.[3] If the trespass consists of depriving the plaintiff of his liberty it is an imprisonment if the deprivation is complete; if the deprivation is only partial the remedy, if any, is an action on the case. It is enough that defendant act negligently.

The deprivation may be either by complete physical enclosure, by arrest or by apprehension of physical restraint. An arrest may be made either by a touching of the person accompanied by words of arrest; or by submission to the apparent power to apply force to take into custody. If the alleged restraint was physical it would seem that it would not be necessary that the plaintiff knew of it; but if the alleged restraint was mental, aliter. It is not necessary that plaintiff be damaged.

If the arrest of the plaintiff was valid he cannot recover in trespass even though he was innocent of the offense for which he was arrested; but if he can show that the defendant acted with an improper motive and without reasonable and probable cause he can recover in an action on the case for malicious prosecution.

§ 4. Essential allegations in the declaration.[4] The declaration in trespass to the person need not describe the trespass with particularity; it is enough to allege that the defendant beat or assaulted or imprisoned the plaintiff. Under these simple allegations the plaintiff may prove any state of facts which, by the substantive law of torts, constitutes the trespass or trespasses complained of.

It is not necessary to allege that the plaintiff was damaged, but unless he alleges and proves substantial damage he can ordinarily recover judgment for only nominal damages. Though mental pain and nervous shock are not such special damage as will support an action on the case, yet when the plaintiff recovers judgment either in battery or assault or imprisonment he may recover also for the mental pain and humiliation. And in most states the jury may, where the defendant has acted in a hostile and insulting manner, include in their verdict an amount in addition to compensation for such mental pain and humiliation, as a deterrent to possible future trespasses; such additional sum is called exemplary or vindictive or punitive damages or "smart money."

B. Trespass to Property

§ 5. Trespass to land—scope.[5] If the defendant interferes directly with land of which the plaintiff is in possession the proper action is trespass

[3] 4 **Am Jur**, Arrest, § 2.
52 **Am Jur**, Trespass, § 9.
Malice and want of probable cause as elements of action for false imprisonment. 19 **ALR** 671–675; s. in 137 **ALR** 504–509.
Charge of larceny and circumstances accompanying same as detention that will support action for false imprisonment. 31 **ALR** 314–323.
Civil liability of judicial officer for false imprisonment. 13 **ALR** 1344–1367; s. in 55 **ALR** 282–284.
Detention as result of dispute over payment of bill for cash service as false imprisonment. 26 **ALR** 1333–1337.
Delay in taking before magistrate or denial of opportunity to give bail as supporting action for false imprisonment. 79 **ALR** 13–29.
Action for false imprisonment or malicious prosecution predicated upon institution of, or conduct in connection with lunacy proceedings. 145 **ALR** 711–735.

[4] 4 **Am Jur**, Assault and Battery, § 140.

[5] 52 **Am Jur**, Trespass, §§ 11–18.
Trespass by acts above surface. 42 **ALR** 945–951.
48 **Harv. L. R.** 216, Aviation under the Common Law.

quare clausum fregit, that is, whereby he broke the close. But it is not necessary that there be any actual enclosure; any direct interference with the possession either below, on or above the surface of the land is enough.

It is enough that defendant acted negligently or that he acted accidentally provided that the trespass was committed while engaged in an act so hazardous that the substantive law impose liability at peril, such as the use of very dangerous explosives in blasting. If defendant's animals escape, even though accidentally, from his own land onto land in the possession of the plaintiff, the latter may maintain trespass for the act of the animals.

It is not necessary that plaintiff's land be damaged; this is because in Anglo-American law the action of trespass to land is used to vindicate a disputed right as well as to force the defendant to pay for damage inflicted upon the land.

If at the time of the defendant's act the land was in the possession of a lessee under a lease, only the lessee can maintain trespass; the lessor's remedy is in case for the damage done to his reversionary interest. If the land was in the possession of a tenant at will the same rule prevails, the right to the immediate possession not being enough. If at the time of defendant's entry the land was not occupied by anyone the plaintiff can maintain trespass if he can prove title to the land at the time of the entry.

If a lessee while in possession commits an act which causes damage to his landlord's interest in the land, he is liable to the landlord in an action on the case in the nature of waste; but if a tenant at will while in possession commits such a destructive act he is liable in trespass.

If the defendant not merely trespasses upon the plaintiff's possession but ousts the plaintiff and enters into possession himself the plaintiff can maintain trespass without first getting back possession; but in such an action he recovers only for the damage done by the ouster, not for being kept out of possession. After he gets back possession, either by re-entry or by bringing ejectment he may then bring trespass with a continuando and recover for mesne profits received by the defendant while in possession; in some states he may also recover for damage done to the land which did not benefit the defendant; in others he must bring an action on the case.

If the defendant's act amounts only to a partial ouster from possession, such as stringing a wire across plaintiff's land the plaintiff may recover either in trespass or ejectment.

If the defendant enters by authority of law and while in possession abuses his legal privilege he thereby forfeits his privilege and becomes a trespasser ab initio.

§ 6. Same—essential allegations of the declaration.[6] The declaration need not particularly describe the land; it is enough to allege that it is in .... county. It is not necessary to allege specifically that the plaintiff was in possession; it is enough to refer to it generally as the land of the plaintiff.

In describing defendant's act of trespass it is enough to allege that the defendant entered upon the land; under this he may prove any state of facts which, by the substantive law, constitutes the trespass. It is not necessary to allege that the land was damaged; but if no substantial damage is alleged he can recover only nominal damages.

6 52 Am Jur, Trespass, § 66.

§ 7. Trespass to chattels—scope.[7] If the defendant's act consists of a direct interference with a chattel in the possession of the plaintiff, either by carrying it away, or by taking possession without removing it, or by causing immediate damage to it without taking possession of it, the plaintiff may bring trespass. If the defendant carries away the chattel or takes possession without removing it the action is called trespass de bonis asportatis and the action will lie though no damage is done to the goods because trespass de bonis, like trespass to land, is used in our law to vindicate a disputed right. If the chattel is not taken out of plaintiff's possession trespass will not lie unless the chattel is damaged; a mere touching of the chattel is not enough, probably because if there is a disputed right the defendant will not be contented with merely touching it but will take possession of it.

If X wrongfully takes a chattel out of the possession of A and then Y wrongfully takes the chattel from X, not only can X maintain trespass against Y but A can maintain trespass against either X or Y. But if X delivers the chattel peaceably to Y neither A nor X can maintain trespass against him.

If defendant's act consists of an indirect interference with the chattel of which the plaintiff is in possession he cannot bring trespass; he must bring case and prove that the chattel was damaged.

If at the time of defendant's act the chattel was in the possession of a bailee for hire for a fixed term which had not yet expired, only the bailee may bring trespass; the bailor must bring case for the damage caused to his reversionary interest and allege and prove such damage. But if the chattel was in the possession of a bailee at will either the bailee or bailor may bring trespass, the bailor's right to immediate possession being held sufficient.

If X takes A's chattel out of the custody of A's servant B, trespass can be maintained by A, not B, because it is A, not B, who is considered to have possession.

If a trespass is committed by A's servant, A is liable in the action of trespass only if he authorized the act to be done; if the act is not authorized and A is rendered liable by the substantive law because the act was within the apparent scope of the servant's employment only the servant is liable in trespass; A must be sued in case.

If the defendant by seduction or by any direct physical tort against the servant causes damage to the master either by way of loss of service or by increasing the master's expenses in caring for the servant, the master can maintain either trespass or case.

§ 8. Same—essential allegations of the declaration.[8] A general description of the chattels is usually enough; but if the defendant can convince the court that the declaration does not give enough information for him to prepare his defense intelligently and that it is very difficult for him to get the information elsewhere the court may, on defendant's motion, compel plaintiff to give a more particular description.

Possession need not be alleged; it is enough to refer to the chattels as the chattels of the plaintiff. Under the usual allegation that the defendant took and carried away the chattels the plaintiff may show either such an asportation or that the defendant merely took possession.

[7] 52 Am Jur, Trespass, § 10.

[8] 52 Am Jur, Trespass, § 66.

CHAPTER II

TROVER

§ 9. **Scope.**[9] In order that a plaintiff may recover in trover for the value of a chattel it is necessary that he be able to prove that at the time of defendant's conversion the plaintiff was in possession of the chattel or that he was entitled to the immediate possession thereof; if he does not have even the right to immediate possession, as when he is a bailor for hire for a fixed period which has not yet expired, he must bring case for any damage done to his reversionary interest and allege and prove such damage. In some cases it is enough to show an equitable right to get back the chattel; for example, a defrauded vendor of a chattel has only an equitable right to get back the chattel from the defrauding vendee or a transferee from such vendee other than a bona fide purchaser for value without notice, but is allowed to bring trover to redress such equitable right.

A conversion may consist of delivering or receiving possession of the chattel upon a purported sale, mortgage, pledge or gift; and a defendant is liable though he was acting as agent and thought that his principal was the true owner. If A's bailee, B, purports to sell the bailed chattel to X and delivers it to him under such purported sale both B and X become liable to A in trover; and this is true even if the bailment was for hire for a fixed period which has not expired, because the purported sale and delivery forfeits B's rights under the bailment and at once revests the right to immediate possession in A; the fact that X paid value in good faith is no defense because he does not get title and is therefore not a bona fide purchaser for value without notice.

If the defendant is in possession or control of plaintiff's chattel and unconditionally refuses to deliver it to the plaintiff on demand, such a detention is evidence of a conversion which is conclusive if not explained. So, if he wrongfully creates a lien on the plaintiff's goods, or fraudulently induces the plaintiff to sell and deliver the goods to himself, or intentionally destroys a chattel of which he is in possession, or takes the goods out of the plaintiff's possession with intent to deprive the plaintiff of them—in all these cases trover may be brought. But if he takes from the plaintiff's bailee who holds under a bailment for hire for a term which has not expired, the proper remedy is not trover but an action on the case for the damage done to his reversionary interest.

If the defendant's act consists merely of a physical intermeddling with the possession without any claim of right in himself or in a third party the plaintiff's remedy is usually either trespass or case, not trover. But in a few cases trover has been allowed though there is no intent to deprive; for example, one in possession who mistakenly delivers the chattel to the wrong person has

[9] 53 **Am Jur,** Trover and Conversion, §§ 1–93.

Nature of property or rights other than tangible chattels which may be subject of trover. 50 **ALR** 1167–1173.

Transfer of possession of personal property with owner's consent, obtained by fraud, as conversion. 95 **ALR** 615–621.

Negative conduct as basis of claim of conversion. 116 **ALR** 870–880.

Mere detention of or failure to deliver chattels after demand as conversion. 61 **ALR** 621–633: s. in 129 **ALR** 638–648.

Voluntary dismissal of replevin action by plaintiff as affecting defendant's right to judgment for the return of value of the property. 2 **ALR** 200–211.

May trover be predicated upon the mere act of purchasing property from some one other than the true owner, without taking actual possession. 38 **ALR** 1096–1102.

21 **Harv. L. R.** 408, The Test of Conversion.

49 **Harv. L. R.** 1084, Qualifying as Plaintiff in an Action for Conversion.

been held liable in trover though the more logical remedy would be case for the damage caused by such intermeddling. So, where a chattel is accidentally destroyed while in the wrongful possession of the defendant trover has been allowed instead of case. No great injustice is occasioned in these two cases because the recovery would be substantially the same whether trover or case be brought.

It is necessary that there be some physical act of intermeddling; a mere intent is not enough; if B, a bailee, wrongfully purports to sell the chattel to X but retains the chattel in his own possession, neither B nor X is liable.

If the defendant's act is merely negligent trover will not lie; the proper remedy is case.

In trespass the plaintiff gets judgment for whatever damage he can prove; in trover he gets judgment for the value of the goods unless the goods have been received back. When the defendant has taken possession under claim of right and the goods have not been received back trespass and trover are concurrent remedies and the measure of damages is the same—the value of the goods.

Trover will not ordinarily lie for any act done to land; but if the defendant enters on land in plaintiff's possession and severs trees or grain or stone or minerals or soil or a building, the articles thus severed become chattels and the plaintiff can recover in trover if the defendant detains them or delivers them upon a purported sale. And if the plaintiff contracts with the defendant to tear down a building on land in defendant's possession and to remove the materials and the defendant refuses to allow the plaintiff to tear down the building, the plaintiff can maintain trover for the value of the materials because the contract treats the building as if it were already severed. But if a defendant while in wrongful possession of land cuts down timber or tears down a building or harvests a crop of grain or removes soil or stone or minerals the plaintiff cannot then maintain trover for the severed chattels; he must first regain possession by self-help or by winning in ejectment and then sue either in trover, trespass for mesne profits or in case for the damage done to the land.

A mere contract right to money or chattels does not entitle the plaintiff to maintain trover.

§ 10. Essential allegations of the declaration.[10] The essential allegations are that the plaintiff had a chattel and that the defendant converted it to his own use. Under the first allegation the plaintiff can prove either possession or the right to immediate possession. Under the second allegation he may prove any state of facts which by the substantive law amounts to a conversion. It is not necessary to allege damage; if no damage is alleged or if damage is alleged and not proved at the trial the plaintiff gets a judgment for only nominal damages.

CHAPTER III

CASE

§ 11. Waste.[1] In the early common law if one rightfully in possession of land but having an estate less than an estate of inheritance should cause dam-

[10] 53 Am Jur, Trover and Conversion, §§ 166–175.

[1] Am Jur, Waste.

age to the inheritance, one who had the immediate estate of inheritance—an estate tail or an estate in fee—could maintain an action of waste against him. If the estate of inheritance did not follow immediately, as where land had been conveyed to A for life, B for life, in fee, C, could not maintain waste unless and until B should predecease A; but an action on the case in the nature of waste could be maintained against A by B as well as by C for damage done to his estate. And today in most states the old action for waste has been superseded by an action on the case in the nature of waste.

§ 12. Damage to land by adverse possessor.[2] If X, while in adverse possession of A's land, cuts timber or gathers crops or severs minerals or tears down a building no action whatever lies for such acts while X remains in possession. After A regains possession either by self-help or by the action of ejectment he can maintain trespass for mesne profits for the value of the benefits received by X from his wrongful possession and, in some states, for any damage to the land which did not benefit X; in other states it is necessary to bring an action on the case to recover for such damage.

§ 13. Damage to reversionary rights in land or chattels.[3] The action of trespass quare clausum can be maintained only by one in possession of the land at the time of the defendant's act; if X is in possession and the plaintiff's interest is in reversion or remainder the plaintiff must bring case and can maintain that action only by showing that the defendant's act in violation of that possession caused damage to the plaintiff's reversionary interest.

The action of trespass de bonis can be maintained only by one who was in possession or had the right to the immediate possession of the chattel at the time of the defendant's act. If the chattel at that time was in the possession of X who was entitled to keep the chattel as against the plaintiff—for example, a bailee whose fixed term had not yet expired—the reversioner must bring case; and that action is not maintainable unless his reversionary interest suffered special damage by defendant's act, just as in the case of land.

The declaration in these cases should set forth plaintiff's exact interest in the land or the chattel, the defendant's act in violation of the possession of the property and the damage to the plaintiff's interest which was caused thereby. A mere general averment that the land or chattel was "of the plaintiff" is not enough.

§ 14. Fraud.[4] If X has caused damage to A by making fraudulent representations to him intending him to act in reliance thereon, the remedy is an action on the case for deceit. The damage usually suffered by A is the loss

2 **Am Jur,** Waste.

3 33 **Am Jur,** Life Estates, Remainders and Reversion, §§ 177, 211, 212.

4 23 **Am Jur,** Fraud and Deceit, §§ 23-94.

Statement or promise as to improvement or development of tract or neighborhood made to purchaser of land as fraud. 27 **ALR** 343-351.

Promises and statements as to future events as fraud. 51 **ALR** 46-177; s. in 68 **ALR** 635-649; 91 **ALR** 1295-1307; 125 **ALR** 879-893.

Application of principle that false representations made to one person with intention that another may act thereon are actionable in favor of latter. 91 **ALR** 1363-1381.

Duty of purchaser of real property to disclose to the vendor facts or prospects affecting the value of the property. 56 **ALR** 429-447.

Fraud predicated upon misrepresentation by grantee or transferee regarding grantor's or transferrer's title. 136 **ALR** 1299-1316.

Necessity for knowledge of falsity of representation as to value, inducing subscription to or purchase of corporate stock, or other securities. 73 **ALR** 1120-1152.

of property transferred by him to X or Y, but it may consist of injury to the plaintiff's person, for example, caused by the explosion of a gun fraudulently represented to be safe; or to rights growing out of contract, business or domestic relations; for example, X induced A to marry a woman whom he had seduced, representing that she was virtuous.

If the fraudulent representations were made to Y and induced Y to inflict damage upon A, the action is case for fraud but it is not called deceit.

In order to maintain an action for deceit it is necessary that X either knew the statement to be false or that he made the statement recklessly without caring whether it was true or false. If he was merely negligent in not knowing the falsity of the statement, case for deceit will not lie but case for negligent misrepresentations should be brought. Silence may amount to a false representation where the defendant is under a fiduciary duty to speak; so may active concealment of a material fact or the partial non-disclosure where one has undertaken to tell all the truth.

It is not necessary that X be benefited or that he even expect to be benefited by making the false representation in order to be liable in deceit. But if X does receive a benefit from A because of the deceit A can maintain trover against X for the value of the benefit or *indebitatus assumpsit* in quasi contract for unjust enrichment.

The declaration in deceit should allege that: (1) X made a representation to A that was not true in fact; (2) X did not believe that the representation was true in fact; (3) X expected A to act upon it; (4) A did so act and was damaged thereby.

§ 15. Nuisance.[5] The common law not only protects one in the peaceable possession of land against direct and indirect physical interference with that possession but also recognizes certain non-possessory rights, such as the right to have the air over the land free from unreasonable pollution by disagreeable vapors and odors and from unreasonable noise and the right to have water in a natural watercourse flow past his land without diminution, deterioration or alteration. Such rights are called natural rights because they exist irrespective of the consent of others. Any violation of these natural rights is called a private nuisance for which the appropriate common-law remedy is an action on the case. There is a conflict of authority as to whether the plaintiff must be able to show damage. The fact that the violation is on

[5] 39 Am Jur, Nuisances, §§ 2–11; 43–116.

Noise from operation of industrial plant as nuisance. 23 ALR 1407–1425; s. in 90 ALR 1207–1214.

Slaughterhouse as nuisance. 27 ALR 329–337.

Gas, water, or electric light plant as a nuisance, and the remedy therefor. 37 ALR 800–813.

Piggery as a nuisance. 50 ALR 1017–1023.

Airport or flight of aircraft as a nuisance. 140 ALR 1362–1369.

Automobile gas-filling or supply station as a nuisance. 124 ALR 383–400.

Garage as a nuisance. 50 ALR 107–113.

Trolley poles in street as nuisance. 2 ALR 496–503.

Dust as nuisance. 3 ALR 312–323; s. in 11 ALR 1401–1402.

Pesthouse or contagious disease hospital as nuisance. 5 ALR 995–1008; s. in 18 ALR 122–123; 48 ALR 518.

Operation of railroad as nuisance to property. 6 ALR 723–736; s. in 69 ALR 1188–1190.

Right of abutting owner to complain of misuse of public park or violation of rights or easements appurtenant thereto. 60 ALR 770–785.

Dogs as nuisance. 79 ALR 1060–1069.

Liability for injury by firearms at rifle range, shooting gallery, military exercise, etc.; use of firearms in such cases as a nuisance. 140 ALR 415–432.

Validity, construction, and application of statute or ordinance declaring plant or establishment which emits offensive odors to be a public nuisance. 141 ALR 285–298.

such a large scale as to amount also to a public nuisance does not, by the better view, modify or impair the plaintiff's remedy.

§ 16. Disturbance of easements.[6] A natural right exists without regard to the consent of others or to the fact of user; a private easement comes into existence either by express or implied grant or by adverse user for the period of the statute of limitations. The most common easements are those of right of way, light and air and right of access to a public way. If the defendant causes damage to the plaintiff by interference with the plaintiff's private easement the proper remedy is an action on the case.

If damage is caused to the plaintiff by the obstruction of a public easement such as the obstruction of a public way, the proper remedy is an action on the case. In some states the plaintiff must prove that he has suffered peculiar damage, that is, damage different in kind from that suffered by the rest of the community, the courts apparently being afraid of a flood of litigation if there was no such requirement.

§ 17. Damage through negligence, by accident or through breach of statutory or customary duty.[7] Where X by his negligent conduct has caused special damage to A, case is always appropriate, special damage here meaning any damage except mental pain or nervous shock. If the special damage has been caused directly to A's person or to land or chattels in his possession he may if he prefers bring trespass; but if the special damage was indirectly caused he must bring case. The same distinction holds where by the substantive law the defendant is liable for damage caused accidentally.

Negligence is the absence of the care required by law. By the common law one is bound to exercise that amount and degree of care which a person of average prudence would exercise under similar circumstances. Sometimes the test of due care is fixed by statute in which instance the remedy is case for negligence. But if the statute imposes a liability entirely apart from negligence the proper remedy is an action on the case, not for negligence, but for damage caused to plaintiff by defendant's violation of the statute. Where a statute creates a liability for wrongfully causing death to a human being, giving a cause of action usually to the executor of the decedent, the proper remedy is case.

In a few cases usually classified as torts there is an affirmative duty; for example, the duty of a land occupier toward a business visitor, to use due care to keep the premises in a safe condition or to warn of any secret dangers of which he knows, or by the exercise of reasonable care could have known. The remedy in such cases is an action on the case.

The obligation of common carriers, innkeepers and others engaged in a public service occupation is not purely tort because the duty is not negative, as it usually is in the law of torts, but affirmative, namely, to serve all at reasonable rates. On the other hand, it is not purely contractual because as long as they remain in the public service occupation they must serve all at reasonable rates; so the duty in such case, which is superficially consensual, is not really

6 17 **Am Jur**, Easements, §§ 114–119; 149–154.

Right and duty of highway contractor as to barricading or obstructing street. 7 **ALR** 1023–1213; s. in 104 **ALR** 955–967.

Personal liability of contractor in respect of injuries sustained by persons other than the contractee during the progress of the stipulated work. 38 **ALR** 403–554.

Liability of independent contractors for injuries to third persons by defects in completed work. 41 **ALR** 8–137.

7 38 **Am Jur**, Negligence, §§ 2–7.

so. The common law did not devise any special writ to enforce such an obligation but allowed the plaintiff to bring either a tort or a contract action; either case for the damage caused by the breach of the customary obligation to serve all at reasonable rates, or special assumpsit for the failure or refusal to carry out the undertaking to serve. Where a common carrier misdelivers a chattel entrusted to him for carriage trover has been allowed though logically it should be case.

§ 18. Same—essential allegations in the declaration.[8] In an action on the case against X for negligently causing damage to land or chattels in A's possession the declaration must contain at least a general allegation that the land or chattels were "of the plaintiff"; and as particular and detailed description of X's act as the circumstances of the case permit. If X's negligent conduct consisted of setting or keeping forces in motion where A had a right to be—for example, on the public highway—or where X knew of A's presence, it is not necessary to allege any further facts showing a duty to use care because such a duty is clear and unmistakable; and it is frequently impossible to describe X's conduct further than to say that he did the act, for example, drove an automobile against A, negligently and wrongfully. Where A was on X's premises A must allege that X knew of A's presence or by the exercise of reasonable care should have known of it in time to avoid causing him damage.

If X's conduct consists of a failure to act, for example, the failure to warn A, a business visitor on his premises, of some hidden danger, A must allege facts showing that he was a business visitor and that the premises were in such a dangerous condition that the law imposed an affirmative duty to warn A.

In case for the damage caused by the breach of an obligation imposed by a domestic statute it is not necessary to set out the statute because the court will take judicial notice of it; it is enough to cite it. But if the obligation is one imposed by a foreign statute the statute itself must be fully set out. There must also be an allegation of a breach of the statutory obligation by X and the damage caused to A thereby.

In case for damage caused by the breach of a customary obligation in refusing to serve A, A must allege that X was engaged in a public service occupation, for example, that of a common carrier or electric light and power company; that A demanded service of X and that X wrongfully refused to serve him, to A's damage in the sum of .... dollars.

There is a conflict of authority on the question whether the defendant must allege contributory negligence or the plaintiff must allege due care on his own part. In those states following the latter rule, if the plaintiff was guilty of contributory negligence but is relying on the last chance doctrine, he should set out the facts showing that the defendant did have the last chance to avoid causing the damage. Wherever the plaintiff is complaining of the defendant's negligent conduct he must allege that such conduct caused special damage but such allegation may be in general terms.

§ 19. Slander and libel.[9] If X makes a false statement or other communication to the mind of Y which tends to bring A into hatred, contempt or ridicule or which tends to injure him in his office, business, trade or profession, the proper remedy is an action on the case. If the defamatory com-

[8] 38 Am Jur, Negligence, §§ 258–275.

[9] 33 Am Jur, Libel and Slander, §§ 3–115.

munication is in oral or other fugitive form the action is case for slander; if in written or other permanent form it is in case for libel.

By the older and better view an action for libel will lie even though there was no special damage; but in an action for slander special damage is necessary unless the communication was one which imputed to A a serious crime, a loathsome disease or tends to disparage him in his office, trade, business or profession.

If X makes a false statement to Y which is not defamatory but which is meant to cause and does cause special damage to A the proper remedy is an action on the case but not for slander or libel.

An action for slander or libel will not lie unless X acted either intentionally or negligently in making the communication to Y; a merely accidental communication is not enough. But it is not necessary that X should have intended the communication to be defamatory or to refer to A or that X should have been negligent in respect thereto; it is enough that Y did understand the communication to be defamatory and to refer to A.

§ 20. Same—essential allegations of the declaration.[10] The declaration in case for slander or for libel should set out, as nearly as possible, the exact words spoken or written by the defendant; it is not enough to give merely the general purport or substance of what was said or written.

If the words in their ordinary meanings were not defamatory but were rendered defamatory by the circumstances under which the words were used, the plaintiff should set forth these circumstances in what is called a colloquium. If the words were rendered defamatory because the hearers or readers attached a particular defamatory meaning to the words this should be set forth in the declaration in an innuendo. When the words did not obviously refer to the plaintiff both a colloquium and an innuendo are usually necessary.

If the words were spoken or written in a foreign language the declaration must allege that the persons who heard or read them understood them. It is necessary to allege that the words were spoken or written "of and concerning" the plaintiff; and that the words were published, but it is not necessary to allege how they were published.

It is apparently still necessary to allege that the defendant spoke or wrote the words falsely and maliciously, but neither allegation needs to be proved. Truth must be set up and proved by the defendant; and malice is of no importance unless the defendant sets up the defense of conditional privilege.

§ 21. Malicious prosecution.[1] If X causes A to be arrested on a void warrant or without any warrant where one was necessary, A's remedy is trespass for false imprisonment; and he may recover even though he was guilty of the crime for which he was thus illegally arrested.

But if A is legally arrested either with or without a warrant he cannot maintain trespass even though he is innocent of the crime for which he is arrested. In such circumstances his only remedy is an action on the case for malicious prosecution; and that action will lie only where A was innocent and where X acted maliciously—that is, from some motive other than the furtherance of justice—and without reasonable and probable cause for believing that A was guilty of the crime charged. In some states the action cannot be maintained without proof of special damage if there was no tres-

10 33 Am Jur, Libel and Slander, §§ 237–242.

1 34 Am Jur, Malicious Prosecution, §§ 2–68.

pass to his person or property and if the charge was such that if made orally outside of legal proceedings an action for slander would not lie without proof of special damage.

The declaration must usually allege: (1) that A was prosecuted in a judicial tribunal by X on a criminal charge; (2) that it terminated in favor of A; (3) that X did not have reasonable and probable cause for such prosecution; (4) that it was done maliciously, that is, with an improper motive.

§ 22. **Interference with contract and business relations.**[2] If X by intimidation or fraud or bribery prevents Y from performing his contract with A thus causing special damage to A the proper remedy is case for interfering with A's contract right. If only peaceable persuasion is used there is a conflict of authority as to X's liability. Where a tortious act of X has unintentionally caused damage to A's contract right with Y there is a similar conflict of authority as to A's right of recovery.

If X by intimidation or other tortious means interferes with A's interest as an employer in the freedom of the labor market; or if X by blacklist interferes with A's interest as an employee in the freedom to sell his services as he wishes; or if X by force, fraud, defamation or disparagement of goods interferes with the interest of a trade rival—in all these cases the proper action is case for the special damage inflicted upon A through interference with his probable expectancies.

§ 23. **Interference with domestic relations.**[3] If X by seduction or by any act which is a tort to A's servant causes special damage to A either by way of loss of service or by increasing A's expense in caring for the servant the logical action is case because A's interest is an intangible one; but A can, if he prefers, maintain trespass against one who seduces his female servant—usually his daughter—or where the damage is caused directly. A parent has no right of action unless he stands also in the relation of master or employer to his child. Where the female seduced is the daughter of A the loss of a very small amount of service is enough to maintain the action.

If X from an improper motive persuades A's wife to leave him; or alienates her affections; or has sexual intercourse with her; or commits any tortious act against the wife which results in the loss of her services to A; in all these four cases the proper remedy is case though apparently trespass may be brought for the seduction.

If X from an improper motive persuades the plaintiff's husband to leave her; or alienates his affections; or has sexual intercourse with him, the proper remedy is case.

CHAPTER IV

COVENANT

§ 24. **Scope.**[4] The action of covenant lies for the breach of a promise under seal; such a promise is also called a covenant. The most common instances of such covenants today occur in conveyances of either freehold or

[2] 31 **Am Jur**, Labor, §§ 295–307.
Liability for procuring breach of contract. 84 **ALR** 43.

[3] 35 **Am Jur**, Master and Servant, §§ 530, 531.
27 **Am Jur**, Husband and Wife, §§ 519–536.
39 **Am Jur**, Parent and Child, § 71–85.

[4] 12 **Am Jur**, Contracts, §§ 60–63.
1 **Am Jur**, Actions, §§ 48, 53.

leasehold interests in land. Some of these covenants are expressly to do or to refrain from doing something in the future, such as covenants for quiet enjoyment or for further assurance. Others are, in terms, undertakings that a certain condition of affairs exists at the time of the conveyance, such as a covenant that the transferor is seised of the land conveyed or a covenant of warranty against incumbrances; such covenants are broken, if at all, as soon as made.

Where the transferee in the conveyance also executes the conveyance he becomes liable to be sued in an action of covenant for breach of his promise in the conveyance such as a covenant to pay rent, not to assign the lease and not to use the premises in a particular way. If the transferee does not execute the instrument but merely assents to its terms the remedy against him must be in assumpsit. Similarly, a landlord can maintain assumpsit, not covenant, against an assignee of the lessee or against a sub-lessee; and a grantee in a warranty deed who signs it but does not seal it is liable for breach of warranty in special assumpsit, not covenant. If one partner undertakes to bind the partnership by executing, in the firm's name, an instrument under seal, only the partner thus executing becomes liable in covenant; the firm is liable only in quasi contract in indebitatus assumpsit or debt on simple contract for the reasonable value of the benefit received by the firm under the contract.

If the plaintiff is suing upon a sealed instrument for a fixed sum of money which the defendant has agreed to pay, the plaintiff may usually, if he prefers, maintain an action of debt on a specialty; common illustrations are an ordinary bond for the payment of money and a lease in which the lessee has covenanted to pay rent. But if the covenant is to do anything else than to pay a fixed sum of money the action of covenant is exclusive; for example, a covenant not to assign the lease. It has also been held—illogically but apparently from analogy to the difference between special assumpsit and indebitatus assumpsit—that debt will not lie on a covenant wherein the defendant has guaranteed the payment to the plaintiff of a debt of a third party.

If there has been a contract under seal which has been later modified by an unsealed contract and the plaintiff is suing for the breach of the contract thus modified he must bring debt on simple contract or special or general assumpsit, not covenant.

It is not necessary that plaintiff be damaged by the breach of covenant.

§ 25. Essential allegations of the declaration.[5] The plaintiff must allege that the defendant made a promise or covenant setting out either the exact words or their legal effect. He must allege also that the contract was under seal and that defendant failed to perform it; if the promise was subject to a condition precedent he must allege performance of the condition or excuse for nonperformance.

He need not allege that the promise was based upon consideration or that the breach caused him any damage; nor need he allege other promises which the defendant made as a part of the same transaction but which are not alleged to have been broken.

5 1 Am Jur, Actions, § 53.

CHAPTER V

DEBT

§ 26. In general.[6] Debt lies in four classes of cases: (1) on a specialty—that is, a sealed instrument; (2) on a statute; (3) on a record; (4) on a simple, that is, unsealed, contract. There is one characteristic common to all four classes of cases: it lies—subject to modern modifications as to class (4)—only for a fixed sum of money.

A. Debt on a Specialty

§ 27. Scope.[7] Where the defendant has promised under seal to pay a sum certain, for example, in an administrator's bond, a sealed bill of exchange or promissory note, a sealed policy of insurance or a sealed lease in which the defendant has promised to pay a fixed rent, the plaintiff may bring debt on a specialty, though he may, if he prefers, bring an action of covenant. If the promise under seal is to refrain from acting or to do anything else except to pay a fixed sum of money the plaintiff must bring covenant, not debt.

§ 28. Essential allegations of the declaration.[8] The plaintiff should allege that the defendant was indebted to the plaintiff in the sum of .... dollars, upon a bond (or lease or other instrument under seal) and that defendant has refused to pay the same upon demand. The promise to pay may be set out in the exact words of the instrument or according to its legal effect. If defendant's liability is subject to a condition which is precedent in form as well as substance the plaintiff must set out the condition and its performance or excuse for nonperformance. But if the condition is subsequent in form the plaintiff may—apart from statute—ignore it and leave it to be pleaded by the defendant even though it be really precedent in effect.

B. Debt on a Statute

§ 29. Scope and essential allegations of the declaration.[9] Where a statute has imposed upon the defendant an obligation to do or not to do a particular act and in default thereof to pay as a penalty a fixed sum of money the proper remedy is debt on a statute. It is also an appropriate remedy to recover unpaid taxes.

Where a statute imposes an obligation to do or not to do a particular act and the purpose of the statute is to protect persons who would likely be damaged by a failure to fulfil the obligation and no penalty is imposed, the proper remedy is not debt but case for the special damage caused to plaintiff by defendant's breach of his statutory duty.

The plaintiff should allege that the defendant was indebted to plaintiff in the sum of .... dollars, upon a statute (setting forth the relevant provisions of the statute) and that the defendant has refused to pay the same on demand.

6 1 Am Jur, Actions, §§ 48, 52.
Liability for injury to pedestrian due to condition of street or highway as affected by his blindness or other physical disability. 141 ALR 721–751.

7 1 Am Jur, Actions, § 52.

8 1 Am Jur, Actions, § 28.

9 1 Am Jur, Actions, § 52.

C. Debt on a Record

§ 30. Scope and essential allegations of the declaration.[10] If a judgment of a domestic court of record has imposed upon the defendant an obligation to pay a definite sum of money to the plaintiff the proper remedy is debt on a record. And because of the full faith and credit clause in the United States Constitution, debt on a record lies upon a judgment rendered by a court of record in a sister state. An equity decree for the payment of money stands upon the same footing as a judgment of a common-law court of record and may be enforced in an action of debt on a record; but if the common-law judgment or equity decree is for anything else except the payment of money debt will not lie.

Upon a judgment of a court not of record—such as the judgment of a justice-of-the-peace court or other inferior court—the proper remedy is not debt on a record but either debt on simple contract or indebitatus assumpsit. And judgments of foreign countries having the common-law system can be sued upon in the same way.

The plaintiff should allege that the defendant was indebted to plaintiff in the sum of .... dollars, upon a judgment or decree, setting forth the name and location of the court that rendered the judgment or decree, and that the defendant has refused to pay the same on demand.

D. Debt on Simple (Unsealed) Contract

§ 31. Scope.[1] Before the development of the action on the case there were two kinds of contract in English law. One was the promise under seal which was enforced by the action of covenant or debt on a specialty; the other was the simple (unsealed) debt or real contract. A simple debt or real contract arose upon the receipt of a res (whence the word *real*) or tangible benefit upon the understanding that a sum certain was to be paid therefor. There was no element of promise involved, the basis of the obligation being the receipt of the res or benefit, upon the understanding that the receiptor was to pay a fixed sum therefor.

The most usual cases in which debt on simple contract lay were for work and labor, goods bargained and sold, goods sold and delivered, money lent, money had and received and interest.

In an action of debt on simple contract the early English law permitted the defendant to have the case tried by wager of law. Under that method of trial, if he swore that he did not owe the debt and could bring in eleven or twelve compurgators to swear that they believed him he was absolved from liability. Such a method of trial was naturally unpopular with plaintiffs and about 1600 the courts began to allow simple debts to be collected in an action of assumpsit in which the plaintiff could insist upon trial by jury. The result of this innovation was that for some two centuries the action of debt on simple contract fell into disuse in England. But trial by wager of law became obsolete and was finally abolished by statute in England in 1833; thereupon debt on simple contract was revived, becoming concurrent with indebitatus assumpsit which had so long superseded it, and being allowed even when the amount sued for was uncertain. The chief advantage of debt on simple contract over indebitatus assumpsit was that the former

10 1 Am Jur, Actions, § 52.

1 1 Am Jur, Actions, § 52.

could and the latter could not be joined with counts in debt on a specialty, on a statute or on a record.

Debt on simple contract has been extended to actions on a promissory note or on a bill of exchange; and in the United States this has been allowed even where the action is not brought for the price of a benefit received by the defendant. It has also been allowed to recover the amount of an award fixed by arbitration.

Where the plaintiff is suing on a contract but not for the price or for the reasonable value of a benefit received by the defendant, debt on simple contract will not lie even though the amount of the plaintiff's demand is certain and the plaintiff has fully performed his own promise; for example, it cannot be maintained to enforce a guaranty or a contract of insurance.

§ 32. Essential allegations of the declaration.[2] The action of debt on simple contract was developed out of the law of property and was based upon property conceptions. If A loaned his horse to B for a month A had a specific property right to get back his horse at the end of the month. If A loaned B £100 for a month A was considered to have a property interest in B's general assets to the extent of £100. The same conception was applied to a debt arising from the sale of goods at a fixed price or the rendering of services at a fixed wage or any other state of facts from which a simple debt arose. Later, of course, courts recognized the fundamental distinction between a lending of a chattel where the title to the chattel remains in the bailor and a loan of money where title to the money passes to the borrower, and regarded the right of the creditor as a personal right against the debtor, to be paid out of his general assets, the right of the creditor in the debtor's property being only indirect, indefinite and intangible.

In view of the proprietary origin of debt on simple contract it is not surprising that in the early history of the action it was necessary for the plaintiff to set forth with considerable particularity the facts out of which the debt arose; for example, if the action was for goods bargained and sold the goods must be carefully described; if it was for money lent the particulars of making the loan must be carefully alleged.

When debt was superseded by indebitatus assumpsit in order to avoid trial by wager of law it was an added advantage of the latter action that it was not necessary to set forth in detail the transaction out of which the debt arose; this was because theoretically the action was brought for breach of the promise to pay the already existing debt and hence it was enough to set out, as an inducement, the existence of the debt in general terms. When, after trial by wager of law was abolished, debt on simple contract was revived, the early requirement of a detailed description of the transaction giving rise to the debt was not insisted upon; it was enough to allege the existence of the debt generally just as in declarations in indebitatus assumpsit; in fact, the declarations in the two actions became identical except that in indebitatus assumpsit a promise to pay the debt and a breach of the promise is alleged.

In the modern action of debt on simple contract the plaintiff should allege that the defendant was indebted to the plaintiff in the sum of .... dollars for work and labor, or for goods bargained and sold, etc., and that the defendant has refused to pay the same on demand. If the defendant can convince the court that the description is so general that he cannot prepare his

[2] 1 Am Jur, Actions, § 52.

defense the court will order the plaintiff to furnish a bill of particulars which will give plaintiff a detailed description of the transactions out of which the debts are alleged to have arisen.

CHAPTER VI

SPECIAL ASSUMPSIT

§ 33. **Scope.**[3] Covenant originally lay for the breach of any promise, even if gratuitous and unsealed, but apparently no action was ever allowed in the kings' courts except upon a promise under seal. The result of this stringent requirement was that although the action of debt on simple contract lay for the collection of debts there was a very long period, down to the rise of assumpsit, during which no action whatever could be brought for the breach of a simple promise; and when that action was finally allowed and the modern simple promissory contract came into existence it was required that such a promise be based upon consideration.

Assumpsit was fashioned out of an action on the case for deceit by substituting promise for false representation, by requiring that there be consideration for the promise and by dropping the requirement of special damage. At first the action was known simply as assumpsit (literally, he undertook); but after the action was extended so as to allow it to be brought for the collection of debts the simple action of assumpsit for the breach of a simple (unsealed) promise came to be known as special assumpsit while assumpsit for the collection of debts came to be called indebitatus assumpsit (literally, having been indebted, he undertook).

Wherever the plaintiff is suing for the breach of a simple (unsealed) promise he may bring special assumpsit whether he is or is not suing for the price or for the reasonable value of a benefit received. If the plaintiff is suing for the breach of the defendant's consensual obligation to pay the price or—if there is no price—for the reasonable value of a benefit received by him, the plaintiff may bring debt on simple contract or indebitatus assumpsit instead of special assumpsit, and will usually do so because the declaration is more easily drawn. If the plaintiff is suing for the breach of defendant's promise to refrain from acting or to do anything else than to pay the price or the reasonable value of a benefit received, special assumpsit must be brought. If the plaintiff is suing in quasi contract for the reasonable value of a benefit received by the defendant, he must bring debt on simple contract or indebitatus assumpsit; special assumpsit will not lie.

Since the obligation of a common carrier or others engaged in a public service occupation is, strictly speaking, neither tort nor contract but is similar to both, a breach of such an obligation may be enforced either by an action on the case based upon the customary obligation to serve all at reasonable rates, or special assumpsit for the failure to carry out the public service undertaking.

§ 34. **Essential allegations of the declaration.**[4] In special assumpsit for the breach of a contract the plaintiff must allege: (1) the promise of the defendant; (2) the consideration for the promise; (3) the performance of conditions precedent and concurrent or excuse for nonperformance; (4) the breach

[3] 4 Am Jur, Assumpsit, §§ 2–17.

[4] 4 Am Jur, Assumpsit, §§ 35, 36, 37.

of the defendant's promise. It is not necessary to allege special damage or to allege anything in regard to conditions subsequent.

In special assumpsit for the breach of a public service obligation the declaration must allege: (1) that the defendant was engaged in a public service occupation, for example, common carrier, supplier of water, gas, etc.; (2) the defendant's undertaking, for example, to carry goods, etc., and that plaintiff demanded service of the defendant; (3) the breach of the defendant's undertaking in refusing or failing to serve plaintiff.

CHAPTER VII

GENERAL ASSUMPSIT

§ 35. Scope.[5] The action of debt on simple contract was unsatisfactory in the early days because a defendant could escape liability by waging his law, that is, by swearing that he did not owe the debt and getting eleven or twelve compurgators to swear that they believed him. After assumpsit was fully developed the courts yielded to the demand for a more satisfactory remedy for the collection of debts by holding that if one who owed a simple debt should later promise to pay it the plaintiff could recover in assumpsit on this promise to pay; since assumpsit was a development from an action on the case the plaintiff was entitled to trial by jury and thus was able to escape the peril of the defendant's waging his law. And since assumpsit grew out of torts instead of property law it later became unnecessary for the plaintiff to show that a sum certain was due. There was no consideration in the ordinary legal sense of exchange but the courts said that in such a case the debt itself was the consideration for the promise to pay it. Later assumpsit was allowed even though no such promise was made, the courts pressing into service the fiction that in all cases of simple debts a later promise to pay the debt would be implied; that is, the defendant was not allowed to deny the allegation that he promised to pay the debt.

When assumpsit to collect debts became established it was distinguished from simple assumpsit by calling the former indebitatus assumpsit (having been indebted, he undertook) and the latter special assumpsit. Debt on simple contract was superseded by indebitatus assumpsit but trial by wager of law, which never gained a foothold in this country, fell into disuse in England, and was finally abolished by statute; whereupon debt on simple contract was revived and became concurrent with indebitatus assumpsit, being allowed even where the amount claimed was not fixed. In the meantime indebitatus assumpsit had been extended so as to allow a plaintiff to recover the reasonable value of a benefit which the defendant had received where there was no understanding that it was to be paid for but where the benefit in equity and good conscience belonged to the plaintiff, thus developing the substantive law of quasi contract for unjust enrichment. While indebitatus assumpsit came to be regarded as the normal remedy in such cases, debt on simple contract can be brought instead.

The most usual benefits for the price or reasonable value of which indebitatus assumpsit is brought are: goods sold and delivered, goods bargained and sold, money lent, interest, land sold and conveyed, money due on account stated, work and labor, materials furnished, money paid to defend-

[5] 4 Am Jur, Assumpsit, §§ 2–17.

ant's use, money had and received, use and occupation of land. By the weight of authority the one last named is confined to contract; the others may be either contract or quasi contract. These counts were in such common use that they came to be known as the common counts.

Two other counts, quantum meruit (what he merited or deserved) and quantum valebant (what the goods were worth) were also known as common counts and within the meaning of general assumpsit but not technically as indebitatus assumpsit because the work done by the plaintiff or the materials furnished by him were alleged as a consideration without first alleging that a debt arose; and the reason for this was that it was impossible to allege that there was a debt in the narrow sense of a sum certain. This distinction ceased to be of importance when the indebitatus counts were allowed where the plaintiff sought to recover the reasonable value instead of a sum certain. Account stated was also originally not included within the term indebitatus assumpsit because the balance due could not be said to be the price of any particular benefit received by the defendant.

If the defendant through the commission of some tort has received a benefit which in equity and good conscience should belong to the plaintiff the latter can usually, instead of bringing the proper tort action, maintain a count for money had and received for the reasonable value of the benefit thus received by the defendant; but if the benefit received consists of chattels not yet converted into money some courts illogically refuse to allow indebitatus assumpsit.

General assumpsit may also be brought upon a bill of exchange or promissory note.

It is often said that general assumpsit lies upon an executed contract, that is, a contract in which the plaintiff has fully performed his part, but such a statement is not accurate. If the defendant's promise is to do anything except to pay money—for example, to convey property—general assumpsit will not lie to enforce the contract even though the plaintiff has fully performed, though it will lie to enforce the quasi-contractual obligation to recover back the purchase money paid if the plaintiff prefers that relief. This exception is sometimes taken care of by limiting the application of the supposed rule to cases where the defendant's obligation is to pay money. But even as amended the rule is still inaccurate because in a contract of warranty or guaranty or insurance the defendant's obligation is to pay money but the plaintiff cannot recover in general assumpsit on the contract because the money to be paid by the defendant is not compensation for benefits received.

§ 36. Essential allegations of the declaration.[6] In indebitatus assumpsit the plaintiff should allege that the defendant was indebted to the plaintiff in the sum of .... dollars for work and labor or money lent, etc., that having been indebted he promised to pay said sum and that the defendant has refused to pay the same on demand. It is not necessary to give more than a very general description of the benefit the receipt of which plaintiff alleges gave use to the debt. If the description is so general that the defendant cannot prepare his defense the court will, upon motion, compel the plaintiff to furnish to the defendant a bill of particulars. Since the basis for

6 4 Am Jur, Assumpsit, § 22.

recovery is the benefit received by the defendant and not the damage sustained by the plaintiff it is not necessary to allege special damage.

CHAPTER VIII

DETINUE

§ 37. Scope.[7] The action of detinue seems to have lain, originally, only where a bailor, at the termination of the bailment, sued his bailee for the return of the chattel bailed, or for the value thereof in case the chattel itself could not be returned. Later the action was allowed against one who received it from the bailee's estate as legatee or next of kin, then against a sub-bailee, then against a finder and finally it was extended to all cases where the defendant wrongfully detained a chattel no matter how he obtained it. Because, as in debt on simple contract, a defendant might wage his law, detinue fell into disuse in England for many years, being replaced by trover.

If goods are bailed by A to B to the use of C, and B refuses to deliver to C the latter can maintain detinue against B. If at the time action is brought the plaintiff is not entitled to the possession of the chattel, or if the defendant never had possession, or without his fault is no longer in possession, detinue will not lie. Nor can it be maintained where the plaintiff's claim is not to specific property or where the chattel has no value.

§ 38. Essential allegations of the declaration.[8] The plaintiff should allege that the defendant detains a certain chattel or chattels "of the plaintiff," giving a description and the value and should demand that the property be turned over to him. It is no longer necessary to allege that the plaintiff bailed the chattel to the defendant even though there was a bailment in the particular case. The description of the property is essential so as to enable the defendant to prepare his defense and in order that it may be identified by the sheriff in case the plaintiff wins. The allegation of value is necessary so that in case the property cannot be found the court may be enabled, by proof of value under this allegation, to render a money judgment for the plaintiff.

CHAPTER IX

REPLEVIN

§ 39. Scope.[9] A landlord to whom rent was due and unpaid was allowed, by the English common law, to distrain on the tenant's chattels and impound them until the rent should be paid. This afforded an unscrupulous landlord the opportunity to oppress his tenant by dishonestly claiming that rent was due and distraining the tenant's work animals and farming implements at the planting or reaping season so that it would be less expensive for the tenant to pay the unjust exaction than to forego planting or reaping his crops. It was apparently to protect tenants against such oppressive acts on the part of landlords that the action of replevin was devised; but if it was originally limited to the redress of wrongful distress for rent it was later extended to all cases of the wrongful taking of chattels but not to cases of mere wrongful detention. But modern statutes have usually thus extended

7 16 **Am Jur**, Detinue, §§ 1–13.

8 16 **Am Jur**, Detinue, §§ 8–10.

9 46 **Am Jur**, Replevin, §§ 9–22.

it with the result that statutory replevin occupies the field of detinue as well as that of common-law replevin.

Since it was highly important that the tenant should have his work animals and farming implements during the seasons of plowing and reaping, it was provided that when the tenant brought replevin to get back the chattels which he claimed had been wrongfully distrained, the sheriff should take the distrained chattels from the landlord and return them to the tenant upon the latter's giving bond to litigate promptly with the landlord the lawfulness of the distress. When replevin was extended to all cases of wrongful taking the right to get back the chattels immediately was likewise extended as incident to the action itself. This characteristic makes replevin different from all the other common-law actions; if the defendant insists that the distress or other taking was not wrongful, he is in the position of a complaining party seeking to get back the chattels which the sheriff has taken from him and delivered to the plaintiff. In many states there are statutes providing that the defendant may, upon giving a counter bond, keep possession of the chattel during the litigation.

As has already been pointed out, a plaintiff in trespass de bonis asportatis or trover may recover even though his possession of the chattels had been wrongful as against a third person. Some jurisdictions apply this rule to replevin, but others have refused to do so, being reluctant to hold that at the very beginning of the litigation the property should be taken from the defendant and turned over to a plaintiff whose possession has been wrongful as against a third person.

Replevin will not lie for land, but it can be maintained for chattels wrongfully severed therefrom, unless the land is being held adversely to the plaintiff.

§ 40. Essential allegations of the declaration.[10] In an action of replevin for a wrongful taking the declaration should allege that the defendant has taken from the plaintiff certain chattels of the plaintiff, and has refused, upon demand, to return them to the plaintiff. In an action of replevin for a wrongful detention the declaration should allege that the defendant is in possession of certain chattels of the plaintiff and has refused, upon demand, to return them to the plaintiff. Under the allegations that the chattels were "of the plaintiff," the plaintiff may prove whatever interest in the chattels may be necessary to maintain the action. Unless provided otherwise by statute the declaration must allege that the property or at least a part of it, was, at the beginning of the action, within the county where action was brought.

The chattels must be described with sufficient particularity and certainty to enable the sheriff to identify them. And in some jurisdictions it is necessary to state the value of the chattels sued for.

CHAPTER X

ACCOUNT

§ 41. Scope and essential allegations of the declaration.[1] The action of account lay against fiduciaries—especially guardians, bailiffs and receivers—who were bound to render an account to their beneficiaries of moneys re-

[10] 46 **Am Jur**, Replevin, §§ 89–97.

[1] 1 **Am Jur**, Accounts and Accounting, § 13.

ceived by them in their fiduciary capacity but have refused to do so. Unless there was an express undertaking to account, the action could not be maintained by a joint tenant or tenant in common against his cotenant for taking more than his share of the rents and profits of the property; but by statute the action was later extended to such cases.

There were two distinct stages in the action; in the first the hearing was before the court and the sole issue was whether the defendant was bound to account to the plaintiff. If this issue was found in favor of the defendant the proceeding came to an end; but if in favor of the plaintiff the judgment rendered was that the defendant account. Then followed the second stage, the actual accounting which took place before auditors. The action was so dilatory and expensive that it was early superseded by a bill in equity for an accounting. Debt or indebitatus assumpsit came also to be allowed in those cases where the sole duty of the defendant fiduciary was to pay over money.

The declaration should allege that the defendant is bailiff, or guardian or other fiduciary of the plaintiff; that the defendant has received certain moneys, naming the persons from whom the moneys were received; that the defendant is under a duty to account to the plaintiff for these moneys, but has refused to do so.

CHAPTER XI

EJECTMENT

§ **42. History.**[2] In the early common law one who claimed a freehold interest in land—i. e., either an estate for life, an estate tail or a fee—could enforce that claim and be restored to his former enjoyment of the land by bringing a writ of right or some other of the old real actions. These actions were called "real" actions because the plaintiff, if successful, recovered the "res" or thing itself for which suit was brought, and were distinguished from personal actions in which the plaintiff recovered only a personal judgment that the defendant pay so much by way of damages. This explains why freehold interests in land came to be called "real" property while other interests in land and movable property came to be called "personal" property.

A term for years in land was not a freehold interest and if a lessee was dispossessed, either by his grantor or by a stranger, his sole remedy before the Statute of Westminster II was an action of covenant on the lease in which he could get only a judgment for damages. After that statute was passed the action of quare ejecit infra terminum was devised; this was maintainable by the lessee against his grantor and all claiming under him, and enabled him to get back possession—if his term had not expired—and damages. For a tenant who had been ousted by a stranger the action of ejectione firmae was later invented and expanded to all cases except where the grantor himself had ousted the tenant; it did not, however, give him back possession but merely damages. But the court of equity interfered and compelled the defendant to restore possession to the wrongfully ousted plaintiff; and the law courts, not to be outdone by equity, came to give judgment that the plaintiff recover possession of the land, and the writ of execution issued upon this judgment ordered the sheriff to turn over possession to him. The plaintiff was thus

[2] 18 Am Jur, Ejectment, §§ 4, 5.

awarded specific relief and the action thus developed came to be called ejectment.

The old real actions for the recovery of freehold interests in land were clumsy, dilatory and expensive; and as soon as courts gave specific relief to tenants for years in the action of ejectment, the next step was to adapt the new actions to cases where the plaintiff claimed a freehold interest and the right to possession. In order to accomplish this result it was necessary that a term for years be created and that the tenant for that term for years be ousted from possession. Consequently, if A claimed a freehold interest and the right to the possession of land in the possession of B, he entered upon the land with his friend X and while there he delivered to X a lease of the premises. X, having a term for years, was then ousted either by B or Y in ejectment. If he was ousted by Y, who came to be known as the casual ejector, and suit was brought against Y, there was danger that B might not know of it, so the courts required that in such circumstances A should notify B of the proceedings; B could then petition the court to be substituted for Y as defendant, which petition would be granted upon condition of his undertaking to indemnify Y against the expenses of the suit. The action then proceeded as an action by X against Y; the courts, however, did not fully recognize A as having been really in possession at the time the lease was executed or X as having been in possession at the time he was ousted by Y, but required X to show his title; this could be done only by showing the title and right to possession of his lessor A, so that in this indirect way the title and right to possession of A against B was put in issue and determined.

The next stage in the history of ejectment was reached about 1650 when, under Lord Chief Justice Rolle, the entry, lease and ouster became mere fictions; the declaration alleged them as facts and when B sought to be substituted as defendant instead of Y the court required him, as a condition of granting their permission, to agree that he would not deny the entry, lease and ouster at the trial but rely for his defense solely upon his title. B would thereupon be substituted and the title of the case would be X on the demise of A v. B. Within recent years statutes in several states have abolished the fictions connected with the action and have required the action to be brought in the name of the real claimant.

§ 43. Scope.[3] Ejectment can be maintained if the plaintiff is entitled to the immediate possession of land which is in the possession of the defendant. The usual case is one of complete possession by the defendant, but even where the plaintiff is only partially ousted, as, for example, by eaves or porches or windows projecting over his land or by wires strung across his land, the action will lie. So, if the plaintiff claims only the minerals under the land or a part of a building he may maintain ejectment. The mere fact that the plaintiff's claim to possession is subject to an easement does not bar him from recovery.

But if the plaintiff's claim is nonpossessory, as, for example, a reversionary right, an easement or a license, or other incorporeal hereditament the action is not maintainable; he must bring either case for the damage caused to his intangible right or a bill in equity.

If the plaintiff recovers judgment in ejectment that judgment entitles him only to be put into possession and to nominal damages. If he wishes to

3 18 **Am Jur**, Ejectment, §§ 7–51.

recover for the benefits received from the land by the defendant during his wrongful occupancy, he must bring a subsequent action of trespass for mesne profits.

§ 44. Essential allegations of the declaration.[4] Before the recent statutes simplifying the action it was necessary that the action be brought in the name of the lessee of the real plaintiff and that the declaration should allege the lease to him and the ouster. Under modern statutes the action is brought in the name of the real plaintiff and there is no allegation of lease or ouster. It is sufficient that the plaintiff allege generally that the land is his or that he is entitled to the possession of it, describing it, that the defendant is in possession and wrongfully withholds it from the plaintiff.

4 18 Am Jur, Ejectment, §§ 81–84.

TORTS

I. TRESPASS.

§ 1. *Accident.*
§ 2. *Mistake.*
§ 3. *Consent.*
§ 4. *Defense of self and others.*
§ 5. *Defense of property.*
§ 6. *Recovery of chattels.*
§ 7. *Recovery of land.*
§ 8. *Arrest without warrant.*
§ 9. *Acts of officer under judicial process.*
§ 10. *Same—privilege to resist service.*
§ 11. *Discipline.*
§ 12. *Trespass to the person to preserve the safety of the plaintiff or others.*
§ 13. *Trespass to property to save life or property or for public or private convenience.*
§ 14. *Trespass in the course of administering justice.*
§ 15. *Trespass ab initio.*

II. CONVERSION.

§ 16. *Excusable conversion—effect of return of chattel.*

III. FRAUD.

§ 17. *Nonactionable representations—intention as to price—"puffing"—price paid.*
§ 18. *Representations of law—negligent misrepresentations.*
§ 19. *Conduct of the plaintiff as a bar to relief—misrepresentations to X.*
§ 20. *Measure of damages.*

IV. NUISANCE AND SIMILAR WRONGS.

A. NUISANCE.

§ 21. *Culpability of defendant—contributory negligence of the plaintiff.*
§ 22. *Motive of defendant—spite fences—percolating waters.*
§ 23. *Joint actors—independent actors.*

B. DISTURBANCE OF PRIVATE EASEMENTS.

§ 24. *Easement of light and air and of way.*
§ 25. *Land occupier's right of access to public way.*

V. DAMAGE THROUGH NEGLIGENCE OR BY ACCIDENT.

A. THE DUTY TO USE CARE—LIABILITY AT PERIL.

§ 26. *Standard of care.*
§ 27. *Degrees of care—degrees of negligence.*
§ 28. *To whom the duty must be owed.*
§ 29. *Affirmative duty to act—duty of those who set or keep forces in motion.*
§ 30. *Duty of land occupiers toward travelers and adjoining land occupiers.*
§ 31. *Same—toward adult trespassers.*
§ 32. *Same—toward trespassing children.*
§ 33. *Same—toward licensee.*
§ 34. *Same—toward invited persons.*
§ 35. *Same—duty in regard to water or other substances escaping from land.*

CHAPTER I

TRESPASS

***For a brief statement of the scope and essential allegations in the declaration in Battery, Assault, Imprisonment, Trespass to Land and Trespass to Chattels, see ante, Forms of Action, Sections* 1-8.**

§ 1. Accident.[1] The most usual legal meaning of accident is an occurrence caused by a non-negligent defendant. In the very early law this was no excuse, the maxim "he that is damaged ought to be recompensed" being applied without reference to whether the defendant was in any way to blame for the occurrence; it was enough that the defendant's voluntary act caused the injury. Later accident was allowed as an excuse where the defendant could show affirmatively that it was utterly without his fault. The modern law is that accident is a defense in denial, the burden being on the plaintiff, whether he brings trespass or case, to show that the defendant acted either intentionally or negligently.

§ 2. Mistake.[2] In its more common legal meaning accident means the negation of intent and negligence; mistake exists where the defendant intended to bring about the result which is damaging to the plaintiff but did it because he acted under a misapprehension as to some material fact. Now that accident is generally a defense one might reasonably expect that a mistake made in good faith and without negligence would similarly be a defense to a tort action on the ground of no culpability, though of course no defense to an action in quasi contract for the reasonable value of any benefit received by the defendant. But such a development was impossible in so far as mistake as to title was concerned because trespass could then no longer be used to vindicate a disputed property right; and since no clear distinction was ever made, except by statute, between an action of trespass brought to enforce compensation for damage suffered and an action of trespass brought for vindication, the rule is well settled that mistake of title to land or chattels trespassed upon is no defense to the action. The law as to mistakes other than mistakes as to title has been in considerable confusion; an officer acting under judicial process is generally held liable if he arrests the wrong party, but in some other cases a non-negligent mistake has been held an excuse, for example, where defendant struck the plaintiff mistakenly thinking that the plaintiff had just struck him.

§ 3. Consent.[3] The general rule is that consent is a complete bar to an action of trespass following the maxim, "volenti non fit injuria," that is, the one who consents is not legally wronged. This applies to battery, assault, imprisonment and trespass to property. If a surgeon cuts off a patient's arm

[1] 52 **Am Jur,** Torts, § 20.
56 **Harv. L. R.** 72, Principles of Torts.
21 **Texas L. R.** 697, A Speculative Inquiry into the Nature of Torts.
17 **Tul. L. R.** 159, Tort Doctrine in Louisiana; The Materials for the Decision of a Case.
16 **Tul. L. R.** 489, Tort Doctrine in Louisiana; From What Sources Does It Derive?
22 **Neb. L. R.** 177, Principles of Torts.

[2] 4 **Am Jur,** Assault and Battery, § 40.
52 **Am Jur,** Trespass, §§ 12, 35.
52 **Am Jur,** Torts, § 20.
28 **Va. L. R.** 26, Advice of Counsel as a Defense.

[3] 52 **Am Jur,** Torts, § 94.
52 **Am Jur,** Trespass, § 39.
Civil liability growing out of mutual combat. 6 **ALR** 388-396; s. in 30 **ALR** 199-200; 47 **ALR** 1092.
Consent as condition of right to perform surgical operation. 76 **ALR** 562-571; s. in 139 **ALR** 1370-1375.
Character and extent of surgical opera-

or takes out his eye with his consent the trespass is excused; so, if the defendant walks across the plaintiff's land or carries away his chattels with the plaintiff's leave the plaintiff cannot recover. The consent need not be to a specific injury; thus, if one consents to play a game he consents to all acts done in accordance with the rules of the game. When consent has been obtained by fraud it is a defense to an action of trespass; the proper remedy is an action on the case for deceit, alleging and proving special damage.

Where a battery complained of by the plaintiff is part of a mutual affray and thus a violation of the criminal law because it is a breach of the peace, the better view is that consent is a bar to the action though of course no bar to a criminal prosecution by the state; but the weight of authority is that it is no bar so that either party may recover from the other. The only justification for the majority view is that giving an action is a greater deterrent to affrays than refusing it; this might happen if one party was pecuniarily responsible and the other not.

§ 4. Defense of self and others.[4] The privilege to defend one's self arises when one has been assaulted; one does not need to wait till the attempt to commit a battery has been successful. On the other hand mere threats or other provocation, such as calling one a thief or liar, gives no legal privilege to use force; the only effect of such provocation would be to reduce exemplary damages.

If the attack upon the defendant is not deadly, that is, does not put life in peril, he may stand his ground and oppose force to force; the force used must not only be reasonable and in proportion to the force used or about to be used by his assailant, but it must also be of a kind calculated to repel the attack; if the attack was made without a weapon it would not usually justify defending one's self by using a deadly weapon and maiming his assailant.

If the attack by the plaintiff is such as to imperil the defendant's life and he can defend himself only by killing his assailant or endangering his life, he must retreat if it is reasonably safe to do so; when retreat is not reasonably safe he may kill in order to save his own life. The doctrine of retreat does not apply if the defendant is in his own dwelling house.

If a person attacked uses unnecessary and excessive force in defending himself this does not forfeit his cause of action for the original attack but he becomes liable to the other party in an action of trespass for such excess. Where the attack was made by an animal belonging to the plaintiff the privilege of self-defense against the animal is greater because of the relatively less value of animal life.

The same amount and kind of force that may be used in defending one's self may be used by a husband to defend his wife, by a wife to defend her husband, by a parent to defend his child and by a child to defend his parent; the privilege probably extends to all near relatives. A servant may defend his master, and it has been contended that the privilege should be extended so as to include the defense of anyone, but this is not the prevailing view.

tion authorized by patient. 26 **ALR** 1036–1042; s. in 53 **ALR** 1056.

Right of seduced female to maintain action for seduction. 121 **ALR** 1487–1496.

4 4 **Am Jur,** Criminal Law, § 328.

21 **Texas L. R.** 17, Defense of Person and Property under Texas Criminal Law.

17 **Tul. L. R.** 60, Unlawful Aggression and Defense.

§ 5. **Defense of property.**[5] There is no privilege to take human life in defense of either land or chattels except when necessary to prevent an attack upon one's dwelling house or to prevent a felony of violence such as highway robbery; each of these is an extension of the privilege of self-defense.

If one sets spring traps in order to prevent a felony and a would-be felon is injured thereby there is no liability; but aliter if one who is rightfully on the land or one who is a mere trespasser is injured.

One may use force to resist an attempt to carry away his chattels; where the chattel is about to be carried away by plaintiff's animals the privilege is much greater and in extreme cases excuses the killing of the offending animal. One who sets traps for animals is excused for injuries inflicted therewith only if he might lawfully have inflicted such injuries by other means.

A person in the possession of land is entitled to use a reasonable amount of force to eject a trespasser, the force used being appropriate in kind and suitable in degree to accomplish the purpose. Generally the trespasser should be pushed or carried off; it is not proper to strike unless there is active resistance. Where the trespasser has entered forcibly there is no need to request him to depart, but aliter if he has entered peaceably.

There is no privilege to kill an animal merely because it is trespassing, but it may be driven from the land and a nonferocious dog may be used for that purpose.

Inanimate property may also be removed from land; for example, chattels left by an outgoing tenant may be stored or impounded by the landlord. Overhanging branches of trees do not constitute a trespass so that the owner of the trees does not acquire any easement by their being allowed to remain; they are a permissive nuisance which may be abated by cutting off the branches up to the boundary line.

§ 6. **Recovery of chattels.**[6] If the loss of possession is only momentary or if the former possessor makes immediate pursuit he has the same privilege to use force as he had when he was in possession to defend his possession.

But where possession has been entirely lost it is an unsettled and difficult question as to whether force may properly be used; the difficulty is in a large measure due to the differences between chattels, especially as to value, perishability and ease of concealment. In some states force may properly be used if plaintiff obtained it wrongfully; in others, if he obtained it by force; in still others no force is allowed even in such cases because it would tend to cause breaches of the peace.

If one can find his chattel in a public place he may retake it peaceably. Whether he may trespass upon the land of A in order to retake it depends upon how it came to be there; if he wrongfully left or placed it on A's land he may not enter to get it; if A will not give him permission and will not himself deliver it over he should bring replevin. But if the chattel is on A's land through A's fault the owner may enter to get it if he can do so peace-

[5] 52 **Am Jur**, Trespass, § 43.

Refusing admission to, or ejecting from, place of amusement. 30 **ALR** 951–964; s. in 60 **ALR** 1089–1091.

Domestic animal or fowl, liability for killing dog to protect. 10 **ALR** 689–697.

Liability for killing or injuring unlicensed or untagged dog. 145 **ALR** 993–997.

Officer's liability for killing or injuring animals, while acting, or professing to act, under a statute in relation to the inspection or destruction of live stock. 12 **ALR** 734–737.

Rights and remedies in case of encroachment of trees, shrubbery, or other vegetation across boundary line. 18 **ALR** 655–667; s. in 76 **ALR** 1111–1114; 128 **ALR** 1221–1223.

[6] 52 **Am Jur**, Trespass, § 42.

Liability for assault or trespass in forcibly retaking property sold conditionally. 9 **ALR** 1180–1189; s. in 105 **ALR** 926–932.

ably and is liable only for unnecessary damage which may be caused to A's property. If the goods have been carried on to A's land by a storm or other act of nature or by the felonious act of X the owner may enter to retake them, being liable for any damage caused to his property in the act of removal and being unable to hold X because the tort remedy against X is suspended by the felony. The same reasoning should apply if X's act was not felonious but the old cases are contra on the ground that the owner may in such a case recover at once against X.

§ 7. Recovery of land.[7] An early English statute made it a misdemeanor for one to take possession of land by force even if he was entitled to its possession and similar statutes are in force in every state. Courts have differed upon the question whether such statutes make forcible entry a tort as well as a crime; the present English law and better view is that it does not make the entry a tort. To compensate for taking away the right of forcible entry which existed at the early common law the statutes usually provide a speedy and summary remedy for getting possession in which a sheriff or constable effects the removal of the one in possession—usually a holdover tenant.

§ 8. Arrest without warrant.[8] The importance of apprehending at once those who have committed serious crimes and of preventing the commission of such crimes is such that arrests may under some circumstances be made without waiting to secure a warrant from a magistrate. Where a felony is about to be committed either an officer or private individual may arrest in order to prevent it. An officer may also arrest where there is reasonable ground for believing that a felony has been committed by some one and reasonable grounds for believing that the plaintiff committed it; a private individual may arrest when some one has actually committed a felony and there is reasonable grounds for believing that the plaintiff committed it.

A breach of the peace is a criminal assault and battery, a mutual affray or any other misdemeanor which tends to excite or alarm the public; either an officer or private citizen may arrest to stop a breach of the peace which is being committed in his presence or to prevent its renewal, but if it is entirely over a warrant must be procured. Flight from a lawful attempt to arrest does not defeat the privilege if pursuit be made at once and continued till the arrest is effected even though at that time the breach is over and there is no danger of its renewal. "Presence" does not require sight; it is enough if the person arresting heard the disturbance in an adjoining room. Where a private person makes an arrest he must with reasonable dispatch deliver him over to a peace officer or take him before a magistrate.

At common law there is no privilege to arrest without a warrant for other misdemeanors but by modern legislation police officers in large cities are allowed to arrest for vagrancy, for misdemeanors committed in their presence and upon mere suspicion of certain minor crimes.

7 22 **Am Jur**, Forcible Entry and Detainer §§ 3–13.

Right to use force to obtain possession of real property to which one is entitled. 141 **ALR** 250–276.

8 4 **Am Jur**, Arrest, §§ 22–51.

Right without judicial proceeding to arrest and detain one who is, or is suspected of being, mentally deranged. 10 **ALR** 488–494; s. in 45 **ALR** 1464, 1465.

Information, belief, or suspicion as to commission of felony, as justification for arrest by private person without warrant. 133 **ALR** 608–621.

48 **W. Va. L. R.** 207, Arrest without Warrant in West Virginia.

§ 9. Acts of officer under judicial process.[9] Judicial process is the written authority given by a court to its ministerial officers—sheriffs or constables—authorizing them to do certain acts such as to attach property or levy upon it or to make arrests. If the process is valid and the officer does as it directs he is protected though the person whom he arrests is later acquitted of the crime for which he was arrested or the property which he attaches is later released from the attachment because its owner was held not liable in the attachment suit.

Even though the process is not valid the officer is protected if it is fair on its face, that is, apparently valid. In order that process be fair on its face it must be (1) issued by a court having jurisdiction of the case; (2) be substantially in legal form; and (3) contain nothing on its face which shows that it is invalid.

The first requirement is satisfied if the court has general jurisdiction of the subject matter; the fact that the officer acted under an ordinance which did not take effect because of failure to publish it in a newspaper is a mere irregularity which does not make the officer liable. Where the jurisdiction of the court is based upon a statute which is later held to be unconstitutional some states hold that this is not a mere irregularity and that the officer is liable; other states excuse him on the ground that it is placing too heavy a burden upon the officer to take the risk of doubtful questions of constitutional law.

A warrant for arrest is not in legal form unless it contains the name of the person to be arrested or, if his name is not known, a description; putting in a fictitious name is usually held not sufficient. Process authorizing the seizure of property may either describe some specific property as in the case of replevin or ejectment; or it may direct the sheriff to levy upon the property of a certain individual without describing it, as in the case of an execution to satisfy an ordinary money judgment.

Where the process is fair on its face but the officer has been informed that it is defective there is a conflict of authority as to whether he should be protected in case he serves it and it turns out to be actually defective. If information that there was a defect were always infallible and hence equivalent to knowledge it would be just to hold the officer liable; but since the information may prove untrue it is the better view that the officer may disregard the information and follow the writ. In a state holding this view if the officer did not serve the writ and it turned out to be invalid he would be protected in not serving it but he would refuse at his peril.

§ 10. Same—privilege to resist service.[10] If process is not fair on its face the officer is of course liable even though he follows the process. He is also liable if he serves valid process upon the wrong person or property; the fact that he made the mistake reasonably and in good faith does not excuse him. Where he is in reasonable doubt he may demand an indemnity bond from the person who is having the process served so that if the process is invalid or should be served upon another person or property and he has to pay damages he may have a remedy over.

Wherever a person who is arrested or upon whom an attempt to arrest is

[9] 4 **Am Jur,** Arrest, §§ 5-16.
Liability for false arrest or imprisonment under a warrant as affected by mistake as to identity of person arrested. 127 **ALR** 1057-1066.
Right of officer to break into building to levy under execution. 57 **ALR** 210-221.

[10] **4 Am Jur, Arrest, §§ 73-92.**

made is entitled to recover in an action against the officer he may resist the officer just as if the latter did not purport to act under a warrant. But where the process is for the attachment of or levy upon property the weight of authority and better view is that if the officer acts reasonably and in good faith in serving the process there is no privilege to resist.

An officer is entitled to call upon anyone to assist him in the service of process; one who is thus called by a known officer is not liable if he acts in good faith even though the officer himself may be liable, because it would place too heavy a burden on the private citizen to take the risk of the officer acting wrongfully, especially where action must be immediate.

An officer may break into a dwelling house to serve criminal process but not to serve civil process; but once he is lawfully inside he may break an inner door if reasonably necessary to the performance of his duty. The officer must have the warrant in his possession at the time he makes an arrest.

§ 11. Discipline.[1] A parent may apply force by way of discipline to his children; a similar privilege may be exercised by a guardian over his ward, a master of a vessel over his mariners and by a teacher over his pupils. It may also be exercised by a captain of a ship over the passengers, but not by a master over an ordinary hired servant, or by husband over a wife. As to whether a teacher or other person standing in loco parentis must reasonably believe that punishment is necessary or whether it is sufficient that he act in good faith, there is conflict of authority. A captain of a ship may imprison a passenger if he thinks and has reasonable grounds for thinking that a mutiny is imminent and that the imprisonment is necessary to avert it.

As to the amount and degree of punishment it seems that the person administering the punishment must act reasonably and not merely in good faith; he cannot inflict death or great bodily harm. A teacher's authority begins when the child leaves home and continues till he returns; a pupil may be punished for an act done at home which is detrimental to the discipline of the school.

§ 12. Trespass to the person to preserve the safety of the plaintiff or others.[2] An insane person may not be imprisoned merely because he is insane; but if because of his insanity his own safety or that of others is endangered, he may be temporarily restrained till he can be handed over to the proper authorities.

A child left without protection and too young to protect himself may be taken charge of temporarily till his parents or guardian be found. A drunken man may be aroused from his stupor and assisted on his way even though such assistance leads to his arrest, if the defendant acted in good faith.

Where a person's life is in danger because of disease or injury and a surgical operation is performed in order to save his life, the defendant should be excused if he acted reasonably and there was no opportunity to obtain consent. And apparently one is justified in causing danger of bodily harm to some persons in order to avert the danger from a much greater number of others.

§ 13. Trespass to property to save life or property or for public or private convenience.[3] Where it is necessary to commit a trespass to property in order to save life or property from imminent danger of destruction the tres-

1 39 Am Jur, Parent and Child, §§ 13, 48–50.

2 52 Am Jur, Torts, §§ 87, 88, 93.

3 52 Am Jur, Torts, §§ 85, 87, 88.

pass is excused if it causes no damage. Even where such a trespass causes damage there is no liability therefor unless the direct and obvious effect of the trespass was to preserve the defendant's property in which case the defendant must probably pay for the damage thus intentionally caused.

Where a ship is in peril it is an excusable trespass to throw overboard a part or all of the cargo if reasonably necessary to save the lives of the persons on board; in such a case the loss is borne proportionally by all whose property was in danger, including the ship, if the remainder of the property is saved.

Where it is reasonably necessary to stop a conflagration buildings may be destroyed; logically the owner of such property should be able to recover contribution from the owners of the property thus saved from destruction but no relief is allowed probably because of the difficulty of determining just what property was saved thereby.

Where a public highway is obstructed a traveler may deviate upon the adjoining land if reasonably necessary; but this does not apply to deviating from a private way.

§ 14. Trespass in the course of administering justice.[4] For trespasses and other torts due to the violation by a judicial officer of purely ministerial duties, such as issuing an execution, the liability is similar to that of sheriffs and constables. Where the duty devolved is judicial instead of ministerial and the judicial officer acts within his jurisdiction there is no liability for errors or irregularities. There is a presumption that a superior court has acted within its jurisdiction but in the case of an inferior court jurisdiction must be affirmatively shown. Where the judge acts clearly beyond his jurisdiction he is liable without regard to his motive; but where the question of jurisdiction is one of doubt and difficulty the weight of authority is that a judge should be excused if the matter was colorably within his jurisdiction.

§ 15. Trespass ab initio.[5] Where consent has been given by a plaintiff to a trespass, such as entry upon land in his possession, which would otherwise be an actionable trespass, misconduct after such entry will make the defendant liable therefor, but does not make the original act wrongful. Where, however, the entry or other trespass has been done under authority of law—such as the privilege of a traveler to be entertained at an inn or the seizure of property by an officer under judicial process—and the authority is later abused, the defendant is liable not only for the abuse of authority, but also for the original trespass; this is called the doctrine of trespass ab initio. It seems to be unsettled whether the abuse must consist of positive acts or may consist of mere omission. There seems to be no justification for the doctrine at the present day and it should be abolished.

CHAPTER II

CONVERSION

For a brief statement of the scope of Conversion, see ante, Forms of Action, Sections 9, 10.

§ 16. Excusable conversion—effect of return of chattel.[6] Most of the instances of excusable conversion are cases of emergencies, for example, throw-

4 52 Am Jur, Trespass, § 41.

5 52 Am Jur, Trespass, §§ 19, 20.

6 53 Am Jur, Trover and Conversion, §§ 114-116.

ing goods overboard in a storm in order to save the lives of passengers on a ship, or selling perishable property of a deceased soldier.

A return of the property after conversion does not cure the tort unless the plaintiff receives it back in full satisfaction of his claim; otherwise it goes merely in mitigation of damages. And the weight of authority is that an unaccepted tender of the goods will not mitigate damages.

CHAPTER III

FRAUD

For a brief statement of the scope of Fraud, see ante, Forms of Actions, Section 14.

§ 17. Nonactionable representations—intention as to price—"puffing"—price paid.[7] Where parties stand in the relation of vendor and purchaser and deal on an equal footing some representations are regarded as not actionable though all the essentials of deceit are present. If a vendor should falsely represent that he did not intend to take less than a certain price or a purchaser that he did not intend to give more than a certain price, such representation would not be actionable even though made with intent to deceive. And representations made by a vendor by way of puffing his wares fall within the nonactionable class for the same reason, namely, that it is "understood the world over, that such statements are to be distrusted."

The exception of "puffing" or "seller's talk" does not, by the weight of authority and the better view, cover false statements as to price paid at a previous sale or as to rental or as to cost of manufacturing. Nor does it apply where the parties have not dealt on an equal footing, as, for example, when the facts are peculiarly within the defendant's knowledge, or where the defendant has thrown the plaintiff off his guard. And apparently the plaintiff can deprive the defendant of the privilege of puffing by expressly telling him that he will rely on the defendant's judgment and not on his own.

§ 18. Representations of law—negligent misrepresentations.[8] It is usually stated to be the rule that an action for deceit will not be sustained for a false representation of law because "every one is presumed to know the law" and therefore the plaintiff could not have relied upon the representation. The phrase quoted above seems to have originated in the unfortunate decision of Lord Ellenborough in Bilbie v. Lumley where it was decided that one who had paid money in ignorance of law could not recover it back, because "every

7 23 **Am Jur**, Fraud and Deceit, §§ 27–34.

Fraud of vendee or buyer inducing vendor or seller to accept less favorable terms as sustaining an action in tort. 52 **ALR** 1153–1160.

Misrepresentation as regards validity of conveyance or transfer of property as fraud. 9 **ALR** 1051–1064.

Validity and effect of stipulation to the effect that vendee or purchaser does not rely upon representations of vendor or seller, or the latter's agent. 10 **ALR** 1472–1480.

Fraudulent misrepresentation or concealment by a contracting party concerning title to property or other subjects which are matters of public record. 33 **ALR** 853–1161.

Opportunity of buyer of personal property to ascertain facts as affecting claim of fraud on part of seller in misrepresenting property. 61 **ALR** 492–548.

Dealings between seller and buyer after latter's knowledge of former's fraud as waiver of claim for damages on account of fraud. 106 **ALR** 172–181.

18 **Notre Dame Lawyer,** 331, Contributory Negligence as a Defense to an Action for Fraud.

8 23 **Am Jur**, Fraud and Deceit, §§ 45, 126–128, 165.

42 **Harv. L. R.** 733, Misrepresentation as Deceit, Negligence, or Warranty.

man must be taken to be cognizant of the law; otherwise there is no saying to what extent the excuse of ignorance might be carried. It would be urged in almost every case." Lord Ellenborough evidently regarded the statement that "every man must be taken to be cognizant of the law" as substantially the equivalent of the maxim that ignorance of the law does not excuse. It has been pointed out repeatedly, both by courts and text writers, that the maxim implies delinquency of some sort—like the commission of a crime or tort or the breach of a contract—and cannot properly apply to one who has done no wrong but merely seeks redress for a wrong committed upon him.

That the rule is unpopular is shown by the willingness of the courts to make exceptions to it. If the parties are not on an equal footing or if the plaintiff is thrown off his guard relief is usually given; and representations of ownership are usually treated as representations of fact.

Where the defendant causes damage to the plaintiff by negligent misrepresentations he should be held liable therefor upon principles of negligence.

§ 19. Conduct of the plaintiff as a bar to relief—misrepresentations to X.[9] It is sometimes broadly stated that the failure of the plaintiff to use ordinary care to discover the falsity of the defendant's representations is a bar to legal relief. Thus stated the rule is open to two just criticisms: (1) Since deceit is an intentional tort, it is illogical to allow what is practically contributory negligence to be a defense and (2) that it ought to be the policy of the law to protect the weak and credulous—to protect the fool against the knave.

There is a class of cases, however, where it is arguable that the plaintiff should be barred, not exactly because of contributory negligence, but on the ground that he cannot be believed when he says that he believed—namely, where the facts were open to his immediate observation, where the parties were on an equal footing and the plaintiff was not thrown off his guard. But even this suggestion is open to the criticism that if the defendant actually intended to deceive, he should not be allowed to say to the plaintiff that the latter was a fool to believe him even if the facts were obvious.

A failure to observe the distinction between immediate observation and later investigation is no doubt responsible for much of the confusion on the subject. If a somewhat extended investigation is necessary to detect the falsity the tendency is to give relief. And whether the rule be stated narrowly or broadly, relief will be given to a plaintiff where he was thrown off his guard or where the parties were on an unequal footing.

Where defendant causes damage to plaintiff by making misrepresentations to X the defendant is ordinarily held liable therefor.

§ 20. Measure of damages.[10] If A sells B a chattel for $300 under a contract of warranty which, if fulfilled, would make the chattel worth $450, but the chattel is actually worth only $200, B is obviously entitled, in an action for breach of the contract of warranty, to a judgment for the difference between $200, the actual value, and $450, the value of the chattel if A's contract of warranty had been performed. If, however, there is substituted for the warranty in the above hypothetical case a fraudulent representation which, if it had been true would have made the chattel worth $450 and A brings an action on the case for deceit, it is obvious that he should logically be entitled to a judgment only for the difference between $200, the actual

[9] 24 **Am Jur,** Fraud and Deceit, § 206.

[10] 52 **Am Jur,** Torts, §§ 217–238.

value of the chattel and $300, the amount he paid for it. Even though he might not have bought the chattel if the representations, if true, would have made it worth only $300 instead of $450, yet the amount he has actually parted with because of the misrepresentation is only the $100 and not the $250; in other words, he should not be entitled to recover, in a deceit action, the loss of prospective profits, but merely the property loss.

A failure to keep the above distinction clearly in mind has in many states led to the erroneous results of holding A liable in a deceit action for the $250.

CHAPTER IV

NUISANCE AND SIMILAR WRONGS

For a brief statement of the subjects of Nuisance and the Disturbance of Easements, see ante, Forms of Action, Sections 15, 16.

A. Nuisance

§ 21. Culpability of defendant—contributory negligence of plaintiff.[1] Liability for private nuisance dates back to a time when apparently all tort liability was absolute, not dependent upon any culpability or blameworthiness on the part of the defendant: "He that is damaged ought to be recompensed." This liability at peril has very largely persisted where injuries to property rather than injuries to the person have been concerned, irrespective of the form of action involved. Hence a defendant may be liable for the creation of a nuisance though done without his knowledge or consent by an independent contractor who has been carefully selected. Where, however, the defendant is a vendee of land upon which a nuisance has been already created he becomes liable only upon principles of negligence, being entitled to a reasonable opportunity to abate the nuisance after knowledge of its existence. But the defendant is not entitled to notice merely because the erection did not become a nuisance till after plaintiff bought and went into possession of his land.

Where the damage caused to the plaintiff by a nuisance is purely personal —having no reference to any injured land—such as injuries to the health of persons having no property interests affected by the nuisance, there is a square conflict of authority as to whether the defendant's liability is at peril or only for negligence.

Where the plaintiff could, by the exercise of ordinary care, have averted damage to himself he will ordinarily be barred from recovery.

§ 22. Motive of defendant—spite fences—percolating waters.[2] Since an easement of light and air may be acquired by prescription in England and the only way of preventing its being thus acquired is by erecting a structure which

1 39 **Am Jur**, Nuisances, §§ 16, 200.
Landlord's liability for damage to property of third person by operations of tenant. 53 **ALR** 327–340.
Liability of purchaser of premises for nuisance thereon created by predecessor. 14 **ALR** 1094–1116.
Contributory negligence as defense against liability for damage from nuisance. 57 **ALR** 7–17.
56 **Harv. L. R.** 772, Nuisances from Land in Its Natural Condition.
37 **Ill. L. R.** 1, Liability for Nuisance.
20 **Tex. L. R.** 399, Nuisance without Fault.

2 39 **Am Jur**, Nuisances, §§ 23, 61.
Spite fences and other spite structures. 133 **ALR** 691–720.
29 **Calif. L. R.** 1, Protection in Means of Diversion of Ground—Water Supplies.
21 **Oreg. L. R.** 113, Analysis of Concepts of Subflow and Percolating Waters.

will shut off the light and air, the erection of any structure for this purpose is permissible; the motive for such erection can be no bar because it is a beneficial use of the property to prevent the acquisition of an easement over it.

In the United States an easement of light and air cannot be acquired by prescription; but on the question of the validity of a structure which is of no beneficial use to the one erecting it, but has been erected from motives of spite, revenge, intimidation, etc., there is a conflict of authority. In some jurisdictions statutes have been passed making unlawful the building of such structures beyond a certain height, and such statutes have been held constitutional. If such structures are held unlawful either with or without a statute, equity will usually enjoin their erection or decree their removal, just as in other cases of private nuisance.

A similar situation exists as to malicious interference with percolating waters. English courts deny relief on the ground that a landowner has an absolute right to the percolating waters which he can intercept in his land and is not liable to an adjoining proprietor, regardless of the quantity of water taken, or the purpose to which it is applied. In this country, by the weight of authority, relief is given against such malicious interference upon the same principles that underlie the spite-fence cases.

§ 23. Joint actors—independent actors.[3] Where a nuisance is caused by several persons intentionally co-operating, each is liable for all the damage done and they may be sued separately or together either at law or in equity. Where, however, the nuisance is caused by several persons acting independently of each other, each is liable at law only for his share of the damage, and apparently each should be sued separately. And this liability exists even though the separate act of each one did not amount to a nuisance; in this latter situation, however, it has been held that the actors must be sued jointly and not separately.

B. Disturbance of Private Easements

§ 24. Easement of light and air and of way.[4] Easements of light and air are quite common in England because they can there be acquired by prescription. This part of the English common law was rejected in the United States as inapplicable to a new country, and easements of light and air by grant are comparatively rare. The mere fact that an action at law will lie for interference with such an easement is not a sufficient reason for an injunction; but the equitable remedy is the one nearly always sought.

One whose private right of way is obstructed is entitled to an action at law for damages, but here also the relief usually sought is an injunction against either an actual or threatened obstruction. Where the obstruction has been caused independently by several defendants the plaintiff is entitled to an action against each one for his share of the damage thus caused.

§ 25. Land occupier's right of access to public way.[5] If the owner of land adjoining a public way owns to the middle of the way, one in the possession of the land may maintain an action of trespass for the use of that part of the way in a manner not authorized by the public easement. But if the fee of the way is in the municipality, the adjoining land occupier has only an easement of access to the way. If this easement is obstructed he is entitled

[3] 39 Am Jur, Nuisances, § 38.

[4] 17 Am Jur, Easements, §§ 114–119.

[5] 38 Am Jur, Negligence, §§ 29–36.

to recover in an action on the case for the damage caused by such obstruction.

Apparently the land occupier has not only a right of access to the adjacent street but also a right to an unobstructed view of the street.

CHAPTER V

DAMAGE THROUGH NEGLIGENCE OR BY ACCIDENT

For a brief statement of the subject of Negligence, see ante, Forms of Action, Section 17.

A. THE DUTY TO USE CARE—LIABILITY AT PERIL

§ 26. Standard of care.[6] Assuming that there is a duty to use care, the question arises as to how much care the law requires. The law on this point as to sane adults is well settled that the standard is that amount and kind of care which the man of ordinary prudence would use under similar circumstances. The standard is thus an artificial, external, objective one; this is justified on the ground that since neither the plaintiff nor the defendant can properly insist that his own standard of care be adopted, the best way to deal with the matter is to ignore the subjective capacity of each person and set up an ideal standard. There is this advantage in the objective over the subjective standard in that it entitles one to assume, in the absence of reasonable notice to the contrary, that the person with whom he deals or is thrown in contact will exercise this objective standard or be responsible for the consequences.

As to the standard required of children, it is not clear whether the test is subjective or objective; some of the decisions seem to say that the capacity

6 38 **Am Jur,** Negligence, §§ 29–42.

Custom as a standard of care. 68 **ALR** 1400–1464.

Admissibility, upon issue of negligence, of evidence of custom or practice of others. 137 **ALR** 611–621.

Liability of private, noncharitable hospital or sanitarium for improper care or treatment of patients. 22 **ALR** 341–359; s. in 39 **ALR** 1431–1436; 124 **ALR** 186–215.

Physicians and surgeons: standard of skill and care required of specialist. 59 **ALR** 1071–1074.

Duty of physician or surgeon to advise patient of the possibility or probability if better results from treatment by specialist or by a mode of treatment which he is not qualified to give. 132 **ALR** 392–404.

Liability of surgeon leaving sponge or other foreign matter in incision. 65 **ALR** 1023–1033.

Duty and liability of physician or surgeon in pregnancy and childbirth cases. 141 **ALR** 111–170.

Duty and liability of dentist to patient. 69 **ALR** 1142–1166; s. in 129 **ALR** 101–130.

"Emergency rule" as applied to automobile or motorcycle drivers. 6 **ALR** 680–689; s. in 27 **ALR** 1197–1208; 79 **ALR** 1277–1304; and 111 **ALR** 1019–1038.

Liability for killing or injuring live stock or fowls in highway by automobile. 11 **ALR** 1405–1407.

Liability for injury to pedestrian struck by automobile as affected by his blindness, deafness, or other physical disability. 62 **ALR** 578–585.

Youth of operator of automobile as affecting his negligence or contributory negligence. 73 **ALR** 1277–1278.

Size or weight of automobile or load involved in accident as factor in determining responsibility. 85 **ALR** 1173–1175.

Distraction of attention of driver of automobile as affecting question of negligence, wantonness, etc., or contributory negligence. 120 **ALR** 1513–1521.

Liability for injury to child playing on or in proximity to automobile. 1 **ALR** 1385–1387; s. in 44 **ALR** 434–435.

Automobiles: cutting corners as negligence. 6 **ALR** 321–327; s. in 115 **ALR** 1178–1184.

Fact that driver of automobile is blinded by glare of light as affecting liability for automobile accident. 10 **ALR** 294–295; s. in 32 **ALR** 887–888; 41 **ALR** 1040–1042; and 62 **ALR** 1531–1534.

Impairment of driver's view through windshield as affecting liability for automobile accident. 10 **ALR** 299.

Existence and condition of lights on automobile as affecting right of owner or operator to recover for negligence. 14 **ALR** 794–796; s. in 40 **ALR** 1243–1246; 113 **ALR** 1260–1267.

41 **Harv. L. R.** 1, Negligence—subjective or objective.

29 **Harv. L. R.** 801, Liability without Fault.

39 **Harv. L. R.** 849, Negligence, Inadvertence and Indifference; the Relation of Mental States to Negligence.

42 **Col. L. R.** 1147, Custom and Negligence.

and experience, as well as the age of the individual child is to be taken into consideration; others take the view that the child should exercise that amount and degree of care which a prudent child of his age would exercise under similar circumstances. For the purpose of determining the standard of care the age at which one becomes an adult is apparently less than 21 years. As far as the question of contributory negligence is concerned a person under mental disability is apparently treated in the same way as a child.

The rule as to infirm persons seems to be that the infirmity is to be taken into consideration as one of the circumstances. The result of this is twofold; a person with an infirmity must generally use greater care because thereof; but if he finds himself without negligence in a position of peril, he cannot be held chargeable with failure to use that amount and kind of care which a person without such infirmity could use. For example, a blind man who is about to cross a street must use greater care than one who can see; but if he does use the proper care, and is unexpectedly placed in peril, he is not required to use the same amount and kind of care which a prudent person with normal eyesight would use.

The above reasoning would apply, apparently, to one who, without his fault, is intoxicated; but where the intoxication is culpable it does not in any way excuse him and furthermore is in itself evidence of lack of care.

Where the circumstances are such as to call for special skill and the defendant professes to have such skill, a failure to use it is negligence; but if he does not pretend to have such skill, he incurs no such professional responsibility.

§ 27. Degrees of care—degrees of negligence.[7] In the law of bailments the degrees of care to be used by bailees is usually stated to be as follows: if the bailment is for the benefit of both bailee and bailor, as in the case where a chattel is let for hire, the bailee is bound to use ordinary care; if the bailment is for the benefit of the bailor alone, as in the case of a gratuitous deposit for safekeeping, the bailee is bound to use only slight care; while if the bailment is for the use of the bailee alone, as in the case of a gratuitous loan for use, the bailee is bound to use extraordinary care. This classification and nomenclature were imported from the civil law into the common law of bailments and attempts have been made to use the distinctions in our law of torts, but without success. As already pointed out, the standard of care in torts is that of the man of ordinary prudence under similar circumstances, the degrees of care in fact being infinite, but only one degree of care in law.

The term "gross negligence" is used in the law of bailments to indicate that the bailee without benefit has not used even the slight care which is required of him; i. e., it is said that he is liable only for gross negligence. The term gross negligence is thus used merely to indicate the degree of care required in the particular kind of bailment. As used in the common law of torts the term means that the defendant has fallen far short of the amount and kind of care required by law; but since his liability is the same whether his default is small or great, the term becomes merely one of description and not of definition; or, as has been frequently said, the term gross as applied to

7 38 **Am Jur**, Negligence, §§ 43–48.

Test or criterion of gross negligence or other misconduct that will support recovery of exemplary damages for bodily injury or death unintentionally inflicted. 98 **ALR** 267–280.

What amounts to gross or wanton negligence in driving an automobile precluding the defense of contributory negligence. 38 **ALR** 1424–1426; s. in 72 **ALR** 1357–1359; 92 **ALR** 1367–1372; 119 **ALR** 654–656.

negligence is only a vituperative epithet.

In statutes where the term "gross negligence" is used it is generally held to indicate a serious and not merely a slight failure to exercise the amount and kind of care required by the common law, so that where a statute provides that one shall not be liable unless he is chargeable with gross negligence it is not sufficient to show merely that he did not exercise the care of a man of ordinary prudence.

§ 28. **To whom the duty must be owed.**[8] If A intentionally and without excuse strikes at B and hits C it has been held that C may recover against A for the battery though there was no intent or negligence as to C. C is thus allowed to take advantage of the unlawful intent to strike B. If, however, A was acting negligently as to B and without negligence or intent as to C should strike C the question is more difficult. If the duty to use care must always be owed to the plaintiff it is obvious that C cannot recover.

Where the injury to the plaintiff has been caused by the defendant's bringing active force to bear against him, the question has rarely arisen except in the following kind of cases. A child is on a railroad track and a train is about to run over it due to the negligence of the servants of the railroad; a bystander at quite a distance from the track sees the child and attempts to save it; he succeeds but in so doing is himself injured. There is no difficulty about causation because the injury is direct and immediate; nor is there any difficulty about contributory negligence or assumption of risk because we will assume that he used due care under the circumstances and it is well settled that one may properly assume considerable risk in order to save human life; but if the bystander was very far away from the track at the moment he saw the peril, in what way is there negligence to him? The answer to this is that it is so probable that some one will attempt to save a person thus imperilled that there is a duty not only towards the person in danger but also towards one who seeks to extricate him from the danger. Where property is in peril of negligent injury there would seem to be likewise a duty towards one who properly endeavors to rescue the property. On this point, however, there is conflict of authority, some cases holding that the value of property being much less than that of human life, a person is not warranted in risking his own life to save it from destruction.

The doctrine that the duty must be owed to the plaintiff is frequently applied in what may be called quasi tort cases, where the plaintiff relies upon a positive duty, such as a duty of a land occupier to keep his premises in repair; in such cases it is well settled that the plaintiff must show that he is the person to whom the duty must be owed—for example, that he is a person invited on business; even though the defendant has allowed the premises to get out of repair so that a business visitor might have recovered, if injured, this will not enable a plaintiff to recover if he is, for example, a trespasser on the defendant's property.

§ 29. **Affirmative duty to act—duty of those who set or keep forces in motion.**[9] By the better view there is no duty, apart from statute, to act affirmatively to prevent damage to others.

8 38 **Am Jur,** Negligence, §§ 37–41.
Liability for death of, or injury to, one seeking to rescue another. 19 **ALR** 4–35.
Failure or delay in sounding crossing signals as affecting liability of railroad company to persons not crossing or about to cross track. 66 **ALR** 811–834.
Rescue, proximate cause of injury to one in seeking to rescue another. See 19 **ALR** 13.

9 38 **Am Jur,** Negligence, § 42.
Duty and liability in respect of sagging

Those who set or keep forces in motion must take ordinary care to prevent such forces from injuring the persons or property of others. This ap-

of electric wire maintained over highway. 84 **ALR** 690–708.

Liability of gas company for injury or damage by escaping gas. 25 **ALR** 262–304; s. in 29 **ALR** 1250–1258; 47 **ALR** 488–494; 90 **ALR** 1082–1108; 138 **ALR** 870–915.

Liability of one maintaining high tension electric wires over private property of another for injuries thereby inflicted. 14 **ALR** 1023–1044; s. in 56 **ALR** 1021–1035.

When automobile is under control. 28 **ALR** 952–960.

Liability for death or injury as result of suction from passing train. 149 **ALR** 907–929.

Liability of railroad company for failing to aid in extinguishing fire set by its engine without negligence. 3 **ALR** 509–515.

Injury to passenger because of lateral space left between station platform and cars. 4 **ALR** 286–298.

Duty of railroad company to maintain flagman at crossing. 16 **ALR** 1273–1286; s. in 71 **ALR** 1160–1177.

State of weather as affecting liability for injury to one struck by train or streetcar. 20 **ALR** 1064–1079.

Failure of signaling device at crossing to operate as affecting liability of railroad for injury. 53 **ALR** 973–985; s. in 99 **ALR** 729–738.

Duty of railroad to maintain gates, gongs, or other safety devices at crossings. 60 **ALR** 1096–1118.

Liability of railroad company where fence or cattle guard becomes ineffective because of snow. 26 **ALR** 679–686.

Liability of a railroad for personal injury and property damage caused by frightening horses. 61 **ALR** 1078–1138.

Liability of railroad company for injury to trespassers or licensees other than employees or passengers struck by object projecting, or thrown, from passing train. 112 **ALR** 850–865.

Duty to run a streetcar or train at a speed that will not prevent its being stopped within the distance covered by its own lights. 29 **ALR** 1045–1053.

Sufficiency as to type of cattle guards at public or private crossings. 75 **ALR** 936–950.

Failure to fence as rendering railroad company liable for damage to or by live stock after leaving right of way. 24 **ALR** 1057–1065.

Duty to guard against danger to children by electric wires. 17 **ALR** 833–857; s. in 41 **ALR** 1337–1345; 49 **ALR** 1053–1057; 100 **ALR** 621–654.

Liability for death of or injury to prisoner. 46 **ALR** 94–116; s. in 50 **ALR** 268; 61 **ALR** 569–572.

Right or duty to turn in violation of law of road to avoid traveler, or obstacle. 24 **ALR** 1304–1317; s. in 63 **ALR** 277–285; 113 **ALR** 1328–1337.

Liability for injuring one engaged about an automobile in highway. 25 **ALR** 134–139; s. in 34 **ALR** 1513–1516; 61 **ALR** 1159–1171.

Liability for injury to pedestrian colliding with side of automobile. 25 **ALR** 1513–1516.

Liability for injuries due to collision between streetcar and automobile at street intersection. 28 **ALR** 217–295; s. in 46 **ALR** 1000–1056.

Liability for injury incident to towing automobile. 30 **ALR** 750–754.

Duty of driver of automobile whose view is obscured by dust, smoke, or atmospheric conditions. 37 **ALR** 587–597; s. in 73 **ALR** 1020–1028.

Liability for injury by automobile to child playing ball in the street. 44 **ALR** 1304–1306.

Reciprocal duty of driver of automobile and person working on highway. 47 **ALR** 807–811.

Liability of owner of motor vehicle for injury to person who has alighted from or is waiting for streetcar. 47 **ALR** 1233–1265; s. in 123 **ALR** 791–843.

Right of way as between vehicles in street or highway and vehicles approaching from private driveway. 50 **ALR** 283–285.

Duty in operating automobile at curve or on hill. 57 **ALR** 589–596.

Automobile crossing street at a point other than a street intersection. 57 **ALR** 1106–1108.

Liability for damage or injury by skidding motor vehicle. 58 **ALR** 264–287; s. in 113 **ALR** 1002–1055.

Driving automobile at a speed which prevents stopping within length of vision as negligence. 44 **ALR** 1403–1407; s. in 58 **ALR** 1493–1495; 87 **ALR** 900–905; 97 **ALR** 546–552.

Physical defect, illness, or drowsiness of operator of automobile as affecting liability for injury. 64 **ALR** 136–140; s. in 138 **ALR** 1388–1397.

Emission of smoke or steam from private premises, or existence of other conditions thereon, as ground of liability of owner or occupant for results of an automobile accident in the highway. 150 **ALR** 371–398.

Injury to one while coasting in street. 20 **ALR** 1433–1441; s. in 109 **ALR** 941–949.

Right of way at street or highway intersection. 21 **ALR** 974–999; s. in 37 **ALR** 493–527; 47 **ALR** 595–635.

Reciprocal duties of drivers of automobiles or other vehicles proceeding in the same direction. 24 **ALR** 507–518; s. in 47 **ALR** 703–720; 62 **ALR** 970–986; and 104 **ALR** 485–545.

Injury by road vehicle to person on sidewalk. 1 **ALR** 840–856; s. in 75 **ALR** 559–577.

Automobiles: effect of defective brakes on liability for injury. 14 **ALR** 1339–1341; s. in 63 **ALR** 398–404.

Automobiles: duty at private crossing or driveway. 24 **ALR** 946–950.

Rights and duties at intersection of arterial (or other favored) highway and nonfavored highway. 58 **ALR** 1197–1208; s. in 81 **ALR** 185–195.

Liability for injury to person who, after falling in street, is struck by automobile. 62 **ALR** 1339–1341.

Liability for collision between streetcar and vehicle driven ahead of or toward it along or close to the track. 63 **ALR** 10–76; s. in 102 **ALR** 716–747.

Right of way of vehicle carrying policeman. 65 **ALR** 140–143.

Liability for injury to pedestrian who

plies not only when the persons or property are where they have a right to be, for example, on the public highway, but also when they are wrongfully where they are, provided the persons setting or keeping the force in motion knew of their proximity. Furthermore, if their presence is to be reasonably anticipated, for example, at street or railroad crossings in cities or villages, there is a duty to use reasonable care to look out for them.

In many jurisdictions there are statutes defining what shall be done under certain circumstances, for example, it is frequently provided that when a locomotive engine shall approach a public crossing the bell shall be rung, or the whistle sounded at a certain distance before crossing.

The duty in regard to setting or keeping forces in motion extends to all cases of active conduct. Thus, if one knows he is afflicted with a contagious disease, such as smallpox, he must use ordinary care not to communicate the disease to others; since his physical condition itself is actively dangerous to those who are close to him, he must keep away from other persons, and if they approach him, he must notify them of the fact so that they may protect themselves. Similar reasoning applies to owners of animals having a contagious disease. Upon principle it would seem that there ought to be a duty upon every one to use ordinary care to find out whether he has a contagious disease.

It would seem that the maintenance of live electric wires should be classified as active conduct but on this point there is a conflict of authority.

§ 30. Duty of land occupiers toward travelers and adjoining land occupiers.[10] While a land occupier does not owe persons using the adjacent

suddenly darts or steps into path of automobile. 65 **ALR** 192–215; s. in 113 **ALR** 528.

Liability for injury or damage resulting from starting of parked automobile without interference of third persons. 66 **ALR** 439–448.

Liability for injury to pedestrian struck by automobile while traveling along street or highway. 67 **ALR** 96–118; s. in 93 **ALR** 551–570.

Liability for damage or injury while automobile is being backed. 67 **ALR** 647–667; s. in 118 **ALR** 242–259.

Liability for injury in collision with automobile standing on wrong side of street or highway. 70 **ALR** 1021–1028.

Overcrowding motor vehicle or riding in unusual position thereon as affecting liability for injury or damage. 104 **ALR** 312–339.

Negligence or contributory negligence in failing to set out flares or lights or station person to warn of motor vehicle stopped on or adjacent to highway. 111 **ALR** 1516–1521.

Liability for injury to person or damage to property from stone or other object on surface of highway thrown by or from passing vehicle. 115 **ALR** 1498–1504.

Collision between automobiles on bridge or approach thereto. 118 **ALR** 1196–1203.

Stopping vehicle on traveled portion of highway as affecting responsibility for collision between vehicles. 131 **ALR** 562–608.

Accelerating speed to prevent car behind from passing. 134 **ALR** 627–629.

Right of way at street or highway intersections as dependent upon or independent of care or negligence. 89 **ALR** 838–840; s. in 136 **ALR** 1497–1499.

Excessive speed of automobile as proximate cause of accident where it or colliding vehicle is on wrong side of road. 77 **ALR** 598–610.

Duty of operator of motor vehicle as affected by barrier placed to indicate that street is closed or undergoing repairs. 78 **ALR** 525–529.

Liability for injury by motor vehicle to one in street directing traffic. 92 **ALR** 1518–1523.

Condition of tires as affecting liability for automobile accident. 79 **ALR** 1218–1221.

11 **Geo. Wash. L. R.** 1. Tort Liability under the Wartime Car Sharing Plan.

10 38 **Am Jur**, Negligence, §§ 129, 130.

Liability of one excavating on his own premises for resulting injury to adjoining building. 56 **ALR** 486–526; s. in 59 ALR 1252–1253.

Liability of abutting owner for injury from ice formed on sidewalk by the discharge of rain or melted snow due to artificial conditions on his premises. 34 **ALR** 409–422.

Liability for injury to person in street by fall of part of structure of completed building. 7 **ALR** 204–215; s. in 138 **ALR** 1078–1097.

Liability of abutting owner or occupant for condition of sidewalk. 41 **ALR** 212–226; s. in 93 **ALR** 799–805.

Liability of owner or occupant for condition of covering over opening or vault in sidewalk. 62 **ALR** 1067–1100.

Liability of adjoining property owner for injury to one deviating from highway or frequented path. 14 **ALR** 1397–1420.

Right of excavating landowner to recover from adjoining owner amount expended by highway any positive duty to keep the highway in front of his premises in repair and in safe condition for travel, he does owe a duty to guard an excavation on his own land which he makes so close to the sidewalk as to render it dangerous to those who are reasonably using the highway. So, if there is a wire fence along the highway, he is under a duty towards travelers to maintain it in a safe condition.

A land occupier making an excavation on his premises must use ordinary care to avoid injury to his neighbor's buildings or land. So, if such danger is likely to result from the erection of a building or a wall, or from allowing an old wall to stand after the burning of a building, or from withdrawing quicksand. If there is a building on the adjoining land notice must be given of an intended excavation in order to afford the owner a chance to protect the building, and failure to do so is negligence. After such notice the responsibility for and cost of shoring up and taking precaution to prevent injury to the building falls upon the owner of the building. Where the occupier has let the contract of erecting a building or wall with proper plans and specifications to an independent contractor, this relieves the occupier of any liability for negligence of the independent contractor, but not of the duty to give notice.

There is such a strong social interest in the cultivation of land that an occupier who cultivates land in the ordinary way is not liable for the spreading of thistle seeds to adjoining land or for a filling up of his neighbor's pond due to cultivating a hillside.

§ 31. Same—toward adult trespassers.[1] Toward adult trespassers there is no duty either to keep the premises in a safe condition or to warn of any perils thereon.

If the owner makes an excavation on his land remote from the highway, there is no duty toward a trespasser to guard the excavation or to warn him in any way of the danger. The occupant is not entitled, however, to set spring guns or other traps in order to catch or injure a trespasser, because the force thus used is not appropriate in kind or suitable in degree for the purpose of removing him.

After the land occupier is aware of the presence of the trespasser he must —by the weight of authority and better view—use due care in changing the conditions of the premises so as to avoid injuring him. Whether the occupier is under any duty to look out for trespassers while changing or when about to change the condition of the premises there is direct conflict of authority. The better view is that he does owe such a duty where trespassing has been so frequent in the past that there is reasonable ground for expecting that there will be trespassers. The same principles apply to the case of trespassing animals.

Where the defendant is not the occupier of the land but is himself a tres-

former to prevent subsidence of soil or collapse of building upon latter's land, or to recover damages caused by such subsidence or collapse. 129 **ALR** 623–633.

6 **John Marshall L. Q.** 33, The Doctrine of Lateral Support in Illinois as Applied to Public Improvements.

1 38 **Am Jur**, Negligence, §§ 109–115.

Poisonous substances or other conditions on premises, injury to stock by. 33 **ALR** 448–464.

Duty of railroad before discovering presence of licensee or trespasser using footpath, along or across track, commonly used, but not a public way. 120 **ALR** 1076–1098.

Duty to check speed of train upon discovering live stock on or near tracks. 23 **ALR** 148–178.

20 **Tex. L. R.** 562, Assumption of Ri . and the Landowner.

passer thereon his position is probably weaker than that of the land occupier.

The fact that the plaintiff is a trespasser as to X is no defense to the defendant.

§ 32. Same—toward trespassing children.[2] As to trespassers who are children the land occupier's duties are in many states greater than to adult trespassers, the doctrine being referred to sometimes as the turntable doctrine because the earliest and most usual cases were those of railroad turntables, and sometimes as the attractive nuisance doctrine because the courts have used this phrase in holding that if a land occupier has on his land something that is attractive and dangerous to children he owes a duty to use due care and to protect the children from the danger. In other states the doctrine has been definitely repudiated.

§ 33. Same—toward licensees.[3] Towards one who is sometimes called a bare or mere licensee or volunteer, i. e., one who is on the land for his own purposes, merely by the sufferance of the occupier, the duty of the latter does not vary much if at all from that toward the trespasser.

Even if permission is given, either expressly or by implication, it is doubtful whether any further duty arises, where the person coming on the premises is doing so for his own use and benefit, except that there can be no question in such a case that the land occupier in setting or keeping forces in motion is under a duty to look out for such a licensee where his presence is reasonably to be anticipated. Upon principle, it would seem that the land occupier should also be under a duty to warn licensees of hidden dangers of which the former knows, and this is apparently the law. By the weight of authority a fireman coming upon premises is treated as a licensee, not as a business visitor.

§ 34. Same—toward invited persons.[4] When a person has been invited but not on business in which the land occupier is or may be pecuniarily interested, the few cases on the point are not in agreement as to the extent of the land occupier's duty. In England such a person has apparently no greater rights than a licensee. In this country what little authority there is seems

[2] 38 **Am Jur,** Negligence, §§ 32, 144-157.

Liability, under attractive nuisance doctrine or related principle, for injury to children jumping or falling from nondefective and stationary object or structure reached by climbing. 145 **ALR** 322-332.

Attractive nuisances. 36 **ALR** 34-294; s. in 39 **ALR** 486-490; 45 **ALR** 982-993; 53 **ALR** 1344-1356; 60 **ALR** 1444-1445.

36 **Harv. L. R.** 826, The Turntable Cases in the Federal Courts.

[3] 38 **Am Jur,** Negligence, §§ 104-108.

Liability of owner or occupier of premises other than store or shop for personal injury to another due to slippery condition of floor. 118 **ALR** 425-458.

Right of one other than owner or lessee of premises to benefit of rule that restricts duty toward trespasser or licensee to abstention from wilful or wanton injury. 90 **ALR** 886-891.

Liability to trespasser or bare licensee as affected by distinction between active and passive negligence. 49 **ALR** 778-800.

Liability for injury to trespassing stock from poisonous substances or other conditions on the premises. 33 **ALR** 448-464.

Duty and liability of owner or occupant of premises to fireman or policeman coming thereon in discharge of his duty. 13 **ALR** 637-651; s. in 141 **ALR** 584-597.

[4] 38 **Am Jur,** Negligence, §§ 96-103.

Liability to spectator at baseball game who is hit by a ball or injured as result of other hazards of the game. 142 **ALR** 868-881.

Liability for death or injury on or near golf course. 138 **ALR** 541-557.

Duty and liability of owner or keeper of place of amusement respecting injuries to patrons. 22 **ALR** 610-685; s. in 29 **ALR** 29-37; 38 **ALR** 357-362; 44 **ALR** 203-210; 53; **ALR** 855-866; 61 **ALR** 1289-1304; 98 **ALR** 557-588.

Duty and liability as regards lighting conditions in theater. 143 **ALR** 61-87.

Duty and liability respecting condition of store or shop. 33 **ALR** 181-231; s. in 43 **ALR** 866-869; 46 **ALR** 1111-1113; 58 **ALR** 136-145; 100 **ALR** 710-767.

27 **U. of Minn. L. R.** 75, Invitees.

to give to the person invited not upon business the same rights as those who are business visitors.

Towards a person who has been invited, either expressly or by implication, upon business which is or may be of pecuniary interest to the occupier, the latter is under a duty to use reasonable care to keep the premises in a safe condition, but is not liable at peril.

§ 35. **Same—duty in regard to water or other substances escaping from land.**[5] In Fletcher v. Rylands the defendant had made a reservoir on his land and filled it with water. The water passed down old mine shafts on the defendant's land, through old mine workings and under intermediate land reached the plaintiff's mine, causing much damage thereto. The court held that the defendant was liable without proof of negligence, an attempt being made to generalize from the liability for nuisances, explosives and trespassing animals. The doctrine was meant to apply to anything which an owner brings on his land and which is likely to escape and to do damage if it escapes; but it has rarely been applied except to cases of escaping water.

The case has been cited in the United States, but not often followed and in some jurisdictions has been definitely repudiated.

§ 36. **Duty of municipality toward traveling public.**[6] Closely analogous to the relation between the ordinary land occupier and the business visitor is the relation between the municipality and the traveling public and the duty in most jurisdictions in the United States is the same, viz., to use ordinary care to keep in repair the places where the traveling public has a right to be, or to warn of hidden dangers of which the municipality knows or can find out by the exercise of ordinary care. In most jurisdictions this obligation rests only upon chartered municipal corporations, i. e., cities, towns and villages, and not upon what are sometimes called quasi municipal corporations, i. e., counties and townships; the reason for this distinction is not conclusive and some states hold the county also liable. In England and Canada, on the other hand, neither county nor city is held civilly liable apart from statute.

The liability is limited to those who are using the street for purposes of travel. If a street is rendered unsafe by the walls of a house left standing after a fire there is a duty to use ordinary care to secure the walls or to have them removed. The liability includes the sidewalks but does not necessarily extend to the whole width of the street.

When the city has caused or authorized the defect in the street, no notice is necessary in order to fix upon it the duty to use ordinary care to repair or warn; but where the city is not in any way responsible for the existence of the defect, it is necessary for the plaintiff to show that the proper city officials either knew of the defect or that by the exercise of ordinary care they

5 38 Am Jur, Negligence, §§ 139–141.

6 25 Am Jur, Highways, §§ 345–349.

Responsibility of county for injury from defect in highway. 2 ALR 721–726.

Duty and liability as to construction or maintenance of bridge as respects weight of load. 68 ALR 605–629.

Liability for injuries due to fall of sign or billboard. 45 ALR 800–812.

Liability for injury by stepping or falling into opening in sidewalk while doors were open or cover off. 70 ALR 1358–1391.

Duty to provide barriers for protection of automobile travel. 27 ALR 937–944; s. in 86 ALR 1389–1407.

Duty of municipality to remedy conditions due to traffic rendering roadway dangerous for automobiles. 63 ALR 208–209.

Liability of public for automobile accident as affected by condition of shoulder of hard surfaced road. 80 ALR 494–496.

Liability of municipality for injury or damage by automobile colliding with temporary obstruction in connection with alteration or repair of street. 100 ALR 1386–1394.

could have discovered it in time to have protected the plaintiff by the exercise of ordinary care.

§ 37. **Duty of vendor or lessor of land.**[7] If one sells land upon which he has erected a nuisance, he does not, of course, escape his liability therefor by such transfer. As to a defect in the condition of the premises which does not amount to a nuisance, the vendor would, upon principle, cease to be liable after the vendee has gone into possession, at least after the vendee knows of the defect.

If one leases to a tenant land on which there is a nuisance he obviously does not thereby escape liability. So, if the premises are in such a condition that ordinary use by the tenant must necessarily create a nuisance, or if the lease contemplates that the lessee will erect a nuisance. Even where the defect in the condition of the premises was not considered to be a nuisance, the lessor may be liable for an injury occurring to a third person properly on the premises after the tenant takes possession. On the other hand, if the premises are in repair at the time of the lease, and no nuisance or negligent act of the lessee is to be reasonably contemplated, the landlord is under no tort liability either to the tenant or a third person to keep the premises in repair.

Where the landlord has rented only part of the premises, as in case of apartment houses, he owes the same duty to tenants and their guests with respect to that part of the premises retained which a land occupier owes to a person invited on business. The tenant stands in the position of a business visitor here because the renting of and the presence of guests invited by the tenant must reasonably have been contemplated by him.

Even where the landlord is under no duty whatever in regard to keeping the premises in repair, if he undertakes to do a particular piece of repair work he must use ordinary care in performing it; if, having so undertaken the work he leaves the premises in a dangerous condition, he will be liable to the tenant or the tenant's guest who is injured thereby. But if the failure of the landlord to carry through his undertaking as planned and expected does not result in leaving the premises in a dangerous condition, there is no liability.

§ 38. **Duty of bailor of chattel.**[8] If one lends a chattel gratuitously and knows that there is a latent defect making it unfit and dangerous for the purpose for which it was lent, he is liable for injuries resulting therefrom to the borrower or those expected to use it. This is analogous to the liability of a land occupier towards persons who have been expressly or impliedly permitted to enter upon the land for their own purposes, and following this an-

[7] 32 **Am Jur**, Landlord and Tenant, §§ 755–757.

Liability of landlord for injury to person or property of tenant, or his privies, from defects in heating or lighting plant or plumbing. 13 **ALR** 837–853; s. in 26 **ALR** 1253–1257; 52 **ALR** 864–868.

Liability of landlord for damage to tenant's goods through negligence in making repairs. 15 **ALR** 971–981.

Permissive character of use as affecting landlord's liability to a tenant, or one in privity with him, for personal injuries received in part of premises remaining in landlord's control. 58 **ALR** 1433–1450.

Liability of landlord for personal injuries due to defective foundation, walls, or roof of building intended for use of different tenants. 43 **ALR** 1273–1279.

Landlord's liability for personal injuries to one who enters as a business patron upon leased premises within tenant's exclusive control. 123 **ALR** 870–884.

Liability of landlord for personal injuries due to defective halls, stairways, and the like, for use of different tenants. 25 **ALR** 1273–1341; s. in 39 **ALR** 294–305; 58 **ALR** 1411–1423; 75 **ALR** 154–172; 97 **ALR** 220–244.

Landlord's liability to one injured while using for a purpose for which is was not intended, property remaining in the former's control. 30 **ALR** 1390–1400; s. in 49 **ALR** 564–565.

[8] 6 **Am Jur**, Bailments, §§ 192–199.

Duty and liability of garage keeper to owner of car. 15 **ALR** 681–701; s. in 42 **ALR** 135–146; 65 **ALR** 431–440.

alogy, there is probably no liability in the absence of actual knowledge of the defect.

If, however, the bailment is for the benefit not only of the bailee but also of the bailor, the duty of the bailor not only to the bailee but to those persons who are likely to use the chattel is to use due care that the chattel so bailed is fit for the purpose for which it was intended. While this principle applies to an initial carrier so that it is under a duty to use care to see that the cars which it furnishes are safe and to a final carrier so that it is under a duty to use care to see that the cars which it receives from the previous carrier are in repair, it is not applied to an intermediate carrier, apparently upon the ground that it is under a duty to receive the car; but the reasoning does not seem conclusive.

Where the bailment is for the purpose of having the bailee repair the chattel for the bailor the bailor is apparently under a duty to notify the bailee of such defects therein as are likely to result in injury during the process of repairing. Where the bailment is by way of lease or hire of a chattel, the benefit to the bailor being the compensation paid for the use of it, the lessor is apparently under a duty to those who would reasonably be expected to use the chattel, to use ordinary care to furnish a chattel reasonably fit for the purpose, just as in the mutual benefit cases just discussed.

§ 39. **Duty of vendor or manufacturer of chattels.**[9] Where the chattel has been sold instead of bailed or leased, the tort liability of a vendor or manufacturer seems to be limited to cases where the vendor or manufacturer knew of the defect unless the chattel is one dangerous to life, in which latter case the vendor or manufacturer is under a duty to use ordinary care to warn prospective users of the chattel of the danger. The distinction between articles dangerous to life and those dangerous in a less degree seems difficult to support as a judicial distinction; it is to be justified, if at all, because of the social interest in free trade in chattels. As a matter of logic it would seem that there should be a duty upon all vendors and manufacturers toward those who might reasonably be expected to use the chattel to warn of all defects of which they might know by the exercise of ordinary care, whether dangerous to life or not. A retailer of goods in a sealed package is not under a duty to warn the purchaser as to the contents of the package.

§ 40. **Duty of keeper of animals—liability at peril of trespasser.**[10] While

[9] 46 **Am Jur,** Sales §§ 799–826.
Liability of druggist for injury in consequence of mistake. 31 **ALR** 1336–1355; s. in 44 **ALR** 1482–1484.
Right of action at common law for damages sustained by plaintiff in consequence of sale of intoxicating liquor or habit-forming drugs to another. 130 **ALR** 352–369.
Liability of manufacturer to ultimate consumer. 17 **ALR** 672–710; s. in 39 **ALR** 992–1001; 63 **ALR** 340–350; 88 **ALR** 527–535; 105 **ALR** 1502–1512; 111 **ALR** 1239–1253; 140 **ALR** 191–251; 142 **ALR** 1490–1495.
Liability of seller of article not inherently dangerous for personal injuries to the buyer, due to the defective or dangerous condition of the article. 13 **ALR** 1176–1189; s. in 74 **ALR** 343–350.
25 **Marq. L. R.** 173, Tort Liability of Manufacturers to Users of Their Goods.
40 **Mich. L. R.** 679, Tort Liability of Suppliers of Defective Chattels.

[10] 2 **Am Jur,** Animals, §§ 102–116; 43–77.
Lien on animal damage feasant, character and extent of claims for which attaches. 26 **ALR** 1047–1052.
Joint liability of several independent owners of trespassing animals. See 91 **ALR** 763.
Liability of owner or occupant of premises for injury to person thereon by dog not owned nor harbored by former. 92 **ALR** 732–737.
Show, liability for injury inflicted by domestic animal exhibited at. 129 **ALR** 431–433.
Doctrine of absolute liability for injury inflicted by wild animal. 69 **ALR** 500–517.
Scienter as condition of liability for damage by trespassing animals other than dogs. 33 **ALR** 1305–1316.
Liability for trespass or damage by fowls. 14 **ALR** 745–747.
Validity, construction, and effect of statute eliminating scienter as condition of lia-

one who drives domestic animals on the public highway is liable only for ordinary care under the circumstances, the English common-law rule was that the keeper of animals was liable irrespective of negligence if his cattle, horses, sheep or swine strayed from his land upon that of his neighbor and damaged his neighbor's land or crops. As the rule was sometimes stated, one was under an absolute duty to fence his live stock in but not to fence others' live stock out. In states of this country which had in pioneer days few inhabitants, few fences for lack of material with which to build them and therefore a large amount of public unenclosed land used for grazing purposes, the common-law rule was held inapplicable, and the reverse rule adopted, viz., that one need not fence his own cattle in but must fence others' cattle out. In many of these prairie states there is legislation either going back entirely to the common-law rule or giving the counties local option on the matter, the reasons for the other rule having disappeared when the prairies were settled.

Where the owner of cattle has put them into the hands of an agister, and they escape into the neighbor's field, the absolute liability attaches to the agister and in some jurisdictions to the owner also; in others the owner is liable only for negligence in selecting an untrustworthy agister.

As to the liability for acts of domestic animals other than trespasses to land, the English common-law rule was that the owner or keeper was liable regardless of the amount of care used where he knew of the dangerous tendency of the animal. In order to prove scienter, i. e., knowledge of vicious propensity, it is not necessary that there should be notice of the particular sort of act which produced the injury to the plaintiff; for example, where the plaintiff has been bitten by defendant's dog it is not necessary that the dog should have bitten another person in order to show scienter; it would be enough if it were known by the defendant that the dog had attempted to bite. That a dog is kept as a watch dog and is kept tied by day and turned loose at night has been held sufficient evidence of scienter.

Where a domestic animal while trespassing commits damage other than damage to the land, the rule appears to be that there is liability without proof of scienter, such damage being considered as aggravation of the trespass and governed by the same rules.

Where one for his own convenience keeps a wild animal which is likely to do damage if it escapes, he is liable at his peril if it does escape and cause damage. But for other damage—for example—the frightening of horses due to the smell of the animal—the defendant is liable only if he fails to use due care.

When X trespasses upon A's land he is liable at peril for any damage done while thus trespassing; and the same reasoning applies where X is in wrongful possession of A's chattel.

§ 41. Duty in regard to explosives, firearms, and fire.[1] The keeping of

bility for injury by dog or other animal. 1 **ALR** 1113–1127; s. in 142 **ALR** 436–463.

22 **Harv. L. R.** 405, The Responsibility at Common Law for the Keeping of Animals.

[1] 22 **Am Jur,** Explosions and Explosives, §§ 15, 27–32, 60–63.

22 **Am Jur,** Fires, §§ 3, 53, 54–97.

Liability of one on whose property accidental fire originates for damages from spread thereof. 42 **ALR** 783–829; s. in 111 **ALR** 1140–1152.

Liability for fire set by sparks from operation of industrial plant. 25 **ALR** 989–999.

Liability of one who sells explosives or firearms to child for injury to child or third persons. 60 **ALR** 434–444.

Liability of one starting bonfire for burning of child. 36 **ALR** 297–301.

Liability for injury to children by explosives left accessible to them. 43 **ALR** 434–475; s. in 49 **ALR** 160–169; 100 **ALR** 451–474.

Liability for spread of fire intentionally kindled on one's premises for a legitimate large quantities of dangerous explosives close to residences may be a private nuisance which may be enjoined at the suit of those whose lives and property are endangered. If under such circumstances an explosion occurs there would apparently be liability regardless of the amount or degree of care used. Where the facts are not strong enough to make out a case of nuisance and an explosion occurs which causes a trespass to adjoining land by throwing rocks or debris thereon, the weight of authority is that there is liability at peril, on the ground that there is a technical trespass; where there is no such invasion of the possession of adjoining land as to amount to a trespass, there is a conflict of authority as to whether the liability is at peril or only for negligence.

By the old English common law the person who kindled a fire was absolutely liable to others whose property was injured by the fire's spreading and there was a presumption that a fire originating upon a man's premises was kindled by him or his servants; this rule was later modified by statutes. In the United States and Canada the liability seems usually to be based upon negligence, apart from statute. In many jurisdictions statutes are in force imposing liability at peril upon railroad corporations for fire communicated by locomotive engines in use on the railroad; in some jurisdictions, the plaintiff is aided in his proof of negligence in such cases by the doctrine of res ipsa loquitur.

§ 42. Liability as affected by statute or ordinance.[2] Liability may be af-

purpose. 45 ALR 870–882.

Liability for damage by concussion from blasting. 92 ALR 741–749.

Violation of statute or ordinance in relation to explosives as ground of action in favor of one injured in person or property by explosion. 12 ALR 1309–1316.

2 38 Am Jur, Negligence, §§ 158–169.

Violation of statute or ordinance regarding safety of building or premises as creating or affecting liability for injuries or death. 132 ALR 863–888.

Liability for injury to person or damage to property as result of "black-out." 136 ALR 1327–1330; s. in 147 ALR 1442–1443; 148 ALR 1401; 150 ALR 1448.

Statute or ordinance requiring abutting owner to remove snow and ice from sidewalk as affecting liability for injuries. 24 ALR 387–394; 28 ALR 1360.

Violation of statute or ordinance regulating movement of vehicles as affecting violator's right to recover for negligence. 12 ALR 458–469.

Dangerous instrumentality doctrine as applied to automobile. 16 ALR 270–274.

Civil rights and liabilities as affected by failure to comply with regulations as to registration of automobile or motorcycle or licensing of operator. 16 ALR 1108–1120; s. in 35 ALR 62–69; 38 ALR 1038; 43 ALR 1153–1154; 54 ALR 374–382; 58 ALR 532–534; 61 ALR 1190–1192; 78 ALR 1028–1032; 87 ALR 1469–1475; 111 ALR 1258–1268.

Automobiles: who is entitled to benefit of "guest" statute. 109 ALR 667–669.

Constitutionality of automobile guest statutes. 111 ALR 1011–1016.

Injury to guest of operator as within statutory or nonstatutory rule which makes owner of automobile liable for negligence of another operating the car with his consent. 131 ALR 891–896.

Automobiles: gross negligence, recklessness, or the like, within "guest" statute or rule, predicated upon position of car on wrong side of road or encroachment across center line. 136 ALR 1256–1260.

Automobiles: gross negligence, recklessness, or the like, within "guest" statute or rule, predicated upon manner of operating car on curve or hill. 136 ALR 1270–1280.

Intoxication of defendant as defense to action under automobile guest statutes. 141 ALR 58–60.

Conduct of operator of automobile at railroad crossing as gross negligence, recklessness, etc., within guest statute. 143 ALR 1144–1147.

Host and guest relationship, within statute or rule regarding liability of driver or operator of motor vehicle for injury to guest, as between parties to "share-a-ride" arrangement. 146 ALR 640–642.

Commencement and termination of host and guest relationship within statute or rule as to liability for injury to automobile guest. 146 ALR 682–687.

Validity, construction, and effect of statutes which make owner responsible or create a lien for injury or death inflicted by another operating an automobile. 4 ALR 361–368; s. in 61 ALR 866–882; 83 ALR 878–887; 88 ALR 174–177; 112 ALR 416–428; 135 ALR 481–497.

Liability of parent who gives automobile or motorcycle to minor child forbidden by statute to operate same, for negligent use thereof by child. 36 ALR 1164–1165; s. in 49 ALR 1523.

Motorcycle as within statute or ordinance in relation to motorcars, motor driven cars, etc. 48 ALR 1090–1092; s. in 70 ALR 1253–1255.

Conflict between statutes and local regulations as to automobiles. 21 ALR 1186–

fected by statute in either of two ways. One is by requiring that under certain circumstances certain things shall be done, the statute being passed for the purpose of avoiding injuries to persons or property. Such a statute does not really create an entirely new cause of action but merely requires specific things to be done instead of leaving the question to the jury to decide whether in the particular case ordinary care under the circumstances was used. Common examples are statutes fixing the lawful speed of motor vehicles and statutes requiring the blowing of a locomotive whistle while approaching a crossing. By the better view, the violation of such a statute is negligence, the defendant being liable not for any damage that may happen but only for such damage as was proximately caused by such violation. Apparently, therefore, an allegation of negligence would be supported by proof of violation of the statute though the statute is not referred to in the complaint or petition.

The other kind of statute affecting the duty to use care is that which makes a defendant liable irrespective of negligence, where, apart from statute, he would be bound only to use ordinary care. An example of such a statute is one which makes a railroad liable absolutely, i. e., without proof of negligence, for property injured or destroyed by fire communicated by a locomotive. If a complaint charges negligence it is a variance for the plaintiff to rely upon such a statute because it is considered as creating a new and different cause of action. And the legislative intent to create a private cause of action in such a case is not ordinarily to be presumed from the mere imposition of a penalty for failing to do something where there was no common-law duty.

As to whether the rule applying to statutes applies also to municipal ordinances there is a conflict of authority. The minority position is that the legislature cannot delegate to the municipality the power to create civil liability between individuals but only the power to fix limited penalties payable to the municipality. The majority view makes no distinction between legislative and municipal enactment holding that since the ordinance is valid

1214; s. in 64 **ALR** 993–1005; 147 **ALR** 522–574.

Liability for injury to or by one operating motor vehicle while under the age prescribed by law. 46 **ALR** 1067–1068.

Liability for damages by vehicle trailers. 3 **ALR** 618–619; s. in 84 **ALR** 281–286.

Constitutionality, construction, and effect of statutes in relation to conduct of driver of automobile after happening of accident. 16 **ALR** 1425–1429; s. in 66 **ALR** 1228–1238; 101 **ALR** 911–919.

Indefiniteness of automobile speed regulations as affecting validity. 26 **ALR** 897–906; s. in 29 **ALR** 1066.

What is street intersection within traffic statute or regulations. 31 **ALR** 488–491; s. in 78 **ALR** 1198–1202.

Constitutionality and effect of statute relating to civil liability of person driving automobile while under influence of liquor. 56 **ALR** 327.

Lack of automobile registration or operator's license as evidence of negligence. 73 **ALR** 162–166.

Parking at improper place as affecting liability for automobile accident. 73 **ALR** 1074–1081.

Unauthorized use of automobile license plates as affecting liability or right to recover for injuries or damages in consequence of automobile accident. 86 **ALR** 236–240.

Liability for accident at crossing as affected by reliance upon or disregard of traffic signals. 75 **ALR** 970–980.

"Assured clear distance" statute or rule as applied at hill or curve. 133 **ALR** 967–971.

What constitutes gross negligence or the like, within statute limiting liability of owner or operator of automobile for injury to guest. 74 **ALR** 1198–1202; s. in 86 **ALR** 1145–1158; 96 **ALR** 1479–1492.

Automobiles: liability of parent for injury or death of child's guest by negligent operation of car. 88 **ALR** 590–595.

Constitutionality, construction and application of statute prescribing special precautions in passing stopped automobile. 108 **ALR** 987–989.

Constitutionality, construction, and application of statute for determination by executive or admistrative board of questions in relation to motor vehicle accidents. 110 **ALR** 826.

Construction, applicability, and effect of traffic regulation prohibiting vehicles from passing one another at street intersection. 78 **ALR** 1206–1208.

for one purpose, it has just the same effect as if the legislature itself had passed it.

§ 43. Duty based upon a private gratuitous undertaking—duty to guard against wrongful acts of others.[3] Where one gratuitously undertakes to do something which he is under no legal obligation to do he must use ordinary care in performing the act not to cause damage to others; and this applies not only to damage which may occur while the act is being performed but also to damage which may result later due to the increased danger which the performance of the act has brought about. Where the danger has not been increased by the defendant's undertaking and the performance or attempted performance thereof, there is no liability. On the other hand, if a plaintiff as a matter of common human experience is entitled to rely and has relied upon the defendant's continued performance of his gratuitous undertaking and a cessation of performance would place plaintiff in danger, the defendant must not cease performance without first using ordinary care to notify the plaintiff of such discontinuance; for example, a railroad that stations a flagman at a crossing for several months must not withdraw such protection without first giving notice to the public.

Apparently there is no duty to guard against the wrongful acts of third parties.

§ 44. Proof of negligence—res ipsa loquitur.[4] The burden of proving

[3] 38 **Am Jur**, Negligence, § 42.
Duty and liability of one who voluntarily undertakes to care for injured person. 5 **ALR** 513–515; s. in 120 **ALR** 1525–1531.
Liability for damage or injury by stranger starting automobile left unattended in street. 26 **ALR** 912–917.

[4] 38 **Am Jur**, Negligence, §§ 295–311.
Applicability of res ipsa loquitur doctrine where person or vehicle is struck by streetcar. 2 **ALR** 1610–1617.
Presumption of negligence from throwing passenger from seat. 5 **ALR** 1034–1041.
Presumption as to due care by person killed at railroad crossing. 84 **ALR** 1221–1264.
Res ipsa loquitur as affected by circumstances tending to negative negligence by defendant. 22 **ALR** 1471–1476.
Applicability of res ipsa loquitur in case of boiler explosion. 23 **ALR** 484–490.
Res ispa loquitur as applicable to injury to passenger in a collision where one of the vehicles is not within carrier's control. 25 **ALR** 690–715; s. in 83 **ALR** 1163–1167.
Liability for injury to one in street by object falling from window. 29 **ALR** 77–92; s. in 53 **ALR** 462.
"Res ipsa loquitur" as a presumption or a mere permissible inference. 53 **ALR** 1494–1519.
Res ipsa loquitur distinguished from characterization of a known condition as negligence, and the establishment of negligence by circumstantial evidence. 59 **ALR** 468–480; s. in 78 **ALR** 731–737; 141 **ALR** 1016–1019.
Res ipsa loquitur in its relation to burden of proof and burden of evidence. 59 **ALR** 486–491; s. in 92 **ALR** 653–658.
Pleading particular cause of injury as waiver of right to rely on res ipsa loquitur. 79 **ALR** 48–71.
Res ipsa loquitur as applicable in action against landlord for injury to person or property due to condition of premises. 145 **ALR** 870–885.
Res ipsa loquitur as applicable to injury to person in street by fall of object in course of construction or repair of building. 146 **ALR** 523–529.
Admissibility of witness's conclusion as to care exercised in driving automobile. 66 **ALR** 1117–1121.
Admissibility of report of operator filed pursuant to law, respecting automobile accident. 69 **ALR** 905–906.
Admissibility of test or experiment after accident as bearing on condition of automobile at time of accident. 72 **ALR** 863–866.
Admissibility as res gestae of statements or exclamations relating to cause of, or responsibility for, automobile or motorcycle accident. 76 **ALR** 1121–1133; s. in 101 **ALR** 1197–1202.
Res ipsa loquitur as applied to automobile accidents. 5 **ALR** 1240–1247; s. in 12 **ALR** 668–669; 64 **ALR** 255–263; 93 **ALR** 1101–1123.
Opinion evidence as to condition of automobile or other motor vehicle. 77 **ALR** 559–566.
Prima facie case or presumption from registration of automobile in name of, or from proof of ownership by, defendant, as applicable to questions other than the master-servant relationship at time of accident. 122 **ALR** 228–229.
Expert or opinion evidence regarding lights on automobiles and the distance at which lights will "pick up" an object. 137 **ALR** 753.
4 **La. L. R.** 70, Res Ipsa Loquitur and Proof by Inference—A Discussion of Louisiana Cases.
15 **Rocky M. L. R.** 220, Res Ipsa Loquitur As Applied in Dental Cases.
17 **S. Calif. L. R.** 187, Res Ipsa Loquitur.

negligence on the part of the defendant is upon the plaintiff. "But where the thing is shown to be under the management of the defendant or his servants, and the accident is such as in the ordinary course of things does not happen if those who have the management use proper care, it affords reasonable evidence, in the absence of explanation by the defendants, that the accident arose from want of care." Where this rule—known as the doctrine of res ipsa loquitur—applies, the plaintiff may submit the issue of negligence to the jury upon proof of the injury only, but by the better view and the weight of authority the burden of establishing negligence does not shift. The doctrine has been most often applied in cases of injuries to passengers by common carriers and to persons on the highway who have been struck by some substance falling from an adjoining building, but the present tendency is toward a wider application. Since the rule is one of human experience based upon probabilities, the fact that the plaintiff is a servant of the defendant should not prevent its application, but in several jurisdictions the rule is otherwise.

But the weight of authority and better view the defendant has the burden of proving contributory negligence of the plaintiff where that is in issue as a matter of substantive law, but in a few jurisdictions the plaintiff must allege and prove that he was in the exercise of due care.

B. Legal or Proximate Cause

§ 45. Negligence and legal cause mixed questions of law and fact.[5] The question of what the defendant's conduct was in a particular case is a pure question of fact; the question of how the defendant should have conducted himself is a pure question of law; but because the law has not undertaken to define exactly and specifically what a person should do in all possible circumstances that may arise but has contended itself with a rule sufficiently indefinite and flexible to apply to all cases, the question of what conduct amounts to due care in a particular case and the question whether the defendant's conduct does or does not equal such conduct are usually not separated. The question of negligence is therefore a mixed question of law and fact. As to whether this mixed question should be decided by the court or jury is not everywhere settled, but the better view is that since the largest and most important ingredient is the question of fact, the jury is the more appropriate tribunal to decide the question under instructions, of course, by the court. If the jury could reasonably find only one way, the court may decide it just as it may decide any other question of fact in such circumstances.

Similarly, the question whether the plaintiff's damage was in any degree whatever caused by the defendant's conduct is a pure question of fact; the question, for what part of the consequences of his conduct the defendant shall be held legally liable is a pure question of law. But since the law has not attempted to define specifically and particularly the consequences for which a negligent defendant is liable, the question of legal cause is also a mixed question of law and fact. And like the question of negligence the question of legal cause is decided—if a doubtful one—by the jury under proper instructions by the court.

5 53 **Am Jur**, Trial, §§ 156–292.
Sufficiency of instruction on contributory negligence as respects the element of proximate cause. 102 **ALR** 411–428.
39 **Col. L. R.** 1087, Of the Teaching of Legal Cause.

§ 46. Defendant not liable for remote consequences.[6] Theoretically and as a matter of strict logic, a culpable defendant should be held liable for all the consequences of his misconduct; but our knowledge of causation is so imperfect that it is often a difficult matter of fact to determine whether the plaintiff's damage is a consequence of the defendant's conduct. In order to secure practical justice, therefore, it has long been settled that a defendant will not be held liable for such consequences as are so far removed in the chain of causation that the causal connection becomes merely conjectural. Such consequences are called remote in contradistinction to near or proximate consequences. While time and distance are always important elements in determining remoteness, they are by no means controlling.

In determining remoteness there is besides time and distance, a third element, viz. the intervention of other agencies, human or nonhuman, between defendant's culpable conduct and the plaintiff's damage. This will be discussed later.

§ 47. The probable consequence rule.[7] A culpable defendant is prima facie liable at least for such consequences as might have been foreseen by a prudent man in the position of the defendant, and a rule of legal cause holds him liable only for such consequences. Strictly applied the probable consequence rule would exempt a defendant from all improbable as well as for all remote consequences; but if the damage follows immediately the fact that it is improbable does not exempt the defendant from liability. One may have been negligent if some damage to another was so likely to happen that a prudent person would either have foregone acting or have guarded against harmful consequences to the other. It is possible that a defendant should have foreseen one particular species of harm and that the plaintiff should actually suffer harm in a different way; for example, a plaintiff sitting on some piles was in danger of being thrown into the water but what actually happened because of defendant's negligent act in striking the piles was that a brace between the piles fell out and the plaintiff fell between the piles and was crushed.

§ 48. The proximate consequence rule.[8] Whether a negligent defendant is liable for improbable consequences which do not follow immediately but which are not so far removed in the chain of causation as to be considered remote or conjectural, seems not to be definitely settled. The only plausible reason for excusing a defendant from liability for such consequences is that although the line between probable and improbable is not a clearly defined

6 38 **Am Jur,** Negligence, § 61.

7 38 **Am Jur,** Negligence, §§ 57–60.

Applicability of "contemplation of parties" rule in tort action. 43 **ALR** 318–327.

Signs warning approaching travelers of presence of crossing, absence, improper location, or insufficiency of, as proximate cause of accident. 93 **ALR** 218–226.

Telephone connection, question of proximate cause as affecting liability for damages for failure to obtain. 10 **ALR** 1456; s. in 19 **ALR** 1419–1421.

Safe deposit box, proximate cause of loss of contents. 40 **ALR** 885; 42 **ALR** 1304–1306; 133 **ALR** 279–304.

Condition of surface of roadway as proximate cause of injury by object thrown therefrom or from vehicle. 115 **ALR** 1498–1504.

Hospital's or sanitarium's negligence as proximate cause of injury to patient. See 22 **ALR** 354; s. in 39 **ALR** 1431–1436; 124 **ALR** 186–215.

Lighting conditions in theater as proximate cause of injury to patron. See 143 **ALR** 75.

Gas company's cutting off of fuel gas upon failure of consumer to pay as proximate cause of resulting illness. See 132 **ALR** 916.

16 **So. Calif. L. R.** 1, 61, 274, Proximate Cause.

8 38 **Am Jur,** Negligence, §§ 49–62.

Poison in article not intended to be eaten or tasted, proximate cause of injury or death in swallowing. 50 **ALR** 1462–1464.

one, it is perhaps easier, on the whole, to determine what is probable than it is to determine what is proximate. This does not, however, seem to be a sufficient reason. Where recovery is allowed for such consequences a culpable defendant is liable for all except remote consequences and hence the rule may properly be called the proximate consequence rule. The rule is apparently the settled law in England; the extent to which it prevails in this country could be determined only after a very careful analysis of many hundreds of cases. In the leading English case the defendant was sued for negligently burning the plaintiff's cottage. The defendant contended that he ought not to be held liable because no reasonable man could have foreseen that the fire would consume a hedge and pass across a stubble field and so get to the plaintiff's cottage, at a distance of two hundred yards from the railway, crossing a road in its passage. The judgment for the plaintiff was affirmed, Channel, B., saying, "When it has once been determined that there is evidence of negligence, the person guilty of it is equally liable for its consequences, whether he could have foreseen them or not." And Blackburn, J., said, "I also agree that what the defendants might reasonably anticipate is only material with reference to the question whether the defendants were guilty of negligence or not, and cannot alter their liability if they were guilty of negligence. . . . If the negligence were once established, it would be no answer that it did much more damage than was expected."

Where a culpable defendant has intended the particular result which happened, he should be held liable therefor even though the result was an improbable one.

§ 49. Concurrent human causes.[9] The fact that the culpable act of X concurs with the culpable act of defendant to produce the damage to the plaintiff does not in any way excuse the defendant; each is prima facie liable to the plaintiff for the full amount of the damage regardless of the relative amount of blame attributable to him; and although each acts independently of the other neither can set up the concurring culpable act of the other in defense for the reason that one cannot escape liability on the ground that his conduct was only a part of the legal cause. The simplest illustration is that of a collision between vehicles negligently driven by defendant and X causing damage to the plaintiff.

Similarly, both are liable if the negligence of one consisted in creating a dangerous passive condition which concurred with active force negligently brought to bear by the other; for example, a passenger was caused by the railroad company's negligence to jump from its train and he alighted upon grease negligently left on the platform by the defendant.

Similarly, liability rests upon both if the negligence of both consists in creating a dangerous passive condition which needs only the nonculpable active conduct of the plaintiff to bring about harmful results; for example, the plaintiff while using a hotel fire escape was injured by an electric wire negligently placed by the hotel owner and negligently allowed to remain by the city.

9 38 **Am Jur**, Negligence, § 64.

Mistake as to chemical or product furnished, or misdescription thereof by label or otherwise, as basis of liability for personal injury or death resulting from combination with other chemical. 123 **ALR** 939–941.

Stopping vehicle on traveled portion of highway concurring with negligence of third person to bring about collision. 131 **ALR** 605.

Liability for injury to child by automobile left unattended in street or highway. 140 **ALR** 538–550.

Joint liability for injury to a third person or damage to his property due to concurring negligence of drivers of automobiles. 16 **ALR** 465–470; s. in 62 **ALR** 1425–1430.

A defendant is not relieved of liability because his negligence concurs with a nonculpable act of X; for example, where X stumbled against the plaintiff and caused plaintiff to fall into a ditch negligently left unguarded.

Similarly a defendant is not relieved because his negligence concurs with a nonculpable act of the plaintiff; for example, where plaintiff slipped on the floor and fell against machinery negligently left unguarded by defendant.

§ 50. **Intervening human cause.**[10] Where, after a dangerous passive condition has been created by the defendant, a third person comes into intelligent control of the situation, and causes damage to the plaintiff, it is a case of intervention and not of concurrence between the defendant's conduct and the plaintiff's damage. Where the defendant's wrongful act has caused the intervening act of the third person, he ought clearly to be held liable for the results of such intervening act; but if he did not cause the intervening act he ought not to be liable for the reason that his conduct becomes thereby a remote cause. As a practical matter, even though the proximate consequence rule were to be followed, it would be difficult, if not impossible, to show that the defendant's culpable conduct caused the conduct of the intervening actor except by showing that the intervening act should have been foreseen. If the intervening actor is also culpable, of course, he, too, will be liable.

The importance of determining whether a cause is concurrent or intervening is obvious for if the defendant's negligent conduct concurred with the conduct of another it is not necessary to show that the defendant should have foreseen the concurring cause; the concurrent human causes may be, and usually are, independent actors.

While cases are comparatively rare where the defendant should have foreseen the neglect of duty of one who later comes into intelligent control of the situation, they are not unknown; for example, where defendant sold liquor to plaintiff's slave knowing he was likely to become intoxicated and the slave became drunk and died of exposure; and where defendant failed to fasten its turntable knowing that it was likely to be revolved by children who were playing on it. Where the third person has not come into intelligent control of the situation, the case is properly classified as one of concurrent and not of intervening cause, even though the third person was negligent in not obtaining such intelligent control.

§ 51. **Operation of nonhuman forces.**[1] In regulating one's conduct so as to satisfy the legal requirement of ordinary care one must take into consideration the ordinary and usual nonhuman forces by which he is sur-

[10] 38 **Am Jur,** Negligence, §§ 67–84.

Intervening act of child as affecting question of proximate cause of damage to the person or property of third person by fire or explosion. 8 **ALR** 1250–1254.

Liability of one causing personal injury for consequences of negligence, mistake, or lack of skill of physician or surgeon. 8 **ALR** 506–522; s. in 39 **ALR** 1006–1008; 56 **ALR** 593–594.

Intervening criminal act as breaking causal chain. 78 **ALR** 471–483.

Burglar, thief, or robber, proximate cause of killing or injuring of servant by. 38 **ALR** 1454–1455.

Parent's intrusting of firearm to child as proximate cause of injury inflicted by latter. 44 **ALR** 1513.

[1] 38 **Am Jur,** Negligence, §§ 71–84.

Liability of carrier responsible for passenger leaving train or car at station other than his destination for subsequent injury to, or illness or death of, passenger. 118 **ALR** 1327–1335.

Injury as proximate cause of death where disease intervenes. 79 **ALR** 351–373.

Delay in transportation or delivery as proximate cause of loss of, or damage to, goods from causes for which carrier is not otherwise responsible. 46 **ALR** 302–313.

Defect in street or highway as proximate cause of injury immediately caused by collision between two vehicles. 104 **ALR** 1231–1238.

rounded, such as gravity, the wind, the rain and the sunshine; nor can he successfully contend that their operation in any way breaks the causal connection between his negligent conduct and the plaintiff's damage. Not only is this true of ordinary inanimate forces; it is also true of the ordinary movements of animals; for example, the kicking of a mule which caused plaintiff to fall into an excavation negligently left by defendant.

Nor is causal connection broken by bodily diseases, such as paralysis following an injury negligently inflicted by defendant. But where the supervening disease is one of the mind instead of the body and the person injured takes his own life while insane many states deny recovery though the better view permits it.

Where defendant's conduct has consisted in creating a dangerous passive condition causal connection is broken by the operation of an extraordinary natural force if the latter is of such a magnitude that it would have produced the same damage even if the defendant had not been negligent; for example, where defendant was negligent in not putting enough culverts through a dam but the storm was so great that plaintiff's building would have been swept away even if defendant had used due care. But if the extraordinary force is not of such magnitude causal connection is not broken.

Where the defendant is a common carrier and its wrongful conduct has consisted merely in failing to perform its public service duty of due diligence in forwarding freight and because of this the plaintiff's goods happen to be left in a place where it is injured by an extraordinary natural force the defendant is properly not held liable. Such conduct is not tort negligence where it is mere delay with no foreseeable danger; and the position of plaintiff's goods due to the delay is merely a nondangerous condition and not a cause of the plaintiff's damage. But if the defendant carrier after actual notice of an impending act of God such as an extraordinary storm or cold weather, could by the exercise of ordinary care, avoid damage to the plaintiff but fails to do so such conduct would be tort negligence and the defendant would be liable for damage caused by the co-operation of such negligence with the act of God.

C. Contributory Misconduct of the Plaintiff

§ 52. **Contributory negligence.**[2] The general rule as to contributory neg-

[2] 38 **Am Jur**, Negligence, §§ 174–211.

Failure to stop, look, and listen at railroad crossing as negligence per se. 41 **ALR** 405–432.

Injury to one while coasting in the street. 20 **ALR** 1433–1441; s. in 109 **ALR** 941–949.

Right of one injured while stopping or loitering in street. 24 **ALR** 766–781.

Intoxication as affecting contributory negligence of one killed or injured at a railroad crossing. 36 **ALR** 336–343.

The doctrine of comparative negligence and its relation to the doctrine of contributory negligence. 114 **ALR** 830–838.

Contributory negligence of children. 107 **ALR** 4–178.

Negligence or contributory negligence of parent in intrusting child to custody of another child. 123 **ALR** 147–161.

Presumption of due care by person killed in accident as supporting or aiding inference of negligence by defendant, or inference that latter's negligence was proximate cause of accident. 144 **ALR** 1473–1479.

Failure to extinguish fire on adjoining property as contributory negligence precluding recovery for damage by fire spreading to plaintiff's property. 27 **ALR** 285–293.

Basis of rule that contributory negligence of person injured precludes recovery by parent or spouse. 42 **ALR** 717–725.

Contributory negligence of one who attempts to cross railroad tracks just after a train, or part of a train, has passed over the crossing. 56 **ALR** 543–577.

Contributory negligence in falling on slippery walk. 13 **ALR** 73–92.

Contributory negligence in disregarding or failing to await complete operation of safety gates or other safety appliance at crossing or draw. 13 **ALR** 942–952.

Failure to stop, look, and listen at railroad crossing as negligence per se. 1 **ALR** 203–218; s. in 2 **ALR** 767; 41 **ALR** 405–432.

Driving automobile across track in front of streetcar that has stopped to take on or let off passengers as negligence or contributory negligence. 14 **ALR** 811–812.

ligence is that even though the defendant was negligent and his negligent conduct was part of the legal cause of the plaintiff's damage, yet if the plaintiff himself did not use ordinary care for the safety of his person or property and if such lack of care was also a part of the legal cause of his damage, he is not entitled to recover. Such negligence on the part of the plaintiff is called contributory negligence. If it is not a part of the legal cause plaintiff is not barred.

The policy of the law behind this doctrine is to place upon all members of society, prospective plaintiffs as well as prospective defendants, the duty to observe such care at all times as will tend to prevent damage. But instead of allowing contributory negligence to defeat recovery altogether, it would be more just to allow it to go only in reduction of damages, thus compelling the negligent defendant to bear a part of the loss and the negligent plaintiff a part. This is the rule in admiralty where there is no jury trial; but in cases where there is a right to trial by jury, such a solution has been thought unwise; probably partly because of the traditional necessity or at least desirability of keeping the issue before the jury simple, and partly because courts have felt that with the admiralty rule it would be difficult to retain the proper control over unreasonable verdicts.

Because of the harsh operation of the doctrine of contributory negligence upon plaintiffs, there has been a strong tendency to mitigate its severity by refusing to apply it in certain classes of cases, thus allowing the plaintiff full recovery in such cases. In a few states statutes allow the jury to divide the damages according to the share of fault of each.

§ 53. Same—the conscious last chance rule.[3] In all jurisdictions there is an exception to the doctrine of contributory negligence but there is confusion and disagreement as to the limits of the exception. According to the prevailing view in this country—which may be briefly designated as the conscious last chance doctrine—recovery is allowed only where the defendant was conscious of the peril to the plaintiff's person or property in time to have avoided the injury by the exercise of ordinary care, the plaintiff being unable to avoid the injury either because he was unconscious of the peril or because he could not by using ordinary care have extricated himself from the peril if he had known it; if the defendant's chance to avoid is no greater than plaintiff's the plaintiff is barred. In many such cases the plaintiff might perhaps be able to recover on the ground that the defendant's negligence was the sole cause of the plaintiff's damage, the defendant having come into complete and intelligent control of the situation and his negligent conduct not being foreseeable by the plaintiff. But cases where the defendant's conduct was foreseeable by the plaintiff are not explainable on the basis of the modern law of legal cause and to that extent the conscious last chance doctrine is an exception to the rule of contributory negligence.

§ 54. The unconscious last chance and humanitarian doctrines.[4] The

Duty and liability to persons struck by automobile while crossing street at unusual place, or diagonally. 14 **ALR** 1176–1200; s. in 67 **ALR** 313–335.

Duty of pedestrian crossing street or highway as regards looking for automobile. 79 **ALR** 1073–1095.

16 **Wis. L. R.** 289, Ten Years of Comparative Negligence.

[3] 38 **Am Jur,** Negligence, §§ 217–222.

Doctrine of last clear chance. 92 **ALR** 47–150; s. in 119 **ALR** 1041–1094.

53 **Harv. L. R.** 1225, The Rationale of Last Clear Chance.

47 **Yale L. J.** 704, The Last Clear Chance: A Transitional Doctrine.

21 **Neb. L. R.** 347, The Last Clear Chance Doctrine.

49 **W. Va. L. R.** 51, Last Clear Chance.

[4] 38 **Am Jur,** Negligence, §§ 223–224.

unconscious last chance doctrine goes further than the conscious last chance doctrine and allows recovery where the defendant was unconscious of the peril but could, by the exercise of ordinary care, have discovered the danger in time to have avoided the injury, the plaintiff, whether conscious of the peril or not, being helpless to avoid it. This represents the English law and there are some cases in this country which seem to be in accord.

The humanitarian doctrine goes even further than the unconscious last chance doctrine and allows recovery even though the plaintiff was not in helpless peril; that is, recovery is allowed if the defendant knew or by the exercise of due care could have known of the plaintiff's peril in time to have avoided the injury though the plaintiff himself may have been negligent in not discovering his peril in time to have avoided the injury. It is thus not a last chance doctrine because defendant's chance to avoid may be only equal to and contemporaneous with that of the plaintiff.

The humanitarian doctrine has been thus called because of its real or supposed influence in preventing the destruction of human life and it is usually spoken of as if it were limited to personal injuries or death caused by dangerous instrumentalities, especially railroad locomotives, streetcars and automobiles, but these limits have not always been carefully observed. The doctrine originated in Missouri and has spread to some three or four neighboring states.

§ 55. Unjustifiable assumption of risk.[5] Another species of plaintiff's misconduct is that of inexcusable or unjustifiable assumption of risk. In cases of contributory negligence the plaintiff is usually unconscious that his person or property is in peril; if he fully realizes the peril and deliberately chooses to encounter it, and such choice is not justified, his misconduct partakes of the nature of consent. It is thus somewhat analogous to recklessness or wantonness in a defendant.

The legal effect of unjustifiable assumption of risk is, however, substantially the same as that of contributory negligence; namely, it enables the defendant to escape liability though his negligence was a part of the legal cause of the plaintiff's damage, unless the defendant is held liable on some one of the doctrines just discussed. Because the legal effect is similar the distinction between contributory negligence and unjustifiable assumption of risk is frequently lost sight of.

§ 56. Same—limits of the doctrine.[6] As already pointed out, one who deliberately chooses to encounter a known risk may be justified in thus choosing and will not be barred thereby, though, of course, he might be barred by contributory negligence if he failed to exercise due care in encountering the risk. Some of the various justifications may be briefly stated as follows: (1) Unless the chance of success is only slight, one is justified in risking his life or bodily safety in order to save the life of another imperiled by the culpable conduct of the defendant even though that other may himself be barred from recovery against the defendant because of contributory

[5] 38 **Am Jur,** Negligence, §§ 171–173.

Liability for injury to one riding on running board of automobile or other place outside body of car. 80 **ALR** 553–561; s. in 104 **ALR** 312–339.

Liability for injury to bicyclist while holding on to moving motor vehicle. 138 **ALR** 1127–1130.

Failure to look or discover automobile approaching on wrong side of road as negligence or contributory negligence. 145 **ALR** 536–537.

Assumption of risk or contributory negligence in riding in defective automobile. 138 **ALR** 838–842.

[6] 38 **Am Jur,** Negligence, § 173.

negligence or assumption of risk. (2) In some jurisdictions one is held to be justified in risking his life or bodily safety in order to save property which has been imperiled by the culpable conduct of the defendant. (3) A traveler on a highway may properly take the risk of injury due to the defective condition of the way where there is no convenient safer way by which he may reach his destination. (4) A tenant of an apartment or office may properly take the risk of injury due to the defective condition of the halls, elevators, stairways and other parts of the premises which remain under the control of the landlord who has culpably allowed them to become dangerous. (5) A land occupier whose access to his premises has been rendered dangerous by the culpable act of the defendant may properly take the risk of injury in order to reach the highway. (6) A business visitor on the premises of a common carrier of goods or passengers may properly take the risk of the defective condition of the premises. (7) One who is employed by a third party may properly take the risk of injury rather than to incur the risk of dismissal from his employment. (8) A land occupier may properly take the risk of injury to his livestock which have been imperiled by the culpable failure of the defendant to build a fence.

§ 57. Plaintiff's violation of statute or ordinance.[7] If the plaintiff at the time of his injury is engaged in the violation of a statute or ordinance he is generally barred from recovery against a negligent defendant if his own misconduct is a part of the legal cause of the damage. In determining the question of legal cause the most important element is the purpose of the statute or ordinance; for example, a plaintiff who failed to obey the statute requiring him to span a bridge with planks before crossing it with his traction engine was denied recovery for damage done to his engine when the bridge broke.

Since the purpose of statutes requiring the registration of automobiles is to raise revenue and to help prevent loss by theft but not to prevent damage through collisions, a plaintiff riding in an unregistered automobile should not be barred thereby from recovery for damage due to defendant's negligent conduct.

Similarly since the purpose of a statute forbidding a common carrier to carry passengers gratuitously is not the prevention of personal injuries to such passengers, one who is injured while being carried gratuitously should not be barred by such fact unless, of course, the statute expressly forbids such recovery. Where a statute or ordinance forbids traveling on Sunday the rule formerly was that a plaintiff thus traveling was barred thereby; the present tendency is to hold otherwise, the purpose of such legislation being to prevent what the legislators considered was the desecration of the Sabbath and not damage to persons or property.

§ 58. Imputed contributory negligence.[8] A master is so far identified

7 38 Am Jur, Negligence, §§ 158–169.

8 38 Am Jur, Negligence, §§ 234–254.

Imputability to rescuer of antecedent negligence of rescued person. 5 ALR 206–210.

Imputing negligence of parent or custodian to child in action by or on behalf of child for personal injury. 15 ALR 414–426.

Negligence of one spouse as imputable to other because of the marital relationship itself. 59 ALR 153–162; s. in 110 ALR 1099–1105.

Presence of young child in street unattended as negligence or evidence of negligence. 51 ALR 209–229.

Contributory negligence of custodian of child as affecting right of parent to recover for its death or injury. 23 ALR 655–661.

Contributory negligence of parent as bar to an action by parent or administrator for death of child. 23 ALR 670–702; s. in 69 ALR 478–482.

with his servant that he is liable for damage done through the negligent conduct of his servant within the apparent scope of his employment and is barred from recovery against a negligent defendant by the contributory negligence of his servant wherever the circumstances are such that the servant himself would be barred. In a few situations a plaintiff has been held barred by the contributory negligence of one who was not his servant. Thus a passenger in X's vehicle who is injured in a collision between defendant's vehicle and that of X has been held barred by the contributory negligence of X; a bailor of chattels that are damaged by defendant while in the possession of the bailee has been held barred by the contributory negligence of the bailee; and a child who has been injured by the concurring negligence of the defendant and the child's parent or custodian has been held barred by the contributory negligence of the parent or custodian. But today it is generally recognized that there is not a satisfactory basis for such identification and the present tendency is contra, either by judicial decision or by statute.

CHAPTER VI

LIABILITY OF EMPLOYERS

A. Liability to Third Persons for Tort of Employees

§ 59. Extent of master's liability.[9] An employer or master is responsible to third persons for the torts committed by his employee or servant in the

Personal care required by one riding in automobile driven by another as affecting his right to recover against third person. 18 **ALR** 309–361; s. in 22 **ALR** 1294–1302; 41 **ALR** 767–781; 47 **ALR** 293–298; and 63 **ALR** 1432–1453.

Liability of guest for injury to third person due primarily to negligence of driver. 18 **ALR** 365–368.

Automobiles: liability of owner or operator for injury to guest. 20 **ALR** 1014–1030; s. in 26 **ALR** 1425–1429; 40 **ALR** 1338–1344; 47 **ALR** 327–332; 51 **ALR** 581–585; 61 **ALR** 1252–1264; 65 **ALR** 952–958.

Negligence of driver of automobile as imputable to passenger. 90 **ALR** 630–637; s. in 123 **ALR** 1171.

Host's inexperience or lack of skill in driving automobile as affecting liability for injury to guest. 91 **ALR** 554–557.

5 **U. of Toronto L. J.** 368, The Rationale of Imputed Negligence.

22 **Neb. L. R.** 264, Gross Negligence under the Guest Statute.

7 **John Marshall L. Q.** 473, The Illinois "Guest Statute."

9 35 **Am Jur**, Master and Servant, §§ 104–115.

Liability for negligence of chauffeur furnished with a car hired for an extended period. 8 **ALR** 484–488.

Liability of master for injury to one whom servant, in violation of instructions, permits to ride on vehicle. 14 **ALR** 145–179; s. in 62 **ALR** 1167–1174; 74 **ALR** 163–165.

Liability of employer for injuries inflicted by automobile while being driven by or for salesman or collector. 17 **ALR** 621–627; s. in 29 **ALR** 470–473; 54 **ALR** 627–634; 107 **ALR** 419–438.

Liability of owner for injury by automobile while being operated by repairman. 18 **ALR** 974–976.

Who is responsible for injury by car during demonstration or instruction by dealer. 20 **ALR** 194–197; s. in 50 **ALR** 1391–1394.

Owner's liability for injury by automobile while being used by a servant for his own pleasure or business. 22 **ALR** 1397–1438; s. in 45 **ALR** 477–498; 68 **ALR** 1051–1061; 80 **ALR** 725–735; 122 **ALR** 858–893.

Liability of owner under "family purpose" doctrine for injuries by automobile while being used by member of his family. 64 **ALR** 844–881; s. in 88 **ALR** 601–616; 100 **ALR** 1021–1030; 132 **ALR** 981–993.

Right, as against vehicle owner, of one not in his general employment, injured while assisting in remedying conditions due to accident to automobile or truck in highway. 72 **ALR** 1283–1285.

Liability of joint owners of automobile for injury or damage resulting from its operation. 109 **ALR** 124–129.

Liability of owner of trailer or semi-trailer attached to motor vehicle owned by another for injury or damage due to negligence in operation of the motor vehicle, 119 **ALR** 1035–1037.

Relation between taxicab company or one holding himself out as furnishing taxicab service, and drivers or owners of cars not owned by company, as regards responsibility for injury or damage. 120 **ALR** 1351–1354; s. in 131 **ALR** 797.

Liability of owner or one in charge of automobile for injury due to its condition, to one, other than his employee or bailee for use, engaged in some service or operation in connection therewith. 122 **ALR** 1023–1025.

course of his employment. This rule is frequently spoken of as the rule of respondeat superior. Whatever its historical development it is today justified upon grounds of expediency.

The rule makes the master liable not only for torts which he specifically authorized and for torts necessarily or usually incident to an authorized course of action but also to unauthorized torts committed in the course of the servant's employment and in intended furtherance of the master's business. Though the torts for which the master is usually thus held liable are those which have been committed by the servant through negligence, he may be held liable for intentional torts as well; and it is no defense that the tort was committed in disobedience of the master's express command.

Where the tort was not committed in the course of the employment or in the intended furtherance of the master's business, the master is not liable unless he was under a positive duty to the plaintiff and the effect of the servant's conduct was that such duty was not performed. Where the master lends or leases his servant to X and during the course of his work for X he injures the plaintiff, the master's liability depends on the nature of the arrangement between him and X as to who shall have control of the servant while he is performing X's work; if he is to obey X's directions as to the manner of performing the work, then the liability is on X; but if X's power to direct the servant is confined to showing him the work to be done, than the master is responsible.

The rule of respondeat superior does not apply to the state or to municipal corporations exercising governmental functions; neither does it apply to pub-

Owner's statutory liability for negligent operation of automobile where he has consented to use by another and car is being driven by a third person. 147 **ALR** 875-882.

Liability for injury or damages resulting from traffic accident on highway involving vehicle in military service. 133 **ALR** 1298-1300; s. in 147 **ALR** 1431.

Automobiles: liability of owner for negligence of one to whom car is loaned or hired. 36 **ALR** 1137-1155; s. in 68 **ALR** 1008-1018; and 100 **ALR** 920-928.

Chauffeur in general employment of owner as servant for time being of owner or of hirer of car. 42 **ALR** 1416-1437.

Chauffeur in general employment of owner as servant for time being of owner, or of borrower of car. 42 **ALR** 1446-1450.

Liability of owner for negligence of one permitted by former's servant or member of his family to drive automobile. 44 **ALR** 1382-1390; s. in 54 **ALR** 851-855; 98 **ALR** 1043-1051; and 134 **ALR** 974-983.

Responsibility of owner of car for negligence of one in general employment of repairman or keeper of garage while getting or delivering car. 46 **ALR** 840-842.

Employer's liability for negligence of employee (or alleged employee) in driving his own car or other vehicle in the employer's business. 57 **ALR** 739-744; s. in 60 **ALR** 1163-1165; 87 **ALR** 787-790; 112 **ALR** 920-931; and 140 **ALR** 1150-1164.

Negligence of driver of automobile as imputed to member of joint enterprise. 62 **ALR** 440-444; s. in 85 **ALR** 630-633.

Responsibility of negligent driver of automobile or his employer for damages immediately inflicted by another car. 62 **ALR** 1181-1195.

Liability of master for injury inflicted by servant with firearms. 10 **ALR** 1087-1103; s. in 75 **ALR** 1176-1191.

Libel or slander of another employee, or former employee, as within scope of employee's authority. 24 **ALR** 133-142; s. in 29 **ALR** 225-226.

Liability of individual or private corporation for false arrest or imprisonment caused by agent or servant. 35 **ALR** 645-714; s. in 77 **ALR** 927-938.

Liability of private employer of police officer for latter's negligence or other misconduct. 55 **ALR** 1197-1218.

Right to join master and servant as defendants in action based on wrongful or negligent act of servant, where master's liability rests on doctrine of respondeat superior. 98 **ALR** 1057-1076.

Status of gasoline and oil distributor or dealer as agent, employee, independent contractor, or independent dealer as regards responsibility for injury to person or damage to property. 116 **ALR** 457-476.

Identity of master, as regards rule respondeat superior, of one loaned or hired out by general employer in connection with WPA or other similar governmental project. 136 **ALR** 525-534.

Rule respondeat superior as applicable to negligent act of employee done within scope of the employment, where injury was the result of a personal collision or accident of a similar nature. 141 **ALR** 683-687.

4 **La. L. Rev.** 1, Respondeat Superior in the Light of Comparative Law.

1 **Loyola L. R.** 25, The Master-Servant Concept and Judge-Made Law.

lic officials. In England charitable corporations are not exempt from the operation of the rule but in this country the weight of authority is that they are, but the courts are not agreed as to the reason for such exemption and there has been much criticism of the position.

In some states there are statutes making the owner of a motor vehicle liable for the torts of his bailee as if the bailee were his servant.

§ 60. Liability for acts and omissions of independent contractor.[10] An independent contractor differs from a servant in that the latter is subject to the control of his employer as to the details of his work, while the former is not subject to such control but is merely under contract to produce a certain result. One who employs an independent contractor is not liable to a third person for injuries caused by him unless (1) an affirmative duty to the third person has already come into existence, the independent contractor has been employed to perform it and the duty has not been performed; (2) the employer authorized the independent contractor to do an act the probable consequence of which is to injure the third person.

Of course an employer may also be liable if he fails to use due care to employ a reasonably competent contractor.

B. Common Law Liability of Master to Servant

§ 61. The fellow servant rule.[1] Prior to 1837 the rule of respondeat superior was usually stated broadly enough to protect servants as well as third persons. In that year, however, the case of Priestly v. Fowler in England and a few years later the cases of Murray v. South Carolina R. R. and Farwell v. Boston, etc., R. R. in this country laid down the rule that a servant could not recover against the master for injuries received in the course of the employment through the negligence of a fellow servant. The analytical reasons usually given for the rule are not convincing and it must therefore be justified, if at all, upon such grounds of expediency as appealed to the courts of that period.

10 27 **Am Jur**, Independent Contractor, §§ 5–51.

Liability of contractee and contractor inter se with respect to injuries sustained while the stipulated work is in course of performance. 44 **ALR** 891–904.

Liability for injuries resulting from failure of independent contractor to guard opening in sidewalk while delivering merchandise, etc. 11 **ALR** 571–575; s. in 53 **ALR** 932–933.

Nonliability of an employer in respect of injuries caused by the torts of an independent contractor. 18 **ALR** 801–864.

General discussion of the nature of the relationship of employer and independent contractor. 19 **ALR** 226–276.

Circumstances under which the existence of the relationship of employer and independent contractor is predicable. 19 **ALR** 1168–1361; s. in 60 **ALR** 303–305.

Elements bearing directly upon the quality of a contract as affecting the character of one as independent contractor. 20 **ALR** 684–808.

Liability of the employer for torts of independent contractor as predicated on the ground that the injury complained of was a direct and necessary result of the stipulated work. 21 **ALR** 1229–1270.

Independent contractor: remedial rights in respect of injuries caused by breaches of positive duties correlative to corporate franchises. 28 **ALR** 122–197.

Liability of employer for acts or omissions of independent contractor in respect of positive duties of former arising from or incidental to contractual relationships. 29 **ALR** 736–817.

Independent contractor: liability of employer as predicated on the ground of his personal fault. 30 **ALR** 1502–1545.

Independent contractor: extent of the employer's liability after he has assumed control of the subject matter of the stipulated work. 31 **ALR** 1029–1045.

Liability of the contractee for injuries sustained by the contractor's servants in the course of the stipulated work. 44 **ALR** 932–1134.

Salesman employed on a percentage or commission basis as a servant or an independent contractor. 61 **ALR** 223–231.

Independent contractor rule as applied to injuries resulting from conditions created by independent contractors in streets. 115 **ALR** 965–990.

Responsibility of operator of place of amusement for negligence of concessionaire or the latter's employees. 145 **ALR** 962–980.

1 35 **Am Jur**, Master and Servant, §§ 334–394.

By its terms the rule does not apply to injuries suffered by the plaintiff while he is outside the course of his employment but the line is not drawn sharply at the time and place of beginning and quitting the work. Nor does it cover injuries inflicted by those who are not fellow servants of the plaintiff, but the question as to who are to be considered fellow servants in this connection has been a difficult one and in some states statutes were passed on this specific subject. One who is rendering compulsory service is not barred by the rule; and the master cannot take advantage of the rule where his own negligence is a part of the cause of the injury.

§ 62. Non-delegable duties of master to servant.[2] The master does not owe any duty to protect the servant from the misconduct of a fellow servant; or from the ordinary risks incident to the employment. There are, however, certain duties of protection owed by the master which must be performed at all events either by himself or a representative and hence are usually referred to as non-delegable duties. These duties are duties to use reasonable care and diligence with reference to the following matters: (1) providing a safe place to work; (2) providing and maintaining safe appliances and machinery; (3) providing inspection and repairs; (4) providing a sufficient force of competent fellow servants; (5) making, promulgating and enforcing rules and regulations; (6) giving special orders in emergencies.

§ 63. Unjustifiable assumption of risk—contributory negligence.[3] It is frequently said that the servant by accepting employment assumes the risk of injury due to the ordinary risks incident to the employment; this is merely an indirect and rather confusing way of saying that as to such risks the master owes no duty to protect the servant similarly, it is also often said that the servant assumes the risk of injuries due to the misconduct of a fellow servant; this properly means that the master owes no duty to protect the servant from such dangers—that the rule of respondeat superior does not apply.

Properly speaking, therefore, the doctrine of assumption of risk in servant cases is limited to cases where the master has defaulted in some of his duties to his servant; if, knowing of such default and the peril thereby occasioned the servant deliberately chooses to encounter the risk of injury and such choice is not justified, he is barred from recovery even though his conduct

[2] 35 **Am Jur**, Master and Servant, §§ 353–363.

Duty of master to care for servant who is stricken or falls sick without fault of the master. 12 **ALR** 909–913; s. in 46 **ALR** 389.

Duty of an employer with respect to the timbering of a mine, under the common law and general statutes. 15 **ALR** 1381–1420.

Duty of an employer with respect to the timbering of a mine under statutes relating specifically to the subject. 15 **ALR** 1432–1506.

Duty of master providing machine of standard make and in common use to equip same with safety device or guard. 36 **ALR** 1477–1487.

Duty and liability of employer to domestic servant. 48 **ALR** 1295–1308.

Liability of employer as predicated on the ground of his being subject to a non-delegable duty in regard to the injured person. 23 **ALR** 984–1014.

Non-delegable duty of employer in respect of work which will in the natural course of events produce injury, unless certain precautions are taken. 23 **ALR** 1016–1081.

Non-delegable duty of employer with respect to work which is inherently or intrinsically dangerous. 23 **ALR** 1084–1135.

Duty of railroad toward employees in respect to telltales or other warning of low bridge or other structure over track. 79 **ALR** 236–249.

Duty and liability of master to servant injured by horse belonging to another. 26 **ALR** 871–891; s. in 42 **ALR** 226–228; 60 **ALR** 468–469.

Nature and extent of master's duty under contract to furnish medical aid to servant. 33 **ALR** 1191–1201.

[3] 35 **Am Jur**, Master and Servant, §§ 243–333.

Contributory negligence or assumption of risk in disobeying rules or directions of master under counterdirections by superior. 23 **ALR** 315–325.

could not properly be described as contributory negligence. The almost uniform refusal of the courts to hold that economic pressure—i. e., the fear of losing his job and being unable to get another one—did not justify his continuing to assume the risk of injury has led to considerable legislation on the matter.

Where the servant complains to the master of the latter's default and the master promises that if the servant will continue in his employ he will remedy the defect, the servant is justified in assuming the risk for a reasonable time unless the situation is so imminently dangerous that a man of ordinary prudence would have refused to do so. And since a seaman on a voyage has no freedom of choice but is subject to discipline, the doctrine does not apply to him.

The doctrine of contributory negligence applies to the same extent as in nonservant cases.

C. Federal Employers' Liability Act

§ 64. Provisions of the Act.[4] The injustice to the employee—under modern conditions—of the fellow servant rule and the doctrines of contributory negligence and assumption of risk led to much remedial legislation both in this country and in England. Much of the early legislation was passed to give special protection to employees engaged in hazardous employments, especially those engaged in the operation of steam railroads. This legislation was so varied in its provisions that in 1908 Congress, acting under its power to regulate interstate commerce, passed what is usually known as the Federal Employers' Liability Act, fixing the duties of employers toward employees engaged in such commerce. The main provisions of the statute were (1) to abolish the doctrine of contributory negligence where the injury was partly caused by the defendant's violation of any statute passed for the safety of employees; (2) in other cases, to allow contributory negligence merely to diminish, not to defeat recovery; (3) to abolish assumption of risk where the defendant had violated any safety statute above referred to.

The effect of this act was not only to supersede existing state legislation of a similar character but is paramount to the Workmen's Compensation Acts which have been passed in all of the states since that time.

D. Workmen's Compensation Acts

§ 65. In general.[5] Workmen's Compensation Acts are now in force in

[4] 35 **Am Jur**, Master and Servant, §§ 398–412.

What employees are engaged in interstate commerce within the Federal Employers' Liability Act. 10 **ALR** 1184–1247; s. in 14 **ALR** 732–738; 24 **ALR** 634–644; 29 **ALR** 1207–1213; 49 **ALR** 1339–1361; 65 **ALR** 613–625; 77 **ALR** 1374–1381; 90 **ALR** 846–852.

Applicability of state statutes and rules of law to actions under Federal Employers' Liability Act. 12 **ALR** 693–718; s. in 36 **ALR** 917–919.

Comparative negligence rule of Federal Employers' Liability Act as supporting recovery where injured employee participated in violation of order or rule of defendant. 72 **ALR** 1345–1351.

[5] See **Am Jur**, Workmen's Compensation Acts.

Workmen's compensation: extent of power of legislature to define hazardous employment. 28 **ALR** 1222–1230.

Who are within provisions of workmen's compensation acts relating to hazardous employments or occupations. 83 **ALR** 1018–1068.

Applicability and effect of Workmen's Compensation Acts in case of injuries to minors. 14 **ALR** 818–828; s. in 33 **ALR** 337–343; 49 **ALR** 1435–1441; 60 **ALR** 847–850; 83 **ALR** 416–426; 142 **ALR** 1018–1033.

Requirement of workmen's compensation act as to notice of accident or injury. 78 **ALR** 1223–1286; s. in 92 **ALR** 505–523; 107 **ALR** 815–827; 145 **ALR** 1263–1314.

May notice of injury or claim contemplated by workmen's compensation act be waived. 78 **ALR** 1306–1317.

Provision limiting time for giving notice of injury or presenting claim as applied to infants. 142 **ALR** 1035–1050.

all American jurisdictions. The motives behind the legislation are various and the provisions of the different Acts are frequently divergent and the legal theory upon which they are based is revolutionary because they substantially ignore the element of blameworthiness; but in spite of a certain amount of criticism the legislation has not only been held constitutional, but on the whole has received judicial approval.

In the following sections will be discussed some of the more important questions which have arisen in connection with the enforcement of the legislation, a large number of them being naturally connected with the judicial construction of the main provisions of the Acts.

§ 66. "Personal injury by accident." [6] The term "personal injury" has been held to include not merely the ordinary cases of obvious physical impact but also any disease of sudden origin, if plainly attributable to the nature of the workman's employment; for example, a heat stroke suffered by a trimmer on a steamship; kidney disease caused by a chill contracted while working waist deep in water. Where the disease is what is known as "occupational disease," there has been a tendency to refuse recovery because it is usually impossible to show that it was an accident in the sense of being an unexpected event the occasion of which can be fixed with reasonable certainty; where the disease is nonoccupational, these difficulties do not arise.

That the workman was under a physical disability when injured does not usually prevent recovery even if the injury would not have happened but for the disability. And it is no objection that the injury was due to the wilful act of a third party.

Payments, or furnishing medical or hospital services, or burial, by employer or his insurer, to employee after injury, as affecting time for filing claim under Workmen's Compensation Act. 144 **ALR** 606–622.

29 **Corn. L. Q.** 176, 353, Insurance Feature of Workmen's Compensation Laws.

16 **Rocky M. L. R.** 60, Employer's Liability for Occupational Diseases.

1 **Mont. L. R.** 1, Workmen's Compensation in Montana.

1 **Loyola L. R.** 169, Workmen's Compensation and Hazardous Occupation Statutes.

2 **Loyola L. R.** 138, Workmen's Compensation for Railroad Employees.

20 **Chicago-Kent L. R.** 193, The Child Labor Act and the W. C. A. of Illinois.

5 **U. of Newark L. R.** 83, Occupational Disease Legislation.

21 **Chicago-Kent L. R.** 209, The Relationship Between Municipal Employment and Workmen's Compensation.

[6] See **Am Jur**, Workmen's Compensation Acts.

Injury to employee while engaged on employer's work, but outside the scope of his usual duty, as arising out of and in the course of the employment. 33 **ALR** 1335–1345; s. in 82 **ALR** 1251–1264.

Compensation for loss or impairment of eyesight within Workmen's Compensation Acts. 8 **ALR** 1324–1331, s. in 24 **ALR** 1466–1470; 73 **ALR** 706–720; 99 ALR 1498–1511; 142 **ALR** 822–841.

Illness or injury due to artificial temperature as compensable. 41 **ALR** 1124–1128; s. in 53 **ALR** 1095–1096; 61 **ALR** 218.

Compensation for disfigurement. 80 **ALR** 970–983; s. in 116 **ALR** 712–720.

Construction and application of specific provisions of workmen's compensation act relating to hernia. 114 **ALR** 1337–1345.

Suicide as compensable under workmen's compensation act. 143 **ALR** 1227–1234.

Workmen's Compensation: injury or death due to the elements. 13 **ALR** 974–982; s. in 16 **ALR** 1038–1039; 25 **ALR** 146–147; 40 **ALR** 400–406; 46 **ALR** 1218–1219; 53 **ALR** 1084–1086; 83 **ALR** 234–240.

Injury or death to which pre-existing physical condition of employee causes or contributes. 19 **ALR** 95–107; s. in 28 **ALR** 204–210; 60 **ALR** 1299–1324.

Lead or other occupational poisoning as within Workmen's Compensation Act. 29 **ALR** 691–698; s. in 44 **ALR** 371–374.

Right to compensation in case of injuries sustained through horseplay, or fooling. 13 **ALR** 540–546; s. in 20 **ALR** 882–884; 36 **ALR** 1469–1473; 43 **ALR** 492–496; 46 **ALR** 1150–1151.

What is casual employment. 33 **ALR** 1452–1467; s. in 60 **ALR** 1195–1204; 107 **ALR** 934–944.

What amounts to loss of member within the meaning of the acts. 18 **ALR** 1350–1360.

What amounts to total incapacity within Workmen's Compensation Acts. 67 **ALR** 785–807; s. in 98 **ALR** 729–741.

Workmen's compensation act as affecting liability of or remedy against employer for injury due to medical or surgical treatment of employee after injury. 127 **ALR** 1108–1120.

§ 67. "Arising in the course of the employment." [7] When the employee's work is to be done entirely upon the employer's premises his employment begins when he enters upon the premises and terminates when he leaves it; where, as in case of commercial travelers, the work is to be done elsewhere, it would seem that he is in the course of his employment from the time he leaves home in the morning until he returns in the evening, because he is hired to travel.

If the employee is on the premises the course of his employment is not limited to the periods during which he is actually engaged upon the work which he is employed to do, nor to the periods for which wages are paid.

When an injury happens while he is outside his regular employment, recovery is usually denied unless there was an emergency and he was acting in furtherance of the enterprise.

§ 68. "Arising out of the employment." [8] Even though the workman was at the time of the accident engaged in the course of his employment, he is not, in most states, entitled to compensation unless the injury also arose out of the employment, i. e., was in some way caused by the employment, or as it is sometimes stated, was reasonably incident to the nature or character of the employment. As to whether it is necessary that the accident be such that the risk of it should have been foreseen as incidental to the employment, or whether it is sufficient that the nature of the employment was such as actually to contribute towards the bringing about of the accident, looking at the matter after the occurrence, there have been conflicting views. Where only nonhuman forces are involved there seems to be no sound reason for requiring that the risk be a foreseeable one; but where the injury was inflicted by the intervening act of third persons it is as a practical matter impossible to show causal connection except by showing that the employer should have foreseen such intervening act. It was formerly held that there must have existed in the employment a special risk not assumed by the public in general or at least a frequency or peculiarity of subjection to a common risk; but the present tendency seems to be away from such requirement.

§ 69. "Is caused to a workman." [9] This phrase is usually construed to refer to causal connection between the accident and the harm suffered by the workman. It is no defense that unknown to the employer, the workman was predisposed to a disease or was suffering from a latent disease which contributed to cause the damage suffered. And full compensation will be awarded where the accident first causes insanity and the insanity causes self-destruction, though such facts may, of course, be difficult to prove. Where

7 See **Am Jur**, Workmen's Compensation Acts.

Injury while riding to or from work in employer's conveyance as arising out of or in course of employment. 10 **ALR** 169–174; s. in 21 **ALR** 1223–1227; 24 **ALR** 1233; 62 **ALR** 1438–1446; 145 **ALR** 1033–1042.

Injuries while entering or leaving place of employment as arising out of or in course of employment. 49 **ALR** 424–445; s. in 82 **ALR** 1043–1050.

Injury to servant who lives on employer's premises as arising out of or in the course of the employment. 31 **ALR** 1251–1261; s. in 56 **ALR** 512–514.

Street risks incurred in course of employment. 51 **ALR** 509–534; s. in 80 **ALR** 126–133.

8 See **Am Jur**, Workmen's Compensation Acts.

Necessity and sufficiency of evidence that disease contracted by applicant for workmen's compensation is attributable to employment. 20 **ALR** 4–83; s. in 73 **ALR** 488–555.

Presumption or inference that accidental death of employee arose out of and in course of employment. 120 **ALR** 683–693.

9 See **Am Jur**, Workmen's Compensation Acts.

there has already been an obvious partial disability, such as the loss of one eye or one hand and the accident causes the loss of the other eye or the other hand, it would seem that compensation should be allowed for total and not merely partial disability. And where the damage to the workman has been enhanced due to the unskilful treatment by a physician of the employer's selection, full compensation is ordinarily awarded.

§ 70. "Serious and wilful misconduct." [10] Even where the accident arose out of and in the course of the employment there are some jurisdictions which provide that there shall be no recovery where the accident was due to the workman's "serious and wilful misconduct." Though the phrase has made considerable difficulty, it seems fairly clear that mere thoughtlessness is not a bar; that whether the misconduct is serious or not is to be determined from its nature and not from its consequences; that acquiescence by the employer prevents him from setting up the bar; and that the workman disobeyed orders and was engaged in the violation of a statute at the time of the accident is not conclusive against him.

§ 71. Who are workmen or employees—dependents—illegal employment. [1] In the absence of an express provision it would seem that policemen and city firemen are not entitled to compensation because they are public officers; but that the employee of a corporation should not be barred merely because he happens also to be a stockholder and officer therein, though there has been some reluctance to grant compensation to an official of high rank. Alienage has been held no bar to relief and unless there is an express provision excluding casual employment from the operation of the Act, one who volunteers in an emergency should be entitled to compensation.

It is probably the better view that dependency in fact is sufficient where there is no legal obligation to support. Whether, upon the death of an employee, the right to compensation vests in his dependent so as to survive to the personal representatives of the latter seems unsettled.

Where the employment was in violation of a statute forbidding the employment of children under a certain age, the prevailing view seems to be that relief, if any, should be at common law or under the death statute and not

[10] See **Am Jur**, Workmen's Compensation Acts.

Injury receved while doing prohibited act. 23 **ALR** 1161–1193; s. in 26 **ALR** 166–170; 58 **ALR** 197–207; 83 **ALR** 1211–1222; 119 **ALR** 1409–1421.

[1] See **Am Jur**, Workmen's Compensation Acts.

"Dependency" within Workmen's Compensation Act. 13 **ALR** 686–724; s. in 30 **ALR** 1253–1277; 35 **ALR** 1066–1081; 39 **ALR** 313–323; 53 **ALR** 218–231; 62 **ALR** 160–177; 86 **ALR** 865–892; 100 ALR 1090–1109.

Workmen's compensation: person in military or naval service. 150 **ALR** 1456–1460.

Applicability to pieceworkers. 38 **ALR** 839–845.

Right of firemen and policemen to recover under workmen's compensation acts. 10 **ALR** 201–205; s. in 81 **ALR** 478–483.

Interest in the business or in corporation or firm owning the business as affecting right to compensation. 15 **ALR** 1288–1297, s. in 81 **ALR** 644–660.

Teamster as independent contractor under workmen's compensation acts. 42 **ALR** 607–622; s. in 43 **ALR** 1312–1319; 120 **ALR** 1031–1056.

Constitutionality of provisions of Workmen's Compensation Law applicable to public officers or employees. 53 **ALR** 1290–1298.

Helper, assistant, or substitute for an employee as himself an employee within contemplation of workmen's compensation act. 80 **ALR** 522–534.

Needy persons put to work by municipality or other public body as means of extending aid to them as within protection of Workmen's Compensation Act. 96 **ALR** 1154–1166; s. in 127 **ALR** 1483–1493.

Who are "workmen" or "operatives" within workmen's compensation act. 129 **ALR** 990–1035.

One temporarily impressed into public service in emergency, as within workmen's compensation act. 142 **ALR** 657–666.

Survival of right to compensation under workmen's compensation acts upon the death of the person entitled to the award. 15 **ALR** 821–829; s. in 24 **ALR** 441–444; 29 **ALR** 1426–1429; 51 **ALR** 1446–1454; 87 **ALR** 864–878; 95 **ALR** 254–258.

under the Compensation Act, though the better view would seem to allow a choice to the plaintiff. An independent contractor is not within the provisions of the Act.

§ 72. **Extra-territorial application of the Acts.**[2] Many of the Acts expressly provide either that they shall apply only to injuries received inside the state or that they shall apply to injuries received outside the state if the contract of employment was made within the state; still others provide that they shall apply to all injuries received in the state regardless of where the contract of employment was made, and also to all injuries received outside the state under contracts of employment made within the state unless provided otherwise in the contract of employment. Under any of these provisions or where there is no provision, some interesting questions are bound to arise. Where the statute is regarded as a substitute for tort liability at common law, the law of the place of injury should logically govern. But where the statute is regarded not only as regulating the contract of employment but as entering into it as a term thereof the law of the place of making the contract should govern except in those jurisdictions which hold that where the contract contemplated performance elsewhere the law of the place of performance should govern. Because of the special procedure necessary, suit can ordinarily be brought successfully only in the courts of the state whose statute is held to create the right.

§ 73. **Rights of workman and employer against culpable third party.**[3] Apart from an express provision in the statute a workman whose injury is due partly to the culpable act of a third party may recover and keep compensation from his employer under the Act and full damages from the third party at common law. This allowance of what is substantially double recovery has been deemed unfortunate and several of the Acts now provide that the workman may recover for himself either from the employer or the third party but not from them both, subrogating the employer to the rights of the workman against the third party to the extent of reimbursing himself.

§ 74. **Relations of the Acts to other legislation.**[4] As already pointed out, the Federal Employers' Liability Act, which applies to injuries received by employees engaged in interstate commerce, is paramount to the Compensation Acts. Under the Federal Judicial Code giving Federal Courts exclusive jurisdiction over admiralty and maritime civil cases "saving to suitors in all cases the right of a common-law remedy, where the common law is competent to give it," the widow of a longshoreman killed while doing work of a maritime nature upon a vessel berthed in the New York harbor was denied the benefit under the New York Act. Thereupon the Judicial Code

2 See **Am Jur**, Workmen's Compensation Acts.
Extraterritorial operation of Workmen's Compensation Statutes; conflict of laws. 3 **ALR** 1351–1365; s. in 18 **ALR** 292–295; 28 **ALR** 1345–1348; 35 **ALR** 1414–1417; 45 **ALR** 1234–1235; 59 **ALR** 735–743; 82 **ALR** 709–719; 90 **ALR** 119–125.

3 See **Am Jur**, Workmen's Compensation Acts.
Rights and remedies where employee was injured by third person's negligence. 19 **ALR** 766–797; s. in 27 **ALR** 493–509; 37 **ALR** 838–849; 67 **ALR** 249–287; 88 **ALR** 665–698; 106 **ALR** 1040–1064.
Constitutionality, construction, and application of provision of Workmen's Compensation Act for deduction in computing compensation on account of recovery from a third person responsible for the injury. 142 **ALR** 170–193.

4 See **Am Jur**, Workmen's Compensation Acts.
What amounts to acceptance or election to come within act by employer as to whom act is not mandatory. 136 **ALR** 899–907.

was amended by adding the clause "and to claimants the rights and remedies under the workmen's compensation law of any State," but this extension of the operation of the State Acts was held unconstitutional.

Where there is a provision in the Act that the remedy provided therein should be exclusive it has been held that the Act took precedence over legislation giving a cause of action for wrongfully causing death; it also deprives the workman of any remedy for an injury which does not affect his earning power, unless the Act makes special provision therefor.

§ 75. **Miscellaneous.**[5] Many of the Acts provide in substance that the administering tribunal shall not be governed by technical rules of evidence; these would seem to allow the admission of hearsay but there has been a tendency to construe this provision strictly and hence to exclude it.

After an award of a weekly or monthly payment has been made the obligation to make the payments ceases upon the death of the employee due to causes other than the accident; but mental or physical illness due to other causes does not defeat the right to the payments; and in the absence of a special provision a workman's widow who has been awarded a weekly sum as compensation does not forfeit it by remarriage.

In determining the amount of compensation to be awarded under the Act "tips" received by the employee should be included as "wages" or "earnings" if expressly or impliedly a part of the consideration for the contract of employment; otherwise not. Where a plumber at the time of the injury which caused his death was assisting, upon request of the village marshal, in apprehending a criminal, it was held that compensation should be based upon the earnings of a policeman and not upon those of a plumber. Where the workman unreasonably refuses to undergo a surgical operation to cure the injury, an award will usually be suspended till compliance.

5 See Am Jur, Workmen's Compensation Acts.

Neglect or improper self-treatment as affecting right to or amount of compensation. 54 ALR 637–644.

Basis for computation of compensation in case of employees who have been intermittently but not continuously employed prior to the injury. 112 ALR 1094–1104.

Right to compensation as affected by the fact that the earnings of the injured employee are as much as, or more than, before the injury. 149 ALR 413–452.

Insurance under workmen's compensation act as coextensive with the insured's liability under act. 45 ALR 1329–1337; s. in 108 ALR 812–820.

Right to compensation for temporary total disability in addition to compensation for permanent partial disability. 88 ALR 385–394.

Res judicata as regards decisions or awards under workmen's compensation acts. 122 ALR 550–620.

Necessity, form, and contents of findings of fact to support administrative determinations relating to workmen's compensation. 146 ALR 123–202.

Liability of general or special employer for compensation to injured employee. 3 ALR 1181–1187; s. in 34 ALR 768–778; 58 ALR 1467–1473.

Liability of property owner for injury to workmen engaged in building or repairing structure. 15 ALR 735–749.

One employed concurrently or jointly by several. 30 ALR 1000–1008; s. in 58 ALR 1395–1398.

Validity, construction, and effect of provisions of statute with respect to rates of workmen's compensation insurance. 82 ALR 943–949.

Cancelation or attempted cancelation of insurance under Workmen's Compensation Act. 107 ALR 1514–1523.

Liability of employer or insurance company for medical and hospital aid furnished to injured employee. 7 ALR 545–553.

Selection or change of physician, surgeon, or hospital. 142 ALR 1205–1237.

Construction and effect of provisions in relation to compensation of physicians or others rendering services to injured employee. 72 ALR 1012–1018; s. in 143 ALR 1264–1273.

Workmen's compensation act: applicability of state compensation act to injury within admiralty jurisdiction. 25 ALR 1029–1044; s. in 31 ALR 518–526; 56 ALR 352–359.

Compensation of attorneys for services in connection with claim under Workmen's Compensation Act. 69 ALR 1317–1329; s. in 103 ALR 906-911.

Proper tribunal for determination of questions relating to insurance under workmen's compensation acts. 127 ALR 473–483.

36 Harv. L. R. 263, The Applicability of Common Law Rules of Evidence in Proceedings before Workmen's Compensation Commission.

CHAPTER VII

DEFAMATION

A. In General

For a brief statement of the scope and essential allegations of the declaration in slander and libel, see ante, Forms of Actions, Sections 19, 20.

§ 76. Definition—libel and slander.[6] The interest protected by the law of defamation is that of security of reputation. Since this interest is intangible the proper form of action is case instead of trespass. One's reputation depends upon the opinion which other persons entertain as to his character, and is therefore damaged by communicating to the minds of third persons something which is disparaging. Defamation therefore consists of a statement or other communication to the mind of another which causes a person to be regarded with hatred, contempt, ridicule, fear or the like; or tends to injure him in his office, business, trade or profession.

Slander is, generally speaking, oral defamation; it includes, however, all defamation in temporary, fugitive form, such as hissing, gestures and the like. Libel is usually written or printed defamation, but it includes all defamation in permanent form, such as painting, caricature, effigy or emblem.

A libel may thus be produced without being communicated, though of course no action would arise until there is communication. Slander, on the other hand, can hardly be said to have any existence unless it is communicated to the mind of another; talking to one's self or to someone who was incapable of understanding would not only not be communication but it would not be slander.

Since the difference between slander and libel is merely one of form it would reasonably be expected that the legal principles applicable thereto would be identical; this is largely true but by historical accident the difference is frequently important.

§ 77. Slander actionable per se—imputations of crime and loathsome disease.[7] Whatever the historical reason therefor, it is well settled that only certain classes of slanderous communications are actionable per se—that is, without proof of special damage; namely, those imputing crime or loathsome disease or disparaging one in his office, business, trade or profession.

Though all jurisdictions agree that statements charging the plaintiff with having committed a crime are actionable per se, there are various divergent views as to the meaning of "crime" in this connection. The English rule is that the crime must be punishable corporally and not merely by a fine, but that it need not be indictable; hence a defendant who spoke to the plaintiff in the presence of others: "I will lock you up in Gloucester gaol next week.

6 33 **Am Jur,** Libel and Slander, §§ 2,3.

Libel and slander; imputing disposition to avoid service in the war. 11 **ALR** 1017–1018.

Libel and slander; imputing disposition labor relations or disputes. 150 **ALR** 932–953.

Liability of master or principal for servant's or agent's libel or slander of one other than servant or agent or former servant or agent. 150 **ALR** 1338–1358.

Motion pictures, law of libel or slander as applied to. 99 **ALR** 878–879.

Abusive words as slander or libel. 37 **ALR** 883–889.

What constitutes variance between pleading and proof of defamatory words. 2 **ALR** 367–399.

24 **Marq. L. R.** 117; 25 **Marq. L. R.** 57, 192, Extemporaneous Defamation by Radio.

7 33 **Am Jur,** Libel and Slander, §§ 11–34.

I know enough to put you there," was held liable without proof of special damage.

In the United States the prevailing view requires that the offense be an indictable one, involving moral turpitude or subjecting the offender to infamous punishment. It is not necessary that the plaintiff would, if guilty of the crime charged, be subject to the punishment at the time of the statement; nor is it necessary that the act charged be a crime at the place where the alleged act was committed; the test is furnished by the law of the place where the words were spoken.

A slanderous charge that the plaintiff is suffering from an existing loathsome disease, such as the plague, leprosy, and venereal disorders is actionable per se. It is not sufficient that the charge be of a malady wholly past, the test being not the moral stigma but the tendency to exclude him from human society.

§ 78. Same—disparagement of one in his office, business, trade or profession.[8] Defamatory charges of this sort may be either that the plaintiff lacks an essential requisite with reference to his trade, business, office or profession, such as honesty, capacity, fidelity or the like or that he has been guilty of actual misconduct in the course thereof. An imputation of insolvency is not ordinarily actionable per se and in some instances may not be defamatory at all, but if it is made with reference to one engaged in trade or business it is actionable per se because a business man must have credit to succeed.

Charges of actual misconduct must apparently have close reference to the conduct of the plaintiff in his calling. In an English case the defendant imputed adultery to the plaintiff, who was a physician. It was held that the plaintiff must show in what manner the charge was connected by the defendant with the plaintiff's profession. Thus, if the adultery were charged as a violation of professional confidence, it would be sufficient, whereas if it were charged as wholly unconnected with the plaintiff's profession, it would not be actionable without proof of special damage. Where the calling is no longer followed by the plaintiff at the time the charge is made, he cannot be defamed with reference to it.

§ 79. Slander not actionable per se but causing special damage.[9] Where

[8] 33 **Am Jur**, Libel and Slander, §§ 63–83.
Notice of cessation of relationship of principal and agent, or business or professional relationship, publication of. 138 **ALR** 671–676.
Matrimonial intentions, false imputation of. 44 **ALR** 1424.
Bank, libel or slander affecting. 37 **ALR** 1348–1352.
Bank's return of check or bill to holder without presentation to drawee as libel upon drawer. 53 **ALR** 800.
Libel and slander: what imputations against clergyman are actionable. 53 **ALR** 637–644.
Libel and slander: imputing disease as actionable per se. 45 **ALR** 1114–1119.
Imputation of mental disorder, impairment of mental faculties, or want of mental capacity, as actionable per se. 66 **ALR** 1257–1264.
Public performers or persons associated with public performances as managers, trainers, etc., reflections on ability of. 72 **ALR** 921–923.
Sufficiency of identification of plaintiff by publication or statement complained of as libelous or slanderous. 91 **ALR** 1161–1175.
Nontrader, listing as unworthy of credit. 3 **ALR** 1590–1593.
Placarding debtor as libel. 3 **ALR** 1596–1598.
Statement or publication respecting physician, surgeon, or dentist as ground of action for libel or slander. 124 **ALR** 553–568.

[9] 33 **Am Jur**, Libel and Slander, § 5.
Oral imputation of sexual immorality to man as actionable per se. 55 **ALR** 175–179.
Libel or slander by charging one with being a bastard or illegitimate. 53 **ALR** 548–550.
Orally charging a women with being a whore or prostitute as actionable per se. 11 **ALR** 669–678.
Libel or slander by imputation of agitating objectionable political or sociological principles. 51 **ALR** 1071–1074.
Libel or slander by imputation of drunkenness. 58 **ALR** 1157–1175.

the slanderous imputation does not fall within any of the three classes just mentioned the plaintiff must allege and prove special damage. This must be something other than mere damage to reputation; and mere loss of society or friends or mental suffering is not enough, though it has been held that loss of such hospitality as the plaintiff would have otherwise enjoyed at her friends' homes is sufficient.

If the person to whom the defendant makes a defamatory statement should repeat the statement and such repetition causes special damage this is sufficient if the defendant authorizes the repetition or if without authorizing it, he intended that the statement should be thus repeated; also, if the person repeating is able to escape liability because of privilege; it ought to be sufficient, upon general principles of legal cause, that the defendant should have foreseen that there would be repetition, but the weight of authority is contra.

§ 80. Libel.[10] Where the defamatory imputation is in permanent form it is not, by English law, necessary to allege or prove special damage in order to make out a prima facie case. The reason for this difference between slander and libel is historical, slander being of common law origin while libel was of civil law origin, coming into the common law soon after the invention of printing through the court of Star Chamber, but several analytical reasons have been suggested; although the distinction has received some judicial approval it has more frequently been criticized as artificial and troublesome; and in this country many states, confusing the phrases actionable per se and libellous per se, require proof of special damage in libel cases unless the charge was libellous per se; that is, libellous on its face.

§ 81. Publication or communication—culpability.[1] No cause of action arises unless the defamation has been published—i. e., communicated to the mind of another; communication to the plaintiff is not enough because what the plaintiff thinks of himself is no part of his reputation. Publication must, apparently, be either intentional or negligent; if a libellous letter is sent to

Methods used in attempting to collect debt, right of action for damages because of. 55 **ALR** 971–975; s. in 106 **ALR** 1453–1457.

Race or nationality as to which there is social prejudice, imputation of association with persons of. 121 **ALR** 1151.

Solicitation of business or fomenting of litigation, imputation of. 112 **ALR** 177–181.

Poverty, imputation of. 137 **ALR** 913–915.

"Slacker," charging one with being. 11 **ALR** 1017–1018.

10 33 **Am Jur**, Libel and Slander, §§ 2, 3.

Libel by headline. 40 **ALR** 583–590; s. in 59 **ALR** 1061.

18 **Wis. L. R.** 331, The Changing Libel Scene.

17 **So. Calif. L. R.** 347, Libel Per Se in California and Some Other States.

1 33 **Am Jur**, Libel and Slander, §§ 96–110.

Customer's conduct, presence of third parties as affecting right of action for defamatory words with regard to, spoken directly to customer. 92 **ALR** 1174–1176.

Accidental communication, not intended by defendant, as a publication. 81 **ALR** 110–114.

Libel and slander: communication of defamatory matter only to person defamed as a publication which will support a civil action. 24 **ALR** 237; 46 **ALR** 562–563.

Employee or business associate of defendant, communication or exhibition to, as publication. 18 **ALR** 776–782.

Liability of one responsible for original libel or slander for its repetition by third persons. 16 **ALR** 726–742; s. in 41 **ALR** 1191–1192.

Mistake in statement or publication as to name or description of person to whom libel or slander relates. 26 **ALR** 454–461; s. in 41 **ALR** 485.

Libel and slander: publisher's liability as affected by his ignorance of writer's libellous intention. 10 **ALR** 672–673

News agency or regular correspondent, libellous or privileged character of publication by newspaper based on matter received from. 86 **ALR** 475–477.

Relevancy of matter contained in pleading as affecting privilege within law or libel. 16 **ALR** 746–754; s. in 42 **ALR** 878–879; 134 **ALR** 483–499.

Telegraph or telephone company's transmission of libellous or slanderous message as privileged. 63 **ALR** 1118–1127.

Libel or slander as affected by mistake in statement or publication as to name or description of person to whom it relates. 26 **ALR** 454–461; s. in 41 **ALR** 485 the plaintiff and is opened by the plaintiff's clerk the defendant is liable only if he should have foreseen that the letter would be thus opened; if such a letter should by mistake of the defendant be addressed to a third party instead of the plaintiff, such mistake will not excuse him.

Where the defendant writes a defamatory letter and then reads it to a third party this is, of course, publication, but there is conflict of authority as to whether it is libel or slander; the better view is that it is only slander since the third party merely hears the words uttered by the defendant. Where the defendant dictates the defamatory statement to a stenographer who then, according to her duty, typewrites it and reads it, it would seem to be libel and not merely slander. Where a libel is written or printed on a post card and sent through the mails it is a publication because almost certainly read by the post-office officials or the plaintiff's employees or members of his family; if the defendant sends a defamatory telegram or has a defamatory statement printed, there is also necessarily a publication.

Though a defendant is liable for a publication only when made intentionally or negligently he is liable at peril if his charge refers to the plaintiff; or if, due to circumstances unknown to him, an apparently innocent statement is defamatory. And all who assist in the dissemination of a libel are liable unless their act is of a purely mechanical or menial type in which case they are liable only if by due care they could have known that they were handling defamatory statements.

§ 82. Who may sue and be sued for defamation.[2] A corporation may maintain such an action.

If the publication of a defamatory charge against X should cause damage to Y, the latter is not entitled to maintain an action for libel or slander; but if such damage were intended it seems clear that Y ought to be allowed a special action on the case, and this is probably the rule.

An interesting situation is presented where a libellous statement is contained in a will. If the plaintiff relies upon a publication during the life of the testator he is met by the rule that tort actions not affecting property die with the tort-feasor; if he sues for a publication after the death of the testator, as, for example, that caused by probating the will, there is the difficulty that at that time the testator is no longer in existence and it would be absurd to hold the executor personally liable for the results of an act which it was his legal duty to do, namely, probate the will. It is obvious, however, that the plaintiff should be granted protection and the few cases on the point have given relief.

B. Justification

§ 83. Truth.[3] Though plaintiffs are still accustomed to allege that the imputation made by the defendant was false, they need not prove it; truth is,

[2] 33 **Am Jur**, Libel and Slander, § 101.
Will, libel by. 87 **ALR** 234–237.
Deceased person, defamatory of, as ground of action by members of his family, or other persons associated with him, in their own right, because of its tendency to subject them to ridicule or contempt. 132 **ALR** 891–895.
Right of individual member of class or group referred to in a defamatory publication to maintain action for libel or slander. 97 **ALR** 281–292.
Action by corporation for libel or slander. 52 **ALR** 1199–1212; s. in 86 **ALR** 442–445.
Servant's personal liability for libel published while acting in capacity of servant. 20 **ALR** 116; s. in 99 **ALR** 408–426.
Wife's joint liability in case of commission of separate slanders by husband and wife. 12 **ALR** 1479.
Stockholder or officer, libel or slander of, by publication or statement reflecting on him as well as on corporation. 58 **ALR** 1233–1236.

[3] 33 **Am Jur**, Libel and Slander, §§ 116–118.

however, a complete defense, but it must be specially alleged and proved by the defendant. This is in harmony with the rule of the criminal law which requires the state to prove the guilt of the accused. In some jurisdictions the defendant is required, if he sets up truth as a defense, in cases where the defamatory statement charged plaintiff with the commission of a crime, to prove beyond a reasonable doubt that the plaintiff committed the crime, but the better view requires merely proof by a preponderance of the evidence.

Where a plaintiff, after having been guilty of the offenses charged by the defendant, has for several years led a law-abiding and useful life the rule that truth is a defense operates harshly and it is perhaps partly for this reason that the defendant must make out his proof with substantial fullness; if he sets up truth and fails to prove it, it is evidence of malice which may be important in the assessing of exemplary or punitive damages allowed in most jurisdictions. That the defendant honestly believed that the statement was true is no defense, but if he knew it was not true, and published it, with intent to cause damage, the jury may consider this in awarding punitive damages.

§ 84. Repetition of another's statement.[4] It seems to have been the early law that if the defendant merely repeated a defamation and at the time of the repetition gave the name of the author, it was a justification, provided the words were given with sufficient exactness to ground an action against the author; this went upon the old scholastic argument that one cause of action against one individual was a sufficient remedy. This doctrine has in recent times been repudiated both as to slander and libel. In an English case the court said: "As great an injury may accrue from the wrongful repetition as from the first publication of the slander; the first utterer may have been a person insane or of bad character. The person who repeats it gives greater weight to the slander. A party is not the less entitled to recover damages in a court of law for injurious matter published concerning him because another person previously published it."

§ 85. Consent—self-defense—illegality—retraction.[5] Upon the general principle that one who consents to the infliction upon him of what would otherwise be a tort cannot later be heard to complain thereof, a plaintiff cannot recover for the publication of a defamatory charge to which he has consented. The difficult question is usually whether what the plaintiff has done really amounts to consent or whether he acted merely for the purpose of investigating and determining whether defamatory charges were in fact being disseminated.

Where the plaintiff has been guilty of defaming the defendant he cannot be heard to complain if in reasonable self-defense defamatory matter about himself is published by the defendant. This is analogous to the privilege of self-defense against a physical attack—i. e. an assault—and is similarly limited.

That the plaintiff was engaged in an illegal act has been held in some cases to be a bar to recovery for defamation.

A retraction is not a defense but it may sometimes be shown in mitigation of damages.

[4] 33 **Am Jur**, Libel and Slander, § 95.
Common report as defense to action **for** libel or slander. 43 **ALR** 887–909.

[5] 33 **Am Jur**, Libel and Slander, §§ 93, 94, 121–123.
Qualified privilege of reply to defamatory publication. 103 **ALR** 476–483.

C. Absolute Immunity or Privilege

§ 86. Judicial immunity.[6] Under some circumstances it is excusable to publish matter which is both false and defamatory. The reason for this is that the interest of the individual in his reputation must sometimes yield to some other interest which the law considers of more importance to the public welfare. In some cases the immunity is absolute—that is, it is not dependent in any way upon the motive of the defendant; in others the defendant is excused only if his conduct was actuated by the proper motive.

In the following cases the immunity is absolute:

(1) Judges, juries, counsel, and witnesses, as to relevant statements made in the course of judicial proceedings.

(2) The chief executive of the United States and of each state and members of the Federal and state legislatures, while acting in their official capacities.

In an English case the defendant, while acting as judge in the trial of a case in which the plaintiff was a party, said of and to the plaintiff: "You are a harpy, preying upon the vitals of the poor." In holding that "no action will lie against a judge for any act done or word spoken in his judicial capacity in a court of justice" the court said: "It is essential in all courts that the judges who are appointed to administer the law should be permitted to administer it under the protection of the law, independently, and freely, without favor and without fear. . . . How could a judge so exercise his office if he were in daily and hourly fear of having an action being brought against him and of having the question submitted to a jury whether a matter on which he had commented judicially was or was not relevant to the case before him. Again, if a question arose as to his bona fides, it would have, if the analogy of similar cases is to be followed, to be submitted to the jury. . . ."

The immunity extends to all courts of whatever grade, either civil or military, but does not extend to administrative officials even though they occasionally exercise some judicial functions.

§ 87. Witnesses, counsel, party and jury.[7] In England the immunity of witnesses, counsel, parties and jury is apparently on a par with that of the judge; but in the United States, it is usually required that all statements be pertinent and material to the issue.

Official statements of superior officers of state are absolutely privileged while those of inferior officers are only conditionally privileged. Petitions to Parliament or other superior legislative bodies are absolutely privileged while petitions to subordinate legislative or other official bodies or to executive or administrative officers are privileged only if they were made in good faith. Legislative officers are absolutely privileged, but of course this privilege does not extend to statements not made while acting in their legislative capacity.

D. Defeasible Immunity or Qualified Privilege

§ 88. Communications in the interest of the maker.[8] Where the public interest in freedom of speech is not strong enough to justify the law in granting absolute immunity as in the cases just discussed it may still be strong

6 33 **Am Jur,** Libel and Slander, §§ 125, 177–182.

7 33 **Am Jur,** Libel and Slander, §§ 125, 179–182.

Libel and slander: scope of absolute privilege of executive officer. 132 **ALR** 1340–1348.

8 33 **Am Jur,** Libel and Slander, §§ 126, 129, 130, 137.

Libel and slander: privilege of communienough to grant immunity dependent upon the absence of an improper motive. The most important occasions where the law gives this defeasible immunity are: (1) communications made in the interest of the maker; (2) communications made in the interest of the maker and recipient; (3) communications made in the interest of recipient; (4) communications made to aid the administration of justice; (5) reports of legislative, judicial and other public proceedings.

A defamatory statement is conditionally privileged if it is made for the purpose of protecting some legitimate interest of the maker. In an English case the plaintiff had sold his stock in trade at auction and the proceeds were in the hands of the auctioneers. The defendant, who had sold goods to the plaintiff on credit, procured his attorneys to send a notice to the auctioneers not to part with the money on the false ground that the plaintiff had committed an act of bankruptcy. In an action for libel the court said: "This case appears to fall within the range of that principle by which a communication made by a person immediately concerned in interest in the subject matter to which it relates, for the purpose of protecting his interests, in the full belief that the communication is true, and without any malicious motive, is held to be excused from responsibility in an action for a libel."

§ 89. Communications in the mutual interest of maker and recipient.[9] In an English case the defendant corporation published of the plaintiff, their manager, in a report of the affairs of the company, the following statement: "The shareholders will observe that there is a charge of £1306, for deficiency of stock which the manager is responsible for; his accounts as such manager have been badly kept and have been rendered to us very irregularly." The court said: "I am quite prepared to hold that a company, having a great number of shareholders all interested in knowing how their officers conduct themselves, is justified in making a communication in a printed report, relating to the conduct of their officer, to all the shareholders that are present or absent, if the communication be made without malice and bona fide." In a few jurisdictions electors are privileged to inform other electors as to the supposed conduct of candidates for public office.

§ 90. Communications in the interest of recipient—in the interest of justice.[10] Common illustrations of privileged communications made in the in-

cations made by private person or concern to public authorities regarding one not in public employment. 136 ALR 543–554.

Relative provinces of court and jury as to privileged occasion and privileged communication in law of libel and slander. 26 ALR 830–863.

Privilege as to communications to one spouse reflecting on other spouse. 69 ALR 1023–1024.

Radio operators, privilege of letter by steamship company to Federal Radio Commission, protesting against conduct of, in demanding new contract just at sailing time. 104 ALR 877.

Allegations contrary to facts as previously adjudicated, privilege as to. 136 ALR 1414–1415.

9 33 Am Jur, Libel and Slander, §§ 129, 130.

Public authorities, privilege of communication by private person or concern to, concerning applicant for position as schoolteacher, or complaining of conduct of pupil in school. 136 ALR 547.

Church matters, privilege as to communications respecting. 63 ALR 649–658.

10 33 Am Jur, Libel and Slander, §§ 129, 137–139.

Libel and slander: privilege regarding communications to police or other officer respecting commission of crime. 140 ALR 1466–1478.

Police or other officer, privilege of communications to, respecting commission of crime, as absolute or qualified. 140 ALR 1471.

Public authorities, privileges of communications made by private person or concern to, regarding one not in public employment. 136 ALR 543–554.

Libel and slander: privilege as to statement reflecting on manner in which public work is performed. 50 ALR 339–347.

Charge of misconduct relating to campaign or public funds. 55 ALR 856.

Libel and slander: defamation of one in his character as a political leader or "boss." 55 ALR 854–865.

terest of the recipient alone are: (1) statements made with regard to a servant to one who is about to give him employment; (2) statements made by commercial agencies in regard to the credit of a business man to one about to extend such credit; (3) statements made in the line of fiduciary duties by an agent to his principal or by an employee to his employer; (4) statements made between near relatives as to the character of a suitor of the recipient of the statement. It is not necessary that the information be asked for by the recipient but the fact that it was volunteered by the defendant may tend to show that he acted officiously and therefore with an improper motive.

In this country it is generally held that if a mercantile agency makes a report only to those of its subscribers who have a present interest in knowing of the condition of the plaintiff's business the occasion is privileged. In England and a small minority of American jurisdictions the privilege is denied on the ground that the agency is conducted for profit.

Where the defendant stood in such a relation to the recipient that he was under a duty to communicate to him information with regard to the plaintiff, the occasion is privileged and courts have been liberal in construing the term duty in this condition.

Defamatory statements with reference to a suitor of the recipient seem to be privileged only if made by a near relative of the recipient; that the defendant was a close friend of the recipient's family is not enough.

When the defendant bona fide believes that the plaintiff has been guilty of a crime he is privileged to make a statement to that effect to the proper officer in order to bring the suspected person to justice.

§ 91. Privileged reports of legislative, judicial and other public proceedings.[1] The general rule is that a report of legislative, judicial and other proceedings should be substantially accurate account of the proceedings as a whole; details may be either omitted or summarized. In Millissich v. Lloyds, the court said: "The question is one for the jury and may be stated as follows: Was the report a fair one, that is, would it give a fair notion to people who were not there of what took place?"

The reason for excusing defamation in reports of court proceedings is "that the balance of public benefit from publicity is great. It is of great consequence that the public should know what takes place in court; and the proceedings are under the control of the judges. The inconvenience, therefore, arising from the chance of injury to private character is infinitesimally small as compared to the convenience of publicity." The privilege extends to reports of even inferior courts not of record; it is no objection that the proceeding was ex parte, or that the court had no jurisdiction to determine the case; but there is probably no privilege if the proceedings are secret.

At the English common law there was no privilege to report proceedings of public meetings, but privilege has been given by Act of Parliament. The decisions in this country have gone almost as far as in the English statute. In Barrows v. Bell the court said: "So many municipal, parochial and other public corporations, and so many large voluntary associations formed for almost every lawful purpose of benevolence, business or interest, are constantly holding meetings, in their nature public, and so usual is it that these

Recall petition, libel by. 43 ALR 1268–1269.

1 33 Am Jur, Libel and Slander, §§ 153–160.

Police investigation as within rule of privilege relative to report of judicial proceedings. 132 ALR 495–499.

proceedings are published for general use and information, that the law, to adapt itself to this necessary condition of society, must of necessity admit of these public proceedings and a just and proper publication of them as far as it can be done consistently with private rights." Proceedings of public bodies may be reported as the proceedings progress, but there is probably no right to comment upon them till the whole is finished; there is no privilege to report a part of a proceeding after it has been entirely closed. Apart from statute newspapers have no peculiar immunity in publishing such reports.

§ 92. **Excess of privilege.**[2] The fact that one is privileged to make a defamatory statement to another person or to a class of persons does not give him the privilege of publishing it to the whole world. On the other hand, the privilege is not necessarily destroyed merely because the statement was communicated to someone other than the one who was entitled to hear it. The test is, whether the privilege was reasonably used; if it was not, the defendant is liable for such excess of privilege. It has therefore been held that under some circumstances it was no excess of privilege to use newspapers or the telegraph, but not a postcard; the modern tendency is to hold that dictation to a stenographer or communication to a printer may be reasonable. Though there are some cases which seem to say that excess of privilege is important only as showing malice the better view is that a defendant will be liable for excess of privilege regardless of his motive. Sending the statement by mistake to one to whom it is not a privileged communication has been held not to make the defendant liable but the case has been criticized.

§ 93. **Malice or improper motive.**[3] Malice ordinarily means ill will or spite. It is still customary for a plaintiff to allege in his declaration or complaint that the defamatory statement was made maliciously; whatever the meaning earlier it is now usually said to mean merely "wrongfully and without just cause or excuse;" such an allegation is, however, a formal one because the plaintiff is not required to negative all excuses at the trial.

The meaning of "malice" in qualified privilege and fair comment, on the other hand, is improper motive; this is frequently called in the cases "malice in fact" or "express malice" to distinguish it from the use of the term in plaintiff's declaration or complaint, in which latter case it is often referred to as "malice in law" or "implied malice." Motive is never material in defamation except in cases of qualified privilege and fair comment; where no question of privilege is raised a defendant is liable though he honestly believed the statement to be true and his motives were of the highest, while in cases of absolute immunity or privilege the defendant escapes liability though actuated by the lowest of motives, such as ill will, spite, revenge, etc.; similarly, the defendant is not liable if he can prove that the statement was true, regardless of his motive.

The burden of alleging and proving a privileged occasion is on the defendant; but the burden of alleging and proving that the defendant was actuated by an improper motive is upon the plaintiff. The evidence of an improper motive is usually circumstantial; evidence of acts or declarations of the defendant even after suit has been brought are admissible, but in the case of a subsequent publication of libel or slander, the jury should be cautioned

2 33 **Am Jur,** Libel and Slander, §§ 183–190.

3 33 **Am Jur,** Libel and Slander, §§ 111–113. Malice, may actual malice which will defeat conditional privilege coexist with belief in truth of imputation. 18 **ALR** 1160.

against giving damages for the later publication as such. In England it is sufficient, in order to disprove improper motive, to show that the defendant acted honestly, but the weight of authority in this country requires also that he should have acted reasonably. The refusal of the defendant to tell the facts upon which his opinion is based is evidence of improper motive.

§ 94. **Criticism or comment.**[4] Anything placed before the public for public consideration—such as a book or play—and the conduct of public men may be commented upon provided that such comment be not malicious—i. e., made with an improper motive, the proper motive in such case being the placing before the public the defendant's honest opinion. It is sometimes said that comment is not a matter of qualified privilege because it is equally open to all and not to a certain favored class; the answer to this is that in no case of either absolute or qualified privilege or immunity is there a favored class; the privilege or immunity is given because of the occasion for the purpose of securing justice—or some other social interest—and not for the purpose of favoring the individual making the defamatory statement.

Privilege to comment or criticize does not include the making of statements of facts which are untrue; for example, that a certain assertion is in a book which is not there, or that a public man said or did something which he did not say or do; nor may comment be made upon such untrue statements of fact. In an English case the court said: "There is no doubt that the public acts of a public man may lawfully be made the subject of comment or criticism not only by the press but by all members of the public. But the distinction cannot be too clearly borne in mind between comment or criticism and allegation of facts, such as that disgraceful acts have been committed, or discreditable language used. It is one thing to comment upon or criticize, even with severity, the acknowledged or proved acts of a public man, and quite another to assert falsely that he has been guilty of particular acts of misconduct."

It is often said that a public man may not be charged with improper motives, but the better view is that he may if his conduct is such as to make natural comment upon his motives.

CHAPTER VIII

WRONGS THROUGH MALICE

A. Malicious Prosecution of Criminal Proceeding

For a brief statement of the scope of this subject, see ante, Forms of Actions, Section 21.

§ 95. **Essentials of the action.**[5] A malicious prosecution of a criminal proceeding may injure a person in three ways: by damaging his reputation, by infringing his personal security, if he has suffered imprisonment, and by

[4] 33 **Am Jur,** Libel and Slander, §§ 162–169.
Libel and slander: doctrine of privilege or of fair comment and criticism as applicable to statement or publication imputing impropriety or dishonesty in bringing or defending civil action or proceeding. 148 **ALR** 1173–1178.
Doctrine of privilege or fair comment as applicable to misstatements of fact in publication (or oral communication) relating to public officer or candidate for office. 110 **ALR** 412–441; s. in 150 **ALR** 358–365.
42 **Col. L. R.** 1085, 1282, Fair Game and Fair Comment.
42 **Col. L. R.** 727, Control of Group Libel.

[5] 34 **Am Jur,** Malicious Prosecution, § 6.
Defendant's acquiescence in, approval of, or silence regarding, acts of another for which he was not otherwise responsible as ground of liability in action for malicious prosecution or false arrest. 120 **ALR** 1322–1331.

causing him expense in defending himself. Hence the interests protected are those of reputation, personal security and of substance.

In order to succeed in an action for the malicious prosecution of a criminal charge the plaintiff must generally allege and prove the following: (a) that the plaintiff was prosecuted on a criminal charge; (b) that the prosecution terminated in favor of the present plaintiff; (c) that there was not probable cause for such prosecution; (d) that it was done maliciously—that is, with an improper motive; (e) in some jurisdictions, that there was special damage, where the charge was such that if made orally outside of legal proceedings, an action for slander would not lie without proof of special damage. If in spite of the plaintiff's proving the above essentials the defendant is able to show that the plaintiff was really guilty of the crime charged the action cannot be maintained.

§ 96. Prosecution on a criminal charge.[6] If the defendant merely gives information to a magistrate without making any charge this is not considered as a prosecution. The test seems usually to be whether the magistrate acts entirely upon his own discretion; but even if he does, the defendant may still be liable if he should mislead the magistrate by furnishing him dishonest evidence.

If a charge is made to a ministerial officer, such as a sheriff or constable, who makes an arrest without getting a proper warrant, the liability, if any, in such a case, is for false imprisonment. But if the charge is made to a police magistrate or other judicial officer, so that the forms of law are properly observed, the liability, if any, is for malicious prosecution. The gist of an action for malicious prosecution, then, is setting a magistrate in motion. The mere preferring a charge not followed by action of the magistrate would not be enough.

The term criminal charge, in this connection, probably covers all charges which subject an offender to loss of liberty or which involve scandal to his reputation. The mere fact that the machinery of the criminal law is used is not enough; thus, a prosecution for the non-repair of a highway would probably not be considered as coming within the meaning of the term.

§ 97. Previous termination of the prosecution.[7] The general rule is that no action will lie for bringing a prosecution until the latter is ended in favor of the accused. This is because otherwise there might be a conflict between the civil and criminal courts. It would allow a sort of informal appeal from the court in which the criminal charge was prosecuted. The rule has been applied even though the conviction was in an inferior court from which there was no appeal.

In some cases the criminal proceeding is of such a nature that it is impossible for it to terminate in favor of the accused. Thus, if his house is unreasonably searched under a search warrant, the proceeding goes no further and can hardly be said to be decided in his favor; all that the plaintiff needs to prove to satisfy this requirement is that nothing was found in the search to incriminate him.

6 34 **Am Jur**, Malicious Prosecution, §§ 7–26.

7 34 **Am Jur**, Malicious Prosecution, §§ 27–43.

Dismissal by magistrate or other inferior court for lack of insufficiency of evidence as a final termination of prosecution as regards action for malicious prosecution. 135 **ALR** 784–796.

Dismissal of criminal proceeding as result of compromise or settlement as precluding action for malicious prosecution. 67 **ALR** 513–521.

According to the better view, a voluntary abandonment of the prosecution seems to be a sufficient termination. On the other hand, an abandonment by way of compromise with the accused is not sufficient.

§ 98. **Lack of reasonable and probable cause.**[8] Reasonable and probable cause has been judicially defined as "such a state of facts as would lead a man of ordinary caution and prudence to believe or to entertain an honest and strong suspicion that the person arrested is guilty." The burden of proving the lack of it,—though a negative proposition—is upon the plaintiff. It is not to be inferred from the existence of malice or improper motive because one might very likely have an improper motive for bringing supposed criminals to justice and yet have reasonable and probable cause for having the prosecution made.

There are three views as to the effect of a conviction in a lower court which is later reversed: (1) it is conclusive evidence of probable cause even though the conviction was obtained by fraud; (2) it is conclusive evidence unless procured by fraud; (3) it is prima facie evidence, which may be rebutted by any competent evidence which clearly overcomes the presumption arising from the fact of the defendant's conviction in the first instance. Waiving examination before the magistrate does not show probable cause.

As to the effect of a favorable termination of the prosecution upon the question of probable cause much depends upon the nature of such termination. Since it is the duty of an examining magistrate to hold an accused for trial if there appears to be probable cause for the prosecution, many courts hold that discharge of the plaintiff by the magistrate is prima facie evidence; other courts hold that such a discharge has no bearing on the question, but the great weight of authority is that an acquittal after the trial is not relevant because it merely tends to show failure to prove the accused guilty beyond a reasonable doubt.

If the defendant before bringing the prosecution laid all the facts before a reputable and competent lawyer and acted honestly upon his advice and opinion, this is usually considered to be conclusive evidence of probable cause, even though the lawyer was mistaken as to the law. If after the prosecution was begun the defendant discovered that the accused was not guilty or had no reason to believe that he was guilty the defendant should be liable if after that he urges on the prosecution and on principle should owe a duty to do what he reasonably can to stop it. Some cases have held that the fact that the plaintiff was indicted is prima facie evidence of reasonable and probable cause.

The question of lack of reasonable and probable cause, though one of fact, is, in most jurisdictions, decided by the court and not by the jury. This rule, which is of early origin, arose from the fear of the courts that prosecutions might be too much discouraged. In England the jury is usually required to give a special verdict; in this country the practice is to instruct the jury as to which possible states of fact in the case would and which would not be probable cause.

8 34 **Am Jur**, Malicious Prosecution, §§ 46–68.

Institution of prosecution on false information without investigation as showing lack of probable cause. 5 **ALR** 1688–1703.

Malicious prosecution: acting on advice of justice of the peace, magistrate or layman. 12 **ALR** 1230–1236.

Acquittal, discharge, or discontinuance as evidence of want of probable cause in action for malicious prosecution. 24 **ALR** 261–294; s. in 94 **ALR** 744–750; 114 **ALR** 885–889.

Actual belief on part of prosecutor as element of probable cause in action for malicious prosecution. 65 **ALR** 225–244.

Even though there was not reasonable and probable cause and the defendant acted from an improper motive and the accused was acquitted the defendant is not liable if the plaintiff was actually guilty of the crime charged.

§ 99. Malice or improper motive.[9] Malice means here, as in qualified privilege in defamation, the absence of the proper motive; in prosecuting supposed criminals the proper motive is the duty to the public and the furtherance of justice.

If lack of probable cause is proved, it is a fair inference of fact, though not a necessary one, that the defendant acted from improper motives; hence the plaintiff is entitled to go to the jury without any other evidence of malice. Evidence as to the conduct of the defendant in the course of the transaction, his declarations on the subject, and any forwardness and activity in exposing the plaintiff by publication are properly admitted to prove malice.

B. Malicious Institution of a Civil Action

§ 100. Development of the rule.[10] One against whom has been instituted a civil action maliciously and without probable cause ought logically to have a remedy just as one who has been maliciously prosecuted on a criminal charge; and a remedy is given him where the civil action has been accompanied by arrest of the person, attachment of his property or other special damage. Where there is not such special damage but where nevertheless the present plaintiff was put to the expense of defending the action, he was likewise allowed an action for such costs by the early English common law; this was changed, however, by the Statute of Marlbridge which provided that in such a case the court in the maliciously instituted suit should award costs to the successful defendant pro falso clamore. Since there is no such legislation in this country the English decisions denying a separate action in such cases are not applicable; this is now being recognized and the present trend of authority is toward allowing recovery.

C. Malicious Abuse of Process

§ 101. Statement of the rule.[1] A legal proceeding, though instituted with reasonable and probable cause, may be employed for some collateral object of extortion or oppression; if in such case there is also an act not proper in the proceeding, the party aggrieved may have relief, though the previous proceeding may not have terminated in his favor. In an English case the plaintiff, who was master and owner of a vessel, had been arrested on civil

[9] 34 **Am Jur,** Malicious Prosecution, §§ 44, 45.

Malicious prosecution: may prosecutor avoid liability on the ground of probable cause or absence of malice, despite the fact that his motive was to collect debt, enforce claim for damages, or recover property. 139 **ALR** 1088–1100.

[10] 34 **Am Jur,** Malicious Prosecution, §§ 9–21.

Prosecution of civil suit, without arrest of person or seizure of property, as ground of action for malicious prosecution. 150 **ALR** 897–916.

Action for malicious prosecution based on institution of involuntary bankruptcy or receivership proceedings. 86 **ALR** 219–225.

Unauthorized prosecution of suit in name of another as ground of action in tort. 146 **ALR** 1125–1130.

[1] 1 **Am Jur,** Abuse of Process, §§ 2–10.

Servant's or agent's personal liability for. 99 **ALR** 415.

Constitutionolity, construction and application of statutory provisions for damages by defendant in wrongful attachment. 125 **ALR** 1219–1228.

Wife's liability for abuse of process by husband. 12 **ALR** 1476, 1484.

Debt, civil liability for use of criminal process to collect. 4 **ALR** 233–238.

Executor's, administrator's or trustee's wrongful legal proceedings, liability of estate for. 44 **ALR** 674; s. in 127 **ALR** 687–694.

Servant's or agent's personal liability for. 20 **ALR** 116; s. in 99 **ALR** 408–426.

process by the defendant, a mortgagee of the vessel, and, under the duress of the imprisonment, was compelled to give up the possession of the ship's register without which he could not go to sea, whereby he lost the profits on four voyages. The court said: "This is an action for abusing the process of the law, by applying it to extort property from the plaintiff, and not an action for a malicious arrest or malicious prosecution. . . . If the course pursued here is such that there is no precedent of a similar transaction, the plaintiff's remedy is by an action on the case, applicable to such new and special circumstances; and his complaint being that the process of the law has been abused to effect an object not within the scope of the process, it is immaterial whether the suit which that process commenced has been determined or not or whether or not it is founded on reasonable and probable cause."

CHAPTER IX

INTERFERENCE WITH VARIOUS RELATIONS

A. Injuries to Contract and Business Relations

§ 102. Compelling or inducing breach of contract.[2] If X by intimidation, or fraud or bribery prevents A from performing his contract with B, X is liable for any damage caused thereby to A and B respectively, and it is no justification that X was acting for his own economic advancement or that he was himself bound by contract to do what he did.

If X uses only peaceable persuasion the better view and probably the weight of authority is that procuring a breach of contract by such means is a prima facie tort which may be justified either by the close family relationship between X and the defendant, or perhaps by other circumstances. The same reasoning has been applied where the defendant has by persuading a fourth party made it impossible for the third party to go on with his contract with the plaintiff.

Where a tortious act of the defendant has proximately though unintentionally caused damage—usually by breach—to the plaintiff's contract right with a third party the defendant should logically be liable therefor and some cases have so held.

The chief reasons for denying recovery in such cases are that it might lead to the manufacturing of contractual relations and thereby increase the recovery against a wrongdoer and the difficulty of properly apportioning damages between the party directly injured and the party indirectly injured.

§ 103. Interference with probable expectancies of an employer—the strike.[3] An employer of labor, even though he does not make contracts of employment with his employees, has obviously an interest in the freedom of the labor market; this interest has received legal recognition and a measure of legal protection. If a defendant—usually a former employee or an official of a labor union—interferes by intimidation or other tortious means with this probable expectancy of a plaintiff employer the latter is entitled to recover.

[2] 30 **Am. Jur**, Interference, §§ 18–36.
Liability for procuring breach of contract. 84 **ALR** 43–100.
Liability for preventing one from making specific contract. 99 **ALR** 12–23.
Liability in damages for inducing the discharge of employee. 29 **ALR** 532–550.
36 **Harv. L. R.** 663, Inducing Breach of Contract.

[3] 31 **Am Jur**, Labor, §§ 178–249.

Where means tortious in themselves have not been used there has been much uncertainty and confusion and several shifts in the judicial attitude. As a matter of logic practically all strikes ought to be held unlawful as amounting to economic intimidation and this was the early law, a strike being indictable as a conspiracy. But since the courts could not undertake to determine the highly complicated question of the wages the employee should receive and the conditions under which he should work and furthermore because of the great economic advantage which the employer had over any one employee, the rule is practically settled now that a strike for higher wages, shorter hours, or better working conditions of the strikers, is lawful. As to whether such a strike may be rendered unlawful by the presence of any other motive there is conflict of opinion. Whether a strike is rendered unlawful because the strikers were employed by a public service company is also a disputed point. Where the strike is a part of a campaign for the unionization of industry it is legal by statute in England and by judicial decision in some states, but illegal in others.

§ 104. Same—the boycott and picketing.[4] It was some time after the ordinary strike had been recognized as a lawful weapon of industrial warfare before any such recognition was accorded to the boycott; the question as to the extent to which there is now such recognition is unsettled and the failure to formulate a definite test of legality or illegality is even more marked than in the case of the strike. Though ordinarily it is easy to distinguish a boycott from a strike, it is not always so; and attempts to differentiate between primary boycotts on the one hand and secondary boycotts on the other have not been entirely satisfactory, the variety and complexity of concrete cases being such as to prevent any such simple classification. Even though it will probably not result in a workable judicial rule it will tend to clarify the situation to recognize the existence of the varying conflicting interests in all trade and labor disputes. As has been pointed out, if the social interest in industrial peace and unimpeded production were the sole interest of society, it might well override the interest of the employees in the freedom of selling on the labor market and thus all strikes as well as all boycotts be held illegal. But there is also the social interest in economic progress which may well be thought to be of even more importance. Since it is impossible to affix any definite weight to the various conflicting interests, the ultimate solution of the problem would seem to lie in some form of legislative regulation which will obviate the waste of industrial warfare.

Picketing for the purpose of peacefully obtaining or giving information is usually regarded as lawful unless carried on in such a way as to become a nuisance.

§ 105. Interference with probable expectancies of an employee—the blacklist.[5] Corresponding to the interest of the employer in the freedom of buying on the labor market is the interest of the employee in the freedom of selling on the labor market. Any forcible interference by the employer with this probable expectancy would no doubt be tortious. Though superficially a combination of employers to blacklist an employee seems analogous to a strike by employees, the relatively greater power wielded by a combination

4 31 **Am Jur,** Labor, §§ 223–249; 250–261. 56 **Harv. L. R.** 180, 513, 532, Picketing and Free Speech. 47 **Yale L. J.** 341, Secondary Boycotts in Labor Disputes.

5 31 **Am Jur,** Labor, §§ 288–294.

of employers makes it more nearly analogous to the so-called secondary boycott by employees and is therefore usually illegal. Where there was no combination of employers but the defendant merely showed his list to another employer, relief was denied.

§ 106. Interference with probable expectancies of a competitor—of a noncompetitor.[6] The infliction of damage upon a trade rival in fair competition is excused because of the social interest in the lowering of prices to the consumer. Competition is not considered fair, however, where the defendant employs force or fraud or defamation or disparagement of goods as a weapon. A difficult question is presented where several combine to drive a plaintiff out of business by underselling him, or where a single defendant, with a dominating desire to damage or ruin the plaintiff, accomplishes or threatens to accomplish the same result.

Where a defendant has intentionally caused loss to one who is not his competitor, it should be held a tort unless he is able to show some other excuse. In a Minnesota case the complaint alleged that the defendant, a banker and a man of wealth and influence in his community, established a barber shop and used his personal influence to attract customers to his shop for the sole purpose of injuring the plaintiff whereby the plaintiff's trade was ruined. This was held to state a good cause of action. The defendant was not in substance a competitor of the plaintiff because he was not seeking his own economic advancement but merely the ruin of the plaintiff.

B. Injuries to Domestic, Social and Political Relations

§ 107. Parent and child—master and servant.[7] The common law of torts does not protect the interest of the parent unless he stands also in the relation of master or employer to his child.

In early English law a master was entitled to an action for enticing away his servant but at the present time no such action lies unless the servant is bound by contract or unless force or other means tortious in themselves are used, as in the case of employees generally.

One who by seduction or by any act which is a tort against the servant causes damage to the master either by way of loss of service or by increasing the master's expense in caring for the servant, is liable to the master; where the female seduced is the daughter of the plaintiff a very small amount of service is enough and the plaintiff is entitled to recover for mental anguish and injury to his feelings.

Though a child has an interest in the support, society and affection of the parent, the common law did nothing to secure it.

§ 108. Husband and wife.[8] A husband had at common law, an interest in his wife's (1) society or consortium, (2) her affections, (3) her chastity and (4) her services, and each interest was recognized and protected by an action on the case. Where by modern statutes a wife is given the legal rights of an unmarried woman, the husband is not entitled to her services and hence cannot recover for loss thereof.

A wife has an interest in (1) her husband's society, (2) his affections, (3)

[6] 30 **Am Jur**, Interference, §§ 43, 44.
Purpose in starting business to injure another as ground of action by latter. 27 **ALR** 1417–1423.

[7] 30 **Am Jur**, Interference, §§ 33–36.

[8] 52 **Am Jur**, Torts, § 38.
27 **Am Jur**, Husband and Wife, §§ 522–536.

his chastity and constancy and to (4) support from him. The failure of the courts to give legal recognition to (4) is due to the practical difficulty of apportioning the damages. The reasons for not giving legal recognition to (1), (2) and (3) were that the wife could not sue without joining her husband and the amount recovered would belong to the husband; these reasons have been eliminated by modern statutes and by the weight of authority and better view in this country she may recover.

§ 109. Social and political relations.[9] One who has been wrongfully expelled from a social club is entitled to maintain an action on the case. Since damages are frequently inadequate, relief is usually sought in equity.

One whose political rights—for example, the right to vote at a regular election or the right to vote at a party primary—have been wrongfully interfered with, is logically entitled to legal redress. There has been, however, considerable reluctance on the part of courts to give full and complete protection.

CHAPTER X

MISCELLANEOUS

§ 110. Interference with monopolies.[10] An action on the case lies for wrongful interference not only with such statutory monopolies as patents and copyrights but also with the common-law right of an author of a literary production to keep it entirely secret or to determine at what time and in what manner it should be published. This right—called variously common-law copyright, right of first publication, copyright before publication—comes to an end as soon as the author publishes or dedicates his production to the public. It is frequently referred to as a property right but similar protection has been given where the right was one of personality rather than of property.

§ 111. Interference with trade interests.[1] An inventor has no absolute property in his invention; there is no common-law patent right to correspond to the common-law copyright in literary and similar productions. Protection is given, however, against the fraudulently obtaining of such a trade secret.

The common law recognizes the right of a manufacturer or vendor of goods to identify them to the buying public by an exclusive trademark. In order to have such recognition, however, words in common use, such as geographical and proper names and descriptive words cannot be used.

Where the means used to identify his goods is not of the kind in which the law recognizes that an exclusive right may be acquired by prior user, relief may still be obtained against a defendant who undertakes to palm off his goods upon the public as those of the plaintiff. In the United States relief

9 4 **Am Jur**, Associations and Clubs, §§ 28–32.

10 40 **Am Jur**, Patents, §§ 150–167.
34 **Am Jur**, Literary Property and Copyright, §§ 8–23; 66–81.
40 **Harv. L. R.** 813, The Rational Basis of Trademark Protection.
28 **Corn. L. Q.** 460, Renewal Rights in Copyright.
19 **Notre Dame Lawyer** 13, Copyright Law Applied to Radio Broadcasting.

1 36 **Am Jur**, Monopolies, Combinations, and Restraints of Trade, §§ 107–109.
52 **Am Jur**, Trademarks, Tradenames, and Unfair Competition, §§ 2–10.
Right to protection against appropriation of advertising matter or methods. 17 **ALR** 760–778; s. in 30 **ALR** 615–618.
Purpose in starting business to injure another as ground of action by latter. 27 **ALR** 1417–1423.
44 **Harv. L. R.** 1210, Traffic in Trade-Symbols.
32 **Georgetown L. J.** 113, Trade-Marks and Restraint of Trade.

in such cases seems to be given only against a defendant who has acted with fraudulent intent, whereas in England it is sufficient that the defendant's conduct does have or is likely to have the result of deceiving customers into buying his wares as and for the plaintiff's wares. A limited protection is thus afforded to a plaintiff in the use of descriptive words, geographical names, and tradenames, including the use of one's own name. The tendency is to deny protection to noncommercial names.

§ 112. Disparagement of property—nondefamatory statements—privacy.[2] One who without excuse misrepresents to third persons, either orally or in writing, the quality of another's property or disparages the latter's title thereto is liable at common law in an action on the case for damages.

Where false statements by the defendant to third persons concerning the plaintiff are not of such a character as to be considered defamatory, an action on the case in the nature of deceit can be maintained if actual damage is caused and the defendant acted with knowledge of the falsity and with intent to cause the damage.

In recent years there has been considerable conflict of authority and opinion as to whether there is a common-law right of privacy, the present tendency being toward the recognition of such a right; in a few states the right has been recognized and protected by statute. Relief is usually sought in equity.

§ 113. Contribution and reimbursement between tort-feasors.[3] Where two or more who are legally responsible are liable in tort to a plaintiff and the plaintiff obtains judgment and satisfaction against one of them, it is the better view and the present trend of authority that the one thus compelled

2 33 **Am Jur**, Libel and Slander, §§ 346–353.

41 **Am Jur**, Privacy, §§ 3–16.

Right of privacy. 138 **ALR** 22–110.

Privacy, protection of right of, under law of libel. 138 **ALR** 33.

Malice as element of action for slander of title. 129 **ALR** 179–192.

Libel and slander: publication of notice of cessation of relationship of principal and agent or employer and employee, or of business or professional relationship. 138 **ALR** 671–676.

Credit association, liability of member of, for reporting person as a delinquent debtor. 48 **ALR** 573–580.

39 **Mich. L. R.** 526, The Right of Privacy.

3 13 **Am Jur**, Contribution, §§ 36–58.

Payment of, or proceeding to collect, judgment against one tort-feasor as release of others. 27 **ALR** 805–822; s. in 65 **ALR** 1087–1092.

Release of one tort-feasor as affecting liability of others. 50 **ALR** 1057–1105; s. in 66 **ALR** 206–214; 104 **ALR** 846–864; 124 **ALR** 1298–1317; 148 **ALR** 1270–1298.

Damages, effect of malice of one of two persons committing an assault on liability of both for punitive or exemplary damages. 16 **ALR** 815; s. in 123 **ALR** 1115–1148.

Master as jointly liable with independent contractor where the former's fault co-operated with that of the contractor. 30 **ALR** 1508.

Highways, joint and several liability for injury by stepping or falling into opening in sidewalk while doors were open or cover off. 70 **ALR** 1384.

Parties, right of defendant in action for personal injury or death to bring in a joint tort-feasor not made a party by plaintiff. 78 **ALR** 580–585; s. in 132 **ALR** 1424–1430.

May acts of independent tort-feasors, each of which alone causes or tends to produce some damage, be combined to create a joint liability. 9 **ALR** 939–955; s. in 35 **ALR** 409–413; 91 **ALR** 759–765.

Slander uttered by agent or employee, joint liability of principal and agent or employer and employee for. 46 **ALR** 1506–1507.

Gas company and plumbing company as jointly liable for injury or damage by escaping gas. 25 **ALR** 280; s. in 29 **ALR** 1250–1258; 47 **ALR** 488–494; 90 **ALR** 1082–1108; 138 **ALR** 870–915.

Joint and several liability of two or more persons guilty of similar acts of misconduct one of which alone caused the injury. 50 **ALR** 361–362.

Constitutionality, construction, and effect of statute relating to exceptions to rule denying indemnity as between joint tort-feasors. 85 **ALR** 1091–1097; s. in 122 **ALR** 520–525; 141 **ALR** 1207–1211.

Master or principal, release of, as affecting liability of servant or agent for tort, or vice versa. 126 **ALR** 1199–1207.

Judgment in action against one or more joint tort-feasors, provision in, to effect that it shall be without prejudice to plaintiff's claim against another joint tort-feasor, or otherwise reserving rights against him, as affecting question of release of latter. 135 **ALR** 1498–1503.

to pay may, if morally innocent, force the other or others to contribute his or their share of such payment; and if the latter are not morally innocent—i. e., are conscious wrongdoers—to pay the whole amount by way of reimbursement. Where the one compelled to pay is himself a conscious wrongdoer, he is not entitled to any relief.

§ 114. Parties to tort actions—infants—parent and child.[4] An infant or minor is in general liable in the law of torts to the same extent as an adult. Where, however, liability is dependent upon proof of negligence the age of the child is apparently taken into consideration in fixing the standard of care required and a similar concession is made where the child is plaintiff and the defense of contributory negligence is relied on. Though it would seem highly desirable to allow an infant to recover for injuries suffered by him before birth, practical difficulties as well as those of legal theory are such that recovery has usually been denied. Where the act of an infant is both a tort and a breach of contract it would seem, upon principle, that he should be liable in tort unless it would amount to holding him responsible for breach of contract; there is, however, much conflict and confusion in the cases.

A parent who uses unnecessary force in disciplining his minor child or who otherwise inflicts bodily injuries upon him may be punished criminally therefor and be compelled to forfeit his right to the custody of the child, but he incurs no tort liability. The reasons usually given are the social interest in preserving domestic harmony and to prevent much petty litigation. Upon the same principle the parent cannot recover against the minor child.

A parent, as such, is not responsible for the torts of his minor child; but if the child is his servant, he may of course be liable therefor as a master for the torts of his servant within the scope of his employment.

§ 115. Same—husband and wife.[5] Apart from statute a husband is alone liable for torts committed by his wife in his presence and under his coercion; for other torts committed by her he is jointly liable with her. This joint liability seems to have been due to the procedural necessity of joining the husband as codefendant with the wife because the husband's liability is terminated either by his own death or that of the wife, and the wife's liability is not affected by her husband's death. These rules have not, however, been affected by general statutes giving a married woman control over her property or enabling her to sue and be sued in her own name; in a few jurisdictions there are statutes expressly abrogating the husband's liability as such and making the wife alone liable where there is no coercion or participation by the husband. The wife, as such, is not liable for torts committed by the husband.

Apart from statute neither husband nor wife can maintain a tort action against the other. This rule seems to have been based not upon procedural reasons but upon the doctrine of the unity of husband and wife, because a wife cannot maintain any action against a third person who co-operated with her husband, even after divorce. Statutes which confer upon the wife the capacity to sue and be sued as if sole have usually been construed as not changing the above rule except as to torts to property, partly because of the fear of interfering with domestic harmony.

[4] 27 **Am Jur**, Infants, §§ 90–96.
39 **Am Jur**, Parent and Child, §§ 89–92.
Liability of parent for injury inflicted by minor child with dangerous instrumentality left accessible to him. 12 **ALR** 812–818.

[5] 27 **Am Jur**, Husband and Wife, §§ 589–600.
43 **Harv. L. R.** 1030, Torts between Persons in Domestic Relations.

§ 116. **Same—insane persons.**[6] In the early law when the current maxim was "he that is damaged ought to be recompensed," insanity was, of course, no defense. Apart from modern statutes based upon economic arguments, most tort liability is now based upon blameworthiness, and logically, insanity should be an excuse but with a few exceptions the old rule of absolute liability is still enforced against insane persons. This is to be justified, if at all, on the ground that such a liability will lead to increased care on the part of the insane person's guardians and relatives and thus protect the public. The weight of authority, however, is that an insane person is not liable for slander or libel and in any case is not liable for punitive or exemplary damages.

§ 117. **Death by wrongful act.**[7] At common law, causing the death of a human being could not be complained of as a tort. Where the action was brought by the personal representative on behalf of the decedent's estate, the plaintiff was barred by the rule that personal actions died with the person, and this reason was illogically given for refusing an action to those who were entitled to the services of the deceased. At the present time there are general statutes in practically all Anglo-American jurisdictions providing for the survival of personal causes of action and also special statutes—following Lord Campbell's Act in England—giving a cause of action to the widow or other relatives. By the better view and probably the weight of authority, two separate and independent causes of action are thus provided for, but in a minority of jurisdictions a recovery under one statute is a bar to recovery under the other.

§ 118. **Mental pain and nervous shock.**[8] As already pointed out, though mental pain and nervous shock may be recovered for where there is an independent tort, the negligently causing of mental pain or nervous shock is not only not an assault, but is not such special damage as to be the basis of an action on the case, though in some jurisdictions it is sufficient if physical—as distinguished from mental—injury results. This is sometimes said to be because such damage is too remote but the sound reason is the practical difficulties of proof and the social interest against imposture. Where the defendant intended the nervous shock or the physical injury resulting therefrom the difficulties of proof are less and by the better view recovery is allowed.

6 28 **Am Jur**, Insane and Other Incompetent Persons, §§ 93–101.

Liability of insane person for tort. 51 **ALR** 833–836; s. in 89 **ALR** 476.

7 16 **Am Jur**, Death, §§ 44–123.

Effect of death of a beneficiary upon right of action under death statute. 13 **ALR** 225–247; s. in 34 **ALR** 162; 59 **ALR** 760–765.

Release by, or judgment in favor of, person injured as barring action for his death. 39 **ALR** 579–592.

Survival of action or cause of action for wrongful death against representative of wrongdoer. 61 **ALR** 830–839.

Division among beneficiaries of amount awarded by jury or received in settlement upon account of wrongful death. 14 **ALR** 516–539; s. in 112 **ALR** 30–39.

Right to maintain action for wrongful death for benefit of nonresident aliens. 138 **ALR** 684–703.

Right of action for death, where deceased left no next of kin, or person within class of beneficiaries named in the state creating the right of action. 117 **ALR** 953–960.

Applicability to limitation prescribed by statute which creates cause of action for death of exception, express or implied, which attach to general statute of limitations. 8 **ALR** 145–154.

38 **Ill. L. R.** 248, Injuries Resulting in Death.

16 **Tul. L. R.** 386, The Survival of Tort Actions and the Action for Wrongful Death —A Survey and a Proposal.

8 15 **Am Jur**, Damages, §§ 175–189.

Recovery for illness, disease, or death claimed to have resulted from worry or mental anguish following breach of contract or tort. 122 **ALR** 1486–1496.

Mental suffering as element of damages for libel or slander of corporation. 90 **ALR** 1180.

49 **Harv. L. R.** 1033, Mental and Emotional Disturbance in the Law of Torts.

22 **Boston U. L. R.** 508, The Lot of the Negligent Frightener.

CONTRACTS

I. IN GENERAL.

§ 1. *Contract obligation distinguished from tort, quasi contract and public undertaking.*
§ 2. *Definition of terms.*

II. FORMATION OF SIMPLE CONTRACTS—OFFER AND ACCEPTANCE.

A. The Offer.

§ 3. *Mistake—"meeting of the minds."*
§ 4. *Definiteness—illusory promises.*
§ 5. *Offer distinguished from an invitation for offers.*
§ 6. *Offer must contemplate legal obligations.*
§ 7. *Offer must be communicated—offers of reward—revocation.*

B. The Acceptance.

§ 8. *When acceptance must be made—effect of counteroffer—options.*
§ 9. *Acceptance must be communicated—the exception.*
§ 10. *Acceptance of offer of unilateral contract—when notice necessary.*
§ 11. *Silence as an acceptance.*

III. FORMATION OF SIMPLE CONTRACTS—CONSIDERATION.

A. In General.

§ 12. *Development of the concept.*
§ 13. *Meaning of legal detriment—past consideration.*
§ 14. *Each promise in a bilateral contract must be based upon consideration.*
§ 15. *Adequacy of consideration—"in consideration of $1."*

B. Promises That Are Binding Without Consideration.

§ 16. *Charitable subscriptions—promissory estoppel.*
§ 17. *Moral consideration.*

C. Promises to Pay Part of What Is Due.

§ 18. *Unliquidated or disputed claim—compromise.*
§ 19. *Undisputed, liquidated claims admittedly due.*
§ 20. *Same—accords.*

D. Promises to Pay for Forbearance to Sue.

§ 21. *Undisputed claims.*
§ 22. *Doubtful and groundless claims.*

E. Promises to Pay for Performance Where Promisee Already Bound.

§ 23. *Performance of an existing contract with promisee.*
§ 24. *Performance of an existing contract with X.*
§ 25. *Performance of other legal duties.*

IV. CONTRACTS UNDER SEAL.

§ 26. *At common law.*
§ 27. *Modern changes.*

V. BENEFICIARIES OF CONTRACTS.

§ 28. *In general.*
§ 29. *The creditor or payment beneficiary.*
§ 30. *Gift or donee beneficiary.*
§ 31. *Miscellaneous.*

VI. ASSIGNMENT OF CONTRACTS.

§ 32. *Non-negotiable choses in action for money.*
§ 33. *Where the performance promised is nonpecuniary.*

CHAPTER I

IN GENERAL

§ 1. Contract obligation distinguished from tort, quasi contract and public undertaking.[1] A contract obligation is consensual, that is, one imposed by law according to the actual or presumed intention of the parties; an obligation in tort or in quasi contract is nonconsensual, that is, one imposed by law without regard to the intention of the parties; a public undertaking obligation is consensual to the extent that no one need enter or continue upon such an undertaking but it is nonconsensual in that as long as one is engaged in such an undertaking his obligation to serve the public at reasonable rates is imposed by law without regard to his consent.

A contract obligation is in personam, that is, it is owed to a particular individual or individuals and not to everybody; so is a quasi-contract obligation. But a tort or public undertaking obligation is in rem, that is, it is owed to the whole world.

A contract obligation may or may not be one to pay money; a quasi-contractual obligation is always to pay money; a tort or public undertaking obligation is never to pay money.

A contract obligation may be either affirmative or negative; a tort obligation is always negative; a quasi-contractual obligation is always affirmative —to pay money; a public service obligation is always affirmative—to serve the public at reasonable rates.

1 12 **Am Jur,** Contracts, §§ 1–6.
46 **Harv. L. R.** 553, The Basis of Contracts.
46 **Harv. L. R.** 1, An Inquiry into the Principles of the Law of Contracts.
51 **Yale L. J.** 893, Conflict Theories of Contracts.
1 **Loyola L. R.** 1, Implied Drilling Obligations in Oil and Gas Leases in Louisiana.

§ 2. Definition of terms.[2] The term parol contract is sometimes used to mean a simple or informal contract, that is, one not under seal; but where the statute of frauds is involved it means an oral contract. Since the term is ambiguous it will not be used in this book.

The term executed contract is sometimes used—especially in the old cases —to mean a conveyance; but it may mean either a contract that has been fully performed on both sides or one that has been fully performed on only one side, the performance on the other side consisting of the payment of money. The term executory contract may mean one where there has been no performance by either party or it may mean one that has not been fully performed by both parties. Since both terms are ambiguous they will not be used in this book.

A unilateral contract is one where only one party promises performance, the performance being in exchange for an act by the other party; a bilateral contract is one where both parties promise performance, each promise being given in exchange for the other.

The term implied contract is sometimes used to mean an actual contract in which a part or all of the offer or acceptance has not been put into express words but is inferred from the conduct of the parties; the term is also used to mean—especially in the older cases—quasi-contract. Since the term is ambiguous it will not be used in this book. Where there is an actual contract not put into express language it will be referred to as a contract implied in fact.

CHAPTER II

FORMATION OF SIMPLE CONTRACTS—OFFER AND ACCEPTANCE

A. The Offer

§ 3. Mistake—"meeting of the minds."[3] Where the language used is unambiguous it is not necessary that the minds of the parties shall meet; if the offeror by mistake of his typist offers to sell his car for $300 when he meant $400 and the offeree accepts there is a contract; if the offeree knew of the mistake when he accepted it, this does not prevent a contract from arising but the fraud of the offeree would be a good defense to any action brought by him to enforce the contract.

Where the language of the offer is ambiguous so that it might reasonably mean either of two things no contract arises unless there was a meeting of the minds, the language having the same meaning to both parties. If in such a case the minds do not meet it is called a misunderstanding.

§ 4. Definiteness—illusory promises.[4] An offer to sell goods need not fix the price because in such case the acceptor of the offer is bound to pay and the offeror is bound to accept a reasonable price for whatever goods are delivered. So an offer to employ the offeree without fixing the salary or wages becomes, when accepted, a contract to pay a reasonable compensation.

But if an offer leaves open other terms—for example, the amount of goods offered for sale—there is no contract unless the offeree fixes the amount in his acceptance. An offer to supply the offeree with all the goods of a certain

[2] 12 **Am Jur**, Contracts, §§ 8–10.

[3] 12 **Am Jur**, Contracts, § 21.
Variance between offer and acceptance in regard to title as affecting consummation of contract for sale of real property. 149 **ALR** 205–215.

[4] 12 **Am Jur**, Contracts, §§ 64–71, 116.

kind which the offeree might need in his business is apparently definite enough but an offer to supply him with all that he might wish is so indefinite that it renders the promise illusory; in such a case there is no contract at all unless the acceptance fixes the amount.

§ 5. **Offer distinguished from an invitation for offers.**[5] An offer may be made by advertisements in newspapers or magazines, by circulars or private letters announcing goods for sale or by signs in shop windows; but the other circumstances in such cases usually show that there was no offer intended but merely an invitation for offers. So, where a prospective vendor is asked to quote prices and he does so, such a quotation is not usually construed as an offer.

Similarly, an auctioneer at an auction is merely inviting offers; even if he promises to sell to the highest bidder, such a promise is not binding because there is no consideration for it and, apart from statute, he may refuse to accept the highest bid. So where advertisements are made for bids, such bids are offers, not acceptances, and no contract arises until a bid has been accepted by the advertiser.

§ 6. **Offer must contemplate legal obligations.**[6] Where the offeror contemplated only social obligations, such as arise upon extending an invitation to dinner or to play a game of golf, there is no offer to contract and no contract comes into existence. So where a candidate for public office promises to do or not to do certain things if elected and a voter thereupon votes for him, no contract arises, the candidate contemplating only political not legal obligations.

Similarly, if the circumstances show that the offeror did not intend to bind himself by contract but merely to make a gift upon certain conditions, no contract arises.

If an offer or an acceptance is made in jest and both parties so understood it, there is no contract; but if the circumstances are such that the offeree reasonably thinks that the offer was meant seriously, and he accepts it on that basis, there is a contract.

Similar reasoning applies where the offeror was laboring under such intense anger or other excitement as to negative any serious intention to be bound.

§ 7. **Offer must be communicated—offers of reward—revocation.**[7] An offer is not effective till it has been communicated to the offeree; hence if A makes an offer to B and B before receiving it makes an exactly similar offer to A so that the two offers cross each other, no contract arises; and this is true even though B had learned from other sources that A had sent him the offer.

Offers are usually made to a specific offeree but they may be made generally to any one who will perform a certain act, such as an offer of reward for the apprehension or conviction of a criminal. If the act requested or any part thereof is done in ignorance of the offer, no contract arises because the actor cannot accept an offer of which he is ignorant. If the actor does know of the offer it is the better view that he is entitled to the reward regardless of the motive which impelled him to perform the act; and it is no objection that the actor had obtained the information requested

[5] 12 Am Jur, Contracts, § 28.

[6] 43 Am Jur, Public Officers, § 374.

24 Am Jur, Gifts, § 11.

[7] 12 Am Jur, Contracts, §§ 26–63.

before learning of the offer. Where the information requested is furnished by two or more persons independently, only the first one is entitled to the reward. If no one person furnishes all the information requested, that person is entitled to the reward who furnishes the last bit of information necessary to bring about the arrest and conviction of the offender and the others contributing get nothing.

Where the state offers the reward, knowledge of the offer has been held not necessary, the actor being allowed to recover not on the basis of a contract, but upon the basis of a legislative offer of a bounty; and in such cases there is usually an apportionment made between those who contribute parts of the information requested.

Where an offer is made to a specific offeree, a revocation does not become effective till the revocation reaches him directly or he learns indirectly that the offeror has changed his mind. Where the offer is made to the public it is not necessary that notice of the revocation shall come to every one who has learned of the offer; it is enough that the offer be withdrawn through the same channel in which it was made.

The death or insanity of the offeror revokes his offer at once so that an acceptance attempted thereafter is ineffectual.

B. The Acceptance

§ 8. When acceptance must be made—effect of counteroffer—options.[8] If an offer is made in the course of a personal interview, acceptance must be made during the course of that interview unless the offeror expressly makes the offer a continuing one.

If an offer is made by mail or telegraph or other means of communication at a distance the acceptance must ordinarily be made within a reasonable time after receipt of the offer; if the offeror stipulates that the acceptance be made by return mail or by a particular date such stipulation must be complied with.

If the offer is expressly made a continuing one, the acceptance may be made at any time during the period stipulated, provided the offer has not in the meantime been revoked; revocation of the offer, like the offer itself, must actually be communicated to the offeree, though apparently the communication need not be made directly. Even though the offeror expressly promises to keep the offer open for a stated time, he may revoke it any time unless such promise is under seal or based upon consideration, in which cases the transaction is called an option and the offeror is liable for breach of contract if he revokes. If the offeree makes a counteroffer this is equivalent to a rejection of the original offer which thus comes to an end.

If the offeree sends his acceptance too late, it becomes in substance a counteroffer which must ordinarily be accepted by the original offeror before a contract comes into existence; but where the acceptance must be made within a reasonable time it seems that the offeror must notify the offeree that his acceptance has come too late.

8 12 **Am Jur,** Contracts, §§ 45–52, 53–59.

Withdrawal of, or right to withdraw, letter from mail as affecting consummation of contract. 9 **ALR** 386–389; s. in 92 **ALR** 1062–1065.

Time and place of consummation of contract on acceptance by telegraph of offer. 47 **ALR** 159–171.

Instrument for purchase of land as a contract or an option. 3 **ALR** 576–605; s. in 87 **ALR** 563–582.

Circumstances supporting inference of original offerer's acceptance of counteroffer or assent to conditions attached by offeree to his acceptance. 135 **ALR** 821–833.

48 **Yale L. J.** 1, On Our Case Law of Contract; Offer and Acceptance.

§ 9. Acceptance must be communicated—the exception.[9] An acceptance, like an offer, must be communicated, but to this rule there is a well-established exception. If A sends an offer to B by mail he impliedly authorizes B to send his acceptance by the same means of communication, and when B mails his acceptance within the stipulated time, or if there be no time stipulated, within a reasonable time, the contract is complete at that moment. This is true even though B, after mailing the acceptance, reclaims his letter from the post office or if for any other reason the acceptance does not reach A.

Similar reasoning applies to offers made by telegraph, the contract ordinarily coming into existence when the offeree delivers his message of acceptance to the telegraph company. If the offeror expressly or impliedly stipulates for a different method of communication from the one used by himself, such method must be employed in order that the contract arise at once. If A make an offer to B orally but B lives in a distant town the circumstances usually warrant B in using the mails to communicate his acceptance.

If the offeror expressly stipulates that the acceptance must be actually received by him, then no contract arises until such receipt. Or, if the offeree does not use the authorized method of communication, no contract arises till the acceptance has actually been received.

Since the revocation of an offer does not take effect till it is actually received, an acceptance sent before that time by the authorized means of communication completes a contract even though the revocation has already been sent.

§ 10. Acceptance of offer of unilateral contract—when notice necessary.[10] If the offer contemplates a bilateral contract, acceptance must be by making a counter promise, not by doing an act.

Conversely, if the offer contemplates a unilateral contract, acceptance must be by performing the act requested, not by making a counter promise. But if, as in the case of an offer by A to X to guarantee the payment for goods to be delivered by X to B, the circumstances are such that A could not easily know whether X had delivered the goods, X must within a reasonable time notify A of his performance if he wishes later to enforce the guaranty. If the offer is for a series of unilateral contracts, it may be withdrawn at any time, thus preventing the arising of any more contracts thereafter.

Where an offer is made for the performance of a single act and the offer is revoked after the act is only partially performed, there is no contract because the offeror contemplated full performance. If the part performance is of benefit to the offeror he will be liable in quasi-contract for the reasonable value of such performance; if it is of no benefit to the offeror there is no liability at all. In order to avoid the hardship which is likely to result in such cases, the courts try to construe such an offer as an offer of a bilateral contract so that they may be able to protect both parties.

§ 11. Silence as an acceptance.[1] The mere decision by the offeree that the terms of the offer are satisfactory and that he will accept it does not amount

[9] 12 Am Jur, Contracts, §§ 46–52.

[10] 12 Am Jur, Contracts, §§ 34, 41–43.
Acting on order for goods as an acceptance thereof. 19 ALR 476–482; s. in 29 ALR 1352–1353.
Private rights and remedies growing out of prize-winning contest. 67 ALR 419–429.

[1] 12 Am Jur, Contracts, § 40.
Silence when offer is made or failure to reject it as an acceptance which will consummate a bilateral contract. 77 ALR 1141–1153.
33 Harv. L. R. 376, Implied-in-Fact Contracts and Mutual Assent.

to an acceptance; the offeree must do something looking toward communication of his decision to the offeror.

If the offeror and offeree agree in advance, expressly or by implication from previous dealings, that silence on the part of the offeree shall amount to an acceptance, then such silence will complete the contract.

If, without any such agreement in advance, the offeror writes in his offer, "unless I hear from you to the contrary I shall assume that you accept," silence by the offeree does not amount to an acceptance; the offeror cannot place on the offeree the burden of rejecting the offer under penalty of accepting it.

If the offeror performs an act and the offeree knows of it and the act is beneficial to the offeree and the offeree knows that the offeror expects to be paid for it, the jury may infer from the silence of the offeree that the latter promises to pay a reasonable sum for such benefit; if, however, the parties are members of the same household the natural inference is that the services rendered were meant to be gratuitous and this inference must be rebutted, either by an express promise or by circumstances, in order to allow recovery.

CHAPTER III

FORMATION OF SIMPLE CONTRACTS—CONSIDERATION

A. In General

§ 12. Development of the concept.[2] In the early common law there were two kinds of contracts. One was the promise under seal where the promise was binding because of the seal without any attention being paid to any concept of consideration. The other was the simple (unsealed) debt which was based upon the receipt of a benefit upon the understanding that a sum certain was to be paid therefor. The debt was not based upon any promise and therefore it can hardly be said that the benefit was the consideration for a promise but there did exist the concept of the exchange of the benefit for the sum certain and exchange is an important part of the modern doctrine of consideration.

The modern doctrine of consideration—of a legal detriment suffered or promised in exchange for a promise—was developed from the action of assumpsit. That action was devised in order to afford a remedy for damage done to a promisee for breach of a simple (unsealed) promise where there was no debt—that is, where no benefit had been received by the promisor. The action of assumpsit was invented by taking the action on the case for deceit, in which the plaintiff alleged that the defendant had knowingly made a false representation to the plaintiff with intent that he act upon it, that the plaintiff did act upon it and was damaged thereby; in this declaration promise was substituted for false representation and legal detriment suffered in

2 12 **Am Jur**, Contracts, §§ 72, 75, 79.

Validity of agreement by parent to surrender custody of child in consideration of promise to leave property to child. 15 **ALR** 223–233.

Surrender of claim against insolvent as consideration for promise by third person. 59 **ALR** 315–323.

49 **Harv. L. R.** 1225, Ought the Doctrine of Consideration be Abolished from the Common Law?

41 **Col. L. R.** 799, Consideration and Form.

41 **Col. L. R.** 863, Common Law Reform of Consideration—Are These Measures?

41 **Col. L. R.** 799, On the Complexity of Consideration—A Foreword.

41 **Col L. R.** 849, Formal Contracts and Consideration—A Legislative Program.

41 **Col. L. R.** 825, The Utility of Consideration—A Comparative View.

exchange for the promise was substituted for damage suffered in reliance upon the representation.

In a few cases today damage suffered in reliance upon the promise has been held sufficient; and in some other cases benefit to the promisor to which he was not already legally entitled has been held to be valid consideration.

§ 13. **Meaning of legal detriment—past consideration.**[3] Legal detriment means doing—or, in a bilateral contract—promising to do, something which the promisee was not legally bound to do, or refraining—or promising to refrain—from doing something which he had a legal right to do. The fact that the act or forbearance asked for might actually be beneficial to the promisee is of no importance; and whether the act or forbearance was or was not beneficial to the promisor is also immaterial.

A promise to pay for services already rendered or goods already received is not binding because it cannot truthfully be said that the services were rendered or goods received in exchange for the later promise. The fact that the promisor was influenced by motives of gratitude in making the promise is of no importance.

§ 14. **Each promise in a bilateral contract must be based upon consideration.**[4] In a unilateral contract it is of no importance whether there was any consideration for the act requested; it is enough if the act requested was consideration for the promise. But in a bilateral contract it is necessary that each promise be based upon consideration; hence, if A promises to supply to B whatever iron B may order during the following year, and B assents without naming any specific amount, there is no contract, not only because the offer and acceptance are defective in not fixing any definite quantity, but also because B's promise, being indefinite or illusory, cannot be consideration for A's promise. And since there is no consideration for A's promise, there is no contract and neither party is bound.

§ 15. **Adequacy of consideration—"in consideration of $1."**[5] Common-law courts pay no attention to the adequacy of consideration. If A sees fit to promise to pay B $10,000 for a letter which later turns out to be worthless, or if B sees fit to promise to sell to A for $2 a stone which later proves to be a diamond worth $1,000, there is a contract in each case.

If A, in writing, bargains and sells to B a piece of land stated to be in consideration of $1, that is a good bargain and sale deed of conveyance, passing title to the land, operating under the statute of uses; and it is of no importance how valuable the land is or that B did not give or intend to give the dollar, or that A did not expect to receive it, the recital of consideration being sufficient. Because of the confusion due to calling deeds of conveyance "executed contracts" some lawyer in drafting a contract reasoned to himself that if the recital "in consideration of $1" was effective in a deed of conveyance, it should be just as effective in a contract, but this is not true; if there was no intent to give or to receive the dollar it cannot be consideration for a contract.

[3] 12 **Am Jur**, Contracts, § 95.
Past services by relative or member of family as consideration for note or other executory obligation. 140 **ALR** 491-506.

[4] 12 **Am Jur**, Contracts, § 72.

[5] 12 **Am Jur**, Contracts, §§ 120-123.

B. Promises That Are Binding Without Consideration

§ 16. Charitable subscriptions—promissory estoppel.[6] If A promises to donate $1,000 to the B church or hospital or school or other charity, and either expressly or impliedly requests the B charity to incur obligations or erect buildings or expressly requests the B charity to obtain additional subscriptions, and the B charity, in reliance upon A's promise, incurs the obligations or starts to erect the building or obtains additional subscriptions, the courts in the United States, though not in England, generally hold that A is bound by his promise.

This doctrine whereby the incurring of legal detriment in reliance upon defendant's promise is substituted for such detriment suffered in exchange for that promise is sometimes called the doctrine of promissory estoppel; it has rarely been applied except in cases of charitable subscriptions.

§ 17. Moral consideration.[7] If after an infant becomes of age he promises to pay an obligation which he incurred while still an infant; if after discharge in bankruptcy the bankrupt promises to pay an obligation which had been barred by the discharge; if, after a surety has been discharged by the creditor's releasing the principal debtor or contracting to extend time to him without the surety's assent, the surety promises to remain liable notwithstanding such discharge, the former infant, the bankrupt and the surety are held bound on their promises. Similarly, if a debtor, after the running of the statute of limitations, makes a new promise to pay the debt, such new promise is binding and if the new promise is made before the complete running of the statute it starts the running of the statute anew.

Partly based upon these cases, and partly based upon the civil law which has no doctrine of consideration, Lord Mansfield held that a widow who promised to pay a bond given by her while married and to which her then coverture was a complete defense, was bound by her promise, Lord Mansfield's reasoning in this and other similar cases being that "the honesty and rectitude of the thing is a consideration." These decisions of Lord Mansfield were overruled after his death and there are only slight traces of this doctrine —usually called the doctrine of moral consideration—left in the law today.

C. Promises to Pay Part of What Is Due

§ 18. Unliquidated or disputed claim—compromise.[8] If A has a claim against B for an unliquidated amount or if his claim for a liquidated amount is disputed by B, and A, in consideration of the payment of a sum of money less than what he claims is due, promises to release the entire claim, he is bound by such promise. It is not necessary that such promise be express; if B sends a check to A with the words written thereon "Payment in full," and A cashes the check he is bound by his implied promise to compromise and release the entire claim.

[6] 12 **Am Jur**, Contracts, § 42.
Consideration for subscription agreements. 38 **ALR** 869–914; s. in 95 **ALR** 1305–1314.
Promissory estoppel. 115 **ALR** 152–162.

[7] 12 **Am Jur**, Contracts, §§ 96–100.
Moral obligation as a consideration for an executory promise. 17 **ALR** 1299–1377; s. in 79 **ALR** 1346–1355.

[8] 12 **Am Jur**, Contracts, §§ 82–87.
Consideration for compromise of family dispute over estate. 38 **ALR** 734–756; s. in 118 **ALR** 1357–1363.
Acceptance of remittance by check purporting to be "in full" or accompanied by indications of debtor's intention that it be so regarded. 34 **ALR** 1035–1059; s. in 75 **ALR** 905–927.

§ 19. Undisputed, liquidated claims admittedly due.[9] If A has against B an undisputed, liquidated claim for $1,000, admittedly due, the payment of any amount less than $1,000 cannot be consideration for A's releasing the entire claim. This rule does not apply if the claim is not yet due or if the part payment is made in another place than that originally stipulated, or if the part payment is made in the note of a third person. But the rule does apply if B gives his own note for part of what is due and it should, logically, apply where B pays one claim which is undisputed, liquidated and admittedly due in consideration that A release another unliquidated or disputed claim, but the weight of authority seems to be contra.

§ 20. Same—accords.[10] If A holds against B an undisputed, liquidated claim for $1,000 and accepts from B a chattel in full satisfaction thereof, A is bound by his promise never to sue on his claim for $1,000, regardless of the value of the chattel. Such a transaction is usually referred to in the old cases, as an accord and satisfaction.

If B does not turn over the chattel but merely promises to do so, and A promises to accept it, the old cases, at a time before the recognition of bilateral contracts, held that this was not a valid contract, calling it an accord executory or unexecuted. Now that bilateral contracts are held to be valid, there would seem to be no sound objection to the unexecuted accord and that is the modern tendency. If in such a case A later refuses to accept the chattel in satisfaction, B can probably compel him to do so by bringing a bill in equity for specific performance. But if B later refuses either to deliver the chattel or to pay the $1,000, it would seem that A should be allowed to choose between suing for the $1,000, or on the promise to deliver the chattel. If A and B agreed that the bilateral contract to transfer and to accept the chattel shall itself be a satisfaction of the claim for $1,000, then A's sole claim thereafter is upon the promise to deliver the chattel.

The above reasoning is equally applicable to a situation where the original obligation was to deliver a chattel and the later agreement was to pay $1,000 in satisfaction of that obligation.

D. Promises to Pay for Forbearance to Sue

§ 21. Undisputed claims.[1] If A has a liquidated, undisputed claim against B for $1,000, and in consideration of the receipt of some property other than money promises never to sue B on the $1,000 claim and then in breach of that promise he later does sue B, equity will give a perpetual injunction against such action in order to avoid circuity of action; in most states today resort to equity is unnecessary because such facts may be set up at law as a complete

[9] 12 Am Jur, Contracts, § 88.

Payment before maturity of part of a liquidated and undisputed indebtedness as a consideration for its acceptance in satisfaction of the entire debt. 24 ALR 1474–1479.

Part payment of liquidated indebtedness by, or with aid of, third person as consideration for its acceptance in discharge of entire debt. 41 ALR 1490–1495.

Acceptance of principal sum as affecting right to interest. 100 ALR 96–121.

[10] 1 Am Jur, Accord and Satisfaction, §§ 1–78.

12 Am Jur, Contracts, § 405.

Rule that promise by creditor to accept, or acceptance of, less than amount due on a liquidated indebtedness in discharge of the whole, is not binding upon creditor as regards unpaid amount. 119 ALR 1123–1129.

Failure to perform act required by new agreement as affecting character thereof as accord and satisfaction. 10 ALR 222–238; s. in 14 ALR 230.

[1] 12 Am Jur, Contracts, § 84.

Payment of undisputed amount or liability as consideration for discharge of disputed amount or liability. 112 ALR 1219–1246.

Validity of promise conditioned upon forbearance or nonexercise of right, without an agreement or other original consideration by promisee. 74 ALR 293–304.

defense to A's action. If the claim is unliquidated, the consideration may consist of money.

If A's promise, in consideration of either money or property, was not to sue for a limited time, and A should, in breach of that promise, bring suit within that time, B's sole remedy is in equity for a temporary injunction restraining A from suing till the expiration of the period fixed. The above reasoning applies where no time is fixed but the circumstances show that A was to forbear for a reasonable time. Where it is doubtful whether A was to forbear perpetually or only for a reasonable time the value of the property turned over to A for the forbearance is likely to determine the interpretation of the contract.

If A merely promises to forbear as long as he chooses to do so, there is no contract at all and A has the right to sue at any time.

§ 22. Doubtful and groundless claims.[2] If A has a claim against B, whether liquidated or unliquidated, and the claim is of doubtful validity and A releases the claim or promises never to sue on it in consideration for B's promise to turn over to A a sum of money or other property and A later sues B for breach of his promise, it will be no defense to B to show that A's claim was actually invalid; it is not important whether A had or had not actually brought suit. The reason for this rule is the policy of the law in favor of compromises of doubtful claims. The above reasoning applies where the promise to pay for forbearance was made by a third person, X, instead of by B.

The above reasoning does not apply if A knew that his claim was invalid; that would be fraud on A's part giving B a complete defense.

Where A acts honestly in making his claim, but the claim is so lacking in validity as to be properly described as groundless, courts differ as to the enforcibility of B's promise, the argument in A's favor being that he has a right to litigate if he is acting honestly. If he has released or promised to release an action which has actually been brought he is more likely to prevail because of a supposed presumption that such a claim is at least doubtful.

E. Promises to Pay for Performance Where Promisee Already Bound

§ 23. Performance of an existing contract with promisee.[3] A contracts with B to build a residence for B according to certain specifications for $10,000; A, either because of unforeseen difficulties or because he made a mistake in his bid or merely because he thinks B will pay more under pressure, threatens not to perform unless B will agree to pay him $500 more; B thereupon agrees and A puts up the building; may A collect the extra $500? The logical answer is that he may not, because he suffered no legal detriment, having been already bound to erect the house, and B gets from the performance no benefit to which he was not already legally entitled.

It has been argued for A that since he had a choice of either performing or paying damages, he suffered legal detriment in giving that choice when he per-

[2] 12 **Am Jur,** Contracts, § 82.
Forbearance to interpose or insist upon defense which is doubtful or known to be unfounded, as sufficient consideration for a promise. 139 **ALR** 854–860.

[3] 12 **Am Jur,** Contracts, §§ 88–90.
Promise of additional compensation for completing building or construction contract. 25 **ALR** 1450–1470; s. in 55 **ALR** 1333–1335; 138 **ALR** 136–141.

Promise by employer to pay bonus as creating valid and enforceable contract. 28 **ALR** 331–338.

Consideration for modification of terms of existing tenancy. 43 **ALR** 1451–1509; s. in 93 **ALR** 1404–1408.

Necessity and sufficiency of consideration for modification of real-estate broker's contract. 42 **ALR** 987–1021.

formed. The answer is that A had no such choice shown by the decisions holding X liable in tort for persuading A not to perform his contract with B.

It has also been argued that if there were unforeseen difficulties in the performance, B should be bound by his promise to pay the additional sum. The answer is that unforeseen difficulties furnished no excuse to A for his nonperformance. Neither does a mistake unless it was shared by B.

A third argument is that the first contract is rescinded and hence A and B are no longer bound by it and are free to enter into a new contract by which B is to pay the larger sum. The answer to this is that although A and B *might* rescind the first contract and then later independently enter into a new one for larger compensation, there is, in actual fact in such cases, either no rescission at all or a rescission under such pressure that it should not be legally recognized.

If B, instead of promising to pay the additional $500, actually pays it, he can probably not recover it back in quasi-contract, the economic duress not being sufficiently strong to prevent it from being a voluntary payment. But if, after such payment, A refuses to perform, it would seem that B may sue for breach of A's second promise to perform because the $500 paid is adequate consideration for that promise; the payment of the $500, being an act and not a promise, does not need consideration.

§ 24. **Performance of an existing contract with X.**[4] Where A is already under a contract with X, but either refuses or is reluctant to perform, and B thereupon promises extra compensation to A if he will perform or promise performance, is is clear that A suffers no legal detriment in exchange for B's promise because A was already under legal obligation to X to perform. It has been suggested that if the contract between A and X is bilateral, there is legal detriment in that A becomes liable to a new party for failure to perform, but this argument begs the entire question as to whether there is any binding contract.

Another argument is that since A has a right to rescind his contract with X he suffers legal detriment by performing instead of rescinding. The answer to this argument is that A has no right to rescind without the concurrence of X. Where the promise of B is made to both A and X who together do have the right to rescind, there is no difficulty in finding legal detriment in their giving up their right to rescind.

Another argument is that if the performance of the contract with X is a benefit to B, he should be held liable on his promise because it is a benefit to which he was not already legally entitled. Decisions holding B liable in such cases recognize benefit to the promisor as an alternative test of consideration.

§ 25. **Performance of other legal duties.**[5] If A is a public official—such as a policeman, fireman or bank director—and as such is already bound to render a particular service and B promises to pay him for the performance of that duty, the promise is not binding because A suffers no legal detriment and B, being a member of the public, receives no benefit to which he was not already legally entitled. But if A is asked to do something outside of his official duty, B is bound by his promise.

4 12 Am Jur, Contracts, § 92.

5 12 Am Jur, Contracts, § 25.

CHAPTER IV

CONTRACTS UNDER SEAL

§ 26. **At common law.**[6] At the early common law, A could bind himself to B by placing a seal upon his written promise to B. At first the seal was an impression upon wax affixed to the parchment or paper; later it was held that an impression on the paper itself was sufficient; still later that any mark on the paper itself was enough if intended as a seal and that any number of people might use the same seal.

§ 27. **Modern changes.**[7] The doctrine of sealed contracts is as old as the simple (unsealed) debt the efficacy of which was based upon the receipt of a benefit upon the understanding that a sum certain was to be paid therefor. Both the sealed promise and the simple debt long antedated the modern contract, which consists of a simple promise based upon consideration which consists usually of legal detriment suffered in exchange for that promise. But after the rise of the modern contract and there was enough spread of education so that most persons could sign their names instead of affixing their seals, contracts under seal so diminished in importance that courts undertook to explain their validity in spite of the lack of consideration by saying that "a seal presumes consideration;" and this concept crept into some statutes. If by "presumes" is meant "conclusively presumes," it is merely an artificial way of saying that no consideration is necessary. But if by the word "presumes" is meant a rebuttable presumption, then the seal becomes of very slight importance because the only real value of a sealed contract is that it furnishes a dignified way of binding oneself without consideration.

In some states seals have been abolished by statute. In so far as these statutes apply to conveyances this is desirable legislation because conveyances are necessarily formal documents even without a seal and the seal serves no useful purpose; the effect of the statutes was to make the conveyances valid without being sealed. But the effect on sealed contracts was the very reverse of this; under these statutes it is impossible to have sealed contracts and therefore there is no dignified way in which one can bind himself without consideration.

CHAPTER V

BENEFICIARIES OF CONTRACTS

§ 28. **In general.**[8] If A sells a bill of goods to B for $600 on thirty days' credit and B agrees that at the end of that period he will pay the $600 to A's creditor X; and if A sells another bill of goods to B for $400 on sixty days' credit and B agrees that at the end of that period he will pay the $400 to A's son Y as a wedding gift from A, may X or Y recover on these promises?

At early common law and in a few jurisdictions today the answer is in the negative, because only a party to a contract may sue on it. Since the situa-

[6] 12 Am Jur, Contracts, § 74.

[7] 12 Am Jur, Contracts, § 74.
Necessity of consideration to support option under seal. 2 ALR 631–637; s. in 21 ALR 137–138.
Right of third person to maintain action at law on sealed instrument. 47 ALR 5–24.
Modification of sealed instrument by subsequent parol agreement. 55 ALR 685–697.

[8] 12 Am Jur, Contracts, §§ 273, 274.
Right of third person to enforce contract between others for his benefit. 81 ALR 1271–1308; s. in 148 ALR 359.

tion is a three-sided one to which the simple common-law procedure is not adapted, the logical thing to have happened—especially in the case of Y, the gift beneficiary—was that equity should allow either the promisee or the beneficiary to bring a suit in equity against the other two persons interested, for specific performance. In such a case the right of the beneficiary would have become a vested, indefeasible right from the moment of contract which could not be modified without his consent.

Except in a very few jurisdictions, equity took no such step; and in the last century and a half the common law has gradually developed so that in the large majority of jurisdictions today X and Y may sue B at common law, the action allowed being usually and logically special assumpsit for the damage suffered because of the breach of B's promise.

§ 29. The creditor or payment beneficiary.[9] In the case put in the preceding section, X, the creditor or payment beneficiary, was not really in need of being allowed to sue B, because he had his original right against A which would be adequate unless A should become insolvent; and even then X could reach A's claim against B based upon B's promise to pay X by filing a bill in equity for equitable execution.

A, the creditor, may also sue B either on the original obligation or on B's promise to pay A's debt to X; in this case the measure of damages would be the amount of the debt. If both A and X should sue B it would seem that the action first filed should be preferred, the other one being dismissed or suspended.

The most usual illustration of the payment beneficiary occurs in the field of mortgages, where the mortgagor transfers his interest in the land to an assignee who expressly undertakes to pay the mortgage debt; another is the promise of a partnership to pay the liabilities of a retiring partner.

§ 30. Gift or donee beneficiary.[10] Since, in the case put in a previous section, Y, the donee beneficiary, has no remedy against A to force him to carry out his intent to make the gift of $400 to him, Y will have no remedy at all unless he can sue B upon his promise either at law or in equity. In England he is allowed to sue in equity, not on the logical theory of specific performance, but upon the erroneous theory of a trust; erroneous because there is no trust res, B being in no sense a trustee of any specific $400 but merely under the obligation of paying some $400 out of his general assets.

Since the assent of a donee to a gift of property is presumed and is effective till he disclaims, it would seem to be the sound view that the donee beneficiary's right should become vested from the moment of contract so that the contract cannot later be released or modified without his consent; but there are some decisions holding that his right does not arise till he knows of the contract and till that time the promisee may effectually release the promisor.

The donee beneficiary is sometimes called a sole beneficiary because only he may collect substantial damages from the promisor. If the promisee sues

[9] 12 **Am Jur**, Contracts, §§ 275–279, 285.
Liability of grantee assuming mortgage debt, to grantor. 21 **ALR** 504–531; s. in 76 **ALR** 1191–1198; 97 **ALR** 1076–1081.
Assumption of mortgage by grantee as affecting right of mortgagee to proceed against mortgagor. 41 **ALR** 317–328.
Liability of grantee assuming mortgage debt to mortgagee or one in privity with him. 21 **ALR** 439–498; s. in 47 **ALR** 339–346.

[10] 12 **Am Jur**, Contracts, § 280.
Rights of beneficiary under obligation or deposit payable to him at death of holder or depositor if not previously paid to latter (United States War Savings Bonds). 131 **ALR** 967–970; s. in 147 **ALR** 1466–1469; 148 **ALR** 1411–1412; 149 **ALR** 1571; 150 **ALR** 1468.

on the contract he can get a judgment for only nominal damages because he would get no benefit from the promisor's performance; in an action in quasi contract, however, he may recover the reasonable value of what the promisor received from the promisee in exchange for his promise.

§ 31. Miscellaneous.[1] If the promisor's promise is expressly conditional the beneficiary is bound by the condition; and if the promisee has not fully performed and is barred by mistake, fraud or failure, the beneficiary is likewise barred. But in the payment beneficiary cases the fact that the debt assumed by the promisor is usurious or otherwise invalid is usually no defense to the promisor.

Apart from statute, one who would only incidentally benefit by the performance of the contract between A and B has no rights against either one; for example, a provision in a building contract that the owner may retain a sufficient sum from the contractor to pay claims for labor and material gives the holders of such claims no rights. Another example is the case where the first transferee of mortgaged land does not undertake to pay the mortgage debt but his transferee does so undertake; the mortgagee cannot collect against the second transferee.

Where a contract is made between A and B, A furnishing the consideration but the promise being made to a third person Z, recovery is allowed to Z; he is a party to the contract and it is no objection that he does not furnish the consideration. A typical case is one when A agrees to name his son as B directs and B gives the son a promissory note for $1,000.

CHAPTER VI

ASSIGNMENT OF CONTRACTS

§ 32. Non-negotiable choses in action for money.[2] In the early law a chose in action even for the payment of money was not transferable except by novation, that is, the substitution of a new obligee with the consent of the obligor. The typical case of such a novation is that of the negotiable instrument where the obligor consents in advance to a transfer, agreeing to pay either to bearer or to the order of the original obligee.

The first step in allowing the assignment of non-negotiable choses in action for money was taken by equity which allowed the assignee to sue in his own name. The next step was taken when common-law courts permitted the use of the power of attorney or agency. The reasoning behind this second step was that although the obligor might insist upon paying no one except

49 **W. Va. L. R.** 132, Sole Beneficiary Problem in West Virginia.

1 12 **Am Jur,** Contracts, § 279.

Conditions of contract with sender as affecting telegraph company's right to insist upon them as against sendee. 94 **ALR** 1056–1067.

12 **Am Jur,** Contracts, § 282.

Right to enforce purchaser's promise to pay mortgage when the grantor or promisee was not himself liable. 12 **ALR** 1528–1542.

Transaction or agreement between mortgagee and purchaser of property who did not assume mortgage as imposing personal obligation on latter for mortgage debt. 94 **ALR** 1329–1337.

Personal liability to mortgagor, as distinguished from mortgagee, of vendee of mortgaged premises who does not in terms assume or agree to pay mortgage. 111 **ALR** 1114–1133.

2 4 **Am Jur,** Assignments, §§ 22–24, 65–70, 84–85.

Creditor's knowledge of, or consent to, assumption by third person of debtor's obligation as release of original debtor of extinguishment of original debt essential to novation. 87 **ALR** 281–285.

Necessity or proof of original obligor's consent to, or ratification of, third person's assumption of obligation, in order to effect a novation. 124 **ALR** 1498–1504.

42 **Mich. L. R.** 789, Assignment of a Life Insurance Policy.

14 **St. John's L. R.** 61, Priority of Assignee of Part Interest in Chose in Action.

the obligee there was nothing to prevent the obligee from appointing an agent or attorney to collect or from telling the agent or attorney to keep what he should collect. As soon as the use of the power of attorney device became established, equity courts declined to give relief in the case of an ordinary assignment because the remedy at law had become adequate—one of the three instances where equity abandoned a field which it had once occupied. In spite of this abandonment the assignment of non-negotiable choses in action is still frequently referred to as an equitable assignment.

In the early cases where common-law courts gave relief to the assignee there was an express power of attorney but later the power of attorney was implied from the words of assignment because that was the only way in which the assignment could be given effect.

The next step was taken by statutes which provided that the action should be brought in the name of the assignee instead of in the name of the assignor to the use of the assignee. These statutes apparently did not change the substantive rights of the parties, the right of the assignee being still regarded as derivative so that if in fraud of the assignment the assignor should collect from an obligor who had no notice of the assignment the assignee's rights would be solely against the fraudulent assignor; after notice of the assignment the obligor is not discharged by paying the obligee; and the assignee takes subject to the equitable defenses of the obligor.

If the obligee sues and gets judgment for less than the amount due, this is a bar to any action for the remainder because it would be unfair to the obligor to compel him to litigate more than once. If the obligee assigns a part of a cause of action to X the courts might have held that X could recover for that part on the power of attorney theory and that such a recovery would bar any action by the obligee for the remainder. But the rule is well settled that X, the partial assignee, has no right at law, unless the obligor agrees to the part assignment, apparently on the theory that the obligee could not be presumed to have intended to throw away the other part of the chose in action. The partial assignee may, however, maintain a suit in equity against the obligee and obligor, thus settling the whole matter in one litigation; and after notice of the part assignment, the obligor is not discharged by paying to the obligee.

An obligor cannot, of course, escape liability by getting X's promise to perform in the obligor's place, unless the obligee agrees to the substitution.

A gift of a chose in action is irrevocable if the donor turns over to the donee a document which so represents it that it must be produced or accounted for in any litigation to enforce it; typical cases are those of life insurance policies and savings bank books. Where there is no transfer of any such document the gift is usually held to be revocable unless there is a formal transfer of it by an instrument under seal or by an unsealed instrument operating under modern statutes. Any attempt to make a gift of part of a chose in action is ineffectual.

§ 33. Where the performance promised is nonpecuniary.[3] Where B contracts to render services to A which are mechanical and do not involve any skill peculiar to B it would seem that A might freely transfer his right to such services to X and that B might freely deputize Y to perform the services, remaining liable to A, of course, in case Y should default.

3 12 Am Jur, Contracts, § 259.

Where the services involve peculiar skill possessed by B, such as is involved in the painting of a picture, B can certainly not deputize Y to do the work though there would seem to be no objection to allowing A to assign to X the right to the picture.

Where the services are to be rendered to A in person, such as valet services, it would seem clear that A cannot transfer to X the right to the services and that B cannot deputize Y to render the services.

Where B has contracted to sell goods to A on credit and A sells out his business to X who assumes A's obligations, B is not bound to extend to X the credit which he agreed to extend to A, and therefore is not bound to deliver the goods to X except for cash.

CHAPTER VII

STATUTE OF FRAUDS

§ 34. **In General.**[4] The English statute of frauds was passed in 1676. At that time the jury system was undergoing a transition from its original function as a group of witnesses to the modern function as a group of nonwitnesses, and the courts had not yet worked out of any satisfactory method of controlling verdicts. Furthermore, parties to a suit and others who were interested in its outcome were not competent witnesses. Parliament therefore interfered by providing that in certain classes of contracts, where there was a strong temptation to commit perjury or other species of fraud by means of oral testimony, there should be a memorandum in writing signed by the party to be charged.

Most of the provisions of the English statute have been copied substantially in most of American jurisdictions. Those dealing with contracts are: (1) A promise by an executor or administrator to pay out of his own funds a claim against the decedent's estate; (2) A promise made in consideration of marriage; (3) On agreement not to be performed within a year from the making thereof; (4) A promise to answer for the debt, default or miscarriage of another; (5) A contract for the sale of any interest in land; (6) A contract for the sale of goods, wares and merchandise for the price of £10 or upwards unless the buyer accepts or receives part of the goods or pays part of the purchase money or gives something in earnest to bind the bargain.

§ 35. **Promises in consideration of marriage.**[5] This section does not apply to mutual promises to marry but does apply to promises to transfer property made in consideration of a promise to marry. Where there is another consideration besides the marriage or promise to marry—for example the dismissal of an action for seduction—the statute does not apply.

§ 36. **Agreements not to be performed within a year.**[6] This section includes only contracts which cannot be performed within a year; if there is a possibil-

[4] 21 **Am Jur**, Executors and Administrators, § 248.

49 **Am Jur**, Statute of Frauds, §§ 1-312.

Oral contract for year's services as within Statute of Frauds. 27 **ALR** 663-673; s. in 114 **ALR** 416-419.

Oral contract of employment terminable by either party at will as within Statute of Frauds relating to contracts not to be performed within year. 104 **ALR** 1006-1008.

Oral contract to enter into written contract as within Statute of Frauds. 58 **ALR** 1015-1023.

When is promise made in consideration of marriage within Statute of Frauds. 10 **ALR** 321-336; s. in 21 **ALR** 311-312.

[5] 49 **Am Jur**, Statute of Frauds, §§ 18, 19.

[6] 49 **Am Jur**, Statute of Frauds, §§ 24, 30, 36, 54.

Statute of frauds against oral contracts not to be performed within year as applicable to contracts susceptible by its terms, or by construction, of performance within year, where performance within that time is improbable or almost impossible. 129 **ALR** 534-549.

ity that full performance may be completed within the year the statute does not apply. Thus a promise to be performed on the death of X or—being of marriageable age—upon his marriage, is not within the statute because his death or marriage may occur within the period; so a promise to support X for his life may be performed within a year because he may die at any time. On the other hand, a promise to support X for two years is within the statute because there will be no complete performance if X should die within a year but merely an excuse for nonperformance. Similarly, the better view is that a promise not to compete with the plaintiff for two years is within the statute because the promisor's death within a year would merely show that he could no longer breach his promise.

An oral contract for a year's service to begin the following day is generally held good on the thory that in such cases the law will not regard fractions of a day, but there are cases contra.

A later oral restatement of the oral contract at a time when the contract could be performed within a year satisfies the statute but not a mere later oral recognition of the existence of the contract.

The mere fact that the contract has been fully performed on one side within the year should not take the case out of the statute where the performance on the other side cannot take place within the year, but there are cases contra.

Where the oral contract is held to be within the statute the plaintiff's sole remedy, if any, is in quasi contract for the reasonable value of any benefit received by the promisor under the contract.

CHAPTER VIII

EXPRESS CONDITIONS

§ 37. Conditions precedent and concurrent.[7] If the defendant promises to pay money or perform services upon the happening of a certain event or upon the previous performance by the plaintiff of some other act, the condition thus imposed by the defendant in his promise is called an express condition precedent if the performance by the plaintiff takes some appreciable time; if the performance by the plaintiff can be practically simultaneous with the performance by the defendant—such as the transfer of property on the one side and the payment of money on the other—the condition is called an express condition concurrent. Strict performance of such express conditions or excuse for nonperformance is necessary to be alleged and proved by the plaintiff to entitle him to recover.

§ 38. Conditions subsequent.[8] Where there is a provision in the defendant's promise whereby upon the happening of a particular event or upon the expiration of a certain time the defendant's liability shall come to an end, such a provision is called an express condition subsequent. The typical illustration is in insurance policies which usually provide that liability shall cease unless action is brought within a certain time—usually six months or a year—from the accrual of the cause of action.

Where, as in the old form of official bonds, the defendant's promise is absolute to pay a certain sum of money, followed by a stipulation that the bond is to become void upon the official's complete performance of his duties, such a promise is in form subject to a condition subsequent but in substance it is

[7] 12 Am Jur, Contracts, §§ 295–297.

[8] 12 Am Jur, Contracts, § 297.

subject to a condition precedent because there is no liability on the part of the obligor unless the official defaults. The advantage of such a bond to the plaintiff is that it places upon the defendant the burden of alleging and proving that the official duties have been performed.

§ 39. **Promises conditional upon satisfaction.**[9] Where the defendant's promise is conditional upon his being satisfied with the plaintiff's performance and the defendant, after giving due consideration to the matter, honestly decides that he is not satisfied he is not liable for breach.

In some states, however, the above statement is true only of performances in which personal taste is an element, such as in the painting of a picture; if personal taste is not involved then the plaintiff need only show that the performance was such as to satisfy a reasonable man.

CHAPTER IX

DEFENDANT EXCUSED BY PLAINTIFF'S DEFAULT— CONDITIONS IMPLIED IN LAW

§ 40. **The early law.**[10] Shortly after bilateral contracts were first recognized the question arose as to whether a plaintiff who had not performed his promise could recover for the breach of the defendant's promise. The early cases held that he could. As it was put in an early case, if A contracted to sell his horse to B for $50, A might recover the $50 without delivering or tendering the horse and B might recover the horse without paying or tendering the $50. A bilateral contract was thus treated as if it were two unilateral contracts, the promise of each being treated as entirely independent of the other.

§ 41. **Later development.**[1] Such a holding was, of course, not consistent with business understanding which conceived of a bilateral contract as an exchange of performances as well as an exchange of promises. It soon seemed clear that the early rule was unfortunate, but it was too explicit to be directly overruled; any change or modification must be by indirection.

An important step in the change was in artificially extending the law of express conditions; thus if A promised to sell the horse to B *for* $50, this was held to be an express condition so that A would not be liable for nondelivery unless B paid or tendered the $50; and if B promised to pay $50 *for* the horse he was not liable for any breach of that promise unless A either delivered or tendered the horse.

The next step in the development was in holding that the promises of A and B were conditional even though the word "for" was not used. The law of express conditions could not, of course, be stretched to cover such cases, so it was said that there was a condition implied in law that neither A nor B could recover for the breach of the other's promise unless there had been performance or tender of performance on the plaintiff's part—not the strict performance required by the law of express conditions but substantial performance or tender thereof.

§ 42. **Implied conditions precedent and concurrent.**[2] Where the performances on each side are such that there can be an immediate exchange, as

9 12 **Am Jur**, Contracts, §§ 340–342.

10 12 **Am Jur**, Contracts, § 327.

1 12 **Am Jur**, Contracts, §§ 333–348.

20 **Chicago-Kent L. R.** 142, Substantial Performance of Building Contracts.

2 12 **Am Jur**, Contracts, § 296.

in the case of a contract to sell property for cash, the implied conditions are said to be mutually concurrent; neither may recover against the other for breach unless there has been performance or tender of performance conditional upon the other's simultaneous performance, or excuse for nontender of performance. But if as in a case of a contract for service, the performance on one side takes time and the business custom is that payment is not to be made in advance, then there is an implied condition precedent that the person who was to render the service may not recover for the breach of the other's promise unless there has been performance or an absolute tender of performance—since an immediate exchange of services for money is not possible—or an excuse for nontender of performance.

The most usual excuse for nonperformance or failure to tender performance is repudiation by the other party; if the plaintiff was in a position where he could have performed but the defendant tells him that he will not accept performance, this is an excuse to the plaintiff; he does not need to tender performance because the law does not require him to do a futile thing.

§ 43. The doctrine of anticipatory breach.[3] The older rule was that a plaintiff could not recover for breach of the defendant's promise until the time had come for the performance of that promise; that if, before the time for the defendant's performance, he should repudiate the contract the plaintiff not only might but must, in accordance with settled rule as to the mitigation of damages, refrain from any further performance and then sue for breach when the time for the defendant's performance had arrived. Furthermore, that if such repudiation should be withdrawn the plaintiff is not excused unless, in reliance upon the repudiation, he has so changed his position that he cannot, without damage to himself, continue to perform.

The above rule is simple and consistent with business understanding. But about 1850 the law on the subject was thrown into considerable confusion by the doctrine of anticipatory breach. The earliest cases in the development of the doctrine were cases of promises to marry upon request where the defendant had married another woman and it was held that action would lie at once without any request. These decisions are easily explained on the ground that there was no fixed date and it would be requiring a futile thing to require plaintiff to make a request before bringing suit; also, a contract to marry is different from an ordinary commercial contract in that it brings into existence an intermediate status which is violated at once when the defendant marries another.

Then came Hochster v. De La Tour. In that case the plaintiff had contracted to serve defendant as courier for three months beginning June 1, 1852. On May 11 defendant wrote to plaintiff saying that his services would not be required. The action was begun May 22. The court held that it had not been brought prematurely because if the plaintiff had not sued at once he would have had to keep himself in readiness to perform up till June 1; and this seems to be the English rule today. Not so much harm was done by merely allowing the plaintiff to sue ahead of time as by the court's unsupported corollary that otherwise the plaintiff must wait and keep himself in readiness to perform on June 1; and in this country the weight of authority

3 12 Am Jur, Contracts, §§ 391–401. 41 Harv. L. R. 340, The Tort Aspect of Anticipatory Repudiation of Contracts.

is that while the plaintiff may sue at once he may wait till time for performance without keeping himself ready to perform.

§ 44. Installment contracts.[4] Where A contracts to sell to B several articles for a lump sum, for example, ten mules for $860, the contract is necessarily indivisible; neither A nor B can insist upon splitting up the contract; A cannot insist upon proportionate payment of $86 for one mule; and B cannot insist upon having one mule upon paying $86. But if the contract was for ten mules at $86 each, especially if they are to be delivered at different times, say, on the first of each month for ten months, then unless by express terms or necessary implication, the parties intend that the contract be indivisible, A is entitled to be paid $86 upon delivery of each mule which satisfies the requirements of the contract, being liable, of course, for breach in failing to make later deliveries. Similar reasoning applies to a contract to render service for ten months at $86 a month.

If A tenders a mule which does not satisfy the requirements of the contract, B may refuse to pay until a satisfactory mule is delivered but such a breach by A will usually be too slight to justify B in refusing to go on with the contract; but if A should fail for three successive months to deliver satisfactory animals this would almost certainly excuse B from further performance; whether the breach by A is sufficient to enable B to declare the contract off is a question of fact depending upon all the circumstances; whether the breach by A is at the very outset or after part performance is usually one of such circumstances to be considered. Where A repudiates the contract B is justified in refusing to go on, at the same time holding A for the damage caused by his breach; though he might rescind the contract thus putting an end to his cause of action for breach he need not do so.

CHAPTER X

IMPOSSIBILITY

§ 45. In general—impossibility due to death or illness.[5] The general rule is that difficulty or even impossibility of performance is no excuse for nonperformance, the argument being that the defendant might have provided against such liability by a stipulation in the contract, but there are several exceptions.

One of the earliest exceptions is that if A contracts to render personal services to B, the death or long-continued illness of A is an excuse. The same reasoning applies where A contracts that X is to render the services and X dies or becomes too ill to perform; and to a case where A contracts to teach Y and Y dies or becomes too ill to be taught. Where the services to be rendered by A are personal to B, such as a contract to teach B or to be a valet to B, the death or illness of B is an excuse to both A and B; but if the services are not personal to B, his death or illness is not an excuse to either A or B.

Where A contracts to marry B and then, without his fault, becomes so seriously ill that a marriage would be dangerous to the life of either A or B or against the social interest in public health both parties are excused from carrying out the contract.

4 12 **Am Jur,** Contracts, §§ 320, 321.

5 12 **Am Jur,** Contracts, §§ 375, 376.

32 **Harv. L. R.** 789, Impossibility of Performance of Contracts Due to Wartime Regulation.

48 **W. Va. L. R.** 189, Excuse of Impossibility in West Virginia Contract Law.

§ 46. Change of law.[6] Where, after A makes a contract with B the act agreed to be performed by A becomes illegal through a change in the domestic law, A's nonperformance is excused unless he expressly assumes the risk of such change. The same reasoning should apply where A's act was to be performed in a foreign country and it has become illegal due to a change in the law of that country but most of the decisions are contra.

§ 47. Destruction of the subject matter of the contract.[7] Where A contracts to build a house on B's land and the house burns before it is completed the increased difficulty due to the fire does not excuse A; he must either build another house or respond in damages. But if A contracts to build a veranda on B's house and after the veranda is partly completed the house burns the impossibility of performing the contract has been held to be an excuse; it is sometimes said that there is an implied condition that the house shall remain in existence. Similar reasoning applies where A contracts to sell a specific chattel to B and the chattel is destroyed before title is passed to B; also where A contracts to carry goods for B by a particular ship and the ship is destroyed, and where A contracts to furnish water to B from a particular spring and the spring fails.

CHAPTER XI

ILLEGALITY

§ 48. Contracts in unreasonable restraint of trade.[8] If A sells to B his business or his practice of a profession such as that of a physician or lawyer, and agrees with B not to engage in the same business or profession in the same locality for a certain time, such a promise is enforceable against A if it is reasonably necessary to protect B; otherwise it is not enforceable because in unreasonable restraint of trade. Similar reasoning has been applied where B employs A in his business and A agrees that he will not, at the conclusion of the employment, compete with A either by setting up a rival business or by entering the employ of one of B's competitors.

§ 49. Wagers.[9] Where A contracts to pay B money or transfer property to him upon the happening of a future event or upon the ascertainment of some fact unknown to both parties such a contract is called a wager. Some wagers are valid because of their social value in that they operate to distribute the risk of loss, as, for example, life, fire, marine, accident and liability insurance contracts. Where there is no such social value, wagers are usually illegal either by statute or judicial decision. In many states there are statutes declaring all gaming and wagering contracts to be void, including contracts for the sale of goods or stocks where the parties do not contemplate delivery but merely a settlement upon the basis of the market price on a particular day.

§ 50. Champerty and maintenance—usury.[10] In most states today there is no objection to a lawyer undertaking to represent an impecunious client

6 12 **Am Jur**, Contracts, § 379.

7 12 **Am Jur**, Contracts, §§ 372–374.

8 36 **Am Jur**, Monopolies, Combinations, and Restraints of Trade, §§ 5–15.

Legality of combination among building or construction contractors. 121 **ALR** 345–353.

Legality of combinations or agreements between insurance companies or insurance agents. 21 **ALR** 543–557.

9 24 **Am Jur**, Gaming, §§ 60–78.

Validity of transactions in futures. 83 **ALR** 522–607.

10 10 **Am Jur**, Champerty and Maintenance, §§ 1, 2, 28, 29.

in return for a certain percentage of what may be recovered in the litigation, provided the percentage stipulated for is not unreasonable and the lawyer does not pay any of the litigation costs or other expenses.

Where A lends money to B upon interest higher than the legal rate the contract is usurious but courts differ widely as to the penalty imposed upon A if B sets up the usury statute in defense; in some states he forfeits only the excess above legal interest, in others he forfeits all interest and in still others he loses all right to both principal and interest.

§ 51. Contracts affecting marriage—Sunday statutes.[1] If A promises B $500 if B does not marry for a year B cannot usually collect against A because the contract is illegal as in restraint of marriage; but where B, in consideration of a promise to provide for her, agreed not to marry and to take care of her uncle during his lifetime and B performed her part of the contract it was held that she was entitled to enforce it against the uncle's estate.

Marriage brokage contracts are illegal, but the rule is made for the protection of clients, so a client may recover back what she has paid to the broker.

In most states there are statutes forbidding work and business on Sunday except as a matter of necessity or charity. Some of these statutes are construed as making illegal contracts made on Sunday, but transfers of property on Sunday are not prohibited and the fact that the contract was made on Sunday gives no ground for rescission of such transfers; hence if A should contract on Sunday to sell a chattel to B and should transfer title to him on that day or later A can neither collect the price nor get back the chattel.

§ 52. Miscellaneous cases of illegality.[2] If A, being the publisher of a newspaper, contracts to support B as candidate for Congress; or being a sheriff, to appoint B his deputy; or being a bank director, to vote to make B president of the bank; in all these cases the contract is illegal because of the public interest that A shall use an unbiased judgment in such matters.

If A contracts not to sue B in a Federal court this is illegal as interfering with the proper administration of justice; formerly contracts to arbitrate were also held illegal because they operated to oust courts of their jurisdiction but today the policy has so changed that in many states there are statutes expressly providing for arbitration.

Where statutes require the payment of a fee for permission to engage in a business and the purpose of the statute is not merely revenue but the protection of the public, for example, statutes requiring a license of innkeepers or

Purchase of cause of action by attorney as champertous. 4 **ALR** 173–185.

Contract by one person to defend litigation that has been or may be instituted against another as champertous or maintenous. 121 **ALR** 847–855.

See **Am Jur**, Usury.

Finance charge in connection with conditional sale contract as usury. 143 **ALR** 238–268.

Construction, application, and effect of provisions of small loan acts regarding fees, charges, etc., in addition to interest. 143 **ALR** 1323–1335.

Usury as affected by repayment, or borrower's option to repay, loan before maturity. 130 **ALR** 73–87.

1 35 **Am Jur**, Marriage, § 283.

50 **Am Jur**, Sundays and Holidays, §§ 43–71.

Sunday law as applicable to contracts signed by guarantor or surety on Sunday but delivered to obligee on weekday. 112 **ALR** 1200–1205.

Ratification of contract invalid because made on Sunday. 68 **ALR** 1487–1497.

2 12 **Am Jur**, Contracts, §§ 186–201.

Agreement conditional upon obligor securing public office. 45 **ALR** 1399–1409.

Validity of contract to influence administrative or executive officer or department. 46 **ALR** 196–219; s. in 148 **ALR** 768–774.

Validity of contract intended or tending to influence location of county seat or public building. 13 **ALR** 734–744.

physicians or lawyers, or of sellers of alcohol, a failure to procure the license is a bar to recovery for services performed or for goods sold; and similar reasoning has been applied to a retailer who uses unsealed measures, scales or weights in making sales of goods. But a defendant cannot set up his own failure to procure a license to give theatrical exhibitions in defense to an action against him for services rendered in giving such an exhibition.

Where A rented a carriage to B, a prostitute, knowing it was to be used as part of her display to attract men, it was held that A could not recover for the rental; and where A sold menhaden to B knowing B expected to retail it as mackerel thus deceiving the public, it was held that A could not collect the price; but where A sold liquor to B in Massachusetts knowing that B expected to resell it in Maine in violation of the Maine statute, A was not barred; nor is A barred from recovering money loaned to B merely because he knew that B expected to use the money in gambling.

CRITICAL LAW

CHAPTER I

IN GENERAL

§ 1. **Sources.**[1] The great body of the criminal law in most states is the English common law which has been gradually modified and supplemented by judicial decisions and by legislation. But in several states the common law of crimes has been expressly abolished so that in those states there is no crime except as provided by statute. Even in such states, however, the statutes must be construed in the light of the common law especially where they use terms like burglary, rape, arson, etc., which have a well-settled common-law meaning.

Since the United States government is one of delegated powers, the Federal courts cannot exercise common-law jurisdiction in criminal cases but only such jurisdiction as has been conferred on them by acts of Congress.

§ 2. **Classification.**[2] A crime may be either treason, a felony or a misdemeanor. Treason against the United States has been defined by the United States Constitution as levying war against the United States or adhering to their enemies, giving them aid and comfort. In some state Constitutions treason against the state has been similarly defined.

A felony at common law was an offense punishable by forfeiture of land or goods and usually also by death. The common-law felonies included murder, manslaughter, larceny, robbery, arson, burglary, rape, and sodomy. In this country there is no forfeiture of land or goods and there is no generally accepted test as to what constitutes a felony. The most common test is whether the offense is punishable by death or imprisonment in the state's prison. Offenses which were felonies at common law are felonies in most states today; besides, some statutes have made other offenses felonies either expressly or by necessary implication, for example, by punishing accessories, the distinction between principal and accessory existing only in felonies.

A misdemeanor is an offense which does not amount to treason or a felony.

§ 3. **Same—interests protected by the law of crimes.**[3] An act is criminal if it so violates or endangers a public interest that the law should furnish protection by punishing the perpetrator of it. There is a public interest in the protection of each individual member of society; hence the law furnishes protection against harms to the person by punishing homicide, rape, mayhem, assault and battery. It protects against interference with freedom of locomotion by punishing kidnapping, and false imprisonment. It protects in one's domestic relations by punishing adultery, abduction and neglect of de-

[1] 14 **Am Jur,** Criminal Law, §§ 14, 15.
43 **Col. L. R.** 753, 967, Interrelations of Criminal Law and Torts.
49 **Yale L. J.** 987, Moral Aspects of the Criminal Law.
18 **Ind. L. J.** 293, Medical and Social Factors in Crime.
32 **Georgetown L. J.** 1, Changing Concepts of Crime and Punishment.
17 **So. Calif. L. R.** 371, Psychiatry in Criminal Trials.

[2] 14 **Am Jur,** Criminal Law, §§ 11-13.

[3] 14 **Am Jur,** Criminal Law, §§ 2-5.

pendents. It protects property interests by punishing larceny, burglary, arson, robbery, forgery, embezzlement and obtaining property by fraud.

The law of crimes also punishes interference with governmental functions. It protects the administration of justice by punishing perjury, barratry, champerty, maintenance, bribery of judicial officers and jurors and the compounding of felonies; and protects the public peace by punishing treason, breach of the peace, disorderly conduct, misconduct in office, illegal voting.

In addition to these offenses directed against the individual and against the government the law recognizes as offenses against public decency such acts as bigamy, incest, seduction, indecent exhibitions and cruelty to animals; and as offenses against the social interest in the well-being of the individual such acts as public nuisances, restraint of trade, abortion and the sale of prohibited drugs and beverages.

§ 4. The act.[4] In order that there be a punishable offense it is usually necessary that there be both an act and an intent. In a few instances no act is necessary in the ordinary sense of the term; some omissions are punishable, for example, the failure to support dependents and the failure of a switchman to throw a switch thus causing the derailment of a train and loss of life. The crime of conspiracy is committed by merely making the agreement and the crime of solicitation by seeking to persuade another to commit a crime; and in some states by statute the mere possession of burglar's tools and counterfeit coin is punishable if with a criminal intent.

§ 5. Effect of consent to the act by the party injured.[5] Consent to the act by the party injured is not a defense unless the crime is one in which such lack of consent is an essential ingredient, for example, rape, larceny, robbery, burglary, arson and embezzlement. In these crimes, however, mere acquiescence does not amount to consent; for example, failing to take precautions against an expected burglary. Consent obtained by fraud is no bar; for example, that entrance to a dwelling house was obtained by fraud is no defense to a prosecution for burglary and that possession of a chattel was obtained by trick is no defense to a prosecution for larceny. Consent obtained by threats of great bodily harm is no bar; for example, that the victim of a robbery consented to the taking of his property because the defendant threatened to kill him if he did not, is no defense to a prosecution for robbery.

Certain persons are regarded as legally incapable of consenting; for example, a female child under a certain age cannot legally consent to sexual intercourse and hence her consent in fact is no bar to prosecution for rape.

§ 6. The intent—negligence—motive—attempts.[6] In some crimes there must be a specific criminal intent; for example, in burglary there must be an intent to commit a felony; in arson there must be an intent to burn the dwelling house of another; in larceny and robbery, an intent to deprive the owner of the goods permanently of his property in them. A specific intent is necessary in all criminal attempts and in assault with intent to murder or

[4] 14 **Am Jur**, Criminal Law, §§ 2, 5, 68.
55 **Harv. L. R.** 615, Criminal Omissions.

[5] 15 **Am Jur**, Criminal Law, § 334.

[6] 14 **Am Jur**, Criminal Law, §§ 12, 23–29, 65–70.
22 **Harv. L. R.** 75, Ignorance and Mistake in the Criminal Law.
45 **Harv. L. R.** 974, Mens Rea.
43 **Harv. L. R.** 689, Criminal Responsibility for the Acts of Another.
41 **Harv. L. R.** 821, Criminal Attempts.
49 **Yale L. J.** 789, Criminal Attempt—A Study of Foundations of Legal Liability.

to rape or to rob. Such an intent need not be shown by direct evidence; it may be inferred from the circumstances; for example, an intent to kill may be inferred from the use of a deadly weapon.

In other crimes no specific intent is necessary; for example, murder may be committed without intent to kill; if the defendant kills while engaged in an independent felony, such as burglary, arson, rape, larceny or robbery, it is murder. In such cases it is usually said that it is enough if there is a general criminal intent.

In still other crimes it is enough if the defendant acted recklessly or wantonly; for example, one may be punished for manslaughter where he caused death while driving recklessly on the highway. In such cases it is usually said that recklessness or criminal negligence is a substitute for general criminal intent.

Finally, there are some common-law offenses which are punishable as crimes though there was neither intent nor negligence; for example, a public nuisance or the obstruction of a public right, such as blocking a highway. These cases, sometimes referred to as cases of malum prohibitum, are more properly classified as public torts, the state using the machinery of the criminal law to give redress for what is really a tort against the public. Statutes also sometimes punish for an act done without either criminal intent or criminal negligence; for example, selling liquor or cigarettes to minors, the defendant being liable though he reasonably and in good faith believed the buyer to be an adult.

The motive or reason for or purpose of committing a crime is not an essential ingredient though the presence or absence of a motive may be considered by the jury especially where the evidence that the defendant committed the act is circumstantial. The presence of a good motive is no defense; for example, it is no excuse for publishing an obscene article that the object was to correct certain social evils.

An act done with intent to commit a crime but which fails of commission is an attempt to commit that crime. Mere preparation is not an attempt because there is no reasonable likelihood of accomplishment but for some obstacle or interference.

CHAPTER II

OFFENSES AGAINST THE PERSON

§ 7. **Homicide.**[7] Homicide, the killing of a human being, may be justified as in the case where it is done by the proper officer in execution of a legal sentence of death. Or it may be excused as in the case of self-defense. Or it may be accidental in which case the person committing it is not liable unless at the time engaged in an unlawful act. Or it may be wrongful—either murder, committed with malice aforethought—or manslaughter, committed without malice aforethought.

It is not necessary that any particular means be used to cause death. Though it is usually done by the use of a deadly weapon it may be by exposing one to inclement weather or to other dangers. It may be by omis-

[7] 26 **Am Jur,** Homicide, §§ 1-8, 45-53.
Homicide: improper treatment of disease. 9 **ALR** 211-223.
Homicide: failure to provide medical or surgical attention. 10 **ALR** 1137-1152.
Criminal homicide or assault by excessive or improper punishment inflicted upon child by parent or one in loco parentis. 37 **ALR** 704-712; s. in 64 **ALR** 292.
37 **Col. L. R.** 701, A Rationale of the Law of Homicide.

sion to act as by failure to furnish food or clothing to helpless dependents or by failure of an employer to ventilate a mine. It may be by using the act of an innocent third person as in having such person administer poison to the decedent or by using the act of the decedent himself as in the case where the decedent discharges a spring gun set by the defendant.

The defendant's act must be a part of the legal cause of the death. If X inflicts upon A a wound which is not mortal the fact that death is partly caused by the negligence of a surgeon or nurse in dressing the wound does not relieve X of responsibility for the death. Nor is X relieved by the fact that A's death was caused partly by his own previously weakened condition. But where X inflicts a mortal wound upon A who is soon thereafter killed instantly by Y, an independent actor, it is Y, not X, who is responsible for the death. In any case apart from statute the death must be caused within a year and a day from the date of the infliction of the wound or other wrongful act.

Apart from statute the destruction of an unborn child is not homicide but abortion.

§ 8. **Same—murder.**[8] Murder is homicide with malice aforethought. The phrase malice aforethought is a technical one and its meaning is determined by the decided cases. Where X, wrongfully and without any extenuating circumstances, intended to kill A and accidentally killed B; or where he intended to inflict great bodily harm upon A or where he intentionally or recklessly committed an act or was guilty of an omission, the natural tendency of which was to cause death or great bodily harm to A, as where he shot in A's direction within shooting distance intending merely to frighten the horse A was riding, or rode a vicious horse into a crowd of persons of whom A was one—in all the above cases there is said to be malice aforethought. In the last class of cases, if X uses no weapon but merely his hands or feet, or if the weapon used is not one likely to cause death or great bodily harm, there is ordinarily no malice aforethought and the homicide is not murder but manslaughter.

There is also said to be malice aforethought if X kills accidentally while resisting a lawful arrest by a known officer or while engaged in the commission of an independent felony such as burglary, rape, arson, robbery or larceny; the crime in this last class of cases is often referred to as a felony murder.

At common law suicide was punishable as self murder, the punishment being the forfeiture of land and goods. Though no longer punishable it is still regarded as criminal so that an attempt to commit suicide is a crime and if X kills A accidentally while attempting to commit suicide it is a felony and probably murder.

The word "aforethought" in the phrase "malice aforethought" does not require either premeditation or deliberation; it is enough that the "malice" exists at the very moment of killing. But in some states, in order to reduce the punishment in the less heinous cases, murder is divided by statute into

8 26 **Am Jur**, Homicide, §§ 9–16, 37–43, 84–88.

Homicide by unlawful act aimed at another. 18 **ALR** 917–929.

Homicide by companion of defendant while attempting to escape from scene of crime as murder in first degree. 22 **ALR** 850–859; s. in 108 **ALR** 847–856.

Homicide by wanton or reckless use of firearm without express intent to inflict injury. 5 **ALR** 603–619; s. in 23 **ALR** 1554–1557.

Suicide or attempt to commit suicide as a criminal offense or as an unlawful act. 92 **ALR** 1180–1185.

17 **Harv. L. R.** 331, Suicide and the Law.

two degrees, murder in the first degree usually requiring both premeditation —that is, a preconceived plan—and deliberation—that is, reflection, or that the homicide be committed while engaged in the commission of certain felonies. Murder in the second degree is usually punishable by life imprisonment and includes those cases of murder which are not in the first degree.

§ 9. **Same—manslaughter.**[9] A wrongful homicide committed without malice aforethought is manslaughter. This may be either voluntary (intentional) or involuntary (unintentional). Where X kills A in sudden passion or heat of blood caused by such reasonable provocation as would cause an ordinary man to act rashly and without reflection, it is voluntary manslaughter. Such reasonable provocation may exist where X has been attacked by A with violence or great rudeness; or where A has made an unlawful attempt to arrest X; or where A and X have been engaged in mutual combat; or where X has seen A committing adultery with X's wife or has just been told of such act. Whether in the particular case X did the act under reasonable provocation is ordinarily for the jury. If they find that although there was heat of blood due to reasonable provocation the blood had actually cooled before X struck the fatal blow they will ordinarily find X guilty of murder, not manslaughter.

Where X was at the time of the killing engaged in a misdemeanor which is malum in se but not naturally tending to cause death or great bodily harm, such as an assault and battery or other breach of the peace, he is guilty of involuntary manslaughter. So if, though engaged at the time in the doing of a lawful act, such as driving an automobile, X causes A's death through recklessness or criminal negligence; or if, charged with a duty to act, such as the duty of a railroad switchman, he is grossly negligent in failing to act by turning a switch, thus causing A's death, X is guilty of involuntary manslaughter.

§ 10. **Mayhem, kidnapping.**[10] If X intentionally and forcibly puts out A's eye or knocks out a tooth or cuts off his hand or finger or castrates him or causes him any other bodily hurt which renders him less able in fighting to defend himself or to annoy his adversary he may be found guilty of mayhem. Modern statutes also punish the causing of serious disfigurement not amounting to mayhem.

At common law kidnapping was a misdemeanor which consisted of wrongfully taking a person from his own country and sending him into another. By modern statutes it is not necessary that the person kidnapped be sent into another country; such statutes usually make the crime a felony and in some states the penalty is death.

§ 11. **Rape, abortion.**[1] Rape is a common-law felony consisting of a man's

9 26 **Am Jur**, Homicide, §§ 18–31.
Homicide or assault in connection with negligent operation of automobile or its use for unlawful purpose or in violation of law. 99 **ALR** 756–843.

10 36 **Am Jur**, Mayhem, §§ 1–6.
31 **Am Jur**, Kidnapping, §§ 1–12.
Mayhem as dependent on part of body injured and extent of injury. 16 **ALR** 955–971; s. in 58 **ALR** 1320–1322.
Kidnapping or other criminal offense by taking or removal of child by, or under authority of, parent, or one in loco parentis. 77 **ALR** 317–323.
Offense of abduction or kidnapping as affected by defendant's belief in legality of his act. 114 **ALR** 870–873.

1 1 **Am Jur**, Abortion, §§ 1–21.
44 **Am Jur**, Rape, §§ 1–137.
Woman upon whom abortion is committed or attempted as an accomplice. 139 **ALR** 993–1003.
Criminal responsibility of one co-operating in offense which he is incapable of committing personally. 5 **ALR** 782–791; 74 **ALR** 1110–1115; 131 **ALR** 1322–1329.
Admissibility in rape cases of evidence of previous unchastity, or reputation for

having illicit intercourse with a woman not his wife, without her consent. It is not necessary that there be emission and the slightest penetration is sufficient. Ordinarily the woman must show her lack of consent by resisting but this is not required where she was asleep or insensible or so insane or feeble-minded as not to understand the nature of the act. Where she understands the nature of the act the better view is that consent is a defense even if obtained by fraud. Modern statutory rape consists of having illicit intercourse with a girl under a certain age with her consent.

Under the common law of crimes an unborn child was not regarded as being in existence till quickening. Destroying the child before quickening was no offense at all; intentionally destroying the child after quickening was a misdemeanor whether committed by the expectant mother herself or by another person with or without her consent, unless believed to be reasonably necessary to save her life. Under modern statutes abortion is usually made a felony whether committed before or after quickening.

§ 12. Assault and battery.[2] The law of crimes as to simple battery or simple assault is apparently the same as the law of torts except that while a tort battery may be committed negligently, either recklessness or criminal negligence is necessary to a criminal battery. In both fields an assault, that is, either an actual or apparent attempt to commit a battery, requires either actual intent or, where the other party is put in reasonable fear of a battery, apparent intent to commit a battery. In both fields it is often said that every battery includes an assault and hence the phrase "assault and battery"; but this is not strictly true because a negligent tort battery or a reckless criminal battery does not necessarily include an assault because in such cases there is no actual intent and there may be no apparent intent to commit a battery.

At common law a criminal battery or assault, whether it was simple or was aggravated by being done with an intent to commit robbery or rape or other felony, was a misdemeanor, though the punishment was different where it was aggravated. But many modern statutes declare to be felonies such aggravated offenses as well as assaults with a deadly weapon; whether, in a doubtful case the weapon used was deadly—that is, likely to produce death —is a matter for the jury to decide; in clear cases, such as in the case of a loaded gun, an ax or brass knuckles the matter is determined by the court.

Though a battery is usually committed with the hand or fist or with a weapon it may be committed by administering poison or by exposing the victim to inclement weather.

CHAPTER III

OFFENSES AGAINST THE HABITATION

§ 13. Burglary.[3] Burglary, a felony at common law, is a breaking and entering the dwelling house of another at night with intent to commit a felony.

unchastity, of prosecutrix 140 ALR 364–392.

[2] 4 Am Jur, Assault and Battery, §§ 31–37.

[3] 9 Am Jur, Burglary, §§ 1–27.

Opening closed but unlocked door as breaking which will sustain charge of burglary for breaking and entering. 23 ALR 112–118.

Burglary without breaking. 23 ALR 288–293.

Construction and application of statute relating to burglars' tools. 103 ALR 1313–1325.

Breaking here is a technical word. It may consist of lifting a door latch, opening a door with a key, raising a closed widow, opening a closed transom or coming down through a chimney which is as nearly closed as its nature permits. Obtaining entrance through trick as by a false pretense of calling on business is enough; so is the breaking of an inner door enough. But there is no breaking if the occupant consents without fraud or where there is merely a breaking out by one who has entered without breaking; nor is there a breaking where there is an entry through an open window or door even though the opening is slight and must be pushed further open by the intruder.

There must be an entry as well as a breaking, but it need not be of the entire body; it may be merely of the hand or head or of a foot or finger; and coming partly down a chimney has been held sufficient.

The term dwelling house includes all outhouses within the common enclosure which are used in connection with the dwelling house proper. The building may be used for a shop or store provided that some one habitually sleeps there. The occupant need not be present when the burglary is committed provided his absence is only temporary. The dwelling house must be that of another but it is not important that the occupant is not the owner of the premises.

Both the breaking and entering must be in the nighttime but they may be on different nights. It is night if there is not sufficient daylight to recognize a man's face, but some statutes have fixed a different test.

Both the breaking and entering must be done with intent to commit a felony, such as rape or larceny; but it is not necessary that the intended felony be committed. A breaking and entering to commit an offense less than felony is not sufficient, for example, to have illicit intercourse with the woman occupant.

Modern statutes have enlarged the scope of common-law burglary either by making a breaking unnecessary or by extending it to other buildings such as stores and warehouses or by making it unnecessary that it be committed in the nighttime.

§ 14. Arson.[4] Arson, a common-law felony, is the wilful and malicious burning of the dwelling house of another, either by night or day. As in burglary, the term dwelling house includes outhouses within the common enclosure and it must be the dwelling house of another not the owner. Burning one's own dwelling house to collect the insurance money is not arson; nor is it arson for a husband to burn the wife's house if it is their home. An accidental burning of A's house is not arson unless it happened as the result of the defendant's wilful and malicious burning of the house of B. It is not necessary that the defendant intend to consume the building; setting fire to a jail in order to escape therefrom has been held sufficient.

There must be an actual burning of part of the house, not a mere scorching; but a charring is sufficient without a blaze.

In most jurisdictions statutes have been passed extending the offense of arson to other buildings, such as shops and warehouses. And statutes also punish the burning of one's own property to collect fire insurance.

4 4 **Am Jur**, Arson, §§ 1–41.
Burning as element of offense of arson. 1 **ALR** 1163–1172.
Ownership of property as affecting criminal liability for burning thereof. 17 **ALR** 1168–1183.

CHAPTER IV

OFFENSES AGAINST PROPERTY

A. Larceny

§ 15. Definition and subject matter of simple larceny.[5] At common law larceny is the taking and carrying away of the personal goods of another of any value with the felonious intent of stealing the same.

Land is not the subject of larceny; hence if X severs and takes away immediately part of the soil or minerals or vegetable growth on the land, such as trees, fruit, vegetables, etc., or fixtures, such as water pipes, windows, etc., it is not larceny. But if X does not take away immediately that which he has severed, or if there has been a severance by the owner or a third person, that which has been severed becomes the subject of larceny. The same reasoning applies to wild animals; if X kills or captures a deer on A's land and immediately removes it, there is no larceny, but if it is killed or captured by X or by the owner or Y it then becomes property and subject to larceny. So, water and gas confined in pipes becomes the subject of larceny. At common law dogs and cats were not the subject of larceny but this has usually been changed by statute.

Abandoned goods cease to be the subjects of larceny and any one may freely appropriate them; but this reasoning does not apply to goods which have been lost or mislaid. Goods are the subject of larceny even though wrongfully in the possession of A or even though they have been stolen by A, and in the indictment the ownership of the goods may be alleged to be in A.

The thing taken must have some value, either to the possessor or another, but the least value is sufficient. A piece of paper, no matter how small, was therefore the subject of larceny; but at common law if a chose in action were written thereon the paper was merged in the chose in action and the chose in action, being intangible, was not the subject of larceny. This has usually been changed by statute making such instruments the subject of larceny.

At common law the use of a chattel was considered to be too intangible to be stolen, so if X takes A's auto merely for a ride and then returns it there is no larceny; but such takings are usually punished by modern statutes.

§ 16. The taking—larceny by trick.[6] At early common law there could be no larceny except by such a trespass as would give rise to an action of trespass de bonis asportatis by the party from whose possession the chattel was taken. But later, by judicial decision, larceny was extended to include the obtaining of possession by fraud or trick. For example, where X hires an auto for a week intending at the time never to return it, or where he shifts checks on trunks intending that A's trunk be delivered by the railroad company to himself—in both these cases there is larceny by trick.

§ 17. Possession and custody—lost goods.[7] One who has received posses-

[5] 32 **Am Jur,** Larceny, §§ 1, 2, 64–84.
Appropriation or removal without payment of property delivered in expectation of immediate cash payment, as criminal offense. 83 **ALR** 441–447.
Larceny of real property or things savoring of real property. 131 **ALR** 146–160.
Dogs as subject of larceny. 92 **ALR** 212–218.

[6] 32 **Am Jur,** Larceny, §§ 26–34, 56–58.
Appropriation of property after obtaining possession by fraud or larceny. 26 **ALR** 381–393.

[7] 32 **Am Jur,** Larceny, §§ 26, 53–71.
Larceny by general owner of property, in which another has a special interest or right of possession. 58 **ALR** 330–339.

sion of a chattel lawfully cannot, by later deciding to appropriate it, become guilty of larceny because there is neither trespass nor trick; but if it was delivered to him by mistake and he then knew of the mistake and received it with intent to appropriate it, it is larceny by trick.

If a box or trunk or other package is delivered to a carrier or other bailee and he breaks it open and takes goods therefrom intending to appropriate them, he is guilty of larceny by breaking bulk.

A servant ordinarily has only custody of goods entrusted to him by his master; hence if he appropriates the goods he is taking from the possession of the master and is guilty of larceny. The same reasoning applies to a guest and to a bailee who has forfeited his right to possession by his misconduct. If a third person delivers a chattel to a servant to be delivered to his master and the servant converts it he is not guilty of larceny because he has possession; but aliter if the servant has placed the chattel in the master's wagon or in any other place where his duty as servant requires him to put them for the master, intending thereby to put them into the master's possession; in such a case he is guilty of larceny if he later appropriates the goods.

Where A hands to X a bill to pay for goods bought, expecting X to give him the change and X appropriates the bill without giving any change, it is larceny because X had only custody; but it is otherwise if with A's consent X goes to another store to get the change.

If X finds a lost chattel and there is no clue to the owner, it is not larceny even though at the time of taking he intends to appropriate it. If there is a clue and X takes the chattel innocently intending to restore it to the owner and later decides to convert it, there is no larceny; but if at the time of taking he intends to appropriate it he is guilty of larceny.

§ 18. The asportation.[8] The slightest asportation is enough. For example, lifting a bag from the bottom of the boot of a coach, lifting a pocketbook three inches from the bottom of a pocket, taking money from a till but not removing it from the room, taking a tub of butter from one end of a car to the open space in the middle of the car, have all been held sufficient. But upsetting a barrel from the end to the side, merely touching a pocketbook in the bottom of a pocket, trying to get a dress off a dummy, have all been held to be insufficient.

The means of removal is not important. For example, it may be by enticing an animal into an enclosure or by connecting a private pipe with a pipe containing water or gas.

§ 19. The intent.[9] The property must be taken and carried away animo furandi; that is, with the fraudulent intent to deprive the owner of his property permanently. If the intent is not fraudulent, for example, if the defendant took the chattel by mistake, thinking it was his own, he is liable in tort in either trespass or trover, but it is not larceny. Nor is it larceny if the defendant took the chattel for a temporary use expecting to

Larceny as affected by distinction between custody and possession. 125 **ALR** 367–393.

Larceny by finder of property. 36 **ALR** 372–387.

8 32 **Am Jur**, Larceny, §§ 10–21.

What amounts to asportation which will support charge of larceny. 19 **ALR** 724–732; s. in 144 **ALR** 1383–1389.

9 32 **Am Jur**, Larceny, §§ 36–42.

Larceny or embezzlement as affected by purpose to take or retain property in payment of, or as security for, a claim. 13 **ALR** 142–147; s. in 13 **ALR** 151–156; 31 **ALR** 1081–1082; 35 **ALR** 1461–1463; 42 **ALR** 741–742; 116 **ALR** 997–1003.

Intent to convert property to one's own use or to the use of third person as element of larceny. 12 **ALR** 804–809.

return it. But it is larceny to take a chattel with intent to return it only upon the payment of a reward or with intent to sell it back to the owner; for example, taking a railroad ticket expecting to use it for a journey and in that way to return the ticket to the railroad company was held to be larceny.

By the better view if there is a fraudulent intent to deprive the owner permanently that is enough without any expectation of gain or benefit to the defendant; for example, taking and intentionally destroying A's horse.

§ 20. Grand and petit larceny—compound larcenies.[10] By an early English statute it was made grand larceny where the value of the property taken was more than twelve pence—that is, one shilling or about twenty-five cents; if the value was not greater than twelve pence it was petit larceny; both were felonies but the punishment was less severe in the case of a petit larceny. In most states there is a similar distinction but petit larceny is usually only a misdemeanor.

In many states there are statutes which make a distinction between simple larceny and larceny committed under certain aggravating circumstances, meriting more severe punishment. The most common of these compound larcenies are larceny from the person and larceny from particular places, such as from a house, or a building, or a shop, or a warehouse or a vessel. The fact that the victim of the larceny was drunk or asleep does not prevent it from being larceny from the person; but in order that there be larceny from a house the chattel must be under the protection of the house and not merely lying on a outside porch or hanging from a nail on the outside of a door.

B. False Pretenses, Embezzlement, Robbery

§ 21. Obtaining property by false pretenses.[1] At common law obtaining possession of a chattel by fraud was punished as larceny by trick; but to obtain title to the chattel by fraud was indictable as a cheat only if a false weight or measure or a false token, such as a ring or key was used. To remedy this defect, statutes have been passed making it a crime to obtain property by false pretenses. The false pretenses necessary to be employed must usually be such as would form the basis for the tort action on the case for deceit. Thus, the representation must be as to an existing material fact; for example, merely giving a false name is not enough. The representation must be a part of the cause of obtaining the property; for example, representing that he

[10] 32 **Am Jur**, Larceny, § 3.

[1] 32 **Am Jur**, Larceny, § 7.
22 **Am Jur**, False Pretenses, §§ 2–29.

May offense of obtaining money or property by false pretenses or confidence game be predicated on obtaining loan or renewal thereof. 24 **ALR** 397–403; s. in 52 **ALR** 1167–1172.

Illegal or fraudulent intent of prosecuting witness or person defrauded as defense in prosecution based on false representations. 95 **ALR** 1249–1262; s. in 128 **ALR** 1520–1522.

False pretense or confidence game through means of worthless check or draft. 35 **ALR** 344–361.

Construction, application, and effect of criminal statutes directed specifically against use of worthless, false, or bogus check or draft. 35 **ALR** 376–396; s. in 43 **ALR** 49–52; 95 **ALR** 486–508.

Criminal offense of obtaining property by false pretenses predicated upon transactions incident to raising of funds for benevolent or charitable purpose. 145 **ALR** 302–308.

Criminal charge predicated upon fraudulently obtaining a check, note, etc., or signature thereon, from the person executing the same. 141 **ALR** 210–244.

Criminal offense of obtaining money under false pretenses, or attempting to do so, predicated upon receipt or claim of benefits under insurance policy. 135 **ALR** 1157–1169.

Failure to deceive prosecutor, or fact that prosecutor did not rely on pretenses, as affecting charge of offense of attempting to obtain property by false pretenses. 89 **ALR** 342–345.

Presentation of and attempt to establish fraudulent claim against governmental agency. 21 **ALR** 180–185.

was an ordained minister was not sufficient where the money obtained was for services actually rendered. But, unlike an action on the case for deceit, buying with intent not to pay is not enough. Nor is the mere fact that damage followed from relying on the representation; it is necessary to show, as in larceny, an intent to deprive the owner permanently of his property.

§ 22. **Embezzlement.**[2] One who obtains possession of a chattel without either trespass or fraud and while thus possessed appropriates it to himself is not guilty of larceny. To remedy this defect statutes have been passed punishing as embezzlement misappropriation of property entrusted to bailees, agents, trustees, attorneys and other fiduciaries. If there has been no relation of trust and confidence, such statutes do not apply; for example, they do not apply to one to whom money has been paid by mistake, or to an ordinary debtor, or to a farm hand who took his employer's wheat and sold it. The last-mentioned case is outside the statute for the additional reason that the defendant did not have possession.

As in larceny and obtaining property by false pretenses there must be, at the time of misappropriation, a fraudulent intent to deprive the owner of his property.

§ 23. **Robbery.**[3] Robbery is a common-law felony consisting of a larceny from the person committed by the open use of force or by intimidation. For example, a pickpocket snatching money from the hand of his victim is guilty of robbery; so is the highwayman who at the point of a gun compels his victim to hand over his valuables.

It is not necessary that the property thus obtained be literally from the person; it is enough that it be taken from his presence; for example, where the defendant, having intimidated his victim, drives away his livestock or compels him to throw down his purse and then picks it up.

It is necessary that the force be used to obtain the property; force used to escape or merely to retain possession is not enough.

C. Receiving Stolen Goods—Forgery

§ 24. **Receiving stolen goods.**[4] At common law the receiver of stolen property knowing it to have been stolen was guilty of misprision of felony because of his failure to prosecute the thief. This was a misdemeanor; but by statute in most states the offense is made a felony which may be committed by receiving the goods either from the thief or from some one other than the thief. But the property must be stolen property at the time that it is received; if it has been returned to the owner it has ceased to be stolen property and receiving it cannot be a crime even if the defendant thought the goods were stolen.

The property must be received with fraudulent intent; one who receives the goods in order to return them to the owner is not guilty of the offense.

2 32 **Am Jur**, Larceny, § 6.
18 **Am Jur**, Embezzlement, §§ 1-27.
Distinction between larceny and embezzlement. 146 **ALR** 532-596.

Larceny or embezzlement by appropriating money or proceeds of paper mistakenly delivered in excess of the amount due or intended. 14 **ALR** 894-903.

What amounts to embezzlement or larceny within fidelity bond. 16 **ALR** 1493-1503; s. in 56 **ALR** 967-969.

3 46 **Am Jur**, Robbery, §§ 1-23.
Threat to arrest or prosecute and acts in connection therewith as force or putting in fear for purposes of robbery. 27 **ALR** 1299-1306.

Retention of property, or attempt to escape, by force or putting in fear as equivalent to taking in that manner for purposes of robbery. 58 **ALR** 656-665.

4 45 **Am Jur**, Receiving Stolen Property, §§ 1-10.

§ 25. **Forgery and uttering.**[5] At common law forgery is a misdemeanor consisting of the false making or altering, with intent to defraud, of some writing or document which, if genuine, would prejudice another's rights; in most states it has been made a felony by statute. Only writings or documents are involved; painting an artist's name in the corner of a picture may help make the defendant liable for obtaining property under false pretenses but it is not forgery. Nor is it forgery if the document, had it been genuine, would have had no legal efficacy; for example, a document purporting to be a lease but ineffective because no time was fixed for the lease to run.

Fraudulent alteration is enough, as by fraudulently increasing the amount of a promissory note; and where X received a check signed in blank with authority to fill in the blank with a certain amount and he fraudulently wrote in a larger amount it was held to be forgery.

By the better view it is not necessary that the forgery cause any damage to any one.

It is also a common-law misdemeanor to utter a forged instrument knowing it to be forged. Uttering usually consists of but does not require the actual delivery of the instrument; it is enough if it is merely presented or offered as genuine.

CHAPTER V

MISCELLANEOUS OFFENSES

§ 26. **Offenses against the public peace.**[6] At common law any act which has a direct tendency to excite or alarm the public is punished as a breach of the peace, a misdemeanor. The most important of these are:

(1) An unlawful assembly, which is an assembly of three or more persons for the purpose of committing some crime of violence or to do any other act likely to cause persons in the vicinity to fear a breach of the peace.

(2) A riot, which is an unlawful assembly which undertakes to carry out its unlawful purpose.

(3) A mutual affray in a public place or an assault and battery committed in a public place.

(4) The publication of a libel which is likely to provoke a breach of the peace. Truth is no defense, apart from statute.

Knowledge imputed to reasonable man as test of knowledge of defendant in prosecution for larceny or receiving stolen property. 147 **ALR** 1058–1071.

May participant in larceny or theft be convicted of offenses of receiving or concealing the stolen property. 136 **ALR** 1087–1104.

5 23 **Am Jur,** Forgery, §§ 1–5, 7–30.

Genuine making of instrument for purpose of defrauding as constituting forgery. 41 **ALR** 229–253; s. in 46 **ALR** 1529–1530; 51 **ALR** 568.

Forgery: use of fictitious or assumed name. 9 **ALR** 407–419.

Altering receipt, canceled check, or other voucher as forgery. 26 **ALR** 1058–1066.

Blanks in paper, filling in, in terms other than authorized. 87 **ALR** 1169–1172.

Alteration of written instrument in order to conform to actual intention as forgery. 93 **ALR** 864–865.

6 8 **Am Jur,** Breach of Peace, §§ 1–16.

46 **Am Jur,** Riots and Unlawful Assembly, §§ 1–12.

33 **Am Jur,** Libel and Slander, §§ 308–316.

What constitutes offense of unlawful assembly. 58 **ALR** 751–757; s. in 93 **ALR** 737–738.

Trespasser, abusive language addressed to, as breach of peace. 34 **ALR** 575.

Group, abusive or insulting language addressed to, as breach of peace. 34 **ALR** 580.

What constitutes breach of peace bond. 54 **ALR** 388–393.

Conduct amounting to offense of disturbing public or religious meeting. 12 **ALR** 650–658.

Words as criminal offense other than libel or slander. 48 **ALR** 83–102.

Character of libel or slander for which criminal prosecution will lie. 19 **ALR** 1470–1543.

Entrapment to commit crime of criminal libel. 18 **ALR** 160.

A trespass upon land was no crime at common law unless attended by a breach of the peace. But by a very early English statute it was made a misdemeanor to make a forcible entry upon the land of another even though the person so entering had a right to the possession; the statute applied chiefly to landlords taking possession at the end of the tenant's term.

§ 27. Offenses against the administration of justice.[7] Any act which tends to corrupt or obstruct the administration of justice is a common-law misdemeanor. The most important of these are:

(1) Perjury and subornation of perjury. Perjury is the wilful and corrupt taking of a false oath with regard to a material matter in a judicial proceeding. In many states statutes have extended it to include false swearing not in a judicial proceeding. Subornation of perjury is procuring another to commit perjury.

(2) Bribery, which is the giving of anything of value to a public official or to any other person performing a public duty, with the intent of influencing him in the discharge of his legal duty; in some states the offense has been made a felony by statute. To offer, to accept or to solicit a bribe is also a common-law misdemeanor.

(3) Misconduct of a public official in the conduct of his office such as extortion or oppression. It is also a misdemeanor to refuse to serve in a public office after being elected or appointed thereto.

(4) Compounding a felony, which is an agreement not to prosecute for a felony.

(5) Breaking prison, or escape from custody after having been lawfully arrested, or rescuing such prisoner or negligently permitting such breach or escape.

(6) If X, having no legitimate interest in the matter and not believing that he has, assists Y to bring a suit against Z, X is guilty of maintenance; and if X makes an agreement with Y whereby X is to receive a part of the recovery, X is guilty of champerty.

§ 28. Offenses affecting public safety, health and comfort.[8] A nuisance on a scale large enough to endanger the safety, health or comfort of the public, such as a large slaughterhouse in a residential community or the pollution

[7] 8 **Am Jur**, Bribery, §§ 1–15.
10 **Am Jur**, Champerty and Maintenance, §§ 1–5.
11 **Am Jur**, Compounding Crimes, §§ 1–3.
22 **Am Jur**, Extortion and Blackmail, §§ 5–8.
39 **Am Jur**, Obstructing Justice, §§ 8–11, 17.
41 **Am Jur**, Perjury, §§ 1, 58, 74–76.
Criminal offense of bribery as affected by lack of legal qualification of person assuming or alleged to be an officer. 115 **ALR** 1263–1268.
Unaccepted offer by or to an official, predicating bribery or cognate offense upon. 52 **ALR** 816–822.
Officer's lack of authority as affecting offense. 122 **ALR** 951–957.
Candidate, statement by, regarding salary or fees of office, as bribery. 106 **ALR** 493–497.
Offense of barratry: criminal aspects of champerty and maintenance. 139 **ALR** 620–653.
Extortion predicated upon statements or intimations regarding criminal liability, in connection with attempt to collect or settle a claim which defendant believed to be valid. 135 **ALR** 728–735.
What constitutes offense of obstructing or resisting officer. 48 **ALR** 746–757.
May conviction of perjury rest on circumstantial evidence. 15 **ALR** 634–641; s. in 27 **ALR** 857; 42 **ALR** 1063–1064.
Offense of perjury by questions relating to jurisdiction of court before which testimony was given. 82 **ALR** 1127–1141.
Rule as to corroborative evidence in prosecutions for subornation of perjury. 56 **ALR** 407–414.
Acquittal as bar to a prosecution of accused for perjury committed at trial. 37 **ALR** 1290–1298.
Perjury or false swearing as contempt. 11 **ALR** 342–357; s. in 73 **ALR** 817–821.
Criminal offense of making false statement or report as to assets or condition of bank. 85 **ALR** 825–844.

[8] 25 **Am Jur**, Health, § 37.
39 **Am Jur**, Nuisances, §§ 178–180.

of a watercourse, is a public nuisance, a misdemeanor. Obstructing a highway or navigable stream is also a misdemeanor. These are not crimes in the narrow sense because they do not require any criminal intent, but public torts which are redressed with the machinery of criminal procedure.

§ 29. Offenses against morality and decency.[9] Where a person already legally married goes through a marriage ceremony with a third person, he is guilty of bigamy. This was not an offense at common law, being punished in the ecclesiastical courts, but was made a felony by an English statute in 1628; there are similar statutes in this country.

In most states there are statutes prohibiting marriage between persons related within certain prohibited degrees, such as brother and sister, ancestor and descendant, etc. Sexual intercourse between such persons with or without a purported marriage is usually punished by statutes as incest.

Some other crimes against public morality and decency are open and notorious illicit cohabitation, the seduction of an unmarried woman of previous chaste character, the keeping of bawdyhouses or of gambling houses, public drunkenness and indecent exposure of the person.

CHAPTER VI

DEFENSES

§ 30. Insanity, intoxication.[10] Though insanity is not usually a defense to a tort action it is a complete defense to a prosecution for crime. If the de-

[9] 7 **Am Jur**, Bigamy, §§ 1–17.
17 **Am Jur**, Disorderly Houses, §§ 6–9.
24 **Am Jur**, Gaming, §§ 12–43.
27 **Am Jur**, Incest, §§ 1–7.
33 **Am Jur**, Lewdness, Indecency, and Obscenity, §§ 1–15.
What amounts to vagrancy. 14 **ALR** 1483–1508.
Criminal offense predicated upon indecent exposure. 93 **ALR** 996–1007.
Coin-operated or slot machine other than slot vending machine which may be played for amusement only or which confines winner's reward to privilege of additional play or other form of amusement, as within antigambling provisions. 148 **ALR** 879–897.
Constitutionality and construction of pandering acts. 74 **ALR** 311–338.
Gifts or prizes or gift enterprises, what transactions are within the purview of statutes or ordinances in relation to. 39 **ALR** 1035–1042.
Trading-stamp schemes as lotteries or gift enterprises. See 26 **ALR** 724; 39 **ALR** 1036; s. in 133 **ALR** 1087–1089.
Numbers game or policy game as a lottery. 105 **ALR** 305–310.
Theaters, etc., scheme for increasing attendance at, as lottery. 48 **ALR** 1115–1122; 57 **ALR** 424–426; 103 **ALR** 866–872; 109 **ALR** 709–714; 113 **ALR** 1121–1124.
Solicitation to crime as substantive common-law offense. 35 **ALR** 961–969.
Subsequent intermarriage of parties, forgiveness, compromise, etc., as defense to prosecution for seduction. 80 **ALR** 833–852.
Valid marriage between prosecutrix and defendant, facts preventing as defense. 85 **ALR** 123–128.
Mistaken belief in existence, validity, or effect of divorce or separation as defense to prosecution for bigamy. 57 **ALR** 792–801.
Place where second or later marriage is celebrated as affecting bigamy. 70 **ALR** 1036–1040.
Isolated acts of sexual intercourse as constituting criminal offense of adultery or fornication or illicit cohabitation. 74 **ALR** 1361–1369.
Single person who has carnal intercourse with married person of the opposite sex as guilty of aiding and abetting adultery. 5 **ALR** 784; s. in 74 **ALR** 1110–1115; 131 **ALR** 1322–1329.

[10] 14 **Am Jur**, Criminal Law, §§ 32–40.
15 **Am Jur**, Criminal Law, §§ 338–341.
Test of present insanity which will prevent trial for crime or punishment after conviction. 3 **ALR** 94–99.
Irresistible impulse as an excuse for crime. 70 **ALR** 659–684.
Investigation of present sanity to determine whether accused should be put, or continue, on trial. 142 **ALR** 961–1015.
Insanity supervening after conviction and sentence of death. 49 **ALR** 804–813.
Voluntary intoxication as defense to homicide. 12 **ALR** 861–904; s. in 79 **ALR** 897–912.
Driving automobile while intoxicated as a substantive criminal offense. 42 **ALR** 1498–1514; s. in 49 **ALR** 1392–1401; 68 **ALR** 1356–1376. See also 142 **ALR** 555–562.
Degree or nature of intoxication for purposes of statute or ordinance making it a criminal offense to operate an automobile while in that condition. 142 **ALR** 555–562.
30 **Harv. L. R.** 535, 724, Insanity and Criminal Responsibility.
57 **Harv. L. R.** 1045, Intoxication and Criminal Responsibility.

fendant at the time the act was committed was incapable of distinguishing between right and wrong, he will not be held criminally responsible in any jurisdiction; some states go further and excuse a defendant who knew the act was wrong but acted under an irresistible impulse. Mere moral perversion is no defense; nor is an insane delusion not connected with the defendant's act.

Involuntary drunkenness is a defense, but voluntary drunkenness is not a defense unless thereby the defendant becomes afflicted with delirium tremens or otherwise unable to distinguish between right and wrong; but it may negative the existence of a specific intent, such as the intent to steal, or to rape or to kill, and it may reduce a crime from murder to manslaughter.

§ 31. **Infancy, coverture.**[1] Infancy is no defense to an action for an intentional tort but in negligent torts the infant is not held to as high standard of care as adults. In the law of crimes a child under seven is held to be incapable; between the ages of seven and fourteen there is a presumption of incapacity; between fourteen and twenty-one there is a presumption of capacity.

At common law a wife was not criminally responsible for any offense, other than treason or murder, committed under the coercion of her husband and there was a presumption of such coercion where the act was committed in his presence or where he was near enough to exert control over her. In many states the presumption has been abolished either by statute or judicial decision.

§ 32. **Mistake, command, necessity, condonation.**[2] Mistake of law is usually no defense even though the defendant acted under the advice of a public official or an attorney; but where specific intent is necessary, as in larceny or embezzlement, a mistake in the application of the law to the facts of the particular case may negative the specific intent so that a defendant who erroneously thought he had a legal right to take the property would not be guilty of larceny.

Where the defendant acted under a mistake of fact which, if true, would render the act innocent or excusable, he is not criminally responsible. For example, though mistake of title is no defense to an action of trespass or trover it is a defense to a prosecution for larceny; and a defendant is excused who erroneously but reasonably thought that it was necessary to kill in self-defense. But the legislature may punish a person regardless of his lack of criminal intent and in such cases mistake of fact is no defense. For example, where a statute punishes as rape having sexual intercourse with a girl under sixteen, or prohibits selling cigarettes to minors, it is no defense that the defendant reasonably thought the girl was over sixteen or that the buyer of cigarettes was over twenty-one.

One who commits an act under threat by a third person of immediate death or great bodily harm is not criminally responsible unless the act consists of killing an innocent person.

The necessity of saving one's own life may excuse the thrusting away of a person who in a shipwreck is trying to get on a plank which is large enough to sustain only the defendant, but it does not excuse deliberate killing of an

[1] 14 **Am Jur,** Criminal Law, §§ 61, 62.
27 **Am Jur,** Husband and Wife, §§ 638–643.
27 **Am Jur, Infants,** §§ 97, 98.

[2] 15 **Am Jur,** Criminal Law, §§ 305, 306.

innocent person in order to sustain life by eating his flesh; nor does it excuse the larceny of food.

Apart from statute it is no defense that the party injured has settled with the defendant or has condoned the offense.

CHAPTER VII

PARTIES IN CRIME—JURISDICTION

§ 33. Parties in crime.[3] The distinction between principals and accessories is important only in felonies. In treason and misdemeanors all who are punishable at all are punishable as principals.

A principal in the first degree is one who actually commits the criminal act either by himself or through an innocent agent, for example, by causing an innocent person to administer poison to another. A principal in the second degree is one who is present, aiding and abetting, for example, keeping a lookout to avoid detection. In order to convict one of being a principal in the second degree it is necessary to show the guilt of the principal in the first degree.

An accessory before the fact is one who procures, commands or counsels the commission of the crime but who is not present when it is committed. Mere knowledge that the crime is to be committed is not enough. An accessory after the fact is one who assists another whom he knows has committed the crime, for example, by receiving him, concealing him and aiding him to escape. Receiving stolen goods from a thief knowing that he stole them is a crime in itself but does not render the receiver liable as an accessory to the larceny. Apart from statute an accessory must be indicted as such and cannot be convicted till the guilt of the principal has been ascertained.

§ 34. Jurisdiction and locality of offenses.[4] A state may punish anyone, except foreign ambassadors and ministers and their servants, for offenses committed within its limits. It may also punish its own citizens for acts committed abroad, but this is rarely done.

Where X, in state A, shoots across the state line and kills Y in state B, the homicide is committed in state B where the shot took effect and it may be punished by state B but not by state A without a special statute, though X might be held guilty in state A of assault with intent to kill. The same reasoning applies if X in state A procures Z, an innocent agent, to administer poison to Y in state B.

Where X steals goods in Clay county and carries them, animo furandi, into Dean county in the same state, he may be punished for larceny in either county, because the carrying into Dean county is a continuation of the original trespass. And either by statute or judicial decision the same reasoning has been applied where X carries the stolen goods into another state.

Where X wounds Y in state A and Y goes into state B and dies there of the wound, X is guilty of homicide in state A because the criminal act was committed there.

[3] 14 Am Jur, Criminal Law, §§ 71–116.

[4] 14 Am Jur, Criminal Law, §§ 221–231.

CHAPTER VIII

CRIMINAL PROCEDURE

§ 35. Extradition.[5] Where X commits a crime in state A and flees into state B, the United States Constitution provides that the governor of state B shall, upon request of the governor of state A, deliver over the fugitive. But since there is no remedy provided in case of the refusal of the governor of state B, the matter lies in his own discretion, and a few years ago, the governor of Indiana refused to surrender a fugitive from Kentucky on the ground that he did not think the fugitive would be given a fair trial in Kentucky.

It is not necessary that X shall be literally a fugitive; if he went into state B for other reasons than escaping prosecution he may still be extradited. But if X committed the crime in state B by shooting across the state line or by using an innocent agent in state B and was never in state B, he may not be extradited.

An extradition warrant, unlike an indictment, need not fully describe the crime.

§ 36. Preliminary examination—bail—commitment.[6] If the accused is not a fugitive from justice and has not already been indicted, and has been lawfully arrested, he is entitled to be brought promptly before a magistrate for a preliminary examination to determine whether a crime has been committed and whether there is probable cause to suspect that the accused is guilty. If the magistrate finds that no crime has been committed or that there is no probable cause to suspect the accused it is his duty to dismiss the charge; but if he finds that a crime has been committed and there is reasonable ground to suspect the accused, he should ordinarily release the accused upon giving bail. If the offense is too serious to be bailable or if bail is not given the magistrate should commit the accused to jail to await trial.

The right to a preliminary examination may be waived by the accused. If either a preliminary examination or bail is wrongfully denied or if excessive bail is required, his proper remedy is a writ of habeas corpus.

§ 37. The indictment or information.[7] In every prosecution there must be

[5] 22 **Am Jur**, Extradition, §§ 1–57.

Extradition of paroled convict. See 78 **ALR** 422.

Determination in extradition proceedings, or on habeas corpus in such proceedings, whether a crime is charged. 81 **ALR** 552–580.

Sufficiency of statements in demanding papers in extradition proceedings as allegation or proof of presence of accused in demanding state at time of commission of alleged crime or that accused is a fugitive. 135 **ALR** 973–988.

Sanity or insanity or pendency of lunacy proceedings as matters for consideration in extradition proceedings. 114 **ALR** 693–697.

Right to try one brought within jurisdiction illegally or as a result of mistake as to identity. 18 **ALR** 509–516.

Surrender of convict to authorities of other jurisdiction as precluding punishment or further punishment under original conviction. 147 **ALR** 941–945.

Right to try one for an offense other than that named in extradition proceedings. 21 **ALR** 1405–1425.

22 **Oreg. L. R.** 60, A Résumé of Decisions of the United States Supreme Court on Federal Criminal Procedure.

12 **Geo. Wash. L. R.** 119, Reform of Federal Criminal Procedure.

[6] 6 **Am Jur**, Bail and Recognizance, §§ 9–39.

14 **Am Jur**, Criminal Law, §§ 240–256.

Amount of bail required in criminal action. 53 **ALR** 399–407.

Factors in fixing amount of bail in criminal cases. 72 **ALR** 801–822.

Induction of principal into military or naval service as exonerating his bail for his nonappearance. 8 **ALR** 371–373; s. in 147 **ALR** 1428–1429.

51 **Yale L. J.** 748, From Suspicion to Accusation.

51 **Yale L. J.** 763, Evidence in Federal Criminal Trials.

51 **Yale L. J.** 723, Objections of the Federal Criminal Procedure Revision.

[7] 14 **Am Jur**, Criminal Law, §§ 232–239.

27 **Am Jur**, Indictments and Informations §§ 2–10, 30–110.

24 **Am Jur**, Grand Jury, §§ 1–50.

a formal accusation. An indictment is a formal accusation made under oath by a grand jury which, apart from statute, is composed of 23 members of whom at least 12 must concur. While ordinarily a grand jury acts upon evidence laid before it by the prosecuting attorney it may act upon its own initiative and its own knowledge. If the crime is a misdemeanor—and in some states even in the case of felonies—the formal accusation may be made by the prosecuting attorney without the intervention of a grand jury; such an accusation is called an information. In most states, by statute, certain minor offenses may be prosecuted by complaint or information under oath by a private person.

The indictment must state the venue, that is, the name of the county; it must state the name of the defendant, if known or, if not known, a description; it must state the offense with reasonable certainty so that the court will know that if the facts stated are true the accused has committed a crime and will know what punishment to impose if the accused should be convicted. It must be certain enough so that the accused will know what particular charge he will be called upon to answer and so that in case of either acquittal or conviction he may plead the proceedings in bar of any other prosecution for the same offense.

Where the crime charged requires a specific intent that intent must be alleged; where it involves request or notice or knowledge that also must be alleged. Where the crime charged requires the use of technical words, such as "feloniously" or "burglariously" or "with malice aforethought," such terms apart from statute, must be used. Where a written instrument forms part of the crime charged, as in case of forgery or criminal libel, such instrument must be set forth, and a similar rule prevails as to spoken words. Where, as in the case of burglary, a building is the subject of the offense charged, it must be adequately described so that it may be identified. A similar rule prevails where personal property is the subject of the offense, and if, as in the case of larceny, the value of such property is important, that too must be stated; but if as in the case of money that has been stolen, it is impossible to identify the coins or bills, such identification is excused.

It must state the day when the offense took place but unless the exact

Power of court to amend indictment. 7 **ALR** 1516–1537; s. in 68 **ALR** 928–940.

Description in indictment for perjury of proceeding in which perjury was committed. 24 **ALR** 1137–1148.

Necessity and materiality of statement of place of death in indictment of affidavit charging homicide. 26 ALR 1342–1349.

Right of prosecution to review of decision quashing or dismissing indictment or information, or sustaining demurrer thereto. 92 **ALR** 1137–1165.

Admissibility of testimony or affidavits of grand jurors for purpose of impeaching indictment. 110 **ALR** 1023–1039.

Quashing indictment for lack or insufficiency of evidence before grand jury. 59 **ALR** 567–583.

Ruling against defendant's attack upon indictment or information as subject to review by higher court, before trial. 133 **ALR** 934–950.

What is "infamous" offense within constitutional or statutory provision in relation to presentment or indictment by grand jury. 24 **ALR** 1002–1016.

Power of court to pass on competency, legality, or sufficiency of evidence on which indictment is based. 31 **ALR** 1479–1489.

Matters within investigating powers of grand jury. 22 **ALR** 1356–1372; s. in 106 **ALR** 1383–1391; 120 **ALR** 437–441.

Duty of secrecy on part of members of, or witnesses or other persons present before, grand jury. 127 **ALR** 272–312.

Jurisdiction or power of courts of respective districts as to subsequent proceedings, as affected by dismissal nolle prosequi or mistrial after change of venue in criminal case. 18 **ALR** 714–716.

State's right to change of venue in criminal case. 80 **ALR** 355–373.

Withdrawal or modification of order granting change of venue, power as to. 59 **ALR** 362–366.

Number of changes of venue, statute limiting. 104 **ALR** 1494–1501.

Certiorari to compel change of venue in criminal case, right of state to. See 109 **ALR** 797.

Right to be tried in county or district in which offense was committed as susceptible of waiver. 137 **ALR** 686–696.

51 **Yale L. J.** 1255, Nolo Contendere—Its Nature and Implications.

date is important the proof of any date within the period of the statute of limitations is enough. It must also state the place where the offense was committed but unless the exact place is part of the offense or is alleged as a matter of local description it is sufficient to prove any place within the jurisdiction of the court. Where murder is charged the time and place of the death of the victim must be alleged.

If the offense is a common-law offense the indictment should conclude, "against the peace and dignity of the state"; if it is based upon a statute, "contrary to the form of the statute in such cases made and provided."

§ 38. Joinder of offenses—of parties.[8] The indictment may, in several counts, charge the offense in several different ways in order to avoid a variance at the trial.

Where as a part of the same transaction two distinct offenses are charged to have been committed, for example, that the accused killed A and B at about the same time, the offenses may, in separate counts, be joined in the same indictment. Similarly, joinder was allowed where three men were charged with having robbed A of his car and at about the same time committed rape on B who had been accompanying A in the car. If the offenses are not a part of the same transaction joinder is not permitted.

If several persons join in the commission of an offense they may be joined in the same indictment and any number may be convicted. If the offense is such that there cannot be joinder therein, such as perjury or drunkenness, they may not be jointly indicted. If the offense is such that it cannot be committed by a single individual, such as conspiracy or riot, one alone may not be convicted.

§ 39. Motion to quash—arraignment—demurrer—pleas—double jeopardy.[9] If the indictment is defective the court should, upon motion made at any time before verdict, sustain a motion to quash it. In some states the motion will lie for defects not apparent on the face of the indictment.

Before the trial starts the defendant must be arraigned—that is, he must be called to the bar of the court and the indictment read to him and he must be asked whether he pleads guilty or not guilty, though in some states a formal arraignment may be waived. If he refuses to plead, a plea of not guilty will be entered for him. If he pleads guilty the court may, in its discretion, permit him to withdraw it and plead not guilty. A plea of nolo contendere has the same effect as a plea of guilty but without any confession of guilt.

After a plea of not guilty the defendant may demur to the indictment on the ground that on its face it is insufficient in law and the defendant should not be required to answer to it. The state may likewise demur to any plea which the defendant may make.

8 27 **Am Jur**, Indictments and Informations, §§ 122–136.
14 **Am Jur**, Criminal Law, §§ 79, 95.

9 27 **Am Jur**, Indictments and Informations, §§ 137–153.
14 **Am Jur**, Criminal Law, §§ 249–256.
15 **Am Jur**, Criminal Law, §§ 359–433.
Acquittal or conviction under Federal statute as bar to prosecution under state or territorial statute based on the same act or transaction, and vice versa. 16 **ALR** 1231–1250; s. in 22 **ALR** 1551–1554; 48 **ALR** 1106–1108.
Conviction or acquittal of larceny as bar to prosecution for burglary. 19 **ALR** 626–631.
Conviction or acquittal upon charge of murder of, or assault upon, one person as bar to prosecution for like offense against another person at the same time. 20 **ALR** 341–351; s. in 113 **ALR** 222–228.
Necessity and sufficiency of pleading by prosecution to contest defendant's plea of former jeopardy. 113 **ALR** 1146–1163.
Acquittal of principal or conviction of lower degree of offense as affecting prosecution of aider or abetter. 24 **ALR** 603–608.

If the defendant wishes to show that he has been already tried and either convicted or acquitted for the same offense or if he wishes to show that he has been pardoned he should do this by a special plea setting forth these facts.

Under the plea of not guilty the defendant may introduce evidence tending to show not only that he did not commit the offense charged but also any defenses in justification or excuse therefor.

By the Constitution of the United States and the different states, no one shall be put twice in jeopardy for the same offense, and in some states this has been construed more broadly than a former acquittal or conviction. Jeopardy begins when the jury has been duly impaneled and sworn, the defendant having been duly arraigned and having pleaded not guilty to a valid indictment so that if after that has taken place a nolle prosequi is entered or the jury is unnecessarily discharged without the defendant's consent, he cannot be again tried for that offense. But he may be tried for a different, even though closely related offense; for example, a former conviction or acquittal on a charge of assault and battery on A is no bar to a later prosecution for the murder of A; a former conviction or acquittal on a charge of burglary is no bar to a prosecution for a larceny committed after entrance into the building, or vice versa, the crime of burglary not involving larceny but merely the breaking and entering in the nighttime with intent to commit some felony; a former conviction or acquittal on a charge of embezzling materials for overcoats is no bar to a prosecution on a charge of embezzling overcoats; and where the accused at the same time killed both A and B, a conviction or acquittal on a charge of murdering A is no bar to a prosecution on a charge of murdering B.

§ 40. Trial—verdict—motion in arrest of judgment.[10] There is a guaranty

[10] 53 **Am Jur,** Trial, §§ 1–1150.
14 **Am Jur,** Criminal Law, §§ 128–213.
15 **Am Jur,** Criminal Law, §§ 434–441.
Racial, religious, social or political prejudice of proposed juror as proper subject of inquiry or ground of challenge on voir dire in criminal cases. 73 **ALR** 1208–1222.
Right of defendant in criminal case to insist, over objection of prosecution or court, upon trial by court without a jury. 79 **ALR** 563–567.
Excusing qualified juror drawn in criminal case as ground of complaint by defendant. 96 **ALR** 508–522.
Irregularity in drawing names for a jury panel as ground of complaint by defendant in criminal prosecution. 92 **ALR** 1109–1124.
Right to consent to trial of criminal case before less than twelve jurors; and effect of consent upon jurisdiction of court to proceed with less than twelve. 70 **ALR** 279–296; s. in 105 **ALR** 1115.
Effect of, and remedies for, exclusion of eligible class or classes of persons from jury list in criminal case. 52 **ALR** 919–931.
Right to waive trial by jury in criminal cases; and effect of waiver upon jurisdiction of court to proceed without a jury. 48 **ALR** 767–778; s. in 58 **ALR** 1031–1032.
Reception of incompetent evidence in criminal case tried to court without court as ground for reversal. 116 **ALR** 558–564.
Prosecuting attorney's reference to defendant's failure to testify as prejudicial. 84 **ALR** 784–802.
Duty of court when appointing counsel for defendant to name attorney other than one employed by, or appointed for, a codefendant. 148 **ALR** 183–187.
Right of accused to have evidence interpreted to him. 140 **ALR** 766–775.
Effect of, and remedy for, infringement of right of accused to communicate with his attorney. 23 ALR 1382–1393; s. in 54 **ALR** 1225–1227.
Right of defendant in criminal case to conduct defense in person. 17 **ALR** 266–274.
What amounts to violation of statute forbidding comment by prosecuting attorney on failure of accused to testify. 68 **ALR** 1108–1166.
Comment by prosecution on failure of defendant to call character witnesses. 80 **ALR** 227–242.
Propriety of conduct of trial judge in propounding questions to witnesses in criminal case. 84 **ALR** 1172–1217.
Comments and conduct of judge calculated to coerce or influence jury to reach verdict in criminal case. 85 **ALR** 1420–1456.
Scope and application of rule which permits judge in criminal case to comment on weight or significance of evidence. 95 **ALR** 785–819; s. in 113 **ALR** 1308–1322.
Right to withdraw plea of guilty. 20 **ALR** 1445–1460; s. in 66 **ALR** 628–645.
Withdrawal of plea of guilty and substitution of plea of not guilty after conviction. 146 **ALR** 1430–1459.
Power and duty of court to direct or ad-

of trial by jury in criminal cases in both federal and state constitutions. In some states jury trial may be waived in all cases, in others only in cases of misdemeanor and in the rest, not at all. Where there may be waiver of jury trial the defendant may validly consent to being tried by less than twelve jurors, but if there can be no valid waiver then there must be twelve jurors, no more and no less.

It is essential that the judge be present throughout the trial, any absence, even with defendant's consent, renders the trial a nullity.

The defendant has a right to be present throughout the trial; by the weight of authority he may not waive this right in felony cases but may do so in cases of misdemeanors. He need not be present when the jurors take a view of the premises where the crime was committed; or when motions are being argued to the court.

The verdict of the jury must be unanimous; it must be unconditional; if a verdict of guilty is brought in on some, but not all of the counts, it must specify which counts. But if a general verdict of guilty is brought in, it is valid even though there is only one valid count in the indictment.

Where upon the face of the record there is no valid count so that the indictment is not sufficient to sustain a judgment, the defendant may take advantage of this by a motion in arrest of judgment.

§ 41. Judgment — sentence — motion for new trial—writ of error or appeal.[1] After the verdict has been accepted and recorded it is the duty of

vise acquittal in criminal case for insufficiency of evidence. 17 **ALR** 910–945.

Separation of jury in criminal case. 34 **ALR** 1115–1245; s. in 79 **ALR** 821–844.

Right to severance where two or more persons are jointly accused. 70 **ALR** 1171–1192; s. in 104 **ALR** 1519–1526; 131 **ALR** 917–927.

Necessity of consistency in verdict in criminal case. 80 **ALR** 171–180.

Right of court to accept verdict upon one or more counts of an indictment or information when jury is unable to reach a verdict on all counts or is silent as to part of counts, and effect of such acceptance. 114 **ALR** 1406–1422.

Participation by defendant in trial on merits after his objection to jurisdiction, made under special appearance, has been overruled, as waiver of objection. 93 **ALR** 1302–1318; s. in 107 **ALR** 1102–1106.

Bail pending appeal from conviction. 45 **ALR** 458–474.

Constitutionality of statute permitting appeal by state in criminal cases. 113 **ALR** 636–649.

Right of municipal corporation to review of an unfavorable decision in an action or prosecution for violation of a municipal ordinance. 110 **ALR** 120–130.

Reference by court or prosecuting attorney to right of defendant in criminal case to appeal to higher court or to apply for executive clemency. 132 **ALR** 679–697.

Reduction by appellate court of punishment imposed by trial court. 29 **ALR** 313–342; s. in 89 **ALR** 295–333.

1 2 **Am Jur,** Appeal and Error, §§ 1–176.
13 **Am Jur,** Criminal Law, §§ 442–504.
3 **Am Jur,** Appeal and Error, §§ 449–458.
39 **Am Jur,** New Trial, §§ 1–176.

Power to impose sentence with direction that after defendant shall have served part of time he be placed on probation for the remainder of term. 147 **ALR** 656–659.

Recommendation of mercy in criminal case. 17 **ALR** 1117–1164; s. in 87 **ALR** 1362–1374; 138 **ALR** 1230–1253.

Loss of jurisdiction by delay in imposing sentence. 3 **ALR** 1003–1021; s. in 97 **ALR** 802–814.

Necessity and sufficiency of recital of, or reference to, the offense in pronouncing sentence or judgment. 14 **ALR** 989–1004.

Constitutionality of statute conferring on court power to suspend sentence. 26 **ALR** 399–407; s. in 101 **ALR** 1402–1405.

Power of court to set aside sentence after commitment. 44 **ALR** 1203–1213; s. in 70 **ALR** 822–823.

Effect of statutory change of penalty or punishment after conviction. 55 **ALR** 443–451.

Constitutionality and construction of statute enhancing penalty for second or subsequent offense. 58 **ALR** 20–114; s. in 82 **ALR** 345–386; 116 **ALR** 209–242; 132 **ALR** 91–118; 139 **ALR** 673–702.

When sentences imposed by same court run concurrently or consecutively; and definiteness of direction with respect thereto. 70 **ALR** 1511–1529.

Defendant's right to elect as to punishment where statutory provision as to punishment is changed after commission of offense, but before conviction. 103 **ALR** 1041–1045.

Necessity and sufficiency of question to defendant as to whether he has anything to say why sentence should not be pronounced against him, and effect of failure to make inquiry. 113 **ALR** 821–840.

Civil effects of sentence to life imprisonment. 139 **ALR** 1308–1325.

Imposition or enforcement of sentence which has been suspended without authority. 141 **ALR** 1225–1237.

the court to render judgment and pronounce sentence. In some states the punishment is fixed by the jury in the verdict; in others by the court, many states providing for an indeterminate sentence thus giving the defendant an incentive to good behaviour while serving the sentence.

A new trial may be granted upon motion of the defendant for any error or irregularity during the trial which prevented substantial justice being done to the defendant. This includes error of the judge in instructing the jury, or in admitting or excluding evidence, misconduct of the jury in determining their verdict by casting lots, or in communicating with outsiders or in separating contrary to the order of the court.

At common law the defendant was entitled to a writ of error to have the proceedings and judgment of the trial court reviewed by an appellate court; it lay only from a court of record and was confined to errors appearing on the face of the record. In many states a statutory appeal has been substituted.

By the great weight of authority the state may not move for a new trial after an acquittal; nor may it take an appeal except—in some states—for the purpose of settling questions of law that arose at the trial.

Character of offense as a felony as affected by discretion of court or jury as regards punishment. 95 ALR 1115–1122.

Consent of convict as essential to a pardon, commutation or reprieve. 52 ALR 835–838.

Power of executive to pardon one committed for contempt. 23 ALR 524–531; s. in 26 ALR 21; 38 ALR 171–172; 63 ALR 226–227.

Formal requisites of pardon. 34 ALR 212.

conditional pardon. 54 ALR 1471–1485;

Right to notice and hearing before revocation of suspension of sentence, parole, or conditional pardon. 54 ALR 1471–1485; s. in 132 ALR 1248–1258.

Fine or penalty imposed in addition to imprisonment, pardon or parole as affecting. 74 ALR 1118–1122.

Public office, pardon as restoring eligibility to. 94 ALR 1011–1012.

Judicial investigation of pardon by governor. 65 ALR 1471–1473.

Brief voluntary absence of defendant from courtroom during trial of criminal case as ground of error. 100 ALR 478–487.

Comments by judge during examination or cross-examination of defendant in criminal trial as ground for new trial or reversal. 65 ALR 1270–1280.

Statements by witness after criminal trial tending to show that his testimony was perjured, as ground for new trial. 33 ALR 550–559; s. in 74 ALR 757–761.

Incompetency, negligence, illness or the like of counsel, as ground for new trial or reversal in criminal case. 73 ALR 1511–1512.

Receipt of document or statement in jury room, constituting new evidence, as ground for reversal or new trial in criminal case. 20 ALR 1187–1203; s. in 67 ALR 1523–1531.

Communications between jurors and others as ground for new trial or reversal in criminal case. 22 ALR 254–276; s. in 34 ALR 103–107; 62 ALR 1466–1474.

Right of indigent defendant in criminal case to aid of state as regards new trial or appeal. 100 ALR 321–339.

Overemphasis in proof of former conviction in connection with habitual criminal law, or unnecessary introduction of evidence in that regard, as prejudicial to accused. 144 ALR 240–251.

Propriety of direction of verdict of guilty or of instruction or requested instruction requiring jury in criminal case to take the law from the court, or advising them as to their duty in that regard. 72 ALR 899–913.

Remark of judge during trial of criminal case as comment on weight of evidence. 10 ALR 1116–1129.

Duty of court to instruct on the subject of alibi. 118 ALR 1303–1318.

Instructions disparaging defense of alibi. 14 ALR 1426–1443; s. in 67 ALR 122–129; 146 ALR 1377–1387.

Absence of evidence supporting charge of lesser degree of homicide as affecting duty of court to instruct as to, or right of jury to convict of, lesser degree. 21 ALR 603–635; s. in 27 ALR 1097–1101; 102 ALR 1019–1031.

Instruction applying rule of reasonable doubt specifically to particular matter or defense as curing instruction placing burden of proof upon defendant in that regard. 120 ALR 591–618.

Duty of court in criminal prosecution for sexual offense to give cautionary instruction to effect that such a charge is easily made and difficult to disprove. 130 ALR 1489–1498.

DOMESTIC RELATIONS AND PERSONS

I. MARRIAGE.

§ 1. *The contract to marry.*
§ 2. *The marriage status or relationship.*

II. DISSOLUTION OF MARRIAGE.

A. Annulment.

§ 3. *Void marriages.*
§ 4. *Voidable marriages—nonage.*
§ 5. *Same—mental or physical incapacity.*
§ 6. *Same—fraud or duress.*
§ 7. *Same—effect of annulment.*

B. Divorce and Separation.

§ 8. *Divorce distinguished from annulment.*
§ 9. *Adultery.*
§ 10. *Cruelty.*
§ 11. *Desertion.*
§ 12. *Other grounds.*
§ 13. *Defenses.*
§ 14. *Alimony and custody of children after divorce.*
§ 15. *Foreign divorce.*
§ 16. *Judicial separation.*

III. HUSBAND AND WIFE.

§ 17. *The wife's property.*
§ 18. *The wife's capacity to contract and to convey property.*
§ 19. *Suits by or against a married woman.*
§ 20. *Antenuptial contracts.*
§ 21. *The wife's earnings.*
§ 22. *Suits between husband and wife.*
§ 23. *Suits for the invasion of the consortium.*
§ 24. *Separation agreements.*
§ 25. *The husband's duty to support the wife.*

IV. PARENT AND CHILD.

§ 26. *Custody.*
§ 27. *Duty to support child.*
§ 28. *Right to child's earnings—emancipation.*
§ 29. *Parent's action for injuries to the child.*

V. INFANCY.

§ 30. *Torts.*
§ 31. *Contracts and quasi contracts—ratification.*
§ 32. *Conveyance by and to infants—disaffirmance.*

VI. ILLEGITIMATE CHILDREN.

§ 33. *Proving illegitimacy—legitimation of children.*
§ 34. *Custody, support, inheritance.*

CHAPTER I

MARRIAGE

§ 1. The contract to marry.[1] A contract to marry is a bilateral contract based upon mutual promises to marry. Where one of the promises is to marry upon obtaining a divorce, or upon the death of one's wife or husband, neither promise is binding; such a contract is illegal because it would tend to weaken the ties of the existing marriage to hold otherwise.

It is a good defense, in an action for breach of promise to marry, that the promise was induced by fraudulent representations so material that otherwise the promise would not have been made. But it is no defense that the defendant was married if the plaintiff was not aware of the fact, impossibility of carrying out the promise being no excuse.

That one of the parties is suffering from a loathsome disease is a good defense to an action for breach brought by such party and a good defense to such an action brought by the other party if the defendant in the latter case did not know that he was afflicted with such a disease.

An action for breach of contract to marry is similar to an action for a tort in two particulars:

1. It dies with the death of either party, like a tort action for assault and battery, libel, slander, or malicious prosecution.

2. In some states punitive damages may be awarded where the defendant's conduct has been outrageous.

The better view is that an oral contract to marry, which is not to be performed within a year is unenforcible because within the statute of frauds, but there are decisions to the contrary, on the ground that in 1676, when the original English statute was passed there was no action in the common-law courts for breach.

§ 2. The marriage status or relationship.[2] Marriage is often referred to as a civil contract, but the emphasis in such a reference is not on the word "contract" but upon the word "civil" as distinguished from ecclesiastical; since there is religious freedom in this country a religious ceremony, and rules of ecclesiastical organizations with regard to marriage have no legal significance.

Though mutual assent is necessary to enter into a marriage the marriage itself is a status or relationship rather than a contract, the rights and obligations of the parties thereto being fixed by the law instead of by the parties themselves. Hence marriages are not within the provision of the United

1 35 **Am Jur,** Marriage, §§ 5–7.
49 **Am Jur,** Statute of Frauds, § 50.
Survival of action or cause of action for breach of contract to marry. 34 **ALR** 1363–1368.
Disease as defense to or in mitigation of action for breach of promise. 33 **ALR** 1238–1249.
17 **Ind. L. J.** 225, Adoption in Indiana.
7 **Md. L. R.** 275, Adoption in Maryland.
22 **Boston U. L. R.** 401, 558, Relationship by Affinity.
28 **Wash. U. L. Q.** 221, Intestate Succession by and from the Adopted Child.

2 35 **Am Jur,** Marriage, §§ 4–9, 28, 35.
Validity of common-law marriage in American jurisdictions. 39 **ALR** 538–559; s. in 60 **ALR** 541–546; 94 **ALR** 1000–1007; 133 **ALR** 758–766.
Habit and repute as essential to common-law marriage. 33 **ALR** 27–45.
Inference or presumption of marriage from continued cohabitation following removal of impediment. 104 **ALR** 6–54.
32 **Harv. L. R.** 473, Marriage by Proxy and the Conflict of Laws.

States Constitution forbidding a state to impair the obligation of contracts.

NOT IN IND.

In most jurisdictions a marriage ceremony before a minister or law officer is not necessary. Parties may enter into what is called a common-law marriage by a contract to become at once husband and wife, usually, but not necessarily, followed by holding themselves out to the public as married. It is not necessary that such an agreement be followed by either sexual intercourse or by cohabitation—that is, by living together. The fact that parties are living together illicitly does not prevent them from entering into a common-law marriage at any time.

Where a supposed marriage is invalid because of an impediment unknown to both parties—for example, one of the parties was married—and the parties continue to live together after the impediment is removed, this has been held to be a good common-law marriage, dating from the removal of the impediment. Where both parties knew of the impediment the above result does not follow. Nor does it follow where one of the parties knew of the impediment; but the party who had such knowledge may be estopped from denying that there was a common-law marriage where he represented to the other party that a remarriage was not necessary.

CHAPTER II

DISSOLUTION OF MARRIAGE

A. Annulment

§ 3. Void marriages.[3] Where one of the parties to the marriage was already married or where the parties are closely related—such as brother and sister or ancestor and descendant—the marriage is void and may be attacked collaterally, even after the death of the parties. And unless the facts are in dispute or there is some question as to whether the case falls within the statute, a decree of annulment should be, and apparently is, unnecessary. But it has been held, illogically, that a plaintiff who knew that he was a bigamist is not entitled to a decree of annulment on the ground that he does not come into court with clean hands; on the other hand, a plaintiff who merely knew that the other party was a bigamist is not thus barred.

§ 4. Voidable marriages—nonage.[4] Where a marriage is voidable but not void, it is valid until declared void by a court decree during the lifetime of the parties thereto; such voidable marriage is not subject to collateral attack and it renders invalid any second marriage by either spouse to a third party.

Where one or both of the spouses is not of the age required by statute, the marriage is voidable. If after both parties become of marriageable age, they continue to live together, the marriage becomes valid and no remarriage between them is necessary.

A suit for annulment may be brought either by the spouse who is underage, or by the parent; but if by the latter, the court may refuse the annul-

[3] 35 **Am Jur**, Marriage, §§ 43–58.

[4] 35 **Am Jur**, Marriage, §§ 56–68, 103–106.
27 **Am Jur**, Husband and Wife, § 568.
By and in whose name suit to annul infant's marriage must be brought. 150 **ALR** 609–617.
Jurisdiction, as between different states, of suit to annul marriage. 128 **ALR** 64–83.
32 **Harv. L. R.** 806, Jurisdiction to Annul a Marriage.

ment if it is against the welfare and wishes of the child. As in the case of commercial contracts, if the other party to the marriage is an adult the adult may not maintain a suit for annulment.

While logically the proper court to pronounce an annulment decree is a court of the state where the marriage was entered into, a court of the state of the matrimonial domicile may also act in the matter.

§ 5. **Same—mental or physical incapacity.**[5] If at the time of the marriage one of the parties was either feeble-minded or insane a suit for annulment may be brought by the incapable party or by the other party where the latter did not know of the incapacity at the time of the marriage. Mere eccentricity does not amount to insanity where it does not prevent the party from understanding the nature, effect and consequences of the marriage. If the insanity might be cured annulment may be temporarily denied, but not if it is regarded as incurable.

If at the time of the marriage one of the spouses was impotent and the impotency is incurable, annulment may be had by the capable party; and it may be had by the incapable party if the latter did not know of the impotency at the time of the marriage. The fact that the incapable party is impotent only with the other party to the marriage and not impotent generally is no bar to annulment. Sterility is no ground for annulment.

§ 6. **Same—fraud or duress.**[6] If the consent of one party to the marriage was procured by the fraud of the other party the defrauded party is entitled to a decree of annulment. The fraud must be such as to go to the very essence of the marriage; for example, the concealment of impotency or sterility or a loathsome disease such as syphilis, the concealment of an intent not to have sexual intercourse after the marriage, the concealment of criminal activities or a false representation of chastity, or that the plaintiff was the father of the defendant's unborn child. On the other hand, a concealment or a false representation as to one's financial condition is usually regarded as not sufficient.

If after discovery of the fraud the defrauded party continues to live with the other party this is a ratification of the marriage and it is too late to ask for an annulment.

Where one is forced into a marriage this is a ground for annulment at the suit of the innocent party. Where after the force has ceased to operate the innocent party continues to live with the other spouse this is ratification of the marriage and it is too late to ask for an annulment. Where the coercion was the bringing of bastardy proceedings against the plaintiff such coercion is regarded as lawful and is not ground for annulment.

§ 7. **Same—effect of annulment.**[7] Where an annulment is decreed it relates back to the beginning of the marriage, but statutes usually provide that the children shall be legitimate. Property which has been accumulated during the marriage should be equitably divided.

[5] 35 **Am Jur,** Marriage, §§ 107–133.
Mental capacity to marry. 28 **ALR** 635–660.

[6] 35 **Am Jur,** Marriage, §§ 86–102.
Concealment of pregnancy as ground for annulment of marriage or divorce. 13 **ALR** 14[illegible].
Concealed premarital unchastity as ground of divorce or annulment of marriage. 82 **ALR** 532–536.
Right to annulment of marriage induced by false claim that husband was cause of existing pregnancy. 11 **ALR** 931–937; s. in 19 **ALR** 80.
Venereal disease as ground for divorce or annulment of marriage. 5 **ALR** 1016–1028; s. in 8 **ALR** 1540.

[7] 35 **Am Jur,** Marriage, §§ 82, 83.
4 **Mont. L. R.** 14, The Status of an Annulled Marriage in Montana.

B. Divorce and Separation

§ 8. **Divorce distinguished from annulment.**[8] Strictly speaking an annulment is decreed because of some state of facts existing at the time of the marriage such as nonage, insanity, impotency, fraud or duress; a divorce, on the other hand, is granted for something happening after the marriage such as adultery or desertion. This distinction, however, is not always observed. In some states divorce is allowed for causes like bigamy which logically should be ground only for annulment.

§ 9. **Adultery.**[9] Causes for divorce vary according to the jurisdiction but with the exception of South Carolina which has a constitutional provision forbidding the granting of divorce, adultery is everywhere recognized as a ground for divorce; and by adultery is meant sexual intercourse by either of the spouses with a third person.

Since it is frequently impossible to have direct evidence of the adulterous act it is usually held that proof of inclination and opportunity is enough. Because of the temptation to perjury testimony given by a detective must usually be corroborated.

§ 10. **Cruelty.**[10] The former rule was that cruelty, in order to be a sufficient ground for divorce, must be physical; but the present tendency is to recognize also mental cruelty, that is, systematic abuse, insults and annoyances such as unjust accusations of infidelity made in the presence of others. But refusal of sexual intercourse is not enough; nor are mere quarrels. And if the cruelty has been provoked by the conduct of the complaining spouse this is a good defense.

§ 11. **Desertion.**[1] If without excuse one spouse abandons the other for the period fixed by statute—usually from one to three years—such conduct is in many jurisdictions a cause for divorce.

8 17 **Am Jur**, Divorce and Separation, §§ 1–3.

Attacking decree of divorce after death of one of the parties on grounds other than original lack of jurisdiction. 30 **ALR** 1466–1481.

Effect of divorce on homestead. 36 **ALR** 431–443; s. in 97 **ALR** 1095–1099.

Interlocutory decree of divorce as affecting marital rights of one spouse in estate of the other. 76 **ALR** 284–296.

Who other than party to divorce suit may attack validity of decree of divorce rendered therein. 99 **ALR** 1309–1318.

Grounds upon which entry of final decree of divorce may be contested after entry of interlocutory decree. 109 **ALR** 1005–1016.

Attack on divorce decree by second spouse of party to divorce. 120 **ALR** 815–830.

28 **U. of Iowa L. R.** 179, A Symposium in the Law of Divorce—Foreword by Dean Pound.

28 **U. of Iowa L. R.** 190, Divorce of Foreigners—A Study in Comparative Law.

28 **U. of Iowa L. R.** 225, Divorce Law and Practice under National Socialism in Germany.

28 **U. of Iowa L. R.** 256, Family Dissolution—Limits of the Present Litigious Method.

28 **U. of Iowa L. R.** 272, Modern Divorce Law—The Compromise Solution.

28 **U. of Iowa L. R.** 321, Recognition by Other States of Decrees for Judicial Separation and Decrees for Alimony.

28 **U. of Iowa L. R.** 286, Legal Problems of Divorce in Italy.

9 17 **Am Jur**, Divorce and Separation, §§ 35–39.

Sufficiency of allegation of adultery in suit for divorce. 2 **ALR** 1621–1637.

Necessity of corroboration of admission or confession of ground of divorce or nullity. 40 **ALR** 630–650.

Adultery by deserted spouse after desertion, as ground of divorce in favor of other spouse. 25 **ALR** 1051–1056.

Birth of child or miscarriage before or after lapse of normal period of gestation since access of husband as evidence of adultery. 21 **ALR** 1457–1460.

10 17 **Am Jur**, Divorce and Separation, §§ 48–86.

Conduct amounting to treatment endangering life within statute defining grounds for divorce. 5 **ALR** 712–723.

Single act as basis of divorce or separation on ground of cruelty. 24 **ALR** 918–929.

Competency of husband or wife to testify in suit for divorce on ground of cruelty. 70 **ALR** 499–506.

Accusation of improper relations as cruelty constituting ground for divorce or separation. 143 **ALR** 623–661.

1 17 **Am Jur**, Divorce and Separation, §§ 87–117.

The desertion is not necessarily physical; if the spouse who leaves is excused in doing so, it is not only not desertion but may amount to desertion by the other party. So, if a spouse who has wrongfully deserted offers, in good faith and within a reasonable time, to return and is refused such refusal will constitute desertion.

As to whether the wrongful refusal of sexual intercourse amounts to desertion there is a conflict of authority. Where there has been an admission of adultery the refusal of intercourse is excused.

The wrongful refusal by the husband to furnish his wife a home has been held to amount to desertion.

§ 12. Other grounds.[2] In many states conviction of crime and sentence to imprisonment in the state prison is a ground for divorce. In some states there are statutes declaring civilly dead a person who has been sentenced to life imprisonment; these statutes automatically put an end to the convict's marriage thus amounting to legislative divorce.

Habitual drunkenness is in many states a ground for divorce; in some states incurable insanity; in still other, nonsupport, and in a number of states causes rendering the marriage void or voidable such as prior marriage, impotence, mental incapacity and fraud. The advantage in the last named class of cases of a suit for divorce rather than annulment is that the court is able, without a statute, to preserve rights which have come into existence during the marriage.

§ 13. Defenses.[3] The actual practice in divorce cases seems to be tending toward granting a divorce regardless of fault where the marriage has been a failure; but the theory behind the law of divorce is that divorce is granted because of some fault of the defendant at the suit of a faultless plaintiff. One defense is that of collusion. Thus if both parties wish a divorce but there are not sufficient grounds for it and they agree that one is to sue and the other is not to set up any defense the legal rule is that a divorce will be refused, such conduct—called collusion—apparently being regarded as a fraud on the court. In actual practice today, however, the defense is rarely set up and it is difficult for the court to find it out of its own motion. But there is as yet no legal sanction to divorce by mutual consent.

Where one spouse, suspecting the other of misconduct, such as adultery, makes opportunities for the other to commit the illegal act, this is called connivance and is a defense. Here there is unilateral consent amounting to

Separation due to husband's refusal or inability to support wife as desertion within divorce statute. 150 **ALR** 991–999.

Refusal of one spouse to live with relatives of other as affecting desertion as ground of divorce or separation. 38 **ALR** 338–347; s. in 47 **ALR** 687–688.

[2] 17 **Am Jur,** Divorce and Separation, §§ 118–171.

Separation within the statute making separation a substantive ground of divorce. 51 **ALR** 763–771; s. in 97 **ALR** 985–989; 111 **ALR** 868–874.

Insanity as substantive ground of divorce or separation. 113 **ALR** 1248–1255.

What amounts to habitual intemperance, drunkenness, etc., within statute relating to substantive grounds for divorce. 120 **ALR** 1176–1188.

29 **Va. L. R.** 771, Insanity as a Ground for Annulment or Divorce in English and American Law.

[3] 17 **Am Jur,** Divorce and Separation, §§ 186–240.

Collusion as bar to divorce. 2 **ALR** 699–717; s. in 109 **ALR** 832–854.

Condonation of cruel treatment as defense in divorce action. 14 **ALR** 931–944; s. in 98 **ALR** 1354–1364.

Knowledge of offenses as condition of condonation as defense to suit or counterclaim for divorce. 109 **ALR** 683–698.

Subsequent adultery as recriminatory defense to desertion or cruelty. 101 **ALR** 646–650.

29 **U. of Iowa L. R.** 527, Divorce without Fault.

a fraud on the court committed by the plaintiff. It is not connivance, however, where the spouse merely watches the commission of the illegal act.

Another defense is that of condonation. If there is a cause for divorce but the other party with full knowledge thereof forgives it, it cannot later be taken advantage of unless the guilty party again commits the offense or otherwise misconducts himself, the condonation being conditional upon the future good behavior of the erring spouse. Condonation may be express or implied from the fact of cohabitation with knowledge of the misconduct. A condonation obtained by fraud is no bar.

If a defendant sets up and proves in defense that the plaintiff was also guilty of such misconduct as would be ground for divorce if the defendant were innocent, neither party is entitled to a divorce. The nearest analogy to this defense of recrimination is found in the law of implied conditions in contracts. The plaintiff charges that the defendant has been guilty of a breach of the marital obligation; the defendant sets up that the plaintiff is not in a position to complain because he has breached his own marital obligation.

§ 14. Alimony and custody of children after divorce.[4] Pending the suit for divorce the wife, whether plaintiff or defendant, is usually awarded temporary alimony, an allowance to be paid by the husband for the support of herself and minor children and for counsel fees to carry on the litigation but if the wife has sufficient funds of her own such an allowance may be refused.

After the divorce is decreed the court may award permanent alimony, either a lump sum or a certain amount per month or per year even if the

[4] 17 **Am Jur**, Divorce and Separation, §§ 495–708.

Power of appellate court to grant alimony, maintenance, or attorneys' fees pending appeal in matrimonial suit. 136 **ALR** 502–516.

Wife's possession of independent means as affecting her right to temporary alimony or allowance for support of children. 15 **ALR** 781–789.

Right of wife to allowance of counsel fees to prosecute or defend appeal in matrimonial action. 18 **ALR** 1494–1509.

Financial condition of parties as affecting allowance of suit money in divorce suit. 35 **ALR** 1099–1108.

Education as element in allowance for benefit of child in decree of divorce or separation. 133 **ALR** 902–914.

Earning capacity or prospective earnings of husband as basis of alimony. 6 **ALR** 192–208; s. in 139 **ALR** 207–257.

Liability of father for support of children awarded to mother by decree of divorce not providing for maintenance. 81 **ALR** 887–895.

Divorce upon constructive service as affecting power to allow alimony upon subsequently obtaining personal jurisdiction over former husband. 42 **ALR** 1385–1398.

Liability of alimony for wife's debts. 55 **ALR** 361–369.

Nonpayment of alimony or suit money as ground for denying right to participate in trial or other proceeding in suit for divorce. 62 **ALR** 663–675.

Propriety and effect of provision in decree in divorce suit in respect of policy of insurance on life of husband. 145 **ALR** 522–530.

Contempt proceedings to enforce payment of alimony or support as affected by security for its payment or availability of other remedy for its enforcement. 136 **ALR** 689–698.

Enforcement of claim for alimony against exemptions. 11 **ALR** 123–129; s. in 106 **ALR** 669–672; 130 **ALR** 1028–1029.

Right of husband to alimony, maintenance, suit money, or attorneys' fees in suit for divorce. 24 **ALR** 491–499.

Bankruptcy as affecting alimony. 39 **ALR** 1283–1289.

Death of husband as affecting alimony. 18 **ALR** 1040–1057; s. in 101 **ALR** 323–329.

Alimony as affected by remarriage. 30 **ALR** 79–92; s. in 64 **ALR** 1269–1277; 112 **ALR** 246–260.

Wife in respect of her right to maintenance or alimony as within protection of statute or rule avoiding conveyances or transfers in fraud of creditors or persons to whom maker is under legal liability. 79 **ALR** 421–434.

Construction and effect of statute or rule that denies alimony to wife guilty of marital fault. 82 **ALR** 539–548.

Propriety of direction that specific property of husband be transferred to wife as alimony, or in lieu of, or in addition to, alimony. 133 **ALR** 860–882.

Power, in absence of reservation by statute or decree, to modify provision in decree of divorce or separation as to alimony or separate maintenance. 71 **ALR** 723–741; s. in 127 **ALR** 741–747.

6 **U. of Newark L. R.** 70, Alimony Pendente Lite in New Jersey.

divorce is awarded to the husband; a decree of temporary alimony is enforced only by holding the husband in contempt of court; a decree of permanent alimony is also enforcible in an action at law or, if the decree is for the conveyance of land, by a suit in equity.

Since the obligation to pay alimony is not only a simple debt but also a social duty it survives the husband's discharge in bankruptcy; but it does not survive his death. In a few states the court may award alimony to the husband.

When there are minor children the court will award custody either to the husband or wife or to a third party according to the best interest of the child; such awards may, of course, be modified later if change of circumstances make it desirable.

§ 15. Foreign divorce.[5] In most jurisdictions the basis of jurisdiction for divorce is the marriage status. If the spouses are domiciled in the same state then the marriage status or relationship is considered to be in that state and a decree of divorce rendered in that state will be recognized everywhere.

If the parties are domiciled in different states then logically a divorce granted by the court of either state should be recognized in all other states because one half of the marriage status is in that state. In the recent Williams cases, 317 US 302, 87 L ed 288, 63 S Ct 207, 143 ALR 1273 (further opinion on retrial 325 US 226, 65 S Ct 1092, 89 L ed 1577, 157 ALR 1366), this position has been adopted with the qualification that the jurisdictional domicile must in fact exist before the foreign decree becomes absolutely binding on the parties under the full faith and credit clause.

§ 16. Judicial separation.[6] In jurisdictions where it is difficult to get an

5 17 **Am Jur,** Divorce and Separation, §§ 740–767.

Jurisdiction on constructive or substituted service, in suit for divorce or alimony, to reach property within state. 29 **ALR** 1381–1399: s. in 64 **ALR** 1392–1396; 108 **ALR** 1302–1306.

Extraterritorial recognition and effect on marital status of decree of divorce rendered upon constructive or substituted service of process. 39 **ALR** 603–674; s. in 86 **ALR** 1329–1343; 143 **ALR** 1294–1318.

Extraterritorial recognition and effect, as regards marital status, of a decree of divorce or separation rendered in a state or country in which neither of the parties was domiciled. 39 **ALR** 677–700; s. in 105 **ALR** 817–824.

What constitutes residence or domicil within state for purpose of jurisdiction in divorce. 106 **ALR** 6–40.

Separate domicil of wife for purposes of jurisdiction over subject matter of suit by her for divorce or separation. 39 **ALR** 710–734.

Extraterritorial effect of provision in decree of divorce as to custody of child. 20 **ALR** 815–827; s. in 72 **ALR** 441–449; 116 **ALR** 1299–1310.

Nonresidence of defendant or cross complainant in a suit for divorce as affecting power to grant divorce in his or her favor. 89 **ALR** 1203–1212.

Injunction against suit in another state or country for divorce or separation. 128 **ALR** 1467–1482.

Inhibition by decree of divorce, or statute of state or country in which it is granted, against remarriage, as affecting a marriage celebrated in another state or country. 32 **ALR** 1116–1146; s. in 51 **ALR** 325–327.

Duty of courts of one state to recognize and give effect to decrees of divorce rendered in other states, as affected by constructive service of process or lack of domicil at divorce forum. 39 **ALR** 603–674; s. in 86 **ALR** 1329–1343; 143 **ALR** 1294–1318.

Public policy of forum against recognition of marriage valid (or voidable only) by the law of the place where it was celebrated, as affected by fact that neither of the parties was domiciled at the forum at the time of the marriage. 127 **ALR** 437–450.

39 **Harv. L. R.** 417, Haddock Revisited.

40 **Col. L. R.** 373, Recognition of Foreign Divorce Decrees in New York State.

41 **Mich. L. R.** 1013, The Bones of Haddock v. Haddock.

39 **Mich. L. R.** 689, Any more Light on Haddock v. Haddock?

18 **Ind. L. J.** 155, Is Haddock v. Haddock Overruled?

16 **U. of Cin. L. R.** 81, Law Applicable to Marriage.

29 **Corn. L. Q.** 1, Williams v. North Carolina.

8 **Mo. L. R.** 177, Jurisdiction and Divorce —A Study in Stare Decisis.

15 **Miss. L. J.** 165, Is Haddock Dead?

7 **Md. L. R.** 29, The Haddock Case Overruled—The Future of Interstate Divorce.

6 27 **Am Jur,** Husband and Wife, §§ 401–434.

absolute divorce the subject of judicial separation or a divorce from bed and board becomes important. A decree for judicial separation is practically always accompanied by a decree for the support of the wife and minor children, if any. It may be revoked by the court upon the joint application of the parties.

CHAPTER III

HUSBAND AND WIFE

§ 17. The wife's property.[7] At common law the husband, upon marriage, became entitled to the rents and profits of the wife's real estate during the coverture and to the wife's chattels and leasehold interests in land; he also received a power of attorney to collect at any time during the coverture any choses in action owned by the wife. And this was equally true of property which the wife acquired after the marriage. In equity, however, it was possible for any donor to the wife or for the wife herself before marriage, to convey property to her for her separate use free from the control of her husband.

Partly influenced by the equity doctrine legislatures have everywhere provided that property belonging to the wife upon the marriage or that acquired by her later shall be hers, not subject to her husband's control.

§ 18. The wife's capacity to contract and to convey property.[8] At common law a married woman's contract was entirely void, but in equity she could by contract bind her separate equitable estate. By statutes everywhere today she may contract almost if not quite as freely as if she were unmarried.

At common law a married woman had no personal property to convey and could convey her land only if her husband joined with her in the conveyance; but her separate equitable estate could not be conveyed at all, equity courts upholding the provision against her power to alien in order to preserve it from falling into the control of her husband. Under modern statutes she may convey her property freely.

§ 19. Suits by or against a married woman.[9] At common law the wife could not sue alone; it was necessary that the husband be joined and any recovery became his property. Today by statutes the wife may sue alone and the recovery is her own property. At common law since the husband upon marriage became entitled to his wife's tangible personal property, to the rents and profits from her real property and to collect her choses in action he became liable for her tort and contract obligations that had come

Jurisdiction of equity courts in the United States, without the aid of statute expressly conferring it, to entertain independent suit for alimony or separate maintenance without divorce or judicial separation. 141 **ALR** 399–445.

Effect of reconciliation on separation agreement or decree. 40 **ALR** 1227–1241; s. in 85 **ALR** 420–424.

7 26 **Am Jur**, Husband and Wife, §§ 34–65.

Marriage settlement or gift from one spouse to other as affected by marital misconduct. 29 **ALR** 198–220.

Misconduct of surviving spouse as affecting marital rights in other's estate. 71 **ALR** 277–290; s. in 139 **ALR** 486–507.

Conveyance of interest in community property by one spouse to other. 37 **ALR** 282–308.

Rights and remedies in respect of property accumulated by man and woman living together in illicit relations. 75 **ALR** 732–742.

Character of interests of husband and wife in purchase-money mortgage on sale of estate by entireties. 30 **ALR** 905–907.

8 26 **Am Jur**, Husband and Wife, §§ 128–202.

9 27 **Am Jur**, Husband and Wife, §§ 601–622.

into existence before marriage, provided they were enforced during the marriage. He also became liable for torts committed by her after the marriage provided they were enforced during the marriage. Today by statute the husband has no such liability; only the wife is liable.

§ 20. Antenuptial contracts.[10] Marriage settlements whereby property was turned over to trustees for the benefit of the parties to the marriage and possible children were valid trusts and governed by equity principles. But today a contract made between husband and wife in contemplation of marriage is governed by the same common-law principles as contracts generally. Hence if the contract has been obtained by fraud it is not enforcible; and the relationship between the parties is such that failure to disclose important facts may be a defense.

§ 21. The wife's earnings.[1] At common law the husband was entitled to the wife's services and therefore to her earnings; but if the husband permitted the wife to work on her own account equity would protect her in the enjoyment of the proceeds. Statutes allowing the wife to have her property to her own separate use are not usually construed as affecting earnings, but in many states there are special statutes applying to earnings.

§ 22. Suits between husband and wife.[2] At common law neither spouse could maintain any action against the other partly because of the unity of husband and wife and partly because the recovery would belong to the husband. In equity and under the married woman's property statutes actions may be brought for injuries to property. Where the tort is for personal injuries the weight of authority is against allowing the action because it would tend to create domestic discord. Where the action is for a negligent tort and the liability will ultimately fall upon an insurance company there is less danger of its causing domestic discord but it is difficult to make a logical distinction on such a ground.

§ 23. Suits for the invasion of the consortium.[3] At common law an ac-

10 26 **Am Jur**, Husband and Wife, §§ 275-294.

Validity of postnuptial agreement releasing or waiving rights of surviving spouse on death of other spouse. 49 **ALR** 116-153.

1 27 **Am Jur**, Husband and Wife, §§ 463-471.

Liability of husband for services rendered by wife in carrying on his business. 23 **ALR** 18-24.

38 **Harv. L. R.** 421, 622, Husband's Right to Wife's Services.

2 26 **Am Jur**, Husband and Wife, §§ 252-273, 589-600.

Right of one spouse to maintain an action against the other for assault and battery, under the Married Women's Acts. 6 **ALR** 1038-1056.

Right of one spouse under Married Women's Acts to maintain an action at law against other, based on tort in respect of property, for damages or recovery of possession. 109 **ALR** 882-887.

43 **Harv. L. R.** 1030, Torts between Persons in Domestic Relations.

3 27 **Am Jur**, Husband and Wife, §§ 499-518.

Admissibility of statements or declarations of plaintiff's spouse concerning acts or conduct of defendant in action for alienation of affections. 4 **ALR** 497-510.

Liability of parent, relative or person in loco parentis in action by husband or wife for alienation of affection. 108 **ALR** 408-429.

Decree of divorce or separation as res judicata or basis of estoppel or evidence in action for alienation of affections or criminal conversation. 20 **ALR** 943-955.

Admissibility of evidence as to character or conduct of plaintiff or reputation of his house in action for alienation of affections or criminal conversation. 63 **ALR** 560-587.

Excessiveness or inadequacy of damages for criminal conversation or alienation of affections. 69 **ALR** 1282-1295.

Constitutionality, construction, and application of statutes abolishing civil actions for alienation of affections, criminal conversation, seduction, and breach of promise to marry. 109 **ALR** 1234-1235.

Husband's right to damages for loss of consortium due to personal injury to wife. 21 **ALR** 1517-1528; s. in 133 **ALR** 1156-1163.

Wife's right of action for loss of consortium. 5 **ALR** 1049-1052; s. in 59 **ALR** 680-681.

tion was allowed to the husband for violating his right to the society, services and conjugal affection of his wife and the right to have sexual intercourse with her. The wife had no corresponding right, but this has been largely changed by decisions or statute. In a few states, however, statutes have abolished actions for alienation of affections, criminal conversation and seduction.

§ 24. Separation agreements.[4] The old English rule was that a separation agreement was invalid as in derogation of the marital obligation, but today it is generally recognized as valid if the parties are already separated or if they contemplate an immediate separation; an agreement to separate in the future is invalid as tending to disrupt the marriage.

The provision for maintenance will be enforced but not the agreement to live apart; and if the parties live together again the entire agreement is abrogated. If the provision fixed for the wife is inadequate it may be set aside in equity. If the wife has been guilty of adultery there is a conflict of authority as to whether this bars her recovery.

§ 25. The husband's duty to support the wife.[5] The husband is under a common-law duty to support his wife according to his means and this duty has been enforced by modern statutes. Where the husband fails in this duty of support she may buy necessaries on his credit, whether she is living with him or is living apart from him through no fault of her own; this is sometimes called agency by necessity. If she is living apart from him through her own fault or if she has agreed to accept a certain amount from him and he pays it, the husband is not liable; nor is he liable where the plaintiff has sold the goods upon the sole credit of the wife; or where the wife is already supplied with necessaries or the money with which to buy them.

Where the wife is compelled to pay for necessaries out of her own separate estate she may recover the amount from the husband and where a third party advances money to the wife with which to buy necessaries the third party may recover the amount of the loan from the husband. Where the husband is in default in supplying necessaries, a notice to tradesmen not to give the wife credit does not prevent them from recovering for necessaries furnished.

Where the spouses are living together it is presumed that the wife has au-

4 17 **Am Jur,** Divorce and Separation, §§ 723–739.

Validity of separation agreement as affected by fraud, coercion, unfairness, or mistake. 5 **ALR** 823–831.

Separation agreement as affecting right of inheritance. 35 **ALR** 1505–1534; s. in 81 **ALR** 693–698.

Right of wife after husband's death to enforce provision of separation agreement for continuance of payments for her support as affected by intervening divorce decree. 147 **ALR** 708–721.

5 26 **Am Jur,** Husband and Wife, §§ 5–9.

Criminal responsibility of husband for abandonment or nonsupport of wife, who refuses to live with him. 3 **ALR** 107–114; s. in 8 **ALR** 1314–1316.

Defenses available to husband in civil suit by wife for support. 6 **ALR** 6–88.

Liability of married woman for necessaries. 15 **ALR** 833–860.

Duty of husband to provide necessaries for wife as affected by her possession of independent means. 18 **ALR** 1131–1140.

Furniture and household goods as necessaries for which husband is liable. 24 **ALR** 1483–1487.

Liability of husband in independent action for services rendered by attorney to wife in divorce suit. 25 **ALR** 354–367; s. in 42 **ALR** 315–316.

Liability of husband for necessaries as affected by question whether or not they were purchased on his credit. 27 **ALR** 554–579.

Liability for funeral expenses of married woman. 31 **ALR** 1499–1509; s. in 108 **ALR** 1226–1233.

Personal liability of married woman for domestic or household services. 36 **ALR** 389–393.

Extent or character of support contemplated by statute making nonsupport of wife or child an offense. 36 **ALR** 866–876.

29 **Va. L. R.** 857, Reconsideration of Husband's Duty to Support and Wife's Duty to Render Services.

thority to pledge the husband's credit for suitable household supplies, but this presumption does not exist if they are living apart; the presumption is that she has no authority to bind him and the person who extends credit has the burden of showing actual authority, or that the husband is estopped by his conduct or that he has ratified her acts.

At common law a wife was under no duty to support the husband but in some jurisdictions statutes have imposed such a duty where the husband is indigent and likely to become a public charge.

CHAPTER IV

PARENT AND CHILD

§ 26. Custody.[6] At common law the father had an almost absolute right to the custody of his children. Today, the court in awarding custody will determine it solely or at least primarily according to the welfare of the child. When there is no statute applicable to the case the proper remedy is in equity, the equity court succeeding to the English chancellor's prerogative as parens patriae. In many states there are statutes creating juvenile courts who have power to award custody of children—usually under a designated age—who are delinquent or neglected, to such persons or institutions or reform schools as the court may determine. Apart from statute a court may award custody to a third party where the welfare of the child requires it.

§ 27. Duty to support child.[7] It is at least doubtful whether at common law there was any legal obligation upon the parent to support the child. But today, either by decision or statute, there is a legal obligation in most states. This is enforcible not by action but by making it a penal offense not to support the child. Support includes not only necessary food, clothing and shelter but education at least through the common schools. There is no obligation of support resting upon the father's estate.

Where the minor child has no independent income the court may, in its discretion, award to the father a reasonable allowance therefrom for the child's support.

§ 28. Right to child's earnings—emancipation.[8] The father is entitled to the services of his minor child and therefore to the child's earnings if he is employed by a third party; where the father is dead the weight of authority is that this right passes to the mother, or to anyone who stands in loco parentis.

6 39 **Am Jur,** Parent and Child, §§ 10–30.
Right of parent to notice and hearing before being deprived of custody of child. 76 **ALR** 242–258.
Nonresidence as affecting one's right to award of custody of child. 20 **ALR** 838–846.
Power of court which denies divorce or legal separation to award custody or make provision for support of child. 113 **ALR** 901–913.

7 39 **Am Jur,** Parent and Child, §§ 35–45.
Bill by or in behalf of child against parent for support. 7 **ALR** 1277–1278; s. in 75 **ALR** 1314–1316.
Liability of father for support of children awarded to mother by decree of divorce not providing for maintenance. 15 **ALR** 569–575; s. in 81 **ALR** 887–895.
Liability of parent for necessaries furnished to adult child. 42 **ALR** 150–154.
Child's ownership of or right to income or property as affecting parent's duty to support, or as ground for reimbursing parent for expenditures in that regard. 121 **ALR** 176–210.
Criminal responsibility of parent under desertion or nonsupport statutes, as affected by child's possession of independent means, or by fact other persons supply his needs or are able to do so. 131 **ALR** 482–502.

8 39 **Am Jur,** Parent and Child, §§ 31, 32, 64–67.
Right of parent as against creditor or lienor to make gift to minor child of latter's own services. 44 **ALR** 876–881.

The right comes to an end upon the child's emancipation which can be effected either by express grant of the parent, by a grant implied from circumstances, by the marriage of the child or by the parent's failure to support. Where the grant is based upon consideration or where it has been acted upon by the child it cannot be revoked by the parent. Since an emancipated child is entitled to his earnings the parent is no longer bound to support him.

§ 29. Parent's action for injuries to the child.[9] The parent of an unemancipated minor child is entitled to recover against a third party who causes loss to the parent by inflicting personal injuries upon the child resulting in loss of services. Where the child has not been emancipated the fact that the child is in the service of another is generally held to be no bar to the parent's action.

Where the defendant has seduced a minor daughter he is liable to the parent not only for the loss of service but also for the humiliation and the stain upon the family honor; in such cases proof of the slightest services rendered by the daughter is enough, and proof of the slightest damage is sufficient.

CHAPTER V

INFANCY

§ 30. Torts.[10] An infant is liable for his torts as if he were an adult unless the tort is so closely connected with a contract made by him that to hold him liable in tort would in substance take away from him his defense of infancy to his liability on his contract.

As regards torts to property an infant is probably liable to his parent even though they are living in the same household; and he probably may sue the parent for a tort to his own property. But an unemancipated infant is not liable to the parent for a tort to the person, nor may he sue the parent for such a tort. The reason usually given for such a holding is that allowing such actions would tend to disrupt the harmony of the home; the answer to this is that where such tortious acts are committed there is likely to be very little harmony left. When the tort is based upon negligence and the liability will ultimately fall upon an insurance company there is less likelihood of disturbing domestic tranquility but it is difficult to draw a distinction between cases where there is insurance and cases where there is not.

Where the infant sues either in tort or contract he must appear by next friend; for an infant defendant a guardian ad litem must be appointed.

The better view is that an infant is as responsible for torts of his servant or agent as if he were an adult.

§ 31. Contracts and quasi contracts—ratification.[1] A contract between an

9 39 **Am Jur,** Parent and Child, §§ 71–85.

Right of parent who consents to or acquiesces in employment of child under statutory age to recover for latter's injury or death while in such employment. 23 **ALR** 635–643; s. in 40 **ALR** 1206–1208.

Right of parent to recover for injury to or death of minor child as affected by award of custody of child to another. 147 **ALR** 482–491.

10 27 **Am Jur,** Infants, §§ 90–96, 113–128.

Right of minor child to sue parent or person in loco parentis for personal tort. 31 **ALR** 1157–1162; s. in 71 **ALR** 1071–1074; 122 **ALR** 1352–1358.

Infant's liability in tort for his own act, or right to recover for another's tort, as affected by its connection with infant's contract. 127 **ALR** 1441–1457.

Infant's appointment of agent, and acts of agent thereunder, as void or voidable. 31 **ALR** 1001–1021.

1 27 **Am Jur,** Infants, §§ 16–22, 30–36, 53, 64–89, 96.

infant and an adult is enforcible by the infant but not against him if he sets up his infancy in defense; the defense is personal to the infant and to his executor or administrator after his death; a third person cannot attack the contract but an undertaking to be bound by it, but by the better view whether the contract was made by the infant directly or through an agent.

Where the contract was induced by the infant's falsely representing his age the weight of authority seems to be that this does not prevent him from setting up his infancy as a defense to an action on the contract but makes him liable in tort for the false representation, if he avoids the contract.

Where a plaintiff has furnished necessaries to an infant the recovery is not really on the contract but in quasi contract because the plaintiff is not entitled to the contract price but to the reasonable value of the necessaries actually furnished.

Where the infant contracts to render services and later disaffirms the contract he is entitled to recover in quasi contract the reasonable value of the services rendered and the employer in such an action is not entitled to a deduction for breach of the infant's contract.

After the infant reaches majority he may then bind himself by ratifying his former promise. Ratification may be either express or implied from conduct. It requires not merely an acknowledgment of the existence of the contract but an undertaking to be bound by it; but by the better view it is not necessary that he understand what his legal rights are in the matter. If he does not ratify his defense remains. Where an infant enters into a partnership he is not liable on any partnership contract if he pleads infancy but he cannot reclaim property taken for the debts of the partnership.

§ 32. Conveyance by and to infants—disaffirmance.[2] If the contract has been performed by the infant conveying either real or personal property to the other party and the infant wishes to take advantage of his legal privilege, it will be necessary for him to disaffirm the transaction. In cases of personal property this may be done either before reaching majority or within a reasonable time thereafter; in the case of real property it must be within a reasonable time after reaching majority. If after majority the infant affirms the transaction it is then too late to disaffirm.

If upon disaffirmance the other party does not return the property received the infant may maintain replevin or trover to get back chattels or their value or a bill in equity to get back land; apart from statutes these actions may usually be brought even against a bona fide purchaser for value from the other party. The infant need not, as a condition precedent to bringing these actions, tender back any of the consideration received by him for the property but the other party is entitled to recover from the infant

Right to recover for money loaned to infant to purchase necessaries. 65 **ALR** 1337–1341.

Liability of infant for medical, dental, or hospital services to him. 71 **ALR** 226–232.

Law of infant's contract as applied to contract of or by partnership. 58 **ALR** 1366–1374.

Misrepresentation as to age as estoppel to plead infancy. 6 **ALR** 416–426; c. in 18 **ALR** 520–523; 90 **ALR** 1441–1446.

[2] 27 **Am Jur**, Infants, §§ 33–62.

Right to allowance for use or depreciation of subject matter, in an action against seller to recover back purchase price upon disaffirmance of infant's contract. 11 **ALR** 491–495; s. in 50 **ALR** 1187–1189.

Return of property purchased by infant as condition of recovery of purchase money paid. 16 **ALR** 1475–1483; s. in 36 **ALR** 782–785; 124 **ALR** 1368–1375.

Power of court or guardian as to mortgaging infant's real property. 95 **ALR** 839–851.

whatever part of the consideration he may still have either in its original or its converted form.

If the contract has been performed by the other party conveying land or chattels to the infant the same principles are applicable. Upon disaffirmance the infant can recover the amount paid and the other party to the transaction may maintain replevin or trover to get back the chattels or their value or a bill in equity to get back the land conveyed; and these actions—apart from statute—are maintainable even against bona fide purchasers for value from the infant. The disaffirmance must be of the entire transaction and not merely of the part prejudicial to the infant.

It is doubtful whether a court of equity has inherent power to order a sale of an infant's real property but in many jurisdictions today there are statutes authorizing the sale, mortgage or lease of the infant's real property where the personal property and the income from his real property are not sufficient to pay his debts and to maintain himself and family, or to avoid waste and dilapidation of the property, or otherwise to better the investment. In order that transactions authorized by the statute shall be valid the statutory provisions must be fully complied with.

CHAPTER VI

ILLEGITIMATE CHILDREN

§ 33. Proving illegitimacy—legitimation of children.[3] There is a strong presumption that a child born to a married woman is legitimate, a presumption that can be overcome only by clear and convincing evidence. The fact that at or near the time of conception the mother had illicit intercourse with another man is not sufficient. But clear evidence that the husband was incapable or that he did not have access to the wife is enough. Nonaccess may not be proved, however, by the testimony of either wife or husband.

When the child is born to an unmarried woman paternity of the child must be proved by a preponderance of the evidence. In some jurisdictions evidence of blood-grouping tests are admitted in order to show non-paternity of the defendant.

In many jurisdictions it is provided that the marriage of the parents shall legitimatize the child.

§ 34. Custody, support, inheritance.[4] At common law the mother of an illegitimate child was exclusively entitled to its custody and services and

[3] 7 **Am Jur**, Bastards, §§ 13–59.

Presumption of legitimacy of child born to married woman as affected by lapse of more than normal period of gestation after access by husband. 7 **ALR** 329–339.

Presumption as to paternity of child conceived or born before marriage. 8 **ALR** 427–434.

Marriage of woman to one other than defendant as affecting bastardy proceeding. 14 **ALR** 974–983.

Competency of husband or wife to testify to nonaccess. 60 **ALR** 380–393; s. in 68 **ALR** 421; 89 **ALR** 911–913.

Degree of proof necessary to overcome presumption of legitimacy. 128 **ALR** 713–726.

What constitutes a "marriage" within meaning of a statute legitimating issue of all marriages null in law. 84 **ALR** 499–508.

16 **Harv. L. R.** 22, Legitimacy and Marriage.

[4] 7 **Am Jur**, Bastards, §§ 60–78, 150–160.

Inheritance by, from, or through illegitimate. 35 **ALR** 570–599; s. in 83 **ALR** 1330–1341.

Illegitimate child as within statute relating to duty to support child. 30 **ALR** 1075–1085.

Nonstatutory duty of father to support illegitimate child. 30 **ALR** 1069–1073.

Validity and enforceability of promise to support or provide for illegitimate child. 39 **ALR** 434–449.

Right of mother to custody of illegitimate child. 51 **ALR** 1507–1517.

Illegitimates as within class in testamentary gift. 120 **ALR** 992–1001.

the father was under no legal duty to furnish support. Today statutes authorize courts to award custody to and also to impose support upon either or both the parents.

At common law the child would not inherit even from his mother and she could not inherit from him. This has been changed everywhere by statutes allowing each to inherit from the other.

AGENCY

CHAPTER I

NATURE AND CREATION OF AGENCY RELATIONSHIP

§ 1. Agent distinguished from servant.[1] The word "agent" is sometimes used in the very general sense of a representative so as to include servants, trustees, etc., but in this book it is used in a narrow, specialized sense excluding such other representative relationships.

An agent is to be distinguished from a servant in that the agent's duty is to create a contractual relationship between his principal and third parties while the servant renders services which do not create such a relationship. To put it briefly, an agent deals with persons while a servant deals with things. While an agent usually exercises discretion and a servant does not, this is not necessarily true and is not a distinguishing characteristic. A person may be both a servant and agent; if A employs B to work on A's farm and to buy feed for A's livestock B is both servant and agent. On the other hand, an insurance agent is not a servant and hence the insurance company is not liable for damage done to X in the operation of his wife's auto. While the same principles underlie the two relationships it is sometimes necessary to distinguish between the two, especially where the interpretation of statutes is involved.

§ 2. Agent distinguished from trustee.[2] An agent is like a trustee in that both are fiduciaries. Therefore an agent may not compete with his principal

[1] 2 **Am Jur**, Agency, § 7.
9 **Harv. L. R.** 507, Of the Nature of Agency.

[2] 2 **Am Jur**, Agency §§ 6, 251–266.
Validity of contract negotiated by agent acting for both parties. 48 **ALR** 917–933.

and must account to him for any secret profit received as agent; and an agent to buy cannot buy from himself. He may not delegate to another any of his duties except those that are merely ministerial; and he may not act as agent for both parties unless both consent. The chief difference is that if a third party contracts with an agent he is able at common law to hold the principal on such contract even though the principal was undisclosed, whereas a third party who contracts with a trustee has a common-law remedy only against the trustee, not against the cestui que trust, even though the existence of the latter is disclosed, but must reach him, if at all, by way of a bill for equitable execution. Hence even if the duties remain similar, an agent who receives the title to property to hold for his principal ceases to be an agent as to such property and becomes a trustee.

§ 3. Agent distinguished from vendee.[3] If A, a wholesaler, sends goods to B, a retailer, to be sold and A retains both title and beneficial interest, B having merely the authority to pass title to customers, then B is an agent of A. But if A transfers the title to B the transaction is either a simple sale or, if B is given the opinion of returning unsold goods to A, the transaction is that of sale and return, not one of agency.

Where A sells and delivers goods to X, a consumer, and transfers to X the beneficial interest in the goods, retaining only the legal title by way of security, the transaction is one of conditional sale, not one of agency.

§ 4. Creation and proof of the agency relationship.[4] Though the phrase "contract of agency" is sometimes used it is not necessary that there be any contract by the principal to pay the agent for his services. It is enough that there is an agreement, express or implied in fact, that A is to act as agent for P.

Where it is sought to prove that A was P's agent in order to charge P therewith, A is a competent witness but his declarations made out of court are not admissible; but where the purpose of the proof is to charge A, a declaration by A that he was the agent of P is admissible as a declaration against interest.

By the better view the fact that an infant P acts through an agent is of no importance. The same reasoning applies where P is insane unless P has been adjudicated insane, when his acts are void whether made through an agent or directly.

Employer's right to earnings or profits made by employee. 13 **ALR** 905–928; s. in 71 **ALR** 933–936.

Right to inventions as between employer and employee. 16 **ALR** 1177–1214; s. in 32 **ALR** 1037–1042; 44 **ALR** 593–598; 85 **ALR** 1512–1525.

Validity of contract by agent for compensation from third person for negotiating loan or sale with principal. 14 **ALR** 464–479.

Right to inventions as between employer and employee. 16 **ALR** 1177–1214.

Acceptance by principal of services of broker with knowledge that he acted for the other party as affecting broker's right to compensation. 80 **ALR** 1075–1101.

Employee's or agent's acceptance of bonus, gratuity, or other personal benefit from one with whom he deals on employer's or principal's account as affecting his right to recover wages, salary, or commissions. 102 **ALR** 1115–1123.

Rights and remedies of principal where agent professes to sell principal's property without disclosing that he is the purchaser. 62 **ALR** 63–77.

3 47 **Am Jur**, Sales, § 837.

4 2 **Am Jur**, Agency, §§ 12, 20–24, 443–447, 449–450.

Admissibility of statements of alleged agent for the purpose of showing that other party dealt with him as agent and not as principal, as distinguished from the purpose of showing the existence or extent of agency. 80 **ALR** 604–608.

Necessity of written authority to enable agent to make contract within Statute of Frauds. 27 **ALR** 606–625.

Infant's appointment of agent and acts of agent thereunder as void or voidable. 31 **ALR** 1001–1021.

CHAPTER II

THE DISCLOSED PRINCIPAL, THE AGENT AND THE THIRD PARTY

§ 5. The agent's express or implied authority to bind the principal.[5] Where the third party seeks to hold P upon a contract made by A on behalf of P it is necessary that T show that A had P's authority to enter into the contract. This authority may be either express or implied from the nature of the agency. Where the authority is express, T must show that it has not been exceeded by A; for example, where P authorized A to buy goods on credit up to $2,000, T must show that when the transaction between A and himself took place, A had not exceeded the limit. But where there is authority to accept payment of a debt due from T to P there is no duty on T to see that A turns the money over to P unless T knew that A was intending to appropriate the money.

Even though the authority is not express, it may be implied in fact from the nature of the agency and the general business understanding as to the authority of certain kinds of agents. For example, an agent with authority to sell real estate has implied authority to promise a marketable title; an agent with authority to collect interest has not implied authority to receive payment of the principal; an agent entrusted with chattels to sell has implied authority to receive payment, unless there is an express prohibition known to the buyer. On the other hand a real-estate broker with authority to seek out purchasers has no implied authority to make a contract with a purchaser; a drummer who has authority to transmit orders to his principal has no implied authority to contract to sell goods to a customer; an agent to sell has no implied authority to borrow money; an agent to receive payment of a note has no implied authority to receive it before it is due; an attorney authorized to prosecute a suit to judgment has no implied authority to indorse a check payable to his client in satisfaction of the judgment; a claim agent for a railroad has no implied authority to promise a life job to an injured employee. It is usually easier for the court to find an implied authority in case of a general agent having large incidental powers than in the case of a special agent.

Where A has been authorized by P to make representations to T and he makes false representations, this is usually held to be within A's implied authority and P is liable even though he has acted honestly. And P has been held liable for a slander uttered against T by A where it has been closely connected with A's employment.

[5] 2 **Am Jur,** Agency, §§ 85–207.

Authority of agent to receive payment for commodities which he is authorized to sell, or for which he is to find market. 8 **ALR** 203–228; s. in 105 **ALR** 718–724.

Authority of agent to indorse and transfer commercial paper. 12 **ALR** 111–144; s. in 94 **ALR** 555–572.

Authority of agent to assent to account stated. 2 **ALR** 71–83.

Implied or ostensible authority of officer, agent, or employee to engage medical services. 71 **ALR** 638–660.

Agent's authority to collect or receive payment as including implied, apparent, or ostensible authority to do so before maturity of obligations. 100 **ALR** 389–400.

Implied or ostensible authority to receive payments of principal of one who has authority to receive payments of interest. 111 **ALR** 578–589.

Acceptance by collection agent, authorized to receive money only, of something else upon which he realizes money, as binding principal. 94 **ALR** 784–800.

Right of broker to repledge customer's securities. 24 **ALR** 452–470.

Power of real-estate broker to execute contract of sale in behalf of principal. 48 **ALR** 634–653.

Authority of real-estate broker to bind employer by representations to purchaser as to the character or condition of the property. 57 **ALR** 111–126.

§ 6. Agency by estoppel or by operation of statute.[6] Even though X has no express or implied authority to act for P, yet if P either expressly or by conduct represents to T that X has authority and in reliance upon that representation T enters into a contract with X as agent purporting to bind P, the latter is bound thereby. Having represented to T that X had authority P is now estopped to deny it; hence it is common to say that X is an agent by estoppel. For example, where P turned an auto over to X with authority for the purpose of selecting buyers and X sold to T, it was held that under the circumstances X had apparent authority to sell and hence T could hold P on the contract. And where P entrusts X with the possession of a bill of lading it is usually held that P is estopped to deny that X had authority to sell the goods represented by the bill of lading.

It is not always easy to determine in a particular case whether P has been held liable on the basis of implied authority or apparent authority, but the distinction is not of practical importance unless there is difficulty in proving reliance upon the part of T; since implied authority is actual authority no reliance by T is necessary.

In some states, by statute, a state official—usually the Secretary of State—is made the agent of nonresidents for the service of process in suits against such nonresidents: for example, in suits against foreign corporations doing business within the state; and in suits against a nonresident automobile owner for damage done by operating his car within the state.

§ 7. Liability of agent to third party.[7] Where A acts within the authority given to him by P he is under no liability to T, unless, of course, such act is a tort against T, in which case the fact that he was acting as agent is no defense.

Where he acts in excess of or without authority, most states hold that he is liable to T for the damage caused to T by the breach of his implied warranty of authority; in some jurisdictions he is held liable on the contract by which he purported to bind P; in still others he is held liable only in a tort action for deceit. Upon principle, whether he is held liable in deceit should turn upon whether or not he knew he was acting outside of or without authority.

Where P is an infant and sets up infancy as a defense to an action by T, this does not make A liable if P actually gave A authority; there is no implied warranty either that P is an adult or that he will not set up his infancy in defense.

§ 8. When principal is bound by notice to agent.[8] Where it is important to determine whether P is to be charged with notice of a particular fact, is it

[6] 2 **Am Jur,** Agency, § 104.
Liability on contract of one who without authority assumes to contract for another. 42 **ALR** 1310–1319; s. in 60 **ALR** 1348–1351.
16 **Harv. L. Rev.** 186–192, Estoppel—Principal and Agent.

[7] 2 **Am Jur,** Agency, §§ 314–334, 343.
Personal liability of one who assumes to contract as agent for a principal who is fictitious or nonexistent. 126 **ALR** 114–123.
Personal liability of broker for breach of contract by his principal. 6 **ALR** 641–669.
Premises of principal, personal liability of agent to third person for injuries or damages due to condition of. 49 **ALR** 521–525.
Personal liability of servant or agent to third person for injuries caused by the performance or nonperformance of his duties to his employer. 20 **ALR** 97–174; s. in 99 **ALR** 408–426.
Liability of the contract of one who without authority assumes to contract for another. 42 **ALR** 1310–1319; s. in 60 **ALR** 1348–1351.
Funds received from third person and turned over to principal not entitled thereto, personal liability of agent in respect of. 82 **ALR** 307–313.
48 **W. Va. L. R.** 96, Some Spadework on the Implied Warranty of Authority.

[8] 2 **Am Jur,** Agency, §§ 368–382.

sufficient to show that his agent had notice of that fact? For example, if A buys property from a trustee knowing that the trustee is acting in violation of his trust, does this prevent A from claiming the rights of a bona fide purchaser for value without notice?

The general rule is that P is bound by A's notice of any fact relating to the subject matter of the agency which A receives while acting as such agent and within the scope of his authority. Where the notice came to A before becoming P's agent or while acting outside the scope of his authority, P is bound if at the time of the transaction in question it was present in A's mind.

The doctrine of implied notice is not applied where A is under a legal duty to some other principal not to disclose, for example, if A is an attorney and he received the information from one of his other clients. Or where A is acting adversely to P in his own interest or in the interest of another, especially if the one seeking to hold P bound by such notice has been acting in collusion with A to defraud P.

CHAPTER III

UNDISCLOSED PRINCIPAL

§ 9. Rights of the undisclosed principal.[9] Where A in making a contract with T acted as if he were the principal but was really acting as agent for P, the latter may enforce the contract against T as if the contract had been assigned to him by A. Thus P takes subject to any right of setoff or to any equities which T may have against A; the mere fact that T would not have entered into the contract had he suspected that A was acting for P is ordinarily no defense; and where the contract contains a personal covenant, for example, to give a warranty deed, P cannot insist upon T's accepting his own covenant as a substitute for that of A.

A may also maintain an action on the contract against T but P's right is paramount to that of A and A's right to sue may be cut off by giving notice to T unless A has some interest of his own which he seeks to protect.

§ 10. Rights of the third party.[10] When A makes a contract with T upon behalf of an undisclosed P and then T discovers this fact, he may recover from P just as if P had taken an assignment of the contract from A and had undertaken with A to perform it.

Imputation of attorney's knowledge of facts to his client. 4 **ALR** 1592–1623; s. in 38 **ALR** 820–824.

Knowledge of agent as imputable to principal in respect of transaction subsequent to agency, or transaction with which agent had no connection. 73 **ALR** 420–427.

Imputing to principal knowledge of agent having adverse interest or acting antagonistically to principal. 104 **ALR** 1246–1253.

26 **Harv. L. R.** 237–252, Notice to Corporation from Entries on its Books.

65 **U. of Pa. L. R.** 1–38, Notice through an Agent.

9 2 **Am Jur,** Agency, §§ 410–421.

Right of defendant in action by undisclosed principal to avail himself of defenses or setoffs that would have been available in an action by the agent in his own right on the contract. 53 **ALR** 414–457.

Exceptions to rule which permits suit by or against undisclosed principal. 130 **ALR** 664–682.

9 **Harv. L. R.** 60, A Problem as to Ratification.

59 **U. of Pa. L. R.** 517–531, 587–596, An Agent's Right to Sue upon Contracts.

10 2 **Am Jur,** Agency, §§ 393–409.

Signing of contract by agent of undisclosed principal as satisfying Statute of Frauds. 23 **ALR** 932–943; s. in 138 **ALR** 330–336.

Liability of undisclosed principal on sealed contract. 32 **ALR** 162–167.

Right to join agent and undisclosed principal in same action. 118 **ALR** 701–708.

Action or judgment against agent as affecting right to maintain action against undisclosed principal. 119 **ALR** 1316–1326.

23 **Harv. L. R.** 513–530, 590–602, Liability of an Undisclosed Principal.

Where, reasonably believing that T looked only to A, P has settled with A, T cannot hold P. And where P furnished money with which to buy goods for cash and A buys from T on credit it has been held that T cannot recover from P.

T may, of course, hold A, and if, in ignorance of the existence of P, T has sued A and obtained judgment, this is no bar to his later recovering from P also. But if T, knowing of the existence of P, sues A and gets judgment he cannot then hold P; or if he sues P and gets judgment he cannot then hold A.

Apart from statute, T may not maintain an action against A and P jointly.

The doctrine of undisclosed principal does not apply to instruments under seal or negotiable paper. In such cases only A may sue or be sued.

CHAPTER IV

RATIFICATION

§ 11. In general.[1] Where A without authority or in excess of authority purported, on behalf of P, to make a contract with T, P, having knowledge of the facts, may, by approving such purported contract, make it valid and binding on both himself and T. P's liability relates back to the date of the purported contract; as to whether T's liability does or does not thus relate back, there is a conflict of authority. If P was not in existence at the time of the purported contract—for example, a corporation not yet organized—the better view is that there can be no ratification.

P may not ratify that part of the transaction between A and T which is beneficial to himself and repudiate the rest. For example, where A purported to act both as agent and servant of P in selling and delivering coal to T, and in delivering the coal negligently damaged T's property and P ratified the sale and delivery it was held that he thereby became liable for the damage suffered by T through A's negligent tort.

Where P refuses to ratify and A's act in purporting to act for P without authority has caused P loss, P may hold A liable for such loss But if P ratifies, A ceases to be liable.

§ 12. Manner of ratification.[2] Ratification may be either express or implied from circumstances, for example, by accepting benefits under the contract or by bringing suit against T to enforce it. There may also be ratification by mere inaction where the circumstances are such as to impose a duty to act. For example, where A was a stockbroker who failed to carry out P's orders to sell his stock it was held that since the stock was fluctuating in value P was bound to act promptly in repudiating A's violation of orders and could not speculate at A's expense.

CHAPTER V

TERMINATION OF AGENCY

§ 13. In general.[3] Where an agency has been created for a definite pur-

[1] 2 Am Jur, Agency, §§ 208-219.

Profession at time of act or contract to be acting for another as a necessary condition of its ratification by latter. 124 ALR 893-897.

What amounts to ratification by owner of unauthorized employment by broker or agent of subagent to procure a sale or purchase of property. 136 ALR 1418-1425.

Ratification by customer of stockbroker's wrongful purchase or sale of securities on his account, or failure to comply with instructions. 87 ALR 794-811.

5 La. L. R. 308-315, What is the Effect of Ratification?

[2] 2 Am Jur, Agency, §§ 225-227.

[3] 2 Am Jur, Agency, §§ 36-76.

pose or for a definite period or until the happening of a particular event, it comes to an end when the purpose is accomplished or when the period expires or when the event happens. It may also be terminated by mutual assent; and, since equity will not give specific performance of a contract of employment, the agency may be terminated by P's revocation or by A's renunciation, the only remedy in each case being an action for damages for breach of the contract; and this is true even though the contract had expressly provided that the agency should be irrevocable or should last for a definite period which had not expired.

Where T has been dealing with A as agent for P and P revokes the agency, A may still bind P in further dealings with T unless and until T actually receives notice of such revocation; mere publication in a newspaper of a notice of such revocation or mailing a notice to T is not enough.

Ordinarily A's authority to bind P and T is terminated by the death of P even though T had no notice thereof; but where T paid off a loan to A after P's death it was held that since such payment could properly be received in A's name, T, acting without notice, should be protected; but on this point there is a conflict of authority.

A contract for personal services is terminated, without liability for damages, by the death of either P or A; and a business agency is usually held to be terminated by the bankruptcy of either P or A.

§ 14. Powers coupled with an interest.[4] Where P transfers to A a present interest in the subject matter of the agency and the agency is created in order to enable A to safeguard that interest, the agency is said to be a power coupled with an interest and cannot be revoked by P in his lifetime and is not revoked by his death. For example, where A, a firm of investment brokers, secured for P a lease for 99 years on some vacant land upon condition that P erect thereon a hotel building worth $250,000, the lease containing many provisions for its forfeiture, and A agreed to finance the building and P agreed to give A a lease of the second floor for twenty years, and made A the agent to collect the rents and manage the building, it was held that A's agency to collect the rents was given to him to enable him to safeguard his rights in the building by preventing any forfeiture of the lease; hence the agency was irrevocable and A was entitled to an injunction against interfering with its exercise. On the other hand, an agency to collect rents is not irrevocable where P does not transfer to A any present interest in the subject matter of the agency. And an agreement by P, a client, to assign to A, his attorney, as compensation for his services, one half of the proceeds of a cause of action belonging to P and to be enforced by A, does not create an agency coupled with an interest because he is not entitled to any interest until the compensation is earned by rendering the services.

Where A has entered upon the execution of his authority before revocation and in so doing has so bound himself that a revocation of his authority would subject him to liability, P must, if he revokes, indemnify A against such liability.

Payment to agent after death of principal. 67 **ALR** 1419–1422.

Right of owner to terminate real-estate broker's employment pending negotiations with prospective purchaser. 88 **ALR** 716–736.

4 2 **Am Jur**, Agency, §§ 77–84.

What constitutes power coupled with interest within rule as to termination of agency. 64 **ALR** 380–391.

PERSONAL PROPERTY

CHAPTER I

ACQUISITION OF PERSONAL PROPERTY

§ 1. Personal property, chattels, real property, land.[1] The distinction between land and chattels is one of fact—the difference between immovables and movables—and in the field of trespass to property this distinction is important.

The distinction between real property, consisting of freehold interests in land, and personal property, including terms for years, chattels and choses in action, arose because centuries ago the only actions by which the res itself, that is, the property in specie, could be recovered, were called real actions, and lay only to recover freehold interests in land. Where other property—including terms for years—was involved, the only action possible was a personal action for damages. The chief importance of this distinction was that upon intestacy the descendible real property went directly to the heir while personal property went to the administrator—or, if there was a will, to the executor—to pay debts and then to distribute to the next of kin. Since in the United States real property has been made subject to the payment of debts and since the tendency of statutes of descent and distribution has been to apply the same rules to real as to personal property the distinction is of steadily decreasing importance. Because of this the tendency is to use the term real property as synonymous with land and personal property as meaning chattels.

1 42 Am Jur, Property, §§ 10-25. 29 Harv. L. R. 374, 501, 731, Property in Chattels.

§ 2. **By pursuit and capture of wild animals.**[2] So long as wild animals, including beasts, birds, fish, etc., remain wild, they are not the subject of property either of the state or of the owner of the land upon which the animal lives. They become property by being captured, dead or alive. Mere pursuit is not enough, though inflicting a mortal wound probably is. If after capture the animal escapes and returns to its former wild state, it ceases to be property.

If A kills or captures a wild animal while trespassing on the land of B, the animal or its carcass belongs to B.

The right to hunt and fish even on one's own land is today regulated by game laws which are meant to preserve wild animals from extinction.

§ 3. **By finding.**[3] If A discovers and takes possession of a chattel that has been lost on the highway or other public place he is under an obligation to return it to the owner on demand, but as to any other person A's right is paramount and he may maintain trespass, trover or replevin against him. A is not entitled to any reward for finding the chattel unless a specific reward has been offered.

If A finds a chattel on land which is not open to the public there is a square conflict of authority as to whether A or the owner of the land is better entitled; if A at the time was trespassing, he is not entitled as against the landowner.

If A at the time of finding the chattel on the land was in the employ of the owner to hunt for lost chattels the owner of the land is better entitled to the chattel than is the servant; but if that was no part of the servant's duty, the servant probably has as much right as if he were a stranger rightfully on the land.

Where goods have been misplaced instead of lost, the tendency has been to hold the owner or proprietor of the land better entitled than the finder even though the chattel was left in a public place, such as a railway train, on the theory that the goods have been left in the care of such owner or proprietor.

§ 4. **By adverse possession.**[4] If A wrongfully takes or detains B's chattel openly claiming it to be his own property and holds it for the period of the statute of limitations, title passes to A, whether A did or did not believe the chattel to be his own. If A acted innocently it is of no importance that B has been unable to find out what has become of his chattel; but if A was a conscious wrongdoer and intentionally concealed the chattel some statutes expressly provide that such concealment prevents the running of the statutory period.

§ 5. **By satisfaction of a judgment for conversion.**[5] If A sues B in trover for converting B's chattel and gets judgment for its value, the better doc-

[2] 2 **Am Jur,** Animals, §§ 5-14.
Cats, property rights in. 33 **ALR** 796-803; s. in 54 **ALR** 92.
Law of bees. 39 **ALR** 352-364.
Rights, title, and remedies of hunter in respect of game which he is pursuing or has killed or wounded. 49 **ALR** 1498-1503.

[3] 34 **Am Jur,** Lost Property, §§ 1-8, 14.
Respective rights of carrier, or of one in similar relation to owner, and of finder of property lost or mislaid. 9 **ALR** 1388-1393; s. in 43 **ALR** 33.
Rights and remedies as to chattels cast upon riparian land. 41 **ALR** 1015-1019.
52 **Harv. L. R.** 1105, Possession and the Law of Finders.

[4] 1 **Am Jur,** Adverse Possession, § 96.
Rule that adverse possession of successive holders may be tacked, in determination of period of limitation, as applicable to chattels. 135 **ALR** 711-718.
32 **Harv. L. R.** 135, Title by Adverse Possession.

[5] 53 **Am Jur,** Trover and Conversion, §§ 202, 203.

trine is that title does not pass to B upon the rendition of such a judgment but only when the judgment is satisfied. Hence if, because of B's insolvency, execution cannot be had on the judgment, A may bring replevin for the chattel against B or anyone else who is in possession of it. But if and when the judgment in the trover action is fully satisfied B's title apparently relates back to the time of the original conversion.

§ 6. **By accession.**[6] Where A takes B's chattel and expends labor and skill upon it, thereby very materially increasing the value of it may B maintain replevin for the chattel or is he limited to an action of trespass or trover for the value of the chattel when taken?

If A's act was consciously wrongful, the weight of authority is that B may maintain replevin for the chattel or trover for the value of it when demanded from A, the conscious wrongdoer thus losing all the benefit of his labor and skill.

If A acted innocently and the value of the chattel has been increased many times by his labor and skill, B cannot maintain replevin but must bring either trespass or trover for the value of the chattel when taken. Where the increase is not so great, the same reasoning should still apply, but courts have been reluctant to apply it except in extreme cases.

Where A takes B's chattel and makes it a part of his land or of the land of X, B cannot maintain replevin, but must sue in trespass or trover even though A's act was consciously wrongful.

§ 7. By confusion.[7] Where A takes B's chattels and mingles them with his own and the mixture is fungible—e. g., grain or oil—A and B become tenants in common of the mixture in the ratio of their respective contributions and by the better view it makes no difference whether A's act was inadvertent, negligent or consciously wrongful. There is the same result where the mixture has been made with B's consent or where it has been made by a third person or where it has happened accidentally.

Where A takes B's goods and mingles them with his own and the mixture is not fungible, the better view is that A loses his own goods unless he can by affirmative proof identify them; and this is true whether A's act was inadvertent, negligent or consciously wrongful.

§ 8. By gift.[8] If A wishes to transfer to B the legal title to a chattel by way of gift he may do so by delivery of the chattel or by delivery of a deed

6 1 **Am Jur**, Accession, §§ 5-11.
Accession of property which is the subject of a conditional sale or chattel mortgage. 68 **ALR** 1242-1246.
16 **U. of Cin. L. R.** 267, Some Applications of Title by Accession.

7 11 **Am Jur**, Confusion of Goods, §§ 1-12.

8 24 **Am Jur**, Gifts, §§ 24-111.
Necessity of delivery where subject of gift is already in possession of donee at time of declaration of gift. 103 **ALR** 1110-1117.
Delivery of key to safe-deposit box or other receptacle as sufficient to consummate gift of contents. 127 **ALR** 780-803.
Delivery of personalty to third person with directions to deliver after donor's death as valid gift. 3 **ALR** 902-928; s. in 60 **ALR** 1054-1060.
Delivery as essential to gift of tangible chattels or securities by written instrument. 63 **ALR** 537-560.
Donor's own check as subject of gift. 20 **ALR** 177-188; s. in 44 **ALR** 625-627; 53 **ALR** 1119.
Delivery of bill or note of third person by way of gift. 25 **ALR** 642-685.
Check or certificate of deposit as subject of gift by payee or indorsee thereof. 40 **ALR** 508-515.
Gift of savings deposit by delivery of passbook. 40 **ALR** 1249-1263; s. in 84 **ALR** 558-566.
Gift or trust by deposit of funds belonging to the depositor in a bank account in the name of himself and another. 48 **ALR** 189-206; s. in 66 **ALR** 881-893; 103 **ALR** 1123-1141; 135 **ALR** 993-1023; 149 **ALR** 879-898.
Gift of interest in estate after decedent's death. 48 **ALR** 223-237.

to the chattel. Mere words of gift are not enough except where the chattel is already in the possession of the donee. After the delivery has taken place, a mere redelivery of the chattel to the donor does not nullify the gift. Where the gift is subject to a condition subsequent the happening of the condition entitles the donor to get back the chattel.

Where a deed of gift is used it is not necessary that the deed be delivered to the donee; a ceremonial delivery in the presence of witnesses is enough. Nor is it necessary that the donee consent to such delivery or even know of it; if upon learning of the gift he disclaims it the title is revested in the donor as of the date of the delivery of the deed.

If A wishes to transfer to B by way of gift the legal title to a chose in action for the payment of money which A holds against X, he may do so if X consents to such transfer. Such consent may be given in advance as in case of a negotiable instrument, the gift in such a case becoming effective upon delivery of the instrument. If no such consent is given by X, A may still make an irrevocable gift to B of a chose in action which is evidenced by some document, such as a non-negotiable note, savings bank passbook, or insurance policy, by delivering to the donee such document; having thus put it out of his power to recover on the chose in action himself because at the trial he must either produce such a document or satisfactorily account for its nonproduction, the law holds the power of attorney to B to collect, and therefore the gift, irrevocable. If there is no such document evidencing the chose in action the power of attorney may be revoked at any time before B collects and is revoked by A's death.

If A wishes merely to transfer to B the equitable interest in a chattel or in a chose in action by way of gift, he may do so by a declaration of trust which may be oral or in writing; if it is in writing it need not be delivered.

CHAPTER II

BAILMENTS

§ 9. A bailee distinguished from a trustee, servant and conditional vendee.[9] A bailee is like a trustee of chattels in that both are fiduciaries; that is, they are both entrusted with or have the care of property for the benefit of another and their duty of care is practically the same—that which is exercised by prudent persons with their own property under similar circumstances. A bailee is unlike a trustee in that the bailee has only possession whereas the trustee has title; if A delivers the possession of a chattel to B for the use of C, C may recover the possession by bringing against B the action of detinue or its code equivalent. If A delivers the title of a chattel to B to be sold and the proceeds held for the use of C, the remedy of C is a bill in equity against B for an accounting.

A servant is different from a bailee in that he has only custody and not possession. If he uses the goods for himself it is larceny whereas in a bailee such an act is embezzlement. A servant cannot maintain any action against a third person for taking the goods away from him and he is not entitled to a retaining lien for labor and skill expended upon the goods.

A bailee is different from an ordinary vendee in that the bailee is a fiduciary while the vendee's obligation is to pay out of his general assets for the goods which he has bought and title to which he has received from his ven-

[9] 6 Am Jur, Bailments, §§ 28–40, 57, 58.

dor. Where the sale is a conditional one, the vendor retaining the title to the goods as security for the payment of the purchase price, the conditional vendee is different from the bailee in that he has not merely possession but also the beneficial interest in the goods for which he is under the same obligation to pay as is the ordinary vendee.

§ 10. **Duty of bailee to bailor.**[10] If the bailment is for the mutual benefit of the bailor and bailee it is well settled that the bailee is under the duty to use ordinary care with regard to the goods, that is, the care which a prudent man would use under similar circumstances. It is usually stated that where the bailment is for the sole benefit of the bailor the bailee need only use slight care and where it is for the sole benefit of the bailee he must use extraordinary care, but it is doubtful whether a jury thus instructed would likely come to a different result than if they were charged that the bailee must in all cases use the care of a prudent man under similar circumstances.

At the termination of the bailment the bailee must return the chattel to the bailor.

§ 11. **Rights of bailor and bailee against a third person.**[1] If during a bailment terminable at will the chattel is taken from the possession of the bailee either the bailor or the bailee may recover in trespass or trover for the full value of the chattel. If the bailee sues and recovers he must account for what he has received to the bailor.

If during a bailment not terminable at will the chattel is taken from the possession of the bailee the bailee may recover in trespass or trover for the full value of the chattel; if he does thus recover he must account to the bailor for the value of the bailor's reversionary interest. If only the bailor sues, he must bring an action on the case because not entitled to the immediate possession of the chattel, and he will recover the value of his reversionary interest.

10 6 Am Jur, Bailments, §§ 171–332.

Duty and liability of gratuitous bailee or mandatory. 4 ALR 1196–1229; s. in 96 ALR 909–924.

Liability of bailee where subject of bailment is stolen. 26 ALR 223–266; s. in 48 ALR 378–393.

Liability for loss of or damage to automobile left in parking lot. 34 ALR 925–927; s. in 131 ALR 1175–1205.

Liability for loss of contents of safe-deposit box. 40 ALR 874–889; s. in 42 ALR 1304–1306; 133 ALR 279–304.

Rights and liability of bailee where there is an adverse hostile title. 43 ALR 149–174.

Liability of bailee for damage to or destruction of subject of bailment by servant acting for his own purposes or in violation of his instructions. 52 ALR 711–722.

Delivery by one in possession of another's property to impostor. 54 ALR 1330–1336.

Presumption and burden of proof where subject of bailment is destroyed or damaged by fire. 9 ALR 559–577; s. in 71 ALR 767–779.

Construction and application of provision of bailment or lease contract relating to cost of repairs or replacements, or damage to chattel. 129 ALR 460–469.

Liability of laundry, clothes presser, dyer, or dry cleaner or third person by whom the work is actually done, for loss of or damage to customer's goods. 130 ALR 1359–1373.

Duty and liability of one in possession of real property in respect of personal property which he finds thereon belonging to another. 131 ALR 165–176.

Duty and liability of fair association, or other bailee, as regards articles entrusted to it for exhibition or display. 139 ALR 931–936.

Status, rights, and liability of parties to bailment for hire where bailee continues in possession after bailment has ended. 144 ALR 1024–1031.

Liability of bailee for loss of or injury to goods kept at a place other than that originally intended. 12 ALR 1322–1334; s. in 17 ALR 979–980.

Duty and liability of garage keeper to owner of cars. 15 ALR 681–701; s. in 42 ALR 135–146; 65 ALR 431–440.

Bailee's express agreement to return property, or to return it in a specified condition, as enlarging his common-law liability. 150 ALR 269–305.

Validity and applicability of stipulation in warehouseman's receipt fixing valuation of property as basis of responsibility. 142 ALR 776–787.

Storage contract as a bailment of chattels, or lease of place where chattels are stored. 138 ALR 1137–1143.

Liability of warehouseman for damage to or destruction of property by fire. 16 ALR 280–305.

1 6 Am Jur, Bailments, §§ 302–310.

CHAPTER III

LIENS

§ 12. Lien distinguished from pledge and chattel mortgage.[2] The holder of a common-law retaining lien has, at common-law, merely the possession with the right to hold until the claim is paid; he has no right to sell. The pledgee has possession with the right to sell upon default. The chattel mortgagee has, in most jurisdictions, title to the property and does not need to be in possession of it and may foreclose the mortgage upon default.

The common-law retaining lien is not the result of any contract; the pledge and chattel mortgage can be created only by contract.

Today, by statute, the holder of a common-law retaining lien is given the right to sell upon default.

§ 13. Liens for improvement by skill and labor.[3] Where A by his labor and skill improves a chattel bailed to him by B for that purpose, A has a right to retain possession of the chattel till his charges are paid. Those who are thus entitled include a racehorse trainer, a shoe cobbler, a blacksmith who shoes a horse, a jeweler who sets a gem, a dyer who dyes cloth, etc. The class does not include an agister or pasturer of animals because, although the animals may be improved by the pasturage furnished, the improvement is not due to skill and labor. Nor does a lien arise where the contract made is inconsistent with a lien; for example, where a carriage maker agreed to repair a physician's carriage and to accept pay therefor in medical services.

The lien given is a specific one, to hold the particular chattel; there is no lien for a general balance due on other transactions where A might have claimed a lien but failed to do so.

§ 14. The lien of the common carrier, innkeeper and warehouseman.[4] The common carrier and innkeeper each has a specific lien, the one on the goods carried and the other on the baggage brought to the inn. The modern justification for these liens is that each is under a public-service obligation to serve all at reasonable rates and, if the goods are lost or damaged, is liable at peril except for an act of God—that is, an extraordinary manifestation of natural forces such as an earthquake or hurricane—or of a public enemy.

If the goods brought to an inn do not belong to the guest the innkeeeper has a lien good against the owner even if the baggage has been taken to the inn without his consent; but the common carrier has no such right as against the owner of goods carried without his authority.

The warehouseman has also a specific lien even though not engaged in a public-service occupation, apparently an extension of the common carrier's lien.

§ 15. Liens by mercantile custom—attorney's lien.[5] In a few cases liens have arisen through mercantile custom. Thus a factor or commission merchant has a lien on goods left in his hands for the purpose of sale to secure any general balance due to him from the customer. A similar general lien

2 33 **Am Jur,** Liens, §§ 3, 43.
Title to securities in possession of broker (or his pledgee) who has purchased them for or sold them to customer. 41 **ALR** 1258–1269.

3 33 **Am Jur,** Liens, § 16.
Lien for repairs to or services in connection with automobile. 62 **ALR** 1485–1497.

4 9 **Am Jur,** Carriers, §§ 636–638.
28 **Am Jur,** Innkeepers, §§ 123–132.
See also 56 **Am Jur,** Warehouses, §§ 1–280.
Lien for storage of automobile. 31 **ALR** 834–840.

5 22 **Am Jur,** Factors, §§ 43–46.
5 **Am Jur,** Attorneys at Law, §§ 209–218.

has been accorded to the packer and wharfinger upon goods in their possession. A banker likewise has a mercantile lien on all money and securities of his depositor for any claim due to the bank from the depositor.

An attorney has a lien upon all the papers of his client in his possession for the general balance due to him from the client.

§ 16. Enforcement and loss of lien.[6] At common law the lienholder had no right to foreclose his lien by sale but could merely hold the chattel. This was a very inadequate remedy especially where the chattel was bulky or had to be fed, because as soon as a lien was claimed, the lienholder was compelled to keep the chattel at his own expense. Statutes today allow the lienholder to sell at public sale after notice and thus to foreclose his lien.

A lien is lost by any conduct of the lienholder which is inconsistent with its continuance. Thus, if he should refuse to deliver up the chattel upon tender of the amount due; or if, without statutory authority he should attempt to sell or pledge it to a third party; or if he should detain it claiming it as his own; or if he should levy an invalid execution upon it; or if he should deliver it to the owner, the lien is lost. But where he delivers only a part of the goods to the owner this does not destroy his lien on the goods still retained.

[6] 33 Am Jur, Liens, §§ 27–32, 42–52.

REAL PROPERTY

CHAPTER I

PRESENT ESTATES IN LAND

A. Freehold Estates

§ 1. **Estates in fee simple.**[1] An estate in fee simple was created at common law by a conveyance "to A and his heirs," whereas a conveyance merely "to A" gave A only a life estate. Today by statute a conveyance "to A" gives him a fee; if it is desired to convey to him only a life estate it must be thus expressly limited.

When the tenant in fee dies without a will, the estate descends to his heirs.

§ 2. **Estates tail.**[2] A conveyance "to A and the heirs of his body" created in A an estate tail. In some states, estates tail have been converted into estates in fee simple; in other states A gets a life estate with remainder in fee to his issue or to those who are his heirs at his death; in still others A gets an estate tail with remainder in fee to his issue.

Where the conveyance is to "A and the heirs of his body by his present wife" and the wife dies, A is not regarded as having a mere life estate but as tenant in tail after possibility of issue extinct, and is not liable for legal but only for equitable waste.

§ 3. **Life estates.**[3] Where an estate is given to A for the life of X or where X, having a life estate, conveys it to A, and A dies before X, some modern statutes give the unexpired portion of the life estate to A's heir, while other statutes give it to A's executor.

Since the duration of a life estate is uncertain, the executor of a deceased life tenant is entitled to emblements. Where the life tenant leases the prop-

[1] 19 Am Jur, Estates, §§ 12–27.

Who entitled to land upon its abandonment for railroad purposes where railroad's original interest or title was less than fee simple absolute. 136 ALR 296–324.

12 Brooklyn L. R. 1, Present Alienage Disabilities under New York State Law in Real Property.

[2] 19 Am Jur, Estates, §§ 46–55.

[3] 19 Am Jur, Estates, § 56.

33 Am Jur, Life Estates, Remainders, and Reversions, §§ 2–18, 423–464.

Duty of life tenant or life beneficiary to pay taxes. 17 ALR 1384–1410; s. in 94 ALR 311–328; 126 ALR 862–876.

Timber rights of life tenant. 21 ALR 1002–1023; s. in 46 ALR 1205–1206.

erty to Y for a term of years and then dies between two rent days, modern statutes apportion the rent for the current period between the life tenant's executor and the remainderman or reversioner.

The life tenant must keep the premises in repair and is liable to the remainderman or reversioner for waste. He must pay ordinary taxes which become due during the tenancy and interest on the amount assessed for permanent improvements. If both the life estate and the remainder in fee are subject to a mortgage, the life tenant must pay the interest on the mortgage and the cost of insurance required by the mortgage. Where there is no such mortgage there is no such burden; the life tenant is under no duty to insure the remainderman's interest.

If the life tenant should buy in an outstanding title the remainderman is entitled to share in its benefit upon his reimbursing the tenant for his proper share of its cost.

B. Estates Less Than Freehold

§ 4. **Tenancies for years.**[4] An estate for any fixed period, no matter how short or how long its duration, is called an estate for years. Apart from statutory modifications as to estates for a very long period, estates for years are regarded as personal property, going to the executor or administrator to pay debts and to distribute the residue to legatees or next of kin.

At common law an estate for years could be created orally, but the English Statute of Frauds, passed in 1676, required leases to be in writing except those for a period not exceeding three years from the making. This part of the statute has been copied more or less literally in most American jurisdictions.

§ 5. **Same—distinguished from licenses.**[5] A tenant for years is to be carefully distinguished from a licensee who has no property right in the land but at most merely a contract right; examples are—a lodger who occupies a room, a servant who occupies a house as incidental to his work as servant and an advertiser who contracts for the use of a wall or signboard for advertising purposes.

One who works land for a share of the crops is usually only a licensee, not a tenant; but if there is a written lease and the ordinary words of letting are used and the intention is clear that the worker is to be in exclusive control of the land, the weight of authority is that he becomes a tenant paying as rent a share of the crops raised.

§ 6. **Tenancies at will.**[6] If A places B in possession of land for no fixed period to be held expressly at the will of A or without reservation of any rent, B becomes a tenant at will. So, if A, having contracted to sell to B, places B in possession, B becomes a tenant at will at law though in equity he may have a right to specific performance of the contract. Where B enters under a void lease, a tenancy at will is temporarily created which is turned into a tenancy from year to year upon the acceptance of rent by A.

Apart from statute, a tenancy at will may be terminated by either landlord or tenant without notice; some statutes require notice by either party, others require it only of the landlord.

4 32 **Am Jur**, Landlord and Tenant, §§ 61-65.

5 33 **Am Jur**, Licenses, § 91.
19 **N. Y. U. Law Q.** 333, Licenses and Tenancies for Years.

6 32 **Am Jur**, Landlord and Tenant, §§ 66-70.
Conveyance or lease by landlord as termination of existing tenancy at will. 120 **ALR** 1006-1019.

If the tenancy is terminated by the landlord, the tenant is entitled to emblements.

§ 7. Tenancies at sufferance.[7] A tenant who wrongfully holds over after his tenancy has expired may be treated by the landlord as a tenant at sufferance. After the landlord has regained possession by self-help or by action he may recover against him in an action of trespass for mesne profits for the value of the use and occupation. The tenant is not entitled to emblements. In some states, statutes require the landlord to give notice before ejecting him.

§ 8. Tenancies from year to year.[8] A tenancy from year to year, quarter to quarter, month to month, or week to week may be created either expressly or by the landlord accepting rent from a tenant who wrongfully holds over or from a tenant who has entered under a void lease. Such a tenancy can be terminated only at the end of a period under which the land is held. Where the tenancy is from year to year, either party may terminate it by giving six months' notice; where the tenancy is from quarter to quarter, month to month, or week to week, the notice must be given for a quarter, month or week respectively.

CHAPTER II

LANDLORD AND TENANT

§ 9. Duties of landlord.[9] In order that the relation of landlord and tenant shall arise, the giving and acceptance of a valid lease is sufficient without the lessee's taking possession.

A lease usually contains express covenants of quiet enjoyment and of right to demise; but today the better view is that such express covenants are not necessary to impose such liabilities on the landlord. There is, however, no implied covenant that the premises are in a tenantable condition.

The landlord is under a duty to pay taxes on the leased land, but he is under no duty to keep it in repair unless he makes an express covenant to that effect or there is a statute imposing such liability.

§ 10. Duties of the tenant.[10] The tenant must keep the premises in re-

[7] 32 Am Jur, Landlord and Tenant, § 75.

[8] 32 Am Jur, Landlord and Tenant, §§ 71–74.

[9] 32 Am Jur, Landlord and Tenant, §§ 268–298, 653–661.

Acts of other tenants as chargeable to landlord. 38 ALR 250–258; s. in 45 ALR 1126; 58 ALR 1049–1051.

Breach of covenant for quiet enjoyment in lease. 62 ALR 1257–1322.

Validity, construction, and effect of landlord's covenant against use or lease of other property for purpose competing with that of lessee. 90 ALR 1449–1472.

Rights and remedies of parties in respect to lease of filling station. 83 ALR 1416–1429; s. in 126 ALR 1375–1401.

What amounts to an option to renew or extend a lease. 26 ALR 1413–1420.

Effect of lessee's failure or delay in giving notice within specified time, of intention to renew lease. 27 ALR 981–1000.

What constitutes sufficient notice of exercise of option of renewal in lease. 1 ALR 343–349; s. in 99 ALR 1010–1019.

When landlord deemed to have assented to renewal by holding over. 64 ALR 309–322.

Right to remove fixtures or improvements placed upon property by one holding under lease as affected by renewal or new lease made to him or his successor without reservation of the right to remove. 110 ALR 480–511.

[10] 32 Am Jur, Landlord and Tenant, §§ 428–430, 478–501, 779–815.

Special assessments as within provisions of a lease requiring lessee to pay "taxes," "taxes and assessments," and variations. 63 ALR 1391–1402.

Extent of lessee's obligation under express covenant as to repairs. 45 ALR 12–84; s. in 106 ALR 1358–1372.

Breach of lessor's covenant to repair as ground of liability for damages for personal injuries to tenant, or one in privity with latter. 8 ALR 765–785; s. in 68 ALR 1194–1205.

Rights and remedies of tenant upon landlord's breach of covenant to repair. 28 ALR 1448–1519; s. in 116 ALR 1228–1240.

pair unless such duty is shifted to the landlord either by express covenant of the landlord, or by statute.

The tenant's chief duty is to pay rent and it is no answer to the landlord's claim for rent that there is an outstanding title paramount to that of the landlord unless the tenant has been ousted by the holder of such a title or there has been a threatened ouster and the tenant has in good faith attorned to such holder.

If the landlord himself ousts the tenant from possession, the liability to pay rent ceases. If the ouster is from only a part of the premises, the rent on the entire premises is suspended during such ouster. If a third party ousts the tenant from a part of the premises the tenant is excused pro tanto from paying rent.

If land is leased upon which there is a building and the building is accidentally destroyed, neither the landlord nor tenant is under any obligation to rebuild unless there has been an express covenant to that effect. Since the tenant is, for the period of his tenancy, the owner of the land, the destruction of the building does not excuse him from paying rent. He is excused, however, if the lease covered only the building or a part thereof, and not the land.

Where the leased property is taken by eminent domain, the landlord and tenant are each entitled to compensation for his interest.

Where the premises become uninhabitable either because of the landlord's maintaining a nuisance on adjoining property, or because of the landlord's

Right of tenant to make alterations in structures on leased premises. 9 ALR 445–459; s. in 13 ALR 824–825.

Construction and effect of statutory provision for double or treble damages against tenant committing waste. 45 ALR 771–776.

Duty of lessee or purchaser of mineral rights other than oil or gas as to development and operation. 60 ALR 901–936.

Liability of lessee who refuses to take possession under executed lease or executory agreement to lease. 54 ALR 1355–1362.

Validity and effect of acceleration clause in lease or bailment. 58 ALR 300–318; s. in 128 ALR 750–757.

Judgment for rent for particular period as bar to action for rent for subsequent period. 24 ALR 885–897; s. in 42 ALR 128.

Rule of estoppel of tenant to deny landlord's title as applicable where landlord affirmatively asserts a title or interest beyond that essential to his right to create the tenancy. 89 ALR 1295–1301.

Estoppel to dispute landlord's title where tenant never was in possession under the lease. 98 ALR 545–553.

Provision in lease as to purpose for which premises are to be used, as excluding use for other purpose. 148 ALR 583–604.

Effect of nonhabitability of leased dwelling or apartment. 4 ALR 1453–1480; s. in 13 ALR 818–819; 29 ALR 52–55; 34 ALR 711–712.

Change of physical conditions on property of landlord, other than that leased, as affecting the rights and liabilities of landlord and tenant. 12 ALR 160–179; s. in 38 ALR 1090–1092; 44 ALR 59–60.

Rights and remedies of tenant who remains in possession of all or part of the premises against landlord for interfering with his possession or enjoyment. 20 ALR 1369–1416; s. in 28 ALR 1333–1337; 64 ALR 900–915.

Time in which to yield possession by tenant after acts or conditions constituting constructive eviction. 75 ALR 1114–1124.

What amounts to permanent improvements within provision of lease against their removal. 39 ALR 1044–1052.

Goods owned by stranger or subject to an encumbrance in his favor as subject to distraint for rent. 62 ALR 1106–1162.

Liability for rent accruing after landlord's institution of action or proceedings against tenant to recover possession. 93 ALR 1474–1483.

Lessee as surety for rent after assignment; and effect of lessor's dealings (other than consent to assignment or mere acceptance of rent from assignee) to release lessee. 99 ALR 1238–1248.

Notice by landlord of change in rent or other modification of tenancy as affecting rights and liabilities incident to tenant's holding over after expiration of term or rent period or time fixed by notice. 109 ALR 197–220.

Landlord's acceptance of rent as waiver of right to forfeit because of tenant's past or future violation of terms of lease. 109 ALR 1267–1293.

Time when rent payable in absence of provision of lease fixing time applicable to all payments. 126 ALR 565–583.

Subject matter covered by landlord's statutory lien for rent. 9 ALR 300–335; s. in 96 ALR 249–270.

Landlord's lien or right of distress on property sold to tenant on conditional sale. 45 ALR 949–961.

Liability of electric light or power company for injury or damage due to condition of service lines or electrical appliance maintained by one to whom it furnishes electric current. 134 ALR 507–531.

breach of some other duty to the tenant and the tenant moves out, his obligation to pay rent ceases; but if he stays in possession, his sole right is to sue the landlord for the nuisance or for breach of covenant.

If the tenant fails to pay rent, the landlord's remedy is to sue or to distrain for the rent due or to oust the tenant under the forcible entry and detainer statutes. The remedy by distraint has in many jurisdictions been either abolished or modified.

§ 11. **Assignments and subleases.**[1] If A leases to B and then B transfers to X all or the residue of his term in the whole or a specific part of the leased premises, X as assignee becomes directly liable to A for the rent reserved in A's lease to B and upon all the other covenants in the lease which run with the land; and such liability continues unless X should in turn assign the lease to Y. It is not necessary that X take possession of the premises or that he expressly undertake the performance of B's covenants; but if he does so undertake he remains liable thereon even after he reassigns his rights to Y. And B remains liable to A on the original lease for any default of either X or any of his successors. If B reserves a reversionary interest in the lease it is a sublease, not an assignment and the sublessee does not become liable to A.

If, in the lease from A to B, there is a covenant by B not to assign without A's consent, this does not prevent B from subletting or from assigning a part of the lease; and a covenant not to sublet does not prevent him from assigning.

If A, the landlord, transfers his reversionary interest in the land, that ordinarily carries with it the right to the rent reserved in the lease; but A may separate the reversion from the right to the rent, transferring either one without the other or transferring the reversion to one party and the right to the rent to another. The transferee of the reversion steps into the shoes of the transferor and may enforce against the tenant or his assigns the various covenants running with the land and becomes himself liable to the tenant or his assigns on the various covenants running with the land against the landlord, though A, the original lessor, still remains liable on such covenants.

§ 12. **Surrender—eviction by summary proceedings.**[2] The tenant may put an end to his rights and obligations under the lease by surrendering the

1 32 **Am Jur**, Landlord and Tenant, §§ 313–426.

Landlord's consent to one assignment or sublease as obviating necessity of consent to subsequent assignment or sublease. 31 **ALR** 153–159; s. in 32 **ALR** 1080–1081.

Right of lessee in absence of covenant to assign lease or sublet premises. 23 **ALR** 135–146; s. in 70 **ALR** 486–488.

Rights of lessee who relets for entire term as against sublessee or person claiming under latter. 32 **ALR** 1429–1461.

Liability of lessee's assignee to lessor for rent accruing after assignment by him, in the absence of assumption of covenants of lease. 89 **ALR** 433–441; s. in 148 **ALR** 196–204.

Period covered by lessee's, sublessee's, or assignee's covenant to pay taxes or assessments. 97 **ALR** 931–946.

2 32 **Am Jur**, Landlord and Tenant, §§ 900–917, 1016–1032.

Right of landlord to dispossess tenant without legal process. 45 **ALR** 313–328; s. in 49 **ALR** 517; 60 **ALR** 280.

Commission of waste as ground for forfeiture of lease. 3 **ALR** 672–679.

When landlord's reletting or efforts to relet after tenant's abandonment or refusal to enter deemed to be acceptance of the surrender. 3 **ALR** 1080–1092; s. in 52 **ALR** 154–158; 61 **ALR** 773–776; 110 **ALR** 368–377.

Surrender of a written lease by parol. 4 **ALR** 666–680.

Death of life tenant as affecting rights under lease executed by him. 6 **ALR** 1506–1517; s. in 15 **ALR** 659.

Surrender and acceptance of term as affecting right to recover rent or on obligation given for rent. 18 **ALR** 957–972; s. in 58 **ALR** 906–907.

Construction of provision for termination of lease in event of sale of property. 35 **ALR** 518–552; s. in 116 **ALR** 931–939.

Computation and requisites of period of notice given to terminate tenancy. 86 **ALR** 1346–1361.

leased premises to the landlord. The Statute of Frauds requires that all express surrenders, except leases of short duration, shall be in writing. But a surrender may be effected without such writing if a new valid lease is made which is inconsistent with the old one; or if the landlord accepts a subtenant or other third person as lessee; or if the tenant abandons the premises and the landlord enters and occupies for himself. But no surrender results if upon abandonment of the property by the tenant the landlord enters and after notice to the tenant relets the property for the rest of the term in order to reduce the tenant's liability for rent.

Where the tenant wrongfully refuses to give up possession the landlord may, by statute, maintain summary proceedings to get possession.

CHAPTER III

CONCURRENT OWNERSHIP

§ 13. Joint tenancies and tenancies in common.[3] In a joint tenancy there are four unities: the unity of interest (the estates held by the joint tenants are similar); of title (the estates are created by the same deed or will); of time (the estates must begin at the same time); and of possession (there is a joint right to possession). If any one of the first three unities is lacking there is a tenancy in common, which requires merely unity of possession. Where a joint tenant conveys, mortgages or leases his interest to X, this destroys the joint tenancy and the parties become tenants in common. But merely making a will does not destroy the joint tenancy.

The chief practical difference between joint tenancy and tenancy in common is that if one joint tenant dies his interest goes to the survivor or survivors; hence the widow of such deceased joint tenant is not entitled to dower.

Where a conveyance is made "to A and B" the presumption today is that unless A and B are trustees they take as tenants in common; if in other cases

Construction and effect of provision of lease or bond saving liability of tenant or sureties in case of forfeiture of lease or re-entry by landlord. 99 **ALR** 42–60.

Provision of lease authorizing its termination by lessor in event of insolvency, bankruptcy, or receivership of lessee. 115 **ALR** 1189–1204.

Waiver or revocation by landlord of notice given to him to terminate tenancy. 120 **ALR** 557–574.

38 **Harv. L. R.** 64. The Element of Intent in Surrender by Operation of Law.

3 14 **Am Jur,** Cotenancy, §§ 6–22.

Rights of cotenants inter se as to timber. 2 **ALR** 993–1005; s. in 41 **ALR** 582–585.

Possession by one claiming under or through deed or mortgage by cotenant as adverse to other cotenant. 27 **ALR** 8–27; s. in 71 **ALR** 444–451.

Accountability of cotenants for rents and profits or use and occupation. 27 **ALR** 184–273; s. in 39 **ALR** 408–410.

Rights and remedies of tenant in common who pays his cotenant's share of taxes or assessments. 48 **ALR** 586–603.

Right of cotenant to acquire and assert adverse title or interest as against other cotenants. 54 **ALR** 874–913; s. in 85 **ALR** 1535–1539.

Partition as affecting pre-existing mortgage or other lien on undivided interest. 93 **ALR** 1267–1285.

Right to partition in kind of mineral or oil and gas land. 143 **ALR** 1092–1107.

Suit for partition as involving freehold or title to real estate within constitutional or statutory provisions relating to jurisdiction. 135 **ALR** 1066–1081.

Allowance and apportionment of counsel fees in suit for partition. 73 **ALR** 16–59; s. in 146 **ALR** 1269–1280.

Respective rights of owners of different parcels into which land subject to oil and gas leases is divided on partition. See 5 **ALR** 1165; s. in 16 **ALR** 588–590; 64 **ALR** 634–640.

Undivided interests held respectively in fee and in life estate, with remainder, voluntary partition of. 12 **ALR** 644–647; s. in 134 **ALR** 661–678.

Judgment creditor of cotenant, right of, to maintain partition. 25 **ALR** 105–107.

Estoppel of one not party to partition by failure to disclose his interest in the property. See 50 **ALR** 791.

Different tracts of land, right to partition of, in same proceeding. 65 **ALR** 893–900.

Pretermitted child's right to maintain partition proceedings. See 123 **ALR** 1092.

Cestui que trust (or one claiming through or under him), right of, to maintain suit for partition. 126 **ALR** 1009–1028.

Parol partition and the statute of frauds. 133 **ALR** 476–515.

it is desired that A and B shall take as joint tenants this intent must be clearly expressed in the instrument.

§ 14. Tenancies by the entirety.[4] Where a conveyance is made to parties who at the time are husband and wife, the parties hold as tenants by the entirety unless the language clearly indicates that they are to take as joint tenants or tenants in common. The spouses do not take by shares but each one is seized of the entire interest; upon the death of one the survivor takes all as in the case of joint tenancy.

Only a husband and wife can hold as tenants by the entirety and if there is a later divorce the former spouses become tenants in common. During the coverture, the husband is entitled to the entire rents and profits; this right is usually abrogated by married women's property acts. Where land is conveyed to husband and wife and to X, the husband and wife together take only one share. In some states the tenancy has never been recognized; in others it has been abrogated by statute.

CHAPTER IV

ESTATES AND INTERESTS ARISING FROM MARRIAGE

§ 15. The husband's right during the marriage.[5] At common law, upon marriage, the title to the wife's chattels passed at once to the husband. He also became entitled to collect, at any time during the marriage any choses in action belonging to the wife; if he failed to do so they were lost to him or to his estate. As to her leasehold interests in land he could sell them and if he survived, he became entitled to them, but if they were not disposed of and the wife survived, she was entitled. As to her real estate the husband became entitled to the rents and profits during the marriage. All these rules applied also to property acquired by the wife after the marriage.

Equity, however, allowed the creation for the wife of a separate estate free from the control of her husband; and, in order to prevent the husband from

Suit for partition as involving freehold or title to real estate within constitutional provisions relating to jurisdiction. 135 **ALR** 1066–1081.

Homestead right of cotenant as affecting partition. 140 **ALR** 1170–1177.

Purchaser at partition sale, rights and remedies of, where sale is void or is set aside because proceedings are imperfect or irregular, or where description of property is defective. 142 **ALR** 310–358.

Fee simple conditional estate, partition of. See 114 **ALR** 615.

Parol partition of real property as between undivided interests held by same person in different capacities. 116 **ALR** 626–627.

Right of party to voluntary partition, or of his successor, as against other parties thereto, or their successors, where title fails as to parcel, or part of parcel, conveyed to him. 123 **ALR** 489–502.

29 **U. of Iowa L. R.** 558, Accountability of Cotenants.

4 26 **Am Jur**, Husband and Wife, §§ 66–86.

Accountability for rents and profits or use and occupation of tenant by the entirety. See 27 **ALR** 264; s. in 39 **ALR** 408–410.

Nature and extent of interest of judgment debtor in estate by entirety subject to lien or execution under judgment against one of the spouses. 27 **ALR** 826–833.

Married Women's Act as abolishing estates by entireties. 141 **ALR** 179–204.

Estate by entireties in personal property. 8 **ALR** 1017–1023; s. in 117 **ALR** 915–924.

Character of conveyance or conveyances necessary to create an estate by entirety. 132 **ALR** 630–644.

Judgment or execution as a lien on estate held by the entireties. 35 **ALR** 147–155; s. in 89 **ALR** 499–504.

Right of murderer in property owned as tenant by entirety with his victim. 51 **ALR** 1106.

Validity and effect of husband's lease of estate by entireties, without joinder of wife. 136 **ALR** 1211–1212.

Creditors of one spouse, right of, either before or after death of other spouse, to attack conveyance or encumbrance of estate by entireties by both spouses as in fraud of creditors. 121 **ALR** 1028–1031.

Incidents of estate passing under deed to persons mistakenly supposed to be husband and wife, as tenants by the entireties 92 **ALR** 1420–1422.

Liens on estate by entirety, right of surviving spouse to exoneration out of the decedent's estate in respect of. 67 **ALR** 1181–1182.

5 26 **Am Jur**, Husband and Wife §§ 34–65

persuading her to convey such separate estate to him, the equity courts upheld provisions taking from the wife the power to alien such property. Such a provision did not prevent the husband from getting curtesy upon the wife's death unless the intent of the creator of the trust was to exclude him.

The equitable separate estate paved the way for married women's property acts which usually provide that a married woman is entitled to keep her property as if she were still unmarried.

§ 16. **Curtesy.**[6] At common law a surviving husband was entitled to a life estate in all his wife's real property, provided that there was a valid marriage, that the wife was seized during the marriage and that issue was born alive capable of inheriting. This right of curtesy existed as to all estates of inheritance and was later extended to real property in which the wife had only a trust or other equitable interest.

By statute in many states curtesy has been either abolished or seriously modified.

§ 17. **Dower.**[7] At common law a surviving wife was entitled to a life estate in one third of her husband's real property provided there was a valid marriage and the husband was seized during the marriage.

This right existed as to all estates of inheritance but, unlike curtesy, it could not be extended by the courts to equitable interests because to do so would have upset many land titles, husbands owning such equitable interests having been accustomed to convey such interests without their wives joining in the conveyances. Today, however, statutes usually give the widow dower in such property.

The right to dower could not be defeated by a conveyance by the husband alone; but the wife might release her inchoate dower right by joining with her husband in the conveyance or by releasing to the husband's grantee by a later conveyance to him.

Where the husband has made a testamentary provision for the wife she is apparently entitled to that in addition to dower unless the husband's intent is that she is to choose one or the other.

Dower should be assigned to the widow within forty days after the husband's death; during that period, called the widow's quarantine, she is entitled to occupy the mansion house and to be supported out of the estate.

Where land is conveyed before marriage either by the husband or a third party in trust for the wife as a provision for her in lieu of dower, this is called a legal jointure and is a bar at law to her dower right. An equitable jointure is any reasonable provision made before marriage and is a bar to dower if the wife assents. The subject of jointures is now usually regulated by statute.

Like curtesy, dower has been either abolished or seriously modified in some states by statutes which make other provisions for her support.

6 15 **Am Jur**, Curtesy, §§ 2–23.
Estate by curtesy in land settled on or conveyed to wife by husband. 30 **ALR** 1057–1065.

7 17 **Am Jur**, Dower, §§ 2–105.
Dower rights of wife who unites with husband in mortgage. 12 **ALR** 1347–1361; s. in 65 **ALR** 963–967.
Validity and effect of alienation or encumbrance of homestead without joinder or consent of wife. 45 **ALR** 395–436.
Outstanding right of dower as breach of covenant of title or against encumbrances in deed or mortgage of real estate. 141 **ALR** 482–513.
Dower in reversion or remainder interest of husband. 21 **ALR** 1073–1080.
42 **Harv. L. R.** 330, Husband and Wife as Statutory Heirs.

CHAPTER V

ESTATES UPON CONDITION, LIMITATION AND CONDITIONAL LIMITATION

§ 18. Estates upon condition.[8] If an estate is given by A to B upon a condition precedent—for example, upon the death of X without issue—such a condition must happen before B's estate vests. But if an estate is given by A outright to B, with the provision that upon the happening of a condition—for example, that B, having a leasehold interest, shall not assign it without A's consent—B's estate is said to be subject to a condition subsequent.

Where there is room for interpretation, courts tend to construe language as creating a condition subsequent rather than a condition precedent; and since a condition subsequent involves a forfeiture of the estate, courts tend to construe language as creating a trust or a covenant rather than a condition subsequent; for example, where there is a restriction upon the use of the premises and there is no provision for re-entry, courts will tend to consider the language as creating a covenant, not a condition, and the remedy will be by an injunction in equity, not by forfeiture. On the other hand, if something affirmative is to be done on the land, such as to build a church, a stipulation that equity would be reluctant to enforce, the court will be inclined to construe it as a condition, not a covenant.

If the court does construe the language as creating a condition subsequent and the condition happens, then the grantor or lessor may enter and eject the grantee or lessee. Apart from statute this right of entry is not assignable and upon the death of the grantor or lessor it goes to the heir instead of to the residuary devisee.

Where, after a condition has been broken—for example, the lessee has failed to pay taxes or has assigned the lease—the lessor, knowing of the breach, accepts rent, this is a waiver of the breach and of his right to terminate the lease. So if before the lessee assigns the lease the lessor assents to such assignment he cannot later take advantage of such breach. It was at one time held that assent to one assignment destroyed the condition but this rule is no longer followed.

Where the breach by the grantee or lessee is innocent and causes little or no damage to the grantor or lessor equity will usually enjoin the latter from taking advantage of it.

Where a condition subsequent is impossible of performance—for example, to support or to marry a person who dies—the estate cannot be forfeited; but where such a condition is precedent the estate will not vest unless the grantor or lessor should be responsible for the performance becoming impos-

[8] 19 **Am Jur,** Estates, §§ 58–74.

Waiver of breach of condition subsequent in instrument conveying title to real property. 43 **ALR** 1049–1059.

Continued use of property for burial purposes as a condition subsequent of a conveyance or dedication of land for that purpose. 47 **ALR** 1174–1186.

Deed in consideration of support of grantor as creating an estate upon condition or a conditional limitation. 76 **ALR** 742–757.

Fee simple conditional. 114 **ALR** 602–627.

Language of lease as creating conditional limitation as distinguished from a condition subsequent, or vice versa. 118 **ALR** 283–297.

Use or exploitation of property for a purpose other than, but not exclusive of, use specified by a deed creating a determinable fee or a fee simple subject to condition subsequent. 137 **ALR** 639–651.

Validity and effect of conveyance of interest remaining in grantor upon conveyance of a fee subject to a conditional limitation, or terminable upon breach of condition subsequent. 109 **ALR** 1148–1162; s. in 117 **ALR** 563–565; 135 **ALR** 576–580.

sible—for example, by interrupting the erection of a building which was required to be finished by a certain date.

§ 19. Estates upon limitation and conditional limitation.[9] Where A conveys land to B till the happening of a certain event—for example, till B's marriage or till Gloversville shall be incorporated as a village—B gets an estate which will terminate upon the happening of the event. Such an estate, sometimes called an estate upon limitation or special limitation, and sometimes—where more than a life estate is intended—a base or determinable fee, differs from an estate upon condition in that the estate comes to an end without the necessity of a re-entry by the grantor or lessor.

Where A conveys to B in fee, but if B should die without issue, then to C in fee, C takes nothing at common law because a remainder could not be limited after a fee. But where the conveyance is by will or by a deed operating under the statute of uses, C's estate is held to be valid and will vest upon B's death without issue. B's estate is therefore an estate upon limitation and since C's estate operates—upon the contingency or condition happening—to put an end to it, C's estate is sometimes called a conditional limitation. Where the conveyance is by will it is also called an executory devise; where it is by deed, it is called a shifting use.

CHAPTER VI

FUTURE ESTATES

§ 20. Reversions and remainders.[10] If A conveys to B a fee upon limita-

9 19 **Am Jur,** Estates, §§ 28–31, 95–97.

10 33 **Am Jur,** Life Estates, Remainders, and Reversions, §§ 44–214.

Reversion of title upon abandonment or vacation of public street or highway. 18 **ALR** 1008–1023; s. in 70 **ALR** 564–569.

Transfer or devolution of reversion as carrying lessee's covenants to repair, or to yield up in repair. 34 **ALR** 782–809.

Inheritable quality of possibility of reverter. 77 **ALR** 344–353.

Grant to one for life, and afterwards, either absolutely or contingently, to grantor's heirs or next of kin, as leaving reversion or creating remainder. 125 **ALR** 548–590.

Necessity of judicial proceeding to vest title to real property in state by escheat. 23 **ALR** 1237–1251; s. in 79 **ALR** 1364–1366.

Right as between life beneficiaries and remaindermen, or successive life beneficiaries, in corporate dividends or distributions during the life interest. 130 **ALR** 492–591.

Right of owner of contingent or defeasible future interest to maintain action for relief in respect of property. 144 **ALR** 769–809.

Distinction between contingent estates and estates vested, subject to defeasance. 131 **ALR** 712–725.

Validity and effect of transfer of expectancy by prospective heir. 17 **ALR** 597–617; s. in 44 **ALR** 1465–1470; 121 **ALR** 450–459.

Release to ancestor by heir expectant. 28 **ALR** 427–461.

Life tenants' and remaindermen's rights as to increase of livestock. See 13 **ALR** 1007; s. in 56 **ALR** 1315–1320; 81 **ALR** 542–547.

Rights and duties of life tenant and remainderman (income and corpus) with respect to repairs and improvements. 128 **ALR** 199–298.

Rights of life tenant and remaindermen inter se as to oil and gas. 43 **ALR** 811–819.

Commutation of life tenant's interest in fund realized from sale of property into estimated present value. 102 **ALR** 696–995.

Provision of will that children, etc., of remainderman who dies before expiration of precedent estate or time fixed for distribution to remaindermen, shall take the share to which he would have been entitled, as affecting character of remainder as vested or contingent. 109 **ALR** 5–66.

Death of life tenant before death of testator as causing lapse or "acceleration" of remainder. 133 **ALR** 1367–1378.

"Divide and pay over" rule, for purpose of determining vested or contingent character of future estate. 144 **ALR** 1155–1172.

Devise of life estate without complete or effective disposition of remainder as negativing right of life tenant to take as heir or next of kin. 128 **ALR** 446–456.

Vested or contingent character of remainder under devise of a remainder to a certain person or persons "or" his or their heirs or other class. 128 **ALR** 306–350.

Words or survivorship in will disposing of remainder upon termination of life or other precedent or intervening estate as referable to time of testator's death or to time of termination of such intervening estate. 114 **ALR** 4–113.

When will, absent explicit provision to that effect, is deemed to confer upon beneficiary of life or lesser estate or interest right to intrench upon principal or cortion or upon a condition subsequent, A has a possibility of reverter or right of entry for breach of condition. In this country today both are generally but illogically held to be vested interests.

If A conveys anything less than a fee, for example, a term for years or a life estate or a succession of life estates, A has a reversion.

If A conveys to B for life and then to C in fee, C is said to have a vested remainder; vested because C is in existence ready to take and his estate will come into possession at once upon the death of B, an event certain to happen. A remainder must be created by the same instrument that created the estate or estates preceding it; if A conveys to B for life and then by a separate instrument conveys the fee to C, C is not a remainderman but the assignee of A's reversion.

If A conveys to B for life, remainder to the heirs of C who is now alive, the remainder is not vested but contingent because the heirs of C cannot be determined till C's death.

If A conveys to B for life and, after the death of C, to D in fee, the remainder to D is contingent because C might outlive B; in such a case if C should outlive B, D's estate would fail at common law because a remainder must arise immediately upon the termination of the preceding estate. Either by statute or decision in most jurisdictions today D's estate does not fail but takes effect upon C's death even though B had already died, just as if it were a springing use.

If A conveys to B for life with remainder in fee to those of C's children who may survive C and at that time C has two children but later has three more, the remainder to the three unborn children is contingent upon their coming into existence and surviving C, but the estate to the two children in existence is held to be a vested remainder subject to its being divested pro tanto by the birth of other children, and also by failure to survive C.

If A devises to B for life and then to executors to divide the property between C and D, the remainders to C and D are vested, the power of the executors to sell and divide not being a contingency.

If A conveys to his children B, C and D for life, and at the death of all of them, to his grandchildren, the intent of A is construed to be that his estate shall go over as a whole and therefore B, C and D each get cross-remainders in the shares of the others.

If A conveys to B for life and later in the same instrument conveys the remainder to B's heirs the rule in Shelley's Case was that B took the fee regardless of A's intent, just as if the conveyance had been simply to B and his heirs. This rule has been abolished by statute in England and in many

pus. 108 **ALR** 542–572.

Devise or bequest which does not state character or duration of estate, but purports to dispose of what remains at death of devisee or legatee, as creating a fee or life estate. 75 **ALR** 71–111.

Rule in Shelley's Case as affected by failure of life estate prior to operative date of instrument. 145 **ALR** 1227–1235.

"Descendants" as a word of purchase or of limitation within rule in Shelley's Case. 13 **ALR** 392–398.

Phrase "from and after" death of life beneficiary as affecting character of remainder as vested or contingent. 103 **ALR** 598–611.

Meaning of term "issue" where used as a word of purchase. 2 **ALR** 930–975; s. in 16 **ALR** 55; 78 **ALR** 1398–1403; 117 **ALR** 691–717; 126 **ALR** 170–174.

Rights as between life tenants and remaindermen to the increase in the value of the estate. 13 **ALR** 1004–1018; s. in 56 **ALR** 1315–1320; 81 **ALR** 542–547.

Burden, as between corpus and income, of inheritance, estate, or succession tax. 117 **ALR** 121–140.

Rights and duties of life tenant with power to anticipate or enjoy principal. 2 **ALR** 1243–1327; s. in 27 ALR 1381–1392; 69 **ALR** 825–840; 114 **ALR** 946–959.

Vested or contingent character of remainder which is subject to be defeated by death of remainderman without issue before termination of particular estate. 109 **ALR** 136–156.

states, B usually taking only a life estate with a contingent remainder to his heirs.

§ 21. Executory devises, shifting and springing uses.[1] If A conveys to B an estate in fee to begin ten years from date, the conveyance failed at common law because no estate could be created in futuro without a particular estate to support it. But if the conveyance was by a bargain and sale deed operating under the Statute of Uses the estate in B was held to be good as a springing use.

If A conveys to X an estate in fee but if X should die without issue then to B in fee, B's estate failed at common law because it would cut short a previous fee; or, as the rule was sometimes expressed, a fee cannot be limited upon a fee. But by a bargain and sale deed operating under the Statute of Uses B's estate was held good as a shifting use.

Where the above conveyances were by will operating under the Statute of Wills, the same result was achieved, B's estate being called an executory devise.

CHAPTER VII

POWERS

§ 22. General powers.[2] If A conveys land to B for life with remainder in fee as B shall appoint, B may make himself owner of the fee by appointing to himself. If he does thus appoint or if he appoints to X by way of gift, his creditors may enforce their claims against the fee, but they cannot compel him to execute the power, apart from modern statutes. Such statutes do not apply where B has merely the power to appoint by will, unless expressly so provided.

If A conveys to B for life with a proviso that C shall have whatever of the property which may remain unconsumed, a general power of appointment in B is implied.

Contingent remainder as subject to levy and sale by creditor. 60 **ALR** 803–814.

Merger of estate for years in fee or lesser estate. 143 **ALR** 93–132.

30 **Harv. L. R.** 226, Contingent Remainders.

55 **Harv. L. R.** 1077, Future Interests Restated; Tradition versus Clarification and Reform.

50 **Harv. L. R.** 749, Fifty Years of Future Interests.

44 **Harv. L. R.** 378; Extinguishment of Contingent Future Interests by Decree and without Compensation.

29 **Calif. L. R.** 290, Classification of Contingent Remainders.

11 **U. of Chicago, L. R.** 82, Argument for Abrogation of Rule in Shelley's Case.

20 **N. C. L. R.** 279; 21 **N. C. L. R.** 284, The Alienability of Non-Possessory Interests.

22 **Boston U. L. R.** 43, Assignability of Possibilities of Reverter and Rights of Reentry.

1 19 **Am Jur,** Estates, §§ 95–134.

33 **Am Jur,** Life Estates, Remainders, and Reversions, §§ 101, 149, 164.

2 41 **Am Jur,** Powers, §§ 4–22.

Property covered by power of appointment as subject to claims of donee's creditors. 59 **ALR** 1510–1528; s. in 97 **ALR** 1071–1073; 121 **ALR** 803–806.

Power of sale as including power to mortgage. 92 **ALR** 882–906.

Devolution of subject of general power of appointment the exercise of which fails as to one or more beneficiaries. 93 **ALR** 967–984.

Nonexclusive powers and illusory appointments. 100 **ALR** 343–357.

Validity of exercise of power of appointment as affected by purpose, request, agreement, or condition that appointee benefit, or knowledge that he intends to benefit, one not an object of the power. 115 **ALR** 930–944.

Effect of partial invalidity of attempted exercise of power of appointment. 121 **ALR** 1226–1263.

Absolute power of disposition in life tenant as elevating life estate to fee. 36 **ALR** 1177–1239; s. in 76 **ALR** 1153–1169.

56 **Harv. L. R.** 757, Release of Powers of Appointment.

42 **Mich. L. R.** 649, Exclusive and Non-Exclusive Powers and the Illusory Appointment.

40 **Mich. L. R.** 337, The Classification of Some Powers of Appointment.

§ 23. **Special powers—powers in trust.**[3] If A conveys land to B for life with power to appoint the remainder among A's relatives or among C's children, the power is described as special. If there is no duty imposed upon B to exercise the power it is called a mere power; but if the power is to appoint among a distinct class, for example, among the childen of C, and it is clear from the instrument that the donor of the power intends that it shall be exercised, it is called a power in trust for the members of the class, so that if the donee of the power fails to exercise it, the property is divided among the members of the class in equal shares.

§ 24. **Execution of powers.**[4] Though desirable it is not necessary for the donee, in exercising the power, to refer to it expressly; it is enough if his intention appears from a fair interpretation of the instrument and the circumstances.

Where the execution of the power is formally defective, as, for example, where the will executing it has only two witnesses instead of three, such defective execution has been held good in equity.

In the absence of a statute a power not in trust must be exercised by all the donees of the power. If the power is in trust and one donee dies, the surviving donee or donees may exercise it, but if all die and the power involves personal discretion, it cannot be exercised by a trustee appointed by the court.

CHAPTER VIII

RULE AGAINST PERPETUITIES

A. At Common Law

§ 25. **The development of the rule.**[5] The development of what is now usually called the rule against perpetuities but which would be more accurately described as the rule against the remoteness of vesting of future interests in property, took place between 1609 and 1832. The rule was the resultant of two opposing forces, the desire of owners of property to control its disposition for a long time after their own lives have come to an end and the policy of the English common law that land shall be freely alienable.

This struggle began long before 1609 with the enactment of the Statute De Donis in 1285. Before that statute, if land was conveyed by A to B and the heirs of his body with a proviso that on the failure of such heirs the land should revert to A and his heirs, B could, upon the birth of issue, convey the land in fee simple. If he had no issue or if he had issue which died without his making any conveyance, or if he conveyed before the birth of issue the land would, upon his death or subsequent failure of issue, revert to A. This was called a fee simple conditional. By the Statute De Donis such estates were turned into estates tail so that neither B nor any of his descendants could convey a fee simple but must allow the land to be enjoyed by the successive generations, or when that failed, by the remaindermen, if any, or by the heirs of A.

The effect of this was such a serious violation of the common law policy of the free alienation of property that some two centuries later, in 1472,

3 41 **Am Jur**, Powers, §§ 3, 4.

4 41 **Am Jur**, Powers, §§ 23–93.

5 41 **Am Jur**, Perpetuities and Restraints on Alienation, §§ 1–18.

51 **Harv. L. R.** 638, Perpetuities in a Nutshell.

Taltarum's Case held that the tenant in tail might, by suffering a common recovery, bar the entail and convey a fee simple.

The next important step was the enactment of the Statute of Uses in 1535. Before that statute, it had been possible for A to create a use in X by a feoffment to B to the use of X; or by a bargain directly with X whereby X acquired the use either at once or at some time in the future, A retaining the legal title. The Statute of Uses provided that wherever A was seized to the use of X the legal title should be adjudged to be in X and not in A. It was now possible by a bargain and sale deed to create a legal estate to begin at any time in the future. If A by bargain and sale conveyed a present fee to B but if B should die before reaching twenty-one, then over to X in fee, the estate of X was called a shifting use because of the shift of the title from B to X upon B's death before reaching twenty-one. If A by bargain and sale conveyed an estate to X to begin twenty years after A's death, with no intervening estate in a third party, then X's estate was called a springing use. The Statute of Wills, enacted in 1540 permitted land to be devised, so that shifting and springing uses could also be created by will; when so created they are called executory devises. Shifting uses and shifting executory devises are also called conditional limitations.

The next important step was taken in 1609 when Manning's Case held that these future estates, unlike contingent remainders, could not be destroyed by the tenant for life levying a fine or suffering a common recovery. Since they were indestructible, it was possible, either by deed or will, to create estates which might not vest till hundreds of years later; so the courts were faced with the problem of placing some time limit upon the control which an owner of land might exercise in creating such estates. This step was finally taken in 1685 in the Duke of Norfolk's Case. In that case land was devised by A to trustees for a long term in trust for C, his second son and the heirs male of his body, but if B, the eldest son of A, should die without issue male in the life of C, or if A's earldom should descend upon C, then the trust should be for D, the third son of A. B died without issue in the lifetime of C. It was held by the House of Lords, affirming the decree of Lord Chancellor Nottingham, that the executory devise to D was good because the contingency upon which it must take effect must happen within or at the end of the lifetime of B.

In 1678, in the case of Taylor v. Biddall, a possible minority was added to the period of a life or lives in being. In 1722 the period was further extended to include any possible period of gestation, a child en ventre sa mere who is later born, being regarded as a life in being from the moment of conception. And in 1832 the case of Cadell v. Palmer held that the term of twenty-one years could be taken in gross without reference to the minority of anyone, so that a bequest by A to all his descendants who may be born within twenty-one years after his death is valid.

Hence the rule is usually stated as follows: "No interest is good unless it must vest, if at all, not later than twenty-one years after some life in being at the creation of the interest."

§ 26. The period—separation of contingencies.[6] In order that the future interest be good it must vest within the period; it is not enough that it will probably so vest even though the probability be so great as to amount to a practical certainty. If A devises to B in trust for C for life, then to B

[6] 41 Am Jur, Perpetuities and Restraints on Alienation, §§ 14–19.

for the life of D, then to the first son of E who shall attain twenty-five, the devise to the son is an executory devise and is bad even though at A's death E had a son who would, of course, attain twenty-five, if at all, in his own lifetime, because that son might die and E might die and a son born after A's death might not attain twenty-five till more than twenty-one years after the death of E.

So if A bequeaths to B in trust to pay the income to C for life, then to pay the income to C's children for their lives and then to pay the principal to the children of such children, the gift to the grandchildren is not good because C may have children after the death of A even though C may be a woman seventy-years old, because of the flat rule that so long as there is life there is possibility of children.

Another example of a possibility which is not a probability is the case where A leaves property to B in trust to pay the income to C for life, then to pay the income to C's widow, if any, for life, and then to pay the principal to the children of C then living. In such a case the gift to the children is bad because although C is fifty years old and has a wife and grown children, his wife might die and C might marry a woman who was not in existence at A's death.

Still another example is the case where A devised property to B "from and after the date of the probate of this will"; the gift was held bad because there was no certainty that the will would be probated within twenty-one years after A's death.

On the other hand, where A devised to B for life, remainder to such children of B as shall be living at B's death who shall attain twenty-five, and B died before A, leaving children all of whom were over four years old, the gift to the children was valid.

The life or lives in being are usually lives of persons to whom the settlor or testator gives—in the deed or will—some interest in the property, but they may be chosen arbitrarily by the settlor or devisor; and there is no limit to the number of persons thus selected provided that the fact of the death of all of them may be readily proved. For example, where A by will directed the accumulation of the income of his property during the lives of his sons, grandsons and great grandsons who might be living at his death and final distribution to be made at the death of the survivor, the will was held valid. So where A died in 1926 having made a bequest to "my descendants who shall be living twenty-one years after the death of all lineal descendants of Queen Victoria now living" the bequest was held valid though at that time there were over a hundred such descendants.

If A bequeaths $1,000 to the first son of B to become a clergyman, but if no son of B shall become a clergyman, then over to C, the gift to C is bad because if B should have sons it might not be known till the death of the last surviving son whether one of them might become a clergyman, an event which might happen much later than twenty-one years after B's death. A should have separated the contingencies, as follows: "To the first son of B to become a clergyman, but if B should have no son, or if B should have sons none of whom shall become clergymen, then over to C." In such a case if B should have no son the gift to C would be valid because that contingency is decided at B's death; but if B should have sons then the gift to C would be invalid because the contingency might not happen till more than twenty-one years after B's death, as already explained.

§ 27. Gifts to classes.[7] If A bequeaths $500 to each child of B who shall reach twenty-one the will is entirely valid because, although B has no child at the death of A, any child he may have later will reach twenty-one within twenty-one years after B's death.

If A bequeaths $500 to each child of B who shall reach twenty-five and B has no children at A's death, the entire bequest fails because later born children might not reach twenty-five within twenty-one years after B's death. But if at A's death B has three children living the bequest to them is valid because they become the lives in being and they must reach twenty-five in their own lifetimes. As to children born to B after A's death the gift fails because they may not reach twenty-five till more than twenty-one years after B's death.

If A bequeaths the residue of his estate to be divided equally among such children of B who shall reach twenty-five, the entire gift fails even though B has children under twenty-five living at A's death because the date of distribution may not come until more than twenty-one years after B's death. But if B has a child living at A's death who has already reached twenty-five, the gift vests immediately in such child and is valid, the rest of the children of B getting nothing, thus partially frustrating the intention of the testator. So, a gift by will to all my nephews and nieces for their lives with remainder in fee to their children equally, was held valid as to those living at the testator's death and their children, after-born nephews and nieces and their children being excluded.

§ 28. Interests affected by the rule.[8] Executory devises, springing and shifting uses are of course within the rule, whether they are legal estates or held in trust, whether realty or personalty; it was because these interests were indestructible that the rule was developed.

Contingent remainders were formerly not within the rule because destructible; now that they are indestructible the rule should and does apply to them, whether they are legal estates or held in trust.

Vested interests, whether remainders or reversions, are not within the rule even though the event upon which such an interest will or may come into possession may be very far in the future. For example, a reversion or remainder after an estate tail or after a term for ninety-nine years; or, where A devises to B, a bachelor, remainder to his children as tenants in common for life, remainder to C in fee, the remainder to C is vested in interest at once though it may not come into possession until more than twenty-one years after B's death.

[7] 41 **Am Jur,** Perpetuities and Restraints on Alienation, §§ 52–54.

When may gift by will or deed of trust be considered as one to a class. 75 **ALR** 773–840; s. in 105 **ALR** 1394–1401.

Living members of class as excluding their children from the class. 83 **ALR** 164–193.

19 **Harv. L. R.** 598, Vested Gifts to a Class and the Rule against Perpetuities.

51 **Harv. L. R.** 1329, The Rule against and Gifts to Classes.

49 **Harv. L. R.** 903, What Constitutes a Gift to a Class?

41 **Col. L. R.** 1, Class Gifts—Definitional Aspects.

22 **N. C. L. R.** 297, Class Gifts in North Carolina.

[8] 41 **Am Jur,** Perpetuities and Restraints on Alienation, §§ 29–51.

Prior estate as affected by remainder void for remoteness. 28 **ALR** 375–406; s. in 75 **ALR** 124–128.

Doctrine as to possibility of issue extinct as affecting property rights or taxation. 67 **ALR** 538–552; s. in 146 **ALR** 794–808.

Violation of rule against perpetuities, or unlawful restraint of alienation or suspension of ownership, by postponement of vesting or alienation of ownership until exercise of discretion as to sale or disposal. 89 **ALR** 1046–1065.

Perpetuities, applicability of rule against, to reverter on breach of condition subsequent. 70 **ALR** 1196–1205; s. in 133 **ALR** 1476–1479.

In this country a possibility of reverter and a right of entry for breach of condition are illogically treated as if they were vested interests and hence not subject to the rule.

Where A leases to B for thirty years with an option to buy the fee at any time before the lease expires upon giving sixty days' notice, B has an immediate equitable right in the land which is conditional only upon his own choice and which, when he exercises the option by acceptance, equity will specifically enforce not only against A but against any transferee from A except a bona fide purchaser for value without notice. It is arguable, therefore, that B has a present vested interest which is not within the rule, but the weight of authority is that it is within the rule. Where, however, the option in B is to renew the lease,—equally a right specifically enforcible in equity—the rule is that it is not within the rule. An option to buy chattels at a future time ordinarily gives no right to specific performance and therefore no property right; hence it is not within the rule.

§ 29. Powers—gifts to charity.[9] A general power to appoint by deed or will is equivalent to ownership and hence is good if the donee must acquire the power within the period of the rule. If A devises in trust for B, a bachelor, for life, remainder to B's eldest son for life, remainder in fee to such person or persons as such son shall appoint, the power is valid because it is acquired at B's death. Whether the appointments actually made by B's eldest son under the power are valid is determined by computing from the date of the exercise of the power and not from the date of its creation.

A general power to appoint by will only or a special power, for example, to appoint among members of a class, is not equivalent to ownership and hence it is invalid if it can be exercised beyond the period. Thus, in the case above stated, if the power given to B's eldest (unborn) son was to appoint among his own children, such a power would be void unless the period of the exercise of the power be limited to twenty-one years after B's death, the time being computed from the date of its creation and not from the date of its exercise. Even though the power itself is valid the appointments made under the power will be invalid unless they must vest within twenty-one years after lives in being at the creation of the power.

Where A by deed creates a trust for himself for life, remainder to his children for life, remainder in fee to his grandchildren, reserving the power to revoke the trust, the remainder to the grandchildren is good because the period is computed from the date of the expiration of the power of revocation, namely, the death of A, the children being regarded as the lives in being, just as if they had taken by will.

A power of sale given to a trustee or mortgagee is not properly within the rule because it in no way tends to interfere with the free transfer of property.

Where there is a gift to an individual and then, upon some contingency, over to a charity; or if, conversely, there is a gift to a charity and then, upon some contingency, over to an individual, the rule applies. But where there is a gift to a charity and then, upon some contingency, over to another

9 41 **Am Jur**, Perpetuities and Restraints on Alienation, §§ 36–39.

Rule against perpetuities as affecting limitation over to charity after a gift of indefinite duration to another charity. 30 **ALR** 594–598.

27 **Harv. L. R.** 705, General Powers and Perpetuities.

28 **Harv. L. R.** 664, Remoteness of General Powers.

17 **Ind. L. J.** 205, Rule against Perpetuities and Gifts to Charity.

charity the rule does not apply, apparently upon the ground that since the property is to be devoted to a public use in any event its transfer, upon some contingency, does not violate any public policy.

B. Statutory Modifications

§ 30. The New York statute.[10] The common-law rule was aimed at the remoteness of the vesting of contingent interests without regard to whether alienation of the property involved was or was not suspended; the rule applied even though there were persons in existence who could unite in conveying a good title. But the New York Legislature in 1830 apparently did not understand this and so aimed their statute at the suspension of alienation, not at the remoteness of the vesting of contingent interests. The present New York statute provides that "every future estate shall be void in its creation which shall suspend the absolute power of alienation by any limitation or condition whatever for a longer period than during the continuance of not more than two lives in being at the creation of the estate; except that a contingent remainder in fee may be created on a prior remainder in fee, to take effect in the event that the person to whom the first remainder is limited dies under the age of twenty-one years, or on any other contingency by which the estate of such persons may be determined before they attain full age." There is no provision for a gross period of years.

Though the New York statute is expressly aimed only at suspending the absolute power of alienation it has been held in New York that even if the contingent interest is alienable it is invalid unless it must vest within two lives in being at the creation of the interest.

§ 31. Application of New York rule.[1] If A devises property to B upon trust to collect the rents and profits and pay them over to C for life and upon C's death to sell and divide equally among such children of C as may survive him, and C has no children at A's death, the gift to his after-born children is bad because it may not vest within two lives in being and also because the absolute power of alienation is suspended till they are born. But if A's will had contained a proviso that the trust must cease upon the death of X and Y, and C dies before the death of X and Y, leaving children, the gift to the children would seem to be valid.

Where A devised property to his widow B upon trust for the support of herself and her six children until the youngest child should reach twenty-one "or would arrive at that age if living" and the youngest child was fourteen years old at A's death, the entire trust was bad as one which would last a flat period of seven years. If A had directed that the trust should cease at all events upon the death of X and Y, then the trust would have been valid.

A in his will created a separate trust for each of his five children, one-half the principal to be paid as each child reached 25, the other half at 30, but if any child should die before all the trust fund vested, leaving no issue, a new trust was to be created for the other four children. The will was held valid because the proviso was only for the death of one child, hence the trust for the other four children must take effect upon the death of that one child.

10 41 Am Jur, Perpetuities and Restraints on Alienation, §§ 10, 15.

1 19 Am Jur, Estates, §§ 96, 105.

CHAPTER IX

RIGHTS IN ANOTHER'S LAND

§ 32. Acquisition of easements.[2] An easement may be acquired in any of the following ways: (a) By express grant or express reservation. Such an easement may accrue either to A for a term of years or during his lifetime or to A and his heirs, in all which cases it is called an easement in gross, and, by the better view, may be assigned by A or his successors. Or it may accrue to A because of his ownership of the piece of land which is benefited by the easement, in which case it passes to A's transferee of the land and is called an easement appurtenant.

(b) By implied grant or implied reservation. If A, owning tract X separates it into tracts Y and Z and conveys tract Y to B and there were visible water pipes leading from a spring on tract Z and supplying water to the house on tract Y, B is entitled to continue the use of the water pipes to supply water to his house, the law thus implying a grant from A to B of an easement. If A had conveyed to B tract Z instead of tract Y, the law would have implied a reservation to A of a similar easement. In order that the above reasoning shall apply the user—whether of water pipes or alleyway or ditch—must be open, notorious and permanent and of such value to the tract conveyed or retained that a reasonable man would regard it as necessary to the full enjoyment of such tract.

If tract Z had been on the highway and tract Y had been remote from the highway with no outlet to it, and A had conveyed tract Y to B, the latter would have a way of necessity over tract Z by way of implied grant; and if A had conveyed to B tract Z instead of track Y, A would have a way of necessity over tract Z by way of implied reservation.

(c) By building a party wall. If A and B own adjoining lots and each erects a building on his lot with a single wall between the buildings, such a wall is called a party wall and in this country A and B are each held to own the half of the wall that is on his lot and to have over the other half of the wall an easement of support. If A had originally owned both lots and erected both buildings with the party wall between and had then conveyed

[2] 17 **Am Jur**, Easements, §§ 18–85.

Right of railroad company to use or grant use of land in right of way for other than railroad purpose. 94 **ALR** 522–536; s. in 149 **ALR** 378–382.

Implied easement upon severance of tract where building is near or encoaches upon the dividing line. 9 **ALR** 488–496; s. in 41 **ALR** 1210–1211; 53 **ALR** 910.

Roadway or pathway used at time of severance of tract as visible easement. 34 **ALR** 233–249; s. in 100 **ALR** 1321–1332.

Easements: way by necessity where property is accessible by navigable water. 38 **ALR** 1310–1312.

Physical conditions which will charge purchaser of servient estate with notice of easement. 41 **ALR** 1442–1452; s. in 74 **ALR** 1250–1252.

Rule of visible easements as applied to easement of light or air. 56 **ALR** 1138–1149.

Implied easement in respect of drains, pipes, or sewers upon severance of tract. 58 **ALR** 824–842.

Right of abutting owner to permanent use of subsurface of street or highway. 7 **ALR** 646–653.

Locating easement of way of necessity. 68 **ALR** 528–538.

Private easement in way vacated, abandoned, or closed by public. 150 **ALR** 644–668.

Character of easement in respect of water as one in gross or appurtenant. 89 **ALR** 1187–1197.

Easement of view from public street. 90 **ALR** 793–805.

Deed to railroad company as conveying fee or easement. 132 **ALR** 142–187.

Express easements of light, air, and view. 142 **ALR** 467–485.

Acquisition by user or prescription of right of way over uninclosed land. 1 **ALR** 1368–1374.

What amounts to use of party wall which will impose obligation to contribute to cost thereof. 113 **ALR** 471–487.

one of the lots to B, the latter would have an easement by implied grant, and A would have an easement by implied reservation.

(d) By adverse user. If A for the period of the statute of limitations makes a tortious use of B's land, for example, by flooding it with water or by driving across it and such user has been open, continuous and adverse —that is, under claim of right—A acquires at the end of the period a right to continue such user indefinitely. Mere verbal protests by B are not sufficient to break the continuity; in order to accomplish that result B must either bring about a physical interruption through self-help or get an injunction in equity or recover a judgment at law for damages.

(e) By a license acted upon by the licensee. In some states if A grants to B a license to use A's land— for example, to build a wall on it—and B in reliance thereon expends money, equity will prevent A from revoking the license and thus will create in B an easement.

§ 33. Division and extinction of easements.[3] If A has over the land of B an easement which is appurtenant to a tract of land owned by himself, and A divides this tract into several lots and sells the lots, each lot owner is entitled to the benefit of the easement.

An easement may be lost by abandonment. If A, having an easement over B's land, such as a right of way, and ceases to use it for a considerable period of time, such cesser is evidence of abandonment which is likely to be held conclusive where it is for a very long period or where it has been so acted upon by B or by third parties that it works an estoppel against A.

A way of necessity comes to an end when the necessity ceases; for example, where the one entitled to the way acquires another access to the highway.

§ 34. Profits a prendre.[4] A profit a prendre is a right to take something from the land of another, such as minerals, grass, wood, turf, ice, etc. A right to take water is an easement since water is not the subject of absolute ownership.

Like an easement, a profit is usually appurtenant to other land, the benefit passing to successive transferees of such land; but it may be created by express grant or express reservation, in which case it may be in gross, for years, for life or in fee.

Where the dominant land is divided and transferred to several different owners, it would seem to be the better view that the benefit of the profit

Right of owner of title to or interest in minerals in place under one tract to use the passages therein for transporting minerals taken from another tract. 15 **ALR** 957–962.

Right of owner of title to or interest in minerals under one tract to use of surface in connection with mining other tract. 48 **ALR** 1406–1420.

Right of railroad company in respect of material or mineral within right of way. 21 **ALR** 1131–1145.

Right to maintain gates or bars across right of way. 73 **ALR** 778–792.

Locating easement of way created by a grant which does not definitely describe its location. 110 **ALR** 174–182.

Acquisition of right of way by prescription as affected by change of location or deviation during prescriptive period. 143 **ALR** 1402–1417.

38 **Harv. L. R.** 180, Exception and Reservation of Easements.

42 **Col. L. R.** 809, An Analysis of Licenses in Land.

30 **Calif. L. R.** 125, Easement novelties.

14 **St. John's L. R.** 1, New York Law on Encroachments and Obstructions upon Streets and Highways.

[3] 17 **Am Jur**, Easements, §§ 134–148.

Assignability and divisibility of easement in gross or license in respect of land or water. 130 **ALR** 1253–1269.

Loss of easement by adverse possession, or nonuser. 1 **ALR** 884–892; s. in 66 **ALR** 1099–1109; 98 **ALR** 1291–1296.

Right of owners of parcels into which dominant tenement has been divided, to use a right of way. 8 **ALR** 1368–1370; s. in 34 **ALR** 972–973.

[4] 17 **Am Jur**, Easements, § 6.

passes to the several transferees provided that the total burden on the servient land is not increased.

Where A had a profit in gross to take away all the iron ore from B's land and A died, it was held that C, who was assignee of only ninety-four ninety-ninths of the rights of A's representatives was not entitled to exercise the profit because it was indivisible.

§ 35. Covenants running with the land.[5] If B owns a tract of land over which there is an easement in favor of a tract of land owned by A, any agreement between the parties at the time of the creation of the easement or later, defining the nature and extent of the user, runs with the land because the easement itself runs with the land, it being enforcible by the subsequent transferees of the covenantee against the subsequent transferees of the covenantor. Where the easement involved is the right to use a party wall and the covenant is to pay part of the cost of the wall if the covenantor should later use it, such a covenant runs with the land till breach; after breach the covenantee has merely a right of action to compel the payment of money; this is a part of his personal estate and does not pass to a transferee of the land.

If A leases to B and either one makes a covenant fixing the terms of the tenancy the benefit of such a covenant may be enforced by successive transferees of the covenantee against successive transferees of the covenantor. The most common covenants running with the land against transferees of the lessee are covenants to pay rent, to repair, to insure, to rebuild, not to use the premises in a certain way and not to assign the lease. Those running with the land against the lessor's transferees are covenants to repair, to rebuild and to renew the lease. If the covenant is purely personal, not fixing the terms of the tenancy, for example. a covenant to pay a sum of money annually to X, it does not run with the land, and if there is a breach and the covenantee is dead, it is enforcible by his personal representatives just as any other cause of action arising out of contract.

If A conveys the fee of a tract of land to B and as a part of the conveyance A covenants to do or not to do something on land retained by him which will benefit the land conveyed or B covenants to do or not to do something on the tract conveyed which will benefit land retained by A, both the benefit and the burden of such covenants run with the land, benefiting and binding successive transferees of the lands involved. In England, however, covenants will apparently not run against a transferee except in case of landlord and tenant.

CHAPTER X

CONVEYANCES

§ 36. Forms of conveyance.[6] Before the Statute of Uses present freehold estates were usually conveyed by livery of seizin, ordinarily accompanied by a deed of feoffment. Incorporeal interests in land, such as reversions, remainders and easements were conveyed by deeds of grant. Where A is in

[5] 14 **Am Jur,** Covenants, Conditions and Restrictions, §§ 19–33.
37 **Harv. L. R.** 301, Party Wall Agreements as Real Covenants.

[6] 16 **Am Jur,** Deeds, §§ 12–18.
Sufficiency of certificate of acknowledgment. 29 **ALR** 919–1028; s. in 72 **ALR** 1290–1303.
16 **U. of Cin. L. R.** 219, History and Development of the Modern Real Estate Deed.

possession having an estate for years or for life, B, the owner of the fee in remainder or reversion, may convey to A by a deed of release, which could also be used to extinguish an easement belonging to the releasor.

After the Statute of Uses, passed in 1535, livery of seizin gradually fell into disuse, being superseded by deeds of bargain and sale the validity of which depended upon containing a recital of consideration, and by covenants to stand seized which were valid if the covenantor and covenantee were related either by blood or marriage. The Statute of Enrolments passed in 1536 required that bargain and sale deeds of freehold interests be enrolled; in order to evade this statute, conveyancers resorted to a bargain and sale of a lease for one year with a release to the bargainee of the reversion. Since the Statute of Enrolments did not become a part of the law in this country conveyances by lease and release have been rarely used here.

In most states today there are statutes providing for short forms of deeds with simple words of transfer like the common-law deed of grant. These may be used, instead of the bargain and sale or covenant to stand seized, to convey any interest in land.

§ 37. Covenants in deeds.[7] The release and the modern quitclaim deed, which is quite similar to it, are mere conveyances; they purport merely to convey only what the transferor may happen to have and contain no element of contract. But the usual modern warranty deed is not merely a conveyance but also binds the transferor by contract. Since deeds were formerly under seal the promises made by the transferor are called covenants. A warranty deed may contain the following six covenants: (1) of seizin, (2) of right to convey, (3) against incumbrances, (4) of quiet enjoyment, (5) for further assurances, and (6) of warranty. The covenant for further assurances is not broken until it is found necessary to execute some further instrument in order to perfect the grantee's title. The covenant of quiet enjoyment and that of warranty are not broken until the grantee or some later transferee is evicted by paramount title. Since they are not broken at once they run with the land into the hands of the successors of title of the covenantee.

The first three covenants, of seizin, of right to convey and against incumbrances are broken, if at all, as soon as made, giving an immediate right of action to the covenantee which was purely personal and which therefore did not run with the land. But since substantial damages cannot be recovered until actual ouster which may not happen till after the covenantee in turn transfers the property, the better view today is that those covenants also run with the land.

§ 38. Rules of construction.[8] In construing the description of the land

[7] 14 **Am Jur,** Covenants, Conditions and Restrictions, §§ 48–114.

Easement as breach of covenant against encumbrances. 64 **ALR** 1479–1507.

Sufficiency of notice or knowledge of pendency of action against covenantee or his privy in order to bind the covenantor by judgment. 34 **ALR** 1429–1444.

Division of the premises by the lessor, or the creation of undivided interests therein, as affecting the enforcement of the lessee's covenants. 12 **ALR** 826–833.

Encumbrance undischarged and unenforced as affecting rights and damages under a covenant against encumbrances. 44 **ALR** 410–425.

Unpaid public improvement as constituting breach of covenant or a defect in the vendor's title. 72 **ALR** 302–323.

Nature of conveyance or covenants which will create estoppel to assert after-acquired title or interest in real property. 58 **ALR** 345–430; s. in 144 **ALR** 554–585.

[8] 14 **Am Jur,** Covenants, Conditions, and Restrictions, §§ 7, 8.

Test of conveyance as quitclaim or otherwise. 3 **ALR** 945–955.

Sufficiency and construction of description in deed or mortgage as "all" of grantor's property, or "all" of his property in certain locality. 55 **ALR** 162–171.

conveyed in a deed the intent of the parties governs in all cases. But where the description is by metes and bounds and there is an inconsistency between the monuments on the one hand and the courses and distances on the other, the boundaries indicated by the monuments usually prevail because of the greater liklihood of error in the courses and distances. But where it appears that there was a mistake made in stating the monuments and that the courses and distances represent the real intent of the parties the courses and distances prevail. Where the description refers to monuments to be erected and they are later erected and acquiesced in by the parties they will prevail over courses and distances.

In most cities today ownership of the streets is in the city, hence conveyances of city land are construed to exclude the street where mentioned as a monument.

In country districts the owner of land bordering on a highway owns usually to the middle of the highway. In conveyances of such land where the highway is mentioned as a monument, as in the phrases "from" or "to the highway" and "along the highway," the strong presumption is that the middle and not the side of the road is meant because retention of such a strip is of no value to the grantor. Such a presumption yields, of course, to clear language showing that the side of the highway was meant.

Character as condition, limitation, covenant, or trust of provision in deed as to purpose for which property is to be used, as affected by introduction with word "provided" or its derivatives. 135 **ALR** 1135–1141.

What are "minerals" within deed, lease, or license. 17 **ALR** 156–168; s. in 86 **ALR** 983–990.

Effect on validity and character of instrument in form of deed, of provisions therein indicating an intention to postpone or limit the rights of grantee until after the death of grantor. 11 **ALR** 25–106; s. in 76 **ALR** 636–653.

Legal significance and effect of phrase "more or less" in a deed of real property. 70 **ALR** 368–381.

Conflict between granting and habendum clauses as to estate conveyed. 84 **ALR** 1054–1078; s. in 111 **ALR** 1078–1086; 131 **ALR** 1239–1246.

Validity and effect of deed which purports to convey specified acreage or quantity of land out of a larger tract, with or without a right of selection expressed. 117 **ALR** 1071–1091.

Validity and effect of reservation in deed of the right to proceeds, or part of the proceeds, of a future sale or condemnation of the property or part thereof. 123 **ALR** 1474–1481.

Validity and effect of deed executed in blank as to name of grantee. 32 **ALR** 737–746; s. in 75 **ALR** 1108–1110.

Effect of omission of words of inheritance from a reservation, exception, or provision for forfeiture in a deed. 34 **ALR** 695–703.

Sheriff's deed as making a prima facie case for one seeking to recover land thereunder. 36 **ALR** 986–1012; s. in 108 **ALR** 667–674.

Rights or interests covered by quitclaim deed. 44 **ALR** 1266–1280.

Effect of unauthorized delivery or fraudulent procurement of escrow on title or interest in property. 48 **ALR** 405–431; s. in 54 **ALR** 1246.

Validity and effect of deed to "heirs" of living person. 22 **ALR** 713–720.

Provision in deed attempting to make reservation or exception in favor of grantor's spouse. 129 **ALR** 310–316.

Deed as conveying fee or easement. 136 **ALR** 379–413.

Statement as to use being made or intended to be made of lands excepted or reserved from conveyance as limiting effect of exception or reservation. 139 **ALR** 1339–1366.

Description with reference to highway as carrying title to center or side of highway. 2 **ALR** 6–36; s. in 47 **ALR** 1276–1281; 123 **ALR** 542–555.

Rule that particular description in deed prevails over general description. 72 **ALR** 410–425.

Which of conflicting descriptions in deeds or mortgages of the extent of the interest conveyed prevails. 115 **ALR** 192–202.

Description of land in deed or mortgage by reference to map, plat, plan, sketch, or diagram as prevailing over description by words. 130 **ALR** 643–657.

Inconsistency between description of land in instrument conveying same or affecting title thereto and description in another instrument referred to therein. 134 **ALR** 1041–1059.

Validity and effect of deed which identifies tract conveyed only by reference to its area and a specified corner or other point of a larger tract from which it is to be taken. 139 **ALR** 1180–1188.

Remedy in case of mistake or fraud respecting actual application on the ground of a correct description in a deed or other instrument. 149 **ALR** 749–755.

Presumption that description by reference to highway carries fee to center thereof, as affected by presence of water system or other apparatus under highway. 147 **ALR** 667–668.

A similar treatment is applied to land bordering on a non-navigable stream where the owner usually owns to the thread of the stream. On the other hand land bounded by public or navigable streams or lakes is treated like land bounded by city streets, the owner owning only to the edge.

§ 39. Delivery—delivery in escrow.[9] In most states today a deed of conveyance must be signed by the grantor but this requirement is satisfied by the grantor making his mark or by another person signing his name in his presence with his assent. Seals are usually not required.

Delivery is necessary before the deed takes effect. This is usually accomplished by the grantor placing the deed in the hands of the grantee or his authorized agent, with intent to deliver. A ceremonial delivery is also effective, the grantor in the presence of witnesses holding the deed in his hand and saying, "I hereby deliver this deed." It is usually held that leaving the deed to be recorded in the registry of deeds raises a presumption of delivery which may, of course, be rebutted.

If A executes a deed of conveyance to B and delivers it to C who in turn is to deliver it to B upon the happening of some event such as the death of A, or the performance of some act by B such as the payment of purchase money, the delivery by A to C is called a delivery in escrow; if, upon the happening of the event or the performance of the act, C delivers the deed to B the delivery in legal effect relates back to the time when the delivery in escrow was made to C; such relation back is, of course, absolutely necessary where the deed was not to be delivered by C to B till after A's death. The escrow doctrine does not apply if A reserves any control over the deed after delivery to C. By the better view, apart from the recording acts, the rights of B are not cut off by a later transfer by A to X even though X bought innocently and for value, B's right being regarded as legal, not merely equitable; if the recording acts are held to apply to the conveyance by A to C and the deed is not recorded then X would of course be protected.

Where C delivers the deed to B without the performance of the conditions, the better view is that no title passes and that a purchaser from B is not protected.

§ 40. Recording acts.[10] Apart from the modern recording statutes if A

[9] 16 **Am Jur**, Deeds, §§ 108–259.
19 **Am Jur**, Escrow, §§ 1–30.
Delivery of deed to third person to be delivered to grantee after grantor's death. 52 **ALR** 1222–1251.
Relation back of title or interest embraced in escrow instrument upon final delivery or performance of condition. 117 **ALR** 69–90.
Delivery of a deed without manual transfer or record. 129 **ALR** 11–54.
Delivery of deed as conditioned on obtaining signature of another as grantor. 140 **ALR** 265–272.
Death, or extinction of corporate existence, of grantee, or one of the grantees, prior to execution of deed. 148 **ALR** 252–260.

[10] 45 **Am Jur**, Records and Recording Laws, §§ 35–173.
Priority as between judgment lien and unrecorded mortgage. 4 **ALR** 434–455.
Record of executory contracts for the sale of real estate. 26 **ALR** 1546–1554.
Priority where senior instrument affecting real property is recorded after execution but before recording of junior instrument. 32 **ALR** 344–353.
Failure properly to index conveyance or mortgage of realty as affecting constructive notice. 63 **ALR** 1057–1066.
Right of one claiming through heir, devisee, or personal representative to protection against unrecorded conveyance or mortgage by ancestor or testator. 65 **ALR** 360–374.
Record of deed to cotenant as notice to other cotenants of adverse character of grantee's possession. 121 **ALR** 1411–1421.
Right of abstracter or insurer of title to inspect or make copies of public records. 80 **ALR** 760–784.
Right of vendee to record title where vendor covenants to furnish abstract showing title. 7 **ALR** 1166–1180.
Neglect or fault of recording or filing officer as affecting consequences of failure properly to record or file instrument affecting property. 70 **ALR** 595–608.

conveys a piece of land to B and later purports to convey the same piece of land to C, the latter gets no title whatever even though he in good faith paid value for the purported conveyance. He stands in the same position as an innocent purchaser from a thief or bailee or any one else who has no title.

The purpose of the recording acts is to require a public record of conveyances so that if B fails to record his conveyance from A according to the recording statute, C's deed will be upheld and B will lose the legal title which he received upon delivery of the deed to him, even though C's deed is not recorded, though the failure of C to record his deed may cause him to lose his title to D if A should later convey to D. The statute usually applies not only to conveyances made by way of sale or gift but also to mortgages and sometimes to transfers of equitable interests in land and to written contracts to convey land. Where the statute does not provide for the recording of a particular instrument, placing it on the record may be effective in conveying actual notice to a prospective buyer or incumbrancer but it does not operate as constructive notice.

Where a legal right arises apart from any instrument, such as title by adverse possession, an easement by adverse user or a way of necessity, the sound doctrine is that the recording acts do not apply and a purchaser takes subject to such rights.

Where a conveyance or mortgage is unrecorded it will be good against purchasers or incumbrancers with notice and every one elso except bona fide purchasers for value without notice; possession under an unrecorded instrument is usually held to operate as constructive notice. In some states innocent judgment creditors as well as bona fide purchasers for value are protected against unrecorded instruments.

In order that the record of an instrument shall be constructive notice it must be in the chain of title so that it may be easily found by consulting the index of grantors or of grantees. If A conveys to B and B does not record the conveyance but conveys to C who does record his conveyance, such record is not constructive notice because it is not in the chain of title. What C should have done was to insist upon B's recording his own conveyance and thus furnish the missing link in the chain.

If A, not owning a tract of land, purports to sell and convey it to B and B records the deed such record is not constructive notice because not in the chain of title. So if A should later acquire title from X and then sell and convey it to C who pays value in good faith, C will be protected against B. What B should have done was to compel A, as soon as he obtained title from X, to make to him a new deed to the tract and have it recorded; such new deed, being in the chain of title from X to B would protect B.

By the better view the mere fact that the second deed is a quitclaim deed does not take away from such a grantee the protection of the recording act.

Since a later transferee is bound by the contents of a recorded deed, he is bound by an easement or equitable servitude stipulated for in such deed.

Right of one otherwise protected by recording law against prior unrecorded deed or mortgage as affected by fact that all or part of the consideration was unpaid at the time he received notice, actual or constructive, of the prior instrument. 109 **ALR** 163–175.

Recording laws as applied to power of attorney under which deed or mortgage is executed. 114 **ALR** 660–671.

Improper insertion or omission of middle initial of one's name as affecting constructive notice from public record. 122 **ALR** 909–919.

CHAPTER XI

ADVERSE POSSESSION

§ 41. In general—constructive possession.[1] If A enters upon the land of B, openly claiming it as his own and occupies it exclusively and continuously for the statutory period—usually twenty years—title passes to him at the end of that period. By the better view it is of no importance whether A did or did not think that the land was his own, but in some states if A intended to occupy only what he thought was his own, his possession is regarded as not being adverse and hence he does not acquire title. If A claimed only a life estate instead of a fee he gets only the life estate which he claimed; but where B claimed a remainder in fee under the same purported will of X, it was held that A's acquisition of title enured to the benefit of B.

It is not necessary that A's possession be under color of title; but if he does claim under color of title, he will get title to the whole tract thus claimed even though he actually occupies only a part of it. This is called the doctrine of constructive adverse possession; it is not applied where the tract covered by the invalid instrument is so extensive as to be totally out of proportion to the tract actually occupied.

§ 42. Tacking—disabilities.[2] If A, having been in adverse possession of B's land, should transfer his interest to X orally or by deed or should die and X enters into possession as A's transferee inter vivos or heir or devisee, X is entitled to tack A's adverse possession to his own so that if A had been in possession for eight years X need occupy only twelve years more in order to acquire title.

If at the time that A's adverse possession of B's land began B was an infant or insane the various statutes of limitation usually provide that B shall have a certain period after the removal of the disability within which to bring his action and this may operate to extend the usual statutory period. But the provision usually does not include subsequent disabilities; thus if B should later become insane or should later die leaving X his infant heir, B's

[1] 1 **Am Jur,** Adverse Possession, §§ 126–222.

Rights as between adverse claimants to improvements placed on public lands. 6 **ALR** 95–108.

Right to crops sown or grown by one wrongfully in possession of land. 39 **ALR** 958–971.

Acquisition of title to mines or minerals by adverse possession. 13 **ALR** 372–383; s. in 67 **ALR** 1440–1446; 93 **ALR** 1232–1239.

Adverse possession based on projection or inclination of wall or other structure. 49 **ALR** 1015–1025.

May adverse possession be predicated upon use or occupancy by one spouse of real property of other. 74 **ALR** 138–148.

Adverse possession due to ignorance or mistake as to boundaries. 97 **ALR** 14–114.

Grantor's continued possession of land after execution of deed as notice of his claim adverse to title conveyed. 105 **ALR** 845–880.

Adverse possession as against remainderman during life estate as affected by fact that conveyance by life tenant purported to cover fee. 112 **ALR** 1042–1051.

Purchase of, or offer to purchase or to settle, outstanding title, interest, or claim as interrupting continuity of adverse possession as regards another title, interest, or claim. 125 **ALR** 825–838.

Property rights in respect of building, fence, or other structure placed upon another's land through mistake as to boundary or location. 130 **ALR** 1034–1053.

Sufficiency of compliance, as regards payment of taxes, with limitation statute requiring payment of taxes as a condition of adverse possession. 132 **ALR** 216–251.

Writing as essential to color of title in adverse occupant of land. 2 **ALR** 1457–1467.

Scope and application of the doctrine that one cannot successfully claim adverse possession under color of title where he has deprived himself or been deprived of the color relied on. 136 **ALR** 1349–1354.

32 **Harv. L. R.** 135, Title by Adverse Possession.

[2] 1 **Am Jur,** Adverse Possession, §§ 19, 151–158.

Right of grantee to tack adverse possession by his predecessor of parcel beyond that called for by deed under which he claims. 46 **ALR** 792–799.

later insanity or X's infancy will have no effect upon the running of the statutory period.

CHAPTER XII

FIXTURES—MISCELLANEOUS

A. Fixtures

§ 43. The annexation.[3] Whether a chattel which is brought onto land becomes a fixture thereon so as to become a part of the land depends upon the intent of the person who places the chattel there. The question may come up in a variety of ways; for example, as between the vendor of land and his vendee; or between the heir and executor of a deceased owner in fee; or between a tenant for years or the executor of a tenant for life and the remainderman. The test is not the secret intent but the intent as would be understood by a reasonable man who is acquainted with the facts.

In determining that reasonable intent there are two main factors—the character of the annexation of the chattel and the character of the chattel itself. If the chattel is physically so attached to a building on the land that its removal would cause serious damage to the building—for example, cold storage rooms put in by a tenant—this is strong but not necessarily conclusive evidence that the chattel was meant to be a fixture; and if the chattel is held to be a fixture then removable parts of it—such as the rolls of an iron rolling mill—become fixtures also. Physical attachment, however, is not necessary; stone fences and other heavy articles such as a statue or sun dial, held in place by gravity alone, have frequently been held to be fixtures.

§ 44. The character of the chattel.[4] If the chattel is so adapted to the use to which the land is put as to make it reasonably necessary to the full enjoyment of the land, this is cogent evidence that it was meant to be a fixture; for example, salt pans used in salt works, hop poles on a farm where hops are raised, a portable grist mill put into a building for the purpose of the occupant's business of grinding grain, farm buildings erected for use on a farm, mirror frames to be set into a building, and doors, sash and trim made to order for a house but not yet attached. Gas and electric light fixtures should be ordinarily regarded as fixtures but the fact that they are substituted for wood and coal stoves and for kerosene lamps and candles which are clearly chattels has tended to influence courts against holding them to be part of the land. Even if the chattels brought on the land are of such a nature as ordinarily to become fixtures, the parties may bind themselves to treat them as chattels and thus permit their removal.

§ 45. Rights of chattel mortgagee or conditional vendor.[5] Where A sells to B a chattel—such as an engine or boiler or power plant or other machinery—expecting it to be annexed to the land, B, a lessee giving a chattel mortgage to A, or A, retaining the title as security for the unpaid purchase

[3] 22 **Am Jur**, Fixtures, §§ 3-10.

Electric fan as fixture. 62 **ALR** 251-256.

Buildings erected by a tenant as "trade fixtures." 107 **ALR** 1153-1165.

Nursery stock attached to the soil as real or personal property, and resulting rights. 125 **ALR** 1406-1417.

[4] 22 **Am Jur**, Fixtures, §§ 49-72.

29 **Calif. L. R.** 21, Classification of Fixtures for Assessment.

[5] 22 **Am Jur**, Fixtures, §§ 32-48.

Right of seller of fixtures retaining title thereto, or lien thereon, as against purchasers or encumbrancers of the realty. 13 **ALR** 448-485; s. in 73 **ALR** 748-775; 88 **ALR** 1318-1348; 111 **ALR** 362-388; 141 **ALR** 1283-1297.

price, A's rights are usually held to be superior to those of a prior mortgagee of the land but subject to those of a subsequent mortgagee of the land, unless the subsequent mortgagee definitely recognizes A's rights.

The proper way to handle this situation is for the recording statute to require that such chattel mortgages and conditional sales be recorded in the record of real-estate mortgages.

§ 46. **Removal.**[6] If a chattel becomes a fixture, there is apparently no right to remove it—apart from express stipulation—except by an owner in fee in possession. But if the chattel does not become a fixture it may be removed. In case it belongs to the tenant for life his executor has a reasonable time after the tenant's death to remove it. But if it belongs to a tenant for years, he must remove it before the end of his term unless the landlord expressly permits him to leave it. Where the tenant has such right to remove he does not forfeit it merely by holding over; and, by the better view, he does not forfeit it by accepting a new lease but the weight of authority is probably contra.

B. Miscellaneous

§ 47. **Trees, perennial and annual crops, manure.**[7] If a tree is growing with its trunk on the land of A but with its branches overhanging the land of B, the latter is not entitled to the branches or to the fruit growing thereon, but he may disencumber his land of both branches and roots. If the tree is growing on the line the parties are tenants in common and if either party cuts it the other may sue him in trespass.

If A contracts to sell to B trees growing on his land the contract, to be enforcible, must ordinarily comply with the fourth section of the statute of frauds because the trees are a part of the land. But if the contract was to sell to B the cordwood to be made from the trees the contract need only comply with the seventeenth section of the statute of frauds because the substance of the contract is that he is buying chattels.

Perennial crops such as timothy or alfalfa are, like growing trees, a part of the land and do not, upon the death of the owner, go to the executor but to the heir or devisee. Annual crops are such as are produced by annual cultivation and industry of the land occupier, for example, corn, wheat, rye, peaches, nursery trees and hops. A contract to sell such crops, even while growing, need only comply with the seventeenth section of the statute of frauds because they are regarded as chattels even before they are harvested, and upon the death of the owner they pass to his executor. Such crops, however, pass to a grantee or mortgagee of the land unless expressly reserved.

Where manure is produced on a farm in the usual course of husbandry, it is considered to be a part of the land; it goes to the heir and not to the executor and a tenant may not remove it at the expiration of his lease. But where the manure has been produced from feed brought onto the land it is regarded as personal property and the above rules do not apply.

6 22 Am Jur, Fixtures, §§ 13, 14.

7 1 Am Jur, Adjoining Landowners, §§ 55–58.
15 Am Jur, Crops, §§ 3–21.
42 Am Jur, Property, § 31.

§ 48. Emblements—accretions and avulsions.[8] If A has an estate for life in land and dies, his executor is entitled to emblements, that is, to the crops growing on the land at the time of A's death. The reason for this rule is to encourage tenants with estates of uncertain duration to use the land beneficially. The same reasoning applies if A had been a tenant for the life of X and X dies; or if A had been a tenant at will or from year to year and the landlord put an end to the tenancy, but not where the tenant terminated it.

A tenant for years it not entitled to emblements but in some states there is a custom allowing a tenant whose tenancy ends in March, to harvest in July the crop of winter wheat or rye which he sowed the previous fall.

Where the waters of the sea or of a lake or of a navigable river gradually recede the new land thus uncovered belongs to the owner of the riparian land. Where land is submerged by water the owner does not lose it; he may erect bulkheads and fill in and thus reclaim it.

[8] 15 **Am Jur**, Crops, §§ 24–27.
See also **Am Jur**, Waters.
Rights, as between landlord and tenant, in respect of crops unharvested at expiration of tenancy (doctrine of emblements). 141 **ALR** 1240–1257.
Rights in respect of crops as between estate of life tenant and remaindermen. 125 **ALR** 280–289.

WILLS, INTESTACY AND ADMINISTRATION

CHAPTER I

WILLS DISTINGUISHED FROM OTHER DISPOSITIONS OF PROPERTY

§ 1. From deeds.[1] A deed requires delivery but need not be attested; a will must be attested but does not require delivery. If an instrument has been attested and has also been delivered the question as to whether it should be treated as a will or deed usually turns upon the intent of the party executing it; and where the instrument on its face is of doubtful character, extrinsic evidence of intent is admissible.

The mere fact that the instrument has been delivered to a third party in escrow to be delivered to the beneficiary upon the death of the party executing it does not make it a will; nor does the reservation of the power to revoke. But if the instrument purports to pass all the property which the maker may have at the time of his death, it will practically always be construed to be a will.

§ 2. From so-called living trusts—joint bank accounts.[2] If property is conveyed by A to X upon trust to pay the income to A for life and then to certain named beneficiaries, the conveyance is valid without attestation even though A reserves the power of revocation or the power to change the beneficiaries; but if the entire beneficial interest remains in A till his death, it is in substance a will and to be valid must be attested as such.

In most jurisdictions the necessity of a will of money may be avoided by a joint bank account payable to the survivor. And in a few jurisdictions A may accomplish a similar result by making a deposit in a savings bank for himself in trust for B, retaining entire control of the deposit during his lifetime.

§ 3. From gifts causa mortis.[3] Where A, in apprehension of impending death, makes a gift causa mortis to B, that is, delivers personalty to B to take effect as a gift to B if A should not recover, the transaction is like a will in that the gift is revocable by A and if it is not revoked, B takes subject to debts just as does a legatee; also, title apparently does not pass till A's death. It differs from a will in that it is a present transaction, delivery being necessary as in case of gifts inter vivos; also a writing is not essential whereas a will must ordinarily be written; and, finally, it applies only to personalty, not to realty.

§ 4. From contracts to devise or bequeath.[4] If A contracts to bequeath to B a chattel or money and dies without having done so, B may recover against A's executor or administrator in an action of special assumpsit the

1 57 **Am Jur**, Wills, § 2.
39 **Mich. L. R.** 1288, Conditions and Limitations in Restraint of Marriage.

2 57 **Am Jur**, Wills, § 45.

2 **Mont. L. R.** 19, The Use in Montana of the Trust as a Substitute for a Will.

3 24 **Am Jur**, Gifts, §§ 4-16.

4 24 **Am Jur**, Gifts, § 14.

value of the promised property. If A contracts to devise land to B and dies without having done so, B may recover either in special assumpsit against A's personal representative or he may maintain a bill in equity against A's heir or devisee of the land to have a constructive trust declared. And if there is danger during A's lifetime that A may convey the land to a bona fide purchaser for value without notice, B may maintain a bill quia timet against A and get a decree entitling him to the land upon A's death; this will operate as lis pendens and prevent any purchaser from A from claiming the rights of a bona fide purchaser for value without notice.

Such contracts are similar to wills in that B becomes entitled to get the property only upon A's death; they are different from wills in that no attestation is required. A contract to bequeath may be oral but a contract to devise requires a memorandum to satisfy the statute of frauds.

CHAPTER II

TESTAMENTARY CAPACITY

§ 5. **Infancy, conviction of crime.**[5] Most states have fixed by statute the age at which one may make a will; the age most commonly fixed is twenty-one but in some states the age fixed is lower. In some the age required for males is greater than that required for females; and in some the age required for devising real estate is greater than that required for bequeathing personalty. Where there is no statute the English law at the time of the separation of this country from England is usually followed, namely, twenty-one years for devises, fourteen and twelve respectively for males and females where personalty is bequeathed.

Apart from a specific statutory provision making civilly dead a criminal sentenced to life imprisonment, conviction for crime does not affect capacity to make a will.

§ 6. **Mental capacity.**[6] In order that one shall possess sufficient mental capacity to make a will it is necessary that he should be able to understand the nature of a will, that he should remember generally the nature and extent of his property and the persons who are the natural objects of his bounty and that he should be able to conceive an intelligent scheme of disposition of his estate. The mere fact that the testator was a member of an unusual religious sect and left much of his property to promote its interests does not render his will void. Nor does even an insane delusion where such delusion did not affect the terms of the will. But an insane delusion that does affect the terms of the will is sufficient to render it void; for example, a groundless belief in a wife's infidelity or groundless hatred of a child. Physical weakness, moral depravity, illness and old age do not necessarily disqualify a testator but they may tend to show, along with other evidence, that the proper testamen-

[5] 57 **Am Jur**, Wills, §§ 55–57.

[6] 57 **Am Jur**, Wills, §§ 63–87.

Admissibility of evidence other than testimony of subscribing witnesses to prove due execution of will, or testamentary capacity. 63 **ALR** 1195–1215.

Testamentary capacity as affected by use of intoxicating liquor or drugs. 67 **ALR** 857–875.

Necessity of affirmative evidence of testamentary capacity to make prima facie case in will contest. 110 **ALR** 675–700.

Relative weight of testimony of attesting witnesses in support of mental competency of testator. 123 **ALR** 88–99.

Illustrations of instructions or requested instructions as to effect of unnaturalness or unreasonableness of provisions of will on question of testamentary capacity or undue influence. 137 **ALR** 989–1003.

Duty of attesting witness with respect to testator's capacity. 35 **ALR** 79–86.

tary capacity was lacking. It is not objectionable that the will is, in the mind of the court and most persons, unjust and unreasonable.

The burden of establishing sanity is upon the proponent of the will, but he is helped out by the presumption of sanity which makes it unnecessary to introduce evidence of sanity until it is put in issue by the contestant.

CHAPTER III

FRAUD AND UNDUE INFLUENCE

§ 7. **Fraud in the execution and in the inducement.**[7] If a testator is deceived by X as to the character or the contents of the instrument that he is signing—for example, where he thought he was signing a burial permit or where he thought the terms were the same as his first will—the will is void and should be denied probate. This is usually referred to as fraud in the execution.

If the testator knew what he was signing but was induced to sign by the fraudulent representations of X and the fraud affects the entire will, the will should be denied probate; but if it affects only a devise or bequest to X, only that part should be denied probate; for example, a bequest "to my wife X" who the testator had been fraudulently induced by X to believe was his wife. Where X by fraud persuaded the testator to leave a bequest to X instead of to A, the remedy of A is to have X declared a constructive trustee of the property thus obtained.

§ 8. **Undue influence.**[8] Where X so influenced the testator that in substance the testator was coerced into making the will—that is, it was the will of X rather than that of the testator—the will should be denied probate on the ground of undue influence. Though this is a frequent basis for contest, comparatively few wills are denied probate on this ground. Threats of force upon or of criminal prosecution of the testator or some one nearly related to him may constitute undue influence. That the property was unfairly distributed, that little or nothing was left to the testator's children, that the person who drew the will was the testator's confidential adviser, and that the will was different from the previously expressed oral purpose of the testator, are each merely evidential and not in themselves enough to show undue influence. That one portion of the will was brought about by such influence does not invalidate the entire will.

CHAPTER IV

MISTAKE

§ 9. **Mistake in the execution—omissions.**[9] Where the testator was mistaken as to the nature of the instrument, the will should be denied probate; for example, where mutual wills or codicils are prepared for A and B, and each one by mistake signs the one prepared for the other there is a mistake in the execution and both documents fail.

If through mistake of the draftsman a devise or legacy to X is omitted

[7] 57 **Am Jur,** Wills, §§ 358-364.

[8] 57 **Am Jur,** Wills, §§ 339-357.

Fraud as distinguished from undue influence as ground for contesting will. 28 **ALR** 787-797; s. in 92 **ALR** 790-794.

Presumption and burden of proof as to undue influence on testator. 66 **ALR** 228-263.

Form and particularity of allegations to raise issue of undue influence. 107 **ALR** 832-841.

[9] 57 **Am Jur,** Wills, §§ 365-370.

from the will this does not affect the validity of the will but X has no remedy; probate of the omitted legacy is denied because as to that part there has not been compliance with the statutory requirements; and, largely for historical reasons, equity courts have refused to reform the will no matter how clear the evidence of the mistake.

§ 10. Mistake in description—striking out words.[10] Where there has been a mistake in describing the property or the beneficiary and the court can, by striking out some of the words of the will, give effect to the intent of the testator, such words will be rejected. For example, where the will read "lot 6 in square 403" and the testator did not own that lot but did own lot 3 in square 406, the court rejected the erroneous "6" and "3" and held that there was enough description left to designate the lot which he owned and intended to devise. And where there was a devise to John William Halston, son of Israel Halston and the latter had no son John William but had a son named John Robert, the court disregarded the middle name and held that John Robert should have the devise.

Similar reasoning has been applied where there has been a mistake in enumerating the number of children of X and the amount owed to the testator by Y.

§ 11. Mistake as to legal effect of language used—equivocation.[1] If the testator used the words he intended to use but was mistaken as to their legal effect, no relief will be granted against such a mistake; for example, where the draftsman so used the word "cancel" as to defeat the testator's intent that his children, to some of whom advancements had been made, should share equally.

Where the description is so ambiguous as to amount to an equivocation, the court will give effect to extrinsic evidence of the testator's intent; for example, where a will contained a legacy to "George Gord, the son of John Gord," and another legacy to "George Gord the son of George Gord," and a devise to "George Gord the son of Gord," the court gave effect to the testator's actual intent as gathered from his declarations.

CHAPTER V

EXECUTION OF WILLS

§ 12. Writing—signature of testator.[2] The ordinary will must be in writing; it may be written in ink or with a lead pencil or typewriter; it need not be on paper but must probably be on some substance that is fairly permanent.

It must be signed by the testator either by his writing his name or his initials or a nickname or making a mark with the intent to make it his signature. Usually it is sufficient that his name be signed by another in the testator's presence and at his request.

10 57 **Am Jur**, Wills, §§ 366, 367.
26 **Harv. L. R.** 212, Striking Words out of a Will.

1 57 **Am Jur**, Wills, § 368.
49 **Harv. L. R.** 689, Interpretation of Wills—Recent Developments.
53 **Harv. L. R.** 207, Construction of Gifts to "Heirs" and the Like.

2 57 **Am Jur**, Wills, § 210.
Retrospective application of statute concerning execution of wills. 111 **ALR** 910–921.
Testator's name in body of instrument as sufficient signature where statute does not require will to be signed at end. 29 **ALR** 891–898.
Validity of will written on disconnected sheets. 30 **ALR** 424–429; s. in 71 **ALR** 530–535.
Manner of signing as affecting sufficiency of signature of testator. 31 **ALR** 682–694; s. in 42 **ALR** 954–955; 114 **ALR** 1110–1116.

If the statute merely requires signature, it may be at any place in the will; but some statutes require that the will be subscribed by him, or that his signature shall be at the foot or end, in which case if there is any dispositive portion of the will after the signature, the entire will is void; but words added after the will has been executed will not invalidate it. Some courts require that the signature be written at the physical end so that if a will is written on pages 1, 3 and 2, a signature at the bottom of page 2 is not valid; other courts regard such a signature as valid because signed at the logical end.

§ 13. **Attestation.**[3] It is usual to require that there be either two or three attesting witnesses who would be competent to testify. If one of the witnesses is a beneficiary under the will it is usually expressly provided by statute that such fact does not render such witness incompetent; the will is not invalidated thereby but the witness loses his own devise or legacy, unless he happens also to be an heir, in which case he can take not more than his share would have been if there had been no will. The fact that a witness was also the attorney who drew the will or that he was appointed executor does not invalidate the will.

In most states the testator must either sign in the presence of the attesting witnesses or acknowledge to them that a signature already made is his own; and in some states it is necessary that he tell them that it is his will.

Usually the witnesses must sign the will and some statutes require that the signature shall be at the end of the will. It is common to require that the witnesses sign in the presence of the testator; presence does not require that the testator see them sign but it is usually necessary either that he be very close to them or that he be so situated—whether in the same room or not—that a person in his position who had sight and looked in the proper direction would be able to see them sign.

Usually the testator signs before the witnesses and sometimes this is expressly required by statute; but by the better view, if the testator signs last but all sign as one transaction the requirement is satisfied. In a few states the witnesses must sign in the presence of each other.

§ 14. **Incorporation by reference—reference to acts.**[4] In most states

3 57 **Am Jur,** Wills, §§ 273–297.

Necessity that attesting witnesses to will subscribe in presence of each other. 99 **ALR** 554–564.

Necessity of, and what amounts to, request on part of testator to the witnesses to attest or subscribe will. 125 **ALR** 414–451.

Necessity that attesting witness to will not signed by testator in his presence shall have seen latter's signature on paper. 127 **ALR** 384–406.

Proof, or possibility of proof, of will without testimony of attesting witness as affecting application of statute relating to invalidation of will, or of devise or legacy, where attesting witness is beneficiary under will. 133 **ALR** 1286–1291.

Character as witness of one who signed will for another purpose. 8 **ALR** 1075–1081.

Place of signature of attesting witnesses. 10 **ALR** 429–435.

Effect of purported subscribing witness's denial or forgetfulness of signature by mark. 17 **ALR** 1267–1276.

Competency of husband or wife of beneficiary as attesting witness to will. 25 **ALR** 308–312.

Effect of witness signing will before testator signs. 39 **ALR** 933–937; s. in 57 **ALR** 833–834.

Admissibility and credibility of testimony of subscribing witness tending to impeach execution of will or testamentary capacity of testator. 79 **ALR** 394–504.

4 57 **Am Jur,** Wills, §§ 223–232.

Incorporation of extrinsic writings in will by reference. 144 **ALR** 714–718.

Codicil as effective to prevent lapse of legacy or devise in consequence of death of legatee or devisee after execution of will and before execution of codicil. 146 **ALR** 1366–1373.

Effect of reference in will to conveyance. 110 **ALR** 261–273.

Reference in will to extrinsic trust instrument for terms of trust created or enlarged by will. 80 **ALR** 103–106.

19 **N. Y. U. Law Q.** 270, incorporation by Reference in New York Wills.

where a will refers to another writing as being in existence and such writing is in existence at the time the will is executed and it is clearly identified as the writing referred to, such writing becomes a part of the will if the will shows that such was the testator's intent. The writing may be a will, a codicil, a deed or a mere memorandum. The reference to it need not be express; for example, the word "codicil" alone may be a sufficient reference to the will which, not being valid itself, thus became incorporated into the valid codicil.

A testator may make the designation of a beneficiary of his will to depend upon the future acts of himself, of third persons or of the beneficiary, provided such acts have independent significance apart from the will. For example, a gift "to the woman whom I may marry" or "to those of my grandchildren who may be living at my death," or "to the person taking care of me at the time of my death."

§ 15. Unusual types of wills.[5] In some states by statute a holographic will—that is, one entirely in the testator's handwriting and signed by him, is valid without any attestation. Unless there is an express provision in the statute, such a will is invalid if any part—for example, part of the date—is printed.

In most states, an oral or nuncupative will of personalty may be valid under certain circumstances. Usually it is required that it should be made during the testator's last illness, at his home or in the house where he died, that he should declare in the presence of witnesses that it is his will and that it be reduced to writing and probated within a certain period.

Soldiers in military service and sailors on the high seas may make informal written wills without attestation or they may make oral wills even though not made in the last illness or reduced to writing as required in the case of nuncupative wills.

Where A and B make a joint will in a single document the result is the same as if each had made a separate will; if it is not revoked it may be probated as the will of A upon A's death and as the will of B upon B's death.

Where A and B by written contract make mutual wills of land, each in favor of the other with remainder to the relatives of each equally, this may be specifically enforced by the beneficiaries; but if the contract is oral there cannot be specific performance, but if A should die and B should in violation of the oral contract devise all the land to his own relatives, A's relatives could have a constructive trust declared of the land received by B from A.

Where a will is expressly made conditional it should be denied probate if the condition has not happened.

5 57 **Am Jur**, Wills, §§ 589–636.
Soldiers' and seamen's wills. 137 **ALR** 1310–1327; s. in 147 **ALR** 1297; 148 **ALR** 1384; 149 **ALR** 1452; 150 **ALR** 1417.
Testamentary character of memorandum or other informal writing not testamentary on its face regarding ownership or disposition of specific personal property. 117 **ALR** 1327–1332.
Letter as a will or codicil. 54 **ALR** 917–939.
Effect on validity and character of instrument in form of deed of provisions therein indicating an intention to postpone or limit the rights of grantee until after the death of grantor. 11 **ALR** 23–106; s. in 76 **ALR** 636–653.
Gift of debts of third person not evidenced by commercial instrument. 3 **ALR** 933–940; s. in 14 **ALR** 707.
Character of instrument as will, or its admissibility to probate as such, as affected by its failure to make any disposition of property or by fact that there is no beneficiary entitled to take thereunder. 147 **ALR** 636–647.
17 **Tenn. L. R.** 440, Holographic Wills.

CHAPTER VI

REVOCATION OF WILLS

§ 16. Revocation by physical act.[6] In most states statutes provide for revocation of a will by some of the following physical acts with intent to revoke: burning, cancelling, tearing, obliterating, destruction, mutilating and cutting. If the act is done with no intent to revoke there is no revocation; for example, where the testator destroyed the document thinking it was not valid. If, after the will has been torn but before the testator has completed the act of destruction, he changes his mind and puts the pieces together again there is no revocation. Nor is there revocation where a third party destroys the will unless done in the testator's presence and at his direction.

Mere intent to revoke without one of the required physical acts is not enough; for example, where the testator wrote on the back of the will, "This will is made void by one of more recent date." By the better view revocation by physical act done to a will does not revoke a separate codicil and vice versa.

Most statutes permit revocation of part of a will by physical act, for example, by the cancellation of separate clauses; but cancelling or erasing the name of a legatee and writing the name of another is not effective.

§ 17. Revocation by operation of law.[7] At common law a man's will was revoked by a later marriage followed by birth of issue, regardless of his intent, and this is still generally true. A subsequent marriage alone did not revoke but in some jurisdictions statutes have provided that it revokes his will absolutely; in others, that it revokes unless the will shows that it was made in contemplation of marriage.

At common law the will of a man made after marriage was not revoked by later birth of issue, but in most states there are statutes either providing that, in the absence of a provision for after-born children, such an event does revoke the will completely, or giving the after-born child an intestate share if not otherwise provided for, thus working a pro tanto revocation.

At common law if a single woman made a will and then married, her will was revoked because she was unable to make a new will after marriage and it was better to have her be intestate than to uphold the will; besides the will was partly revoked by the marriage giving to the husband all her chattels and the power to reduce her choses in action to possession. Today, however, the wife has power to make a valid will and to keep her property so that her will made while unmarried is not revoked by her marriage unless there is express legislation to that effect.

Divorce does not revoke a will but where there is an agreement with regard to property, such an agreement is usually held to revoke any devises or bequests that had been made to the divorced spouse.

6 57 **Am Jur**, Wills, §§ 476–483.

Effect of testator's attempted physical alteration of will after execution. 62 **ALR** 1367–1410; s. in 115 **ALR** 710–725.

Interlineations or changes appearing on face of will. 67 **ALR** 1138–1152.

7 57 **Am Jur**, Wills, §§ 497–512.

Divorce as affecting will previously executed by husband and wife. 25 **ALR** 49–55; s. in 37 **ALR** 312–313; 42 **ALR** 1289.

When will deemed to have provided for, or contemplated, contingency of future birth or adoption of children, marriage, or other event which by statute wholly or partially revokes or otherwise renders such will inoperative. 127 **ALR** 750–773.

Rule regarding revocation of will by marriage as affected by antenuptial agreement or settlement. 92 **ALR** 1010–1023.

40 **Mich. L. R.** 406, Implied Revocation of Wills.

7 **Md. L. R.** 101, The Maryland Statute Relating to the Lapsing of Testamentary Gifts.

§ 18. Revocation by subsequent instrument.[8] In most states a later will or codicil with express words of revocation operates to revoke an earlier will in whole or in part; and a codicil may merely revoke a will without undertaking to dispose of any property. The words "I revoke my former will" also revokes the codicils thereto. The words "my last will and testament" are not usually construed to be words of revocation.

Where there is no clause of revocation, the later will or codicil revokes the earlier instrument only to the extent that it is inconsistent with it. A later will that disposes of all the testator's property necessarily nullifies the effect of an earlier will.

§ 19. Conditional or dependent relative revocation.[9] Where the testator expressly says that he revokes only upon a certain contingency, there is no revocation unless or until such contingency happens.

The so-called doctrine of dependent relative revocation is apparently based upon what the testator would probably have intended if he had not been mistaken as to the facts upon which he acted in executing his will. Thus, where a testator cancels an earlier will upon the supposition that he has made a valid later will, and the later will is invalid, such cancellation is held ineffective, apparently on the ground that the testator would probably have preferred to have the earlier will than to die intestate. And where the testator revoked legacies to his grandchildren "they all being dead" and they were alive, it was held that the legacies were not revoked because he would not have revoked them if he had known that the grandchildren were still alive.

Where the revocation is by subsequent instrument, it is usually held that the mistake must appear upon the face of the instrument, but this is not always required. Thus, where the testator had page 5 of his will re-written, leaving out the name of his sister, and the new page, not being attested, was invalid, the court held that the attempted revocation of the original page was not effective.

Where the testator destroys his will, expecting promptly to make a new one and the new one is not made, the better view is that the revocation stands.

It has been argued that in every case the court should try to find out what the testator's intent would have been rather than to follow what the court thinks was his probable intent.

CHAPTER VII

REPUBLICATION AND REVIVAL OF WILLS

§ 20. Republication.[10] Where a valid will has been destroyed as part of the process of revocation and the testator then changes his mind again and decides that he wishes that to be his will, he can do so only by executing a new will with the same terms as the revoked will. Where the revoked will is still in existence physically he may re-execute it by again signing it or re-

[8] 57 Am Jur, Wills, §§ 442-468.
Revocation of earlier will by revoking clause in a lost will or other lost instrument. 94 ALR 1024-1033.
Possibility of avoiding or limiting effect of clause in later will purporting to revoke all former wills. 125 ALR 936-947.
Implied revocation of will by later will. 51 ALR 652-731; s. in 123 ALR 1395-1409.
Revocation of will by writing not testamentary in character. 3 ALR 833-844; s. in 14 ALR 1018.

[9] 57 Am Jur, Wills, §§ 490-494.
Revocation of later will as reviving earlier will. 28 ALR 911-926; s. in 53 ALR 521-522.
33 Harv. L. R. 337, Dependent Relative Revocation.

[10] 57 Am Jur, Wills, §§ 572-588.

tracing or adopting his original signature and having such signature attested.

Where the purported will was not valid because it was not properly attested or because there was undue influence or the testator was incapacitated and a later will or codicil is properly executed, referring to the purported will, the latter is thereby—in most states—incorporated by reference into the new valid instrument. This is frequently spoken of as a republication, though it is difficult to see how an instrument which was never valid can be really restored or revived or republished.

In some jurisdictions there is a doctrine that where the original will was valid the effect of a codicil thereto is to republish the original will so as to make it read as of the date of the codicil. Thus, where the original will released all debts and is later republished by codicil, the effect is to release all debts incurred down to the date of the codicil. The doctrine should not be applied so as to defeat the testator's intent; for example, to render invalid gifts to charity made in the original will where the codicil was executed less than thirty days before the death, the codicil itself being in violation of the death bed gift statute.

§ 21. Revival—revocation of a revoking will.[1] Where A, the testator, executes will X and later executes will Y, expressly revoking will X, and still later revokes will Y by destroying it, and then dies, is will X, which has not been destroyed, valid? If the revoking part of will Y is considered as not taking effect till the death of A, then will X has never been revoked and is valid regardless of A's intent in the matter and this is the view taken in some states. In other states, while the dispositive part of will Y does not, of course, take effect till the death of A, the revoking clause is considered to take effect as soon as will Y is executed and in those states it becomes a question in each case as to whether, by revoking will Y it was A's intention to revive will X. In still other states there is a presumption against revival. In a few states, statutes have provided that there shall be no revival unless there is a codicil showing an intent to revive; still other statutes provide that there shall be no revival unless the terms of the revocation of will Y show that A intended such revival.

CHAPTER VIII

INTESTACY

§ 22. Descent and distribution—realty and personalty.[2] At common law upon the death of an intestate his realty—that is, his descendible freehold interests in land—went to his heir; his personalty—that is, his chattels, choses in action and terms for years in land—went to the administrator to pay debts and then to distribute to the next of kin. Under the English canons of descent, the heir was the eldest son. Males were preferred before females,

1 57 **Am Jur**, Wills, § 587.

2 16 **Am Jur**, Descent and Distribution, §§ 5–11, 36–73.

Family settlement of intestate's estate. 6 **ALR** 555–567; s. in 38 **ALR** 759–763; 54 **ALR** 976–979.

Ancestral character of property which came to interstate by deed. 122 **ALR** 820–831.

Heirs or next of kin who take upon intestacy resulting from failure of contingent remainder after life estate as determinable as of date of death of the testator or of life tenant. 132 **ALR** 1069–1077.

Nature of, and remedies for enforcement of, the interest which a pretermitted child takes by virtue of statute where parent leaves will. 123 **ALR** 1073–1093.

5 **U. of Newark L. R.** 1, Proposed Legislation Amending the Intestate Succession Laws of New Jersey.

lineal ancestors and the half-blood were excluded. Today, both in England and in this country these doctrines have been abolished and persons who are entitled to the realty are those who are entitled to the personalty.

In most states today the next of kin are the issue, if any; if no issue they are determined by the civil law method adopted by the English Statute of Distribution of 1670. By that method the number of steps from the claimant up to the nearest common ancestor of the claimant and intestate is added to the number of steps from the common ancestor down to the intestate. Thus parents take before brothers and sisters because a parent is only one degree removed while brothers and sisters are two degrees removed. A nephew or an uncle takes before a cousin or great uncle because a nephew or uncle is only three degrees removed while a cousin or great uncle is four degrees removed.

§ 23. Share of the surviving spouse.[3] At common law a widow was entitled to dower, that is, a life estate in a one-third part of the decedent's freehold estates and a surviving husband was entitled—if issue was born alive—to a life estate in all of the decedent's freehold estates. Neither was an heir of the other though the widow was entitled to a share in the personalty of her deceased husband. Today this has been changed everywhere by statute. In many states the surviving spouse has been made an heir of some proportion of the realty and an equal proportion of the personalty, the proportion usually varying according to whether there is also surviving issue of the marriage.

§ 24. Ancestral property—the half-blood—illegitimates.[4] If H marries W to whom an uncle conveys a piece of land by deed or will and H and W die intestate, leaving only one child X who dies intestate without issue, the English canons of descent provided that the land should go to W's relatives because X had inherited the land from W. This doctrine of ancestral property still prevails in some states by judicial decision, in others by statute; in still other states it has been abolished by statute.

Under the English canons of descent, if A died intestate without issue having a brother B and a half brother C, B was entitled to inherit all of A's land. In most states today C would inherit equally with B; in others he would inherit a smaller portion and in still others he would inherit only if there is no brother or sister of the full blood.

Many states today provide that an illegitimate child may inherit from the mother.

3 17 **Am Jur**, Dower, §§ 1–12.

Compensation of legatees disappointed by another's election against the will. 99 **ALR** 230–236; s. in 125 **ALR** 1013–1016.

What amounts to election by widow to take under or against will. 82 **ALR** 1509–1558.

Direction in will that provision for wife shall be in lieu of other rights or claims as requiring election as between provisions of will and her rights in respect of property or property not validly disposed of by the will. 93 **ALR** 1384–1393.

Who must bear loss occasioned by election against will. 99 **ALR** 1187–1198.

Effect of election to take under will on right of widow to fixed statutory allowance, or allowance for support. 4 **ALR** 391–400; s. in 140 **ALR** 1220–1226.

Election on behalf of incompetent to take under or against will. 74 **ALR** 453–467; s. in 147 **ALR** 336–352.

Revocation of election to take under or contrary to will. 81 **ALR** 740–763.

When is widow put to her election between provision made for her by her husband's will, and her dower, homestead, or community right. 22 **ALR** 437–524; s. in 68 **ALR** 507–520.

19 **N. Y. U. Law Q.** 343, "Life, Liberty—and Dower," Disherison of the Spouse in New York.

4 16 **Am Jur**, Descent and Distribution, §§ 62–73.

CHAPTER IX

PROBATE AND CONTEST OF WILLS

§ 25. Necessity, place and effect of probate—lost wills.[5] In all states a will of personalty and in most states a will of realty must be probated, not in order that title may pass to the executor or heir but to enable such title to be proved if called in question in litigation. If the attesting witnesses are dead or incompetent or absent from the state the will may be probated upon proving the signature of the testator and of the witnesses.

The proper place for probating a will is in the state and county where the decedent was domiciled at the time of his death; later the will may be probated in any other state in which the decedent left property.

Neither probate nor administration can ordinarily be granted till after the death, though some states provide for a testator depositing his will with the probate court. In some states statutes authorize the administration of the estate of one who has been absent and not heard from for a certain number of years, but a statute authorizing the administration of the estate of one who is civilly dead because sentenced to imprisonment for life would probably be unconstitutional as authorizing the taking of property without due process of law. It is no objection to the probate of a will that it is in breach of a contract.

After a will is probated it becomes free from collateral attack on the ground of improper execution, forgery, lack of testamentary capacity or revocation; it may be attacked on these grounds only by way of appeal or contest as provided for by statute. If a later will is discovered, it may be probated and thus supersede the earlier will but transactions entered into upon the basis of the earlier will—such as the purchase of land from a devisee—will be protected.

In most states if an unrevoked will be lost or destroyed, it may be probated, the court requiring clear proof of its contents and execution.

Apart from statute there is no limit of time within which a will must be offered for probate.

§ 26. Contest of wills.[6] Any one in the possession of a will at the time of the decedent's death is under a duty to produce it and if he suppresses it or destroys it he may be held liable in damages to the beneficiaries under the will.

[5] 57 **Am Jur,** Wills, §§ 676, 887–908.

Revocation of probate of will as affecting title of purchasers from beneficiaries under will. 26 **ALR** 270–278.

Establishment of will lost before testator's death. 34 **ALR** 1304–1315.

Who entitled to appeal from decree admitting will to probate or denying probate. 88 **ALR** 1158–1175.

Power of court to refuse letters testamentary to one named in will as executor, absent specific statutory disqualification. 95 **ALR** 828–836.

Probate in state where assets are found of will of nonresident which has not been admitted to probate in state of domicil. 119 **ALR** 491–512.

42 **Mich. L. R.** 961, Preparation of a Model Probate Code.

[6] 57 **Am Jur,** Wills, §§ 693–703.

Right to allowance out of the estate of attorney's fees in attempt to establish or defeat a will. 10 **ALR** 783–809; s. in 69 **ALR** 1052–1059; 128 **ALR** 1002–1013.

Contract to refrain from contesting will. 55 **ALR** 811–818.

Right to jury in will contest. 62 **ALR** 82–95.

Validity of provision of will for forfeiture in case of contest. 67 **ALR** 52–67.

Right of one who takes under a will to attack its validity. 72 **ALR** 1134–1143.

Prima facie case for proponent in will contest as shifting burden of proof. 76 **ALR** 373–386.

Validity and applicability of provision of will or trust instrument forfeiting share of contesting beneficiary as affected by probable cause and good faith in contest. 125 **ALR** 1135–1143; s. in 146 **ALR** 1211–1212.

The will may ordinarily be propounded or offered for probate by any person interested in having it probated; and it may be contested by any one who is interested in not having it probated. Any serious contest of the will is usually not in the probate court because the probate judge is not always a lawyer and because there is no right to jury trial in such a court; the contest proceedings are usually in the ordinary trial court either upon appeal from the probate court or upon objections raised in that court.

The usual grounds of contest are (1) the mental incapacity of the testator, (2) lack of proper execution, including forgery, (3) fraud, undue influence and mistake, and (4) revocation. While there is no constitutional right of trial by jury, statutes usually provide for it. The right to open and close to the jury is, by the majority view, given to the proponents upon whom is the burden of establishing testamentary capacity and the due execution of the will by a preponderance of the evidence. On the issue of fraud, undue influence and revocation, the burden of establishing is on the contestant.

Since it is the executor's duty to uphold the will, his costs and attorney's fees are usually allowed from the estate even though the will is not admitted to probate; and some courts treat contestants in the same way where there was probable cause for the contest.

CHAPTER X

GRANT OF ADMINISTRATION

§ 27. Purpose and necessity of administration.[7] The purposes of administration of a decedent's estate are to collect the personal assets, pay the debts and distribute whatever may be left to the legatees under the will or to the distributees if there is no will. If the personal assets are not sufficient to pay the debts, the executor or administrator may petition the court to have enough of the real estate sold to make up the deficiency.

Administration is not always necessary. If there is no real estate and no will and no dispute as to who are legally entitled to be distributees and the latter are of full age and they all agree upon a settlement and the rights of creditors are taken care of and no one petitions for administration, there is no reason why such a settlement should not be upheld.

§ 28. Appointment of personal representatives—executor de son tort.[8] If there is a will appointing an executor and he is willing to act the court will usually confirm the appointment unless he is unfit to act. If there is no

[7] 21 **Am Jur,** Executors and Administrators, §§ 13, 15–22.

Dispensing with, or revoking grant of, administration of decedent's estate on ground that administration is not necessary. 70 **ALR** 386–399.

Allowance out of decedent's estate for costs and attorneys' fees incurred by parties interested in granting or revoking of letters of administration or letters testamentary. 90 **ALR** 101–116.

32 **Harv. L. R.** 315, Problems in Probate and Administration.

[8] 21 **Am Jur,** Executors and Administrators, §§ 54, 55, 825–848.

Judgment or order in connection with appointment of executor or administrator as res judicata, as law of the case, or as evidence, on questions other than the validity of the appointment. 119 **ALR** 594–627.

Right of guardian of infant or incompetent to appointment as executor or administrator as representative or substitute for infant or incompetent. 135 **ALR** 585–595.

Person to be appointed as special or temporary administrator pending will contest. 136 **ALR** 604–616.

Administration of estate of one the fact of whose death rests upon presumption or circumstantial evidence. 140 **ALR** 1403–1419.

Relation back of letters testamentary or of administration. 26 **ALR** 1359–1371.

Personal interests of executor or administrator adverse to or conflicting with those of other persons interested in estate as ground for revocation of letters or removal. 119 **ALR** 306–326.

will the court will appoint an administrator to settle up the intestate estate. If there is a will but no executor is named or the person named as executor does not act, the court appoints an administrator with the will annexed to carry out the provisions of the will. If either an executor or administrator administers only a part of the estate, his successor is called an administrator de bonis non.

At common law if before the appointment of a personal representative X intermeddled with the goods of the decedent he was called—even though there was no will—an executor de son tort (of his own wrong) and held liable not only to the subsequently appointed personal representative but also to creditors. In so far as his liability to creditors is concerned the doctrine is inconsistent with the modern requirement that claims against the estate must be duly proved and in some states this part of the doctrine is rejected. The executor de son tort is charged with all the burdens of a personal representative but with none of his rights, but if he himself is later appointed administrator his right relates back to the time of death.

§ 29. Ancillary administration.[9] If A, the decedent, died domiciled in state X, but owning tangible property and having debtors in state Y and it becomes necessary to bring an action to get hold of the property or to enforce payment of the debts, this cannot be done by the executor or administrator appointed in state X; this is apparently because of the desire to protect any creditors of A's estate living in state Y. So it is necessary that ancillary letters of administration be taken out in state Y; in some states, the personal representative of state X will be appointed; in other states only a resident of state Y is eligible. Where the debtor of state Y voluntarily pays the personal representatives of state X before ancillary administration is taken out it is a good payment and by the better view it is a good payment even after such letters have been issued but before the debtor knows of it. If the estate as a whole is insolvent, the better view is that the ancillary administrator should pay local creditors an amount which will make all the creditors share equally.

§ 30. Miscellaneous.[10] By statute the one best entitled to be appointed administrator is usually the surviving spouse; next, the closest of kin and if there are several equally related, then the most suitable one, in the court's discretion; next, to a creditor or creditors and lastly, to a suitable stranger. Letters of administration with the will annexed are likely to be granted to a residuary legatee because of his self-interest in having the estate efficiently administered.

One named as executor or one entitled to be named administrator may renounce his right, but such renunciation may be withdrawn if letters have not been granted to any one else in the meantime.

In all jurisdictions an administrator must furnish bond and in most juris-

9 21 **Am Jur,** Executors and Administrators, §§ 849–893.

Remission of assets by ancillary administrator to domiciliary executor or administrator. 90 **ALR** 1043–1060.

Accountability of domiciliary executor or administrator, to court of domicil, in respect of personal assets subject, or susceptible, to ancillary administration. 132 **ALR** 1369–1381.

10 21 **Am Jur,** Executors and Administrators, §§ 58–78, 150–161, 716–748.

Selection of administrator from among members of class equally entitled. 1 **ALR** 1245–1255.

Appointment as administrator of one not a member or nominee of a member of the class of persons designated by statute as eligible to appointment, where no one in better right has applied. 119 **ALR** 143–153.

16 **U. of Cin. L. R.** 401, Ohio's "Half and Half" Inheritance Statute.

dictions an executor must give bond unless this has been dispensed with by the testator.

Letters of administration may be revoked where they should not have been granted and courts may remove an executor or administrator whose subsequent conduct shows him to be unfit. By the better view a court may accept the resignation of a representative who wishes to be relieved.

CHAPTER XI

POWERS AND OBLIGATIONS OF PERSONAL REPRESENTATIVES

§ 31. The collection of assets.[1] The first duty of the personal representative is to file an inventory of the personal assets and have them appraised by persons appointed by the court for that purpose. Personal assets include chattels and choses in action which survive. Where there are not enough other assets to satisfy the creditors, the personal representative may sue to recover back property given by the decedent causa mortis and in most jurisdictions property transferred by the decedent in fraud of creditors; but next of kin or distributees are not entitled to share in such assets.

Choses in action owned by the decedent which are based upon contract or quasi contract, survive, except a right of action for breach of contract to marry. Tort actions for or affecting property survive; tort actions for assault and battery, false imprisonment, malicious prosecution, slander and libel, usually do not survive; a statutory tort action for wrongfully causing the death of the decedent does not survive because it did not belong to the decedent but the statute frequently provides that the personal representative shall enforce an action for the benefit of the widow and children.

If there are two or more personal representatives any one has the power to sell chattels belonging to the estate and to receive payment of claims due to the estate; but if it becomes necessary to bring suit, all the joint representatives should join.

Title passes to the personal representative as soon as he qualifies as such but it relates back to the death so as to enable him to recover for any tort committed to the personal assets after the death.

§ 32. Contracts and torts of the personal representative.[2] A contract

1 21 **Am Jur,** Executors and Administrators, §§ 171–204.

Bond of executor or administrator as covering debt due from principal to decedent. 8 **ALR** 84–97.

What effects removal of executor or administrator. 8 **ALR** 175–187.

Power of those who accept executorship or trusteeship to exercise right to sell real property, conferred by will on several named as executors and trustees, some of whom fail or refuse to accept. 36 **ALR** 826–850.

Implied power of executor or testamentary trustee to sell real property. 134 **ALR** 378–420.

Liability of executor or administrator, or his bond, for loss caused to estate by acts or default of agent or attorney employed by him. 144 **ALR** 875–887.

Power of sale of real estate given to executor as impliedly conferring a right to possession. 94 **ALR** 1140–1149.

Right of an administrator with the will annexed, or trustee other than person named in will as such, to execute power of sale conferred by will. 116 **ALR** 158–204.

Right of executor or administrator to commissions as affected by faults in administration. 83 **ALR** 726–744.

Power and responsibility of executor or administrator in respect of waiver or compromise of claim due estate. 85 **ALR** 176–196.

Liability of executor or administrator for loss by depreciation in value of securities, through retaining or deferring sale thereof. 92 **ALR** 436–469.

Right of executor or administrator to resign. 91 **ALR** 712–722.

Power to sell decedent's real estate to pay commissions of executor or administrator or expenses of administration. 95 **ALR** 1143–1150.

2 21 **Am Jur,** Executors and Administrators, §§ 205–249.

Liability of estate for torts of executor, administrator, or trustee. 44 **ALR** 637–681; s. in 127 **ALR** 687–694.

Liability of executor or administrator or

made by the personal representative—for example, to pay funeral expenses, or to pay for taking care of the personal assets—does not bind the estate, but binds him personally even though he signs the contract "as executor." But if the contract has been properly entered into, he is entitled to be reimbursed from the estate or to have the claim paid out of the assets of the estate; and if he is insolvent his right thus to be exonerated can be reached by a bill in equity for equitable execution.

If in the course of administration the personal representative should commit a tort he and not the estate becomes responsible therefor; but if he has been guilty of no negligence and no conscious wrongdoing he will usually be allowed reimbursement, especially where the estate has benefited from the tort.

§ 33. **Performance of decedent's contracts.**[3] If the decedent left unperformed a contract for other than services of a personal nature—for example, to put up a building for X according to certain specifications, or to have Y put up a building for the decedent according to specifications—should the personal representative continue to put up the building for X or to allow Y to put up the building on the land of the decedent, or should he in each case refuse and pay damages for breach? Whichever course he pursues the heirs or next of kin or distributees or creditors may complain that he should have pursued the other. He should try to come to some agreement with the parties interested and if he fails, he should seek authority from the proper court.

CHAPTER XII

PAYMENT OF DEBTS AND DISTRIBUTION

§ 34. **Priority of claims—overpayment to creditors.**[4] Statutes everywhere provide that certain claims against the estate shall have priority; this becomes quite important if the estate is insolvent. While the statutes vary, most of the following claims are usually given priority: (1) An allowance to the family for support during the administration. (2) Funeral expenses. (3) Expenses of the last illness. (4) Costs of administration. (5) By federal statute, taxes owed to the United States. (6) Wages of servants for a fixed period before the death. (7) Judgments against the decedent. Such statutes do not, of course, prevent a secured creditor from realizing on his security.

If the personal representative, mistakenly thinking that the estate is solvent, pays a creditor in full, the better view is that he is entitled to compel the creditor to refund enough to place all the ordinary creditors on the same basis.

§ 35. **Advancements—release and transfer of expectancies.**[5] If A transfers to his child B a piece of land or a sum of money and then dies intestate and the transfer was intended by A to be an advancement to B of a part of his prospective share in A's estate, such transfer must be taken into account if B wishes to share in A's estate. For example, if A thus transferred to B $1,000 and left an estate of $8,000 and three children, B, C and D, the $1,000

his bond for loss of money deposited in bank in his representative capacity. 60 **ALR** 488–601.

[3] 21 **Am Jur,** Executors and Administrators, §§ 255–263.

[4] 21 **Am Jur,** Executors and Administrators, §§ 389–490.

[5] 1 **Am Jur,** Advancements, §§ 1–151. 4 **Am Jur,** Assignments, §§ 47–64.

must be brought into hotchpot; that is, in computing what each of the children is to receive the $1,000 must be added to the $8,000, making $9,000; of this sum each will receive $3,000, but from B's share of $3,000 will be deducted the $1,000 already advanced to him. If, instead of advancing $1,000, A had advanced $5,000 to B, it would not, of course, be advantageous to B to claim any share of the estate because one-third of $8,000 plus $5,000, would be less than $5,000.

Of course, it may always be shown that A did not intend an advancement but an absolute gift; the amount of the sum or the value of the land transferred, the surrounding circumstances, and express declarations of A are all evidence on the question of his intent.

If A had left a will disposing of all his property the sum received by B will not be regarded as an advancement unless the will so provides; and in most states the same result follows even though the will does not dispose of all his property.

In most states if B had released to A his expectant interest in A's estate, this would bar B if he had received a fair consideration for such release. The most common theory upholding such a transaction is that it is an advancement liquidated by the agreement as amounting to B's entire share. Where the other children C and D were living at the time of the release but both predeceased A, B is not barred by the release.

If B had transferred his expectant interest in A's estate to X, the latter would be entitled to B's share upon A's death intestate, if B were still living. But such transfers are closely scrutinized by the courts as to the amount of consideration received by B, and some courts refuse to enforce the transaction unless A consented to it.

§ 36. Ademption and satisfaction.[6] If A makes a will bequeathing to B a specific chattel or specific shares of stock or devises to him a piece of land and later the chattel is lost or destroyed or A transfers it and the piece of land and then dies, the legacy and devise are said to be adeemed or destroyed. And this result follows regardless of A's intent in the matter, for example, where A set apart the money received for the property and regarded it as belonging to B. If only part of the property is destroyed or transferred the rest of it passes under the will.

If A makes a will bequeathing to B a sum of money and later gives to B an equal or greater sum intending it to be in satisfaction of the legacy, B will not be entitled to the legacy which is frequently said to be adeemed or destroyed by the gift. If A stood in loco parentis to B, there is a presumption that A meant the gift to be in satisfaction, but in any case A's actual intent may be shown. Where the amount of the gift is less than the legacy, it will go in partial satisfaction thereof if A so intended. Since it is the testator's intent that is important there would seem to be no reason why the doctrine of satisfaction should not be applied to specific bequests and to devises, but the weight of authority is contra.

§ 37. Abatement—refunding—renunciation.[7] If there are not enough

[6] 57 **Am Jur,** Wills, §§ 1496–1509.

Ademption of specific devise or bequest by guardian or conservator of incompetent testator. 30 **ALR** 676–681.

Legacy or devise to creditor of testator as satisfaction in whole or part of debt. 86 **ALR** 6–40.

18 **Wis. L. R.** 11, Ademption by Extinction: Its Practical Effects.

[7] 57 **Am Jur,** Wills, §§ 1372–1380, 1481–1488.

Right of recovery against person to whom, by mistake of law, property of decedent's estate has been improperly distributed. 147 **ALR** 121–134.

assets to pay the debts and legacies and the will does not specify any order of abatement to be followed in such a contingency, the first to be abated is the property, if any, not covered by the will. Next in order are the residuary legacies and devises, then the general legacies and devises, and finally the specific legacies and devises and the demonstrative legacies, that is, legacies that are payable primarily out of a particular fund, but if that is not available, then out of the general assets.

If through mistake the personal representative overpays a legatee or distributee, the better view is that there is an obligation to refund the excess.

If a legatee renounces his legacy and there is a residuary clause in the will, the legacy renounced goes to the residuary legatee, not to the next of kin.

DAMAGES

CHAPTER I

IN GENERAL

§ 1. Terminology.[1] The word "damage" means loss or harm suffered; the word "damages" usually means the money compensation awarded for such loss but it is sometimes used to mean both the harm and the compensation; when it is said that A sued B for the damages inflicted upon A's land by B, what is meant is that A sued B for compensation for the harm or loss inflicted by B upon A's land.

In some tort actions, for example, in an action on the case for deceit or for negligent conduct, it is necessary for the plaintiff to allege and prove special damage as a part of his cause of action; and in this connection special damage means any actual damage except mental pain or nervous shock. But the term special damage is often used with another meaning. Where damage would usually follow from the cause of action alleged by the plaintiff it is not necessary for him to allege it in his declaration, and such damage is frequently referred to as general damage. But where the plaintiff expects at the trial to prove an item of damage which would not usually but which did actually follow from the cause of action alleged, then, in fairness to the defendant, he must specifically allege such damage in his declaration so that the defendant will be warned of such a claim; such damage is often referred to as special damage, though it would be better to call it specific damage.

[1] 15 Am Jur, Damages, §§ 1–12.
Right to discovery as regards facts relating to amount of damages. 88 ALR 504–521.
Duty of jury to follow instruction as to amount of party's liability if liable at all. 23 ALR 305–309.

Unless the defendant violates some right of the plaintiff the infliction of damage gives rise to no cause of action. On the other hand, a breach of contract and a large number of torts, including trespass to land and conversion are actionable without any damage being shown.

§ 2. Certainty.[2] Where, as in actions based upon negligent conduct, liability at peril, deceit and most cases of slander, etc., special damage is an essential element of the tort, the question as to whether the defendant's misconduct was the legal cause of the plaintiff's damage is a part of the substantive law of torts; but where special damage does not need to be proved in order to make out a cause of action, for example, in actions for trespass to land or to the person, for conversion, for libel and for breach of contract, rules of legal cause are important only in determining the amount of damages to which a plaintiff is entitled; questions arising as to such rules belong, therefore, to the law of damages.

Under any rule of legal cause the damage claimed by the plaintiff must not be conjectural or speculative but reasonably certain. However, if the fact of damage be shown with reasonable certainty, the extent of the damage may be left to reasonable inference by the jury; and if the uncertainty of the damage has been caused by the defendant's wrong he cannot take advantage of it.

Where the plaintiff claims that the defendant's wrong has resulted in loss of commercial profits to the plaintiff, he must specifically allege such loss in his declaration; if so alleged and the plaintiff's business was an established one, he will usually be able to recover for such lost profits because there is available the record of past profits from which the jury may draw a reasonable inference; where the business is a new one with no past records of profits, courts have sometimes allowed the records of profits of other businesses similarly situated to be shown and this is justified if the conditions shown indicate a fair chance of success rather than failure. Where there are no businesses similarly situated, lost profits are usually not allowed; for example, where there were no other glass factories in Kansas, the defendant's wrong consisting of failure to perform its contract to supply enough natural gas to run the factory, it was held proper to allow the plaintiff only the rental value of his idle factory. Where the defendant's wrong consists of refusing to allow the plaintiff an exclusive agency for which the plaintiff contracted, evidence as to the profits made by the one who displaced the plaintiff has been received. If in any case there are data upon which to base an inference, an expert witness may be allowed to interpret the data, but he usually is not allowed to testify as to his opinion if no data are available.

In a few cases the plaintiff has been awarded the value of a chance; for example, where the defendant railroad delayed shipping the plaintiff's hogs so that, because of the condition of the hogs, plaintiff received only second instead of first prize at a stock show, the plaintiff was entitled to have the jury award him the value of his lost chance.

5 **U. of Newark L. R.** 371, Decrees for Damages in New Jersey.

[2] 15 **Am Jur,** Damages, §§ 20–23, 149–158.

Distinction between uncertainty as to whether substantial damages resulted and uncertainty as to amount. 78 **ALR** 856–866.

§ 3. Avoidable consequences.[3] After B has breached his contract with A or has committed a tort against him, A will not be able to collect for any damage which he might have avoided by the exercise of ordinary care. Unlike contributory negligence, this rule of avoidable consequences does not defeat A's cause of action but merely reduces the amount of his recovery and hence does not need to be pleaded. It is often said that there is a duty to reduce damages by using due care to avoid the consequences of the defendant's tort or breach of contract, but it is not such a duty as gives rise to a cause of action in favor of the defendant against the plaintiff.

Where a landlord breached his contract with his tenant by furnishing poor seed wheat and the latter knew of its poor quality before he sowed it, he was not allowed to recover for the damage due to the poor crop which was harvested. And where defendant railroad company negligently set fire to and burned plaintiff's fence, it was held that if the plaintiff, after notice of the destruction of the fence, could, by the exercise of ordinary care, have prevented the escape of his hogs, he cannot recover for the hogs which escaped and were lost.

But a plaintiff is not required to exercise more than ordinary care; he is not bound to do anything unreasonable. For example, a plaintiff who has suffered personal injuries due to defendant's negligence is not bound to undergo a serious and expensive surgical operation; a plaintiff is not bound to abandon his dairy to avoid the consequences of the operation of defendant's nearby smelter; and a plaintiff who, by his contract, is entitled to credit is not bound to pay cash wrongfully demanded by the defendant in order to lessen the damages due to defendant's breach of contract.

Where a defendant refused to complete a contract for the installation of a fire extinguisher system by the plaintiff and the latter sued for lost profits it was held that since it was not a contract for personal services and the subject matter was not in the plaintiff's possession, the rule of avoidable consequences did not apply; if the defendant should be allowed to take advantage of the profit which plaintiff could have made on other contracts he would be bound also to assume the risk of loss.

Where a plaintiff does exercise due care in attempting to reduce the amount of the damage he is entitled to recover for the expense reasonably incurred in making such attempt. And where defendant's wrong has resulted in a benefit to the plaintiff, the value of such benefit must be deducted from the amount of the plaintiff's damage in determining the amount of the plaintiff's recovery.

[3] 15 **Am Jur**, Damages, §§ 27–41.

Workmen's compensation: duty of injured employee to submit to operation or to take other measures to restore earning capacity. 6 **ALR** 1260–1266; s. in 11 **ALR** 230–233; 73 **ALR** 1303–1319; 105 **ALR** 1470–1483.

Duty to mitigate damages. 81 **ALR** 282–286.

Contracts within the rule which requires one to use reasonable effort to obtain other employment in order to minimize damages from breach of contract. 15 **ALR** 751–774.

Compensation from other source as precluding or reducing recovery against one responsible for personal injury or death. 18 **ALR** 678–689; 95 **ALR** 575–582.

Duty to refrain from improving or using one's property in anticipation of flooding of the property by another's wrong. 19 **ALR** 423–429.

Duty of landlord, on abandonment of premises by tenant before expiration of term, to use diligence to procure another tenant. 40 **ALR** 190–199; s. in 126 **ALR** 1219–1224.

Right of defendant to diminution of damages to real property on account of interest of plaintiff's cotenant who is not a party to the action. 80 **ALR** 992–997.

Presumption and burden of proof regarding mitigation of damages. 134 **ALR** 242–286.

Insurance on property as precluding or reducing recovery of damages from one responsible for loss of or injury to such property. 81 **ALR** 320–326.

27 **U. of Minn. L. R.** 483, The Rule of

§ 4. **Value.**[4] The question of value arises in a large variety of cases; for examples, where trover is brought, or an action on the case for the value of property negligently destroyed by the defendant, or special assumpsit for the refusal of a buyer of property to accept and pay for it, or for the refusal of a seller to allow the buyer to have the property, or special assumpsit on an insurance policy for the value of goods accidentally destroyed, indebitatus assumpsit on the contract for the reasonable value of goods transferred or services rendered where no price was fixed by the contract, indebitatus assumpsit in quasi contract for the reasonable value of goods or services of which the defendant would otherwise be unjustly enriched.

Usually value of goods means not the retail value of the separate articles but the market value of the property as a whole. Where the market value would be quite inadequate, as in the case of clothing or furniture in actual use, the plaintiff is entitled to recover the value as to him; in fixing such value the jury may consider its original cost, the use which the plaintiff has had of it, its present condition and the cost of replacement. Market value may also be inadequate because the property can no longer be legally used for its original purpose as in the case of an action on a policy of fire insurance for the value of a brewery which could not, at the time of the fire, be legally used to manufacture malt.

Where B contracts to deliver goods to A at town X or if B wrongfully destroys A's goods at X, the market value at X is used as the basis for assessing damages; if there is no market for the goods there, then the value at the nearest market.

Where trover is brought for the conversion of goods or special assumpsit for refusal to deliver or to accept goods, the value at the time of conversion or at the agreed time and place of delivery is the basis for computing damages. Where the goods are of fluctuating value the better view is that the plaintiff is entitled to the highest value reached during the period from the time he learned of the conversion or breach of contract down to the expiration of a reasonable time for securing similar goods on the market; but some courts allow the highest intermediate value down to the time of trial and still others disregard entirely any subsequent change in the value of the goods.

The value of personal property or of land or of services is usually proved by the opinion evidence of persons who are familiar with such values.

Where action is brought in this country upon a contract obligation to pay money in a foreign country and the value of the currency of that country has fluctuated, the prevailing and better rule is that the plaintiff is entitled to judgment in dollars according to the rate of exchange on the day when the money was due—the breach day rule; the minority doctrine gives judgment in dollars according to the rate of exchange on the day judgment is rendered—the judgment day rule.

§ 5. **Interest.**[5] Where a plaintiff, suing either for a tort or breach of contract or in quasi contract, claims a sum certain due in money and becomes entitled to judgment, he is entitled to recover as damages legal interest from

Avoidable Consequences and Blameworthiness of the Defendant.

17 **Tenn. L. R.** 821, Plaintiff's Duty to Minimize Defendant's Liability by Surgery.

4 15 **Am Jur**, Damages, §§ 114, 122–128.

5 15 **Am Jur**, Damages, §§ 159–174.

Reduction of claim under contract as affecting right to interest. 3 **ALR** 809–819; s. in 89 **ALR** 678–680.

Rate of interest chargeable against guardians, executors or administrators, and trustees. 37 **ALR** 447–473.

the time the money should have been paid; and by the better view this is true even though the defendant disputed the amount due.

Where the amount of money to which the plaintiff is entitled is not certain but is based upon the valuation of property or services which have a market value, he is usually held entitled to recover as damages legal interest from the time when the defendant should have settled, but in some states the matter is left to the uncontrolled discretion of the jury.

Where the plaintiff's claim is for pecuniary loss but is not based upon market value, some courts deny interest while others permit the jury to use their discretion in allowing it.

Where the jury awards compensation for such wrongs as personal injuries, libel, slander, seduction, malicious prosecution or breach of promise to marry, interest is not allowed, though no doubt juries often take into consideration the delay suffered by the plaintiff in getting compensation for the wrong committed by the defendant.

§ 6. Expenses of litigation.[6] In a common-law action the loser usually pays the costs of that litigation; these are fixed by statute and ordinarily include the fees of the sheriff or constable and clerk of court but not counsel fees or other expenses, but in some states counsel fees have been allowed to successful plaintiffs in certain classes of cases; for example, in actions on insurance policies and actions against railroads for loss or damage to freight.

In probate, receivership and bankruptcy proceedings the executor or administrator or receiver or trustee in bankruptcy who is compelled to litigate to preserve the estate or fund in the hands of the court is entitled to his reasonable expenses to be deducted from the estate or fund; and, by statute, the same privilege has been accorded to petitioning creditors in bankruptcy proceedings and, without a statute, to minority stockholders who have brought suit to recover corporate property where the directors have failed to protect the interests of the corporation. In most states a wife who sues for divorce or separation is entitled, even though unsuccessful, to recover from her husband reasonable attorney's fees. And equity courts have in some cases allowed counsel fees to a defendant where the suit brought was groundless and vexatious.

Where X has recovered against the plaintiff city for a tort—for example, for personal injuries due to the failure to keep a street in repair—the plaintiff may not only recover against the defendant whose negligent conduct had directly caused the injury, the amount which it was compelled to pay X, but also counsel fees and other expenses reasonably incurred in the previous litigation. And similar reasoning has been applied where B fraudulently induced A to contract to buy land from B which B did not own and A brought a fruitless suit for specific performance against B.

Where A sells and conveys land to B with a covenant of warranty and B in turn sells and conveys it to C with a similar covenant and B is held liable for breach in an action brought by C, it has been held that B may recover from A not only the amount of the judgment which he was compelled to pay C but also the counsel fees and other expenses reasonably incurred in that

Power of court to add interest to verdict returned by jury. 72 **ALR** 1150–1162.

Interest on damages for period before judgment for injury to, or detention, loss, or destruction of, property. 96 **ALR** 18–245; s. in 111 **ALR** 1299–1309.

16 **Rocky M. L. R.** 162, Interest as Damages in Colorado.

6 15 **Am Jur,** Damages, §§ 141–144.

previous litigation. And the same reasoning has been applied to a similar case where goods were sold by A to B and by B to C with a warranty of title or quality, and C recovered a judgment against B for breach of warranty.

Where A wrongfully obtained an injunction against B and B is compelled to sue A for dissolution of the injunction bond given by A and for damages, B is entitled, by the weight of authority, to recover reasonable counsel fees and other expenses incurred in prosecuting the suit.

CHAPTER II

DAMAGES IN TORT ACTIONS—EMINENT DOMAIN

§ 7. Personal injuries.[7] Where the plaintiff has suffered a permanent personal injury he is entitled to recover both past and future medical and nursing expenses, damages for both past and future physical pain and mental suffering, and damages for both past and future earnings. The better view is that it is no defense that medical and nursing services were or will be rendered or paid for gratuitously by members of the plaintiff's family or by his employer or by an insurance company. Where plaintiff is nursed by a member of his family the value of his services is to be computed on the basis of value as a nurse.

The physical pain and mental suffering includes not only the pain and shock at the time of the injury and during medical treatment but fear of future inability to work and embarrassment due to any scars or disfigurement; where the plaintiff was a pregnant woman she was allowed to recover for mental worry that the child would be marked though there is no scientific basis for such apprehension.

[7] 15 **Am Jur,** Damages. §§ 70–105.

Excessiveness of verdict in action by person injured for injuries not resulting in death (For the years 1916–1926). 46 **ALR** 1230–1423; s. in 102 **ALR** 1125–1579.

Excessive or inadequate damages for personal injuries resulting in death (For period beginning 1916). 48 **ALR** 817–876.

Excessiveness or inadequacy of verdict in action for false imprisonment or for malicious prosecution. 40 **ALR** 297–334; s. in 47 **ALR** 312–314.

Right to recover for mental pain and anguish alone, apart from other damages. 23 **ALR** 361–392; s. in 44 **ALR** 428–430; 56 **ALR** 657–660.

Damages for mental anguish on account of mutilation of corpse. 12 **ALR** 342–349.

"Sentimental" losses, including mental anguish, loss of society, and loss of marital, filial, or parental care and guidance, as elements of damages in action for wrongful death. 74 **ALR** 11–116.

Mental distress from pregnant woman's apprehension or realization of injury to or loss of child, as element of damages in action for personal injury. 145 **ALR** 1104–1113.

Recovery for illness, disease, or death claimed to have resulted from worry or mental anguish following breach of contract or tort. 122 **ALR** 1486–1496.

Recovery for physical consequences of fright resulting in a physical injury. 11 **ALR** 1119–1144; s. in 40 **ALR** 983–987; 76 **ALR** 681–686; 98 **ALR** 402–406.

Measure of damages in action by female for assault upon her. 6 **ALR** 1062–1067.

Excessive or inadequate damages for an assault or assault and battery upon a female. 6 **ALR** 1074–1081.

Liability of person causing injury for aggravation thereof by accident. 9 **ALR** 255–262; s. in 20 **ALR** 524.

Future pain and suffering as element of damages for physical injury. 81 **ALR** 423–472.

Instructions regarding measurement of damages for pain and suffering. 85 **ALR** 1010–1053.

Damages on account of medical expenses, past or future, due to injury to wife, as recoverable by her or by the husband. 66 **ALR** 1189–1197.

Loss of enjoyment as an element of, or factor in determining, damages for bodily injury. 120 **ALR** 535–543.

Admissibility, as against objection of remoteness, of evidence as to past earnings, upon issue as to amount of damages in action for personal injury or death. 130 **ALR** 164–178.

What items of damage on account of personal injury to infant belong to him and what to parent. 37 **ALR** 11–85.

Measure of damages for loss of earning capacity of person engaged in business for himself. 9 **ALR** 510–520; s. in 27 **ALR** 430–436; 63 **ALR** 142–156; 122 **ALR** 197–320.

In determining the amount of the probable loss of future earnings, the jury should take into account not only the probable expectancy of life as calculated by mortality tables but also the amount of wages the plaintiff had been receiving, his habits and the condition of his health before and after his injury; in determining the present worth of such probable future earnings the annuity tables are ordinarily used, making allowances for probable diminution of wages due to increased age. Where the plaintiff was engaged on his own account in the practice of a profession, evidence of his past earnings are used as a basis of computation; if he was employed by others, his wages or salary or commissions; if he was the owner of a small business where the profits of the business were dependent chiefly upon his own efforts, then the past profits of the business.

Where the person injured is a minor he is entitled to recover for past and future pain and suffering and for probable future earnings after majority shall have been reached; the parent is entitled to recover for expenses incurred for medical treatment and nursing, and for increased cost of maintenance and for loss of services till majority.

Where the person injured is a married woman, she is entitled to recover for physical pain, mental suffering and humiliation due to disfigurement; also the cost of treatment where she has paid it or it is charged to her, and impairment of earning capacity where she was employed outside the household. Her husband is entitled to recover the cost of treatment where he has paid it or it has been charged to him, for the loss of her services in the household, and for the interference with his enjoyment of her society.

§ 8. Death by wrongful act.[8] At common law where B wrongfully caused personal injuries to A later resulting in A's death, A's right of action for pain and suffering, for expenses incurred in treating the injury and loss of earnings died with him unless reduced to judgment before his death. In most states today, by what are called Survival Acts, this action survives to A's executor or administrator, the recovery becoming part of A's estate. In all the states there are statutes, usually called Death Acts, which give a new cause of action for wrongfully causing death, the recovery usually not going to A's estate but to his widow and next of kin.

Where, as in most states having both statutes, both actions may be brought, the damages in survival actions are limited to those that accrued before A's death; where, as in some states, there is no recovery under the Death Act where the death does not follow at once, recovery under the Survival Act includes also the loss to A's estate of A's earning power during the period of his life expectancy. This, according to the better view, consists of the probable earnings which A would have made during the rest of his life less his personal living expenses.

8 16 Am Jur, Death, §§ 176–200.

Duty to instruct, and effect of failure to instruct, jury as to reduction to present worth of damages for future loss on account of death or personal injury. 77 ALR 1439–1466.

Right of jury to allow substantial damages in action for death of minor child not gainfully employed. 149 ALR 234–271.

Increase in cost of living as affecting damages for personal injuries or death. 3 ALR 610–612; s. in 10 ALR 179–180; 18 ALR 564–567; 60 ALR 1395–1397.

Measure of damages for death in action for benefit of decedent's estate. 7 ALR 1314–1335; s. in 26 ALR 593–600.

Funeral expenses as element of damages for wrongful death. 94 ALR 438–448.

Damages in action for personal injuries or death as including value of care and nursing necessitated by the injury, rendered by one spouse to another or by a third person gratuitously or as a result of hospitalization insurance previously carried. 128 ALR 686–704.

Pecuniary value of services rendered by deceased without legal obligation as element of damages for his death. 53 ALR 1102–1105.

Where action is brought under the Death Act some states allow recovery for loss to the estate and the recovery goes to the estate; in other states, where the recovery goes to the surviving members of the family, recovery is allowed for their pecuniary loss due to the death but not for loss of society and companionship.

In a few states punitive damages are allowed where the defendant's act was wanton or malicious.

§ 9. Damage to interests in personal property.[9] Where B wrongfully destroys A's personal property he is liable for its value at the time of destruction, with interest. Where the property is not destroyed but is wrongfully damaged to such an extent that it cannot be satisfactorily repaired, the measure of recovery is the difference between its value just before and its value just after the damage was inflicted. If satisfactory repair is possible—and especially if A has already repaired it—he recovers the reasonable cost of repairs plus the difference between its value just before and its value just after it was repaired if there has been depreciation; if the repaired article is of more value, then the difference should be deducted; and if during the period of repair A has been compelled to use a substitute for the damaged chattel, then the reasonable cost of such rental should be added.

Where A succeeds in an action of replevin against B and during the action B has given a counter bond and kept the chattel, A is entitled to recover damages for such detention; similar reasoning applies in the converse case where A fails in the action and was in possession of the chattel during the action. Where the chattel is turned over to A at the end of the trial or where it is not available and A is compelled to accept the value of the chattel as if he had brought trover, his damages for detention will ordinarily be measured by the value of the use during the period plus depreciation; but where the property is valuable only for consumption, legal interest for the period will be allowed.

§ 10. Damage to interests in land.[10] Where B has wrongfully destroyed A's growing crops, either by fumes or fire or water, A is entitled to the value

[9] 15 **Am Jur,** Damages, §§ 121–128.

Measure of damages for destruction of or damage to automobile other than commercial vehicle. 78 **ALR** 917–923.

Measure of damages for destruction of or injury to commercial vehicle. 4 **ALR** 1350–1364; s. in 32 **ALR** 706–707; 78 **ALR** 910–914.

Recovery for depreciation of property between the date it was replevied and final judgment. 24 **ALR** 1189–1196.

Damages for killing or injuring dog. 94 **ALR** 729–738.

Measure of damages for fraud inducing the purchase of corporate securities. 57 **ALR** 1142–1154; s. in 108 **ALR** 1060–1067.

Constitutionality, construction, and application of statutory provisions for recovery of damages by defendant in attachment or garnishment. 125 **ALR** 1219–1228.

Injury to credit as element of damages for wrongful attachment. 54 **ALR** 451–457.

Allowance as damages for conversion of commodities or chattels of fluctuating value, of increase in market value after the time of conversion. 40 **ALR** 1282–1304; s. in 87 **ALR** 817–820.

Measure of damages for carrier's conversion of goods. 56 **ALR** 1171–1186.

Measure of damages for loss or conversion of, or injury to, wearing apparel or household goods. 63 **ALR** 240–263.

[10] 15 **Am Jur,** Damages, §§ 107–120.

Cost of building or repairs thereto as necessary or proper element in fixing damages for its destruction or injury. 7 **ALR** 277–303.

Nuisance as entitling owner or occupant of real estate to recover damages for personal inconvenience, discomfort, annoyance, anguish, or sickness, distinct from, or in addition to, damages for depreciation in value of property or its use. 142 **ALR** 1307–1337.

Measure of damages for pollution of pated Injury to Land.
stream. 38 **ALR** 1388–1401.

Right of trespasser to credit for expenditures in producing, as against his liability for value of, oil or mineral. 7 **ALR** 908–933; s. in 23 **ALR** 193–194.

Damages recoverable by owner or occupier of surface on account of subsidence due to mining operations. 35 **ALR** 1137–1149; s. in 56 **ALR** 310–313.

37 **Harv. L. R.** 574, Damages for Antici-

which the crop would have had if it had matured and been harvested, less the cost of the labor of cultivating the crop and harvesting it. If B has merely damaged the crop A is entitled to the difference between the value of the crop just before and just after the damage was inflicted.

Where B has wrongfully cut A's trees which are chiefly valuable for timber he is usually allowed to choose between suing for the damage to the land and suing for the value of the trees as timber. Where the trees are too immature to be valuable for timber or where they are fruit or shade trees, the better view allows the plaintiff to choose between recovery for the damage to the land and recovery for the value of the trees to A.

Where B has destroyed a building on A's land which was in good condition A is apparently entitled to choose between the damage to the land as a whole and the value of the building which is usually computed upon the cost of replacement less depreciation; if the buildings are merely damaged and can be easily repaired, then the reasonable cost of the repair plus the value of the use of the building during the repair period. If the buildings are old and dilapidated A should be entitled to choose between the diminution in the value of the land and the diminution in the value of the building itself because the building might have considerable value to A and yet be of slight or no value to the land.

Where B has wrongfully caused damage to A's land by a permanent structure—usually on B's land—the weight of authority is that A may recover not only for the damage done down to the date of bringing his action but also for prospective damages. The difficulty here is chiefly in determining whether the structure should be regarded as permanent; for example, it was held that a dam was not a permanent structure because it might be reconstructed while in another case a railroad embankment and bridges were held to be permanent even though openings could be made in them which would put an end to flooding plaintiff's land.

§ 11. Defamation.[1] A nuisance per se means a clear case of nuisance such as a slaughter house or soap factory near a residential district; similarly, a libel per se or slander per se means a clear case of defamation such as calling the plaintiff a thief or murderer. Actionable per se, on the other hand, means actionable without proof of special damage, for example, trespass to land, trover and actions for breach of contract. Under the old law of defamation a slander was not actionable per se unless the plaintiff was charged

1 33 **Am Jur,** Libel and Slander, §§ 199–223.

Evidence of wealth or reputed wealth of defendant in action for libel or slander. 34 **ALR** 3–25.

Retraction as affecting right of action or amount of damages for libel or slander. 13 **ALR** 794–802.

Sufficiency of allegations of loss of patronage or profits to permit recovery of special damages from false publication. 86 **ALR** 848–858.

Mental or physical suffering as element of damages for libel or slander. 90 **ALR** 1175–1203.

Provocation as mitigating damages in action for libel or slander. 132 **ALR** 932–956.

2 15 **Am Jur,** Damages, §§ 265–300.

Actual damages as a necessary predicate of punitive or exemplary damages. 33 **ALR** 384–417; s. in 81 **ALR** 913–919.

Punitive or exemplary damages in action for alienation of affections or criminal conversation. 16 **ALR** 1316–1322.

Liability of telegraph company for punitive damages for wrongful or negligent acts of employees as regards messages. 89 **ALR** 356–373.

Exemplary or punitive damages as recoverable in action for death. 94 **ALR** 384–401.

Applicability of statutes providing for multiple damages or penalty for wrongful trespass as affected by the defendant's purpose or intent. 111 **ALR** 79–102.

Punitive or exemplary damages for assault. 16 **ALR** 771–856; s. in 123 **ALR** 1115–1148.

44 **Harv. L. R.** 1173, Punitive Damages in Tort Cases.

6 **John Marshall L. Q.** 477, Can Damages Properly Be Punitive?

with a crime or a loathsome disease or was disparaged in his office, business, trade or profession, whereas all libels were actionable per se. But apparently because of confusing libelous per se with actionable per se a large number of states now require proof of special damage in libel cases unless the written charge was libelous per se.

Special damage in defamation cases must be pecuniary; humiliation, mental pain, even physical illness have been held insufficient. In any defamation case where the damage claimed by the plaintiff would not usually follow from the defamatory charge it must be specifically alleged in the declaration. Where special damage is not necessary or where it is alleged and proved the plaintiff is entitled to recover, without specific allegation, for damage to his reputation, loss of business, mental pain and physical suffering resulting therefrom.

Where the defamatory charge is actionable and has been made maliciously or with reckless indifference to consequences, most states allow the jury to assess exemplary or punitive damages. On the other hand, the defendant is entitled to show, in mitigation of damages, that before the defendant published the defamatory charge the plaintiff's reputation was already tarnished.

§ 12. Exemplary or punitive damages.[2] In almost all states a jury may, in its discretion, in any tort action or action for breach of contract to marry where the conduct of the defendant was malicious, wanton, oppressive or insulting, assess against him exemplary or punitive or vindictive damages as a deterrent to wrongdoing. The fact that the defendant has already been punished criminally for the offense is no defense and in most states does not even reduce the amount of recovery. By the majority view a verdict for exemplary damages may be given if a cause of action is proved even though there is no finding of substantial damage.

In some states there may be a verdict for exemplary damages against an employer even though he does not participate in or ratify the employee's conduct but the weight of authority seems to be contra.

§ 13. Eminent domain proceedings.[3] Where plaintiff's property is taken by eminent domain proceedings, either by the state or by a public utility so authorized by the state, he is entitled to its market value for the highest and best available use, less any increase of value to the plaintiff's other land due to the public improvement, plus any damage done to the plaintiff's other land by the prospective construction or operation of the improvement.

[3] 12 **Am Jur,** Constitutional Law, § 658.
18 **Am Jur,** Eminent Domain, §§ 240–303.
Deduction of benefits in determining compensation or damages in eminent domain. 145 **ALR** 7–299.
Increment to value, from project for which land is condemned, as a factor in fixing compensation. 147 **ALR** 66–103.
Profits derived from business conducted on property taken by eminent domain as evidence of market value. 7 **ALR** 163–175.
Income as an element in determining value of property taken in eminent domain. 65 **ALR** 455–466.
Measure of damages or compensation where property is taken to widen street. 64 **ALR** 1513–1535.
Measure of damages for injury to land caused by obstruction of highway. 128 **ALR** 780–792.
Special value or adaptability of property for purposes for which it is taken, as an element of, or matter for consideration in fixing, damages in condemnation proceedings. 124 **ALR** 910–937.
Measure and items of compensation or damages for flooding property under the right of eminent domain. 106 **ALR** 955–996.
Compensation in eminent domain in respect of fixtures or chattels used in connection with real property taken or damaged. 90 **ALR** 159–166.
Measure of owner's damages for temporary appropriation of or injury to real property by municipality or other public authority. 87 **ALR** 1384–1392.
Expense of building and maintaining fences as element in determination of damages in eminent domain. 10 **ALR** 451–462.

The fact that it is especially adapted for the use for which it is taken may be taken into consideration where the land could have been thus used by the plaintiff or others without the exercise of eminent domain; otherwise, probably not, though it has been argued that since owners of property are usually allowed to profit by socially useful efforts a plaintiff should be allowed compensation for the "strategic value" due to the likelihood that the land, being especially adapted, will be taken in eminent domain proceedings.

Where the land taken has been devoted to a noncommercial purpose such as a college or church or clubhouse the plaintiff is entitled to the amount which a buyer needing property devoted to such a use would pay for it.

Where the ownership of the land is divided among various holders, for example, A has a life estate, B the fee in remainder and both subject to an easement belonging to C, each is entitled to compensation for his interest unless a statute requires compensation to be assessed on the property as a whole.

CHAPTER III

DAMAGES IN CONTRACT CASES

§ 14. In general—liquidated damages.[4] Where A brings an action against B for breach of contract the general rule as to damages is that A is entitled to be placed in the position he would have occupied if B had performed his promise. This rule was modified by Hadley v. Baxendale which held that there could be no recovery for damage which was not reasonably foreseeable by the parties when the contract was made. This means that if the damage was unusual B must have been notified of the special hazard before the contract was made and in some states it has been held also that B must have expressly or impliedly agreed to be liable for such damage if it should occur. In determining whether there has been sufficient notice to B in the particular case courts are likely to be influenced by the proportion between the risk imposed upon B and B's expected profit on the transaction and by whether B's breach was or was not wilful and deliberate.

For example, where A claimed loss of profits on his saw mill because of B's failure to perform his contract to lend money to A, it was held that he was not entitled because B had no notice that A could not borrow money elsewhere; and when A claimed loss of a prospective resale of goods because of B's breach of warranty of title or of equality, A could not recover for such loss unless B had notice of what A expected to do with the goods. The doctrine of Hadley v. Baxendale has also been applied to actions against common carriers for damage to, delay in, and failure to deliver freight and to actions against telegraph companies for mistakes in messages or for delay or failure to deliver them.

Damages for mental pain are not allowed even though foreseeable, except in

[4] 15 **Am Jur,** Damages, §§ 240–264.

Rate of foreign exchange to be taken into account in assessing damages for breach of contract. 11 **ALR** 363–374; s. in 33 **ALR** 1285–1291; 43 **ALR** 520–522; 50 **ALR** 1273–1276; 105 **ALR** 640–646.

Right to amount stipulated in contract for breach where it appears there were no actual damages, or there was no proof of such damages. 34 **ALR** 1336–1350.

Punitive or exemplary damages for breach of contract, other than contracts to marry and actions on statutory bonds. 84 **ALR** 1345–1354.

Right to recover, and measure of recovery, for breach of obligation to drill wells in search for oil or gas or other obligation of a prospecting or exploratory character. 122 **ALR** 458–479.

"Out of pocket" or "benefit of bargain" as proper rule of damages for fraudulent representations inducing contract. 124 **ALR** 37–82.

Measure of damages for breach of contract to lend money. 36 **ALR** 1408–1435; s. in 44 **ALR** 1486–1487.

actions for breach of contract to marry and actions against public service companies where, of course, the action might have been brought in tort instead of contract; but in some states where a breach of contract involves the relations of A to his family, damages for mental distress have been permitted.

Where the amount of profits lost by A because of B's breach of contract is so uncertain that no recovery can be had for them courts usually allow as the measure of damages the reasonably necessary expenditures and services rendered by A in his preparation for performance and in his part performance.

Where A and B provide in their contract that in the case of breach a certain amount shall be paid this stipulation will fix the amount of recovery if A and B intended it as an estimate of the probable loss and the amount fixed was not unreasonable at the time of contract; otherwise it will be ignored as a mere unenforcible penalty. Whether the parties use the term liquidated damages or penalty is not important. Provisions for liquidated damages are often used in contracts to sell land, or goods or a business, construction contracts and employment contracts.

§ 15. Construction contracts.[5] Where, after A has partly performed, B repudiates the contract, A is logically entitled to recover the contract price less what it would have cost him to complete the work; but where it is difficult for A to prove with reasonable certainty the cost of completion he has sometimes been allowed the profit upon the entire contract plus the cost to him of the work already done; other cases have allowed him such part of the contract price as the cost of completing part bears to the cost of com-

Measure of damages for breach of duty by bank in respect to collection of commercial paper. 19 **ALR** 555–601; s. in 67 **ALR** 1511–1519.

Measure of damages for tenant's failure to surrender possession of rented premises. 39 **ALR** 386–397.

Measure of damages for breach by lessor of contract to lease or to put lessee into possession. 104 **ALR** 132–167.

Provision in lease for pecuniary forfeiture where lease is prematurely terminated as one for liquidated damages. 106 **ALR** 292–318.

Measure of damages for buyer's repudiation of or failure to accept goods under executory contract. 44 **ALR** 215–285; s. in 108 **ALR** 1482–1504.

Provision for liquidated damages in contract for sale of goods. 138 **ALR** 594–633.

Stipulation as to damages in case of breach of contract for purchase of goods to be manufactured by other party, as penalty or liquidated damages. 79 **ALR** 188–195.

Damages for breach by seller or former employee of covenant, express or implied, not to engage in like business or enter employment of competitor of covenantee. 127 **ALR** 1152–1179.

Stipulation as to amount recoverable for breach of contract against entering certain business or employment as a provision for liquidated damages or for a penalty. 59 **ALR** 1135–1145.

Liability of seller for special damages based on resale by buyer, as affected by his knowledge or ignorance of the resale. 88 **ALR** 1439–1480.

Expense of caring for personal property prior to its resale upon failure of sale contract. 29 **ALR** 61–73.

Measure of seller's damages under executory contract as affected by his resale of the property. 44 **ALR** 296–340; s. in 119 **ALR** 1141–1151.

Loss of anticipated profits as damages for breach of seller's contract as to machine for buyer's use. 32 **ALR** 120–156.

Anticipatory repudiation of contract for sale of goods by buyer as affecting time as of which damages are to be computed. 34 **ALR** 114–132.

Extent of liability of seller of live stock infected with communicable disease. 51 **ALR** 498–507.

Damages for breach of telegraph company's agreement to transmit money. 80 **ALR** 298–307.

Measure of damages for failure, delay, or mistake in transmitting or delivering telegram in cipher. 55 **ALR** 1146–1153.

Measure of damages for breach of contract to will property. 31 **ALR** 129–146.

5 9 **Am Jur**, Building and Construction Contracts, §§ 150–156.

Measure of owner's damages for delay of contractor, or breach resulting in delay, where performance of other contract or work was necessary to complete project. 125 **ALR** 1242–1251.

Cost of correction or completion, rather than loss in property value, as measure of damages recoverable for breach of building contract or other contract to change condition of real property. 123 **ALR** 515–537.

Wilful or intentional variation by contractor from terms of contract in regard to material or work as affecting measure of damages. 6 **ALR** 137–145.

31 **Col. L. R.** 1286, Builder's Measure of Recovery for Breach of Contract.

pleting the whole contract, plus the profit that would have been made on the uncompleted part. The advantage of the last two formulas is that A will usually be allowed to recover something for the part already done.

Where there would have been no profit on the entire contract it is much better for A to sue in quasi contract because, by the weight of authority, he is not limited to the contract rate on the part already performed but may recover for the actual cost of the work done.

Where, after part performance by A, it is A instead of B who defaults and the default is not wilful, many states allow A to recover in quasi contract for the reasonable value of the work done, not to exceed the contract rate, less a reasonable allowance for the damage caused to B by A's breach. Where B uses A's breach by way of recoupment or counterclaim or independent action and A's default consists of defective construction, B is entitled to the reasonable cost of remedying the defect; but if the defect is such that it cannot be satisfactorily remedied at reasonable cost, then B is entitled to the difference between the value of the building as it is and the value it would have had if it had been completed according to contract. Where A's default consists of abandoning the contract after part performance, B is entitled to recover for the delay plus the reasonable cost of completion. Where A's default consists merely in delay B is entitled to recover for the rental value of the completed building.

§ 16. Employment contracts.[6] Where A, an employee, has been discharged by B in breach of the contract of employment, A is entitled to sue at once, and to recover what he would have earned for the full term of the contract, less the amount which B can show that A has earned or could have earned in other employment during that period, plus reasonable expenses incurred in seeking other employment. If A has secured employment of any sort before suing, what he has earned goes in reducing his recovery; if he has not secured employment he is chargeable only with what he could have earned in another position of the same rank and grade, in the same kind of work, in the same locality.

Where by the employment contract A was entitled to commissions on sales or to a percentage of profits of the business, recovery may be had therefor if the amount of what he would have received can be established with reasonable certainty.

§ 17. Contracts to sell land—covenants of title.[7] Where A contracts to sell land to B and B wrongfully refuses to perform, A is entitled to recover

6 35 **Am Jur**, Master and Servant, §§ 55–57.

Wrongful discharge of servant—doctrine of "constructive service." 8 **ALR** 338–351; s. in 17 **ALR** 629–650.

Kind of other employment within rule which requires discharged employee to seek or accept other employment or credit earnings in such employment. 28 **ALR** 736–758; s. in 141 **ALR** 662–674.

Recovery by commission salesman given exclusive territory where employer breaches contract of employment. 41 **ALR** 1175–1184.

Employer's offer to take back employee wrongfully discharged as affecting former's liability. 72 **ALR** 1049–1059.

Expenses incurred in seeking or in obtaining other employment as element of damages in an action for wrongful discharge of employee. 84 **ALR** 171–176.

7 14 **Am Jur**, Covenants, Conditions, and Restrictions, §§ 140–190.

See also **Am Jur**, Vendor and Purchaser.

Measure of damages for purchaser's breach of contract to buy real property. 52 **ALR** 1511–1533.

Measure of recovery by buyer where seller breaches agreement to repurchase at selling price. 50 **ALR** 325–335.

Measure of recovery by vendee under executory contract for purchase of real property where vendor is unable or refuses to convey. 48 **ALR** 12–72; s. in 68 **ALR** 137–152.

Measure of damages for breach of covenants of title in conveyance or mortgages of real property. 61 **ALR** 10–190; s. in 100 **ALR** 1194–1204.

the excess of the contract price over the market price at the time fixed for performance. If A has in the meantime sold the land to X for a less price than B was to pay, this resale price is merely evidential of the market price in A's favor, but it fixes the top limit of A's recovery.

Where it is A who defaults, B should logically be allowed the excess of the market price at the time of performance over the contract price and this is the rule in about half of the states; but in the other half, the courts substantially follow the English rule which limits recovery against an innocent vendor who is unable to convey to the amount of the deposit paid by the buyer and the expenditures made by him, unless the vendor has assumed the risk of his inability to convey good title. The expenditures usually include the reasonable cost of investigating the title.

Where A has conveyed the land to B by deed with covenants of title and the title wholly fails so that B is compelled to give up possession to X, B should logically be entitled to recover the value of the land at the time of eviction and this is the rule in England and a few states in New England; but in the other states B is allowed to recover only the price paid by him to A just as if he were suing in quasi contract instead of in contract. The prevailing rule grew up during pioneer days when values of land were increasing so rapidly that the courts thought that the English rule would work great hardship on vendors.

When B buys in an outstanding title or an incumbrance he is entitled to recover the amount paid therefor, not exceeding the price received by A from B for the land. Where B reasonably defends his title in court he is entitled to recover also the amounts thus expended in his unsuccessful attempt.

PART II EQUITY AND COMMERCIAL

EQUITY

I. LIMITS AND NATURE OF EQUITY JURISDICTION.

§ 1. *Equity acts in personam, not in rem.*
§ 2. *Decrees involving affirmative acts abroad.*

II. SPECIFIC PERFORMANCE OF CONTRACTS.

A. In General.

§ 3. *Is there a right to break a contract?*
§ 4. *Alternative performance—liquidated damages—penalty.*

B. Affirmative Contracts.

§ 5. *Contracts for the sale of interests in land—mutuality.*
§ 6. *Contracts relating to property other than land.*
§ 7. *Damages at law conjectural.*
§ 8. *Contracts for continuous performance.*
§ 9. *Miscellaneous cases.*

C. Negative Contracts.

§ 10. *Defendant's promise entirely negative.*
§ 11. *Defendant's undertaking partly affirmative—Lumley v. Wagner.*

D. Relief for and against Third Persons.

§ 12. *The creation of a property right in P.*
§ 13. *Bankruptcy of V; of P.*
§ 14. *Contracts to devise—right of a beneficiary to sue in equity.*

E. Equitable Servitudes.

§ 15. *Tulk v. Moxhay.*
§ 16. *Who are bound by and who may enforce.*
§ 17. *Miscellaneous matters.*

F. Consequences of Right of Specific Performance.

§ 18. *Devolution of rights and obligations of P; of V.*
§ 19. *Options.*
§ 20. *Transfers of rights of V; of P.*
§ 21. *Risk of loss.*

G. Partial Performance with Compensation.

§ 22. *Suit by V; by P.*

H. Defenses.

§ 23. *Lack or inadequacy of consideration.*
§ 24. *Title not marketable.*
§ 25. *Statute of frauds—part performance.*
§ 26. *Plaintiff's default or laches.*
§ 27. *Fraud, misrepresentation and concealment.*
§ 28. *Mistake, sharp practice, hardship.*
§ 29. *Lack of mutuality.*

III. REFORMATION OF INSTRUMENTS.

§ 30. *The invulnerability of instruments at common law.*
§ 31. *Bilateral transactions—mutual mistake.*
§ 32. *Same—defendant's knowledge of plaintiff's mistake—collateral matters.*
§ 33. *Unilateral transactions.*

CHAPTER I

LIMITS AND NATURE OF EQUITY JURISDICTION

§ 1. Equity acts in personam, not in rem.[1] After the Norman conquest of England in 1066 the king became the fountainhead of justice which was administered by the judges of the king's courts. The jurisdiction of these common-law courts was limited by the original writs issued by the king's secretary or chancellor. The jurisdiction of the equity court, gradually developed by the chancellor, was limited only by the chancellor himself. There were two important limitations, both adopted to avoid any clash with the common-law courts. One was that equity would not interfere where there was an adequate remedy at common law; the other was that equity would act merely against the person of the common-law plaintiff or defendant and would therefore affect the legal right only in that indirect fashion. For example, an injunction against negotiating a negotiable note does not destroy the negotiability of the note; an injunction against enforcing a common-law judgment does not affect the validity of the judgment; if the defendant is willing to remain in prison for contempt he may have execution on the judgment. And a decree that the defendant convey land does not affect legal title to the land; hence if the defendant is insane, all that the equity court can do—unless it assumes in rem jurisdiction—is to decree that the defendant convey when he shall have recovered from his insanity. Now that there is no longer any danger of a clash with common-law courts there is no reason why equity should not assume such jurisdiction without a statute and a few states have done so; but the general understanding has been that legislation is necessary and in most states such statutes have been passed.

§ 2. Decrees involving affirmative acts abroad.[2] If the defendant has been properly served with process or has submitted to the jurisdiction of the equity court a decree may be given though it affects property outside the state; for example, a decree that the defendant convey land outside the state, which may be performed anywhere and does not involve the defendant's

[1] 19 **Am Jur**, Equity, §§ 3, 23.

Jurisdiction of equity to sequester, seize, enjoin transfer of, or otherwise provisionally secure assets for application upon money demand which has not been reduced to judgment. 116 **ALR** 270–320.

Jurisdiction to enjoin trespass upon real property in another state or country. 113 **ALR** 940–944.

Power to enjoin party from prosecuting or commencing an equitable suit. 102 **ALR** 308–320.

Constructive service of process against nonresident in suit for specific performance of contract relating to real property within state. 93 **ALR** 621–632.

Remedies in respect of mortgage on real property in another state or the debt secured thereby. 42 **ALR** 470–487.

Meritorious defense as a condition of injunction against judgment for want of jurisdiction. 39 **ALR** 414–428; s. in 118 **ALR** 1498–1505.

He who comes into equity must come with clean hands. 4 **ALR** 44–107.

Decree granting injunction as bar to action at law for past damages on account of thing enjoined. 14 **ALR** 543–547.

18 **Notre Dame Lawyer** 119, Aristotle's Conception of Equity.

[2] 19 **Am Jur**, Equity, §§ 23–25.

Jurisdiction and propriety of its exercise, to require real property in another state or country to be applied in satisfaction of debt (including the setting aside of a fraudulent conveyance thereof). 144 **ALR** 646–663.

leaving the state. Similarly, such a defendant may be enjoined from doing any act anywhere in the world since he may obey the decree anywhere by merely doing nothing: for example, a decree that defendant refrain from committing a trespass in another state. But where the carrying out of a court's decree would involve affirmative acts abroad, either of the defendant or of its own officers, relief will usually be refused; for example, the abatement of a foreign nuisance.

CHAPTER II

SPECIFIC PERFORMANCE OF CONTRACTS

A. In General

§ 3. Is there a right to break a contract? [3] Equity's giving specific performance of contracts was stoutly resisted by common-law courts, Lord Coke insisting that a party to a contract had a right to break it and pay damages. The answer to this argument is that each party to a contract has a right to have the other party perform in specie and that it is merely because the common law is defective in its machinery that it gives only damages; there is no right to break a contract even though there happens to be the power to do so. Even at common law the right to performance in specie is recognized in some cases and given effect to indirectly. For example, if X wrongfully induces A not to perform his contract to render services to B, the latter may hold X liable in an action of tort. If A had a right to break his contract with B, it is difficult to see how inducing him to break it could be a tort.

§ 4. Alternative performance—liquidated damages—penalty. [4] Where defendant's promise is in the alternative, either to do or to refrain from doing certain acts or to pay money at his option, equity will not give specific performance because that would be taking away defendant's option and thereby making a contract for the parties substantially different from the one into which they entered. But where the parties contemplate that the payment of money is not performance but is merely a fixing of liquidated damages or a penalty for nonperformance, this does not bar the giving of specific performance even though the defendant is willing and offers to pay the amount.

B. Affirmative Contracts

§ 5. Contracts for the sale of interests in land—mutuality. [5] The great weight of authority is that equity will give specific performance of a contract to sell any interest in land without regard to the size, value or loca-

[3] 49 Am Jur, Specific Performance, § 2.
Dismissal of suit as affecting election of remedies as between damages and specific performance. 26 ALR 111-116.

[4] 19 Am Jur, Specific Performance, §§ 43-45.
Provision in land contract for pecuniary forfeiture or penalty upon default of the purchaser as affecting the vendor's right to maintain an action for the purchase price. 32 ALR 617-627.
A provision in land contract for pecuniary forfeiture or penalty by a party in default as affecting the right of the other party to specific performance. 32 ALR 584-609; s. in 98 ALR 887-897.
Stipulation in land contract for payment of specified sum by vendor in case of default as provision for liquidated damages or penalty. 48 ALR 899-913.

[5] 49 Am Jur, Specific Performance, §§ 34, 35.
Specific performance of a contract as a matter of right. 65 ALR 7-110.
Specific performance of written executory contract for lease of real property. 31 ALR 502-571.

tion of the land or the possibility of getting other land substantially equivalent, there being a hard and fast rule that land is unique and that in such cases damages are inadequate; for example, a contract to give or to renew a lease, a contract to sell an easement or a mere possessory interest in the land, or a contract providing to sell standing trees which are not to be severed at once, are all specifically enforcible. Nor is it an objection that the purchaser does not expect to keep the land or that he has already agreed to sell it to a third party. And not only may the buyer get specific performance; if the case is one where the buyer could have had specific performance, the vendor may also, though of course all that the vendor asks is money. The justification for this hard and fast affirmative rule of mutuality is that there is not an open market for land and wherever it is important for the vendor to sell the land it is likely to be very difficult to find another buyer.

§ 6. Contracts relating to property other than land.[6] Where there is a contract to sell a chattel which is procurable on the open market, the common-law remedy of damages is obviously adequate and equity will not give specific performance, for example, all the ordinary agricultural and manufactured products. Where the subject matter of an entire contract is partly ordinary chattels and partly an interest in land equity will give specific performance of the whole contract.

Equity will also give specific performance where the chattel is unique and cannot be duplicated—for example, a painting by one of the old masters; or where it has a sentimental value, such as an heirloom; or where the circumstances are such that it is procurable only from the vendor, for example, stone from a particular quarry to finish a partly constructed building. Similar reasoning applies to property protected by a legal monopoly such as a patent or copyright.

The weight of authority is that specific performance of a contract to sell shares of stock in private corporations will be given unless there is an open market for such stock so that its value can be easily ascertained and the purchaser may be able to buy elsewhere.

Where the vendor of an ordinary chattel has been paid all or a substantial part of the purchase price and has become insolvent without delivering the chattel it is obvious that damages are inadequate and specific performance has been given in a few cases; the objection to it is that it is usually unfair to other creditors of the vendor.

§ 7. Damages at law conjectural.[7] If an action at law is brought for the breach of a contract to sell an annuity the market value of the annuity will be computed according to one of the recognized mortality tables which are based upon the expectancy of life of the average human being. The plaintiff, whether vendor or purchaser, may properly insist that he had in mind not the life of the average person but the life of the particular individual; it is obvious that damages in such a case would be conjectural. Similarly,

6 49 **Am Jur**, Specific Performance, §§ 125–133.

Specific performance of contract for sale of corporate stock. 22 **ALR** 1032–1073; s. in 130 **ALR** 920–937.

Specific performance, or injunction against breach, of contract for sale of tangible personal property. 152 **ALR** 4–87

31 **Harv. L. R.** 702, Insolvency and Specific Performance.

7 49 **Am Jur**, Specific Performance, §§ 10–13, 82–86.

Specific performance of contract to lend or borrow money. 41 **ALR** 357–362.

2 **Wash. and Lee L. R.** 210, The Enforcement of Oral Promises to Give Real Estate Security.

in a contract to sell dividends against a bankrupt's estate the uncertainty of the percentage of dividends which the estate will pay makes damages at law so conjectural that specific performance will be decreed to either seller or buyer.

A contract to give a mortgage on specific land would be specifically enforcible merely because an interest in land is involved. But a contract to give a mortgage on specific property of any kind will be specifically enforced because damages are conjectural. If the debtor should remain solvent there would be no damage and the damages recoverable would be only nominal; but if the debtor should become insolvent the damage might be the total amount of the debt depending upon the seriousness of the insolvency.

If an insurance company contracts to insure and then refuses to issue a policy, equity will give specific performance because damages are conjectural, varying from a nominal amount up to the full amount of the policy in case of a total loss.

If a seller contracts to deliver property which fluctuates greatly in value, the deliveries to be made in installments covering a relatively long period of time, equity will usually give specific performance because damages would be conjectural.

§ 8. Contracts for continuous performance.[8] Where the defendant has agreed to erect a building according to plans and specifications on the plaintiff's land, damages at law are usually more satisfactory than specific performance because the plaintiff can usually find some one else who will do the work substantially as well and it is better to have a builder who works willingly than one who works under compulsion; furthermore there is the difficulty of supervising defendant's performance, so that specific performance will not be decreed unless the hardship on the plaintiff would be very great. But where the defendant has agreed to erect on his own land a building of a certain type to cost not less than a stated sum, the benefit to the plaintiff consisting of an expected enhancement of value to his other land in the vicinity, equity will usually give specific performance because damages would be conjectural and no supervision by the court would be necessary.

A contract to render personal services will not be affirmatively enforced against the party who agreed to perform the services even though such services are unique because personal services rendered under compulsion are not likely to be satisfactory and if the services to be rendered are those of manual labor through long hours and for a considerable period of time an order of court requiring the defendant to perform them would be in violation of the United States Constitution.

§ 9. Miscellaneous cases.[9] A contract to lend money cannot be specifically

8 49 **Am Jur,** Specific Performance, §§ 69–71.

Specific performance of contract for services. 135 **ALR** 279–317.

9 49 **Am Jur,** Specific Performance, §§ 72, 86.

Contract for exclusive distribution or sales agency as subject of suit for specific performance. 145 **ALR** 684–694.

Right of vendee to enforce specific performance where his vendor holds equitable title under executory contract or deed in escrow executed by owner of legal title. 141 **ALR** 1432–1440.

Specific performance of contract to adopt. 27 **ALR** 1325–1360; s. in 142 **ALR** 84–129.

Uncertainty as to terms of mortgage or note contemplated by contract for sale of real property as affecting right to specific performance. 37 **ALR** 365–378.

Validity and enforceability of provision for renewal of lease at rental not determined. 30 **ALR** 572–587; s. in 68 **ALR** 157–161.

Right to specific performance, or injunction against breach, of lease or sublease or of contract to make lease as affected by right of complainant to cancel lease before expiration of term for which other party is bound. 117 **ALR** 256–262.

enforced by either party even though the loan is to be with security. In most cases damages at law are adequate because there is ordinarily an open market for the lending and borrowing of money upon good security. If the loan were to be made without security or with insufficient security, specific performance should be denied because there is no way of assuring that the lender will get back his money at the maturity of the debt.

If a contract is made to submit a matter to arbitration and the arbitrators make an award the award is treated as if it were a contract between the parties, so that if the award is to convey land, specific performance will be given. But if after the agreement to arbitrate is made, one of the parties refuses to appoint an arbitrator, equity will not interfere because the acts expected of an arbitrator involve so much discretion that it is unlikely that a command by a court of equity would bring about the desired result. But in many states statutes have been passed providing for compulsory arbitration.

A contract to enter into a partnership for an indefinite period will not be specifically enforced because such a partnership could be immediately dissolved and the equity decree rendered futile. A contract to enter into a partnership for a fixed time will not be enforced for the same reason that equity will not give specific performance of contracts to render personal services; no court would undertake to compel the partners to work together as such.

C. Negative Contracts

§ 10. Defendant's promise entirely negative.[10] Where A has contracted never to sue B on a certain cause of action, equity will give specific performance by a perpetual injunction in order to avoid circuity of action. In most states today the same facts may be set up as a so-called equitable defense at law. If the contract not to sue was for a limited time, equity will give specific performance by a temporary injunction till the time has expired. If a common-law court in such a case should allow B to recover back the full

Vendor's or vendee's lien against realty in case of combined sale of realty and personalty. 88 **ALR** 92–104.

Validity of agreements to arbitrate disputes generally as a condition precedent to the bringing of an action. 26 **ALR** 1077–1085.

Power of equity to decree that party perform obligations of contract within fixed time upon pain of forfeiture. 114 **ALR** 1389–1401.

Deed of one acquiring vendor's title as meeting vendor's obligation. 109 **ALR** 182–190.

Waiver of, or estoppel to assert, or election not to assert, forfeiture of executory land contract because of default in payment. 107 **ALR** 345–409.

Remedies for breach of decedent's agreement to devise, bequeath, or leave property as compensation for services. 69 **ALR** 14–219; s. in 106 **ALR** 742–767.

Vendor's remedy by foreclosure of contract for sale of real property. 77 **ALR** 270–294.

Specific performance of contract to lend or borrow money. 41 **ALR** 357–362.

Right of vendee under an executory land contract to a lien for amount paid on the purchase price. 45 **ALR** 352–370.

Right of purchaser to acquire and assert outstanding title as against vendor. 40 **ALR** 1078–1081.

Judgment as lien on judgment debtor's equitable interest in real property. 30 **ALR** 504–532.

Right of vendor and purchaser respectively to possession pending performance, but before default, of executory contract for sale of real estate. 28 **ALR** 1069–1089.

Liability for taxes accruing after execution of contract for sale of land and before conveyance. 12 **ALR** 411–426.

Adverse possession as against vendor by one who enters under executory contract. 1 **ALR** 1329–1352.

Interlocutory mandatory injunction to compel surrender of possession. 32 **ALR** 894–918.

Arbitration agreement made pending action. 42 **ALR** 727.

10 35 **Am Jur,** Master and Servant, § 97.

36 **Am Jur,** Monopolies, Combinations, and Restraints of Trade, § 202.

45 **Am Jur,** Release, § 3.

Enforceability of agreement not to compete as against a nonsigner or a signer who had no interest as owner in property or business sold. 94 **ALR** 341–351.

Validity and enforceability of contractual restrictions on right to practice as physician, surgeon, dentist, etc. 58 **ALR** 156–175.

amount of the judgment there would be circuity of action as in the case of a promise never to sue; if it should allow recovery of less than the full amount the common-law remedy would be inadequate because of the difficulty of estimating the amount of damages in such a case.

If A sells out his business to B and agrees, as a part of the consideration, not to engage in competition with B, equity will give specific performance to B if the contract is not illegal as in unreasonable restraint of trade, the value of the goodwill of a business being conjectural. Similar reasoning applies where A's promise not to compete is based upon a consideration other than the sale of a business.

If an employee agrees, as a part of the consideration for his employment, not to divulge his employer's trade secrets, equity will give specific performance of such a contract, damages being wholly inadequate because of the difficulty of estimating them, and because irreparable damage would usually result. Even if there is no express promise the circumstances may be such as to show an implied promise.

§ 11. Defendant's undertaking partly affirmative — Lumley v. Wagner.[1] In the leading case of Lumley v. Wagner, 42 Eng Reprint 687, the defendant, Joanna Wagner, a singer of great ability, agreed to sing at plaintiff's theater in London for a certain period and not to sing elsewhere during that time. Later the defendant refused to sing for the plaintiff and entered into a contract to sing during that period at a rival theater. The court specifically enforced defendant's promise not to sing elsewhere during the time of her contract with the plaintiff by giving a temporary injunction. There were the following elements in the case:

(1) The affirmative promise was not specifically enforcible because it was a contract to render personal services. If it had been specifically enforcible there would have been no difficulty in giving negative relief.

(2) There was no separate consideration for the negative promise; if there had been, so as to make the contract a divisible one, there would be no objection to specific performance, damages being inadequate.

(3) The negative promise was incidental to the affirmative; that is, the main thing the plaintiff wanted was that defendant should sing for him but he also wished to be protected against business being attracted away from his theater to that of a rival by her singing at the latter's theater; and he wanted specific performance of the negative, not only because it would prevent his rival from increasing his share of the theater patronage, but in order to bring pressure upon the defendant to perform her affirmative undertaking. In other words, performance of the negative is being sought not merely for its own sake but in order to bring about performance of the affirmative which the court would not directly enforce. It has been urged in criticism of the decision that it is an unwarranted extension of equity jurisdiction because the court is attempting to do indirectly what it cannot do directly. If the court had no jurisdiction to compel the performance of the affirmative the criticism would be sound, but equity does have jurisdiction, the objection being one merely going to its exercise because of the difficulty of supervision. In

1 49 **Am Jur**, Specific Performance, §§ 134–137.

Injunction to prevent employment of, or contract with, another, as available remedy for defendant's breach of contract to employ plaintiff or give him an exclusive right to promote or sell defendant's product or invention. 125 **ALR** 1446–1455.

Validity and enforceability of restrictive covenant in contracts of employment. 9 **ALR** 1456–1484; s. in 20 **ALR** 861–870; 29 **ALR** 1331–1334; 52 **ALR** 1362–1373; 67 **ALR** 1002–1010; 98 **ALR** 963–990.

enjoining a breach of the negative there was no difficulty about supervision.

(4) Defendant had broken both promises; plaintiff had been damaged by the breach of the affirmative and would have been damaged further by the breach of the negative. If instead of contracting to sing at a rival theater in London she had contracted to sing in a city so far distant that such singing could not damage the plaintiff, the better view is that equitable relief should not be given.

(5) Miss Wagner could not have obtained specific performance of a promise by Lumley not to employ anyone else during the period of her engagement because damages would have been adequate to her; but if she were a comparatively unknown singer in England and a London appearance was of great importance to her, she should logically be given relief. The few decisions on the point have given relief to the employee.

(6) If after giving Lumley his decree he refused to accept Miss Wagner back to the performance of her contract or refused to pay her for her services, she would be entitled at once to have the injunction dissolved.

(7) In Lumley v. Wagner, the defendant's promise was express but this was not necessary; a promise to do anything necessarily involves a promise not to do anything inconsistent with it. But merely making an express promise not to quit the employment is not sufficient.

(8) If Miss Wagner had merely made a contract to sing for Lumley's rival in the afternoons while she sang for Lumley at night, Lumley would probably be entitled to an injunction because of the damage it would do to his business. If the contract were to sing in the afternoons in a remote section of London so that his business would not be damaged thereby he should be denied relief unless such singing made her less effective in the evenings.

(9) Miss Wagner's services were unique. If an employee's services are not unique the employer is not entitled to an injunction even though the employee in his contract admitted that they were.

D. Relief for and against Third Persons

§ 12. The creation of a property right in P.[2] The purchaser's specifically enforcible right to get specific property is of necessity a specific property right and not a mere contract right. One might reasonably expect that equity would consider that this property right came into existence at the time set by the parties for performance, because it is not till then that the purchaser can get a conveyance; but the rule is well settled that equity regards the purchaser as having a specific property right from the moment of making the specifically enforcible contract. There were two reasons for this: (1) If no time is set for performance a purchaser is entitled to performance after a reasonable time has elapsed. It would be highly inconvenient to have the time of coming into existence of important property rights open to such an uncertainty. Since it is fairly easy to determine the date of completion of a contract the advantage of having the equitable property right date from that time is obvious. (2) If a time is set for performance and the vendor keeps the property till that time it might not be objectionable to regard the purchaser as having only a common-law contract right till that time and to regard the equitable property right as coming into existence at that time if the vendor failed to convey. But to hold that the purchaser has

[2] 49 Am Jur, Specific Performance, § 149.

no property right till the time set for performance would make it possible for the vendor to prevent him from ever getting it by merely conveying it away before the time set. In order to give the purchaser adequate protection the equity courts were compelled to regard the purchaser as having a property right from the moment of contract.

The situation between V and P is as follows: From the moment the contract is entered into which equity would enforce on behalf of both parties, V is treated in equity as a fiduciary of the land, holding the legal title as security for the payment of the purchase money while P is treated as the equitable owner with the right to become the legal owner upon paying or satisfactorily securing the price. But though the equitable property right comes into existence at the moment of contract it is postponed as to enjoyment till the time for performance, the situation being analogous to the relation between the tenant of a particular estate and the holder of a shifting use.

It is often said that P is trustee of the purchase money; all this means is that equity will compel him to pay the full amount of the purchase money. If, as is usually the case, he does not have the sum set aside, there could be no trust because there would be no trust property. And even though he does have it set aside, there could be no trust till V assents to it.

§ 13. Bankruptcy of V; of P.[3] If after making a specifically enforcible contract to sell land V should transfer the land to a third person or should die and the land should descend to his heir or should go by will to a devisee, the transferee would take subject to P's equity unless he were a bona fide purchaser for value without notice. If V should become bankrupt the assignee in bankruptcy, not being a bona fide purchaser, takes subject to P's rights; P, having an equitable property right and not merely a contract right is entitled to the property in specie and need not come in with the general creditors. Also specific performance may be enforced by V's assignees in bankruptcy against P.

But if it is P who becomes bankrupt V cannot enforce specific performance against P's assignees in bankruptcy because V's right is not a right to any specific property of P's but merely to a sum of money out of P's general assets, hence there is no specific property for him to claim. And although his remedy at law is not adequate, it would inflict too great a hardship on the other creditors to throw upon P's assignee in bankruptcy the burden of getting rid of the property. V's remedy is to sue for breach, reduce his claim to judgment and then prove with the other creditors.

Though P's assignees in bankruptcy cannot be compelled to take the property and pay the purchase price, they may, if they prefer, enforce specific performance against V, for example, where the property has increased greatly in value.

Similar reasoning applies where P assigns his rights to X without becoming bankrupt; V cannot specifically enforce the contract against X unless X has expressly or impliedly assumed to pay the purchase price; the assignment passes rights to X but imposes no liabilities. If X does not undertake to pay the purchase price, V's remedy is to have the property sold on a foreclosure sale, equity treating V as if he were a mortgagee.

§ 14. Contracts to devise—right of a beneficiary to sue in equity.[4] A contract to devise land is treated like a contract to convey by deed; from the

[3] 49 Am Jur, Specific Performance, §§ 147–158.

[4] 57 Am Jur, Wills.

moment of making the contract the owner is regarded as a fiduciary thereof, so that if he devises it to another or allows it to descend to his heir or transfers it by deed to anyone except a bona fide purchaser for value, specific performance will be granted and the transferee declared a constructive trustee of the property.

Where V contracts with P to convey the land to X as either payment or gift beneficiary, X is entitled to specific performance against V.

E. Equitable Servitudes

§ 15. Tulk v. Moxhay.[5] In Tulk v. Moxhay (1848) 2 Phillips 774, 41 Eng Reprint 1143, the plaintiff, who was the owner of a piece of vacant land in Leicester Square and also of several of the houses forming the square, sold it to one Elms, the deed contained a covenant by Elms that he, his heirs and assigns would keep the piece of ground in its then state. The piece of land passed by several conveyances into the hands of the defendant whose deed contained no similar covenant with his vendor but he had notice of the original covenant when he made his purchase. The defendant having asserted a right to build on the land, the plaintiff sought and obtained an injunction.

The court placed its decision upon the ground that otherwise the defendant would be unjustly enriched; but it is clear that there would be no unjust enrichment unless there was a misapprehension of the law because the price of the property would be fixed according to whether the covenant was or was not enforcible. The decision has been uniformly followed because there was need—in the rapid growth of modern cities—for some way to control the use of property. A specifically enforcible right that the land of another shall not be used in a certain way is of course a property right; but though it originated because the legal remedy was not adequate it developed into a technical property right not dependent upon the rules of specific performance of contracts, the plaintiff not being required to show any damage at all. Hence equitable servitudes are to be sustained, not upon the ground of the inadequacy of the common law of contracts, but upon the inadequacy of the common-law of property.

§ 16. Who are bound by and who may enforce.[6] A common-law easement or profit is enforcible against any successor in title though he paid value in good faith; but, like other equitable rights, the benefit of an equitable servitude cannot be enforced against a bona fide purchaser for value, though —unlike a common-law covenant running with the land—it can be enforced against one who does not succeed to the estate of the covenantor. One who obtains title from a trustee by adverse possession is entitled to hold it against the cestui que trust even though he knew of the trust; but one who by adverse possession obtains title to property subject to an equitable servitude is bound by it even if he had no notice of it. The only way he can get

[5] 14 **Am Jur,** Covenants, Conditions, and Restrictions, §§ 192–194.

Garage, or filling station, as breach of restrictive covenant. 54 **ALR** 659–699; s. in 99 **ALR** 541–551.

Part of structure that must be beyond line to amount to violation of building-line restriction. 55 **ALR** 332–349.

Mandatory injunction as remedy for breach of restrictive covenant affecting real property. 57 **ALR** 336–346.

Multiple-residence structures as violations of restrictive covenants. 18 **ALR** 451–468; s. in 57 **ALR** 244–253.

[6] 14 **Am Jur,** Covenants, Conditions and Restrictions. §§ 308–335.

Who may enforce restrictive covenant or agreement as to use of property. 21 **ALR** 1281–1327; s. in 33 **ALR** 676–678; 60 **ALR** 1223–1233; 89 **ALR** 812–819.

28 **Va. L. R.** 951, 1067, The Enforcement of Equitable Servitudes in Land.

rid of it by adverse action is by violating it and having the statute of limitations run in his favor.

This is the reason for the distinction—the owner of the benefit of the equitable servitudes is not interested in the ownership of the servient property, but merely in the way the property is used. While it is a breach of trust for the trustee to convey trust property without the consent of the cestui que trust, or an order of court, because he owes a fiduciary duty to protect and administer the property for the cestui, the holder of property subject to an equitable servitude is not a fiduciary to that extent; he may alien freely except that he must not destroy the servitude by conveying it to a bona fide purchaser for value. And if he has made no covenant, he does not become liable for any infringement by his alienee unless he authorizes it.

In determining the question as to who may enforce equitable servitudes, equity will usually carry out the intentions of the parties. While it is usually the intent to benefit a particular piece of land into whosoever hands it may come the parties may intend that the servitude shall last only so long as the covenantee continues to hold the land. It would seem that the courts should not be inclined to infer such an intent because such a limitation very largely wipes out the commercial value of the servitude to the covenantee; if the transferee knows that he will not be able to enforce the servitude he will pay his transferor nothing for it.

While one having an estate in possession in the dominant property can get an injunction without showing any damage to such property, one who has an estate in reversion or remainder after a life estate and is not the promisee must show that the breach would cause damage to his estate in order to get injunctive relief.

§ 17. **Miscellaneous matters.**[7] Though equitable servitudes are treated as technical property rights, no particular formality is required for their creation and in some states there need be no memorandum to comply with the statute of frauds; it is not important whether the restrictions take the form of covenants, reservations or conditions. Mutual covenants in general building schemes are frequently inferred from the circumstances surrounding the sale of the group of lots, but it is safer to have an express stipulation that each of the various transferees is to have the benefit of the restriction upon the other lots.

Where the character of the neighborhood has so changed that giving an injunction would be futile, equitable relief will be denied; and it will also be denied to a plaintiff who has acquiesced in its violation or who has himself violated the restriction. Though most equitable servitudes are in the nature of restrictions, a few cases have upheld servitudes requiring affirmative action on the part of the owner of the servient property.

Most of the cases of equitable servitudes consist of restrictions imposed upon one piece of land for the benefit of another piece of land, but they may be imposed upon a business or upon chattels.

[7] 14 **Am Jur,** Covenants, Conditions, and Restrictions, §§ 210–288.

Change of neighborhood in restricted district as affecting enforcement of restrictive covenant. 54 **ALR** 812–837; s. in 85 **ALR** 985–996; 103 **ALR** 734–739.

Right of manufacturer, producer, or wholesaler to control resale price. 7 **ALR** 449–493; s. in 19 **ALR** 925–931; 32 **ALR** 1087–1088; 103 **ALR** 1331–1343; 125 **ALR** 1335–1367.

41 **Harv. L. R.** 945, Equitable Servitudes on Chattels.

F. Consequences of Right of Specific Performance

§ 18. Devolution of rights and obligations of P; of V.[8] Upon the death of P intestate his equitable right to get real property goes to his heir, but his right to sue at law for damages goes to his executor who may enforce only if the heir declines to sue for specific performance. If the heir does sue he should join the executor as codefendant so as to compel him to pay for the property out of the personal assets. If P devises his right to the land to X, the rights of X are the same as those of the heir in case of intestacy.

Upon the death of V his equitable right to obtain the purchase price and his right to sue at law for damages both go to his executor; but if the contract fixes a time in the future for performance his right to the rents and profits during that period go to V's heir. If after V's death P seeks specific performance his suit is primarily against V's heir because he has the title, but V's executor should be joined because the money is to be paid by him.

§ 19. Options.[9] Where a specifically enforcible express option to buy land has not been exercised before the option holder's death and the period for exercising the option has not yet elapsed the more logical view is that since it is a right to get the land at a desirable price it should pass to the heir who must, however, pay for it out of his own pocket because the executor is not bound; the few cases on the point are in conflict, some holding that it passes to the executor.

Where the owner of land, subject to an option to buy, dies before the holder of the option has exercised it and thereafter it is accepted, the purchase money should go to the heir because his ancestor had no right to the purchase money but held the land subject to its being turned into money; and this is the modern trend. But the older cases gave it to the executor with the unfortunate practical result that the heir's right to the land could be destroyed at the whim of the option holder and nothing left in its place.

§ 20. Transfers of rights of V; of P.[10] When V transfers to X his right to the purchase money, usually evidenced by a note or bond, X is entitled to have the land held for him as security, but a transfer to X of the land—that is, the security—does not carry with it the right to the purchase money; in such a case X's rights, if any, are to show that the transfer of the right to the purchase money had been omitted by mistake.

Where V has wrongfully sold the land to a bona fide purchaser for value P cannot, of course, get specific performance of the contract, but he may still get equitable relief against V by way of an accounting for the value of the land or by having a constructive trust declared. Where the purchase money notes recite that

8 49 **Am Jur,** Specific Performance, § 147.
Obligation of assignee to vendor to perform contract on assignment by purchaser of contract to sell real property. 59 **ALR** 954–969.
Right or duty of executor or administrator to complete or enforce decedent's executory contract for purchase of real property. 58 **ALR** 436–457.
Rights and remedies of vendor under executory contract for the sale of land as affected by vendee's death. 35 **ALR** 927–938.

9 49 **Am Jur,** Specific Performance, §§ 117–120.
Option to purchase at price offered to optionor by third person. 136 **ALR** 138–151.
Instrument for purchase of land as a contract or an option. 3 **ALR** 576–605; s. in 87 **ALR** 563–582.
Exercise of option as affecting rights intervening between giving and exercise of option. 50 **ALR** 1314–1329.
Who may enforce option contained in lease for purchase of property. 38 **ALR** 1162–1180.

10 49 **Am Jur,** Specific Performance, §§ 147–158.
Remedy of specific performance as available to vendee's assignee. 138 **ALR** 205–220.

they are given for the purchase money, this is notice to any transferee of the notes of P's equitable claim to specific performance and if good title to the land cannot be made the notes cannot be enforced.

At common-law the land is liable for the debts of V, but since in equity V is merely a fiduciary of the land from the moment of contract, P may enjoin V's creditors from levying on the land.

P's equitable right to the land and his common-law right to sue for damages are both freely alienable; if P undertook to assign them to different parties the equitable property right would almost certainly take precedence. The remedy of P's creditor is by a bill in equity for equitable execution but in many states P's equitable property right can be sold at common-law execution.

§ 21. **Risk of loss.**[1] Where a building on the land has accidentally burned after the making of a contract specifically enforcible against P, the great weight of authority is that V may compel P to pay the full purchase price on the ground that since he has the equitable property right from the moment of contract he should bear the loss. That this reasoning is unsound is shown by the fact that if because of V's default, he cannot enforce the contract, he cannot shift the loss to P even though P, not being in default, has the equitable right to the property. The rule does not apply if the vendor agrees to deliver the premises in the condition then existing.

The rule works badly practically because it is the general understanding among laymen that the risk does not pass till P gets title and hence he does not insure. Logically he is not entitled to the insurance money received by V because the insurance contract is one of personal indemnity, but in many states the hardship of the illogical general rule has been mitigated by illogically allowing P to get the insurance money. Persons who are in the habit of drawing up sale contracts usually avoid the rule by providing that the risk of loss shall be upon V till he conveys the title.

G. Partial Performance with Compensation

§ 22. **Suit by V; by P.**[2] If V brings suit for specific performance and is unable to perform fully—usually because of a deficiency in acreage—the court may in its discretion award him specific performance with compensation to P for the deficiency. If the suit is brought by P instead of by V the court may likewise in its discretion award specific performance to P with compensation, the court being more liberal in its attitude where P is suing and is willing to accept whatever performance V is able to give. The criticism of the doctrine is that unless it is carefully limited in its application it may work a hardship upon the defendant by making over his contract and compelling him to perform it as thus made over, when he would never have made such a contract if he had known that complete performance could not be made.

1 49 **Am Jur**, Specific Performance, §§ 105–110.

Rights of vendor and purchaser inter se in respect of proceeds of insurance. 37 **ALR** 1324–1331; s. in 40 **ALR** 607–608; 51 **ALR** 929–930.

Who must bear loss due to destruction or deterioration of real property pending contract for its conveyance. 22 **ALR** 575–585; s. in 41 **ALR** 1272–1273; 46 **ALR** 1126–1127; 101 **ALR** 1241–1247.

2 49 **Am Jur**, Specific Performance, §§ 102–114.

Right of vendor to specific performance with abatement from purchase price where he is unable to perform as to part of property. 81 **ALR** 900–908.

Specific performance with abatement from purchase price of the value of the wife's dower interest. 46 **ALR** 748–772; s. in 148 **ALR** 292–300.

Dower rights of wife of purchaser under executory contract. 66 **ALR** 65–77.

Where the defect in V's title is known by P at the time of contract he cannot get compensation unless V agreed to remove the defect and then failed to do so. Where it is of such a nature that it is difficult to estimate the proper compensation to be allowed, for example, where land was subject to restrictive covenants, compensation will be refused. Where V's wife refuses to release her inchoate dower right, some courts refuse to allow P any compensation therefor, some figure compensation according to mortality tables and some direct that part of the purchase price be retained by P to indemnify him in case V's wife should survive V.

H. Defenses

§ 23. Lack or inadequacy of consideration.[3] Though the common-law action of covenant may be maintained by either V or P where the contract to convey was under seal the weight of authority seems to be that neither may get specific performance of the contract if there was no consideration for it. But a sealed gratuitous option to convey land is specifically enforcible by P because, though he pays nothing for the option, he must pay for the land.

Mere inadequacy of consideration is no defense to an action for specific performance, but where it is so great as to shock the chancellor's conscience or where it is coupled with insufficient evidence of fraud or unfair conduct or coercion, relief may be denied.

§ 24. Title not marketable.[4] Though V's title is one which a court or a trained lawyer would regard as good, equity will not compel P to accept it if the average layman would regard it as doubtful unless the court, having all the necessary parties before it, is able to and does remove the doubt. It is no objection that the title was acquired by adverse possession. In some states the equity rule has been adopted at law.

§ 25. Statute of frauds—part performance.[5] A contract to convey an interest in land either by deed or will is not, by the statute of frauds, usually enforcible unless there is a memorandum signed by the party to be charged therewith. But certain acts have been held sufficient to take the case out of

[3] 49 **Am Jur**, Specific Performance, §§ 26, 65.

[4] 49 **Am Jur**, Specific Performance, § 95.

Necessity of tender of performance by vendee as condition of specific performance where vendor's title is defective. 79 **ALR** 1240–1249.

Marketability of title derived from or through tax proceedings. 115 **ALR** 140–147.

Right of vendee prior to time fixed by contract for conveyance to complain of encumbrances or defects in title. 109 ALR 242–272.

Opinion of court or counsel or other person learned in law as a factor in determining marketability of title. 90 **ALR** 609–616.

Marketability of title derived from or through infant. 90 **ALR** 87–96.

Marketable title. 57 **ALR** 1253–1554.

Duty of vendor as to abstract of title. 52 **ALR** 1460–1504.

Taking or remaining in possession under executory contract for the purchase of land as waiver of right to complain of defects in or failure of vendor's title. 34 **ALR** 1321–1330.

[5] 49 **Am Jur**, Statute of Frauds, §§ 149–235, 313–478.

Part performance to take oral contract of lease out of statute of frauds predicated upon acts or conduct of one in possession of the property under another contract or right. 125 **ALR** 1468–1482.

Doctrine of part performance in suits for specific performance of parol contract to convey real property. 101 **ALR** 923–1115.

Doctrine of part performance as sustaining action at law based on contract within Statute of Frauds. 59 **ALR** 1305–1318.

What constitutes part performance sufficient to take agreement in consideration of marriage out of operation of Statute of Frauds. 48 **ALR** 1356–1364.

Character and extent of improvements necessary to constitute part performance. 33 **ALR** 1489–1543.

Accepting paid employment or remaining in such employment as part performance which will take oral contract to convey or devise real property out of Statute of Frauds. 40 **ALR** 223–229.

the statute; courts are accustomed to say that the act must be unequivocally and solely referable to some contract with reference to the land. In some states it is enough if P takes possession under the oral contract; in others he must take possession and make valuable improvements. Continuance in possession and making valuable improvements is enough. If the case is taken out of the statute in favor of P it is also taken out in favor of V.

Even full payment of the purchase price is not enough, whether that consists of money, labor, material or other land. But irreparable change of position without change of possession has been held sufficient; where personal services have been rendered in return for an oral promise to devise, the weight of authority is against giving relief where there has been no change of possession.

Where A orally promises to make a gift to B of a tract of land and B in reliance thereon takes possession and erects valuable improvements thereon, B may get specific performance of the oral promise though by the modern law of contracts there is no contract because the legal detriment was not suffered in exchange for but merely in reliance upon A's promise.

The doctrine of part performance is not recognized at common law; hence if A conveys away the promised property to a bona fide purchaser for value, B's sole relief is in equity for an accounting of the value of the property thus sold; he cannot recover at law on the contract.

§ 26. Plaintiff's default or laches.[6] Where there is an express condition precedent with which plaintiff has for any reason failed to comply, the plaintiff is ordinarily barred in equity as well as at law. Where a plaintiff has failed to accept an option within the time fixed for acceptance he cannot get specific performance because no contract has come into existence. And a plaintiff may be barred because he has made a substantial default in the performance of his own promise. Where P has become insolvent after making the contract he cannot insist upon the credit provided for in the contract.

If after making the contract P first learns of a defect in V's title, he is justified, after waiting a reasonable time for V to remedy the defect, to repudiate the contract; and if he does so and changes his position upon the supposition that he cannot get the land, V cannot, by repairing the defect later, insist upon performance.

In the ordinary land contract a delay of weeks or even months may not give rise to a defense by the other party; but if in the meantime the property has changed considerably in value, the court is likely to refuse relief. If the circumstances are such as to show that prompt performance is very important, for example, if the property involved is fluctuating in value, a very slight delay on the part of the plaintiff is likely to be fatal.

Contracts frequently stipulate that time shall be of the essence and earlier cases have enforced such a stipulation against a purchaser who has paid a large part of the purchase price and then made a slight default in paying a later instalment, quite ignoring the fact that in such a case P is substantially in the position of a mortgagor and should be protected against such a for-

6 49 **Am Jur**, Specific Performance, §§ 73–76.

Right of party who has once refused to perform to have specific performance of contract. 2 **ALR** 416–422.

Right of purchaser under land contract to anticipate time of payment fixed by contract. 17 **ALR** 866–873.

Vendor's acceptance of payment tendered after time specified as waiver of provision making time of essence of contract. 9 **ALR** 996–1006.

Time for performance of contract for sale or exchange of land where time fixed by contract has been waived. 4 **ALR** 815–827.

feiture. Later cases are not inclined to take such a stipulation seriously except where P has paid nothing or only a small part of the purchase price.

Where P delays a long time V is entitled to foreclose P's right outside of court by a notice to P to complete the purchase by a particular date, provided the time thus allowed is reasonable; but it is usually safer for V to apply to a court of equity to set the time.

§ 27. **Fraud, misrepresentation and concealment.**[7] Misconduct of a plaintiff which is not serious enough to bar an action at law or to serve as a basis for rescission of the transaction in equity may be a bar to a suit for specific performance; in such a case if the plaintiff does sue at law the jury is not likely to award him full damages.

Though innocent misrepresentation by itself is not likely to be a bar to specific performance, it may be a bar if coupled with the fact that great hardship would result to the other party if specific performance should be granted.

Ordinarily a nonfiduciary is under no duty to disclose what he knows to the other party to the transaction, but nondisclosure by a fiduciary to his beneficiary may amount to fraudulent concealment and be a bar to relief.

§ 28. **Mistake, sharp practice, hardship.**[8] When defendant's mistake is not serious enough to justify a court of equity in rescinding a contract or a conveyance it may still be used as a defense to a suit for specific performance especially when it is combined with sharp practice on the part of the plaintiff or when specific performance would result in great hardship to the defendant. The fact that the plaintiff innocently caused the mistake will make the courts less likely to give him relief; and the fact that the defendant was negligent in making the mistake will tend to influence the court in favor of the plaintiff. Though hardship alone is rarely, if ever, a ground for rescission, it may be, if very great, a bar to specific performance.

§ 29. **Lack of mutuality.**[9] Where an infant makes a contract to buy or sell a piece of land and while still an infant sues for specific performance, it is the well-settled and sound rule that he cannot get it for the very good reason that he could later make the decree futile by rescinding the transaction. Fry, in his book on Specific Performance, ignoring the real reason for the decision, generalized from this one particular by laying down the rule that "when, therefore, whether from personal incapacity, the nature of the contract or any other cause the contract is incapable of being enforced against one party, that party is equally incapable of enforcing it against the other. . . ."

The rule, as thus laid down, is subject to a large number of exceptions, for example: (1) where the infant sues after he becomes an adult; (2) where the defendant has, but the plaintiff has not, complied with the statute

[7] 49 **Am Jur**, Specific Performance, §§ 46–53.

Concealment of fact that one of parties to land contract was acting for third person, or misrepresentation as to identity of party for whom he was acting as reason for denying specific performance or for rescission of contract. 121 **ALR** 1162–1179.

Fraud or misrepresentation not sufficient to prevent or support other forms of relief as ground for refusing specific performance of land contract. 87 **ALR** 1345–1356.

[8] 49 **Am Jur**, Specific Performance, §§ 54–64.

Ignorance of, or mistake as to, terms of existing mortgage upon the property as ground for relief from a contract for the purchase of real property. 26 **ALR** 528–537.

[9] 49 **Am Jur**, Specific Performance, §§ 34–39.

Infancy of party to contract as affecting his right to specific enforcement. 43 **ALR** 120–136.

of frauds; (3) where there has been complete performance by the plaintiff; (4) options; (5) where the vendor fails to get title but later procures it before the purchaser learns of the defect. The true principle was first laid down by Professor Ames and may be stated as follows: a defendant should not be compelled specifically to perform his promise unless he has already received the plaintiff's performance or the equity court is in a position to give him such performance either at the time of the decree or later. The Fry doctrine is usually referred to as that of lack of mutuality of remedy; the Ames rule is usually known as that of lack of mutuality of performance.

CHAPTER III

REFORMATION OF INSTRUMENTS

§ 30. The invulnerability of instruments at common law.[10] At common law if a transaction, whether contract or conveyance, was reduced to a written instrument, the instrument was conclusive as to the terms of such contract or conveyance. This so-called parol-evidence rule was a valuable rule of convenience but it resulted in much injustice if the instrument did not express the actual intent of the parties thereto. In order to relieve from this injustice an equity court will rectify or correct the written instrument so as to make it conform to the actual intent.

All instruments except wills are subject to reformation, but not mere memoranda. If the transaction is a business or bilateral one the standard of rectification is the intent of both parties; if it is unilateral, it is the intent of the transferor, who is usually a donor.

§ 31. Bilateral transactions—mutual mistake.[1] If A contracts to convey eighty acres of land to B and by mistake the scrivener includes another tract of twenty acres, A may have the deed rectified; and this right, like other equities, is good against any transferee of B except a bona fide purchaser for value. If A should sell and convey to B a farm supposed to contain 200 acres at $100 an acre but the farm contained only 180 acres and B has paid the full purchase price his proper remedy is ordinarily at law in quasi contract to get back the excess payment; but if the mistake has been made in the deed also so that it is necessary or desirable to have the deed corrected, his remedy is in equity for reformation.

§ 32. Same—defendant's knowledge of plaintiff's mistake—collateral matters.[2] If at the time plaintiff thinks he is making a bargain with defendant

10 20 **Am Jur,** Evidence, §§ 1091-1141.

45 **Am Jur,** Reformation of Instruments, § 113.

Pendency of suit for cancelation, reformation, or rescission of a contract as abating subsequent action to enforce it or to recover damages for its breach, and vice versa. 118 **ALR** 1240-1252.

When does limitation or laches commence to run against suit to reform an instrument. 106 **ALR** 1338-1353.

Effect of alteration intended merely to correct mistake in instrument so as to conform it to original understanding. 73 **ALR** 652-669.

Right to reformation of conveyance as depending upon consideration. 69 **ALR** 423-443; s. in 128 **ALR** 1299-1305.

Right to reformation of contract or instrument as affected by intervening rights of third persons. 44 **ALR** 78-120; s. in 102 **ALR** 825-837.

Reformation as condition of assertion of right of action or defense predicated on the true contract differing from that evidenced by the written instrument; and right to both reformation and other relief in same action or suit. 66 **ALR** 763-793.

1 45 **Am Jur,** Reformation of Instruments, §§ 45-49.

Reformation on ground of mutual mistake regarding character or extent of estate or title imported by language used in instrument. 141 **ALR** 826-843.

Reformation of instrument on ground of mutual mistake as to legal significance of the terms used. 135 **ALR** 1452-1458.

23 **Harv. L. R.** 608, Mistake of Fact as a Ground for Affirmative Equitable Relief.

2 45 **Am Jur,** Reformation of Instruments, §§ 48, 57-62.

Right of insurer to reformation of policy

the latter knows that the plaintiff is suffering under a misapprehension as to the terms of his offer or acceptance, the defendant's fraudulent conduct entitles the plaintiff to have the transaction rescinded because there was no real bargain and hence no basis for reformation. But if the bargain had actually been entered into, the fraud of the defendant either in reducing the bargain to writing or in performing the contract will not prevent the plaintiff from getting reformation. Where, however, the defendant is entirely innocent of the plaintiff's mistake, reformation will be refused. It will also be refused if the mistake is as to some extrinsic or collateral matter going merely to the motive for entering the transaction; for example, where the plaintiff accepted a quitclaim deed thinking that there were no incumbrances on the land.

§ 33. **Unilateral transactions.**[3] If a donor by mistake conveys eighty acres when he meant to convey only sixty, he is entitled to have the deed reformed; the intent of the donee is not important.

If a donor by mistake conveys sixty acres when he meant to convey eighty, the donee is not entitled to any relief. But if a debtor conveys sixty acres when he meant to convey eighty in payment of or as security for a pre-existing obligation, the creditor is entitled to reformation because, although the creditor could not have compelled the transfer of any property, he stands in a stronger position than a mere donee.

Where the donor's mistake is not discovered till after his death, some cases have allowed reformation to the donee against the representatives of the deceased on the ground that as between volunteers equity is justified in giving reformation in order to carry out the intent of the donor.

§ 34. **Mistake of law—amount of proof required.**[4] Following Lord Ellenborough's unfortunate holding in Bilbie v. Lumley (1802) 2 East 469, 102 Eng. Reprint 448 the rule is frequently laid down that equity will not grant reformation where the mistake is one of law, but there are very few decisions to that effect and the modern trend is the other way.

Because in giving reformation equity disregards the parol evidence rule, clear and convincing evidence of the mistake is required.

§ 35. **Statute of frauds.**[5] Where A by mistake conveys to B more land than the contract called for there is no difficulty about the statute of frauds because B's obligation to return the excess is in the nature of a constructive trust. But where A conveys too little, A's obligation to convey the omitted portion is in the nature of specific performance of the contract and a minority of states refuse to give relief because to do so without a memorandum would be a violation of the statute of frauds. But the weight of authority is that B is entitled to relief, the statute being "uplifted" by the fact that a conveyance of part was actually executed.

§ 36. **Plaintiff's conduct as a defense.**[6] If the plaintiff has been in un-

or other relief because of its own error, not due to misrepresentation by insured, in computing premiums, indemnity, or other benefits or options under policy. 125 **ALR** 1058–1075.

[3] 45 **Am Jur**, Reformation of Instruments, §§ 28–33.

[4] 45 **Am Jur**, Reformation of Instruments, §§ 50–53, 116.

[5] 45 **Am Jur**, Reformation of Instruments, §§ 16–18.

[6] 45 **Am Jur**, Reformation of Instruments, §§ 75–85.

Attempt to reform contract as election of remedies precluding action to enforce contract as written, or vice versa. 49 **ALR** 1513–1518.

Negligence in executing contract as affecting right to have it enforced. 45 **ALR** 700–711.

disturbed possession of the tract which was mistakenly added to or omitted from the conveyance, no length of delay will bar him; the burden is upon the other party to bring ejectment.

In most states today there are statutes specifically applying to equity suits. It is usually held that the statutory period begins to run from the time when the plaintiff could have discovered the mistake by the exercise of ordinary care; but a plaintiff may be barred by unreasonable delay under all the circumstances for less than the statutory period—the doctrine of laches. The fact that the plaintiff was negligent at the beginning in failing to discover the mistake may, in the discretion of the court, be sufficient to bar him, but the effect of such negligence may be overcome by the fact of the plaintiff's illiteracy. If the defendant acted fraudulently in reducing the transaction to writing, the plaintiff's failure to discover the error should not ordinarily bar relief.

Where the parties have entered into a compromise of disputed questions of fact or law, this is a bar to any equitable relief either of reformation or rescission. Similarly, if the plaintiff, knowing of the mistake, has ratified the transaction, for example, by bringing an action on it, this is a bar to reformation.

CHAPTER IV

RESCISSION

§ 37. Distinguished from reformation.[7] The effect of reformation is to rectify the transaction; the effect of rescission is to cut off or remove the attacked transaction leaving the parties in the same position as they were before such transaction took place. Reformation can be had only in equity; but where it is not necessary to have instruments cancelled, rescission can ordinarily be had at law.

§ 38. Mistake of fact.[8] In order to obtain rescission for mistake in bilateral transactions, it is necessary to show either that it was mutual, that is, common to both parties, or that defendant innocently caused plaintiff's mistake, or that the parties misunderstood each other. If the plaintiff alone was mistaken, and the defendant did not cause the mistake and did not know of it rescission is ordinarily refused. If defendant knew of plaintiff's mistake, rescission is granted on the ground of fraud.

The mistake must be one as to an intrinsic, not as to a collateral matter; for example, rescission was refused of a release given under the belief that defendant was insolvent because the mistake as to insolvency was not as to an intrinsic matter; similar reasoning has been applied where plaintiff bought a note mistakenly thinking that it was secured by mortgage.

If the erroneous transaction was such as to involve the act of the plaintiff only and the effect of the transaction would be the unjust enrichment of the defendant the plaintiff is entitled to have the transaction rescinded though he was the only party mistaken—for example, when the plaintiff cancelled a mortgage thinking that the mortgage debt had been paid.

7 9 **Am Jur,** Cancelation of Instruments, § 7.
19 **Am Jur,** Equity, §§ 100, 160.

8 9 **Am Jur,** Cancelation of Instruments, §§ 32–35.
Mistake in lease as ground for relief. 26 **ALR** 472–523.
Unilateral mistake as basis of bill in equity to rescind the contract. 59 **ALR** 809–834.

§ 39. **Mistake of law.**[9] Because of the unfortunate decision in Bilbie v. Lumley, 2 East 469, 102 Eng. Reprint 448, the rule has been laid down that rescission will not be granted for mistake of law. A few courts have thrown the rule overboard entirely, others seek to make exceptions, holding, for example, that mistake of ownership of property is to be treated as a mistake of fact.

Where A sues B and gets judgment which is upheld by the highest court in the state and on the basis of this decision a transaction is entered into between X and Y, that transaction will not be affected by a later decision of the highest court overruling the case of A v. B. This is because of the social interest in the security of transactions and the holding is sound whether we consider that X and Y acted under a mistake of law or not; for all practical purposes the last decision of the highest court in the state is the law of that state.

§ 40. **Fraud.**[10] Upon the principle that having once acquired jurisdiction over a certain field, equity will not usually abandon the jurisdiction even though the common law later gives a complete and adequate remedy, English courts apparently regard all cases of fraud as entitling the party defrauded to equitable relief though only damages be sought. In this country the prevailing view is that where the party defrauded may get an adequate remedy at law, equity will not give relief; but equity will give relief if a constructive trust is asked to be imposed or an accounting is sought.

Where a plaintiff has been induced by fraud to part with chattels, he may recover either in trover for the value of the chattels or replevin for the chattels themselves, trover and replevin being used here to redress the equitable right to get back the chattels; and in most states equity will not give relief in such cases. It is usually said in such cases that the plaintiff rescinds before bringing his action at law whereas in an equity suit the proceeding is brought for a rescission. If there is no rescission either at law or in equity the defrauded party may maintain an action on the case for deceit.

Ordinarily the burden of proving fraud is on the plaintiff; but where there are two of the following three elements present, there is a presumption of fraud: (1) plaintiff in financial distress; (2) sale at an inadequate price; (3) defendant a fiduciary or possessing some other advantage over the plaintiff.

§ 41. **Placing defendant in statu quo.**[1] Acting upon the equitable principle that a party who seeks equitable relief should be required as a condition thereto to do equity to the other party, one who asks rescission, whether on the ground of mistake or fraud, is usually required to place the defendant in statu quo. Though occasionally there is a tendency to apply the principle mechanically by denying relief if such restoration is impossible the better view is that the principle never requires more than substantial restoration and that the impossibility of giving even substantial restoration may be excused by countervailing circumstances. Since an equity court may make a

9 9 **Am Jur,** Cancelation of Instruments, §§ 36, 37.

Mistake as to one's interest in land under law of descent as subject of relief. 39 **ALR** 194–206.

Relief in equity from mistake of law. 75 **ALR** 896–902.

10 9 **Am Jur,** Cancelation of Instruments, §§ 21–23.

Fraud or undue influence in conveyance from child to parent. 11 **ALR** 735–752.

1 9 **Am Jur,** Cancelation of Instruments, §§ 39–43.

conditional decree it is not indispensable that the plaintiff should tender restitution at or before suit.

§ 42. Duress and undue influence.[2] If instead of using deception to attain his ends the defendant uses constraint to induce the plaintiff to part with property or to enter into an obligation, equity will just as readily give rescission as in fraud cases. The test of duress includes such threats as would put in fear a person of ordinary courage. Usually duress on a third person affords no basis for relief; but where the family relationship between the plaintiff and the third person is very close so that the plaintiff is really constrained to enter into the transaction because of the duress equity will grant rescission.

Most of the cases where equity has given rescission because of undue influence are cases of gifts to persons who because of close family or fiduciary relationship are in a position to exercise strong influence on a donor who is very old or ill or very young. Gifts from clients to attorneys are closely scrutinized and are usually set aside if the client did not have independent professional advice.

§ 43. Miscellaneous.[3] If property has been transferred in consideration of future unlawful cohabitation equity will give no relief unless it be shown that the plaintiff at once abandoned the immoral purpose.

If the loser in a gambling transaction gives to the winner a check for the amount lost it would seem that public policy would be better served by allowing the loser to stop the payment of the check and by awarding him cancellation thereof; this is because he is in substance a defendant till payment of the check is actually made; hence cancellation merely preserves to him his common-law defense. But relief has occasionally been refused on the mechanical ground that the plaintiff must allege the illegal transaction in order to make out a prima facie case.

Where the promise of a grantee of land is to do something other than pay money and the common-law remedy would for any reason be inadequate, equity properly gives rescission and orders a reconveyance—for example, where land is conveyed by an aged person in exchange for support during

[2] 9 **Am Jur,** Cancelation of Instruments, §§ 19, 20.

[3] 9 **Am Jur,** Cancelation of Instruments, §§ 28–31, 49.

Does right of grantor to maintain a suit in equity to set aside his conveyance for cause survive to his heir? 2 **ALR** 431–438; s. in 33 **ALR** 51–53.

Relief in equity from deed on ground of intoxication. 6 **ALR** 331–348.

Return or tender of consideration for release or compromise as condition of action for rescission or cancelation, action upon original claim, or action for damages sustained by the fraud inducing the release or compromise. 134 **ALR** 6–178.

Independent advice as essential to validity of transaction between persons occupying a confidential or fiduciary relationship. 123 **ALR** 1505–1520.

Rescission as essential to cancelation of instrument or lien voidable for fraud or failure of consideration. 109 **ALR** 1032–1045.

Pecuniary damage as essential to rescission of contract for purchase of real or personal property. 106 **ALR** 125–166.

Action involving rescission or right to rescind contract and to recover amount paid thereunder as one at law or in equity. 95 **ALR** 1000–1019.

Right of vendor in contract for sale or exchange of real property to bring suit for forfeiture, foreclosure, or rescission, or to quiet title or recover possession, without first giving notice, or making demand for possession. 94 ALR 1239–1264.

Remedy of grantee in possession under deed with covenants of title, independently of those covenants, where the grantor's title is defective. 50 **ALR** 180–206; s. in 65 **ALR** 1142–1145.

Avoidance of release of claims for personal injuries on ground of mistake or fraud relative to the extent or nature of the injuries. 48 **ALR** 1462–1523; s. in 117 **ALR** 1022–1048.

Rights and remedies in respect of the property upon the death, in the lifetime of grantor, of the grantee in a deed in consideration of future support. 34 **ALR** 136–145.

Remedy of rescission for grantee's breach of agreement to support grantor. 112 **ALR** 670–724.

the rest of the grantor's life. In such a case not only are the damages conjectural because of the uncertainty of the duration of the grantor's life, but if the homestead has been conveyed, there are additional reasons for giving rescission where the grantee has defaulted.

Ordinarily a grantee who accepts a conveyance of land is not entitled to rescission for mere breach of warranty of title; but if a judgment at law for damages would be inadequate because of the insolvency of the grantor, rescission will be granted.

Where the transaction was illegal and the parties in equal fault rescission will ordinarily be denied.

CHAPTER V

BILLS QUIA TIMET AND TO REMOVE CLOUD ON TITLE

§ 44. Bills quia timet.[4] In the narrow technical sense a bill quia timet lies where a plaintiff who is obligor on a written instrument fears that the obligee may postpone bringing his action thereon so long that the equity plaintiff will lose the evidence of his defense to the instrument; or, if the instrument is negotiable and not yet due, that the obligee may transfer it to a bona fide purchaser for value and thus cut off the obligor's equitable defense; hence the equity plaintiff asks that the instrument be delivered up and cancelled.

Courts have often been slow to give this relief, arguing that the equity plaintiff has an adequate remedy in a bill to perpetuate testimony or its statutory equivalent, but such evidence is usually read by the court stenographer and is not an adequate substitute for the testimony of the witnesses themselves in open court.

The fact that the equity defendant has already begun his common-law action on the instrument is no defense because he might dismiss such an action at any time.

§ 45. Bill to remove cloud on title.[5] By the better view a cloud on title is any claim which actually does affect marketability by depreciating the market value of the property even though the court which orders the can-

4 44 **Am Jur,** Quieting Title, § 3.
19 **Am Jur,** Equity, § 78.
Right to quiet title or remove cloud on title to personal property by suit in equity or under declaratory judgment act. 105 **ALR** 291–299.
Right to jury trial in suit to remove cloud, quiet title, or determine adverse claims. 117 **ALR** 9–61.
Requiring security from life tenant for protection of remainderman. 14 **ALR** 1066–1083; s. in 101 **ALR** 271–275; 138 **ALR** 440–448.
Injunction against bringing or prosecuting action in another state or country because of the danger that result would be different from that which would be reached in the jurisdiction whose law is the proper governing law as regards matters of substance. 69 **ALR** 591–598.
Remedies during promisor's lifetime for breach of agreement to give property at death. 66 **ALR** 1439–1447.
Power to enjoin bringing or prosecution of action under Federal Employers' Liability Act in another jurisdiction. 85 **ALR** 1351–1361; s. in 113 **ALR** 1444–1447; 136 **ALR** 1232–1236; 146 **ALR** 1118–1119.
18 **Wis. L. R.** 229, The Right of an Owner of a Future Interest in Personalty to Security.

5 44 **Am Jur,** Quieting Title, §§ 11–33.
16 **Am Jur,** Depositions, §§ 8–10.
What constitutes cloud on title removable in equity. 78 **ALR** 24–313.
Jurisdiction of suit to remove cloud or quiet title upon constructive service of process against nonresident. 51 **ALR** 754–759.
Right of one not in possession to maintain suit to remove cloud on title in case of fraud. 36 **ALR** 698–717.
Remedies of grantor who has conveyed with covenants against third person asserting title or interest hostile to covenants. 97 **ALR** 711–720.
Avoidance of multiplicity of suits as ground of jurisdiction in equity of a suit by one out of possession to quiet title against persons in possession of different portions of the land in severalty. 30 **ALR** 109–114.

cellation can see that the claim is invalid, the test being the mind of the average purchaser rather than the mind of one learned in the law.

Apart from statute, relief is given only to the holder of the legal title. If the defendant is in possession and the plaintiff claims a right to immediate possession he may bring ejectment and does not need equitable relief; but if for any reason ejectment cannot be brought, either because the plaintiff claims as reversioner or remainderman or mortgagee not entitled to possession, or is a mere warrantor of title without any possessory right, or because neither party is in possession, then equitable relief is proper.

A bill to perpetuate testimony is of slight value here because such testimony would probably not reach and would certainly not convince prospective purchasers.

The fact that plaintiff's title was gained by adverse possession is no bar to giving cancellation even against the former owner who holds the record title.

By the better view the doctrine applies to personalty as well as realty. If the claim made by the defendant is oral the proper relief is by injunction instead of by cancellation. Where the claim has been recorded it is no defense to having the record expunged that the registry statute did not provide for its recording and that it would therefore not be constructive notice, because prospective purchasers would see it on the record and would be impressed by the fact of registry. The Torrens system of registering land titles requires the removal—as far as possible—of all clouds on title by a proceeding in rem.

CHAPTER VI

SPECIFIC REPARATION AND PREVENTION OF TORTS

A. Waste

§ 46. Common-law waste.[6] Common-law waste consists of any act done or omission suffered by one who is in rightful possession of land but who has an estate less than an estate of inheritance, which results in damage to the inheritance. Where the harm is caused by an omission it is called permissive as distinguished from active or voluntary waste. Permissive waste consists in failing to use due care to prevent damage to the land or buildings by fire, water, etc.; by the modern view the tenant is not liable for accidental damage or for the unauthorized act of a stranger. Where the act of the tenant, though wrongful, results in an increase of value to the property, it is called ameliorating waste.

The common-law action of waste could be brought only by one who had an immediate estate of inheritance; hence if land be conveyed to A for life, B for life, C in fee, neither B nor C could bring an action against A during B's lifetime, but C could bring it after B's death. But an action on the case was allowed to anyone whose estate was injured by the act of waste.

There is some doubt as to whether at common law tenants who were in by act of the parties were liable for waste; but in 1267 the statute of Marlbridge made lessees liable for full damage and in 1278 the statute of Gloucester provided for treble damages and forfeiture of the tenant's estate.

[6] 32 Am Jur, Landlord and Tenant, §§ 779, 780.

Right of holder of tax or other lien on real property, other than mortgage, to restrain waste. 103 ALR 384–391

34 Harv. L. R. 388, Equitable Relief against Torts.

At common law the only relief which plaintiff could get for common-law waste was damages; where the damage threatened was very serious equity would enjoin but not where the damage was trivial or the waste ameliorating; where the waste was permissive equitable relief would involve an affirmative decree and supervision, so it was rarely given.

§ 47. **Equitable waste.**[7] In order to avoid the forfeiture imposed by the statute of Gloucester it became common for the instrument creating an estate for life or for years to provide that the tenant shall be without impeachment of waste thus giving him the same power and immunity in dealing with the land as if he were the owner in fee in possession. But equity placed a limit to this common-law immunity by enjoining an unreasonable destruction of the property and such an abuse by a tenant unimpeachable at law came to be known as equitable waste. The more common instances of such abuse are the cutting of ornamental timber or of very young timber or an unreasonable amount of timber and the destruction of buildings. The real basis of the doctrine seems to be the public and social interest in the beneficial use of the land.

The doctrine of equitable waste was later extended to include all those whose estates were considered of greater dignity than a simple life estate but whose self-interest might lead them to abuse the property; for example, a tenant in tail after possibility of issue extinct, jointress in tail and tenant in fee subject to an executory devise over. A somewhat similar jurisdiction was exercised to protect the interest of a mortgagee against a mortgagor in possession to prevent the latter from so using the land as to impair the mortgagee's security, and to protect the interest of an unpaid vendor against a purchaser in possession.

§ 48. **Right to the proceeds of waste.**[8] Where timber has been cut by order of court the proceeds of the timber become a trust fund for the benefit of the tenant or tenants for life in succession until the first tenant for life without impeachment for waste is reached, who takes the principal. Such a result would seem to be the most desirable in all other cases where the tenant in possession is not in fault, for example, where the timber has been wrongfully cut by a stranger or has been blown down by a storm; and this principle has been recognized to the extent that if the timber is thus severed while a tenant unimpeachable for waste is in possession, the latter, not being in fault, is entitled to the timber just as if he had cut it himself. But where the tenant in possession is impeachable for waste and timber is destroyed by himself or by a stranger or by a storm and there is no ground for getting into equity the proceeds must go as a lump sum; since, therefore, the estate of a succeeding tenant for life may never come into possession, the one holding the first estate of inheritance is entitled.

B. Trespass

1. Trespass to Land

§ 49. **Common-law and equitable remedies.**[9] The common-law action of trespass to land lay only in favor of one in possession of land against one who directly interfered with such possession; if the land was in the possession of the holder of a particular estate and the plaintiff wished to recover

7 Am Jur, Waste.

8 Am Jur, Waste.

9 28 Am Jur, Injunctions, §§ 128–131.

damages for the injury to his interest in remainder or reversion he was compelled to bring an action on the case; and if the land was in the possession of the defendant himself the plaintiff must bring ejectment. In all of these cases equity calls the act of the defendant a trespass and under some circumstances will enjoin threatened trespasses and give specific reparation for trespasses already committed.

§ 50. Requiring plaintiff to establish his right at law.[10] The early rule was that if the defendant disputed the plaintiff's title or in any other way claimed a right to do the act threatened the mere fact that there was a dispute precluded equitable relief. This was probably due to the fact that common-law courts sat in various parts of England but equity was administered only at Westminster, and to the further fact that trial in equity was by deposition, not in open court. Now that the reasons have disappeared the rule should also disappear but it still persists in modified form in many states briefly as follows: If there is a bona fide and reasonable dispute as to title equity will give a temporary injunction to preserve the status quo till the legal right can be settled at law; if the defendant is in possession the burden will be upon the plaintiff to bring ejectment; if the plaintiff is in possession and the defendant has actually committed a trespass, the burden will be upon plaintiff to bring trespass quare clausum; if no trespass has been committed the burden will be upon defendant to bring ejectment.

§ 51. Plaintiff in possession.[1] Where plaintiff is in possession the legal remedy may be inadequate because (1) a serious physical injury to the land is threatened, for example, cutting ornamental trees or cutting off part of plaintiff's house; or (2) there have been repeated trespasses in the past and are likely to be repeated in the future and thus ripen into an easement; or (3) there is a continuous trespass which threatens to deprive the plaintiff of the enjoyment of all or part of his land—for example, leaving large amounts of rock on plaintiff's vacant city lot, maintaining permanent structures such as overhanging eaves or waterpipes under the surface or wires strung above the surface; or (4) taking possession of part of plaintiff's land—for example, constructing a building which encroached several inches upon plaintiff's adjoining land; or (5) erecting a barrier on plaintiff's land so as to interfere seriously with plaintiff's business. In all these cases equity will give relief by injunction.

§ 52. Defendant in possession—defendant insolvent.[2] If defendant is in possession of all the land involved and is committing seriously destructive acts, equity will ordinarily give a temporary injunction until the plaintiff can establish his title by getting a judgment in ejectment. If the plaintiff's estate in the land is a reversion or remainder, he is not entitled to relief either at law or in equity unless he can prove special damage thereto. Where the plaintiff's sole remedy at law is either trespass or case for damages, the fact that it would be impossible to collect a judgment at law because of defendant's insolvency is frequently the deciding factor in the giving of an in-

[10] 28 **Am Jur**, Injunctions, §§ 132, 133.

[1] 28 **Am Jur**, Injunctions, §§ 135, 136.

Injunction against repeated or continuing trespasses on real property. 32 **ALR** 463–556; s. in 92 **ALR** 578–590.

Injunction against removal of, or interference with, remains interred in burial lot. 21 **ALR** 651–658; s. in 33 **ALR** 1432–1433.

Mandatory injunction to compel removal of encroachments by adjoining owner. 14 **ALR** 831–841; s. in 31 **ALR** 1302–1303; 96 **ALR** 1287–1294.

[2] 28 **Am Jur**, Injunctions, §§ 136, 137.

junction, but it is no reason for allowing it as a substitute for ejectment if defendant is in possession.

2. Trespass to Chattels

§ 53. Remedies at law and in equity.[3] For a wrongful taking of chattels under claim of right, the plaintiff may bring either trespass or trover; in either action he will ordinarily get a judgment for the value of the chattel. If there has been a wrongful detention he may ordinarily maintain either trover or replevin. If the chattel is unique, equity will command the defendant to deliver it over to avoid its being secreted from the sheriff; if the defendant is threatening to seize and carry away a unique chattel, equity will enjoin such seizure. If the chattels are not unique, equitable relief is usually refused unless the defendant is insolvent or the defendant's threatened act would cause serious damage to plaintiff's business, for example, levying upon a stock of goods.

C. Private Nuisance

§ 54. Remedies.[4] The common-law remedy is an action on the case. Where the plaintiff could have recovered substantial damages at law, equity will usually order the defendant to abate the nuisance. Such a remedy is more advantageous than the action for damages because if the plaintiff recovers damages only to the date of the action he will be compelled to bring an action every few years to prevent the acquisition of an easement; and if he recovers prospective damages also his land becomes at once subject to an easement. The equitable remedy is preferable to private abatement because if the injured party abates he loses his cause of action for damage already suffered; he cannot abate if the nuisance is only threatened and he takes the risk of being able to show that there was a nuisance and that he did nothing not reasonably necessary to his protection.

The rule requiring the plaintiff first to establish his right at law has had much the same development as in the field of trespass.

§ 55. Balance of convenience.[5] In determining whether there is a nuisance, whether damages at law are adequate or whether to give a preliminary injunction, the courts will balance the inconvenience to the plaintiff if relief is refused, against the inconvenience to the defendant if relief is given. Where the act complained of is proved or admitted to be a nuisance and where, furthermore, damages therefor are conceded to be inadequate, it would seem to follow logically that the plaintiff should be entitled to a permanent injunction as of right, regardless of any further question of balancing conveniences. This is probably the prevailing rule, but in some states courts have refused injunctions in such cases if giving relief would result in great hardship to the defendants and to the public, for example, where the nuisance consists of an expensive manufacturing plant employing a large number of

[3] 28 **Am Jur,** Injunctions, § 140.

[4] 39 **Am Jur,** Nuisances, §§ 128–138, 146–162.
Injunction against pollution of stream by private persons or corporations. 46 **ALR** 8–79.
Right to enjoin threatened or anticipated nuisance. 7 **ALR** 749–787; s. in 26 **ALR** 937–956; 32 **ALR** 724–726; 55 **ALR** 880–891.
Nuisance resulting from smoke alone as subject for injunctive relief. 6 **ALR** 1575–1584.
Effect of delay in seeking equitable relief against nuisance. 6 **ALR** 1098–1111.
Constitutionality of statute conferring on chancery courts power to abate public nuisances. 5 **ALR** 1474–1483; s. in 22 **ALR** 542–545; 75 **ALR** 1298–1305.

[5] 39 **Am Jur,** Nuisances, §§ 155–161.
Doctrine of comparative injury in suit to enjoin nuisance. 61 **ALR** 924–937.

men. To give an injunction in such a case usually results practically in forcing defendant to buy the plaintiff's property at a high price; to deny the injunction, in forcing plaintiff to sell out to the defendant at a low price.

D. Miscellaneous

§ 56. Disturbance of private easements, obstruction of public rights, public nuisances.[6] The remedy at law for the disturbance of a private easement is an action on the case for damages; where this is not adequate equity grants relief by either a negative or affirmative decree. In most of the cases where equitable relief has been granted the easement disturbed has been either one of light and air, right of way or right of access to a public way.

In order that a private individual may recover at common law for the disturbance or obstruction of a public right, many states illogically require that he must suffer damage peculiar to him and different in kind from that to which the public is subjected and if the plaintiff could not recover at law he can get no relief in equity. The remedy of the public is by indictment or injunction at the suit of the attorney general.

A private nuisance which affects a considerable portion of the public becomes thereby a public nuisance; the most common illustrations are nuisances which affect the health and comfort of the community. The remedy of the public is by indictment or by injunction at the suit of the state or municipality. The fact that a private nuisance is also a public nuisance because it affects a large portion of the public should not in any way diminish what would otherwise be the rights and remedies of the private individual and this seems to be the prevailing view. But in some states the confusion resulting from calling the obstruction of a public right a public nuisance has caused the courts to require the private individual to show some peculiar damage not suffered by the public in general.

§ 57. Common-law copyright—statutory monopolies.[7] The author of a literary production has a right to keep it secret or to determine at what time and in what manner it shall be published. For a violation of this right, usually called common-law copyright, damages are usually inadequate and equity will protect by injunction.

The common-law remedy for infringement of a patent right is an action on the case for damages. Unless the patent is about to expire a plaintiff usually prefers an injunction against the continuance of the infringement and an accounting of profits as incidental thereto. Since the damage caused by the infringement may be much greater than the profits made by the infringer, a plaintiff who is entitled to an injunction should be allowed to choose damages instead of profits, and this is now provided for by statute in England.

The rules applicable to patents apply substantially to statutory copyright.

6 19 **Am Jur,** Easements, §§ 150–153.
39 **Am Jur,** Nuisances, §§ 124–126.
Relief in injunction suit in respect of easement as affected by doubt as to right to, or extent or location of, easement; necessity of first establishing easement at law. 139 **ALR** 165–201.
Right to injunction to protect easement of light and air. 93 **ALR** 1180–1196.
Right to injunction to protect water rights as affected by fact that party seeking injunction contemplates no immediate use of rights, or by doctrine of comparative injury. 106 **ALR** 687–701.
Who, other than abutting owner, may maintain a suit to enjoin closing or obstructing street or highway. 68 **ALR** 1285–1302.

7 34 **Am Jur,** Literary Property and Copyright, §§ 18–23.
40 **Am Jur,** Patents, §§ 177–182.

§ 58. Interference with trade interests.[8] If the defendant has contracted not to disclose plaintiff's trade secret or if he has obtained it by fraud or by means of a fiduciary relationship, equity will give protection; but a bona fide purchaser from the defendant would probably be protected.

Where the defendant has infringed upon plaintiff's trademark, equity will enjoin and require an accounting of the profits made. Similar relief will be granted against unfair competition in the use of trade names.

§ 59. Interference with contract and business relations.[9] Wherever there is a wrongful interference with the performance of a contract between plaintiff and a third person; or with the probable expectancies of an employer in obtaining labor on the labor market by means of strikes, boycotts or picketing; or with the probable expectancies of an employee by means of the black list, damages are practically always inadequate and, in the absence of a statute, equity will give relief. But today there is much legislation seriously restricting the right of the employer to equitable relief in labor disputes.

§ 60. Defamation.[10] Logically equity should give relief against disparagement of character wherever damages would be inadequate but there has been considerable reluctance to do so because there is a notion that equity should protect only property rights and that an injunction would interfere with freedom of speech. The answer to the first argument is that although in the past equity courts limited their protection to property rights, there is no reason for such a limitation today; the answer to the second argument is that the right to free speech is not violated by injunctions in the case of non-political libels. Because of the tendency to confuse disparagement of character with disparagement of property—trade libel and slander of title—equity courts have also been reluctant to give relief in the latter class of cases.

§ 61. Interference with domestic, social and political relations.[1] Where defendant's act has consisted of interfering with domestic relations, equitable relief has rarely been given unless a property right was involved. There is a similar reluctance to give relief against interference with social and political relations.

[8] 28 **Am Jur**, Injunctions, §§ 110-115.
52 **Am Jur**, Trademarks, Tradenames, and Trade Practices, § 142.
Injunction against acts or conduct, in street or vicinity, tending to disparage plaintiff's business or his merchandise. 144 **ALR** 1181-1189.
Right of one not a party to a combination or contract in restraint of trade to maintain a suit to enjoin the same or to recover damages he suffers by reason thereof. 92 **ALR** 185-193.
Right to enjoin competitor from selling his produce to dealers with whom plaintiff has exclusive contract or in such form as to enable dealers to palm off competitor's produce on customers as that of plaintiff. 84 **ALR** 472-490.
Right to enjoin use of name of defunct corporation. 27 **ALR** 1024-1032.
Right, in absence of express contract, to enjoin former employee from soliciting complainant's customers. 23 **ALR** 423-432; s. in 126 **ALR** 758-770.
55 **Harv. L. R.** 595, Unjust Enrichment in the Law of Unfair Competition.
42 **Col. L. R.** 955, Erie v. Tompkins and Trade Marks.
37 **Col. L. R.** 582, Non-Competing Goods in Trademark Law.
36 **Col. L. R.** 60, Fog and Fiction in Trademark Protection.

[9] 31 **Am Jur**, Labor, §§ 320-405.
53 **Harv. L. R.** 1289, Unfair Competition.

[10] 28 **Am Jur**, Injunctions, §§ 117-119.

[1] 28 **Am Jur**, Injunctions, §§ 121, 122.
Jurisdiction of equity to protect personal rights. 14 **ALR** 295-311.
Determination of controversies within political party. 20 **ALR** 1035-1061.
Power to enjoin holding of election. 33 **ALR** 1376-1388; s. in 70 **ALR** 733-740.

CHAPTER VII

PREVENTION OF CRIMES AND CRIMINAL PROCEEDINGS

§ 62. Prevention of crimes.[2] In the early days of English equity when the state was weak and unable thoroughly to enforce peace, the chancellors undertook to protect persons and property from violence. As the state became stronger the need for relief from this source decreased so that by the end of the fifteenth century the jurisdiction of equity to prevent crimes had been practically abandoned. But the mere fact that an act was a crime has not ordinarily, apart from statute, prevented equity from giving an injunction if there are other well-recognized grounds for exercising jurisdiction.

§ 63. Prevention of criminal proceedings.[3] The general rule is that because of the pre-eminent appropriateness of trial by jury in criminal cases equity will not enjoin a criminal proceeding even if property interests are incidentally affected. But where there would be irreparable injury to property or business caused by the prosecution and the sole question involved is one of law there would seem to be no valid reason why equity should not give relief and the modern tendency is to give injunctions in such cases. Where a question of fact is involved only a preliminary injunction should be given pending the trial of such question by a jury. Where no irreparable damage is threatened but a large number of prosecutions have been begun, equity may enjoin all save one in order to prevent a multiplicity of actions.

CHAPTER VIII

BILLS OF INTERPLEADER

§ 64. Definition and general requirements.[4] A bill of interpleader is a proceeding devised to enable a person who is ready to perform a duty but is unable to determine to whom such duty is owed, to compel the adverse claimants to such performance to litigate the matter between themselves and thus relieve him from the suits which have been or might otherwise be brought against him.

The applicant for interpleader must establish that the adverse claims have a reasonable foundation and that there is a reasonable doubt as to whether the applicant would be safe in satisfying either claim. It is not necessary that one claimant be entitled; for example, where a reward has been offered several may claim it but there may be none able to prove his claim.

[2] 28 **Am Jur,** Injunctions, § 183.
Jurisdiction, at the instance of governmental agency, to enjoin an act amounting to a crime. 40 **ALR** 1145-1171; s. in 91 **ALR** 315-323.

[3] 28 **Am Jur,** Injunctions, §§ 233-240.
Power to enjoin officers from enforcing liquor laws. 3 **ALR** 1484-1492.

[4] 30 **Am Jur,** Interpleader, §§ 2-13.
When insurance company deemed to be a disinterested stakeholder for purposes of bill of interpleader. 108 **ALR** 267-277.
Constitutionality, construction, and application of Federal statutes regarding interpleader by insurance company. 106 **ALR** 626-639.
Warehouseman's right to interplead rival claimants to goods stored or their proceeds. 100 **ALR** 425-435.
Interpleader where one claimant asserts an adverse and paramount title. 97 **ALR** 996-1012.
Right of owner to maintain bill of interpleader against contractor and lien claimants and others in respect of fund arising from construction contracts. 70 **ALR** 515-518.
Right of bank to interplead rival claimants to deposit. 60 **ALR** 719-730.
56 **Harv. L. R.** 541, Broadening the Second Stage of Interpleader.
56 **Harv. L. R.** 929, Broadening the Secong Stage of Federal Interpleader.
51 **Yale L. J.** 924, Historical Origins of Interpleader.
49 **Yale L. J.** 377, Federal Interpleader and the Act of 1936.
16 **U. of Cin. L. R.** 117, Interpleader.
7 **Mo. L. R.** 203, Interpleader in Missouri.

The applicant must file an affidavit that he has not colluded with either claimant. If he claims a limited interest in the res this is usually a bar unless both claimants concede such an interest though it is arguable that he might be allowed interpleader and then litigate his claim with the winner. By the better view it is no bar that the claimants claim different amounts, for example, where claims for taxes are based upon the domicile of the applicant. If one of the claimants is a nonresident who does not voluntarily submit to the jurisdiction of the court, it is very difficult to give interpleader unless the court has, and is exercising, jurisdiction over the res in dispute.

§ 65. **Claims mutually exclusive—the same debt, duty or thing.**[5] Usually interpleader will be denied unless the claims mutually exclude each other. If the applicant is under an admitted liability to one of the claimants which is in no way dependent upon his liability or nonliability to the other, interpleader will not reduce the amount of litigation; he should satisfy the admitted liability to the one claimant and litigate with the other. The claimants must claim the same debt, duty or thing, but the requirement should have a liberal interpretation and be considered satisfied if the claims are mutually exclusive; the mere fact that the claimants must bring different actions or claim in different capacities should be held immaterial if their claims are substantially the same.

§ 66. **Miscellaneous.**[6] It is frequently stated that there must be privity between the adverse claimants which means that one claim shall be derived from the other or that both shall be derived from the same source. This seems to have been based upon the rule of policy that a tenant should not be permitted to deny his landlord's title, but equity might easily have overcome the objection by imposing the burden of proof as to title upon the claimant making the paramount claim.

By the better view the fact that the applicant is a tort-feasor, for example, a sheriff who has levied upon the disputed property, should not be a bar to relief. Nor should it be a bar that one of the claimants has obtained a judgment against the applicant, such fact being merely evidence of laches.

The applicant is not allowed to appeal on behalf of the losing claimant; nor is a claimant allowed to interplead or to compel a stakeholder to do so.

Where the applicant is unable to satisfy the requirements for a strict bill of interpleader he can still get interpleader relief if there is some other ground for getting the case into equity, such as cloud on title, trust, mortgage, bill of peace, etc.; in such a proceeding he need not be disinterested and need not deny collusion.

CHAPTER IX

BILLS OF PEACE

A. To Avoid or Prevent Numerous Actions between One and Many

§ 67. **Scope—claim of exclusive property right.**[7] The purpose of a bill of peace is to prevent useless litigation by settling in one equity suit a question which would be common to many actions at law or in equity—either repeated actions between one plaintiff and one defendant or numerous actions between

5 30 **Am Jur**, Interepleader, § 8.

6 30 **Am Jur**, Interpleader, §§ 9–15.

7 28 **Am Jur**, Injunctions, §§ 49–53.

several plaintiffs and one defendant or between one plaintiff and several defendants. One who seeks interpleader must be a stakeholder and is ordinarily not interested in the litigation except to get his discharge from the court; one who seeks a bill of peace is not a stakeholder and is always interested in the final outcome of the litigation either to fix liability on the other party or parties or to escape it himself. A bill of peace may be sought by either a plaintiff or a defendant.

In the early cases that arose between one and many there was a claim of an exclusive property right in the one against the many; this makes a strong case for relief and courts have been reluctant to go beyond these early decisions, regarding them as determining not only the principles but also the limits of the remedy.

§ 68. No claim of exclusive property right.[8] Where there is no claim of an exclusive property right but merely a community of interest in common questions of law and fact, for example, in many actions for personal injuries due to the alleged negligence of a railroad company, there would seem to be sound reasons for giving relief if the common questions were important, but the weight of authority is probably contra.

If any one taxpayer is allowed to enjoin the collection of an illegal tax, several taxpayers may join in the suit as a matter of equity pleading. If a single taxpayer is not thus allowed to sue, the weight of authority is that equity will allow several to join on bill of peace grounds.

B. To Avoid or Prevent Numerous Suits of One against One

§ 69. Bill to quiet title—ejectment.[9] An action of ejectment was unlike other common-law actions in that the person named as plaintiff was fictitious; hence if the defendant won the verdict and judgment the matter did not become res judicata because the real plaintiff need only to name another fictitious lessor as plaintiff and begin again, ad infinitum. The sole relief of the law defendant was a bill in equity to enjoin further ejectment actions after there had been enough verdicts in his favor to indicate that there had been a fair adjudication of the controversy. Statutes requiring a plaintiff in ejectment to sue in his own nome have not affected the matter; but in some states statutes limit the number of ejectment actions that may be brought.

§ 70. Same—repeated actions of trespass.[10] Though a judgment on the merits for the defendant in an action of trespass quare clausum is conclusive as to the particular act of trespass alleged by the plaintiff, it does not prevent the latter from bringing another action for an alleged act of trespass upon the same land, raising the identical property question as the first action; and there is no limit to the number of actions which may thus be brought if the law plaintiff remains unconvinced. In these circumstances, if there has been a fair adjudication of the merits of the case at law, equity should and

8 28 **Am Jur,** Injunctions, §§ 49–53.
Propriety of suit in equity by or against several insurers under fire policies covering same risk. 98 **ALR** 181–187.
Power of equity upon ground of avoiding multiplicity of suits to enjoin prosecution of independent actions at law against same defendant by different persons on contracts. 90 **ALR** 554–569.
Right to enjoin enforcement of illegal tax, local assessment, or license fee, upon joinder of several affected thereby. 32 **ALR** 1266–1284.
Pendency of action in Federal court as ground of injunction against action in state court. 24 **ALR** 1084–1107; s. in 122 **ALR** 1425–1431. See also 137 ALR 983.
45 **Harv. L. R.** 1297, Bills of Peace with Multiple Parties.

9 28 **Am Jur,** Injunctions, § 224.

10 28 **Am Jur,** Injunctions, § 52.

does interfere just as in ejectment cases in order to prevent vexatious and endless litigation.

§ 71. Numerous criminal prosecutions.[1] Where the equity plaintiff is being subjected to numerous prosecutions for alleged infractions of a statute or ordinance and he insists that he has not committed the acts alleged or that the statute or ordinance is invalid, equity will usually interfere to prevent such vexation and oppression.

CHAPTER X

MISCELLANEOUS

§ 72. Equitable conversion.[2] Where there is a peremptory direction in a will or deed that land shall be sold or money invested for the benefit of certain beneficiaries, equity regards—especially for purposes of devolution—the prospective sale or investment as if it had taken place at the time the will or deed took effect; this is usually called the doctrine of equitable conversion. Historically, the adoption of such a rule owed much to the influence of the maxim that equity regards that as done which ought to be done; were it not for this maxim equity might very well have regarded the right of the beneficiaries as being realty till the sale actually took place or as personalty till the investment actually took place, just as in the case where the direction to sell is not imperative. By strict logic equity—in following the maxim—should have regarded the conversion as taking place at the time when the trustees should have converted it; but unless there was a time fixed for such conversion it would be the duty of the trustees to make the sale or the investment within a reasonable time and it would be obviously undesirable to have the question of the coming into existence of equitable property rights open to such an uncertainty as the lapse of a reasonable time. Hence courts were compelled—consciously or unconsciously—to fall back upon the certain time of the taking effect of the will or deed.

Since the rule is at least dependent upon if not caused by the right of the beneficiaries to compel the trust to be carried out, it is usually limited in its operation to the carrying out of the purposes of the trust. Hence, if the trust comes to an end because of the death of all the beneficiaries without issue, so that there is a resulting trust to the representatives of the creator of the trust, the rule does not apply to the resulting trust; and the same reasoning has been applied where there has been only a partial failure of the trust if created by will, but not where the trust was created by deed. The rule does not apply so as to change the requirement that all the trustees shall execute a deed of realty; but as to whether it prevents the attachment of a judgment lien on land before the actual sale takes place there is a con-

1 28 **Am Jur,** Injunctions, §§ 233–240.

2 19 **Am Jur,** Equitable Conversion, §§ 1–31.

Equitable conversion by will as affected by total or partial failure of testator's purpose. 144 **ALR** 1236–1258.

Doctrine of equitable reconversion. 130 **ALR** 1379–1427.

Doctrine of equitable conversion as affected by discretion as to time, manner or other circumstances of sale, where the duty to sell is mandatory. 124 **ALR** 1448–1459.

Doctrine of equitable conversion in relation to taxation. 112 **ALR** 23–27.

Proceeds of sale or condemnation of real property of infant or incompetent as real or personal property. 90 **ALR** 897–915.

Doctrine of equitable conversion as affecting succession tax as to real property situated in a state or country other than the domicile. 42 **ALR** 426–435.

flict of authority. The better view is that the rule does not operate to deprive a widow of her dower right.

Where the beneficiaries are all sui juris and agree to do so, they may—before the conversion actually takes place—elect to take the property in its original form, because the trustees in such a case must obey the beneficiaries rather than the directives of the creator of the trust; this is usually referred to as the doctrine of equitable reconversion.

The doctrine of equitable conversion has been applied where an unconditional direction to sell has proceeded from a court of competent authority and the owner dies before the sale actually takes place. And where the property of one who is not sui juris has actually been sold or invested by order of court during such disability, it is usually held that equity will protect the interests of such incompetent and his representatives by regarding his property right as if no conversion had taken place, till such disability is removed.

§ 73. Penalties and forfeitures.[3] Two important fields of early equity jurisdiction were the prevention of the forfeiture of the estate of a mortgagor who failed to pay on the day and the prevention of the enforcement of penalties in bonds. At the present time common law courts have adopted this equitable principle and generally refuse to enforce such stipulations. But in many cases relief must still be sought in equity, as in the case of covenants in leases providing for forfeitures and in the case of judgments obtained through fraud, mistake or accident.

It is often said that equity will never enforce a forfeiture, but an exception has been made where forfeitures are justly enforceable but the legal remedy is inadequate; for example, where the lessee under a gas and oil lease defaults in developing the property so that very serious injury would result to the lessor.

Where contracts for the sale of land expressly provide that time shall be of the essence of the contract equity courts have too often acquiesced in and indirectly enforced an injust forfeiture of the vendee's interest by refusing specific performance after payment of a large proportion of the purchase money.

[3] 23 Am Jur, Forfeitures and Penalties, §§ 1–94.
Power of equity to relieve against forfeiture for nonpayment of rent. 16 ALR 437–450; s. in 24 ALR 724–725; 56 ALR 800–801.

TRUSTS

CHAPTER I

ORIGIN, HISTORY AND CLASSIFICATION

§ 1. Origin and history of uses.[1] During the twelfth century so much land had been given to religious corporations and thus taken off the land market that, in 1217, Parliament passed the Statute of Mortmain, forbidding such bodies to hold land. In order to evade this statute, land was usually conveyed to a close friend of the religious body who allowed the corporation to use the property as if it were theirs. At first his obligation to allow this was only moral, but about 1450 equity gave a remedy against him if he did not carry out his undertaking; thus what had been merely a moral obligation became a juridically binding one. The person thus receiving and holding legal title was called the feoffee to uses and the beneficiary the cestui que use. Once established, uses were employed for other purposes. Since the law of forfeiture of property for treason applied only to the legal title and not to the equitable use it became common for the English landed gentry who were frequently engaged in civil wars, to convey the legal title to some reliable elderly bachelor to hold for the use of themselves and their families and thus avoid the loss of their property in case they should be defeated in war and later convicted of treason.

§ 2. Statute of uses—trusts.[2] The employment of uses led to many evils, so Parliament in 1534 passed the Statute of Uses. But instead of forbidding the conveyance of land in use or declaring the use void it provided that whenever A should be seised to the use of B, the legal title should be in B and not in A. The statute was effectual—at least for the time and so far as it was construed to extend—in preventing the separation of the legal title and the equitable interest, but its most important result was in the law of conveyances. To convey a legal title after the statute, it was necessary merely to create a use in the person to whom it was intended to convey title, either directly by a bargain and sale or by a feoffment to a third person to his use; the statute of uses then operated to vest the legal title in him.

The statute was construed as not affecting uses in personalty, uses for married women and uses where the conveyance imposed active duties upon the transferee to uses. These active uses came to be called trusts in order to distinguish them from uses which had become so important in the law of conveyancing.

About a century after the statute was passed it was held that if land was conveyed to A to the use of B to the use of C the statute would operate only once, to place the legal title in B and that the second use in favor of C took effect as a passive trust. In some states today there is legislation forbidding the creation of passive trusts in land.

[1] 54 **Am Jur**, Trusts, §§ 9–14.
42 **Harv. L. R.** 1048, Trusteeship in Modern Business.
16 **U. of Cin. L. R.** 191, When Is a Trust Not a Trust?
26 **Marq. L. R.** 57, Problems in the Drafting and Administration of Trusts.
21 **Chicago-Kent L. R.** 275, Modification of Trusts for Children.

[2] 54 **Am Jur**, Trusts, § 9.

§ 3. Creation of express trusts—classification of trusts.[3] Express trusts may be created in any one of three ways: (1) A conveys property to B in trust for A; (2) A conveys property to B in trust for C; (3) A declares himself trustee of property for C. In every express trust there are three elements: a trustee, trust property and a beneficiary or cestui que trust.

According to form, trusts are either express or not express, the second class including resulting and constructive trusts; the distinction is important because the statute of frauds applies only to express trusts.

A logical classification of trusts according to substance or intent would result in the following divisions: (1) Actually intended trusts; whether the intent is expressed or inferred from circumstances; (2) trusts—so called—where the obligation is imposed by equity to prevent unjust enrichment, without regard to the intention of the parties and often contrary to such intent; (3) a middle class in which the obligation is imposed by equity according to what would probably have been the intent of the creator of an express trust if he had thought about the factual situation which later developed. The second class is always called constructive trusts; the term resulting trusts is usually applied to those trusts in which the obligation is imposed according to the real or to the supposed probable unexpressed intention of the parties, thus including class (3) and part of class (1).

CHAPTER II

TRUSTS COMPARED WITH SIMILAR RELATIONS

4. With a debt.[4] A trust is similar to a debt in that the obligation of either trustee or debtor may arise upon receiving title to property. The chief difference is that a trustee is a fiduciary, his obligation being to hold for the benefit of the cestui que trust, while a debtor may usually do as he likes with the property received, his obligation being to pay out of his general assets. Hence if trust property be lost or damaged without the trustee's fault he will not be liable; whereas if the property received by the debtor be lost this does not lessen his liability to the creditor. If a trustee should become insolvent or bankrupt the cestui is entitled to get the property so held in trust and need not come in with the general creditors of the trustee; but if a debtor becomes bankrupt the creditor must share with the other creditors even though the debtor still has the property he received from the creditor. In an otherwise doubtful case, the fact that the one who receives

[3] 54 **Am Jur**, Trusts, §§ 4, 5, 15–92.

Degree or intensity of parol proof necessary to establish a trust. 23 **ALR** 1500–1550.

Preference in event of debtor's insolvency in respect of funds designated or set apart by him for payment of specified obligation. 32 **ALR** 950–974.

Gift or trust by deposit in bank in another's name or in depositor's name in trust for another, without his knowledge. 59 **ALR** 975–983.

Effect of deed in which the word "trustee" follows the name of grantee, but does not set out terms of trust or name the beneficiary. 137 **ALR** 460–473.

Life tenant in possession as implied or quasi trustee. 137 **ALR** 1054–1058.

Validity of trust created by nontestamentary instrument reserving benefit to settlor for life with power of revocation. 73 **ALR** 209–224; s. in 118 **ALR** 481–485.

Devise or legacy upon promise of devisee or legatee that another shall benefit as creating trust. 66 **ALR** 156–172.

[4] 54 **Am Jur**, Trusts, § 6.

Bank deposit for purpose of meeting certain checks or classes of checks. 24 **ALR** 1111–1115; s. in 39 **ALR** 1138–1140; 86 **ALR** 375–381.

Liability of forwarding bank for proceeds of collection by correspondent bank which becomes insolvent after crediting proceeds to account of forwarding bank. 99 **ALR** 510–515.

Trust in proceeds of collections made by charging debtor's account in collecting bank. 24 **ALR** 1152–1159; s. in 42 **ALR** 754–757; 47 **ALR** 761–765; 77 **ALR** 473–483.

the property is to pay interest out of his own pocket shows that he is a debtor, not a trustee.

If a creditor consents, the debtor may change his obligation into that of trustee if he has the money and sets it aside for the creditor. And the trustee may, with the consent of the cestui, change his obligation into that of debtor. Because of commercial usage, a bank which undertakes, as trustee, to collect paper for a depositor may, upon collection, even without his consent, place the money in its general funds and credit the depositor therewith.

The remedy against a debtor is debt or indebitatus assumpsit; the usual remedy against a trustee is a bill in equity for an accounting; but if the trustee's sole duty, according to the terms of his trust, is to pay over money, the cestui may recover against him in debt or indebitatus assumpsit.

§ 5. With contract for the benefit of a third person.[5] If X receives money from A and undertakes to pay a substantially equivalent amount out of his general assets to B, there is no trust because there is no trust property. B is merely the beneficiary of the contract between A and X but by the great weight of authority in this country B—whether payment or gift beneficiary—may recover in special assumpsit for the breach of X's promise and he is not entitled to any preference in case of X's bankruptcy. In England where the beneficiary of a contract may not sue thereon, equity has illogically given a remedy to a gift beneficiary by imposing a trust obligation upon X though there is no trust property set aside and no intent to become a trustee.

§ 6. With an equitable charge.[6] If A grants land to X, reserving a charge thereon or if, keeping the land, he grants a charge thereon to X, the charge thus created is a legal charge. But if A conveys the land to X subject to a charge in favor of Y, the latter, not being a party to the transaction but merely a beneficiary, was denied any remedy at law; equity gave Y relief and hence Y is said to have an equitable charge. Such a charge differs from a trust in that X is not a fiduciary, owing Y merely the negative duty not to destroy the charge by conveying the land to a bona fide purchaser for value without notice.

§ 7. With the assignment of a chose in action.[7] If A assigns a non-negotiable chose in action against X to B, legal title does not pass—apart from statute—unless X assents to the transfer, agreeing to pay B instead of A, B thus getting merely the beneficial interest. If A instead of assigning the chose in action to B had declared himself trustee of it for B, the case would be similar in that A has the legal title and B the beneficial interest.

The chief difference between the two cases is that in the case of the assignment, A is not a fiduciary, owing to B merely the negative duty of not interfering with B's collecting the chose in action. In the case of the trust, however, A is the proper person to collect and B has no remedy against X so long as B performs his duty as trustee. Before it was changed by

[5] 54 **Am Jur**, Trusts, § 6.
Trust or preference in respect of money placed in bank for purpose of transaction with third person where bank subsequently becomes insolvent. 31 **ALR** 472–485; s. in 93 **ALR** 881–896.
39 **Mich L. R.** 59, Deposits to Pay Dividends.

[6] 54 **Am Jur**, Trusts, § 6.
See also 57 **Am Jur**, Wills.
Provision in devise requiring devisee to pay money as creating a charge or a condition. 62 **ALR** 589–620.
Rights and remedies in respect of legacy charged upon land devised. 116 **ALR** 7–67; s. in 134 **ALR** 361–366.

[7] 4 **Am Jur**, Assignments, § 2.

statute, B was compelled to sue in the name of A; now he is generally allowed to sue in his own name but he still sues as representative of A; he has no remedy in equity unless A threatens to collect from the obligor or there is some other special circumstance requiring equitable interference. In case of the trust X will be protected in paying A unless he knows that A is about to commit a breach of trust; in case of the assignment, X will not be protected in paying A unless he was ignorant of the assignment.

§ 8. With the relation of vendor and purchaser of land.[8] A vendor of land under a specifically enforcible contract is frequently called a trustee or a constructive trustee. The relation is similar to a trust in that the vendor has the legal title and the purchaser the equitable interest. If the purchase money has been paid or secured according to the contract the vendor is under a duty to turn over the land to the purchaser, but this is not a constructive obligation but one which the common law imposes and for which equity gives specific redress according to the intention of the parties. The obligation in such a case is similar to that of an express passive trustee whose duty is merely to convey, but it is not exactly that because there is no intention to become a trustee. Where the purchase money has not been paid it is still further from being an express passive trust because the vendor has an interest in holding the land as security till he is paid.

CHAPTER III

ESSENTIALS TO CREATION OF THE TRUST RELATION

§ 9. Language necessary—subject matter of trust.[9] If the words "upon trust" are used or words of command, a trust will ordinarily arises if the property involved has been properly described and there are no conditions imposed which would be inconsistent with a trust such as the payment of interest. Formerly precatory words such as "wish", "hope", etc., were held sufficient where used in a will, but the great weight of authority today is contra.

Purely personal rights, such as peerages and offices, cannot be assigned and cannot be held in trust; but everything on which one may predicate property may be held in trust including land, chattels and choses in action; even the cestui's interest, being an equitable chose in action, may be held in trust.

§ 10. Consideration—the law of uses.[10] It was the law of uses before the statute of uses that consideration was necessary to create a use. If A conveyed property to B to the use of C, the receipt of the property by B was consideration for his obligation to hold it to the use of C. If A desired to create a use in C without conveying the legal title, his having the property could not be consideration because he already had the property, and therefore unless A received something of value in exchange for his promise to hold to C's use, such a promise was ineffectual.

After the statute of uses was passed and uses become important in the law of conveyancing the rule requiring consideration was so modified that one might create a use in favor of a near relative by blood or marriage by a mere declaration under seal without receiving anything in exchange; the stat-

8 Am Jur, Vendor and Purchaser.

9 54 Am Jur, Trusts, §§ 17, 18, 32, 37–40. Precatory trusts. 49 ALR 10–103; s. in 70 ALR 326–334; 107 ALR 896–924.

10 54 Am Jur, Trusts, § 41.

ute of uses would then operate to transfer the legal title to the relative in whom the use had been created. Such a conveyance is called a covenant to stand seised; the near relationship upon which it is based usually referred to as "good consideration", but there is no consideration in the true sense of exchange. Sometimes consideration in the true sense is called "valuable" consideration to distinguish it from the so-called "good" consideration. Where a use is raised by a valuable consideration or by the recital of a valuable consideration the conveyance is called a bargain and sale.

§ 11. Same—the law of trusts.[1] Until 1811 a valuable consideration was essential to the creation of a trust. In that year it was decided that if A declares himself trustee for C, this mere declaration is sufficient to make A trustee and to vest the equitable interest in C even though C is a stranger, and there need be no delivery of the instrument creating the trust.

It has long been the law of gifts that the donor must either deliver the property or make a conveyance by deed or will, a mere declaration of intent being insufficient. After it was held that a mere declaration of trust was enough, it was natural that the disappointed donee of every imperfect gift would try to induce the court to construe the transaction to be a declaration of trust which for most purposes would be as satisfactory as a transfer of the legal title. In a few English cases the donees were successful, but the great weight of authority and better view is that the doctrine is applicable only to cases where there is a clear intent to become a trustee and therefore does not apply to imperfect gifts.

§ 12. Statute of frauds.[2] Apart from statute a trust either of real or personal property may be created orally. In a few states the statute of frauds provides that trusts in land shall be created in writing, but by the English statute, which has been copied substantially in many states, the requirement is that "all declarations or creations of trust or confidences of any lands, tenements or hereditaments shall be manifested and proved by some writing signed by the party who is by law enabled to declare such trusts." It does not apply to trusts of chattels and resulting and constructive trusts are expressly excepted.

Unless the statute expressly requires that the creation of the trust shall be in writing, the writing is not necessary to the creation of the trust but merely to its enforcement. Hence the memorandum is sufficient if made at any time before it is necessary to make proof at the trial and is effectual even if made after the trustee's bankruptcy, if the trust was created before the bankruptcy.

If A conveys land to B upon trust for C, A may comply with the statute by expressing the trust in the conveyance, whether by deed or will. If he fails to do this, then only B can comply with the statute since he is the party to be charged with the trust. If A declares himself trustee of land for C, only A can comply with the statute.

§ 13. The cestui que trust—public or charitable trusts.[3] Any person capable

1 54 **Am Jur**, Trusts, § 41.
May unconsummated intention to make a gift of personal property be made effective as a voluntary trust. 96 **ALR** 383–391; s. in 123 **ALR** 1335–1337.

2 54 **Am Jur**, Trusts, §§ 43–51.
Validity, as against creditors of trustee or one deriving his right from trustee, of conveyance or transfer to carry out terms of unenforceable parol trust. 64 **ALR** 576–582.
Applicability of Statute of Frauds to contracts to surrender, rescind, or abandon trusts. 106 **ALR** 1313–1320.

3 10 **Am Jur**, Charities, §§ 4–11.
54 **Am Jur**, Trusts, §§ 136–146.

of holding the legal title to property may be a cestui que trust of such property.

A charity has been defined as anything which tends to the improvement of mankind in general, including schools, churches, lodges, hospitals, libraries, etc. The rules as to charitable trusts differ in two important respects from the rules as to private trusts; the cestuis need not be definite and the trust may last forever. A devise of property to X upon trust to apply the income each year for the benefit of the worthy poor of Z county is valid though the parties to be benefited are not specified and though the income is to be applied perpetually. In fact it is one of the essential features of a charity that the person to be ultimately benefited thereby should not be specified because it must be for the benefit of the public.

In two other respects, a charitable trust differs from a private trust. Largely because it is doing the work of the state, it is not liable in tort for the acts of its employees, but the present tendency is to limit this doctrine so as to bar only the beneficiaries of the charity. And if it becomes impossible or highly difficult to carry out the original charitable intent on the part of the settlor, the property will be devoted to a similar charity; this is called the doctrine of cy pres.

If a charitable corporation is named as the immediate cestui it is the proper party to enforce the trust; otherwise the state will enforce it, usually through the attorney general.

§ 14. Same—private trusts.[4] If a trust is for a private purpose it is a fatal objection if it is to last indefinitely; for example, a trust to apply the income from £200 to the upkeep of a monument. If the trust had been limited to the period permitted by the rule against perpetuities, it would probably have been good.

The fact that there is no cestui capable of enforcing a private trust is not objectionable provided the purpose of the trust is definite; for example, a trust to erect a monument to the first husband of the testator's wife was

Liability of privately conducted charity for personal injuries. 14 **ALR** 572–604; s. in 23 **ALR** 923–925; 30 **ALR** 455–457; 33 **ALR** 1369–1370; 42 **ALR** 971–973; 62 **ALR** 724–729; 86 **ALR** 491–499; 109 **ALR** 1199–1205; 133 **ALR** 821–833.

Validity of charitable trust to promote change in laws or system or methods of government. 21 **ALR** 951–956.

Validity of trust for religious purposes not limited by sect or denomination. 22 **ALR** 697–708.

Gift for public school as a valid charitable gift. 48 **ALR** 1126–1137.

Determination by the civil courts of property rights between contending factions of an independent or congregational church. 8 **ALR** 105–133; s. in 70 **ALR** 75–90.

Who may maintain suit or proceedings to enforce or administer benevolent or charitable trusts. 62 **ALR** 881–904; s. in 124 **ALR** 1237–1242.

General charitable intent as essential to application of cy pres doctrine. 74 **ALR** 671–684.

Effect on certainty of purpose or beneficiaries of a charitable gift, of the possible, but not required, inclusion of a noncharitable object. 115 **ALR** 1123–1146.

Power of trustees of charitable trust to mortgage trust property. 127 **ALR** 705–711.

Want of trustee as invalidating charitable trust. 5 **ALR** 315–345.

Nature of estate created by, and enforceability of, provision in devise or bequest to charitable, religious, or educational corporation as to particular purpose of the corporation for which it shall be used. 130 **ALR** 1101–1141.

Provision for relief or education of member of family or relatives as creating charitable trust. 131 **ALR** 1277–1292.

Charitable trust as affected by lack of territorial limitation as regards beneficiaries. 141 **ALR** 346–356.

Failure of trustee to carry out purposes of charitable trust, or diversion of trust property to other purposes, as ground of suit by trustor or his heirs for adjudication of title to him or them. 143 **ALR** 395–407.

17 **Tenn. L. R.** 838, Tort Liability of Hospitals.

[4] 41 **Am Jur**, Perpetuities and Restraints on Alienation, § 43.

54 **Am Jur**, Trusts § 31.

Devise or bequest for upkeep of cemetery lot as a violation of rule against perpetuities. 4 **ALR** 1124–1128; s. in 14 **ALR** 118–119.

held valid, the trustee being willing to perform; if the trustee had been unwilling, there would have been a resulting trust for the next of kin. But where the object of the trust is indefinite, the trust has been illogically declared invalid even though the trustee is willing to carry it out; for example, a trust to "dispose of the ultimate residue to such objects of benevolence and liberality as the Bishop of Durham shall most approve." The testator in that case might have accomplished the desired result by bequeathing the property to the next of kin subject to a power in the Bishop of Durham to appoint to such objects of benevolence and liberality as he should most approve.

§ 15. The trustee—appointment, removal, disclaimer.[5] The creator of a trust may validly appoint anyone a trustee, for example, an infant, an insane person, a bankrupt or an alien, but a court is likely to remove them if objection is made and incompetency shown. At one time it was thought that a corporation could not be a trustee because it had no conscience, but today most trust property is held and administered by corporations.

If for any reason a trusteeship should become vacant and the trust instrument does not provide for filling the vacancy, the duty devolves upon the court. In performing this duty the court will try to appoint one who will be capable of managing the trust estate and who will be fair to all the cestuis. Hence a court would never appoint an infant or insane person and would not appoint a nonresident of the state, an insolvent or one of the cestuis unless there should be exceptional circumstances to justify such an appointment.

If a trustee is guilty of serious misconduct or is for any reason incapable of performing the trust duties he should be removed. Ordinarily the proper equity court will command the trustee to convey the trust property to a person designated by the court to be the new trustee. If the trustee should be an infant or insane, a transfer by him would not be binding even if made by order of court; in such a case equity will not order a transfer but will issue an injunction against the trustee's further handling the trust property and will appoint a conservator who will manage the trust property till a valid transfer can be made. In most states statutes have been passed which enable a court to vest the title in a new trustee without a transfer by the old trustee.

No one is under any obligation to accept the office of trustee. If a conveyance be made to T upon trust for C, the title passes as soon as the conveyance is made without waiting for the consent of T; but if T upon learning of the conveyance, refuses to accept, such disclaimer places the title back in the transferor or his representatives just as if the conveyance had never been made. If T once accepts, it is too late to disclaim; he must then, in order to be re-

5 54 **Am Jur**, Trusts, §§ 112–135.

Power of municipal corporation or other political body to accept and administer trust. 10 **ALR** 1368–1388.

Hostility between trustee and beneficiary as ground for former's removal. 45 **ALR** 331–338.

Provisions of will or other trust instrument exempting trustee from or limiting his liability. 83 **ALR** 616–629.

Right to double commission where same person, natural or corporate, is named as executor and trustee. 84 **ALR** 667–678.

Compensation of trustee as affected by neglect or violation of his duties. 110 **ALR** 566–578.

Right of surviving or remaining trustee or trustees to act without substitution of another trustee in place of one who has died or resigned or been removed, where the will or other trust instrument provides for substitution or replacement. 142 **ALR** 1099–1105.

7 **Md. L. R.** 1, Duration of the Trustee's Interest Where the Trust Property Is Personalty.

lieved of the trust, persuade a court to accept his resignation or, if the cestuis are all sui juris get their consent.

Neither disclaimer by the trustee or his refusal to act after acceptance will defeat the interest of the cestui. Equity will not allow a trust to fail for want of a trustee but will appoint some one who is willing to serve. The cestui's interest is likewise saved where the person or corporation is forbidden by law to hold the legal title or where the person named in a will dies before the testator, or where the conveyance is upon trust, but no trustee is named.

CHAPTER IV

NATURE OF CESTUIS' INTEREST

§ 16. Remedies of C against T and T against C.[6] If by the terms of the trust or by T's stating an account to C, the sole duty of T is to pay over money, C may maintain debt or indebitatus assumpsit. Where the duty of T is to do anything else, C must proceed in equity to enforce it.

If T should execute an instrument under seal agreeing to carry out the terms of the trust C could maintain against T the action of covenant. If the promise to perform the trust is not under seal, special assumpsit should be allowed against T wherever there was consideration for his undertaking the trust provided the beneficiaries of a contract are allowed to sue thereon; receipt of the trust property from the creator of the trust would, of course, be sufficient consideration. But the jurisdiction of equity over trusts was so well settled before the action of special assumpsit came into general use that the latter remedy has rarely been brought.

Since the legal title is in T, he may recover against C in ejectment for trust land or in trover or replevin for trust chattels; C's only remedy, if any, is to get a decree in equity forbidding T to continue with his action at common law and for the termination of the trust. But in some states statutes permit C to plead his equitable interest in defense to the common-law action and a resort to equity is unnecessary.

If C wishes to sue T for an accounting of the trust property it is not necessary that he sue in a court having jurisdiction over the property. Since equity acts in personam it is enough that T be subject to the jurisdiction of the court by being served with process or by entering a voluntary appearance. Furthermore, not only may C sue T wherever he can get jurisdiction of him, he must do so there if at all; apart from statute, jurisdiction over the property is not enough. To meet this situation, statutes have been passed giving to the equity court of the situs of the property the power to confiscate T's title and vest it in a new trustee.

§ 17. C's remedies against X.[7] Where the trust property has been wrongfully interfered with by X so as to give rise to an action either at common law or in equity, T is the proper person to bring the action unless C is in possession of the trust property, in which case he may bring the proper remedy against X for a violation of such possession. Similarly T is the proper person to collect a contractual chose in action due to the trust estate. If T refuses to sue, it is a breach of trust and C's remedy is to sue T therefor and get an equitable decree commanding him to bring the appropriate action at law or suit in equity; if X is within the jurisdiction C may have X joined with T and have both suits settled in one; if X is beyond the jurisdiction it

[6] 54 Am Jur, Trusts, §§ 570–575, 592–595. [7] 54 Am Jur, Trusts, §§ 586, 587.

will be necessary for C to get an assignment from T of his chose in action against X and then, as T's assignee, sue X where he can get jurisdiction over him. If T is beyond the jurisdiction and X within it, equity will allow C to sue X without joining T.

Where T is properly performing his duties by suing X, it is not necessary that C be joined as party plaintiff. If T neglects to sue X and the statute of limitations bars T's action, C is also barred. But where T, in violation of his trust, conspires with X and conveys to him the trust property, T may repent of his wrong and maintain a suit to get back the property from X for C; but in such a case the running of the statute in X's favor against T will not bar C, because C may sue X directly because of the fraud and the statute would not begin to run till C's discovery of the fraud.

Only T can give to X a release which will be valid at common law; but if such a release is in fraud of C's rights, C may enjoin X from taking advantage of it unless X is a bona fide purchaser for value without notice. A release by C, though no bar at common law, is effective in equity if C was sui juris, equity giving X an injunction against T in order to avoid circuity of action.

At one time it was illogically held that a purchaser of trust property from T, even though he had no reason to suspect a breach of trust, was under obligation to see that the purchase money was properly applied by T for the benefit of C, but this has been changed in most, if not all, the states either by statute or by judicial decision.

§ 18. Remedies of X against T and C—setoff.[8] Suits, whether at law or in equity, brought by X with respect to the trust property are properly brought against T alone. It is T, not C, who is usually liable for the taxes and for damage caused to X by a nuisance on trust land. In entering into contracts with X, T may by express stipulation limit his liability to the amount of trust funds in his hands; in such a case X will properly get a judgment against T, but will levy execution only against trust property.

At the early common law, if A sued B on one cause of action and B had another cause of action against A, B could not use this is any way as a defense, but was compelled to bring a separate suit. In order to remedy this, statutes have been passed, usually limited to liquidated claims, allowing B in such a case to set off his claim against A's claim and thus settle both cases in one litigation. Where T sues X upon an obligation due the trust estate, X may set off against it a claim which he has against T, because setoff statutes have been construed to apply to parties to the record and not to parties who are ultimately to be benefited. But equity protects C by giving him an injunction against X's relying on such a setoff unless at the time he became bound to T he was ignorant of the trust and thus substantially in the position of a bona fide purchaser for value without notice. If X's claim had been against C instead of against T, he could not have set off because C is not a party to the record; but in equity X is usually allowed to take advantage of such a claim by what is known as equitable setoff.

[8] 54 Am Jur, Trusts, §§ 583, 588–595.

CHAPTER V

RESULTING AND CONSTRUCTIVE TRUSTS

§ 19. **Distinction between resulting and constructive trusts.**[9] The chief practical difference between resulting and constructive trusts arises in the field of conflict of laws. Whether there is a resulting trust in a particular case depends upon the law of the place where the property is situated regardless of where the parties live or where the transaction took place or where the suit was brought. But whether a constructive trust, being nonconsensual, will be declared will depend entirely upon the law of the place where the suit is brought—the law of the forum.

§ 20. **Purchase money resulting trusts—origin.**[10] During the century prior to the passing of the statute of uses, most of the land in England was held in use; it was therefore natural for a purchaser of land to have the title conveyed to a third person to hold to the use of the purchaser. And so general was this practice that even if the use were not expressed in the conveyance, there was a presumption that such a conveyance was for the use of the purchaser. Later, when the modern passive trust arose the same presumption was applied though in the meantime the conveyancing customs had changed and it was not usual for land to be held in trust; hence the only argument for the modern presumption is that a purchaser is more likely to intend the stranger to hold in trust for him than he is to make the stranger a gift.

§ 21. **Same—extent of the rule.**[1] In order that a purchase money resulting trust arise the purchase money must be furnished not later than the time of the conveyance. This requirement is satisfied if the person seeking to have the trust declared binds himself to pay the purchase money; the later payment of the purchase money which he is obligated to pay is not a later furnishing of it. Hence if A borrows from B the money wherewith to buy the land and has the land conveyed to B, there is a presumption of a resulting trust of the equity of redemption, B being entitled to hold the land merely as security for the repayment of the loan. Where A furnishes not all but some definite part of the purchase money and B furnishes the rest there is a presumption of a resulting trust pro tanto.

It is not necessary that B have any knowledge of the transaction; if he did know of it and make an oral promise to hold in trust, such promise would not be binding but would tend to show that no gift was intended.

If A buys land and has the conveyance made to B in order to defraud A's creditors, A is prevented by the fraud from taking advantage of any resulting trust, but this does not bar A's creditors from having a trust—whether called resulting or constructive—declared for themselves to the extent of their claims against A.

[9] 54 **Am Jur**, Trusts, §§ 187–192.

Payments made or obligations incurred by a constructive trustee or a trustee ex maleficio as a charge upon or a liability of the trust estate. 124 **ALR** 1409–1422.

Rights and remedies against persons who have frustrated intention of another to make a gift or bequest to, or permit intestate succession to, third person. 98 **ALR** 474–480.

27 **Harv. L. R.** 437, The Classification of Trusts as Express, Resulting and Constructive.

[10] 54 **Am Jur**, Trusts, §§ 193–195, 203–205.

[1] 54 **Am Jur**, Trusts, §§ 206–217.

Complainant's purpose to defraud creditors as defense to suit to recover property paid for by him but conveyed to defendant. 117 **ALR** 1464–1476.

40 **Harv. L. R.** 669, Resulting Trusts Arising upon the Purchase of Land.

Where the conveyance is taken in the name of one not dependent, the presumption of a resulting trust may be rebutted by showing that a gift was intended. Where the conveyance is taken in the name of a dependent, such as a wife or child there is no presumption of a resulting trust and the burden is upon the one furnishing the purchase money to show that a trust was intended.

The presumption of a purchase money resulting trust is difficult to justify either on the score of probability or convenience and should be abolished by statute; but statutes abolishing the entire doctrine, except in favor of the purchaser's creditors, are unfair to the purchaser because they allow the grantee upon an oral trust to enrich himself at the former's expense unless the court can find some basis for imposing a constructive trust.

§ 22. Intended trust fails.[2] If A devises or bequeaths property to T upon trust for C and C dies before A there is, apart from statute, a lapse of C's equitable interest and there is a resulting trust for the heirs or next of kin of A. And there is a similar resulting trust for the transferor or his heirs or next of kin, where a gratuitous conveyance is made upon trust for a purpose which has been declared illegal by statute or decision; or where property is conveyed gratuitously upon trust but no purpose is mentioned or the purpose mentioned is too indefinite to be accorded legal recognition; or where the trust fails to exhaust the entire property conveyed to the trustee.

These resulting trusts are imposed upon the theory that if the grantor or devisor had thought about the possibility of the failure of the intended trust, he would probably have preferred that the beneficial interest should vest in himself or his successors rather than in the trustee. Such a rule seems justified both on the score of probability and fairness. If in any of the cases the transferor received pay for the property there is no resulting trust.

§ 23. Gratuitous conveyance by deed upon oral trust.[3] It was the general custom, during the century before the statute of uses to have land held in use. Hence if A made a gratuitous conveyance without declaring any use it was presumed that a use was meant to result to the grantor. After the statute of uses, such conveyances would be utterly futile because the legal title would at once revest in the grantor and hence it was decided that no resulting use arose. After the modern passive trust was recognized it was held not only that there was no presumption of a resulting trust but that no resulting trust could be recognized. It is obvious, however, that the transferee in such a case should not be allowed to keep the land thus conveyed to him and hence the English courts impose a constructive trust as a specific remedy for the wrongful retention of the land. In this country many courts, being misled by the fact that imposing a constructive trust would lead to the same result as enforcing the oral trust, have refused to follow the English rule on the ground that it would violate the statute of frauds, but the present tendency is the other way.

[2] 54 **Am Jur,** Trusts, §§ 196–200.

Avoidance or reverter of valid charitable trust, purpose of which has failed, in absence of express provision therefor. 38 **ALR** 44–71.

Devolution of property under will giving property to one "in trust" (or containing terms indicative of possible trust), where trust fails for uncertainty or there is failure to show intent to create trust. 96 **ALR** 958–973.

37 **Harv. L. R.** 653, Conveyances upon Trusts Not Properly Declared.

17 **S. Calif. L. R.** 144, Gifts for Masses Are Restricted by State Statutes and Church Laws.

[3] 54 **Am Jur,** Trusts, § 202.

Grantee's oral promise to grantor as giving rise to trust. 35 **ALR** 280–321; s. in 45 **ALR** 851–856; 80 **ALR** 195–209; 129 **ALR** 689–697.

§ 24. Conveyance by will upon oral trust.[4] If A makes an absolute devise to B but with an intention not expressed in the will that B shall hold the land upon trust for C, B will hold beneficially unless notice of such intent is communicated to him before the death of A. But if notice does reach B before that event B is not allowed to hold beneficially, though instead of imposing a constructive trust for the heirs of A—as would be expected in analogy to the case of a conveyance by deed to B upon an oral trust for C—the courts impose a constructive trust for C. This is squarely in violation of the statute of frauds but it is probably justified by the strong desire of the courts to carry out A's intent; the doctrine has now been extended to the case of a conveyance by deed in contemplation of death. And where A's heir orally promised A to hold in trust for C if A would refrain from making a will C may have a constructive trust declared for himself.

§ 25. Property acquired by homicide.[5] If a beneficiary under a will should murder the testator in order to prevent the latter from revoking the will, it would seem that either by statute or decision the beneficiary should be prevented from profiting by his crime. But there are three different lines of authority. In some states it has been held that the commission of the crime does not affect the rights of the beneficiary the latter retaining both the legal and beneficial interests in the property. In other states the beneficiary does not get even the legal title so that a bona fide purchaser from him would not be protected. The objection to this view is that it seems a plain violation of the statute of wills which makes no such exception. The third and sound view is that although the legal title passes to the beneficiary according to the terms of the will, equity will impose upon him a constructive trust for the benefit of the heir or next of kin of the testator in order to prevent him from profiting by his crime.

If an ancestor is murdered by a prospective heir in order to prevent his making a will which would destroy or reduce the heir's share in the estate, it is clear that he should not be allowed to profit by his wrongful act. Where it is known whom the will was intended to benefit, it would seem the best solution to impose a constructive trust for the benefit of such intended beneficiaries. Where it cannot be shown who the intended beneficiaries were, the constructive trust should be for those next entitled after the murderer. Similar reasoning should be applied where the beneficiary of a life insurance policy murders the insured in order to collect on the policy; the insurance company should be held liable to the insured's estate.

§ 26. Purchase by fiduciary, converter or disseisor.[6] If a trustee or other fiduciary misapplies the property held by him in the purchase of other property for his own benefit he may be declared constructive trustee of such property for the benefit of the cestui or other beneficiary. If such a remedy

[4] 54 **Am Jur,** Trusts, §§ 243–244.
43 **Harv. L. R.** 521, Trusts and the Statute of Wills.

[5] 54 **Am Jur,** Trusts, § 247.

[6] 54 **Am Jur,** Trusts, §§ 233–238.
Effect of purchase by cotenant in possession of common property at foreclosure sale thereof. 6 **ALR** 297–307.
Right of beneficial owner to recover property or funds transferred by trustee or fiduciary to pay or secure his own antecedent indebtedness. 12 **ALR** 1048–1057.
Rights of parties under oral agreement to buy land or bid it in at judicial sale for another. 42 **ALR** 10–126; s. in 135 **ALR** 232–262.
Duty of joint adventurers inter se in respect of acquisition or renewal of property rights or interests related to the enterprise. 62 **ALR** 13–31.
Adverse possesssion by third party or stranger of property held in trust. 2 **ALR** 41–57.
Right of trustee, executor, administrator, or guardian to purchase property of estate or trust at sale brought about by third person. 77 **ALR** 1513–1539.

will not make the beneficiary whole he has a personal claim for the difference; if the property thus purchased should increase in value the constructive trust remedy enables the beneficiary to avail himself of such increase.

If X, a stranger, disseises T of trust land or converts trust chattels, he cannot be held as constructive trustee of such property because he does not claim through T but adversely to him, and may insist upon having the question of title between himself and T tried at common law. Similarly, if the land and chattels were not held in trust, the disseisor or converter cannot be held as constructive trustee by the owner but must be sued at law in ejectment or trover or replevin. But if, in either of these cases the disseisor or converter should sell the property whose possession he has acquired and should invest the proceeds in other property there is no common-law action to obtain such newly acquired property—because as to such property he gets title from his vendor—and equity should declare a constructive trust thereof. For though the right to bring ejectment, or trover, or replevin for the original property is not cut off by any transfer made by the disseisor or converter, such property may have depreciated in value and the disseisor or converter may now be insolvent and the newly acquired property may have increased in value. The authorities, however, are in conflict on the matter.

§ 27. **Tracing trust funds.**[7] If T wrongfully mingles trust money with his own, the trust attaches to the entire amount C having an equitable lien on it or any part of it for the amount of the trust money thus commingled; hence if part of the mixture be lost the lien may be enforced against the residue. If T deposits trust money in a bank with his own in his own name and later withdraws part of it and dissipates it, such withdrawals are charged against his own interest so that so long as enough is left in the bank account to equal the amount of the trust funds, C is protected by giving him an equitable lien. But if all is withdrawn or if it is reduced below the amount of the trust funds, C will lose entirely or pro tanto respectively, if T becomes insolvent; for while T is liable personally for his breaches of trust to the full extent of C's loss, yet in a contest between C and the general creditors of an insolvent trustee, C cannot ordinarily be a preferred claimant unless he is able to trace the trust funds. Where the amount withdrawn by T has not been dissipated by him but has been invested in property, C is entitled to an equitable lien on this property; this is highly important to C if the balance of the account has been dissipated by T.

The above reasoning applies also to cases where there is a constructive trust based upon other wrongs besides breaches of trust. It is fraud for bank officials to accept deposits after they know of the bank's insolvency; hence if the depositor can trace his money in such a case he is entitled to claim it as against the general creditors of the bank; but if it has been dissipated—for example, paid out again to meet other checks—he is not entitled, apart from statute, to any such preference.

If at any time T should invest the commingled funds or any part thereof in property, C's equitable lien will attach to this property so that if the prop-

[7] 54 **Am Jur,** Trusts, §§ 248–273.

Following trust funds deposited in mixed bank account of trustee. 26 **ALR** 3–16; s. in 35 **ALR** 747; 55 **ALR** 1275–1276; 102 **ALR** 372–379.

Remedy of one whose money is fraudulently used in the purchase or improvement of real property. 43 **ALR** 1415–1447; s. in 47 **ALR** 371–372; 48 **ALR** 1269.

Right of one party to a joint bank account to follow money withdrawn by the other. 77 **ALR** 799–807.

Following or identifying trust funds in assets of insolvent bank. 82 **ALR** 46–288.

39 **Col. L. R.** 172, Swollen Assets Theory.

erty should increase in value he should be allowed to avail himself of his proportional share of the profit.

§ 28. Taking renewal of lease—gratuities.[8] A fiduciary is not allowed to make a profit out of his fiduciary position so that even if he uses his own funds in acquiring property, his duty in respect thereto may be such that the beneficiary may compel him to hold it upon a constructive trust. For example, a trustee of leasehold property who takes a renewal of the lease for his own benefit may be compelled to hold it for the benefit of C even though the landlord had refused to renew it for the benefit of C. Similar reasoning applies to any gratuities which come from third parties to the fiduciary because of the latter's position, even though no harm is done the beneficiary thereby. And when a fiduciary compromises a claim against the estate of his beneficiary he is entitled only to reimbursement, not to the face value of the claim.

§ 29. Fiduciary with authority to sell or to buy.[9] If a fiduciary has authority to sell property for his beneficiary and he conducts a public sale of it there is a flat rule that if he buys at the sale he may be compelled to hold it for the benficiary; if he was anxious to bid at the auction he should have asked the court to appoint some one else to conduct the sale. But there is no flat rule forbidding his buying at a private sale from the beneficiary; but such sale may be set aside unless the fiduciary shows that he divested himself of every advantage which he had gained from his fiduciary position, by disclosing to the beneficiary whatever knowledge he had acquired relative to the value of the property.

Where A entrusts B with money with which to buy property and to take title in A's name and B in violation of his instructions buys the property with his own funds and takes title to himself A may have a constructive trust declared subject to his reimbursing B. By the better view it is not important that A's instructions to B were oral.

CHAPTER VI

TRANSFER OF TRUST PROPERTY

A. By Act of T

§ 30. Bona fide purchase for value—(1) paying value.[10] In 1450 equity gave a remedy against a trustee or feoffee to uses but not against his transferee unless he too expressly undertook the trust. This obviously was not a complete protection to C, so the equity court took the further step that the transferee would be presumed to have taken the property upon the original use or trust. This presumption soon hardened into a rigid rule that the transferee was bound whether he did or did not undertake the trust; the obligation thus being imposed or constructed by equity in order to protect C more fully it came to be called a constructive trust and the doctrine was extended to all cases where a defendant would be unjustly enriched with specific property at

[8] 54 **Am Jur**, Trusts, §§ 229, 233, 239.

[9] 54 **Am Jur**, Trusts, § 228.

Principle which condemns transactions in which trustee or other fiduciary acts in his own interest adversely to beneficiaries or others whom he represents, as applicable to transactions in which spouse or relative has a part. 131 **ALR** 990–1003.

Power of testamentary trustee to purchase at his own sale. 1 **ALR** 747–753.

[10] 54 **Am Jur, Trusts,** §§ 266–273.

Unperformed obligation as value, as regards one's status as a bona fide purchaser freed from prior equities. 124 **ALR** 1259-1263.

the plaintiff's expense including cases where the conveyance was in fraud of the equities of specific performance, reformation of instruments, equitable mortgage and rescission.

But the doctrine of constructive trust has an important limitation: it is not enforced against a transferee who had both paid value and received title before notice of the trust or other equity. If the transferee has bought and received the conveyance in good faith but receives notice of the trust or other equity before actually paying any of the purchase price C may at his option have him declared a constructive trustee even though he has given his notes and a mortgage. Where he has paid enough of the purchase money in cash that the mortgage is good security for the rest it is certainly arguable—now that mortgages are so common—that he should be protected; but the rule is usually stated that he must pay all. Where he has paid part in good faith and is then required by C to surrender the property, he is entitled to an equitable lien on the property to secure what he has paid.

One who gives up a pre-existing claim against T in exchange for trust property should be and is considered as having given up present value; and the tendency is toward protecting one who merely accepts trust property as collateral security for a pre-existing debt, the value being found in the forbearance to sue.

A judgment creditor is not a bona fide purchaser for value because he gives no present value for the property upon which his judgment is a lien and also because he gets no title to it; but if he buys the property at the execution sale he is regarded as then giving value because he credits the amount of the purchase price on his claim.

A purchaser from a known trustee who has the authority to sell need not see to the proper application of the purchase money.

§ 31. **Same.—(2) getting title.**[1] Though the purchaser has paid all the purchase price before notice of the trust he is not protected if he has failed to get title. In such a case he has, of course, an equitable right to call upon T for a conveyance, but C has a similar equitable right, equally meritorious, which is prior in time; as between equal equities the prior one prevails. Furthermore, to allow the purchaser to improve his position by obtaining a conveyance after knowledge of the equity would place a premium on dishonesty.

Though the purchaser has not actually received the legal title it is enough if the act of transfer is a ministerial one which he may compel by a writ of mandamus. Also he need not have the legal title conveyed to himself; he may have it transferred to a third person in trust for himself, provided the third person receives it in good faith.

If instead of selling the trust property T mortgages or pledges it the mortgagee or pledgee, if he advances his money and receives the mortgage or pledge in good faith, will be protected to the extent of his advances; this is true even though the pledgee gets merely possession and in many states the mortgagee gets only a legal lien.

§ 32. **Same.—choses in action, equitable interests.**[2] If T instead of transferring land or chattels should transfer negotiable choses in action the doctrine of bona fide purchase for value may apply because T can transfer title. If the chose in action is not negotiable he cannot pass title unless the obligor assents; he can give only a power of attorney to his transferee to collect the

1 54 Am Jur, Trusts, § 266.

2 54 Am Jur, Trusts, § 31.

chose in action for his own benefit. There is a conflict of authority as to whether the doctrine of bona fide purchase for value should apply so as to protect such a purchaser against C's equity. The argument in favor of protecting him is that although he does not have title he has a legal as distinguished from a merely equitable right and hence he should not be deprived of it if he has, by paying value, acquired an equity equal in merit to that of C.

If the owner of a non-negotiable chose in action is induced by fraud to assign it to X who in turn assigns it to Y who pays value for it in good faith without notice of the fraud, the situation is similar, the equity of fraud being substituted for breach of trust; and there is a similar conflict of authority.

If T, in violation of his trust, mortgages trust property to X and then gives a second mortgage—that is, mortgages the equity of redemption—to Y, it is clear that the doctrine of bona fide purchase for value applies to X because he gets either legal title or a legal lien, but there is conflict of authority as to whether it applies to Y. Decisions which support C against Y are usually supported on the basis that C's right has ceased to be merely that of a claimant against T and has become a property right which can be cut off only by a transfer of the legal title by T. Decisions which protect Y against C are usually justified on the ground that the doctrine of bona fide purchase for value is a salutary one and should be extended to the protection of property rights other than the legal title.

A similar question arises where C declares himself trustee of his equitable interest for A and then assigns it to B; or where C is induced by fraud to assign his trust interest to D who in turn assigns it to E who pays value without notice of the fraud. B and E will be protected only if the doctrine of bona fide purchaser for value is extended to equitable interests.

§ 33. Same—(3) without notice.[3] Ordinarily one must both get the legal title and pay value before notice of the trust or other equity in order to be protected. But if the property has once passed into the hands of a bona fide purchaser for value the equities are cut off and do not reattach unless the property comes again into the hands of the trustee or some one else who once held the property and fraudulently transferred it instead of continuing to hold it for C; other transferees even if they pay no value and have notice of the equity are protected. If such transferees were not protected the bona fide purchaser might find it very difficult to sell his property—especially land—where the breach of trust or other misconduct had become well known.

In order to be chargeable with notice it is not necessary that the purchaser should have had actual knowledge of the breach of trust or other misconduct; it is enough if he knew such facts as would put a prudent man upon inquiry. If he knows that his vendor is a trustee he is usually chargeable if it turns out that the trustee had no authority to sell. One who accepts a quitclaim deed cannot usually claim to be without notice; and a purchaser who asks his vendor to do an act which amounts to a fraud on another has been held chargeable with notice thereof.

B. By Act of C

§ 34. Successive assignments.[4] If C by sale or mortgage conveys his

3 54 **Am Jur**, Trusts, §§ 267, 268.
Right of one who, with knowledge of outstanding equity, derived his interest in real property from or through a bona fide purchaser, to same protection as latter. 63 **ALR** 1362–1375.

4 54 **Am Jur**, Trusts, § 270.

equitable interest in realty to X and later fraudulently purports to convey, by sale or mortgage, his interest in the same realty to Y, X will be protected everywhere against Y because his equity is prior. But when the trust property involved is personalty, there is square conflict of authority. The prevailing view in this country protects X, but in England and in a minority of states Y is protected if he took his assignment without notice of the previous assignment to X and notified T thereof before T learned of the assignment to X. The minority rule would be good legislation because similar to the registry statutes, but there seems to be no satisfactory ground for a nonstatutory duty upon X toward Y to notify T.

In any jurisdiction if the second assignment by C is made to T the latter is protected if bona fide because he has the legal title and as good an equity as X. Similarly if Y has not merely notified T but has in good faith obtained from T an assignment of the legal title he is entitled to protection everywhere against X.

C. Other Transfers

§ 35. **By death.**[5] Upon the death of a sole trustee leaving heirs the legal title to real estate—apart from statute—passes to such heirs, but since they pay nothing for it, they take subject to the trust; if the trust property consists of personalty it passes to the executor or administrator who likewise takes subject to the trust. If one of several co-trustees dies his title survives to the others, the statutes abolishing the rule as to survivorship applying only to property held beneficially.

Where the trustee of allodial realty dies without heirs the title goes to the state, but since the state is a volunteer it takes subject to the trust in the same way as does a private individual, the remedy being by petition rather than by subpoena. But if the realty is held in feudal tenure the state takes as reversioner free from the trust because the grant to T and his heirs having terminated for want of heirs C's interest, which is dependent for its existence upon T's title, also terminates. In many states statutes preserve C's rights against the possibility of T's dying without heirs.

If C dies leaving heirs and next of kin his equitable interest descends just as the legal title would have descended if he had had it. Equity follows the law here because there was no occasion for a different rule.

If C dies without heirs or next of kin his equitable interest in allodial realty and in personalty goes to the state which is entitled to enforce the trust against T. In case of feudal land it was formerly the English rule that T was entitled to keep the property because there was no one to take it away from him. C's interest did not escheat because C was never a part of the feudal system which regarded only the legal title. In England, by statute, equitable interests in land now escheat to the state; in this country the same result has been reached by judicial decisions which have applied the rule of bona vacantia (goods without an owner) to all kinds of property.

§ 36. **By marriage.**[6] Before C's right in equity to the beneficial use of the trust property became well settled, the widow or widower of a deceased feoffee to uses or trustee was entitled to dower or curtesy respectively in trust land; but after C's right was recognized the constructive obligation

Priority as between different assignees of same chose in action as affected by notice to debtor. 31 ALR 876–883; s. in 110 ALR 774–778.

[5] 19 Am Jur, Escheat, § 11.
54 Am Jur, Trusts, § 133.

[6] 15 Am Jur, Curtesy, §§ 16, 19, 22.
16 Am Jur, Dower, § 20.

which was imposed upon T's other transferees was extended after T's death to T's widow or widower.

The early rule was that C's widow or widower was not entitled to dower or curtesy because C had not been seised of the land. But as soon as dower or curtesy was denied to T's widow or widower it was the logical theory for equity to give dower or curtesy to C's widow or widower. In the case of curtesy this could be and was done by judicial decision because husbands had been joined in transfers made by a female cestui because of the disability of coverture and land titles would not be upset; but it had not been customary for the wife of a male cestui to join in a conveyance of trust land, so statutes were necessary to give her dower without upsetting land titles.

Where land is conveyed upon trust for a married woman for her separate use free from the control of her husband this does not prevent him from getting curtesy unless that was expressly excluded by the trust instrument.

It was the common-law rule that upon marriage the husband received title to all the wife's chattels and the right to collect all her choses in action as her assignee. If he should fail to collect the choses in action or otherwise reduce them to possession during the coverture his power of attorney to do so was revoked by the termination of the coverture and the choses in action would not become a part of his estate. If C's right be regarded as merely an equitable chose in action against T, then, in order to make trust chattels a part of his estate C's husband would need to get a conveyance of the legal title from T. Such was the early holding, but it was later overruled on the ground that equity should follow the law and hold the same as to equitable interests in chattels as the law would hold if the wife had had the legal title to the chattels. If part of the trust estate consists of legal choses in action they must be collected or otherwise reduced to possession by T before the husband's right to them will be perfected.

§ 37. By bankruptcy—spendthrift trusts.[7] Where T becomes bankrupt, title to the trust property does not pass to the assignee in bankruptcy unless T had some beneficial interest therein, for example if he had a lien on it for advances or was also one of several cestuis. In any event the assignee in bankruptcy takes subject to C's equity as does an assignee for the benefit of creditors.

It has been the policy of the common law that property should be freely alienable either by the act of the owner or of his creditors; hence any provision by the grantor of property that the grantee of the legal title should not alien or that it shall be free from the claims of his creditors is void. On this point equity has, by the great weight of authority, followed the law where C's interest is in fee; where C's interest is only for life the weight of

[7] 54 **Am Jur**, Trusts, §§ 152–185.

Validity of spendthrift trust for life or shorter period for benefit of one to whom fee simple or absolute estate is given. 91 **ALR** 1084–1092.

Validity of spendthrift trusts. 119 **ALR** 19–71; s. in 138 **ALR** 1319–1330.

Subjecting income directed to be paid to or used for the benefit of the beneficiary of a trust, to the maintenance of his wife or children. 52 **ALR** 1259–1263; s. in 104 **ALR** 779–784.

Validity of provisions of instrument creating legal estate attempting to exempt it from claims of creditors. 80 **ALR** 1007–1028.

Provision in trust instrument making solvency of beneficiary, or discharge of his debts, a condition precedent to his receipt of trust property. 138 **ALR** 1336–1344.

Authority conferred by will or trust instrument upon trustee to determine amount of income or principal that beneficiary shall receive as exercisable by substituted or successor trustee. 126 **ALR** 931–942.

44 **Harv. L. R.** 203, Spendthrift Trusts Created in Whole or in Part for the Benefit of the Settlor.

43 **Harv. L. R.** 63, Reaching the Interest of the Beneficiary of a Spendthrift Trust.

authority upholds such a provision as valid. The arguments in favor of this doctrine are that the creator of the trust should be allowed to do what he pleases with his own property; that it ought to be possible to protect those who are incompetent to take care of their property in much the same way that infants and insane persons are protected; and that upholding such trusts will tend to prevent such cestuis from becoming public charges. In no jurisdiction may the owner of property make such a settlement on himself.

Where the trust instrument provides that T shall have an uncontrolled discretion in applying the income for the maintenance of C, the latter has no enforcible interest in the property and there is nothing that he can assign or that his creditors can reach.

§ 38. By act of creditors.[8] Since T has the legal title to trust property it is liable at common law for all his debts even though not incurred in the management of the trust property and the creditors may have it sold on execution. But unless T has some beneficial interest in the property, equity will usually, at the suit of C, enjoin the creditors from levying thereon. If no injunction is asked and the property is sold to a bona fide purchaser for value at the execution sale, C's equity is cut off.

If the creditor's claim against T is for property or services of which the trust estate has properly received the benefit and T is a nonresident or insolvent the creditor may reach, by a bill for equitable execution T's right of exoneration, that is, his right to pay for such property or services out of the trust estate instead of out of his own pocket; if T is in arrears to the trust estate this will reduce pro tanto the claim which the creditor can reach.

Since C's interest, from the standpoint of procedure, is only a chose in action against T, it could not be reached by an ordinary common-law levy any more than could a legal chose in action; apart from statute a sheriff can sell only tangible property, possession of which could be delivered over to the purchaser. To remedy this defect in common-law procedure equity allows a judgment creditor who has tried but who cannot get satisfaction through common-law execution, to file a bill against his debtor asking that enough of the latter's intangible property be assigned to the creditor to pay the latter's claim; the creditor can then collect the chose in action as the debtor's assignee. If the obligor of the chose in action sought to be reached is within the jurisdiction of the court he may be joined as a codefendant and thus settle the whole matter in the equity suit. Such a bill is called a creditor's bill for equitable execution and enables a creditor to reach both legal and equitable choses in action. Hence if a creditor of C is unable to get complete satisfaction at law out of tangible property of C, he may file a bill in equity asking that C's trust interest be subjected to the payment of his claim. By statute in some states equitable interests in land have been subjected to common-law execution.

At common law creditors who levied upon the property of an insolvent debtor were entitled to preference according to the time of their respective levies; equity follows the law here by giving preference to creditors according to the time of filing their respective bills in equity for equitable execution.

8 21 Am Jur, Executions, §§ 447, 586, 664, 694.

CHAPTER VII

EXTINGUISHMENT OF A TRUST

§ 39. **Methods of extinguishment.**[9] A trust may be extinguished in any one of four ways:

(1) By revocation where by the terms of the creation of the trust a power to revoke has been reserved.

(2) By merger of the equitable interest into the legal title, either by transfer by T to C or by C to T or by either one inheriting from the other.

(3) In some jurisdictions, by statute, where the purposes of the trust have been accomplished, the title of T is passed to C.

(4) By accidental destruction of the entire trust property.

If T is responsible for the destruction of the trust property there is not a complete extinguishment of the trust because T's obligation still remains.

CHAPTER VIII

DUTIES OF TRUSTEE

§ 40. **As to conveyance of the trust property.**[10] If C is sui juris, T must ordinarily convey at his direction either to C himself or to a third party. If there are several cestuis they must all concur in order to be entitled to a conveyance; T is not bound to convey less than all. Where the instrument creating the trust directs T to convert land into money or invest money in land C, if sui juris, may object to the proposed conversion and compel T to convey the property in its original form; this is called the doctrine of equitable reconversion.

Though ordinarily a sole cestui is entitled to a conveyance of the trust property as soon as he becomes sui juris, some jurisdictions hold valid a provision in the trust instrument that the corpus of the estate shall not be transferred to him till some time after reaching majority. Though the purpose of the provision is similar to the purpose of creating a spendthrift trust—to prevent persons of slight business ability from wasting the property—the mere postponement of control does not make the property inalienable.

§ 41. **As to possession, information and custody.**[1] The cestui for life

[9] 54 **Am Jur**, Trusts, §§ 127–135.

Right of creator to revoke or procure cancelation of voluntary trust. 38 **ALR** 941–1032; s. in 91 **ALR** 102–121; 131 **ALR** 457–478.

Termination of trust by consent of all beneficiaries. 45 **ALR** 743–751; s. in 123 **ALR** 1427–1450.

Resignation or removal of executor, administrator, guardian, or trustee, before final administration or termination of trust, as affecting his compensation. 94 **ALR** 1101–1112.

Construction and application of provision in trust instrument relating to amendment or modification. 128 **ALR** 1173–1186.

57 **Harv. L. R.** 362, Effects of a Power to Revoke a Trust.

42 **Harv. L. R.** 849, Parol Extinguishment of Trusts in Land.

[10] 54 **Am Jur**, Trusts, §§ 300–305.

[1] 54 **Am Jur**, Trusts, §§ 338–345, 356.

Individual liability of trustee or other fiduciary for injury to person or property of third person due to negligence, or violation of statute or ordinance, in management of trust estate. 7 **ALR** 408–416; s. in 123 **ALR** 458–465.

Responsibility of fiduciary for loss of funds deposited in bank in his own name or other form not indicating fiduciary character. 43 **ALR** 600–610.

Care required of trustee or guardian with respect to retaining securities coming into his hands as assets of the estate. 77 **ALR** 505–524; s. in 112 **ALR** 355–368.

Liability for interest or profits on funds of estate deposited in bank or trust company which is itself executor, administrator, trustee, or guardian, or in which executor, etc., is interested. 88 **ALR** 205–218.

Liability of trustee or other fiduciary for loss on investment as affected by the fact that it was taken in his own name without indication of fiduciary capacity. 106 **ALR** 271–284; s. in 150 **ALR** 805–809.

has no right to demand possession of trust property unless it is clear from the trust instrument or from special circumstances that the settlor intended him to have possession.

T must keep clear and accurate accounts of the trust property and produce them for the benefit of C; and if he procures opinions of counsel to guide him in the administration of the trust he must produce them at the request of C.

Like other fiduciaries a T, while properly performing his duties is liable only for failure to use due care of the trust property; he is not liable as an insurer. Hence if it be lost by theft or is destroyed or depreciates while it is rightfully in his custody he is not liable unless negligent; nor is he liable for loss if he has rightfully placed the property in the hands of another; but he cannot escape liability for a breach of trust of a cotrustee by merely remaining passive. It is frequently his duty not to keep personal charge of trust funds; it would not usually be due care for him to keep large sums of money on his person or at his residence; he should deposit them in a reputable bank at the earliest opportunity and if he fails to do so he will be liable if they are stolen or destroyed. In making the deposit he must use the word "trustee" or some similar word to indicate his fiduciary position so that the bank will not be able to acquire the rights of a bona fide purchaser of the money. The bank is not liable for the misappropriation of money withdrawn by T unless it has notice of such intended misappropriation.

By the weight of authority a public officer who has charge of public funds is liable as an insurer; the reason usually given for this heavy liability is the great public interest in preserving public funds.

§ 42. As to investment.[2] In making investments T must use such care as

Personal liability of trustee, executor, administrator, or guardian, as affected by terms of contract or form of signature. 138 **ALR** 155–198.

Contract of trustee as basis of suit to reach the trust estate or to charge the trustee personally or as trustee. 139 **ALR** 134–159.

2 54 **Am Jur**, Trusts, §§ 370–428.

Liability, as between life tenant and remainderman, for a premium paid for bonds. 4 **ALR** 1249–1255; s. in 16 **ALR** 527; 48 **ALR** 684–710; 101 **ALR** 7–55; 131 **ALR** 1426–1465.

Right of trustee to invest trust funds in stock of private corporation. 12 **ALR** 574–592; s. in 26 **ALR** 812; 122 **ALR** 657–665.

Rights of life tenant and remainderman respectively as to discount at which securities are purchased. 48 **ALR** 684–710; s. in 101 **ALR** 7–55; 131 **ALR** 1426–1465.

Rights as between life beneficiaries and remaindermen in corporate dividends or distributions during the life interest. 130 **ALR** 492–591.

Right of trustee to retain unauthorized securities held by testator or creator of trust. 37 **ALR** 559–572; s. in 122 **ALR** 801–814; 135 **ALR** 1528–1533.

Power of trustee and court as regards term of lease of trust property. 61 **ALR** 1368–1385.

Power of trustee to mortgage trust property for the purpose of making improvements or repairs. 63 **ALR** 795–805.

Allocation to capital or income of testamentary trust of interest, dividends, or other earnings, during settlement of estate or pending conversion directed by testator. 70 **ALR** 636–654; s. in 105 **ALR** 1194–1197.

Sale or exchange of property which is subject to life estate and remainder, where it is unproductive, or income is insufficient to pay taxes and upkeep. 76 **ALR** 540–551.

Right as between life tenant and remainderman in respect of property, estates, or securities of a wasting, consumable, or perishable nature. 77 **ALR** 753–782; s. in 109 **ALR** 234–236; 113 **ALR** 1193–1195.

Liability of trustee, guardian, executor, or administrator for loss of funds invested, as affected by order of court authorizing the investment. 88 **ALR** 325–340.

Investment of trust funds in share or part of single security or group or pool of securities. 103 **ALR** 1192–1208; s. in 110 **ALR** 1166–1173; 125 **ALR** 669–674.

Allocation between principal and income of amount received on disposition or liquidation of defaulted securities or other unproductive trust property. 103 **ALR** 1271–1301; s. in 115 **ALR** 881–889; 116 **ALR** 1354–1357; 129 **ALR** 1314–1337; 142 **ALR** 264–269; 149 **ALR** 1376–1378.

Payment to one of two or more trustees, executors, or administrators. 106 **ALR** 109–117.

Provisions of will or trust instrument contemplating advice, request, or consent of person other than one named as executor or trustee as regards exercise of powers conferred upon latter. 120 **ALR** 1407–1419.

Share of beneficiary of trust or of decea prudent man would exercise in his own affairs, not with a view to speculation but to the preservation of the corpus of the fund. If the creator of the trust directs T to make or continue certain investments, T will ordinarily be justified in following such directions even though they would not otherwise be approved by an equity court.

At the present time investments in government securities or in first mortgages on real estate are the only ones permitted in most states apart from statute. But in Massachusetts and a minority of states T may, in the exercise of a sound discretion, invest a part of the trust funds in the stocks and bonds of business corporations. But even in states having the more liberal rule there are certain investments that would usually not be approved, for example, loans on personal security, the purchase of land, loans on a participating mortgage or on a second mortgage, or on leasehold mortgages or on foreign mortgages and loans where there is a large element of speculation. If the property placed in trust by the creator of the trust is invested in unauthorized securities T should convert it, within a reasonable time, into authorized securities in the absence of any direction by the testator.

If T has trust money in his hands for which he cannot find a proper investment he should deposit it in a reputable bank temporarily in his name as trustee; it should not be for a fixed time and if T leaves it there an unreasonable time and the bank fails he is liable for the loss. If the deposit is made without adding the word "trustee" or otherwise indicating his fiduciary position it is a breach of trust because if the bank is not informed of his fiduciary obligation it might give him personal credit on the security of such a deposit and thus become entitled to the rights of a bona fide mortgagee for value.

§ 43. As to collection and payment—liability for breach.[3] T should ordinarily collect debts due the trust estate as soon as they become due; if loss occurs because of unreasonable delay he must bear it. It is no defense that it would have ruined the debtor to press him for payment even where a good business man might have delayed or even where the creator of the trust would have granted indulgence. But he may excuse himself by showing that

dent's estate, who is also trustee or executor or administrator, as subject to charge in respect of his liability in his fiduciary capacity. 123 **ALR** 1320–1331.

Expenses of trust administration, such as court costs, costs of litigation, bond premiums, attorneys' fees, etc., as payable from income or corpus. 124 **ALR** 1183–1210.

Right or duty of trustee to withhold income as a reserve against future charges, anticipated loss, or reduction of future income or other emergencies. 125 **ALR** 629–641.

Duty of trustee to diversify investments, and liability for failure to do so. 131 **ALR** 1158–1170.

Right of corporate trustee to invest in or retain its own stock. 134 **ALR** 1324–1330.

Power of trustee or court to intrench upon corpus when income is insufficient to pay amount which the trust instrument directs to be paid to beneficiary out of income. 136 **ALR** 69–101.

Liability of trustee, guardian, executor, or administrator for loss of funds as affected by failure to obtain order of court authorizing investment, in absence of mandatory statute. 116 **ALR** 437–449.

Surchargeability of trustee, executor, administrator, or guardian, in respect of mortgage investment, as affected by matters relating to value of property. 117 **ALR** 871–884.

Trustee's compensation as payable from income or corpus. 117 **ALR** 1154–1160.

Right of cestui que trust (or one claiming through or under him) to maintain suit for partition. 126 **ALR** 1009–1028.

Apportionment of income where right to income commences or ends during accrual period. 126 **ALR** 12–55.

Effect of beneficiary's consent to, acquiescence in, or ratification of, improper investments or loans (including failure to invest) by trustee or other fiduciary. 128 **ALR** 4–56.

57 **Harv. L. R.** 601, Retention of Its Own Shares by a Corporate Trustee.

20 **Chicago-Kent L. R.** 331, Investments by Trustees.

[3] 54 **Am Jur**, Trusts, §§ 338–345.

Right of guardian to expend principal of ward's estate for maintenance and support. 5 **ALR** 632–655.

43 **Harv. L. R.** 63, Reaching the Interest of the Beneficiary of a Spendthrift Trust.

41 **Col. L. R.** 1332, Tort Liability of Trust Estates.

more was to be gained by temporary indulgence than by prompt legal proceedings; or if he can show that there were no reasonable grounds for believing that anything could be realized by suing.

Where it is the duty of T to make payments out of the trust funds he is liable at peril if he pays to the wrong person.

If T is guilty of any misconduct and the trust funds are thereby wholly or partially lost he is liable for the amount thus lost with simple interest. If an investment wrongfully made by T should be successful C has the option of taking the investment and calling upon T for an accounting of the profits. If T has wrongfully invested in a business venture, he is chargeable with compound interest unless he can prove that profits to that amount were not realized.

§ 44. As to delegating trust duties.[4] After once accepting the office of trustee T cannot by merely conveying the trust property to another, rid himself of any part of his trust duties. If he wishes to be relieved he may either get the consent of the cestuis if they are all sui juris or secure a release from the proper equity court.

While T's transferee is bound by the trust, unless he is a bona fide purchaser for value, he is not entitled by the transfer to perform the duties of the trustee's office; this applies to the heirs, devisees or executor of a deceased trustee as well as to a transferee inter vivos. But the creator of the trust may appoint the successors to the first appointees or provide that they shall choose their own successors. If property is conveyed to A "his heirs and assigns," A's devisee has been held entitled to act, but not an assignee inter vivos.

In a private trust all the trustees must concur in order that their acts may be valid; if one is unable to agree with the rest he should resign and the court should appoint a substitute. A majority is not competent to act unless the trust instrument so provides; and if a majority attempts to act without the consent of the minority the latter should ask for an injunction because their mere refusal to concur will not excuse them from liability for a breach of trust committed by the majority. In trusts for a public purpose a majority of the trustees may act unless the trust instrument provides otherwise.

While T may not delegate to another an act which requires discretion, such as the supervision of an auction sale of real estate or the purchase of a mortgage security, he may employ subordinates to perform mechanical duties which require technical skill rather than discretion, such as advertising a sale, auctioneering, etc. Furthermore, if in selling trust property or in making investments in public securities it is the usual course of business to employ a broker, he may do so and will not be liable for loss if he uses due care in selecting the broker.

4 54 Am Jur, Trusts, §§ 360, 361.

QUASI CONTRACTS

CHAPTER I

IN GENERAL

§ 1. When a quasi-contractual obligation arises.[1] Where a benefit has been received by the defendant from the plaintiff under such circumstances that in equity and good conscience the defendant should compensate the plaintiff therefor the law imposes upon the defendant a nonconsensual obligation—usually called today quasi contractual—to pay to the plaintiff the reasonable value thereof. Where the plaintiff seeks to get back specifically the benefit itself either in its original or in its changed form he will usually do this by bringing a bill in equity to have a constructive trust declared.

The benefit may be conferred or received either (1) through mistake; (2) in the performance of a contract; (3) through the commission of a tort; or (4) through duress. If a benefit is conferred under any other situation it is usually said to be conferred voluntarily and no quasi-contractual obligation arises.

There are two special difficulties inherent in the subject of quasi contracts. The question as to what is or is not unjust is one which deals with the com-

[1] 12 Am Jur, Contracts, § 6. 4 Am Jur, Assumpsit, § 10.

plexity of human conduct and, like many of the questions arising in the administration of equity, could be better dealt with by a court exercising its discretion without the necessity of laying down a rule as must be done where trial is by jury. The other special difficulty springs from the fact that procedurally quasi contract grew out of contract and courts do not always recognize the fundamental difference between the consensual obligations imposed by the law of contracts and the nonconsensual obligations imposed by the law of quasi contracts.

CHAPTER II

BENEFITS CONFERRED THROUGH MISTAKE

§ 2. Mistake of intrinsic fact.[2] If A, owing B $200 should pay him $300, or if A should pay him $200 and B should credit him with $300; or if A supposing that his son X had defaulted in his obligation to B had paid B $600 in satisfaction thereof; or if A, administrator of X's estate had paid B, a creditor, the full amount of his claim thinking that the estate was solvent whereas it was insolvent paying only sixty cents on the dollar; or if A, thinking that B had conveyed to him 160 acres of land, paid him therefor, whereas the conveyance covered only 143 acres; in all these cases the mistake is as to an intrinsic fact and there is a quasi-contractual obligation to pay the reasonable value of the benefit mistakenly conferred either where both parties were mistaken or where the plaintiff alone was mistaken and the defendant knew it. If the plaintiff alone was mistaken and the defendant was innocent there can be no recovery.

Where A owed B $50 but mistakenly thought he owed him $150 and turned over to B in payment a horse worth approximately the latter sum it would seem that where B refuses to return the horse and accept the $50 or to pay the difference between $50 and the value of the horse, that A should be allowed to choose either to tender the $50 and replevin the horse on principles of constructive trust, or to sue in quasi contract for the difference between $50 and the value of the horse; but the law is unsettled.

§ 3. Mistake of collateral fact.[3] If A should sell to B for $1 an uncut diamond worth $1000, both mistakenly thinking it to be a topaz; or if A should sell to B for $480 a note on X for $500 both mistakenly thinking X to be solvent or that the note was secured by mortgage; or if A should sell bank stock to B at par both mistakenly thinking that the bank's capital had not been impaired;—in all these cases no quasi-contractual obligation arises because the mistake is as to a collateral or extrinsic fact such as characteristic or quality or value affecting merely the motive for entering the trans-

[2] 4 **Am Jur**, Assumpsit, § 24.
40 **Am Jur**, Payment, §§ 187–204.
Right to return of premiums paid upon insurance policy which is void ab initio. 129 **ALR** 57–95.
Recovery by vendee of money paid under mistake of fact as to vendor's title. 36 **ALR** 482–486.
Right of maker to recover payment or overpayment made by mistake to transferee of paper in good faith. 41 **ALR** 588–591.
Good faith in receiving payment made under mistake of fact as affecting its recovery. 87 **ALR** 649–660.
Right of one who by mistake pays taxes to recover against person benefited by payment. 91 **ALR** 389–393.

[3] 4 **Am Jur**, Assumpsit, § 23.
Rights and remedies as to premium where insured was under mistaken belief regarding value, nature, or existence of property subject of insurance. 138 **ALR** 924–932.
Rights of buyer and seller inter se as affected by invalidity of, or subsequent changes or developments with respect to, tax. 115 **ALR** 667–675; s. in 132 **ALR** 706–714.

action and not the transaction itself. If the defendant was not mistaken but knew of the plaintiff's mistake he is liable in quasi contract on the ground of fraud.

§ 4. **Mistake of law.**[4] As a matter of sound reasoning there should be no difference between mistake of fact and mistake of law and such was the holding of the early English cases; but in 1802 Lord Ellenborough in Bilbie v. Lumley, 2 East 469, 102 Eng. Rep. 448, held that where A paid money to B under a mistake of law he could not maintain an action in quasi contract because "every one is presumed to know the law." There is no such maxim and the rule that ignorance of the law is no excuse does not properly apply because A has done no wrong for which he seeks to be excused. Nevertheless Bilbie v. Lumley represents the weight of authority, but the rule is so unpopular with the courts that a plaintiff is not barred by mistake of foreign law and a mistake of private right is in some states classified as a mistake of fact regardless of the nature of the mistake; it has also been held that where the payment was made to or by an officer of court the rule does not apply and relief is granted.

§ 5. **Plaintiff's negligence—defendant's change of position.**[5] The mere fact that A was negligent in making the mistake is no bar to his recovery in quasi contract; but if, in reliance upon such negligent mistake, B has irrevocably changed his position A is barred. That B has in the meantime surrendered or otherwise lost a right which might have been enforced against X has been held to be such an irrevocable change of position but not merely spending the money or other benefit received from A. Where B received the money as agent of C and in ignorance of the mistake and in performance of his duties as agent has paid the money over to C, this has been held to be such a change of position as to relieve B and compel A to seek his remedy against C; but this does not apply if B was the agent of an undisclosed principal.

§ 6. **Notice and demand—accrual of cause of action.**[6] Where, at the time when A through mistake transfers money or other benefit to B, the latter knows of the mistake, it is not necessary for A to give him notice thereof before bringing suit, but such notice is necessary if B was also mistaken because B might promptly correct the mistake as soon as it is called to his attention. By the great weight of authority, however, such notice is merely

[4] 4 **Am Jur**, Assumpsit, § 24.
40 **Am Jur**, Payment, §§ 205–212.
Action to recover for improvements made on land, taxes or interest paid, or lien discharged, by one who mistakenly believed himself the owner. 104 **ALR** 577–619.

Exception as regards payments to officers of court to rule preventing recovery back of payments made under mistake of law. 111 **ALR** 637–642.
Liability of public corporation for money received by it for unlawfully issued instrument of indebtedness. 6 **ALR** 355–358; s. in 105 **ALR** 80–102.
Recovery of tax paid under unconstitutional statute or ordinance. 48 **ALR** 1381–1396; s. in 74 **ALR** 1301–1306.
Right to recover money voluntarily paid with knowledge of facts but under misapprehension as to legal rights or obligations. 53 **ALR** 949–964.
Recovery back of public money paid by mistake. 63 **ALR** 1346–1356.
Character of action or proceeding in which purchaser at invalid sale for taxes or local improvement assessment may secure reimbursement from owner; and provisions of decree or judgment as to relief. 86 **ALR** 1208–1236.

[5] 12 **Am Jur**, Contracts, § 352.
19 **Am Jur**, Estoppel, § 84.
Personal liability of agent in respect of funds received from third person and turned over to principal not entitled thereto. 82 **ALR** 307–313.
45 **Harv. L. R.** 1333, Change of Position in Quasi Contracts.

[6] 4 **Am Jur**, Assumpsit, § 37.

a condition precedent to bringing action but not to the arising of a cause of action because the statute of limitations begins to run from the date of receiving the benefit, not from the date of receiving notice of the mistake

§ 7. Putting defendant in statu quo.[7] Where A is suing B in quasi contract for the reasonable value of a benefit received by B from A, his recovery should be reduced by the reasonable value of any benefit received by him from B in the same transaction, following the maxim, he who seeks equity should do equity; but unfortunately some decisions have applied the maxim, he who comes into equity must come with clean hands, and thus have barred A where he either refused or failed or was unable to return the benefit which had been received by him from B.

§ 8. Compromise.[8] If A contends that B owes him $500 and B contends that the amount is only $300 and B finally pays $400 in full settlement under a compromise agreement, this bars any recovery by A even though he is later able to show clearly that B did owe him $500. But compromise is a good defense only as to points covered by the compromise agreement; for example, where A paid the B county $50 toward the support of an illegitimate child of which X was supposed to be pregnant and it later turns out that X was not pregnant, A is not barred from recovery, because pregnancy was assumed, the only points compromised being the amount paid and the paternity of the child.

§ 9. Mistake as to title or as to the existence of the subject matter of a contract.[9] If A pays B $200 for a chattel which both think belongs to B but which is later reclaimed by the true owner Y, A may recover in an action of special assumpsit for breach of the implied warranty of title the reasonable value of the chattel, but he may, if he prefers, sue in quasi contract for the recovery of the amount which he paid for the chattel—$200.

If A pays B $1,000 for a piece of land which both mistakenly think belongs to B and the conveyance is by quitclaim deed instead of by warranty deed there is no recovery for breach of contract because there is no implied warranty in such a case. Where $1,000 was the approximate value of the land conveyed it would seem that A should be allowed to recover back the $1,000 in quasi contract in case the title failed; but the weight of authority is contra, most courts not distinguishing between a case where the grantor merely undertakes to convey whatever interest he may happen to have for a small fraction of the value, and the case where the grantor undertakes to convey the land for substantially the full value but gives a quitclaim deed because he is a fiduciary and does not wish to bind himself by a personal covenant of warranty; in the latter case the recovery, if allowed, should be against the beneficiary who actually received the money.

If A pays B for an annuity on the life of X, mistakenly thinking that X is alive; or for a chattel which he mistakenly thinks is still in existence, or for a land lease held by B which he mistakenly thinks is valid;—in all these cases A may recover back from B the amount paid. The same reasoning

7 4 Am Jur, Assumpsit, § 10.
12 Am Jur, Contracts, § 451.
Duty of innocent creditor to restore to third person money or other property of the latter received as result of fraud or mistake in transaction between debtor and third person. 114 ALR 382-395.

8 11 Am Jur, Compromise and Settlement, §§ 23-28, 32.

9 46 Am Jur, Sales, § 754.

would logically apply to money paid by A to B for the use of a patent mistakenly supposed to be valid, but the law is apparently contra on the ground that the subject matter of the contract was not a valid patent but freedom from interference by B.

§ 10. **Mistake as to the existence of a contract—misunderstandings.**[10] Where A confers a benefit upon B mistakenly thinking that there is a contract between them, A is logically entitled to recover the reasonable value of the benefit thus conferred. For example, where A and B have attempted to enter into a contract but have failed to do so because the language used is so equivocal that it can be reasonably understood in two different ways, A understanding it in one way and B in another, B is liable for the reasonable value of the benefit conferred under the supposed contract.

A misunderstanding between A and B may be brought about by the fraud of X. Where X, owing B a debt, made arrangements with B to deliver to him in satisfaction thereof two tons of coal and then ordered the coal from A fraudulently pretending that the order was made by B and A delivered the coal, B should either allow A to take the coal away upon principles of constructive trust, or to pay him its reasonable value. Where the coal has been consumed before the fraud of X is discovered, it would seem that since coal is a staple product which B would need to buy in any event that A should be allowed to recover in quasi contract, but such recovery has unfortunately been denied.

CHAPTER III

BENEFITS CONFERRED IN THE PERFORMANCE OF A CONTRACT

§ 11. **Further performance impossible.**[1] Where, after A partly performs a contract with B, further performance is stopped by the state, A is entitled to recover either on the contract on the ground that he has fully performed the abbreviated contract, or in quasi contract for the reasonable value of the benefit received by A.

Where A partly performs for B a contract for personal service and further performance is rendered impossible by A's illness or death, A or A's personal representative may—unless there is an express contract for full performance—recover for the reasonable value of the service rendered and by the better view this is not to be diminished by any damage caused to B by A's failure to perform because that would be indirectly holding A or A's personal representative liable for an excusable breach.

Where A has contracted to build a house for B on B's land and after the house is partly built it is destroyed by fire, this is not considered as a case of impossibility, because the land is still there and A is still under obligation to erect a complete house. But if A should contract to add a porch to B's complete house and after part performance the house and partly completed porch are destroyed by fire, A is held to be excused from further performance because it is impossible now to add any porch to the destroyed house and, by the better view, A is entitled to recover the reasonable value of the partly completed porch on the ground that it had become a part of B's property before the fire.

[10] 12 **Am Jur**, Contracts, §§ 352, 353.

[1] 12 **Am Jur**, Contracts, §§ 67, 352.
Right to recover consideration paid or performed upon contract, performance of which by other party is excused by reason of supervening impossibility. 144 **ALR** 1317–1335.

Where A undertakes to carry goods for B from New York to San Francisco, he is entitled to recover for part performance if part, but not all, of the goods are delivered at the latter place or if B accepts part or all of the goods at some intermediate place; if no part of the goods is received by B or delivered at San Francisco A is not entitled to recover anything even though the goods were destroyed within only a very short distance of the destination.

§ 12. Contract illegal.[2] Where A turns over to B, his agent, money to be used by B in furtherance of some illegal purpose, A may at any time compel B to return to him that part of the money which B still has, because it is more important to compel an agent to be loyal to his principal than to penalize the principal for being engaged in an illegal transaction.

Where A makes a wager with B and A loses the wager, B cannot force A to pay because of the illegality of the contract, and if A has paid he cannot—apart from statute—recover back from B, because they are in pari delicto. Where both parties have turned over the money wagered to X, a stakeholder, either A or B may, before the event is decided, give notice to X and recover from him the amount received; but, apart from statute, it is too late if X has paid the stake to the winner or if merely the event has been decided.

Where there is not a real but only a pretended wager used for the purpose of perpetrating a fraud, like the case of the three acorn cups and a ball or the case of the fake footrace, the victim of the fraud has been allowed to recover in quasi contract on the ground that it is better for the administration of justice to protect one who is part fool and only part knave against one who is entirely knave.

Where A confers a benefit upon B in performing a contract which A mistakenly supposed was legal A may recover for the reasonable value of the benefit thus received by B.

Where a transaction is made illegal in order to protect one of the parties, that party is not barred by illegality in recovering in quasi contract; for example, a statute making illegal a marriage brokage contract in order to protect the client, or a statute making it illegal to charge more than $10 to obtain a soldier's pension from the United States government.

§ 13. Defendant in default.[3] Where, after A has conferred a benefit upon

[2] 12 **Am Jur,** Contracts, §§ 212–219.

Rule that denies relief to party in pari delicto as applicable to transaction with a public officer or an official of the court. 116 **ALR** 1018–1031.

Right to return in specie of the consideration received by a political subdivision under an invalid or unenforceable contract, or to declaration of trust or other right in respect of property into which consideration has been converted. 93 **ALR** 441–454.

Necessity, as condition of action at law, or a defense thereto, based on rescission of contract, of return or tender before action, of securities, commercial paper, or documents evidencing property or contractual rights received as consideration. 105 **ALR** 1003–1017.

Margin transactions or dealings in futures as within constitution or statutes providing for recovery back of money paid on gaming consideration. 49 **ALR** 1085–1091.

[3] **Am Jur,** Work and Labor.

Amount or basis of recovery by attorney who takes case on contingent fee where client discontinues, settles, or compromises. 3 **ALR** 472–495; s. in 40 **ALR** 1529–1539.

Right of vendee who enters under parol contract, to recover for improvements where vendor refuses to convey. 17 **ALR** 949–952.

Vendee's right to recover amount paid under executory contract for sale of land. 59 **ALR** 189–275; s. in 102 **ALR** 852–911; 134 **ALR** 1064–1099.

Rights and remedies of tenant who takes possession of land under agreement in violation of statute of frauds. 119 **ALR** 1225–1235.

Nontort liability of third person who receives money or property in supposed performance of contract, to party to contract who was entitled thereto. 106 **ALR** 322–335.

Contract which violates Statute of

B in the performance of a contract with B, the latter refuses to go on or is guilty of a substantial breach of contract, A has a choice of two remedies; he may maintain special assumpsit to recover for the damage done by B's breach of contract or he may recover in indebitatus assumpsit for the reasonable value of the benefit conferred. Where B has received no benefit there is no liability in quasi contract even though B was in default in refusing to receive it. Where A has fully performed his part of the contract and B's obligation is to pay money therefor, probably the weight of authority is that A may not recover more than the contract price even though that is less than the reasonable value of the benefit conferred. Where the contract was within the statute of frauds, for example, a contract not to be performed within a year or a contract to convey land or chattels in excess of the statutory limit of price, A's remedy is of course entirely in quasi contract.

The fact that the benefit contracted for turned out to be unprofitable to B is no defense whether A rendered full or only part performance.

By the better view any benefit which has been received by A under the contract goes merely in reduction of A's recovery.

Where A accepted from B an oral lease on some land and transferred to him a gold watch in payment of the first month's rent of $100 and B later repudiated the oral lease it was held that B could not compel A to receive back the watch but that A was entitled to recover its value in quasi contract. But since the default was B's it would seem that A should be able to get back the watch if he preferred, upon principles of constructive trust.

§ 14. **Plaintiff in default.**[4] Where A has conferred upon B a benefit in the performance of a contract with B and then defaults in further performance, the weight of authority is that if B is willing to go on with the contract, A can recover nothing, whether the contract is or is not within the statute of frauds. Where the contract is within the statute, A is in the position of being compelled—in order to escape forfeiture—to complete performance and then be content with recovery in quasi contract for the reasonable value of the benefit conferred, not being able to recover against B on the contract.

By the minority view—chiefly based upon cases of contracts of personal service—A's refusing to complete performance does not prevent his recovery in quasi contract for the reasonable value of the benefit conferred less the amount of damage suffered by B for A's breach.

CHAPTER IV

BENEFITS RECEIVED THROUGH THE COMMISSION OF A TORT

§ 15. **Trespass, fraud.**[5] If B seduces A's servant, A may maintain either trespass or case for the damage occasioned to him by the seduction; if B received a benefit by using the services of a seduced or kidnapped servant, for example, an apprentice, A may, if he prefers, maintain an action in quasi contract for the reasonable value of such services. Similar reasoning applies to a case where A was convicted of a crime in a court having no jurisdiction and served B under a labor contract made by B with the state.

Frauds as evidence of value in action not based on the contract. 49 ALR 1121–1129.

Contract price as limit of attorney's recovery on quantum meruit in event of his discharge without fault on his part. 108 ALR 674–678.

4 Am Jur, Work and Labor.

5 4 Am Jur, Assumpsit, §§ 14, 23.

If B causes A damage by means of a fraudulent representation, A may maintain an action on the case for deceit even though B was not benefited by the fraud; but if B does receive a benefit thereby A may, if he prefers, maintain an action in quasi contract for the reasonable value of such benefit; for example, if B, already married, fraudulently persuades A to go through a marriage ceremony with him and live with him as his wife, the better view is that A is entitled to recover from B the reasonable value of services rendered to B before the fraud was discovered.

Where B buys goods from A upon credit with a preconceived design not to pay for them, A may recover in quasi contract from B at once upon discovery of the fraud, though it is not clear that he may maintain an action on the case for deceit.

§ 16. Conversion of chattels and disseisin of land.[6] If B converts A's chattel, the usual remedy is trover; but if B has purported to sell the chattel, A may, if he prefers, maintain an action based upon quasi contract for the money received upon such purported sale. Where B still has the chattel or has disposed of it, A should be allowed to maintain an action in quasi contract for its reasonable value but on this point there is a conflict of authority.

If B wrongfully takes and holds possession of A's land, A may maintain an action of trespass for the original entry, or ejectment to get back possession of the land, but he cannot maintain any action for any benefit derived by B from the wrongful occupancy till he regains possession either by self-help or by an action of ejectment; then he may maintain an action of trespass for mesne profits which is in essence quasi contractual.

CHAPTER V

BENEFITS RECEIVED THROUGH DURESS

§ 17. Duress of the person.[7] If B by threats of prosecuting A or one of A's near relatives for a crime extorts money from A, the latter is entitled to recover the amount thus paid, even though A or the near relative was guilty of the crime charged. But where A is the party who takes the initiative in the matter, the better view is that he is not entitled to recover.

Similar reasoning applies where the payment of an illegal tax or license fee is extorted from A by threats of immediate arrest or seizure of his goods.

§ 18. Economic duress.[8] Where B takes advantage of A's economic necessities to extort money from him, A is entitled to recover in quasi contract. For example, a common carrier or other public service company that refuses service unless an illegal exaction is paid is thus liable. So where A threatened to levy upon B's carts loaded with ice ready to deliver to his customers early Monday morning and thus forced B to pay a debt for which he had received a discharge in insolvency proceedings, it was held that A might recover back the amount paid; and there was a similar holding where A was compelled to pay boomage not due in order to get his logs down the river.

6 53 Am Jur, Trover and Conversion, § 162. 4 Am Jur, Assumpsit, § 14.
Waiver of tort and recovery in assumpsit for conversion as dependent on or affected by sale of the goods by the converter. 97 ALR 250-277.

7 4 Am Jur, Assumpsit, § 23.

8 17 Am Jur, Duress, §§ 3, 6, 7.

CHAPTER VI

MISCELLANEOUS

§ 19. Benefits conferred voluntarily or incidentally.[9] Where A confers a benefit upon B without involving any intrinsic mistake or contract or tort or duress, the benefit is said to be conferred voluntarily and—apart from statute—no quasi-contractual obligation arises. For example, services rendered by a surgeon to a supposed pauper, or by a charitable institution to orphans supposed to be without funds or temporary unprofessional services rendered during an emergency. But where professional services are rendered in an emergency by a physician in case of personal injuries suffered in an accident or by an undertaker who is called in to take charge of a corpse, compensation is ordinarily allowed.

Where one member of a family renders ordinary services to other members of the family there can be no recovery in quasi contract, any liability must be based upon a contract, either express or implied in fact from the circumstances; but if the services are unusual recovery may be allowed in quasi contract, for example, where, at the suggestion of the physician in charge, the defendant's intestate, ill and unconscious, was taken to the home of the plaintiff, a foster child who took care of her for nearly a year.

Where B dies leaving livestock with no one to care for them, a former servant of B or a near neighbor is entitled to compensation for services rendered till an administrator takes charge of the estate.

Where A found B's boat between high and low tide in danger of destruction and took care of it and repaired it in order to preserve it, A was held entitled to compensation in quasi contract, but not to a lien, for the reasonable value of the services thus rendered.

Where A for his own purposes does an act which incidentally benefits B, no quasi-contractual obligation arises; for example, where A in draining his own quarry incidentally drained B's quarry also, it was held that B was under no obligation to pay A for the benefit thus received.

Where A knows that he has paid his debt to X but has lost the means of proving that fact and he pays again and then finds the lost proof he may not recover back because there was no mistake and apart from fraud, X's demand does not amount to duress.

§ 20. The test of benefit.[10] The better view is that benefit does not require enjoyment thereof; it is enough that the benefit was added to the defendant's estate. For example, if A contracts to add a porch to X's house and after the porch is partly built the house burns A is entitled to recover

[9] 40 **Am Jur,** Payment, §§ 22, 23.

Liability for services of child taken into home without express agreement for compensation. 10 **ALR** 139–144.

Servant's right to compensation for extra work or overtime. 25 **ALR** 218–239; s. in 107 **ALR** 705–714.

Right to recover back fine or penalty paid in criminal proceeding. 26 **ALR** 1523–1538.

Right of jury to apportion or sever damages as between joint tort-feasors. 30 **ALR** 790–798; s. in 108 **ALR** 792–801.

Request of surgeon or physician to attend relative as creating an implied obligation to pay for the services. 114 **ALR** 1252–1261.

Restitution as remedy for wrongful injunction. 131 **ALR** 878–885.

Right of municipality or other public body, or taxpayer, to recover back payments made under invalid or unenforceable contract. 140 **ALR** 583–615.

Liability of municipality or other governmental body on implied or quasi contract for value of property or work. 84 **ALR** 936–980; s. in 110 **ALR** 153–166.

Who other than borrower may avail himself of latter's right to recover back usurious payments or penalties therefor. 82 **ALR** 1008–1021; s. in 134 **ALR** 1335–1337.

[10] 12 **Am Jur, Contracts,** §§ 352, 353.

the reasonable value of the incomplete porch because it had become a part of X's land. And where A, an agent, being in default to his principal P, obtains money by fraud from X and deposits the money in P's bank account in order to cover the defalcation and then, still without P's knowledge, checks the money out again and absconds with it, apparently X may recover from P because the money did become temporarily a part of P's estate.

SALES

CHAPTER I

IN GENERAL

§ 1. A sale distinguished from similar transactions.[1] A sale is like a gift of chattels in that in both cases title passes; in a gift, delivery of the chattel

[1] 46 **Am Jur,** Sales, §§ 10–12.

Validity and mutuality of agreement to buy where there is no express agreement to sell. 60 **ALR** 215–232.

When transfer of accounts or other choses in action is deemed a sale rather than a pledge as security for a loan, and vice versa. 95 **ALR** 1197–1209.

Express provisions in contract of sale, or for supply of a commodity, for relief from the obligation in certain event. 51 **ALR** 990–1020.

Use of conditional sale contract to secure debt in addition to the purchase price. 148 **ALR** 346–353.

52 **Harv. L. R.** 725, Across Sales on Horseback.

52 **Harv. L. R.** 873, The First Struggle to Unhorse Sales.

41 **Mich. L. R.** 445, Conflict of Laws Relating to Installment Sales.

7 **Md. L. R.** 177, Caveat Emptor versus Caveat Venditor.

or of a deed to the chattel is necessary; in a sale it is necessary that there be a consideration in money paid or promised to be paid, but delivery is not necessary.

Where A delivers merely the possession of a chattel to B, the transaction is a bailment and B's obligation is that of a fiduciary, to return the chattel to A upon demand; if the chattel is destroyed without his fault the loss falls upon A; but if title also passes to B and B is to pay a consideration therefor the transaction is a sale and B must pay at all events no matter what happens to the chattel.

Where A delivers a chattel to B in exchange for another chattel the transaction is a barter or exchange; if A delivers the chattel to B for cash paid on the spot it is a sale without contract as in the ordinary sale of goods over a counter; but most sales are preceded or accompanied by a contract to sell, the transaction ripening into a sale upon the passing of title; if title does not pass, the transaction remains a mere contract to sell.

§ 2. Subject matter of a sale—potential existence.[2] A may make a valid contract with B to sell him a chattel which A does not own or which is not even in existence; but if both parties thought that A owned the chattel but in fact it had already been sold by A's agent to X or it had been destroyed without A's fault there is neither a sale nor a contract to sell because the subject matter of the contract is not in existence.

If A purports to sell to B chattels which he does not now have but which he expects to acquire in the future—for example, the fish he expects to catch on a contemplated fishing trip—the transaction is valid as a contract to sell but there is no sale; title cannot pass at the time of the purported sale because A does not have the title, and it has been held that title does not pass when A later acquires it. But to this rule there is the exception of potential existence: if the chattels consist of crops to be grown upon A's land or of the future offspring of animals owned by A, title to such chattels passes to B as soon as they come into existence.

CHAPTER II

TRANSFER OF TITLE OR BENEFICIAL OWNERSHIP

§ 3. Sales of specific goods—fungible goods.[3] Where A sells specific goods to B for cash and the goods are delivered to B on that understanding and B then fails or refuses to pay the price, the title has not yet passed and A may maintain replevin for the goods or trover for their value; but A may waive his right to cash thus making the transaction a sale, and maintain indebitatus assumpsit for goods sold and delivered. A failure to sue promptly in replevin or trover is evidence of such waiver.

Where A contracts to sell to B upon credit specific goods which are ready for delivery, title passes to B at the time of contract unless the parties have a different intent. But where the goods are not ready for delivery because something remains to be done by A, for example, where the goods are to be weighed or measured in order to determine the price, title does not pass at the time of contract unless there is affirmative evidence that the parties intended title to pass at once.

[2] 46 **Am Jur,** Sales, §§ 20–32.

[3] 46 **Am Jur,** Sales, §§ 410–423, 426–429.
Liability for loss of or damage to property delivered on trial or with privilege of return. 31 **ALR** 1365–1372.
35 **Harv. L. R.** 797, Delivery as a Requisite in the Sale of Chattel Property.

Where A delivers goods to B with the provision that B may later return the goods, title passes at once to B subject to its being revested in A upon the return of the goods; such a transaction is called a sale or return. But when A delivers goods to B subject to B's approval within a fixed time, title does not pass to B until such approval which may be done either expressly or by conduct inconsistent with his rejecting the goods.

If A, having 500 or an unknown number of bushels of wheat or other grain in a granary, contracts to sell to B 200 bushels of the mass and the intention of the parties is that title shall pass at once, B becomes at once the owner of 200 bushels as tenant in common with A; and the same reasoning has been applied wherever the parties regarded the units of the mass as of equal value and interchangeable; for example, oil in a cistern, barrels of pork, hay in a stack, flour in barrels, cattle in a herd, wine in bottles and sugar in sacks. Where there is no such intent on the part of the parties, title to the amount sold does not pass until A, with B's consent, appropriates specific goods to the carrying out of the contract.

§ 4. **Sales of unascertained goods—appropriation.**[4] Where A contracts to sell chattels to B according to description, title does not pass until there is a later appropriation by A, assented to by B, of specific chattels to the performance of the particular contract. This appropriation may be accomplished by delivery by A and acceptance by B; or by A's setting the chattels aside with B's assent given either before, at, or after the time of such setting aside; merely setting the chattels aside and marking them with B's name is not enough without such assent. Where A contracted to build a house for B, materials bought for the house did not pass to B until they were delivered to and accepted by B or were affixed to the house. Where A sold a certain quantity of barley to B and sent sacks to be filled, title passed to the barley as each sack was filled. And where A sold four barge loads of oil to B and B sent barges for the oil, title passed as each barge was completely filled.

§ 5. **Sales of goods to be sent by carrier.**[5] Where A contracts to sell to B goods to be sent to him by carrier and the goods are shipped in conformity with the contract, title passes to B upon delivery to the carrier unless a contrary intention is shown; as, for example, where the contract provides that A is to transport the goods to a particular place, the presumption is that title is not intended to pass till the goods have reached that place. On the other hand the mere fact that the goods are to be shipped and are shipped "c.o.d." (collect on delivery) does not prevent title from passing at once but merely preserves A's vendor's lien; nor does the fact that the goods are to be shipped and are shipped "c.i.f." (cost, insurance, freight to be paid by buyer) or "f.o.b." (free on board) or "f.o.b. point of shipment;" but if they are shipped "f.o.b. destination" the presumption is that title is not intended to pass till the destination is reached.

§ 6. **Same—bills of lading—warehouse receipts—trust receipts.**[6] Where A sells goods to B on credit and takes out a bill of lading from the carrier for

[4] 46 **Am Jur**, Sales, §§ 424, 425, 430, 431.

[5] 46 **Am Jur**, Sales, §§ 440-445.
Failure to ship by carrier designated by buyer as affecting passing of title. 31 **ALR** 955-960.

[6] 46 **Am Jur**, Sales, §§ 453-456.
47 **Am Jur**, Sales, § 838.
F.o.b. provision in sale contract as affecting time or place of passing of title. 101 **ALR** 292-304.
Time and place of passage of title to

the goods in the name of B, both the beneficial interest and legal title to the goods pass to B at once even though A retains possession of the bill of lading; but if the sale is not on credit, retention of the bill of lading will be construed as retaining possession until B has paid or otherwise settled with A; when that has been done, B is entitled to the possession of the goods and may maintain replevin against the carrier.

Where A takes out the bill of lading in his own name but he intends to appropriate the goods to the performance of his contract with B, he reserves title to himself by way of security, the beneficial interest in the goods and the accompanying risk of loss passing to B; upon B's paying or tendering the price B may maintain replevin against the carrier for the goods.

The most common practice is for A to take out the bill of lading to himself or order or to bearer and send to a bank the bill of lading with a sight or time draft upon B for the price attached to it, with directions to notify B to come in and either pay, if it is a sight draft or accept, if it is a time draft. Upon such payment or acceptance, the bill of lading is turned over to B and thus he is able to get the goods from the carrier; but if B defaults A is in a position to sell the goods to another buyer and indorse the bill of lading to him. A's taking the bill of lading in his own name by way of security is frequently called the reservation of the jus disponendi (power and right of disposal).

At common law a bill of lading was regarded as a symbol of the goods and since the goods were not negotiable, neither was the bill of lading; so that if A should entrust a bill of lading endorsed in blank or deliverable to bearer to his agent X and X without authority should transfer the bill of lading for value to Y, the latter would not be protected even though he accepted it in good faith thinking that X had authority; but under the Uniform Bills of Lading Law, Y is protected in such a case and even where there was no entrusting by A, for example, where the bill of lading had been stolen by X.

Where B expects to resell the goods which he has ordered from A, but is unable to pay A for the goods till the resale is actually made, it has become a common practice for C, a bank or other financing house, to advance the purchase money to A who endorses the bill of lading to C, and for C to endorse the bill of lading to B upon B's signing a trust receipt in which B agrees that he will, out of the proceeds of the resale, reimburse C for the advances made, with interest, C being regarded as in the position of holding a claim to the goods or the proceeds as security for its advances; in such a case the risk of loss throughout the entire transaction is upon B, the beneficial owner of the goods. The trust receipt usually provides that C may at any time cancel the trust receipt and take possession of the goods.

§ 7. Factors' acts and bulk sales acts.[7] Since a bailee has merely possession and not title, a purchaser from him is not protected as against the

goods shipped under bill of lading, with draft attached, consigning them to shipper's order. 60 **ALR** 677–693.

Validity as to creditors of the buyer or consignee of reservation of title to goods delivered under implied or express authority to resell. 63 **ALR** 355–384.

Trust receipts. 49 **ALR** 282–316; s. in 87 **ALR** 302–323; 101 **ALR** 453–465.

53 **Harv. L. R.** 792, c. i. f. Contracts in International Commerce.

7 22 **Am Jur**, Factors, §§ 54–63.

24 **Am Jur**, Fraudulent Conveyances, §§ 238–260.

Validity of factor's pledge of his principal's property. 14 **ALR** 424–449.

Presumption of fraud under Bulk Sales Act as prima facie or conclusive. 75 **ALR** 674–687.

Character or class of creditors within contemplation of Bulk Sales Law. 84 **ALR** 1406–1420; s. in 102 **ALR** 565–570.

bailor unless the bailor has given him authority to sell or has estopped himself by holding the bailee out as having such authority. But in many states there are factors' acts which provide that where the owner of goods turns them over to a factor or commission merchant, a purchaser in good faith from such factor is protected even though the sale was without authority of the owner.

To protect wholesalers against a retailer's disposing of his entire stock of merchandise in bulk and disappearing with the proceeds many states have bulk sales statutes which make such sales void as against creditors unless notice of the details of the sale are given to creditors a certain number of days in advance.

§ 8. Conditional sales—retention of possession by vendor.[8] Especially where the purchase price of goods is to be paid in installments, it is common practice for the seller to require the buyer to sign a conditional sale agreement—frequently called a lease—whereby the seller retains the title to the goods as security for the complete performance of the buyer's undertaking, the seller to have the right, upon default of the buyer, to take possession of the goods. Though the transaction is similar to an ordinary sale with the buyer giving the seller a chattel mortgage on the goods, a conditional sale is not usually held to be covered by statutes requiring the recording of chattel mortgages. Some states have adopted the Uniform Conditional Sales Act which requires the recording of such sales in order to be valid as against creditors of or purchasers from the buyer.

The buyer under a conditional sale agreement has the beneficial interest in the goods and upon tender of the sum due he may maintain replevin for the goods and such a property right may be attached by his creditors.

Where B buys goods from A but allows A to retain possession, the transaction is held in some states to be fraudulent as against A's attaching creditors; but in most states there is only a presumption of fraud which may be rebutted by showing that the sale and retention of possession were made in good faith. Where A sells and delivers the retained goods to X who pays for them in good faith without notice of the previous sale to B, the Sales Act provides that X shall be protected as against B just as if A had authority from B to sell the goods.

§ 9. Risk of loss.[9] The risk of loss from accidental damage to or destruc-

Right of a factor, commission merchant, or produce broker to sell property to protect advances. 40 **ALR** 387–398.

[8] 47 **Am Jur**, Sales, §§ 827–980.

Requisites and sufficiency of description of property in conditional sales contract. 65 **ALR** 714–724.

Rights and duties in respect of property as between seller and seller's assignee on conditional sale of property. 65 **ALR** 783–794.

Interest of vendee under conditional sales contract as subject to attachment, garnishment, or execution. 61 **ALR** 781–793.

Rights as between conditional seller and one claiming under or through sale or mortgage by buyer which is subject to the seller's reservation of title. 87 **ALR** 941–952.

Conditional sale contract as affected by seller's acceptance of a chattel mortgage from the buyer covering the same property. 95 **ALR** 332–351.

Validity as against third persons of sale or pledge of goods, or receipts issued for goods, retained in warehouse on premises of seller or pledgeor (field warehousing). 133 **ALR** 209–254.

What amounts to a conditional sale. 17 **ALR** 1421–1497; s. in 43 **ALR** 1247–1263; 92 **ALR** 304–337.

Right as between landlord and conditional seller of property to tenant. 45 **ALR** 967–972; s. in 98 **ALR** 628–634.

Right of purchaser from party to conditional sale as affected by actual or apparent authority in party to sell property. 47 **ALR** 85–105; s. in 88 **ALR** 109–123.

[9] 46 **Am Jur**, Sales, §§ 270, 280.

tion of the goods ordinarily falls upon the holder of the legal title unless the legal title has been reserved to the seller merely to secure the payment of the price as in the case of a conditional sale or of taking the bill of lading in his own name, in which case the loss falls upon the buyer as the one who has the beneficial interest in the goods. But the parties may expressly or impliedly determine which of them shall bear the risk; for example, an express provision that the goods shall be at the seller's risk for two months implies that after that time the risk shall be on the buyer.

CHAPTER III

OBLIGATIONS OF SELLER AND BUYER

§ 10. Express warranties—sales by description or sample.[10] In earlier days when sales were infrequent and the buyer usually had a good opportunity to inspect the goods there was no obligation on the seller with regard to the quality of the goods sold unless the buyer stipulated for an express undertaking or promissory warranty; a mere affirmation was not a warranty and if the affirmation was as to a mere matter of opinion—that is, seller's talk—or if the seller believed his statement of fact to be true, there was no liability whatever.

Modern law is much more liberal to the buyer; an affirmation regarding the goods is treated as an express warranty if the buyer justifiably relies upon it and such reliance is usually justified where the seller is or pretends to be better informed about the goods than is the buyer. And where there is a sale by description or by sample the seller is under an obligation—similar to the old express warranty—to furnish goods that conform to the description or to the sample.

§ 11. Implied warranty of title.[1] Where A purports as owner of goods to sell them to B, the modern law is that A impliedly warrants the title to the goods unless he expressly stipulates against such an obligation. Under the Uniform Sales Act such a seller not only warrants the right to sell and quiet possession but also warrants against undeclared or unknown incumbrances. Where A does not purport to be the owner, as in case of a sale by a pawnbroker of a forfeited pledge or a sale by a sheriff under an execution, there is no implied warranty of title.

§ 12. Implied warranty of quality.[2] Where A, a manufacturer or wholesaler, sells goods to B, a retailer, there is ordinarily an implied warranty

[10] 46 **Am Jur**, Sales, §§ 299–331.
Warranties and conditions upon sale of seed, nursery stock, etc. 16 **ALR** 859–902; s. in 32 **ALR** 1241–1248; 62 **ALR** 451–456; 117 **ALR** 470–484.
Construction, application, and effect of statutory provisions requiring notice of breach of warranty on sale of goods. 71 **ALR** 1149–1156.
Right of dealer against his vendor in case of breach of warranty as to article purchased for resale and resold. 22 **ALR** 133–138; s. in 64 **ALR** 883–895.
Seller's advertisements as affecting rights of parties to sale of personal property. 28 **ALR** 991–1011.
21 **Harv. L. R.** 555, What Constitutes an Express Warranty in the Law of Sales.

[1] 46 **Am Jur**, Sales, §§ 403–409.
Doctrine of caveat emptor as applied to purchaser at judicial or executor's sale. 68 **ALR** 659–684.

[2] 46 **Am Jur**, Sales, §§ 337–381.
Implied warranty or condition as to quality of timber or lumber. 52 **ALR** 1536–1547.
Implied warranty of fitness on sale of article by trademark, tradename, or other particular description. 59 **ALR** 1180–1232; s. in 90 **ALR** 410–423.
Implied warranty of merchantability under Uniform Sales Act in case of sale of goods by patent or tradename. 135 **ALR** 1393–1399.
Express or implied warranty of quality, condition, or fitness of automobile or truck sold by retail dealer. 34 **ALR** 535–550; s. in 43 **ALR** 648–651.
Implied condition or warranty of merchantability on sale of goods without particular description or warranty, or present

that the goods shall be merchantable, that is, fairly salable on the market; by the Uniform Sales Act, where B inspected the goods, there is no implied warranty as to defects which such inspection should have revealed.

Where X, a consumer, buys goods from B, a retailer, and makes known to B the particular purpose for which he is buying them and X relies upon B's skill or judgment, there is an implied warranty that the goods shall be reasonably fit for such purpose. Where X asks B for an article under its patent or trade name and B supplies the article, there is no implied warranty of fitness for purpose; but if X buys the article on B's recommendation as to its fitness for X's purpose, the fact that B identifies the article by its patent or trade name should not, by the better view, negative a warranty of fitness for purpose.

Where B, a retailer, sells unpackaged food to X for human consumption there is ordinarily an implied warranty that the food is wholesome; but where the food is in the original packages as it came from A, the manufacturer or wholesaler, so that B cannot know the actual contents of the packages, there is some difficulty in holding B because X usually relies upon A rather than upon B. But X cannot hold A for breach of an implied warranty because there is no contractual relation between them, A's liability, if any, being in tort for negligent misrepresentation; furthermore A is not likely to be easily accessible to X; hence, as a matter of expediency it would seem to be the better view to allow X to recover from B for breach of an implied warranty of wholesomeness and for B in turn to hold A for breach of an implied warranty of merchantability.

§ 13. Delivery and payment.[3] Unless A in selling to B agrees to extend credit to him, he is entitled to insist upon payment of the price at the time of delivery. Unless otherwise stipulated for, B must accept delivery at A's place of business; but if the goods are known by B to be located elsewhere, then at that place. Where the goods are in the possession of a bailee, assent by the bailee to hold for B is equivalent to delivery but not the mere giving of a delivery order by A; the bailee's assent may be given in advance by the bailee's issuing a negotiable bill of lading or warehouse receipt. Unless there is an express stipulation otherwise, A is bound to make and B to receive delivery within a reasonable time after the making of the contract.

When A delivers a larger quantity of goods than required by the contract, B is not bound to accept any, but he may accept all or he may merely reject the excess. If A delivers less than is required by the contract B need not accept; if he accepts expecting to receive the rest later and no further deliveries are made he is liable for the reasonable value of the amount received, but not in excess of the pro rata contract price. Where A is to deliver in installments to be separately paid for and the breach by either A or B with respect to one installment is sufficiently serious to constitute a breach of the entire contract, the other party may, by the prevailing view in this country, refuse to go on with the contract.

opportunity for inspection. 21 **ALR** 367–385.

Warranty or misrepresentation as to character of article as new, where seller fails to disclose that article has been used or is secondhand. 104 **ALR** 551–556.

27 **U. of Minn. L. R.** 117, The Implied Warranty of Merchantable Quality.

3 46 **Am Jur**, Sales, §§ 112–192.

What constitutes delivery of goods sold under "c.i.f." contract. 10 **ALR** 701–705; s. in 20 **ALR** 1236–1238.

§ 14. **Inspection.**[4] Unless B has already inspected the goods he is entitled to a reasonable opportunity to inspect before A can require him to pay for them; and where it is necessary he may consume a small amount of the goods to determine whether they conform to the contract. Where the contract provides for inspection as a condition precedent to the passing of title, no title passes until such inspection even though the goods conform to the contract; where B postpones inspection till after delivery to him apparently the title passes upon such delivery subject to its being passed back to A if, upon inspection, it is found that the goods do not conform to the contract.

§ 15. **Acceptance.**[5] Acceptance of the goods by B may be shown by words or by conduct inconsistent with A's being still the owner. If B rejects the goods, he is permitted to resell them on A's account without A's consent only where the goods are so perishable or the market so fluctuating that such resale is necessary to protect A against serious loss.

Under the Uniform Sales Act, B's acceptance of the goods does not prevent his later holding A liable for breach of warranty provided he gives A notice of such breach within a reasonable time after B knows or should know of such breach.

CHAPTER IV

RIGHTS OF UNPAID SELLER AGAINST THE GOODS

§ 16. **Liens.**[6] If A sells goods to B without extending credit but retains possession, he has a seller's lien on the goods till the purchase price is either paid or tendered. Where credit is extended but A is still in possession when the period of credit expires and B is then insolvent A's seller's lien is automatically revived.

A loses his lien by unconditionally surrendering the goods to B; or, if the goods are in the possession of a bailee, by the bailee's agreeing, with A's consent, to hold for B. He also loses his lien by refusing to deliver to B on grounds inconsistent with the existence of a lien or on other grounds without mentioning the lien. But he does not lose his lien by taking additional security or by suing B to recover the price.

§ 17. **Stoppage in transit.**[7] If B becomes insolvent after A has transferred title to B and has delivered the goods to a carrier to be shipped to B, A may stop the goods in transit and revest himself with the seller's lien which

[4] 46 **Am Jur,** Sales, §§ 246–266, 338–340, 342.

[5] 46 **Am Jur,** Sales, §§ 47–55.

Duty of purchaser of goods "on trial" or "on approval" regarding notice of rejection. 78 **ALR** 533–544.

Acceptance of instalment of goods as affecting buyer's right to rescind because of defects in that instalment. 29 **ALR** 1517–1526.

Acceptance after agreed time of delivery as waiver of damages on account of seller's delay. 80 **ALR** 322–339.

[6] 46 **Am Jur,** Sales, §§ 518–525.

Repossession of chattels by seller upon their return or abandonment by buyer as effecting a mutual rescission or as evidence thereof. 106 **ALR** 703–710.

[7] 46 **Am Jur,** Sales, §§ 526–562.

When right of stoppage in transitu terminates. 7 **ALR** 1374–1422.

Rights of seller of fixtures retaining title thereto, or a lien thereon, as against purchasers or encumbrancers of the realty. 13 **ALR** 448–485; s. in 73 **ALR** 748–775; 88 **ALR** 1318–1348; 111 **ALR** 362–388; 141 **ALR** 1283–1297.

Seller's rights in respect of the property, or its proceeds, upon dishonor of draft or check for purchase price, on a cash sale. 31 **ALR** 578–589; s. in 54 **ALR** 526–527.

Right of conditional seller to retake property without legal process. 146 **ALR** 1331–1344.

Who bears loss incident to destruction of goods sold conditionally. 38 **ALR** 1319–1331.

Demand for payment or for possession as a condition of seller's right to retake property or otherwise enforce forfeiture under conditional sale. 59 **ALR** 134–148.

be had before delivery to the carrier. This right prevails over a purchaser from B unless A has transferred to B a negotiable bill of lading and B has in turn transferred it to such purchaser who gives value without notice of A's stoppage.

The transit comes to an end upon delivery to B before the goods arrive at their destination or upon the carrier's agreeing, at the destination, to hold for B; or if the carrier wrongfully refuses to deliver to B. Where only a part of the goods has been delivered to B, the rest may be stopped by A unless the part delivery was made under such circumstances as to show an intent to hold the rest for B.

A's right may be exercised either by resuming possession or by merely notifying the carrier of his claim. Where the goods are perishable or B has been in default an unreasonable time A may resell the goods either at public or private sale; or he may, upon giving reasonable notice to B, rescind the sale and keep the goods and then maintain an action against B for any loss due to B's breach of contract.

CHAPTER V

REMEDIES OF THE SELLER

§ 18. **Recovery of the price.**[8] If the title or, if the title has been reserved by A by way of security, the beneficial interest in the goods has passed to B, an action for the price may be maintained by A. Where the beneficial interest in the goods has not passed because B wrongfully refuses to receive it, A may recover the price and thus compel B to take the goods where they cannot readily be resold by A at a reasonable price. The Uniform Sales Act also provides for recovery of the price where the price is payable at a day certain irrespective of delivery or transfer of title unless before judgment in such an action the seller has shown an inability or unwillingness to perform.

§ 19. **Damages for nonacceptance—rescission.**[9] Where B wrongfully refuses to accept and pay for the goods, A may maintain an action against him for such refusal. The measure of damages in such a case is ordinarily the difference between the contract price and the market price at the time and place where the goods should have been accepted.

Where the goods have not been delivered to B and B has shown his unwillingness or inability to perform or has committed a substantial breach thereof, A may rescind the contract to sell or the sale by giving notice thereof to B.

§ 20. **In conditional sales.**[10] If upon default of the buyer under a conditional sale the seller gets back possession of the goods either by self-help or by an action of replevin, may he keep all the payments made by the buyer? If the amount paid is very small it would seem fair not only to allow him to do so but if the amount paid is less than the depreciation in the value of the goods he should be allowed to hold the buyer for the deficiency; but if the buyer has paid almost the full amount of the purchase price and the

[8] 46 **Am Jur**, Sales, §§ 583-607.

[9] 46 **Am Jur**, Sales, §§ 608-610, 563-565.

[10] 47 **Am Jur**, Sales, §§ 938-969.

Bringing action for price as waiver by conditional vendor of right to reclaim property. 12 **ALR** 503-520; s. in 56 **ALR** 238-241; 113 **ALR** 653-657.

Rights and remedies as between parties to a conditional sale after the seller has repossessed himself of the property. 37 **ALR** 91-115; s. in 83 **ALR** 959-989; 99 **ALR** 1288-1303.

Rights of parties to conditional sale as affected by breach of warranty. 48 **ALR** 969-985; s. in 130 **ALR** 753-763.

goods have not depreciated seriously in value it would seem unfair to the buyer to allow the seller to keep all the payments. The Uniform Conditional Sales Act meets the situation by requiring the seller, where the buyer has paid at least half the purchase price and fails to redeem in ten days, to resell the goods at public auction within thirty days after the retaking; if there is a surplus after all expenses are paid such surplus goes to the buyer; if there is a deficiency the seller may recover such deficiency from the buyer or from anyone who has succeeded to his obligations.

CHAPTER VI

REMEDIES OF THE BUYER

§ 21. Where the title has not passed.[1] Where A has wrongfully neglected or refused to transfer the title to the goods to B the latter may maintain an action of special assumpsit for such breach and recover the difference between the contract price and the market price at the place of delivery. If the chattels are unique he may maintain a bill in equity to compel specific performance of the contract. And under the Uniform Sales Act the court may, if it thinks fit, give specific performance to B of any contract to deliver specific or ascertained goods.

If there has been a breach of warranty by A, B may rescind the contract and recover back in quasi contract any payments made on account.

§ 22. Where the title has passed—breach of warranty.[2] If title has passed to B, he may maintain either replevin or trover against A or anyone else who wrongfully withholds possession.

Where there has been a breach of warranty by A and A sues for the price, B may use such breach by way of recoupment of damages or by way of counterclaim or he may maintain an independent action thereon; or, finally, he may—if he acts within a reasonable time—rescind the sale, restoring the goods to A and maintain an action in quasi contract to recover back any payments made to A. If the goods have been destroyed or seriously depreciated in value there is no right to rescind unless such destruction or depreciation was due to the defect warranted against. If B offers to return the goods but A refuses to receive them, the Uniform Sales Act gives B a lien on the goods as security for the repayment of the amounts paid by him. By the Uniform Sales Act the buyer is permitted only one of the above remedies.

CHAPTER VII

STATUTE OF FRAUDS

§ 23. "Contract for the sale of goods, etc." [3] The English statute passed in 1677 provided that "no contract for the sale of goods, wares and merchandize,

1 46 **Am Jur,** Sales, §§ 673–688.

2 46 **Am Jur,** Sales, §§ 711–769.
Time for rescission by purchaser of chattel for fraud or breach of warranty. 72 **ALR** 726–797.
Use of article by buyer as waiver of right to rescind for fraud, breach of warranty, or failure of goods to comply with contract. 77 **ALR** 1165–1191.

3 49 **Am Jur,** Statute of Frauds, §§ 236–248.
Contracts relating to corporate stock as within provisions of Statute of Frauds dealing with sales of goods, etc. 14 **ALR** 394–405; s. in 59 **ALR** 597–599.

Statute of Frauds as applied to agreements of repurchase or repayment on sale of corporate stock or other personal property. 121 **ALR** 312–340.

Provision in sale contract to effect that only conditions incorporated therein shall be binding. 75 **ALR** 1032–1082; s. in 127 **ALR** 132–163; 133 **ALR** 1360–1364.

for the price of ten pounds sterling or upwards, shall be allowed to be good, etc." The Uniform Sales Act provides that "a contract to sell or a sale of any goods or choses in action of the value of five hundred dollars or upward shall not be enforceable by action, etc."

A contract to sell or a sale of trees which are not to be severed promptly is not within this section of the statute but within the section with regard to interests in land; but if trees or buildings are to be severed promptly they are within this section and so are contracts to sell or sales of growing crops which are of course to be severed at maturity.

Before the Uniform Sales Act there were three different views as to the boundary line between a contract for goods and one for work and labor. Under the Act "the provisions of this section apply to every such contract or sale notwithstanding that the goods may be intended to be delivered at some future time or may not at the time of such contract or sale be actually made, procured or provided, or fit or ready for delivery, or some act may be requisite for the making or completing thereof, or rendering the same fit for delivery; but if the goods are to be manufactured by the seller especially for the buyer and are not suitable for sale to others in the ordinary course of the seller's business, the provisions of this section shall not apply."

In some states adopting the Act the limit is set at $50 or $100 instead of $500. Where several articles are sold at one time at a separate price for each one but the parties intended that there should be only one transaction and the sum of all the items is greater than the statutory limit the case is within the statute.

If the statute is not complied with, the result is merely that the contract cannot be enforced by action and third parties cannot take advantage of this fact; for example, in an action to enforce a contract of insurance, it is no defense that the plaintiff had only an oral contract to purchase the goods insured.

§ 24. Acceptance and receipt of part of the goods.[4] The language of the Uniform Sales Act is: "unless the buyer shall accept part of the goods or choses in action so contracted to be sold or sold, and actually receive the same, etc." If at the time of the oral contract the goods are specific the oral contract itself is an acceptance, that is, an assent to take the goods as owner. If the goods are not specific there must be an assent either by words or conduct of B to a later appropriation by A. A resale of the goods by B is such an unequivocal act as to amount to an acceptance and so is the use of a portion of the goods in the manufacture of other goods. If B assents conditionally it is not effective unless the condition happens. A cannot act as B's agent in making such an acceptance as will satisfy the statute; hence a mere appropriation of the goods to B, even though they conform to B's prior order, is not enough. The actual receipt of the goods means that possession has passed to B with A's assent. This may be done by A physically handing over the goods to B or to some one authorized by B to accept them; or if the goods are in the hands of X, a bailee, by X agreeing to hold for B instead of for A; where the goods are already in B's possession, A's assent to B's holding as owner instead of bailee is enough; and where

4 49 **Am Jur**, Statute of Frauds, §§ 272–300.

When goods remaining in custody of seller or some third person deemed to have been received by buyer, within exception to Statute of Frauds. 4 **ALR** 902–924.

Acceptance which will satisfy Statute of Frauds where purchaser of goods is in possession at time of sale. 36 **ALR** 649–658; s. 111 **ALR** 1312–1313.

A has taken out a negotiable bill of lading or other document of title and indorses it to B, that has been held sufficient.

Both acceptance and receipt must be under the contract sought to be enforced.

§ 25. Earnest or part payment.[5] The language of the Uniform Sales Act is "or give something in earnest to bind the contract, or in part payment." Formerly earnest money was a small sum given by B in addition to the purchase price; today any sum paid is regarded as part payment—a part of the purchase price. Money put up to be forfeited in case B should later default is not regarded as part payment.

Part payment may consist of money, goods or services. If B's note or check is given, it should be regarded as part payment, but it is apparently so regarded only if it is shown to have been accepted in absolute payment. By the weight of authority, B's oral discharge of a claim which he has against A is not sufficient.

§ 26. The note or memorandum.[6] The language of the Uniform Sales Act is: "or unless some note or memorandum in writing of the contract or sale be signed by the party to be charged or his agent in that behalf." The memorandum may be given at any time before action brought and the motive for giving it is of no importance; it may consist of a written cancellation or repudiation of the oral contract, amounting to an admission of its existence. It may be found in letters, telegrams or any other writings and may consist of several writings only the last of which is signed, provided the former writings are incorporated by reference or there is sufficient internal evidence to connect them.

The memorandum must indicate the subject matter of the contract and the parties thereto; it must state the price if there was a price and the time for delivery if there was a time for delivery fixed in the oral contract. It must be signed but need not be subscribed by the party to be charged in the particular litigation and may be either printed or written; it is not necessary that the other party sign it. If it is signed by the defendant's agent, his authority need not be in writing. Neither party may sign for the other but a third person may be authorized to sign for both, as in the case of an auctioneer or his clerk at an auction sale.

5 49 Am Jur, Statute of Frauds, §§ 265–271.

6 49 Am Jur, Statute of Frauds, §§ 313–418. Necessity of statement in writing of consideration or price for sale of goods or choses in action in order to satisfy Statute of Frauds. 30 ALR 1163–1169; s. in 59 ALR 1422–1424.

BILLS AND NOTES

CHAPTER I

ESSENTIALS OF A NEGOTIABLE INSTRUMENT

§ 1. Words of negotiability—signature.[1] In order to be negotiable the instrument must be payable to order or to bearer, though a statement in a note that "this note shall be negotiable" has been held to be enough. If the

1 7 **Am Jur,** Bills and Notes, §§ 20, 47, 79, 80.

When negotiable instruments deemed payable to fictitious or nonexistent persons within statute or rule that makes such paper payable to bearer. 74 **ALR** 822–833; s. in 118 **ALR** 15–50.

40 **Col. L. R.** 836, Development of State Statutes on Negotiable Paper Prior to N.I.L.

7 **John Marshall L. Q.** 327, Changes Needed in the Illinois Negotiable Instruments Law.

instrument is not negotiable in its inception it cannot be made negotiable later, for example, by an indorsement to order or to bearer.

The instrument must be in writing and signed by the drawer or maker; it need not be subscribed. Placing a seal on the instrument does not render it non-negotiable.

§ 2. The promise or order to pay—consideration.[2] A note must contain a promise and a bill of exchange an order to pay. The words "promise" or "order" need not be used; it is sufficient that such is the fair meaning of the words used, but a mere acknowledgment of indebtedness is not enough.

The promise or order must be unconditional. If payment is to be made out of a particular fund then the order or promise is conditional upon the continued existence and availability of the fund and hence the instrument is not negotiable. But merely indicating a fund from which reimbursement may be had or stating the transaction which gave rise to the instrument does not make the promise conditional; for example, a statement in a note that it is secured by a mortgage on land or by reserving title upon the sale of goods.

Where the promise is conditional and hence the instrument is non-negotiable, the remedy is special assumpsit for breach of the conditional promise.

A negotiable instrument, like a simple contract, is not enforcible as between the original parties thereto without consideration, but consideration in such a case is presumed. And even though there is no consideration, a bona fide purchaser for value without notice may enforce it.

§ 3. Time of payment.[3] In order that an instrument be negotiable it must be payable at a certain time. Usually the instrument fixes a calendar date but that is not necessary; it is enough if payment is to be made upon the happening of an event that is sure to happen, for example, "upon the death of A." If the event is not sure to happen, for example, "upon confirmation by Congress of a land grant to X" or "when A reaches 21," the instrument is not negotiable, because Congress may not act and A may die before reaching 21.

It is not objectionable that the instrument is to be paid "on or before" a certain date; that merely gives an option to pay earlier. Nor is it objectionable that it is to become payable upon default in the payment of inter-

[2] 7 **Am Jur,** Bills and Notes, §§ 105–119.

Negotiability of municipal bonds as affected by reference to fund from which they are to be paid. 42 **ALR** 1027–1032.

Negotiability of note as affected by provision therein, or in mortgage securing the same for payment of taxes, assessments, or insurance. 45 **ALR** 1074–1108.

Negotiability as affected by provisions of instrument in relation to collateral other than mortgage. 102 **ALR** 1095–1105.

Negotiability of bill or note as affected by provision authorizing confession of judgment. 117 **ALR** 673–678.

Validity and effect of anticipatory provision in contract in relation to rate of interest in the event of default. 12 **ALR** 367–378.

Writing on the margin or on the back of a bill or a note at the time of its execution as a part thereof. 13 **ALR** 251–267.

Reference to extrinsic agreements as affecting negotiability of bill or note. 14 **ALR** 1126–1133; s. in 33 **ALR** 1173–1175; 37 **ALR** 655; 61 **ALR** 815–820; 104 **ALR** 1378–1387.

Negotiability of title-retaining note. 28 **ALR** 699–713; s. in 44 **ALR** 1397.

Duplicate or substitute drafts, notes, or checks. 87 **ALR** 1480–1492.

Burden of proof as to consideration for a bill or note, when plaintiff not protected as a holder in due course. 35 **ALR** 1370–1409; s. in 65 **ALR** 904–909; 127 **ALR** 1003–1008.

2 **Wash. and Lee L. R.** 44, Ambiguous Payees of Negotiable Paper.

[3] 7 **Am Jur,** Bills and Notes, §§ 143–169.

Negotiability as affected by provisions for extension of time. 77 **ALR** 1085–1099.

Acceleration provision as affecting negotiability. 34 **ALR** 872–894; s. in 72 **ALR** 268–275.

est; or that there may be a confession of judgment if the instrument is not paid at maturity. But a stipulation in a note that it shall become "due and payable at the option of the payee when it shall deem itself insecure" has been held to render the note non-negotiable, the court refusing to treat it as a demand note, which—in spite of the language used—is payable at once without any demand and therefore payable at a time certain.

§ 4. **Payment in money.**[4] In order to be negotiable the instrument must be payable in money, that is, in currency, either domestic or foreign. A promise to pay an ounce of gold or any other chattel is not negotiable.

The amount to be paid must be certain; but the amount is not rendered uncertain by a provision for attorney's fees or for "current exchange on New York City." A promise in a note to pay 9% interest but if paid at or before maturity 7% does not make the note non-negotiable because the provision is not effective till after maturity at which time the prevailing rule is that the instrument ceases to be negotiable anyway.

CHAPTER II

TRANSFER

§ 5. **Delivery.**[5] The transfer of the legal title to a negotiable instrument requires delivery. Handing over the possession of a note by the maker to his agent is not a delivery of the note because it is still within the maker's control. But where an instrument properly indorsed is sent to the payee by mail according to the latter's direction title passes upon mailing.

Where a note is delivered to the payee upon an oral condition that title is not to pass until the payee obtains a loan for the maker the condition is effective; the parol evidence rule is not violated because the condition does not affect the terms of the instrument but merely the transfer of title to it.

§ 6. **Indorsements—in general.**[6] An indorsement is usually on the back of the instrument, but it may be on its face; and if there is no room on the back for further indorsements a separate paper, called an allonge, may be attached to the instrument upon which indorsements may be written.

An instrument payable to bearer may be transferred by mere delivery without indorsement; an instrument payable to order must first be indorsed. But where an instrument payable to order has been indorsed in blank it

[4] 7 **Am Jur**, Bills and Notes, §§ 120–142.
Negotiability of instrument payable in "current funds," "currency," etc. 36 **ALR** 1358–1374.
2 **Loyola L. R.** 1, Sum Certainty in Negotiable Paper as Affected by Interest and Discount Provisions.

[5] 7 **Am Jur**, Bills and Notes, §§ 31–41.
8 **Am Jur**, Bills and Notes, § 1050.
Admissibility of parol evidence to show that a bill or note was conditional or given for a special purpose. 20 **ALR** 421–502; s. in 54 **ALR** 703–719; 105 **ALR** 1346–1360.

[6] 8 **Am Jur**, Bills and Notes, §§ 317–320.
Undertaking of one who indorses a note without recourse. 2 **ALR** 216–222; s. in 91 **ALR** 399–408.
Indorsement of bill or note in form of guaranty of payment. 21 **ALR** 1375–1391; s. in 33 **ALR** 97–98; 46 **ALR** 1516.
Transfer of notes as carrying the original claim for which note was given. 11 **ALR** 449–454.

Necessity of proof of title by one in possession of a negotiable instrument bearing his indorsement. 30 **ALR** 328–347.
Indorsement by one of several joint payees or indorsees not partners. 38 **ALR** 799–807.

Indorsement of bill or note by writing not on instrument itself. 56 **ALR** 921–926.
Construction, applicability, and effect of provisions of Negotiable Instruments Law as to delivery of order paper without indorsement. 87 **ALR** 1178–1191.
Validity and effect of note payable by its terms to maker or order and not indorsed by maker. 126 **ALR** 1309–1318.

becomes, like a bearer instrument, transferable by mere delivery, even though a later holder may indorse it specially.

Where A, the holder of a negotiable instrument, payable to order, indorses it in blank and delivers it to B who indorses it specially to C and delivers it to C, no indorsement by C is necessary to transfer title back to B; title passes by mere delivery to B who may strike out the indorsement of B to C, and maintain an action on the instrument. The holder of a note once indorsed in blank is presumed to be a holder in due course.

Where the holder of a negotiable instrument indorses it "without recourse" these words do not prevent title to the instrument from passing, but they do prevent any liability arising upon the indorsement; it is called a qualified indorsement and operates like a quitclaim deed to land. It does not impair the negotiability of the instrument.

Where A the holder of a negotiable instrument indorses it to B upon condition, for example, "upon my name appearing in the Gazette as ensign," the payor may by the Negotiable Instruments Law pay B whether the condition has been fulfilled or not; if the condition has not been fulfilled, B must, of course, account to A for the amount thus received.

The possession of an indorsed negotiable instrument raises no presumption of title; the possessor must prove affirmatively that the indorsement was made by the rightful holder or with his authority. The possession of an unindorsed order instrument does not raise a presumption of even beneficial interest in the possessor. He is just as likely to be a mere bailee of the instrument.

§ 7. Same—restrictive indorsements—collection cases.[7] Where A, the holder of a negotiable instrument indorses it (1) to B as A's agent for collection or (2) to B as trustee for C or (3) with the stipulation that payment is to be made to B only, such indorsements are called restrictive and the presumption in (1) and (3) is that B is not a bona fide purchaser for value, whereas if the indorsement is not restrictive, that is, in blank or merely "to B," or "to B in trust for C," the presumption is that the indorsement is for value. B, the restrictive indorsee, may receive payment and may maintain any action on the instrument that A could bring; if he transfers his rights his transferee takes subject to the restriction. Where the indorsement is to B for collection A may revoke the indorsement and collect the instrument himself and not be liable to B.

Where A indorses to B as trustee for C the payor, knowing of the trust, cannot set off a claim which he has against B the trustee personally.

Where A deposits in his own, the B, bank a check or note or draft on X payable at another bank, the presumption seems to be that the B bank is in the position of a buyer of the instrument, in which case the B bank may hold A on his indorsement of the instrument in case it is not paid.

If the B bank receives the instrument for collection only and transmits it to its correspondent bank C to collect from X and there is loss due either because of the negligence of the C bank in failing to collect from X or to the insolvency of the C bank after collection but before remittance, the

[7] 8 **Am Jur,** Bills and Notes, §§ 324, 545.

Title to commercial paper deposited by customer of a bank to his account. 11 **ALR** 1043–1075; s. in 16 **ALR** 1084–1085; 42 **ALR** 492–503; 68 **ALR** 725–736; 99 **ALR** 486–498.

Crediting the proceeds of negotiable paper to holder's deposit account as constituting bank a holder in due course. 6 **ALR** 252–275; s. in 24 **ALR** 901–904; 60 **ALR** 247–251; 80 **ALR** 1064–1066.

weight of authority is that the B bank must bear the loss, A being allowed to maintain an action against it for the full amount of the instrument. This was sometimes placed upon the ground that since the C bank was the agent of the B bank, payment to the agent was payment to the principal; while this statement is true from the standpoint of X in paying the instrument to the C bank it is hard to see how it is true from the standpoint of the B bank which does not in fact receive the money. Another ground for the majority doctrine was that the B bank should be responsible for the default of its agent the C bank.

The minority doctrine is that since A impliedly authorized the B bank to select a correspondent bank, the B bank should not be liable for loss due to the correspondent bank except for failure to use due care in such selection and therefore if such care was used the loss should fall on A.

As soon as the C bank or the B bank receives the money it may, following the usual custom of banks, make itself a debtor of the money unless A expressly stipulates to the contrary.

If, after the C bank receives the instrument from the B bank, it becomes bankrupt before collection, A may insist that the C bank was merely trustee of the instrument for collection and that the assignee in bankruptcy of the C bank turn over to A the instrument itself or the proceeds. But if the instrument is sent directly to the bank upon which it was drawn and that bank sends worthless paper in payment and then becomes bankrupt, A must come in with the general creditors of the drawee bank; there is no basis for any preference.

§ 8. Transfer of unindorsed order instruments.[8] If A the holder of an instrument payable to his order delivers it to B for value without indorsing it B gets the beneficial interest therein and may, in the absence of agreement, require A to make an unqualified indorsement of it, just as one who contracts to buy land may insist upon having a warranty deed to it. Where no indorsement was bargained for or intended the transferee is a mere assignee taking subject to all the equitable defenses good against his transferor.

Where a note is drawn to the order of the maker it must be indorsed by him before it becomes a complete instrument.

CHAPTER III

HOLDERS IN DUE COURSE

§ 9. The doctrine of bona fide purchase for value without notice—title.[9] There are usually three essential elements in the doctrine: (1) the purchaser must get title; (2) he must pay value; (3) he must do both without notice of any equitable defense. If he gets title after he has notice of the equitable defense he is not protected even though he paid value before.

[8] 8 **Am Jur,** Bills and Notes, §§ 315, 316.

Liability of seller to purchaser of invalid non-negotiable public warrants, bonds, certificates, etc., 139 **ALR** 1426–1436.

[9] 7 **Am Jur,** Bills and Notes, § 19.

Crediting the proceeds of negotiable paper to holder's deposit account as constituting bank a holder in due course. 6 **ALR** 252–275; s. in 24 **ALR** 901–904; 60 **ALR** 247–251; 80 **ALR** 1064–1066.

Payee as a holder in due course under the Negotiable Instruments Law. 15 **ALR** 437–446; s. in 21 **ALR** 1365–1367; 26 **ALR** 769; 32 **ALR** 289–299; 68 **ALR** 962–968; 97 **ALR** 1215–1221.

Effect of fraud in the inception of a bill or note to throw upon a subsequent holder the burden of proving that he is a holder in due course. 18 **ALR** 18–63; s. in 34 **ALR** 300–310; 57 **ALR** 1083–1091.

Usually if one does not have title he cannot pass it; but though a thief or bailee of money or negotiable instruments payable to bearer does not have title, he may pass it to a bona fide purchaser for value without notice; this exception is due to the desirability of having such instruments pass freely from hand to hand.

Where a complete instrument is not delivered but is taken wrongfully by the payee the view before the Negotiable Instruments Law was that since no title passed even a bona fide purchaser for value would not be protected; but the Negotiable Instruments Law provides that "where the instrument is in the hands of a holder in due course a valid delivery thereof by all parties prior to him so as to make them liable to him is conclusively presumed."

But where the instrument is incomplete, for example, a check signed in blank, and the instrument is stolen, there is no liability either at common law or under the Negotiable Instruments Law unless the drawer of the check was negligent in making the check accessible to the thief.

Where A signs an instrument leaving blank the place for the name of the payee and entrusts the instrument to B to negotiate a loan and turn over the proceeds to A, and B fraudulently sells the note to X whose name is inserted as payee, and converts the proceeds to his own use, the rule of the Negotiable Instruments Law is that A is not liable because he became a party to the instrument before negotiation and his authority was not followed.

§ 10. Same—value.[10] One who accepts a negotiable instrument either in payment of or as security for a pre-existing debt is regarded as giving value even though, in the second case, there is no express promise to forbear suing to collect the debt.

Where a negotiable instrument subject to an equitable defense is deposited by the holder in the X bank and the bank discounts it and pays him cash therefor, or accepts it in payment of or as security for a pre-existing debt, the bank is of course protected. Merely giving credit to the depositor on the books is not considered as value, but where the depositor later checks against such deposit and the bank pays it, then the bank is considered as giving value. Where the depositor has made several deposits and several withdrawals, how can it be determined whether the bank has paid out money against the particular credit? On this point there is conflict of authority. Some states, following the "first in, first out" rule, hold that the withdrawals are to be checked against the credits in chronological order and if, on this basis, the bank has honored checks against the particular credit, then it is a bona fide purchaser for value to that extent. Other courts reject this rule and hold that if the balance in the bank has been at all times greater than the amount of the particular credit, the bank is not a bona fide purchaser because it has not paid out money against the particular credit.

§ 11. Same—in good faith without notice.[1] Under the Negotiable Instruments Law a purchaser of a negotiable instrument must have acted in good

10 8 **Am Jur,** Bills and Notes, §§ 328–330.

Taking negotiable paper as collateral security for or in payment of pre-existing indebtedness as sustaining one's character as holder in due course under Uniform Negotiable Instruments Act. 80 **ALR** 670–685.

1 8 **Am Jur,** Bills and Notes, §§ 383–442.

Effect of bona fides of purchase of promissory note of fact that there is interest due and unpaid upon it. 11 **ALR** 1277–1283; s. in 40 **ALR** 832.

High rate of discount upon sale of negotiable paper as affecting one's status as holder in due course. 91 **ALR** 1139–1158.

Character as holder in due course of con-faith without actual knowledge of any infirmity or defect or knowledge of such facts that his action amounted to bad faith; for example, accepting a draft from an utter stranger or a negotiable bond from one who was known to be a thief and a degenerate or a note from one known in the business community to be engaged in a fraudulent business.

By the better view knowledge of a contemporary collateral agreement that under certain conditions the note was not to be paid is not notice provided there is no knowledge of any breach of that agreement.

One who buys from a known trustee is bound by the instrument creating the trust; but a bank in which a trustee has deposited trust funds may safely honor the trustee's check unless it has notice of a contemplated breach of trust.

The fact that an instrument is being negotiated before its date is not notice of any defect but the fact that there has been a default in the payment of interest is a fact to be considered by the jury on the question of notice.

§ 12. Same—before maturity.[2] The fact that a negotiable instrument is overdue is ordinarily enough in itself to prevent one from becoming a holder in due course because query at once arises, why does not the transferor collect it instead of selling it? But where a note and mortgage were overdue in the hands of a payee and X fraudulently represented to the payee that the mortgagor wished to pay off the mortgage and induced the payee to assign the note and mortgage to him and then he assigned the note and mortgage to Y who paid value without notice of X's fraud it was held that Y should be protected because there was nothing in the transaction to suggest suspicion.

A negotiable instrument payable on demand is, from the standpoint of bringing an action thereon, due at once without any demand; but from the standpoint of negotiation it is regarded as overdue only after the lapse of a reasonable time after its issue. What is a reasonable time depends upon the nature of the instrument, the usage, if any, in the trade or business and the facts in the particular case. For example, it was held in one case that under the extraordinary circumstances a demand note was not overdue four and a half years after issue, whereas in another case a draft payable on demand was held to be overdue after four months and twenty-three days.

A stipulation in a note that nonpayment of interest should cause the note to become due at once makes the note overdue as soon as there is a default; but a mere option in the holder to declare the note overdue has no such effect.

§ 13. Transferee with notice from holder in due course.[3] In order to protect a bona fide purchaser for value of a negotiable instrument in his right to dispose of his property his transferee will be protected even though at the

cern which takes paper from its dealers or agents. 61 **ALR** 694–706.

Addition of word indicating representative or fiduciary capacity after name of payee, indorser, or indorsee on commercial paper as charging transferee with notice of trust in favor of third parties or of defenses in maker. 61 **ALR** 1389–1407.

[2] 8 **Am Jur**, Bills and Notes, §§ 423–430.

Rights of transferee after maturity of accommodation paper. 48 **ALR** 1280–1291.

Transferee of demand note as a purchaser before maturity. 60 **ALR** 649–652.

Right of purchaser of past-due paper to protection as against defenses or equities between parties to intermediate transfer. 68 **ALR** 982–993.

Rights as between one who buys bill or note after maturity and third person legally or equitably entitled thereto. 33 **ALR** 699–711.

[3] 8 **Am Jur**, Bills and Notes, §§ 379–382.

Right of purchaser of negotiable paper to the benefit of the position of a former holder who was a holder in due course as affected by notice or purchase after maturity. 98 **ALR** 296–319.

time of the transfer he knew of the equitable defense and paid no value; he gets all the rights which his transferor had. But such protection is not extended to a transferee who had been a party to any fraud or illegality affecting the instrument. Nor can one who is primarily liable on a note acquire the rights of a bona fide purchaser by buying it from him.

CHAPTER IV

DEFENSES

§ 14. Real defenses.[4] There are some defenses that are good against even a holder in due course; these are called real or legal or absolute defenses to distinguish them from defenses which are not good against such a holder, which are called personal or equitable defenses.

Forgery or the lack of authority of a supposed agent to sign his principal's name is always a real defense; and so is duress if it consists of taking the party's hand and compelling him to sign his name, thus being similar to forgery. While infancy is a personal defense in the sense that only the infant or, after his death, his personal representative, may set it up, it is usually—apart from statute—held to be a real defense, good against every one.

Where the negotiable instrument has been given in a transaction which a statute expressly declares is void, the illegality is a good defense against even a holder in due course; the most common example is that of notes given for gambling debts which are usually held to be void. In some jurisdictions usury is also a real defense; though a note already in existence may be sold at any price it may not be so negotiated if the transaction is really a loan instead of a sale.

That the defendant at the time of the execution of a negotiable instrument had already been adjudged insane is a real defense, and in some jurisdictions insanity is a real defense although there had been no such adjudication.

Fraudulent material alteration of an instrument by the holder thereof is a real defense and so is want of completion and delivery as to any person whose signature was placed thereon before delivery.

Where a party to an instrument signed it relying upon a fraudulent representation that it was a mere receipt or memorandum, this also is a real defense—fraud in the execution—but the party may as in cases of forgery, fraudulent material alteration by a holder and lack of completion and delivery, render himself liable either by negligence in contributing to the creation of the defense or by estoppel in representing to the plaintiff that the void instrument is valid.

4 8 **Am Jur,** Bills and Notes, §§ 578, 604–621.

Estoppel by delay, after knowledge, in disclosing forgery of commercial paper, 25 **ALR** 177–186; s. in 50 **ALR** 1374.

Addition of maker or other obligor to commercial paper as material alteration discharging nonconsenting party. 119 **ALR** 898–914.

Memorandum on negotiable instrument as an alteration. 96 **ALR** 1102–1113.

Liability of party to commercial paper so drawn as to be easily alterable as to amount. 22 **ALR** 1139–1153; s. in 36 **ALR** 327; 39 **ALR** 1380.

Alteration of note before delivery to payee as affecting parties who do not personally consent. 44 **ALR** 1244–1255.

Renewal of bill or note as precluding defenses available against the original. 35 **ALR** 1258–1289; s. in 72 **ALR** 600–611.

Liability on note given to bank to aid in evading law. 64 **ALR** 595–606.

Ratification of forged or unauthorized signature on negotiable instrument under the provision of the Negotiable Instruments Act negativing effect of such signature unless the party against whom it is sought to enforce a right thereunder is precluded from setting up the forgery or want of authority. 150 **ALR** 978–986.

47 **Yale L. J.** 883, Forged Indorsements.

§ 15. Personal or equitable defenses.[5] The following defenses are always personal or equitable, not good against a holder in due course:

(1) Fraud in the inducement—that is, the party understood that he was signing a negotiable instrument but was induced to do so by fraudulent representations.

(2) Duress not amounting to forgery—that is, the party signs his own name because of threats of violence.

(3) Lack of consideration.

(4) Failure of consideration—that is, the consideration promised to the party in return for his signature to the instrument was not performed.

(5) Illegality other than where the transaction or the instrument is declared void by statute.

(6) Ultra vires of a corporation where the corporation had statutory authorization to execute negotiable paper for some purposes but not for the particular purpose.

Where the instrument has been materially altered, the holder in due course may recover thereon according to its original tenor.

It is no defense that the plaintiff has collateral which he has not tendered but upon payment the collateral must be surrendered.

CHAPTER V

RIGHTS AND LIABILITIES OF PARTIES

§ 16. The maker.[6] The maker of a negotiable note undertakes to pay it to the holder according to its tenor. So far as liability on the note is concerned he is primarily liable and is bound to pay at all events, even though he is an accommodation maker and, apart from the note, has the rights of a surety over against the accommodated party—usually the payee. He admits the existence of the payee and his capacity to indorse so that if the payee is an infant his indorsement will be good to pass title though not to bind the infant on his indorsement.

§ 17. The drawer and drawee.[7] The drawer of a bill of exchange in substance says to the payee that if he or a later holder will take it to the drawee and the latter refuses to accept or pay it, he himself will pay it if the payee or later holder will give him (the drawer) seasonable notice so that he may protect himself.

The drawee of a bill of exchange or check is not liable on the instrument until he accepts it, though he may be liable to the drawer for breach of contract in not accepting it. Hence the holder of a check which is dishonored has no right against the drawee bank but only against the drawer of the check.

§ 18. The acceptor—the rule of Price v. Neal.[8] If the drawee accepts he becomes liable to the payee or subsequent holder who presents it for ac-

[5] 8 **Am Jur,** Bills and Notes, §§ 571–586.
Setoff or counterclaim between prior parties to a negotiable instrument as available against one not a holder in due course. 70 **ALR** 245–263.

[6] 8 **Am Jur,** Bills and Notes, §§ 518–520.
Discharge of accommodation maker or surety by extension of time or release of collateral security, under Negotiable Instruments Law. 48 **ALR** 715–728; s. in 65 **ALR** 1425–1427; 108 **ALR** 1088–1094.

[7] 8 **Am Jur,** Bills and Notes, §§ 521–528.

[8] 8 **Am Jur,** Bills and Notes, §§ 524–528.
Construction, application, and effect of provision of Negotiable Instruments Law to effect that accommodation party is liable to holder for value notwithstanding that

ceptance. His liability to such holder is like that of a maker of a negotiable note to his payee, so that even if he is an accommodation acceptor he is the one primarily liable on the bill of exchange. The acceptor agrees to pay according to the tenor of his acceptance and admits the existence of the drawer, the genuineness of his signature and his capacity and authority to draw the instrument, the existence of the payee and his then capacity to indorse. Thus, though ordinarily there may be recovery back of money paid under mistake of fact, the acceptor of a bill of exchange or check who pays the holder thereof in ignorance that the name of the drawer has been forged thereto cannot recover back from the holder. The reason usually given today for this rule, first announced in Price v. Neal ((1762) 3 Bun. 1354, 97 Eng. Reprint 871), whereby the acceptor takes the risk of the genuineness of the drawer's signature, is business convenience. The rule does not protect one who was not a holder in due course; and it does not apply to a case of a forged indorsement even though the instrument paid was a check and the supposed indorser was a depositor in the payor bank. Nor does it apply to a case where the body of the bill has been forged or materially altered.

§ 19. The indorser.[9] One who indorses a negotiable instrument thereby warrants that he has good title thereto and the right to indorse it, that it is valid, that the parties thereto are competent and undertakes that if it is not accepted or paid after due presentment or demand and after notice to him, he will pay. Each indorser becomes liable to those who succeed him as holders of the instrument and has a right, if he is also an indorsee, against those prior indorsers except as against those who indorsed without recourse.

§ 20. The anomalous indorser—the agent.[10] One who, not being a holder of a negotiable instrument, indorses it before delivery in order to give it the credit of his name, is now, by the Negotiable Instruments Law, held liable, not as a comaker or guarantor but as if he were a regular indorser. If he signs for the accommodation of the payee he is liable to all parties subsequent to the payee but not, of course, to the payee himself; on the contrary, he stands in the position of a surety to the payee and has the rights of a surety against him. The matter is dealt with similarly where he signs for the accommodation of the drawer or for the maker or for some third person.

The Negotiable Instruments Law provides that if an indorser is the accommodated party and therefore the principal debtor it is not necessary that he be given notice that the instrument has been dishonored; but this, of course, does not apply to the anomalous indorser who is an accommodating party and therefore in the position of a surety.

latter knew of accommodation character. 95 **ALR** 964–990.

Who must bear loss as between drawer induced by fraud of employee or agent to issue check payable to nonexisting person or a person having no interest in the proceeds thereof, and one who cashes or pays it on the forged indorsement by such employee or agent of the name of such ostensible payee. 99 **ALR** 439–453.

9 8 **Am Jur**, Bills and Notes, §§ 529–532.

Liability of indorser of non-negotiable commercial paper. 79 **ALR** 719–772.

10 8 **Am Jur**, Bills and Notes, §§ 452–453, 468–476.

Admissibility, under Negotiable Instruments Law, or parol or extrinsic evidence for purpose of relieving from personal liability one to whose signature are added words indicating his agency or representative capacity, where name of his principal does not appear on face of instrument. 111 **ALR** 650–657.

Parol evidence as to liability of irregular indorser to payee. 37 **ALR** 1222–1238.

If A is acting as agent for B in signing a negotiable instrument and wishes to escape personal responsibility thereon, the safest form of signature is "B, per A, agent." Merely adding the word "agent" after his own signature is usually not effective, the word being regarded as merely descriptive.

CHAPTER VI

PRESENTMENT, DISHONOR AND PROTEST

§ 21. **Presentment.**[1] In order to charge parties secondarily liable on a negotiable instrument—indorsers on a promissory note and drawer and indorsers on a bill of exchange—it is necessary for the holder to present a note to the maker for payment, or a bill of exchange to the drawee or acceptor for payment. The Negotiable Instruments Law also provides that presentment must be made to the drawee for acceptance where expressly stipulated for, where such presentment is necessary to fix the maturity of the instrument and where the bill is drawn payable elsewhere than at the residence or place of business of the drawee.

Presentment need not be made where it cannot be done by the exercise of reasonable diligence, where the drawee is a fictitious person or where there has been express or implied waiver.

§ 22. **Dishonor and protest—acceptance for honor.**[2] Where an instrument is duly presented for acceptance or payment and acceptance or payment cannot be obtained, or where presentment has been excused and the instrument is overdue and unpaid it is said to be dishonored. It then becomes necessary for the holder, in order to hold those secondarily liable on the instrument, to give them either oral or written notice of such dishonor. Such notice should contain a sufficient description of the instrument, a statement that it has been presented for acceptance or payment and has been dishonored, a statement that it has been protested, if such protest is necessary, and finally, an announcement of the holder's intent to look to the party addressed for payment. Such notice must ordinarily be given to the drawer and to each indorser and each drawer or indorser to whom notice is not given is discharged. But it is not necessary to give such notice to a drawer or indorser who is the principal debtor.

In order to prove that the regular legal steps have been taken by the holder to fix liability upon parties secondarily liable, it is necessary, in case of a foreign bill of exchange and frequently desirable, in case of an inland bill or note, to have the testimony of some responsible person, usually a notary, that the proper procedure has been followed. This is called a protest; it is usual for the notary himself to make a second presentment of the instrument on the day of dishonor and upon refusal to accept or pay, to make

1 8 **Am Jur**, Bills and Notes, §§ 623–695.

Necessity of possession and exhibition of paper at time of demand in order to make a valid presentment. 11 **ALR** 969–980; s. in 50 **ALR** 1200–1202.

2 8 **Am Jur**, Bills and Notes, §§ 696–779, 895–898.

Insolvency or bankruptcy of party primarily liable on commercial paper, as excusing demand and notice of dishonor. 25 **ALR** 962–971; s. in 87 **ALR** 1394–1396.

Presentment and notice of dishonor as condition of holding one who appears on paper as indorser but was in fact primarily liable. 62 **ALR** 116–130.

Indorsement of renewal note, or offer or promise to renew, as waiver by indorser of presentment and notice of nonpayment. 110 **ALR** 1149–1157.

Necessity of notice of nonpayment of note or bill upon which corporation is primary obligor, in order to hold officer, director, or stockholder as indorser. 123 **ALR** 1367–1378.

a minute thereof on his official record or an initialed minute on the instrument itself, showing the date of dishonor. Later he executes a certificate of these facts under his official seal and sends notice of it to all the parties to the instrument.

Where a bill of exchange has been protested for dishonor by nonacceptance, any person not a party to the bill may, with the consent of the holder, intervene and accept the bill for the honor either of the drawee or of any party liable on the bill, in order to protect his credit. Such acceptance must be in writing, signed by the acceptor for honor in the presence of a notary, and must indicate that it is an acceptance for honor. Such an acceptor does not become liable till after the bill has been protested for nonpayment; if he later pays the bill he has recourse against the person for whose honor he made the acceptance and all parties against whom the latter would have recourse.

CHAPTER VII

DISCHARGE

§ 23. Payment—payment for honor.[3] It would seem that payment either by the principal debtor or by the party primarily liable on the instrument would be a valid discharge of it, because the principal debtor would necessarily have no rights over against anyone, and the rights of the party primarily liable—not being the principal debtor—are not on the instrument.

Payment by one secondarily liable who is not the principal debtor does not discharge the instrument which remains in existence for the purpose of holding the prior parties liable thereon.

Though ordinarily one who voluntarily pays the debt of another acquires thereby no right of reimbursement against the latter, the N. I. L. provides that in case of a bill of exchange protested for nonpayment, one who is not a party to the bill may pay it for the honor of any person liable thereon or for the honor of the person for whose account it was drawn. In such a case the payor for honor becomes subrogated to all the rights of the holder against the person for whose honor he pays and all parties liable to the latter, as in case of sureties generally.

The N. I. L. provides that an absolute renunciation of his rights against the principal debtor discharges the instrument.

§ 24. Cancellation and surrender—novation.[4] Where the holder of an instrument with the intention of destroying and cancelling it does destroy it, the instrument is discharged; however, where the instrument, payable to bearer, was merely torn into two pieces and a person present stuck the two pieces together with some adhesive and negotiated it to a holder in due course, it was held that the latter was protected because of the negligence of the party who attempted to destroy it.

3 8 **Am Jur**, Bills and Notes, §§ 825–851, 899–902.

Discharge of drawer or indorser of check by holder's acceptance therefor of something other than money. 52 **ALR** 994–1007; s. in 87 **ALR** 442–448.

Rights and remedies of accommodation party to paper as against accommodated party after payment. 36 **ALR** 553–598; s. in 77 **ALR** 668–675.

Renewal note as discharging original obligation of indebtedness. 52 **ALR** 1416–1432.

Trade acceptance or unsecured note or bill of debtor as accord and satisfaction. 62 **ALR** 751–762.

Payment to payee, indorser, or guarantor of bill or note not in possession thereof. 103 **ALR** 652–677.

4 8 **Am Jur**, Bills and Notes, §§ 574, 781, 789, 831.

Where the holder of an instrument delivers it up to a party liable thereon for the purpose of discharging his liability thereon, this operates as a discharge of such party.

Where the holder of an instrument receives from a party liable thereon a new instrument covering the same liability, the presumption is that it is received merely by way of collateral security; but it may—if so intended—operate as a novation by substituting the new instrument for the old.

CHAPTER VIII

CHECKS

§ 25. **Distinguished from bills of exchange.**[5] A check is a bill of exchange drawn on a bank payable on demand and most of the rules regarding bills of exchange apply also to checks, but there are a few differences. A bill of exchange must, but a check need not, be presented for acceptance. A check is drawn against a deposit but a bill of exchange usually is not. The death of the drawer of a bill of exchange does not revoke the authority of drawee to pay but knowledge of the death of the drawer of a check is usually held to revoke the authority of the bank to pay.

A check must be presented for payment within a reasonable time after its issue and failure to do so will discharge the drawer to the extent of the damage caused by such failure due to the bank becoming insolvent; failure to make proper presentment of a draft discharges the drawer even if no damage is done.

§ 26. **Certification—check as payment.**[6] A bank is not under obligation to accept or certify a check but if it does do so for the holder it becomes liable directly to him and the drawer and indorsers are discharged. If the check has been raised and the bank pays the larger amount it may recover back the difference from the holder. If a check is postdated, the bank will not be bound by a certification made before such date.

A check does not operate as a partial assignment of the drawer's claim against the bank and therefore if the bank refuses to pay, the remedy of the holder is not against the bank but against the drawer and the indorsers; if the refusal of the bank to pay the check was wrongful the drawer is entitled to recover against the bank for breach of its promise—usually implied in fact—to honor its depositor's checks.

A check given in payment of an obligation is presumed to be only in conditional payment, but it may be accepted as absolute payment if so intended.

[5] 7 **Am Jur,** Bills and Notes, §§ 9, 10.

Time within which check must be presented to prevent discharge of drawer in event of bank's insolvency. 91 **ALR** 1181–1206.

Rights and obligations between depositor and bank which pays forged check, as affected by provisions of Negotiable Instruments Act. 146 **ALR** 840–859.

Right of drawee of forged check or draft to recover money paid thereon. 12 **ALR** 1089–1116; s. in 71 **ALR** 337–345; 121 **ALR** 1056–1062.

Examination of account, pass book, or canceled checks by bank depositor. 15 **ALR** 159–170; s. in 67 **ALR** 1121–1127; 103 **ALR** 1147–1155.

Liability of bank to depositor for dishonoring check. 126 **ALR** 206–249.

Who must bear loss as between drawer who delivers check to an impostor and one who cashes or pays it upon latter's indorsement. 22 **ALR** 1228–1253; s. in 52 **ALR** 1326–1329; 112 **ALR** 1435–1441.

Time of negotiation of check as affecting one's character as a holder in due course. 23 **ALR** 1205–1211.

[6] 7 **Am Jur,** Banks, §§ 557–573.

Banks: effect of overcertification of check. 2 **ALR** 86–90.

Tender by check. 23 **ALR** 1284–1298; s. in 51 **ALR** 393–398.

Where the amount due was unliquidated or in dispute the acceptance of a check marked "In full payment" operates as a compromise, but not where the amount due was liquidated and undisputed.

CORPORATIONS

CHAPTER I

FORMATION OF CORPORATIONS

§ 1. The statutory requirements.[1] Unless prohibited by constitution, a state legislature may create corporations by a special statute, but nearly all corporations today are organized under a general statute. Such a statute usually requires that each of the persons forming a corporation shall prepare and sign a memorandum or certificate or articles of association and acknowledge it before a notary. The incorporators must be adults but they need not be shareholders or residents or even citizens unless the statute so stipulates nor need there be any fixed number of incorporators unless the statute so provides. Some statutes require that a certain amount of the capital stock be subscribed; others require that a certain amount be paid in.

The statute usually requires that some officer issue to the incorporators a certificate of incorporation and that this certificate be filed with the Secretary of State or some other officer either as a condition precedent to the existence of the corporation or to its right to do business. Finally, the certificate must be accepted by the corporation; such acceptance is usually inferred from its election of officers and—in case of the business corporation—its beginning business.

§ 2. Corporation de facto.[2] If there has been substantial compliance with the statutory requirements the result is a corporation de jure—one whose existence cannot be successfully questioned even in a direct proceeding brought by the state for that purpose.

If there has not been such substantial compliance with statutory requirements, the result may be a corporation de facto which is like a corporation de jure except that its existence may be successfully questioned by a direct proceeding brought by the state for that purpose.

In order that there be a de facto corporation, there must be (1) a law under which a corporation with the powers assumed by the association in question might have been organized; (2) a bona fide attempt to organize as a corporation under such law; (3) the user of corporate powers. Such a corporation can hold property, make valid conveyances and contracts and, by the better view, can exercise the power of eminent domain as if it were a corporation de jure; and such acts will not be invalidated in any

[1] 13 **Am Jur,** Corporations, §§ 20–44.
Effect upon the corporate existence of failure to file certificate in organizing a corporation. 22 **ALR** 376–397; s. in 37 **ALR** 1319.
Binding effect of subscription to stock in corporation to be formed. 61 **ALR** 1463–1523.
Form of pleading necessary to raise issue of corporate existence. 55 **ALR** 510–525.
Protection of business or trading corporation against use of same or similar name by another corporation. 66 **ALR** 948–1033; s. in 115 **ALR** 1241–1255.
Individual liability of stockholders, directors, or officers on corporate contracts improperly entered into before subscription of requisite amount of stock. 50 **ALR** 1030–1043.
31 **Georgetown L. J.** 381, Industrial Combinations and the Law.

[2] 13 **Am Jur,** Corporations, §§ 45–62.
Liability of officers, directors, or members of defectively organized corporation to one of their number of advances, commissions, etc. 115 **ALR** 658–664.
Conclusiveness of charter as regards character, kind, or purposes of corporation. 119 **ALR** 1012–1028.
Organization sought to be incorporated under an unconstitutional statute as a de facto corporation. 136 **ALR** 187–204.
40 **Harv. L. R.** 733, A Note on Partnership Liability of Stockholders in Defectively Organized Corporations.

way by a later ouster by the State in a quo warranto proceeding; there is no relation back.

If the incorporators have not acted in good faith but for purposes of fraud, no corporation de facto results and the incorporators are liable personally.

§ 3. **Corporations by estoppel.**[3] Where the requirements for a corporation de facto have not been met—that is, where there is no valid law under which the association might have organized as a corporation, or where there has been no colorable compliance with statutory requirements, or where there has been no user of corporate powers—an association may in a particular case be treated as if it were a corporation. This doctrine is called the doctrine of corporation by estoppel though the usual requirements of estoppel—damage suffered in reliance upon a misrepresentation—may not be present.

If A participates either as promoter or director or shareholder in holding out an association as a corporation and thereby induces X to deal with it as such, A is estopped to deny that it is a corporation if such denial would cause damage to X; for example, if X is a creditor seeking to hold the supposed corporation on a statutory liability for debts. This is genuine estoppel.

If B contracts with a supposed corporation which later sues B for breach of the contract, B may not deny his liability on the ground that the association was not really a corporation. The basis of B's liability is not, however, true estoppel because it cannot be said that B has represented to the association that it is a corporation, but rather that since B has in business dealings recognized the association as a corporation he should not be allowed to raise an immaterial issue which does not in any way affect his rights or obligations.

If C makes a contract with X and Y and later seeks to hold them liable as individuals or as partners for breach of that contract, may X and Y set up in defense that C dealt with X and Y as a corporation and therefore has rights only on that basis? On this question there is a conflict of authority. In favor of C it is argued that it is not fair for X and Y merely by assuming a corporate name and pretending to be a corporation to escape individual responsibility, and that allowing them to escape such liability would encourage them to form illegal or prohibited corporations. On the other hand, it is argued for X and Y that there is no real estoppel because they did not hold themselves out as individual contractors; that they did not undertake to become liable individually and that it is making over their contract thus to hold them. Under this, the better view, C's right is merely against the corporate assets and against the officers and agents of the supposed corporation either as principals or for breach of their implied warranty of authority.

CHAPTER II

CHARACTERISTICS OF A CORPORATION

§ 4. **Corporation distinguished from other forms of business association.**[4] A corporation differs from an ordinary partnership chiefly in that apart from

[3] 13 Am Jur, Corporations, §§ 63–69.

[4] 13 Am Jur, Corporations, § 3.

statute the shareholders in a corporation are not personally liable for the debts of the corporation whereas the members of a partnership are liable for the debts of the partnership; and the death of a shareholder does not dissolve the corporation whereas the death of a partner dissolves the partnership. In some states statutes provide for the organization of a special form of partnership usually called a joint stock company; shares in such companies are made transferable but each shareholder is liable for obligations incurred by the company while he is a shareholder. Such companies are usually treated as if they were corporations for purposes of taxation and bankruptcy. Where a corporation received as collateral for a loan some shares in a partnership this did not make the corporation a partner and hence it was not liable for the partnership debts.

In a business trust the shares of the cestui are transferable; the cestuis are not liable personally for the obligations incurred by the trustees in conducting the business and the trustees may escape their responsibility therefor by express stipulation with the persons with whom they deal. But a business trust is not an entity, and the trustees deal with the trust property as principals while the corporation directors deal with corporate property as agents of the corporation.

§ 5. Corporation distinguished from its shareholders.[5] One who buys all the stock of a corporation does not thereby acquire the title to the corporation's property and hence cannot maintain replevin to recover a chattel belonging to the corporation. And where the United States owned all the stock in a corporation it was subject to suit as such stockholder and was not entitled to immunity as a sovereign.

Where A conveyed land to B, the latter covenanting not to convey it to a colored person or persons, it was held that the covenant was not violated by a transfer to a corporation though the purpose of the corporation was to use the land as an amusement park for colored persons.

CHAPTER III

THE CORPORATE ENTITY

§ 6. The general rule.[6] The corporation is an entity separate from the shareholders; it holds the title to the corporate property and is the proper party to sue and be sued upon contracts made by the corporation or for torts committed upon or by the corporation. The shareholder has only an intangible right to share in the profits and in the surplus upon dissolution after debts are paid; he has no right to the corporate property itself and cannot recover for torts committed upon it. And if X sues the corporation to collect a debt due him from the corporation the shareholder is not entitled to set off a debt claim which he has against X.

§ 7. One-man companies—subsidiary companies.[7] The mere fact that one individual owns all the stock in a corporation is not objectionable because

5 13 **Am Jur,** Corporations, §§ 171–176.

6 13 **Am Jur,** Corporations, §§ 6–8.
28 **U. of Minn. L. R.** 341, The Corporate Entity Concept (or Fiction Theory) and the Modern Business Organization.

7 13 **Am Jur,** Corporations, § 6.
51 **Harv. L. R.** 1373, The Incorporated Individual: A Study of the One-Man Company.
41 **Harv. L. R.** 874, Subsidiary Corporations and Credit Manipulation.

limited liability is regarded as a legitimate object of incorporation and a creditor of the corporation cannot reach the individual assets of the sole shareholder. But if the sole shareholder confuses the corporation business with his individual affairs the person who deals with him may properly be in the position of being able, at his option, to hold either the one-man corporation or its sole shareholder.

The mere fact that corporation X—or its directors or shareholders—owns all or a majority of the stock in a subsidiary corporation Y is not objectionable; but if such ownership and control is used for its own purposes and interests to the prejudice of innocent third persons or the public generally, corporation X may be held responsible for the contracts and torts of its subsidiary and if it has advanced money to it may not be allowed to compete with the other creditors of the Y corporation.

CHAPTER IV

CORPORATE CAPACITY

§ 8. Implied powers.[8] A corporation may legally do not only all the various things enumerated in the certificate of incorporation, but also the things which are reasonably necessary to enable it to exercise the powers which are expressly granted and thus to accomplish its main objects. For example, a railroad company may maintain restaurants along its route for the accommodation of its passengers; and a mining company may operate a railroad or steamboat to convey its ore to market or to a smelter, but not to transport passengers for hire. A manufacturing company may buy land on which to erect factories and for the purpose of erecting dwellings for its employees, but not for the purpose of holding for speculation.

A corporation may enter into a contract of suretyship or guaranty if it is a proper means of accomplishing an authorized purpose; and the same reasoning applies to holding stock in another corporation.

§ 9. Ultra vires—the early view.[9] If a corporation is about to do something which is not within its express or implied powers any stockholder is entitled to get an injunction against such action. But suppose no injunction is sought and the corporation does enter into transactions—conveys property, makes contracts or commits torts—which are ultra vires, that is, not authorized by its certificate of incorporation, what is the legal effect of such transactions?

The early view was that since a corporation was created only for certain purposes, it had no existence beyond the limit of those purposes and any act outside such limit was a nullity.

§ 10. Same—the modern trend.[10] The modern trend is toward treating a corporation in much the same way as if it were an individual. The individual has the power to do many things which it has no right to do—to breach a

8 13 Am Jur, Corporations, § 740.

9 13 Am Jur, Corporations, § 754.

10 13 Am Jur, Corporations, §§ 752-758.
Necessity of showing authority or qualification of affiant in affidavit made in behalf of corporation. 3 ALR 132-146.

Right of corporation to perform or to hold itself out as ready to perform functions in the nature of legal services. 73 ALR 1327-1337; s. in 105 ALR 1364.

Assumption of mortgage or lien by bank or other corporation as ultra vires. 91 ALR 177-188.

contract, to commit a tort or crime—and is liable for such wrongful acts. So, it is now argued, a corporation has the power to do many things which it has no legal authority to do and should be held liable for such wrongful acts unless they are also illegal or in violation of the public interest.

§ 11. Ultra vires contracts.[1] Where the A corporation enters into an ultra vires contract with X and it is fully performed on both sides, the great weight of authority is that the transaction stands. If there has been no performance on either side, the weight of authority is that neither the A corporation nor X may maintain any action on the contract either at law or in equity; that is, neither party is barred from asserting that the contract is ultra vires.

Where the contract has been fully performed by only one of the parties, resulting in a benefit to the other, there is a conflict of authority as to whether the liability is on the contract for the contract price or is merely in quasi contract for the reasonable value of the benefit received. Under the former view, the party receiving the benefit is barred from setting up ultra vires in defense. In a few jurisdictions there is no liability on the A corporation unless the benefit received by it was used for some legitimate purpose.

Where the A corporation has only partly performed, X cannot hold A for failure to perform the rest; and similar reasoning applies to a partial performance by X. The one rendering the partial performance is ordinarily entitled to recover in quasi contract for the reasonable value of the benefit received through such part performance.

Where the contract between the A corporation and X is apparently within the authority of the A corporation but is ultra vires because of extrinsic facts not known to X, ultra vires is no defense to A. For example, if the A corporation having the authority to become an accommodation indorser of negotiable paper to a reasonable amount, does so in excess of that amount, it cannot set up ultra vires as against a bona fide purchaser of such paper.

It has sometimes been argued that X should not be able to hold the A corporation on an ultra vires contract where it is plainly beyond the authority granted by the charter because the charter is a matter of record and X should be held to have constructive notice of its contents; but the better view is that this is too heavy a burden to place upon X without express legislation to that effect and that X should be held only to know the nature of the A corporation and the usual scope of the business of such corporations. If X knew or should have known that his contract with the A corporation was ultra vires he cannot hold the A corporation on the contract but can usually compel it to pay the reasonable value in quasi contract for the benefits received under the contract.

The better view is that the shareholders of the A corporation may bind the corporation by ratification of or acquiescence in an ultra vires contract unless it would prejudice creditors or the public.

Right of corporation or individual, not himself licensed, to practise medicine, surgery, or dentistry through licensed employees. 103 **ALR** 1240–1248.

Power of corporation to guarantee for accommodation the contracts of the customers or vendors with third persons. 11 **ALR** 554–560.

Power of corporation after expiration or forfeiture of its charter. 47 **ALR** 1288–1569; s. in 97 **ALR** 477–504.

Necessity and manner of authenticating paper purporting to be act of private corporation. 65 **ALR** 329–344.

[1] 13 Am Jur, Corporations, §§ 753–758.

§ 12. **Conveyances by or to corporations.**[2] Unless a corporation is expressly prohibited by statute from receiving or holding property, an inter vivos conveyance to it either of land or chattels or choses in action passes title and only the state in a quo warranto proceeding can object that such taking or holding was ultra vires. Where by conveyance inter vivos a corporation undertakes to transfer property ultra vires, title passes and the corporation has no right to have such a transfer set aside.

Since bequeathed personal property does not go directly to the legatee but to the executor whose assent is necessary for the legatee to get it, the executor may apparently refuse to assent if the corporation legatee has no authority under its charter to hold the property. And since a devise of real property is effective only under the statute of wills, a devise to a corporation is void if the statute of wills does not permit such a devise.

§ 13. **Corporation's liability for torts.**[3] Where B, an employee of the A corporation, while acting within the apparent scope of his employment, commits a tort upon X, the A corporation is liable to X for compensatory damages, just as an individual employer would be. Where an employee's conduct is wanton or malicious he may be held liable for exemplary or punitive damages but his employer, if an individual, would not be liable for such damages unless he had authorized or later ratified the employee's act. It would seem that similar reasoning should apply to a corporation employer unless the employee was the corporation manager or high official. Apparently the present trend is toward holding the corporation liable for such damages.

The fact that a tort is committed by the employee while engaged in an ultra vires business or transaction is not, by the better view, a defense to the corporation.

§ 14. **Corporation's liability for crimes.**[4] Where a manager or other primary representative of a corporation, in the course of conducting the corporation business, commits a crime the weight of authority is that the corporation may be punished therefor, whether the criminal offense be a public nuisance, the violation of a police regulation, negligent manslaughter or offenses requiring specific criminal intent, such as larceny. Where the crime is committed by an employee of minor importance, it would seem that the corporation should not be held liable unless it authorized or ratified the act. Though a corporation cannot be imprisoned it may be punished by a fine or by forfeiture of its charter.

Where a criminal statute uses the word "persons" it will be construed to include corporations if they are within the purpose of the act—for example, a statute forbidding any person to employ children under 14 in a factory.

CHAPTER V

PROMOTERS

§ 15. **Promoters' contracts.**[5] Where B, the promoter of the A corporation,

[2] 13 **Am Jur,** Corporations, §§ 773–779.
Right of business corporation to use its funds or property for humanitarian purposes. 3 **ALR** 443–447.

[3] 13 **Am Jur,** Corporation, §§ 1118–1131.
Doctrine of ultra vires as applied to torts of private corporations. 57 **ALR** 302–310.
14 **Miss. L. J.** 190, Tort Liability of Power Companies.

[4] 13 **Am Jur,** Corporations, §§ 1132–1145.

[5] 13 **Am Jur,** Corporations, §§ 97–1141.
Liability of corporation on contracts of promoters. 17 **ALR** 452–512; s. in 49 **ALR** 673–680; 123 **ALR** 726–738.

enters into a contract with X—for example, for services—on behalf of the expected corporation, the latter is not bound by the contract unless it adopts it expressly or by conduct. The word "ratification" is deemed to be inappropriate in this connection because at the time when B and X made the contract the A corporation was not yet in existence.

It has been suggested, in explanation of such adoption, that the A corporation is the intended beneficiary of the contract between B and X; this theory might well be applied if the A corporation were suing X on the contract but could hardly apply if X were suing the A corporation because beneficiaries of contracts do not, as such, become liable thereon.

Where the intention of B and X is that upon adoption of the contract by the A corporation B is to be released from any further liability on the contract, then the case would seem to be one of novation by substituting the A corporation for B. Where there is no such intention, then the case would seem to be one of assignment by B to the A corporation of B's rights under the contract and an assumption by the A corporation of B's obligations; where there are no rights assigned, however, it is difficult to find any consideration for the A corporation's assumption of B's obligations.

§ 16. The promoter's fiduciary duty.[6] If a promoter causes damage either to the corporation or to stockholders by making fraudulent representations, he may be held liable therefor in an action on the case for deceit or the fraudulent transactions may be rescinded and set aside in equity.

Even where the promoter makes no fraudulent representations, he may be made to account in equity for secret profits made at the expense of the corporation or of the shareholders. Because he is in a position of power which enables him to take an unfair advantage of the corporation or the shareholders, the courts hold that he is a fiduciary. He differs from an agent in that he is self appointed, and from a trustee in that he has executed no declaration of trust. But as the trustee is under a duty in his dealings with his cestui que trust to disclose facts which are peculiarly within his knowledge as trustee, so the promoter must make a similar disclosure when he deals with the corporation or the shareholders. Such a disclosure is effective if made, before the transaction, to an independent board of directors of the corporation or to each of the original subscribers; he may also be protected by making a disclosure after the transaction to the shareholders if the latter vote to adopt the transaction.

Where the promoters issue all the stock to themselves and later sell it without making a disclosure to such purchasers of secret profits, the better view and weight of authority is that the corporation may rescind or it may hold the promoter liable for secret profits; the minority view is that if there is any right of action it belongs to those who bought stock from the promoters because at the time of the transaction the promoters were the sole stockholders and therefore were the corporation, and there was assent to the transaction by them. Under the minority view the best remedy of the shareholders is a representative suit in which all the defrauded shareholders may join.

By the better view there is a duty of disclosure even if the property turned

38 **Harv. L. R.** 887, The Promoter: A Legislative Problem.

42 **Harv. L. R.** 748, Compensation of Bankers and Promoters through Stock Profits.

6 13 **Am Jur,** Corporations, §§ 115–130.

5 **U. of Toronto L. J.** 21, The Liability of Promoters for Secret Profits in English Law.

over to the corporation had been acquired by the promoters without any idea of forming a corporation, but some courts hold that in such a case the promoters are liable only for fraudulent representations.

CHAPTER VI

DIRECTORS AND OFFICERS

§ 17. Powers of directors and officers.[7] The management of the regular business affairs of the corporation is usually vested by the charter in a board of directors. The directors must usually act as a board at a regular or specially called meeting; hence they cannot act by proxy and mere concurrence of even all the directors without a meeting is usually not valid because they are expected to meet, discuss and deliberate before acting. Fundamental changes in the corporation such as amending its charter, merging with another corporation or selling all its assets must be made by the shareholders, not by the directors.

A trustee may employ persons to render professional services, such as lawyers, accountants and auctioneers, but may not delegate to anyone matters involving the exercise of discretion in the management of the trust. But a board of directors, even without express authorization, may delegate to an executive committee or president or vice-president the power to perform any act which they themselves can legally perform though it involves the exercise of discretion, such as entering into a contract. Such a rule is based partly upon usage and partly upon necessity, the directors being unable themselves to attend to all the details of the corporation's business.

While each partner is an agent of the partnership, a director, as such, is not an agent of the corporation. Since the authority of a president is not always broad, the fact that he is president does not imply that he has any greater power than any other director. A corporation, like a natural person, may be estopped to deny the authority of an officer or agent where it has clothed such officer or agent with apparent authority to act for it in a particular business or transaction. And where the officer or agent acted without authority, the corporation may later bind itself by either express or implied ratification.

While an officer or agent is acting within the apparent scope of his employment, notice to him is ordinarily notice to the corporation; but this does not apply where the interest of such officer or agent is adverse to that of the corporation.

The by-laws usually require that notice of all meetings be sent to each director, but the failure to send such notice becomes of no importance if all the directors attend. Unless provided otherwise, a majority of the board constitutes a quorum, excluding any who are disqualified by reason of personal interest in the matter to be acted upon at the meeting.

§ 18. Duties and liabilities of directors and officers.[8] Directors and other

7 13 Am Jur, Corporations, §§ 889–971.

8 13 Am Jur, Corporations, §§ 985–1117.

Corporation's payment of bonus to officers or employees. 40 ALR 1423–1442; s. in 88 ALR 751–756.

Right of court to interfere with amount of salaries voted to officers of private corporations by directors. 27 ALR 300–310; s. in 44 ALR 570–572.

Power of president of a corporation to employ, control, or discharge agents or subordinates. 5 ALR 1485–1495.

Authority to employ attorney for corporation. 130 ALR 894–915.

Ratification by corporation of unauthorofficers are liable to the corporation for any losses resulting from their negligence, from acts in excess of their authority and from fraudulent acts; but they are not liable for losses due to mere mistakes of judgment or to the default of subordinate employees where due care has been used in selecting them.

Where A, an officer, acting within his authority on behalf of the corporation, makes a contract with X who knows that A is so acting, the corporation and not X becomes liable on the contract. But if, in contracting with X, A does not disclose that he is acting for a corporation or if he purports to act for a nonexistent corporation, or if he acts outside his authority and X is ignorant of these facts, A becomes personally liable to X; in some states his liability is in tort for misrepresentation, in others for breach of an implied warranty of authority or on the contract itself.

§ 19. Directors and other officers as fiduciaries.[9] Directors and other officers are fiduciaries and hence, like agents, trustees, promoters, and other fiduciaries, must account to the corporation for any secret profit made out of their position; they may not, without the consent of the corporation, buy at a public sale of corporate property and if they buy from or sell property to the corporation or enter into any other transaction with it, they must divest themselves of any advantage which they have by virtue of their position.

Where the directors of A corporation enter into a transaction with B, one

ized contract entered into by officer, by acceptance and retention of benefits. 7 **ALR** 1446–1495.

Personal liability of directors as affected by terms of contract or form of signature. 33 **ALR** 1353–1361; s. in 51 **ALR** 319–320.

Power of directors of private corporation to remove officers or fellow directors. 63 **ALR** 776–783.

Informality of meeting of directors as affecting action taken thereat. 64 **ALR** 712–730.

Right of officer or director of private corporation to purchase in his own interest at a judicial or other public sale of the corporate property. 76 **ALR** 439–460.

Validity of contract between corporations as affected by directors or officers in common. 114 **ALR** 299–318.

Construction and application of statutes making corporate officers or directors liable in respect of loans or advances to stockholders or officers. 129 **ALR** 1258–1268.

Liability of director of bank or loan company for losses on bad debts. 45 **ALR** 678–697; s. in 77 **ALR** 543–553.

Right of stockholder as individual to complain as against officers, directors, or large stockholders, of their transactions in corporation's outstanding stock involving its control or other purpose. 132 **ALR** 260–282.

Statute of limitations in stockholder's derivative suit against directors or officers. 123 **ALR** 346–371.

Recovery against corporate directors or officers for fraud or mismanagement as affected by releases, ratification, waiver, or consent by some, but not all, of the stockholders. 120 **ALR** 238–250.

Request that stockholders as a body sue directors as a condition of right of individual stockholders to bring the action in the interest of the corporation. 72 **ALR** 628–638.

Proceeding by stockholder in behalf of corporation for relief from judgment taken against it through fraud of officers or directors. 135 **ALR** 838–849.

Laches as affecting right of corporation or its stockholders to relief against directors for violation of trust. 10 **ALR** 370–380.

Abatement upon death, of cause of action to enforce personal liability of corporate officer, director, or trustee. 79 **ALR** 1517–1528.

Duty of officer or director of corporation toward one from whom he purchases stock. 84 **ALR** 615–635.

Personal liability of corporate directors or officers under statute imposing such liability in respect of excessive indebtedness as affected by payment by the corporation (or its receiver, assignee in insolvency or trustee in bankruptcy) of all or part of the excessive indebtedness. 130 **ALR** 824–830.

Statute relating to liability of officers or directors of private corporation as penal within principle that penal laws will not be enforced extraterritorially. 25 **ALR** 1428–1442.

Liability of directors for defalcations by executive officer or employee. 2 **ALR** 867–879.

Personal civil liability of corporate officers and directors in case of sale of bonds or stock in violation of statutory requirement. 144 **ALR** 1356–1371.

9 13 **Am Jur**, Corporations, §§ 889–971.

44 **Harv. L. R.** 1049, Corporate Powers as Powers in Trust.

47 **Harv. L. R.** 1305, Directors Who Do Not Direct.

45 **Harv. L. R.** 1145, 1365, For Whom Are Corporate Managers Trustees?

18 **Ind L. J.** 293, Director's Power to Compete with His Corporation.

of the directors, and B's vote is necessary to make a quorum or to make a majority of those voting, the corporation may repudiate the transaction without regard to its fairness; where there were enough disinterested votes, without B's, to make a quorum or a majority, the better view is that such a transaction is valid if entirely fair to the corporation. Where the A corporation enters into a transaction with the X corporation and the two corporations have common directors who are in control, the transaction may later be avoided; where the common directors are only a minority, the transaction will stand if it is fair to both corporations.

In any case where a transaction might be avoided by the corporation because of the adverse interest of directors, the transaction may, of course, be ratified either expressly or by acquiescence.

Where a director buys from or sells shares to a stockholder, there is a conflict of authority as to whether he must divest himself of the advantage of his position by making disclosures to the shareholder, the modern tendency being in the affirmative.

CHAPTER VII

SHAREHOLDERS AND SHARES

§ 20. Subscription for shares.[10] Where B subscribes unconditionally to shares in the A corporation which is already in existence and the A corporation assents, B becomes at once a shareholder and bound to pay the full par value of the shares for which he subscribed. If the A corporation is not yet in existence the subscription takes effect when it comes into existence and assents, either by vote of the directors or by treating him as a shareholder; until such assent the weight of authority is that, apart from statute, the purported subscription is a mere offer which may be revoked by B. If B merely agrees to subscribe in the future, this does not make B a shareholder; he is not liable for the par value of the shares but only for the damage caused by his breach of contract, the difference between the par value and the market value of the shares.

Where B, C and D contract with each other to form the A corporation, this makes the subscription of each one irrevocable from the date of the contract; but the mere fact that they sign together a subscription agreement

[10] 13 **Am Jur**, Corporations, §§ 221–318.

Effect upon the validity of subscription to corporate stock, of failure to comply with statutory requirement of payment at the time of subscribing. 6 **ALR** 1116–1134.

Validity and effect of agreement by a corporation contemporaneously with issue or sale of stock, to repurchase or redeem the stock or to cancel the subscription therefor and refund consideration paid. 101 **ALR** 154–180.

Validity of release, cancelation, or compromise of unpaid subscription for stock by corporation or its representatives. 101 **ALR** 231–265.

Validity and effect of extrinsic agreement absolving one, in whole or part, from liability on subscription to corporate stock. 81 **ALR** 198–215.

Note as consideration for issuance of corporate stock under statute forbidding issuance of stock except for money paid, property received, etc. 58 **ALR** 708–717.

Stockholders' privilege as to acquisition of new issue of stock by corporation. 52 **ALR** 220–244; s. in 138 **ALR** 527–538.

Insolvency of corporation as barring stockholder's right to rescind subscription on ground of fraud. 41 **ALR** 674–717; s. in 46 **ALR** 484–485.

Admissibility of oral evidence as to proceedings at meetings of stockholders or directors of private corporations or associations. 66 **ALR** 1328–1342.

Informality of meeting of stockholders as affecting action taken thereat. 51 **ALR** 941–966.

Power of corporation to change obligations to stockholders. 105 **ALR** 1452–1466; s. in 117 **ALR** 1290–1293.

57 **Harv. L. R.** 295, The Relative Rights of Preferred and Common Shareholders in Recapitalization Plans under the Holding Company Act.

29 **Va. L. R.** 460, Pre-incorporation Subscriptions.

does not necessarily mean that they are making any such contract with each other; they may be merely making an offer to the corporation.

Where B subscribes conditionally, the condition is valid if it is not unfair to other shareholders or creditors; for example, a stipulation that the shares were to be paid for out of future earnings of the corporation.

Usually the obligation to pay for shares subscribed is subject to the implied condition that the full amount of the capital or the percentage thereof required by the charter shall have been unconditionally subscribed.

A subscriber is not released from his obligation by mere mismanagement or abandonment of the business but he is released where, without his consent, the charter has been fundamentally altered or there has been consolidation with a corporation of a different character.

§ 21. Shareholders' right of inspection.[1] In order that a shareholder may be able to protect his interests, he is entitled at common law to inspect the books and papers of the corporation at a reasonable time and for a proper purpose, such as to find out the financial condition of the corporation and the value of his stock, to ascertain whether the corporation is being mismanaged and whether a receivership should be sought. Where, however, his purpose is to find out business secrets, or to get a list of business prospects, so as to aid a competitor of the corporation, he has no right to inspect. The proper remedy for wrongful refusal is mandamus. In many states the right has been regulated by statute.

§ 22. Voting rights and duties of shareholders.[2] At common law each shareholder was entitled to one vote no matter what the size of his holdings but it is now almost universally provided by charter or by-laws that each share is entitled to one vote. The right to vote, apart from statute, is in those who on the day of the corporate meeting are registered on the corporation books as owners, except that shares which have been purchased by the corporation are not entitled to vote; nor can shares held by another corporation ultra vires. The fact that the one registered as owner holds the shares as trustee or executor does not prevent him from voting. If the charter provides for cumulative voting, this right may not be abrogated by a by-law.

At common law there is no right to vote by proxy, but such right is usually given by statute or by-law and when thus given, it cannot be taken away without consent. A proxy may not vote for a fundamental change in the charter unless expressly authorized to do so. There is a conflict of authority as to whether proxies may be made irrevocable as in voting trusts.

A shareholder as such is not an agent of the corporation; he can bind the corporation only by his vote at a legal meeting. At such a meeting he is not rendered ineligible to vote because of his personal interest in the matter being voted on, but the modern tendency is to hold that the majority is under a fiduciary duty not to act fraudulently or oppressively toward the

[1] 13 **Am Jur,** Corporations, § 1025.
Stockholders' right to inspect books and records of corporation. 22 **ALR** 24–106; s. in 43 **ALR** 783–791, 1373–1384; 80 **ALR** 1502–1520.

[2] 13 **Am Jur,** Corporations, §§ 485–509.
Voting corporate stock title of which is held jointly. 134 **ALR** 989–995.
Who may exercise voting power of corporate stock pending settlement of estate of deceased owner. 114 **ALR** 1057–1065.
Validity of voting trust or other similar agreement for control of voting power of corporate stock. 105 **ALR** 123–148.
41 **Mich. L. R.** 38, 225, Corporate Proxies.
21 **Texas L. R.** 139, Voting Trusts, Their Abuses and Regulation.
5 **U. of Toronto L. J.** 282, Preference Shareholders in the Reconstruction of English Companies.

minority. If the corporate business can no longer be carried on profitably the majority may, acting in good faith, abandon the enterprise and dissolve the corporation; but they may not do so if the business is a going concern, as against the wishes of a minority.

§ 23. The right to dividends.[3] The shareholders are not the owners of the corporate property; their sole right is to a share in the profits and in the surplus, upon dissolution, after the corporate debts are paid. Where the corporation is steadily making profits it is the duty of the directors to declare dividends from such profits—a duty which a court of equity will enforce in flagrant cases. If they declare a dividend out of capital, the corporation creditors may hold liable both the directors who declared the dividend and the shareholders who received it.

As soon as a dividend is properly declared, the shareholder becomes to that extent a creditor of the corporation and entitled to the same rights and remedies as other creditors; if there is a fund set aside for the payment of dividends, the shareholders are entitled to share in the fund to the exclusion of other creditors.

Where the corporation may lawfully issue more stock it may, in place of a dividend payable in cash or property, declare a stock dividend, thus transferring part of the accumulated surplus to capital. Since the proportional interest of the shareholder in the corporation remains the same, a stock dividend is not taxable as income.

When a cash or property dividend is properly declared, the holders of noncumulative preferred stock are entitled, before the holders of common stock, to be paid not only the dividend for that year, but also the dividends on previous years where such dividends were earned but not declared; and the holders of cumulative preferred stock are entitled also to be paid dividends for previous years where no dividends were declared whether or not there were profits during those years.

Where shares are held upon trust for X for life with remainder to Y, there are two views as to the way in which dividends should be apportioned. Under the Massachusetts rule all stock dividends go to Y and all cash dividends go to X. Under the Pennsylvania rule, which seems to be the majority view, dividends, whether stock or cash, are apportioned according to whether the profits out of which they were declared were earned during the testator's lifetime, in which case they go to Y, or whether they were earned during the life estate, in which case they go to X.

[3] 13 **Am Jur,** Corporations, §§ 683–738.

33 **Am Jur,** Life Estates, Remainders and Reversions, §§ 371–422.

Right as between seller and purchaser of stock to dividends declared thereon. 60 **ALR** 703.

Right as between life beneficiaries and remaindermen in corporate dividends or distributions during the life interest. 24 **ALR** 9–122; s. in 42 **ALR** 448–460; 50 **ALR** 375–380; 56 **ALR** 1287–1303; 72 **ALR** 981–997; 83 **ALR** 1261–1273; 101 **ALR** 1379–1393; 130 **ALR** 492–591.

Rights of holders of preferred stock in respect to dividends. 6 **ALR** 802–835; s. in 67 **ALR** 765–780; 98 **ALR** 1526–1531; 133 **ALR** 653–673.

Right or duty of corporation to pay dividends; and liability for wrongful payment. 55 **ALR** 9–147; s. in 76 **ALR** 885–897; 109 **ALR** 138–1401.

Right as between seller and purchaser of stock to dividends declared thereon. 60 **ALR** 703–712.

Conclusiveness of assessment of statutory liability of stockholders of national banks. 90 **ALR** 1063–1071.

Statutory added liability of stockholders of bank or other corporation as affected by sale of, or other transaction in relation to, assets. 89 **ALR** 790–797; s. in 100 **ALR** 1276–1283.

42 **Harv. L. R.** 186, The Pre-emptive Right of Shareholders.

18 **Ind. L. J.** 111, Dividend Rules and Mistaken Precedent.

§ 24. Unpaid subscriptions—watered stock.[4] Where X has subscribed for shares in the A corporation and has not paid his subscription in full, that is, has not paid par on the par value shares or has not paid the price fixed by the directors on nonpar shares, the corporation may compel X to pay the remainder of his subscription unless the subscription was obtained by fraud or there has been a substantial amendment of the charter without his consent. If the corporation has gone into bankruptcy or into the hands of a receiver the trustee in bankruptcy or receiver may enforce the unpaid subscription after showing the amount necessary to be recovered to pay the debts of the corporation. Where the corporation is insolvent but not bankrupt or in the hands of a receiver the corporation creditors, after exhausting their remedy at law against the corporation may bring a creditor's bill for equitable execution against the corporation and thereby reach the corporation's claim for unpaid subscriptions. By the better view such a bill should be brought on behalf of all the creditors who wish to come in. The fact that unpaid for stock has been issued as fully paid does not prevent the creditors from forcing the subscriber to pay the difference between what he has paid and the par value; but usually the creditor cannot impose any such liability upon a bona fide purchaser of such stock.

The usual method of watering stock is to issue it for property at a gross over valuation of the property. There are two views as to determining the value of such property, the true value rule and the good faith rule, the courts following the latter rule recognizing that value is a matter about which men may honestly differ and taking the position that if the directors have acted in good faith their judgment should stand.

While ordinarily par value stock must be issued at par, yet if a corporation is active but unfortunate, it may, for the purpose of paying its debts and prosecuting its business successfully, sell its stock for the best price that can be obtained.

§ 25. Transfer of shares.[5] Where B, a shareholder in the A corporation, delivers to C his stock certificate indorsed in blank, either by sale or gift, the better view is that legal title to the shares passes to C even without a transfer on the corporation's books; but until the corporation has notice of the transfer it may safely treat B as the owner of the shares; and C's title may be defeated by B's transferring his shares to D who pays value without notice of C's rights and has the transfer to himself registered on the cor-

[4] 13 **Am Jur**, Corporations, §§ 279–318, 172, 558–569.
40 **Mich. L. R.** 1125, Current Phases of Derivative Actions against Directors.
29 **Cinn. L. Q.** 431, Further Phases of Derivative Actions against Directors.

[5] 13 **Am Jur**, Corporations, §§ 329–378.
Right of pledgee of corporate stock to have it transferred to him on books of company. 116 **ALR** 571–581.
Rights, powers, and duties in respect of sale or transfer of corporate stock in which one holds a legal life estate. 126 **ALR** 1298–1305.
Right or duty of corporation to refuse to transfer stock on books to one presenting properly indorsed certificate, because of knowledge or suspicion of conflicting rights of registered holder or of third person. 139 **ALR** 273–297.
Duty of corporation upon presentation for transfer of stock standing in one's name as trustee or other fiduciary. 56 **ALR** 1199–1208.
Issuance by corporation of new stock certificates without requiring surrender of old 61 **ALR** 436–448; s. in 150 **ALR** 148–152.
Validity of restrictions by corporation on alienation or transfer of corporate stock. 65 **ALR** 1159–1186; s. in 138 **ALR** 647–657.
Effect of intrusting another with stock certificate indorsed or assigned in blank to estop owner as against a bona fide purchaser or pledgee for value. 73 **ALR** 1405–1421.
Constitutionality, construction, and application of statute relating to lost, destroyed, or stolen certificate of corporate stock. 125 **ALR** 997–1008.
Priority as between lien of corporation and rights of pledgee or bona fide purchaser of corporate stock. 81 **ALR** 989–1000.

poration books, but by the better view E, an execution or attaching creditor of B, acquires no rights good against C.

Apart from statute a stock certificate is not negotiable; hence if B, a shareholder, should indorse his stock certificate in blank and should entrust it to his agent F, or if G should steal it, or if B should lose it and H should find it, Y, a purchaser from G or H, even though innocent and paying value would not be protected because he would not get title; but Z, a purchaser from F, might be protected if B's allowing possession to be in F were held to be clothing him with such apparent ownership as to work an estoppel against B. Under the Uniform Stock Transfer Act, both Y and Z would be protected if they bought in good faith, the Act making certificates of stock negotiable.

Where F or G or H procures a transfer to J of B's stock on the corporation book and the corporation issues a new certificate to J who pays value therefor in good faith without notice that the transfer has not been authorized by B, J will be protected because he gets title from the corporation. In such case B's remedy is to compel the corporation to replace his shares if it has not already issued all the stock authorized by its charter, or to compel the corporation to pay him the value of the shares, thus destroyed by the corporation, the corporation acting at its peril in making the transfer on its books. The remedy of the corporation is against the person who presented the certificate with the unauthorized assignment for breach of an implied warranty that his title was good.

One who in good faith purchases from a trustee or executor who is registered on the corporation books as owner is of course protected as a bona fide purchaser for value without notice even though the sale was wrongful, because he gets title.

Where B in good faith transfers his shares to C who is in a position to assume the obligations of a shareholder and the transfer is registered on the corporation books, there is a complete novation, C standing in B's shoes and succeeding to B's rights and obligations. If by the charter or by a statute the corporation has a lien on B's shares for a claim against B, C takes subject to such a lien even if he had no notice of it; but by the better view C takes free from any lien created by contract or by law if he pays value without notice of such lien.

Where B transfers his shares to C but the corporation wrongfully refuses to register the transfer on its books, C may maintain an action of special assumpsit for damages as the beneficiary of the contract between the corporation and B that it will register transfers. Or C may maintain a bill in equity to compel the registration. In some jurisdictions he may maintain mandamus to compel registration. The corporation is not bound, however, to register the transfer and issue a new certificate unless the old certificate is surrendered or is shown to have been destroyed; in case the certificate has been lost the corporation is entitled to exact a bond of indemnity against the possibility that the old certificate may be sold to a bona fide purchaser for value who would be entitled to hold the corporation thereon.

§ 26. Shareholders' suits against the corporation.[6] A shareholder may maintain an individual suit against the corporation for a wrong done to him individually, such as an action to recover an unpaid dividend, or for refusal to recognize a valid transfer of stock to him, or for recognizing an

[6] 13 Am Jur, Corporations, §§ 450–471.

invalid transfer thus depriving him of his stock, or for refusal to allow him to inspect the corporate books. He also may individually maintain a suit to enjoin the corporation from embarking upon an ultra vires undertaking or other misapplication of assets where such acts could not be ratified even if all the shareholders except himself should thus vote.

Where the ultra vires or other illegal act has already been accomplished and the corporation has a cause of action therefor against some third person, or if the directors have been guilty of fraud or negligence causing loss to the corporation, action should be brought by the corporation. If it refuses to bring suit, then the shareholder may bring a representative suit in equity on behalf of himself and other shareholders who wish to join him, against the corporation and the third persons who have caused it loss, asking for a decree that the third persons compensate the corporation for the loss inflicted by them. Unless the shareholder is in substance suing on behalf of a rival corporation, his motive in bringing the suit is apparently immaterial.

§ 27. Statutes regulating the marketing of shares.[7] Since 1911 Blue Sky Laws have been passed requiring dealers in shares to procure licenses and requiring permits for the shares to be sold. Where these statutes have not been complied with, the purchaser may usually rescind the sale.

The Federal Securities Act of 1933 requires registration with the Securities and Exchange Commission of statements with regard to the issue of shares offered in interstate commerce or through the mails. The Public Utility Holding Act of 1935 instructed the Securities and Exchange Commission to prevent such holding companies from issuing securities without provisions to safeguard investors.

CHAPTER VIII

CORPORATION CREDITORS

§ 28. The trust fund theory.[8] Courts have frequently said that the corporate assets are a trust fund for the benefit of creditors. This does not mean that there is a trust in the narrow sense but that a corporation does not have the same freedom in dealing with its assets as has a solvent individual, but must, in its transactions, always consider its present and future creditors. Many of the cases laying down the trust fund theory were merely cases of conveying the corporate assets in fraud of creditors, so that it was unnecessary to lay down any such doctrine. Where the corporation has been dissolved or has gone into the hands of a receiver, the assets will, of course, be distributed for the benefit of all the creditors, but the trust fund theory is not necessary to such a holding.

§ 29. The creditors' remedies.[9] A creditor cannot maintain a suit for an injunction against the corporation to interfere with the management of its

[7] 13 **Am Jur,** Corporations, §§ 1264–1265.
Blue Sky Laws. 87 **ALR** 42–164.
Market manipulation of securities. 115 **ALR** 271–291.

[8] 13 **Am Jur,** Corporations, §§ 1264–1265.

[9] 13 **Am Jur,** Corporations, §§ 1279–1284.
Creditor's knowledge that stock is unpaid as affecting stockholders' liability. 7 **ALR** 972–986; s. in 69 **ALR** 881–883.
Payments to stockholders applicable upon double liability. 23 **ALR** 1367–1373; s. in 45 **ALR** 1216; 56 **ALR** 527–529; 83 **ALR** 147–149; 120 **ALR** 511–517.
Effect of stockholder's bankruptcy upon his liability as stockholder. 82 **ALR** 988–999.
When does Statute of Limitations begin to run against an action by, or in behalf of, creditors of a corporation on unpaid stock or subscriptions. 35 **ALR** 832–856.
Right of stockholder to set off indebtedness of corporation against statutory superadded liability. 40 **ALR** 1183–1200; s. in 98 **ALR** 659–665.

business unless he is able to show some fraud or breach of trust as against him or the violation of some lien or other right which he has acquired against the corporation. He may, of course, get a judgment at law and levy execution upon the ordinary assets of the corporation but he cannot reach the franchises of the corporation or, in case of a public utility, the property which is necessary for the corporation to perform its duties to the public. Where there are no tangible assets that can be reached on common-law execution he may, having exhausted his common-law remedies, maintain a creditor's bill to reach choses in action due to the corporation. He may also, by a creditor's bill based upon fraud, reach assets which have been fraudulently withdrawn and distributed among shareholders.

Apart from statute, a corporation, even though insolvent, may voluntarily prefer some creditors by payment or mortgage or confession of judgment or the creditor may, by action on his part obtain such preference against the corporation. The better view, however, is that no such preference can be obtained by a creditor who is an officer, but may be obtained by a creditor who is merely a stockholder because the officers stand in a fiduciary position.

Where the corporation is being so fraudulently mismanaged that its assets will be lost or fraudulently disposed of, the court may, at the suit of a creditor, appoint a receiver for the corporation; such appointment, made in the sound discretion of the court, suspends the ordinary remedies of the credi-

Liability of transferrer of corporate stock for calls or assessments as affected by insolvency, fraud, or illegality in transfer. 45 ALR 99–127; s. in 86 ALR 57–63.

Failure to enter transfer of stock on corporate books as affecting liability of transferrer for calls or assessments. 45 ALR 137–160; s. in 104 ALR 638–649.

Implied obligation of purchaser of corporate stock to indemnify vendor against future calls or assessments. 45 ALR 168–180; s. in 141 ALR 1351–1358.

When limitation begins to run against action to enforce stockholder's superadded liability. 55 ALR 1068–1098; s. in 137 ALR 788–803.

Applicability of constitutional or statutory provisions relating to added liability of stockholders to corporate debts contracted prior to the adoption of the provision. 105 ALR 165–168.

Who is an employee, laborer, or servant, etc., of corporation within statute relating to liability of stockholders to that class of persons. 104 ALR 765–773.

Liability under trust-fund doctrine of subscribers of stock of corporation the charter of which has been canceled for reason other than insolvency. 71 ALR 103–106; s. in 90 ALR 1350–1355.

Preference of wages over lien creditors of corporation in hands of receiver, in absence of statutory provision therefor. 5 ALR 690–709.

Priority as between creditors and holders of preferred stock. 29 ALR 254–267.

Right to bring action against corporation, or prosecute pending action, as affected by the appointment of a receiver for the corporation. 8 ALR 441–460.

Right of creditor of corporation to maintain personal action against directors or officers for mismanagement. 50 ALR 462–473.

Validity, construction, and application of express restrictions on right of action by individual holder of one or more of a series of corporate bonds or other obligations. 108 ALR 88–133.

Transfer of property by debtor to corporation, in consideration of its stock, as a fraud on creditors. 85 ALR 133–148.

Failure to enter transfer of stock on corporate books as affecting liability of transferee for calls or assessments. 60 ALR 112–128.

Applicability of constitutional or statutory provisions relating to added liability of stockholders to holders of stock issued, or stockholders of corporations organized, before their enactment. 72 ALR 1252–1267.

Stockholder's statutory added liability as affected by death of stockholder. 79 ALR 1537–1558; s. in 96 ALR 1466–1470.

Construction, application, and effect of statutes giving corporation a lien on shares of its stockholders for debts due from stockholders to corporation. 80 ALR 1338–1359.

Liability of pledgee of stock as shareholder. 82 ALR 565–582.

Exclusiveness of statutory remedy of sale or forfeiture of stock to enforce liability for assessment. 83 ALR 892–910.

Statutory superadded liability of stockholders as affected by reorganization, consolidation, or merger of corporation. 89 ALR 770–783.

Liability of stock held by one as trustee or in other fiduciary capacity. 91 ALR 257–285; s. in 97 ALR 1250–1252; 117 ALR 653–658.

Statutory liability of stockholder of bank or other corporation as affected by change in or renewal of corporation's obligation. 97 ALR 630–643.

Right to set off liability of stockholder of insolvent corporation against corporation's debt to him. 98 ALR 647–656.

tors, the receiver representing the rights of the general creditors as well as those of the corporation and the shareholders.

CHAPTER IX

MISCELLANEOUS

§ 30. Increase or reduction of capital stock.[10] A corporation cannot lawfully increase its capital stock without legislative authorization; and if it does do so the stock thus issued is void and the right of an innocent purchaser for value of such stock is against the corporation in an action for damages.

Where a corporation lawfully increases its capital stock, each shareholder has a right to subscribe for such new stock in proportion to his present holdings so that he may retain the same proportionate interest in the corporation. By the weight of authority such right of pre-emption exists as to stock that is held in the treasury for a long time before issue.

A corporation cannot lawfully reduce its capital stock without legislative sanction. In most jurisdictions a corporation may lawfully buy back shares of its own stock if it pays for them out of surplus, provided the rights of creditors are not prejudiced; but this is not a real reduction of capital stock but is similar to the situation where these shares were authorized but not issued.

§ 31. Succession of corporations.[1] Where corporation B buys all the assets of corporation A either at an ordinary sale or at an execution sale or on foreclosure of a mortgage, or succeeds to its assets by way either of a legally authorized merger or consolidation, corporation B does not become liable for the debts of corporation A unless it assumes them; but where, upon merger or consolidation no property is left for the payment of the creditors of corporation A they may reach the assets thus transferred as property transferred in fraud of creditors.

§ 32. Foreign corporations.[2] It was formerly held that since a corporation was not a citizen within the privileges and immunities clause of the United States Constitution, a state might exclude a foreign corporation from doing

[10] 13 **Am Jur,** Corporations, §§ 182–185, 194–198.

Reduction of capital stock and distribution of capital assets upon reduction. 44 **ALR** 11–54.

Validity, construction, and effect of provisions of articles of incorporation or certificates of stock relating to redemption or retirement of stock. 88 **ALR** 1131–1148.

Construction and effect of provision for preference or redemption of preferred stock in respect of capital value. 33 **ALR** 1257–1267; s. in 124 **ALR** 1069–1077.

42 **Harv. L. R.** 516, Incorporation, Multiple Incorporation and the Conflict of Laws.

[1] 13 **Am Jur,** Corporations, §§ 1175–1203.

Liability of corporation for debts of predecessor. 15 **ALR** 1112–1193; s. in 149 **ALR** 787–824.

Constitutionality, construction, and effect of statutory or charter provisions relating to the sale of all or substantially all, of the assets of corporation or division or distribution of proceeds. 79 **ALR** 624–651.

Extension or renewal of period of corporate existence. 108 **ALR** 59–77.

Construction and effect of provisions for payment of dissenting stockholders in statutes relating to merger, consolidation, or reorganization of banks or other corporations. 87 **ALR** 597–609.

Power to require nonassenting creditors or bondholders to accept securities of, or shares in, new or reorganized corporation. 28 **ALR** 1196–1207; s. in 88 **ALR** 1238–1251.

Extraterritorial effect of confiscations of property and nationalization of corporations. 37 **ALR** 726–754; s. in 41 **ALR** 745–750; 65 **ALR** 1494–1497; 89 **ALR** 351–352; 91 **ALR** 1431–1432; 139 **ALR** 1209–1224.

[2] 23 **Am Jur,** Foreign Corporations, §§ 260–383.

Rule that in general inhibits foreign corporation which has failed to comply with conditions of doing or continuing business in state, or domestic corporation which has forfeited its charter, from maintaining action, as applicable to action at law to vindicate corporation's property rights against tort-feasor. 136 **ALR** 1160–1174.

Personal liability of stockholder, officer, or agent for debt of foreign corporation doing business in the state. 51 **ALR** 376–391.

Who, other than public official, may be served with process in action against foreign corporation doing business in state. 113 **ALR** 9–172.

business within its limits and therefore might lay down any conditions whatever to the doing of such business. But this has been modified by holding that the state may not exact the surrender of any privilege granted by the Constitution, such as the right to sue in the federal courts, the right to due process, the equal protection of the laws and the right to have the obligation of contracts remain unimpaired. But the state may discriminate between foreign and domestic corporations for tax purposes if the tax is based upon a reasonable classification; and it may insist that a resident agent be kept within the state till the statute of limitations has run on all actions arising out of business done in the state.

To the extent that a foreign corporation is doing foreign or interstate business it is not subject to local regulation because of the constitutional provision as to interstate commerce. As to intrastate business the phrase "doing business" means something "substantial and continuous in character and not merely casual or occasional." For example, it must be something more than acts which are merely preliminary to doing business such as the appointment of a resident agent; it must be something more than merely collecting debts due it and more than any isolated transaction which does not indicate continuity of purpose.

The statute usually requires, as a condition of doing business, that the foreign corporation first obtain a certificate of authority from the Secretary of State. In order to obtain this certificate it must present to the Secretary of State a statement setting forth usually the name of the corporation, the state or country of its incorporation, the place where its office within the state is to be located, the business which it proposes to do within the state, and the designation of the Secretary of State as its agent upon whom process

Constitutionality, construction, operation, and effect of retaliatory statutes against foreign corporations doing business within state. 91 **ALR** 795–817.

Character or class of claims protected by deposit by foreign corporation as condition of doing business, and rank or priority of such claims. 104 **ALR** 748–761.

Subsequent compliance with conditions of doing business in state as affecting enforceability of contract of foreign corporation made before compliance with such conditions. 75 **ALR** 446–469.

Right of foreign corporation to plead statute of limitations. 59 **ALR** 1336–1341.

Service of process upon actual agent of foreign corporation in action based on transactions outside of state. 30 **ALR** 255–292; s. in 96 **ALR** 366–375.

Statute providing for service of process upon designated state official, in action against foreign corporation, as applicable to action based on transaction outside the state. 145 **ALR** 630–667.

Foreign railway corporation as subject to service of process in state in which it merely solicits interstate business. 46 **ALR** 570–589; s. in 95 **ALR** 1478–1484.

Constitutionality, construction and effect of statute providing for service of process upon statutory agent in action against foreign corporation as regards communication to corporation of fact of service. 89 **ALR** 658–670.

Cessation by foreign corporation of business within state as affecting designation of agent for service of process. 45 **ALR** 1447–1456.

Right of foreign corporation or its assignee to maintain an action in Federal court which it could not have maintained in state court because of noncompliance with conditions of doing business in state. 133 **ALR** 1171–1186.

Right to revoke license of foreign corporation for bringing suit in, or removing suit to, Federal court. 21 **ALR** 188–193.

What constitutes doing business within state by foreign insurance corporation. 137 **ALR** 1128–1148.

Jurisdiction to garnish a debt due from a foreign corporation doing business within the state to a nonresident, arising from business outside the state. 27 **ALR** 1396–1410.

Solicitation within state of orders for goods to be shipped from other state as doing business within state within statutes prescribing conditions of doing business or providing for service of process. 60 **ALR** 994–1039; s. in 101 **ALR** 126–143; 146 **ALR** 941–966.

Soliciting subscriptions to or selling corporate stock as doing business within state. 35 **ALR** 625–637.

Jurisdiction of action or proceeding involving internal affairs of foreign corporation. 18 **ALR** 1383–1406; s. in 89 **ALR** 736–747.

Effect of domestication of foreign corporations. 18 **ALR** 130–143; s. in 126 **ALR** 1503–1525.

Power to regulate activities of foreign corporation without state as condition of its doing business within. 132 **ALR** 482–486.

may be served. The effect of noncompliance with the prescribed conditions are fixed by statute and may be either a fine imposed upon the corporation or its agent or a general liability imposed on its officers or shareholders, a prohibition against suits by the corporation in the courts of the state till the conditions have been complied with or a declaration that contracts made by the corporation shall not be enforceable till the statute has been complied with.

PARTNERSHIP

CHAPTER I

IN GENERAL

§ 1. The entity theory and the aggregate theory.[1] There are two theories as to the nature of a partnership. One is the mercantile theory that it is an entity or legal person distinct from the individuals who compose it, in much the same way that a corporation is an entity, or legal person distinct from its shareholders. A businessman who advances money to a partnership considers that he is lending it to this entity, not to the members of the firm. The other, the common law, theory, regards the partnership not as a separate entity but as the aggregate of its members.

As far as the actual decisions go, most of them can be reconciled with either theory but this is not always true. For example, where a court holds that a partnership made up entirely of infants cannot disaffirm its transactions because of infancy, this is consistent only with the entity theory. And where a court holds that a partnership is not liable for a tort committed by one of its members upon his wife, this is consistent only with the aggregate theory.

1 40 Am Jur, Partnership, § 18.

The existing statutes affecting partnerships do not follow either theory consistently. For example, the Uniform Partnership Act does not always treat a partnership as an entity but does so in permitting the holding of title to property in the partnership name; state statutes follow the entity theory in permitting a partnership to be sued in the partnership name, and so does the United States Bankruptcy Act in providing that a partnership may be adjudged a bankrupt without reference to the bankruptcy of the partners as individuals; and so does the Uniform Fraudulent Conveyance Act in making fraudulent a transfer by the partnership to a partner or partner's creditor while the partnership is insolvent.

§ 2. Test of existence of partnership.[2] A partnership has been defined as an association of two or more persons to carry on as co-owners a business for profit. If it is not conducted for profit it is not regarded as a partnership. On the other hand, the fact that it is conducted for profit and that A receives part of that profit raises a presumption that A is a partner in the business; but this presumption is rebutted by showing that A was merely a creditor who received a share of the profits in payment of a claim against the person or persons conducting the business; or that A was a business employee who received part of the profits as wages; or that A was a landlord who received part of the profits as rent for the land on which the business was conducted; or that A was a widow or representative of a deceased partner to whom an annuity is paid out of profits in consideration for the share of the deceased partner in the business; or that A was a vendor of property which he sold to the partnership, receiving a share of the profits in settlement therefor.

§ 3. Special forms of partnership.[3] In nearly all the states there are statutes permitting the formation of limited partnerships and twenty states have adopted the Uniform Limited Partnership Act. Such a partnership consists of general partners who have the same powers and duties as have members of an ordinary partnership, and limited partners who have no part in the management of the business, who share in the profits but do not share losses beyond the capital which they invest in the enterprise.

[2] 40 **Am Jur**, Partnership, §§ 32–70.
Partnership as distinguished from employment (where rights of parties inter se or their privies are concerned). 137 **ALR** 6–174.
Validity of partnership agreement between husband and wife. 20 **ALR** 1304–1317; s. in 38 **ALR** 1264.
What creates partnership relation between cotenants of property. 150 **ALR** 1003–1047.
Lease or tenancy agreement as creating partnership relationship between lessor and lessee. 131 **ALR** 508–558.
What amounts to a joint adventure. 48 **ALR** 1055–1086; s. in 138 **ALR** 968–998.
Applicability of Statute of Frauds to joint adventure or partnership to deal in real estate. 18 **ALR** 484–500; s. in 95 **ALR** 1242–1246.
Who must sign and form of signature, in case of partnership, in order to comply with statute of frauds. 114 **ALR** 1005–1010.
Liability of special partner who has withdrawn his capital, to creditors of the firm. 67 **ALR** 1096–1101.
Personal liability of member of voluntary association not organized for personal profit on contract with third person. 7 **ALR** 222–234; s. in 41 **ALR** 754–756

[3] 40 **Am Jur**, Partnership, §§ 505–518.
Co-operative marketing of farm products by producers' associations. 25 **ALR** 1113–1128; s. in 33 **ALR** 247–260; 47 **ALR** 936–956; 77 **ALR** 405–423; 98 **ALR** 1406–1421.
Liability of unincorporated labor organization to suit. 27 **ALR** 786–799; s. in 149 **ALR** 508–525.
Construction and effect of statutes as to doing business under an assumed or fictitious name or designation not showing the names of the persons interested. 45 **ALR** 198–280; s. in 59 **ALR** 455–461.
Basis of settlement between building and loan association and borrowing member during solvency of association. 98 **ALR** 6–68.
Status of holder of withdrawn, matured, prepaid, and preferred stock in building and loan association and resulting rights and liabilities. 98 **ALR** 89–134.
Right of building and loan association to transfer to third person loan made to borrowing member. 112 **ALR** 459–471

Where A, B and C form a partnership with a provision that the shares shall be transferable and that the business be managed by representatives chosen for that purpose, the organization is called a joint stock company. Each shareholder is liable personally for obligations incurred by the company while he is a shareholder and such liability continues after he transfers his share. For purposes of taxation and bankruptcy the company is usually treated as if it were a corporation.

Where a business venture is of limited scope and duration not requiring the entire attention of the persons engaged therein it is likely to be classed as a joint adventure, not a partnership. Most of the law of partnership is applicable; the associates are fiduciaries toward each other and each one represents the others within the scope of the business. But the partnership rules as to priority of creditors do not apply and the associates could not be adjudicated a bankrupt as a separate entity.

Where A, a member of the firm of A, B and Co. makes an agreement with X, a nonpartner, for the sharing of the profits and losses received by A, the relationship between A and X is called a sub-partnership. The term is misleading; X is not a partner with A because they are not carrying on any business together as co-owners. And X is not a partner with A, B and Co. because there is no partnership agreement between them. But where X is an undisclosed principal of A, furnishing all the capital contributed by A and expecting to receive all of A's share of the profits he may be held liable as partner when his identity is discovered.

Where X by words or conduct falsely represents to Y that he is a partner with A or that he is a member of the firm of A, B & Co., and in reliance thereon Y extends credit to the supposed firm of A and X or to A, B & Co., Y may hold X as if he were a partner with A or a member of the firm of A, B & Co., X being estopped to set up the truth. The same result follows if X consents to the false representation being made by someone else. Where the representation has been made publicly the presumption is that Y knew of it.

Where A, B and C attempt to organize a corporation but do not succeed even in organizing a de facto corporation the tendency is to hold them not merely liable individually for the debts of the purported corporation but liable as partners though there was no intent to form a partnership.

CHAPTER II

PARTNERSHIP PROPERTY

§ 4. Title to partnership property.[4] Whether a certain piece of property belongs to the partnership or to one or more of the partners individually is a matter for the partners themselves to decide, subject, of course, to the possibility that if individual property is represented to be partnership property and partnership creditors extend credit in reliance thereon the partners will be estopped to set up the truth.

Where, before the partnership is formed, one of the partners owned land which is later used by the firm, the presumption is that it remains individual

4 40 Am Jur, Partnership, §§ 90–112.
Partnership land as real or personal property for purposes of descent and distribution. 25 ALR 389–414.
Validity and effect of chattel mortgage on partner's interest in firm. 54 ALR 534–537.
Partition of partnership real property. 77 ALR 300–305.

property. On the other hand, the presumption is that property bought with partnership funds is partnership property.

At common law a partnership could acquire legal title to personal property in the name of the partnership. If there was a conveyance of real property to the partnership in the firm name legal title did not pass to the partnership. If the surname of one or more of the partners appeared in the partnership name legal title passed to such partner or partners, upon a resulting trust, of course, for the partnership; in some jurisdictions legal title passed to all the partners as tenants in common even if no surname of any partner appeared in the firm name. The Uniform Partnership Act expressly provides that a conveyance to the partnership in the partnership name passes legal title to the partnership and that title so acquired can be conveyed only in the firm name.

§ 5. Rights of partners, partnership creditors and separate creditors.[5] Whether the legal title to partnership property is held by the partnership as an entity or by one or more partners as trustees for the partnership, each partner is entitled, in equity, to have the partnership property applied first to pay the partnership debts, and the partnership creditors have the right—usually regarded as derivative—to insist upon this priority of application. To give the partnership creditors a prior right to partnership assets and to allow them also to share proportionally with the individual creditors in the partners' individual property would give them too great an advantage over the separate creditors; therefore, as a corollary to the priority of partnership creditors in partnership property the separate creditors are given a prior right to the individual property of the partners.

At common law a partner could assign his share in specific partnership property or it could be levied upon by his creditor subject to the right of the other partners and partnership creditors to have the property applied for partnership purposes. Under the Uniform Partnership Act a partner's right in specific partnership property is not assignable except in connection with the assignment of the rights of all the partners in the same property; and such right is not subject to attachment or execution except upon a claim against the partnership.

Upon the death of a partner the rule at common law was that the title to specific partnership personal property passed to the surviving partners for the purpose of winding up; and the legal title to his share in the partnership real property passed to his heirs or devisees subject to the rights in equity of surviving partners and partnership creditors to have it applied for partnership purposes. Under the Uniform Partnership Act the partner's right to specific partnership property, real or personal, passes to the surviving partners free from any claim by the heirs, widow or next of kin.

5 40 **Am Jur,** Partnership, §§ 399–428.

Right of individual partner to exemption in partnership property. 4 **ALR** 300–343.

Right of partnership creditor to proceed against estate of deceased partner. 61 **ALR** 1410–1441.

"Business sign" statute as affecting order of priority among creditors of person transacting business. 124 **ALR** 169–176.

Liability of incoming partner for existing debts. 45 **ALR** 1240–1323.

Right of one who accepts firm assets or obligation upon account of an individual indebtedness of, or transaction with, a partner. 50 **ALR** 432–444.

Indebtedness to partnership as subject of attachment or garnishment by creditor of individual partner. 71 **ALR** 77–91.

Relative rank of judgment, attachment, or execution based on partnership liability and judgment, attachment, or execution based on liability of individual partner. 75 **ALR** 997–1017.

§ 6. Fraudulent conveyances by partnership.[6] Unless a partnership is insolvent or will be rendered insolvent thereby, it may dispose of its property as it sees fit. In determining whether a partnership is insolvent there must be added to the value of the partnership property the value of the individual assets of each partner beyond the amount necessary to satisfy his individual debts. If the partnership is insolvent or would be rendered insolvent thereby, a conveyance of partnership property for less than its fair value is not fraudulent as to partnership creditors in those states that regard the rights of the partnership creditors as purely derivative from the rights of each partner to have partnership assets applied in payment of partnership debts; but such a transfer is regarded as fraudulent in those states which hold that the rights of partnership creditors are not purely derivative but have an independent existence and also in those states which have adopted the Uniform Partnership Act which in this respect has treated the partnership as a legal entity. Where the partnership property is conveyed to one of the partners in consideration of his promise to pay the partnership debts such promise is probably not such fair value as to render the transaction free from attack.

CHAPTER III

MANAGEMENT OF THE PARTNERSHIP ENTERPRISE

§ 7. Power of a partner to act as agent.[7] Each partner has the power to bind the other partners or—according to the entity theory—the partnership, within the scope of the partnership business, and this power is not affected by the dissent of a minority partner. The Uniform Partnership Act uses the phrase "for apparently carrying on in the usual way the business of the partnership;" the word "usual" here probably includes what is usual for the particular partnership and also what is usual for similar partnerships.

Whether borrowing money, buying or selling property and hiring employees are such partnership acts as may be done by a partner depends upon the nature of the firm business. A partner does not have implied power to bind the partnership as surety or guarantor, or to pay individual debts with firm assets or to subscribe for stock in a corporation. Where the partnership has expressly restricted the authority of a partner by forbidding him to do some usual act this restriction is effective only if the other party to the transaction knows of it.

Where the partners disagree, the majority has the power to manage the firm business; the minority must acquiesce or petition for dissolution. Where the partners are equally divided, the better view is that where this disagreement is known to third persons no new action can be taken by the partnership till the deadlock is broken. The Uniform Partnership Act has provided that less than all the partners have no authority to assign the partnership property in trust for creditors or on the assignee's promise to pay the firm debts, to dispose of the good will of the business, to do any other act which would make it impossible to carry on the ordinary business of the partner-

6 40 Am Jur, Partnership, §§ 419–425.

7 40 Am Jur, Partnership, §§ 137–189.
Admissions of partner as to past transactions or events as evidence against firm or other partner. 73 ALR 447–473.
Discharge or settlement by, or payment to, one partner or co-obligee, as affecting rights of others. 142 ALR 371–385.

ship, to confess a judgment or to submit a partnership claim or liability to arbitration or reference.

§ 8. Power of a partner to subject partnership to tort liability—admissions and notice.[8] Where a partner, acting within the scope of the partnership business, commits a tort upon X or upon X's property, X is entitled to hold liable all the members of the partnership. It is often a difficult question to determine whether the partner was acting within the scope of the business. For example, where R and W were partners in the drug business and R, without W's knowledge, concealed himself in the store to catch burglars and by mistake shot and killed X, it was held that since R's dominant purpose was to catch burglars and not to protect partnership property, W was not liable. The partnership is not liable for a tort committed by one partner upon another; and where one partner while acting within the scope of the business negligently injured his wife it was held that his immunity as husband protected the firm from liability, the court rejecting the entity theory.

The Uniform Partnership Act provides that the partnership shall be liable for the misapplication of property received by a partner from a third person.

Admissions made by a partner concerning the firm business, within the scope of his authority, are admissible against the partnership. And notice given to one partner or knowledge obtained by him as to matters relating to the business usually operates as notice to or knowledge of the partnership unless he is engaged in committing a fraud on the partnership.

CHAPTER IV

PARTNERSHIP RIGHTS AND LIABILITIES

§ 9. Enforcement of partnership rights.[9] At common law partnership rights can be enforced only by actions brought in the name of all the active, known partners; a dormant partner, like an undisclosed principal, need not but may be joined. This includes actions for trespass to partnership property, replevin for partnership chattels (by the better view), deceit causing loss to firm business, assault and battery on a partner causing loss to the business and actions for libel or slander of the partnership. In some states statutes permit actions to be brought in the partnership name.

§ 10. Enforcement of partnership liabilities.[10] At common law where X enters into a contract with a partnership, the obligation is joint and if X sues less than all of the active known partners he may be required, by a plea in abatement, to join the others; and if X should release any one partner, without reserving his rights against the others, all the others, including dormant partners, are discharged. In some states statutes have made partnership obligations joint and several; under such statutes X may maintain an action against any one partner.

At common law, where one of the partners dies, the obligation of the contract rests entirely upon the survivors, but where they are insolvent, X may proceed in equity against the estate of the deceased partner; in some states statutes permit such an action to X even where the surviving partners are solvent.

[8] 40 **Am Jur**, Partnership, §§ 190–195, 275, 276.

[9] 40 **Am Jur**, Partnership, §§ 430–433.

[10] 40 **Am Jur**, Partnership, §§ 434–438.

Where X brings his action against all the partners but is unable to get service upon all, he may—either by judicial decision or under joint debtor acts—get a judgment which is good against the partnership property and against the individual property of those served, but not against the individual property of those not served. In many states there are statutes permitting actions against the partnership in the partnership name; judgments in such actions are collectible out of partnership assets and the individual property of such partners as are served with process or appear. Other statutes provide that if a nonresident partnership does business within the state jurisdiction may be obtained by service upon a resident agent and a judgment obtained in that way may be satisfied out of the partnership property within the state; such a judgment may be sued on in another state and reach partnership property in that state.

Since tort obligations of partners are joint and several it is not necessary to sue all the partners.

CHAPTER V

RIGHTS AND DUTIES OF PARTNERS TOWARD EACH OTHER

§ 11. Repayment of contributions, sharing profits and losses—management.[1] Where the partnership agreement makes no provision as to such matters as sharing profits and losses or management or right to compensation other than profits, the rights and duties of the partners are fixed by mercantile usage.

Upon dissolution a partner who has advanced money to the partnership beyond his capital contribution is entitled to be repaid such amount, with interest, after the partnership creditors are satisfied. Next in order of repayment are the capital contributions which do not bear interest till the time when such repayment should have been made.

Unless there is an express provision that partners shall share equally in profits and losses, the share is proportional to capital contributions. If A contributes $12,000, B $8,000 and C $4,000, A's share of profits and losses is one half, B's one third and C's one sixth. But if there is a provision that they shall be equal partners, does this mean that if half the capital, i. e., $12,000, is lost, that A, B and C are each to lose one third—i. e. $4,000, A getting back $8,000, B getting back $4,000, and C nothing? Such is the provision of the Uniform Partnership Act; apart from the Uniform Partnership Act, there is a conflict of authority.

Each partner is entitled to share in the management and receives nothing for his services, but in joint stock companies the management is usually concentrated in a small group who are paid for their services.

§ 12. Partners as fiduciaries toward each other.[2] Like other fiduciaries, such as agents, trustees or executors, each partner, or the representative of a deceased partner, is liable to account to the partnership for any secret profits acquired through his status as such partner; he may not compete with the

[1] 40 **Am Jur**, Partnership, § 113–135.
Right of partners inter se in respect of interest. 66 **ALR** 3–58.
Effect of failure of party to joint adventure to contribute his share of expenses. 11 **ALR** 432–437.

[2] 40 **Am Jur**, Partnership, §§ 132–135.
Duty in respect of good faith and disclosure of information upon sale of member's interest in a partnership adventure to other member. 120 **ALR** 724–742.
Accountability of partner or joint adventurer for profits earned subsequently to death or dissolution. 80 **ALR** 12–98.

partnership, and if he secretly takes to himself a renewal of a lease on property held by the partnership, he may be held by the partnership as constructive trustee of such lease.

Each partner or the representative of a deceased partner is entitled, upon demand, to inspect the partnership books and to receive full information respecting the partnership enterprise.

§ 13. Contracts between partners.[3] Where A and B make a contract to form a partnership and B later refuses to do so A cannot get specific performance because, if no time is set for the duration of the partnership equity would not give a decree that could so easily be rendered futile; and if a time is fixed equity will not give relief because of the supervision required to make the contract effective. Unless B was already engaged in business A's remedy in special assumpsit for breach is not likely to give him substantial damages because there would be no satisfactory basis for computing the loss to A. If B has received from A any benefit under the contract A is of course entitled to recover the reasonable value thereof in quasi contract.

Where A and B form the partnership any contract made between them which does not affect the partnership—for example, if A lends money to B—is enforcible as if they were not partners. But if the contract affects the partnership—for example, if B defaults in making his contribution to the contract—A's remedy is in equity for an accounting after the partnership is dissolved; and the same is true where B wrongfully refuses to allow A to participate in management or profit.

§ 14. Contracts between the firm and a partner.[4] Where the firm of A and B enters into a contract with A which affects the partnership the proper remedy is by an accounting after dissolution. Where it is clear that the contract was not to affect partnership relations, it should be enforced just as if the contract had been made with X instead of with A; there is, of course, the difficulty that at common law the same person cannot be both a plaintiff and a defendant, but this can be obviated by either A or A and B making an assignment to Y, at least where the contract is in the form of a negotiable instrument. Similar reasoning applies to a contract between the firm of A and B and the firm of B and C.

CHAPTER VI

DISSOLUTION AND WINDING UP—BANKRUPTCY

§ 15. The various grounds for dissolution.[5] A partnership may be dissolved without breach of contract when (1) the time fixed for its duration has expired; (2) by agreement of all the partners; (3) by the election of any

[3] 40 **Am Jur**, Partnership, §§ 460-503.

Validity, construction, and effect of agreement for disposition of interest in partnership in event of death of partner. 73 **ALR** 983-1006.

Right of one partner in action at law against him by another partner on a personal claim to set up by counterclaim or otherwise claim arising out of partnership transactions. 93 **ALR** 293-300.

[4] 40 **Am Jur**, Partnership, §§ 465, 475-484.

Right to set off claim of individual partner against partnership. 5 **ALR** 1541-1552; s. in 55 **ALR** 566.

Actions at law between partners and partnerships. 21 **ALR** 21-133; s. in 58 **ALR** 621-634.

Right to set off claim of firm against indebtedness of individual partner. 27 **ALR** 112-119; s. in 60 **ALR** 584, 585.

[5] 40 **Am Jur**, Partnership, §§ 241-263.

Misconduct of or dissensions among partners or joint adventurers as ground for dissolution by court. 118 **ALR** 1421-1440.

of the partners not to continue where no time was fixed for the duration of the partnership.

The ordinary partnership, not having transferable shares, is dissolved by the death of one partner; an express agreement that in such case the business shall continue does not prevent dissolution but merely avoids the necessity of winding up the partnership affairs. Where a partner becomes bankrupt his interest in the firm passes to his assignee in bankruptcy, thus dissolving the partnership and making it necessary that its affairs be wound up; the winding up is done by the nonbankrupt partners.

Upon application by or on behalf of a partner a court may decree a dissolution where a partner has become insane or otherwise incapable of performing his part of the partnership contract, or has acted fraudulently in inducing the plaintiff to enter into the partnership, or has been guilty of such conduct that it is not practicable to continue the business, or where the business can only be carried on at a loss, or where there are other circumstances making a dissolution equitable. Where a partner has assigned his interest, his transferee is entitled to a decree of dissolution.

Where one partner has wrongfully brought about a dissolution by a breach of the partnership agreement, he is liable to the other partner or partners in an action at law for damages.

§ 16. The effect of dissolution on existing liabilities.[6] Ordinarily the dissolution of a partnership does not affect the accrued liability of any of the partners; but where the dissolution is caused by the death of a partner, an employment contract with X which involved personal relations on the part of the deceased partner is discharged.

Where the dissolution has been caused by the retirement of a partner and the business is continued by the others, the retiring partner may be discharged by a novation either express or implied from the circumstances, made between the partnership creditor, the continuing partners and the one who has retired. Where the continuing partners merely contract with the retiring partner to assume his obligations, the latter—by the Uniform Partnership Act and the better view—becomes a surety to the continuing partners, and a creditor who knows of the arrangement must treat him as such.

Where the partnership has been dissolved and the partnership business is continued by some of the partners the modern tendency is to hold that this does not terminate policies of insurance held by the partnership unless the risk has been substantially altered.

Where the dissolution has been caused by the death of a partner, his individual property remains liable for the payment of firm debts subject to the claims of his individual creditors.

§ 17. The effect of dissolution upon the powers of the partners—the winding up.[7] Unless the dissolution is due to the death of a partner and there is a provision in the partnership agreement for the continuance of the part-

[6] 40 **Am Jur,** Partnership, §§ 264–272.

Dissolution of partnership as affecting efficacy of service on single partner in action against partnership or partners before partnership affairs have been wound up. 131 **ALR** 1071–1077.

Remedy where additional assets or liabilities are discovered after settlement of partnership affairs as at law or in equity. 41 **ALR** 1454–1465.

Accountability for good will on dissolution of partnership. 44 **ALR** 517–526.

Applicability of statute of nonclaim or limitation statute as between surviving partner and estate of deceased partner. 96 **ALR** 441–449.

[7] 40 **Am Jur,** Partnership, §§ 264–284, 294, 295.

nership business by the surviving partners, a dissolution must be followed by a winding up. In the absence of statute this is done by the surviving partners. As to existing obligations not affected by the dissolution the powers of the partners to continue and complete performance remains unchanged but there is no power to bind firm property by undertaking new business. Each partner may reduce assets to cash and collect debts owing to the firm. There is no power to borrow money, but if it is borrowed and the other partners receive the benefit of it they may be held liable in quasi contract for the benefit thus received.

Each partner has the power to pay firm creditors. Where he makes a partial payment the prevailing and better view is that this starts the statute of limitations to running anew only as to himself, not as to the other partners. If a statute entrusts the winding up to the personal representative of a deceased partner or if the partners themselves choose one or more of their number to do the winding up the power of the other partners in the matter ceases.

At common law if dissolution was due to the death or bankruptcy of a partner it was effective at once without any notice to or the knowledge of other persons; but the Uniform Partnership Act in both cases requires that actual notice be given to those persons who have had dealings with the partnership and that publication in newspapers be made in order to bind those persons who knew of the partnership but not of its dissolution. This does not apply to dealings between X and the bankrupt partner because X takes the risk of the status of the person with whom he is dealing.

§ 18. Retiring and incoming partners—sale of the business.[8] Where A retires from the firm of A, B and C, he will become liable upon new partnership undertakings to persons who are not aware of his retirement unless he gives actual notice to those persons with whom the firm had been dealing and publishes in newspapers a notice of his retirement thereby binding other persons who knew of his membership in the firm but not of his retirement therefrom.

At common law where D was admitted to membership in the existing firm of A, B and C, he did not thereby become liable on old obligations of the partnership; but the Uniform Partnership Act provides that he shall become liable on such obligations to the extent of his interest in the partnership property, and he may, of course, become liable without any such limitation by a novation or by contracting with his co-partners or with a retiring partner that the old creditors shall be paid.

Where the firm of A, B and C sells out its assets and business to D or to a corporation formed by A, B and C, it is usual for the transferee to assume the firm debts and in such case the creditor as payment beneficiary may in most states enforce the contract; and where the sale is to the corporation, the majority view is that the corporation is liable without an express assumption, at least to the extent of assets received, either on the ground of an assumption implied in fact or that the conveyance is in fraud of firm creditors.

8 40 **Am Jur**, Partnership, §§ 197–232.
Liability of former partners as such in respect of transactions subsequent to incorporation of their business. 89 **ALR** 986–993.
Sale of business and "good will," or of interest in partnership and "good will," as implying restriction against competition in absence of provision in that regard. 82 **ALR** 1030–1040.

§ 19. Distribution upon winding up.[9] The assets of a partnership consist of its tangible property, the good will of the partnership business, claims against third parties and claims against the partners individually for contributions necessary for the payment of partnership obligations. Partnership obligations in the absence of express agreement otherwise, are satisfied in the following order: (1) those owing to creditors other than partners; (2) those owing to partners other than for capital and profits, such as claims for advancements; (3) those owing to partners in respect of capital; (4) those owing to partners in respect of profits.

§ 20. Adjudication of partnership as bankrupt.[10] Where the partnership is insolvent and has committed an act of bankruptcy a creditor of the partnership may file a petition under the United States Bankruptcy Act to have the partnership adjudicated a bankrupt; and this petition will be granted though one of the partners is an infant or insane, or a farmer or wage earner and hence not subject individually to involuntary bankruptcy. A petition for voluntary bankruptcy must apparently be filed by all the partners. If the entity theory were applied to the question of insolvency a partner might be adjudicated a bankrupt even though the partners themselves were individually solvent, but the present view is that a partnership is not insolvent unless all the partners are insolvent.

The act of bankruptcy must be committed by the partnership; for example, a conveyance of partnership property in fraud of partnership creditors or paying or giving security to a partnership creditor. A conveyance by a partner of his separate property in fraud of partnership creditors or as a preference to a partnership creditor is not an act of bankruptcy of the partnership.

Even if there are no bankruptcy proceedings against the partners as to their individual estates the trustee in bankruptcy of the partnership is entitled to administer the separate estate of each partner in order to produce a surplus therefrom with which to pay the partnership creditors; and this may be done though a partner, being a farmer or wage earner, is not subject to involuntary bankruptcy proceedings.

The rule that partnership creditors are entitled to priority against partnership property applies to a partnership with a dormant partner but it cannot apply unless there is an actual partnership and hence does not apply where there is only a partnership by estoppel. It a partnership creditor wishes to avoid the rule that separate creditors are entitled to priority out of separate property, he should stipulate for a joint and several obligation or for a separate undertaking by the partners individually; in such a case if both the partnership and the separate partners are thrown into bankruptcy the creditor can prove against each one. By the better view a statute making partnership obligations joint and several does not operate to permit such double proof.

A discharge in bankruptcy of the partnership does not discharge the individual partners from their separately undertaken obligations to the partnership creditor and probably does not discharge their obligations as partners to partnership creditors. Where there are bankruptcy proceedings against a partner but not against the partnership and the partner gets a discharge, this covers his obligation as partner to the partnership creditors if they had an opportunity to prove their claims.

9 40 Am Jur, Partnership, §§ 398–428.

10 6 Am Jur, Bankruptcy, §§ 32, 39, 81.

SURETYSHIP

CHAPTER I

IN GENERAL

§ 1. Terminology—construction.[1] The word "surety" is sometimes used in a very broad sense to include every case where, there being two persons who are responsible for the same burden, one of them should, either as a matter of contract or of fairness, bear the burden rather than the other. This includes the surety co-obligor on a note, the accommodation maker or indorser on a note, the accommodation drawer, acceptor or indorser on a bill of exchange, a regular indorser on a note or bill of exchange who has a right over against prior indorsers, one who contracts to indemnify or save harmless, a guarantor, a guarantor of collectibility, and the case where property insured against loss by fire is tortiously destroyed, the insurance company having a right to be subrogated as a surety to the rights of the owner against the tortfeasor.

In a narrow sense the word "surety" may be used to mean any kind of surety except a guarantor or in the still narrower sense of a surety co-obligor on a note; the obligation of the surety co-obligor is an absolute one to pay the note when due, while that of the guarantor is collateral, that is, conditional upon the default of the principal obligor.

Where a surety receives no compensation for undertaking the suretyship obligation the contract is construed strictly in his favor; but this rule does not apply to a compensated surety.

§ 2. Formation of guarantor's contract.[2] Where P (principal obligor) is contemplating buying goods at various times from C (creditor or obligee)

1 50 **Am Jur**, Suretyship, § 2.
Liability of surety company as distinguished from that of gratuitous surety. 12 **ALR** 382–390; s. in 94 **ALR** 876–885.

2 24 **Am Jur**, Guaranty, §§ 8–19, 34–39.
Who may enforce guaranty. 1 **ALR** 861–878; s. in 48 **ALR** 1041–1043.
Limitation of actions: availability of

on credit and to induce such sale G, without compensation, offers to guarantee payment by P, the offer is for a series of unilateral contracts; the offer may be revoked at any time and is revoked by G's death or at least by C's knowledge of G's death. Logically each unilateral contract comes into existence whenever C sells goods to P but in some jurisdictions it is necessary that C notify G of such sale. Where G receives compensation for his guaranty, the contract fixing the limit of G's liability, any attempted withdrawal of his guaranty before reaching the limit is, of course, a breach of his contract.

CHAPTER II

SURETY'S DEFENSES

§ 3. Statute of frauds.[3] One of the provisions of the English statute of frauds required a written memorandum in order to charge a defendant upon "any special promise to answer for the debt, default or miscarriage of another person." Similar statutes have been passed in most, if not all, the states.

The statute applies to a promise to become a surety in the future, for example, by becoming a party to a negotiable instrument. But its chief application is to guaranties. A guarantor's undertaking being one to pay C upon P's default has been construed to be a promise to answer for the debt or default of P. But there are several apparent or real exceptions. If G's contract is in form a guaranty but there is no principal obligor, it is not within the statute; for example, where C had P arrested and G orally agreed to pay P's debt to C if C would release P and thereupon C did release P, the statute of frauds did not apply because the release of P from custody discharged P's debt to C; since G was the only one liable it is obvious that he could not be a surety.

If G's undertaking is in form a guaranty but he is in substance the principal obligor the case is properly held not to be within the statute. Where C sold P a chattel for $100 payable in installments and then, having paid $25, P sold the chattel to G for $100, G paying $25 in cash and orally agreeing with P to pay to C the $75 which P still owed C, G is in substance the principal debtor and P the surety and the statute does not apply.

statute, and time when it begins to run, where one assumes and agrees to pay another's debt. 31 **ALR** 1056–1063.

Guarantor's death as terminating guaranty. 42 **ALR** 926–937.

Validity, construction, and application of guaranty of corporate stock, or dividends thereon, by one other than corporation. 107 **ALR** 1171–1188.

Language used by owner or other person interested in building or construction contract, importing a promise to pay a subcontractor, materialman, or employee of contractor or subcontractor, or one making advances to him, as a promise to answer for the debt or default of another. 99 **ALR** 79–123.

3 49 **Am Jur,** Statute of Frauds, §§ 60–72.

Statute of Frauds: validity of oral promise by stockholder to pay debt of corporation. 8 **ALR** 1198–1213; s. in 52 **ALR** 787–794; 67 **ALR** 506–509.

Statute of Frauds: warranty or guaranty in respect of the subject matter of a contract between third persons, which does in terms embrace such an obligation. 19 **ALR** 1033–1038.

Discharge of existing debt (or crediting indebtedness) as part payment which will take contract out of Statute of Frauds. 23 **ALR** 473–479.

Promise to pay another's antecedent debt in consideration of agreement to cancel it as within Statute of Frauds as a promise to pay debt, default or miscarriage of another. 74 **ALR** 1025–1039.

Promise of landlord or tenant to pay for supplies furnished to tenant or subtenant as within Statute of Frauds in relation to contracts to answer for the debt, default, or miscarriage of another. 59 **ALR** 179–185.

Oral promise to pay debt of decedent, in consideration of creditor's forgoing claim against the estate, as within provision of Statute of Frauds relating to contract to answer for debt of another. 144 **ALR** 1110–1116.

Promise by other than the principal to indemnify a surety, as one to answer for the debt, default, or miscarriage of another. 1 **ALR** 383–392; s. in 68 **ALR** 347–350.

41 **Harv. L. R.** 689, Contracts of Indemnity and the Statute of Frauds.

Where G holds a note against P for $200 and sells and assigns the note to C for $190 orally guaranteeing to C that P will pay the note at maturity, G is a guarantor both in form and substance and logically the case should be held to be within the statute, C's proper remedy being in quasi contract to get back the $190 received by G if G refused to make his oral guaranty good. The cases hold, however, that because of the benefit received by G from C, G's oral promise is not within the statute and that C may recover the full $200 from G in special assumpsit for breach of his oral contract. And the same decision has been reached where the benefit to G has been much less concrete than the receipt of money or other property; for example, getting ore transported from P's mine to G's furnace, G being already entitled to such ore by his contract with P.

It is sometimes said, in support of these decisions, that the promise, to come within the statute, must have been made to the creditor, not to the debtor, but there is no hint of such a limitation in the statute and in most jurisdictions the creditor may recover as payment beneficiary on a promise made to the debtor. It is also sometimes said that the statute should not apply where the guaranty was merely incidental to another transaction—the "main purpose" argument—for example, the transfer of the note from G to D; but here again there is no trace in the statute of any such limitation.

Where G's oral promise to C is to pay P's debt to C out of money or property belonging to P which is in G's hands the guaranty is properly held not to be within the statute because G is not undertaking any obligation to pay out of his own pocket and hence the case is not within the evils at which the statute was aimed.

Where P in order to induce S to become surety for him to C, orally promises P to indemnify him against loss the promise is held not to be within the statute, because even without such a promise P would be bound to exonerate S. But where S, about to become surety for P on a bond to C, induces X to become co-surety with him by orally agreeing to indemnify him against loss the above reasoning does not apply because S's obligation to X apart from his promise is merely to contribute his share with X in case P defaults. Logically, therefore, S's promise should be held to be within the statute, but by the weight of authority it has been held otherwise. Sometimes this is put on the ground that the statute does not apply to any promise to indemnify; it might be put on the ground that it is a promise made to a prospective debtor but X is also a prospective creditor, so probably the best argument in support of the majority view is that there is no great likelihood of perjury in such a case.

A del credere agent is one who undertakes to sell goods on commission and in consideration of extra compensation promises to become responsible for the purchase price in case of a sale. It is well settled that such a promise is not within the statute. This is sometimes put on the ground that since the principal may recover against him in indebitatus assumpsit for the price as purchaser and need not bring the special assumpsit which must be brought against guarantors, the obligation of the del credere agent is not a guaranty at all but an independent, unconditional undertaking. Sometimes it is put on the ground that the promise is merely incidental to the promise to sell on commission and sometimes on the ground that the danger of perjury in such cases is slight.

The memorandum necessary to satisfy the statute must contain a statement of the promise and of the parties but there is a conflict of authority as to whether the consideration must be stated; by the better view it need not be unless the consideration has not yet been performed.

§ 4. **Defect in P's obligation.**[4] Where P and S execute a promissory note to C, the fact that P was insane or that P was a corporation and the giving of the note was an ultra vires act is no defense to S. It would seem that the same reasoning should apply where P was an infant, but the weight of authority is that if the infant disaffirms and returns to C what he has received S is discharged in spite of the fact that it may have been P's infancy that caused C to require a surety. S may not set up usury; and the bankruptcy of P does not release S.

Where C has been guilty of fraud in inducing P to contract with him and S becomes surety without knowledge of such fraud, the better view and weight of authority is that S is discharged because C's concealment of the fraud on P is a fraud on S himself and also because C by his fraud has rendered valueless S's right to be subrogated to C's rights against P. The minority view is that the defense of fraud is personal to P and unless he sets it up it is no defense to S.

Where S signs an instrument as surety and the instrument shows that P was expected to sign it as principal but P does not sign it, the weight of authority is that S is discharged unless P is liable to C as principal in some other way, for example, on a separate contract, because, in the latter case, S's rights against P are substantially the same as if he had signed.

Where P's name is on the instrument but his signature has been forged by X or placed there by X without authority, S is discharged; the same reasoning is not applied where it is the signature of a co-surety that has been forged.

§ 5. **Extinguishment or suspension of P's obligation.**[5] It is well settled that if C unconditionally releases P without S's consent, this discharges S also, unless he has been indemnified by P. The reason usually given is that such a release destroys the value of S's right of subrogation against P; and this reasoning applies where C voluntarily enters into a composition agreement with other creditors to discharge P, but not to a discharge of P in bankruptcy because that does not involve any act of C. Where C releases P, reserving his rights against S, the courts, in order to give effect to the reservation, construe the release as a covenant never to sue and construe the reservation of rights against S as reserving all of S's rights against P; hence since S's position is not impaired in any way he is not discharged. The

[4] 50 **Am Jur**, Suretyship, §§ 141–152.
Incapacity of principal to contract as affecting liability of guarantor or surety. 24 **ALR** 838–850; s. in 43 **ALR** 589, 590.

[5] 50 **Am Jur**, Suretyship. §§ 58–78, 126–129.
Remission or waiver of part of principal's obligation as releasing surety or guarantor. 121 **ALR** 1014–1022.
Release of mortgagor (or intermediate grantee who has assumed the mortgage) by subsequent dealings between his grantee and mortgagee. 41 **ALR** 277–314; s. in 72 **ALR** 389–400; 81 **ALR** 1016–1061; 112 **ALR** 1324–1345.
Acceptance of interest in advance as consideration for, or evidence of, an extension of time which will release a guarantor, surety, or indorser. 59 **ALR** 988–1015.
Construction and effect of anticipatory agreement by indorser or surety consenting to extension or extensions of time or waiving objection thereto. 94 **ALR** 1447–1459.
Extension of time for payment of obligation or agreement to forgo enforcement thereof as consideration for a new promise by a third person as affected by nonenforceability of the obligation at time extension or agreement was made. 114 **ALR** 1203–1210.
Creditor's reservation of rights against surety in releasing or extending time to principal debtor. 139 **ALR** 85–126.
50 **Yale L. J.** 387, Discharge of Latent Sureties on Negotiable Instruments Because of Release or Extension of Time.
15 **U. of Cin. L. R.** 58, Extension Agreements in the "Subject-To" Mortgage Situation.

above reasoning also applies where C releases a surety; if absolute the co-surety is released, but not if C reserves his rights against the co-surety.

Payment by P ordinarily discharges S; but if it was made within four months of P's bankruptcy and C is compelled to return it, S remains liable unless C at the time that he accepted payment knew of P's insolvency.

Legal tender of payment by either P or S discharges S because S's undertaking is that C shall be paid and if he refuses a tender his failure to receive payment is his own fault.

Where C contracts to extend time to P without S's consent this discharges S unless he has been indemnified by P, because it suspends and therefore impairs his right of subrogation; but if C reserves his rights against S, this is construed as reserving S's rights against P and S is not discharged. S is also not discharged if the contract for extension of time was obtained by fraud because in such case C would not be bound by the contract. S is likewise not discharged if he did not know of the suretyship relation; and recently there has been a tendency not to discharge a compensated surety where the extension of time was made in good faith and not in excess of reasonable, customary credit unless S was damaged thereby.

Where C sues P and P wins on the merits, this operates to discharge S; where C wins and then sues S, the weight of authority is that the judgment against P is prima facie evidence against S but in some jurisdictions it has no weight at all and in others it is conclusive against S.

It is no defense to S, in whose favor the statute of limitations has not run because of absence from the state, that C has allowed the statute to run in favor of P; but payments made by P do not set the statute to running again as to S.

§ 6. Surrender or loss of security rights by C.[6] Where C has in his hands securities for P's performance, for example, a mortgage or pledge or judgment lien, and he releases them without S's consent, S is discharged to the extent of the value of the securities thus released even if S did not know of their existence. The same reasoning applies if C levies upon the securities held by him to satisfy a claim against P for which S was not surety, or if he exchanges securities held by him for some of less value.

Ordinarily S is not released by mere inaction of C; for example, failure to sell a depreciating security even after maturity of the debt, failure to insure the property or to redeem it from a prior incumbrance; but where the burden is slight, as where he fails to record a mortgage given by P, so that the property is lost to a bona fide purchaser for value without notice, S is discharged pro tanto.

Where a construction contract provides that P shall be paid as the work progresses but that C shall retain a certain percentage of the amount due as security for further performance by P and C fails to make such retention, the modern rule is that a compensated surety is discharged only to the extent of damage done to him by C's premature payment; the earlier cases, where S was not compensated, gave him a complete discharge.

§ 7. Claims held by P against C.[7] If C sues P and S together and P has a claim against C which he might use in his defense S may also avail himself of P's claim.

If C sues S alone, the weight of authority is that S may not use any claim

[6] 50 **Am Jur,** Suretyship, §§ 109–120. [7] 50 **Am Jur,** Suretyship, § 138.

which P has against C without P's consent. This is sometimes put on the ground that P has a right to determine whether to use his claim defensively or in a separate action against C. In view of P's obligation to pay C's claim and save S harmless the reasoning does not seem conclusive and the hardship on S is especially great, if P is insolvent; it would seem fairer to regard such a claim as a security held by C of which S may avail himself. Furthermore, where P's claim against C arises out of the same transaction, for example, a claim for breach of warranty of the quality of the goods sold by C to P, it is arguable that S should be totally discharged because by C's breach of warranty he has made it less likely that P will perform; but if any discharge is allowed to S it is only to the extent of the damage suffered by him because of C's breach of warranty.

§ 8. Other defenses.[8] Where, without S's consent, C does an act which varies S's risk, for example, where C and P enter into a new agreement in substitution for the old, S is totally discharged. So, where S undertook to answer for P's performing his duties as bookkeeper and C required him to act also as teller so that he could not and did not properly perform his duties as bookkeeper; and where P was employed to sell on commission and C required him to extend credit freely in the hope of increasing the business, S was held discharged.

Where C is a bank and when P's note payable there becomes due P has sufficient funds on deposit to meet the note, S is discharged if C fails thus to apply the funds. But if the funds are not sufficient, C is not bound to apply pro tanto or to apply deposits made later.

Where, when S becomes surety, C knows that P has been guilty of fraudulent conduct, and fails to disclose such fact, S is discharged; for example, where C accepted S's bond guaranteeing faithful performance of P as employee of C, and C knew that P had misappropriated funds belonging to himself. But C need not tell S that P has merely been dilatory in making remittances or is insolvent, unless S asks for information in regard to such matters. Similar reasoning applies where, after P enters upon the performance of his

[8] 50 **Am Jur,** Suretyship, §§ 40–57, 82–96, 163–171.

Duty of employer to notify surety that employee was dilatory, slow, or negligent in settling account. 60 **ALR** 160–166.

Extrajudicial admissions by principal as evidence against surety. 60 **ALR** 1500–1547.

Obligee's concealment of facts or evasive answers as fraud against surety. 8 **ALR** 1485–1508.

Language or purport of notice to proceed against principal, noncompliance with which will relieve surety. 30 **ALR** 1285–1299.

Surety's liability as affected by the addition, without surety's knowledge or consent, of the personal obligation of a third person. 144 **ALR** 1266–1278.

Right of surety on bond of trustee, executor, administrator, or guardian to terminate liability as regards future defaults of principal. 118 **ALR** 1261–1276; s. in 150 **ALR** 485–490.

Misrepresentations by principal obligor to surety or guarantor as affecting obligee. 71 **ALR** 1278–1287.

Liability on bond of public official or employee as affected by change in principal's duties. 94 **ALR** 613–628.

Liability of sureties on bond of executor or administrator in respect of property or funds not assets of estate coming into hands of principal. 104 **ALR** 180–209.

Liability of sureties as affected by actual, constructive, or asserted transfer of property or funds by fiduciary acting in one capacity to himself acting in another capacity. 111 **ALR** 267–305.

Payments or advancements to building contractor by obligee as affecting rights as between obligee and surety on contractor's bond. 127 **ALR** 10–84.

Accounting by guardian, executor, administrator, or trustee as a necessary condition of action on his bond. 119 **ALR** 83–123.

Validity, construction, and application of provision of fidelity bond as to giving of notice of loss or claim within specified time after close of bond year. 149 **ALR** 945–964.

Bail: stage of proceeding at which sureties are discharged in criminal case. 20 **ALR** 594–639.

Liability of sureties on bond of guardian, executor, administrator, or trustee for defalcation or deficit occurring before bond was given. 82 **ALR** 585–600.

contract with C; when the latter discovers that P is dishonest C must notify S. But when P's default consists merely in failing to complete a building on time, S is discharged only to the extent that the delay caused damage to him.

Where S has offered to guarantee that P will pay for goods to be purchased at various times from C, the better view is that where S would not ordinarily find out whether the goods had been furnished, C is under a duty to notify him of such fact.

The great weight of authority is that C is under no obligation to S to sue P before proceeding against S; but in some states, either by decision or statute, C must sue P if S requests him to do so and if C fails to sue or to prosecute the suit with due diligence, S will be discharged to the extent of the resulting loss.

If a note is signed by P under duress, S, who signed as comaker, may set it up.

CHAPTER III

RIGHTS OF THE SURETY AND OF THE CREDITOR

§ 9. Subrogation.[9] After C has been paid in full, either wholly by S or partly by S and partly by P, S is entitled, in equity, to compel C to assign

[9] 50 **Am Jur,** Subrogation, §§ 2–132.

Payment of entire claim of third person as condition of subrogation. 9 **ALR** 1596–1610; s. in 32 **ALR** 568, 569; 46 **ALR** 857; 53 **ALR** 304–306; 91 ALR 855–863.

Right of surety who discharges obligation due to government to be subrogated to priority or preference of latter. 24 **ALR** 1502–1519; s. in 83 **ALR** 1131–1137.

Right of surety who discharges obligation due to government, to be subrogated to rights of latter against third persons. 24 **ALR** 1523–1530.

Subrogation of insurer to insured's rights against the carrier where shipping contract provides that carrier shall have benefit of insurance. 39 **ALR** 1116–1125.

Right of building contractor's surety who completes contract to moneys earned by contractor but unpaid before default. 45 **ALR** 379–388; s. in 134 **ALR** 738–747.

Right of insurer which has paid loss, as against the insured who has released or settled with third person responsible for the loss. 36 **ALR** 1267–1280; s. in 55 **ALR** 926–928.

Right of subrogation of fiduciary's surety to claim of the estate against third person who knew or was chargeable with notice that fiduciary's transaction with him involved breach of fiduciary's obligation. 134 **ALR** 997–1006.

Surety's right to be subrogated to obligee's right against third person as affected by equities in favor of latter which are insufficient to prevent his liability to obligee. 137 **ALR** 700–713.

Right of insurer, in absence of subrogation clause, to be subrogated to claim of mortgagee (or conditional vendor) to whom it paid loss, under loss-payable or mortgagee clause, after policy had been canceled as against insured or had become unenforceable by him. 146 **ALR** 442–448.

Proper party plaintiff to action against tort-feasor for damage to insured property where insurer is entitled to subrogation to extent of loss paid by it. 96 **ALR** 864–889.

Right of subrogation in respect of encumbrances paid by third person under mistake or in order to protect his interest in property as affected by Statute of Limitations or laches. 103 **ALR** 1182–1186.

Scope and extent of subrogation in favor of one entitled to be subrogated to mortgage lien. 107 **ALR** 785–792.

Claim of obligee or surety on supersedeas bond, or other bond given in course of litigation, as entitled to preference over mortgage bondholders of railroad or other corporation. 113 **ALR** 494–505.

Surrender of principal by sureties on bail bond. 3 **ALR** 180–198; s. in 73 **ALR** 1369–1376.

Right of one who pays taxes for which another is bound, to subrogation to the right of the taxing power. 61 **ALR** 587–615; s. in 106 **ALR** 1212–1227.

Rights and remedies incident to subrogation to one but not both elements of a single cause of action for injury to person and damage to property. 140 **ALR** 1241–1249.

Rights and liabilities as between sureties on successive bonds given in course of litigation. 117 **ALR** 583–599.

Subrogation to prior lien of one who advances money to discharge it and takes new mortgage, as against intervening lienor. 70 **ALR** 1396–1426.

Right of surety or guarantor who pays judgment to preservation thereof as against his cosureties or coguarantors. 71 **ALR** 300–310.

Right of surety on supersedeas or appeal bond to subrogation. 77 **ALR** 452–465.

Right and remedy of mortgagee who for the protection of his security pays taxes on, or redeems from tax sale of, mortgaged property. 84 **ALR** 1366–1400; s. in 123 **ALR** 1248–1266.

Right of principal, cosureties, or coguarantors to benefit of discount at which an obligation is purchased or discharged by a surety or guarantor. 118 **ALR** 416–422.

to him the claim itself and all the securities which C has received from P or from co-sureties, the latter being liable to S only for their pro rata share.

The basis of equity jurisdiction here is substantially that of constructive trust: since C has been fully paid he is not entitled to enforce the claim or the securities for his own benefit; since P has not paid he is not entitled to have the claim or the securities delivered up and cancelled; S, who has paid, has, therefore, the best right to them even though he did not bargain for the right and did not know that any securities were being held.

The right does not arise till after C has been paid in full because it might embarrass P if S could compel a part assignment of C's claim and it would be unfair to C to allow S, who has paid only a part, to compete with him. Nor does it arise where, even though S has paid all that he agreed to pay, it would be unfair to C; for example, where P bought land from C for $3,000, payable in three equal annual installments, and S became surety on the note first due, S is not entitled till C has been paid all the notes.

Anyone who stands in the position of surety, using that term in the broadest sense, is entitled to subrogation. It is not necessary that P know of S's existence and a fire insurance company which has paid a fire loss is entitled to be subrogated to the right of the insured to recover against the tort-feasor responsible for the loss.

The rights to which S may be subrogated include a mortgage, pledge or lien of any sort, the right to collect attorney's fees upon a note, the right to confess judgment against P, the right to trace trust funds, and the right, where C is the state, to the state's priority over the other creditors of P.

In some jurisdictions by statute, a surety who pays is entitled, without bringing a suit in equity against C, to sue P or a cosurety as assignee of C. Even without such a statute the better view is that S is not barred by the statute of limitations in enforcing, as assignee of C, his claim against P or against the co-surety unless C himself would have been barred.

§ 10. **Reimbursement.**[10] In addition to the equitable right to the assignment of all C's rights against P as soon as the entire debt has been paid, S has also the right to proceed directly against P for reimbursement as soon as he has paid any part of the debt. This right was first recognized in equity, but later the common-law courts allowed an action for money paid to the defendant's use. This right was at first regarded as quasi-contractual, to prevent P from being unjustly enriched at S's expense; but later the right became so well settled and understood that wherever S became surety at P's request or with his consent, it became a contract right arising at the moment S became bound though of course no cause of action arose till S paid some of the debt. Where S becomes surety without the consent of P the right still remains quasi-contractual as where C pays S to guarantee the performance of P's obligation to C. It is also quasi-contractual where a morally innocent tort-feasor recovers reimbursement from his joint tort-feasor who is not morally innocent.

Though the doctrine has been much criticised as being too liberal to S, it

10 50 **Am Jur**, Suretyship, §§ 221–232.
Liability of contractor and contractee inter se in respect of damages paid to third persons for injuries sustained during the progress of the stipulated work. 38 **ALR** 566–591.
Construction and application of contractual provision regarding payment by surety of claim as evidence of principal's liability to surety ("conclusive evidence" clause). 144 **ALR** 521–528.

has been held that where C accepts S's note in full satisfaction of the debt, S may at once recover from P without paying the note.

Where the statute of limitations has run against C in favor of P but not in favor of S, for example, because S has been absent from the state, and S pays, he is entitled to reimbursement from P because S was bound to pay. And in the converse case, where C is barred as to S but not as to P it has been held that if S pays he may recover from P, it being regarded as a proper payment, and the same reasoning has been applied where S has been discharged by C's contract to extend time to P. But if C is barred as to both P and S and S pays he is not entitled to reimbursement.

§ **11. Contribution.**[1] In addition to the equitable right of S to stand in C's shoes as to all of C's rights against the co-sureties, S has a direct right to compel contribution from them as soon as he has paid more than his share of the debt, to the extent of the excess beyond his share. Like reimbursement, it was at first recognized in equity and then later at law, being quasi-contractual except where S became surety at the request of or with the consent of the cosurety. The equitable remedy is frequently more advantageous because he may join the co-sureties in one suit—which he cannot do at law—and may recover according to the number of solvent sureties within the jurisdiction while at law he can recover only the proportion fixed by the number of sureties who became liable.

In order to be entitled to contribution it is not necessary that the sureties should have signed the same instrument or should have known of each other; it is usually enough that they should be equally liable for the same burden though not necessarily in equal shares. Where S and X both sign an instrument as sureties for P but X agrees with S to save him harmless, S becomes a subsurety and if he pays his right against X it is not merely for contribution but for reimbursement.

Except that the statute of limitations does not begin to run against a surety till he has paid more than his share, the reasoning applied to the running of the statute as to S's right of reimbursement against P applies also as to the running of S's right of contribution against his cosureties. The better doctrine is that S's partial payment does not set the statute to running anew as to C's right against the cosureties.

Where S has received securities from P he must account for them in any action for contribution; but this does not apply to securities received from another.

The better view and the tendency of the authorities is to allow contribution between joint tort-feasors who are morally innocent, for example, between partners who are liable for an unauthorized tort committed by an employee of the firm.

[1] 13 **Am Jur**, Contribution, §§ 3–15.

Necessity of express agreement between indorsers to be jointly and not successively liable, in order to give a right of contribution as between themselves. 11 **ALR** 1332–1337; s. in 90 **ALR** 305–308.

Proportion of obligation enforceable by way of contribution between joint obligors. 64 **ALR** 213–238.

Oral agreement between joint obligors as to extent of liability inter se. 65 **ALR** 822–832.

Right to contribution or indemnity of executor, administrator, guardian, testamentary trustee, or sureties against a cofiduciary or sureties, in respect of losses or defaults for which the fiduciaries are answerable. 66 **ALR** 1147–1154.

Rights of coparties against whom judgment has been rendered to contribution or indemnity as affected by statute providing that under certain conditions judgment shall remain in effect for benefit of party who pays it, or more than his share thereof. 114 **ALR** 178–181.

§ 12. Exoneration.[2] In order that S be entitled to subrogation, reimbursement or contribution, he must have paid, either all or part of the debt. If S has plenty of ready money with which to do this these remedies are ordinarily adequate; but where he does not have the ready money and would suffer irreparable damage by being compelled to raise the money by a sale or incumbrance of his own property or by withdrawing it from his business, these remedies are not adequate and he is therefore entitled, in equity, to a decree against P that he exonerate S entirely from having to pay and to a decree against his cosureties that they exonerate him except as to his own share, the decrees being enforcible by being levied against the property of P and the cosureties respectively. The right arises as soon as C's claim is due; S need not wait till he is sued. And while the inadequacy of S's other remedies was the reason for recognizing his right to exoneration, he need not allege or prove such inadequacy today.

The enforcement of the right must not in any way hinder or embarrass C; he may, notwithstanding S's suit for exoneration, proceed to judgment and execution against him; hence realization upon the right is dependent upon the inaction of C against S.

The right is sometimes placed upon quia timet grounds; and where there is an actual contract to exonerate and S's other remedies are inadequate it is properly based upon the specific performance of contracts.

§ 13. C's right to S's securities.[3] The court in the early English case of Maure v. Harrison (1692) 1 Eq. Abrdg. Cases 94, 21 Eng. Reprint 904, laid down the rule, by way of dictum, that C is entitled, in equity, to have any securities given by P to S applied in payment of the debt, but the dictum was later repudiated in England. In this country, in spite of the fact that there is no satisfactory basis for the doctrine, it represents the weight of authority. Of course, if P creates a trust for C there is no reason why this should not be enforced, but merely placing securities in S's hands does not show any intent to create a trust. Even where C's right is recognized, he cannot complain if, before he takes any steps to assert his right, S in good faith releases or impairs the securities turned over to him.

2 50 Am Jur, Suretyship, §§ 44, 225–229.

3 50 Am Jur, Suretyship, §§ 177–182.

MORTGAGES

CHAPTER I

IN GENERAL—ELEMENTS OF THE MORTGAGE

§ 1. The mortgage at common law and in equity.[1] Since the fifteenth century a mortgage at common law has been, in form, a conveyance of the legal title upon a condition subsequent; if the mortgagor should on a certain day do some act—usually pay a certain sum of money—the conveyance was to be void; if he should fail to meet the condition the conveyance would become absolute and the land would belong unconditionally to the mortgagee.

Where through accident or other unexpected misfortune the mortgagor was unable to pay on the day but was able to pay later and the amount of the mortgage debt was much less than the value of the land the hardship on the mortgagor was so great that the English equity court interfered to prevent such a forfeiture by insisting that since the substance of the transaction was that the mortgagee should hold the land as security for the mortgage debt the mortgagee was under an equitable obligation to reconvey the title to the mortgagor upon payment, after the day, of the mortgage debt with interest; and this right could be destroyed only by foreclosure proceedings brought by the mortgagee. This right of the mortgagor to get back his land upon payment after the day came to be called his equity of redemption, a term which is in common use today to describe generally the mortgagor's right whether it is recognized and enforced in equity or at law.

§ 2. The title theory and the lien theory.[2] In a majority of states the treatment accorded to mortgages by equity courts has prevailed to such an extent that in spite of the express words of the mortgage the mortgagee is consid-

[1] 36 **Am Jur**, Mortgages, §§ 2, 12.
Validity and construction of statute allowing penalty and damages against mortgagee refusing to discharge mortgage on real property. 56 **ALR** 335–348.
4 **Harv. L. R.** 1, The Story of Mortgage Law.
92 **U. of Pa. L. R.** 179, The Common Law Mortgage and the Conditional Bond.
92 **U. of Pa. L. R.** 53, Mortgage Moratoria since 1933.
12 **Brooklyn L. R.** 103, Rights of Mortgagees in Condemnation Proceedings.
17 **Temple U. L. Q.** 315, Developments in Mortgage Law and Practice.

[2] 37 **Am Jur**, Mortgages, § 917.

ered as not having the legal title but only a legal lien, the legal title and right to possession remaining in the mortgagor till after sale upon foreclosure. One important result of this is that in states following the lien theory the mortgagee cannot enter and avail himself of the rents and profits of the land; but if the mortgagee is allowed by the mortgagor to take possession he must apply the rents and profits to the payment of the mortgage debt.

In states which still hold the title theory a mortgagor who is allowed by the mortgagee to remain in possession may—on the strength of that possession—recover in trespass or ejectment against a third party. In those states, if the mortgagee wishes to assign the legal right to the mortgage he must make a formal conveyance of the land, whereas in lien states a transfer of the mortgage debt apparently carries with it the legal right to the lien of the mortgage. In title states only a tender of payment on the day will discharge the mortgage debt and place title back in the mortgagor, while in most lien states a mere temporary tender after the day will discharge the lien; in other lien states such a tender will not discharge the debt unless the tender is kept good because of the hardship on the mortgagee in compelling him at his peril—on a day when he is not expecting payment—to determine whether the amount tendered is correct. In any event the mortgagor is not entitled to have the mortgage cancelled of record unless he makes a permanent tender of the amount due, depositing the amount in a bank subject to the order of the mortgagee and then paying it to the clerk of court as soon as suit is brought.

§ 3. Absolute conveyance by way of security—deeds of trust.[3] After equity interfered to create the equity of redemption money lenders sought to evade the necessity of foreclosure by requiring the borrower to make an absolute conveyance of the legal title, the defeasance clause being in a separate instrument, but courts of equity held that any conveyance by way of security was in substance a mortgage, the grantor having the right to redeem even if there was no separate instrument with a defeasance clause but merely an oral agreement or an unexpressed understanding that reconveyance was to be made upon payment of the mortgage debt. If the conveyance was not by way of security the promise to reconvey must be in writing to satisfy the statute of frauds. Similar treatment was accorded to deeds of trust used as a means of providing security to the lender.

§ 4. After-acquired property—equitable mortgages—future advances.[4] Where a mortgage is given of crops to be raised on the mortgagor's land—especially if they have been planted—or of wool to be grown on the mortgagor's sheep, or of the future offspring of his animals, either title or a legal lien passes to the mortgagee as soon as the property comes into existence.

[3] 36 **Am Jur**, Mortgages, §§ 16–31.

Value of property as factor in determining whether deed intended as mortgage. 90 **ALR** 953–967.

Exemption to rule of admissibility of parol evidence to show that deed absolute on its face was intended as a mortgage. 111 **ALR** 448–462.

Lapse of time as affecting rights and remedies of parties to absolute deed intended as mortgage. 28 **ALR** 554–582.

Change of deed intended as mortgage by subsequent agreement into an absolute deed. 65 **ALR** 771–780.

Deed absolute on its face, with contemporaneous agreement or option for repurchase by grantor, as a mortgage vel non. 79 **ALR** 937–958.

Duty and liability of trustee under mortgage or deed of trust to holders of bonds, or other obligations secured thereby. 57 **ALR** 468–483; s. in 71 **ALR** 1413–1417.

Removal, substitution, and succession of trustee under deed of trust or mortgage securing bonds or other obligations. 98 **ALR** 1132–1181.

[4] 36 **Am Jur**, Mortgages, §§ 13, 33, 63–67, 82–85.

But where the mortgagor undertakes to mortgage property to be later acquired to which this doctrine of potential existence does not apply, the mortgagee gets an equitable right to such property as soon as it is acquired by the mortgagor whether by sale or gift or inheritance, the equitable right being based upon the right to specific performance of contracts to give security on definite property. This doctrine of equitable mortgages has also been applied to an attempted legal mortgage which has been defectively executed and to contracts by which the debtor in terms agrees to give as security a mortgage on property which he now has or which he expects to acquire in the future. Where the debtor undertakes to mortgage a shifting stock of goods the weight of authority is that even if such a mortgage is recorded it is void as to the mortgagor's creditors because of the power of sale reserved in the mortgage.

In England an owner of land may create an equitable mortgage on his land by depositing his title deeds as security; but in this country, because of our recording acts the possession of title deeds is of almost no importance so an equitable mortgage cannot be created in that way.

If in the mortgage transaction the mortgagee contracts to make future advances and the mortgage is recorded he is protected as to such advances against any subsequent purchaser, mortgagee or creditor. But if the mortgage merely provides that the mortgage shall be security for any advances which the mortgagee may make then he is not protected as to such advances against any intervening mortgage or other lien of which he has actual notice; but he is not bound by merely record notice of such intervening lien.

§ 5. The mortgage debt.[5] Though a mortgage may be executed by way of gift it is nearly always given to secure a debt either of the mortgagor or of another. The debt is usually evidenced by a note or bond; if there is a good defense to the note or bond such as usury, fraud, mistake, lack or failure of consideration, the mortgage cannot ordinarily be enforced; nor can it be enforced for any greater amount than the mortgage debt though the note or bond may call for more. Ordinarily the mortgagee may sue on the note or bond and at the same time bring a suit to foreclose the mortgage though of course he is entitled to only one satisfaction; and the fact that the statute of limitations has barred the remedy on the note or bond does not operate to bar the remedy on the mortgage.

§ 6. Transfer by the mortgagee.[6] If the mortgagee assigns the note or bond without assigning the mortgage the assignee is entitled to an assignment of the mortgage even though he did not know of its existence. This is because he is the one best entitled to it, the mortgagee not being able to enforce it because he no longer owns the note or bond it was given to secure, and the mortgagor not being entitled to have it delivered up and canceled because he has not paid the mortgage debt.

In lien states if the mortgagee assigns the mortgage without assigning the note or bond the assignee is not entitled to an assignment of the note or bond unless such transfer was omitted by mistake, in which case the assignee is

5 36 **Am Jur**, Mortgages, §§ 57–77.

Union of title to mortgage and fee in the same person as affecting right to personal judgment for mortgage debt. 95 **ALR** 89–111.

50 **Yale L. J.** 224, Creation and Effect of Personal Liability on Mortgage Debts in New York.

6 37 **Am Jur**, Mortgages, §§ 1202–1219, 1241–1262.

27 **Va L. R.** 853; 28 **Va. L. R.** 445, Purchasing Subject to Mortgage.

entitled in equity to have the transaction reformed so as to include the transfer of the note or bond. He is not entitled to foreclose the mortgage without producing the note or bond in court. If the note or bond is assigned to A and then the mortgage to Y the latter gets nothing.

In title states a transfer of the land by the mortgagee in possession entitles the transferee to an assignment of both note and mortgage.

§ 7. Transfer by the mortgagor—marshalling.[7] If A the mortgagor transfers to X his equity of redemption in the land warranting the land to be free from incumbrances the mortgagee may still recover against A on the note or bond and also foreclose his mortgage but the land occupies the position of a surety to A. If the transfer was subject to the mortgage the amount of the mortgage debt being deducted from the purchase price the land becomes the primary debtor and A becomes the surety; but if X assumes the payment of the mortgage debt the mortgagee may, in most states, recover as payment beneficiary against X who becomes the primary debtor, A being the surety, and entitled to a decree of exoneration against X. The mortgagee may also, of course, foreclose the mortgage.

If A the mortgagor conveys a part of the land to X and X assumes the mortgage debt he becomes the primary debtor and A becomes a surety. If X assumes a part of the mortgage debt contribution will be enforced between them on that basis. Usually, however, X will pay part of the purchase price to the mortgagee and secure a release from the mortgage. If X pays the full value of the land purchased to A and—usually because of ignorance or negligence—does not get a release, X stands in the position of a surety to A and can insist upon the part of the land retained by A being applied first to the payment of the mortgage debt in exoneration of the piece which he purchased.

Where A, after selling part of the land to X, sells and conveys another part to Y who also pays full value without getting a release, he takes his part subject to X's equity that the part retained shall be the primary fund, so in such case his part will be applied to the payment of the mortgage debt before the part purchased by X. This sale in inverse order of alienation is a rule of equity and should not be applied in any case where it would work unfairly.

§ 8. Rights and duties of mortgagee and mortgagor.[8] A mortgagee in possession is liable for any waste which he may commit and is entitled to be reimbursed for any expenses incurred in keeping the premises in reasonable repair. In title states a mortgagor in possession is liable for legal waste but in lien states he is liable only in equity and only for such waste as will impair the mortgagee's security.

Taxes must be paid by the mortgagor; if he fails to pay them the mortgagee may pay and add the amount to the principal of the mortgage debt. If he buys the premises at a tax sale he acquires the same rights as would any other purchaser. If the property is sold under condemnation proceedings the mortgagee's right attaches to the proceeds.

The mortgagee and mortgagor each has an insurable interest in the buildings on the premises, the mortgagee to the amount of the mortgage debt and the mortgagor to the full value of the buildings without deducting the mort-

[7] 37 **Am Jur**, Mortgages, §§ 977–1015.
35 **Am Jur**, Marshaling Assets and Securities, §§ 32–35.

[8] 36 **Am Jur**, Mortgages, §§ 324–362.

gage debt. Neither one is under any duty to insure for the benefit of the other but the mortgage usually provides that the mortgagor shall keep the buildings insured for both mortgagee and mortgagor as their interests shall appear.

The mortgagor may sell and convey his interest in the property to the mortgagee but it is usual for courts to say that such a transaction will be closely scrutinized and will be set aside at the suit of the mortgagor unless the transaction was a fair one. But as long as the mortgage relation continues any agreement that the mortgagor shall not redeem the property from the mortgage will not bind him. Furthermore any agreement made in the mortgage transaction or later which would unfairly clog or fetter the right of redemption will be held invalid; for example, an option given by the mortgagor to the mortgagee to buy the property at a stated price; or a provision in the mortgage that upon foreclosure the mortgagor is to be charged with an excessive sum as attorney's fee; or a promise by the mortgagor of a leasehold public house that neither he nor his successors would sell any malt liquors during the term of the lease except those purchased from the mortgagee.

If the mortgagor inherits the mortgage or if the mortgagee inherits the equity of redemption the two interests are merged and the mortgage is extinguished unless such merger would bring about an inequitable result.

CHAPTER II

PRIORITIES—FORECLOSURE

§ 9. Priorities—the recording acts.[9] If A gives a legal mortgage to Y who knows of a previous equitable mortgage held by X, Y takes subject to such

[9] 36 **Am Jur,** Mortgages, §§ 234–239.
45 **Am Jur,** Records and Recording I ws, §§ 40, 41, 85–104.
Right to receive rent as between mortgagor and mortgagee of leased premises. 14 **ALR** 640–658; s. in 105 **ALR** 744–755.
Effect on note of acceleration of mortgage securing note. 34 **ALR** 848–861; s. in 56 **ALR** 185, 186.
Chattel annexed to realty as subject to prior mortgage. 41 **ALR** 601–622; s. in 88 **ALR** 1114–1122; 99 **ALR** 144–147.
Duty of mortgagee to account for rents and profits or for use and occupation for benefit of owner of equity of redemption or junior lienor. 46 **ALR** 138–155.
Validity of mortgage securing unlimited future advances. 81 **ALR** 631–638.
Omission of amount of debt in mortgage or in record thereof (including general description without stating amount) as affecting validity of mortgage, its operation as notice, or its coverage with respect to debts secured. 145 **ALR** 369–392.
Doctrine of inverse order of alienation as affected by release of part of property covered by mortgage or other lien. 110 **ALR** 66–82.
Extension of existing real estate mortgage or deed of trust by subsequent agreement to cover additional indebtedness. 76 **ALR** 574–591.
Rights in mortgage security, of mortgagor or intermediate grantee who pays the mortgage debt after conveying the property. 2 **ALR** 242–251.
Recording laws as applied to assignments of mortgages on real estate. 89 **ALR** 171–200; s. in 104 **ALR** 1301–1309.
Priority as between mortgage for future advances and mechanics' liens. 5 **ALR** 398–406; s. in 53 **ALR** 580–583.
Discharge of mortgage and taking back of new mortgage as affecting lien intervening between the old and new mortgage. 33 **ALR** 149–165; s. in 98 **ALR** 843–851.
Priority as between holders of different notes or obligations secured by the same mortgage or mortgages executed contemporaneously. 50 **ALR** 543–584; s. in 108 **ALR** 485–498; 115 **ALR** 40–56.
Grantee of mortgagee by quitclaim deed or mortgage in quitclaim form as within protection of recording laws. 59 **ALR** 632–649.
Priority as between mechanic's lien and purchase-money mortgage. 72 **ALR** 1516–1531.
Deed from mortgagor to mortgagee as merger of real estate mortgage as regards intervening liens. 95 **ALR** 628–651; s. in 148 **ALR** 816–834.
Duty and liability of trustee under mortgage or deed of trust securing debt to mortgagor, subsequent purchaser, or lienor. 117 **ALR** 1054–1066.
Right of holder of negotiable paper secured by mortgage or of trustee in mortgage to protection as regards defenses against mortgage. 127 **ALR** 190–216.
Optional advance under mortgage as subject to lien intervening between giving of the mortgage and making the advance. 138 **ALR** 566–589.
Right of mortgagee or other lienor to

equitable mortgage; but, apart from recording acts applying to X's equitable mortgage, if Y advances his money and takes his mortgage in good faith without notice of X's rights he takes priority over X. If X's equitable mortgage was the result of a specifically enforcible contract to give security and the recording act provided that such contracts be recorded and X did record his contract then Y is bound by such record and X is entitled to priority.

If A after giving the mortgage to Y should convey or mortgage the land to Z and Y fails to record his mortgage as required by the recording act, Z takes priority over Y if Z advanced his money and took his mortgage in good faith without notice of Y's mortgage, though some states require that in order to have such priority he must record his own mortgage. In any event, if he does fail to record his own mortgage he may in turn be postponed to a subsequent mortgage given to Z. In some states the recording acts protect not only subsequent bona fide purchasers and mortgagees but also bona fide judgment creditors. Apart from recording acts a judgment creditor takes subject to equities and hence to equitable mortgages. In order that the record of a mortgage be constructive notice it must, of course, be in the chain of title. Some states require that an absolute deed given as security shall be recorded as a mortgage; and that a bill of sale given by way of security shall be recorded as a chattel mortgage.

If A buys land from B who conveys it to A upon A giving a mortgage for the purchase money such purchase money mortgage takes priority over any other mortgage given by A even though executed before the execution of the purchase money mortgage; it also takes priority over any mechanic's lien or judgment or other right which attaches to his interest upon his getting title.

§ 10. Foreclosure.[10] The remedy sought and given in the earliest suits for foreclosure of the mortgagor's equity of redemption was what is now

acquire and hold tax title in his own right as against persons owning other interests in or liens upon property. 140 **ALR** 294–331.

[10] 37 **Am Jur,** Mortgages, §§ 529–557.

Strict foreclosure as remedy where claimant of title, interest, or lien subordinate to mortgage was not made party to prior judicial foreclosure and sale. 118 **ALR** 769–783.

Necessity in suit to foreclose mortgage on property of decedent of joining as parties devisees or heirs of decedent, and effect of failure to do so. 119 **ALR** 807–815.

Judgment for debt without foreclosure of mortgage securing it as affecting mortgage, or right to foreclose the same, where no execution or attachment is levied under the judgment. 121 **ALR** 917–931.

Creditor or encumbrancer redeeming from mortgage sale as acquiring title and rights of sale purchaser. 135 **ALR** 196–209.

Personal representatives, or nonlien creditors, of deceased mortgagor or of deceased grantee of premises subject to mortgage (with or without assumption of mortgage debt), as necessary or proper parties to foreclosure suit. 124 **ALR** 784–808.

Deed from mortgagor or privy to mortgage holder as extinguishing equity of redemption. 129 **ALR** 1435–1540.

Right of mortgagor or purchaser of equity of redemption to defeat lien of mortgage by acquisition of title at sale subsequent to mortgage for nonpayment of taxes, or of assessment for local improvement. 134 **ALR** 289–312.

Right of junior lienor in respect of redemption as affected by failure to make him a party to suit to foreclose senior mortgage or property to serve him with process in such suit. 134 **ALR** 1490–1519.

Validity, construction, application, and effect, in case of failure to maintain insurance, of acceleration provision in mortgage or deed of trust. 142 **ALR** 1120–1131.

Application of insurance moneys received by mortgagee. 11 **ALR** 1295–1304.

Breach of policy by mortgagor as affecting mortgagee under a loss-payable clause which does not provide for that event. 38 **ALR** 367–379; s. in 48 **ALR** 1245.

Effect of foreclosure of mortgage as terminating lease. 14 **ALR** 664–680.

Right to jury trial of issues as to personal judgment for deficiency in suit to foreclose mortgage. 112 **ALR** 1492–1506.

Waiver of right to foreclose mortgage. 53 **ALR** 525–534; s. in 148 ALR 687–704.

Rights and remedies of purchaser under foreclosure sale where foreclosure proceedings are imperfect or irregular. 73 **ALR** 612–648.

Protection of mortgagor or owner of mortgaged property, on foreclosure sale, by fixing upset or minimum price, requiring credit of specified amount on mortgage debt, or denying or limiting amount of deficiency judgment. 85 **ALR** 1480–1488; s. in 89 **ALR** 1087–1091; 90 **ALR** 1330–1338; 94

called strict foreclosure; the equity court decreed that unless the mortgagor should pay by a certain date the mortgagee's title should become absolute, and the mortgage debt should be discharged. Such relief is given today only where the value of the mortgaged property is less or very little more than the amount of the mortgage debt or where a subsequent lienholder has not been joined in a previous foreclosure and sale proceeding against the mortgagor and it is desired to put an end to his right to redeem.

In a very few states a mortgagee is allowed to foreclose by peaceable entry on the mortgaged land and holding possession for three years.

The usual foreclosure proceeding in this country is by a suit in equity or under a statute asking that the property be sold and the proceeds applied to the payment of the mortgage debt and costs of the proceeding, the surplus, if any, going to the mortgagor.

In the foreclosure proceeding it is not necessary to join any prior incumbrancer, the sale being made subject to his incumbrance. But if such incumbrance is due the prior incumbrancer may be joined and the property sold free from his incumbrance; in such case he has a prior right to be paid out of the proceeds. It is also desirable to join a prior incumbrancer if there is any doubt as to the extent of his rights in order that such a question shall be adjudicated. Similar reasoning applies to any other rights which are prior to those of the plaintiff, for one who claims title adversely to both mortgagor and mortgagee is not a proper party to the foreclosure proceeding but if he voluntarily appears and litigates his claim he is barred by the court's decision.

In the foreclosure proceeding it is necessary and proper to join all holders of rights in the property subsequent to the mortgage including subsequent mortgagees and other lienholders in order that their rights to redeem may be foreclosed along with those of the mortgagor; the only exception is the holder of a subsequent mortgage who has failed to record it and the mortgagee had no actual notice of it before starting his foreclosure suit. If the mortgagor has conveyed away all his interest in the property and is not bound personally to pay the mortgage debt he is not a proper party to the foreclosure proceeding; but if he is personally liable for the mortgage debt he should be joined in order to obtain a deficiency judgment against him, and the same reasoning applies to any transferee of the mortgagor who assumed to pay the mortgage debt and then conveyed away his interest in the property.

Where a first mortgagee has filed a suit to foreclose making a junior incumbrancer a party and the mortgagor pays off the first mortgage the junior incumbrancer is entitled to have the proceeding continued so that he may obtain payment of his claim.

A provision in either the note or the mortgage that upon default in the payment of interest the entire debt becomes due is valid, not being regarded as

ALR 1352–1359; 96 **ALR** 853–858; 97 **ALR** 1123–1128; 104 **ALR** 375–388.

Interest of trustee in debt secured under deed of trust (or association with or relationship to one having interest in debt) as affecting validity of deed or exercise of trustee's power of foreclosure or sale. 138 **ALR** 1013–1034.

Right to attack voidable sale under power in mortgage, as personal to mortgagor (or owner of equity of redemption), or as exercisable by his heir, grantee, creditor, or other person claiming under or through him. 153 **ALR** 528–540.

Validity and effect, as against mortgagee or purchaser upon foreclosure, of mortgagor's assignment of rents to third person. 146 **ALR** 1133–1146.

Redemption from mortgage or judicial sale as affecting lien intervening that under which property was sold and that under which it was redeemed. 26 **ALR** 435–450.

Financial depression as justification of moratorium or other relief to mortgagors. 90 **ALR** 1330–1338; s. in 94 **ALR** 1352–1359; 96 **ALR** 853–858; 97 **ALR** 1123–1128; 104 **ALR** 375–388.

29 **Va. L. R.** 519, A Study on Strict Foreclosure.

either a penalty or forfeiture; foreclosure proceedings may be begun at once and the statute of limitations begins to run from that time; but if the mortgage debt becomes due only at the option of the mortgagee the statute does not begin to run till the mortgagee exercises his option which is usually done by beginning suit. Most states today have statutes expressly fixing a time within which suits to foreclose must be begun.

Pending the suit for foreclosure the court may, in its discretion, appoint a receiver to take charge of the rents and profits of the property where the security of the mortgaged property is not adequate and especially if the mortgagor is insolvent; a receiver may also be appointed to preserve the property from waste or deterioration during the foreclosure proceedings.

After the sale upon foreclosure has taken place the proceeds are distributed in the order of priority of the liens of the various lienholders who are parties to the foreclosure suit. If the mortgagors were tenants by the entirety the surplus is similarly held.

In most states today if the proceeds of the sale upon foreclosure are not sufficient to pay the mortgage debt and the mortgagor is personally liable therefor the mortgagee may get a deficiency judgment against the mortgagor in the foreclosure proceeding and need not institute a separate action for that purpose. In recent years because of the serious decline in land values and the consequent lack of any land market, the mortgagee usually bids in the property at a very low figure and hence is usually in a position to get a large deficiency judgment; to remedy this situation statutes have been passed providing for the elimination or reduction in the amount of deficiency judgments.

Mortgages frequently give to the mortgagee a power of sale upon the mortgagor's default, thus evading the necessity of foreclosure by suit. These have usually been held valid and many states have statutes regulating the procedure to be followed by the mortgagee. Since the mortgagee is not properly regarded as the agent of the mortgagor in making the sale the death of the mortgagor does not revoke the power. And by the better view the power may be exercised by an assignee of the mortgagee or by his personal representative after his death. The power must of course be exercised with due regard to the interests of the mortgagor and the mortgagee may not—apart from statute—bid at the sale without consent of the mortgagor. Statutes usually provide that the sale must be properly advertised in order to be valid.

INSURANCE

CHAPTER I

MAKING THE CONTRACT—INSURABLE INTEREST

§ 1. Making the contract.[1] The purpose of insurance is to distribute and equalize losses due to death, to fire, to accident, to storm, to floods or to any of the many other vicissitudes of life, the distribution being made—through the payment of premiums or assessments—among those who are subject to similar perils. A contract for the mere shifting of risk, such as the ordinary suretyship contract, is not a contract of insurance.

The contract of insurance is usually unilateral, the insurer undertaking the risk in consideration for the payment, in advance, of the premium by the insured, but occasionally the risk is undertaken though the insured has merely promised to pay the premium. This is the only real promise made by the insured; the application for insurance or the insurance policies may contain stipulations which are in form promises by the insured, but the breach of such

[1] 29 **Am Jur,** Insurance, §§ 3–21, 127–155.

What constitutes insurance. 63 **ALR** 711–773; s. in 100 **ALR** 1449–1460; 119 **ALR** 1241–1250.

Oral contracts of insurance. 15 **ALR** 995–1021; s. in 69 **ALR** 559–574; 92 **ALR** 232–240.

Rights and remedies arising out of delay in passing upon application for insurance. 15 **ALR** 1026–1034; s. in 75 **ALR** 952–962.

Divisibility of fire insurance policy covering building and contents. 47 **ALR** 650–667.

Right in proceeds of insurance taken out by warehouseman on goods stored. 53 **ALR** 1409–1415.

Temporary life, accident, or health insurance pending approval of application, or issuance of policy. 81 **ALR** 332–342; s. in 107 **ALR** 194–201.

Substitution by common agent of two or more insurance companies of policy of one company for policy of another. 83 **ALR** 298–315.

Insurance by agent on his own property. 83 **ALR** 1509–1536.

Binding effect of application not signed by insured. 91 **ALR** 1127–1133.

Death of insured or other loss pending application not effectively granted, for reinstatement of life or accident insurance, after lapse. 105 **ALR** 478–493.

57 **Harv. L. R.** 937, Insurance as Commerce in Constitution and Statute.

33 **Harv. L. R.** 198, The Delivery of a Life Insurance Policy.

50 **Yale, L. J.** 959, Insurance and Interstate Commerce.

43 **Col. L. R.** 825, Apportionment of Losses between "Blanket" and "Specific" Insurance Policies.

92 **U. of Pa. L. R.** 347, Indemnification against Tort Liability.

"promises" does not give rise to any cause of action against the insured but at most gives the insurer a defense.

It is sometimes said that in the ordinary life insurance contract the contract is only for one year with an option of perpetual renewal at the end of each year upon the payment of another premium; but the better view is that it is a contract to insure for life with a condition subsequent for forfeiture for the nonpayment of premiums.

Since in making the insurance contract the insurer must rely largely, if not entirely, upon the statements of the applicant for insurance, such applicant is required, in making such statements, to exercise a high degree of good faith; and since the insurer is the one who draws up the contract, and the contract is usually long and detailed, and the insurer is in a position to protect himself therein, a high degree of good faith is required of him so as to prevent him from taking an unfair advantage of the insured.

Even though a contract for insurance extends over many years it is not within the statute of frauds as to contracts not to be performed within a year and unless some other statute forbids, the contract may be oral; but it is usually embodied in a formal written instrument—the policy—which becomes effective only upon delivery and upon the happening of any conditions precedent to its taking effect. Since most persons today do not read insurance policies the failure to read does not prevent them from having the policy reformed if the policy, through mistake, does not express the real contract.

§ 2. Insurable interest—life insurance.[2] Since the purpose of insurance is the distribution and equalization of loss a contract of insurance usually requires that the insured shall have an insurable interest in the subject matter of the insurance contract; otherwise it is a mere wager and illegal.

One may insure his own life, either because the continuance of his life may be of pecuniary value to his estate or because the question of insurable interest is immaterial since there is usually no question that the insurance is being taken out in good faith. And he may name any one as beneficiary even though the one named has no pecuniary interest in the continuance of the life insured, the danger that the beneficiary might murder the insured being too slight to invalidate the policy. Similarly, he may take out the insurance to himself and assign it to one who has no insurable interest in his life if the transaction is entered into in good faith. Where it is assigned to a creditor to secure a debt the interest of the creditor is limited to the amount of his claim.

A husband may insure the life of his wife because he usually has a reasonable expectation of receiving her services even though he no longer has a legal right to them. A wife may insure the life of her husband because legally entitled to have him support her; and the reasonable expectation of receiving such support is probably enough where the marriage turns out to be

[2] 29 **Am Jur,** Insurance, §§ 353–375.

Application of community property system to problems arising in connection with life insurance policies. 114 **ALR** 545–562.

Divorce of insured and beneficiary as affecting the latter's right in life insurance. 52 **ALR** 386–454; s. in 59 **ALR** 172, 173.

Rights in respect of proceeds of life insurance under policy naming creditor as beneficiary. 115 **ALR** 741–750.

Validity and enforceability of promise by beneficiary of life insurance to insured to pay proceeds, in whole or part, to third person. 102 **ALR** 588–600.

Insurable interest of foster child or stepchild in life of foster or step-parent, or vice versa. 25 **ALR** 1547–1551.

Effect of erroneous designation of beneficiary of insurance as "wife." 32 **ALR** 1481–1490.

Right of insolvent to insure life for benefit of relatives. 31 **ALR** 51–78; s. in 34 **ALR** 838.

Eligibility of brother or sister of insured as beneficiary in life insurance policy. 45 **ALR** 1181–1192; s. in 61 **ALR** 917, 918.

invalid but was thought to be valid. Where there is a valid insurance policy as between husband and wife a later divorce does not invalidate it. And a woman may insure the life of her fiance.

A parent may insure the life of his minor child because of his legal right to services and the minor child may insure the life of a parent who is under a legal obligation to support him. Where the child is an adult there is an insurable interest between him and the parent only if the circumstances are such that there is a reasonable expectation of services or of support; and the same reasoning applies between brother and sister or any other relationship, though there are dicta that where the relationship is close it is not necessary to show any further insurable interest. Where there is held to be an insurable interest, the amount of the insurance is not limited to the value of that interest; it may be in any amount; though life insurance is founded upon the general principle of indemnity the contract itself is not a contract of indemnity.

A creditor may insure the life of his debtor provided the amount of the policy is not so much greater than the amount of the debt as to show a want of good faith in the creditor; the fact that before the death the debt has been paid does not invalidate the policy. Similarly, a surety may insure the life of his principal; and where there is a real pecuniary interest to be protected a partner may insure the life of his copartner, a corporation the life of its president or director and an employer the life of his employee. It is the better view that apart from small policies taken out on the lives of infants the consent of the person whose life is insured is necessary to the validity of the contract.

§ 3. Same—other insurance.[3] Generally one has an insurable interest in property when the destruction of or damage to the property would result in loss to him. This includes: (1) The holder of the legal title to property whether in fee or a life estate or term for years or in reversion or remainder and whether he holds beneficially or as trustee; in the latter case it is his duty to insure for the benefit of the cestui que trust and whatever he recovers in case of loss he will hold subject to the trust.

(2) The holder of an equitable property right such as that of a purchaser under a specifically enforcible contract to buy the property; the purchaser also has an insurable interest where the contract may be specifically enforced against him but not by him. Where property is pledged or mortgaged both the pledgor and pledgee and the mortgagor and mortgagee have insurable interests. In case of a mortgage on land the usual custom today is for the mortgagor to keep the property insured the proceeds to be paid to the mortgagee "as his interest shall appear."

(3) One who has a lien on property or who has merely possession of prop-

[3] 29 **Am Jur,** Insurance, §§ 322–352.

Validity of insurance on property possessed in violation of law or used for unlawful purpose. 18 **ALR** 1084–1089; s. in 132 **ALR** 125–137.

Insurable interest of husband or wife in other's property. 68 **ALR** 362–371.

Extent of recovery by insured who has only a partial or limited interest in the insured property. 68 **ALR** 1344–1353.

Right of lessor or lessee or his privies to benefit of insurance taken out by other or his privies. 66 **ALR** 864–870.

Vendee or vendor under executory contract as having exclusive ownership or interest, within the meaning of condition in insurance policy requiring interest of insured to be that of "unconditional and sole ownership," or the like. 60 **ALR** 11–87.

Reacquisition or extinguishment of title or interest as affecting provision in fire insurance policy against change of title, interest, or possession, or against encumbrance. 52 **ALR** 843–851.

Mortgage as breach of condition in insurance policy as to sole and unconditional ownership or as to change of title or interest, or similar terms. 126 **ALR** 473–501.

erty has an insurable interest; so has one who has a contract to buy chattels which is not specifically enforcible.

On the other hand, a prospective heir, who has a mere expectancy, has no insurable interest in the property which he expects to inherit; nor has a creditor any insurable interest in the property belonging to his debtor.

The insurable interest must exist at the time of loss but the better view is that it need not exist at the time the policy was issued provided the policy was issued and accepted in good faith and not as a wager. It has long been settled that an open marine policy may cover a return cargo which may be bought long after the policy is issued, a ship may be insured "lost or not lost" if the parties are both ignorant of the loss and a floating policy on a fluctuating stock of goods is valid.

CHAPTER II

DEVICES FOR ASCERTAINING AND CONTROLLING RISK AND LOSS

§ 4. **Concealment.**[4] In marine insurance the insured is under an obligation to disclose to the insurer every material fact that is or should, in due course of business, be known to the insured. In other insurance concealment does not affect the validity of the contract unless the fact concealed was known by the insured to be material and he concealed it in order to defraud the insurer. In order that the fact concealed be regarded as material it is not necessary that it increase the risk; it is enough that knowledge of such fact by the insurer would influence him not to undertake the risk. The insured need not disclose facts discovered by him after the contract was made; or facts which are known to the insurer or reasonably believed by the insured to be known by him, or facts which relate to risks excluded by warranties or excepted by the policy. But the policy will be invalidated by the failure to disclose material facts known to the insured's agent where the latter was under a duty to disclose them to his principal and had a reasonable opportunity to do so.

§ 5. **Representations.**[5] If the insured makes either an oral or written representation about a material fact to the insurer to induce him to undertake the insurance the contract is voidable unless the statement is substantially true, even though the representation was made innocently, the representation being construed liberally in favor of the insured. If he makes a representation as

[4] 29 **Am Jur**, Insurance, §§ 540–544.
Effect on insurance of mere failure to disclose encumbrance on property. 28 **ALR** 801–815.

[5] 29 **Am Jur**, Insurance, §§ 523–528.
Insurance: incorrect statement of age. 1 **ALR** 459–470; s. in 14 **ALR** 926–928.
Statements by applicants for life insurance as to use of intoxicating liquor. 26 **ALR** 1279–1295.
Materiality of false representation, in application for policy of insurance, as to whether applicant has consulted physician. 131 **ALR** 617–655.
False answer in application for life insurance to question regarding previous rejection. 120 **ALR** 1424–1440.
Kind of insurance or insurer contemplated by provision in policy of life, health, or accident insurance, or by question asked in application therefor, in regard to other or additional insurance or prior application therefor. 119 **ALR** 765–788.
Admissibility as against the beneficiary of life or accident insurance of statements or declarations by the insured outside of his application. 86 **ALR** 146–166.
Overvaluation in proof of loss of property insured as fraud avoiding fire insurance policy. 20 **ALR** 1164–1179; s. in 56 **ALR** 390–392.
28 **U. of Minn. L. R.** 14, Innocent Misrepresentation of Health in Insurance Applications.
27 **Wash. U. L. Q.** 30, 196, Conflict of Laws; Treatment of Warranties and Representations in Life Insurance Policies.

to his intention, opinion or belief—for example, as to the value of his property or as to whether he is afflicted with a particular disease—the contract is rendered voidable only if he acted fraudulently. Whether a representation is material is usually a question for the jury; the fact that a statement is made in response to a question raises a strong presumption that it is material.

§ 6. **Warranties—conditions—exceptions.**[6] If in the policy itself or in a separate instrument expressly incorporated therein, there is attributed to the insured a statement of fact or a promise that certain things shall be done or that certain conditions shall exist during the time covered by the policy, the falsity of such a statement or a breach of such a promise renders the policy voidable even though such statement or promise was not material; but the parties must have intended the statement or promise to be a warranty—a mere stipulation to that effect is not enough. By the weight of authority a statement in a fire policy that books of account are to be kept in an iron safe is construed as a warranty and if they are not so kept no recovery can be had.

The doctrine, when applied to immaterial matters, is so artificial and harsh

[6] 29 **Am Jur,** Insurance, §§ 529–539, 901–1088.

Provision in life insurance policy excluding or limiting liability if insured is not in sound health on date or delivery of policy as confined to change in condition after making or acceptance of application. 136 **ALR** 1516–1530.

Provisions of insurance policy as to watchman, and warranties and representations in that regard. 87 **ALR** 1074–1149.

Automobile insurance: exclusion clause relating to age of driver, etc. 72 **ALR** 1070–1096; s. in 115 **ALR** 827–836.

Sufficiency of bookkeeping to satisfy conditions of insurance policy. 39 **ALR** 1443–1458; s. in 62 **ALR** 630–637; 125 **ALR** 350–360.

Noncompliance with statutory requirement that insurance policy contain entire contract, or that application be attached to, incorporated in, indorsed upon, or delivered with, the policy as affecting right of insurer to show initial fraud or misrepresentations by insured. 93 **ALR** 374–395.

What amounts to medical or surgical attendance or consultation within contemplation of contract of life or accident insurance. 63 **ALR** 846–860.

Provision in insurance policy as to means of extinguishing fire. 23 **ALR** 27–37.

Accident insurance: provision exempting from or limiting liability where death or injury results from poison. 2 **ALR** 61–67; s. in 110 **ALR** 1276–1279; 131 **ALR** 1061–1063.

Provision of accident or health insurance policy that insured shall be under care of physician or surgeon. 115 **ALR** 1062–1071.

Construction and application of provision of accident policy or accident feature of life policy extending benefits to one disabled from engaging in any occupation or employment for wage or profit. 149 **ALR** 7–186.

Validity, construction, and effect of provisions in life or accident policy in relation to military service. 137 **ALR** 1263–1285; s. in 143 **ALR** 1513; 147 **ALR** 1294, 1295; 150 **ALR** 1414–1416.

Attempt to board or alight from moving train, car, or locomotive, as within general provisions of accident policy avoiding liability for policyholder's negligence or exposure to obvious danger. 29 **ALR** 712–720.

Construction and application of provision of insurance policy in case of injury or death while on public conveyance. 36 **ALR** 811–820.

Construction and effect of specific provision in accident or life insurance policy in relation to homicide or intentional injury by third person. 56 **ALR** 685–697.

Scope and application of provisions of accident policy, or accident feature of life policy, relating to accident in connection with automobile or other motor vehicle. 138 **ALR** 404–426.

Validity and effect of provision in insurance policy for forfeiture upon foreclosure, or commencement of foreclosure, or other proceeding to enforce a mortgage. 50 **ALR** 1117–1129; s. in 57 **ALR** 1044–1046.

What amounts to a "delivery" or an "actual delivery" to insured within express provision of insurance policy. 53 **ALR** 492–515; s. in 145 **ALR** 1434–1457.

Test or criterion of "actual cash value" under insurance policy insuring to extent of actual cash value at time of loss. 56 **ALR** 1155–1167.

What amounts to a sale within forfeiture provision of insurance policy forbidding property to be sold or conveyed without assent of insurer. 38 **ALR** 316–331.

Physical condition which in itself is not within, or is expressly excluded from, the coverage of an insurance policy, as within such coverage when it results from or is directly attributable to a cause within coverage. 108 **ALR** 6–37.

Provisions for autopsy in policy of life or accident insurance. 15 **ALR** 614–620; s. in 88 **ALR** 984–991.

Assignment by insured of life policy reserving right to change beneficiary, as affected by failure to comply with provisions of policy respecting change of beneficiary. 135 **ALR** 1040–1058.

that in many states there are statutes which either modify the doctrine or abolish the distinction between warranties and representations, treating warranties as if they were representations and requiring either that the warranty be material or that it be made with a fraudulent intent.

Where the policy provides that no risk shall attach if the insured does not have sole and unconditional ownership of the property such a provision is a condition precedent performance of which must be alleged and proved by the insured. But if the condition is subsequent, for example, that no gasoline be kept on the premises, the burden of allegation and proof is upon the defendant, just as it is in case of warranties.

Where the policy expressly excepts certain risks this merely limits the application of the policy and does not otherwise affect the relation of the parties. The breach of a warranty or of a condition may be waived by the insurer but an exception can not be waived unless new consideration is given.

CHAPTER III

ESTOPPEL—WAIVER—SUBROGATION

§ 7. Estoppel.[7] Where A has a life policy in the X Co. and tells the agent of the company that he is about to enter military service and the agent assures him that the stipulation against his entering military service will not be enforced and A thereupon enters such service and is killed, the X Co. will be estopped to take advantage of the stipulation if the agent was acting within the apparent scope of his authority.

Similar reasoning applies where B has a fire policy with the Y Co. and notifies the agent that he has been violating the stipulation against keeping gasoline on the premises and the agent tells him that the policy is still good and B in reliance thereon does not take out other insurance and there is a loss by fire due to the gasoline.

If at the time that A's life policy was delivered to him he was already in military service and the agent knew it; or if when B's fire policy was delivered to him he was storing gasoline on the premises and the agent knew it, the weight of authority and better view is that the insurers are estopped, having received premiums for supposedly valid policies; but in Massachusetts, New Jersey and the federal courts there is no estoppel because of the parol evidence rule and New York has vacillated on the point. A similar situation is presented where the insurer's agent has, without the knowledge of the insured, falsified answers to questions put to the insured in his application for insurance; and where the agent has falsely stated to the insured that certain acts necessary to the validity of the policy, such as indorsement of consent by the insurer, have been performed.

[7] 29 **Am Jur**, Insurance, §§ 799–879.

Denial of liability as waiver of proofs of loss required by insurance policy. 22 **ALR** 407–428; s. in 108 **ALR** 901–911.

Agent's promise to make indorsement upon policy as a waiver or estoppel to assert provision that any privilege or permission shall be void unless in writing. 38 **ALR** 636–651.

Liability insurance: insurer's assumption of, or continuation in, defense of action brought against the assured as waiver, or estoppel, as regards defense of noncoverage, or other defense existing at time of accident. 81 **ALR** 1326–1402.

Insurance agent's misrepresentations to applicant, insured, or beneficiary, as basis of action by them, other than on policy itself, or as defense to action against them. 136 **ALR** 5–61.

Insertion by insurer's agent in application of false answers to questions correctly answered by insured, or answers suggested by agent. 81 **ALR** 833–875; s. in 117 **ALR** 790–798; 148 **ALR** 507–516.

§ 8. Waiver.[8] In the case of an ordinary bilateral contract the operation of the doctrine of waiver is usually not difficult to understand. If there is an express condition in the contract which is exclusively for the benefit of the plaintiff he may waive it—that is, throw it away—and he will almost certainly do this if it is to his advantage to do so. For example, A contracted to buy B's crop of tobacco, then growing in the field, at 10 cents a pound but if as much as one fourth of the tobacco when harvested should be frostbitten, A might cancel the contract. When the crop was harvested one fourth of it had been frostbitten so that A might have cancelled the contract but it was not to his advantage to do so because the price of tobacco had then advanced to 15 cents a pound, so A waived the condition and insisted upon getting the tobacco. In such a situation there is, of course, no element of estoppel.

Where an insurance contract is bilateral—for example, where there is merely a promise to pay the premium—and there is a proviso that the insurance company may cancel the policy upon default, the insurance company may waive its right to cancel and maintain an action for the premium because the stipulation is for its exclusive benefit.

Where the insurance company is a defendant, the action being brought to enforce the policy, and the defendant sets up breach of a condition, if the plaintiff can show a promise to waive the condition based upon consideration, such a contract is a good reply to the defense of breach of condition and the insurance company will be held liable on the policy.

Where there is no contract to waive but there is an express assurance, either at the time of the delivery of the policy or later, that the insurance company will not take advantage of a breach of condition and the insured acts upon such assurance the insurance company is estopped by its assurance. Such cases of estoppel are frequently called waivers and probably a majority of courts hold that waiver and estoppel are synonymous. And the cases are very few where an insurance company has been held liable in spite of the breach of a condition unless there was either a contract to waive the breach or an assurance that it would not be taken advantage of, followed by action in reliance thereupon.

§ 9. Subrogation.[9] If A insures his building against fire with the B Insurance Company and then the building is burned through the negligent conduct of X and the B Insurance Company pays the loss, it is subrogated to the rights of A against X because, as between one who is bound merely by a contract of indemnity and one who is liable as tort-feasor, the latter should, as a matter of fairness, bear the loss. If the B Insurance Company should re-

[8] 29 **Am Jur,** Insurance, §§ 799–879.

Action of insurer in regard to unpaid premium note after maturity as waiver of, or estoppel to claim, forfeiture for nonpayment. 83 **ALR** 846–868.

Representation by insurer's agent as to nonliability as fraud avoiding release. 96 **ALR** 1001–1015.

Practice of fraternal or mutual benefit society of accepting late payment of premiums or assessments as waiver of right to insist upon forfeiture for nonpayment of other premiums or assessments at time due. 108 **ALR** 681–693.

Waiver or estoppel in respect of scope or limitation of coverage of insurance policy as distinguished from waiver or estoppel of grounds of forfeiture or defense. 113 **ALR** 857–871.

Delivery of policy of life insurance without payment of premium as waiver of condition that policy shall not be in force until payment of first premium. 118 **ALR** 1072–1078.

Necessity and sufficiency, or waiver, of demand as a condition of statutory liability of insurer for failure to pay or delay in paying loss. 145 **ALR** 343–349.

[9] 29 **Am Jur,** Insurance, §§ 1335–1358.

Insurer's right of subrogation to insured's claim against wrongdoer as affected by existence of defense, or possibility of defense, to action on policy. 138 **ALR** 1170–1187.

47 **Harv. L. R.** 976, Some Recent Subrogation Problems in the Law of Suretyship and Insurance.

cover more from X than the amount of the insurance it must account for that to A. The doctrine of subrogation applies also to indemnity insurance.

But it does not, apart from statute, apply to life insurance. If A takes out insurance on his life for $10,000 with the C Insurance Company and then is killed through the negligent conduct of Y, the C Insurance Company is not entitled to be subrogated even though there is a statute providing for the survival of the tort action against Y. And there is a similar holding with regard to insurance against accident causing personal injuries. But the Workmen's Compensation Acts usually provide for subrogation of the employer or his insurer to any claim of the employee against a tort-feasor responsible for the injury.

CHAPTER IV

MISCELLANEOUS

§ 10. Suicide—incontestable clauses—rights of beneficiary.[10] Where A takes out a policy on his own life and later kills himself while insane the insurance company is everywhere held liable. If he kills himself while sane and the policy was taken out with the intention of committing suicide the insurer is everywhere held not liable because of the fraud. If there was no such fraud the weight of authority is that the insurer is liable; and if there is a clause in the policy excepting death by suicide it is construed to include only cases of self-destruction while sane. As to what constitutes sanity in this connection the minority doctrine is that the insured is insane only when he is unable to understand the physical consequences of his act; the majority rule is that he is insane when he does not understand the moral quality of his act. In order to escape the operation of the majority rule policies frequently include a provision against suicide "sane or insane" and under this any intentional act of self-destruction has been held to excuse the insurer.

In order to reassure the prospective policyholder that after his paying pre-

[10] 29 **Am Jur,** Insurance, §§ 880–900, 912–926, 983–985.

Provision of policy of insurance regarding other insurance as applicable to a policy the indemnity or coverage of which is limited to the excess over other insurance carried by insured. 122 **ALR** 1204–1210.

Failure or refusal of insured to submit to corrective surgical or medical treatment as affecting right to recover insurance benefits, or to avoid payment of premiums. 126 **ALR** 136–145.

Rights and remedies of beneficiary after death of insured who had pledged policy to secure debt. 83 ALR 77–85.

Insurance: incontestable clause as excluding a defense based upon public policy. 6 **ALR** 448–456; s. in 13 **ALR** 674, 675; 35 **ALR** 1491–1493.

Time when incontestable clause in life insurance policy becomes effective; death of insured before end of contestable period. 31 **ALR** 108–118; s. in 85 **ALR** 234–241; 105 **ALR** 992–999.

Insanity as affecting the applicability of "suicide" clause, with the words "sane or insane," in life insurance contract. 35 **ALR** 160–188; s. in 138 **ALR** 827–832.

Insurance: what amounts to a contest within contemplation of incontestable clause. 36 **ALR** 1245–1250; s. in 64 **ALR** 959–962; 101 **ALR** 868–871.

Right of insurer to directed verdict on issue of suicide. 37 **ALR** 171–180.

Provision in policy of life or accident insurance as to "self-destruction," "death by own hand," and other forms not employing term "suicide," as applicable to death by accident. 39 **ALR** 1088–1094.

Suicide clause in policy of life or accident insurance as affected by incontestable clause. 55 **ALR** 549–555; s. in 67 **ALR** 1364, 1365.

Express exception in incontestability clause as negativing other exceptions thereto. 88 **ALR** 773–782.

Rights as between mortgagor and insurance company where policy avoided as to mortgagor, but not as to mortgagee. 52 **ALR** 278–284.

Who entitled to proceeds of life insurance under policy naming two or more beneficiaries, in event of death of one or more but less than all of them before insured. 112 **ALR** 729–744.

Respective rights of insured and beneficiary in endowment, accumulation, and tontine policies. 19 **ALR** 654–664.

Disposition of benefit fund in benefit society on failure of beneficiary in absence of specific provision for such contingency. 31 **ALR** 762–781.

miums for several years the beneficiary, after loss of testimony of the insured and others, may have to contest in an expensive lawsuit the validity of the policy there is a provision in many policies making the policy incontestable either from date of issue or after a certain period, usually one or two years. Such a provision does not, of course, prevent the insurer from showing that the insured had no insurable interest or that the loss was due to an excepted risk, or that conditions to be performed by the insured after loss, such as giving notice of loss, have not been complied with. Nor does it, where the provision is that the policy shall be incontestable from date of issue, prevent the insurer from setting up that the policy was procured by fraud. The contest which must be made by the insured within the prescribed period must be in a court action either in a suit in equity by the insured to have the policy cancelled or in an action at law on the policy to which the insurer puts in his defense. The death of the insured during the prescribed period does not prevent the incontestable clause from becoming operative at the end of the period.

Though there is no satisfactory reason for so holding, if A takes out insurance on his life naming X the beneficiary, X's rights in almost all states become vested as soon as the insurance contract is made so that they can not be defeated by any acts of either A or the insurer though of course they can be defeated by the failure of A to continue to pay premiums; and if the beneficiary dies before the insured the prevailing but not the better view is that the policy becomes the property of the beneficiary's estate beyond the control of the insured. Where, as is frequently the case, A reserves the right to change the beneficiary, any action brought on the policy during A's lifetime belongs to A, but if no such action is brought the right of A to the cash surrender of the policy can not be reached by his creditors, nor can they reach the proceeds of the policy after A's death unless the premium payments were in fraud of creditors; the beneficiary is also entitled as against A's personal representatives.

Where the beneficiary murders the insured in order to collect on the insurance policy he will be held as constructive trustee of the proceeds for the benefit of the insured's estate, equity not permitting him to profit by his crime.

§ 11. Construction of the insurance contract—formalities.[1] Because the insurance contract was formerly drawn up by the insurer and usually printed

[1] 29 **Am Jur**, Insurance, §§ 156–167.

Wrongful termination of policy by insurer, or false information to insured in that regard, as excusing further tender and payment of premiums or assessments. 122 **ALR** 385–417.

Liability of policyholders in mutual insurance companies to assessments. 137 **ALR** 945–957.

Validity, construction, and application of automatic premium loan provision in life insurance policy. 129 **ALR** 1105–1114.

Validity, construction, and effect of provisions in life or accident policy in relation to military service. 137 **ALR** 1263–1285; s. in 140 **ALR** 1533; 141 **ALR** 1510.

Requirement of "positive" proof of death of insured as excluding circumstantial evidence. 60 **ALR** 592–595.

Applicability to limitation prescribed by policy of insurance or by special statutory provision in relation to insurance of provisions of Statute of Limitations extending time or fixing time when action deemed commenced. 23 **ALR** 97–109; s. in 149 **ALR** 483–492.

Disposition of life insurance which, by terms of policy, is dependent upon survivorship, where there is no presumption or proof of survivorship. 5 **ALR** 797–804; s. in 113 **ALR** 881–889.

Inclusion or exclusion of first or last day in computing period of time prescribed by insurance contract. 137 **ALR** 1155–1174.

Validity, construction, and effect of provisions in life or accident policy in relation to military service. 137 **ALR** 1263–1285; s. in 143 **ALR** 1513; 147 **ALR** 1294, 1295; 150 **ALR** 1414–1416.

Necessity and sufficiency of consent by or notice to insured employee or beneficiary in order for insurer and employer or other representative of group validly to cancel, modify, or substitute a master group policy before expiration of term for which issued. 142 **ALR** 1288–1303.

Appraiser's award in insurance cases as subject to attack because appraiser had in small type the courts construed the contract strictly against the insurer and this rule of construction has been carried over to standard policies required by statute. For example, words of description of the property covered by a fire insurance policy are construed liberally in favor of the insured, and the phrase unconditional and sole ownership has been held to be satisfied even though the interest was merely equitable and subject to incumbrances.

Apart from statute an insurance contract need not be formal or even in writing and it is the custom of insurance companies to issue binders which gives the insured protection while the insurer investigates the risk and determines whether to issue the policy; such a binder includes all the obligations covered by the policies in customary use by the insurer.

§ 12. Extent of insurer's liability.[2] An insurer against fire is liable only for damage directly caused by hostile fires; this includes damage caused by water used to extinguish the fire, to the expense of removing insured goods to a place of safety and to thefts committed during such removal. It is no defense that the fire was caused by the negligent conduct of the insured or of a third party. If ignition takes place it includes damage due to charring or blistering. The insurer is not liable for loss caused by friendly fires such as burn in a stove or furnace unless the friendly fire escapes, for example, sets fire to soot in a chimney.

If the insured reserves the option to rebuild and later exercises the option there is a new, substituted agreement and no action can be maintained on the policy.

In some states the standard fire policy provides that the insurer may cancel the policy five days after giving notice of cancellation.

Fire policies frequently provide that satisfactory proofs of loss must be made within sixty days; in some states an inexcusable failure to comply avoids the policy, in others it merely postpones the right of action against the insurer. It is quite common to provide that action must be brought within one year from the date of loss and this stipulation is usually held valid.

Standard life policies usually provide that the insurer must mail notice as to the amount of premiums due, where payable and that the policy will be forfeited unless the premium is paid.

If there has been a mistake in drawing up the policy the proper remedy is a bill in equity for reformation.

previously acted for party naming him. 104 **ALR** 563–572.

Apportionment of annuities in respect of time. 116 **ALR** 135–151.

What persons or corporations, contracts or policies, are within statutory provisions allowing recovery of attorneys' fees or penalty against insurance companies or against companies dealing in specified kinds of insurance. 126 **ALR** 1439–1465.

24 **Harv. L. R.** 119, The Meaning of Fire in an Insurance Policy against Loss or Damage by Fire.

[2] 29 **Am Jur**, Insurance, §§ 1150–1238.

Date from which life insurance premium periods are to be computed. 6 **ALR** 774–788; s. in 32 **ALR** 1253–1258; 80 **ALR** 957–968; 111 **ALR** 1420–1431.

Provision suspending insurance during default in payment of premiums or assessment as affected by failure of insurer to declare a suspension before loss. 8 **ALR** 395–413.

Life insurance: forfeiture for nonpayment of premiums or assessments as affected by physical or mental disability. 15 **ALR** 318–326.

Notice to insured of insufficiency to meet premiums of cash or loan value, reserve, or dividends. 140 **ALR** 683–694.

Liability of property insurer as affected by explosion. 13 **ALR** 883–895; s. in 65 **ALR** 934–939.

Forfeiture of life or accident insurance for nonpayment of premium due to failure or neglect of one authorized by insured to pay same. 67 **ALR** 180–196.

Insurance agent's right to commissions or renewal premiums. 79 **ALR** 475–492; s. in 136 **ALR** 160–177.

Person to whom payment of insurance premium may be made (or tendered) so as to charge insurer. 85 **ALR** 749–776.

Acceptance by insurance agent of something other than money or insured's money obligation in payment of premium. 93 **ALR** 654–660.

In insurance against accident the bankruptcy or insolvency of the insured is no defense to an action brought by the injured person against the insurer: but the insurer may set up any defenses which could have been set up in an action by the insured.

CREDITORS' RIGHTS AND BANKRUPTCY

X. DEBTOR RELIEF WITHOUT LIQUIDATION.

XI. CORPORATE REORGANIZATION UNDER CHAPTER TEN.

PART I. CREDITORS' RIGHTS

CHAPTER I

JUDGMENTS

§ 1. Common law executions—judgment liens—exemptions.[1] Where a judgment is that the plaintiff, having brought an action of ejectment, is entitled to the possession of certain land or, having brought an action of replevin, is entitled to the possession of a certain chattel, it becomes the sheriff's duty, in executing the judgment, to place the plaintiff in possession of the land or of the chattel. But where a judgment is that the plaintiff is entitled to recover a certain sum of money it becomes the sheriff's duty, in executing the judgment, to sell enough of the judgment debtor's tangible property—land or chattels—to satisfy the judgment.

In some states as soon as the judgment is rendered, however, without any levy of execution, it becomes a lien on whatever land the debtor may have within the jurisdiction of the court. If at that time the debtor has no land there but acquires some later—either by purchase or by inheritance—the judgment lien attaches the moment the land is acquired, and if there are several judgments they all attach at once and nothing turns upon the order in which the judgments were rendered. If the creditor wishes to reach land of his debtor in another jurisdiction and he is able to get personal service of the debtor

[1] 21 **Am Jur,** Executions, §§ 16–26.
31 **Am Jur,** Judgments, §§ 296–380.
22 **Am Jur,** Exemptions, §§ 2–12.
Municipal funds and credits as subject to levy under execution or garnishment on judgment against municipality. 89 **ALR** 863–870.
Debtor's exemption of proceeds of insurance on property itself exempt. 63 **ALR** 1286–1307.
Decree or order directing or confirming sale of homestead for payment of debts as subject to collateral attack. 66 **ALR** 926–934.
Inclusion of different tracts or parcels in homestead. 73 **ALR** 116–148.
Waiver of, or estoppel to assert, debtor's exemption, by laches or delay. 82 **ALR** 648–658.
Time as of which, and extent to which, homestead exemption attaches to property received in exchange for homestead. 83 **ALR** 54–62.
Estate or interest in real property to which a homestead claim may attach. 89 **ALR** 511–563.
Direction in will for payment of debts and expenses as subjecting exempt homestead to their payment. 103 **ALR** 257–264.
Creation of homestead right in real estate as affecting existing judgment lien. 110 **ALR** 883–898.
Character of property as homestead as affected by its use for business as well as residence purposes. 114 **ALR** 209–244.
Recital in deed or mortgage disclaiming homestead as respects property described or affirming homestead in other property. 128 **ALR** 414–427.
Creation of homestead right in real estate as affecting previous mortgage, trust deed, or purchase money or vendor's lien. 123 **ALR** 427–441.
Multiple dwelling house part of which is occupied by owners as subject of homestead. 128 **ALR** 1431–1437.
Debtor's exemption (other than homestead) as applicable in favor of nonresidents or of residents absent or about to remove from the state. 119 **ALR** 554–584.
Validity of contractual stipulation waiving debtor's exemption. 47 **ALR** 300–308.
17 **Temple L. Q.** 217 Execution Sales: Lien Divestiture and Distribution of Proceeds in Pennsylvania.

in the second jurisdiction he may sue on his judgment in that jurisdiction and get a judgment there which will at once become a lien on the land.

In some states there are statutes requiring judgments to be registered before they become a lien on the land of the judgment debtor; and by federal statute such state statutes may apply also to decrees of federal courts but no state may require federal judgments to be registered without making the same requirement of judgments of state courts.

Where the judgment debtor has chattels within the jurisdiction the judgment becomes, in most states, a lien thereon from the moment of delivery of the writ to the sheriff for execution and if there are several judgments levied, priorities are reckoned on that basis without regard to the dates of the rendition of the different judgments. But where A puts a writ in the hands of the sheriff with instructions not to levy and later B puts a writ into the hands of the sheriff with instructions to levy at once and B's judgment is thereupon levied before A's, B is entitled to priority over A's because A's conduct is regarded as a fraud upon B.

In all states a judgment debtor is entitled to a personal property exemption, either of certain enumerated chattels or personal property up to a certain fixed value. This exemption is much lower in the eastern states—usually around $300—than it is in the western states where a high exemption was fixed by statute in the early days as a means of attracting settlers from the east who were in embarrassed circumstances. In nearly all states judgment debtors are entitled also to a homestead exemption. In some states all that is necessary for such an exemption is that the homestead be the actual abode of the judgment debtor; in others it is necessary for the homestead to be registered in the office of the county clerk or recorder. A judgment lien on the land takes precedence over a later acquired homestead exemption therein.

Apart from statute, a sheriff can levy only upon land or tangible personal property, but in many states there are statutes enabling him to levy upon negotiable notes or bonds.

§ 2. Creditor's bill for equitable execution—supplementary proceedings.[2] If a debtor has no property which is subject to common-law execution but does have a chose in action against a third party, the creditor may reach such intangible property by a creditor's bill for equitable execution. In order to maintain such a bill he must ordinarily prove that he has exhausted his common-law remedies by showing that he obtained a judgment against his debtor, that he had execution issued and that it was returned, "no property found." Where the creditor is able to convince the equity court that the judgment debtor is so hopelessly execution proof that the levy of execution would be obviously futile, he need not go to the useless expense of having execution levied. After fulfilling these requirements the debtor is entitled to an equity decree that the debtor assign to him the debtor's choses in action against third parties so that the creditor may be enabled to realize upon such choses in action by suing thereon as assignee of the judgment debtor. If the third parties are in the same jurisdiction in which the creditor's bill is brought, they may be

[2] 14 **Am Jur,** Creditors' Bills, §§ 14–44.
21 **Am Jur,** Executions, §§ 657–696.
Nonresidence or absence of debtor as obviating necessity of procuring judgment as condition of creditors' bill. 38 **ALR** 269–285.
Right of creditor who institutes supplementary proceedings to priority over other creditors in respect of property disclosed thereby. 92 **ALR** 1435–1450.
39 **Col. L. R.** 139, Execution Process and Life Insurance.
36 **Col. L. R.** 1061, Collection of Money Judgments: Experimentation with Supplementary Proceedings.

joined as parties defendant and thereby become subject to an equitable decree that they satisfy their obligations to the judgment debtor by paying them to the judgment creditor.

As soon as the creditor's bill is filed and process is served on the judgment debtor, the judgment creditor becomes entitled to an equitable lien on the debtor's intangible property.

In some states—notably New York—there are statutes which provide the judgment creditor with proceedings supplementary to judgment under which the creditor may have his debtor and his debtor's debtors examined, under oath, with regard to choses in action belonging to the judgment debtor. If nonexempt property is thereby found the court may order a receiver to take charge of it or it may order the debtor's obligor to pay his obligation directly to the judgment creditor.

§ 3. Garnishment—attachment—imprisonment.[3] In many states there are garnishment statutes—called trustee statutes in New England—which in simple cases afford a cheap and convenient substitute for a creditor's bill for equitable execution. Under these statutes the judgment creditor, A, serves notice on his debtor's (B's) debtor, C, not to pay his obligation to B; having proved his judgment against B and the obligation of C to B, the judgment creditor is entitled to a judgment that C pay to him (A) the obligation which C owes to B. Where C is B's employer who is indebted to C for wages, statutes frequently exempt a certain percentage of such wages. If the facts are not relatively simple the garnishment statute may not apply; thus, if A has a claim against B and X and B alone has a claim against C, A may not garnishee C but must resort to a creditor's bill for equitable execution.

In some states statutes permit a creditor to attach property of his debtor at the commencement of an action against him to collect the debt; in other states such a remedy is limited to cases where the debtor is about to remove his property from the state or is himself continuously absent from the state. Other statutes, usually called foreign attachment statutes, authorize a creditor to attach the property of a nonresident debtor and then, by an in rem proceeding based on such attachment, enforce his claim against such property. Similar statutes, called foreign garnishment statutes, permit a creditor of a nonresident debtor, to garnishee the nonresident debtor's obligor resident within the state and then, with this as a basis, enforce his claim against such intangible property of his debtor. For a discussion of foreign attachment and foreign garnishment statutes, see Conflict of Laws §§ 12, 13.

[3] 4 **Am Jur,** Attachment and Garnishment, §§ 3–13.

21 **Am Jur,** Executions, §§ 697–703.

Leaving property in custody of debtor as abandonment of levy under attachment or execution. 86 **ALR** 1412–1442.

Right of one to summon or charge himself as garnishee. 31 **ALR** 711–721; s. in 61 **ALR** 1458, 1459.

Liability of obligor to garnishment in respect of obligation to contractor under construction contract. 82 **ALR** 1115–1124.

Right of surety on bond given to prevent or secure the release of, attachment, to attach attachment proceedings after recovery by plaintiff of judgment in attachment action. 89 **ALR** 266–279.

Attachment proceedings as affected by officer's failure to comply with statutory requirements as to return or inventory. 93 **ALR** 748–773.

Garnishment of bank deposit as affected by bank's right, or waiver of right, to set off depositor's indebtedness to it against deposit or apply deposit to such indebtedness. 106 **ALR** 62–72; s. in 110 **ALR** 1268, 1269.

What amounts to a contingency within statute or rule permitting garnishment or similar process before an obligation is due or payable, if payment or delivery is not dependent upon a contingency. 134 **ALR** 853–872.

Priority of assignment of chose in action over subsequent garnishment as affected by lack of notice to debtor of assignment. 52 **ALR** 109–126.

Formerly, especially in England, a judgment creditor was allowed execution against the body of his debtor, the sheriff being required to keep him in custody till the debt was satisfied. This was later modified in practice so that in most cases the debtor was not actually put in jail but was required to stay within a certain territory, usually referred to as the jail limits. Some states have completely abolished imprisonment for debt; in other states the remedy is limited to cases where the debtor is about to leave the state or is concealing his property.

CHAPTER II

TRANSFERS IN FRAUD OF CREDITORS

§ 4. **Creditor's bill in equity to set aside transfer.**[4] If a debtor, in order to defraud his creditors, transfers his property to another—usually a relative or close friend—usually upon a secret understanding that the property is to be held for the debtor, the creditor may maintain a bill in equity to set aside such transfer and have the property applied in payment of his claim

Since the basis of equity jurisdiction here is the debtor's fraud and not the failure of common-law execution to reach the debtor's intangible property, there would seem to be no satisfactory reason why the creditor should be required, as a condition precedent to his obtaining relief, that he get a judgment, have a levy made and the execution returned unsatisfied; but the fact that a creditor's bill for equitable execution and a creditor's bill to set aside a fraudulent transfer are both called briefly creditor's bills, has led to such confusion that it has frequently been laid down, in cases where a bill has been brought by a creditor to set aside a fraudulent transfer, that he must first get a judgment and exhaust the possibilities of common-law execution before being able to maintain his bill. But courts that make such a require-

[4] 24 **Am Jur,** Fraudulent Conveyances, §§ 169–181.

Conveyance in consideration of future support as fraudulent against creditors. 2 **ALR** 1438–1453; s. in 23 **ALR** 584–587.

Right of grantee or transferee to be reimbursed for expenditures in payment of taxes or encumbrances on property where conveyance of transfer is in fraud of creditors. 8 **ALR** 527–543.

Necessity of participation by the grantee or transferee in the fraud of the grantor or transferor in order to avoid a voluntary conveyance of transfer as against creditors. 17 **ALR** 728–743.

Gift of debtor's services to third person as fraud on creditors. 28 **ALR** 1046, 1065.

Right of tort claimant to attack conveyance or transfer as fraudulent. 39 **ALR** 175–188.

Right to set aside, for benefit of heirs and distributees, a conveyance or transfer by decedent in fraud of his creditors. 148 **ALR** 230–243.

Conveyance pursuant to antenuptial agreement as fraud on creditors. 41 **ALR** 1163–1172.

Gift by husband as fraud on wife. 64 **ALR** 466–499; s. in 112 **ALR** 649–657.

Absolute conveyance or transfer with secret reservation as fraudulent per se as against creditors. 68 **ALR** 306–321.

Doctrine of lis pendens as applicable to actions to avoid conveyance or transfer in fraud of creditors or to prevent such conveyance or transfer. 74 **ALR** 690–701.

Right of grantee, mortgagee, or transferee in instrument fraudulent as to creditors to protection to extent of consideration paid to him. 79 **ALR** 132–149.

Principle which denies relief to party who has conveyed or transferred property in fraud of his creditors, as affected by execution, as part of, or as contemplated at time of, the fraudulent transaction, of reconveyance or retransfer of the property to him. 89 **ALR** 1166–1180.

Validity as against creditors of conveyance in trust for settlor for life with remainder to his appointees. 93 **ALR** 1211–1223.

Right of creditor of decedent, before perfecting his claim or after loss of recourse against decedent's estate, to pursue remedy against property conveyed by the decedent in fraud of his creditors. 103 **ALR** 555–568.

Fact that debt to pay or secure which conveyance was made was barred by limitation as affecting attack made upon it as a fraud upon creditors. 109 **ALR** 1220–1229.

Right of individual creditor or creditors of debtor in liquidation or receivership to maintain bill to set aside conveyances or transfers in fraud of creditors. 119 **ALR** 1339–1348.

Excessive security for debt as affecting question of fraud upon creditors. 138 **ALR** 1051–1065.

ment usually make an exception where the circumstances are such that the creditor must act promptly. In some states the requirement has been abrogated by statute. Wherever the requirement is enforced it is obviously impossible for a creditor to get any equitable relief unless his claim has matured —an obviously undesirable result.

§ 5. The Statute of Elizabeth—Uniform Fraudulent Conveyance Act.[5] In 1570 Parliament passed a statute, commonly referred to as the Statute of Elizabeth, which permitted—in case of a fraudulent transfer by a debtor— the creditors to ignore such transfer and have common-law execution levied on the property just as if no such transfer had been made, with a proviso protecting bona fide purchasers for value from the debtor.

The advantage of the proceeding under the statute over bringing a bill in equity to set aside the transfer was its cheapness and promptness. The disadvantage was that if a creditor was unable to prove that the transfer was fraudulent he might he held liable in an action of trespass or trover for having an unlawful execution levied upon the property.

The Statute of Elizabeth was substantially re-enacted in most if not all of the states. But in the last quarter of a century nearly half of the states have adopted a Uniform Fraudulent Conveyance Act. That statute provides that as against all but bona fide purchasers a creditor whose claim has matured may have a fraudulent transfer set aside or he may disregard the conveyance and either attach or levy execution upon the property conveyed; if his claim has not matured he may ask the court to restrain the defendant from disposing of the property, or to appoint a receiver to take charge of the property or to set aside the conveyance.

Though transfers of choses in action were held not to be within the Statute of Elizabeth because choses in action could not be reached by common-law execution, such transfers come within the fraudulent conveyance statutes of most states and within the Uniform Fraudulent Conveyance Act.

§ 6. Badges of fraud—retention of possession by transferor.[6] Twyne's Case, decided in 1601, named several badges of fraud: (1) that the transfer of goods was of everything the transferor had; (2) that the transferor continued in possession and used the goods as his own; (3) the transfer was made secretly; (4) the transfer was made while a creditor of the transferor was trying to reach the goods; (5) the transfer was made subject to a trust in favor of the transferor; (6) the deed of transfer contained a clause that the transfer was made honestly.

In Twyne's Case (1602) 3 Co. R.(b), 76 Eng. Reprint 809, the transfer was made by way of gift. But whether the transfer is by way of gift or sale or pledge, the retention of possession by the transferor is, in some states, regarded as fraudulent as against attaching creditors; in other states the retention of possession is regarded as raising a presumption of fraud, and in still others as merely evidence of fraud.

In all the states there are bulk sales acts which protect wholesalers and other creditors against a retailer's disposing of his entire stock of goods and disappearing with the proceeds of such a sale, by requiring notice to be given to creditors of the details of such a sale a certain number of days in advance; if such notice is not given the sale is not good as against creditors. A chattel mortgage is not a sale or transfer within the meaning of such bulk sales act

[5] 24 Am Jur, Fraudulent Conveyances, §§ 4–6.

[6] 24 Am Jur, Fraudulent Conveyances, §§ 41–61.

but comes, of course, within the statute requiring registry of the chattel mortgage. In many states a bill of sale given by way of security must be registered as a chattel mortgage in order to be good against creditors.

§ 7. **Same—transfer of possession to bailee or to conditional vendee.**[7] Where goods are sent by the vendor to an agent on consignment for purpose of sale on behalf of the principal such a consignment is not regarded as fraudulent and the creditors of the agent are not entitled to reach the goods.

Where a vendor of goods retains title by way of security until the full purchase price is paid, the transfer of possession to the conditional vendee is not regarded as fraudulent and apart from statute the conditional vendor prevails against the creditors of the conditional vendee. Such transactions are not covered by the Chattel Mortgage Registry Act but in many states there are special statutes requiring the registry of such conditional sales to be good against the vendee's purchasers and creditors.

§ 8. **Same—transfer upon promise to reconvey.**[8] Where A, while insolvent, borrows money from B and conveys to B property worth much more than the sum borrowed, upon a promise by B to reconvey upon repayment of the loan, courts differ as to whether such a conveyance is good as against A's creditors. Some hold that the conveyance is fraudulent both as to existing and subsequent creditors, others hold it fraudulent only to existing creditors, still others hold it presumptively fraudulent as to existing creditors and, some states hold that there is no presumption of fraud in such a transaction but that fraud must be affirmatively shown.

Where A loaned money to B, known to him to be insolvent, and took a chattel mortgage to secure that and a previous debt, the transaction may be a preference but is not in itself a fraudulent conveyance. Where A loans money to B and takes a mortgage on property of much greater value than the loan, such a transaction is not in itself fraudulent as to B's creditors, but it may furnish evidence of fraudulent intent.

CHAPTER III

GENERAL ASSIGNMENTS—CREDITOR'S AGREEMENTS

§ 9. **General assignments.**[9] Though named as an act of bankruptcy in the bankruptcy statute, a general assignment by a debtor of all his property for the equal benefit of all his creditors is valid at common law. If it is not for the benefit of all creditors it is regarded as a fraudulent conveyance as to the creditors not provided for. For example, where A and B, partners, both insolvent, assigned the partnership personal property and real property held in common, to be used to pay partnership debts only the transfer was held to be fraudulent as to individual creditors for whom no provision was made.

Where the general assignment is made for the purpose of carrying on the debtor's business for a definite period it is not valid because it is regarded as

[7] 24 **Am Jur,** Fraudulent Conveyances, §§ 48, 55.

[8] 24 **Am Jur,** Fraudulent Conveyances, § 122.

[9] 4 **Am Jur,** Assignments for Benefit of Creditors, §§ 4, 8–30.

Setoff by surety of claim paid for insolvent principal whose assets are being administered for the benefit of creditors, against own indebtedness to principal. 40 **ALR** 1096–1110.

Validity and effect of provisions in assignments for creditors authorizing assignees to continue assignor's business. 23 **ALR** 119–222.

an assignment not for the benefit of creditors but a transfer for the purpose of hindering and delaying creditors and therefore a fraudulent conveyance.

Apart from statute a debtor making a general assignment may provide for preferring some creditors above others unless the preference is used as a means of coercing the preferred creditors into agreeing to execute releases of their respective demands. In some states statutes have been passed regulating the making of preferences in general assignments.

The weight of authority is that a general assignee for the benefit of creditors stands in the shoes of the debtor and is not a bona fide purchaser for value.

§ 10. Creditors' agreements.[10] Where the creditors of a debtor in embarrassed circumstances believe that the debtor's financial embarrassment is only temporary they may work out together a friendly arrangement under which the business is continued as a going concern usually with a change of management. If the arrangement succeeds the creditors may be able to realize very much more than if a receiver is appointed or the debtor is thrown into bankruptcy.

If under such an arrangement some of the creditors or some outsiders undertake to manage the business, this does not make the other creditors partners either with the debtor or with the managers, because their participation in the profits of the business is not for the purpose of making profits but merely for the purpose of getting their claims paid. Nor do the managers of the business become the agents of the creditors so as to render the creditors liable for their undertakings.

Where the arrangement made by the creditors of a corporation debtor is necessary and fair and assented to by all the creditors and nearly all the stockholders, a stockholder holding only a small amount of stock is not entitled to have the arrangement set aside as a fraud on him.

If under a creditor's arrangement the manager of the business property contracts new debts in order to carry on the business, but the arrangement fails and a receiver is appointed and the assets distributed, the new creditors are entitled to priority over the old creditors who are regarded as having consented to having the business assets put up as capital and authorized the manager to contract debts upon the faith of such assets.

Where the creditors enter into a composition agreement with their debtor, consenting to accept payment of a percentage of their claims in full satisfaction thereof and the agreement is carried out, the debtor is completely discharged; if it is not carried out and the debtor later becomes bankrupt, the creditors may prove in the bankruptcy proceedings only for the unpaid balance due, not for the full amount of their claims.

CHAPTER IV

RECEIVERSHIPS

§ 11. Scope of receivership jurisdiction.[1] A receivership is merely an ancillary and incidental remedy, not final relief. It does not determine any

10 11 **Am Jur**, Composition with Creditors, §§ 1–8.

1 45 **Am Jur**, Receivers, §§ 7–80.

Friendly or consent receiverships. 84 **ALR** 1443–1466; s. in 90 **ALR** 406.

Power of court to appoint receiver in a suit for divorce or separation. 95 **ALR** 902–913.

Inherent power of equity, at instance of a stockholder, to appoint receiver for, or substantive right; it is not even a step towards the determination of such a right but is merely a means of preserving property which may ultimately be applied toward the satisfaction of substantive rights.

A receiver is often appointed upon the application of a secured creditor who fears that his security will be wasted; or upon application of a judgment creditor who has exhausted his legal remedy; or in a proceeding to foreclose a mortgage. Apart from statute it is usually held that a receiver will not be appointed upon the application of an unsecured simple contract creditor or of a corporation stockholder. But in many states there are statutes allowing the appointment of a receiver of the corporation upon the application of a stockholder, in order to bring about a reorganization of the corporation. And after 1908, consent receiverships became a common method of reorganizing embarrassed corporations. The practice was for the corporation and its larger creditors to work out a plan of reorganization, then induce a simple contract creditor to file a petition asking for a receivership; in this petition the corporation would join, waiving the requirement that a simple contract creditor must first reduce his claim to judgment and exhaust his legal remedies before asking for the appointment of a receiver. The tendency today is toward using reorganization proceedings under § 77B (Chapter 10) of the Bankruptcy Act instead of equity receiverships.

The doctrine of consent receiverships has not been applied to an individual debtor, so a receiver will not be appointed upon petition of an unsecured simple contract creditor, even if consent is given by the debtor, though the purpose is to prevent the depletion of the debtor's estate by the judgment, attachment and secured creditors.

Where a corporation was still solvent the appointment of a receiver was sought in order to compel the minority stockholders to agree to a reorganization; this was held to be an improper purpose and the appointment was refused.

§ 12. Status of the receiver.[2] The appointment of the receiver of a corporation does not put an end to the corporation which can still sue and be sued as to matters not placed within the authority of the receiver.

Since a receiver is the officer of the court appointing him, a receiver appointed in the state is not entitled as of right to bring suit in another state to collect assets of the estate, but he is usually permitted to do so. If there are considerable assets to be collected in other states, however, the usual practice is for each of such states to appoint an auxiliary or ancillary receiver. Whether such ancillary receiver will distribute the assets collected by him to the creditors in the state of his appointment or will transmit them to the primary receiver will depend upon the discretion of the court that appoints him. After the appointment of an ancillary receiver all creditors who have not acquired some priority of lien upon its assets stand on the same footing.

Since a receiver is an officer of the court appointing him any wrongful dis-

to wind up, a solvent going corporation, on ground of fraud, mismanagement, or dissensions. 43 **ALR** 242–318; s. in 61 **ALR** 1212–1224; 91 **ALR** 665–683.

Right of mortgagee to receiver. 26 **ALR** 33–85; s. in 36 **ALR** 609–613; 55 **ALR** 533–537; 87 ALR 1008–1015; 111 **ALR** 730–7 6.

Appointment of receiver of property of individual debtor or partnership on application of simple contract creditor without lien. 109 **ALR** 279–297.

Right to appointment of receiver in action between persons owning or claiming to own undivided or successive interests in property or fund. 127 **ALR** 1228–1263.

2 45 **Am Jur**, Receivers, §§ 126–134.

Operation of railroad by receiver at expense of prior lienors. 50 **ALR** 146–174.

Right of receiver to take property in summary manner or by summary proceedings from strangers to the record. 40 **ALR** 903–921; s. in 43 **ALR** 1340.

turbance of the property held by him is a contempt of court and punishable as such.

Where a receiver's duty is merely to preserve assets but not to make any distribution among creditors, the latter may proceed as if no receiver had been appointed.

Where a receiver has been appointed for a corporation, he, and not the stockholders, is the proper party to bring suit against directors of the corporation for negligence.

§ 13. Respective liabilities of the debtor and receiver.[3] Where the debtor for whom a receiver has been appointed is a lessee of property the receiver may go into posssssion of such property for a reasonable time in order to determine whether to adopt the lease; if he then rejects it, he is liable only for the fair rental value for the time he occupied it.

As to contracts other than leases, a receiver is likewise entitled to a reasonable time in which to decide whether to adopt or reject it. Where, after the appointment of a receiver, the employment contract of a debtor's employee expires and the employee is kept on by the receiver there is no implication of any new contract because the acts of a receiver must be ratified by the court appointing him.

Where a receiver elects to reject a contract, the other party to the contract is entitled to damages for breach thereof and is entitled to share with those whose contracts were breached before the receiver was appointed; and in determining the amount of the damages for the breach of such rejected contracts the breach is considered as having taken place at the time of the receiver's appointment. Unless the receiver affirmatively adopts a contract he is considered to have renounced it.

Unless the receiver is personally at fault, his liability ceases when his office as receiver comes to an end. On the other hand, except by statute, the debtor is not liable for the acts of the receiver, except to the extent of the profit received therefrom.

Where a receiver is authorized to borrow money up to a certain amount and is not authorized to buy on credit he may not, by buying on credit, exceed the amount authorized, because buying on credit is the equivalent of borrowing money to pay for such goods.

§ 14. Priority and distribution.[4] Where gasoline taxes due to the state were mingled by the receiver with receivership assets it was held that the state was entitled to priority and that tracing the funds was not necessary.

Since usually the main purpose of having a receiver appointed is to prevent borrowing he has no authority to borrow unless expressly authorized by a court.

Since it is important that a railroad or other public service be continued, receivers' certificates may displace the lien of public utility bondholders; but

[3] 45 **Am Jur**, Receivers, §§ 342–353.
Liability of one procuring appointment of receiver for expenses of receivership. 68 **ALR** 878–892.
Failure to obtain permission to sue receiver as affecting jurisdiction of action. 29 **ALR** 1460–1471.
Claim in receivership for breach of contract which was still executory when receiver was appointed. 33 **ALR** 508–520.
Conduct pending receivership as contempt of court. 39 **ALR** 6–37; s. in 45 **ALR** 241, 242.
Liability of receiver in his official capacity for torts or negligence of receivership employees. 10 **ALR** 1055–1079.
Continuance of business by receiver at loss. 12 **ALR** 292–304.

[4] 45 **Am Jur**, Receivers, §§ 236–241, 250–274.
43 **Harv. L. R.** 336, Conflict of Equities under the "Deep Rock" Doctrine.

this may not be done in the case of an ordinary industrial corporation, unless it is for the purpose of saving corporate property from destruction.

Where a railroad corporation goes into the hands of a receiver, wage earners are usually given priority over bondholders in respect of wages earned with a short period—usually six months—before the appointment of the receiver; and it would seem to be the better view that the same rule should be applied to other corporations.

Since in a receivership the title to the debtor's property remains in the debtor, any amount already received by a secured creditor must first be deducted in determining the amount for which he may prove in the receivership proceedings.

PART II. BANKRUPTCY

CHAPTER V

INTRODUCTION

§ 15. History of bankruptcy legislation.[5] Before the present Federal Bankruptcy Act was passed in 1898 there had been three statutes, all of them short lived. The first was passed in 1800, confined to merchants and traders; there was no provision for voluntary petitions and no provision for discharge except by consent of two-thirds of the creditors. The statute was criticized by the Republican-Democratic party as in derogation of the powers of the states and soon after Jefferson was elected the act was repealed, after an existence of three years.

The second act was passed in 1941, partly due to the financial panic of 1837. It provided for voluntary petitions and for discharge and in the eighteen months of its existence some 28,000 debtors took advantage of its provisions.

The third statute was brought on by the Civil War. It was enacted in 1867 and lasted for eleven years. One of the objections to the law was that it was too easy for creditors to prove the insolvency of a debtor.

The present statute, passed in 1898, was due in large measure to the financial depression, which lasted from 1893 till 1896, and produced a very large number of business failures. It has been amended eleven times, thereby adding new sections dealing with the problems of farmers, railroads, municipal corporations and wage earners, and has apparently become firmly imbedded now in our jurisprudence.

§ 16. Constitutionality of the present act.[6] The constitutionality of the present act has been questioned on the ground that it is not uniform because it excepts from its operation such property as is exempt from execution by the varying laws of the different states, but this objection has been answered by pointing out that one of the effects of the act is that of a general execution issued in favor of all the creditors and it is quite proper to confine its legal operation to such property as other legal process could reach. There is also the argument from necessity; there is such a variance in the provisions of the various state exemption laws that a Federal bankruptcy act would be impossible if it undertook to impose the same exemption in bankruptcy proceedings in all the states.

Provisions for reorganization under § 77B—later Chapter 10—have been justified because of the unsatisfactory results obtained by equity receiverships

[5] 6 **Am Jur**, Bankruptcy, §§ 1–3.
16 **Tul. L. R.** 339, A Primer on Bankruptcy.
8 **Mo. L. R.** 85, Security Devices as Preferences under the Bankruptcy Act.
5 **U. of Toronto L. J.** 324, International Bankruptcy Law—Its Present Status.
17 **Temple U. L. Q.** 115, Section 270 of the Federal Bankruptcy Act.

[6] 6 **Am Jur**, Bankruptcy, § 4.
Constitutionality, construction, and effect of § 74 of Bankruptcy Act (with outline of procedure, and forms). 99 **ALR** 1325–1369.

Constitutionality, construction, and effect of § 75 of Bankruptcy Act (with outline of procedure, and forms). 99 **ALR** 1379–1438; s. in 112 **ALR** 1467–1485.

Construction and application of provisions of § 77B of Bankruptcy Act relating to allowance for expenses and services. 107 **ALR** 537–564.

and because it was a logical development of bankruptcy legislation to give relief where there is no insolvency in the modern sense and where debts may be met if time to do so be sufficiently extended. Such reorganization proceedings are also similar to the composition with creditors which had been authorized by the Act of 1867; and a similar justification has been made for the schemes of arrangement provided for by the present statute.

The constitutionality of section 75(8), as amended by the Frazier-Lemke Act was attacked by a mortgagee as depriving him of property without due process, but it was upheld on the ground that the three-year stay granted to the mortgagor was an emergency measure and not absolute and that giving to the mortgagor control over the property after default was not unfair because the mortgagor was assumed not to be a wrongdoer but the victim of general economic conditions and his possession was not worse for the mortgagee than that of a receiver or trustee would be.

The constitutionality of the provision, in Chapter 10, for the composition of indebtedness of taxing agencies or instrumentalities was attacked, in its application to an irrigation district, as a violation of the Fifth and Tenth Amendments; but it was upheld on the ground that the state had consented to the application of the act to irrigation districts, that the state retained control of its fiscal affairs and that the state could give no relief to the irrigation district against the financial depression due to the low price of agricultural products because it could not pass a valid law impairing the obligation of contracts.

§ 17. Effect of a National Bankruptcy Act on state laws.[7] When there is a national bankruptcy act in force, it supersedes all state insolvency laws undertaking to give a discharge to a debtor as to all claims of creditors resident within that state and of nonresident creditors who prove their claims in the state insolvency proceeding. The reason for this is that otherwise there would be intolerable confusion. On the other hand state laws as to voluntary assignments for the benefits of creditors are not superseded because no discharge of the debtor is provided for.

When there is no national bankruptcy act in force old state insolvency laws are revived and the way is open for the states to pass new insolvency laws if they wish. The defect of such laws is that they can not bind nonresident creditors who do not prove their claims.

CHAPTER VI

BANKRUPTCY ADMINISTRATION

§ 18. Jurisdiction—territorial, ancillary.[8] Bankruptcy proceedings may be held in that district in which the debtor had his or its principal place of business, residence or domicile for the greatest portion of the preceding six months or in which a foreign debtor has property. Where petitions are filed against the same debtor in different districts each of which has jurisdiction "the cases shall, by order of the court first acquiring jurisdiction, be transferred to and consolidated in the court which can proceed with the same for the greatest convenience of parties in interest."

7 6 Am Jur, Bankruptcy, §§ 5, 6.
27 U. of Minn. L. R. 1, Garnishment and Bankruptcy.

8 6 Am Jur, Bankruptcy, §§ 23–31, 339, 354.

Section 2(20) provides that bankruptcy courts may "exercise ancillary jurisdiction over persons or property within their respective territorial limits in aid of a receiver or trustee appointed in any bankruptcy proceedings pending in any other court of bankruptcy."

§ 19. Same—summary and plenary—appellate.[9] Where property is either actually or constructively in the possession of the debtor at the time the bankruptcy petition is filed the trustee in bankruptcy may bring informal summary proceedings in the bankruptcy court to get control of it. But if there is an adverse claim made to property claimed by the trustee in bankruptcy that must be formally litigated in a plenary proceeding, for example, where the debtor had a deposit in a bank and the bank claimed a right to hold the deposit; or when a creditor had obtained a lien within four months while the debtor was still solvent, because the property might have come into the hands of a bona fide purchaser for value or inchoate rights by way of lien might have been acquired before the four-month period.

Plenary suits should—under Section 23—be brought in the same court where the debtor would have sued if there had been no bankruptcy proceedings, except suits for the recovery of property, under sections 60, 67 and 70.

There is no right to take an appeal from an interlocutory decision of the bankruptcy court; but if there is any doubt whether the decision is interlocutory or final it is better to take an appeal because the right to appeal may be lost in case the decision is held to have been a final one.

Where an involuntary petition is filed and the debtor insists upon his common-law right to a jury trial on the issues of insolvency and the commission of the acts of bankruptcy alleged there can be no appeal from the decision of the lower court, thus taking up questions of both law and fact; the remedy is by writ of error which brings up merely matters of law. Where there has been no jury trial there may be an appeal as provided in section 25a.

§ 20. Stay of proceedings—administrative officials.[10] Where at the time of petition filed a suit is pending against the debtor upon a claim dischargeable in bankruptcy, such suit is stayed till there has been an adjudication or a dismissal of the petition; and if the debtor is adjudged a bankrupt there is a further stay till the question of his discharge is decided.

The term "judge" does not, but the term "court" does, include "referee." A referee, as well as a judge, may grant, deny or reject discharges. An important part of the judge's duties is to pass upon the records, findings and orders certified to him by a referee. Referees are appointed for two years but are usually reappointed; they may not hold any other federal or state office of importance.

The trustee or trustees in bankruptcy—not exceeding three—may be elected by the creditors in ordinary bankruptcy proceedings; if they fail to elect or if there is a failure to qualify, the court appoints. In reorganizations and arrangements the court appoints. A court should not appoint any one selected, directly or indirectly, by the debtor. The trustee is vested with the title to the debtor's unexempt property as of the date of the petition.

Upon the application of the parties in interest the bankruptcy court may appoint a receiver to take charge of the debtor's property and protect the interest of the creditors till the petition is dismissed or the trustee qualifies.

[9] 6 **Am Jur,** Bankruptcy, §§ 326–369, 536–556.

[10] 6 **Am Jur,** Bankruptcy, §§ 136–143, 487, 518–520.

The receiver may be authorized to carry on the debtor's business temporarily and to prosecute or defend any action brought by or against the debtor.

§ 21. Initiatory procedure—persons subject to bankruptcy.[1] The bankruptcy proceedings are begun by petition which is in the nature of a pleading. A voluntary petition need not allege insolvency or an act of bankruptcy. Section 59(b) provides that "three or more creditors who have provable claims, fixed as to liability and liquidated as to amount against any person, which amount in the aggregate in excess of the value of securities held by them, if any, to $500 or more; or if all of the creditors are less than twelve in number, then one of such creditors whose claim equals such amount may file a petition to have him adjudged a bankrupt."

Any person except municipal, railroad, insurance or banking corporations or a building and loan association may become a voluntary bankrupt. Any natural person except a wage earner or a farmer or any moneyed business or a commercial corporation, except a building and loan association, a municipal, railroad, insurance or banking corporation, owing debts to the amount of $1,000 or over may be adjudged an involuntary bankrupt.

A co-operative milk association, though nonprofit, may be adjudged an involuntary bankrupt because it is engaged in business or commerce as those words are ordinarily understood. A joint stock company or partnership with transferable shares, engaged in the insurance business, is a corporation within the meaning of the Bankruptcy Act and therefore cannot be put into involuntary bankruptcy.

A partnership may be adjudged a bankrupt as a separate entity and a discharge of the partnership does not discharge the individual general partners from liability for the firm debts. On the other hand, where all the general partners are individually adjudged bankrupt the partnership entity is also adjudged bankrupt without further petition.

A wage earner is one who works for wages, salary or hire at a rate of compensation not exceeding $1500 a year. A music teacher who gave lessons at fifty cents an hour was held not to be a wage earner.

Whether one who is personally engaged not only in farming but also in other activities is a farmer within the Bankruptcy Act depends upon whether, under all the circumstances, he is engaged primarily in farming or whether the principal part of his income is derived from such farming operations.

§ 22. Discharge.[2] A natural person need not apply for a discharge; a corporation must apply within six months after the adjudication.

[1] 6 **Am Jur,** Bankruptcy, §§ 32–39, 53–56.
Voluntary or involuntary bankruptcy proceedings in case of incompetent or infant. 125 **ALR** 1292–1301.

[2] 6 **Am Jur,** Bankruptcy, §§ 457–535.
What amounts to promise to pay which will avoid effect of discharge in bankruptcy. 75 **ALR** 580–603.
Grant of injunction or stay by Federal court to protect discharge in bankruptcy. 141 **ALR** 1380–1394.
Failure to keep books as ground for refusal of discharge in bankruptcy. 73 **ALR** 1157–1170.
Right to and form of judgment against one discharged in bankruptcy in order to sustain attachment or garnishment or to perfect a right of action against one secondarily liable as surety on a bond given to dissolve the same. 81 **ALR** 81–97.
Conversion as wilful and malicious injury to property within provision of Bankruptcy Act preventing discharge from liability for such injury. 98 **ALR** 1454–1461.
Exceptions in discharge provisions of Bankruptcy Act as applicable to debts arising from extension of credit incident to sale of property. 133 **ALR** 440–467.
False statement of partner or other agent of bankrupt as ground for refusal of discharge. 133 **ALR** 676–684.
Imputation of agent's knowledge to bankrupt or to creditor as satisfying conditions of provisions of Bankruptcy Act excepting unscheduled debts from discharge. 134 **ALR** 185–192.
Validity and effect of promise made after

A discharge may be waived by a writing filed in the bankruptcy proceedings or by inexcusable failure to appear at the first meeting of creditors or at a meeting specially called for his examination. A discharge may be opposed either by creditors or by the United States Attorney for the district. A second discharge may not be granted within six years, the period being computed between the first discharge and the filing of the petition for the second discharge. Various acts of misconduct which will prevent discharge are set out in Section 14(b); they include obtaining property or credit by fraud and making conveyances in fraud of creditors within one year before the filing of the petition. Where the discharge has been obtained by fraud it may be revoked. The policy of the bankruptcy law is to allow a fresh start only to honest debtors.

Generally, all provable debts are dischargeable, but there are many exceptions, including federal and state taxes, liability for fraudulently obtaining money or property, for malicious injury to persons or property, for alimony and debts due to employees for services. Whether liability for converting personal property is dischargeable depends upon whether it was or was not morally innocent.

The discharge does not entirely obliterate the obligation; if the debtor promises to pay a provable debt he will be bound by it even though made before discharge if it was made after the filing of the petition.

CHAPTER VII

ACTS OF BANKRUPTCY

§ 23. In general.[3] Section 3 enumerates six acts of bankruptcy. They are, briefly: (1) conveyance in fraud of creditors; (2) voluntary preferences while insolvent; (3) involuntary preferences while insolvent; (4) allowing, while insolvent, a creditor to obtain a levy, attachment, judgment or other lien; (5) made a general assignment for creditors, or, while insolvent, a receiver or trustee has been put in charge of his property; (6) admitted in writing his inability to pay his debts and his willingness to be adjudged a bankrupt on that ground.

The common-law test of insolvency was the inability to pay debts as they mature and that seems to be the test where debtor relief is sought by way of composition, extension and reorganization. For the purpose of ordinary bankruptcy proceedings it seems to be uncertain whether the common-law test applies or the assets and liabilities test. The stopping-payment test may be too harsh on the debtor where he has plenty of assets; and the assets and liabilities test may be too harsh on him because unmatured obligations are included in the computation. In determining assets, exempt assets are included because they may be used by the debtor to pay debts.

An adjudication in bankruptcy does not establish conclusively, as against a creditor to whom a preference was supposed to have been made, that the debtor was insolvent at the time of the alleged preference.

§ 24. The separate acts of bankruptcy.[4] A surety who as such has a contingent claim against the principal debtor is regarded as a creditor of such

filing of petition in bankruptcy, but before discharge, to pay existing debt. 83 ALR 1295–1301.

3 6 Am Jur, Bankruptcy, §§ 47–52.

4 6 Am Jur, Bankruptcy, §§ 48, 49.
What constitutes a "general assignment

principal debtor from the standpoint of a conveyance in fraud of creditors.

The fact that the property transferred by the debtor to a creditor has been purchased in good faith from a thief does not prevent it from being a preferential transfer. But substituting, within the four months' period, a new mortgage on the same property in place of an old mortgage given before the four month period, is not a preference.

There need not be an actual, subjective intent to prefer; as is usual in the common-law system, the objective test is applied; if the natural and actual result of a transaction is a preference, that is sufficient.

Where a debtor, while insolvent, permitted a creditor to obtain a judgment and to make a levy on a stock of goods and failed to vacate it at least five days before sale under execution and a sale was had, it was an act of bankruptcy.

A general assignment to a trustee for the benefit of creditors is an act of bankruptcy even though the debtor was solvent. If it is made within four months of filing a petition in bankruptcy the assignment is avoided by an adjudication in bankruptcy; but this does not forfeit the right of the general assignee to compensation for his services or to litigate the question in plenary proceedings as an adverse claimant; he cannot be dealt with in summary proceedings.

CHAPTER VIII

ASSETS OF THE ESTATE

§ 25. In general.[5] As soon as a trustee in bankruptcy qualifies, his title relates back to the time of the filing of the petition.

The property which passes to the trustee includes expectancies and contingent and executory interests which vest or become assignable within six months after bankruptcy; and the trustee may avoid any fraudulent transfer made during the year prior to the date when the petition in bankruptcy was filed.

For the purpose of avoiding preferences and fraudulent transfers made by the debtor, a transfer shall not be deemed to be made till it is so far perfected that no bona fide purchaser from the debtor and no creditor could thereafter have acquired any right in the property superior to the right of the transferee therein.

§ 26. Causes of action in contract or tort—expectancies.[6] Where the debtor at the time of petition filed was a party to an unperformed contract the

for the benefit of creditors" within provisions of the Bankruptcy Act which make such an assignment an act of bankruptcy. 57 **ALR** 859–865.

[5] 6 **Am Jur**, Bankruptcy, §§ 144–149.

Life insurance as assets under Bankruptcy Act. 68 **ALR** 1215–1239; s. in 103 **ALR** 239–251.

Right of trustee in bankruptcy as regards property held in trust for bankrupt. 16 **ALR** 552–564; s. in 138 **ALR** 1349–1354.

Right of receiver, assignee, or trustee in bankruptcy to possession and administration of collateral validly pledged by his insolvent. 28 **ALR** 409–420.

Trademark or tradename as asset in case of bankruptcy, insolvency, or assignment for benefit of creditors. 44 **ALR** 706–713.

Future estate or interest in property as asset in bankruptcy. 48 **ALR** 784–797; s. in 65 **ALR** 773–775.

Right to rescind sale and reclaim goods for buyer's fraud as to his financial condition as against trustee in bankruptcy under American act. 59 **ALR** 418–430.

What claims against the government pass to trustee in bankruptcy. 102 **ALR** 159–170.

Rights in respect of assets undisclosed at the time of bankrupt's discharge. 111 **ALR** 835–856.

Voidable preference within meaning of Bankruptcy Act as created by payment or transfer to bankrupt's creditor by a third person, or with funds or property furnished by him. 130 **ALR** 956–962.

Growing crops as part of land or as a chattel asset, in farm debtor proceedings under Bankruptcy Act. 150 **ALR** 1175–1178.

[6] 6 **Am Jur**, Bankruptcy, §§ 159, 169–176.

trustee in bankruptcy is entitled to the benefit of the contract without giving notice of adopting it, whether the other party has been guilty of a breach thereof or not.

A right of action for a purely personal tort such as slander, malicious prosecution, assault and battery and negligent injury to the person do not pass to the trustee in bankruptcy; but an action for deceit in the sale of property does pass because the fraud was an injury to the debtor's property.

Apart from the recent change in the statute giving the trustee in bankruptcy expectancies and contingent or executory interests which vest or become assignable within six months after bankruptcy, the possibility of a debtor inheriting from an ancestor does not go to his trustee in bankruptcy even though the ancestor should die shortly after petition filed. Where a will gave a remainder after the death of the testator's wife to three children in equal shares, giving to descendants of any child the parent's portion in equal shares, it was held that the interest of a child who became bankrupt before the death of the mother passed to the trustee in bankruptcy because it was assignable.

§ 27. Exemptions—insurance—leaseholds.[7] Property which by the state law is exempt from execution does not go to the trustee in bankruptcy. If the debtor has waived his exemption the remedy of the creditor is in the state court. If the debtor conceals from the trustee in bankruptcy assets exceeding in value the amount of the state exemption he thereby forfeits his exemption because exemption laws are not meant for the protection of dishonest debtors.

Where the debtor has a life insurance policy on his own life payable to his estate or where he has reserved an absolute right to change the beneficiary, the trustee in bankruptcy is entitled to the cash surrender value of the policy. If this is forthcoming from the debtor or his friends, the policy may be preserved for the debtor. This is of considerable importance where, because of ill health, the debtor cannot get new insurance. In some states, by statute a policy taken out by the debtor in favor of another—usually a wife or near relative—is exempt and the beneficiary is entitled to the exclusion of creditors.

Where a lease held by the debtor provides for forfeiture of the lease if the lessee should assign without the consent of the lessor, this applies also to a voluntary assignment by the lessee and does not prevent his trustee in bankruptcy from selling it for the benefit of creditors. If a lease provides for a right of re-entry in case the lessee becomes bankrupt and the trustee in bankruptcy decides not to adopt the lease because not beneficial, the lessor may not re-enter because the condition has not happened.

The debtor's membership in a board of trade passes to the trustee in bankruptcy and the court can order the bankrupt to do what is necessary to transfer the membership.

§ 28. Property held in trust—liens acquired by legal proceedings.[8] Where the debtor holds the bare legal title to property subject to a trust or similar equity, the title to such property does not pass to the trustee in bankruptcy because, not being a bona fide purchaser for value he would take it subject to the equity and the property would be of no value to the creditors.

Where a lien is given by statute, such as a mechanic's lien or a lien given

[7] 6 **Am Jur,** Bankruptcy, §§ 153, 163–168, 181–189.

[8] 6 **Am Jur,** Bankruptcy, §§ 161, 162, 298–310.

to a landlord on property of his tenant, the trustee in bankruptcy takes subject to such a lien. He also takes subject to a lien obtained on the debtor's property by legal proceedings more than four months before the filing of the bankruptcy petition, a lien obtained by creditor's bill relating back to the time of filing the bill. But if such lien has been acquired either by levy or attachment at law or by a creditor's bill in equity within the four-month period the trustee in bankruptcy may, in plenary proceedings, have such lien declared void.

§ 29. Interests adverse to the bankrupt.[9] Upon qualifying, the trustee in bankruptcy gets title to all the debtor's property no matter where it is located and the court may order the sale of land outside the district and enjoin the foreclosure of a mortgage thereon.

Where a creditor sues in a state court to have a fraudulent conveyance set aside and after more than four months after the beginning of such suit the debtor becomes bankrupt, the trustee in bankruptcy may assert the creditor's right and have the conveyance set aside but if he does not do so the creditor may continue the proceedings in the state court.

After the filing of the petition no one can acquire an interest in the property; but a mere entry by a mortgagee to foreclose a mortgage is not the acquiring of an interest but merely the assertion of one already acquired.

Where some of the debtor's property is subject to valid liens it should ordinarily be sold subject to those liens; it should not be sold free from liens unless there is a reasonable prospect that after the lien holders are paid out of the proceeds there will be a surplus for creditors.

Where by the state law an unrecorded conditional sale is void only as to creditors who file their liens before the sale contract is recorded, a conditional sale made long before bankruptcy but filed within four months is good against the trustee in bankruptcy whose lien dates only from the filing of the petition.

A present pledge of securities to be completed as soon as the securities are capable of delivery is valid as against the trustee in bankruptcy of the pledgor, but not a mere agreement to give security in the future.

Where the debtor assigns to X accounts receivable, reserving an unrestricted power of disposition, this creates in X no right which is good against the debtor's trustee in bankruptcy because such a transaction is regarded as a fraud on creditors. But where the debtor while solvent assigned accounts receivable to X the contract providing that X was to have a lien on merchandise returned or refused by customers, this was a pledge of the merchandise and good against the trustee in bankruptcy as to merchandise taken possession of by X before petition filed.

Where a chattel mortgage is, because of failure to observe the requirements of the registry act, void as to existing creditors and those who became such later but before recording, the property thus mortgaged goes to the trustee in bankruptcy free of the mortgage for the benefit of the estate.

Where a debtor makes a conveyance to X in fraud of creditors and the conveyance is recorded and a creditor of X attaches the property in good faith, the attaching creditor's right is good against the trustee in bankruptcy.

Where an insolvent debtor, in order to avoid a criminal prosecution, transfers all this property to X as security for a small loan, such a transfer is not

9 6 **Am Jur,** Bankruptcy, §§ 356–358.
Pendency of bankruptcy proceedings as affecting nonjudicial foreclosure or enforcement of valid liens. 112 **ALR** 508–526.

a preference because of the present consideration but the trustee in bankruptcy may have it set aside as a conveyance in fraud of creditors.

§ 30. Preferences.[10] One who accepts a security with reasonable cause to believe that it is a preference does not thereby act fraudulently because the transaction was only voidable and not void; and if the trustee in bankruptcy does not act to avoid the preference he cannot later when the one receiving the preference goes into the hands of a receiver, maintain a claim to have a constructive trust declared.

A suit to recover a preference is not a part of the bankruptcy proceedings but is based on a controversy arising out of those proceedings and may be brought either in a state court or in the bankruptcy court. If it is merely a suit to recover money paid the remedy is at law, not in equity.

Where the debtor became entitled to a homestead in land burdened with a lien issuing out of a state court and levied within four months of bankruptcy the trustee is entitled to treat the lien as a preference and to enforce it for the benefit of all the creditors.

If the payee of a note accepts payment from the maker and such payment is later declared to be a preference and avoided as such, this does not discharge the indorsers because the payee was bound to accept payment and the indorsers are no worse off than if payment had not been made.

A bank which collects a draft as an agent and not as owner, is not a creditor so as to make it liable for a payment received and turned over to its principal though the payment was a preference to the principal.

The fact that the debtor pays only a part of his debt does not prevent the transaction from being a preference because it enables that creditor to obtain a larger percentage of his claim than the other creditors of his class.

Where an insolvent debtor gives a mortgage to a creditor and the latter persuades the debtor not to file a petition in bankruptcy till after the four months' period has expired, the trustee in bankruptcy may not have the mortgage avoided as a preference.

Where a debtor more than four months before bankruptcy gives a chattel mortgage to a creditor who takes possession within four months of bankruptcy the transaction may not be avoided by the trustee in bankruptcy as a preference even though by the state law an attaching or judgment creditor would not be bound by it.

Where, long before bankruptcy a debtor set aside securities for his drawing account, the creditor authorizing him to substitute other securities of equal value, the transaction, having been entered into in good faith, was held valid as creating a property right in the creditor even though he did not get possession of the securities till within the four months' period.

[10] 6 **Am Jur,** Bankruptcy, §§ 264–297.

Applicability to transaction between principal and surety of provision of American Bankruptcy Act avoiding preference. 39 **ALR** 120–126.

Right of corporation to prefer creditors. 19 **ALR** 320–380; s. in 38 **ALR** 90–94; 48 **ALR** 479–481; 56 **ALR** 207–209; 62 **ALR** 738–740.

Character of service contemplated by statutes giving a lien or preference, in event of insolvency, to servants, employees, laborers, etc. 54 **ALR** 567–594; s. in 111 **ALR** 1453–1460; 142 **ALR** 362–367.

State's prerogative right of preference at common law 51 **ALR** 1355–1376; s. in 65 **ALR** 1331–1334; 90 ALR 184–191.

Bankruptcy: lessor's right, upon bankruptcy of lessee, to enforce lien or retain security for future rentals. 22 **ALR** 1307–1312; s. in 45 **ALR** 717–718.

Setoff by bank against bankrupt's deposit as a preference within the Bankruptcy Law. 85 **ALR** 369–390.

Statute or rule relating to preferences by insolvent debtor as applicable to new security given in renewal of, exchange or substitution for, or addition to, existing security. 132 **ALR** 1407–1421.

If a debtor within the four months' period gives a mortgage to secure an antecedent debt the mortgage is a preference there being no present consideration.

Where a debtor assigned to a creditor a large amount of bills receivable most of which were forgeries and the creditor, discovering this, and knowing the debtor to be insolvent, forced the debtor within the four months' period to assign valid bills receivable in place of the forgeries the latter transaction was a voidable preference; even though the creditor had a right to the valid receivables, because of the forgeries he had no right to collect damages against the trustee in bankruptcy of a known insolvent.

Where a creditor turns over to his debtor certain chattels upon a trust receipt, getting back possession of the chattels within the four months' period is not a preference since the trust receipt is a valid reservation of title.

CHAPTER IX

CLAIMS AGAINST THE ESTATE

§ 31. What are provable claims.[1] Where a debtor is liable on a note not only may the payee prove his claim but also the surety co-maker or guarantor or indorser of the note; and this is true even if the note is not due till after the year allowed for the proof of claims. Since one of the purposes of the Bankruptcy Law is to give the honest debtor a fresh start it would be highly undesirable that the contingent claim of a surety comaker or guarantor or indorser should not be held to be provable and therefore barred by the discharge. The payee in such a case need not give notice of dishonor in order to share in the debtor's estate because the only purpose of such notice is to charge the indorser.

If a creditor has received a preference, even if it is in another transaction, he must surrender it before he is allowed to prove his claim.

Where the debtor is liable on a contract such a claim is provable even though the damages are unliquidated, because it would be undesirable to have such a claim survive discharge. By express provision of the Act if an action for a negligent tort is pending at the time of petition it is provable, otherwise not. Other tort claims are not provable as such but a judgment founded on such a claim is provable.

Where a lease provided that upon the filing of a petition in bankruptcy of the tenant the landlord should forthwith be entitled to damages in an amount equal to the difference between the rent reserved and the rental value, the landlord's claim was held to be provable because it arose at the moment the petition was filed. But where a lease contained a covenant that if the tenant

1 6 **Am Jur,** Bankruptcy, § 101.

Bankruptcy: double proof of claim against estate of firm and individual partner. 10 **ALR** 851–858.

Right of creditor to interest after bankruptcy, declared insolvency, or appointment of receiver, where assets are more than sufficient to pay the principal of all claims. 39 **ALR** 457–467; s. in 44 **ALR** 1170, 1171.

Provability of claims by lessors under Bankruptcy Act since amendments of 1934 and 1938. 129 **ALR** 701–724.

Creditor's right of appeal from decision or allowance in favor of another under Bankruptcy Act. 133 **ALR** 1383–1389.

Setoff as between claims by or against bankrupt or insolvent in claims by or against trustee in bankruptcy, receiver, assignee, or trustee in insolvency, arising from transaction after bankruptcy or insolvency. 71 **ALR** 804–820; s. in 128 **ALR** 809–816.

Power of Bankruptcy Court to adjudicate equities among creditors in distribution of dividends. 100 **ALR** 660–667.

What amounts to "penalty or forfeiture" within provision of Bankruptcy Act against allowance of claim of that character by governmental body. 104 **ALR** 884–888.

91 **U. of Pa. L. R.** 601, Foreign and Domestic Creditors in Bankruptcy Proceeding.

should default in the payment of rent and should become insolvent or bankrupt the landlord might re-enter and relet as the agent of the tenant and charge the tenant with the difference, the landlord cannot prove for loss of future rentals because the covenant was not breached by the bankruptcy but by the failure later to indemnify the landlord after the inception of the bankruptcy proceedings.

§ 32. Reclamation proceedings—secured claims.[2] Where the debtor, after knowing that he was insolvent, that his chance of being able to pay is only slight, buys goods on credit, the seller may rescind and get back the goods from the trustee in bankruptcy; but apparently mere knowledge of the debtor that he was insolvent is not sufficient.

If a creditor is secured by a mortgage given by a third party this does not prevent him from proving for the full amount against the debtor's estate. Where a creditor is secured by property of the debtor he may not apply the proceeds of the secured property in payment of interest accruing after the filing of the petition because interest ceases at that moment.

§ 33. Claims having priority.[3] The following claims are preferred: (1) debts due to the United States; (2) taxes due to the State; (3) compensation for services rendered and expenses incurred by an assignee for creditors where the same were beneficial to the estate; (4) the reasonable value of the use and occupation of premises—presumptively the rent reserved in the lease—used by the receiver or trustee in bankruptcy during the administration of the estate; (5) employees' wages for services rendered during the four-month period; (6) mechanics' liens. It has also been held that the owners of stock that had been wrongfully pledged by the debtor are entitled to priority over the owners of stock which had been rightfully pledged.

§ 34. Proof of claims—setoff and counterclaim.[4] Claims must be proved within the six months' period provided for by statute; the court may shorten this period but cannot extend it. Where a preference has been set aside this does not forfeit the right of the creditor to prove against the estate.

Where the debtor at the time of petition filed has funds deposited in a bank which has a claim against the debtor and there is no suspicion of bad faith in making the deposit, the bank may use the funds toward the payment of its claim against the debtor, because a deposit in a bank is not a payment and hence not a preference but merely substitutes for currency a medium of exchange in universal use.

Where a debtor is heavily indebted to a creditor for goods sold and the creditor, knowing of the debtor's insolvency, insists upon being paid in advance for the next order of goods and then, without sending the goods, keeps the payment to apply on the previous indebtedness, the creditor is considered to have received a preference. Similarly a pledgee who insists upon keeping the security after his claim is paid, may not use the security toward the payment of an unsecured claim against the debtor. Also, a trustee in bankruptcy of a partnership cannot set off a debt owed to one partner against a claim of a partnership creditor.

Where a lessor files a claim for rent the trustee in bankruptcy cannot set off a claim for damages for negligently allowing water to come upon the

2 6 **Am Jur,** Bankruptcy, §§ 324-365.
Bankruptcy: effect of filing secured debt as an unsecured claim. 46 **ALR** 922-928.

3 6 **Am Jur,** Bankruptcy, §§ 392-397.

4 6 **Am Jur,** Bankruptcy, §§ 90-98, 232-238

premises of the bankrupt lessee because it is a tort claim and because it arises out of a different transaction.

Setoff does not work automatically simply because of bankruptcy proceedings and the filing of schedules and proofs; the court has the primary duty of determining whether there are "mutual debts and credits" within the meaning of the Act.

§ 35. **Compositions—compromise—distribution.**[5] Common-law compositions of creditors were upheld on the theory that the promise of each creditor to forgive a part of his claim was consideration for a similar promise by each of the others. They were rendered voidable by secret preferences and other unfair practices.

In bankruptcy compositions a majority of the creditors binds the minority but the court exercises supervisory jurisdiction to protect against fraud and to see to it that the composition is for the best interests of the creditors. The Act provides for the proof of disputed claims. When the debtor gets back his property it is subject to any liens that could not have been defeated by a discharge in bankruptcy. If a composition is confirmed it is like a discharge in bankruptcy and there cannot be another within six years. Where a composition is entered into it is binding upon the creditors even if it is not carried out so that if there is a later bankruptcy proceeding the creditors are limited in their proof to the amount of the composition notes as a matter of fairness to subsequent creditors.

A claim of the debtor against X may be validly compromised if it is approved by the trustee in bankruptcy and by the court; approval of the creditors is not sufficient.

Where funds are in the custody of the bankruptcy court they may be reached by attachment or garnishment only by order of the court.

CHAPTER X

DEBTOR RELIEF WITHOUT LIQUIDATION

§ 36. **Farm debtor relief under Section 75.**[6] Section 75 deals only with farmers and is emergency legislation. The farmer, instead of filing a petition in bankruptcy, may ask the aid of the court to secure a voluntary adjustment with all his creditors which will enable him to continue to farm, the will of a majority in number and amount controlling the minority. If such an adjudgment cannot be accomplished he can either drop the matter or amend his petition and ask to be declared a bankrupt, and at the same time, under subsection S, petition the court that all his property be appraised, his exempt property be set aside to him and he be allowed to retain possession of the rest, under the supervision of the court; and he may ask this relief even though he has no equity in his farm and is actually insolvent.

§ 37. **Arrangements and wage earner plans.**[7] An arrangement under Chapter XI can affect only unsecured creditors. The petition of the debtor for an arrangement can be filed either before or after an adjudication in bankruptcy or independently of any bankruptcy proceeding. The plan of arrangement

5 6 **Am Jur,** Bankruptcy, §§ 384-405, 415-456.

6 6 **Am Jur,** Bankruptcy, §§ 443-456.

40 **Col. L. R.** 1133, Bankruptcy Reorganizations for Farmers.

7 6 **Am Jur,** Bankruptcy, §§ 426-443.

must be accepted by a majority in number and amount of unsecured creditors and after such acceptance must be confirmed by the court.

Chapter XIII enables wage earners, at low court costs, to liquidate debts out of future earnings where the wage earner wishes to avoid the stigma of a bankruptcy discharge.

CHAPTER XI

CORPORATE REORGANIZATION UNDER CHAPTER TEN

§ 38. Corporations eligible.[8] Any corporation which could become a bankrupt, and also certain railroad corporations, may file an original petition or, in case an involuntary petition in bankruptcy is filed, an answer stating the requisite jurisdictional facts, the nature of the debtor's business, its assets, liabilities, capital stock and financial condition, facts showing need for relief, that the corporation is insolvent or unable to meet its debts as they mature and that it desires to effect a plan of reorganization. Since an insurance corporation may not become a bankrupt it may not take advantage of Chapter X; but a fraternal benefit organization is not considered as being in the insurance business and therefore it is so entitled.

Where a corporation has been dissolved and its charter forfeited by proceedings in a state court it may not take advantage of Chapter X even though by the state statute the corporation is considered as being in existence for two more years for the purpose of finishing pending litigation; but apparently an involuntary petition will lie in such a case.

§ 39. Jurisdiction—approval or dismissal of petition.[9] An involuntary proceeding for corporate reorganization must be based upon an act of bankruptcy, a bankruptcy or receivership or loss of possession of the debtor's property by reason of default on a mortgage. Jurisdiction is acquired through approval of the petition by the court, attaching to the debtor and its property wherever situated. If both a voluntary and an involuntary petition are filed in the same court, the one first approved by the court determines whether the proceedings are to be voluntary or involuntary.

Where a corporation organized in one state had its principal place of business in another and its manufacturing plant in a third with a receiver appointed in each one so that relief under Chapter X was desirable, it was held that the preferences of bondholders as to which district court should have jurisdiction were entitled to be considered.

8 6 **Am Jur,** Bankruptcy, §§ 567, 568.

56 **Harv. L. R.** 1037, 1193, A Decade of Railroad Reorganization under Section 77 of the Federal Bankruptcy Act.

48 **Harv. L. R.** 1100, Reorganization through Bankruptcy: A Remedy for What?

48 **Harv. L. R. 39,** Some Comment on the Corporate Reorganizations Act.

45 **Harv. L. R.** 233, Remedies of Dissenting Stockholders under Appraisal Statutes.

43 **Col. L. R.** 317, Rent Claims in Bankruptcy and Corporate Reorganization.

39 **Col. L. R.** 907, Claims against Affiliated Companies in Reorganization.

38 **Col. L. R.** 256, Democratization of Corporate Reorganizations.

38 **Col. L. R.** 1199, Corporate Reorganization under the Chandler Act.

51 **Yale L. J.** 1057, Findings of "Value" in Railroad Reorganization.

48 **Yale L. J.** 1334, Competing Systems of Corporate Reorganizations.

40 **Mich. L. R.** 624, The New Schoolmaster in Finance.

18 **N. Y. U. Law Q.** 367, Tort Claims in Bankruptcy and Reorganization.

18 **N. Y. U. Law Q.** 161, Present Status of Railroad Reorganizations and Legislation Affecting Them.

18 **N. Y. U. Law Q.** 352, Some Recent Developments in Corporate Reorganizations.

9 6 **Am Jur,** Bankruptcy, §§ 562–566, 572–584.

A voluntary petition must not only be bona fide but the plan presented must be reasonable and practicable; if there is no reasonable prospect of effecting a reorganization this tends to show bad faith. The mere fact that a corporation has been recently organized does not prevent relief, but where the original debtor was not a corporation and a corporation was organized for the purpose of getting certain things done which could not be done in the case of an individual this tended to show bad faith. A corporation is not entitled to relief merely because it is unable to pay cumulative dividends on preferred stock. Where over two thirds of the bondholders favored a plan proposed by the debtor this shows the good faith of the debtor even though the plan may be disapproved by a bondholders' committee, a body not recognized in Chapter X.

Where a plan would permit the corporation to pay large salaries to officers and thus deplete the assets it is likely to operate unfairly to first mortgage bondholders. Where there are two competing plans, the fact that a very large majority of bondholders favors one plan tends to render the other one not feasible. The mere fact that a plan has not yet been presented by the debtor does not justify a court in finding a lack of good faith. It is not necessary for the debtor to show a reasonable prospect for successful rehabilitation if it can show instead that it is in a position to obtain a slow, beneficial and orderly liquidation.

§ 40. Persons and property subject to reorganization court.[10] Since the jurisdiction of the United States district court is exclusive of all other courts in bankruptcy and reorganization proceedings, the trustee in bankruptcy need not apply to the state court for an order to turn over the debtor's property in the hands of an officer of that court, but the receivers appointed by the state court may apply for payment of expenses and compensation for services. Until a valid plan of reorganization is presented, accepted and approved the receivers should be allowed to continue in possession and management. And where a state statute authorized the state to forfeit to the state crude oil produced in violation of the statute it was held that the reorganization court should have allowed the state to sue to have the debtor corporation's oil confiscated.

§ 41. Unsecured claims.[1] Proof of claims may be allowed after the time limit unless the proceedings have reached such a point that their purpose would be frustrated or the rights of other creditors impaired.

Where a trustee of debenture bonds issued by the debtor had an option to accelerate the date of maturity of the bonds for nonpayment of interest, the reorganization court may not enjoin such acceleration.

A landlord of the debtor is entitled to prove in reorganization proceedings for damages for rejecting the lease even if there is no covenant therein to indemnify the landlord against loss. If there is such a covenant, the landlord's claim for indemnity is limited to an amount not exceeding three years rent.

Where the debtor is subsidiary to another corporation which exercises a

10 6 **Am Jur**, Bankruptcy, §§ 566, 569, 570.
Judgment against bankrupt or debtor, after filing of petition in bankruptcy, composition, or reorganization proceedings under the Bankruptcy Act, as liquidation of claim for purpose of proof. 106 **ALR** 1121–1133.
Constitutionality, construction, and application of provisions of Bankruptcy Act regarding composition of claims against municipalities or other taxing agencies or instrumentalities. 124 **ALR** 696–708; s. in 136 **ALR** 867–883.

1 6 **Am Jur**, Bankruptcy, § 588.

dominating control over the subsidiary, the reorganization court may refuse to allow the parent corporation to share with other creditors on a basis of equality.

Where A loaned money to the debtor corporation, A to receive one half the net profits of the debtor corporation's business as compensation for the use of the money that did not make A a joint adventurer and does not prevent him from sharing with other creditors.

Where the reorganization proceeding superseded a bankruptcy proceeding a creditor whose claim had finally been allowed in the bankruptcy proceeding is not entitled to be paid at once but may receive payment under any plan of reorganization that may be confirmed.

§ 42. Secured claims.[2] Where by the state law a mortgagee in possession after default is regarded as owner he may not be compelled to surrender that possession even in plenary proceedings.

A trustee representing a large number of mortgage bondholders is entitled to intervene in the reorganization proceeding and is entitled to the net income of the mortgaged property from the date of the approval of the debtor's petition even though the debtor is continued in possession.

A mortgagee who, upon giving up the right to insist upon forfeiture, receives payment from a receiver appointed in an equity suit may not be required to repay the money even though the payment was made just before an involuntary petition for reorganization was filed.

An attorney for a debtor in reorganization proceedings has been held entitled to hold books and papers of his client as security for his fees even though it may thwart the reorganization proceedings.

§ 43. Voting by security holders.[3] The judge determines the divisions of creditors and stockholders into classes according to the nature of their respective claims and interests. All creditors of equal rank with claims against the same property should be placed in the same class but creditors of different ranks or creditors of the same rank but with claims against different properties should ordinarily be placed in different classes; but the latter part of the rule need not be followed where no substantial injustice results. The judge also determines the fairness and feasibility of any plan finally agreed upon by a majority of the various classes of creditors and stockholders, and may suggest changes in the plan submitted. No change in the voting should be allowed later unless a good reason is given for it. Where a mortgage provides for a two-thirds vote of the bondholders as being necessary for changes in the security of the mortgage, the trustee of the mortgage may not vote to the exclusion of the bondholders.

§ 44. Communication with creditors and stockholders—protection of proceedings.[4] The list of creditors and stockholders should be available to all creditors and stockholders and parties in the proceeding. The right to examine the corporation books is not affected by the reorganization proceedings.

A reorganization court may not release a guarantor of an old bond issue of the debtor's in consideration of his guaranteeing a new bond issue because the guarantor is not subject to the court's jurisdiction.

Where an action had been brought against the debtor in a wrongful death

[2] 6 **Am Jur,** Bankruptcy, § 588.

[3] 6 **Am Jur,** Bankruptcy, §§ 590–594.

[4] 6 **Am Jur,** Bankruptcy, § 590.

action and the debtor is covered by liability insurance, leave should be granted to prosecute the action because of the importance of jury trial and because there will be no serious interference with the reorganization proceedings or with the rights of the other creditors.

Where a school filed a reorganization petition and an official of the school continued to collect pledges from graduates of the school, it was held proper to enjoin him from thus interfering with the reorganization proceedings.

§ 45. Examination of witnesses—investigation.[5] Where the trustee in reorganization proceedings instituted three suits in a state court against former officers, directors and bankers of the debtor seeking to recover money for the debtor's estate, it was held proper to order an examination of a large number of witnesses under section 7(9) and 21(a) of the Bankruptcy Act.

Where a voluntary petition alleges that the good will of the debtor is being impaired by an involuntary reorganization proceeding, an injunction suit and a separate bill in equity for a receiver, it was held proper for the court to appoint independent investigators, their report being for the benefit of all the parties.

§ 46. Fairness and feasibility of plans submitted.[6] Even though there is no protest made against a plan the court may reject it either because it is visionary and impractical or because it is unfair to some of the parties interested. But if all the parties interested vote in favor of a plan the court may approve even though it will give nothing to the stockholders because it may be better than foreclosure. The fact that the debtor has no equity in the assets does not prevent giving reorganization relief.

A plan may be disapproved because it is unfair to mortgagees in heavily reducing the amount of the mortgage; or because stockholders, though not furnishing additional capital, are preferred at the expense of creditors; or because preferred stockholders are favored at the expense of first mortgage bondholders.

5 6 **Am Jur**, Bankruptcy, § 591.

6 6 **Am Jur**, Bankruptcy, § 593.

18 **N. Y. U. Law Q.** 375, The Third Year of Arrangements under the Bankruptcy Act.

CONFLICT OF LAWS

CHAPTER I

IN GENERAL

§ 1. Scope—meaning of "conflict."[1] The subject of Conflict of Laws deals mainly with two questions: the question whether a particular court is a

[1] 11 **Am Jur,** Conflict of Laws, § 2.
49 **Yale L. J.** 1027, Public Policy and the Political Crisis in the Conflict of Laws.
40 **Mich. L. R.** 781, Developments in the Conflict of Laws 1902–1942.
5 **U. of Toronto L. J.** 133, Choice-of-Law Policies in Multiple Contract Cases.

proper one to take jurisdiction of and try a case and the question of what rule shall be applied to determine the rights and obligations of the parties.

The word "conflict" is unfortunate because it is likely to convey the notion of actual strife between courts; such strife does sometimes occur where one court takes jurisdiction and another court refuses to recognize the right of the first court to do so, but for the most part the only conflict is in the minds of the judges as to whether to take jurisdiction or as to what rule to apply to the case. The courts in all civilized countries try to avoid clashes by laying down such rule as will meet with general approval.

The subject is sometimes called Private International Law because it deals with the enforcement in ordinary judicial tribunals of private rights created abroad; but the word "international" is unfortunate because while in Public International Law the unit is a political one—the nation—the unit in Conflict of Laws is legal, not political. Each of the states in the United States is a legal unit; and with some exceptions due to some clauses in the United States Constitution such as the one requiring full faith and credit to be given to judgments of sister states and the one giving to the citizens of each state the privileges and immunities of citizens of other states, each state is as foreign to the other states as it is to Canada or Mexico.

§ 2. Tribal and territorial law.[2] Law and organized society came into existence together; neither can exist without the other. As long as the organized society wandered from place to place its law was the law of the people and not of the land; only the members of the society or tribe were bound by it. But when farming becomes the chief occupation instead of hunting and stock raising and the society permanently occupies a certain territory the law tends to become territorial instead of tribal, extending to the boundaries of the territory and governing all persons and property within it but not beyond. In those countries where the law is based upon the English common law the law is territorial; in continental European countries whose law is based upon the old Roman law the territorial idea predominates but traces of the earlier tribal notion still persist.

§ 3. Introduction and change of law.[3] A territory without an organized community has no law unless it is under the control of an organized community in another territory. If a previously uninhabited territory is settled by immigrants coming from other organized communities the law which is introduced is that which the settlers or a majority thereof brought with them. Hence when Oklahoma was settled chiefly by persons from other parts of the United States the law which was introduced was "the established rules and principles of the common law as recognized and promulgated by the American courts . . . unmodified by American and English statutes."

A mere change of sovereignty or political control does not change the law; when the United States acquired control of the Philippine Islands the old law continued except, of course, the law of allegiance. But the law may be changed either by legislation or—in the common-law system—by judicial decision. Or it may be changed by a change in the character of the inhabitants; for example, when the Dutch settled what was then called New Amsterdam they carried Dutch law with them; the mere conquering of the colony by the English did not change the law but the coming in of English settlers in such numbers as greatly to outweigh the influence of the Dutch

[2] 11 Am Jur, Conflict of Laws, §§ 2, 3. [3] 30 Am Jur, Conflict of Laws, §§ 44-47.

colonists did effect a change of law. Where the newcomers are conquerors but not numerous enough to displace the old law there may be a divided law; in India the English, being only a small minority, have never displaced the old law; the English are subject to English law, the Hindus to Hindu law and the Mohammedans to Mohammedan law; all three together form one law—the law of the territory known as India.

§ 4. Meaning of "general law" or "general common law." [4] Under the territorial idea of law there can be no law apart from a certain piece of land; hence the word "law" in such phrases as the "general law" or the "general common law" is being used in a different sense—not as positive law which creates rights and imposes obligations—but as a method of legal thinking; such phrases are similar to the phrase, "weight of authority", meaning that on some particular question of law there is a more or less complete agreement among courts under the common law system.

§ 5. Meaning of "comity"—nature of the law of conflict of laws.[5] Where A sues B in a New York court for damages for an act committed in Pennsylvania the general rule is that in order to determine whether the act was a tort the New York court will look to the law of torts of Pennsylvania, not to the law of torts of New York. In such a case it is frequently said that it is through comity that the New York court thus recognizes the rights of A acquired under Pennsylvania law. The use of the word "comity" is unfortunate because the ordinary meaning of comity is courtesy and the impression conveyed is that the law of Pennsylvania is—through the courtesy of the New York courts—given an extraterritorial operation. The real situation is quite different. The law of Pennsylvania is not given any extraterritorial operation, but as a matter of justice to litigants the New York court adopts—for the case of A v. B—the Pennsylvania rule of the law of torts as a part of its own law; that is, it is a part of the New York law of conflict of laws that when an action is brought in a New York court for damages for an act committed in any other state or country the court will apply—as a part of its own law—the rule of such other state or country in order to determine whether the act is a tort. And similar reasoning applies wherever any court looks to the rule established in another state or country to determine whether rights—either tort or contract or property—have arisen in that state or country.

§ 6. The renvoi doctrine.[6] In a Michigan case a Michigan married woman signed a note in that state and on the basis thereof a loan was made in Illinois by an Illinois corporation. Under Illinois law such a note, given by a married woman, was valid; under Michigan law it was invalid. The Michigan court found that the place of contracting was Illinois where the loan was made and that the capacity of a married woman to contract was governed by the Illinois law as the place of contracting. But by the Illinois law of conflict of laws the capacity of a married woman to contract is governed by the law of the place where the instrument was executed—here,

[4] 11 **Am Jur,** Common Law, § 2.

[5] 11 **Am Jur,** Conflict of Laws, §§ 4-15.

[6] 11 **Am Jur,** Conflict of Laws, § 3.
31 **Harv. L. R.** 523, The Doctrine of Renvoi in Anglo-American Law.
51 **Harv. L. R.** 1165, Renvoi Revisited.
52 **Harv. L. R.** 747, A Survey of the Characterization Problem in Conflict of Laws.
51 **Yale L. J.** 191, Characterization in the Conflict of Laws.
50 **Yale L. J.** 743, Qualification, Classification or Characterization Problem in Conflict of Laws.

Michigan. If the Michigan court had applied only the internal law of Illinois—excluding its law of conflict of laws—judgment would have been given for the plaintiff; but the Michigan court—following what is known as the renvoi doctrine—applied also the Illinois law of conflict of laws and, applying the internal law of Michigan, gave judgment for the defendant. The weight of authority is, however, against the renvoi doctrine, the critics of the doctrine pointing out that since the Michigan court looked to the Illinois law of conflict of laws there was no logical reason why they should not also look to the Michigan law of conflict of laws and thus have an endless chain of references—a legal merry go round.

§ 7. Conflict of laws and constitutional law.[7] Where a state court goes badly astray in refusing to adopt as part of its law of conflict of laws the law of another state such a decision may be overruled by the United States Supreme Court. Thus in Hartford Accident and Indemnity Co. v. Delta and Pine Land Co., 292 US 1143, 78 L ed 1178, 54 Sup Ct 634, 92 ALR 928, the H. Co. contracted with the D. Co. in Tennessee to make good any losses suffered by the D. Co. through embezzlement by its employees, the contract stipulating that all claims must be made within fifteen months after the loss; the stipulation was valid in Tennessee but not in Mississippi. A loss occurred in Mississippi and D. Co. sued there after the fifteen months period had elapsed. The Mississippi court allowed recovery applying its own rule that the stipulation was invalid. The United States Supreme Court held that the refusal of the Mississippi court to apply the Tennessee rule to determine the validity of the stipulation was a violation of the due process clause of the Fourteenth Amendment and reversed the judgment. Such supervision by the United States Supreme Court will tend toward bringing about uniformity among the various states in deciding conflict of laws questions.

Another recent United States Supreme Court decision making for uniformity in the law of conflict of laws is that of Erie R. Co. v. Tompkins, 304 US 64, 82 L ed 1188, 58 S Ct 817, 114 ALR 1487, which by overruling Swift v. Tyson, 16 Pet. 1, 10 L ed 865, requires a federal court to follow the law of the state in which it sits.

§ 8. Criminal and penal laws.[8] If A commits a crime in Ohio and then goes into Indiana the latter state is not enough interested in preserving public order and discipline in Ohio to punish A; all that it will do is to surrender him up to the Ohio public authorities on extradition proceedings.

It is usually said that a penalty imposed in one state—either by legislative or by judicial decree—will not be enforced in another but there is not entire agreement as to the exact meaning of penalty in this connection. The following have been held to impose penalties unenforcible abroad: a statute imposing treble damages for rate discriminations, a statute imposing a fine

7 11 **Am Jur,** Conflict of Laws, § 7.
11 **Am Jur,** Constitutional Law, § 343.
Federal Constitution and conflict of laws as to rights not based on judgments. 74 **ALR** 710–722; s. in 100 **ALR** 1143–1152; 134 **ALR** 1472–1485.

Duty of courts to follow decisions of other states, on questions of common law or unwritten law, in which the cause of action had its situs. 73 **ALR** 897–918.

39 **Harv. L. R.** 533, The Power of the Supreme Court to Review State Decision in the Field in Conflict of Laws.
27 **U. of Minn. L. R.** 500, Constitutional Aspects of the Conflict of Laws.
22 **Oreg. L. R.** 109, State Decisions in Conflict of Laws and Review by the United States Supreme Court under the Due-Process Clause.

8 11 **Am Jur,** Conflict of Laws, § 6.
46 **Harv. L. R.** 193, Extrastate Enforcement of Penal and Governmental Claims.

for causing death by wrongful act, a statute making one convicted of larceny incompetent to testify, a statute declaring civilly dead one sentenced to life imprisonment, a statute imposing double damages for injuries to live stock, a statute making corporation directors liable for all debts of the corporation upon failure to file a required report, and a statute requiring a father to support an illegitimate child. It would seem that by the same reasoning the imposition of punitive damages should be regarded as a penalty but the law on this point is not settled; and in a case decided by the United States Supreme Court it was laid down by way of dictum that no obligation is to be regarded as penal in the conflict of laws sense if it merely affords a private remedy to a person injured by the wrongful act.

CHAPTER II

JURISDICTION

§ 9. Jurisdiction over the person.[9] Since the law of any particular territory extends to its borders every person in it is subject thereto. Hence if one is served with process while only temporarily there the court acquires jurisdiction over his person and is in a position to render a valid personal judgment against him.

Even though one has never been within the territory he makes himself subject to the jurisdiction of a court in that territory by consenting thereto either at the time action is brought or in advance. Many states by statute stipulate that if a foreign corporation wishes to do business within its borders it must consent in advance to being sued in the courts of that state; in such a case the usual provision is that service be made upon one of the corporation's agents who represent it within the state. And in some states there are statutes providing that a personal judgment may be rendered against the nonresident driver of a motor vehicle for a tort committed upon the highways of the state. Here by statute consent to being sued is found in voluntarily driving upon the highways of the state and the usual provision is that personal service of process may be made upon some state official such as the secretary of state.

If one has his domicile within a state he is subject to the jurisdiction of its courts; in such a case if he has a residence in the state service of process by leaving it at that residence is enough even though he be absent from the state at the time. If, although domiciled within a state he has no place of residence there, then service of process at his last place of residence within the state is probably sufficient.

If a court once acquires jurisdiction over a person in any of the ways just discussed such jurisdiction continues until the case is finally disposed of. Hence if A gets a judgment in an Ohio court and then A removes to Tennessee and X takes a writ of error to a higher court in Ohio it is not necessary that A be served with process. Even if A had never been a resident of Ohio bringing suit in an Ohio court subjected him to that court's jurisdiction and that jurisdiction continued until the end of the litigation.

[9] 11 **Am Jur,** Conflict of Laws, § 188.

Jurisdiction to entertain suit · render judgment against foreign executor or administrator who appears or submits to jurisdiction of court. 77 **ALR** 251–259.

Construction, application, and effect of statutes providing for constructive or substituted service of process on nonresident motorists. 82 **ALR** 768–775; s. in 93 **ALR** 574–599; 125 **ALR** 457–474; 138 **ALR** 1464–1478.

§ 10. Jurisdiction over property.[10] The jurisdiction of a country covers all property—movable or immovable—within its boundaries. The territory includes not only all its land but adjacent portions of water such as small inlets and bays, and by general international agreement the jurisdiction also extends over the ocean as far as three miles from shore. If disputes arise involving rights in land within a country the courts of that country will always exercise their jurisdiction; but in case of a controversy between subjects of another country as to movable property only temporarily within the territory, such as a merchant vessel in port, the court may, in its discretion, refuse to try the case.

Actions to obtain possession of property or to determine questions of title to property must be brought in the courts of the state where the property is located. For example, if one wishes to obtain possession of land in Delaware he must bring his action of ejectment in a Delaware court because only a Delaware court could put him in possession; so, if he wishes to obtain possession of movables in Delaware he must bring his action of detinue or replevin in a Delaware court.

§ 11. Same—proceedings in rem.[1] Actions of ejectment, detinue and replevin are brought against a specific person or persons and the judgment binds only them and the persons who claim through them. If A brings ejectment against X in a Maryland court to get possession of a piece of Maryland land and wins this binds only X and those who may claim under him, that is, his heirs or assigns; it would not prevent Y, a stranger, from suing A in ejectment and showing that he (Y) had a better right to the land than A, thus getting judgment against A for the land. Such a judgment would, of course, bind only A, his heirs and assigns.

But in certain cases it is possible to bring suit against every one claiming any interest in the property and thus settle the right of the plaintiff therein as against the whole world. In such a case the basis of the court's jurisdiction is the property within its control; hence it is not necessary to serve those who may have an interest in the property with personal process. This is quite important where part or all of the defendants are nonresidents and beyond the reach of personal process because beyond the reach of the arm of the court. All that is essential is that the proceedings be sufficiently advertised so that those who claim an interest in the property may have a reasonable opportunity to find out about the proceedings and come in and assert their claim. The most common proceeding of this sort is a libel in admiralty brought against all who may be interested in a ship, for example, for wages due to a sailor or for damage caused to another ship by collision. Notice of such proceedings is usually given by affixing a printed notice for a reasonable time to some part of the ship.

Proceedings to determine absolutely and finally the title to land by a bill in equity to remove clouds on title held by all nonresidents are not uncommon, the outstanding example being the proceeding authorized by the statutes modeled on the Torrens Act. A state might authorize similar proceedings in regard to ordinary chattels within its borders, but apparently no state has done so.

[10] 11 **Am Jur**, Conflict of Laws, §§ 29–98. 49 **Yale L. J.** 241, Situs of Intangibles in Suits against Non-Resident Claimants.

[1] 11 **Am Jur, Conflict of Laws, §§ 29–98.**

§ 12. Same—foreign attachment.[2] Suppose that X of Illinois owes A of Indiana $500. As long as X remains in Illinois A will not be able to get a personal judgment against him unless A sues him in an Illinois court where personal process can be served on X. But if X owns land or chattels in Indiana A may have such property applied to the payment of his claim. The jurisdiction of the court is based upon the property being within the control of the court; hence suit must be begun by attaching the property and it must be carried on in a reasonably public manner in order to give X a reasonable opportunity to find out about it and have some one look after his interest in the property and in the litigation. Since the jurisdiction of the court depends upon the control over the property the attachment must take place at the very beginning of the suit. Publicity for the suit is usually obtained by publication of notice in a newspaper of general circulation in the community where suit is brought and the sending of such notice by mail to X's last known place of residence in Illinois.

A foreign attachment statute might authorize the suit to be brought not only against X but also against all who claimed any right in the property but the existing statutes provide only for a suit against X, so that if the property turned out to be the property of Y the judgment would not be binding upon Y. Because the proceedings are not brought against and are not binding upon the whole world they are sometimes called proceedings quasi in rem. Furthermore, though the judgment is binding upon X to the extent of his interest in the property, yet since the jurisdiction is based upon the property and not upon the person of X there can be no personal judgment; so, if the property brings only $400 at the execution sale at the end of the proceedings A cannot get a personal judgment for the other $100 against X; it will be necessary for him either to attach other property or to sue in an Illinois court where he can get personal service and relitigate the matter there.

§ 13. Foreign garnishment.[3] If instead of X owning some tangible property in Indiana, Z, living in Indiana owed X $400, A may, by a process similar to foreign attachment, maintain a garnishment suit in Indiana to compel Z to pay the $400 to A instead of to X and thus get part payment of his claim against X for $500. Since the place where X will usually collect his claim against Z is in Indiana it is not inaccurate to say that although X lives in Illinois the situs for the purpose of his claim against Z is in Indiana and therefore the Indiana court has jurisdiction to compel Z to pay A rather than X. Such a garnishment proceeding is started by a notification to Z not to pay X and this is considered to give the court jurisdiction just as did the attachment of the tangible property in the preceding section. Here, as in attachment proceedings, a personal judgment against X cannot be recovered and for the same reasons.

If A's claim against X is not a valid one but Z pays A the $400 according to the court's order the weight of authority is that X cannot compel Z to pay a second time. The result of this is that X must not only look after his tangible property in other states but he must also look after his intangible property in the shape of claims owing him by foreign debtors; if his debtor

[2] 4 **Am Jur,** Attachment and Garnishment, §§ 47, 72.
5 **Am Jur,** Attachment and Garnishment, § 959.

[3] 4 **Am Jur,** Attachment and Garnishment, § 47.
5 **Am Jur,** Attachment and Garnishment, § 959.

is being garnisheed on a false claim he must contest the claim in the garnishment proceeding if he wishes to take advantage of its being invalid.

§ 14. Taxation—tangible property.[4] Land is taxable where it is located and nowhere else. It is usually taxed as a whole but if there are divided interests in it each interest may be taxed separately; the domicile of the owner is immaterial.

The old common-law view was that all movables were taxable at the domicile of the owner, no matter where the movables were; this did not work badly when chattels were not often separated from the owner. The modern and better view is that movables, like land, should be taxed only where they are actually located. It is obvious that if one state should follow one theory and another state should follow the other theory some movable property would be taxed twice and some not at all.

Since taxation of property is compensation charged by the state for protection to such property a chattel that is in the state for only a week or a day might be charged for a week or a day's protection. But taxes are ordinarily imposed only for a year and a certain day is picked out as tax day; if on that day property is seeking protection for the coming year it is taxable and the fact that it is unexpectedly moved out of the state the next week does not entitle the owner to any rebate.

If the property is only temporarily within the jurisdiction, for example, if it is passing through on a railroad train and merely happens to be there on tax day it is not in the United States legally taxable there because an attempt to tax would be invalid as not due process of law. But where a sleeping car company had within the state at all times an average of one hundred cars it was held that the state might tax the company for a hundred cars even though no particular hundred cars remained within the state.

§ 15. Taxation—intangible property.[5] If Z of Indiana owes X of Illinois $400, for purposes of garnishment by A of Indiana, a creditor of X, the chose in action held by X against Z is treated as having a situs in Indiana where X would ordinarily collect it. Upon similar reasoning it has been urged that Indiana is the proper state to tax X's claim, one argument being that it would be easy to collect the tax there because Z would pay it and deduct it from his debt to X. But the great weight of authority is that X's chose in action against Z is taxable only by Illinois, the domicile of X; this is not on the theory that there is any property in Illinois but that the tax is a tax on X's person; a chose in action is a power over property rather than property itself and X is taxed according to the amount of power he has.

If X's chose in action against Z is in the form of a bond or note and X leaves it with his agent in Kentucky it has been held that Kentucky may tax the instrument as if it were an ordinary chattel; but the present day view is against this, holding that only Illinois, the state of the domicile of the creditor X, may tax. And the same reasoning applies to ordinary de-

4 51 **Am Jur,** Taxation, §§ 443–462.
52 **Harv. L. R.** 1246, Immovables and the Law of the Situs.

5 51 **Am Jur,** Taxation, §§ 463–474.
48 **Harv. L. R.** 911, The Administration of Intangibles in View of First National Bank v. Maine.
45 **Harv. L. R.** 777, The Passing of Situs—Jurisdiction to Tax Shares of Corporate Stock
40 **Mich. L. R.** 806, Multiple Taxation of Intangibles.
29 **Calif. L. R.** 706, Problem of Residence in State Taxation of Income.
18 **Wis. L. R.** 352, Business Situs on Basis for Taxation of Intangibles.
8 **Mo. L. R.** 155, State Jurisdiction to Tax Intangibles: A Twelve Year Cycle.

posits made by X in a bank outside Illinois, the relation between X and the bank being that of creditor and debtor. But where X sends money to his agent B in Kentucky to be invested there and B there lends the money to Kentucky borrowers, makes periodical remittances of income to X, collects the principal of the loans as they come due and reinvests the proceeds in Kentucky through new loans, apparently Kentucky may levy a tax upon such business credits even though the notes taken from the Kentucky debtors should be sent by B to X till time for collection and reinvestment. If Illinois as the state of the creditor's domicile should also tax X upon such business credits double taxation would result.

If X's chose in action against Z consists of shares in Z, an Indiana corporation, the rule seems to be that only Illinois, the state of X's domicile, may tax, as in the case of bonds and notes owned by X; there can be no valid taxation of them either by Indiana, the incorporating state, or by Kentucky, the state where the certificates of shares are kept by X's agent.

If X is engaged in a mercantile business which extends over several states and the business has an established good will it seems that each state may tax a fair share of such intangible value.

§ 16. Divorce, annulment and judicial separation.[6] Theoretically, at least, the basis for jurisdiction for divorce is not the person but the marriage status. Where the spouses are domiciled in the same state the marriage status is of course in that state. But the prevailing view in this country is that the wife may have a separate domicile for the purpose of bringing a divorce action so that a part of the marital status may be in one state and part in another. Logically a divorce granted in either state should be entitled to recognition everywhere but it has been held that if the defendant in such a suit has not been served with process or entered appearance the decree is not within the full faith and credit clause of the United States Constitution.

As a matter of strict logic a suit for annulment, which relates back to the beginning of the marriage or supposed marriage, should be brought in the state where the marriage or supposed marriage was entered into, but the rule is well settled that a court of the matrimonial domicile may act in the matter though, if the decree is that there never was a marriage it would seem that they should apply the law of the state where the supposed marriage was entered into. Such a decree is entitled to recognition everywhere.

The rules as to judicial separation or limited divorce would seem to be the same as those applying to absolute divorce.

In many states, either by statute or judicial decision, a wife may acquire a separate domicile not only for the purpose of suing for a divorce but for several other or for all purposes.

CHAPTER III

DOMICILE

§ 17. Definition—domicile of origin and domicile of choice.[7] If a person has only one home that home is his domicile; but whether he has no home

[6] 17 **Am Jur,** Divorce and Separation, §§ 244–266.
35 **Am Jur,** Marriage, §§ 60–68.

[7] 17 **Am Jur,** Domicil, §§ 12–34.
Domicil while in itinere from old to new home. 5 **ALR** 296–303; s. in 16 **ALR** 1298.

at all or several homes the law requires that he shall have a domicile because it is the law of his domicile that determines many important questions—for example, the validity of his will of personal property, how his personal property shall be divided if he dies intestate, the validity of a personal tax upon him and his right to vote.

As soon as a child is born he has the domicile of his father, if legitimate or of his mother if illegitimate, and this domicile continues until it has been changed either by himself or by others. In order to acquire a new domicile the English rule is that there must be the taking up of a new place of residence with the intent to reside there an unlimited or indefinite time. In this country where economic and social conditions are less settled and removals from place to place are more common the rule is not so strict; a day laborer who abandons his home and intends to have a home wherever he works probably acquires a domicile in each successive town where he lives as a laborer as long as he remains there; and similar reasoning would apply to the followers of any occupation who change their abode several times during their lives, such as ministers and school teachers.

In order to show a change of domicile from one town to another stronger evidence of intent would usually be required than if it were a change from one house to another in the same town, but less evidence than to prove a change of domicile from one state to another or from one nation to another. And there seems to be no reason why one may not be domiciled in a particular town or country without being domiciled in a particular house; if A goes from New York to England intending to make England his home and continues to stay in England it would seem that he may acquire a domicile in England though it might be impossible to determine in what particular house he was domiciled; the fact that he spends his time traveling from place to place or that he lives only in lodgings would not prevent his acquiring a domicile in England.

In the case just put, suppose A's domicile of origin was Ohio, New York being a domicile of choice; what is his domicile after he abandons his New York home but before he arrives in England? According to the law in this country the result is the same as if the New York domicile had been the domicile of origin—the old domicile remains till a new one is acquired; but according to English law the domicile of origin revives. This difference is due to the fact that in a newly settled country much less importance is attached to one's domicile of origin than in an older country like England.

One cannot acquire a domicile of choice unless there is freedom of choice; one who is arrested and put in jail does not acquire a new domicile at the jail. On the other hand the fact that one is prevented from living in

Acquisition of domicil in countries (such as China, Turkey, and Egypt) granting extraterritorial privileges to foreigners. 39 **ALR** 1155–1168.

Separate domicil of married woman or divorced woman as affecting citizenship, domicil, residence, or inhabitancy of children. 53 **ALR** 1160–1165.

Governing law of will as affected by change of domicil after its execution. 57 **ALR** 229–238.

Change of domicil as affecting character of property previously acquired as separate or community property. 92 **ALR** 1347–1355.

Domicil or residence of person in the armed forces. 148 **ALR** 1413–1422; s. in 149 **ALR** 1471; 150 **ALR** 1468, 1469.

Law of domicil or of place of ancillary administration as governing rights and priorities of creditors of decedent in respect of assets in ancillary jurisdiction. 124 **ALR** 1281–1292.

Change of domicil by public officer or employee. 129 **ALR** 1382–1404.

What suits at domicil of corporation involving corporate stock or rights and obligations incident thereto are in rem, jurisdiction in which may rest upon constructive service of process against nonresidents. 145 **ALR** 1393–1410.

53 **Harv. L. R.** 68, Death and Taxes Are Certain—But What of Domicile?

a place does not forfeit a domicile already acquired there; for example, a political exile or refugee or one who is unable to live at his old home on account of health.

Though a corporation does not have a home it is regarded as having a domicile in the state in which it is incorporated.

§ 18. Having more than one home.[8] If one has two homes the one first acquired will in doubtful cases usually take precedence. If a merchant came originally from the country and he keeps up his household establishment there his residence in the city will usually not be his domicile; but if his original domicile was in the city and he buys or builds a country house chiefly for a place to spend the summer his domicile will usually remain in the city.

If a town, county or state boundary line runs through the house in which he is domiciled any rule of determining on which side of the boundary line his domicile is must necessarily be artificial where the house is about equally divided. It has been suggested that the place where the occupant usually slept would decide the question; another suggestion is that since actual residence with intent to make the house his home creates a domicile, the first place of entry into the house with intent to remain there would be decisive. The place where he has been in the habit of paying personal taxes might have some bearing on the matter.

§ 19. Change of domicile by others—"residence" in statutes.[9] The domicile of the wife ordinarily follows that of the husband and that of the minor child follows that of the father; and after the father's death that of the mother while she remains a widow. If the mother marries again and thereby acquires the domicile of her second husband it was formerly held that she loses the power to change the domicile of her children so that the domicile they had before her second marriage remains, but the modern tendency is contra. The domicile of an illegitimate child follows that of the mother till she marries.

If a father abandons his minor child he loses the power to change the child's domicile; a similar result follows if the minor enters into a valid marriage or is emancipated.

If the minor is an orphan and has a guardian of the person the latter can change the orphan's domicile within the state in which the guardian is appointed; if he has no guardian it would seem that he ought to be able to change his domicile just as if he were an adult.

Though it is not necessary, in order to change one's domicile, to sleep in the house in which domicile is claimed, it has usually been held that there must be actual physical presence in the place where domicile is to be established; one cannot change domicile by agent.

Where statutes use the word "residence" or "resident" the usual but not universal meaning is that of domicile.

[8] 17 **Am Jur,** Domicil, §§ 5, 82–85.
Diverse adjudications, actual or potential, by courts of different states, as to domicil of decedent as regards taxation, administration, or distribution of estates. 121 **ALR** 1200–1218.

[9] 17 **Am Jur,** Domicil, §§ 9–11, 57–72.

CHAPTER IV

THE CREATION OF RIGHTS

§ 20. Tort rights.[10] Whether a particular act gives rise to a tort cause of action depends upon the law of the place where the act was committed; and that is the place where the last event occurs which is necessary to make the actor liable. For example if a slander is uttered in state X but heard only in State Y the latter state is the place where the tort was committed.

The measure of damages in tort actions is also governed by the law of the place where the tort was committed because it is considered to be a part of the right of action and not merely of the remedy. But if there is a statute limiting the amount of recovery in certain actions it applies to all actions of that sort brought in the courts of that state no matter where the cause of action arose and it thus becomes a limitation on the remedy.

The statutory right to recover damages for wrongfully causing death is also governed by the law of the place where the injury was committed which resulted in the death; if the right is given by way of punishment imposed upon the wrongdoer it is enforceable, like other penal obligations only in the state where the obligation arose; but if it is given by way of compensation it may be enforced elsewhere.

The Workmen's Compensation Acts of most states provide for special tribunals to make the awards and hence awards are rarely made under the provisions of a foreign statute.

Whether a tort claim survives the death of the tort-feasor or the injured person depends upon the law of the place where the tort was committed.

§ 21. Contract rights—capacity and formalities.[1] The place of contracting is the place where the last act is done which makes the agreement operative as a contract. Whether the parties had capacity to enter into the contract is governed by the law of the place of contracting except that limitations imposed upon a corporation by the state of incorporation are applicable to contracts made anywhere.

The formalities required in a contract are usually determined by the law of the place of making because the parties will presumably get forms and

[10] 11 **Am Jur,** Conflict of Laws, §§ 180–184.

Conflict of laws as to joint tort-feasors 77 **ALR** 1108–1110.

Extraterritorial operation of workmen's compensation acts; conflict of laws. 28 **ALR** 1345–1348; s. in 35 **ALR** 1414–1417; 45 **ALR** 1234, 1235; 59 **ALR** 735–743; 82 **ALR** 709–719; 90 **ALR** 119–125.

Power of court, in exercise of discretion, to refuse to entertain action for nonstatutory tort occurring in another state or country. 32 **ALR** 6–82.

Conflict of laws as to contributory negligence. 32 **ALR** 796–804.

Jurisdiction of action at law for damages for tort concerning real property in another state or country. 42 **ALR** 196–221.

Conflict of laws as regards statutory or contractual provisions relating to right of injured person to maintain action against tort-feasor's insurer. 120 **ALR** 855–862.

Nature of differences between lex loci and lex fori which will sustain or defeat jurisdiction of a cause of action for death arising under the law of another state or country. 77 **ALR** 1311–1327.

Right of personal representative appointed at the forum or in a jurisdiction where decedent was domiciled or where the tort occurred, to maintain action for death under foreign statute which provides that the action shall be brought by executor or administrator. 85 **ALR** 1231–1251.

State or country deemed to be the place of tort causing personal injury or death, as regards principle that law of place of tort governs. 133 **ALR** 260–270.

Conflict of laws regarding contribution between tort-feasors. 148 **ALR** 1130, 1131.

18 **Wis. L. R.** 145, Conflict of Laws, Problems in Automobile Accidents.

[1] 11 **Am Jur,** Conflict of Laws, §§ 99–115, 128–130.

Conflict of laws as to capacity of married women to contract. 18 **ALR** 1516–1567; s. in 71 **ALR** 744–749.

Conflict of laws as to whether an instrument is to be regarded as one under seal, and as to effect of seal. 109 **ALR** 479–488.

legal advice at that place. If at the place of making there is a statute providing that all agreements should have a stamp in order to be valid, all agreements made there must have a stamp. But if the statute provided that agreements must bear stamps in order to be admitted into evidence, such a requirement would apply to contracts sought to be enforced in that state no matter where the contracts were made but would not apply to contracts made there and sued on elsewhere. The same distinction is made in questions arising under the statute of frauds, the more usual statute requiring merely a certain kind of proof and applying to all contracts sued on in that state no matter where made.

§ 22. Same—essential validity.[2] As to matters other than capacity and formalities the law is in confusion. Three theories have been advanced: (1) The law of the place of making governs; (2) The law of the place of performance governs; (3) The law intended by the parties governs.

Prima facie it would seem that the law of the place of making should govern because logically it is only that law that can annex a legal obligation to an agreement; is there any good reason for applying the rule of any other place? It may be urged that if an agreement constitutes a valid contract by the law of the place of performance, it ought to be valid even though the law of the place of making does not ordinarily annex an obligation to such an agreement. Suppose A and B enter into an agreement in Ohio the agreement to be performed entirely in Michigan; by the law of Michigan such an agreement constitutes a valid contract; by the law of Ohio it does not. Is there any good reason why A and B should be compelled to go to Michigan in order to make a valid contract? That is, should not Ohio, as to agreements to be performed entirely in another state, uphold the agreement as a valid contract if by the law of the place of performance such an agreement is a valid contract? Should not Ohio, as to agreements valid by the law of the place of performance, adopt and make a part of its own law the law of the place of performance?

In usury cases the above argument has prevailed in most states the result being that if a loan of money is made in Ohio to be repaid in Michigan the contract is not usurious if it is valid by the law of either state provided that the place of repayment has not been chosen merely to evade the usury law of the place of making. And if any other rule than the simple one that the law of the place of making should apply to all questions of validity, the rule of the usury cases that the contract should be upheld if valid either by the law of the place of making or by the law of the place of performance has the next claim for recognition, there being much to be said for it on the score of convenience.

But in many cases the rule is laid down that that law governs validity

[2] 11 **Am Jur,** Conflict of Laws, §§ 116-127.

Validity of contractual provision limiting the place where, or the courts in which, an action may be brought. 59 **ALR** 1445-1457; s. in 107 **ALR** 1060-1063.

Validity and effect, and remedy in respect, of contractual stipulation to submit disputes to arbitration in another jurisdiction. 93 **ALR** 1073-1082.

Validity and effect of stipulation in contract to the effect that it shall be governed by the law of a particular state which is neither the place where the contract is made nor the place where it is to be performed. 112 **ALR** 124-134; 114 **ALR** 1461-1471; s. in 149 **ALR** 1083.

Conflict of laws as to usury. 125 **ALR** 482-502.

Law of place of performance, other than that of place where contract is made and transportation commences, as the governing law of carrier's contract. 72 **ALR** 250-265.

23 **Harv. L. R.** 1, 79, 194, 260, What Law Governs the Validity of a Contract.

which the parties intended should govern it. From a practical standpoint this is objectionable because it is so uncertain in its application. Ordinarily the parties have no intent in the matter and if there were such an intent and the contract is written no direct evidence of such intent outside the written instrument could be given any effect because of the so-called parol evidence rule. Hence the courts have been compelled to fall back upon presumptions of intent, thus making the rule artificial. As might be expected, the courts differ as to what the presumption is in such cases, some saying that the parties are presumed to have intended the law of the place of making to govern, and others that the presumption is in favor of the law of the place of performance. Where the contract is to be performed in several states the laws of which differ on the question of validity it is obviously impossible to apply the law of the place of performance. The doctrine is also objectionable because it seems to be based upon the notion that rights depend upon the will or intent of the parties and not upon the law.

§ 23. **Same—interpretation—performance—assignment—discharge.**[3] Interpretation of a contract is ordinarily a matter of the usage of language rather than a question of law; since the party using the language was presumably most familiar with the usage of his domicile that usage should govern.

On the question as to whether a contract has been performed the law of the place of performance is the one to be applied; for example, whether a note given for the purchase price of chattels some months after the purchase was made operated as payment for this antecedent debt should be determined by the law of the place where the purchase price was to be paid not by the law of the place where the note itself was payable.

The validity of an assignment of a contract is determined by the law of the place where the assignment is made.

As a matter of logic the question as to whether a contract has been discharged should depend upon the law of the place of performance, the discharge making the contemplated performance unnecessary and hence a substitute for performance. But where an indivisible contract is to be performed in two or more states the laws of which differ on the point it is necessary to fall back upon the law of the place of making.

Logically discharge in bankruptcy should be treated as any other sort of a discharge but in this country it is well settled that a state bankruptcy law is effective only as to those creditors who are domiciled in that state or who submit themselves to the jurisdiction of its courts by making their proof in bankruptcy proceedings; this is the potent reason for the existence of the federal bankruptcy act.

§ 24. **Personal rights.**[4] Capacity to marry is ordinarily governed by the law of the place where the marriage is entered into; if valid there it is recognized as valid everywhere. But if A should come to the United States bringing with him more than one lawful wife he would not be allowed to live with more than one; this would not deny the validity of the marriage but merely one of its incidents.

If a divorce decree is so worded that it does not become operative till a certain time has elapsed neither party may marry anywhere during that pe-

[3] 11 **Am Jur**, Conflict of Laws, §§ 131–134.
Conflict of laws regarding deficiency in respect of debt secured by mortgage or deed of trust. 136 **ALR** 1057–1068.

[4] 11 **Am Jur**, Conflict of Laws, §§ 16–28.
44 **Harv. L. R.** 501, Marriage and the Domicil.

riod; but if the provison is so worded as to operate only against the guilty party it is considered to be in the nature of a penalty and by the weight of authority does not prevent the guilty party from marrying in another state unless he goes into the other state merely to avoid the penalty.

Where one of the spouses is white and the other colored and they go and are married in a state where a marriage between them is not forbidden and then return to their domicile where such a marriage is invalid the southern states hold such marriages invalid as against their public policy against mixed marriages.

Where a marriage is celebrated on the high seas according to the law of the vessel's home port such marriage is valid; but if celebrated on a boat so small as to have no port of registry it would seem that there is no marriage unless there was a separate organized community on board.

One who is born illegitimate may later be made legitimate either by special statute or by a statute giving such an effect to intermarriage between the parents; since status is thereby created it would seem that the only state that could make the child legitimate as to the father would be the state of the father's domicile; if the state of the father's domicile takes such a step it would seem that this might well make the child the legitimate child of the mother also, assent on the part of the state of the mother's domicile being presumed. In some countries, without a statute, subsequent intermarriage of the parents makes the child legitimate; in order for the marriage to have such an effect it would seem to be necessary that such effect be given it by the law of the domicile of the party to whom the relation of legitimate child is claimed.

The proper state to act in case of an adoption is the state of the domicile of the adopting parent or the state of the domicile of the adopting child.

§ 25. Property rights—tangibles.[5] The creation of rights in immovables depends generally upon the law of the place where the land is located. Though capacity to enter into contracts, including contracts with reference to land, depends upon the law of the place where the contract was made, capacity to transfer any property interest in land either by contract, deed or will depends upon the law of the situs of the land; similarly all other questions with reference to the validity of a conveyance of an interest in land, such as the requirement of witnesses, are determined by the law of its situs. If land is located in a state which gives specific performance of an oral contract to convey where there had been part performance the buyer will get a property right in the land the moment that such part performance takes place; but if the land is located in a state which would not grant specific performance in such a case but suit is brought in a state which would do so the buyer will get no right in the land till the seller conveys the land in pursuance of the court's decree and such conveyance must comply with the law of the situs.

The creation of rights in movables by transactions inter vivos depends upon the law of the situs of the movable at that time regardless of the domicile

[5] 11 **Am Jur,** Conflict of Laws, §§ 29–83.

Conflict of law as to conditional sales of chattels. 25 **ALR** 1153–1173; s. in 57 **ALR** 535–541; 87 **ALR** 1308–1315; 148 **ALR** 375–390.

Conflict of laws as to chattel mortgages. 57 **ALR** 702–733.

Conflict of laws as regards validity of fraudulent and preferential transfers and assignments. 111 **ALR** 787–821.

Conflict of laws as to exercise of power of appointment. 150 **ALR** 519–551.

Extraterritorial effect of confiscation of property and nationalization of corporations. 37 **ALR** 726–754; s. in 41 **ALR** 745–750; 65 **ALR** 1494–1497; 139 **ALR** 1209–1224.

of the owner. If A lends $500 to X and takes a mortgage of movables in New York and complies with the New York registration statute and then X should take the movable into New Jersey without A's consent A will not lose the right given him by New York law. But if X removes the chattel into New Jersey with A's consent it is competent for New Jersey to require A to register his mortgage in that state within a reasonable time after the arrival of the chattel in the state; but A's right will not be affected unless New Jersey has a statute specifically requiring such registration because the ordinary recording statute will be construed as affecting only movables within the state when the mortgage was executed.

§ 26. Same—intangibles—trusts—marital property.[6] A transfer of corporation stock is governed by the law of the state which chartered the corporation because it is only by a transfer on the corporation books that the assignee becomes complete owner. The assignment of an ordinary chose in action is governed by the law of the place where the assignment is made.

As to whether the law creates a trust right in property as the result of some transaction depends upon the law of the situs of the property; this applies not only to express trusts but to resulting trusts—that is, trusts imposed upon the property in accordance with the real or probable intent of the parties. But where a trust obligation is imposed merely as a matter of remedy irrespective of the intention of the parties, the law of the place where the remedy is sought determines whether such a remedy shall be given and no interest in foreign property will arise in such a case till the transfer is made according to the court's decree.

In this country the right of one spouse in the property of the other spouse is treated as a part of the law of property and not as a part of the law of the marriage; hence the law of the situs applies as to land and probably applies as to movables but the matter has been clouded by the frequent repetition of the fiction that the situs of movables is at the domicile of the owner.

§ 27. Same—intestacy—testacy.[7] If A dies intestate the law of the situs determines the succession of his immovable property, and the courts of the situs apply their own succession rule. As to his movables the courts of the situs might equally insist upon applying their own succession rule, but the advantage of treating the whole movable estate of the deceased as a unit is so great that in most states the rule of distribution is not that of the situs of the property but that of the decedent's domicile at the time of death.

The law as to testate succession to immovables is similar to the law as to intestate succession; the law of the situs applies as to the capacity of the testator, the extent of his power of disposition and the forms and solemnities necessary to give the will its authority and effect.

As to movables, the desirability of having all the movables governed by one rule is so great that in most states the law of the domicile at the time of

6 11 **Am Jur,** Conflict of Laws, §§ 85–98.

Conflict of laws as to trusts inter vivos. 89 **ALR** 1023–1034; s. in 139 **ALR** 1129–1138.

Conflict of laws as to administration of testamentary trusts, and proper forum for judicial proceedings relating thereto. 115 **ALR** 802–822.

44 **Harv. L. R.** 161, Trusts Inter Vivos and the Conflict of Laws.

7 11 **Am Jur,** Conflict of Laws, §§ 82, 83, 169–179.

Conflict of laws as to construction and effect of will devising real property. 79 **ALR** 91–112.

Governing law as to rights of spouse in estate of deceased spouse. 88 **ALR** 861–871.

Conflict of laws regarding election for or against will; and effect in one state of election in another. 105 **ALR** 271–288.

15 **Miss. L. J.** 77, The Dual Relationship of the Rules of Conflict of Laws in the Succession Field.

death is applied as to the capacity of the testator, the extent of his power of disposition and to the formalities necessary to make the will valid. Where the will does not comply with the requirements of the law of the domicile at the time of death but does comply with the law of the domicile at the time of making the will or with the law of the place where the will was executed the present tendency is to uphold the will in order to carry out, not frustrate, the intent of the testator. Where there has been an attempted revocation it would seem the law of the domicle at the time of death should govern; but where there is a question of the interpretation of a will the usage of the testator's domicile at the time of making the will should govern.

CHAPTER V

RECOGNITION AND ENFORCEMENT OF RIGHTS

§ 28. Remedies—local and transitory actions.[8] The general rule is that if a legal right has come into existence by the proper law it will be recognized everywhere and will be enforced as far as the machinery where enforcement is sought is adapted to such enforcement unless there is some good reason against it.

Actions in which the relief sought is the recovery of the possession of property—for example, ejectment, detinue and replevin—or the determination of title to it—for example, a suit in rem to remove all clouds from title—must be brought where the property is located. Logically it ought to be possible to bring all actions seeking a personal judgment for damages, or seeking a personal decree in equity, whether based upon tort, breach of contract, or unjust enrichment in any court where jurisdiction over the defendant can be obtained. This is the general rule but there is one illogical and unfortunate exception; by the weight of authority an action for trespass to land can be brought only where the land is located. The result is that if X trespasses upon A's land in Maine and then removes from Maine permanently without leaving any property in Maine which might be attached it is obviously impossible for A to get any relief. It is not a sound objection to giving relief that the court may be compelled to determine who owns the land because such a finding is only incidental to giving a judgment for the damages sought and could not in any way bind the land or bind the parties in a later local litigation over the land in a court which has jurisdiction over it.

§ 29. Same—procedure.[9] If A sues X in Iowa on a cause of action which arose in Kansas all matters relating to procedure are governed by the law of

[8] 11 **Am Jur**, Conflict of Laws, § 186.

Refusal on grounds of public policy of forum to enforce stipulation in carrier's contract limiting its liability, valid according to the proper law of the contract. 57 **ALR** 175-185.

Assumption of or refusal to assume jurisdiction by court of one state or country, of action on contract involving foreign elements. 87 **ALR** 1425-1449.

Conflict of laws as to title and transfer of corporate stock. 131 **ALR** 192-208.

Conflict of laws, with respect to trademark infringement or unfair competition, including the area of conflict between Federal and state law. 148 **ALR** 139-169.

[9] 11 **Am Jur**, Conflict of Laws, §§ 187-205.

Lex loci or lex fori as the governing law as to whether the case or question is to be submitted to the jury or determined by the court. 89 **ALR** 1278-1284; s. in 149 **ALR** 775-779.

Determination of question relating to foreign law as one of law or of fact. 34 **ALR** 1447-1476.

Conflict of laws as regards survival of cause of action and revival or pending action upon death of party. 87 **ALR** 852-862. s. in 92 **ALR** 1502-1508.

Law of the forum as governing the right to and rate of interest as damages for delay in payment of money or discharge of other obligation. 78 **ALR** 1047-1067.

Extraterritorial effect and recognition of

Iowa where the remedy is sought. If by the law of Iowa a creditor plaintiff is entitled to have his debtor arrested for debt A may have X arrested for debt even though no such remedy would have been allowed to A if he had sued in Kansas. And, if, by the law of Iowa the statutory period of limitation is six years that statute will govern even though the statutory period in Kansas is only four years, unless by the Kansas statute the cause of action is extinguished at the end of the four year period and X had lived in Kansas for that period after the action against him had accrued. Some of the statutes that create a cause of action for wrongfully causing death furnish an illustration of such extinguishment.

All matters relating to evidence are determined by the law of the forum. This includes the law as to presumptions because a presumption is a substitute for evidence. Whether a witness is competent or not, whether a partnership should be sued in its firm name or in the name of all its partners, the amount of exemption from execution allowed to a debtor, whether a defendant is entitled to set off in a particular case—all these are questions of procedure and determined by the law of the forum.

§ 30. Legitimation—adoption.[10] If an illegitimate child has been legitimated by the proper law the weight of authority is that he may inherit land and succeed to movables everywhere as if he had been legitimate at birth. Where the word "child" or "son" or "daughter" occurs in a will or in a statute the word should be construed to cover a legitimated child but there are some cases contra.

The great weight of authority is that an adopted child may inherit land in any state which has substantially the same provision for adoption as has the state where the adoption took place. But where there is a limitation upon inheritance in the state where the land is located—for example, that he can inherit only from the adoptive parents—the tendency is to apply such a limitation to children adopted in another state.

§ 31. Administration of decedent's estates.[1] A personal representative—that is, an executor or administrator—gets title to all the movables within the state in which he is qualified or is appointed and in order that the property shall at all times be within legal protection, his title relates back to the death of the decedent. Having title he may sue to recover the possession of the movables not only in the state of his appointment but in other states to which the movables may have been taken after the decedent's death. As to movables which are outside the state of his appointment at the death of the decedent he gets no title.

As to claims in favor of and against the estate a personal representative

adjudication of competency or incompetency, sanity or insanity. 102 **ALR** 444–454.

Statute of Frauds and conflict of laws. 105 **ALR** 652–681.

Conflict of laws as to period of limitation to enforce stockholders' statutory liability. 113 **ALR** 510–523; s. in 143 **ALR** 1442–1450.

[10] 11 **Am Jur,** Conflict of Laws, §§ 19–24.

1 **Am Jur,** Adoption of Children, § 10.

Conflict of laws as to legitimacy or legitimation, or as to rights of illegitimates, as affecting descent and distribution of decedents' estates. 73 **ALR** 941–960.

Conflict of laws as to adoption as affecting descent and distribution of decedent's estate. 73 **ALR** 964–980.

[1] 21 **Am Jur,** Executors and Administrators, §§ 45–53.

Judgment against executor or administrator qualified in one state as binding upon an executor or administrator of the same decedent, qualified in another. 3 **ALR** 64–71.

Law governing capacity of legatee or devisee to take, or of testator to give, to charitable or religious institutions. 91 **ALR** 491–508.

28 **U. of Iowa L. R.** 422, 613, Conflict of Laws in the Administration of Decedent's Intangibles.

cannot sue or be sued as such outside the state in which he is appointed; but if there are claims on contracts which the personal representative himself has made he may sue or be sued on them anywhere. If he sues upon a claim due the estate and gets a judgment thereon the old claim is merged in the judgment, he becomes the owner of the judgment, and he may sue on it as owner anywhere. But if action is brought against him on a claim against the decedent and judgment is rendered thereon such a judgment does not become a personal judgment against the personal representative and no suit thereon can be brought in any other state.

§ 32. Same—principal and ancillary adminstrations.[2] Where a decedent dies leaving personal property in several states an administrator will usually be appointed in each state. The one appointed in the state of the decedent's domicile is called the principal administrator; those appointed in other states or countries are called ancillary administrators. The administrator of the domicile is frequently appointed ancillary administrator in other states but the two adminstrations are kept separate just as if the ancillary adminstrator were a different individual. For assets which he has received in one state he is not accountable in another.

§ 33. Same—collection of choses in action.[3] For purposes of administration a simple contract debt is treated as if it had a situs at the residence of the debtor to the extent that a payment to the administrator appointed in that state is a good discharge and that the existence of such a claim at the time of the grant of administration is sufficient ground for the appointment of an administrator though there is no tangible property within the state the place of residence of the debtor at the time of the decedent's death is of no importance. But the administrator in the state where the debtor resides is not the only one entitled to collect; if the debtor pays any administrator either involuntarily or voluntarily in good faith such payment is a good discharge.

Where a debt is in the form of a negotiable instrument the debtor is entitled, upon paying, to the surrender of the instrument; hence only an administrator who has the instrument can sue upon it. If the debtor resides in a state other than that of the administrator who has the instrument the simplest method is for the administrator to endorse the instrument in blank, thus making it payable to bearer; he may then sue upon it anywhere not as administrator but as bearer—owner, being accountable for the proceeds to the court that appointed him.

§ 34. Same—proof of claim—distribution.[4] In order to protect its own citizens who may be creditors each state usually exercises its power to grant administration of the assets within its borders. While a state might insist

[2] 21 **Am Jur,** Executors and Administrators, §§ 849-893.

Necessity and sufficiency of assets to justify appointment of administrator at domicil of decedent. 59 **ALR** 87-95.

Right of foreign domiciliary, or of ancillary, personal representative to maintain an action for death, under statute of the forum which provides that the action shall be brought by the personal representative. 65 **ALR** 563-573.

Right of foreign executor or administrator to discharge or assign debt. 10 **ALR** 276-286.

Liability of insurer under policy payable to representatives or estate as between domiciliary and ancillary representative. 24 **ALR** 148-155.

42 **Harv. L. R.** 597, Voluntary Payment to a Foreign Administrator.

39 **Harv. L. R.** 797, Problems of Foreign Administration.

[3] 21 **Am Jur,** Executors and Administrators, §§ 981-987.

[4] 21 **Am Jur,** Executors and Administrators, §§ 875, 876, 884-893.

upon its own citizens being paid first to the exclusion of other creditors the general rule is that a creditor may prove his claim in every state which grants administration. He is not likely to do this unless the estate is insolvent and in any event he is entitled to only one satisfaction; and a creditor who has already received part payment in state X should not be allowed to share in the assets in state Y till the creditors in state Y have received payment to the same extent. Questions of priorities and other questions relative to the payment of debts are governed by the law of the forum just as in the case of collecting and paying the debts of a living person.

After the debts have been paid by the ancillary administrator to the local creditors and to such other creditors as have proved their claims there, and it is shown that all the creditors of the estate have been paid, the court of the ancillary administration may, in its discretion, either distribute the surplus or order the ancillary administrator to transmit it to the principal administrator for distribution; in either case the rule of distribution followed is that of the decedent's domicile. But if the debts are not all paid the court must order the surplus to be transmitted to the principal administrator for the purpose of paying the rest of the debts because until all the debts are paid there is nothing to distribute.

After the ancillary administrator has complied with the order of court directing him to transmit the surplus to the principal administrator he is relieved of any responsibility therefor, and if he is sued by a distributee he may plead the order of court in defense. If the ancillary administrator happens to be also the principal administrator the same principles apply, payment being made by charging himself as principal administrator with the receipt of the surplus so as to make himself accountable for it to the court of the principal administration.

§ 35. Receivers.[5] Jurisdiction to appoint a receiver depends upon control over the property. If the corporation, partnership or individual has property in several states the usual procedure is to have a receiver appointed in each state, the one appointed at the domicile being called the principal receiver, the others, ancillary receivers. The appointment of an ancillary receiver will not be made if there are no creditors residing in the state to object to the principal receiver's taking over the assets because it would only add to the expense. If the principal receiver asks to be appointed in the other states where there are assets and creditors he will usually be appointed, but the assets in each state will be separately administered.

If assets are assigned to the receiver he may sue in regard thereto anywhere just as any other assignee. If no assignment is made to him the general rule is that, having no title, he cannot sue outside the state in which he has been appointed; but in some states he may do so either as statutory successor to a corporation or as quasi assignee of the corporation's creditors. As to rights acquired by him he may sue anywhere even though they were acquired on behalf of the estate.

Generally a receiver cannot be sued as such outside the state in which he has been appointed; nor can he be sued there without leave of court because

[5] 45 **Am Jur**, Receivers, §§ 419–424.
When receiver of corporation deemed to be vested with title to assets so as to entitle him to sue in a foreign jurisdiction. 3 **ALR** 262–268; s. in 29 **ALR** 1495–1497.
Local property of insolvent foreign corporation for which a liquidator or receiver has been appointed in another state as subject to sequestration or seizure under execution or attachment. 98 **ALR** 351–386.
45 **Harv. L. R.** 429, Extraterritorial Powers of Receivers.

he is an officer of the court. But if the receiver is engaged in the business of a common carrier he is liable as such in any jurisdiction.

§ 36. Judgments.[6] In order that a judgment be enforced in another state it must comply with the following requirements: (1) There must be a tribunal distinct from the parties—one cannot be a judge in his own case; (2) There must be a complaining party to set the legal machinery in motion; (3) The adverse party must be given a reasonable opportunity to be heard; (4) The judgment must be responsive to the issues; (5) If the judgment is personal the court must have had jurisdiction of the person; if it is a judgment in rem the court must have had jurisdiction of the property; and a finding by the court that it has jurisdiction is not conclusive. If any of the five requisites is lacking the judgment is not entitled to enforcement abroad.

There is a provision in the United States Constitution requiring that each state shall give full faith and credit to the judgments of the courts of any other state; this does not name the federal courts but their judgments are accorded full faith and credit by the state courts and vice versa. The fact the cause of action upon which the judgment was based was against the public policy of the state in which full faith and credit is sought is no defense.

§ 37. Same—suit on a foreign judgment or decree.[7] In common-law countries a judgment can be executed only in the state or country in which the judgment was rendered; if it is wished to have, in New Jersey, execution of a judgment of a New York court, action must be brought upon it in a New Jersey court and a New Jersey judgment obtained. If the New York court had jurisdiction to render the judgment there is, in the New Jersey suit, no examination into the merits of the suit in New York; the New York judgment becomes res judicata, that is, it is accepted as final and binding upon the parties thereto and their privies. And all this is just as true of equitable decrees for money as it is of common law judgments for money. Where A obtains in New York an equity decree against X for the conveyance of land—whether in New York, New Jersey or elsewhere—and X leaves New York without complying with the decree and A then finds him in New Jersey and sues him there, will the New Jersey court regard the New York decree as res judicata and issue a decree for the conveyance of the land or will it insist upon A's proving his case all over again? The better view and the trend of the decisions is in favor of the New Jersey court recognizing the New York decree as final.

A judgment or decree for the payment of money is frequently sued on in the same state or country in which it has been rendered; this is usually done to avoid the running of the statute of limitations; the new judgment is a new cause of action and the statute of limitations; the new judgment is a new cause of action and the statute begins to run all over again. The better doctrine is that if there is a suit in New Jersey on a New York judgment the New Jersey judgment does not merge the judgment of the New York court

6 31 **Am Jur,** Judgments, §§ 530–575.

Refusal to entertain an action upon a judgment rendered in another state upon a cause of action which it would have been contrary to statute or public policy of the forum to have entertained. 4 **ALR** 968–975; s. in 10 **ALR** 719; 24 **ALR** 1437, 1438.

Judgment entered in sister state under warrant of attorney to confess judgment. 40 **ALR** 441–458; s. in 89 **ALR** 1503–1510.

Conclusiveness as to merits of judgment of courts of foreign country. 46 **ALR** 439–456; s. in 148 **ALR** 991–1002.

29 **Va. L. R.** 557, The Supreme Court and the Full Faith and Credit Clause.

92 **U. of Pa. L. R.** 401, Workmen's Compensation Award—Commonplace or Anomaly in Full Faith and Credit Pattern?

7 31 **Am Jur,** Judgments, §§ 530–575.

because the judgment creditor might later find some property in New York which—if there is no merger—could promptly be reached to satisfy the judgment creditor's claim.

In civil law countries there is no such thing as a suit on a judgment, either domestic or foreign; after an examination into the merits the judgment is declared executory and execution is issued without a new judgment being rendered. By the better view this difference in procedure should not prevent an action being brought in a court in this country upon a judgment rendered in a civil law country, but there is a decision in the United States Supreme Court that since no execution of a judgment in an American court could be obtained in France without an examination into the merits of the original cause of action, a judgment obtained in France should not be accepted as final in a suit brought on a French judgment in this country because of a "want of reciprocity."

PART III—PUBLIC LAW

PUBLIC UTILITIES

CHAPTER I

IN GENERAL

§ 1. The old and the new public utilities.[1] From very early times till the present day the common carrier and the innkeeper have been regarded as engaged in callings in which the public had such a direct and immediate interest that there was imposed upon both a duty to serve the public at reasonable rates. In the early days there may have been others who were sub-

1 43 **Am Jur,** Public Utilities and Services, § 22.

Duty to extend electrical service or supply individual applicant as affected by cost involved. 58 **ALR** 537–554.

Irrigation company as a public utility. 8 **ALR** 268–289; s. in 15 **ALR** 1227–1234.

Telegraph ticker service. 1 **ALR** 1286–1298; s. in 45 **ALR** 1379.

Right and duty of telephone companies to make physical connection of exchanges or lines. 11 **ALR** 1204–1219; s. in 76 **ALR** 953–957.

Duty of telegraph company to notify sender of message in case of inability to transmit or deliver promptly. 17 **ALR** 109–119; s. in 55 **ALR** 639, 640.

Right of public utility company to discontinue its entire service. 11 **ALR** 252-259.

Measure and amount of damages for breach of duty to furnish water, gas, light, or power service. 108 **ALR** 1174–1197.

Right of one neither sender nor addressee to recover against telegraph company because of delay or mistake. 72 **ALR** 1198–1211.

Right of telephone company to refuse, or discontinue, service because of failure to pay bills or other violation of conditions of use. 70 **ALR** 894–904.

Duty of telegraph company as to delivery of message where sendee is found absent from the address given. 63 **ALR** 808–819.

What telephone companies are within public utilities acts. 21 **ALR** 1162–1172.

43 **Harv. L. R.** 379, The Federal Courts and State Regulation of Public Utilities.

41 **Harv. L. R.** 277, The Public Utility Concept in American Law.

41 **Mich. L. R.** 1, Integration under Sec-

ject to the same obligation—the common surgeon, the common tailor, the common smith, the common victualer, the common baker and the common miller—but in these last named occupations if there ever was such an obligation the number of persons employed therein increased to such an extent that the public interest was protected by competition, and it became unnecessary in those occupations to continue to impose the legal duty to serve.

Within the last century there has arisen—beginning with the telegraph—a new group of callings in which the public interest is not protected by competition so that the law has imposed the obligation to serve at reasonable rates. At first the duty was imposed by way of analogy to that of the well-established public service occupations of the common carrier and the innkeeper; thus the telegraph and telephone were said to be common carriers of messages and the sleeping cars and steamboats were thought to be analogous to inns. But later these four, together with many more, were recognized as merely members of a large modern class of public utilities which includes also such well-known utilities as waterworks, irrigation systems, gas works, electric light and power plants, steam heat and refrigeration.

§ 2. Unusual burdens and an unusual privilege.[2] The common law as to common carriers and innkeepers developed in England at a time when there was comparatively little commerce or travel and when the forests were infested with robbers. In order, therefore, to protect senders of goods and travelers the law imposed upon the common carriers of goods for hire and upon innkeepers the burden of liability for any damage done to the goods being entrusted to the carrier or to the goods of the guest, except that inflicted by an act of God or of the public enemy. The purpose of the strict rule was to prevent collusion between carriers or innkeepers with highwaymen or robbers and this purpose explains the exceptions. The danger of collusion with a public enemy was slight and furthermore, if there should be an invasion of England such an event would be so well known throughout the kingdom that it would be easily capable of proof and could not easily be pretended.

As to the "act of God" exception—according to the theology of that period, the universe had been created some fifty-five hundred years earlier and at that time God had set in motion the ordinary physical forces of the universe, such as the sunshine, the rain and the tides and these continued to operate automatically without any further divine impetus; but occasionally God did interfere by sending a hurricane, an earthquake, a tidal wave or other unusual manifestation of natural forces. The reason for excluding these as due to an "act of God" was that any such unusual manifestation of physical forces would be so well known as to negative any collusion or any pretense of such a happening. In more recent years the origin of the term has been lost sight of and it has been extended to mean any natural force acting without human agency, which is very nearly the same as inevitable accident. A further unusual burden imposed upon public utilities is that of statutory regulation.

tion 10(c) of the Public Utility Holding Company Act.

48 **W. Va. L. R.** 226, Profits à Prendre and Interstate Price-Fixing.

17 **Tenn. L. R.** 308, Social Performance of Public Utilities.

17 **Temple N. L. Q.** 153, History of Public Utility Rate Regulation in Pennsylvania.

19 **Notre Dame Lawyer** 85, Problems of Our Domestic Air Transportation.

2 9 **Am Jur,** Carriers, § 4.

28 **Am Jur,** Innkeepers, § 29.

As at least a partial compensation for the duty to serve the public at reasonable rates, for the liability at peril for all damage done unless by act of God or the public enemy and for statutory regulation, some public utilities—especially railroads—have been given the power of eminent domain by which they can take private property for public use upon paying reasonable compensation therefor.

§ 3. What makes an occupation a public utility.[3] There is no definite test by which to determine whether a particular occupation is or is not a public utility. Some public utilities, such as ferries and bridges, have an exclusive franchise granted by the legislature, thus giving them a legal monopoly. Others, such as electric and gas companies, have been granted the use of public highways for their poles, wires and pipes. Others, such as oil pipe lines, have been granted the right of eminent domain. Others, such as grain elevator companies and dock companies, have a virtual monopoly due to scarcity of advantageous sites. Still others, such as telegraph and telephone companies, have a virtual monopoly due to the difficulty and frequently the undesirability of effective competition. But there are some public utilities, such as innkeepers and messenger service which have none of the above privileges or advantages.

There is, however, in addition to the requirement that the public interest must be affected in order to make an occupation a public utility, a further characteristic that is common to practically all public utilities, and that is that it renders service and does not merely sell commodities. Thus the grocer who sells candles and lamps and electric light bulbs, is not engaged in a public service occupation but the electric company that brings to the customer electric current through a wire and a gas company that brings gas through a pipe are both public utilities.

While undertaking to serve the public indiscriminately is not enough in itself to make an occupation a public utility, such an undertaking is essential. A railroad which was constructed merely as a war measure and not for the use of the public generally was not a common carrier; nor was an amusement company that ran a ferryboat from Detroit to its amusement park on an island; a motor bus line which makes special arrangements to carry passengers beyond their line is not a common carrier as to such passengers; and a liveryman who hires out vehicles has been held not to be a public utility. One who merely forwards goods has been held not to be a common carrier, but one who solicited goods from different persons having less than a carload expecting to send them in carload lots has been held to be a common carrier though he owned no railroad line himself. The mere fact that X carried for one common carrier did not make X a common carrier; but a terminal company that serves all railroads at the terminal has itself been held to be a common carrier.

Formerly, in order to hold the proprietor of a hotel liable as an innkeeper it was necessary that he furnish his guests with room and food and a stable for his horses, but today neither the food nor the stable is necessary. On the other hand an apartment or family hotel, obviously not conducted for the convenience of travelers, is not an inn.

[3] 43 **Am Jur,** Public Utilities and Services, §§ 2–6.

§ 4. Same—effect of legislation.[4] Some occupations not recognized as public utilities at common law have been so recognized by legislation undertaking to regulate such occupations on the ground that they are affected with a public interest. The outstanding illustration is the grain elevator. The Illinois constitution of 1820 declared all elevators or storehouses where grain or other property is stored for a compensation to be public warehouses and provided that the general assembly should pass laws for the inspection of grain, for the protection of producers, shippers and receivers of grain or produce. Legislation under this constitutional provision fixing the maximum charges for the storage of grain in warehouses was attacked as being in violation of the United States Constitution but was held valid in the famous case of Munn v. Illinois, 94 US 113, 24 L ed 17.

Since that decision legislation has been upheld regulating stockyards, tobacco warehouses, cotton gins, coal mining, insurance and theaters and other places of amusement; and a statute has been held valid which authorized a fuel yard to be maintained by a city or town to sell fuel at cost. Emergency housing legislation regulating the business of renting houses has been held valid as well as a statute levying a tax of 1% of a bank's average daily deposits to create a depositors' guaranty fund. But a Kansas statute declaring the manufacture and preparation of food, the manufacture of clothing and fuel and the transportation of food, clothing and fuel to be affected with a public interest was held to be invalid in so far as it applied to the business of slaughtering hogs and cattle.

CHAPTER II

SERVICE

§ 5. Excuses for refusal or failure to serve.[5] A common carrier of goods is not liable for failure to accept goods for carriage until the goods and the freight charges have been tendered at the proper time and place. Express companies may fix reasonable limits for collecting and delivering shipments and a telegraph company may fix reasonable limits for the free delivery of messages.

A railroad may refuse to honor a limited passenger ticket after the limit has expired and may eject a passenger who refuses or fails to pay his fare. The fact that a passenger is colored is no excuse for failure to provide accommodations equal to that provided for white passengers. The fact that a passenger is unchaste is no excuse for failure to carry but it has been held that the keeper of a bawdy house is not entitled to have a telephone in the house. However, the mere fact that a shipper of cattle plans to offer the cattle for sale in violation of a Sunday statute has been considered no excuse for refusal to carry the cattle.

Apart from statute a common carrier is not bound to carry a circus; and an innkeeper may exclude boisterous and disorderly persons from his inn.

§ 6. Adequacy of service.[6] Although it is not clear that there is a common-law duty on public utilities to use care to furnish reasonably adequate facilities, such a duty is practically always imposed today by legislation.

[4] 43 **Am Jur,** Public Utilities and Services, §§ 10-15.

[5] 43 **Am Jur,** Public Utilities and Services, §§ 31, 32.

[6] 43 **Am Jur,** Public Utilities and Services, §§ 47, 48.

What is reasonably adequate depends, of course, upon the circumstances. If a railroad runs through a territory in which lumber or coal or iron or grain or livestock is produced for shipment it must use due care to supply a reasonable number of suitable cars to carry such commodities; but apparently, apart from special statute, it need not furnish tank cars in which to transport oil. If the territory produces for shipment perishable products such as meat, butter, fruits, berries or vegetables it must use due care to furnish a reasonable number of refrigerator cars for such commodities. And where livestock is being carried it must use due care to furnish the necessary water and feed during the transit, but not at the stock pens while such livestock is awaiting shipment.

Where suit is brought against a common carrier for failure to use due care to provide adequate facilities the burden of going forward with the evidence is upon the carrier because the facts are peculiarly within its knowledge.

§ 7. Equality of service.[7] The early common-law rule seems to have been that as long as a public utility did not charge anyone more than a reasonable amount for its service it might discriminate between customers by charging some a less amount or nothing at all. This rule was taken advantage of by large shippers who became still larger and sometimes achieved a monopoly by insisting upon rebates which gave them an advantage over their competitors who had to pay the regular rate or who had to be contented with a lower rebate. Largely because of this well-known usage courts came to take the view that such discrimination tended to show that the regular rate was unreasonably high. Today, usually by statute, the rule seems to be well settled that arbitrary discrimination is itself unlawful, so that contracts for rebates are not enforcible and even if an undercharge was made by mistake the carrier may recover the deficiency from the shipper—or, if it was a passenger carrier, from the passenger.

Some discrimination, however, has been held to be lawful. A common carrier of passengers may validly sell commutation tickets and party rate tickets. A common carrier of goods may charge a higher rate for expedited service provided that such rate is published and thus made available to all; where there are not enough facilities to transport all the goods offered for shipment it may and should give preference to those which are perishable; it may charge a higher rate to transport livestock than packing house products; but it is doubtful whether it may extend credit to some shippers and not to others.

A railroad may make an exclusive arrangement with one express company to handle express on its lines; and it may make an exclusive arrangement with one taxicab company to handle passengers entering or leaving the station, the rival taxicab companies having the right to solicit passengers merely on the sidewalks adjacent to the station.

Most of the decisions on the subject of discrimination involve common carriers; but it has been held that an electric light company may not charge for a transformer only those customers who did not employ the company to wire the house.

7 43 Am Jur, Public Utilities and Services, §§ 22, 42–46.

CHAPTER III

LIABILITY

§ 8. Common carriers of goods.[8] As the rule is usually stated a common carrier of goods is liable for any loss or damage to the goods except that caused by an act of God or the public enemies. But there is no liabilty at peril if the loss or damage is due to some act of the shipper, for example, where the loss was due to his faulty crating of the goods; or to his misrepresenting the value of the goods in order to get a lower rate; or if the loss or damage is due to some inherent quality of the goods, for example, where stoves rusted due to the quality of the material used in them; or if the goods have been taken from the carrier by a lawful attachment. Nor does liability at peril apply against an owner of a tugboat who merely furnishes motive power and does not take possession of the boat towed. Or against the owner of a ferryboat where the vehicle on board the boat remains under the control of the driver of it.

Where loss or damage is due merely to delay, the common carrier is liable only if negligent. But where goods have been wrongfully sent on a different route from the one authorized by the shipper and the goods are lost or damaged during such wrongful deviation the carrier is absolutely liable as an insurer without any exceptions made in its favor.

8 9 **Am Jur,** Carriers, §§ 660–812.

Carrier's liability as affected by improper packing or preparation of goods for shipment. 81 **ALR** 811–821.

Carrier's right or liability in respect of excess of lawful charge over charge understated where discrimination is forbidden. 83 **ALR** 245–268.

Right to maintain action against carrier on ground that rates which were filed and published by carrier pursuant to law were excessive. 97 **ALR** 406–431.

Assumption of risk and contributory negligence in connection with injuries arising from improper manner of loading or fastening load on freight car. 106 **ALR** 1140–1151.

Right to damages because of abandonment or relocation of railway line, station, or sidetrack. 23 **ALR** 555–565.

Person or corporation transporting goods on the public highways as a common carrier, or private or contract carrier, as regards liability for loss of or damage to goods. 112 **ALR** 89–102.

Waiver of rights by carrier under interstate shipments as constituting unlawful discrimination among shippers. 135 **ALR** 611–624.

Status, rights, and obligations of freight forwarders. 141 **ALR** 919–938.

Carriers: sufficiency of compliance with stipulation requiring notice of claim for damages to shipment. 1 **ALR** 900–913.

Car shortage as affecting liability of carrier for failure to furnish cars. 10 **ALR** 342–363.

Who may maintain action to recover back excessive freight charge. 13 **ALR** 289–302.

Right of railroad company to discontinue or reduce service on branch line or part of road which is unprofitable. 123 **ALR** 922-933.

Duty of carrier to shipper as to condition of stock pens or yards. 15 **ALR** 200–212.

Strike as defense against claim for demurrage. 21 **ALR** 1473–1484.

What constitutes delivery of freight to carrier. 22 **ALR** 970–1006; s. in 113 **ALR** 1459–1471.

Liability for freight charge as affected by delivery without collecting charge as stipulated or directed. 24 **ALR** 1163–1171; s. in 78 **ALR** 926–930; 129 **ALR** 213–216.

Special services or facilities afforded by shipper as a factor in carrier's rates. 25 **ALR** 191–211.

Demurrage as affected by impossibility of performing shipper's obligation, due to act of God or weather conditions. 26 **ALR** 1431–1445.

Carrier's liability for delay, or damages incident to delay, in transportation, due to strike. 28 **ALR** 503–511; s. in 45 **ALR** 919–922.

Validity, construction, and effect of provision of contract for carriage of livestock whereby shipper assumes responsibility for condition of car. 28 **ALR** 526–536.

Liability of carrier which negligently delays transportation or delivery for loss of or damage to goods from causes for which it is not otherwise responsible. 46 **ALR** 302–313.

Demurrage as affected by insurrection or act of public authorities. 44 **ALR** 829–848.

Presumption and burden of proof as to carrier's responsibility for goods received in good condition and delivered to consignee in bad condition. 53 **ALR** 996–1019; s. in 106 **ALR** 1156–1169.

Liabilities of the parties to a contract of towage with respect to injury sustained by the tow or tug during the performance of the towage service. 54 **ALR** 104–260.

Liability of one not named as consignor or consignee for freight on goods delivered to and accepted by him. 61 **ALR** 422–433.

Logging or mining road as a common carrier. 67 **ALR** 588–599.

§ 9. Common carriers of passengers.[9] Partly due to the fact that a common carrier of passengers is not in possession of the passengers and that the latter are usually in a position to do something in regard to their own safety, and partly to the fact that there is very little, if any, danger of collusion between such a carrier and third persons, the liability is not one at peril for the safety of the passengers. But since the safety of human beings is at stake the carrier must use a high degree and amount of care, which is substantially the same as that of a man of average prudence under similar circumstances.

Where the passenger turns baggage over to the carrier the latter becomes responsible therefor as a common carrier of goods.

The extraordinary liability of a common carrier of goods applies only when the goods are carried for hire. But the fact that a passenger is

[9] 10 **Am Jur,** Carriers, §§ 948, 949.

Liability of motorbus carrier for death of or injury to discharged passenger struck by vehicle not within its control. 145 **ALR** 1206–1216.

Liability of motor carrier for injury to passenger by sudden stopping, starting, or lurching of conveyance. 138 **ALR** 224–235.

Liability of common carrier by motorbus or taxicab for personal injury to or death of passenger where condition of highway was the cause or a contributing factor. 126 **ALR** 1084–1092.

Liability of motor carrier for personal injuries to or death of passenger due to structural conditions of interior of conveyance. 126 **ALR** 461–469.

Duty and liability of carrier of passengers for hire by automobile. 4 **ALR** 1499–1509; 31 **ALR** 1202–1211; 45 **ALR** 297–309; 69 **ALR** 980–998; 96 **ALR** 727–772.

Liability of carrier by water for injury to passenger while embarking or disembarking. 59 **ALR** 1355–1368.

Liability of carrier for giving misinformation to passenger as to running of train. 8 **ALR** 1183–1195.

Liability of carrier for injury due to casual or temporary condition of station or its approaches. 10 **ALR** 259–271.

Liability of carrier to passenger for assault by third person. 15 **ALR** 868–894; s. in 42 **ALR** 168–176; 43 **ALR** 1035.

Duty and liability of carrier toward one accompanying departing passenger or present to meet incoming one, with respect to conditions at or about station. 92 **ALR** 614–626.

Liability of carrier for injury to passenger as result of ice, snow, or rain on exposed or interior portions of car or vessel. 117 **ALR** 522–538.

Duty of carrier to discover abnormal condition of passenger. 124 **ALR** 1428–1443.

Loss or theft of passenger's ticket or other token of right to transportation as affecting rights and duties of carrier and passenger. 127 **ALR** 222–233.

Carrier's liability for conduct of passenger (other than assault) causing injury to other passenger. 140 **ALR** 1194–1206.

Means of preventing overcrowding of streetcars. 6 **ALR** 124–134.

Duty and liability of carrier to passenger attempting to leave moving streetcar. 56 **ALR** 981–1011.

Status of, and liability of street railway company to, person approaching to board streetcar. 75 **ALR** 285–296.

Liability of carrier operating in street to passenger struck by other vehicle while on platform, step, or running board of car. 77 **ALR** 429–448.

When relation of carrier and passenger commences as between railway or interurban company and one intending to take train or car not at a regular stopping place. 116 **ALR** 756–766.

Liability of sleeping-car company for refusal to furnish accommodations. 23 **ALR** 1302–1317.

Liability of carrier for baggage not accompanied by passenger. 23 **ALR** 1446–1460.

Liability of carrier for injury to passenger by car door. 25 **ALR** 1061–1076; s. in 41 **ALR** 1089–1092.

Use of emphatic words, like "great care," "utmost care," or "highest care," in instructing jury as to duty of carrier to passengers. 32 **ALR** 1190–1215.

Duty of carrier to heat car. 33 **ALR** 168–175.

Duty and liability to passenger temporarily leaving train. 35 **ALR** 757–774; s. in 61 **ALR** 403, 404.

Carrier's liability to passenger for consequences of ejection or threatened ejection by one employee due to fault of another employee. 36 **ALR** 1018–1063.

Dispute over payment of fare as justifying arrest of passenger by carrier. 39 **ALR** 862–867.

Carrier's liability to passenger for failure to keep trains to schedule time. 52 **ALR** 1332–1344.

Duty and liability of carrier as to assisting passenger to board or alight from car or train. 55 **ALR** 389–406; s. in 59 **ALR** 940.

Duty of carrier as to notifying passenger of approach to or arrival at destination. 58 **ALR** 1064–1119.

Liability of railroad company for acts of employees in ejecting trespassers from train. 72 **ALR** 536–571.

Validity, construction, and application of municipal ordinances relating to loading or unloading passengers by interurban busses on streets. 144 **ALR** 1119–1127.

Liability of motorbus carrier for death of or injury to discharged passenger struck by vehicle not within its control. 145 **ALR** 1206–1216.

carried gratuitously does not, in the absence of contract, affect the duty of a common carrier of passengers.

§ 10. Innkeepers.[10] The common-law liability of an innkeeper for a guest's luggage is similar to that of a common carrier of goods;—he is liable for any loss or damage except that which is caused by an act of God or the public enemies or by the guest himself. Regulations made by the innkeeper that he will not be responsible for valuables unless deposited in the office have been usually upheld as to very valuable jewelry and large amounts of money but not as a watch, inexpensive jewelry and such moderate amounts of money as are accustomed to be carried by persons in the guest's station in life.

In practically all states today there is legislation regulating the liabilities of innkeepers and the keepers of hotels which do not fall within the definition of a common-law inn.

§ 11. When liability begins and ends.[1] The extraordinary liability of a common carrier of goods begins when the goods are received and accepted for carriage even though no bill of lading has been issued therefor; and it continues until the consignee has had a reasonable time, after notice, to remove the goods at the destination. After such reasonable time has elapsed, or after the goods have been tendered and refused, the common carrier becomes liable merely as a bailee for the failure to use ordinary care of the goods. Placing goods on a car on a siding is not delivery to the carrier unless there is an agent in attendance. An express company whose duty it usually is to deliver goods to the consignee remains liable as a common carrier until such delivery or until reasonable efforts have been made to find the consignee.

One becomes a passenger on a railroad when he enters the railroad station not more than a reasonable time before the scheduled departure of the train he expects to take and ordinarily he continues to be a passenger until he has had a reasonable time at his destination to claim his baggage. But if, after boarding the train, he tenders only an invalid ticket he ceases to be a passenger and may be ejected from the train.

One becomes a passenger on a streetcar, not from the time that he signals for the car to stop but from the time he places his foot on the car step to enter the car and ordinarily continues to be a passenger until he alights from the car. One who is descending the stairway of an elevated railway has been held to have ceased to have the rights of a passenger thereon.

One ordinarily becomes a guest at an inn when he registers as such on the hotel register, or upon the receipt and acceptance of his baggage as such, expecting to occupy a room therein; and he ordinarily continues to be a guest even after he has paid his bill till he has had a reasonable time to remove his baggage. But if he should continue at the inn for several months so that he can no longer be considered as a traveler he ceases to have the rights of a guest. Merely eating a banquet at an inn as a guest of a club does not make one a guest of the inn.

§ 12. Limitation of liability.[2] Common carriers of goods may validly stipulate against their extraordinary common-law liability by offering a

[10] 28 Am Jur, Innkeepers, §§ 40-147.

[1] 9 Am Jur, Carriers, § 661.
10 Am Jur, Carriers, §§ 955-966.

[2] 9 Am Jur, Carriers, §§ 732-777.
10 Am Jur, Carriers, §§ 1134-1143.
52 Am Jur, Telegraphs and Telephones, § 143.

lower rate. And, by the prevailing view, they may limit their liability, in case of loss or damage to the goods, to a specified amount unless the shipper pays a higher rate for an additional valuation; and such limitation has been held valid though the shipper does not sign any stipulation to that effect.

Similarly, by the better view, a telegraph company may limit its liability for damage caused by a mistake in the message to the price paid for sending the message where the sender fails to pay an additional sum to have the message repeated.

As to whether a common carrier of passengers may validly, in issuing a free pass or a ticket at reduced rates, provide against liabilty for damage to person or property caused by its negligence there is a square conflict of authority. Some courts permit the carrier to stipulate against liability for the negligence of its servants but not its own, while others permit it to stipulate against liability for more than ordinary care.

§ 13. Liability where there is a connecting carrier.[3] Where goods shipped must be sent over two or more lines each line is of course responsible—apart from stipulation—for any loss or damage to the goods while in its possession. Where the goods have been delivered in good order to the inital carrier and they have been delivered by the last carrier in bad order the presumption is that they were in good order when the second or subsequent carrier received them.

Where the initial common carrier contracts to deliver beyond its own line it is liable as common carrier for the entire distance. Where there is no such contract to deliver at destination the prevailing view in this country is that the initial carrier is not liable, apart from express stipulation, for loss or damage except on its own line. But the Carmack Amendment to the Interstate Commerce Act makes the initial carrier liable beyond its own line as to interstate shipments where the loss has been caused by it or by the connecting carrier, with a provision that the act "shall not affect any remedy which the shipper has by existing laws". Under this provision an initial carrier was held liable for loss due to the explosion of munitions. The Carmack Amendment has been construed not to affect the common-law presumption against the delivering carrier.

CHAPTER IV

RATES

§ 14. Judicial review—utility commissions.[4] Since a court is not a legislative body it has no authority to fix the rates which a public utility may

[3] 9 **Am Jur,** Carriers, §§ 862–946.
10 **Am Jur,** Carriers, §§ 1691–1705.

[4] 43 **Am Jur,** Public Utilities and Services, §§ 81–191.

Power of Public Service Commission with respect to regulation of street railways. 5 **ALR** 36–79; s. in 39 **ALR** 1517–1542.

Power of Public Service Commission in respect to alteration or extension of passenger service. 70 **ALR** 841–854.

Power of Public Service Commission to increase franchise rates. 3 **ALR** 730–748; s. in 9 **ALR** 1165–1177; 28 **ALR** 587–609; 29 **ALR** 356–358.

Power of state to change private contract rates for public utilities. 9 **ALR** 1423–1437.

Regulating issuance of securities by public utilities through Public Service Commissions. 41 **ALR** 889–925.

Profit factor in determining rates for municipally owned or operated public utility. 90 **ALR** 700–704.

Membership corporation or association or co-operative group furnishing to its members electric, telephone, or other service commonly supplied by public utility, as subject to governmental regulation or to jurisdiction of Public Service Commission. 132 **ALR** 1495–1514.

charge but may merely declare that the rates fixed are so excessive as to be unfair to the public or so low as to amount to a confiscation of the utility's property.

Today rates are sometimes fixed directly by the legislature but more often by a public utility commission. The existence of a franchise or even of a contract which has fixed rates seems to be no bar to the action of a commission in fixing lower rates but such a contract has been held to be a bar to fixing higher rates. The action of the legislature or the commission seems to be a bar to any complaint made by the public that the rates are too high, but no bar to a complaint by the utility that the rates thus fixed are so low as to be confiscatory.

§ 15. **Fair value.**[5] The public utility is entitled to charge reasonable rates based upon the fair value of its property. But how is such fair value to be determined?

Some half century ago it was held that fair value means fair exchange value—that is, what a purchaser would pay for all the tangible and intangible property of the utility. There are two difficulties with this test; as long as the public utility is a going concern it does not ordinarily sell out; and if it did sell, the purchase price would be determined largely according to the net income of the utility, which is dependent directly upon the rates which the utility is charging, thus involving reasoning in a circle.

Another test that was strongly urged a few decades ago was the reproduction cost. In an era of declining prices when there had been reckless financing, unconscionable construction contracts and watered stocks this test was vehemently advocated by the consumer; later, where prices of labor and material soared it was the utility that urged it. Because our price level is changing every few years reproduction cost is not satisfactory as a single test though it may be considered as one of several elements, in arriving at a fair valuation.

Now that modern utility regulation has greatly reduced, if it has not entirely wiped out, reckless financing and watered stocks, and more reliable and accurate accounts of untility expenditures are being used, probably the best single test is that of prudent investment, that is, the amount of money that has been prudently invested in the utility enterprise.

Where in the past the rates have provided for depreciation and such depreciation has been paid by the consumer that amount should be deducted

Regulations or provisions upon requiring physical connection of telephone lines. 16 **ALR** 352–362.

Federal control of public utilities. 4 **ALR** 1680–1721; s. in 8 **ALR** 969–990; 10 **ALR** 956–976; 11 **ALR** 1450–1463; 14 **ALR** 234–236; 19 **ALR** 678–711; 52 **ALR** 296–363.

Reasonableness of regulation of speed of railroad train. 20 **ALR** 1222–1232.

Power to require railroads or street railways to permit use of tracks in street by other companies. 28 **ALR** 969–979.

Forfeiture of street railway franchise for breach of condition. 34 **ALR** 1413–1425.

Service contract by public utility, in consideration of conveyance of property, by individual or private corporation, as affected by public utility acts. 11 **ALR** 460–466; s. in 41 **ALR** 257–263.

Public utility rate valuations as affected by advance in price conditions due to World War. 20 **ALR** 555–589.

Power of Public Service Commission to increase freight rates. 28 **ALR** 587–609; s. in 29 **ALR** 356–358.

38 **Col. L. R.** 959, Conflicting Judicial Criteria of Utility Rates.

38 **Col. L. R.** 1037, Public Utility Depreciation.

[5] 43 **Am Jur**, Public Utilities and Services, §§ 105–140.

43 **Harv. L. R.** 1249, Valuation as a Requirement of Due Process of Law in Rate Cases.

41 **Harv. L. R.** 593, The Economic Merits of Original Cost and Reproduction Cost.

38 **Col. L. R.** 978, Due Process Requirement of a Fair Hearing in a Rate Proceeding.

42 **Mich. L. R.** 1049, Demise of Fair Value.

11 **U. of Chicago L. R.** 297, History of Rate Determination under Due Process Clauses.

in fixing fair valuation in the future. On the other hand if the property of the utility has appreciated in value the better view seems to be that such appreciation should be taken into consideration in fixing a fair valuation for the purpose of rate making.

§ 16. **Fair return.**[6] In fixing the rates to be charged so that the utility may realize a fair return various matters are to be considered. These include labor costs and other current expenses, income taxes, the risk of loss in the particular utility and therefore the problem of attracting sufficient capital. In order to encourage efficiency in managing the utility a share of the savings due to efficiency should ordinarily go to the management and part to the employees. There must also be taken into consideration that lower rates may mean such a large increase in the amount of business that the net income will be increased instead of diminished.

While a public utility cannot be compelled to operate permanently at a loss a street railway which has several branches may not discontinue one because it does not show a profit provided the system as a whole shows a fair return. But where a railroad has both interstate and intrastate business it is entitled to a fair return on each one; it may not be compelled to carry either at a loss merely because its whole business shows a fair return.

Since there seems to be no escape from having business cycles, a utility should be allowed sufficient return so that in good years it may accumulate a surplus to carry it over the lean years that are almost certain to come. And the same reasoning applies in fixing the rates of an irrigation company that must face the likelihood of seasons with a reduced water supply.

Sometimes, in fixing rates, the effect upon competitors should be considered. Thus a steamboat company which ran only one boat was compelled to increase its rates so as not to injure the business of a competitor that offered the public a complete service. And where rates were made uniform for several railroads serving the same territory and this results in some of the roads receiving more than a fair return it has been held that as to the excess the railroads receiving it are to be considered as trustees thereof, under the order of the commission.

6 43 Am Jur, Public Utilities and Services, §§ 156–170.

MUNICIPAL CORPORATIONS

CHAPTER 1

CREATION, CORPORATE CHANGES, DISSOLUTION

§ 1. Incorporation.[1] In the narrowest and most proper sense the term municipal corporation applies only to cities and towns of a compact establishment, with chartered rights adequate for the general conduct of local public affairs; in a broader sense the term applies also to such local subdivisions of the state—frequently called quasi-municipal corporations—as counties, townships and parishes, while in a still broader sense the term includes school districts and districts for such purposes as fire, drainage or irrigation, which are also sometimes referred to as quasi-municipal corporations.

At the English common-law municipal corporations could be created either by the Crown or by Parliament; but in this country they may be created only by the state legislature or by the Congress in the case of municipal corpora-

[1] 37 **Am Jur**, Municipal Corporations, §§ 7–9.
30 **Calif. L. R.** 1, 272, Municipal Home Rule in California.
17 **Ind. L. J.** 375, Municipal Home Rule in Indiana.

tions in the District of Columbia or in the national territories which have not reached statehood. While formerly municipal corporations were sometimes created by special statute they come into existence today only under the operation of a general legislative act.

Though consent of inhabitants is not necessary and they acquire no rights from incorporation, at a time when incorporation was by special charter it was usual to grant it subject to consent of a majority of the inhabitants and this was held not to be a delegation of legislative authority.

§ 2. Prescription—legislative recognition—corporations de facto.[2] Though today a municipal corporation can be created in this country only by the legislature, it has been held that proof that a community for over forty years had held school meetings, chosen trustees, kept a school and erected school buildings raised the presumption that a school district had been duly organized.

It has also been held that legislative recognition of a municipal corporation is sufficient to preclude inquiry into its existence. And even without such legislative recognition it has been considered a sufficient answer to quo warranto proceedings to show acquiescence by the state for nine years, during which time officers had been elected, ordinances had been passed and enforced, taxes levied, public improvements made and commissions issued by the governor to persons elected as mayor. And where an honest but ineffectual attempt was made to incorporate, it was held proper for the legislature by special curative act to validate the defective incorporation.

Where there has been no recognition either by the legislature or other state officials and no legislative validation a defective corporation may be immune from any but a direct attack by the state in quo warranto proceedings if there was a law—even if unconstitutional—under which incorporation might have been made, a bona fide attempt to incorporate and acts done thereunder. If there was no such law there cannot be even a de facto corporation.

§ 3. Corporate changes and regulation—dissolution.[3] After a municipal corporation has once been created its boundaries may be enlarged or made smaller only by the legislature. They may be enlarged so as to include farming land though they should not include land that is suitable only for farming. In the case of cities or towns it is usually held that the added territory must be contiguous, but this is not true in case of drainage districts.

While the legislature, in its regulation of municipal corporations, may not usually legislate with regard to a particular city, it is permissible and usual for it to reach a somewhat similar result by classifying cities—usually according to population—such classification being valid if reasonable, and it is no objection that at the time of the classification there is only one city in one or more of the classes.

Since both territory and inhabitants are necessary for the existence of a municipal corporation, if the territory should be wholly destroyed by flood or earthquake or if it should be entirely abandoned by its inhabitants, the

[2] 37 **Am Jur,** Municipal Corporations, §§ 10–12.

[3] 37 **Am Jur,** Municipal Corporations, §§ 18–39.

Power to extend boundaries of municipal corporations. 64 **ALR** 1335–1384.

Facts warranting extension or reduction of municipal boundaries. 62 **ALR** 1011–1043.

Power to detach land from municipal corporations, towns, or villages. 117 **ALR** 267–299.

Discretion of administrative officers as to changing boundaries of school district. 65 **ALR** 1523–1552; s. in 135 **ALR** 1096–1123.

corporation would come to an end. It can also come to an end through dissolution by the legislature, but not through mere surrender or non-user of its charter, or through failure to elect corporate officers; in the last mentioned eventuality process may be legally served upon the officer last in office.

Where a municipal corporation has come to an end through a change of sovereignty and is then reorganized under a new sovereign the new corporation, in the absence of express legislative provision to the contrary, succeeds to the property, the contracts and obligations of the old.

§ 4. Effect of corporate changes on property rights and obligations.[4] Where the legislature creates new counties out of the territory of an existing county the new county becomes the owner of the sewers and all the other property affixed to the land within its confines, but in the absence of legislative provision it does not become entitled to any of the personal property of the old county and does not become liable for any of the old county's debts. But the legislature may apportion both the personal property and the debts.

Where a corporation is dissolved and a new one created by the legislature embracing all or practically all the territory of the old corporation the new corporation succeeds to the property of the old and becomes liable for its debts. And where two or more municipalities are consolidated into one, each part of the new corporation is entitled to its proportionate share of the property and liable for its proportionate share of the debts of the old corporations.

CHAPTER II

THE CORPORATE ORGANIZATION

§ 5. Binding the corporation—government by commission—city managership.[5] In order to bind a New England town it is necessary that there be either original authority, ratification or estoppel. Where original authority is relied on it must be shown that authority was given by vote in a town meeting after the purpose of the meeting had been set forth in the notice of the meeting.

Where the municipal form of government is by mayor and common council, authority is given only by resolution of the council which is either signed by the mayor or passed over his veto.

In many states statutes authorize the establishment, by popular vote, of a commission form of government, thereby vesting the power ordinarily exercised by the mayor and common council in a board of commissioners—usually five—each one being in charge of a department or departments to be determined by the board. Such a board has power to abolish any office existing under the mayor and council and transferring its duties to another corporate agency.

There are also statutes in many states authorizing the establishment, by popular vote, of the city manager form of government, the city manager being not a mere employee of the city but an officer clothed with administrative and executive functions, and, as such, having the authority to appoint the

4 37 **Am Jur**, Municipal Corporations, §§ 40–42.

5 37 **Am Jur**, Municipal Corporations, §§ 72–75.

38 **Am Jur**, Municipal Corporations, §§ 493–523.

Constitutionality of city manager or commission form of municipal government. 67 **ALR** 737–758.

members of such administrative boards as the board of health, the purely legislative functions of the municipality being exercised by the mayor and council.

Finally, since the people have no inherent power to select their municipal officers, the legislature may authorize the governor to appoint them, such officers having the sole power to bind the municipality. Similarly, the legislature may create a new system of taxation and commit power of assessment to a state board of tax experts and thereby deprive municipal officers of such power; and it may erect a metropolitan fire district or health district or excise district or police district transferring to state officials functions ordinarily belonging to local officers; and it may authorize state officials to construct public buildings, parks and highways though the expense is to be paid locally and though the power to make such improvements had been previously vested in the local authorities.

§ 6. Same—judicial and ministerial functions.[6] Where the act of a municipal officer is judicial, the municipality is not liable therefor, but only where it is ministerial. Where the act could be as well done by another as by the officer himself, it is a ministerial act even if it involves skill and education. Thus, when a road supervisor determines whether certain road work should be done he is acting judicially and the municipality is not liable if he should err in his judgment, but the performance of the road work is a ministerial act though it may require a high order of engineering and mechanical skill and involve discretion in the selection of materials, because it is an act which can be done as well by another as well as by the road supervisor himself; hence the municipality is liable if the work is done so negligently as to cause personal or property damage.

CHAPTER III

POWERS

§ 7. In general—public utility and other public service.[7] A municipal corporation may exercise those powers which are granted by its charter either

6 38 **Am Jur,** Municipal Corporations, §§ 572–580.

7 37 **Am Jur,** Municipal Corporations, §§ 111–138.

Right to enjoin removal of or interference with trees in highways. 116 **ALR** 95–116.

To what uses may park property be devoted. 18 **ALR** 1246–1272: s. in 64 **ALR** 484–493; 144 **ALR** 486–513.

Implied or inherent power of municipal corporation to sell its real property. 141 **ALR** 1447–1462.

Power of municipal corporation to lease or sublet property owned or leased by it. 63 **ALR** 614–631; s. in 133 **ALR** 1241–1254.

Disposition of revenues from operation of revenue-producing enterprise owned by municipal corporations. 103 **ALR** 57^–588.

Pledge or appropriation of revenue from utility or other property in payment therefor, as indebtedness within constitutional or statutory limitation of indebtedness of municipality or other political subdivision. 72 **ALR** 687–701; s. in 96 ALR 1385–1399; 146 **ALR** 328–356.

Power of municipality to sell, lease, or mortgage municipal waterworks, gas or electric plant, or interest therein. 39 **ALR** 216–229.

Power of municipality to agree to abide by conditions or regulations imposed by Federal authority in respect of construction, maintenance, or operation of a municipal public utility plant or enterprise. 128 **ALR** 620–627.

Discrimination in the operation of a municipal utility. 50 **ALR** 126–138.

Donations, by state or municipal subdivision, to community chest or other nongovernmental charity. 142 **ALR** 1076–1088.

Power of municipal corporation to submit to arbitration. 40 **ALR** 1370–1382.

Power of city, town, or county or its officials to compromise claim. 105 **ALR** 170–181.

Power of municipal council to correct its minutes. 3 **ALR** 308–1323.

Power of municipality to consent to judgment against itself. 67 **ALR** 1503–1509.

Property of one municipality within territorial limits of another as subject to taxation by latter. 81 **ALR** 1518–1527; s. in 99 **ALR** 1143–1145.

expressly or by necessary implication and also those which are incidental to those powers and essential to their efficient operation. Though the charter is to be strictly construed against the municipality, especially to protect the public against heavy burdens, this strict construction should not be allowed to prevent the exercise of a power which is clearly implied.

For example, under general welfare clause, a city may build a city hospital or it may issue bonds for money to be turned over to a charitable hospital. It may appropriate a small sum for a public band concert where it had express authority to do so for the celebration of holidays and other public purposes. And under a charter providing that "no money shall be expended for any celebration procession, funeral ceremony, reception or entertainment of any kind or on any occasion unless by the votes of four fifths of all the members of the board of alderman" it was held that the city of New York might issue $400,000 in bonds for the celebration of the twenty-fifth anniversary of the Greater City of New York.

It may offer a reward for the arrest and conviction of persons who set fire to municipal buildings, but probably not for the arrest and conviction of incendiaries generally; and it may pay the expenses of some of its officers to attend a meeting of an association of municipal officers. And a charter provision was held constitutional which authorized a municipality to regulate the elections of its board of freeholders since the subject of elections comes within the term "municipal affairs" and was therefore not special legislation.

On the other hand, a municipality may not, without express authorization, contract for the construction of a levee or pay for the loan, from Philadelphia, of the Liberty Bell; nor may it require private garages to be licensed. It may not engage in the business of brickmaking but it may buy a rock quarry to supply crushed rock for city streets.

Statutes today commonly authorize cities to own, maintain and operate electric light and power plants, water plants, aviation fields and other public utilities; and in fixing rates it has been held proper for the legislature to discriminate between public service corporations and municipal corporations operating public utilities on the ground that only the former are operated for profit.

A statute authorizing a city to erect houses to replace slums has been held valid and so has a statute authorizing the maintenance of a public library. It has also been held proper to authorize a city to engage in the business of selling gasoline and lubricating oil to its inhabitants but there is conflict of authority as to whether it may maintain a coal and wood yard. In New England a town may erect a public hall without express authorization; but outside New England there must be express legislative authority therefor.

§ 8. Police power.[8] In the exercise of its police power a municipal corporation may pass and enforce ordinances reasonably necessary to public

[8] 37 **Am Jur**, Municipal Corporations, §§ 276–318.

Power of municipal corporation to require railroad to eliminate grade crossings. 35 **ALR** 1322–1331; s. in 36 **ALR** 1122.

Power of municipality as to billboards and outdoor advertising. 72 **ALR** 465–481.

Power of county or municipality to exempt from taxation or otherwise aid or subsidize private enterprises conducted for recreational, exhibition, or entertainment purposes. 116 **ALR** 889–900.

Effect of unreasonableness, or variance from constitutional, charter, or statutory provision, of penalty prescribed by ordinance. 138 **ALR** 1208–1222.

Power of municipal or school authorities to prescribe vaccination or other health measure as a condition of school attendance. 93 **ALR** 1413–1442.

Conflict between statutes and local regulations as to automobiles. 21 **ALR** 1186–1214; s. in 64 **ALR** 993–1005; 147 **ALR** 522–574.

Validity of municipal ordinance prohibiting or regulating keeping of livestock. 32

health and safety. Thus it may regulate traffic on its streets by means of speed and parking regulations; it may forbid the burning of bricks or the storing of gasoline or the selling of impure milk or the keeping of a house of ill fame within the city limits; it may forbid the sale of vegetables during certain hours or prohibit keeping a private market within a certain distance of a public market; it may prohibit advertising by the use of "sandwich" man on the street; it may declare a millpond to be a nuisance; it may contract to dispose of city garbage; it may regulate the erection of new buildings by fixing fire limits; it may require living rooms in residences to have a certain area of window-space; it may regulate amusements such as dance halls and miniature golf courses.

On the other hand, it may not declare smoke to be a nuisance where it was not a nuisance at common law; it may not, without legislative authority, censor moving pictures or prohibit the maintenance of billboards which do not endanger public safety merely on the ground of aesthetics; if it wishes to get rid of such billboards it must pay reasonable compensation therefor. As to whether it may impose upon adjoining landowners the burden of removing ice and snow from sidewalks in winter or sprinkling the streets in summer there is a direct conflict of authority.

§ 9. Same—city planning and zoning.[9] From 1850 to 1900 it was common practice for grantors of land, especially where it was desired to build up residential districts in or near cities, to impose restrictions upon its use—restrictions which were enforceable in equity as equitable servitudes. Since about 1900 there has been a gradual development of legislative restrictions, statutes empowering municipal corporations to pass and enforce zoning ordinances; these have supplemented and largely supplanted equitable servitudes.

This zoning legislation has been uniformly held constitutional, but ordinances have sometimes been held invalid as to a particular piece of land on the ground that it has been unfairly classified. Thus a zoning ordinance was held to be invalid as to the plaintiff because her land was well adapted to apartments and business and not to residences and hence it was unreasonably classified as residential; another was held unreasonable in excluding from a residential district a Jewish orphanage built on a cottage plan; and

ALR 1372–1385; s. in 40 **ALR** 566.

Validity of municipal ordinance as affected by motive of members of council which adopted it. 32 **ALR** 1517–1526.

Validity of statute or ordinance relating to place of sale of food. 52 **ALR** 669–681.

Extension of police power of municipal corporation beyond territorial limits. 55 **ALR** 1182–1190.

Authorization, prohibition, or regulation by municipality of the sale of merchandise on streets or highways, or their use for such purpose. 105 **ALR** 1051–1063.

Municipal license as affecting municipality's exercise of police power adversely to licensee. 124 **ALR** 523–542.

Power to limit weight of vehicle or load thereon with respect to use of highways. 26 **ALR** 747–754; s. in 72 **ALR** 1004–1007.

Power of municipal corporation to legislate as to Sunday observance. 29 **ALR** 397–427; s. in 37 **ALR** 575, 576.

29 **Va. L. R.** 617, Validity of Parking Meter Ordinances.

9 **Am Jur,** Zoning.

Validity of "stopgap" statute or ordinance, or refusal of building permit which in effect prevents, the use or improvement of property in a way or for a purpose contrary to a contemplated zoning regulation. 136 **ALR** 844–853.

Constitutionality of variation of provisions of zoning statutes or ordinances. 86 **ALR** 714–719.

Attack upon validity of zoning statute or ordinance as affected by provisions for variations, permits, etc. 136 **ALR** 1378–1398.

Rezoning or amendment of zoning regulations as affecting persons who have purchased or improved property in reliance upon original regulations 138 **ALR** 500–509.

Changes, after adoption of zoning regulations, in respect of nonconforming existing use. 147 **ALR** 167–183.

37 **Harv. L. R.** 834, Constitutionality of Zoning.

41 **Col. L. R.** 451, Retroactive Zoning and Nuisances.

12 **Geo. Wash. L. R.** 1, Constitutionality of Federal Airport Zoning.

still another was held unreasonable in excluding from a residential district a proposed home for aged poor without getting consent of owners of two thirds of the property within four hundred feet of the proposed building. An ordinance has also been held to be unreasonable in excluding a public garage or filling station from any city block in which sixty per cent of the frontage of said block was used exclusively for residence purposes; and another was held invalid in not permitting a building to cover more than twenty-five per cent of the area of any lot or parcel of ground in a residential district.

On the other hand, a city may not only impose reasonable conditions as to width of street, building lines, etc., before approving the plat of a new addition to the city, but it may have the map of subdivision canceled because it is not approved by the planning board. Statutes authorizing cities to take land by eminent domain for the purpose of establishing a city park or residential district have been held constitutional; and it has been held that passing a zoning law did not create such an incumbrance on the property affected by it as to make the title unmarketable.

A zoning ordinance is not rendered invalid because it exempts from its operation businesses already established or because it reserves authority to deal specially with unusual cases.

§ 10. Power to contract—quasi-contractual liability.[10] A municipal corporation has inherent power to enter into such contracts as may be essential and suitable to the ends for which it was created. Thus, where a city council has authority to construct sidewalks, schoolhouses and other municipal buildings it may make contracts for such construction and issue bonds therefor. And where a city in its proprietary capacity owns and operates water works or electric light plant or gas plant, it may bind itself by contract to buy supplies with which to run such plant and may take out insurance for its protection against fire, liability or other casualty the same as if it were a private corporation; and if in operating an electric light plant it produces a surplus of energy it may market such energy outside its own limits. If it does not have a water plant of its own it may contract for a water supply at reasonable price for a reasonable period.

Statutes frequently provide that in awarding contracts for erecting buildings, procuring material and supplies, etc., the municipality must advertise for offers and let the contract to the lowest bidder. If this is violated the contract is void and cannot be ratified by the municipality and there is no liability in quasi contract. Such statutes are usually not construed as applying to the services of an architect who is usually employed on a percentage

[10] 38 **Am Jur,** Municipal Corporations, §§ 493–523.

Power of municipal corporation to employ attorney. 83 **ALR** 135–141.

Validity of contract between governmental unit and attorney which makes compensation contingent upon results accomplished. 136 **ALR** 116–130.

Power of board to appoint officer or make contract extending beyond its own term. 70 **ALR** 794–806; s. in 149 **ALR** 336–344.

Estoppel of municipality to deny that it gave its consent to street franchise. 7 **ALR** 1248–1258; s. in 89 **ALR** 619–625.

Sale of municipal or other public bonds at less than par or face value. 91 **ALR** 7–73.

Right to call governmental bonds in advance of their maturity. 109 **ALR** 988–1001.

Liability of municipality in consequence of its inability, refusal, or failure to collect the cost of local improvements from the property benefited. 38 **ALR** 1271–1306; s. in 51 **ALR** 973–975.

Rights and remedies of creditor of municipal corporation which is dissolved or combined with another municipal body. 47 **ALR** 128–146.

Estoppel by recitals in municipal bonds as to lawfulness of issue. 86 **ALR** 1057–1101.

47 **Harv. L. R.** 1143, Quasi-Contractual Liability of Municipal Corporations.

basis; but some courts have applied the statute so as to prevent a municipality from specifying a patented article even though the owner of the patent agrees to furnish the article at a fixed price to the successful bidder; and most courts have construed the statute as rendering invalid other statutes requiring that all labor employed on the performance of the contracts shall be union labor, or that the work of cutting and preparing stone for construction of public buildings shall be done within the city.

If the one contracting with the city is also a city official the contract cannot be enforced against the city; and if there is a statute forbidding such a contract there may not be recovery even in quasi contract. And where an official buys property and then sells it to the city at an advance in price the city may recover back the excess from the official.

Statutes frequently require that bonds must be authorized by resolution of the governing body of the municipality; if this requirement is not met the bonds are void even in the hands of a bona fide purshaser for value. Statutes requiring that the prevailing wages shall be paid upon public works are upheld when there is a satisfactory method of determining such wages.

If a contract is reasonable in its terms it is no objection that it covers a time greater than the lifetime of the governing board.

Where a contract is not enforceable against a municipality but benefit thereunder has been received by it, recovery is sometimes allowed, the courts being influenced by a desire to do justice in the particular case, and sometimes it is disallowed, the courts being influenced by a desire to protect the municipality in the future. In the following instances recovery in quasi contract has been allowed: (1) for the money received from the sale of bonds rendered invalid because the city attempted to evade provisions of a registration law; (2) for crushed stone received by city and used on its streets; (3) for legal services rendered to village defending it against action in quo warranto questioning its legal existence; (4) where needed goods were bought at reasonable price from municipal official and used; (5) where money loaned to city in good faith had been spent for an authorized purpose; (6) for gas furnished to city for three years where not possible to find the contract; (7) for services and material used in constructing a highway, plaintiff not being bound at peril to know the authority of village selectmen; (8) for taxes paid on land not within city limits.

On the other hand, in the following instances recovery in quasi contract has been refused: (1) where statute forbade contract with city official; (2) where statute required contract to be awarded to lowest bidder; (3) where plaintiff did extra work on bridge made necessary by unauthorized change of location of bridge by bridge commissioners; (4) where a plaintiff rendered services in selling city bonds.

In some cases where relief in quasi contract has been refused, the court has suggested that the plaintiff might be able to reclaim the exact chattels or money turned over to the municipality; but where plaintiff sought to trace the money received into property in which such money was invested by the city relief has been refused.

Though a municipality is usually held to have no authority to issue a negotiable note for borrowed money, it is frequently authorized to issue negotiable bonds because otherwise the bonds would have only a local market. In the absence of express power a municipality may not usually borrow money for ordinary expenses.

§ 11. Limitations on municipal indebtedness.[1] In practically all the states there are constitutional provisions limiting the amount of indebtedness which a municipality can voluntarily incur; such provisions do not prevent a tort obligor from enforcing a tort obligation against the municipality; they do not render invalid warrants issued for ordinary expenses or for services of city officials because such services are necessary to the existence of the municipality; nor do they prevent a municipality from making a long-term contract for the supply of gas or water at an annual rental, because no debt arises till they are furnished.

The most usual limitation forbids indebtedness in excess of a fixed percentage of the assessed value of taxable property within the limits of the municipality or other taxing district. Where a city borrowed money to construct waterworks the creditor to be repaid merely out of receipts from the waterworks, such obligation was held not to be a "debt;" but where a city borrowed money to extend its waterworks the creditor to be paid out of a special fund but the city gave to creditor a mortgage in its then existing waterworks and the proposed extension as security, this did create a "debt." And it is generally held that contracts for the construction of local improvements the use of which is to be met entirely by special assessments on local land owners do not create a "debt;" though it is of course otherwise if the city's credit is pledged to repay the money thus borrowed.

The fact that money borrowed to erect a public building is to be repaid out of a special tax levy over a term of years does not prevent such borrowing from creating a "debt;" but where X contracted with a city to erect on city land a building suitable for a city hall, the city to pay rent for it with an option to buy, such option was held not to create a "debt." That land is conveyed to a city for park purposes without other consideration except that the city spend a certain amount per year for maintenance does not prevent such expenditure from being a "debt."

In the absence of a constitutional or statutory provision to the contrary a debt incurred by a city's board of education is not a debt of the city itself; and where a sinking fund has been set aside to meet some specific indebtedness the amount of such fund is to be deducted in estimating the debts of the municipality.

Where the indebtedness which a municipality may incur in any one year is limited to the income and revenues provided for that year, such limitation may not be evaded by incurring debts to be met and discharged from the revenues of a subsequent year.

1 38 **Am Jur,** Municipal Corporations, §§ 408–482.

Obligation for local improvements as within municipal debt limit. 33 **ALR** 1415–1427.

Funding or refunding obligations as subject to conditions respecting limitation of indebtedness or approval by voters. 97 **ALR** 442–462.

Instalments payable under continuing service contract as present indebtedness within organic limitation of municipal indebtedness. 103 **ALR** 1160–1177.

Pledge or appropriation of revenue from utility or other property in payment therefor, as indebtedness within constitutional or statutory limitation of indebtedness of municipality or other political subdivision. 72 **ALR** 687–701.

Failure to comply with constitutional or statutory requirement that municipality, or other political subdivision, at or before incurring indebtedness, shall provide a tax for its payment as affecting validity of indebtedness or obligations issued therefor. 90 **ALR** 1240–1260.

Obligation to meet which money is appropriated at the time of its creation as an indebtedness within limitation of indebtedness. 92 **ALR** 1299–1315; s. in 134 **ALR** 1399–1404.

CHAPTER IV

MUNICIPAL PROPERTY

§ 12. Acquisition.[2] A municipality may acquire land by dedication which becomes effective upon acceptance thereof, but neither the dedication nor the acceptance needs to be in writing or to be otherwise formal. It may acquire property by purchase and a contract thus to acquire is valid and enforceable if the acquisition is for a proper municipal purpose. And land thus acquired need not be within its limits; it may acquire land outside its limits for the purpose of supplying its inhabitants with water or for obtaining rock to be crushed and used on its streets.

It may, of course, acquire any kind of property by gift. By the better view it may accept a gift upon trust for any charitable purpose and if it does so accept it is bound by the terms of the trust.

Statutes may authorize a municipality to take property by eminent domain for a public purpose, but it may not take over a public utility unless such power has been specially conferred. While a statute may authorize it to take land for a highway to be used merely for pleasure travel, it may not be authorized to condemn land merely for the purpose of preventing the erection of an unsightly building near a parkway. A statute may not authorize it to take more land than is needed and then to sell the excess, but such excess condemnations have been authorized in a few states by constitutional amendment.

§ 13. Alienation.[3] Where a municipality has accepted property upon trust —for example, land to be used as a park or a public square—such property may not be aliened or used for other purposes.

Where no such trust is involved a municipality may sell property which is no longer needed, such as an abandoned city hall or jail; and it may lease a small part of a public park for a hotel if such lease would be advantageous to the public. Where a statute authorizes it to sell a public square such sale does not violate the rights of a land owner on the other side of the street.

A municipality may not ordinarily transfer a public utility to a private corporation without statutory authority, but it has been held that where such sale was acquiesced in by all the inhabitants it was estopped later to attack the transfer.

While as to its privately owned property the statute of limitations applies, it is not barred by delay from complaining of encroachments on its streets.

§ 14. Streets and highways.[4] A city may not vacate a street merely for the private benefit of owners and lessees of the abutting lots. On the other hand, if a municipality discontinues a highway thereby depriving an abutting owner of access to any highway, such discontinuance amounts to a taking for which compensation must be made.

2 38 **Am Jur,** Municipal Corporations §§ 483-486.

Injunction, rather than quo warranto, as available to restrain enforcement of tax against real property upon ground involving attack upon legal existence of municipality, or upon inclusion of property within its boundaries. 129 **ALR** 255-265.

3 38 **Am Jur,** Municipal Corporations, §§ 487-490.

4 25 **Am Jur,** Highways, §§ 345-360.

Right to deposit goods in street as incident of loading or unloading. 23 **ALR** 816-826.

Right of abutting owner to use street including sidewalk, for the deposit, exhibition, or sale of goods. 6 **ALR** 1314-1321.

Dedication: time for acceptance. 66 **ALR** 321-338.

Where an obstruction in a street amounts to a public nuisance the city may be compelled by mandamus to remove it; but formerly hitching posts and watering troughs and more recently gasoline pumps on sidewalks are not usually considered to be public nuisances.

A city may restrain the erection of a building with pillars in the street because the view of the street would be obstructed; it may cut down shade trees inside the street line of the sidewalk without making compensation therefor; and if the construction of a bridge over a highway connecting buildings would damage neighboring property the owner thereof is entitled to enjoin it.

Where the city does not own the fee in the streets the maintenance of telephone and telegraph wires and poles, water mains and gas pipes therein is an added burden which entitles abutting property owners to compensation. But where the city owns the fee such uses may be permitted as long as the public easement for street purposes is not prejudiced thereby.

CHAPTER V

APPROPRIATION OF MUNICIPAL FUNDS—SPECIAL ASSESSMENTS

§ 15. Appropriation of municipal funds.[5] A municipality is authorized to levy taxes to raise funds for public purposes, and the following purposes have been held valid within that rule: police pensions and group insurance for teachers, under express statutory authority; traveling expenses of president of board of education and superintendent of schools to visit technical schools; determining the practicability of a canal between the city and Lake Erie; extension of university campus in order to keep the state university within the city.

On the other hand, the following purposes have been held to be invalid: lobbying before the state legislature; making contribution to a private denominational college; issuing bonds as donation to a private corporation to induce it to establish a factory in the city; subscribing to capital stock in a private corporation; building a bridge five miles outside city limits; contribution to civic opera company; reimbursing a defeated candidate for expenses of election contest.

There is direct conflict of authority as to whether the following purposes are valid: advertising the city; paying for fireworks display on July 4; reimbursing a municipal official for expenses incurred in defending himself against legal proceedings brought against him for some act done in the performance of his duties.

[5] 38 **Am Jur,** Municipal Corporations, §§ 441–448.

Application to permanent improvements of constitutional or statutory provision against county or municipality exceeding current revenue. 41 **ALR** 790–814.

Constitutionality of statutory provisions as to political corporations or divisions which shall bear cost of establishing or maintaining highways. 2 **ALR** 746–758.

Compensation of tenure teacher. 145 **ALR** 408–436.

What amounts to waiver of status or rights under teachers' tenure statute. 145 **ALR** 1078–1091.

Extent of power of school district to provide for the comfort and convenience of teachers and pupils. 7 **ALR** 791–799; s. in 52 **ALR** 249–259.

Schools: free textbooks and other school supplies for individual use of pupils. 17 **ALR** 299–304; s. in 67 **ALR** 1196–1199.

Transportation of school pupils at expense of public. 63 **ALR** 413–428; s. in 118 **ALR** 806–822; 146 **ALR** 625–638.

Teachers' tenure statutes. 110 **ALR** 791–811; s. in 113 **ALR** 1495–1504; 127 **ALR** 1298–1335.

Unionization, centralization, or consolidation of school districts as affecting indebtedness and property of the individual districts. 121 **ALR** 826–841.

Funds raised by taxation for one purpose may not be used for another purpose. A municipality may not exempt from taxation any property it is authorized to tax; but it may not tax an electric light plant within its limits which belongs to another municipality.

There is conflict of authority as to whether a city may impose upon an abutting owner the burden of removing snow from the sidewalk.

§ 16. Special assessments.[6] Where a municipality decides that it is desirable to make a local improvement such as grading or paving a street or constructing a sidewalk, it may make the improvement and assess the cost thereof against the property benefited thereby; and if the assessment does not produce enough revenue to cover the cost, the legislature may authorize a reassessment to meet the deficiency.

In order that the special assessment be valid the ordinance must have been passed before the improvement was made; and the owners of the property assessed must be given a fair opportunity to raise objections to the assessment; but if such opportunity is given and no objection is raised, the property owner is barred from later getting a decree cancelling the assessment or from enjoining the sale of the property to pay the assessment, unless he can show that the property was not subject thereto. Where, upon the hearing, the assessment is proved to be unfair and discriminatory it will be set aside and a new assessment ordered. Unless the ordinance describes the work to be done with sufficient definiteness to enable the property owner to determine what effect the improvement will have upon his own interest and that of the public it is not considered that he has a fair opportunity to object.

In making the assessment a wide latitude is allowed the assessors; the benefit must be more than speculative but it need not be direct or immediate. It is usually fair to assess according to front footage unless some of the lots are very shallow. If the burden imposed is clearly in excess of the benefit, as to such excess it amounts to taking property without compensation.

In some states the municipality may impose a personal liability on the owner of the property assessed; but if the owner is not a resident of the state this cannot be done unless he makes a voluntary appearance at the hearing.

Where the improvement is not local the burden may not be specially assessed; for example, building a bridge over a ravine to connect the two ends of a street bisected thereby. As to whether street sprinkling in residential districts may be assessed locally there is conflict of authority.

CHAPTER VI

TORT LIABILITY

§ 17. Governmental and proprietary functions.[7] If a municipal employee commits a tort while engaged in a governmental activity the municipality

[6] 38 **Am Jur,** Municipal Corporations, §§ 381-394.

[7] 37 **Am Jur,** Municipal Corporations, §§ 114, 115.

Liability of municipality as affected by license issued by municipal officer. 42 **ALR** 1208-1218.

Duty of municipality to prevent obstruction of drains or sewers. 43 **ALR** 964-971.

Liability of municipality for injury by or incident to fireworks display. 93 **ALR** 1356-1363.

Liability of municipality for enforcement of an unconstitutional or void ordinance. 118 **ALR** 1054-1060.

Constitutionality of statute which relieves municipality from liability for torts. 124 **ALR** 350-359.

Construction and application of statute making municipal corporation liable for damages due to negligence of official or employee while operating vehicle. 136 **ALR** 582-595.

Tort liability of municipality or other

is not liable therefor, because it benefits by the immunity of the state itself. The clearest illustration is that of a tort committed by a police officer, such as making a search without a warrant or making an illegal arrest, the municipality not being liable even though, at the time of the appointment, the mayor knew the officer had a violent temper.

On the other hand, if a municipal employee commits a tort while engaged in a proprietary activity, such as the maintenance and operation of a waterworks plant, the municipality is liable just as if it were a private corporation.

Partly because of the difficulty in drawing the line between governmental and proprietary, partly because of a growing feeling that the group—whether the state or the municipal corporation—should bear such tort burdens rather than to allow them to rest upon the tort-feasee, the tendency is away from immunity toward liability, the courts being inclined to seize upon any distinction which will enable them to impose tort liability upon the muncipality. Thus while a city is not liable for a tort arising in the maintenance and operation of a building used exclusively for public bathing or as a city hall, or for school purposes, yet if the building is used partly for profit the city is likely to be held liable in tort; and a similar distinction has been taken where a city made an incidental profit in the removal of garbage. Sometimes the city is held liable because, while engaged in a governmental activity such as education, it maintains a public nuisance such as a wall alongside a school yard; or a diving board over shallow water at a place maintained for public bathing. In some cases a city has been held liable because the negligence was not that of a mere employee but that of the city board of education itself. Although the maintenance of a fire department is a governmental function so that the city was held not liable where an employee ran over a pedestrian with a hose cart while trying to put out a fire, a city was held liable to a pedestrian who was run over by the fire chief's auto on the way to a fire. And although education is a governmental activity it was held not to prevent recovery by a pupil injured by an unguarded buzz saw while doing school work in the manual training department.

governmental subdivision in connection with poor relief activities. 134 **ALR** 762–770.

Municipal immunity from liability for torts. 120 **ALR** 1376–1382.

Liability of municipality for mob or riot. 13 **ALR** 751–779; s. in 23 **ALR** 297–301; 44 **ALR** 1137–1143; 52 **ALR** 562–564.

Liability of school district, municipal corporation, or school board for injury to pupil. 9 **ALR** 911–921; s. in 14 **ALR** 1392, 1393; 21 **ALR** 1328–1330; 24 **ALR** 1070–1072; 56 **ALR** 164–169; 66 **ALR** 1281–1284.

Use of municipal automobile as a corporate or as a governmental function. 110 **ALR** 1117–1132.

Liability of municipal corporations and their licensees for the torts of independent contractors. 25 **ALR** 426–490; s. in 52 **ALR** 1012–1014.

Fire department as pertaining to the governmental or to the proprietary branch of municipality. 9 **ALR** 143–157; s. in 33 **ALR** 688–691; 84 **ALR** 514–520.

Liability of municipal corporation for tort of officer or employee of water department. 24 **ALR** 545–553; s. in 28 **ALR** 822–823; 54 **ALR** 1497, 1498.

Liability of municipality or waterworks company for injury due to condition of service line, meters, etc., which supply individual consumer with water. 142 **ALR** 243–257.

Sufficiency of notice of claim against municipality as regards identity, name, and residence of claimant. 130 **ALR** 139, 147.

Sufficiency of description of personal injury in notice given thereof as a condition of municipal liability. 106 **ALR** 855–875.

Necessity of presenting claim against municipality for damaging property. 52 **ALR** 639–663.

Incapacity as excuse for failure to give, or delay in giving, notice of accident or injury as condition of holding municipality liable. 31 **ALR** 619–632; s. in 59 **ALR** 411–413; 109 **ALR** 975–978.

Construction, application, and effect of statutory provisions avoiding effect of inaccuracy or omission in notice of injury required as condition of municipal liability. 103 **ALR** 298–305.

18 **Ill. L. R.** 355, Municipal Liability for Tort.

25 **Marq. L. R.** 116, School District Responsibility for Negligent Supervision of Pupils.

§ 18. Tort liability for maintenance of streets and highways.[8] In this country incorporated cities, towns and villages are usually held liable at common law for damage caused by failure to keep streets in repair; but, following an old English case, unincorporated municipalities such as counties and townships are usually held not liable, but there is a minority of states imposing such liability and in many states the liability is imposed by statute. In England, Canada, the New England states and a few other jurisdictions there is no liability even on incorporated municipalities apart from statute, but such statutes are now quite general in those jurisdictions.

Where a city is liable at common law, a statute requiring notice of a highway defect to be given to some city official at least twenty-four hours before the occurrence of the damage complained of was held to be invalid as amounting to a denial of due process.

CHAPTER VII

MISCELLANEOUS

§ 19. Estoppel by recitals in municipal bonds and notes.[9] Where negotiable municipal bonds have come into the hands of a bona fide purchaser for value may the municipality escape liability by showing that the bonds were invalid because a necessary election was not held or was not properly conducted or that the bonds were issued in order to make a subscription to a private corporation or that the bonds were issued in violation of the debt limit?

Where there was a recital in the bonds that they had been issued in accordance with the vote of electors it has been held that a bona fide purchaser

[8] 25 **Am Jur,** Highways, §§ 345–358.

Liability of municipal corporations for injuries due to conditions in parks. 29 **ALR** 863–880; s. in 42 **ALR** 263–265; 99 **ALR** 686–700; 142 **ALR** 1340–1383.

Liability for injury to pedestrian predicated upon slope or contour of sidewalk or crosswalk, or slippery nature of material of which it is constructed. 133 **ALR** 1026–1033.

Liability for injury on park strip between sidewalk and curb. 59 **ALR** 387–404; s. in 61 **ALR** 267.

Liability of municipality for injury resulting from slippery condition of walk, concurring with defect therein. 3 **ALR** 1130–1145; s. in 48 **ALR** 1154; 80 **ALR** 1170–1173.

Liability of municipality for injury or damage due to pole maintained by third person in street or highway. 128 **ALR** 1269–1284.

Liability of municipality for injury to person or property due to improper plan for or defects in original construction of street or highway. 90 **ALR** 1502–1529.

Liability of municipality for injury or damage by automobile colliding with temporary obstruction in connection with alteration or repair of street. 100 **ALR** 1386–1394.

Degree of inequality in sidewalk which makes question for jury or for court, as to municipality's liability. 119 **ALR** 161–174.

Liability of municipality or other governmental body to pedestrian for injury in street closed or partially closed during construction or repairs. 119 **ALR** 841–855.

Liability of a municipal corporation for injuries caused by the unsafe condition of a street resulting from or incidental to work performed under a permit authorizing the construction, alteration, repair, or demolishing of a building or its appurtenances. 11 **ALR** 1343–1386.

Liability of municipal corporation for injuries from snow or ice on sidewalk. 13 **ALR** 17–71; s. in 80 **ALR** 1151–1165.

Liability for injury due to condition of trees in or overhanging highway. 19 **ALR** 1021–1029; s. in 49 **ALR** 840–842.

Liability of municipality for act of employee engaged in sprinkling or cleaning streets or removing garbage or rubbish. 14 **ALR** 1473–1481; s. in 32 **ALR** 988, 989; 52 **ALR** 187, 188; 60 **ALR** 101, 102.

Duty to provide barriers for protection of automobile travel. 27 **ALR** 937–944; s. in 86 **ALR** 1389–1407.

Liability of municipality for interfering, in raising grade of street, with flow of surface water from abutting property. 27 **ALR** 970–976.

Duty of towns and townships as to snow and ice in highways. 27 **ALR** 1104–1117.

Liability of municipality for injury from ice or snow on crosswalk. 32 **ALR** 1293–1313.

Liability of street railway company or municipality for injury due to condition of part of street occupied by street railway. 54 **ALR** 1291–1327.

54 **Harv. L. R.** 437, Municipal Tort Liability in Operation.

29 **Va. L. R.** 960, Liability of Virginia Municipalities for Defects in Streets and Sidewalks.

[9] 43 **Am Jur,** Public Securities and Obligations, §§ 197–212.

should be protected even if no election was held or if the bonds were in excess of the debt limit because it would be difficult for a purchaser at a distance to determine the fact. And where there was a recital that the bonds had been issued for a municipal purpose a city has been held estopped to show that they were issued to aid a private enterprise. On the other hand, it has been held that if the facts concerning which an estoppel is asserted—for example, that the debt limit has been exceeded—has been made a matter of public record the city is not estopped; nor is it estopped by a mere recital that the bonds have been issued "under and pursuant to law."

The doctrine does not apply in favor of one who is not a bona fide purchaser for value; nor does it apply unless the bonds are negotiable; but it has been applied to negotiable notes.

§ 20. Franchises.[10] Where a franchise is granted to a public utility such as the right of a water company to use the streets, the city may not later impose license fees; and if the ordinance granting the franchise fixes no time limit thereto, this does not mean that it is revocable at will. But where a streetcar company had been given permission to lay double tracks in a street this was held revocable where there was a strong public interest against it because of the narrowness of the street. And where a franchise was granted to a streetcar company specifying a five cent fare this was held to be not binding on the company where the fare had become confiscatory.

§ 21. Licenses.[11] Under statutory authorization a city may impose a license fee either by way of regulation under the police power or for purposes of taxation. Even if valid only as a regulatory measure the fee may be large enough to include not only the expense of issuing the license but also a reasonable amount for supervision of the activity of the licensed. An ordinance exacting a license fee of $300 a year on auctioneers was held to be entirely unauthorized as a tax and unreasonably high for mere regulation. On the other hand a license fee of $2,000 on liquor dealers was held not to be unreasonable as a regulatory measure because of the large profits made by such dealers and because of additional police expenses due to the use of liquor.

While a city may not be authorized to tax sales of goods outside the city limits it may be authorized to regulate them as an exercise of the police power; but in issuing licenses to peddlers it may not discriminate between residents of the city and nonresidents. While a city may revoke the license of a moving-picture exhibitor for good cause shown it may not revoke the licenses of all exhibitors indiscriminately since there is no authority to deal with the matter arbitrarily.

10 38 Am Jur, Municipal Corporations, §§ 524–558.

11 38 Am Jur, Municipal Corporations, §§ 319–380.

CONSTITUTIONAL LAW

I. IN GENERAL.

§ 1. *Making and amending constitutions.*
§ 2. *Separation of powers.*
§ 3. *Delegation of legislative power.*
§ 4. *Power of courts to declare statutes unconstitutional.*

II. POLITICAL RIGHTS—PERSONAL AND RELIGIOUS LIBERTY.

§ 5. *Citizenship—naturalization.*
§ 6. *Suffrage.*
§ 7. *Personal and religious liberty.*
§ 8. *Miscellaneous political rights.*

III. PROTECTION TO PERSONS ACCUSED OF CRIME.

§ 9. *Bills of attainder.*
§ 10. *Ex post facto laws.*

IV. DUE PROCESS AND EQUAL PROTECTION OF LAW—PROCEDURE.

§ 11. *Due process—jurisdiction.*
§ 12. *Same—notice and fair hearing.*
§ 13. *Equal protection of the laws.*

V. DUE PROCESS AND EQUAL PROTECTION OF LAW—POLICE POWER.

§ 14. *In general.*
§ 15. *Public health.*
§ 16. *Public morals.*
§ 17. *Public safety.*
§ 18. *Public order and comfort—aesthetics.*
§ 19. *Licensing occupations—domestic relations—miscellaneous.*
§ 20. *Protection against fraud or oppression.*
§ 21. *Regulation of ownership and use of property.*
§ 22. *Regulation of business—public utilities.*

VI. DUE PROCESS AND EQUAL PROTECTION OF LAW—TAXATION.

§ 23. *In general—lands and chattels.*
§ 24. *Corporate assets.*
§ 25. *Pecuniary choses in action.*
§ 26. *Shares of stock—franchises.*
§ 27. *Inheritance or succession taxes—transfers inter vivos.*
§ 28. *When is a purpose public?*
§ 29. *Classification—progressive and confiscatory taxation.*

VII. DUE PROCESS AND EQUAL PROTECTION OF LAW—EMINENT DOMAIN.

§ 30. *In general.*
§ 31. *The public use—the property that may be taken.*
§ 32. *Taking property—damaging property.*
§ 33. *Compensation—condemnation proceedings.*

VIII. STATE LAWS IMPAIRING THE OBLIGATIONS OF CONTRACTS.

§ 34. *"No state shall pass a law."*
§ 35. *"Of a contract."*
§ 36. *"Impairing the obligation."*

IX. OTHER CIVIL RETROACTIVE LAWS.

§ 37. *Constitutional provisions.*
§ 38. *Validating or curative statutes.*

X. REGULATION OF COMMERCE.

A. IN GENERAL.

§ 39. *Exports, imports and tonnage.*
§ 40. *Foreign and interstate commerce.*

CHAPTER I

IN GENERAL

§ 1. Making and amending constitutions.[1] A constitution is a body of precepts the purpose of which is to control governmental action until modified in some authorized manner. These precepts may be either written or unwritten. For the most part the English Constitution is unwritten. Its written parts consist of documents affecting executive action such as Magna Charta, the Bill of Rights of 1689 placing certain restrictions upon the acts of the sovereign and the Act of Settlement of 1701 regulating the tenure of judges and the succession to the crown.

In this country there are written constitutions securing certain fundamental personal, property and political rights. During the War of the Revolution most of the revolting colonies adopted written constitutions and the experience gained thereunder was a valuable asset in the formation and adoption of the United States Constitution in 1787.

The English Constitution may be amended by Parliament. In this country most constitutions expressly provide for their own amendment. The United States Constitution contains in Article V an express provision for proposing amendments by a two-thirds vote of each house of Congress or by a convention called by Congress upon an application of the legislature of two thirds of the states, such amendments to become effective when ratified by the legislatures of three fourths of the states or by conventions in three fourths thereof. Following the former method of proposal, twenty-one amendments have thus far been adopted. The Constitution did not set any time within which

1 11 **Am Jur**, Constitutional Law, §§ 19–34.
38 **Col. L. R.** 555, Constitutional History and Constitutional Law.
39 **Mich. L. R.** 189, Present Status of the Sherman Act.
39 **Mich. L. R.** 213, Constitutional Interpretation and Judicial Self-Restraint.
18 **N. Y. U. Law Q.** 482, Constitutional Protection of the Alien's Right to Work.
10 **U. of Chicago L. R.** 142; 11 **U. of Chicago L. R.** 374, A Study in Constitutional Rigidity.
92 **U. of Pa. L. R.** 238, New Theories of Constitutional Construction.
21 **Oreg. L. R.** 285, The Passing of the Old Dissent.
29 **Ky. L. J.** 143, Disloyalty and Denaturalization.
29 **Ky. L. J.** 172, Delimitations of Erie Railroad v. Tompkins.
30 **Ky. L. J.** 1, Amendment by Decision—More on the Erie Case.
11 **Brooklyn L. R.** 1, 155, The President over the Judiciary.
26 **Marq. L. R.** 1, Has Congress the Power to Modify the Effect of Erie Railroad Co. v. Tompkins?
25 **Marq. L. R.** 1, A Symposium on Freedom.
6 **John Marshall L. Q.** 74, In Search of Freedom.
11 **Fordham L. R.** 133, The Bethlehem Steel Case—A Test of the New Constitutionalism.
6 **U. of Newark L. R.** 1, How Can New Jersey Get a New Constitution?

ratification must take place; but in submitting the 18th amendment Congress stipulated that ratification must be made within seven years and this limitation was held to be valid. Where Congress does not fix a time limit, the ratification must take place within a reasonable time.

If a constitution expressly provides that it may be amended only in a certain way and another way is followed, such an attempted amendment is illegal; but if it is acquiesced in it becomes effective as a peaceful revolution such as took place when the United States Constitution took effect upon the ratification by nine states in spite of the fact that the old Articles of Confederation provided that they should not be amended without unanimous consent of the states.

§ 2. Separation of powers.[2] The framers of the United States Constitution had before them the words of Blackstone and of Montesquieu each of whom had emphasized the importance of a general separation of the legislative, executive and judicial departments of government and this separation was observed by them in framing the United States Constitution without including therein any formal statement of the theory. Such formal statement does exist, however, in the constitutions of forty states while in the other eight such separation is actually made. But there is no requirement in the United States Constitution that the states shall have governments organized into the three departments, and unless the state constitution forbids, a state legislature may clothe an officer or agency created by it with functions involving the exercise of powers executive, legislative and judicial.

Because of the general recognition of the separation of powers a legislature may not grant a new trial, such power belonging exclusively to the judiciary. In a state which has a constitutional restriction as to separation of powers a legislature may not confer upon a court the legislative power of fixing public utility rates, or of adopting and approving a location for the tracks of a street railway.

On the other hand, the separation of powers has never been absolute. Under the United States Constitution and many state constitutions the chief executive has a limited right to veto legislation, thus exercising a certain amount of legislative power. Treaties and certain appointments by the President must be confirmed by the Senate, which thus exercises a limited executive power. In connection with the framing and passing of legislative acts legislatures may make investigations, thus exercising incidentally a small amount of judicial power. And because of the necessity of protecting their own existence, courts have the inherent right to punish summarily for contempt and a statute requiring a jury trial in such cases was held to be invalid.

In recent years there has been a strong tendency to modify the application

[2] 11 **Am Jur,** Constitutional Law, §§ 180–213.

Power of legislature to set aside or impair judgment. 3 **ALR** 450–458.

Relation of treaty to state and Federal law. 4 **ALR** 1377–1396; s. in 134 **ALR** 882–888.

Validity of statute or ordinance vesting discretion in public officials without prescribing a rule of action. 12 **ALR** 1435–1455; s. in 54 **ALR** 1104–1116; 92 **ALR** 400–419.

Constitutionality of statutes for formation or change of political districts or municipal corporations as affected by objection that they confer nondelegable powers, or impose nonjudicial functions, on a court. 69 **ALR** 266–295.

Jurisdiction of courts to determine election or qualifications of member of legislative body, and conclusiveness of its decision, as affected by constitutional or statutory provision making legislative body the judge of election and qualification of its own members. 107 **ALR** 205–238.

Injunction against legislative body of state or municipality. 140 **ALR** 439–455.

Statute conferring power upon administrative body in respect to the parole of prisoners, or the discharge of parolees, as unconstitutional infringement of power of executive or judiciary. 143 **ALR** 1486–1503.

of the doctrine of separation of powers by clothing administrative tribunals with powers executive, legislative and judicial. For a discussion of this, see post, Administrative Law, p. 492.

§ 3. Delegation of legislative power.[3] The general rule is that a legislature may not delegate its power to legislate. Thus in the famous Schechter case it was held that Congress could not delegate to the President the power to prescribe a code of fair competition, fixing minimum wages and maximum hours of labor, for an industry having no approved code, the statute supplying no standards for action by the President. On this ground the decision was distinguished from the case upholding the flexible tariff act because under that statute a standard was supplied, and the President was merely empowered to ascertain and declare the event upon which the declared will of Congress was to take effect. If Congress cannot set up a specific standard it may, as in the case of the Interstate Commerce Commission, prescribe a procedure which makes the standard specific in the particular cases to which it is to be applied.

Upon historical grounds legislative powers over local affairs may be delegated to municipal corporations and to territorial legislatures; and it is proper to delegate to a supreme court the power to regulate procedure because at the time of the adoption of the constitution it was not considered a strictly legislative power.

Though there is conflict of authority as to whether, apart from a constitutional provision authorizing referendums, general legislation may be submitted to popular vote, it is usually held that a legislature may allow local communities to determine by popular vote whether or not they will take advantage of a legislative act. It has also been held that a statute affecting growers of tobacco might stipulate that it should not go into operation till two thirds of the tobacco growers should vote in favor of it.

§ 4. Power of courts to declare statutes unconstitutional.[4] As already indicated, the English Constitution, largely unwritten, may be changed at any time by Parliament; in other words the English courts have no power to declare an act of Parliament unconstitutional. In this country, on the other hand, with its written constitutions, shorter traditions and less homogeneous population, courts may declare statutes unconstitutional. The reasons for this are political rather than logical. The judiciary is the weakest of the three departments of government, controlling neither the sword nor the purse, and the judges, with their legal training and experience, are likely to be more conservative and less influenced by fluctuating changes in popular opinion than the legislators and are therefore better qualified to construe both written constitution and statute so as to ensure consistency and constitutional stability.

While the existence of the power is well settled it is equally well settled that it should be exercised only in clear cases; that it should not be exercised merely because the court thinks the statute unwise; that it should be exercised only in cases where there is actual litigation so that both sides of the question of constitutionality will be adequately presented to the court which is not bound by any advisory opinion it might have given before the

[3] 11 **Am Jur**, Constitutional Law, §§ 214–231.
39 **Col L. R.** 751, Constitutionality of the Trade Agreements Act.

[4] 11 **Am Jur**, Constitutional Law, §§ 86–167.

statute was passed; and that it does not extend to political acts of either the executive or the legislative departments. Thus the United States Supreme Court refused to hold unconstitutional the reconstruction statutes passed by Congress after the Civil War, just as it had in earlier days refused to determine which of two rival state governments was entitled to recognition.

Where a part of a statute is held to be unconstitutional the entire statute will fall where it is clear that the legislature would not have passed that part by itself.

Where a statute is declared unconstitutional such declaration does not affect the result of earlier cases where no question of constitutionality was raised; and where the statute declared unconstitutional was one providing for a municipal government such declaration did not invalidate the previous acts of the municipal officers thereunder.

CHAPTER II

POLITICAL RIGHTS—PERSONAL AND RELIGIOUS LIBERTY

§ 5. Citizenship—naturalization.[5] Since the adoption of the fourteenth amendment to the United States Constitution "all persons born or naturalized in the United States and subject to the jurisdiction thereof are citizens of the United States and of the state wherein they reside." The purpose of this was to give citizenship to the ex-slaves but it also had the effect of giving citizenship to Chinese children born in this country even though, under the Chinese Exclusion Act then in force, their parents could not become citizens.

By act of Congress, citizens of Puerto Rico, Hawaii and the Virgin Islands have been declared to be citizens of the United States, but inhabitants of the Philippines have been declared to be citizens of the Philippines.

The phrase "subject to the jurisdiction thereof" excludes five classes of persons born within the territorial limits of the United States:

(1) Children of diplomatic representatives of foreign countries but not children of their consuls or other agents whose duties are not diplomatic.

(2) Children born to foreign parents on foreign public vessels while in United States waters.

(3) Children of public enemies in hostile occupation of United States territory.

(4) Expatriated persons—that is, those who though born or naturalized in the United States, have renounced allegiance to the United States government.

(5) Tribal Indians. By act of Congress of 1887, citizenship was conferred upon such Indians as should separate themselves from their tribes and adopt the habits of civilized life.

Corporations are not citizens within the meaning of any part of the Constitution except that clause giving the federal courts jurisdiction of suits between citizens of different states, the courts deciding that for this purpose the stockholders of the corporation would be conclusively presumed to be citizens of the state in which it was incorporated.

Before the fourteenth amendment, a state might confer local citizenship upon any person it pleased but this would not entitle such person to be treat-

[5] 12 **Am Jur,** Constitutional Law, §§ 451, 452.
2 **Am Jur,** Aliens, §§ 175–249.
39 **Col. L. R.** 563, Our Equivocal Constitutional Guarantees.

ed as a citizen in other states—that was for the federal government. Under the fourteenth amendment which declares that all persons born or naturalized within the United States shall not only be citizens of the United States but also citizens of the state wherein they reside, there is now little or no occasion for the states to act in the matter, but the amendment did not take away from Congress the power to confer citizenship upon persons who were not born in this country or subject to its jurisdiction, for example, children born abroad of American parents.

Until the rule was changed recently as to Chinese, naturalization was limited to persons of the white and African races and to inhabitants of our colonies who become residents of a state or organized territory; this has been held not to include high caste Hindus. Congress may determine the conditions upon which naturalization may take place and it has been denied to one who refused to promise to take up arms in defense of the country, however necessary the war may seem to be to the government of the day.

§ 6. **Suffrage.**[6] Apart from the fifteenth amendment, the privilege of voting for state officers is within the absolute control of each state, so that a state may enfranchise persons who are not citizens and many states formerly did so. The qualifications of electors who vote for members of Congress are fixed by the Federal constitution as the same as those required for electors of the most numerous branch of the state legislatures. And the qualifications of those who vote for presidential electors are expressly put within the power of the states, the phrase in the Constitution being, "Each state

[6] 11 **Am Jur**, Constitutional Law, § 311.

Validity of statute requiring information as to age, sex, residence, etc., as condition of registration or right to vote. 14 **ALR** 260–263.

Voting by persons in the military service. 140 **ALR** 1100–1117; s. in 147 **ALR** 1443–1445; 148 **ALR** 1402; 149 **ALR** 1466; 150 **ALR** 1460, 1461.

Residence or domicil of student or teacher for purpose of voting. 37 **ALR** 138–146.

Constitutionality of statutes in relation to registration before voting at election or primary. 91 **ALR** 349–379.

Remedy and procedure for purging voters' registration lists. 96 **ALR** 1035–1052.

Basis for computing majority essential to the adoption of a constitutional or other special proposition submitted to voters. 131 **ALR** 1382–1419.

Result of election as affected by votes cast for deceased or disqualified person. 133 **ALR** 319–360.

Construction and application of statute regarding statement by candidate as to his expenses, or his interest in, or the financial value of publicity through, newspapers or other publicity sources. 103 **ALR** 1424–1435.

Costs or reimbursement for expenses incident to election contest or recount. 106 **ALR** 928–942.

Constitutionality, construction, and application of constitutional or statutory provisions which make payment of poll tax condition of right to vote. 139 **ALR** 581–614.

Constitutionality, construction, and application of statute which declares a defeated candidate for nomination ineligible as a candidate at general election, or prohibits printing his name on official ballot. 143 **ALR** 603–617.

Construction and application of statutes relating to filling vacancies in nominations for election to public office. 143 **ALR** 996–1016.

Constitutionality of election laws as regards nominations by petition or otherwise than by statutory convention or primary election. 146 **ALR** 668–680.

Validity of public election as affected by fact that it was held at time other than that fixed by law. 121 **ALR** 987–993.

Incompatability of offices or positions in the military and in the civil service. 26 **ALR** 142–149; s. n 132 **ALR** 254, 255; 147 **ALR** 1419–1426; 148 **ALR** 1399; 150 **ALR** 1444–1446.

Induction or voluntary enlistment in military service as creating a vacancy in, or as ground for removal from, public office or employment. 143 **ALR** 1470–1473; s. in 147 **ALR** 1427, 1428; 148 **ALR** 1400; 150 **ALR** 1447.

Constitutionality of statute requiring, or limiting, selection or appointment of public officers or agents from members of a political party or parties. 140 **ALR** 471–484.

Referendum of general legislative act to people in absence of constitutional requirement in that regard. 76 **ALR** 1053–1063.

Construction and application of constitutional or statutory requirement as to short title, ballot title, or explanation of nature of proposal in initiative, referendum, or recall petition. 106 **ALR** 555–566.

Character or subject matter of ordinance within operation of initiative and referendum provisions. 122 **ALR** 769–793.

Construction and application of constitutional or statutory provisions expressly excepting certain laws from referendum. 146 **ALR** 284–314.

shall appoint (electors) in such manner as the legislature thereof may direct," etc.

The fifteenth amendment, though passed in order to enfranchise the ex-slaves, does not undertake to confer the privilege of voting upon any one but merely provides that suffrage may not be denied by the states on account of race, color, or previous condition of servitude. In order to evade this amendment, several southern states passed statutes imposing certain educational qualifications with what is usually referred to as a "grandfather clause," exempting from the educational requirement the lineal descendants of any person who could vote in any state prior to a certain date—usually January 1, 1866 or January 1, 1867. Such statutes have been held to violate the fifteenth amendment, so that today many southern states rely upon the requirement of a poll tax in order to discourage negroes from voting. There would seem to be no valid constitutional objection to such a tax because the requirement affects poor whites as well as negroes.

The nineteenth amendment, though passed in order to extend the franchise to women who had not been enfranchised in some states, does not undertake to confer the privilege of voting upon them but merely provides that "the right of citizens of the United States to vote shall not be denied or abridged by the United States or by any state on account of sex."

§ 7. Personal and religious liberty.[7] The thirteenth amendment abolishing "slavery and involuntary servitude," has been construed to cover the compulsory enforcement of an agreement to render service in discharge of a debt whether the enforcement is specific or merely by the imposition of the penalty of fine and imprisoment for breach. Such compulsory enforcement of agreements to labor are usually called peonage. On the other hand the amendment does not cover cases where a sailor who has deserted after having voluntarily agreed to complete a voyage, has been compelled to return to his ship. Nor does it interfere with military and naval enlistments or the right of parents and guardians to the custody of minor children.

The first amendment provides that "Congress shall make no law respecting the establishment of religion or prohibit the free exercise thereof;" a similar provision is found in most of the state constitutions and the fourteenth amendment has been construed to protect religious liberty against state action. These provisions have usually been held not to prevent the reading of the Bible in public schools without sectarian comment, or to prevent the enforcement of statutes prohibiting polygamy or to forbid laws regarding the

[7] 11 **Am Jur,** Constitutional Law, §§ 311, 312, 333.

Constitutional guaranty of freedom of religion as applied to license taxes or regulations. 141 **ALR** 538–548; s. in 146 **ALR** 109–116.

Use of streets or parks for religious purposes. 133 **ALR** 1402–1423.

Sectarianism in schools. 5 **ALR** 866–908; s. in 141 **ALR** 1144–1157.

Manner of inflicting death sentence as cruel or unusual punishment. 30 **ALR** 1452–1457.

Constitutional guaranties against unreasonable searches and seizures as applied to search for or seizure of intoxicating liquor. 3 **ALR** 1514–1522; s. in 13 **ALR** 1316–1320; 27 **ALR** 709–761; 39 **ALR** 811–851; 74 **ALR** 1418–1517.

Plea of former jeopardy where jury discharged because of misconduct or disqualification of one or more of their number. 38 **ALR** 706–719.

Constitutional right to jury trial in proceeding for adjudication of incompetency or insanity. 91 **ALR** 88–99.

29 **Va. L. R.** 440, A Turning Point for Religious Liberty.

28 **U. of Minn. L. R.** 209, The Debt of Constitutional Law to Jehovah's Witnesses.

22 **Neb. L. R.** 1, Free Speech and Fair Trials.

28 **Wash U. L. Q.** 251, Liberty under the Fourteenth Amendment.

18 **Wash. L. R.** 90, American Bill of Rights.

21 **Chicago-Kent L. R.** 156, Religion and the Law.

11 **Brooklyn L. R.** 125, From Seditious Libel to Freedom of the Press.

17 **Tenn. L. R.** 706, Civil Rights during and after the War.

observance of Sunday, or the calling of a physician to treat minor children who are ill, or to require students at a state university to take military training. But a state may not require children to accept instruction from public school teachers only, or to require school children to salute the flag.

§ 8. Miscellaneous political rights.[8] The first amendment provides that Congress shall make no law abridging the freedom of speech or of the press, and the fourteenth amendment, with its due process clause, has been construed to protect these freedoms against encroachment by the states. This provision does not permit the publication of libels, blasphemous articles or other publications injurious to public morals or private reputations, Congress having the power to forbid the use of the mails for the circulation of obscene matter or of lottery advertisements. In time of and under the influence of war freedom of speech and the press may be still further curtailed, a conviction of criminal anarchy being sustained for circulating a communist manifesto because it incited to violence even though there was no concrete result and the words were not addressed to any particular persons.

While a state may punish for the publication of malicious and defamatory matter, a state statute authorizing the enjoining as a public nuisance of a paper, magazine or other periodical for publishing malicious, scandalous and defamatory matter, was held unconstitutional as an infringement of the liberty of the press guaranteed by the fourteenth amendment.

The first amendment protects "the right of the people peacefully to assemble, and to petition the government for a redress of grievances" against any violation by the federal government and the fourteenth amendment gives similar protection against state action, but this was held not to entitle "Jehovah's Witnesses" to violate a state statute prohibiting a parade or procession upon a public street without a special license, the state having a right, as a matter of public order, thus to regulate street parades without violating freedom of the press or assembly or freedom of worship.

CHAPTER III

PROTECTION TO PERSONS ACCUSED OF CRIME

§ 9. Bills of attainder.[9] The United States Constitution, Article I, section 9, prohibits the United States from passing any bill of attainder or ex post facto law and the following section forbids any state from doing either of these things. A bill of attainder is a legislative act which inflicts punishment without a judicial trial. A statute in West Virginia denied the right to bring certain suits in the courts of that state to persons who were unable to take an oath that during the Civil War they had never supported any government hostile to the United States. This was held unconstitutional as a bill of attainder because it sought to inflict punishment, without trial, for having engaged in rebellion against the United States.

§ 10. Ex post facto laws.[10] Though the phrase ex post facto, meaning merely "after the fact," would prohibit retroactive legislation affecting either

[8] 11 **Am Jur**, Constitutional Law, §§ 310, 319–326.

Power of legislature or school authorities to prescribe and enforce oath of allegiance, salute to flag, or other ritual of a patriotic character. 110 **ALR** 383, 384; s. in 120 **ALR** 655–657; 127 **ALR** 1502–1505; 141 **ALR** 1030–1035; 147 **ALR** 698–700.

[9] 11 **Am Jur**, Constitutional Law, § 347.

[10] 11 **Am Jur**, Constitutional Law, §§ 348–382.

Constitutional or statutory changes affecting grand jury or substituting information for indictment as an ex post facto law. 53 **ALR** 716–722.

civil rights or criminal punishments, it applies, not only in the United States Constitution but in the English law prior thereto, only to penal statutes. The Constitution thus prohibits the passing of any statute which by its necessary operation and in its relations to the offense or its consequences, alters the situation of the accused to his disadvantage. This includes any statute which makes criminal an act which was innocent when done and punishes such act; any statute that makes a crime greater than it was when committed; any statute that inflicts a greater punishment than the law annexed to the crime when committed; and any statute that allows less or different testimony than the law required at the time of the commission of the offense in order to convict the offender.

Thus, a statute authorizing a jury of eight persons instead of twelve in criminal cases was held bad because it would be easier for the prosecution to secure the unanimous vote of eight jurors than of twelve. As to whether changing the penalty for a crime from death to life imprisonment is bad because it is such an entirely different punishment or is valid as merely a mitigation since most men desire to live as long as they can, there is a conflict of authority. A law imposing a heavier penalty upon second offenders, passed between the two offenses, has been held valid. And so has a statute permitting the use in evidence of other writings of the accused in order to show whether or not some document in the case was in his handwriting, since it did not give to the prosecution any right that was denied to the accused. Statutes changing the number of appellate judges, or the place of trial, or requiring more intelligent jurors have been held valid as not changing the situation of the accused to his disadvantage. And a statute forbidding any person after conviction of a felony to practice medicine in the state was upheld as against a physician who had been convicted of abortion before the statute was passed. On the other hand, a provision in a state constitution adopted just after the Civil War, disqualifying all persons who took part in the rebellion from holding any office in any corporation in the state, being professors or teachers in any educational institution, acting as attorneys at law or as priests or clergymen of any religious denomination under penalties of fine and imprisonment, was held bad as ex post facto because there was no reasonable connection between the conduct sought to be punished and the qualifications for the vocations named.

CHAPTER IV

DUE PROCESS AND EQUAL PROTECTION OF LAW—PROCEDURE

§ 11. Due process—jurisdiction.[1] The fifth amendment to the United States Constitution forbids the United States government to deprive any per-

[1] 12 **Am Jur**, Constitutional Law, §§ 567–579.

Substituted service, service by publication, or service out of the state, in action in personam against resident or domestic corporation, as contrary to due process of law. 126 **ALR** 1474–1498; s. in 132 **ALR** 1361, 1362.

Necessity that hearing be allowed before imposition of punishment for contempt. 57 **ALR** 545–554.

Validity of statutory provision for attorneys' fees. 11 **ALR** 884–910; s. in 90 **ALR** 530–539.

Constitutionality of statute permitting state to take or use in evidence depositions in criminal case. 90 **ALR** 377–384.

Constitutionality of statute which predicates criminality upon repute or reputation. 92 **ALR** 1228–1236.

Constitutionality, construction, and application of statutes empowering court to require judgment debtor to make payment out of income or by instalments. 111 **ALR** 392–406.

20 **Chicago-Kent L. R.** 287, Service of Process upon Foreign Corporations.

son of life, liberty or property without due process of law; the fourteenth amendment enacts the same prohibition against the states. If either a state or the United States undertakes to give or to enforce a judgment which is not based upon jurisdiction such action is invalid as a violation of the United States Constitution. As to what constitutes jurisdiction, see Conflict of Laws §§ 9–16.

§ 12. Same—notice and fair hearing.[2] In addition to jurisdiction, due process of law ordinarily requires a fair hearing before some impartial tribunal, with due notice to the parties to be affected, an opportunity to be heard and a trial based upon some orderly course of proceedings, procedure according to settled usage, however, being valid.

Thus, where a trial court forced a defendant charged with a serious misdemeanor to be tried within five hours after his arrest; where three ignorant negroes were whipped and tortured till they confessed murder and were at once put on trial and convicted without other evidence than the confessions; where a Federal statute provided that Chinese persons wrongfully in the United States could be sentenced to prison at hard labor; where a state statute imposed a presumption of negligence upon railroads in actions for injuries to person and property; and where a notice to defend a suit in Texas regarding land there was served on a defendant in Virginia, which gave but five days in which to appear and answer the suits; all these cases were held to be violations of the due process clause.

On the other hand, it was held not to be a violation for a state statute to provide that persons charged with crime might be tried therefor without an indictment upon an information lodged before a magistrate; or for a state statute to allow an appeal to the state on questions of law in criminal cases though under it a defendant was sentenced to life imprisonment on the first trial and to death on the second trial, the provision against double jeopardy appearing only in the fifth amendment, not in the fourteenth; or for a state statute to declare nets used in illegal fishing to be a public nuisance and to provide for summary destruction thereof, the property involved being of slight value; or for a federal statute to authorize the issue of a distress warrant against a federal revenue collector for balance due to treasury department, such summary method having been used in England to collect debts due to the crown; or for a state statute to abolish jury trial in both civil and criminal cases provided that the new proceeding affords a fair trial; or for a federal statute to provide that any person not a native-born or naturalized citizen of the United States who may not appear to the examining immigration inspector to be clearly entitled to land, be detained for examination by a board of special inquiry, with final decision in the Secretary of Labor, though result of statute was that X, who had never resided in the United States but who claimed to be the son of Y, a native-born Chinese citizen of the United States, was not entitled to a judicial hearing on the question of his citizenship, a fair hearing having been provided for.

Since it is only the fifth and not the fourteenth amendment which protects one from being compelled in a criminal case to be a witness against himself, a state may validly require self-incrimination since it is not considered to be a violation of the due process clause, the practice of compulsory incrimination having existed in England several centuries after Magna Charta.

[2] 12 Am Jur, Constitutional Law, §§ 594–647.

If the parties to a litigation have been given a fair hearing in their case neither of them can complain that his property has been taken without due process merely because a court has erroneously decided against him; similarly an erroneous decision in a criminal case does not deprive the defendant of his liberty without due process. But a litigant is entitled to an honest tribunal and if he is injured through fraud or corruption of the court his constitutional right to due process has been violated.

§ 13. Equal protection of the laws.[3] Usually the question of equal protection of the laws comes up in substantive law, not in procedure; but a state statute making colored men ineligible for jury service was held invalid on that ground. This does not mean that a jury trying a negro must be composed, in whole or in part, of negroes, but merely that negroes shall not be excluded from jury service on account of their color. Nor does it mean that lawyers, ministers, physicians, teachers, railroad engineers and firemen may not be excused from jury duty in order not to interrupt their regular work; or that persons may not be excluded because through age or other incapacity they may reasonably be considered not well qualified for such service.

CHAPTER V

DUE PROCESS AND EQUAL PROTECTION OF LAW—POLICE POWER

§ 14. In general.[4] In order to promote and protect the social and economic interests of the public, each of the states and the United States, in their re-

3 12 **Am Jur,** Constitutional Law, §§ 468–566.

Rights and protection of innocent persons where property in which they are interested is seized because of its illegal use in connection with intoxicating liquor. 47 **ALR** 1055–1084; s. in 61 **ALR** 551–561; 73 **ALR** 1087–1111; 82 **ALR** 607–622; 124 **ALR** 288–315.

Construction and application of constitutional provisions prescribing requisites or conditions of passage of local or special law relating to property, affairs or government of municipality. 106 **ALR** 1471–1475.

18 **Wash. L. R.** 120, Privileges and Immunities under the Fourteenth Amendment.

4 11 **Am Jur,** Constitutional Law, §§ 245–254.

Constitutionality of vagrancy statutes and ordinances. 111 **ALR** 68–75.

Validity of legislation directed against political, social, or industrial propaganda deemed to be of a dangerous tendency. 20 **ALR** 1535–1550; s. in 73 **ALR** 1494–1501.

Constitutionality of statute to prevent cruelty in trapping animals. 79 **ALR** 1308–1310.

"Dog laws," constitutionality of. 49 **ALR** 847–855.

Power of state to prohibit or restrict exportation of natural resources. 32 **ALR** 331–342.

Constitutionality, construction, and application of criminal statutes specifically denouncing offenses affecting cemeteries, burial lots, tombstones, and the like. 132 **ALR** 557–568.

Selective Training and Service Acts. 129 **ALR** 1171–1226; s. in 147 **ALR** 1313–1365; 148 ALR 1388–1395; 149 **ALR** 1457–1462; 150 **ALR** 1420–1427.

Exemption of member of armed forces from service of civil process. 137 **ALR** 1372–1379; s. in 149 **ALR** 1455, 1456; 150 **ALR** 1419.

Suits and remedies against alien enemies. 137 **ALR** 1361–1371; s. in 147 **ALR** 1309, 1310; 148 **ALR** 1386, 1387; 149 **ALR** 1454.

Federal Espionage Act. 148 **ALR** 1442–1479; s. in 149 **ALR** 1474; 150 **ALR** 1481.

Right of nonresident alien subject of enemy nation to institute suit after commencement of war. 137 **ALR** 1355–1360; s. in 147 **ALR** 1307, 1308; 148 **ALR** 1385; s. in 149 **ALR** 1454.

Right of resident alien who is a subject of an enemy country to prosecute suit during war. 137 **ALR** 1347–1354; s. in 147 **ALR** 1303–1307; 149 **ALR** 1453.

Effect of war on litigation pending at the time of its outbreak. 137 **ALR** 1335–1346; s. in 147 **ALR** 1298–1303; 148 **ALR** 1384, 1385; 149 **ALR** 1452; 150 **ALR** 1418.

Constitutionality of statute for relief of parties to public contract because of war conditions. 137 **ALR** 1256–1262.

Who is "enemy" within Trading with the Enemy Act. 148 **ALR** 1423–1428; s. in 149 **ALR** 1472.

Constitutionality, construction, and application of Emergency Price Control Act. 146 **ALR** 718–732; s. in 148 **ALR** 1429–1441; 149 **ALR** 1472, 1473; 150 **ALR** 1470–1480.

Constitutionality and construction of Emergency Price Control Act as relating to rent. 147 **ALR** 1446–1465; s. in 148 **ALR** 1403–1410; 149 **ALR** 1467–1470; 150 **ALR** 1462–1468.

Price ceiling, adopted as war measure, as affecting pre-existing contract. 147 **ALR** 1286–1293; s. in 149 **ALR** 1451.

spective spheres, have a power of regulation which is usually called the police power. The most important of these social interests are public health, public morals, public safety and public order and comfort; and the most important things to be guarded against in protecting economic interests are fraud and oppression.

§ 15. **Public health.**[5] Wide latitude is permitted by the courts to the legislative department of the government in its bona fide efforts to safeguard the public health. Thus a state may grant for twenty-five years a city wide monopoly of slaughtering animals to be sold for meat in the city in order to secure more effective sanitary control of the meat business; it may impose a heavy tax or absolutely prohibit the sale of oleomargarine if such product can reasonably be considered detrimental to the public health; it may restrict the hours of labor of children in any employment and of adults, especially women, in unhealthful employments such as laundries or underground mines, and in the construction of public works; it may require vaccination; it may require property owners to raise the grade of their land and thus put an end to nuisances affecting public health; it may require garbage to be delivered at city crematories in closed trucks; it may authorize the destruction of cattle having a communicable disease; and one of the reasons for upholding the Pure Food and Drugs Act of Congress is the safeguarding of the public health.

On the other hand, if the legislation bears no reasonable relation to protecting the public health it will not be upheld on that ground; for example, a statute forbidding more than ten hours a day labor in bakeries was held invalid because the court thought bakeries were not sufficiently unhealthful places to work to justify such a regulation.

§ 16. **Public morals.**[6] The principal subjects of regulation in this field have been gambling in various forms, intoxicating liquors and sexual vice.

Curfew in wartime. 147 **ALR** 1270–1272.
Constitutionality, construction, and application of statutes regarding rate of interest during "emergency." 147 **ALR** 1023–1028.
Constitutionality and construction of state farm aid laws. 92 **ALR** 768–784.
Governmental powers in peacetime emergency. 86 **ALR** 1539–1557; s. in 88 **ALR** 1519–1524; 96 **ALR** 312–314, 826–836.
Constitutionality of statutes imposing absolute liability on private persons or corporations, irrespective of negligence or breach of a specific statutory duty, for injury to person or property. 53 **ALR** 875–884.
40 **Harv. L. R.** 943, Due Process of Law, Police Power and the Supreme Court.
50 **Yale L. J.** 778, Trial by Ordeal, New Style.
28 **Va. L. R.** 761, The Evolution of Smyth v. Ames.
29 **Va. L. R.** 152, New Relationship Between Due Process of Law and the States' Police Power.
29 **U. of Iowa L. R** 383, Judicial Protection of Civil Rights.
21 **N. C. L. R.** 253, Compulsory Vaccination and Sterilization: Constitutional Aspects.

[5] 11 **Am Jur,** Constitutional Law, § 271.
Construction and application of regulation as to milk. 122 **ALR** 1062–1135.
Constitutionality of regulations as to milk. 18 **ALR** 235–258; s. in 122 **ALR** 1062–1135.
Decisions under the "Lever Act" (Act of August 10, 1917, amended in 1919). 11 **ALR** 1265–1273; s. in 14 **ALR** 1059–1060.
Constitutionality of statute in relation to oleomargarin or other substitute for butter. 53 **ALR** 474–481.
Constitutionality of anticigarette legislation. 20 **ALR** 926–936.
Harrison Narcotic Act. 13 **ALR** 858–875; s. in 39 **ALR** 236–252.
Validity of statutory or municipal regulation as to garbage. 15**ALR** 287–304; s. in 72 **ALR** 520–526; 135 **ALR** 1305–1311.
Constitutionality and construction of statutes and ordinances for protection of municipal water supply. 72 **ALR** 673–682.
Constitutionality of statute regulating the time of payment of wages. 12 **ALR** 612–640; s. in 26 **ALR** 1396, 1397.
Constitutionality of child labor laws. 12 **ALR** 1216–1226; s. in 21 **ALR** 1437–1438.
Constitutionality of statute or ordinance relating to rate of wages of persons employed on public work. 50 **ALR** 1480–1495; s. in 132 **ALR** 1297–1308.
Constitutionality of statutes limiting hours of labor in private industry. 90 **ALR** 814–842.

[6] 11 **Am Jur,** Constitutional Law, § 272.
Public regulation of dancing, dance halls, dancing schools, etc. 48 **ALR** 144–182; s. in 60 **ALR** 173–184.

Gambling includes not only ordinary betting but also lotteries, trading stamps, and business transactions of a highly speculative character, such as sale of corporation stock on margin. The liquor traffic may not only be regulated but prohibited, even including liquor lawfully owned before the law went into effect; and in one state the selling of liquor is made a government monopoly. An ordinance forbidding the granting of liquor licenses except to persons who obtained written consent of majority of city board of police commissioners was held valid.

Legislation designed to prevent or limit sexual immorality are usually held valid, for example, ordinances fixing the limits of what is ordinarily called red light districts. Statutes prohibiting marriage or cohabitation of a man and woman either of whom is an epileptic, imbecile or feeble-minded are sustainable either on the ground of public health or public morals. A few states authorize the sterilization of criminals; such statutes may be upheld either on the ground of public health, public morals or public safety.

§ 17. Public safety.[7] There is a large amount of legislation designed to protect the public against the hazards and perils of dangerous property such as automobiles and explosives and dangerous businesses such as factories, mines, railroads, navigation and building construction. For example, a state statute making railroad companies liable for any injuries to an employee resulting from the negligence of a fellow employee under whose direction the injured employee was hurt, was held valid. So was a state statute making injuries inflicted by running of locomotives or cars prima facie evidence of negligence on the part of the railroad; and a statute allowing a reasonable attorney's fee to successful plaintiffs in actions against a railroad for damage due to the negligent escape of fire. And so was an ordinance forbidding the washing and ironing of clothes in public laundries and wash houses within certain parts of the city from 10 P.M. till 6 A.M. the next day because of the danger of fire to wooden buildings.

On the other hand, an ordinance forbidding any person to carry on a laundry

Power to prohibit the possession of intoxicating liquor, irrespective of any intention to traffic therein. 2 **ALR** 1085–1095.

Constitutionality, construction, and application of statutes designed to prevent or limit control of retail liquor dealers by manufacturers, wholesalers, or importers. 136 **ALR** 1238–1251.

Provisions of statute regarding personal qualifications necessary to entitle one to license for sale of intoxicating liquor, as denial of equal protection of laws. 145 **ALR** 509–517.

Constitutionality of corrupt practices acts. 69 **ALR** 377–387.

7 11 **Am Jur**, Constitutional Law, § 271.

Validity, construction, and effect of statutes which make owner responsible, or create lien, for injury or damage inflicted by another operating the automobile. 4 **ALR** 361–368; s. in 61 **ALR** 866–882; 83 **ALR** 878–887; 88 **ALR** 174–177; 112 **ALR** 416–428; 135 **ALR** 481–497.

Power to require closing of place of amusement or other place of public assembly because of fire hazard or unsanitary conditions. 140 **ALR** 1048–1054.

Power to forbid or restrict repair of wooden building within fire limits. 26 **ALR** 1219–1232; s. in 56 **ALR** 878, 879.

Indefiniteness of automobile speed regulations as affecting validity. 26 **ALR** 897–906; s. in 29 **ALR** 1066.

Construction and effect of statute in relation to conduct of driver of automobile after happening of accident. 16 **ALR** 1425–1429; s. in 66 **ALR** 1228–1238; 101 **ALR** 911–919.

Constitutionality of automobile guest statutes. 111 **ALR** 1011–1016.

Validity of statute or ordinance relating to granting or revocation of license or permit to operate automobile. 71 **ALR** 616–618; s. in 108 **ALR** 1162–1168; 125 **ALR** 1459–1465.

Validity of automobile registration or license fee as affected by classification or discrimination. 126 **ALR** 1419–1430.

Constitutionality of statute or ordinance imposing upon abutting owners or occupants duty in respect of care or condition of street or highway. 58 **ALR** 215–231.

Constitutionality of statute for control of diseases of livestock. 65 **ALR** 525–553.

Power of state to require changes in buildings previously erected in order to comply with new requirements and standards for protection of health and safety. 109 **ALR** 1117–1123.

Constitutionality of levee and flood control acts. 70 **ALR** 1274–1299.

within the city except in buildings of brick or stone was held bad because, as it was administered it discriminated against a Chinese who had conducted a laundry in a wooden building for twenty-two years and was not justified on the ground of public safety. And a statute forbidding the mining of coal under cities so as to cause subsidence of dwellings or places where labor was employed was held bad because purchasers of such property deliberately took the risk of subsidence.

§ 18. Public order and comfort—aesthetics.[8] Legislation regulating the use of streets and other public places in order to secure quiet, especially in the vicinity of hospitals, is quite common. Zoning ordinance provisions as to grocery stores in residential sections are sometimes sustained because of the increase of fire and police hazards. Statutes providing for the separation of races in public conveyances and schools have been upheld on the ground of the promotion of public order, and so have statutes forbidding the soliciting for certain kinds of business on trains. But an ordinance forbidding occupancy of a lot by persons of color in a block where the greater number of residences was occupied by white persons was held bad.

On the other hand an ordinance regulating signs and billboards not affecting public safety but based merely upon aesthetic grounds have been held invalid; if a community wishes to get rid of unsightly billboards already erected it may perhaps do so under the power of eminent domain, making compensation to the owner; and an ordinance forbidding the sale of provisions or liquor in places where dry goods, clothing, jewelry and drugs were kept for sale was held bad, public health and comfort not being involved.

§ 19. Licensing occupations—domestic relations—miscellaneous.[9] Where an occupation, such as selling liquors, may be forbidden altogether, the state may obviously require licenses. It may also require them where the occupation is of such a character as to require a special course of study or training or experience to qualify one to pursue it with safety to the public interests; on this basis licenses may be required in a large number of occupations—

8 11 **Am Jur**, Constitutional Law, §§ 277, 280.

Constitutionality, construction, and application of statutes or governmental projects for improvement of housing conditions (slum clearance). 130 **ALR** 1069–1092.

9 11 **Am Jur**, Constitutional Law, §§ 284–296.

Statute regulating banks and trust companies as special or class legislation, or as denying the equal protection of the laws. 111 **ALR** 140–152.

Exception of existing buildings or businesses from statute or ordinance enacted in exercise of police or license taxing power, as unconstitutional discrimination. 136 **ALR** 207–226.

Construction and application of constitutional provision against special or local laws regulating practice in courts of justice. 135 **ALR** 305–383.

Refusal of amusement license or permit as subject to judicial review. 124 **ALR** 247–272.

Making payment for water or light a charge upon the property or against the present owner or occupant, irrespective of the person who enjoyed the service. 13 **ALR** 346–355; s. in 55 **ALR** 789–791.

Licensing and regulation of pool and billiard rooms and bowling alleys. 20 **ALR** 1482–1497; s. in 29 **ALR** 41, 42; 53 **ALR** 149–163; 72 **ALR** 1339–1341.

Regulation of junk dealers. 30 **ALR** 1427–1441; s. in 88 **ALR** 970–974.

Constitutionality of statute regulating barbers. 20 **ALR** 1111, 1118; s. in 98 **ALR** 1088–1096.

Constitutionality of statute regulating newspapers or magazines. 35 **ALR** 7–14; s. in 110 **ALR** 327–333.

Validity of regulations as to plumbers and plumbing. 36 **ALR** 1342–1353; s. in 137 **ALR** 1065–1072.

Grounds for revocation of valid license of physician or surgeon or dentist. 54 **ALR** 1504–1522; s. in 82 **ALR** 1184–1189.

What offenses involve moral turpitude within statute providing grounds for denying or revoking license of dentist, physician or surgeon. 109 **ALR** 1459–1464.

Validity of statute or ordinance fixing closing hours for certain kinds of business. 55 **ALR** 242–252.

such as those of the physician, the lawyer, the engineer, the dentist and the teacher.

In the exercise of its police power, the state may regulate the requirements for marriage and for divorce. It may forbid marriage between persons closely related or between persons of different races, and it may entirely forbid divorce. It may make the education of children compulsory; it may take care of persons who are dependent; or those who are defective, such as the insane or feeble-minded; or those who are delinquent, having abnormal tendencies markedly injurious to the social order such as truants, habitual criminals and vagrants.

Legislation which may not be easily classified under the foregoing headings may sometimes be upheld as a valid exercise of the police power. For example, a statute invalidating the assignment of future wages without consent of wage-earner's wife and employer; a statute allowing appeals from certain counties only to an intermediate court and not to the supreme court of the state; a statute imposing a penalty for allowing Johnson grass to go to seed; a statute imposing a penalty on insurance companies for vexatious refusal to pay certain claims promptly; a statute forbidding any kind of legal or equitable ownership of land by aliens other than those who have in good faith declared their intent to become citizens; a statute forbidding banking by anyone except a corporation; a statute making the malicious erection of a fence over six feet high for the purpose of annoying adjoining occupants a private nuisance.

§ 20. Protection against fraud or oppression.[10] In the exercise of its police power, the state may legislate to prevent fraud by fiduciaries and by the use of short weights, imitations or adulterations; and to this end it may make and enforce inspection laws and regulate businesses so as to prevent fraudulent practices. But under the guise of such legislation, the state may not unreasonably restrict competition; for example, it may not prohibit the sale of healthful oleomargarine for the mere purpose of protecting the butter industry against competition.

The state may also protect honest but unfortunate debtors against oppression by forbidding excessive interest and annoying practices in the collection of debts and by giving them discharges in bankruptcy. It may protect employees by requiring that wages shall be paid in cash, at certain intervals, and by giving claims of employees for wages priority where the employer dies or becomes bankrupt. And it may prevent economic oppression of small businesses by laws forbidding combinations in restraint of trade.

§ 21. Regulation of ownership and use of property.[1] The state may forbid long-time leases of agricultural lands or the creation of contingent interests in property which will vest far in the future. It may regulate the appropriation and use of certain kinds of property such as game, fish, natural gas and oil and may forbid wanton waste of gas and oil and forest trees, even by private owners of such property.

It may create land irrigation or drainage systems and compel the owners of land benefited thereby to share the cost. It may authorize the develop-

[10] 11 **Am Jur**, Constitutional Law, § 273.
Constitutionality of rent laws. 11 **ALR** 1252–1261; s. in 16 **ALR** 178–180.

[1] 11 **Am Jur**, Constitutional Law, §§ 297 et seq.
43 **Am Jur**, Public Utilities, §§ 10–15, 83–97.
Fair Labor Standards Act, judicial questions regarding. 130 **ALR** 272–285; s. in 132 **ALR** 1443–1459.

ment of water power by damming a stream and flooding the upper riparian land, compelling the owner of such land to submit thereto upon being paid therefor by the owner of the dam.

§ 22. Regulation of business—public utilities.[2] Where a business is of such a nature as to render such important service to the state as to be affected with a public interest it may be regulated by the legislature. The most important of these businesses are usually called public utilities and include the furnishing of transportation, telegraph and telephone service, gas, water and electricity. Sometimes the regulation is based upon the existence of a public franchise, such as the use of streets, sometimes on the existence of a virtual monopoly. In all these cases the state may prescribe maximum charges for service and the details of the service to be rendered, the public utility being generally entitled to a fair return on the business. The state may also regulate banking and insurance in order to protect the public against loss due to dishonesty or imprudent management.

Where a business is of such a nature as to require special supervision or exposes persons or property to special hazard the cost of such supervision and burden of such hazard may be placed upon the owners of the business; for example, the cost of inspecting mines may be placed upon the mine owners and the cost of maintaining a railroad commission may be placed upon the railroads. The state may make railroads absolutely liable for damage done by fire from their engines and a liquor seller liable for damage done by intoxicated persons to whom he has sold liquor; and railroads may be compelled to install safety devices and to pay for elevating tracks to avoid grade crossings in thickly populated districts.

CHAPTER VI

DUE PROCESS AND EQUAL PROTECTION OF LAW—TAXATION

§ 23. In general—lands and chattels.[3] In order that a tax may be valid, under the fifth and fourteenth amendments, the taxing power—whether federal, state or municipal—must have jurisdiction of the subject of taxation, the tax must be levied for a public purpose and it must not be arbitrary or unreasonable, or discriminatory.

Any interest in land, whether possessory or intangible, such as an easement or mortgage thereon, may be taxed only in the jurisdiction where the

[2] 11 Am Jur, Constitutional Law, §§ 279-283.

Statutes or ordinances which apply to railroads, but not to carriers on public highways, or vice versa, as denying equal protection. 139 ALR 977-987.

11 Am Jur, Constitutional Law, §§ 284-296.

Constitutionality of statutes affecting riparian rights. 56 ALR 277-303.

Abandoned animals, constitutionality of statute or ordinance providing for destruction of. 8 ALR 67-79.

Constitutionality of statute providing for destruction of dogs as affected by property rights in dogs. 8 ALR 77.

Constitutionality of fencing and stock laws. 6 ALR 212-234; s. in 18 ALR 67-69.

Constitutionality of statutes for protection of vegetation against disease or infection. 12 ALR 1136-1146.

Constitutionality of statute limiting or controlling exploitation or waste of natural resources. 24 ALR 307-318; s. in 78 ALR 834-843.

Constitutionality of statute making presence of brand on animal prima facie evidence that animal belongs to owner of brand. 51 ALR 1168; s. in 86 ALR 179-190.

Validity, construction, and application of statutes or ordinances penalizing one who enters or remains in dwelling after having been forbidden to do so. 146 ALR 655-660.

[3] 12 Am Jur, Constitutional Law, §§ 640-647.

51 Am Jur, Taxation, §§ 441-462.

Statutory enactment or repeal subsequent to tax sale or issuance of tax certificates as affecting rights of holders of tax certificates or purchasers at tax sale. 111 ALR 237-261.

land is located. The same rule applies to tangible chattels located permanently in one place; but if, like refrigerator cars, the chattels are employed by the owner part of the time in his own state and part of the time in another state, the latter state may tax the average number of chattels within it during its tax year.

§ 24. Corporate assets.[4] The assets of a corporation consist not only of its tangible property—land and chattels—but also of its intangible property, such as its good will, its franchises and its contracts; both kinds of assets may be taxed and usually their value is found by adding together the amount of bonds and stock outstanding.

Where the corporation has its home office in state X but does business in states X, Y and Z, Y may tax any land or chattels of the corporation located in state Y and also that part of the corporation's intangible assets which may fairly said to be based upon the business done by the corporation in state Y. In the case of a railroad this is usually arrived at by deducting the value of its large terminals not located within state Y and the value of bonds held by it merely for investment and not used in its general business and then taxing the rest upon a proportionate mileage basis, so that if the railroad's mileage is one tenth in state Y, that proportion of its intangible property is taxable by state Y. Where practically the entire business is so localized in state Y that the corporation may be said to have a commercial domicile in state Y, the latter state may tax the corporation on its entire intangible property.

§ 25. Pecuniary choses in action.[5] Where A, living in state X, owes a simple debt to B who lives in state Y, A's chose in action is taxable as property only by state Y, not by state X, because its value is with B, the creditor. But if A had given to B a bond and B kept the bond in state Z it may be taxed by state Z, the bond being regarded as the chose in action itself and not merely evidence of it. On the other hand, if A had given B a negotiable note and B turned the possession of the note over to his agent or bailee in state Z merely for safekeeping, state Z may not tax it. But if B keeps money on deposit in state Z, that may be taxed by state Z, even though the money consisted of bank notes, payable to bearer, because bank notes, like bonds, are considered as property.

Where B insurance corporation located in state Y, loaned money to its policy holders in state X, the business being done through its agent in state X, it was held that these loans made in state X were taxable by state X as capital employed in a business, although the notes given by the debtors and the insurance policies held by B corporation as security were kept in state Y till the notes were paid.

§ 26. Shares of stock—franchises.[6] A corporation, being the legal owner of all the corporate assets, is taxable thereon just as an individual owner would be. The corporation stockholders have the right to any dividends that may be earned and the right to share in what is left of the assets upon dissolution after payment of debts. Though the same property, tangible and intangible, gives the value to the corporate assets and to the shares of stock, both may be taxed.

Where A, living in state X, owns stock in corporation B of state Y, both

[4] 51 **Am Jur**, Taxation, §§ 793–802.

[5] 51 **Am Jur**, Taxation, §§ 463–474.

[6] 51 **Am Jur**, Taxation, §§ 487–494.

states may tax, state X on the ground that the stock, like any other chose in action, has a situs where A the owner lives, and state Y on the ground that the stock has a situs at the domicile of the corporation.

A franchise is a privilege granted by the government. All corporate franchises, whether it be a franchise to be a corporation, a right to exercise the power of eminent domain, a right to occupy public streets with poles or pipes or conduits for gas and electric wires or a right to take tolls for a highway—all those are taxable as privileges where they are exercised; they may also be taxed as intangible property either separately or in common with all the other corporate assets. In every state in which a corporation does business its franchise to be a corporation may be taxed as property.

§ 27. Inheritance or succession taxes—transfers inter vivos.[7] Where A dies domiciled in state X owning land and chattels in state X and claims against debtors living in state X, that state may tax A's estate for the privilege of permitting the devolution of A's property, either by deed or will.

As to A's land and chattels located in state Y and claims against debtors living in state Y, state X cannot tax the succession to the land, that being dependent entirely upon the law of state Y. As to the chattels, if state Y permits the law of state X to govern its devolution, then state X, as well as state Y may levy a succession tax; otherwise only state Y may do so. As to succession to the claims of A against debtors living in state Y, state X may tax; and although state Y may not tax such claims as property it may tax succession to such claims because B, a creditor of A, might have come into state Y and compelled the debtor in state Y to pay his obligation to B instead of to A. As to A's stock in a corporation in state Y, state X may tax the succession to it as a part of A's intangible property; and state Y may also tax the succession, because of its control over the transfer of the stock at the domicile of the corporation. Where notes and bonds against debtors in state Y or stock in a state Y corporation are permanently kept in state Z, the latter state may also levy a succession tax thereon.

Where a legatee or distributee of A's estate lives in state R, he may be taxed in state R upon whatever he may receive from the estate, the privilege of receiving being as taxable as the privilege of transmitting.

A state may also tax transfers inter vivos of shares of corporation stock or other personal property when made within its limits, regardless of the situs of the property or of the corporation.

§ 28. When is a purpose public?[8] Taxes may not be levied in support of a purpose which the courts regard as private; for example, to make a donation to a bridge company planning to establish a bridge making factory in the city; or to lend money to owners of land whose buildings have been destroyed in a conflagration; or to provide homes for mechanics, laborers or other wage earners.

On the other hand, taxes may be levied to support public charities and to

[7] 28 **Am Jur**, Inheritance, Estate, and Gift Taxes, §§ 16–33.
50 **Am Jur**, Stock Transfer Taxes, § 2.

[8] 51 **Am Jur**, Taxation, §§ 321–386.
Constitutionality of statutes providing for bounty or pension for soldiers. 7 **ALR** 1636–1657; 13 **ALR** 587–589; 15 **ALR** 1359, 1360; s. in 147 **ALR** 1432–1441.
Constitutionality of statute authorizing state to loan money or engage in business of a private nature. 14 **ALR** 1151–1173; s. in 115 **ALR** 1456–1464.
Use of public funds or exercise of taxing power to promote patriotism. 30 **ALR** 1035–1043.
Construction and effect of soldiers' bonus and bounty laws. 13 **ALR** 594–608; s. in 147 **ALR** 1438–1441; 148 **ALR** 1401.

give pensions to soldiers, sailors, firemen, policemen and teachers as part of their compensation for services already rendered or being rendered. At a time when railroads were being built, it was held to be a valid public purpose for counties and townships to levy taxes in aid of railroad construction. In arid states, taxes may be levied to support irrigation and in an agricultural state which had had a succession of poor crops it was held proper to lend public money to farmers with which to buy grain.

Logically, the power to make tax exemptions should be treated on the same basis as the power to levy taxes; but in some states tax exemptions have been upheld as a means of encouraging some kinds of private industries; and in all states property devoted to sectarian purposes has been exempted from taxation though the levy of a tax in aid of such purposes would be invalid, the reason for the exemption in such cases being chiefly that they always have been made.

§ 29. Classification—progressive and confiscatory taxation.[9] In order to be valid under the fifth and fourteenth amendments, a tax must not be confiscatory, discriminatory or disproportionate. This means that the classification of objects for taxation shall be reasonable, not arbitrary, but this is construed with great liberality in favor of the tax.

Thus, a license tax on persons or corporations engaged in refining sugar and molasses based on annual receipts, excepting planters and farmers grinding and refining their own sugar and molasses was held valid the purpose of the exception being to encourage agriculture. A tax levied by state X upon a state Y manufacturing corporation doing business in state X measuring the tax by a certain percentage on their entire capital stock, state X having absolute power to exclude the corporation from its borders; though such power would not justify state X, after permitting the foreign corporation to do business within the state, in imposing a new and additional franchise tax for the privilege of doing business, the corporation having already paid the license tax demanded for the privilege.

Since a succession tax is not a tax on property but upon the privilege of succession, such a tax may be graded as to whether the succession was lineal or collateral. A special assessment is valid though some of the property in the assessment district is not benefited and although property outside the assessment district does receive some benefit therefrom; and an assessment of the cost of a sidewalk to the abutting land is valid though the land is not benefited thereby. And where the original assessment was void and there was a reassessment, the fact that A bought land without notice does not relieve him of the reassessment.

A stamp tax of two cents on each $100 of face value or fraction thereof on all sales of stock in associations or corporations was held valid, the classification being regarded as reasonable. And land valuable only for farming may be annexed to a city and compelled to pay city taxes though receiving no benefit therefrom.

On the other hand, while it is ordinarily proper to apply the front foot rule in special assessment cases, it was improper where a single property

[9] 51 **Am Jur**, Taxation, §§ 173–201.
Discrimination by state against foreign corporations in imposition of taxes and license fees. 49 **ALR** 726–755; s. in 77 **ALR** 1490–1497.
Validity of license statute or ordinance which discriminates against nonresidents. 61 **ALR** 337–351; s. in 112 **ALR** 63–70.
Condemnation of premises or part thereof as affecting rights of landlord and tenant inter se. 43 **ALR** 1176–1184; s. in 53 **ALR** 686.
Condemnation by de facto corporation. 44 **ALR** 542–557.

would bear the entire cost of opening a street including the cost of condemnation proceedings. And a stamp tax of two cents for each share of $100 face value or fraction thereof on all transfers of stock was held bad because it imposed the same tax whether the transfer was of $100 shares or $1 shares.

A rate of taxation and of exemption therefrom may be made progressively larger according to the amount involved both in the field of income taxes and of inheritance and succession taxes. It has rarely, if ever, been applied to direct taxes on land or chattels.

It has been said that the power to tax is the power to destroy; it is not, however, the right to destroy except those things which—apart from the power of taxation—the government has the right to take or destroy without compensation, such as the liquor traffic. Thus, since Congress had the right to prohibit state banks it could tax them out of existence.

CHAPTER VII

DUE PROCESS AND EQUAL PROTECTION OF LAW—EMINENT DOMAIN

§ 30. In general.[10] The fifth amendment forbids the United States to take private property for public use without just compensation. There is a similar provision in all but a few of the state constitutions and in those few the fourteenth-amendment provision forbidding the states to take property without due process of law has been interpreted to reach the same result. The clear implication from these provisions is that private property shall not be taken for private use even with compensation and it has been so held.

In the exercise of its police power, however, some kinds of private property may be taken for public use without compensation; for example, buildings may be destroyed to prevent the spread of a conflagration; land may be used to prevent a river from overflowing its banks; diseased cattle may be destroyed to prevent the spread of the disease; the sale of liquor already legally manufactured may be prohibited and a brewery already legally in existence may be forbidden to manufacture beer; a minor nuisance such as bell ringing to summon factory employees may be legalized by the legislature. The United States government may, in order to improve navigation of a stream, interfere with the right of adjoining property owners to develop water power from the flow of the stream. And in the exercise of war powers in time of war property may be seized and used for war purposes if reasonably necessary in the interests of public safety.

Like the taxing power and the police power, the power of eminent domain is not given by any constitutional provision but is inherent in all governments, being necessary for the preservation of governmental effectiveness. It may be exercised by the government not only directly but also indirectly by authorizing it to be done by any enterprise that discharges public functions, such as railroad, telegraph, telephone, water, gas and electric companies.

[10] 11 **Am Jur**, Constitutional Law, §§ 248, 266, 394.
12 **Am Jur**, Constitutional Law, §§ 618, 634, 658, 673.
Right of body having power of eminent domain to enter upon or explore land, before proceeding to acquire it. 29 **ALR** 1409–1418.
Power of eminent domain as exercisable by state or one of its political subdivisions for benefit of Federal Government, or by Federal Government exclusively under state authority. 143 **ALR** 1040–1050.

§ 31. The public use—the property that may be taken.[1] If a purpose is recognized as public so that public money may be appropriated to it, it may be furthered by the exercise of eminent domain. But there must always be the necessity of accomplishing some public good. Thus, where a dam had been built and lands flooded to develop water power but later the reclamation of the lands was of more value to the public than the continuance of the water power, the state was permitted to reduce the height of the dam, making compensation to the owner of the dam and the owners of the mills affected thereby. Land may be taken for a public but not for a private cemetery; or for the purpose of building a spur railroad track to a private industry. Placing telephone poles and wires in a street is a public purpose because it relieves the street of messengers. In a mining state, a mining corporation was held entitled to condemn a right of way across a placer mining claim for an aerial bucket line; and in an arid state it was held permissible to authorize giving a private individual an easement of a ditch across intervening land in order to conduct water from a stream to irrigate his land. A statute limiting the height of buildings around Copley Square in Boston in order to preserve the architectural symmetry of the square and thereby promote its beauty and attractiveness as a public park was held a valid exercise of the power of eminent domain, compensation being made to the property owners affected, though it would probably have been sustainable, even without compensation, as an exercise of police power.

On the other hand, land may not be taken for the purpose of developing water power for the use of private factories; or for the purpose of constructing a scenic railway in the gorge of the Niagara river below the falls, the railway not being a real highway. Nor may the right of fishing in certain fresh-water lakes be taken merely for the sport and amusement of a few people.

Where the purpose is public there is no rule limiting the amount taken to cases of necessity, but if the power is authorized to be exercised by a public utility or municipality the courts will construe the authorization strictly. In taking land for a highway a city may take the fee or merely a public easement over the land.

Any kind of property may be taken. Where X has a franchise from the state or a contract with the state or with a municipality or with third parties,

[1] 12 **Am Jur,** Constitutional Law, § 658.

Exercise of eminent domain for purpose of irrigating land of private owner. 9 **ALR** 583–590; s. in 27 **ALR** 519, 520.

Right to condemn property previously condemned or purchased for public use, but not actually so used. 12 **ALR** 1502–1512.

Right of owner of fee burdened with easement in nature of street, private or public, to compensation on condemnation of property for public street. 17 **ALR** 1249–1263.

Compensation for property confiscated or requisitioned during war. 137 **ALR** 1290–1309; s. in 147 **ALR** 1295–1297; 148 **ALR** 1384; 149 **ALR** 1451.

Furnishing electricity to public as public use or purpose for which power of eminent domain may be exercised. 44 **ALR** 735–754; s. in 58 **ALR** 787, 788.

Right of owner of property not abutting on closed section to compensation for vacation of street or highway. 49 **ALR** 330–375; s. in 93 **ALR** 639–646.

Eminent domain: combination of public and private uses or purposes. 53 **ALR** 9–36.

Public benefit or convenience as distinguished from use by the public as ground for the exercise of the power of eminent domain. 54 **ALR** 7–45.

Right to take property under eminent domain as affected by fact that property is already devoted to cemetery purposes. 109 **ALR** 1502–1509.

Eminent domain for development or operation of mines and mining industries. 54 **ALR** 56–75.

Right of public body to compensation where property held by it is taken for another public purpose. 56 **ALR** 365–379.

Exercise of power of eminent domain for purposes of logging road or logging railroad. 86 **ALR** 552–563.

the state may not impair the obligation of the franchise or the contracts but it may take the contracts, making compensation to X therefor.

§ 32. Taking property—damaging property.[2] The simplest act of taking is that where the fee of a piece of land is taken and used for the construction of a schoolhouse or city hall, all the owners of the fee being entitled to compensation, including those who had easements over the land. Another simple case is that where either the fee of or a public easement over land is taken for a public highway or for a railroad right of way. Where the fee of the street is taken the later use of the street for streetcar tracks, telegraph and telephone poles, gas and water pipes and conduits for telephone wires is usually held not to entitle the owners of the land taken to additional compensation. It is also a taking if a dam is built or a protecting ridge is cut, or a street's grade is altered so as to flood A's land permanently.

Where property has not been taken but merely damaged by noise and the pollution of the atmosphere the owner is not entitled to compensation unless —as in about half the state constitutions—there is an express provision for compensation in such cases. Under such express provisions, a steam railroad is liable for annoyance from smoke, noise, dirt, cinders and danger from fire to one from whom no property is taken; a street railway has been held liable for damage to land caused by inconvenience of access due to a cable road being placed between its tracks and the sidewalk; and a city which constructed a viaduct which cut off traffic between two of its important streets except by a flight of stairs and thereby reduced the value of X's property from $5000 to $1700 was held bound to compensate X for the damage.

§ 33. Compensation—condemnation proceedings.[3] The constitutional requirement is not merely for compensation but just compensation. Hence it

[2] 12 **Am Jur,** Constitutional Law, §§ 658, 673, 676–678.

Limitation applicable to action for consequential damage as result of taking or damaging of property for public use. 30 **ALR** 1190–1212; s. in 139 **ALR** 1288–1301.

Obstruction or diversion of, or other interference with, flow of surface water as taking or damaging property within constitutional provision against taking or damaging without compensation. 128 **ALR** 1195–1210.

Right of abutting owner to compensation for railroad in street under constitutional provision against damaging property for public use without compensation. 22 **ALR** 145–187.

[3] 12 **Am Jur,** Constitutional Law, §§ 634, 658.

Eminent domain: what is sufficient attempt to agree on compensation. 8 **ALR** 471–478.

Right and measure of compensation to owner of fee when telegraph or telephone line is erected along railroad right of way or highway. 8 **ALR** 1293–1311; s. in 19 **ALR** 383.

Liability upon abandonment of eminent domain proceedings for loss or expenses incurred by property owner. 31 **ALR** 352–376; 121 **ALR** 84.

Right to compensation for improvements made under authority, or color thereof, by body having power of eminent domain, before exercise of that power. 34 **ALR** 1082–1102.

Right to and remedy, in respect of damages due to negligent or delayed prosecution of condemnation proceedings. 92 **ALR** 379–386.

Validity, construction, and effect of specific provision of lease or statute relating to rights and compensation of lessee in event of condemnation. 98 **ALR** 254–262.

Right of owner or occupant of property to damages, and measure and elements thereof, because of temporary closing or obstruction during repairs or reconstruction of street or highway, under statutes in that regard. 120 **ALR** 896–906.

Right to abandon and effect of abandonment of eminent domain proceedings. 121 **ALR** 12–98.

Provision for taking or retaining possession pending appeal in condemnation proceeding. 55 **ALR** 201–220.

Injunction against exercise of power of eminent domain. 133 **ALR** 11–175.

Protection of rights of mortgagee in eminent domain proceedings. 58 **ALR** 1534–1548; s. in 110 **ALR** 542–554.

Constitutionality of provisions as to tribunal which shall fix the amount of compensation for taking of property in eminent domain, otherwise than objections that a trial by jury is necessary. 74 **ALR** 569–583.

Lack of diligence to contest a public use on ground that compensation has not been made for private property or rights as affecting right to relief. See 133 **ALR** 133–146.

was a violation of the United States Constitution for a city to take for street purposes part of a railroad right of way where only $1 was allowed therefor by the jury and state court.

Where only a part of X's tract is taken he is entitled to the value of the part taken plus any diminution in value of the rest, for example, that due to prospective noise, vibration and smoke of a steam railroad; but if the part remaining is not diminished but enhanced in value, that enhancement must be deducted unless there is an express constitutional requirement providing that there shall be no deduction.

Unless there is a constitutional requirement to that effect, compensation need not be tendered in advance of condemnation proceedings. Those proceedings need not be before a jury because they are not suits at law or in equity. Nor is it necessary that they be before a court; they may be before an administrative officer. Where attempts are made to use the land without taking any proceedings the owner may ordinarily secure an injunction till the proceedings are taken or until the aggressor will pay what the equity court decides is a fair value for the property.

CHAPTER VIII

STATE LAWS IMPAIRING THE OBLIGATIONS OF CONTRACTS

§ 34. "No state shall pass a law." [4] Section 10 of Article I of the United States Constitution provides that "No state . . . shall pass any . . . law impairing the obligation of contracts." There is no corresponding prohibition against the federal government but the fifth amendment requiring due process of law gives a measure of protection against arbitrary interference by the federal government with contracts.

Since the language is "no state shall pass a law" it refers, not to a change of judicial decision with regard either to the common law or to the construction of a state statute, but merely to an act of the state legislature or to an ordinance or bylaw passed by a municipal corporation under the authority of the legislature.

§ 35. "Of a contract." [5] The term "contract" in this connection does not include a judgment even though it is based upon breach of contract, judgments not being classified as contractual but as quasi contractual, not depending upon consent; hence a state may change at will the rate of interest to be paid on a judgment. Nor does it include a purported contract which is not enforceable because of lack of consent, or lack of consideration, failure to satisfy the statute of frauds or because of illegality. Nor does it include

[4] 12 **Am Jur**, Constitutional Law, §§ 386–388.

Paving ordinance as impairment of obligation of street railway franchise. 10 **ALR** 897–904.

Statutes in relation to interest as obnoxious to constitutional provision against impairing obligation of contracts. 87 **ALR** 462–478.

Debtor's exemption statutes as impairing obligations of existing contracts. 93 **ALR** 177–186.

Validity and construction of war legislation in nature of moratory statute. 137 **ALR** 1380–1439; s. in 147 **ALR** 1311.

Constitutional provision against impairing obligation of contracts as applied to rights or remedies of owners of property subject to assessment for local improvements. 100 **ALR** 164–179.

Constitutional provisions against impairment of obligations of contract as applied to sinking funds for retirement of municipal or other public bonds. 115 **ALR** 220–231.

Constitutionality of statute for relief of parties to public contracts because of war conditions. 137 **ALR** 1256–1262.

57 **Harv. L. R.** 512, 621, 852, The Supreme Court and the Contract Clause.

[5] 12 **Am Jur**, Constitutional Law, §§ 403–416.

marriage which is not regarded as a contract in the narrow sense but a status; hence a legislature may authorize the giving of a divorce for causes that were not grounds for divorce when the marriage was entered into.

On the other hand, the word "contract" does include a grant. This is justifiable historically because at the time the constitution was adopted a grant was called an executed contract; but a better justification is that as a matter of sound policy a grant, being entirely consensual, should receive the same protection against impairment as an ordinary contract. Hence where a state granted land to X and later, after X had conveyed the land to Y, the state undertook to annul the grant because of fraud, it was held that this did not affect Y who was ignorant of the fraud.

In 1819, in the famous Dartmouth College case, 4 Wheat 518, 4 L. Ed. 629, it was decided that the charter of a private corporation was a contract within the meaning of the constitutional prohibition and, in spite of much pertinent and forceable criticism the decision has never been overruled, but it has never been applied to charters of municipal corporations. In order to avoid the effect of the decision, most states usually provide, either by constitution or legislative enactment that all corporation charters thereafter granted shall be subject to amendment, alteration, or repeal by the legislature. Under such a statutory reservation it was held permissible to repeal the charter of corporation X and then to charter corporation Y to do the the same thing; and to enforce a prohibition against the manufacture of malt liquor. But where, before the repeal of a charter on the ground of fraud in obtaining a franchise most of the corporation stock had come into the hands of innocent purchasers, such purchasers were protected.

§ 36. ". . . Impairing the obligation. . . ." [6] Because of the police power of the states in the protection and promotion of public morals, public safety and public health the impairment of the obligations of contracts interfering therewith has been justified. Thus a state may abrogate a previously granted charter to conduct a lottery, or a slaughterhouse, or to run a railroad without being liable for the death of any person even if caused by its negligence. On somewhat similar reasoning, a grant to the Illinois Central Railroad Company by the Illinois legislature of the state's right and title to the submerged lands under Lake Michigan in the Chicago harbor for a distance of one mile from shore could be abrogated by the state because of the tremendous importance of the property to the people of the state.

On the other hand, where no such paramount public interests are involved the constitutional prohibition is applied. Thus, while a state may pass an insolvency or bankruptcy law which will validly affect contracts with its own citizens made thereafter, it cannot affect contracts already made; it cannot affect noncitizens who do not appear, not because of the constitutional prohibition but because of lack of jurisdiction.

Where a city under statutory authority issued bonds in aid of a railroad and a later statute reduced the city's taxing powers to one half of one per cent, leaving no margin to pay bonds, the act was held unconstitutional as far as the bonds were concerned. A contract made with banks exempting them from taxation may not be impaired by a later statute abrogating the exemption. An exclusive grant to a corporation to supply gas to a city by pipes in the street for fifty years was held entitled to constitutional pro-

[6] 12 Am Jur, Constitutional Law, §§ 390–398.

tection; and so was a grant to a steam railroad company to lay a double track in a wide street, public safety not being involved. But in determining whether the obligation of a corporation charter has been impaired, courts are inclined to a strict construction against the corporation. Thus a state may authorize a new bridge to compete with a bridge already built, there being no express provision that no other bridge shall be built. And an express agreement against another ferry does not bind the state as to a bridge. Also, a provision in the charter of a water company that "said company shall charge the following rates" was held to be merely a command to the company not to exceed those rates, and not a contract that the state would not reduce them.

The remedy for the enforcement of a contract is so important that any state statute reducing the effectiveness of the remedy of the obligee is prima facie unconstitutional; but mortgage moratorium laws extending the period of redemption from mortgage sales have been upheld on the ground of the emergency created by the depression beginning in 1929. On the other hand, a denial of a deficiency judgment to the mortgagee where the value of the land bid in at the foreclosure sale was equal to the mortgage debt was held not to be even a prima facie impairment of the obligation of the contract.

CHAPTER IX

OTHER CIVIL RETROACTIVE LAWS

§ 37. Constitutional provisions.[7] Apart from the prohibition to the states of passing laws impairing the obligations of contracts there is no provision in the United States Constitution against civil retroactive laws, but in the constitutions of some eight states there are express prohibitions of retroactive legislation in general. In one of those states—New Hampshire—it was held that a retroactive statute as to causes for divorce was a violation of the state constitution; and a statute authorizing amendments to existing suits to recover statutory penalties by striking out the names of improper plaintiffs was not valid because it "would be an inroad upon the conservative constitutional ideas that have prevailed in this state."

§ 38. Validating or curative statutes.[8] In the absence of constitutional provisions courts are inclined to refuse to give a retrospective operation to statutes unless the legislative language is clear. But if the language is clear, a statute will be ordinarily upheld where the effect of it is to cure a merely formal irregularity and to carry out the intention of the parties. Thus a statute undertaking to cure the invalidity of marriages where the ceremony was performed by itinerant Methodist ministers was held valid so as to make a village liable for the children of the marriage of paupers.

7 11 **Am Jur**, Constitutional Law, §§ 365–371.
Power of legislature to revive a right of action barred by limitation. 36 **ALR** 1316–1327; s. in 133 **ALR** 384–394.
Retrospective effect of statute relating to causes of action for death dependent upon prior statute. 77 **ALR** 1338–1350.
Withdrawal by constitutional amendment or legislative act of power under which political body acted in punishing act as crime, as affecting prior offenses. 89 **ALR** 1514–1521.
Character of defenses that may be cut off by retrospective legislation. 113 **ALR** 768, 769.
Constitutionality of retroactive statute curing defect in private instrument purporting to convey title or create interest in property or as to filing or recording thereof. 57 **ALR** 1197–1218.
Validity and effect, as to previously recorded instrument, of statute which places or changes time limit on effectiveness of record of mortgages or other instruments. 133 **ALR** 1325–1332.

8 11 **Am Jur**, Constitutional Law, §§ 373, 374, 379–382.

So, where judicial proceedings were irregular because land supposed to be in the county was in an adjacent county, a statute curing the irregularity was held valid. Similarly, it was held permissible for a statute to cure a formal irregularity in a tax levy where the taxpayer had an opportunity to be heard before any final judgment was rendered against him. And a federal statute increasing the tax on gifts already made was upheld where the donor, at the time the gift was made, was warned of the possible increase.

On the other hand, where the rights of third parties would be injuriously affected, the statute is likely to be held invalid as a violation of due process. Thus a statute undertaking to cure a defect in a tax assessment was held invalid as against the intervening rights of a mortgagee. Similarly, a statute which undertook to cure the defective acknowledgment of a prior trust deed was held to be invalid as against the intervening rights under a later properly acknowledged trust deed. Also a statute which undertook to declare a tax deed conclusive as to matters essential to jurisdiction was held invalid as depriving the owner of the land of his vested defense to the tax deed.

CHAPTER X

REGULATION OF COMMERCE

A. In General

§ 39. Exports, imports and tonnage.[9] Article I, section 9 of the United States Constitution provides that "No tax or duty shall be laid on articles exported from any state." But the federal government may tax exports to territorial dependencies, like Puerto Rico; and it may lay an excise tax on such articles as tobacco even though some of the goods should be later exported. A stamp tax upon bills of lading for any goods exported from the United States has been held to be a tax on exports because a bill of lading in such cases is a commercial necessity. But a federal income tax on net income of a domestic corporation is valid though part of that income is derived from the export business.

Section 10 of Article I provides that "No state shall, without consent of Congress, lay any imposts or duties on imports or exports, except what may be absolutely necessary for executing its inspection laws; and the net produce of all duties and imposts, laid by any state on imposts or exports, shall be for the use of the treasury of the United States; and all such laws shall be subject to the revision and control of the Congress."

Under this provision, if an article is imported into a state for sale therein, it was held in 1827 that the state may not tax it so long as it remains in the original package; but it was later decided that the importer cannot take advantage of this doctrine by making the package very small—for example, a package of 10 cigarettes—in order to evade the laws of the state into which the goods are being imported.

The provision as to inspection laws has been construed to apply only to property, not to persons, and hence a state may not require foreign immigrants to pay a fee for inspection to determine whether they were criminals, paupers or orphans. The inspection fees may only be high enough to cover the reasonable cost of inspection; it may not include the cost of policing; and if it is largely in excess of the cost of inspection it may be held invalid as a violation of the power of Congress to regulate interstate commerce; for

9 15 Am Jur, Customs Duties, §§ 3, 60. 48 Am Jur, Shipping, §§ 650, 651.

example, where the fee for inspecting cement was sixty times the cost of inspection in order to prevent the importation of the article into the state.

Section 10 of Article I provides that "no state shall, without the consent of Congress, lay any duty of tonnage." This refers merely to a tax where no service is performed by the state for which the tax is reasonable compensation; it does not apply where wharfage rates for the use of a wharf are graduated according to tonnage. Nor does it prevent a state from levying a general property tax on vessels having a situs within the state for taxation, though apparently such a tax may not be proportioned to tonnage.

§ 40. Foreign and interstate commerce.[10] Section 8 of Article I gives Congress power to "regulate commerce with foreign nations, and among the several states and with Indian tribes." This has been construed to mean that as far as foreign commerce is concerned, the power of Congress is exclusive but that in case of interstate commerce, it is exclusive only where the matter admits of only one uniform system or plan of regulation; in other cases it is concurrent with the states but paramount, so that if Congress acts in any field of interstate commerce this supersedes at once any state legislation even if the act of Congress is not to take effect till later.

The term "commerce" has always been construed to include not only the transportation of goods but of persons, and this includes today such transportation by railroads, automobiles, ferries or toll bridges. It was formerly apparently confined to transportation for trade purposes; but this limitation no longer applies because the free passing of persons across a bridge between two states is now regarded as commerce without regard to the purpose of their passing. The sending of telegraphic messages has been held to be commerce; and so is the business of correspondence schools. Quite recently it has been held that insurance is commerce. On the other hand, neither agriculture nor mining nor fishing nor manufacturing is commerce.

B. State Legislation

§ 41. Discrimination against interstate commerce.[1] A state statute discriminating against interstate commerce is unconstitutional. For example, a statute requiring a license fee from those peddling goods produced outside the state but not from those peddling domestic goods was held bad. So was a statute requiring animals to be slaughtered for sale to be inspected within twenty-four hours before each slaughter because it practically prohibited sales of animals slaughtered outside the state. Also, a New York statute prohibiting the sale of milk in New York if the price paid for it outside New York was less than would be paid to New York farmers in like circumstances. And a North Carolina statute which imposed an annual privilege tax of $250 on any one who, not being a regular retail merchant, displayed goods in a hotel room for the purpose of securing retail orders. Similarly an Arkansas statute forbidding the driving into the state of any automobile carrying over twenty gallons of gasoline in its gasoline tank until the state tax thereon had been paid was held bad as an interference with interstate commerce.

10 11 **Am Jur,** Commerce, §§ 2, 4–6.
51 **Harv. L. R.** 846, The Regulation of Interstate Telephone Rates.
52 **Harv. L. R.** 617, The Sales Tax in Interstate Commerce.

1 11 **Am Jur,** Commerce, §§ 20, 22.

§ **42. Nondiscriminatory taxes affecting transportation and sales.**[2] Even if there is no discrimination against interstate commerce, a state tax may be unconstitutional if it places a burden upon interstate commerce, especially if it operates to place interstate commerce at a competitive disadvantage with intrastate commerce. Thus a state tax of two to five cents a ton upon interstate freight was invalid even though there was a similar tax upon intrastate freight. A Pennsylvania tax on all corporations doing business within the state was invalid as to a corporation operating a ferry between Philadelphia and New Jersey even though all the ferry did in the state was to land passengers in Philadelphia. A tax of $8/10$ per cent upon the gross receipts of every transportation company incorporated or doing business within the state was invalid as to gross receipts from foreign or interstate commerce. An ordinance imposing an annual license tax on telegraph companies doing business in the city was invalid as a tax on an occupation engaged in interstate commerce. And a statute imposing a tax on a telegraph company on its total authorized capital as a condition of doing business in the state is also invalid.

But a bonus paid to a state for a corporate franchise may be measured by its total receipts, including receipts from interstate business; but this may not be done if there is a separate tax on the property of the corporation. A state may tax a railroad on the average number of cars in the state during the taxable year. Similarly, a state may tax a sleeping car company upon business done in the state, computing interstate business on a pro rata mileage basis, tax to be in lieu of all other taxes on property. A tax on net income of the corporation was held valid though much of its business was interstate because it was like a tax on property measured by net income. And it may tax property brought into the state for later resale to purchasers inside or outside the state if the property is there at rest on the regular taxing day.

Where Tennessee taxed interstate busses on the state highways according to their carrying capacity, this was invalid; it would have been valid if the tax had been for the use of the highways or for the expense of regulating motor traffic. But a tax by a city on wholesale dealers in soft drinks whether manufactured within or without the state was held valid there being no discrimination against drinks brought from outside the state.

Where an ice making plant was sent from Pennsylvania to Texas and set up under supervision of the vendor, such setting up was a part of the entire transaction and Texas may not require a license fee of the vendor as a condition to his suing for the price.

Where a corporation of state X keeps merely a selling office in state Y and all the business done in state Y is the soliciting of orders, such business may not be taxed by state Y. A Tennessee statute requiring a license of all drummers and persons not having a licensed house of business in Memphis but offering goods for sale by sample was held invalid as in substance a tax on interstate commerce.

§ **43. Nondiscriminatory state regulation.**[3] A nondiscriminatory regulation may be valid even though it affects interstate commerce if the court

[2] 28 **Am Jur**, Inspection Laws, § 3.
57 **Harv. L. R.** 40, Gross Receipts Taxes on Interstate Transportation and Communication.

[3] 11 **Am Jur**, Commerce, §§ 18–26.
40 **Mich L. R.** 49, The Supreme Court, the Commerce Clause and State Legislation.

thinks it is reasonably necessary for the protection of the interests of the people of the state. For example, a Texas statute forbidding the transportation into the state of cattle, horses and mules in order to prevent the spread of anthrax; a Maryland state requiring both resident and nonresident motorists before using the state highways to register their cars, attach a numbered plate and obtain operator's license; an Ohio statute requiring a license of a dealer in corporate securities, even as applied to securities sent in from other states to be sold; a North Carolina statute imposing a charge of 25 cents a ton on fertilizer to cover the cost of inspection so as to protect against fraud, a Michigan statute forbidding telegraph companies to limit their liability for nondelivery of the message to fifty times the cost of the message; a Massachusetts statute forbidding the sale of oleo colored to look like yellow butter.

In some cases the court expressly points out that the state legislation is valid until Congress acts in the matter. For example, a Kentucky statute regulating ferries between Ohio and Kentucky was held valid, the states having regulated ferries for seventy-five years and there being no action by Congress. Similarly it was held proper for Philadelphia to build a bridge across the Schuylkill River, a navigable stream within the state until Congress should act in the matter. A Minnesota statute fixing intrastate rates was held valid till Congress, because of the interdependence of intrastate and interstate railroad operations, should regulate both. So was a Georgia statute requiring speed of railroad trains to be checked at railroad crossings. And a New York statute regulating rates at which natural gas should be furnished from Pennsylvania wells to domestic consumers was held valid there being no congressional action in the matter.

On the other hand some state statutes have been held invalid without regard to any possible future action of Congress. For example, a Washington statute operating to exclude an interstate auto stage line on the ground that there were already adequate facilities, the purpose being not to protect highways but to prevent competition; a Kansas statute requiring all foreign corporations to file reports, as applied to International Correspondence Schools; a South Dakota statute requiring all foreign corporations, as a condition precedent to suing in the courts of the state, to file a copy of its charter with the Secretary of State, appoint a resident agent upon whom process may be served and pay a fee of $25, the requirements having no natural or reasonable relation to the right to sue; an Illinois statute penalizing unjust discrimination against shippers, as applied to interstate shipments. Where Congress had already acted, a Wisconsin statute requiring all corn syrup containing over 75% of glucose to be labelled "glucose, flavored with . . ." was held invalid as requiring a label not required by the federal Pure Food and Drug Act, and therefore an interference therewith.

Since the power of Congress over foreign commerce is exclusive, a city ordinance exacting a license fee for each boat engaged in ferrying from the city over to Canada was held invalid.

C. Power of Congress and the Federal Courts—Maritime Power

§ 44. Power of Congress and the Federal courts.[4] The power of Congress over interstate commerce seems to be limited only by the due process clause of the fifth amendment. It may authorize the construction of interstate railways and bridges and the exercise of the power of eminent domain in aid

4 11 **Am Jur,** Commerce, §§ 9–17.

thereof; it may regulate interstate railway rates throughout the country, and while it has no general power to regulate intrastate rates it may do so if interstate and intrastate commerce are so mingled together that Congress may not make its regulation effective without incidentally regulating intrastate rates. Under the Anti-trust Act it may forbid a combination of railroads to maintain interstate rates and may forbid a single corporation to own the stock of two competing railways. It may compel railways to use safety appliances on interstate traffic. It may regulate the liability of interstate railroads to their employees even where the employee was injured by a negligent employee engaged only in intrastate traffic. It may regulate the hours of labor of interstate railroad employees engaged in moving trains. It may forbid the transportation of lottery tickets from one state to another; and it may enact, meat inspection and pure food and drug laws designed to exclude from interstate traffic unhealthful or adulterated food and drug products.

In aid of congressional legislation affecting interstate commerce the federal courts may decree the dissolution of a combination of corporations controlling the tobacco business. And even if there has been no express legislation on the matter, federal courts may enjoin the obstruction of trains engaged in interstate commerce or in carrying the mails.

§ 45. Maritime power.[5] Section 2 of Article III of the United States Constitution provides that the federal judicial power shall extend to all cases of admiralty and maritime jurisdiction, which has been construed to extend to all the navigable rivers, canals and lakes that are accessible by water from any other state. The result is that even intrastate commerce on such waters is subject to the control of Congress. Thus a federal statute limiting liability of owners of American vessels for certain losses to the value of their interest in the vessel and cargo was held valid as part of maritime law without regard to the power of Congress over foreign commerce. An Indiana statute imposing liability for tortious death resulting from a collision on the Ohio river within Indiana was held valid till Congress should legislate on the subject. But a state may not create liens upon foreign vessels where such liens are not authorized by general maritime law. And a New York state court may not give a workmen's compensation award against a steamship company for the death of a stevedore while unloading a ship in New York harbor because it would interfere with uniformity of maritime law.

CHAPTER XI

JURISDICTION OF FEDERAL COURTS—PRIVILEGES AND IMMUNITIES CLAUSES

§ 46. In general—in Federal questions.[6]—The federal courts are given jurisdiction over all cases involving federal questions, that is, all questions in law and equity arising under the United States Constitution, laws or treaties and all cases of admiralty or maritime jurisdiction. They are also given jurisdiction over cases having the following parties, regardless of the questions involved: (1) when ambassadors, public ministers or consuls are parties; (2) when the United States is a party; (3) where the suit is between two or more states; (4) where the suit is between state and citizens of another state; (5) where the suit is between citizens of different states; (6)

[5] 48 **Am Jur**, Shipping, §§ 6–16.

[6] 54 **Am Jur**, United States Courts, §§ 6–141.

where the suit is between a state or its citizens on one side and foreign states or aliens on the other.

While a contest of a will is within the language "suits of a civil nature at common law or in equity," it has been held that a proceeding to probate a will is not, because there is no contest.

§ 47. Diverse citizenship.[7] Where jurisdiction is based upon diverse citizenship of the parties, since the District of Columbia is not a state, the federal courts have no jurisdiction over a contest between the citizens of a state and citizens of the District. Where a corporation is a party it is regarded—for this purpose—as a citizen of the state in which it was incorporated, the usual statement being that there is a conclusive presumption that the members of the corporation are citizens of the state creating the corporation.

Where jurisdiction is based upon diverse citizenship, Congress has limited the jurisdiction of the federal courts to cases involving $3,000 or more. While there is no constitutional provision for removal of such cases from the ordinary state courts, it is well settled that if A of state X sues B of state Y in the state courts of state X, B may have the case removed to the federal courts if $3,000 or more is involved.

Where jurisdiction of the federal courts is based upon diverse citizenship of the parties, the federal court is bound to follow the decision of the state court in which it is sitting unless the state law on the point is unsettled. The rule was formerly otherwise, under the decision of Swift v. Tyson, as to questions of general or commercial law, but that decision was overruled in 1938 by Erie Railroad v. Tompkins.

§ 48. The Eleventh Amendment—immunity of a sovereign state from suit.[8] The Constitution provided for suits "between a state and citizens of another state." In 1792, a creditor of Georgia living in another state brought suit against Georgia in the United States Supreme Court and it was held that he was entitled to do so. This led to the eleventh amendment providing that "the judicial power of the United States shall not be construed to extend to any suit at law or in equity, commenced or prosecuted against one of the United States by citizens of another state, or by citizens or subjects of any foreign state." Where, in order to evade the eleventh amendment A, having a claim against state X assigned it to state Y for purpose of suit and state Y sued state X in the United States Supreme Court on the assigned claim, it was held that the action did not lie, state Y not being the real party in interest; but it has been held otherwise where it was an absolute assignment to state Y.

About sixty years ago a citizen of Louisiana brought suit in the federal courts against Louisiana seeking to collect certain bonds, arguing that he was entitled to do so because not covered by the eleventh amendment. But it was held that this suit was not maintainable because of the well-established doctrine that no sovereign may be sued without its consent.

Although a suit may not be brought against a state by a citizen of that or any other state, a suit may be brought in the federal courts by a state against the citizens of another state. Thus Georgia was held entitled to an injunctions against citizens of Tennessee discharging noxious gases across the state line into Georgia causing damage to property in Georgia.

[7] 54 **Am Jur,** United States Courts, §§ 57–135.

[8] 11 **Am Jur,** Constitutional Law, § 311.

§ 49. Suits by and between states and the United States.[9] Though a state may not be sued in any court by any citizen, it may be sued by the United States in the United States Supreme Court under the provision as to cases to which the United States is a party and such a suit was brought by the United States against Texas in regard to the boundary line between Texas and Oklahoma Territory. But a state, being a subordinate sovereign may not sue the United States without the consent of the latter.

Under the provision for suits in the United States Supreme Court between states, a suit was maintained between Virginia and West Virginia to compel the latter to contribute her share of the public debt which Virginia had at the time the state was divided, but the exact way in which the judgment should be enforced was expressly left undecided.

§ 50. Privileges and immunities of citizens.[10] Section 2 of Article IV of the Constitution provides that "The citizens of each state shall be entitled to all the privileges and immunities of citizens of the several states." Because of this provision, a state may not impose a heavier tax on nonresidents than upon residents on transfer of property by will. Nor may it deny equality of right to nonresident creditors in the distribution of assets of a corporation which has been doing business in the state. But it may protect its own citizens by forbidding nonresidents from gathering oysters within the state, and by forbidding the killing of game for transportation out of the state. And it may deny the right to practice medicine to physicians who have practiced for ten years in another state but allow the right to those who have practiced for that period within the state.

It is well settled that a corporation organized in state X is not entitled to do business in state Y because a corporation is not a citizen within the meaning of this provision.

The fourteenth amendment to the Constitution provides that "No state shall make or enforce any law which shall abridge the privileges or immunities of citizens of the United States." These privileges and immunities are those derived from the United States government, such as the right to use navigable streams, the right to demand government protection when out of the country, the right to engage in foreign and interstate commerce, and the rights secured by the various provisions of the thirteenth, fourteenth and fifteenth amendments. It has been held that this provision was aimed only at state action and hence the act of Congress passed in 1875 known as the Civil Rights Act, providing that all persons in the United States should be entitled to equal privileges in inns, public conveyances and places of amusement, without discrimination on account of race, color or previous condition of servitude, was unconstitutional because it was not aimed at discriminations by any of the states but at discriminations by individuals.

9 49 **Am Jur,** Statutes, §§ 80-90.

10 12 **Am Jur,** Constitutional Law, §§ 446-467.

ADMINISTRATIVE LAW

CHAPTER I

IN GENERAL

§ 1. The need for administrative tribunals.[1] Since the creation of the Interstate Commerce Commission in 1887 and especially since 1933 there has

[1] 42 **Am Jur,** Public Administrative Law, §§ 4, 5.

Jurisdiction of Public Service Commission over carriers transporting by motor trucks or busses. 1 **ALR** 1460–1463; s. in 9 **ALR** 1011–1014; 51 **ALR** 820–828; 103 **ALR** 268–295.

Constitutionality, construction, and application of Emergency Price Control Act. 146 **ALR** 718–732; s. in 148 **ALR** 1429–1441; 149 **ALR** 1427–1473; 150 **ALR** 1470–1480.

Power of Public Service Commission with respect to regulation of street railways 5 **ALR** 36–79; s. in 39 **ALR** 1517–1542.

Validity and construction of statute creating Federal Trade Commission. 6 **ALR** 366, 367; s. in 11 **ALR** 797–799; 18 **ALR** 549–554; 30 **ALR** 1129–1144; 32 **ALR** 792, 793; 51 **ALR** 331–336; 68 **ALR** 847–850; 79 **ALR** 1200–1207

Power of Public Service Commission to require public utility to extend gas service into new territory. 31 **ALR** 333–337.

Regulating issuance of securities by public utilities through Public Service Commissions. 41 **ALR** 889–925.

Constitutionality, construction, application and effect of statute requiring or authorizing judicial or administrative approval before issuance or sale of municipal bonds. 87 **ALR** 706–720; s. in 102 **ALR** 90–111.

Right of attorney general to represent or serve administrative officer or body to exclusion of attorney employed by such officer or body. 137 **ALR** 818–829.

36 **Harv. L. R.** 405, 583, Administrative Tribunals.

42 **Col. L. R.** 89, Dean Pound and Administrative Law.

42 **Col. L. R.** 804, Dean Pound's Errors about Administrative Agencies.

41 **Col. L. R.** 589, Administrative Law Investigation Comes of Age.

41 **Col. L. R.** 628, Administrative Technique—The Report on Administrative Procedure.

41 **Col. L. R.** 617, Effect in Practice of the Report on Administrative Procedure.

37 **Col. L. R.** 1, The Supreme Court and Administrative Law.

47 **Yale L. J.** 603, Administrative Law and Federal Expenditures.

47 **Yale L. J.** 577, Administrative Law and the Role of Discretion.

47 **Yale L. J.** 519, Administrative Policies and the Courts.

been a large increase in the number of administrative tribunals—boards, commissions and bureaus. For the most part the increase has been due to sheer necessity, precipitated by the growing complexity of modern life and to the inability of legislatures and the ordinary courts to deal effectively therewith.

The advantage of the administrative tribunal over the ordinary court lies in its flexibility, its promptness of decision, its greater ability to take advantage of expert knowledge, especially in technical fields, and to lay down rules for the future only. The advantage over the legislature lies in its substantial avoidance of political partisanship, its greater ability to take advantage of expert knowledge, its greater flexibility in dealing with local variety, with details, with unknown future conditions and with emergencies.

Administrative tribunals have been criticized upon various grounds. The most important of these are: they violate the doctrine of the separation of powers and the doctrine forbidding the delegation of legislative power and because they tend toward the legalizing of arbitrary and irresponsible action.

§ 2. Separation of powers.[2] It is conceded that the establishment of administrative tribunals does violate any strict statement of the doctrine of separation of powers but advocates of the tribunals point out that there never has been any such strict doctrine and that while there are a few state constitutions that expressly state the doctrine, there is no statement in the United States Constitution or in the constitution of the other states in regard to the matter. Where there was an express provision in a state constitution the state supreme court, in an advisory opinion, stated that it was not permissible to set up a court of justice in the executive department of the state government.

47 **Yale L. J.** 538, Concepts and Policies in Anglo—American Administrative Law Theory.

51 **Yale L. J.** 367, "When 'Omer Smote 'is Bloomin' Lyre."

42 **Mich. L. R.** 51, The Administrative Crime, Its Creation and Punishment by Administrative Agencies.

41 **Mich. L. R.** 269, If there Were Angels.

40 **Mich. L. R.** 378, Parties to Administrative Proceedings.

40 **Mich L. R.** 501, Reform of Administrative Procedure.

30 **Calif. L. R.** 507, Court Review of Administrative Decisions in California.

11 **U. of Chicago L. R.** 91, Implied Limitations on Regulatory Powers in Administrative Law.

29 **Va. L. R.** 82, Comparative Administrative Law.

29 **Va. L. R.** 347, Practice before the Industrial Commission.

91 **U. of Pa. L. R.** 118, Comparative Administrative Law—The Continental Alternative.

91 **U. of Pa. L. R.** 36, Administrative Law and Droit Administratif.

92 **U. of Pa. L. R.** 412, Administrative Agencies under Fire.

28 **Corn. L. Q.** 177, The Authority Plan—Tool of Modern Government.

30 **Ky. L. J.** 137, Administrative Hearings under the Federal Constitution.

14 **Miss. L. J.** 412, The Literature of Administrative Law.

22 **Boston U. L. R.** 1, The President as Chief Administrator.

12 **Fordham L. R.** 130, Personal Tort Liability of Administrative Officials.

[2] 42 **Am Jur**, Public Administrative Law, § 28.

Constitutionality of legislative delegation of powers to prescribe or vary regulations concerning motor vehicles used on highways. 87 **ALR** 546–555.

Constitutionality, construction, and application of statute for determination by executive or administrative board of questions in relation to motor vehicle accidents. 110 **ALR** 826.

Delegation to board or officer of police power to require vacation, destruction, or repair of individual building deemed by such officer or board unsafe or insanitary, apart from noncompliance with specific regulation. 114 **ALR** 446–450.

Power or discretion of civil service commission in respect of classifying or grading positions in civil service. 134 **ALR** 1103–1120.

Statute relating to closing of bank and assessment of stockholders as subject to constitutional objection of conferring judicial power upon administrative or executive officers. 78 **ALR** 774–779.

Statute conferring power upon administrative body in respect to the parole of prisoners, or the discharge of parolees, as unconstitutional infringement of power of executive or judiciary. 143 **ALR** 1486–1503.

Delegation by municipality of its powers as to building regulations. 43 **ALR** 834–839; s. in 46 **ALR** 88, 89.

§ 3. Delegation of legislative power.[3] While there is no prohibition of the delegation of legislative power in the federal or in any of the state constitutions, such delegation has frequently been held invalid because inconsistent with the doctrine in the law of agency that a delegated power cannot be redelegated; that is, since the legislature's power has been delegated to it by the people it cannot be delegated by it to another body or to an individual.

It is conceded, of course, that the legislature may not entirely alien its power. And where Congress authorized the President to prohibit the transportation in interstate and foreign commerce of petroleum and products thereof; and later where it authorized him to prescribe a code of fair competition in any industry in which no such code existed, both attempts were held invalid because Congress furnished no standard to guide the President in his action. On the other hand, where Congress authorized the President to reduce the compensation of civil service employees according to the cost of living index, and in the Tariff Act of 1922 to adjust the tariff on imported articles according to a comparison of the costs of production of such articles here and abroad, such statutes were held valid on the ground that they did furnish a standard of action for the President, in spite of the fact that the question of cost of production is very difficult and complicated.

As to what amounts to a standard of action sufficiently definite to validate a delegation of power, the cases are not harmonious. Thus, where a New York statute authorized the governor to appoint a commission to determine the maximum price to be charged to consumers by gas and electric light companies within the limits fixed by law, this was upheld because the law requires that rates be reasonable and this was a sufficiently definite standard. Similarly, where the Food and Drug Act required that the quantity of contents of packages be plainly marked on the outside with a proviso that the administrative officers might validate reasonable variations and tolerances and exemptions as to small packages, the proviso was held valid. Where the Secretary of War was authorized to suppress bawdyhouses within such distance of military camps as he might deem needful and he fixed a distance of five miles, both the statute and the action thereunder were upheld. And movie censorship has been upheld though the censors had no standard except sense and experience.

On the other hand, a city ordinance directing that wages on a city construction job should be not less than the prevailing wages to be determined by wages paid to members of labor unions was held invalid as a delegation of legislative power to labor unions. A statute providing that licenses of soft drink stores may be revoked by the Commissioner of Public Safety in his discretion for disorderly or immoral conduct or gambling on the premises was held bad because there was no specifically prescribed rule of action. A statute authorizing the state fire marshal to decide whether a building is a fire hazard and to order its removal was held bad because it did not fix any rules by which the official was to be guided. And a New York statute authorizing the Alcoholic Beverage Control Board to adopt rules for the

3 42 **Am Jur,** Public Administrative Law, §§ 43–52.

Delegation of legislative or judicial power to housing authorities. 130 **ALR** 1082.

Validity of statute or ordinance vesting discretion in public officials without prescribing a rule of action. 12 **ALR** 1435–1455; s. in 54 **ALR** 1104–1116; 92 **ALR** 400–419.

Discretion of administrative officers as to changing boundaries of school district. 65 **ALR** 1523–1552; s. in 135 **ALR** 1096–1123.

Discretion of civil service commission as regards promotional examinations for eligible list. 75 **ALR** 1234–1237.

regulation of the manufacture and sale of beer, violation of any such rule to be a misdemeanor if such rule should so provide, was held bad as an attempt to delegate to the board whether a violation of their rules should constitute a crime.

It has long been settled that a legislature may delegate legislative power to municipal corporations because municipal needs can be better perceived by the inhabitants of the locality and it has been argued that the same argument should apply to a delegation of power to an administrative body which is better acquainted than is the legislature with the needs of the particular industry.

While the 14th Amendment does not require a separation of powers—because due process does not necessarily mean judicial process—and does not prohibit the delegation of legislative power, yet if the delegation by the legislature is of uncontrolled discretion the statute may be held to be a violation of the due process provision because it might be descriminatory and oppressive in its operation.

§ 4. Suggested safeguards against arbitrary action.[4] The fundamental objection to administrative tribunals is not that they violate the letter of the Constitution but that where—as usual—the tribunal acts as legislature, prosecuting attorney, judge and sheriff, there is so much possibility of arbitrary and irresponsible action, especially since the personnel have little or no legal training. Several possible safeguards against such arbitrary and irresponsible action have been suggested. One is that legislation be delegated not to the administrative tribunal but to a sublegislature so as to achieve uniformity in procedure among the various tribunals. Another is that in certain fields, like the field of labor, advisory committees representing the specially affected interests should be appointed to assist in the drafting of rules. Another is that findings by the tribunal should precede legislation. Still another is that the decisions of the tribunal should be subject to review either in the already established courts or in courts to be established for that purpose. But in the long run perhaps the most effective single safeguard would be to place the administrative personnel in the civil service so that its members could look forward to their work as a career and gradually develop a professional attitude comparable to that of lawyer and judge.

CHAPTER II

NOTICE

§ 5. The right to notice.[5] When the legislature acts, neither fair hearing nor notice to the parties to be affected by the legislation is necessary. When courts act, both fair hearing and notice are practically always necessary. To what extent should there be notice or fair hearing before an administrative tribunal which exercises both legislative and judicial powers?

When either a constitution or a statute requires fair hearing and notice such requirement must be observed. Where there is no such requirement usage may determine that no fair hearing or notice is necessary. For example, where a state tax commission decides that all the property throughout

4 42 **Am Jur,** Public Administrative Law, §§ 186–250.
56 **Harv. L. R.** 704, Administrative Procedure Re-examined.

5 42 **Am Jur,** Public Administrative Law, §§ 119, 120, 135.

a county has been undervalued it may, without notice, raise the valuation so as to equalize it with the rest of the state; and fish and game commissioners may, without notice, declare that putting sawdust in a stream is a nuisance and order it stopped even though it has been done for many years. So, health officers may order the arrest of a prostitute, examine her to determine whether she has a venereal disease and quarantine her; and cheap gambling devices like musical slot machines may be seized and confiscated.

Or usage may determine that the administrative agency may act without giving notice, subject to being held liable in damages later if such action cannot be justified. Sometimes this is because of emergency; for example. the destruction of milk from supposedly tuberculous cows or other supposedly unwholesome food; or the destruction of horses supposedly afflicted with glanders; or of steers supposedly afflicted with anthrax. Sometimes such summary action is justified because of the small value of the property involved and the proportionally large expense of a hearing; for example, officers may be authorized to destroy fish nets being illegally used, each net being worth about fifteen dollars. Usage also permits dirt to be taken to repair a street, compensation therefor to be fixed later; and to permit a street to be paved if opportunity is given to be heard later.

§ 6. **Adequacy of notice.**[6] If notice is expressly required either by constitution or by statute or if the court decides that notice is required as a matter of due process of law the question then arises as to adequacy of the notice. If the statute requiring notice provides for the form and manner of giving notice—whether personal or by publication—such provision must be rigidly carried out.

If there is no express provision as to notice in either constitution or statute but the court decides that notice is necessary in order to satisfy the due process of law requirement, it is usually sufficient if all the parties to be affected by the decision of the administrative tribunal have actual notice of the proceedings and the issues to be decided; but actual notice merely to the parties to the proceeding is not enough where, if due notice had been given, other persons interested in the matter might have come in.

If the persons upon whom notice has been served reasonably think that the notice served upon them is not adequate they may be able to get an order of the tribunal for a bill of particulars, as in case of the ordinary judicial proceeding.

Where there are so many persons to be affected by the proceedings that it is impractical to serve notice on all of them it is usually enough to serve notice on some members of a class as representative of the entire class. If indispensable parties have been omitted they should be added later regardless of the expense; merely proper parties should be added later only if the expense of doing so would be relatively small.

Persons not entitled to notice may be allowed to intervene in the proceedings if they can convince the administrative tribunal that they have a substantial interest in the outcome; where such intervention is allowed the interveners have most, if not all, of the rights of parties.

In some classes of cases where no personal liability will result notice need not be personal; for example, in special assessment proceedings it is sufficient to notify the person who paid taxes on the land the preceding year.

6 42 **Am Jur,** Public Administrative Law, §§ 119, 120, 135.

Where personal notice is necessary it would seem that notice by registered mail should be sufficient.

CHAPTER III

FAIR HEARING

§ 7. In general.[7] Assuming that a fair hearing has been made necessary either by constitution, by statute or by judicial interpretation of the due process clause the question arises as to what constitutes a fair hearing.

The statutes establishing administrative agencies have the goal of cheap, expeditious, informal justice, but courts have sometimes been inclined to forget this and to impose the standards of fair hearing which have developed during the long history of the ordinary judicial courts. However, it seems to be agreed that while the proceedings may be summary and informal they must usually be unbiased and dispassionate and conducted in an honest and reasonably intelligent attempt to ascertain the truth.

In holding that there has not been a fair hearing in a particular case a court may come to that conclusion not because of any one particular defect but because the proceedings as a whole show bias and arbitrariness, as in the 1920 Boston wholesale raid upon alien communists, where citizens were arrested and held over night, private rooms were searched without warrants and the law enforcing officials acted like a mob.

Even though a hearing might not otherwise have been demanded as of right yet if the regulations of the administrative agency provide for one, it may be insisted on.

The right to a hearing usually includes the right to be represented thereat by counsel, especially where, as in deportation proceedings, the general prejudice against aliens is likely to be intensified. As to whether the administrative agency may determine who shall act as counsel, as to whether only lawyers may so act, as to whether evidence of special fitness may be required—on all these questions there is conflict of authority due partly to diversity between the various agencies and partly to the fact that many lawyers have not and many nonlawyers have become acquainted with administrative law practice.

There seems to be no constitutional right to insist that the testimony be under oath or to have compulsory process to procure testimony. While the opportunity to cross-examine is regarded as of great importance in the judicial courts and may usually be insisted upon, the requirement is not enforced as rigidly in administrative proceedings. For example, in a production costs hearing under a flexible tariff proceeding there is no right to cross-examine a competitor in order to find out his production costs, the hearing in such a case being regarded as legislative in character; and in rate-fixing proceedings before a public utility commission affidavits are accepted without the personal appearance of the affiant.

§ 8. Official records—official knowledge—expert testimony.[8] While general official records may be used to check testimony without according the right to cross-examine the authors, records of a special ex parte proceeding may not be thus used and no official records may be used unless they are introduced in evidence. And a decision based upon the investigation of the

7 42 **Am Jur**, Public Administrative Law, §§ 134–144.

8 42 **Am Jur**, Public Administrative Law, §§ 128–133.

tribunal rather than upon the testimony of witnesses should not be upheld.

On the other hand the tribunal of an administrative agency may, like the judge in an ordinary court, take judicial notice of matters of common knowledge and to some extent it may act upon the specialized knowledge acquired through official experience in agency work. For example, an industrial accident board was entitled to act upon its specialized knowledge that an income of $26 a week was not adequate for a family of five persons; and a workmen's compensation board, that inguinal hernia was not traumatic though the physician testified to the contrary.

Like a court an administrative tribunal can take judicial knowledge that there had been a financial depression and a decline in market values but may not take judicial notice of the extent of such a decline as a basis for reducing public utility rates.

Where expert testimony runs strongly in one direction and the tribunal decides the other way its decision is likely to be set aside; but the wisdom of such a holding has been questioned where the testimony was in regard to a matter highly conjectural and uncertain, such as value.

§ 9. **Hearsay.**[9] It is common for statutes to provide that administrative tribunals shall not be bound by "technical rules of evidence" or by "common law and statutory rules of evidence." Under such provisions it would seem logical to hold that such tribunals might base their findings entirely on such hearsay as responsible persons are accustomed to rely upon, especially since the exclusion of hearsay in Anglo American law stems from trial by jury, an unlearned tribunal likely to be misled by such testimony. But such has been the vitality of the rule that it is usually held that while it is not reversible error to admit hearsay there must be a residuum of legal evidence sufficient to support the tribunal's decision; but there is no requirement that such legal evidence shall consist of other than circumstantial evidence. Where the tribunal is permitted to act upon hearsay alone the personnel of the tribunal should be selected carefully and mere rumor or uncorroborated hearsay should be excluded.

§ 10. **The tribunal personnel.**[10] Ordinarily administrative proceedings, must be held before an unbiased tribunal. Thus an owner of adjacent premises is not qualified to sit on a commission while it is passing upon the application for a liquor license; and bias shown by the legal examiner in a hearing before the National Labor Relations Board was held sufficient to invalidate his findings.

On the other hand, the necessities of the situation may be such that bias in the tribunal will not affect its decision. Thus a state medical board was entitled to revoke A's license to practice medicine for diagnosing cases over the radio though the members of the board were prejudiced against him, there being no other tribunal to act in the matter, the court pointing out that if the rule were otherwise then "any lawyer or doctor who commits an offense so grave that it shocks every right thinking person has an irrevocable license to practice his profession if he can get the news of his offense to the court or board before the trial begins." And where a public service

[9] 42 **Am Jur**, Public Administrative Law, § 129.
Hearsay in proceeding for suspension or revocation of license to conduct business or profession. 142 **ALR** 1388–1392.

[10] 42 **Am Jur**, Public Administrative Law, §§ 18–24.

commission was the only tribunal that could pass upon public utility rates, opinions expressed by a member during his campaign for election were held not sufficient to disqualify him. But where disbarment proceedings were brought against X before the Federal Communications Commission and an affidavit was filed by X that the chairman of the commission, having helped to formulate the charges against X, was biased against him, it was held that the commission had no choice except to disqualify its chairman.

It is, of course, desirable that the one who makes the decision at the end of administrative proceedings should have heard the testimony; and that "the one who decides must hear" was stated by the United States Supreme Court in what is usually referred to as the first Morgan case, which held that an allegation that the Secretary of Agriculture had fixed maximum rates of commission to be charged by brokers in buying and selling livestock at the Kansas City stockyards, without his hearing or reading any of the testimony, must be answered. On the other hand, it is the established practice before such large administrative tribunals as the Interstate Commerce Commission, the Securities and Exchange Commission, and the Federal Communications Commission that the hearings are conducted before legal examiners, in somewhat the same way as hearings before an equity court are sometimes conducted by special masters or referees appointed for that purpose by the court.

CHAPTER IV

FINDINGS

§ 11. Intermediate.[1] Must an administrative tribunal, before making its decision, make a statement of its findings and give an opportunity of examination thereof to the parties before it? It was thus held by the United States Supreme Court in what is usually referred to as the second Morgan case, the court remarking that "the proceeding had all the essential elements of contested litigation, with the Government and its counsel on one side and the appellants and their counsel on the other." In criticism of this decision the Secretary of Agriculture argued that such a requirement was a serious interference with the promptness so necessary to prompt action by administrative agencies. And the United States Supreme Court later refused to impose the requirement on the National Labor Relations Board in an unfair labor practice proceeding against a telegraph company for refusing, because of union activity, to receive back strikers after the strike was over, no harm to the company because of failure to file an intermediate report having been shown.

§ 12. Final.[2] Where a statute expressly finds that a final decision by an administrative tribunal shall be accompanied by a statement of findings of fact, such statute must, of course, be complied with. In the absence of such express requirement, courts are inclined to read the requirement into the statute as a means of protection against arbitrary action by the tribunal. Thus, where a statute provided that certain aliens be deported "if the Secre-

[1] 42 **Am Jur,** Public Administrative Law, §§ 147–185.

[2] 42 **Am Jur,** Public Administrative Law, §§ 147–185.

Necessity, form, and contents of express finding of fact to support administrative determinations. 146 **ALR** 209–239.

11 **Fordham L. R.** 30, Administrative Findings of Fact.

27 **Wash. U. L. Q.** 62, 169, Administrative Findings of Fact.

tary of Labor, after hearing, finds that such aliens are undesirable residents of the United States" a statement of his findings was necessary to give him jurisdiction. Where a statute authorized the Interstate Commerce Commission to order the installation of safety devices to eliminate "unnecessary peril to life and limb," and the commission ordered railroads to substitute power reverse gear for hand reverse gear, it was necessary for it to state its findings that hand reverse gear caused "unnecessary peril to life and limb." And where a Kansas statute authorized the Public Utilities Commission to fix and order a variation of existing electric rates if it found such rates to be unjust, unreasonable, unjustly discriminatory or unjustly preferential, the United States Supreme Court held that the commission's rate order was defective because it contained no statement of its finding that the rates were unreasonable or otherwise within the terms of the statute. But the Kansas Supreme Court declined to follow this case on the ground the action of the commission fairly implied the existence of rates that were unreasonable or otherwise covered by the language of the statute.

Where such a statement of findings of fact is held to be necessary it is sufficient to state ultimate, not evidential, facts. Where the range of the investigation is very broad, detailed and technical as in case of proceedings before the Securities and Exchange Commission it has been argued that making a statement of findings is so burdensome that it should not be insisted upon.

CHAPTER V

JUDICIAL CONTROL OF ADMINISTRATIVE ACTION

§ 13. Scope.[3] A statute may expressly make administrative action final as to questions of fact and limit review on questions of law unless such action has violated the constitutional requirements of due process and just compensation, in which case there is a right to a judicial determination.

Where there is no such express statutory provision it is usually held that findings of fact are final if there was evidence to support them, the courts' attitude in this respect being somewhat similar to their attitude toward a jury verdict. If the findings of fact are in a highly technical field the courts are likely not to disturb them, but it is otherwise if a question of fraud or unfair conduct is involved.

If a public utility contends that the rates fixed by a public service commission are so low as to be confiscatory, the utility is entitled to have this

3 42 **Am Jur,** Public Administrative Law, §§ 206–208.

Member of governmental board voting on measure involving his personal interest. 133 **ALR** 1257–1270.

Assumption of jurisdiction by court before completion of administrative procedure as ground of prohibition. 132 **ALR** 738–741.

Refusal of amusement license or permit as subject to judicial review. 124 **ALR** 247–272.

Practice or procedure for testing validity or scope of the command of subpoena duces tecum in proceedings before legislative bodies, administrative tribunals, etc. 130 **ALR** 339.

Approval of or refusal to approve bond of public officer as subject of judicial review. 134 **ALR** 1359–1374.

Justiciable controversy within Declaratory Judgment Act as predicable upon advice, opinion, or ruling of public administrative officer. 149 **ALR** 349–369.

Conclusiveness of governor's decision in removing officers. 52 **ALR** 7–33; s. in 92 **ALR** 998–1002.

Conclusiveness of official determination of existence of emergency within the contemplation of constitutional or statutory provisions permitting excess of maximum limit of tax or indebtedness in an "emergency." 90 **ALR** 328–330.

Conclusiveness of assessment of statutory liability of stockholders of national banks. 90 **ALR** 1003–1071.

Right to maintain action against carrier on ground that rates which were filed and published by carrier pursuant to law were excessive. 97 **ALR** 406–431.

48 **Yale L. J.** 981, Exhaustion of Administrative Remedies.

question passed upon judicially, but whether there should be a retrial of the issue of confiscation or merely an independent judicial consideration of the record does not seem to be settled. If there is a retrial the result may be that the judgment of the court will be substituted for that of the administrative tribunal.

§ 14. Remedies and methods of control.[4] Judicial review is sometimes expressly provided for by statute; apart from such a statute there are several remedies, one or more of which may be available. If the administrative action has resulted in imprisonment the person so detained may raise the question of the legality of the imprisonment by a writ of habeas corpus.

If threatened administrative action would allegedly result in irreparable damage to the petitioner, such as the imposition on a public utility of confiscatory rates, the usual way of raising that question is by a suit in equity against enforcement of the rates by the public utility commission.

If the administrative action would result in the waste of public funds or property an appropriate remedy would be a taxpayers' suit.

An administrative official who is uncertain of his duties and powers and does not wish to risk liability for unauthorized acts may raise the question of the constitutionality of the interpretation of the statute under which he acts by an action for a declaratory judgment.

In some states the constitutionality of the statute under which the administrative officer is acting may be tested by quo warranto proceedings brought against the officer demanding to know by what warrant or authority he is acting.

§ 15. Same—mandamus.[5] Where it is the duty of the administrative officer to perform a ministerial act, such performance may usually be compelled by utilizing the extraordinary common-law remedy of mandamus. In such an action the officer may not raise the question of the constitutionality of the statute imposing the duty unless, perhaps, his action would result in the waste of public funds and he is the only one to raise the question.

Where a question of fact is involved the applicant should seek an alternative writ which will be made peremptory after the question of fact is decided favorably.

Where it is the duty of an administrative tribunal to act judicially mandamus lies to compel it to act but not to act in a particular manner.

Where an administrative official states in advance that he will not do his duty, mandamus may lie though the time for action has not yet come.

In the following cases the duty was held to be ministerial and mandamus lay: to correct a mistake of including plaintiff's lot in special assessment proceedings for repaving a street; to issue hotel barroom license to one who may have been guilty of keeping a disorderly place but who had not been

[4] 42 **Am Jur**, Public Administrative Law, §§ 227–237.

Injunction against legislative body of state or municipality. 140 **ALR** 439–455.

Availability of writ of prohibition as means of controlling administrative or executive boards or officers. 115 **ALR** 3–35.

Right of public officer or board to appeal from a judicial decision affecting his or its order or decision. 117 **ALR** 216–222.

Judicial review of decision, on merits, of claim upon public pension fund. 117 **ALR** 1408–1413.

Necessity of some evidence as hearing to support decision of public board or official required to be made after or upon hearing. 123 **ALR** 1349–1352.

56 **Harv. L. R.** 1125, Discovery against Federal Administrative Agencies.

[5] 42 **Am Jur**, Public Administrative Law, § 229.

Change of incumbent of office or of personnel of board or other official body as affecting mandamus proceeding previously commenced. 102 **ALR** 943–964.

convicted thereof; to issue permit to construct a hospital though it might impair property values in the vicinity; to compel a sewer commissioner to pay for work done under contract to construct a sewer system; to compel a mayor to sign bonds for the purchase of fire apparatus; to compel the United States Treasurer to pay interest on certificates that had been received by him; to compel the Comptroller General and Chief of Finance to place applicant, after thirty years of service in the Philippine Scouts, on the retired list of the Army at three-fourths pay; to issue a license to operate an X-ray machine, the license having been refused because applicant was a chiropractor who would attempt to use the pictures in connection with the diagnosis and treatment of disease; to compel a board of dental examiners to give a license to a graduate of a reputable dental college, the license having been refused merely because of dental college rivalry.

On the other hand, mandamus was refused in the following cases: to compel the examining board of a city police department to change the grading of examination papers and to change the applicant's rating; to compel a city mayor to enforce the law against keeping saloons open on Sunday, such enforcement being a governmental function; to compel a mayor and police commissioner to stop the illegal operation of bus lines; to compel the Secretary of War and Chief of Army Engineers to authorize the construction of a wharf in the Potomac River, because of the expense it would place on the government, mandamus being governed by equitable principles; to compel the Commissioner of Water Supply, Gas and Electricity to permit a dentist to have an illuminated sign, the commissioner having a limited discretion to discourage unprofessional advertising; to compel refund of taxes, there being no clear duty to refund without an adjudication and the ordinary action being an adequate remedy; to compel the Interstate Commerce Commission to vacate its orders in regard to applications before it of several railroads with regard to the use of terminals of other railroads.

§ 16. Same—certiorari.[6] Where an administrative tribunal has acted judicially the person aggrieved by such action may avail himself of the extraordinary common-law remedy of certiorari under which a court will order the administrative tribunal to turn over its proceedings to the court for judicial review. In such a review the court will consider and decide the question of the jurisdiction of the tribunal and such legal questions as the sufficiency of the evidence before it and its alleged errors in the admission or exclusion of evidence.

Where the action of the tribunal has not been judicial, certiorari will not lie; for example, the forming of a new school district, the revocation of a certificate of public convenience by a public service commission, the revocation of a license to sell ice at retail and an order denying the use of mails in furtherance of a fraudulent scheme. On the other hand, the determination of damages where domestic animals were killed by a dog was held to be judicial and certiorari lay.

[6] 42 **Am Jur,** Public Administrative Law, § 229.

Propriety of certiorari to review decisions of public officer or board granting, denying, or revoking permit, certificate, or license required as condition of exercise of particular right or privilege. 102 **ALR** 534–549.

Propriety of certiorari to review decisions of tax boards. 77 **ALR** 1357–1366.

29 **Calif. L. R.** 586, Certiorari and the Local Board.

TAXATION

CHAPTER I

IN GENERAL

§ 1. Theories of taxation—source of the taxing power.[1] The older theory of taxation is that taxes are imposed as compensation for the protection furnished to the taxpayer by the state. But in recent years the tremendous increase in the expenses of government have caused a shift of emphasis to the theory that taxes should be imposed according to ability to pay, with little or no attention being paid to the benefit received by the taxpayer.

The power of each of the states to tax is inherent, limited only by the 14th Amendment and its own Constitution. Since the federal government is one of delegated powers its power to tax is found in the Federal Constitution which also contains—especially in the 5th Amendment—certain limitations on its taxing power.

[1] 51 **Am Jur**, Taxation, §§ 9, 40, 41.
57 **Harv. L. R.** 1153, The Need for a Court of Tax Appeals.
42 **Col. L. R.** 356, Federal Taxation in the Pre-War Decade.
38 **Col. L. R.** 49, Sales and Use Taxes.
38 **Col. L. R.** 809, Foreign Investment and Extraterritorial Taxation.
36 **Col L. R.** 382, The Franco-American Convention Relative to Double Taxation.
40 **Mich. L. R.** 207, Federal Taxation of Insurance Trusts.
28 **Va. L. R.** 488, Protecting the Taxpayer During a Period of Defense Spending.
15 **Rocky M. L. R.** 8, Intergovernmental Tax Immunity.
12 **Geo. Wash. L. R.** 245, Taxability of the Government Subsidy.

§ 2. Constitutional limitations on the taxing power—classification—uniformity.[2] The general effect on the taxing power of the constitutional provisions requiring due process and equal protection of the law has already been considered; see ante, Constitutional Law, §§ 23 to 29.

It is well settled that the equal protection clause does not prevent reasonable classification. Thus a state may tax anthracite and not bituminous coal because anthracite can be used only for fuel whereas bituminous has a variety of other uses. It may impose a heavier license tax on chain than upon individually owned stores because of differences in organization, management and type of business transacted. And it may impose a heavier tax on bank deposits held by its own citizens in banks outside the state than on deposits held by them in banks within the state because of differences in the difficulties and expense of tax collection.

On the other hand, a state may not tax gross receipts from taxicabs owned by corporations without imposing a similar tax on gross receipts from taxicabs owned by individuals or partnerships. It may not tax the recording of deeds and mortgages, exempting mortgages where the indebtedness does not mature within five years, though such fact might have been a valid basis for varying the amount of the tax; the exemption of building and loan association mortgages was held valid because of the quasi-public purpose of such associations. Nor may it impose a graduated gross sales tax because the volume of transactions does not necessarily show a greater profit or a greater ability to pay.

In several states there are constitutional provisions requiring uniformity in taxation of property. Under such a provision a tax of fifty cents a gallon on every person engaged in the business of owning, storing or manufacturing whisky was held bad because it was a property tax and whisky was also subject to a general property tax. A graduated income tax was held bad as to income from real estate, stocks, bonds and securities, because not uniform. And a floor tax of $2 a gallon on all liquors stored in the state till the twenty-first amendment should be ratified was held bad because the value of the liquor, ranging from 40 cents to $16 a gallon, was disregarded.

On the other hand, a tax on some but not all intangibles was upheld as an excise tax and not within the uniformity provision, the court evidently being influenced by the fact that the effect of the statute had been to increase twelve times the state's revenue from intangibles.

§ 3. Same—limitations on taxation affecting governmental instrumentalities.[3] While a state tax on a branch of the United States Bank was held unconstitutional, United States bonds are subject to state inheritance, succession and estate taxes; a legacy to the United States may be taxed as such by a state and a legacy to a municipal corporation is subject to a federal succession tax.

It was formerly held that the salary of a state official was not subject to a

[2] 51 **Am Jur**, Taxation, §§ 73–149, 151–201.
Liability for license fee or occupation tax of one who has conducted business without required license or payment. 5 **ALR** 1312–1319; s. in 107 **ALR** 652–657.
Tax on cigarettes or tobacco, or dealers therein, as violating requirement of uniformity or equality in taxation. 62 **ALR** 105–113.
Constitutionality of tax on corporations in nature of, or purporting to be, excise or privilege tax measured by income or receipts. 71 **ALR** 256–271.
What is a property tax as distinguished from excise, license, and other taxes. 103 **ALR** 18–107.
State excise, privilege, or franchise tax upon foreign corporation as affected by commerce clause. 105 **ALR** 11–67; s. in 139 **ALR** 950–960.

[3] 51 **Am Jur**, Taxation, §§ 218–283.

federal income tax and the salary of a federal official was not subject to a state income tax but the law is now contra in both cases, the immunity of the federal and state governments not extending to employees.

§ 4. Same—special limitations on federal taxation—taxes on interstate commerce.[4] The United States Constitution gives Congress the power to levy duties, imposts and excises but requires that they shall be uniform throughout the United States. This was held not to be violated by a graduated succession tax though the testamentary and intestacy laws of the various states varied in their provisions, just as duties may be validly levied on articles which are not uniformly consumed throughout the United States. And a federal inheritance tax statute which allowed a partial deduction of sums paid under state inheritance tax laws was not rendered invalid by the fact that three of the states imposed no inheritance taxes.

The United States Constitution requires that, like representatives, all direct taxes—such as taxes on land or other property—shall be apportioned among the several states according to population. Apparently Congress has never attempted to apportion any taxes and the federal income tax statute of 1895 was held to be unconstitutional because it included income from land and it was not apportioned. That decision led to the adoption of the 16th Amendment which permitted Congress to pass a statute covering income from land, the statute reading "from whatever source derived."

The Corporation Tax Law of 1909 was held valid as an excise tax on the privilege of doing business as a corporation; and the gift tax of 1924 was held valid as an excise tax upon a particular use of the property, not a direct tax on the property itself. Hence in neither of these cases was an apportionment necessary.

The subject of limitations upon the power of the United States and of the states to tax commerce has already been treated; see ante, Constitutional Law §§ 39–43.

CHAPTER II

PROPERTY TAXES

§ 5. Divided interests in property—taxing day.[5] Where A owns unincumbered land worth $10,000 there is only one property tax to be paid; but if A

[4] 12 **Am Jur,** Constitutional Law, § 518.
51 **Am Jur,** Taxation, §§ 203–217.

[5] 51 **Am Jur,** Taxation, §§ 29–37, 284–286.
Rights of insured or beneficiary under insurance policy as subject to property tax. 150 **ALR** 788–798.
Constitutionality, construction, and application of statute or ordinance imposing license fee or tax upon automobiles or trailers used for habitation. 150 **ALR** 853–855.
Review of decisions of United States Supreme Court since Union Refrigerator Transit Co. v. Kentucky (1905) 199 US 194, 50 L ed 150, 26 S Ct 36, on situs of personal property for purposes of taxation. 123 **ALR** 179–199; s. in 139 **ALR** 1463–1465.
Taxation of insurance reserves. 13 **ALR** 186–204; s. in 78 **ALR** 562–566.
Oil and gas rights or privileges as independent subject of taxation, or as tangible property for purposes of taxation. 16 **ALR** 513–520.
Shares owned by a resident in a foreign corporation as subject of property tax. 43 **ALR** 686–726; s. in 48 **ALR** 997, 998.
Taxation of foreign-owned railroad rolling stock temporarily within the taxing state. 49 **ALR** 1099–1115.
State tax on goods purchased by, or for the benefit of, the Federal Government, or on the privilege of conducting the business in connection with which the sales are made. 56 **ALR** 587–590; s. in 140 **ALR** 621–642.
Leasehold interest as real property within tax laws. 59 **ALR** 701–707.
Situs as between different states or countries of bank deposits for purposes of property taxation. 59 **ALR** 1046–1056.
Situs for property taxation as between different states or countries, of personal property, or interests therein, held by trustees, executors, or administrators. 67 **ALR** 393–413; s. in 127 **ALR** 379–381.
Tax on automobile or on its use for cost of road or street construction, improvement, or maintenance. 24 **ALR** 937–942; s. in 68 **ALR** 200–209.

borrows $6,000 from B, giving B a note therefor and a mortgage on the land to secure it, A may still be required to pay the same taxes on the land without deduction for the mortgage, and B must pay taxes on the $6,000 note. Though such double taxation is unfair it has the sanction of long-settled taxing habits and is not unconstitutional.

If A should give to C an ordinary lease on his land for agricultural purposes, C is usually not taxed on his interest in the land and A's taxes remain as before; and the fact that a lease was made at a rental which, due to an increase in the value of the property, was low, is no defense to A, if his land is assessed as neighboring land is assessed.

But if the lease is for mineral rights over a long period then C and not A will be taxed on the value of the minerals thus leased to C.

Where a lease on land is for so long a period as to amount to a fee the land is assessed to the lessee not to the lessor. And where a lease is given on lands owned by the state, such as tide lands, the lessee is taxed for the value of his leasehold interest, the reversion in the state not being taxable.

Where A is a citizen of the state where the land lies he might be made personally liable for the taxes thereon; but for the most part taxes on land and chattels are impersonal and collectible only out of the property taxed.

Most taxing statutes fix a taxing day—usually the first day of March or April or May—so that all property owned by A on that day and on no other is taxable to him. If just before taxing day A should take $10,000 which he had on deposit in a bank and invest it in nontaxable government bonds, he may escape taxation thereon if it was a bona fide and not a colorable transaction even though a few days later he sells the bonds and deposits the money in the bank. In order to meet this situation the tax may be levied on the average monthly deposits instead of the deposits on taxing day.

§ 6. The assessment.[6] Property is usually assessed each year but in some states land is assessed less often; if land is not assessed against the owner but

Constitutionality of statutes or ordinances for taxation of common carriers by automobile. 75 **ALR** 13–47.

"Business situs" for purposes of property taxation of intangibles in state other than domicil of owner. 76 **ALR** 806–829; s. in 143 **ALR** 361–389.

What property is within provision in relation to local taxation of certain railroad property under statute or constitution providing for assessment or taxation of railroad property by state commission or board. 80 **ALR** 252–279.

Situs as between different states or countries of tangible chattels for purposes of property taxation. 110 **ALR** 707–732.

Constitutionality, construction, and application of statutes relating to ad valorem or property taxation of motor vehicles. 114 **ALR** 847–859.

Who is liable for tax in case of conditional sale, or option for purchase, of personal property. 116 **ALR** 325–332.

Taxation in same state of real property and debt secured by mortgage or other lien thereon as double taxation. 122 **ALR** 742–747.

Different parts or parcels of land in same ownership as single unit or separate units for tax assessment purposes. 133 **ALR** 524–549.

Situs for property taxation as between different governmental units within state of personal property or interests therein held by trustees, executors, or administrators. 129 **ALR** 273–294.

Personal liability of property owner to pay assessments for local improvements. 127 **ALR** 551–595.

Taxation of property owned by public body but not devoted to public use. 3 **ALR** 1439–1457; s. in 101 **ALR** 787–793; 129 **ALR** 480–487.

Public school property as subject to assessment for local improvements. 36 **ALR** 1540–1544.

Public property as subject to special assessment for improvement. 90 **ALR** 1137–1169.

Manner of enforcing special assessments against public property. 95 **ALR** 689–702; s. in 150 **ALR** 1394–1402.

4 **La. L. R.** 469, Some Plain Talk about the Louisiana General Property Tax.

6 51 **Am Jur**, Taxation, §§ 647–695.

Assessment of corporate property at full value according to law when valuations generally are illegally fixed lower. 3 **ALR** 1370–1379; s. in 28 **ALR** 983–986; 55 **ALR** 503, 504.

Notice to property owners of increase in assessment or valuation by board of equalization or review. 24 **ALR** 331–382; s. in 84 **ALR** 197–211.

Prospective value as basis for valuation

by description alone there is no right to collect against the owner personally. Tangible personal property must be listed separately; it may not be assessed in a lump sum.

In fixing the valuation a very wide latitude is allowed to the assessor. He should keep in mind not only the price at which the property could be sold on the market but also the value to the owner; and in case a business depression seriously affecting sales price and business property is involved he may properly take into consideration the original cost, the reproduction cost and the capacity to earn money for the owner, and thereby arrive at a compromise evaluation. Where, however, the statute expressly provides that the property shall be assessed at the full value which could ordinarily be obtained at private sale, then such sales value governs.

In agricultural districts and in the towns and smaller cities where usually the market for land is not active, and the property is not uniform, the assessor relies on his own individual judgment; but in the larger cities a standardized method is usually followed, the land and the improvements being valued separately. In valuing the land under this standardized method the assessor first fixes on the frontage value of a vacant lot in the particular block and consults the previous tax assessments, previous sales, mortgage loans and rentals. In valuing the building a classification of urban buildings is used with tables of costs for each type and tables for depreciation so that all the assessor does is to classify the particular building, ascertain its age and make an estimate of its size.

Sometimes the taxing statute requires that evaluations shall be made at the full value, sometimes at a fixed percentage of the full value. If the assessments are made on a fixed percentage of the full value, say 60%, then each taxpayer is entitled to have his property assessed at that rate; it is no answer to say that it is not assessed at more than its full value.

Where railroads and other large public utilities are involved the unit rule of assessment is ordinarily used, the assessment being made not by the local assessor but by the State Tax Commission which is strongly influenced by the amount of income received by the utility.

§ 7. **Same—remedy of the aggrieved taxpayer—local assessments.**[7] Where a taxpayer is dissatisfied with the assessment it is usually provided that he may appeal to the county board, thence to the State Tax Commission or to the courts. The only notice to which he is entitled is found in the statute prescribing the time when such complaint will be heard.

of land for purposes of property taxation. 24 **ALR** 649–655.

Assessment of railroad right of way for local improvements. 37 **ALR** 219–265; s. in 82 **ALR** 425–433.

Assessments for improvements by the front-foot rule. 56 **ALR** 941–953.

Prior judgment as precluding reassessment for public improvement. 60 **ALR** 513–525.

When may payment of tax or assessment be regarded as involuntary or made under duress. 64 **ALR** 9–132; s. in 84 **ALR** 294–298.

Income or rental value as a factor in valuation of real property for purposes of taxation. 95 **ALR** 442–452.

Original cost of construction or reproduction cost as proper factors in assessing real property for taxation. 104 **ALR** 790–802.

Name under which property of decedent should be assessed. 119 **ALR** 383–410.

Sufficiency of description of property on tax rolls or in tax proceedings, by reference to map, plat, or survey. 137 **ALR** 184–201.

Discrimination in state taxation of national banks or national bank shares. 59 **ALR** 10–46; s. in 81 **ALR** 502–511; 87 **ALR** 846–848.

Lack of or defects in petition of property owners for local improvement as affecting validity or enforcement of assessment. 95 **ALR** 116–146.

Construction or improvement of sewers as a local or district improvement within provisions authorizing or requiring special assessments or other specified means of defraying expense. 134 **ALR** 895–908.

7 51 **Am Jur**, Taxation, §§ 728–733.

The mere fact that the assessor undervalues some property or omits it entirely from the assessment roll does not invalidate assessments on other property which have been properly made.

Where a taxpayer is able to show that his property has been valued too high as compared with other property in the vicinity the better remedy is to reduce his assessment rather than to have all the property reassessed, a procedure which is usually quite expensive to the public.

Where property in one section of the state has been consistently undervalued the state tax board may order all assessments in that section to be raised a fixed percentage and on this matter the individual taxpayer has no right to be heard and no right to an injunction.

Local assessments need not be uniform but there must be some benefit to the land assessed. Where the legislature determines directly what property shall be included, no notice or hearing is necessary and such an assessment will be upheld unless the result thus reached is arbitrary and confiscatory; as, for example, where 60% of the cost of a reclamation project was assessed against a railroad which would be benefited only by increased traffic after the completion of the project. But if the matter is left to a local agency there must be notice and a hearing at some point even if only when the owner of the land assessed is sued for the tax.

CHAPTER III

DEATH AND GIFT TAXES

§ 8. In general.[8] The federal government and a few of the states impose, upon the death of a decedent, an excise tax upon the estate for the privilege of transmitting property, an estate tax. In most of the other states the death tax imposed is an excise tax upon the privilege of receiving the decedent's property, and is levied upon the share of each devisee, legatee, heir or distributee of the decedent. This tax, which developed earlier than the estate tax, is usually called an inheritance or succession tax, is less simple in administration than the estate tax especially where the decedent has left a will devising contingent future estates.

[8] 28 **Am Jur,** Inheritance, Estate, and Gift Taxes, §§ 2, 315.

Estate and succession tax: constitutionality, construction, and application of specific provisions taxing property transferred, by trust or otherwise, subject to a power to alter, amend, or revoke. 139 **ALR** 517–557.

Ultimate burden or incidence of estate tax. 142 **ALR** 1135–1146.

Whole estate or individual shares as basis of computation of inheritance tax. 7 **ALR** 688–696: s. in 11 **ALR** 825, 826.

Consideration as affecting the liability to a succession or inheritance tax. 7 **ALR** 1046–1067: s. in 58 **ALR** 1143–1146.

Retrospective operation of succession tax. 26 **ALR** 1461–1484; s. in 66 **ALR** 404–416; 109 **ALR** 858–877; 114 **ALR** 518–521.

Time of assessment of succession tax on future contingent interests. 30 **ALR** 478–491.

Constitutionality of discrimination in succession tax based on relationship or amount of estate. 39 **ALR** 504–513.

Succession tax at domicil of decedent as to personal property located elsewhere, or the obligations of nonresidents or foreign corporations. 42 **ALR** 327–341; s. in 86 **ALR** 741–746.

Succession tax at domicil of debtor or corporation as to credits or corporate stock belonging to the estate of a nonresident. 42 **ALR** 354–372; s. in 60 **ALR** 565–569; 65 **ALR** 1008, 1009; 72 **ALR** 1310, 1311; 77 **ALR** 1411, 1412; 139 **ALR** 1458–1463.

Succession tax in state or country in which personal property (or evidence thereof) belonging to the estate of a nonresident decedent is found. 42 **ALR** 378–399; s. in 86 **ALR** 760–765.

When transfer deemed to take effect in possession or enjoyment at or after death within the Inheritance Tax Law. 49 **ALR** 864–903; s. in 67 **ALR** 1247–1258; 100 **ALR** 1244–1257; 121 **ALR** 359–374.

37 **Harv. L. R.** 691, Retroactive Excise Taxation.

22 **Neb L. R.** 70, Federal Estate and Gift Taxes.

§ 9. **Transfers at death.**[9] Where A died leaving two sons X and Y, and X died later on the same day, Y was compelled to pay a succession tax on property inherited from X though X's estate was also bound to pay a succession tax on property inherited from A. But the present tendency is to provide expressly for a reduction of the second inheritance tax when it follows closely upon the first.

Where A died leaving a will but his widow elected to take her dower interest, the better view is that she must pay a succession tax because though dower may be inchoate before A's death, yet in a broad sense she takes under the intestate law of the state.

Where A died having bequeathed the residue of his estate to X, a stranger, and Y, a nephew of A, contested the will and forced a compromise approved by the court it was held that Y's tax should be computed according to the will and not according to the terms of the compromise.

Where A by antenuptial contract with X agreed to adopt X's daughter Y and to leave her his property if he should have no children by X, and A defaulted and Y obtained a decree for specific performance against A's devisees and legatees, it was held that the succession tax must be paid because devolution of the property had taken place under the will.

And where Jay Gould bequeathed to his son George $5,000,000 in stocks and bonds as compensation for services rendered, it was held that George must pay the New York succession tax because the New York statute was not limited in its application to amounts left gratuitously by will.

§ 10. **Transfers before death.**[10] In order to prevent the avoidance of death taxes by transfers made by the decedent in contemplation of death it became necessary to extend the application of estate and succession taxes to such transfers. It is frequently so difficult to prove that a particular transfer was made in contemplation of death that statutes frequently provide that all gratuitous transfers made within a fixed period—usually two years—before death, are presumptively made in contemplation of death, thus giving the laboring oar to the taxpayer, and such statutes have been upheld. But when Congress undertook to make the presumption conclusive this was held to be unconstitutional as a violation of the due process clause of the 5th amendment.

The fact that in transferring property upon trust the transferor reserved a life interest to himself is at least some evidence that the transfer was in contemplation of death and Congress has expressly provided that such transfers should be taxable. But where the conveyance is made in exchange for an annuity to the transferor such a transfer is not taxable. The distinction between the two cases is not easily drawn.

Where a transfer upon trust is made revocable in the sole discretion of the transferor, this tends to show that it was made in contemplation of death and in some states such a transfer is expressly made taxable. Where the transfer is made revocable only with the consent of the trustee or the beneficiaries or a majority thereof the transfer is not taxable because the power

9 28 **Am Jur,** Inheritance, Estate, and Gift Taxes, §§ 159–180.
54 **Harv. L. R.** 10, Apportionment of Death Taxes.

10 28 **Am Jur,** Inheritance, Estate, and Gift Taxes, §§ 138–158.
When transfer deemed to be one in contemplation of death, within the meaning of the Inheritance Tax Law. 4 **ALR** 1523; 7 **ALR** 1028–1041; 21 **ALR** 1335–1340; 41 **ALR** 989–991; 75 **ALR** 544–555; 120 **ALR** 170–201; 148 **ALR** 1051–1071.

of revocation is not absolute; but Congress has expressly made such transfers taxable.

§ 11. Same—joint interests—powers of appointment.[1] Where A and B each conveyed real estate to X who thereupon conveyed it to A and B jointly and A later died it was held that B need not pay an inheritance tax because nothing passed to B upon A's death. But in the federal code and in the statutes of many states there are express provisions, varying in terms, imposing death taxes upon the death of a joint tenant.

Where A paid the entire purchase price for land which was conveyed to him and B, his wife jointly and A died it was held that B must pay the federal estate tax on the full value because it was not till the death of A that she had the sole right to sell the land without risk of loss which might have resulted from partition or separate sale of her interest while A lived.

And where A bought land and had it conveyed to himself and wife as tenants by the entirety this was held to be a gift to the wife and she must pay the federal gift tax thereon, because it was the conveyance and not the death of A that created the estate in her.

Where A devises land to B for life with remainder in fee to such persons as B should appoint by deed or will and in default of appointment to C in fee, B is dominus of the property; he has a general power of appointment and may appoint to himself. If he fails to appoint the property will usually descend as intestate property of A. If he undertakes to appoint to D his creditors may reach the property as property conveyed in fraud of their rights.

If the creditors do not object does D receive the property from A, the donor of the power, or from B, the donee of the power? As a matter of simplicity of tax administration it is preferable to regard D as receiving the property from B, and such is the tendency of legislation in most of the states. Under such a statute it was held that where a conveyance was made by A to B for life with general power to appoint by will and in default of appointment to A's grandchildren, it was held that the inheritance tax applied to the property thus received by the grandchildren because it was not certain till B's death how the property would go. And where A died in 1876 leaving land to his son B for life with power to convey to his sisters or their issue and in 1911 in pursuance of his power, B by deed transferred the entire property including his life estate to his sisters, the transfer was held taxable though the appointment was by deed.

But where A devised to B for life with power to appoint by will and in default of appointment to her issue and if no issue, to her next of kin, and B appointed to her sisters who elected to take under the will of A, the property was held not taxable because it did not pass under B's will.

§ 12. Same—life insurance.[2] Where A insured his life naming B as beneficiary the money received from the insurance company upon A's death was

[1] 28 **Am Jur,** Inheritance, Estate, and Gift Taxes, §§ 122–126. 131–137.

Succession, inheritance, or estate tax in respect of decedent's interest in partnership. 144 **ALR** 1134–1144.

Inheritance or succession tax on property covered by power of appointment. 18 **ALR** 1470–1492; s. in 23 **ALR** 738; 64 **ALR** 740–753; 124 **ALR** 653–667; 141 **ALR** 954–965; 150 **ALR** 730–739.

52 **Harv. L. R.** 929, Powers of Appointment and the Federal Estate Tax.

56 **Harv. L. R.** 739, Powers of Appointment and the New Revenue Act.

56 **Harv. L. R.** 742, Taxation of Powers of Appointment.

[2] 28 **Am Jur,** Inheritance, Estate, and Gift Taxes, §§ 69–73.

Federal estate tax in respect of life insurance. 150 **ALR** 1268–1273.

not a gift from A within the meaning of a succession tax statute because the right which B received arose when the policy was taken out and all A had was a contract right against the insurance company.

The United States estate tax statute expressly covers the amount received by the decedent's executor under policies taken out by the decedent on his own life payable to his estate and to the extent of the excess over $40,000 of the amount receivable by all other beneficiaries under policies taken out by the decedent payable to them. This has been held not to be a property tax and therefore did not need to be apportioned, but a tax upon the transfer from the insurance company to the beneficiary. And it has been held that the statute could not be successfully evaded by the decedent's assignment to his wife of policies payable to himself though the policies had been taken out in 1925 before the statute was passed, life insurance being testamentary in character.

Where A took out a single premium policy payable to himself and then made an irrevocable gift of it to B it was held taxable as a gift to B, not merely of the surrender value of the policy but of the cost of the policy to A.

§ 13. Valuation and assessment—exempt transfers.[3] The federal statute provides for the purpose of determining the value of a decedent's gross estate the executor may elect to have it determined as of one year after the decedent's death; but where he does so elect it has been held that income received during the year must be included.

In determining the "value of the property" it is not the value which it had to the decedent but the value to the new owners and the best evidence of that is the market price.

Where the estate includes a large block of shares of stock the tax commissioner should take into consideration not only the condition and trend of the market for such shares but also the difficulty, which ordinarily exists, of disposing of such large blocks.

Where a will creates a life estate in X and a vested remainder in Y, both estates are valued—for the purpose of assessing a succession tax—as of the date of the decedent's death, and become payable at once. Where a will creates a contingent remainder it is usual to require immediate payment based on the contingency which would yield the largest return to the state and later make any necessary adjustments when the contingency is determined.

Where A devised to B for life with remainder to C in fee and during B's life C transferred his interest to D and D then transferred to E, the transfers by C and D were taxable as such, the date of B's death not being important.

The federal statute exempts from estate taxes all devises, legacies or transfers for public, charitable or religious purposes. Where A made a pledge to a charitable institution which was legally enforceable against A's estate it was held that this was not exempt because no actual transfer was made by A. And where A promised to give $100,000 to a church for the erection of a building upon condition that the church would contribute an equal amount, and

State succession, transfer, inheritance, or estate tax in respect of life insurance and annuities. 150 **ALR** 1285–1299.

43 **Harv. L. R.** 724, Proceeds of Life Insurance Policies under the Federal Estate Tax.

52 **Harv. L. R.** 1037, Life Insurance and the Federal Estate Tax.

55 **Harv. L. R.** 226, Taxes and Insurance: A Suggested Solution to the Uncertain Cost of Dying.

3 28 **Am Jur**, Inheritance, Estate, and Gift Taxes, §§ 191–200, 216–277.

the condition was not fulfilled before the death of A, the $100,000 was held to be part of A's gross estate.

§ 14. Deductions.[4] The federal estate tax statute provides that in fixing the value of the net estate there shall be deducted from the gross estate the expenses for the funeral, for the administration of the estate and for the support of those dependent upon the decedent, and also the claims against the estate where contracted bona fide and for an adequate and full consideration in money or money's worth. Where the decedent had entered into agreements, valid under the state law, with charitable organizations to establish a fund as a memorial to her husband and to pay professors' salaries, sums paid by the executor in performance of these agreements were held not to be deductible because not based on adequate and full consideration in money or money's worth. On the other hand, claims against the estate which could not be paid in full because of insolvency were held to be deductible in full. Where a will fixed the compensation of a trustee for managing a liquor business at $5,000 a year for ten years that sum was held not to be deductible in fixing a state inheritance tax, because not an administration expense.

State inheritance tax statutes sometimes provide for the deduction of amounts paid in settlement of the federal estate tax but a statute is not rendered invalid by a provision that no such deduction be made.

CHAPTER IV

INCOME TAXES

§ 15. In general—concepts of gross and net income.[5] Since the adoption of the sixteenth amendment in 1913 the subject of federal income tax has

[4] 28 **Am Jur,** Inheritance, Estate, and Gift Taxes, §§ 238–260.

Deduction of commissions of executors, administrators, or trustees in computing succession or estate tax. 92 **ALR** 537–554.

[5] 27 **Am Jur,** Income Taxes, § 7.

Income tax in relation to stock dividends (including character of corporate distributions as stock dividends). 105 **ALR** 761–789; s. in 130 **ALR** 408–416; 143 **ALR** 231–235; 144 **ALR** 1337–1341.

Income tax in respect of salaries of public officers and employees. 11 **ALR** 532–539; s. in 82 **ALR** 989–995; 108 **ALR** 1439–1449; 114 **ALR** 1190–1196; 120 **ALR** 1477–1486; 122 **ALR** 1393–1396; 125 **ALR** 1421–1423.

Income tax on nonresident. 15 **ALR** 1326–1344; s. in 90 **ALR** 484–494.

Assignment of right to future earnings, commissions, or benefits as affecting income tax of assignor 83 **ALR** 88–100; s. in 131 **ALR** 661–683.

Motive to avoid, limit, or postpone income tax by transaction which otherwise affects incidence of that tax. 101 **ALR** 204–216.

Income tax in respect of exchange of properties. 102 **ALR** 6–23.

Method or formula for determination for income tax purposes of value of corporate stock absent sufficient basis in transactions of purchase and sale. 103 **ALR** 955–977.

Payment to one performing services as compensation subject to income tax or gift exempt therefrom. 110 **ALR** 285–306.

Liability on bond given as condition of extension of time for payment of income tax. 117 **ALR** 452–466.

Right to use inventories, for income tax purposes, in respect of transactions in securities. 118 **ALR** 462–474.

Method of computing income tax, or failure to report taxable income, in earlier year as precluding or estopping taxpayer in computation of tax for later year. 118 **ALR** 302–313; s. in 149 **ALR** 1150–1164.

Question whether gift is valid, or a mere sham, as regards income tax of donor. 125 **ALR** 779–787.

State income tax in respect of business that extends into other states. 130 **ALR** 1183–1220.

Income tax: constitutionality, construction, and application of statutory provisions allowing credit for income tax paid to another state or country. 134 **ALR** 1433–1462.

Income tax on income of taxpayer who dies during taxable year. 142 **ALR** 213–238.

What constitutes a trust, for income tax purposes. 113 **ALR** 457–467.

Constitutionality, construction, and application of statutory provisions for taxation of grantor on income of revocable trust and trust income distributable to him. 106 **ALR** 798–813; s. in 132 **ALR** 785–814; 143 **ALR** 1116–1141.

Liability of settlor for income tax in respect of trust income applied to relieve him of financial obligation or burden. 101 **ALR** 397–405; s. in 109 **ALR** 1048–1054; 132 **ALR** 819–839.

been of steadily increasing importance. After the depression of 1929 most of the states adopted a general income tax largely following the federal model but they have been unable to obtain very much revenue therefrom because the federal tax had already made such a heavy drain upon the national tax resources, and this has now been accentuated by the greater national need due to World War II.

Income for the calendar year might logically be considered as the increase of net worth of the taxpayer from January 1 to December 31, but this would be too complicated to be practical. Income is therefore regarded as something that must have been realized in some way during the taxable year, not merely increase in net worth.

Since each taxable year is a unit, if A suffers a net loss during 1944 of $10,000 and during 1945 makes a net gain of $25,000 he may not use a part of the net gain to offset the loss of the previous year.

Where A received a subsidy from the Cuban government to aid in constructing a railroad this was held not taxable as income because the purpose of the subsidy was to reimburse A for capital expenditures. And where the X Corporation received from the Y city a factory owned by the city in consideration of the X Corporation locating its plant in the city for ten years, the X Corporation was held not liable to pay either income or gift tax on the factory.

At the outset it is important to become familiar with the concepts of gross and net income. Gross income for tax purposes includes all income except (1) life insurance and the major portion of annuities; (2) property acquired by gift, devise, bequest or inheritance; (3) interest on certain governmental obligations and on obligations of corporations which are instrumentalities of the United States; (4) compensation in the nature of insurance or damages for personal injuries or illness.

In order to arrive at net income within the meaning of the federal statutes, the following items are deducted from gross income: (1) ordinary and necessary business expenses; (2) interest; (3) taxes; (4) losses in business or in transactions entered into for profit and any losses arising from fire, storm, shipwreck or other casualty or from theft; (5) capital losses; (6) bad debts; (7) depreciation of business property through wear and tear and obsolescence; (8) depletion or exhaustion of wasting assets such as minerals; (9) certain charitable contributions.

Construction and application of statutory provisions taxing legatees, heirs, or trust beneficiaries on income distributable or distributed to them. 141 **ALR** 1055–1113.

When corporations deemed affiliated within contemplation of income tax law. 69 **ALR** 1271–1279; s. in 85 **ALR** 153–160.

What amounts to "reorganization" of corporation within income tax statutes. 97 **ALR** 1359–1399.

Premium or discount at which a corporation issues or sells, or purchases or retires, its stock, bonds, or other obligations as income, or as deductible in computing income tax of corporation. 112 **ALR** 186–220.

When dividends on corporate stock become taxable as income to a taxpayer making his return on a cash basis. 120 **ALR** 1280–1297; s. in 143 **ALR** 596–598.

What is a "personal holding company" within income tax acts. 140 **ALR** 649–658.

51 **Harv. L. R.** 40, Ascertainment of "Earnings or Profits" for the Purpose of Determining Taxability of Corporate Distributions.

52 **Harv. L. R.** 1077, Public Utility Depreciation and the Income Tax.

53 **Harv. L. R.** 977, Discharge of Indebtedness and the Federal Income Tax.

53 **Harv. L. R.** 1322, The Federal Income Tax in Short Term and Revocable Trusts.

55 **Harv. L. R.** 329, Annuity Trusts under the Federal Tax Laws.

51 **Yale L. J.** 1143, Present Method of Taxing Trust Income.

48 **Yale L. J.** 1315, Federal Income Tax Problems of Mortgagors and Mortgagees.

20 **Tex. L. R.** 150, Federal Income Tax on the Family.

20 **Tex. L. R.** 532, Community Property and the Taxation of Family Income.

29 **Corn. L. Q.** 28, Alimony and the Income Tax.

22 **Neb. L. R.** 252, Federal Income Tax Problems of the Small Business Man.

In order to arrive at the tax base for assessing the normal tax there must be subtracted from net income certain credits or exemptions: (1) interest on obligations of the United States or of a federal instrumentality if such interest has not already been excluded as tax free; (2) earned income credit; (3) personal exemption and credit for dependents.

§ 16. Gifts, devises, bequests and inheritances.[6] Gifts may be subject to a gift tax but are expressly excluded from the federal income tax. Where A bought shares worth $1,000, held them till they were worth $2,000 and then gave them to his daughter B who later sold them for $5,000, B's taxable income on the transaction was not $3,000 but $4,000 because the statute expressly provides that in such a case "the basis shall be the same as that which it would have been in the hands of the donor or the last preceding owner by whom it was not acquired by gift."

Where the X Company had been unusually successful, had reorganized into the Y Company to which its assets were transferred and the Y Company distributed $600,000 to the employees of the X Company as a "gift or honorarium" and "not as payment for services" such distribution was held not to be income to the recipients but a gift.

Devises and bequests as well as distributive shares of an intestate's estate may be subject to an estate or an inheritance tax but not to an income tax. Where A devised her residuary estate to a charity and A's grandson X contested the will and recovered by way of compromise a part of what he claimed, this was held to be an inheritance to X and not taxable as income.

§ 17. Stock dividends—bonds—miscellaneous.[7] Where the A corporation distributes to its shareholders a dividend of money or shares of X corporation which it owns, such a dividend is taxable to the stockholders as income. But where the A corporation, being capitalized at $100,000 and having a surplus of $200,000, declares a 100% stock dividend, this stock dividend has been held not taxable as income to the stockholders because they get no more than they had before and mere increase in the value of capital is not income. If a stockholder should sell the new stock he would of course be taxable on the selling price as income, but if he makes such a sale he no longer has as large a share in the corporation as he had before.

The exact line of demarcation between these two situations has not been easy to draw. Where the stockholders of A corporation formed a new company, the B corporation, and distributed the shares of the B corporation to the stockholders of the A corporation, such new shares were held to be income because they could be disposed of without reducing the share of the stockholder in the A corporation. But where X corporation having stock of $5,000,000 par value was dissolved and Y corporation was formed with stock having par value of $25,000,000, and the Y corporation took over the assets paying the old stockholders $7,500,000 in cash and $12,500,000 in stock, it was held that only the cash was taxable income.

6 27 **Am Jur**, Income Taxes, §§ 85–89.
56 **Harv. L. R.** 337, A Plan for the Coordination of the Income, Estate and Gift Tax Provisions with Respect to Trusts and Other Transfers.
55 **Harv. L. R.** 1, Correlation of Gift and Estate Taxes.
38 **Col L.R.** 1393, Administrative and Judicial Procedure for Federal Income, Estate and Gift Taxes.
40 **Col. L. R.** 773, Federal Gift Tax.

7 27 **Am Jur**, Income Taxes, §§ 65, 75.
40 **Mich. L. R.** 1005, Taxation of Annuity Contracts.
22 **N. C. L. R.** 1, 85, Present Taxable Status of Stock Dividends in Federal Tax Law.

Where a corporation issued bonds at par and later bought some on the open market at less than par it would seem that the difference should be taxable income to the corporation if the corporation is solvent and the bonds are extinguished and the corporation did not lose the money borrowed on the bonds; but the matter cannot be said to be settled.

Where a corporation paid income tax for an employee it was held that this constituted additional taxable income to the employee. Whether, if the employer should pay this additional tax, such payment would also become taxable income to the employee, was expressly left undecided.

Where A leased land to X who erected a building thereon and then forfeited the lease, it was held that although the building could not be profitably severed A was taxable on the increase to the value of the land due to the addition of the building thereto.

Where A conveyed property on trust for his wife B with power to revoke, the income from the trust property was held to be taxable to A though he allowed B to collect and use it.

Where A created a trust in order to maintain life insurance policies for the benefit of third persons it was held constitutional for Congress to tax to A the income from such a trust though the trust was irrevocable because the device had been used as a means of avoiding heavy surtaxes, and the obligation to provide for one's family in some way is well recognized.

There are two widely different concepts of taxation; one is the expenditure concept, that is, the taxation of spendings. This is recognized occasionally in taxes on retail sales and in allowing exemptions from income tax for certain amounts for personal and family consumption. The other is the accrual concept which is the recognized basis for the income tax.

Capital gains are not taxable under the British income tax law; the chief argument for taxing them in this country is that the average layman thinks of such gains as income.

§ 18. Deductions—credit for dependents.[8] The federal statute expressly provides that the following shall not be deductible: (1) personal, living or family expenses; (2) cost of new buildings or improvements to property; (3) cost of restoring property or in making good the exhaustion thereof for which an allowance is or has been made; (4) premiums paid on insurance on officer or employee for the benefit of the employer. The list of deductions has already been given, ante § 15.

Where the X corporation wished that the nine members of its executive committee should have a financial interest in the corporation but could not

[8] 27 **Am Jur**, Income Taxes, §§ 94–129.

Right of beneficary of trust (and correlative right of trustee) to deduction, in determining income tax, for loss, depreciation, or depletion. 141 **ALR** 1117–1135.

"Obsolescence" for which deduction may be claimed in computing income tax. 120 **ALR** 446–460.

Deduction of salaries, commissions, or bonuses to officers or employees in computing income tax. 145 **ALR** 834–861.

Income tax: what constitutes a sufficient "charge-off" to entitle taxpayer to "bad debt" deduction. 130 **ALR** 212–225.

Income tax: deduction of loss on sale or demolition of residential property. 139 **ALR** 815–828.

Income tax: deduction for "losses." 11 **ALR** 500–510; s. in 51 **ALR** 536–542.

Income tax: deductibility of amount paid or expense incurred by taxpayer on account of his liability or alleged liability for tort, crime, or statutory violation. 104 **ALR** 680–692.

57 **Harv. L. R.** 129, The Tax Benefit Rule Today.

57 **Harv. L. R.** 175, The Tax Benefit Rule Tomorrow.

40 **Col. L. R.** 1326, Cancellation of Indebtedness and Its Tax Consequences.

41 **Col. L. R.** 61, Cancellation of Indebtedness and Its Tax Consequences.

38 **Col L. R.** 80, Tax Evasion and Tax Avoidance.

3 **Wash. and Lee L. R.** 1, Deductions from Gross Income.

12 **Fordham L. R.** 8, Legal Expenses as Deductions.

issue the stock without first offering it to existing stockholders, and A, a large stockholder, in order to sell the shares to them, borrowed the shares from the X corporation under a ten-year agreement, the expenses incurred in the transaction by A were held not to be an ordinary and necessary business expense but an extraordinary one and hence not deductible.

Interest paid by a corporation on its debenture bonds was held to be deductible even though the holders of such bonds were subordinated to the rights of the general creditors. But where in one transaction A made a pretended gift to his wife and then pretended to borrow back the money it was held that he was not entitled to deduct interest thus pretended to be paid.

Where land taxes were paid by A to discharge the obligation of A's predecessor in title such taxes were not deductible by A.

Where A contracted to buy ore from B and paid B $30,000 in advance and only $3,000 worth of ore was delivered, A's loss was properly deductible when it became apparent that he would be unable to collect anything as damages for breach of contract.

Where A's debtor X was in financial straits and was forced into bankruptcy in 1920, but the prospects were that something would be realized and in 1922 A received a dividend of 15 per cent and in 1923 a dividend of 12½ per cent, A was not entitled to deduct the claim as a bad debt in 1920 even though he reported the dividends as income in 1922 and 1923; the claim less the dividends should have been deducted in 1923.

Where A supported sixty-four orphans or quasi orphans none of whom were related to her, she was not entitled to credit for their support, the arrangement being merely a private charity with no semblance of family or clan relationship.

§ 19. Taxable periods—accounting methods.[9] The taxpayer may treat as the taxable period either the calendar year or any other twelve-month period ending on the last day of any month except December.

He may keep his accounts upon either a cash or accrual basis, and in case of a very large business the second method is preferable, but whichever method is chosen, it must be consistently followed.

Where accounts are kept on an accrual basis and a claim has accrued which is uncertain in amount the taxpayer should report the amount approximately and correct it in an amended return when the amount is later fixed. But if not merely the amount of the claim but the claim itself is wholly unpredictable it should not be reported; for example, where A corporation made an 18-year contract with F as sales manager and discharged him four months later and it was quite uncertain whether the discharge was or was not justified, the liability should not have been reported by A until it was determined.

§ 20. The taxable person.[10] Where the owner of negotiable bonds detached therefrom negotiable interest coupons and made a gift of them to his son who in the same year collected them at maturity, it was held that they remained taxable income to the donor because he had enjoyed the economic benefits thereof. And where a husband assigned to his wife the income to be earned as a member of a partnership it was still taxable to the husband. On the other hand, where a beneficiary of an ordinary trust assigned the in-

9 27 Am Jur, Income Taxes, §§ 195–217.

10 27 Am Jur, Income Taxes, §§ 161–182. 53 Harv. L. R. 1, Five Years with Douglas v. Willcuts.

come therefrom to his children this was held to relieve him from tax liability.

It was held to be not due process for a state to assess against a husband income received by his wife from a partnership with which he had no connection. In most of the community property states community income is chargeable equally between the spouses, each one having a vested interest therein; but in California such income is taxable entirely to the husband the wife having only an expectancy and not a vested interest.

Where an irrevocable trust is created and the beneficiary has a vested interest therein the income therefrom is chargeable to the beneficiary. Where the settlor of a trust reserves the power to revoke either by himself or with the concurrence of some one not having a substantial adverse interest in the disposition of the property the income is chargeable to the settlor. And where the trust is irrevocable but the trustee has absolute discretion as to paying the income to the beneficiary, the latter is not chargeable because he has no vested interest and the income is therefore taxable to the trustee.

In the case of an ordinary partnership, the income is taxable proportionally to each partner; one of the results of this provision is that an individual with a large income from his profession or business will frequently form a partnership with his wife or with one or more of his children in order to avoid the large surtaxes and such action is apparently legal if there is a real and not merely a pretended intent to form a partnership.

Where a partnership or a business trust is composed of a large number of persons the federal income tax statute classifies them, along with corporations, as associations, and this classification has been held to be constitutional.

LABOR LAW

CHAPTER I

THE NATIONAL LABOR RELATIONS ACT—DUTIES OF THE EMPLOYER

§ 1. In general.[1] The common law as to labor relations has already been discussed in Torts §§ 102–106 and equitable relief in Equity § 59. Most of the following pages will deal with the effect of modern statutes on labor law.

The most important statute is the National Labor Relations Act, passed in 1935. That statute undertook to deal with such unfair labor practices by employers as affected interstate commerce, and was held to be constitutional

[1] 31 **Am Jur,** Labor, §§ 136–154.

Construction and application of National Labor Relations Act. 112 **ALR** 959-968; s. in 115 **ALR** 314–322; 123 **ALR** 612-661.

State labor legislation as affected by N. L. R. A. 117 **ALR** 414, 415.

Subpoenas duces tecum issued by National Labor Relations Board. 136 **ALR** 890–894.

Unfair labor practice, within National Labor Relations Act or similar state statute, predicated upon expressions of opinion or statements by employer concerning labor unions. 146 **ALR** 1024–1045.

Unfair labor practice, within National Labor Relations Act or similar state statute, predicated upon statements or acts by employees not expressly authorized by employer. 146 **ALR** 1062–1095.

39 **Col. L. R.** 339, Politics and Labor Relations.

49 **Yale L. J.** 461, Unemployment Compensation and Labor Disputes.

41 **Mich. L. R.** 66, N. L. R. B. Back Pay.

41 **Mich. L. R.** 595, N. L. R. B. Fair Procedure.

40 **Mich. L. R.** 24, Federal Intervention in Labor Disputes and Collective Bargaining.

16 **Wis. L. R.** 211, Employer Freedom of Speech and the N. L. R. B.

17 **Ind. L. J.** 517. The Social Problem: Legal Principles Involved in Its Solution.

29 **Corn. L. Q.** 203, A Slave Trade Law in a Contemporary Setting.

22 **Oreg. L. R.** 1, The National War Labor Board, Its Powers and Duties.

8 **Mo. L. R.** 25, Freedom of Speech in Labor Controversies.

11 **Geo. Wash. L. R.** 399, Wartime Wage Control.

5 **U. of Toronto L. J.** 403, The N. L. R. A.

12 **Fordham L. R.** 252, Guaranteed Wages under New York State Minimum Wage Legislation.

even as applied to manufacturing establishments whose activities were so extensive as to obstruct or unduly to burden the freedom of such commerce. The failure of the statute to deal with unfair conduct of employees was held to go only to the policy of the act, not to the power of Congress to pass it.

§ 2. Duty of employer to bargain collectively—the appropriate bargaining unit.[2] Because experience has shown that much labor trouble could be eliminated if the employer and the representative of the employees would try, sincerely and fair-mindedly, to reach an agreement, both the N. L. R. A. and the Railroad Labor Act make it the duty of the employer, enforceable in equity, to bargain collectively with the employees. As a corollary to this it has been held proper to enjoin the employer from entering into a contract with individual employees.

The N. L. R. A. does not undertake to define what is meant by "appropriate bargaining unit" thus leaving the employees free to organize themselves on either a craft, industrial, plant or other basis, as they deem best, without any interference from their employers. Under the rulings of the National Labor Relations Board the appropriate bargaining unit might be several plants in different cities owned and operated by different employers; or it might be the technical engineers and draftsmen in a single plant.

§ 3. Same—choosing the employees' representative—negotiation requirements.[3] In choosing a representative the N. L. R. A. provides that this shall be decided by a majority vote; where there is no majority, the affirmative votes being almost equally divided between two candidates and a substantial vote for "neither," it is the usual practice, though there is no express authority in the Act, to have a run off election with no chance to vote for "neither." But where one candidate received 2454 votes, another 688 and there were 2774 votes for "neither" it was held that no run off election was necessary. Though the Board might, within its discretion, refuse to certify an election where only a small number of the eligible voters cast their votes, yet where this was due to the fact that the employer discouraged voting, it was held that the Board was justified in certifying where most of the votes cast were for one candidate.

Where the contract between the employer and the union provided that employees who had worked at least 60 days and had then been laid off, through no fault of their own, were entitled to seniority rights for a year it was held that such employees were entitled to vote. And where there was a strike over a current labor dispute and an election held during the strike it was held that the strikers were entitled to vote; where there has been no unfair labor practic on the part of the employer it has been held that strikebreakers are also entitled to vote but this holding has been criticised.

Though the Act does not expressly impose upon the employees any duty

[2] 31 **Am Jur**, Labor, § 98.
What amounts to "collective bargaining" within National Labor Relations Act. 147 **ALR** 7–55.
43 **Col. L. R.** 731, Compulsory Contracts in the Crystal Ball.
43 **Col. L. R.** 586, The Scope of Compulsory Contracts Proper.
43 **Col. L. R.** 705, Duty to Bargain in the Motion Picture Industry.
43 **Col. L. R.** 603, Bargaining, Duress and Economic Liberty.
43 **Col. L. R.** 688, New Conceptions of Contract in Labor Relations.
39 **Col. L. R.** 1110, The Appropriate Unit.
39 **Mich. L. R.** 1065, The Evolution of the "Duty to Bargain." Concept in American Law.
10 **U. of Chicago L. R.** 177, Union Peacetime Restraints on Collective Bargaining.

[3] 31 **Am Jur**, Labor, §§ 100, 151–154.
38 **Ill. L. R.** 41, "Representatives of Their Own Choosing."

to negotiate with the employer, they must indicate to the employer their willingness to negotiate before he can be considered in default.

The employees may insist upon personal conferences at the plant, the employer not being entitled to insist upon negotiation by letter or at their main office located a long distance from the plant. And the employees may insist upon having the contract reduced to writing and signed by the employer.

§ 4. Duty of employer not to interfere with or to dominate union.[4] In order to evade the statutory requirement of sincere and open-minded bargaining with an employees' representative, employers have resorted to various devices all of which have been held to be unfair labor practices: for example, planting spies and bribing union leaders in order to undermine the solidarity of the union members; importing laborers for the purpose of obstructing or interfering by force or threats with peaceful picketing by employees during a strike affecting wages, hours or conditions of labor; circulating blacklists of individual laborers to prevent them from obtaining employment elsewhere; requiring employees to relinquish the right to strike or to demand a closed shop; fostering and assisting and dominating a company union as an employees' representative. And where the employer solicited leading men of one union in order to beat a rival union in an election it was held that the winner did not represent an uncoerced majority of the employees.

On the other hand, where an employer had in 1927 put into effect an employees' representation plan, revised it several times and in May 1937 revised it to comply with the N. L. R. A., and the Board found that the plan of joint control vested in management and employees had functioned well for ten years, it was held not to be necessary to require its disestablishment.

§ 5. Duty of employer not to discriminate.[5] After a lawful strike has been terminated it is the duty of the employer to reinstate all the strikers without discrimination unless the work formerly done by strikers is now done by old employees, not by strikebreakers, in which case all that such strikers are entitled to is to be put on the preferential list for future employment.

After the termination of an unlawful strike, for example, a sit-down strike or a strike by seamen, the strikers are not entitled to insist upon reinstatement and the fact that the employer invites some to return does not work an estoppel against him. Where employees refused to work overtime except upon their own terms but did not cease their regular work, the court, apparently influenced by the sit-down strike cases, held that the employer

4 31 Am Jur, Labor, § 148.
41 Mich. L. R. 1037, In Defense of the Supreme Court's Picketing Doctrine.

5 31 Am Jur, Labor, § 148.
Violation or alleged violation of collective bargaining agreement as "unfair labor practice" within jurisdiction of labor relations boards. 137 ALR 867–870.
Amount which employee, or one wrongfully denied employment, has earned, or might have earned, in other employment as affecting computation of amount to compensate him for loss of time due to unfair labor practice. 133 ALR 1235–1237; s. in 144 ALR 399–401.
Treatment of strikebreakers or others employed pending strikes as affecting question of compliance by employer with order of board or decree of court regarding reinstatement of strikers, and validity of such orders. 135 ALR 565–567.
National Labor Relations Act: right of employer by agreement or compromise with employees or former employees to avoid compliance with board's order for their reinstatement or other order in relation to them. 129 ALR 879, 880.
Nonprofit hospitals or other charitable institutions as within contemplation of Federal or state legislation regarding relation of employers and employees. 132 ALR 1153–1157.

was entitled to discharge the recalcitrant employees. The reasoning is not convincing because if the employees had gone on a strike they would have apparently been entitled to reinstatement upon the strike's termination.

Though there is no excuse provided in the N. L. R. A. for an employer who is compelled to discriminate because of an emergency it has been held that where because of rivalry between two unions of radio operators and the need for keeping its ships moving, the employer was compelled to discharge three employees, it need not reinstate them though such discharge was technically an unfair labor practice. On the other hand, it was held that where an employer newspaper discharged some employees in order to get its papers delivered this was no excuse for failing to reinstate them.

It is well settled that an employer may not discharge an employee because the latter is a member of a labor union; and it has also been held that in hiring men the employer may not discriminate against a candidate for employment because he is a unionist, so that if the laborer thus discriminated against is unable to get other employment the employer may, within the Board's discretion, be compelled to give him employment and back pay; and even if he has obtained equivalent employment elsewhere the Board may undo the discrimination and thus require the employer to furnish employment. But this position has been severely criticised as unduly drastic against employers.

CHAPTER II

OTHER LEGISLATION AFFECTING LABOR

§ 6. Anti-injunction statutes—"labor disputes."[6] Long before 1914 there had been agitation against allowing the employer the highly effective weapon of the injunction against strikes, boycotts and picketing. In that year Congress passed the Clayton Act forbidding any federal court to give an injunction or restraining order in a dispute concerning terms and conditions of employment unless necessary to prevent irreparable injury to property or to a property right. This Act was so strictly construed and so many injunctions were issued in spite of it that in 1932 there was passed the Norris-La Guardia Act confirming the earlier statute, and providing that if there is a labor dispute no injunction shall issue except after findings of fact by the court that unlawful acts have been committed and will be continued unless restrained. Similar anti-injunction statutes have been passed in several states.

[6] 31 **Am Jur**, Labor, §§ 178–286, 363–405.

Suit between labor organizations or members thereof as involving a labor dispute within anti-injunction statutes. 138 **ALR** 287–300.

Liability of labor union or its members for circulating false statements with respect to industrial disputes. 1 **ALR** 1149–1151.

Liability for procuring breach of contract. 84 **ALR** 43–100.

Liability of unincorporated labor organization to suit. 27 **ALR** 786–799; s. in 149 **ALR** 508–525.

Liability of labor organization for inducing breach of contract to furnish or accept material. 29 **ALR** 562–566.

Power of labor union to bind individual members by contracts or arrangements with employers. 95 **ALR** 10–56.

Legality of rule of labor organization operating to discriminate between employers and localities. 47 **ALR** 391–394.

Liability of labor union or its members for unlawful suspension or expulsion of member. 62 **ALR** 315–318.

Validity of stipulation in contract of employment against connection with labor union or employers' association, and power of legislature to prohibit such contract. 68 **ALR** 1267–1273.

42 **Harv. L. R.** 766, Labor Injunctions and Federal Legislation.

21 **Oreg. L. R.** 63, The Anti-Injunction Acts and Our State Constitutions.

11 **Geo. Wash. L. R.** 428, The Norris-La Guardia Act in the Constitution.

These statutes do not apply to situations where there is no labor dispute but as to whether or not in a particular case there is a labor dispute is often a difficult question for the courts to decide. In the following cases it was held that there was a labor dispute within the meaning of the statute: where the union picketed plaintiff's place of business to bring pressure on plaintiff to coerce his employees into joining the union; where a negro organization picketed a new grocery store to compel the employment of negro clerks; where the X union picketed an employer to compel him to recognize it instead of the Y union as employees' representative; where thirteen truck drivers went on a strike for higher wages and the four employers, brothers, did the work themselves, whereupon the union picketed the premises; where the union picketed a retail meat dealer to bring pressure upon the wholesaler to pay his employees union wages; where A's employees, being out on strike, picketed his store with placards stating that A was unfair in not employing union labor to maintain his burglar alarm system.

On the other hand, in the following cases there was held to be no labor dispute and the anti-injunction statute did not apply: where the union tried to coerce a motion picture proprietor to employ a projectionist instead of doing the work himself; where A ordered an electric sign for his store specifying that the sign work was to be done by union labor, Local 304, and after its erection two other unions picketed the store claiming that the sign was nonunion manufactured; where a musicians' union induced stage hands union to join in a combination to destroy A's "opera on tour" business because A used canned music; where a fish dealers' association demanded that A, a fish canner, agree not to buy fish except from members of the association and when A refused, induced its members not to sell fish to A; where X, a general contractor, employed Y, a subcontractor, on a job where only union men worked but X had other jobs on which he did not employ union men exclusively and the union called a strike on Y in order to bring pressure on X to employ only union labor on all his jobs.

Where the action of the union is attended with deliberate violence and intimidation the anti-injunction statutes do not prevent the issuance of an injunction against such acts even if there is a labor dispute. And where the American Federation of Musicians demanded that members of the American Guild of Musical Artists resign therefrom and become members of the American Federation before a certain date or they would not be permitted to fulfil any engagements, it was held that the American Guild was entitled to an injunction because the objective was not a lawful one.

Where A and B were peddlers of baked goods working seven days a week and unions picketed their customers in order to compel them to work only six days a week and employ a union man for the seventh day it was held that even if there was no labor dispute the unions were entitled to the protection of the Fourteenth Amendment in disseminating information.

And where an employee of X agreed not to act as laundry driver for himself or any other laundry for two years after his employment with X should cease the Anti-injunction Act prevented giving an injunction against him.

§ 7. The Sherman Anti-trust Act—miscellaneous.[7] The Sherman Act, passed in 1892, was aimed at combinations of capital in restraint of inter-

[7] 31 **Am Jur,** Labor, §§ 38-42.

Validity of legislation directed against political, social, or industrial propaganda deemed to be of a dangerous tendency. 1 **ALR** 336-338; s. in 20 **ALR** 1535-1550; 73 **ALR** 1494-1501.

Constitutionality of statute regulating the time of payment of wages. 12 **ALR** 612-640; s. in 26 **ALR** 1396-1397.

Constitutionality of child labor laws. 12 **ALR** 1216-1226; s. in 21 ALR 1437, 1438.

What employers are within "hours of labor" statutes. 16 **ALR** 537-546.

Validity of minimum wage statutes relating to private employment. 24 **ALR** 1259-1262; s. in 47 **ALR** 217, 218; 103 **ALR** 1466, 1467; 108 **ALR** 1345, 1346.

Constitutionality of the "Service Letter" Acts. 27 **ALR** 39-41.

Constitutionality of statute relating to absence of employee in private employment. 28 **ALR** 616.

Waiver of statutory right to immediate payment of wages on discharge. 41 **ALR** 445.

Constitutionality of statute regulating employment agencies. 56 **ALR** 1340-1345; s. in 133 **ALR** 1505-1510.

Construction and application of child labor law as regards exhibitions or entertainments by children. 72 **ALR** 141-143.

Necessity in indictment charging violation of statute regarding wages, or hours, of naming particular employers. 81 **ALR** 76, 77.

Constitutionality of statutes limiting hours of labor in private industry. 90 **ALR** 814-842.

What is a "manufacturing establishment" within meaning of regulatory statutes. 96 **ALR** 1351-1358.

Waiver of statutory right to minimum wage or benefit of regulation as to hours of labor. 102 **ALR** 842-846; s. in 129 **ALR** 1145-1148.

Constitutionality, construction, and application of statutes relating specifically to hours of service or other conditions affecting drivers of motor trucks. 120 **ALR** 295-297.

Judicial question regarding Federal Fair Labor Standards Act (Wage and Hour Act) and state acts in conformity therewith. 130 **ALR** 272-286; s. in 132 **ALR** 1443-1459.

Intrastate transportation of goods after they are shipped in interstate commerce and warehoused, as constituting a part of interstate commerce, within contemplation of Federal Fair Labor Standards Act. 149 **ALR** 386-407.

Construction and application of provisions of Fair Labor Standards Act (Wage and Hour Act) regarding investigatory subpoenas duces tecum. 149 **ALR** 194-201.

Conduct of employees or labor union as unfair labor practice within labor relations acts. 149 ALR 464-476.

What constitutes a "service establishment" within exemption provision of Fair Labor Standards Act. 150 **ALR** 700-713.

Janitors, elevator operators, watchmen, and other service or maintenance employees, as engaged in "commerce" or in "production of goods for commerce" within Fair Labor Standards Act. 150 **ALR** 589-601.

Construction and application of provisions of Federal Railway Labor Act regarding the method of choosing representative for purpose of negotiation with employer. 109 **ALR** 353-355.

Validity and effect of the provisions of the Federal Transportation Act for settlement of disputes between carriers and their employees. 47 **ALR** 836-840.

Validity, construction, and application of statute designed to prevent discrimination between male and female employees as regards wages or other conditions of work. 130 **ALR** 436.

Statutes presenting medium of payment of wages or salary as prohibiting compensation by corporate stock or other interest in business. 137 **ALR** 846-849.

Provision of Fair Labor Standards Act for increased compensation for overtime. 140 **ALR** 1263-1269.

Validity, construction, and application of provision of Fair Labor Standards Act that no provision of the act shall justify an employer in reducing a wage which is in excess of the applicable minimum wage of the act. 144 **ALR** 1375, 1376.

Constitutionality, construction, and application of statutes prohibiting agreements to refund wages under employment contracts ("kickback" agreements). 149 **ALR** 495-505.

Validity of statute, or administrative regulation thereunder, which in effect guarantees to part-time employees minimum wages regardless of the time of their actual employment. 143 **ALR** 1086, 1087.

Claims based on provisions of statutes relating specifically to rights, duties, and obligations between employer and employee as subject to arbitration provisions of contracts or statutes. 149 ALR 276-281.

Judicial questions regarding Federal Social Security Act and state legislation adopted in anticipation of or after the passage of that act, to set up "state plan" contemplated by it. 100 **ALR** 697-699; s. in 106 **ALR** 243; 108 **ALR** 613-618; 109 **ALR** 1346-1348; 118 **ALR** 1220-1225; 121 **ALR** 1002-1010.

Who is an independent contractor rather than an employee within social security acts or unemployment compensation acts. 124 **ALR** 682-685.

Construction and application of provision of Federal Social Security Act that makes one's status as wife, widow, child, or parent, etc., dependent upon state law respecting devolution of intestate personal property. 147 **ALR** 598.

What amounts to vendor-vendee or lessor-lessee relationship as distinguished from employment or service relation, within social security or employment compensation acts. 129 **ALR** 525, 526.

Exhaustion of administrative remedies as condition of resort to court in respect of right claimed under social security or old age acts. 130 **ALR** 882, 883.

Test of independent contractor relationship in the field of workmen's compensastion and social security acts. 134 **ALR** 1029-1033; s. in 147 **ALR** 828-830.

Construction and application of provisions of social security or unemployment compensation acts relating to exemptions of corporations or institutions of a restate or foreign commerce, but the language was broad enough to cover also combinations of labor; and in the famous Danbury Hatters case, decided in 1908, a complaint alleging that the United Hatters of America, a union with 9,000 members and affiliated with the American Federation of Labor, conspired to interfere with the carrying out by the plaintiff hat manufacturer, of contracts with wholesalers of hats outside the state, was held good on demurrer.

This case was followed in 1921 in a case where the defendant union maintained a boycott against the shipping of plaintiff's printing presses, manufactured in Michigan, to New York City where its principal market was located; and in 1926 in a case where the defendants conspired to prevent manufacturing plants outside Chicago from selling and delivering nonunion made building material in Chicago, and it was no defense that the purpose was also to shut out nonunion made material from inside Illinois, outside of Chicago. These decisions were followed in 1927 by a case where the defendant labor union called a general strike to coerce local employers not to buy limestone products of Indiana operators because such products had been processed by nonunion labor, even though the avowed purpose of the defendants was to compel unionization.

On the other hand, relief has been refused in cases where the defendant had not "directly" interfered with interstate commerce, the defendant's mere knowledge that plaintiff's products would be shipped in interstate

ligious, charitable, or educational character. 136 **ALR** 1467, 1468.

Construction and application of provisions of unemployment compensation acts relating to seasonal employment. 136 **ALR** 1480–1485.

Insurance agents and solicitors of mutual benefit associations as within the coverage or exclusionary provisions of social security or unemployment compensation acts. 137 **ALR** 625–628.

Salesman on commission as within unemployment compensation or social security acts. 138 **ALR** 1413–1423.

Construction and application of state social security or unemployment act as affected by terms of the Federal act or judicial or administrative rulings thereunder. 139 **ALR** 892–895.

Officer of corporation or member of firm as an employee for purposes of social security act. 139 **ALR** 925–927.

What constitutes "agricultural labor" or "farm labor" within social security or unemployment compensation act. 139 **ALR** 1164–1171; s. in 146 **ALR** 1318–1323.

Rank or priority of lien or claim for unpaid employer's contribution under social security or unemployment compensation act. 140 **ALR** 1042, 1043.

Circumstances of abandonment of employment, or nature of excuse for refusing re-employment, as affecting right to unemployment compensation. 141 **ALR** 101–104.

Validity, construction, and application of provisions of social security or unemployment compensation acts as to employment units which are affiliated or under a common control. 142 **ALR** 918–932.

Industrial homeworkers as within social security unemployment compensation, fair labor standards or workmen's compensation acts. 143 **ALR** 418–421.

Receiver as within social security and unemployment compensation acts. 143 **ALR** 984-987.

One who uses his own truck as an independent contractor or an employee of concern for which he transports goods, within social security or unemployment compensation act. 144 **ALR** 740–743.

State banks, insurance companies, or building and loan associations, which are members of Federal Reserve Bank or similar Federal agency, or national banks, as within state social security or unemployment compensation act. 145 ALR 1074–1075.

What amounts to "misconduct" which precludes benefits under unemployment compensation act to discharged employees. 146 **ALR** 243–245.

Construction and application of self-employment provisions of social security or unemployment compensation acts. 146 **ALR** 748, 749.

Construction and application of provision of Federal Social Security Act that makes one's status as wife, widow, child, or parent, etc., dependent upon state law respecting devolution of intestate personal property. 147 **ALR** 598.

57 **Harv. L. R.** 183, The National War Labor Board and the Maintenance-of-Membership Clause.

40 **Col. L. R.** 14, The Sherman Act and Labor Disputes.

29 **Va. L. R.** 272, 395, Organized Labor and the Clayton Act.

41 **Mich. L. R.** 1060, Coverage of the Fair Labor Standards Act.

21 **Oreg. L. R.** 37, Trade Unions under the Wagner Act.

29 **Ky. L. J.** 413, Labor Warfare and the Anti-Injunction Laws.

31 **Georgetown L. J.** 115, The Practical Administration of the Wage and Hour Act.

commerce not being sufficient to show an intent to interfere; or where plaintiff's enterprise was too small to affect interstate commerce substantially. And a jurisdictional dispute between a carpenters' union and a machinists' union over the erection and dismantling of machinery was held not to be a violation of the Act.

Ordinances requiring a license to distribute circulars, hand books, etc., have been held invalid as an infringement of the freedom of the press though the purpose of the ordinances was to keep the streets clean. And a statute forbidding loitering or picketing was held invalid on its face because an infringement of the constitutional right to disseminate information about labor disputes, peaceful picketing being the laborer's means of communication.

Ordinarily where there has been picketing with violence an injunction will issue only against the violence but where there has been much violence in the past it has been held proper to enjoin all picketing.

CHAPTER III

THE TRADE AGREEMENT

§ 8. Contracts fixing wages and hours—right of the union and the individual employee.[8] Where an employer enters into a trade agreement with a representative of his employees, and the employer later, in violation of the agreement, substitutes piece work for weekly wages, the union is entitled to an injunction, increased cost of production making the business unprofitable to the employer being no excuse.

On the other hand, where protests against the retention of married women resulted in a new agreement between the union and the employer as to discharging married women regardless of the seniority rights provided for in the old agreement, it was held that the plaintiff, a married woman who had been discharged, could not rightly complain because both agreements were for the benefit of all the members of the union and hence the union could validly consent to the abrogation of the plaintiff's seniority rights in the interest of all.

Where the trade agreement provided for payment for overtime and some six months later X, an employee, quit work, and then some three weeks later became a member of the union it was held that he was not entitled to the benefit of the provision in the trade agreement because the union was not his agent when the agreement was made and the provision had never been made a part of his contract with the employer; and apparently it would have made no difference if the employer had voluntarily given the benefit of the provision to other nonunion employees.

8 31 **Am Jur**, Labor, §§ 96-127.
Continuance or termination of labor union's status or authority as bargaining agent. 144 **ALR** 444-471.
Validity, construction, and application of statute or ordinance regarding solicitation of persons to join an organization or society or to pay membership fees or dues. 144 **ALR** 1346-1351.
Collective labor agreements. 95 **ALR** 10-56.
Right of member to recover against union where, without fault on his part, he has been damaged by its act, not specifically directed against him. 117 **ALR** 823-825
Withdrawal of a local labor union or part of its membership from the parent organization or from a general association as affecting property rights. 131 **ALR** 902-908.
Right of labor union to publicize that commodity is nonunion-made, or that competing commodity is union-made. 131 **ALR** 1068-1074.
44 **Harv. L. R.** 572, Collective Labor Agreements in American Law.
50 **Harv. L. R.** 1071, A Half Century of Legal Influence upon the Development of Collective Bargaining.
17 **Wash L. R.** 181; 18 **Wash. L. R.** 1, The Collective Bargaining Agreement and Its Legal Effects.

§ 9. **Same—rights of the employer.**[9] Where a union calls a strike in violation of its trade agreement the employer is entitled to a decree of specific performance and the anti-injunction statute is no defense. Where a union insisted that the employer could not operate its shop in accordance with the trade agreement, it was held that the employer was entitled to close the factory. And where three foremen truculently demanded straight time in violation of the trade agreement, it was held that the employer was entitled to discharge them.

§ 10. **Contract for a closed union shop.**[10] Where there is an agreement between the employer and the local union that only members of that union be employed a change of affiliation of the local from the A. F. of L. to the C. I. O. does not change the rights and liabilities of the local. Where there is no change of affiliation but a majority of the members of the local withdraws and forms a new, previously nonexistent union, the employer is justified in carrying out its contract with the old union.

Where the employees have selected a labor union to represent them and a closed shop contract has been entered into, they are not entitled to a certificate that they have selected another union to represent them in order to repudiate the contract. On the other hand, where an employer corporation became dissatisfied with the contract because it paid one and a half for overtime while its competitors did not, and the stockholders formed a new corporation which took over all of the assets of the old corporation and the old corporation discharged its union employees and the new corporation employed nonunion men, it was held that neither corporation was liable on the contract.

Where a closed shop contract was entered into with an A. F. of L. union, comprising about 85% of the employees it was held that the employer was justified in shutting down its plant in order to prevent the entrance of a rival C. I. O. union and the consequent disruption of industrial peace.

Where a three-year contract was entered into in New York City, the employer agreeing not to remove beyond the five-cent-fare limits and it later removed to Pennsylvania and locked out the former employees, the employer was compelled to move back to New York, re-employ the old workers and pay them compensatory damages.

CHAPTER IV

UNION MEMBERSHIP

§ 11. **The right to join a union—classification of members.**[1] While apart from legislation a court of equity will not compel a union to admit a new member thereto, it will enjoin the union which so refuses membership, from

9 31 **Am Jur,** Labor, § 121.

10 31 **Am Jur,** Labor, §§ 108, 109.

Constitutionality, construction, and application of statute prohibiting employer from deducting from wages of employees dues or assessments payable to labor organization, or otherwise assisting in collection thereof. 108 **ALR** 1133.

Deduction or collection of labor union dues from wages of employees. 135 **ALR** 507-511.

43 **Col. L. R.** 42, The Closed Union and the Right to Work,

1 31 **Am Jur,** Labor, §§ 31-37, 65.

Validity and construction of contract by labor unions to continue salary or wages in whole or in part to pay benefits if other party loses employment or position because of joining union. 114 **ALR** 1300-1302; s. in 125 **ALR** 1260, 1261.

50 **Yale L. J.** 621, Civil Liberties and the Trade Union.

91 **U. of Pa. L. R.** 275, Union Security: A Study of the Emergence of Law.

interfering with the work of such applicant; and if the union should force the applicant's discharge, will enjoin the union from interfering with his reinstatement.

Since the union may entirely refuse membership it may give only temporary membership. But where a theatrical stage employees and moving-picture machine operators union gave all the votes to seniors who paid $80 annual dues while juniors, who were just as competent, paid $454 dues per annum, it was held that the juniors were entitled to have those provisions of the constitution and by-laws annulled in the public interest.

§ 12. Same—"yellow dog" contracts.[2] In 1917 it was decided in the famous Hitchman case that where a mining company employed mine workers on a strictly nonunion basis and the defendant union, knowing this, persuaded about sixty of the workers to agree to join the union, planning that as soon as enough agreed they would go on strike and unionize the mine, the employer was entitled to an injunction because the purpose was unlawful. Following this decision employers frequently stipulated with their employees that they should not join a union and such employment contracts came to be known as yellow dog contracts. Such stipulations in employment contracts were expressly declared unenforceable in the Norris-La Guardia Act of 1932.

§ 13. The union's right to punish members.[3] Where, after a fair trial, a union expels or suspends a member for a violation of its rules he has no redress for such loss of membership; but where as such member he held a certificate of insurance and the ground for his expulsion was that in a vote directed by a government agency to determine whether the members of the union desired that union or another union to represent them and he voted against his own union this was held not to be sufficient ground for forfeiting the insurance certificate.

Though the union may be justified in expelling a member it is liable in damages for procuring his discharge from his employment. But where plaintiff became in arrears in dues to the union and under the closed shop contract became ineligble to work, and was suspended therefor and the unions picketed the employer till he discharged the plaintiff, it was held that the plaintiff has no cause of action against the union.

On the other hand, where the employee in arrears to the union is not expelled or suspended the union is not entitled to deprive him of his employment merely in order to collect the arrears, the ordinary remedies of a creditor being open to the union.

§ 14. Judicial review over punitive measures taken by the union.[4] The rule usually laid down is that a member who contends that his expulsion or suspension was wrongful must first exhaust his remedies within the union before appealing to the courts, even though it may be difficult for him to prosecute the necessary appeals provided for by the union constitution. But

[2] 31 **Am Jur,** Labor, § 11.

[3] 31 **Am Jur,** Labor, § 50.
Validity of trade union's classification of members. 97 **ALR** 609-612.

[4] 31 **Am Jur,** Labor, §§ 66, 67.
Mandamus to compel reinstatement of suspended or expelled members of labor union. 141 **ALR** 617-623.
Controversy within labor union regarding seniority rights as subject of litigation in civil courts. 142 **ALR** 1055-1071.
48 **Yale L. J.** 195, Collective Labor Agreements in the Courts.
49 **Yale L. J.** 424, Inter-Union Disputes in Search of a Forum.
38 **Ill. L. R.** 128, Federal Control of Collective Bargaining.

this rule was not applied where five successive appeals were provided for, the last being to the general convention of the union, the appeals not being of right but of grace only.

Nor is the rule enforced where the procedure provided for by the union rules has not been followed; for example, where the required charges in writing were not made; or where it is obvious to the court that in other respects the disciplined member did not have a fair trial. An anti-injunction statute has been held to be no bar to giving relief against an arbitrary expulsion because no labor dispute is involved.

PART IV—PROCEDURE

COMMON LAW PLEADING

CHAPTER I

INTRODUCTION

§ 1. Origin of forms of action.[1] Before the Norman conquest of England in 1066 the people were the fountainhead of justice. The Anglo-Saxon courts of those days were composed of large numbers of freemen, and the law which they administered was that which had been handed down by oral tradition from generation to generation. In competition with these popular, nonprofessional courts the Norman king, who insisted that he was the fountainhead of justice, set up his own tribunals. The judges who presided over these royal courts were the agents or representatives of the king, not of the people; but they were professional lawyers who devoted most of their time and energy to the administration of justice, and the courts over which they presided were so efficient that they gradually all but displaced the popular, nonprofessional courts.

The Anglo-Saxon tribunals had been open to all; every freeman could appeal to them for justice. But there was no corresponding right to sue in the king's courts. That was a privilege which had to be purchased by any suitor who wished to avail himself of the superior efficiency of royal justice. These privileges were issued to suitors by the king's secretary or chancellor, and the document which evidenced the privilege was called an original writ. Since it was necessary that the writ be issued before the king's courts were authorized to hear the case, the royal judges had only a limited, not a universal jurisdiction.

The form of the writ depended upon the case which the suitor wished to present to the court. It would vary according to the fact alleged and the relief sought by the complaining party. If the suitor complained that the defendant had trespassed on his land the writ issued to him would not be the same as if he had alleged that the defendant had refused to return a borrowed horse. And a writ for the recovery of the possession of land would be quite unlike a writ in trespass for false imprisonment. At first these writs were issued by the king's secretary or chancellor himself; later, after the devising of new kinds of writs became infrequent, the task of issuing writs became a matter of routine and was attended to by the chancellor's clerks.

Some two centuries after the Norman conquest the issuance of writs had become so mechanical that suitors were unable to induce the clerks in chancery to formulate new writs to meet new states of fact arising out of changed economic and social conditions. To remedy this situation Parliament in 1285 enacted the Statute of Westminster II commanding the

1 41 **Am Jur**, Pleading, § 5.
51 **Yale L. J.** 951, Fundamental Legal Concepts as Applied in the Study of Primitive Law.
51 **Yale L. J.** 1269, In Defense of an Unsystematic Science of Law.

clerks in chancery to issue new writs *in consimile casu,*—that is, in cases that were similar but not exactly like those that were covered by the old writs. Under the authority of this statute a large number of new writs were devised. They were formulated in analogy to the writ in trespass and were therefore called trespass upon the special case, a name which was successively abbreviated to trespass on the case, action on the case, and finally, case.

Of the large number of writs which had been issued prior to the Statute of Westminster II, only six were in common use as late as 1800; these were trespass, debt, covenant, detinue, replevin and account. One other, ejectment, seems to have been developed after but largely independently of the Statute of Westminster II. The action on the case became a large family of actions, with two members of the family so important and so different from the rest that they came to be known as separate actions; these were trover and assumpsit. The most important of those that continued to be called actions on the case are those for deceit, nuisance, negligence, libel, slander, malicious prosecution, and interference with contract, business and domestic relations. The action on the case is today the growing part of the common law; if unprecedent circumstances arise in which courts administering the common law feel that redress should be granted, relief will be awarded in analogy to some one or other of the numerous actions on the case that have already been recognized.

§ 2. The effect of codes of procedure.[2] The wide development of the action on the case went far toward adapting the common law to changing conditions, but not far enough. Partly because of the rigidity of common law rules, partly because common law courts could not issue a direct command to a defendant, partly because common law procedure could not be adapted to complicated cases it became increasingly necessary for the king, as the fountainhead of justice, to administer relief to his subjects directly through his secretary or chancellor as well as indirectly, through his agents of limited authority, the judges of the common law courts. As time went on the chancellor gradually developed a separate court known as the court of chancery. And since this supplementary system of justice which the chancellor administered was claimed to be more just and fair and equitable that the older system enforced in the common law courts, the rules and principles of the chancery court came to be known as equity.

In the common law courts in the early days there were several modes of trial which have since become obsolete—by battle, by ordeal, by wager of law. These were all gradually superseded by trial by jury which, at least after 1600, became the usual method of trial. Since the jury was an unlearned tribunal it was necessary that the issues of fact which it was called upon to decide should be simple, presenting a situation in which one of the parties to the litigation affirmed and the other party denied some material fact. Hence the fundamental aim of common law pleading was to require the parties to arrive at such an issue. This insistence upon simplicity of issue combined with the conservatism of the bench and bar in holding tenaciously to various fictions which had been employed to adapt the common law actions to new social and economic conditions, resulted in making various parts of the system of pleading in common law courts so technical and

[2] 41 Am Jur, Pleading, § 5.

arbitrary that a thoroughgoing revision of the system was very much needed. In England this revision was done by the Common Law Procedure Act of 1873, the actual work of revision being done or supervised by the bench and bar. In the United States things turned out differently. The lead was taken by the New York Legislature. In 1848, without making any serious attempt to win the concurrence of bench or bar, it adopted a code of civil procedure which in terms abolished all the forms of action at common law and the distinction between law and equity and provided for one civil action. Many other states followed the lead of New York and have today what is usually called code pleading. The states which did not adopt a code of procedure have all made statutory modifications of common law pleading, so that the system of pleading which was in existence during the golden age of the common law—from 1800 to 1873—is nowhere followed today.

Even in states which have code pleading a knowledge of common law pleading is still important. For this there are three reasons. The first is that most of our substantive law has grown up around the various forms of action and the attempt, by statute, to abolish them did not and could not put an end to substantive law distinctions which had either come into existence because of their forms or were closely entwined with them. It is therefore necessary to have a knowledge of forms of action in order to understand thoroughly the substantive law. The second reason is that a lawyer—even in a code pleading state—cannot draft his petition or complaint intelligently unless he knows the scope and essential allegations of the declarations in the various common law actions. Finally, a knowledge of the proceedings subsequent to the declaration is highly desirable because it was in the light of those proceedings that many provisions of the codes of civil procedure were interpreted.

§ 3. Acquiring jurisdiction.[3] The authority of the common law court to give relief to a plaintiff was strictly limited by the original writ. Under a writ in trover for the intentional destruction of a chattel in the defendant's possession the court would not listen to a complaint that the defendant owned money to the plaintiff; and a writ in special assumpsit for breach of contract did not authorize a court to award a judgment for damages for an assault and battery. The declaration and all the subsequent proceedings must correspond to the writ.

There was still another requirement that must be met before the court was ready to hear the plaintiff's complaint: it must get jurisdiction of the defendant. This was accomplished by having him served by the sheriff or constable with a summons to appear before the court on a certain day and answer the plaintiff's complaint. Originally it was also necessary that the defendant actually appear and plead before the court acquired jurisdiction over him, but later the courts worked out what appears to us now as the natural, if not inevitable, procedure of entering judgment by default if the defendant, after being served with process, did not appear to defend. If the plaintiff won, either upon default or after the defendant appeared and contested the plaintiff's right to recover, the judgment would be for money damages and costs, except in replevin and ejectment where the main judgment was for the specific chattel or the specific piece of land demanded by him. In detinue the plaintiff recovered either the chattel itself or its value.

3 14 Am Jur, Courts, §§ 159–196.

In replevin, ejectment and detinue the action must ordinarily be brought against the one in possession of the chattel or of the land at the time of bringing the action.

Today, where the plaintiff's debtor is out of the jurisdiction but has property within the jurisdiction, statutes quite generally authorize courts to attach the property and thereby acquire jurisdiction; after giving sufficient publicity to the proceedings to furnish a reasonable notice to the debtor to come in and defend his property against the plaintiff's demand, and the plaintiff wins either upon default of the debtor to appear or after a contest, the court will order the property sold to satisfy the plaintiff's demand. In such a case the proceeding must start with the attachment of the property and the court's jurisdiction is limited to the property; it cannot render a personal judgment against the debtor. But such a proceeding is only by statute, not at common law.

§ 4. Arriving at an issue.[4] Having been authorized by the original writ to hear the case and having acquired jurisdiction of the defendant, the next step is the filing of the pleadings and reaching an issue. The pleading in which the plaintiff states his case is called the declaration. The defendant —if he appears—has a choice of three ways in which to meet the plaintiff's declaration. First, he may demur to it, awaiting the decision of the court as to whether the facts stated in the declaration are such that he is under a legal obligation to answer it. A demurrer raises an issue of law to be decided by the court.

Secondly, he may deny one or more of the facts alleged in the declaration. Such an answer in denial is called a plea and raises an issue of fact, to be decided ordinarily by the court under instructions by the court as to the law applicable to the various possible findings of fact by the jury.

Thirdly, the defendant may confess all the facts properly pleaded in the declaration, but seek to avoid liability thereon by urging other facts not alleged in the declaration. Such a plea in confession and avoidance obviously does not raise an issue and the plaintiff in turn has a choice of three ways in which to meet the facts alleged in the defendant's plea: he may demur to the plea, raising an issue of law as to the legal sufficiency of the facts alleged in it to make out a valid answer to the declaration; he may deny one or more of the facts stated in the plea, or he may confess and avoid them thus giving the defendant a choice of demurring, denying or confessing and avoiding. This process goes on until finally one or the other parties either demurs, raising an issue of law, or pleads in denial, raising an issue of fact. The second pleading of the plaintiff is called a replication; the second pleading of the defendant is called a rejoinder; the third pleading of the plaintiff is called a surrejoinder; the third pleading of the defendant is called a rebutter and the fourth pleading of the plaintiff is called a surrebutter. No name has ever been given to any pleadings beyond a surrebutter and in only a few cases in the books have the pleadings gone far enough to include a surrebutter.

The scope and essential allegations of the declarations in the eleven important common-law actions—Trespass, Trover, Case, Covenant, Debt, Special Assumpsit, General Assumpsit, Detinue, Replevin, Account and Ejectment—have already been slated. See the chapters on Forms of Actions, §§ 1–34.

4 41 Am Jur, Pleading, §§ 362–364.

CHAPTER II

DILATORY PLEAS

A. Pleas to the Jurisdiction and in Suspension of the Action

§ 5. **Pleas to the jurisdiction.**[5] Dilatory pleas are such as tend merely to delay the plaintiff's action instead of dealing with the merits of his claim. While they can often be used to perform a useful function they have been frequently employed merely for the purpose of delaying and thereby discouraging the plaintiff in the pursuit of his remedy; for this reason they have been unpopular with the courts who have consequently required that they be pleaded at once, before demurring to or answering the declaration and have insisted that they be pleaded with strict accuracy.

They are usually classified as follows: (1) Pleas to the jurisdiction; (2) Pleas in suspension of the action; (3) Pleas in abatement.

If the plaintiff has brought his action in a court that does not have jurisdiction of the subject matter of the suit—for an extreme example, in a court that has only criminal jurisdiction—and the want of jurisdiction appears upon the face of the declaration, the defendant may raise the objection by demurrer or motion in arrest of judgment; if it does not appear on the face of the declaration, the defendant may take advantage of it by motion to dismiss or the court may, of its own motion, dismiss or stay the proceedings. Where the court has jurisdiction of the subject matter but because of some defect in the proceedings it does not have jurisdiction in the particular case the defendant must object promptly by a dilatory plea to the jurisdiction, otherwise the right to object is lost.

Example of Plea to the Jurisdiction.

John Doe
v.
Richard Roe

And the said John Doe, in his proper person, comes and defends the wrong and injury, when, etc., and says that this court ought not to have or take further cognizance of this cause, because he the said John Doe was before and at the time of the commencement of this action, and from thence hitherto has been, and still is, a resident of the county of Chester, in the State of Pennsylvania, and that during all of said time he did reside and still resides in the said county of Chester, and did not reside and does not now reside in the said county of York, in the said State of Pennsylvania as in said writ is supposed and alleged; that he, the said John Doe, was not found or served with process in the said county of Chester, but was found and served with process in the said county of York; that the supposed cause of action herein did not, nor did any part thereof, arise in the said county of Chester, but that said supposed cause of action and every part thereof did arise within the said county of York; and this the said defendant is ready to verify: wherefore he prays judgment whether the court here will or ought to have or take further cognizance of this action.

John Doe, Defendant.

(Verification)

[5] 41 Am Jur, Pleading, § 129.

§ 6. Pleas in suspension of the action.[6] If the plaintiff has been declared an outlaw and the judgment of outlawry has worked a total forfeiture of his property, such facts should be pleaded in bar of the action; but if there is no such forfeiture then the fact of outlawry should be set up in suspension of the action.

Similarly, if at the time of bringing action the plaintiff was an alien enemy, such fact may be pleaded in bar; but if he has become an alien enemy since the beginning of the suit, such fact should be pleaded in suspension of the action.

Where a defendant wishes to set up that the plaintiff has contracted to extend time to the defendant and that such time has not expired at the beginning of the suit, the usual method of taking advantage of these facts is by a bill in equity for a temporary injunction. It has been held, however, that it may be set up by a plea in abatement of the writ, though it would seem more appropriate, if allowed to be set up at common law, to have it go in suspension of the action till the time should elapse. Where, by the terms of the contract sued upon, the cause of action had not matured at the time of bringing suit, the defendant may show this under the general issue.

Plea in Supension of the Action—Plaintiff an Alien Enemy.

John Doe
v.
Richard Roe

And the said John Doe, defendant in this cause, by ...., his attorney (or in his proper person), comes and defends the wrong and injury, when, etc., and says that the said plaintiff ought not to have or maintain his action against the defendant, because he says that the plaintiff is an alien, born in foreign parts, out of the allegiance of the United States of America, and within the allegiance of a foreign state, to wit, of the United Kingdom of Great Britain and Ireland, and has not become a citizen of the United States of America by naturalization or otherwise, to wit, at, etc., and that the persons exercising the powers of government in the said foreign state, the United Kingdom of Great Britain and Ireland aforesaid, are at open war with and enemies of the United States of America, to wit, at, etc., and that the said plaintiff being such alien as aforesaid, and an enemy of the United States of America, and not a citizen thereof by naturalization or otherwise, entered and came into the United States of America, and still remains therein, without any letter of safe-conduct from the President of the said United States of America, or any license to be, reside, or remain in the said United States of America, but that the said President ordered and directed him the said plaintiff to quit and leave the United States of America (or set out some other matter showing affirmatively that he has no license to remain); and that the defendant is ready to verify: wherefore he prays judgment whether the plaintiff ought to have or maintain his said action against him.

B. Pleas in Abatement

§ 7. In general.[7] A plea to the jurisdiction asks judgment as to whether the defendant should answer or the court take cognizance of the case; a

6 41 Am Jur, Pleading, § 115.

7 41 Am Jur, Pleading, §§ 124-128.

plea in suspension of the action usually concludes with the prayer that the plaint remain without day; a plea in abatement, in the narrow sense, asks that the writ be abated or quashed. Since a plea in abatement attacks the writ rather than the declaration, a demurrer to such a plea does not reach the declaration.

If the plaintiff demurs to a plea in abatement and the plea is held bad, the judgment of the court is that the defendant shall answer over—i. e., shall answer the declaration. After such a judgment the defendant may either demur to the declaration or plead in bar to the merits. But if the plaintiff puts in a replication to the plea in abatement and the verdict of the jury is in favor of the plaintiff on the issue of fact, the plaintiff is entitled to judgment just as if the defendant had defaulted; in such a case the defendant is not allowed to demur to the declaration or plead in bar to the merits. This is sometimes put on the ground that the defendant is presumed to know whether his plea be true or false in fact; another reason given is that the common law admits of only one issue to the jury; but probably the real reason is the court's dislike of all dilatory pleas and their desire to discourage them.

If the defendant wins on his plea in abatement, either upon an issue of law or of fact, the judgment is that the writ be quashed, in which case, of course, the declaration based thereon is thereby rendered useless. The plaintiff in such case must procure a new writ and it is usually required of the defendant that he supply, in his plea in abatement, the information which will enable him to procure the proper writ and draw up the proper declaration; but this requirement is not enforced where the plaintiff cannot have a better writ.

§ 8. Disability of parties.[8] That the plaintiff is an infant who has undertaken to sue in his own name without a next friend who would become responsible for costs in case the suit should fail, is properly pleaded in abatement. So, if two plaintiffs falsely pretend to be husband and wife the defendant should take advantage of this fact by plea in abatement. And if a supposed plaintiff falsely pretends to be a corporation, the defendant may plead this in abatement though it is also possible to plead the same fact in bar.

Where a defendant is sued as a corporation and it wishes to set up that it is not a corporation, it must do so by a plea in abatement, therein informing the plaintiff whether it is a joint stock company, partnership, or other aggregation of individuals.

Plea in Abatement—Infancy of Plaintiff.

John Doe
v.
Richard Roe

And the said John Doe, the defendant in this suit, by ...., his attorney, comes and defends the wrong and injury, when, etc., and prays judgment of the said writ and declaration, because he says that the said plaintiff is an infant under the age of twenty-one years, to wit, of the age of nineteen years, to wit, at, etc., in the county aforesaid; and this he is

[8] 27 Am Jur, Infants, § 142.

ready to verify: wherefore, inasmuch as the said plaintiff has sued in his own person, and not by his guardian or next friend, the said defendant prays judgment of the said writ and declaration, and that the same may be quashed.

................, Defendant's Attorney.

(Verification)

§ 9. **Nonjoinder of parties.**[9] If the declaration shows on its face that another party should have been joined as plaintiff the defendant may demur, move in arrest of judgment or bring a writ of error. If the defect does not appear on the face of the record the defendant may—in contract actions—take advantage of it either by plea in abatement or may show it under the general issue and ask that the plaintiff be nonsuited; whereas in tort actions the defendant must plead such nonjoinder in abatement.

If the declaration in a contract action shows on its face that the defendant and X contracted jointly with the plaintiff and that X is still alive and therefore should have been joined in the action, the defendant may demur, move in arrest of judgment or bring a writ of error. If the defect does not appear on the face of the writ or declaration, then the defendant must plead such fact in abatement, furnishing to the plaintiff the names and addresses of those who should have been joined. In a tort action the question does not ordinarily arise because the obligation arising from a joint tort is usually not merely joint but joint and several, so that the defendant cannot validly object that he alone has been sued.

Plea in Abatement—Nonjoinder of Parties Defendant.

John Doe
v.
Aaron Brown

And the said John Doe, the defendant in this suit, by ...., his attorney, comes and defends the wrong and injury, when, etc., and prays judgment of the said writ and declaration, and that the same may be quashed, because he says that the said several supposed promises and undertakings in the said declaration mentioned, if any such were made, were, and each of them was, made by the said defendant jointly with one .... (here disclose the names of all the contracting parties), who is still living, and who at the time of the commencement of this suit was, and still is, resident within the jurisdiction of this court, and not by the defendant alone; and this the defendant is ready to verify: wherefore, inasmuch as the said .... is not named in the said writ and declaration together with said defendant, he the said defendant prays judgment of the said writ and declaration, and that the same may be quashed.

§ 10. **Misjoinder of parties.**[10] If action—either contract or tort—is brought by two or more parties and one or more of such parties should not have been joined as plaintiffs, and the defect appears on the face of the declaration, the defendant may demur, move in arrest of judgment or bring a writ of error. If it does not appear on the face of the record but is disclosed by the evidence at the trial it is a proper ground for a nonsuit or a verdict for the defendant; the defendant need not plead in abatement.

9 41 **Am Jur**, Pleading, § 230.

10 39 **Am Jur**, Parties, §§ 118-120.

If a contract action is brought against two or more defendants and one or more of them should not have been joined, the defect, if it appears on the face of the declaration, may be taken advantage of by demurrer, motion in arrest of judgment or writ of error; if it does not thus appear but is disclosed by the evidence it is a proper ground for nonsuiting the plaintiff. In tort actions, on the other hand, the general rule is that misjoinder of parties defendant is no defense at all; the verdict is merely divided, the plaintiff getting a verdict against those defendants who are liable and a verdict being given for those defendants who should not have been joined.

§ 11. **Another action pending.**[1] When the defendant wishes to show that at the time action was brought there was already another action pending in the same jurisdiction between the same parties for the same cause of action, he must do this by plea in abatement; an action brought subsequently, or in another jurisdiction, is no defense at all.

Plea in Abatement—Another Action Pending.

Richard Roe
v.
John Doe

In the Court of .... county, No. ...... of .... Term, A. D.

And the said defendant, John Doe, by his attorney, ..., says that this action was commenced in the court here, on the .... day of ...., A. D. 18...., and not before; and that theretofore, to-wit, etc., he the said plaintiff commenced a certain other action in this court against him the said defendant, in a certain plea of trespass on the case, for the non-performance of the very same promises and undertakings in the plaintiff's declaration in this action set forth; which said former suit so brought and prosecuted against him the said defendant by the said plaintiff is still pending in the said court, and not discontinued, tried, or determined; and this the said defendant is ready to verify.

Wherefore he prays judgment that the writ in the present suit and the proceedings thereon may be quashed.

(Verification)

CHAPTER III

DEMURRERS

§ 12. **The nature and purpose of general and special demurrers.**[2] As already stated, the sufficiency of a declaration or of any subsequent pleading may be promptly tested by the other party interposing a demurrer thereto. The purpose of permitting this prompt objection is to make it easy to avoid the expense of a jury trial where the plaintiff has not stated a cause of action or where the defendant has not pleaded a sufficient defense. The attitude of a demurrant is that even supposing that the facts alleged in the pleading demurred to are true they are not sufficient to sustain any action on the part of the plaintiff, or—if the plaintiff is the demurring party—

[1] 1 Am Jur, Abatement and Revival, §§ 14-44.

[2] 41 Am Jur, Pleading, §§ 204-210, 223-227.

any defense to such an action; and consequently that there is no necessity that he should plead. In other words, he is in substance saying, "even if it is true, what of it?" A demurrer is thus an excuse for not pleading.

In the early common law it was apparently not necessary for the demurrant to point out the defects in the pleading except where he was demurring the duplicity; a demurrer on the ground of duplicity thus came to be known as a special demurrer while any other demurrer was called a general demurrer because under it the demurring party could take advantage of all defects except duplicity. As long as pleadings were made orally in open court this practice produced no inconvenience because the pleadings were then comparatively flexible and informal. But when pleadings came to be written, the forms of the pleadings—under successive judicial rulings—gradually crystallized into a rigid, formal system; and since the party defending his pleading in an argument before the court on general demurrer was not aware, in advance, of what attack would be made upon it, the result was that litigating parties frequently lost a meritorious cause of action or a meritorious defense merely because the exact form of approved precedents had not been followed in every particular.

To remedy this injustice, Parliament in 1585 by Statute 27 Eliz. Chap. V, § 1, reciting that "upon some small mistaking or want of form in pleading, judgments are often reversed upon writs of error, and oftentimes upon demurrers in law given otherwise than the matter in law and very right of the cause doth require" enacted that "after demurrer joined . . . the judges shall proceed and give judgment according as the very right and cause of the matter shall appear unto them, without regarding any imperfection, defect or want of form in any writ, return, plaint, declaration or other pleading, process or course of proceeding whatsoever, except those only which the party demurring shall especially and particularly set down and express together with his demurrer."

This statute thus introduced a distinction in pleading between matters of substance and matters of mere form and changed entirely the meaning of the terms general and special demurrers. The term special demurrer came to be applied to a demurrer which, in addition to testing matters of substance, raised certain specially pointed out objections as to form, while the term general demurrer came to mean a demurrer which did not raise any objection of form and therefore tested only matters of substance.

§ 13. Grounds for general and special demurrers.[3] There is no test by which to determine whether a defect in a pleading is one of substance or one of mere form. If any of the essential allegations have been omitted from the declaration; or if by the substantive law the plea or any subsequent pleading does not state a sufficient answer to the pleading it purports to answer; or if the plaintiff has brought the wrong form of action; or has made a discontinuance; or has made a misjoinder of counts; or if either party has made a departure, such defects are treated as defects of substance and may be reached by either a general or a special demurrer.

But if a pleading is duplicitous; or if, being an affirmative pleading it should conclude with a verification; or a declaration in trespass should omit the phrase vi et armis or if a pleading is an argumentative instead of a direct denial; or if a party has pleaded in confession and avoidance

[3] 41 **Am Jur**, Pleading, §§ 211–222.

when he should have pleaded in denial; or if a defendant has pleaded a specific traverse instead of the general issue; all these defects are treated as matters of mere form, which can be reached only by a special demurrer which specifically points out the formal defect to which objection is being made.

A demurrer reaches only those defects that are apparent on the face of the record, and cannot be used to state new facts not alleged in the "pleading demurred to." Or to take the place of a plea in abatement; or of a plea in bar.

If there are two or more counts in a declaration and a single demurrer is put into the whole declaration the demurrer will be overruled if only one of the counts is good; the defendant should have demurred to each count separately. Similarly, if there are several pleas and a single demurrer to all of them, the demurrer will be overruled if any one plea is good. And where there are two defendants and a declaration is good against one and the two defendants put in a joint demurrer the court will overrule the demurrer.

§ 14. Searching the record.[4] A defect of form in a pleading can be taken advantage of only by a special demurrer of the opposite party specifically objecting thereto; if he fails to do this his right to object is lost. As it is usually expressed, defects of form are waived by pleading over.

But not so with defects of substance. Upon a demurrer to a plea or replication or any subsequent pleading the court will search the record and usually give judgment against the one who committed the first substantial fault in his pleading. As it is sometimes expressed, a bad replication is good enough for a bad plea and a bad plea is a sufficient answer to a bad declaration. The rule is not applied where a substantial defect in a pleading is supplied by a later pleading of the opposite party. But this exception is limited to the supplying of defects; it does not permit a plaintiff to rely upon a cause of action which he has not alleged in his declaration but which is disclosed by the defendant's plea.

Where a defendant puts in two or more pleas to a single count, as he may do under the statute of Anne, the plaintiff may either demur or plead to each of the pleas; if one of these lines of pleading should end in a demurrer it has been held that such a demurrer reaches the declaration even though another of the lines of pleading ended in an issue of fact; but it does not reach any of the other pleadings in another line, with which, of course, it has no connection. It has been held, also, that the fact that there was a demurrer to a declaration which was overruled does not prevent a demurrer to a plea from reaching the declaration.

The two preceding paragraphs apply, however, only if the defendant has put in a plea or pleas in bar; if he pleads in abatement and the plaintiff demurs to it such a demurrer does not reach the declaration.

§ 15. Admission by demurrer or by failure to plead.[5] As already stated in § 12, the attitude of a demurring party is that even conceding the truth of the facts stated in the pleading demurred to, they are not sufficient to state a cause of action or to answer effectively the preceding pleading. For the sake of the argument on the demurrer the demurrant thus admits all the facts in the pleading demurred to which are material and well pleaded.

4 41 Am Jur, Pleading, §§ 232–237.

5 41 Am Jur, Pleading, §§ 238–244.

It does not admit the truth of statements which the court knows are not facts. For example, that the defendant threw stones *molliter*, i. e., gently; or that a child less than two years old rendered services; or that satin suits with gold lace costing £44 were necessaries for an infant. Nor does it admit the truth of statements which are shown by the rest of the pleading to be false.

It does not admit the truth of statements which are not on the record; for example, a note which was the basis of suit but not made a part of the declaration. Nor does it admit the truth of immaterial averments. For example, in an action against a common carrier for negligently transporting goods the exact date of undertaking the transportation was not material and hence not admitted; and in an action of trespass *quare clausum* the allegation of the plaintiff's ownership of the property was not material because possession was sufficient to maintain the action.

A demurrer does not admit the truth of an averment in which the facts are not well pleaded. An averment of a conclusion of law—though regarded as bad only in form—is usually regarded as not well pleaded and therefore not admitted by demurrer. For example, that the property in question was subject to a lien of the plaintiff; or that the defendant's conduct was negligent; or that the local law is thus and so, because the court takes judicial notice of the law that it administers. Similarly, an argumentative averment and an averment which the party had stipulated should not be made are both regarded as not well pleaded and therefore not admitted by demurrer.

In the preceding paragraphs the admissions referred to have been merely for the sake of argument on the demurrer. If there should be a later trial of the issue of fact arrived at by the pleadings, the pleading demurred to cannot be introduced as evidence; it does not have the effect of an ordinary admission by the party.

On the other hand, if the demurring party loses on his demurrer and then fails to plead, judgment goes against him by default. In such a case it will be unnecessary for the other party to prove the material facts well pleaded; the demurring party has admitted them, not by his demurrer, but by his failure to plead thereafter.

General Demurrer to Declaration.

Caption:

Richard Roe
v.
John Doe

And the said Richard Roe, by ...., his attorney, comes and defends the wrong and injury when, etc., and says that the said declaration (or the said first count of the said declaration) and the matters therein contained, in manner and form as the same are above stated and set forth, are not sufficient in law for the said John Doe to have or maintain his aforesaid action thereof against him, the said Richard Roe, and that the said Richard Roe is not bound by the law of the land to answer the same, and this he is ready to verify: wherefore for want of sufficient declaration (or first count of the said declaration) in this behalf, the said Richard Roe prays judgment, and that the said John Doe may be barred from having or maintaining his aforesaid action thereof against him, etc.

Special Demurrer to Declaration.

(Add to above form) And the said Richard Roe, according to the form of the statute in such case made and provided, states and shows to the court here the following causes of demurrer to the said declaration (or to the said first count of the said declaration), that is to say, for that, etc., (Here state the particular causes, and conclude thus:) and also for that the said declaration (or first count of the said declaration) is in other respects uncertain, informal, and insufficient, etc.

CHAPTER IV

PLEAS IN BAR

A. In General

§ 16. Negative and affirmative pleas.[6] If the defendant has omitted to put in either a dilatory plea or a demurrer, or having done so, has not succeeded in so meeting the plaintiff's writ or declaration as to put an end to or suspend the litigation, he must—in order to avoid a judgment against him by default—put in a plea in bar, which usually goes to the merits of the plaintiff's case.

As pointed out above in Section 4, the defendant may plead either negatively or affirmatively—i. e., either in denial or in confession and avoidance. The pleas in denial are called traverses and apparently, in the early days of common-law pleading, each traverse denied a specific fact alleged in the declaration. But in most of the actions one of these traverses developed into what is called a general traverse which denied two or more facts alleged in the declaration and thus led to a general issue of fact between the parties. For this reason the general traverse itself came to be known as the general issue.

Affirmative pleas, i. e., pleas in confession and avoidance, admit the truth of all the facts alleged in the declaration, but set up new facts which avoid, i. e., show that there is no liability. These new facts might be such as excuse or justify the defendant's conduct or they might show that he had discharged or had been released from a liability which at one time came into existence.

§ 17. Pleading several pleas to one count—the Statute of Anne.[7] In the very early days of common-law pleading the plaintiff was probably allowed to state only a single cause of action in his declaration; if he had two or more causes of action against the same defendant he must have a separate writ and declaration for each one. But a long time ago the practice grew up of allowing a plaintiff to seek redress in one declaration for two or more causes of action which were so similar that they could be easily and conveniently tried together. The declaration might thus contain two or more counts in trespass; one for entering the plaintiff's land, another for committing a battery on the plaintiff and a third for carrying away the plaintiff's goods. Similarly, he might join in one decalaration a count for work and labor with another for money lent and a third for goods sold and delivered.

Still later there was developed another use for separate counts. Since

6 41 Am Jur, Pleading, §§ 138–144, 156–160. 7 41 Am Jur, Pleading, § 162.

the plaintiff's lawyer might be uncertain as to what he would be able to prove at the trial, he was permitted to state a single cause of action in two or more different ways so as to avoid, if possible, the misfortune of a variance, i. e., of proving at the trial a cause of action but not the one stated in the declaration. Thus, if his client had contracted to supply the defendant with a carload of potatoes and he was uncertain whether he could prove a delivery or even that title passed he would naturally plead one count in general assumpsit for goods sold and delivered, another for goods bargained and sold and still a third in special assumpsit for refusal to accept the potatoes when tendered.

But no such liberality was shown by the courts towards defendants. To be sure, a defendant was usually able, under the general traverse, to put in issue two or more facts alleged in the county or declaration; but he was allowed only one plea to each count. He must choose between the general issue or a specific traverse or a plea in excuse or one in justification or one in discharge; he could not plead any two of them. But Parliament, recognizing that the defendant's lawyer might lose his case merely because the defense which he was able to prove at the trial was not the one which he thought he would be able to prove when he filed his plea, allowed him, by the statute of Anne, to plead any number of pleas to a single count. As a matter of strict logic any plea in denial is inconsistent with one in confession and avoidance. If, for example, the defendant did not commit the assault and battery alleged in the declaration, how could he have committed it in self-defense, or with the consent of the plaintiff or while making a lawful arrest? Nevertheless, such pleas were allowed, for the reason before mentioned, namely, that the defendant's lawyer, not being omniscient, could not be sure what he could prove at the trial. But the confession involved in any plea in confession and avoidance was limited strictly to the purpose of that plea; it could not be introduced in evidence to prove the plaintiff's case on the issues raised by defendant's pleas in denial.

§ 18. The English Hilary Rules of 1834.[8] In some of the common-law actions the scope of the general traverse—or issue—was gradually so broadened that when it was pleaded by the defendant the plaintiff was under the necessity of proving every fact alleged in his declaration; in still other actions, as trover and case, he was required to prove also many matters which were logically matters in confession and avoidance. The result was that a plaintiff suffered under the disadvantage of not knowing which one of many possible defenses would be relied upon at the trial and must be prepared to meet them all. To remedy this situation the English courts in 1834 adopted certain rules of pleading which narrowed the scope of the general issue in many of the actions, requiring that the negative defenses thus excluded from its scope be set up by way of specific traverse and the affirmative defenses by way of pleas in confession and avoidance. These rules of court went into effect at the Hilary term of court, 1834, and thus came to be called the Hilary Rules. They were in force in England till 1873 when the Judicature Act entirely abolished general issues.

In the United States the Hilary Rules were never adopted, though some of the English decisions under the rules have been followed.

8 41 **Am Jur,** Pleading, § 190.

B. Scope of the Various Pleas in Bar in Each of the Common Law Actions

§ 19. **Trespass.**[9] The general issue in trespass is not guilty. This requires the plaintiff to prove not only that the defendant committed the act of trespass alleged in the declaration, but also, in case of trespass to land or trespass to chattels, that he had such a property right as entitled him to bring the action.

Matters in excuse or in justification must be pleaded specially in confession and avoidance. And likewise matters in discharge.

Trespass—Not Guilty.

Caption:

Richard Roe
v.
John Doe

And the said Richard Roe, by ...., his attorney, comes and defends the force and injury, when, etc., and says that he is not guilty of the said supposed trespasses above laid to his charge or any part thereof, in manner and form as the said John Doe hath above thereof complained against him. And of this the said Richard Roe put himself upon the country, etc.

§ 20. **Trover.**[10] The general issue is not guilty. Under it the defendant may show that he did not commit the act of conversion relied upon in the declaration; or that the plaintiff had no such property interest in the goods as entitled him to maintain the action. Furthermore, since trover is a specialized form of action on the case the conversion alleged in the declaration has been construed to mean a wrongful conversion and matters in excuse or justification have been considered as being in denial of such wrongful conversion and hence can be shown under the general issue. Even matters in discharge can be similarly shown, except that release and the statute of limitations must be pleaded in confession and avoidance, but it has been held that a defendant may, if he prefers, plead any matter in discharge affirmatively.

§ 21. **Case.**[1] The general issue in case is not guilty. Under this plea the defendant may deny not only the conduct attributed to him in the declaration but also the plaintiff's right—property or otherwise—entitling him to maintain the action. Furthermore, since the plaintiff is required to aver such facts in his declaration as would show the defendant's conduct to be wrongful and inexcusable,—the defendant may, under not guilty, take advantage of all defenses in justification or excuse, except that of truth in slander or libel. All defenses in discharge, except that of the statute of limitations, may also be taken advantage of under not guilty.

§ 22. **Covenant.**[2] The plea of *non est factum* ("it was not executed") is sometimes called the general issue in covenant, but it has only a limited scope, denying merely the legal execution of the instrument. Under this plea the defendant can deny that he signed or delivered the instrument, or he can

[9] 41 Am Jur, Pleading, §§ 140–144.

[10] 41 Am Jur, Pleading, §§ 140–144.

[1] 41 Am Jur, Pleading, §§ 140–144.

[2] 41 Am Jur, Pleading, §§ 140–144.

show that at the time of such signing or delivery he was under such legal disability as to render the instrument void. If the defendant wishes to deny the breach or that the plaintiff has performed the conditions precedent he must use a specific traverse; while all pleas in excuse or discharge or those which tend to show the instrument to be voidable only must be pleaded affirmatively in confession and avoidance.

§ 23. Debt on a specialty.[3] As in covenant the plea of *non est factum* puts in issue only the legal execution of the instrument, not the breach or the performance of conditions precedent. Matters in excuse, such as duress or fraud in the inducement, or matters in discharge, such as payment, or accord and satisfaction, must be pleaded affirmatively.

§ 24. Debt on a statute.[4] The general issue in debt on a statutory obligation is *nil debet* (he does not owe). Under this the defendant is apparently able to take advantage of any defense, except the statute of limitations, which must be pleaded affirmatively. In a few cases it has been held proper for the defendant to plead not guilty in preference to *nil debet.*

§ 25. Debt on a record.[5] In debt on a record the plea of *nul tiel* record ("no such record"), frequently referred to as a general issue, puts in issue the legal existence of the record. If the action is on the judgment of a court of record of a sister state and the defendant wishes to set up the defense of want of jurisdiction over the subject matter or over the person he must do so by a special plea setting forth all the facts tending to show lack of jurisdiction. Matters in discharge must be pleaded in confession and avoidance.

§ 26. Debt on simple (unsealed) contract.[6] The general issue in debt on simple contract is *nil debet* ("he owes nothing"). Taken literally, the defendant under this plea would be able to show not only that no debt ever arose but also that although a debt did come into existence it has since been paid, released or otherwise discharged; but it has been held that accord and satisfaction must be specially pleaded in confession and avoidance.

§ 27. Special assumpsit.[7] The general issue in special assumpsit is *non assumpsit* ("he did not undertake or promise"). Taken literally the plea would merely deny the defendant's promise or at most, the existence of the contract; but its scope was gradually extended until it not only put in issue the existence of the contract, the breach and the fulfillment of conditions precedent, but also allowed to be shown all matters in excuse, and almost all matters in discharge. But the defendant may, if he prefers, plead specially all matters in excuse or discharge but not matters which deny the allegations of the declaration.

§ 28. General assumpsit.[8] It is a necessary allegation in every declaration in general assumpsit that the defendant promised to pay either a sum certain or a reasonable sum. But the promise thus alleged is a mere fiction, the sole purpose of the averment being that it affords the only certain method by which to distinguish a declaration in general assumpsit from one in debt on simple contract. It is obvious, therefore, that *non assumpsit,* which is the gen-

3 41 **Am Jur,** Pleading, §§ 140–144.

4 41 **Am Jur,** Pleading, §§ 140–144.

5 41 **Am Jur,** Pleading, §§ 140–144.

6 41 **Am Jur,** Pleading, §§ 140–144.

7 41 **Am Jur,** Pleading, §§ 140–144.
4 **Am Jur,** Assumpsit, §§ 42, 43.

8 41 **Am Jur,** Pleading, §§ 140–144.
4 **Am Jur,** Assumpsit, §§ 42, 43.

eral issue in general assumpsit, does not deny the fictitious promise. On the other hand, the real basis of the action of general assumpsit is the receipt of a benefit by the defendant upon either a contractual or *quasi*-contractual obligation to pay therefor and it might reasonably have been expected that *non assumpsit* would put in issue merely the facts from which such contractual or *quasi*-contractual obligation arose. But, as in special assumpsit, the scope of the general issue was gradually extended until it put in issue the breach of the obligation and allowed the defendant to set up all defenses in excuse and almost all the defenses in discharge.

§ 29. Detinue.[9] The general issue in detinue is *non detinet* ("he does not detain"). This puts in issue both the fact of detention and the plaintiff's right to the goods alleged to be detained, and it has been held that the statute of limitations may also be taken advantage of under this plea.

§ 30. Replevin.[10] As explained in Forms of Action § 39, replevin differs from all the other actions in that the sheriff, at the very outset of the litigation, turns over the chattels to the plaintiff upon the latter's giving bond to litigate diligently his right thereto, and to deliver back the chattels if he loses in the litigation; and the pleas in bar have been considerably influenced by this difference.

The plea of *non cepit* ("he did not take") is sometimes classified as a general traverse, but its scope is limited to denying the taking at the place alleged; and the defendant's success on such a plea does not entitle him to have the goods turned over to him. If the defendant wishes to deny the right of the plaintiff to the chattels he must do so by a specific traverse to that effect.

If the defendant cannot successfully deny the taking or the property right of the plaintiff in the chattels, he will usually plead in justification that he lawfully seized the chattels either for rent in arrear or for taxes or for damage feasant. If he justifies in his own right, such a plea is called an avowry; if in the right of a third party for whom he has been acting as representative, a cognizance. If he succeeds in maintaining his avowry or cognizance he will be entitled to have the goods returned to him. Such a plea is therefore not a mere plea in justification but is substantially a cross declaration asking for affirmative relief, and must therefore set forth all the essential facts entitling him to seize the goods. In recognition of this, if the avowry or cognizance is for rent in arrear the most common answer put in, no rent in arrear, is called a plea and not a replication; and if such a plea sets up new matter the answer to it is called a replication and not a rejoinder.

§ 31. Account.[1] As already explained in Forms of Action § 41 there were originally two distinct stages in the action of account. All pleas in bar must be filed during the first stage; it is too late after the court has rendered its judgment that the defendant must account before the auditors. There is no general issue. If the defendant wishes to deny that he was ever a bailiff or receiver of the plaintiff he must do so by a specific traverse. And if he wishes to set up that he has fully accounted, or a release, or that the statute of limitations has fully run, he must do so by a plea in confession and avoidance.

§ 32. Ejectment.[2] The general issue in ejectment is not guilty. Under it the defendant may deny the plaintiff's right or his own possession, or may

9 41 Am Jur, Pleading, §§ 140-144.

10 41 Am Jur, Pleading, §§ 140-144.

1 41 Am Jur, Pleading, §§ 140-144.

2 18 Am Jur, Ejectment, § 90.

take advantage of the statute of limitations, or any other defense. Disclaimer of any interest in the premises is not classified as a defense; if the defendant does disclaim and the plaintiff is not satisfied with such disclaimer and insists upon a trial, at which he proves the defendant to be in possession, the plaintiff will be entitled to judgment, but if he fails the defendant will be entitled to judgment for his costs.

CHAPTER V

MOTIONS BASED ON THE PLEADINGS

§ 33. **Motions in arrest of judgment.**[3] As explained above in § 12 and § 14, a declaration may be attacked for defects of substance either promptly by a demurrer thereto or somewhat less promptly, by a demurrer to a subsequent pleading. If it is not thus attacked or, if it is attacked unsuccessfully, defects in substance therein may still be reached, after verdict for the plaintiff and before judgment, by a motion in arrest of judgment. There is this difference, however, between a demurrer and a motion in arrest of judgment; upon demurrer to a declaration the court construes the declaration strictly against the pleader whereas upon a motion in arrest of judgment the court takes into consideration the fact that there has been the expense of a trial and makes every presumption in favor of the declaration in order to uphold the verdict; this is usually called the doctrine of aider or cure by verdict.

Since defects of form are cured by pleading over, they cannot be reached by a motion in arrest of judgment. But all defects of substance which have not been cured by verdict can be reached; for example, if the plaintiff has omitted an essential allegation from the declaration; or if the plaintiff has brought the wrong form of action; or made a misjoinder of counts. Like a demurrer it does not reach defects that do not appear on the face of the record. And if there are several counts, some of which are good and some bad and the plaintiff gets a general verdict, the proper procedure is not to arrest the judgment but to award a *venire de novo* so that the new jury may restrict its verdict to the good counts.

If the motion in arrest of judgment is sustained the case is not necessarily at an end; it does not become *res judicata* as it would in a case where a verdict is directed for the defendant. The plaintiff must pay at least his own costs and in some jurisdictions the defendant's costs also; but he may continue the litigation by getting leave of court to amend his declaration or, if the statute of limitations has not run against his cause of action he may file an entirely new declaration.

Apparently a motion in arrest of judgment will be sustained only if the declaration is bad; if the declaration and plea are both good and the plaintiff wins his verdict on a bad replication it would seem that the defendant should be entitled to have the judgment arrested; but it has been held that in such a case the court will merely award a repleader.

§ 34. **Motion for judgment non obstante veredicto (notwithstanding the verdict).**[4] If the declaration is good and the plea is one in confession and avoidance but with an insufficient avoidance, upon which, however, the defendant gets a verdict, the plaintiff is entitled to have judgment by confession

[3] 41 **Am Jur**, Pleading, § 330.

[4] 41 **Am Jur**, Pleading, §§ 335–337.

Right to move for judgment notwithstanding verdict after entry of judgment. 95 **ALR** 429–434.

notwithstanding the verdict; the avoidance being insufficient the issue thereon is immaterial and a verdict on an immaterial issue is obviously worthless. This was the beginning of the doctrine but it has since been extended to cases where the confession is in a plea other than the one on which there was a verdict on an immaterial issue. But it has never been extended to cases where there is merely a verdict for the defendant upon an immaterial issue; in such cases the court will award a repleader.

Like a motion in arrest of judgment, a motion for judgment notwithstanding the verdict will not be sustained for merely formal defects or for matters not appearing on the face of the record.

There seems to be no reason why a motion for judgment *non obstante* made by a defendant should not be sustained in a proper case, especially where there is a good plea and a replication in confession and avoidance with an insufficient avoidance, and there are a few decisions to that effect; but the weight of authority and general understanding is that the defendant can move only for an arrest of judgment or for a repleader, not for judgment *non obstante.*

§ 35. Motion for a repleader.[5] Where there has been a verdict on an immaterial issue and the state of the whole record is such that the court cannot determine the merits of the case so as to arrest the judgment or give judgment *non obstante veredicto,* the court will award a repleader. It is usually said that the party who has made the first fault in pleading which occasioned the immaterial issue is not in a position to ask for a repleader, but this applies only where the verdict on the immaterial issue is found against him. Where a repleader is awarded, the faulty pleadings are ignored and the parties begin pleading anew just after the last good pleading, each party usually paying his own costs.

CHAPTER VI

MISCELLANEOUS TOPICS

§ 36. Special or absque hoc traverse.[6] A specific traverse must ordinarily express its denial directly, not indirectly or argumentatively, else it will be bad on special demurrer. For example, if the plaintiff alleges that he was in the possession of a certain chattel and the defendant with force and arms took the said chattel from his possession and the defendant answers that X was in possession of the said chattel, this would be bad in form because it denies the plaintiff's possession only indirectly and argumentatively. But there were a few instances where it has been considered necessary and in still others where it has been considered desirable to put into a traverse some affirmative matter which is not in confession and avoidance but in argumentative denial. In such cases the pleader is allowed to state the affirmative matter which constitutes the argumentative denial in the inducement, i. e., the beginning of his pleading; but he must follow this with a direct denial of the same averment. This direct denial is said to "cure" the formal defect of argumentativeness in the inducement. In the illustration given *supra* the affirmative statement that X was in possession of the chattel should have been followed by a direct denial that the plaintiff was in possession. The usual form is, to put it very briefly, "X was in possession of the chattel, *absque hoc*

[5] 41 Am Jur, Pleading, § 250.

[6] 41 Am Jur, Pleading, §§ 190–203.

that the plaintiff was in possession." The literal translation of *absque hoc* is "without this," a very awkward negative in English. A more liberal rendering is "and . . . not." Thus, in the illustration the plea would be "X was in possession *and* the plaintiff was *not* in possession."

If the direct denial part of the special traverse is in proper form and puts in issue a material allegation, the other party must join issue; he is not allowed to plead to the inducement either by way of traverse or confession and avoidance. But if the denial part is bad because it puts in issue an immaterial averment and the inducement is good in substance, the other party may ignore the ineffective denial and the uncured argumentativeness of the inducement, and traverse the inducement.

§ 37. Duplicity.[7] The original conception of common-law pleading seems to have been that the plaintiff in his declaration should state a single cause of action, with a single ground therefor; that the defendant, if he did not demur, should plead a single plea setting up a single defense either in confession and avoidance or in denial; that the replication—if the plea was in confession and avoidance—should set up a single reply to the plea, and so on until a single issue should be reached. In the course of time, however, this conception came to be modified in several particulars. The declaration might contain several counts, each stating a different cause of action; by the Statute of Anne a defendant was allowed to plead several pleas to each count; in most of the actions there were developed general traverses which put in issue two or more averments in the declaration and under some of which the defendant might take advantage of matters in confession and avoidance; and the replication *de injuria* was allowed in some actions to put in issue all the essential averments in a plea in excuse. But if a plaintiff should state several grounds for a single cause of action; or if a defendant in a single plea other than a general traverse should undertake to deny more than one fact in a count or should otherwise state two or more defenses in one plea; or if a replication other than a replication *de injuria* should undertake to deny more than one fact stated in a plea or otherwise state two or more replies to a single defense, the count or plea or replication would be bad for duplicity. The defect, however, is regarded as one in form only which can be taken advantage of only by a special demurrer and is cured by pleading over.

§ 38. Replication de injuria.[8] The Statute of Anne which permitted a defendant to plead any number of pleas to each count in the declaration made no provision for replications or for any subsequent pleadings. If the defense set up in a plea consisted of several facts and the plaintiff wished to plead in denial it was still necessary for him to traverse only one of these facts. Since a defense in excuse frequently consisted of several facts this operated to the disadvantage of the plaintiff, whose lawyer might be unable to tell in advance which of the facts could be successfully denied at the trial. Consequently the courts, in several actions, permitted a plaintiff to put in issue all the facts constituting a defense in excuse by what was called a replication *de injuria*. The full phrase was *de injuria sua propria absque tali causa*, i. e., concerning the wrong done it was the defendant's own fault, without such cause or excuse as alleged by the defendant.

The scope of the replication *de injuria* is limited. It can be used only in tres-

[7] 41 **Am Jur**, Pleading, §§ 44-46. [8] 41 **Am Jur**, Pleading, §§ 174-189.

pass, case, replevin, covenant and assumpsit. It cannot be used to deny matters of record or title to property or the authority of the plaintiff. There seems to be some doubt as to whether it can be used to reply to a plea in justification. It would seem clear that it should not be used where the defendant has put in a setoff; and if it is used to reply to a defense in discharge it will be held bad in form for duplicity.

§ 39. Departure.[9] The main purpose of common-law pleading is to arrive promptly at an issue. If a plaintiff in his replication should rely upon a cause of action which has not been set forth in his declaration or if a defendant in his rejoinder should allege a defense different from that upon which he relied in his plea, such conduct would obviously postpone the reaching of an issue and thus seriously interfere with the chief purpose of the whole system of pleading. Such a shifting of ground is called a departure; it is regarded as a defect of substance to the extent that it may be reached by either a special or general demurrer, but not by motion in arrest of judgment; the verdict is said to "cure the fault."

If a plaintiff should shift from a cause of action based upon the common law to one based upon a statute; or from an action against an infant for goods bargained and sold to an action for fraudulently misrepresenting his age to the plaintiff; or from a debt due to plaintiff's testator to a new promise made to the plaintiff himself; or from alleging performance by himself of conditions precedent to alleging an excuse for nonperformance; or if a defendant should allege in his plea that he has performed his covenants and in his rejoinder an excuse for nonperformance;—in all these cases the later pleading will be held bad in substance as a departure. But if the subsequent pleading merely re-enforces and fortifies the position taken in the earlier pleading it is not regarded as a departure. It is apparently on this ground that a replication to a plea of the statute of limitations that the defendant has made a new promise within the statutory period is not regarded as a departure.

§ 40. New assignment.[10] If a declaration is framed in such general terms that it can be understood to refer to a cause of action other than the one upon which the plaintiff is suing, and the defendant in his plea does thus understand it, the plaintiff should disregard the plea and make what is called a new assignment, i. e., he should so explain his declaration as to leave no room for doubt as to the cause of action which he meant to state.

If the plaintiff in trespass *quare clausum* should allege merely that the defendant trespassed upon the plaintiff's close in a certain township and the defendant pleads *liberum tenementum,* i. e., that the close, naming it, was his own, the plaintiff must, by new assigning, describe accurately the close which he had in mind in drawing his declaration. Similarly, if the defendant pleads to trespass *quare clausum* that he entered by consent of the plaintiff, and the plaintiff is seeking to recover not for the original entry, but for some act other than the entry, he should new assign, explaining that he is suing for the excess. Or if to trespass for imprisonment the defendant pleads a justification the plaintiff must new assign if he wishes to recover only for imprisoning him longer than was justifiable. If the declaration alleges several trespasses and the defendant pleads in justification, and some of the trespasses were justifiable and others not, the plaintiff must new assign and spec-

9 41 Am Jur, Pleading, §§ 184–189.

10 41 Am Jur, Pleading, §§ 288–315.

ify the trespasses for which he is suing. But if there is a single act of trespass sufficiently described in the declaration, there is no room for new assignment.

Most of the decisions are in cases of trespass, but the doctrine is not confined to that action. If to an action of debt the defendant pleads payment and it is true that the defendant did owe the plaintiff a debt which he has paid, the plaintiff must new assign and more particularly describe the debt which he is seeking to collect. And if to an action for slander the defendant pleads justification as a witness giving testimony, the plaintiff must new assign if he is basing his action on the speaking of the words on another occasion where there was no such justification.

§ 41. Bills of particulars.[1] When the action of general assumpsit was devised as a substitute for debt on simple contract, the debt was considered as merely the inducement for the promise upon which the action was purported to be based. Consequently the courts required only the most general statement of the facts which gave rise to the debt. The result of this was that—especially where there had been numerous transactions between the parties—a defendant was often put to a serious disadvantage in not knowing what facts the plaintiff expected to prove at the trial. To relieve defendants in such cases courts adopted the practice of requiring a plaintiff, upon application by the defendant, to furnish to the latter a bill of particulars showing more specifically the claim or claims upon which his action was founded. After the doctrine was established in general assumpsit it was extended to the other actions in those cases where the circumstances of the case made it necessary, in the judgment and discretion of the court, for the proper protection of the defendants.

Though the bill of particulars does not become a part of the declaration so as to make the latter bad on demurrer, it restricts the plaintiff in his proof to the matters therein specified.

If the defendant puts in an affirmative defense which is too general in terms the court may, upon application of the plaintiff, require the defendant to make his pleading more specific.

§ 42. Time, place, description and value.[2] If a declaration undertakes to describe a dated document it must do so accurately, otherwise the plaintiff may be nonsuited at the trial for a variance. In other cases, for example, in alleging a trespass or other tort committed by a defendant, the plaintiff must allege some date before the beginning of the suit, though he does not need to prove the exact date at the trial; any date before suit brought will be sufficient unless the statute of limitations should be relied upon as a defense in which case it must be some date within the statutory period.

In the early English law when jurors were witnesses chosen from the vicinage it was obviously important in all actions that the writ and declaration state accurately the place where the facts transpired upon which the cause of action was based. But jurors are no longer witnesses and most actions today are transitory, i. e., they need not be brought in the same jurisdiction where the cause of action arose; in such actions the averment of place is usually a mere matter of form which need not be proved as alleged and may

1 41 **Am Jur**, Pleading, §§ 268–277.
Effect of bill of particulars on proof. 8 **ALR** 550–563.

2 41 **Am Jur**, Pleading, § 376.

be omitted, the venue in the margin of the declaration being regarded as sufficient. But wherever the action is regarded as local the allegation of place is regarded as one of substance and must be proved as alleged.

In most of the actions it is not necessary to describe in detail the property involved or allege its value. But in detinue and replevin the chattels must be described with sufficient definiteness to enable the sheriff to identify them, and in detinue the value must be alleged so that in case the plaintiff wins and the property cannot be found at the end of the litigation the court may be enabled to render a money judgment for the plaintiff.

§ 43. Plea puis darrein continuance (since the last continuance).[3] In the English common-law courts it was the practice, after issue had been joined in an action, to set a day for the parties to appear in court and this was entered on the record of the case. This was called a continuance because the proceedings were thereby continued without interruption from one adjournment to another. If new matter of defense arose after the last continuance and before the day set for the reappearance of the parties, the defendant was not allowed to take advantage of such matter at the trial unless he should plead it as a matter which had happened after the last continuance. Later, by act of Parliament, it became unnecessary to make any entry of the continuances on the record and the time after which the defendant must make such a plea was shifted to the day when the last pleading was filed, but the name of the plea has not been changed.

The effect of such a plea is to waive all former pleas, so that if the defendant should be unable to prove the new defense at the trial the plaintiff would be entitled to judgment. Since such pleas are frequently used merely for the purpose of delay they, like dilatory pleas, must be drawn with great strictness and be verified by affidavit.

If a matter of defense should arise after action brought but before the defendant puts in his plea such matter is not a proper subject for an ordinary plea in bar or for a plea *puis darrein* continuance but must be pleaded to the further maintenance of the suit.

The above discussion, however, does not apply to actions on the case, because such actions are equitable in their nature and hence any matter arising at any time before trial which tends to show that in equity and conscience the plaintiff ought not to recover, may be shown under the general issue.

§ 44. Splitting a cause of action.[4] In order to protect a defendant from unnecessary and vexatious litigation a plaintiff who sues to enforce only a part of an entire cause of action cannot later enforce the other. For example, if the defendant is liable on a contract to pay plaintiff by installments the plaintiff may bring a separate action as each installment falls due; but if he allows two or more installments to fall due without suit he must sue for all the installments which are then due or forfeit his right on the installments not thus included.

Similarly, a plaintiff who has brought an action for personal injuries and recovered judgment cannot later sue for new items of damage even though such items could not have been discovered at the time of the trial.

So, if a defendant has by a single wrongful act damaged two or more pieces of property, only one cause of action arises so that if the plaintiff sues for the damage done only to one he is barred from later recovering for the

[3] 41 **Am Jur,** Pleading, §§ 115, 168–170. [4] 1 **Am Jur,** Actions, §§ 96–121.

damage done to the other or others. But if by a single wrongful act the defendant damages both the plaintiff's property and his person, two causes of action arise which should be separated into different counts and may be enforced in separate actions.

§ 45. Misjoinder of counts.[5] As pointed out above in § 17, there are two distinct uses of separate counts in one declaration. One use is to state a single cause of action in several ways in order to have at least one count which will correspond with the proof at the trial and thus avoid a nonsuit on the ground of variance. The other use is to join in one action two or more causes of action which are so similar that they may be conveniently and efficiently tried together. As long as the different counts are all in the same form of action there seems to be no difficulty as to joinder. One count in trespass may be joined with another count in trespass; and the same is true of case, debt, special assumpsit and general assumpsit.

But when the counts are in different forms of action there are several limitations upon joinder. No action clearly in tort, such as trespass, trover, case or replevin, can be joined with any contract action, such as covenant, debt, special assumpsit or general assumpsit. Furthermore trespass cannot be joined with trover or with case; covenant cannot be joined with debt and debt cannot be joined with assumpsit.

But trover may be joined with case, debt with detinue, and special assumpsit with general assumpsit.

Misjoinder may be taken advantage of by a demurrer to the whole declaration, or by motion in arrest of judgment, or writ of error.

§ 46. Set off and recoupment.[6] In the early common law if a defendant had a claim against the plaintiff the only way in which he could enforce it was by another action; there was no way in which he could take advantage of it in the same litigation. This involved unnecessary expense and might entail considerable hardship upon the defendant, especially where the plaintiff was insolvent. Consequently, if an equity court, upon some equitable ground, obtained jurisdiction of the case it would, whenever the result would be fair and just, allow a defendant to set off his claim against that of the plaintiff and thus reduce the amount of the plaintiff's recovery. Following the lead of equity statutes were passed permitting a set off in case of mutual

5 1 **Am Jur**, Actions, § 69.

6 47 **Am Jur**, Setoff and Counterclaim. §§ 2–14.

Right to set off deposit in insolvent bank against indebtedness to bank. 25 **ALR** 938–959; s. in 82 **ALR** 665–673; 97 **ALR** 588–594.

Setoff as between dividends from assets of insolvent bank or other corporation and liability of creditors as stockholders. 91 **ALR** 326–334.

Setoff as between judgments. 121 **ALR** 478–542.

Right to interpose setoff or counterclaim against municipal claims. 90 **ALR** 431–438.

Prior action in which claim might have been asserted by counterclaim, setoff, or cross petition, as barring or abating subsequent independent action thereon. 8 **ALR** 694–745.

Availability as setoff or counterclaim of claim in favor of one alone of several defendants. 10 **ALR** 1252–1268; s. in 81 **ALR** 781–785.

Claim barred by limitation as subject of setoff, counterclaim, recoupment, or cross bill. 16 **ALR** 326–343; s. in 73 **ALR** 574–582.

Setting up counterclaim, setoff, or recoupment in reply. 42 **ALR** 564–570.

Immaturity of claim against insolvent at time of insolvency proceedings as affecting right of setoff. 43 **ALR** 1325–1331; s. in 51 **ALR** 1477, 1478.

Character of claims available by way of setoff, counterclaim, or recoupment in action on construction contract. 46 **ALR** 393–413.

Equitable setoff of claim of one person and claim of his debtor against another. 57 **ALR** 778–786; s. in 93 **ALR** 1164–1170.

Cause of action in tort as counterclaim in action on contract. 68 **ALR** 451–481.

Judgment in action in which matter was asserted as a defense without seeking affirmative relief as precluding use of such matter as basis of an independent action, offset, or counterclaim. 83 **ALR** 642–655.

debts, usually allowing the defendant to get an affirmative judgment if he should be able to prove that the plaintiff owed him a larger amount than he owed to the plaintiff.

Apart from statute, however, courts gradually developed the doctrine of recoupment or reduction of damages. This doctrine is limited in its application to cases where the claims of both plaintiff and defendant arise out of the same transaction, a limitation which does not apply to set off. In further distinction from set off, the claims may be in either contract or tort for an unliquidated amount.

Set off must usually be specially pleaded. but recoupment may be ordinarily taken advantage of under the general issue.

CODE PLEADING

CHAPTER I

INTRODUCTION

§ 1. The defects of common law pleading.[1] There were two main characteristics of common-law pleading. One was that the issue was formulated by the parties themselves, in contradistinction to the procedure in civil law countries, where the issue was determined by the court. The issue might be an issue of law to be decided by the court or an issue of fact, to be decided by the jury Since the jury was an unlearned tribunal it was necessary that the issue be a simple one and one of the main purposes of common-law pleading was to aid or force the parties to arrive at this simple issue.

The other main characteristic of common-law pleading was the system of forms of action which were developed partly for the purpose of raising revenue for the king for the privilege of suing in the king's courts instead of in the popular Anglo-Saxon courts which were thereby largely, but not en-

[1] 41 **Am Jur,** Pleading, § 5.
20 **Tex. L. R.** 16, Scope and Function of Pleading under the New Federal and Texas Rules.
20 **Tex. L. R.** 4, Texas and Federal Rules of Procedure.
21 **Oreg. L. R.** 319, What is a Single Cause of Action for the Purpose of the Doctrine of Res Judicata?
7 **Mo. L. R.** 1, The Proposed Code of Civil Procedure for Missouri—The Parties and Pleadings.
14 **St. John's L. R.** 253, Discovery and Inspection under the New York Civil Practice Act.

tirely, superseded. Though the scope of these forms of action was extended under the stimulus of the Statute of Westminster the Second, passed in 1285, whereby the various actions on the case, including trover and assumpsit, were developed. the system was never completely satisfactory and the various technical refinements that were introduced into it ultimately brought about a wave of pleading reform which started in this country with the adoption of the New York Code of 1848.

§ 2. The main characteristics of code pleading.[2] Under code pleading there is only one form of action either for actions at law or suits in equity, the distinction between the various common-law forms of action and the distinction between actions at law and suits in equity being expressly abolished.

The other main characteristic of code pleading is that the parties were to plead facts without their being required to arrive at an issue, the modern requirement being that the pleading shall give fair notice of the pleader's case to the court and to the opposing party, the issue or issues being frequently arrived at during the trial.

§ 3. The "one form of action" of the codes.[3] Under common-law pleading if a plaintiff brought an action of trover when he should have sued in trespass or case, or if he sued in debt on simple contract when he should have brought covenant, or special assumpsit or a bill in equity, his action failed, he had to pay costs and begin over bringing the right action. The codes undertook to make this unnecessary by providing for only one form of action so that in that one action he could obtain whatever relief, legal or equitable, the facts of the case entitled him to receive. Thus if the pleader thought he was entitled to recover for breach of contract but the facts proved at the trial showed no breach of contract but did show damage caused by fraud, he was not turned out of court to begin another suit but was given damages to compensate him for the loss caused by the fraud. In some code states, however, the courts carried over from common-law pleading the notion that each pleading must have been drawn according to some theory and denied relief if the facts proved did not correspond to the theory of the pleading.

In all the states there are constitutional provisions guaranteeing trial by jury in common-law cases. This makes it impossible for law and equity to merge completely in this country and makes it necessary for courts in code states to have two dockets—a jury docket and an equity docket. If a plaintiff brings an action at law and the defendant sets up thereto an equitable defense, trial by jury can be demanded only of common-law issues; the issues raised by the equitable defense are triable by the court.

CHAPTER II

PARTIES

§ 4. The real party in interest.[4] Before the codes a common-law action could be brought only for the violation of a common-law right and a suit in equity only to enforce an equitable right. Most of the codes provide that with certain exceptions the one form of action under the code shall be brought by the real party in interest.

(a) The assignee of a chose in action.

[2] 1 **Am Jur**, Actions, § 47.

[3] 41 **Am Jur**, Pleading, §§ 79, 145.

[4] 39 **Am Jur**, Parties, §§ 16–22.

Apparently the chief reason for the real party in interest provision was that the assignee of a chose in action was still required to sue in the name of his assignor instead of in his own name. By the better view this provision has made no change in the substantive law. Though the assignee sues in his own name he still sues as the representative of the assignor. And whether he may sue at all depends upon whether, by the substantive law, the chose in action is assignable.

(b) The subrogee of a chose in action.

Where one who stands in the position of a surety has fully paid the obligee he is entitled, in equity, to an assignment of the obligee's claim against the obligor. By the better view and great weight of authority, the real party in interest provision should enable the subrogee to sue the obligor without getting an assignment from the obligee. Where, in insurance cases, the insurer is entitled, by the substantive law of insurance, upon payment of the full amount of the policy, which is less than the total loss, to partial subrogation against the tort-feasor who is liable for the loss, the better view is that the insurer is entitled to join with the insured in an action against the tort-feasor.

(c) The beneficiary of a contract.

In this field the real party in interest provision has had no effect. If by the substantive law the beneficiary of a contract has a right to enforce it he may sue thereon in his own name, entirely apart from the statute; otherwise he may not sue at all.

(d) The "trustee of an express trust."

Before the codes a trustee, as long as he was performing the duties of his office, was the only party who could maintain an action against third parties and in bringing such an action it was not necessary for him to join the beneficiaries of the trust. By express terms this situation remains unchanged under the codes. Where the trustee was in default in performing his duties as such, the beneficiary's remedy was to call him to account in equity; under the codes he may still do that, bringing the "one form of action" for that purpose.

(e) Executors or administrators.

The exception in the real party in interest provision of the code, allowing an executor or administrator to sue without joining beneficiaries of the estate is similar to the trustee exception and has been treated by the courts in a similar manner, the executor or administrator being usually the sole party to sue third parties in the process of settling the estate. Where the estate is entirely free from debt it is arguable that the beneficiaries of the estate should be allowed to maintain an action against an obligor to the estate, but on this point there is conflict of authority.

(f) Agents.

Before the codes an agent might maintain an action against a third party only if the principal was undisclosed. In some of the codes there is a provision that "a person with whom or in whose name a contract is made for the benefit of another is a trustee of an express trust within the meaning" of the real party in interest provision, this does not, by the better view, allow an agent of a disclosed principal to sue. As before the codes a disclosed principal may always sue and an undisclosed principal may sue except where prevented by the rules of sealed or of negotiable instruments.

§ 5. Joinder of parties plaintiff.[5] At common law only those who were jointly interested in property or contract rights could join as plaintiffs and they were compelled to join; there was no permissive joinder. If one of the joint owners or joint obligees died the cause of action survived to the others. If there was misjoinder and it was apparent on the face of the declaration defendant could take advantage of it by demurrer, motion in arrest of judgment or writ of error; if not apparent, by a motion to nonsuit. If there was nonjoinder in contract actions and this was apparent on the face of the declaration, defendant could take advantage of it by demurrer, motion in arrest of judgment or writ of error, or if not so apparent, by motion to nonsuit. In tort actions if the defect was not apparent defendant could only plead in abatement.

In equity every one whose interests would be directly affected by the decree was a necessary party and if he refused to join as plaintiff he could be made a defendant, the reason being stated in the bill. And all persons might join as plaintiffs if they were interested in the subject of the action or in obtaining the relief demanded. If there was misjoinder appearing on the face of the bill defendant could take advantage of it by demurrer, otherwise by plea or answer. If there was nonjoinder appearing on the face of the bill defendant could take advantage of it by special demurrer designating the omitted parties; otherwise by plea or answer. The plaintiff could at any time amend by adding omitted parties and the court could, of its own motion, refuse to go on until necessary parties were brought in.

The codes followed substantially the equity rules. Thus, most of them provide that those who are united in interest must be joined as plaintiffs or defendants; that all persons having an interest in the subject of the action and in the relief demanded may be joined as plaintiffs, and that if the consent of any one who should be joined as plaintiff cannot be obtained he may be made a defendant, the reason being stated in the complaint. If there is misjoinder appearing on the face of the record, the defendant may take advantage of it by special demurrer, otherwise, by plea in abatement. If there is nonjoinder apparent on the face of the record defendant may take advantage of it by special demurrer; otherwise, by answer designating the omitted parties.

Where plaintiffs are jointly interested the codes regard them as necessary parties; for example, joint obligees in a contract to convey land or joint obligees on an injunction bond or joint owners of property who sue in ejectment or trover or trespass. Where there is not joint ownership but tenancy in common, the tenants in common may join in suing in ejectment, trover or trespass and in a few cases it has been held that they must join. Where a mortgagor took out an insurance policy payable to the mortgagee as his interest may appear it was held that while the mortgagor might sue alone the mortgagee could not sue without joining the mortgagor.

Where the plaintiffs are not joint tenants but tenants in common they may join as plaintiffs. Also, where suit is brought against a tort-feasor for burning a building the owner and the insurer of the building may join, and where cosureties unite in compromising with the creditor they may join in an action against the principal debtor.

On the other hand, except under later code provisions adopted in a few states, mere community of interest in questions of law or fact is not sufficient

[5] 39 **Am Jur,** Parties, §§ 29–33.

29 **U. of Iowa L. R.** 3, Joinder of Parties and Actions.

to permit joinder. For example, a suit to abate a nuisance to individual owners of several tracts of land, a suit to set aside separate deeds executed at different times by different grantors, a suit to set aside a conveyance of land as a fraud upon separate creditors; a suit for malicious prosecution brought by plaintiffs who were not partners or otherwise united in interest, and a suit on an insurance policy in which the insurer agreed to pay varying amounts to different individuals.

§ 6. Joinder of parties defendant.[6] At common law it was ordinarily necessary to join all joint obligors; but if one should be out of the jurisdiction or was an infant or had died it was sufficient to join the others. Joint tortfeasors could be sued either jointly or severally; if one joint tort feasor died it was not possible to join his personal representative with the other joint tort feasors.

In contract actions if the misjoinder appeared on the face of the record defendant could take advantage of it by demurrer; otherwise, by motion to nonsuit. In tort actions, by a motion to dismiss those improperly joined.

If there was nonjoinder in contract actions appearing on the face of the record defendant could take advantage of it by demurrer; otherwise, by a plea in abatement, giving the name of the omitted joint contractor. Since joint tort feasors could be sued separately no question of nonjoinder arose.

Where tort feasors were not joint but several, as, for example, a servant and a master who did not authorize the tort, joinder was not permitted. But where the acts of two independent defendants combine to produce a single injury to the plaintiff, as in collision cases, courts in this country generally permit joinder.

In equity none of the common law rules against joinder prevailed. All parties must be joined if without their joinder the transaction could not be satisfactorily settled. If one should have joined as a plaintiff but refused, he could be made a defendant, and all parties who were interested in the subject of the action and the relief demanded were proper parties defendant.

Under the codes the common law and equity rules as to compulsory joinder of defendants generally prevail. Hence where the plaintiff was employed by several persons to render services to them as an attorney in a litigation, the obligation was construed to be joint and all the obligors were necessary parties; and where suit was brought in equity to compel the removal of a dam it was held that all property owners whose interests would be affected by such removal were indispensable parties defendant. Also, where suit was brought by the equitable owners of a fire insurance policy to restrain the insurer from paying to the insured or his assignee, such assignee was a necessary party to the suit. On the other hand, where suit was brought to foreclose a mortgage without asking for a deficiency judgment, the mortgagor and other prior owners of the land are not necessary parties to the suit. However, the codes, following the equity rule, usually provide that where a question is one of common or general interest or when the parties are so numerous that it would be impractical to bring all of them into court, one or more may sue or defend for the benefit of all. Such suits are usually called representative or class suits.

6 39 **Am Jur**, Parties, §§ 34–43.
Joinder, in one action at law, of persons not jointly liable, one or the other of whom is liable to the plaintiff. 41 **ALR** 1223–1252.
Joinder in one action of sureties on different bonds relating to same matter. 106 **ALR** 90–101; s. in 137 **ALR** 1044, 1045.

On the subject of permissive joinder of defendants, most of the codes adopted the equity rule that any person may be made a defendant who has or claims an interest in the controversy adverse to the plaintiff or who is a necessary party to the complete determination of the question involved therein, but courts have been reluctant to advance much beyond the common law rules. Successive warrantors of title may be joined by the warrantee; so may joint possessors of trespassing cattle be joined in an action for the trespass. The survivors and the personal representative of the deceased coobligor on a note may be joined in an action on the note and the purported seller and buyer of plaintiff's chattels may be joined in an action for conversion because it was construed to be a joint conversion. Where a lessee of land and a guarantor of the rent thereunder are bound by the same instrument they may be joined but usually not if bound by separate instruments. On the question of joining in a tort action a servant and his master who did not authorize the tort there is a conflict of authority. And independent underwriters who insure the same property may not be joined in an action by the insured.

In a few states later code provisions have undertaken to liberalize the practice by providing that—within the discretion of the trial court—"all persons may be joined as defendants against whom any relief is alleged to exist, whether jointly, severally or in the alternative; and judgment may be given against such one or more of the defendants as may be found to be liable, according to their respective liabilities." The provision allowing joinder in the alternative is a desirable innovation because it avoids the difficulties which frequently result from the necessity of bringing separate actions.

The equity practice permitted the bringing in of new parties at the instance of either the plaintiff or the defendant or the court, where the controversy could not be satisfactorily determined otherwise; this practice has been provided for by the codes. And in a few states a defendant may have brought in a party who is liable over to him in order to secure a complete adjudication of the defendant's rights and liabilities.

Finally, the codes have followed and liberalized the equity practice of permitting one not a party to intervene and become such under certain conditions; for example, where an interest is claimed by the intervenor in property in the hands of a receiver or in property the right to possession of which is being litigated.

CHAPTER III

SPLITTING AND JOINDER OF CAUSES OF ACTION

§ 7. Splitting a cause of action.[7] The common law pleading rule against what is usually called the splitting of a cause of action has been stated already, and in this field the codes have made little change. There is a tendency to treat the running account as analogous to the sale with the purchase price payable in installments, and to treat in a similar way the annual flooding of the plaintiff's land because the damage is temporary. There is a conflict of authority where the same negligent act causes damage to the plaintiff's property and his person. And while a partial assignee of a chose in action could not sue at all at common law, under the codes the defendant may merely demand that the partial assignor be joined as party plaintiff.

[7] 1 Am Jur, Actions, §§ 96–121.

§ 8. Joinder of actions.[8] As already explained the question of joinder of causes of action in common law pleading was almost entirely determined by the form of action, so that the code abolition of forms of action carried with it the common law rules as to joinder. In equity there were no specific rules except the one against multifariousness, the courts having discretion to allow the joinder of claims arising out of the same transaction or out of a series of transactions which formed a connected whole.

The codes, though tending to follow the equity situation, devised new rules of joinder based upon similarity of claims but cutting across the old common law forms of action and the distinction between law and equity. Thus the codes usually allow joinder of claims based on "contracts express or implied," which include not only suits in equity based upon a contract but also claims arising under sealed contracts, claims based upon a judgment and those based upon a quasi contractual obligation. Other common groupings were: injuries to the person, injuries to character, injuries to property, actions to recover real property with or without damages, claims against a trustee by virtue of a contract or by operation of law, and, finally, actions arising out of the same transaction or transactions connected with the same subject of action. But there was usually a requirement that the claims must affect all parties to the suit and must not require different places of trial.

A plaintiff who suffered personal injuries because of the unsafe condition of a sidewalk due to the negligence of the city, the owner of the adjacent land and the lessee in possession of it was allowed to join in one action his claims against all three. Similarly, a plaintiff who suffered personal injuries because of the failure of four physicians in succession to set properly an injured shoulder was allowed to join them in one action. And a plaintiff who had suffered personal injuries due to the negligence of a railroad company and a depot company was allowed to join them though the liability of the former was based upon the common law and those of the latter upon statute. But where A was negligently injured by X and was then negligently treated by Y, both together causing death, joinder was denied.

Where several defendants independently polluted a canal causing damage to the plaintiff's property the plaintiff was allowed to join them in a suit for an injunction, the court following the old equity practice in such cases.

Where by the same negligent act the defendant caused damage to plaintiff's property and his person the actions could be joined because both arose out of the same transaction. Where defendant committed an assault and battery on the plaintiff and then made a fraudulent conveyance of his property to defeat the collection of any judgment which might be recovered against him the action for assault and battery and the suit to have the conveyance set aside could be joined because they arose out of the same transaction or transactions connected with the same subject of action. An action to quiet title to land and an action for trespass to the same land could be joined because

[8] 1 **Am Jur,** Actions, §§ 65–91.

Injury to person and property occurring at same time as giving rise to single cause of action. 64 **ALR** 663–674; s. in 127 **ALR** 1081–1084.

Propriety of consolidation for trial of actions for personal injuries, death, or property damage arising out of same accident. 104 **ALR** 62–76.

Tort damaging real property as creating a single cause of action or multiple causes of action in respect of different portions of land of the same owner affected thereby. 117 **ALR** 1216–1224.

Joinder of claims to separate parcels in suit to quiet or to remove cloud on title, or to determine adverse claims to land. 118 **ALR** 1400–1415.

May acts of independent tort-feasors, each of which alone causes or tends to produce some damage, be combined to create a joint liability? 9 **ALR** 939–955; s. in 35 **ALR** 409–413; 91 **ALR** 759–763.

the subject of the two actions was the same. And an action in tort may be joined with an action for breach of contract if they arose out of the same transaction and are not inconsistent; for example, an action for breach of a charter party contract to pay the plaintiff demurrage and an action based upon fraudulent representations whereby the plaintiff was induced to enter into the contract. But not if the claims are inconsistent; for example, where plaintiff contracted to buy an auto, trading in his old car and the defendant was unable to deliver the new one, a claim for breach of contract in failing to return the purchase price was held to be inconsistent with a claim in tort for the refusal to return the old car.

On the other hand, where a collision caused damage to goods and personal injuries, joinder was not allowed because the action for personal injuries could not be brought in the county where the goods were to be delivered. An action against X alone cannot be joined with an action against X and Y or with an action against X as administrator because the parties are not the same.

If causes of action are misjoined the defect can be taken advantage of only by demurrer pointing out specifically the ground of objection.

In recent years a few states have abolished some of the rules of joinder and others have abolished all of them.

§ 9. Same—separate statement.[9] The codes require that where several causes of action are joined in one complaint they shall be separately stated and numbered, so that the allegations in one division of the complaint cannot be used to help out the allegations in another division unless they are specifically incorporated therein. Where a plaintiff sues as an individual and also in a representative capacity there are two causes of action and they should be separately stated and numbered; similarly, where a plaintiff sues because of damage done to his property and to his person by the same negligent act of the defendant. But where action is brought by an employee against his employer for personal injuries there is only one cause of action though it may be based upon the common law, the state employers' liability act and the federal employers' liability act, and the requirement does not apply. However, even though there is only one cause of action stated in more than one paragraph, it may be desirable to number each paragraph.

As already stated, it was the common law practice for a plaintiff who was uncertain as to what he would be able to prove at the trial to state a single cause of action in several ways in different counts in order to avoid a variance by proving at the trial a cause of action not alleged in the declaration. Though code pleading decisions have criticised this practice it is generally permitted and is especially desirable where the pleader wishes to present to the court two or more legal theories of his case.

CHAPTER IV

THE COMPLAINT

§ 10. In general.[10] The scope and essential allegations in each of the common-law actions have already been stated. Although under the codes there is only one form of action they have brought about comparatively few changes in this portion of the field. Under the codes, as at common law it is

9 41 **Am Jur**, Pleading, §§ 106–108.

10 41 **Am Jur**, Pleading, §§ 73–88.

necessary that the pleader state ultimate facts, not evidence or legal conclusions, and he must allege positively and directly, not hypothetically or contingently or by way of recital; and, generally, a complaint will be sufficient if it would have been a good declaration at common law.

But the codes have made some new provisions. Under common law pleading the word "verification" was used in describbng the conclusion of all affirmative pleadings— "and this the plaintiff (or defendant) is ready to verify"—that is, ready to prove. Under the codes the word "verification" is used more literally in referring to pleadings that have been verified or sworn to, usually by the party pleading. Under some of the codes no such verification is required; others require it of all pleadings, while still others provide that the pleader may compel the verification of all subsequent pleadings by verifying his own. Where the pleader, because of lack of definite knowledge of the facts alleged in the pleadings, is unable to verify positively, the codes permit him to verify upon information and belief.

The codes also permit the pleader to incorporate into his complaint by express references exhibits attached thereto; and to incorporate by express reference allegations made in another count in his complaint. A few codes permit pleading in the alternative if the pleading gives reasonable notice of the pleader's position.

Under common law pleading if a plaintiff brought the wrong form of action—if, for example, he brought trespass for false imprisonment when he should have brought case for malicious prosecution—there was nothing for him to do but to begin over and bring the right form of action, which he could do if in the meantime the statute of limitations had not run. The codes undertook to change this, their underlying concept being that the pleader was to state the facts and he was to be given whatever relief those facts entitled him to receive, regardless of the theory upon which the pleader proceeded in drawing his pleading. But in some states it has been held that if the pleader drew his pleading upon the wrong theory he must, as under common law pleading, begin over; he cannot shift at the trial to another theory.

§ 11. Contract actions.[1] Under common law pleading, as already stated, if a plaintiff wished to sue for the price or for the value received, based either upon contract or quasi contract, he might bring the common counts either in debt or indebitatus assumpsit; or, if he was suing on a contract, he might also bring special assumpsit. Though the practice has been criticised the common counts are equally good under the codes as at common law.

Under common law pleading, as already stated, if a plaintiff wished to sue on a contract for anything else except the price or value of a benefit received he must bring special assumpsit, alleging the defendant's promise, the consideration therefor, the performance or excuse for nonperformance of conditions precedent or concurrent, either express or implied by law. This practice, also, remains practically unchanged under the codes. If the plaintiff sues as assignee he must still state facts showing the assignment; in alleging performance of conditions he must still do it with particularity unless the code permits a general allegation of performance, in which case the statute must be followed exactly; and by the weight of authority consideration must still be alleged factually, a statement that defendant's promise was based upon "legal consideration" not being sufficient. Where a fact is presumed it is un-

1 41 Am Jur, Pleading, §§ 95–105.

necessary to allege it; for example, consideration in an action on a negotiable note.

§ 12. Tort actions.[2] The scope and essential allegations in a common law action on the case for damage caused by negligence have already been set forth: the codes have caused almost no change. He must allege that defendant's conduct caused plaintiff's damage. There is the same distinction observed between cases where the defendant's conduct was active and those where he was under an affirmative duty to use care toward particular classes of persons, for example, business visitors. There is the same conflict as to whether the plaintiff must allege due care on his part. By the better view, though he relies on the last clear chance doctrine he need not allege anything about it and under an allegation of wanton or—as it is sometimes called—wilful negligence he may prove ordinary negligence.

There is similarly little or no change in actions for deceit, slander, libel or malicious prosecution; and where, as in trespass or trover, it becomes necessary to prove a property right in the plaintiff it is still sufficient to allege generally that the plaintiff owned the property though it is sufficient to prove merely the possession of it or the right to its immediate possession.

§ 13. Miscellaneous.[3] A corporation plaintiff need not allege that it is a corporation so that it has capacity to sue; nor need an executor or administrator allege his appointment as such if the caption of the complaint shows that he is suing in that capacity.

Where the plaintiff's action is based on a statute and there is an exception in that part of the statute which confers the right he must allege that his case does not come within the exception.

If the plaintiff's action is based upon the common law of another state which is different from the common law of the forum he must allege the rules of the other state which he contends give him a cause of action.

Under common law pleading a defendant might in case of reasonable doubt as to what the plaintiff expected to rely upon at the trial, demand a bill of particulars, especially where the action was on the common counts. Though under the codes the defendant may achieve the same result by a motion to have the complaint made more definite and certain, he may still ask for a bill of particulars as at common law.

At common law a pleading was construed—in case of reasonable doubt as to its meaning—strictly against the pleader. The codes usually provide that the pleading shall be liberally construed so as to carry out the pleader's real intent.

CHAPTER V

THE DEMURRER, ANSWER AND REPLY

§ 14. The demurrer.[4] In many respects the code demurrer is like the common law demurrer. It reaches only defects apparent on the face of the pleading; it admits the material allegations in the pleading demurred to, not as a matter of evidence but merely for the purpose of argument; a demurrer to a subsequent pleading searches the record for the first defect of substance; if the decision goes against a demurrant and he refuses to plead fur-

[2] 41 **Am Jur**, Pleading, §§ 72, 77–88.

[3] 41 **Am Jur**, Pleading, § 63.

[4] 41 **Am Jur**, Pleading, §§ 204–255. Conclusiveness of judgment on demurrer. 13 **ALR** 1104–1123; s. in 106 **ALR** 437–447.

ther, judgment is entered against him as on default; and where there is a joint demurrer and the pleading is good as to any one of the demurrants the demurrer will be overruled.

But the common law pleading distinction between general and special demurrers does not exist. The codes specify the grounds for demurrer to a complaint and the demurrant must point out the ground for demurring. These grounds usually include lack of jurisdiction of the action, that the complaint does not state a cause of action, another action pending, defect of parties, misjoinder of causes of action and that the plaintiff has not legal capacity to sue. Of these six, the last four are waived by failure to demur. There is square conflict of authority as to whether the statute of limitations or the statute of frauds may be taken advantage of by demurrer. The codes also specify the grounds for demurring to an answer or reply.

In most code states the dilatory plea has been superseded either by demurrer or motion if the objection appears on the face of the complaint, otherwise by answer in abatement. In some code states the demurrer itself has been superseded by the motion or objection in point of law as a means of expediting litigation by eliminating one of its stages, the motion being considered just before the trial. In England the objection in point of law may be taken up by the court before the time for trial where the court thinks that the entire case may in that way be disposed of.

§ 15. The answer—general and specific denials.[5] The common law general traverse or general issue, which in some forms of action put in issue matters not alleged in the declaration, and the specific traverse, have been superseded, under most of the codes, by a general denial which puts in issue only the allegations in the complaint, and the specific denial which puts in issue only those specifically pointed out. Where the defendant wishes to deny most, but not all, of the allegations in the complaint the present practice allows him to do so by putting in a general denial definitely excepting the allegations which he is not in a position to deny.

Under the codes an argumentative denial or one which contains a negative pregnant seems to be quite as objectionable as under common law pleading, though the better view would seem to be that such a denial should be held good where the pleader's meaning is clear.

Where the code requires the defendant to verify his answer but he does not have definite knowledge as to the truth of the plaintiff's allegations yet is not willing to admit them, he may deny that he has any knowledge or information sufficient to form a belief; if he has some but not sufficient grounds for believing the allegations false he may deny "according to information and belief."

§ 16. The same—pleading new matter—equitable defenses.[6] Under common law pleading if a defense to the merits could not be shown under a specific or general traverse it was necessary to plead it affirmatively as a plea in confession and avoidance, either by way of justification or excuse or in discharge. Similarly, under the codes, if a defense to the merits cannot be shown under a specific or general denial of the allegations of the declaration he must plead it affirmatively as new matter. And as at common law a defendant may at the same time plead in denial and affirmatively, because although technically inconsistent in fact, the pleader, not being omniscient,

[5] 41 Am Jur, Pleading, §§ 114–120, 190–196. [6] 41 Am Jur, Pleading, §§ 155–160.

should be able to safeguard himself against unforeseen failure of proof at the trial.

Where under the old practice a defendant had no defense at law but was in a position to go into a court of equity and on some basis such as fraud or mistake, get a permanent injunction against the plaintiff's continuing with his action, the codes allow him to set up such facts at law. Such defenses are called equitable defenses at law, the word equitable merely indicating that the facts could formerly be made use of only in an equity court; however, the code provision that a defendant might plead as many defenses as he had "both legal and equitable" has helped to crystallize the phrase.

§ 17. **Same—counterclaims.**[7] The codes provide not only for defenses "both legal and equitable" but for counterclaims. Their provisions go far beyond the setoff and recoupment possible under common law pleading but are not uniform. While the setoff permissible under common law pleading was limited to setting off one debt against another the codes usually provide that "in an action arising upon contract any other cause of action arising also upon contract and existing at the commencement of the action" may be used set up by a defendant. The other usual provision is that the defendant may set up "a cause of action arising out of the contract or transaction set forth in the complaint as the foundation of the plaintiff's claim, or connected with the subject of the action."

The word "transaction" permits a counterclaim in tort actions; for example, in an action for assault and battery the defendant may counterclaim either for an assault and battery committed upon himself at the same time or for slander of the defendant which provoked the defendant's attack. But to an action for false imprisonment the defendant cannot counterclaim for trespass to land not connected therewith; and for the same reason to an action of replevin against a conditional vendee the defendant cannot counterclaim for fraud and breach of warranty. Even if the claims arise out of the same transaction some courts are reluctant to permit counterclaims between tort claims and contract or quasi contract claims; for example to an action for conversion the defendant cannot set up a counterclaim in quasi contract. But to an action on a note given for a thresher the defendant was allowed to counterclaim for damages for personal injuries caused to the defendant's minor son by the plaintiff's servants while undertaking to repair the thresher.

Under the contract provision the defendant cannot counterclaim on a cause of action which is not yet in existence; for example, a surety's claim for contribution where he has not yet paid the creditor. Nor can a defendant counterclaim on any cause of action which does not tend to defeat or diminish plaintiff's recovery; for example, to an action on a judgment defendant cannot counterclaim to set aside a deed. But since, under the codes, a defendant may get an affirmative judgment on his counterclaim there would seem to be little reason for the latter limitation.

A few codes provide for counterclaims against codefendants.

§ 18. **The reply.**[8] Since the chief purpose of common law pleading was that the parties should arrive at an issue there was no limit to the number of pleadings though only the first seven had names. Since the purpose of the

[7] 47 **Am Jur,** Setoff and Counterclaim, §§ 11, 26–35, 43–47.
3 **Wash and Lee L. R.** 47, Counterclaim and Equitable Defense in Virginia.
3 **Mont. L. R.** 33, Counterclaim in Montana.

[8] 41 **Am Jur,** Pleading, §§ 174–180.

codes is to get each party's statement of the facts placed on the record promptly whether an issue is thereby arrived at or not, they usually do not provide for more than three pleadings. All of them provide for a reply where the defendant has filed a counterclaim, the reply being an answer to the counterclaim, and most of them also provide for a reply where the defendant has set up an affirmative defense. If no reply is provided for the facts alleged in the affirmative defense are assumed to be denied, so that the defendant must prove them; but if a reply is provided for and the plaintiff does not file one, the facts alleged in the affirmative defense are held to be admitted. In a jurisdiction which does not provide for a reply to an affirmative defense it is therefore important to determine whether an answer is a counterclaim or is merely an affirmative defense and this is often difficult where the answer can easily be construed to be a counterclaim or an equitable defense at law.

Like an answer a reply may consist of either denials or new matter, including equitable defenses, but usually it may not contain a counterclaim except in answer to a counterclaim set up by the defendant.

Under common law pleading if a pleader in a later pleading shifted from the position which he had taken in an earlier pleading such a shift of position was called a departure which was regarded as a defect of substance which could be taken advantage of only by demurrer, the defect being cured by verdict. On this point the codes follow the common law practice but since amendments are freely allowed the rule is rarely invoked. The codes also follow the common law pleading rules as to new assignment.

Objections to a reply may be taken by the defendant by demurrer or motion in much the same way as he may object to a complaint or as the plaintiff may object to an answer.

CHAPTER VI

MISCELLANEOUS

§ 19. Motions.[9] Under common law pleading if a pleading was defective in form the defect could be taken advantage of by a special demurrer specifically pointing out the defect. Under the codes such defects may be taken advantage of by motion; thus if the pleading is indefinite and uncertain the opposing party should move to have the pleading made more definite and certain.

But motions have a much wider use. They may be used to compel an adversary to elect between actions or defenses which the mover contends are inconsistent; or to expunge or strike from the files whole pleadings or parts thereof because they are irrelevant or redundant; or to add or drop parties; or to compel a plaintiff to separately state and number his causes of action. And in some states demurrers have been entirely superseded by motions.

Under common law pleading a defendant might, after verdict for plaintiff, move in arrest of judgment on the ground that the declaration was bad in substance; if the declaration was good in substance and there was a plea in confession and avoidance and a verdict for the defendant on an immaterial issue, the plaintiff might move for judgment notwithstanding the verdict. Apparently such motions may also be made under the codes but some codes also provide that a plaintiff with a good complaint may, even before trial, move for summary judgment on the pleadings, the motion being supported

9 41 **Am Jur**, Pleading, §§ 326–361.

by affidavit that the answer presents no real defense. In some states such a motion may be made only where the action is based upon a liquidated demand; in other states its scope has been more widely extended. In some states a defendant may move for summary judgment on the pleadings where the complaint is insufficient.

§ 20. Amendments.[10] Under common law pleading statutes provided for amendments where a pleading was held bad in form on special demurrer. If the pleading was bad in substance amendments were within the discretion of the court; in practice the courts were usually liberal in allowing amendments; but not, according to the prevailing view, permitting a change in the cause of action.

The codes usually provide for amendments without leave of court if made within a certain period, and after that period with leave of court where the court, in its discretion, decides that such action will be in furtherance of justice. While the decisions are in conflict the present tendency seems to be to allow a plaintiff by amendment to change the cause of action or a defendant to change his defense.

The farther a case has progressed the less willing are the courts to permit amendments. But in unusual cases courts have permitted amendments at the trial and even after the trial, for example, to conform the pleadings to the proof. Where the judgment of a lower court has been reversed the parties are placed back as they were before trial and therefore it is proper to allow amendments as freely as before.

§ 21. Supplemental pleadings.[1] As a substitute for the common law plea *puis darrein* continuance the codes permit supplemental pleadings to either party. These are usually limited to setting forth facts occurring after the filing of a previous pleading by the same party but some codes permit the pleader to set forth facts of which the pleader was ignorant when he filed his earlier pleading.

The prevailing view is that a supplemental pleading, like an amendment, is not allowed to change a cause of action; and if a complaint has failed to state a cause of action the plaintiff cannot remedy the defect by such a later pleading.

10 41 Am Jur, Pleading, §§ 288–315.

1 41 Am Jur, Pleading, §§ 261–267.

EVIDENCE

CHAPTER I

JUDICIAL NOTICE

§ 1. Matter of fact.[1] Where a fact is one the existence of which is a matter of common knowledge no evidence need be offered to prove it; the court will take judicial notice of it. For example, the alternation of day and night and of the seasons, the usual time for the planting and harvesting of crops; that tomatoes are vegetables, that gin is intoxicating, that pure gasoline is almost colorless, that dynamite is an explosive, that iodine and spirits of camphor are drugs but that cigars and tobacco are not, that one cannot

[1] 20 **Am Jur,** Evidence, §§ 16–28, 50–134.
Distinction between judicial notice and judicial knowledge. 113 **ALR** 258–264.
Evidence contrary to scientific principles or laws of nature. 21 **ALR** 141–156.
Right of judge trying case without jury to base findings on result of personal observations. 97 **ALR** 335–339.
29 **Va. L. R.** 679, Scientific Proof in Law and Medicine.
57 **Harv. L. R.** 269, Judicial Notice.
47 **Yale L. J.** 194, Evidence and the New Federal Rules of Procedure.
40 **Mich. L. R.** 174, Congressional Enactment of Uniform Judicial Notice Act.
41 **Mich L. R.** 872, Scientific Proof and the Relations of Law and Medicine.
10 **U. of Chicago L. R.** 243, Scientific Proof and the Relations of Law and Medicine.
91 **U. of Pa. L. R.** 581, Our "Model Code of Evidence:" How Shall It Be Adopted?
20 **Tex. L. R.** 661, The New Code of Evidence of the American Law Institute.
23 **Boston N. L. R.** 143, Scientific Proof and Relations of Law and Medicine.
16 **So. Calif. L. R.** 119, Symposium Series on Scientific Proof and Relations of Law and Medicine.
17 **Tenn. L. R.** 10, Modern Thinking upon Evidence.

throw a stone gently, that a child less than two years old cannot render valuable services, that an automobile being driven on the highway is a dangerous agency, that it is a heavy burden for a railroad to defend an action in a state remote from where the action arose, that a particular section of a city is a business district, that lumber piled in a street would attract children, that a mule has a propensity to kick and that potatoes and onions are perishable vegetable products.

A court will also take judicial notice of the time of the rising and setting of the sun and moon and that a particular day of a certain month was on a particular day of the week, though it is usually necessary to consult a calendar or almanac to get the exact information. It will take judicial notice of the location of important cities and of the existence of foreign governments, though it may be necessary to consult the Department of State at Washington to find out recent developments.

Taking judicial notice of a fact is not conclusive; the opponent is not prevented from disputing it by evidence.

A jury may also take notice, without proof, of matters of common knowledge which they actually know, and it is proper for a court to instruct that the members of the jury should bring to their assistance their experience as men of affairs.

If a matter is not one of common knowledge neither the court nor the jury is entitled to go upon their own knowledge—or what they think is their knowledge; for example, that a bridge is not in disrepair. In such a case the judge or the juryman should take the stand as a witness and testify as to his knowledge so that it may become a part of the record and the jury may pass upon it; but if such evidence is highly important it is likely to be known beforehand and the judge should disqualify himself or the juror should be excused from serving.

A court may take judicial notice even when it may not be compelled to do so; and the tendency is to extend the operation of the doctrine as a salutary means of reducing the time required for litigation.

§ 2. **Matter of law.**[2] A court will take judicial notice of the law that it administers. A state court will take judicial notice of the United States Constitution, treaties with foreign governments, public acts of Congress, decisions of the United States Supreme Court and of the various federal courts, the state constitution, public acts of the state legislature and the decisions of its own courts of last resort. The same is true of the United States Supreme Court upon appeal from a state court upon some question of constitutional law.

A state court will not take judicial notice of municipal ordinances or of the law of a foreign country. Nor will it take notice of the law of a sister state; such law must be proved like any other fact, by the testimony of an expert or by official publications of statutes or decisions so that it becomes a part of the record. In cases where its jurisdiction is based upon the diverse citizenship of the parties, a federal court—including the United States Supreme Court—will take judicial notice of the laws of all the states, but it has been held that it is not error for such a court to fail to take judicial notice of a state statute which counsel had not brought to its attention.

[2] 20 **Am Jur**, Evidence, §§ 29–49.
Judicial notice of banking customs or other matters relating to banks or trust companies. 89 **ALR** 1336–1356.
Judicial notice of municipal ordinances where action originates in a municipal court. 111 **ALR** 959–966.

In some states there are statutes authorizing the taking of judicial notice of private acts of the legislature; and it has been strongly urged that state courts should be authorized by statute to take judicial notice of the laws of sister states.

There is a presumption that the common law of a sister state or of any country that administers Anglo-American law is the same as that of the forum, but this does not apply to statute law.

A court will take judicial notice that the common law has never prevailed in France or in any other country that does not have the Anglo-American system of law. There is no presumption that the law of such countries is the same as that of the forum.

CHAPTER II

WITNESSES

A. Examination of Witnesses

§ 3. Knowledge, recollection, belief, impression—maps—interpreter.[3] Ordinarily a witness testifies as to his knowledge or his recollection. But neither knowledge nor recollection need be positive; a statement of his belief or his impression is admissible if founded upon actual observation and not upon hearsay, and is not a mere opinion or conclusion; it is not rendered inadmissible merely because his observation or his recollection of his observation is faint. It is the privilege and duty of opposing counsel in cross examination to ask the witness the basis of his belief or impression.

In order to help a witness make his testimony as clear as possible he may use maps, diagrams, models, photographs, etc. And if he is a deaf mute or is unable to speak English, a sworn interpreter is used to translate the testimony into audible English.

§ 4. Present recollection revived—past recollection recorded.[4] The common use of the phrase "refreshing one's memory or recollection" has tended to cause confusion between present recollection revived and past recollection recorded.

In order to revive or refresh his present recollection of past events the witness may use any writing whatever provided it does produce that result. The writing may have been made at any time, by any person, and it may be a copy of the writing originally made.

Where the witness is not able to speak from present recollection he may introduce into evidence a writing which, he testifies, contains an accurate record of his past recollection of the event. Such a record need not have been made by the witness himself, but it must have been made when the recollec-

[3] 20 **Am Jur**, Evidence, §§ 741, 1186–1188.
See also **Am Jur**, Witnesses.
Effect of witness qualifying his testimony with "I think," "I believe" or the like, when expressing thereby indistinct observation or recollection. 4 **ALR** 979–990.
Right of witness to give summary based on inspection of number of documents. 66 **ALR** 1206–1225.
Comparative value of positive and negative testimony. 98 **ALR** 161–169.
Use of photograph, plan, map, cast, model, etc., as evidence as affected by marking or legends thereon. 108 **ALR** 1415–1428.
41 **Harv. L. R.** 860, Some Observations on the Law of Evidence—Memory.

[4] 20 **Am Jur**, Evidence, § 964.
See also **Am Jur**, Witnesses.
Use of memorandum by witness to refresh recollection as affected by the time when it was made. 65 **ALR** 1478–1490.
Refreshment of recollection by use of memoranda or other writings. 125 **ALR** 19–250.
40 **Harv. L. R.** 712, The Relation between Hearsay and Preserved Memory.

tion of the event was fairly fresh, which usually means that it must have been made soon after the event; a copy of the original record can be introduced only if the original is not available. Whether the original writing or a copy of it is introduced the opponent is entitled to inspect it for use in cross examination.

The application of both the foregoing rules should be subject to the discretionary control of the trial court.

§ 5. **Leading questions—friendly and hostile witnesses.**[5] A witness is not permitted to read to the jury a prepared statement; he must give his testimony orally.

Occasionally he is allowed to give his testimony in narrative form; the advantage of this is that it is more likely to be coherent and easy to follow and understand; the disadvantage is that he is likely to include inadmissible material such as hearsay; and striking out such matter upon motion of the opposing counsel does not entirely erase it from the minds of the jury. So ordinarily the witness testifies in answer to questions put by counsel. If he is a friendly witness—whether called by the examining counsel or by his opponent—it is the duty of the trial court to restrain counsel from putting leading questions—that is, questions which suggest the desired answer—but a failure to perform this duty is not a ground for reversal, the matter being left entirely to the discretion of the trial court.

Where the witness is hostile, biased or unwilling—whether called by the examining counsel or by his opponent—leading questions may be put freely. So as to preliminary, undisputed matters such as the name, age, residence and occupation of a witness; also if the witness's recollection is exhausted or he is illiterate or very young or too ill to speak. And if the court puts a question to a witness it is no objection that it is leading in form, the court being impartial, not partisan.

If in his answer to a question put by counsel a witness makes statements which are hearsay or otherwise inadmissible the remedy is to have such statements stricken from the record and the jury instructed to ignore them.

§ 6. **Cross examination—scope.**[6] The right to cross examine a hostile witness—one usually called by opposing counsel—is a powerful aid in arriving at the truth in a litigation and is an outstanding characteristic of Anglo-American law. So important is it regarded that if, after direct examination a witness dies or becomes too ill to be cross examined it is reversible error not to strike out the direct testimony.

The original doctrine was that cross examining counsel may question the witness not only on matters covered by the direct examination but upon any matters embraced within the issues of the case so that it might be possible for a defendant to establish his defense without calling a single witness. This would seem to be the sounder view; but due largely to the influence of Story and Greenleaf the weight of authority in this country is that if the

[5] See also **Am Jur**, Witnesses.

[6] See also **Am Jur**, Witnesses.

Cross-examination of character witness for accused with reference to particular acts or crimes. 71 **ALR** 1504–1546.

Cross-examination as to sexual morality for purpose of affecting credibility of witness. 65 **ALR** 410–426.

Right to cross-examine accused as to previous prosecution for, or conviction of, crime, for purpose of affecting his credibility. 6 **ALR** 1608–1648; s. in 25 **ALR** 339–348; 1^3 **ALR** 350–367.

Cross-examination of witness called to testify on particular point or under order of court. 7 **ALR** 1116–1128.

Extrajudicial statements by witness who is subject to cross-examination as evidence of facts to which they relate. 133 **ALR** 1454–1466.

cross examiner wishes to question the witness as to matters not covered in the direct examination he must make the witness his own at the proper time. The latter rule is objectionable because it is inconsistent with the witness's oath to tell the whole truth, it is often difficult for the trial court to tell what is and what is not new matter and in most jurisdictions it reduces the right of the cross examining counsel to impeach the witness, because the witness becomes his own.

The manner and extent of cross examination is largely within the discretion of the trial court but abuse of such discretion may be reversible error.

§ 7. Impeachment of opponent's witness—(1) reputation for veracity.[7] A witness called by one's opponent may be impeached by calling other witnesses who are acquainted with his general reputation for truth and veracity in the community where he lives; if such witnesses testify that his reputation for truth telling is bad some jurisdictions allow the further question, "would you believe him upon oath?" Other jurisdictions do not allow this on the ground that it is a mere opinion of the witness.

It is not the better view but in some states the bad general character of the witness may be shown. Where the charge is that of a sexual crime it is the better view that the reputation of the complaining witness for chastity may be shown but the authorities are in hopeless conflict. [See § 30.]

Where a witness has been impeached by testimony that he has a bad reputation for truth telling in the community where he lives the party who has called him may call other properly qualified witnesses to testify that his reputation for truth telling is good or that it is so good they never heard it questioned.

If the accused in a criminal prosecution takes the witness stand, he is subject to impeachment as a witness in the same ways that other witnesses may be impeached.

§ 8. Same—(2) prior conviction of a crime.[8] An opponent's witness may be impeached by showing that he has been convicted of a crime. That he was arrested or indicted or that he was tried and acquitted or that there was a verdict of guilty upon which judgment was not entered is not enough; nor is it enough that he was convicted of the violation of a local ordinance or traffic violation where no moral turpitude is involved. But the fact that sentence was suspended or that he was pardoned does not prevent the conviction from being shown; nor does the fact that the conviction took place in another jurisdiction. The impeached witness may explain the circumstances surrounding the conviction.

That the witness confessed to having committed a crime of which he was not convicted is not admissible to impeach him.

[7] See also **Am Jur,** Witnesses.

Admissibility of evidence of good reputation for truth and veracity of witness who has not been impeached. 15 **ALR** 1065–1076; s. in 33 **ALR** 1220–1222.

Admissibility of evidence of good character of party for truth and honesty on issue of fraud in civil action. 78 **ALR** 643–654.

Right to impeach accused as a witness by proof of general bad moral character or reputation. 90 **ALR** 870–880.

Evidence of character or reputation as embracing character or reputation as exhibited in place where one works or carries on his profession or business as distinguished from the general community or the particular community in which he lives. 112 **ALR** 1020–1031.

Admissibility in support of general credibility of an accomplice-witness who has not been impeached, of evidence from non-accomplice witness not otherwise relevant or of probative value as against defendant. 138 **ALR** 1266–1273.

Admissibility, for purpose of supporting impeached witness, of prior statements by him consistent with his testimony. 140 **ALR** 21–186.

[8] See also **Am Jur,** Witnesses.

§ 9. Same—(3) by cross examination as to specific instances of misconduct.[9] An opponent's witness may be asked as to whether he has committed specific acts of misconduct either criminal or merely disgraceful. In those states which allow a witness to be impeached by evidence of general bad character there would seem to be no reason for requiring the acts to be such as would tend to show lack of veracity such as fraud, perjury or forgery but might include such crimes as assault or incest; but even in states which limit proof of reputation to truth telling there has been a tendency not thus to impose this limit on cross examination.

The act or conduct inquired about may be either criminal or merely disgraceful, such as being engaged in a disreputable business or frequenting houses of ill fame. If the witness denies that he committed the act the negative answer is theoretically conclusive; the cross examiner may not contradict him by evidence from other witnesses that the act, being entirely collateral to the main issue, was committed; but in the hands of a skilful cross examiner the putting of such questions may influence the jury against giving full credit to the witness. This may result in great unfairness to the witness and to the party who called him and it is the duty of the trial court to hold such a cross examiner in check. As to the privilege of the witness not to testify because his answer may tend to incriminate him, see post § 26.

§ 10. Same—(4) by showing prior contradictory statements.[10] An opponent's witness may be impeached by showing, by other witnesses, that on a previous occasion he had made a statement inconsistent with all or with some material part of his present testimony. If such statement was oral he must first be asked—by way of laying a foundation—whether he had made such a statement, specifying time, place, language used and the person to whom the statement was made, so that he may have an opportunity to change his present testimony or to explain the contradiction. If he denies making the statement or says he does not remember making it, the fact that he did make such a statement may then be shown by other witnesses in order to discredit his present testimony; but such prior statement does not become positive evidence—that is, it has no independent testimonial value.

If such statement was in writing it is merely necessary to show the writing to the witness and to ask him whether he wrote or signed it. If he admits the genuineness of the writing he may be able to explain the contradiction; if he does not admit it, its genuineness may then be shown, usually by proving his signature.

If the oral or written statement does not contradict on a material point it is regarded as collateral and not admissible, because it would waste time and tend to confuse the main issue.

Where the witness is a party to the action, inconsistent statements are treated as admissions and admissible without any foundation being laid.

Where apparently inconsistent statements have been introduced the party calling the witness may, upon re-examination, give the witness the oppor-

9 See also **Am Jur**, Witnesses.

10 See also **Am Jur**, Witnesses.

Testimony tending to show that party or witness has made contradictory statements as ground for evidence as to his truth and veracity. 6 **ALR** 862–887.

May a witness who testifies to facts be impeached by showing of prior inconsistent expressions of opinion by him. 66 **ALR** 289–304.

tunity to harmonize the statements. And where the testimony of the witness has been attacked as a recent fabrication, proof of consistent statements made at a time when there was no motive to falsify may be shown on re-examination.

§ 11. Same—(5) by showing bias or interest or abnormal mentality.[1] An opponent's witness may be impeached by the testimony of other witnesses as to acts or declarations of the witness tending to show bias—that is, that the witness is friendly to the party calling him or hostile to the adverse party—or tending to show that the witness has a financial interest in the outcome of the litigation. It is usual, but not necessary, in most states, to lay a foundation for such testimony by asking the appropriate questions on cross examination.

An opponent's witness may also be impeached by showing, by other witnesses, that at the time of the occurrence about which he has testified or at the time of giving his testimony he was mentally deranged or under the influence of liquor or drugs; or, in the case of a woman complaining of a sex offense committed by a defendant, that she is suffering from nymphomania or sex suppression. Such testimony is ordinarily given by psychiatrists or other medical experts.

§ 12. Impeachment of one's own witness—in general.[2] The general rule is that, apart from statute, one may not impeach his own witness. This has been traced historically to the time centuries ago when those who attended trials were not witnesses in the modern sense but compurgators or oath helpers who did not pretend to be neutral but were out and out partisans of the party for whom they appeared; therefore the rule has no proper application to the modern testifying witness who is not supposed to be a partisan. The only logical justification for the rule is that if a party could freely impeach his own witness he might use the power to coerce his witness into testifying favorably but the chance of this actually happening is very slight and only rarely has it been urged as the reason for the rule. The reason most commonly given is that by calling a witness a party guarantees his credibility and therefore may not impeach him; but if this were really true the party would not be able to show by other witnesses that the facts were otherwise, but this mild, indirect form of impeachment is allowed everywhere, though it is not allowed for the sole purpose of contradiction.

§ 13. Same—scope of the doctrine.[3] The rule prevents a party from attacking the credibility of his witness either by introducing testimony as to his bad reputation for truth telling or by showing that he has made prior inconsistent statements or by showing bias or interest.

The rule applies where a party makes the adverse party his own witness but it does not apply where the law requires the calling of the witness, as in the case of attesting witnesses to a will.

For the purposes of the rule merely putting a witness on the stand and

1 See also **Am Jur**, Witnesses.

Necessity of laying foundation for evidence showing bias or prejudice of witness. 16 **ALR** 984-996.

2 See also **Am Jur**, Witnesses.

3 See also **Am Jur**, Witnesses.

Right of party surprised by unfavorable testimony of own witness to ask him concerning previous inconsistent statements. 74 **ALR** 1042-1070.

Proper practice and relief on development of hostility by party's own witness. 117 **ALR** 326-329.

Competency of physician or surgeon of school of practice other than that to which defendant belongs to testify in malpractice case. 78 **ALR** 697-709.

asking him preliminary questions does not make him one's own witness but only the giving of relevant testimony. Where a witness is called by and testifies for both parties neither party may, apart from statute, impeach him. And in states which do not permit cross examination on new matter a party who undertakes to cross examine as to new matter thereby makes the witness his own; but by the better view this does not prevent the putting of leading questions because the test of that privilege is the hostility of the witness and not the identity of the party calling him.

In some states prior self contradictions may be shown where the witness surprises the party calling him by unexpectedly giving adverse testimony; and in some other states the entire rule forbidding impeachment has been either abolished or modified by statute.

B. Competency

§ 14. Judge, counsel, jurors.[4] A judge may testify in a case which is being tried before him but except as to formal and undisputed matters he should not do so as a matter of the decent administration of justice unless the trial can go on without his returning to the bench, and this is not possible where, as usually happens, he is the only judge sitting. He should not attempt to occupy the dual position of judge and witness; and hence should not have undertaken to try the case at all. But there is no objection to a judge who is not the trial judge testifying as to what took place in previous trials over which he presided.

An attorney who is acting as counsel in the case may, but should not, also be a witness except as to formal matters because it is so likely to create in the public mind the impression that he has been employed to manufacture testimony; if he does testify he should at once retire from the case.

A juror may testify and should do so rather than to go upon his personal knowledge in rendering a verdict; but except as to formal matters the question rarely arises because his knowledge of the facts involved in the case are so likely to be brought out upon his *voir dire* and on that basis he will be excused from service as juror.

§ 15. Mental, moral and theological incapacity.[5] In the early law mentally deranged persons were not allowed to testify; today they may do so unless the derangement is such as to negative trustworthiness upon the specific subject of the testimony, and this is to be determined by the trial court. Even if the testimony is admitted the fact of mental derangement may be shown to affect credibility. It has been urged by text writers that since the question of derangement is a difficult one of degree there should be no exclusion of a witness on this ground. Though it is usual to stress the existence of mental derangement at the time of giving testimony the fact of such derangement at the time of the event testified about is also important.

In the early law the competency of a child to testify was determined largely by deciding whether he understood the meaning of an oath. Today the emphasis is shifting to a question of testimonial trustworthiness, to be determined within the discretion of the trial judge; sometimes children as

[4] See also Am Jur, Witnesses.

[5] See also Am Jur, Witnesses.
Mental condition as affecting competency of witness. 26 ALR 1491–1505; s. in 148 ALR 1140–1159.
Religious belief or lack of it as affecting credibility of witness. 95 ALR 723–727.

young as six years have been allowed to testify. Here, as in the case of mental derangement, it has been urged that there should be no exclusion on this ground, the jury to be allowed to listen to the testimony and give it whatever weight it might seem to merit.

Formerly the fact that one had been convicted of a serious crime made him incompetent to testify, but this disqualification has been almost entirely abolished by statute. However, the fact of such conviction may be shown in order to affect his credibility.

Formerly the fact that one did not profess to believe that if he should tell a falsehood he would be punished for it "either in this world or the next" disqualified him from taking an oath and therefore prevented him from testifying; but in most states this theological requirement has been abolished either by constitution or by statute.

In any case where an oath is required the requirement may be waived either expressly or by failure to object.

§ 16. Interest—civil cases.[6] About 1600, parties in civil actions were excluded from testifying and about 1650, this disqualification was extended to those who had an interest in the outcome of the litigation; the reason given for this exclusion was that such persons would be so likely to commit perjury. About a century ago this disqualification was abolished by statute, the interest of the witness merely affecting his credibility. But in one instance the disqualification has survived, either being provided for in the statute abolishing the disqualification or in another statute passed shortly thereafter: where the basis of the suit is a transaction between a person since deceased and one who still survives, the latter may not testify in an action by or against the decedent's estate unless the personal representative waives the disqualification by himself taking the stand, or by introducing testimony given by the decedent at a previous trial. Objection should be made to the competency of the witness, not to the competency of the testimony.

The theory of the exception is that in the absence of the other party to the transaction the survivor is almost certain to commit perjury, but this overlooks the privilege of a rigid cross-examination which would seem to be a sufficient check. It has been strongly urged that the exception should be abolished as doing more harm than good and in a few states the exception has been modified by statute either by allowing the evidence if corroborated, or—in other states—if the trial court thinks that otherwise injustice will be done, or, in still other states, by permitting also any writings or declarations of the decedent in regard to the matter to be introduced into evidence.

[6] See also **Am Jur**, Witnesses.

Release or assignment of interest by witness as removing disqualification to testify in action by or against estate of decedent. 28 **ALR** 6–32.

Competency of witness in actions for death as affected by statute disqualifying one person as a witness because of death of another. 36 **ALR** 959–970; s. in 41 **ALR** 345, 346; 45 **ALR** 1477.

Examination of witness as waiver of his incompetency as to transactions or conversations of decedent. 64 **ALR** 1148–1184; s. in 107 **ALR** 482–497.

Statute excluding testimony of one person because of death of another as applied to testimony in respect of lost or destroyed instrument. 79 **ALR** 785–802.

Statutes excluding testimony of one person because of death of another as applicable in proceeding to probate will. 115 **ALR** 1425–1435.

Statute excluding testimony of one person because of death of another as applicable to attorneys. 116 **ALR** 1323–1334.

Statute disqualifying one person as witness because of death of another as applicable to executor or administrator of decedent. 117 **ALR** 606–639.

Statute rendering witness incompetent because of death of other person as applicable to latter's mental condition. 146 **ALR** 250–279.

§ 17. Interest—criminal cases.[7] Some fifty years after the abolition of the disqualification of parties and interested parties in civil cases, the accused in a criminal prosecution was by statute made a competent witness in his own behalf. Perhaps the chief reason for this tardiness was that if the defendant was permitted to testify and did not do so the jury would draw the inference that he was guilty whereas if he could not testify such inference could not be drawn. Permitting the accused to testify is desirable because it usually operates in his favor if innocent but against him if guilty. In no state can he be compelled to testify.

In most states it is reversible error for the prosecuting attorney or the court to comment to the jury upon the failure of the defendant to testify.

§ 18. Husband and wife.[8] Formerly a husband or wife of a party was incompetent to testify for each other during the existence of the relationship but this has been changed by statute almost everywhere as to both civil and criminal cases; and in the federal courts a wife was held competent without a statute to testify for her husband in a criminal prosecution.

As to the privilege of a husband and wife not to testify against each other, see post § 25. As to privileged communications between husband and wife see post § 21.

C. Privileged Communications

§ 19. In general.[9] The mere fact that A makes a communication to B expressly in confidence does not give A any privilege to prevent B from testifying as to such communication. But there are some relationships where such a privilege does exist. It is usually said that there are four conditions that must be satisfied in order that there be such a privilege:

(1) Though the communication need not be expressly confidential there must be an intention that it be not disclosed.

(2) Confidentiality must be essential to the maintenance of the relationship.

(3) The relation must be one which deserves such protection.

(4) Disclosure of the communication on the witness stand would cause greater harm than non-disclosure.

§ 20. Attorney and client.[10] Though the attorney and client privilege arose at common law as that of the attorney, being based upon his oath and honor as such, it has for the last two centuries been held to be that of the client who is entitled to insist that his attorney shall not disclose on the witness stand any confidential communications made by himself to the attorney or by the attorney to himself in giving legal advice.

All the four conditions are here present. In order that the attorney may satisfactorily represent his client it is desirable that the client be protected in making a full disclosure to his attorney; and non-disclosure by the attorney does not cause much harm because, in civil cases, the client himself

[7] See also **Am Jur**, Witnesses.

[8] See also **Am Jur**, Witnesses.
Rule rendering husband or wife incompetent as a witness for the other in a criminal case as changed without the aid of a statute expressly abrogating it or comprehensively removing disqualification of witnesses. 93 **ALR** 1144–1147.

[9] See also **Am Jur**, Witnesses.
Privilege against use as evidence of communications made to reporter, editor, or publisher of ne spaper or magazine. 102 **ALR** 771–773.

Evidence: privilege of communication made to public officers. 9 **ALR** 1099–1119; s. in 59 **ALR** 1555–1561.

Evidence: statement or report by servant or agent to master or principal, in respect of matters then or afterward involved in litigation, as a privileged communication. 146 **ALR** 977–993.

may now be put on the witness stand and compelled to disclose what he knows.

In order that the privilege exist it is necessary that the attorney be licensed to practice and that he should be consulted as such by the client, even though the attorney be not later employed by him. It is also necessary that the communication be confidential; hence if a third person is present other than employees of the attorney there is no privilege; and if a third person overhears the conversation, he may be compelled to testify. If X and Y jointly consult A there is no privilege in any litigation between X and Y, but there is a privilege in litigation between X or Y and Z. If a client consults his opponent's attorney there is, of course, no privilege.

If advice is sought with regard to a criminal or illegal act already committed by the client the communication is privileged, but there is no privilege if advice is sought as to a criminal or illegal act to be performed in the future.

The privilege may be waived only by the client, not by the attorney, but if not waived it lasts even after the death of the client; but by the better view it may be waived by the deceased client's personal representative. If the client voluntarily testifies to the communication the privilege is thereby waived but this does not apply to testimony brought out by cross examination of the client, or to his testimony on matters other than the communication. If the client is not a party to the litigation the party may not waive the privilege.

§ 21. Husband and wife.[1] The four conditions for the existence of a privilege are all satisfied in the relation of husband and wife; confidence is essential to the relation, the relation deserves such legal protection and more harm would probably ensue by disclosure than by nondisclosure. Hence neither the husband nor the wife may, without the consent of the other, testify as to any confidential communications, oral or written, made during the marriage; and this privilege is permanent, outlasting divorce or the death of one of the parties, and may be waived only by the concurrence of both spouses.

The communication need not be expressly confidential; it is enough that it was of a confidential character, not made in the presence of a third party. Even if confidential, if a third party overhears it, he may be compelled to testify to it.

The privilege does not exist where action is brought for alienation of af-

[10] See also **Am Jur,** Witnesses.

Attorney-client privilege as affected by wrongful or criminal character of contemplated acts or course of conduct. 125 **ALR** 508–531.

Impropriety of attorney testifying for client as ground of exclusion of testimony otherwise admissible. 118 **ALR** 954–965.

Disclosure of name, identity, address, occupation, or business of client as violation of attorney-client privilege. 114 **ALR** 1321–1333.

Privilege as to communications to attorney in connection with drawing of will. 64 **ALR** 184–202.

Persons other than client or attorney rendered incompetent by the privilege attaching to communications between client and attorney. 53 **ALR** 369–375.

Evidence: attorney-client privilege as applicable to communications between attorney and client's agent, employee, spouse, or relative. 139 **ALR** 1250–1261.

Attorney-client privilege as applied to communications in presence of two or more persons interested in the subject matter to which the communications relate. 141 **ALR** 553–565.

[1] See also **Am Jur,** Witnesses.

Effect of knowledge of third person acquired by overhearing or seeing communication between husband and wife upon rule as to privileged communication. 63 **ALR** 107–132.

Applicability and effect in suit for alienation of affections of rule excluding confidential communications between husband and wife. 36 **ALR** 1068–1081; s. in 82 **ALR** 825–865.

fections or for criminal conversation, and some statutes except also criminal prosecutions for family desertion.

§ 22. Jurors—witnesses before a grand jury.[2] The relationship between petit jurors is one that satisfies the four conditions for the existence of a privilege: confidence that the deliberations in the jury room shall not later be disclosed on the witness stand by a fellow juror is essential to the satisfactory maintenance of the relation, the relationship merits legal protection and more harm would probably come from disclosure than from nondisclosure. Hence a petit juror is entitled to object to having any communication from himself to a fellow juror disclosed upon the witness stand by the latter. As the rule is usually stated, a juror is incompetent to impeach his own verdict. But the privilege does not protect a juror who is being prosecuted for a crime alleged to have been committed by him in connection with his jury service, such as criminal contempt for not disclosing on his *voir dire* his connection with one of the parties to the litigation.

The privilege of a grand juror is similar to that of a petit juror and for the same reasons; he is entitled not to have his vote or expression of opinion in the jury room disclosed on the witness stand by a fellow grand juror.

A witness or complainant who appears before a grand jury is entitled not to have his testimony or complaint disclosed on the witness stand by a grand juror until after the hearing has been terminated either by indicting or discharging the person or persons accused.

§ 23. Clergyman and penitent.[3] Though the four conditions present in the relation of jurors, attorney and client, and husband and wife are also present in the relation of clergyman and penitent there is no common law privilege that the confession made by the penitent be not disclosed on the witness stand by the clergyman. But in about half the states there are statutes bestowing the privilege.

These statutes usually exempt the penitent as well as the clergyman from disclosure but limit the privilege to confessions of sin made in pursuance of church discipline which requires the layman to make confession, or which merely requires the clergyman to receive it; it does not cover other confidential communications.

§ 24. Physician and patient.[4] A patient has no common law privilege against the disclosure by his physician on the witness stand of communications made to him by the patient. But in 1828 a statute was passed in New York granting such a privilege to the patient and since that time about half the states have passed similar legislation.

Of the four conditions present in the four relations previously discussed only one is completely present here: the relation is one that merits legal protection. Usually the communication is not confidential—unless it has to do with venereal diseases—and even where it is, it would have been made though no privilege existed; this is shown by the fact that in this respect there seems

[2] See also **Am Jur**, Witnesses.

[3] See also **Am Jur**, Witnesses.

[4] See also **Am Jur**, Witnesses.

Who may waive privilege of confidential communications to physician by person since deceased. 31 **ALR** 167-182; s. in 126 **ALR** 380-386.

Waiver of privilege as regards one physician as a waiver as to other physician. 62 **ALR** 680-689; s. in 90 **ALR** 646-648.

When testimony by patient deemed to waive physician-patient privilege. 114 **ALR** 798-806.

Physician-patient, attorney-client, or priest-penitent privilege as applicable in nonjudicial proceeding or investigation. 133 **ALR** 732-738.

to be no dfference between medical practice in the states which have granted the privilege and those which have not. Finally, very little if any harm follows from disclosure but considerable harm from nondisclosure. The question arises chiefly in three classes of cases: (1) actions to enforce a policy of life insurance where the defense is that the insured misrepresented his health; (2) personal injury actions where the question is as to the extent of the plaintiff's injuries; and (3) actions involving a will where the question is as to the sanity of the testator. Nondisclosure in (1) and (2) frequently results in the enforcement of fraudulent claims; nondisclosure in (3) sometimes results in preventing an innocent plaintiff from enforcing a just claim.

The privilege does not exist unless there was the relation of physician and patient, though it is not necessary that the patient should have called the physician, or that a fee was paid or expected. Nor does it exist unless the communication was confidential though confidentiality is presumed. It need not be in words but covers information acquired by the physician through observation; but it must be necessary in order that the physician prescribe remedies; and it does not cover information which is open to the observation of any layman. The privilege does not operate to excuse a physician who is being charged civilly or criminally with malpractice and statutes as to insurance against industrial accidents usually provide against any privilege in such cases.

The privilege is that of the patient, not of the physician or of the party to the suit where the patient is not the party. It may be waived by the patient either expressly or—by the better view—by testifying as to his physical condition or by calling the physician to testify thereto, in which latter case the waiver extends to knowledge obtained of the patient's physical condition by other physicians. A waiver once made is waived permanently and for all purposes. After the death of the patient the privilege may be waived by his personal representative.

In some states statutes have been passed making void any contract to waive the privilege, the legislation being aimed chiefly at waivers inserted in life insurance contracts.

D. Other Cases of Privilege

§ 25. Not to testify against one's wife or husband.[5] For the last three centuries it has been held that neither husband nor wife may testify against the other without the latter's consent. The two reasons for the rule which are usually given are (1) that it tends to preserve domestic harmony; (2) that there is a natural repugnance toward compelling a wife or husband to be the means of condemning her or his spouse.

The privilege does not exist unless there is a valid marriage and ceases upon divorce or the death of one of the spouses. It exists even though neither spouse is a party to the action. Logically it should not exist where the action is for criminal conversation or alienation of affections because there is no domestic harmony left to be preserved, but the courts have not always held thus.

The privilege apparently belongs to both spouses and can be waived only by both. If one spouse calls the other as a witness this is usually regarded as a waiver.

About half the states have abolished the privilege in civil cases and a few in criminal cases; in several states statutes have modified the rule by making

[5] See also **Am Jur**, Witnesses.

exceptions, for example, in proceedings involving a crime or personal injury or crime committed by one spouse against the other.

§ 26. Not to incriminate oneself—scope of privilege.[6] Partly because of the resentment in England against the inquisitorial proceedings in the Court of Star Chamber and partly because of the experience of the American colonists with high handed prerogative courts before the American Revolution, there is, in the United States Constitution and in the constitutions of nearly all the states, a provision—varying in phraseology but not in legal effect—that no one shall be compelled to give testimony which would tend to incriminate him.

The privilege exists in any proceeding whatever in which testimony is taken, whether the person involved is a party to the proceeding or merely a witness, where the answer to the question might tend to make the answerer subject—by the law of the forum—to a penalty of fine or imprisonment or the forfeiture of some privilege. There is no objection to asking about a prior conviction where the penalty has been imposed and suffered; or about an act where the statute of limitations has run against its prosecution or the witness has received a pardon; or about an act supposed to have been committed by a third person. The privilege cannot be claimed by a corporation.

The privilege does not apply to a record required by law to be kept, of acts not criminal in themselves, such as a druggist's record of sales of narcotics; or to an oral report required by law to be made, of acts not criminal in themselves, such as an auto driver's report of a traffic accident.

The privilege protects the witness not only from testifying orally but also from producing documents in his possession; but it does not protect him from the seizure of such documents without the use of process against him as a witness, or from being compelled to stand up to be identified or to roll up his sleeve so that the jury may see his arm, or to take off his shoes so that it may be seen whether they fit into certain foot prints.

§ 27. Same—waiver—inferences—immunity statutes—policy of the privilege.[7] The privilege is that of the witness, not of counsel or the party calling him, and must be claimed by him at the time the question is asked, otherwise it is waived. And it is for him alone to decide whether the answer would incriminate him unless the court is of the opinion that no direct answer to the question *could* incriminate the witness. If the court should erroneously allow the privilege and excuse the witness from answering, the party asking the question may take advantage of the error on appeal.

If the witness is the accused in a criminal prosecution and he goes on the stand he places himself in the position of an ordinary witness and may be

[6] See also **Am Jur**, Witnesses.

Privilege against self-incrimination before grand jury. 27 **ALR** 139–154.

Privilege against self-incrimination as applicable to answer to pleadings. 52 **ALR** 143–149.

Power to require plaintiff to submit to physical examination. 51 **ALR** 183–192; s. in 108 **ALR** 142–153.

Footprint evidence as violating rule against self-incrimination. 64 **ALR** 1089–1103.

Calling upon accused in the presence of jury to produce document in his possession as violation of privilege against self-incrimination. 110 **ALR** 101–119.

Adequacy of immunity offered as condition of denial or privilege against self-incrimination. 118 **ALR** 602–629.

Privilege against self-incrimination as justification for refusal to comply with order or subpoena requiring production of books or documents of private corporation. 120 **ALR** 1102–1117.

Necessity and sufficiency of assertion of privilege against self-incrimination as condition of statutory immunity of witness from prosecution. 145 **ALR** 1416–1426.

15 **Harv. L. R.** 610, The Privilege against Self-Incrimination—Its History.

30 **Calif. L. R.** 547, Privileges against Self-Incrimination in California.

[7] See also **Am Jur**, Witnesses.

cross examined and impeached as such. If he claims the privilege or if he refuses to go on the witness stand the jury is likely to draw the inference that he is guilty, but in most states neither the court in its charge nor the prosecuting attorney in his address to the jury may comment on the fact. If the accused does not go on the stand the modern rule permitting him to testify thus operates to his disadvantage.

In order to secure convictions in certain cases, especially such as bribery and gambling, where evidence is otherwise difficult to obtain, modern statutes grant immunity from prosecution to certain classes of persons if they will testify; in such cases the privilege ceases as soon as the witness testifies because the criminality of his act has been taken away by the statute.

The privilege has been criticised because it tends to prevent the conviction of a guilty witness; it has been defended on the ground that without it an innocent witness might be compelled, on cross examination, to disclose discreditable facts which might make him the victim of blackmail, and because it would tempt the prosecuting officers not to hunt diligently for other evidence.

CHAPTER III

REAL EVIDENCE AND RELATED TOPICS

§ 28. Real evidence.[8] Instead of having witnesses give testimony from which the court or jury may, either directly or indirectly, draw inferences of fact, the fact to be proved may be of such a nature that the court or jury may use their own senses upon persons or objects in their presence; for example, whether a party to the action who claims that he is an infant is really such, whether the complaining witness in a prosecution for statutory rape is under the age of consent, whether clothes are blood stained, whether, in a paternity case, the child resembles the defendant. Because the person or thing itself is passed upon by the jury such evidence is usually called real evidence (from "res," meaning "thing"); it is sometimes called autoptic profference—that is, offered to the sight—because it is usually the sense of sight rather than feeling, hearing, taste or smell that is employed by the jury.

Where it is impossible to bring the object into court the jury may, in the court's discretion, be permitted to view it outside of court; for example, land which is the subject of litigation or which is the place where the crime charged was committed. This matter is usually regulated by statute.

Occasionally the presentation of objects in court has been refused because it would tend to prejudice the jury; for example, the exhibition of plaintiff's bodily injuries in a personal injury suit against a corporation or a wealthy individual. In some states statutes permit a defendant in a personal injury case to require the plaintiff to submit to a physical examination.

It is not a legitimate objection to admitting real evidence that there is no way of transmitting it to a higher court upon appeal or bill of exceptions, there being no way of getting it into the record, because there is equally no way of getting into the record the appearance, tone of voice, mode and manner of expression and general demeanor of a witness while he is testifying—matters which may and frequently do have a considerable influence upon the jury's verdict.

8 20 Am Jur, Evidence, §§ 718–762.

§ 29. Illegally obtained evidence.[9] Down to about fifty years ago the fact that evidence—usually consisting of documents, weapons or other chattels—was obtained by an illegal search was no objection to its admissibility, and that is still the rule in about two-thirds of the states; in those states the remedy for such illegal search is solely against the one making the search. But in the other states, following the lead of the United States Supreme Court in Boyd v. United States and Weeks v. United States evidence obtained in violation of the Fourth Amendment to the United States Constitution prohibiting unreasonable search and seizure, may not be introduced in evidence if the illegality of the search and seizure be established before trial and the articles be reclaimed, though the Fourth Amendment does not provide for any such reclamation.

This minority doctrine has been much criticised as an inexcusable obstruction of the administration of justice and in the Federal courts the doctrine has been strictly limited. It does not apply where the search was made by anyone who was not a Federal officer, or if the search was made by a Federal officer upon premises not owned or occupied by the party defendant, or if made in an automobile not on defendant's premises, or if made with the consent of the party defendant, or if made lawfully.

If the Federal rule were sound it would, upon principle, logically apply to evidence obtained against the accused by illegally tapping telephone wires and listening in to conversations, but the United States Supreme Court has refused to hold such evidence inadmissible because wire tapping is not literally a search.

§ 30. Circumstantial evidence—character evidence.[10] Where there are no eye witnesses to an act—as frequently happens in prosecutions for such crimes as murder, conspiracy and forgery—resort must be had to nontestimonial evidence usually called circumstantial evidence.

If Y is upon trial for the murder of X and no one was present when X was killed the prosecution will necessarily be compelled to rely upon such circumstantial evidence as that Y was in the vicinity about the time when the killing occurred or that the knife or gun used was the property of Y. The defendant, on the other hand, may rely upon the circumstantial evidence that he had a reputation in the community for being a peaceable, law abiding citizen who would not likely commit murder. If the defendant thus puts his character in issue by calling witnesses who swear that his reputation for peaceableness is good, the prosecution may then introduce the testimony of other witnesses that his reputation for being peaceable is bad. If the crime charged is one not of violence but of fraud, the evidence must be of reputation for veracity.

Where the defendant is accused of murder he may, in order to show that he acted in self defense, prove that the reputation of the deceased was that of a quarrelsome man and that defendant knew of such reputation and hence acted in the honest belief that his life was in peril. Where the defendant did not know of such reputation evidence of decedent's threats are admissible merely to show that he was the aggressor.

Where the defendant is accused of rape he may show in defense the bad reputation for chastity of the prosecuting witness. In a prosecution for bas-

9 20 Am Jur, Evidence, §§ 393–402.

10 20 Am Jur, Evidence, §§ 270–273, 319–331. 23 Boston U. L. R. 277, Circumstantial Evidence in Poisoning Cases.

tardy the defendant may show specific instances of sexual intercourse between the mother and men other than the defendant at or near the beginning of the period of gestation.

Neither the character of the plaintiff nor of the defendant may ordinarily be put in issue in civil actions, but the nature of the action may be such as to raise such an issue.

There is no rule as to the respective weight of testimonial and circumstantial evidence. In spite of the fact that in many cases innocent persons have been found guilty and executed where the testimony was circumstantial, courts frequently say that circumstantial evidence is more reliable than testimonial.

§ 31. Remote and prejudicial evidence.[1] In order to be admissible, evidence must be relevant to the issue. While relevancy is, strictly speaking, a matter of logic rather than law, courts are frequently called upon to determine whether some particular evidence offered is relevant enough to be admitted or is so remote that it should be excluded. For example, in an action against a buyer for refusal to accept iron, the defense was inexcusable delay by the seller; defendant's evidence that the delay was due to the seller's delivering to others at a higher price than he was to pay was held admissible. In an action for personal injuries due to lead poisoning it was held permissible for plaintiff to show that other employees who had worked in the same room had suffered from lead poisoning. And in an action for negligence be-

[1] 20 **Am Jur,** Evidence, §§ 248, 249, 253.

Experimental evidence as affected by similarity or dissimilarity of conditions. 8 **ALR** 18–59; s. in 55 **ALR** 479–501.

Proof of other defamatory statements in civil action for libel or slander. 12 **ALR** 1026–1040; s. in 86 **ALR** 1297–1301.

Use of photographs in examination and comparison of handwriting or typewriting. 31 **ALR** 1431–1441.

Evidence of other forgeries or alterations on issue as to forgery or alteration in civil cases. 33 **ALR** 427–439.

May demonstration before jury, otherwise proper, be permitted outside of courtroom. 60 **ALR** 574–580.

Valuation for purposes of taxation as evidence of value of property for other purposes. 17 **ALR** 170–179; s. in 84 **ALR** 1485–1488.

Admissibility on question as to quality, condition or capacity of articles, machines, or apparatus, of evidence in regard to similar things manufactured or sold by the same person. 66 **ALR** 81–101.

Admissibility and weight on issue of mental capacity or undue influence in respect of will or conveyance, of instruments previously executed by the person in question. 82 **ALR** 903–975.

Habit, custom, or reputation of one injured or killed as evidence of his own negligence or freedom from negligence. 15 **ALR** 125–145; s. in 18 **ALR** 1109, 1110.

Admissibility and weight of mortality tables as evidence as affected by lack of normal health. 116 **ALR** 416–432.

Admissibility on issue of value of real property of evidence of sale price of other real property. 118 **ALR** 869–914.

Evidence which indirectly or incidentally suggests poverty or wealth of party not in itself proper matter of proof. 122 **ALR** 1408–1415.

May proof of delivery essential to gift rest upon subsequent declarations of donor. 124 **ALR** 1391–1403.

Admissibility of statements by one who claimed to have met with an accident, as evidence of fact of accident. 130 **ALR** 291–310.

Nature, extent, and conduct of physical examination of party to action or proceeding to recover for personal injury or disability. 135 **ALR** 883–900.

Admissibility, on issue of negligence or contributory negligence, of statement or comment in respect of conduct of driver of car, or other person, shortly afterwards involved in an accident. 140 **ALR** 874–881.

Evidence of trailing by dogs. 94 **ALR** 413–427.

Admissibility in rape cases of evidence of previous unchastity, or reputation for unchastity, of prosecutrix. 140 **ALR** 364–392.

Admissibility of evidence, and propriety and effect of questions, statements, comments, etc., tending to show that defendant in a personal-injury or death action carries liability insurance. 56 **ALR** 1418–1550; s. in 74 **ALR** 849–874; 95 **ALR** 388–417; 105 **ALR** 1319–1338.

Admissibility of evidence as to prior or subsequent accidents on issue of negligence respecting condition of street or highway. 65 **ALR** 380–404.

Admissibility on issue of defendant's negligence in respect of condition of place where plaintiff was injured, of evidence of prior accidents or injuries at same place. 128 **ALR** 595–608.

Admissibility on issue of negligence or contributory negligence of statements warning one of danger. 125 **ALR** 645–656.

46 **Harv. L. R.** 954, The Rule of Exclusion of Similar Fact Evidence.

51 **Harv. L. R.** 988, The Rule of Exclusion of Similar Fact Evidence.

cause of a failure to provide adequate safety devices evidence of general usage in the same kind of business may be introduced to establish a standard by which ordinary care may be judged.

On the other hand, where action was brought to recover damages for the value of a truck which had been negligently overturned by the defendant and had then caught fire and burned, it was held error for the plaintiff to ask the city fire chief if he knew of trucks which caught fire after being damaged because defendant could have offered evidence that other trucks were overturned and did not catch fire. And in an action for negligently causing personal injuries or death it is not permissible to show that the plaintiff's intestate was an habitually careful person or that the defendant's employee was an habitually careless person.

Even though evidence is relevant enough from a logical standpoint it may be excluded because it would tend to confuse or mislead the jury or because it would otherwise be unfair. For example, evidence that after the alleged negligent act occurred repairs were made and precautions taken by the defendant is inadmissible because it would tend to mislead the jury and would operate to penalize unusually careful defendants and hold out inducements for continued negligence.

Similarly, in a criminal prosecution it is not usually permissible to show that the defendant had committed other crimes because it would unduly prejudice the jury against him. But such evidence is allowed in order to show motive, or intent or the absence of accident or mistake or the identity of the defendant or a common scheme embracing two or more crimes so closely related to each other that the proof of one tends to prove the other.

CHAPTER IV

OPINION

A. Nonexpert Testimony

§ 32. The general rule of exclusion.[2] Three centuries ago an ordinary, nonexpert witness could not testify merely as to his opinion but must state facts that had come within his personal observation; he must state what he knows, not what he thinks or believes; mere opinion was rejected on about the same ground that hearsay was rejected. But if he did state facts he might also give his opinion on those facts. Later, however, partly because of the constant repetition of the phrase, "opinion is not evidence" the witness was required to state only facts and not opinion.

This was sometimes placed on the ground that to allow the witness to state his opinion would allow him to usurp the function of the jury—especially an opinion which happened to be on the very point at issue in the case, such as legal cause or the negligence of the defendant or damages or the contributory negligence of the plaintiff, though it is difficult to see how allowing the witness to state his opinion prevents the jury from having their own opinion, especially since the jury freely passes on the matter after the witness has testified.

The only rational ground for the rule excluding opinion as supplementary to testimony based on personal observation is that it is sometimes superfluous and of no help to the jury. This occurs where the facts are such that the witness can fully and accurately reproduce them. But the mere fact that

[2] 20 Am Jur, Evidence, §§ 765-772.

the witness's opinion in such a case might be superfluous does not seem to be an adequate reason for excluding it; and it seems likely that the rule of exclusion will ultimately be abrogated by legislation.

§ 33. The exceptions.[3] Where the facts cannot be fully and accurately reproduced by the witness he may, after stating the facts as well as he can, supplement such testimony by giving his opinion. The following are the most important examples:

(a) On the question of identity
(b) On the question of sanity
(c) On the question of intoxication
(d) On the question of the genuineness of handwriting
(e) On the question of apparent physical condition
(f) On the question of emotional state
(g) On the question of the value of property or services
(h) On the question of the ownership of property
(i) On matters involving taste, smell or touch
(j) On matters of color, size, weight, etc.
(k) On the speed of railroad trains, automobiles, etc.

In most states the fact that the defendant had been convicted in a criminal prosecution is *prima facie* evidence against him in a civil action for damages which is based upon the same wrongful act. In such a situation the jurors do not appear as witnesses in the civil action but their verdict, based upon their nonexpert opinion, is admitted.

B. Expert Testimony

§ 34. Opinion based upon the expert's own observation.[4] Where there is a question before a jury which involves technical knowledge and experience beyond the capacity and understanding of the average juror, either party may place on the witness stand persons who have such technical knowledge and experience and, where it is necessary for the jury's understanding of the matter, ask their opinion upon the question at issue. Whether the particular person thus called to the witness stand has such technical knowledge and experience as qualifies him to give an expert opinion is a preliminary question which must first be passed upon by the trial court and is usually

[3] 20 **Am Jur,** Evidence, §§ 769–775.
Opinion evidence as to distance within which automobile can be stopped. 135 **ALR** 1404–1414.
Right of witness to state his opinions or conclusion, based on examination of books and accounts, as to solvency or insolvency. 81 **ALR** 1431–1436.
Competency of testimony of nonexperts on question of sanity or insanity in criminal cases. 72 **ALR** 579–587.
Opinion evidence as to condition of automobile or other motor vehicle. 77 **ALR** 559–566.
Opinion evidence directly as to the ultimate question of the amount of damage to property. 86 **ALR** 1449–1493.
Right of witness to testify as a conclusion or as an ultimate fact to existence or nonexistence of agency or relationship of master and servant. 90 **ALR** 749–765.
Admissibility and effect of testimony of lay witness as to existence of a particular disease, or as to apparent physical condition of a person, on the issue of existence of particular disease. 93 **ALR** 482–488.
Necessity of laying foundation for opinion of attesting witness as to mental condition of testator or testatrix. 93 **ALR** 1049–1055.

[4] 20 **Am Jur,** Evidence, §§ 775–797.
Admissibility of opinion of medical expert as affected by his having heard the person in question give the history of his case. 65 **ALR** 1217–1232.
Expert testimony to interpret or explain or draw conclusion from photograph. 77 **ALR** 946–956.
Testimony of expert witness as to ultimate fact. 78 **ALR** 755–759.
54 **Harv. L. R.** 1105, The Use of Experts by the Courts.
10 **U. of Chicago L. R.** 285, Suggested Remedies for Obstructions to Expert Testimony by Rules of Evidence.
10 **U. of Chicago L. R.** 323, A Ministry of Justice as a Means of Making Progress in Medicine Available to Courts and Legislatures.

not subject to review. The mere fact that the proposed witness has more knowledge on the matter than the jury is not enough to warrant such a person in expressing an opinion.

Where the expert witness can speak from personal observation—for example, on the question of the sanity of a person whom he has examined or the extent of personal injuries—he may first testify as to what he knows from personal observation and then give his expert opinion based upon his own testimony and upon his technical knowledge and experience; or the fact basis may later be brought out either upon direct or cross examination.

A medical expert who has knowledge of the particular case may testify as to the cause and the probable permanence of a personal injury, but he may not express a purely speculative opinion as to such permanence or an opinion as to future consequences which are of a speculative nature.

Testimony of experts on the question of identity which is based upon fingerprints is freely admissible because conceded to be accurate and reliable, and so are the results of blood group tests to establish identity and lack of kinship. In several criminal cases the state has sought to introduce, as evidence of guilt, the expert opinion of one skilled in the use of what is popularly known as the lie detector—a machine which records changes in blood pressure due to emotional disturbances when the person being tested is questioned about the crime; but the evidence has usually been rejected because there are not yet enough data to demonstrate its accuracy and reliability.

§ 35. Opinion given in answer to hypothetical questions.[5] Where the expert is not acquainted with the facts in the particular case and is therefore not able to give an opinion based upon personal observation, his opinion must be based upon hypothetical questions stated to him by either or both parties. The hypothetical question may assume the existence of any facts not in dispute or any state of facts which the evidence fairly tends to justify; but it may not be based upon "all of the evidence in the case," partly because it is too vague and partly because facts in dispute are practically always included.

[5] 20 **Am Jur**, Evidence, § 788.

Questions of evidence involved in the inspection and examination of typewritten documents and typewriting machines. 106 **ALR** 721–737.

Right of expert witness to testify as to "total disability" or other physical condition contemplated by specific provision of insurance policy. 111 **ALR** 603–618.

Necessity of expert evidence to warrant submission to jury of issue as to permanency of injury or as to future pain and suffering, or to sustain award of damages on that basis. 115 **ALR** 1149–1158.

Right to test qualifications of witness to testify as to genuineness of handwriting by cross-examining him as to the genuineness of other handwriting not the subject of his direct examination. 128 **ALR** 1329–1351.

Expert and opinion evidence as regards fire. 131 **ALR** 1113–1141.

Opinion or expert testimony as to materiality of misrepresentation in application for insurance or as to increase of risk or as to practice or usage of insurance companies regarding acceptance or rejection of certain class of risk. 135 **ALR** 411–423.

Sufficiency of expert evidence to establish causal relation between accident and physical condition or death. 135 **ALR** 516–546

Admissibility of opinion evidence as to cause of death, disease, or injury. 136 ALR 965–1007.

Necessity of expert evidence to support an action for malpractice against a physician or surgeon. 141 **ALR** 5–50.

Right of expert to give an opinion based on testimony of other witnesses not incorporated in a hypothetical question. 82 **ALR** 1460–1492.

Competency of physician or surgeon as an expert witness as affected by the fact that he is not a specialist. 54 **ALR** 860–869.

Medical books or treatises as independent evidence. 65 **ALR** 1102-1112.

Use of medical or other scientific books or treatises in cross-examination of expert witness. 82 **ALR** 440–462.

Safety of condition, place, or appliance as proper subject of expert or opinion evidence in tort actions. 146 **ALR** 5–57.

Most expert witnesses to whom hypothetical questions are put are either medical experts or handwriting experts. The handwriting expert bases his opinion upon a comparison between genuine writings and the writing whose genuineness is in dispute. The genuineness of the standard writing may be conceded or it may be established by witnesses who saw it written or by witnesses who are familiar with the handwriting of the person in question or by evidence that such person recognized the writing as his own.

In order to qualify as a handwriting expert one must have been either a teacher of writing or one engaged in the work of a bank cashier or clerk or in any other employment which requires them frequently and regularly to scrutinize writings. One who has testified as a handwriting expert may be tested upon cross examination by showing him other writings and asking him if they are genuine.

CHAPTER V

EXCEPTIONS TO THE HEARSAY RULE

§ 36. Basis of the hearsay rule.[6] The general rule excluding hearsay became established about two centuries ago. The modern basis of it is that testimony should not be received unless there has been an opportunity to cross examine the person whose statement is offered in evidence. The rule is applied so strictly that if a witness has been examined in chief and then, because of illness or death there is no opportunity to cross examine, the testimony in chief is stricken out.

Where, as in an action for slander the matter in issue is not the truth of what the defendant said but whether he said it, a statement by a witness as to what the defendant said is not considered as hearsay at all. Similarly, in an action for malicious prosecution, statements made by X upon which defendant relied in starting the prosecution of the plaintiff are regarded not as hearsay but as original evidence on the question of probable cause.

To this general rule of exclusion there are several exceptions which will be discussed in the following sections.

§ 37. Declarations in matters of pedigree.[7] Statements about family history on such matters as birth, legitimacy, illegitimacy, marriage, death, descent and relationship are admissible in evidence provided that (1) the declarant was related by blood or marriage to the family and of this there must be proof independent of the declarations; (2) the declaration was made before any controversy about the matter arose; and (3) by the weight of authority, the declarant is dead. Such declarations are frequently the only evidence available.

The declaration may be either oral or written, it need not have been made upon the knowledge of the declarant but the question of pedigree must be directly in issue. The weight of such evidence will depend upon varying circumstances.

[6] 20 **Am Jur**, Evidence, §§ 450–476.

Inadmissible hearsay evidence introduced without objection as proper for consideration in determining facts. 104 **ALR** 1130–1135.

Constitutionality, construction, and application of statutes making statements of deceased persons admissible in evidence. 96 **ALR** 686–706.

48 **Harv. L. R.** 1138, Hearsay and Non-Hearsay.

26 **Harv. L. R.** 146, An Exception to the Hearsay Rule.

17 **Harv. L. R.** 437, The History of the Hearsay Rule.

[7] 20 **Am Jur**, Evidence, §§ 468–476.

Entries in family Bible as evidence. 29 **ALR** 372–391.

Competency of witness to testify as to his own age. 39 **ALR** 376–382.

It is well settled that a witness may testify as to his own age and family relationship, though such testimony is, of course, based on hearsay. Sometimes this rule is placed upon the ground that it is a pedigree declaration but in such cases it is not necessary that the declarant, upon whose statement the witness relies, be dead.

§ 38. **Dying declarations.**[8] In a prosecution for homicide the dying declarations of the victim as to the facts and circumstances of the homicide are admissible in evidence provided that (1) the declarant was *in extremis,* that is, at the point of death; (2) the declarant was conscious of impending death without hope of recovery; and (3) the declarant, if living, would have been a competent witness. The declarant may be impeached in the same way as if he were alive and testifying. The chief reason for admitting it is the frequent difficulty of getting other evidence.

At the time when the dying declaration exception became established it was thought that the declarant's fear of punishment after death if he should make a false accusation was a sufficient substitute for an oath and cross examination; but waning belief in such punishment has not yet affected the admissibility of the evidence.

§ 39. **Parties' shop or account books.**[9] The exception allowing a party to the litigation to introduce into evidence in support of his claim, his account book, kept by himself, was established at a time when the party could not be a witness in his own behalf. Had it not been for this exception it would have been impossible for the small business or professional man to collect for goods sold or for services rendered. Now that parties may, by statute, testify on their own behalf the exception is no longer so necessary but such evidence is still held to be admissible.

There are two lines of authority on the use of parties' shop books, one of which is known as the New York rule and the other as the New England rule. Under the New York rule, in order for the exception to apply, it must appear that (1) the party kept no clerk; (2) some of the services charged for have been performed or some of the goods charged for have been delivered; (3) the books are fair and honest, as testified to by those who have had dealings with the party and who have settled with him on the basis of his accounts; (4) the books are the account books of the party.

The exception does not apply to entries of cash transactions or to a case where there is a single transaction, there being no regular course of dealing between the parties. It applies to all professions and businesses kept by individuals.

The weight of the account books in evidence will depend upon their appearance, the manner of their keeping and the character of the party who offers them.

[8] 20 **Am Jur,** Evidence, §§ 611, 612, 450–452.
Admissibility of dying declaration with respect to transaction prior to homicide. 14 **ALR** 757–760.
Impeaching or discrediting dying declarations. 16 **ALR** 411–423.
Dying declarations involving an opinion or conclusion. 25 **ALR** 1370–1402; s. in 63 **ALR** 567–572.
Admissibility of dying declarations in cases not involving homicide. 49 **ALR** 1282–1291; s. in 91 **ALR** 560–562.
Admissibility of oral testimony as to dying declarations which had been reduced to writing. 112 **ALR** 43–52.

[9] 20 **Am Jur,** Evidence, §§ 1051–1090.
Death of adverse party as affecting evidence with respect to book account. 6 **ALR** 756–766.
Admissibility of loose-leaf systems of accounts. 83 **ALR** 806–822.
Admissibility of book accounts to prove loans or payments by person by or for whom they are kept. 84 **ALR** 147–165.
Admissibility of books of account as affected by mutilation, erasures, or alterations. 142 **ALR** 1406–1417.

Under the New England rule the shop book is admitted in evidence with a suppletory oath by the party that it was the book in which his accounts were usually kept, that the entries were made at or about the time of the transactions and were the originals and were correctly made, that the goods were delivered or that the services were performed and that the sums charged had not been paid. Under the New York rule such suppletory oath is not required or admitted.

The practice in New York has now been modified by statute providing that the entrant need not have had personal knowledge of the transaction.

§ 40. **Entries made in the regular course of business.**[10] Where a series of entries has been made in the regular conduct of an occupation such entries are admissible in evidence provided that (1) the entrant is dead or outside the state or otherwise unavailable; (2) the entries have been made in the discharge of his duty or in the regular course of his employment; (3) the entries were made at or near the time of the transaction; (4) the entrant had personal knowledge of the facts recorded or the data were furnished to him by those who had such personal knowledge. Where, as in the modern large business numerous persons, such as clerks, salesmen, teamsters, etc., co-operate in making reports directly or indirectly to the entrant, it would seem to be the better practice merely to require that the method of compiling the information be verified by a single witness instead of requiring the attendance of so many.

In some states the matter has been regulated by statute.

§ 41. **Declarations made as a part of the res gestae and related topics.**[1] When an event takes place, the event itself being admissible in evidence, and the party or parties therein make declarations at that time or so soon thereafter as to preclude the possibility of the story being fabricated, such declarations are admissible as a part of the event itself; as the courts usually state it, as a part of the res gestae. To be admissible the declaration

[10] 20 **Am Jur**, Evidence, §§ 1043–1048.
Necessity of verification by one who furnishes data for book entries made by another having no personal knowledge of the transactions. 27 **ALR** 1439–1465.
Death certificate as evidence. 17 **ALR** 359–372; s. in 42 **ALR** 1454, 1455; 96 **ALR** 324–341.
Statute providing for admissibility as evidence of records or entries in the regular course of business (Model Act) as applicable to reports of accidents. 144 **ALR** 727–735.

[1] 20 **Am Jur**, Evidence, §§ 661–685.
Admissibility of expressions of pain or suffering by person injured. 64 **ALR** 557–573.
Admissibility as res gestae of statements or exclamations relating to cause of, or responsibility for, automobile or motorcycle accident. 76 **ALR** 1122–1133; s. in 101 **ALR** 1197–1202.
Admissibility of statements or declarations of plaintiff's spouse in an action for alienation of affections for the purpose of showing his or her mental state. 82 **ALR** 825–865.
Admissibility of testator's declarations upon the issue of the genuineness or due execution of purported will. 62 **ALR** 698–716; s. in 119 **ALR** 1366–1370.
Admissibility of declarations of testator on issue of undue influence. 79 **ALR** 1447–1488; s. in 148 **ALR** 1225–1228.
Admissibility of declarations by testator on issue of revocation of will. 79 **ALR** 1493–1511.
Admissibility of declarations by donor subsequent to alleged gift, on issue as to gift. 105 **ALR** 398–413.
Extrajudicial declarations of agent as admissible in action against principal for personal injuries for purpose of showing knowledge of relevant fact or condition at or prior to time of injury. 141 **ALR** 704–718.
Admissibility of statements made by deceased with reference to purpose or destination of a journey or trip he was about to make. 113 **ALR** 268–310.
Statute which disqualifies one person as a witness because of death of another, as applicable to testimony as to statements or acts of deceased, offered as part of res gestae or to show mental condition ("verbal act" theory). 146 **ALR** 250–279.
Admissibility of statements by injured or diseased person to physician while latter is treating him or examining him to qualify himself as a witness. 67 **ALR** 10–41; s. in 80 **ALR** 1527–1530; 130 **ALR** 977–989.

must be a spontaneous exclamation and not a mere narrative of something which has already occurred. In some states the spontaneous exclamations of bystanders are also admissible even though such bystanders would not be competent witnesses.

Since it is difficult otherwise to determine whether and to what extent a party suffers pain, declarations of such party as to the pain then being suffered are admissible to show his physical condition at that time. The rule became established as a matter of necessity at a time when the party could not testify, but in most jurisdictions such declarations are still admissible because, being contemporary, they are likely to be more trustworthy than statements made later by the party on the witness stand. That the statements were made after the controversy arose does not render them inadmissible but goes only to their credibility.

Where the declarant's intention at a particular time is in issue his declarations tending to show his intent at that time are admissible; for example, statements made by the declarant that he intended to commit suicide, or that he intended to change or to retain his domicile. Similar reasoning applies where the declarant's reason or motive for doing an act or his emotional state is in issue. The fact that the complainant in a rape case made prompt complaint, as testified to by her or a third party, is admissible as bearing upon the credibility of her testimony.

As to whether declarations of an intent to do an act are admissible to show that the act was done, the law is quite unsettled. In a will contest the assertion by the testator that he does or does not intend to make a particular will in the future is admissible as tending to show that it was or was not done; but an assertion that he has or has not made such a will or has or has not revoked such a will or that a particular will has been obtained by fraud or undue influence, would logically seem to be inadmissible as mere hearsay, except to show testamentary capacity or the lack thereof; but some courts allow it, by way of corroboration of other evidence, though there is danger that—being in testimonial form—it will be given greater credence by a jury than a mere declaration of intent, and greater than it deserves.

§ 42. Declarations as to matters of public or general interest—ancient documents.[2] Declarations of persons now deceased concerning the general reputation in their community with respect to matters of public or general interest are admissible in evidence provided that the declarant had sufficient opportunity to acquire knowledge of the matters in issue and the declarations were made before any controversy arose The most common topics covered by this exception are land boundaries and land customs.

A document, such as a will or deed, which is more than thirty years old, which comes from the proper custody and which is free from any appearance to excite suspicion is admissible without any proof of its execution. The basis for this exception to the hearsay rule is, of course, necessity. The most common use of such documents is to establish land titles.

§ 43. Reported testimony.[3] Testimony given at a former trial is admissible (1) where the witness has since died or, by the modern trend of au-

[2] 20 **Am Jur**, Evidence, §§ 582, 941.

Recital in ancient deed as evidence of facts recited against stranger to title. 6 **ALR** 1437-1452.

Dispensing with proof of proper custody as condition of admission of ancient document. 29 **ALR** 630-636.

[3] 20 **Am Jur**, Evidence, §§ 686-715.

Use in criminal case of testimony given on former trial, or preliminary examinathority, has become ill, insane or a nonresident of the state, and (2) where the parties and the issues are substantially identical. In such a case the important requirement or opportunity for cross examination has been substantially satisfied so that the testimony thus admitted is an exception to the hearsay rule only in that in the present proceeding there is no opportunity to cross examine. The former testimony may be proved by any one who heard it; and it may be objected to even if the objection was not made at the former trial or was made and overruled.

§ 44. **Declarations against interest.**[4] Since it is unlikely that a person would make a statement of fact against his own interest unless it was true, declarations of that sort are admissible in evidence provided that (1) the declarant is now dead or otherwise unavailable as a witness; (2) the declarant had knowledge of the facts; (3) the declaration when made was known by the declarant to be against his pecuniary or proprietary interest; and (4) there was no motive to misrepresent. If part of the declaration is against interest, the entire declaration is admissible.

Admissibility is not affected by the fact that the declarant is an entire stranger to the parties to the litigation. Where the declaration is made by a former owner of property claimed by the party it becomes an admission good against the party and admissible as such. That the statement was against one's penal interest is not enough but this limitation of the exception has been criticised as arbitrary.

CHAPTER VI

ADMISSIONS AND CONFESSIONS

A. Admissions

§ 45. **In general—relation to the hearsay rule.**[5] An opponent's admissions made out of court are admissible in evidence against him not only to discredit the position now taken by him in the litigation and thus to discredit his testimony therein if he does testify, but also as proof of the facts stated in the admissions. This is not an exception to the hearsay rule because

tion, by witness not available at present trial. 15 **ALR** 495–564; s. in 79 **ALR** 1392–1423; 122 **ALR** 425–446.

Conviction or acquittal as evidence of facts on which it was based, in a civil action. 31 **ALR** 261–283; s. in 57 **ALR** 504–506; 80 **ALR** 1145–1147; 130 **ALR** 690–703.

Identity of parties as condition of admissibility in civil case of testimony or deposition in former action or proceeding of witness not available in present action or proceeding. 142 **ALR** 673–721.

Admissibility of plea of guilty at preliminary hearing. 141 **ALR** 1335–1345.

[4] 20 **Am Jur,** Evidence, §§ 542–660.

Admissibility as against interest of statement or report made out of court regarding accident as affected by the fact that it relates to or includes matters of opinion or conclusion. 118 **ALR** 1230–1237.

Admissibility of subsequent declarations of vendor on issue whether sale was in fraud of creditors. 64 **ALR** 797–830.

Admissibility of declarations of grantor or transferrer on issue as to whether conveyance or transfer was in fraud of creditors. 83 **ALR** 1446–1498.

Evidence of declarations of accused on issue of insanity. 8 **ALR** 1219–1226.

[5] 20 **Am Jur,** Evidence, §§ 542–561.

Admission of bankrupt or insolvent before or during bankruptcy or insolvency proceedings as evidence against trustee in bankruptcy or assignee in insolvency. 53 **ALR** 650–661.

Conclusiveness of testimony of a party favorable to adverse party. 80 **ALR** 624–637.

Admissibility of admissions made during discussion of compromise. 80 **ALR** 919–935.

Admissibility of inculpatory statements made in the presence of accused, and not denied or contradicted by him. 80 **ALR** 1235–1286; s. in 115 **ALR** 1510–1521.

Admissibility in favor of writer of unanswered letter not part of mutual correspondence. 8 **ALR** 1163–1170; s. in 34 **ALR** 560, 561; 55 **ALR** 460.

Admissibility as evidence of pleadings as containing admissions against interest. 14 **ALR** 22–93; s. in 90 **ALR** 1393–1411.

Admissibility in action for death of statements against interest by decedent. 114 **ALR** 921–940.

only the opponent could logically insist upon cross examination and he is not likely to insist upon cross examining himself, though of course he has the right to explain the making of the admission.

Where it is desired to introduce, in cross examination, evidence of prior oral inconsistent statements made by an ordinary witness in order to discredit him, a foundation must first be laid by asking whether he made such statements, but there is no such requirement as to an opponent's admissions.

It is not necessary that the admission be based upon personal knowledge; it may be based on hearsay. But a mere statement by the party as to what he had heard is not an admission.

An admission must be against the opponent's interest at the time of trial but it need not have been against his interest at the time of making it.

§ 46. Judicial admissions.[6] Where facts are admitted in the pleadings in a case or in an agreed statement of facts or in open court they are conclusive on the party in that litigation in that they narrow the issues to be litigated; as such they are not really evidence but take the place of evidence. Such statements may be introduced in evidence in the litigation of other cases as an admission of the pleader if the pleading was verified or if it is shown that the facts were inserted with the pleader's knowledge and approval. And admissions made on the witness stand by a party in the prior litigation may be testified to by any one who heard the testimony.

§ 47. Implied admissions.[7] An admission may be implied from certain kinds of conduct. For example, if the party now accused of a crime fled the scene of the crime shortly after it was committed, or if he attempted to resist arrest therefor; or if a party tries to bribe or coerce a witness.

Where a statement was made in the presence of a party and the circumstances were such that a normal person would naturally reply unless he admitted the truth of the statement, his failure to reply may be introduced as an implied admission. And where a creditor sends a bill to his debtor the latter's failure to reply and object within a reasonable time is an implied admission of the validity of the creditor's claim; but this does not apply to an ordinary letter received by the party; his failure to reply is not an admission of the facts stated in the letter.

An admission made in an offer to compromise is admissible against the party who made it; but in itself an offer to compromise is not an implied admission because it might have been made merely to avoid the trouble and expense of litigation. Nor is the offer of help made by an employer to an injured employee an implied admission of liability because it might have been made merely as an act of benevolence.

Where after an accident has happened a land occupier repairs the premises where the injury occurred or an employer repairs the machinery which caused the accident, such repairs might logically be regarded as an implied admission of negligence; but they are not necessarily so and the policy of encouraging land occupiers and employers to take the utmost precautions to avoid injury is distinctly against regarding such conduct as an admission. Nor is the discharge of an employee after an accident an implied admission of negligence.

[6] 20 **Am Jur**, Evidence, §§ 630–636.
Judicial stipulation or formal admission of facts by counsel as available upon a subsequent trial. 100 **ALR** 775–788.

[7] 20 **Am Jur**, Evidence, §§ 562–577.

Where the admission is received in evidence, the party against whom it operates is entitled to have the entire writing containing the admission introduced in order to explain or modify the admission.

§ 48. Admissions by agent, servant, partner, co-obligor or conspirator.[8] Declarations made by an agent accompanying an act done within the scope of his authority are admissible against his principal, but not if made outside the scope of his authority or after the relation of principal and agent has terminated. The same reasoning applies to declarations made by a servant accompanying an act done within the scope of his employment. Neither the relationship of principal and agent nor employer and servant is implied from the relationship of husband and wife or from the relationship of parent and child. Merely referring to another person for information does not make him an agent.

During the existence of a partnership declarations made by one partner within the scope of the partnership business are admissible against the others because as to such matters each partner is the agent of the others, and this continues after the partnership comes to an end as to matters necessary to wind up the partnership.

A declaration made by an agent is not admissible, in an action by the agent against his principal, to prove the agency; nor is an admission by a partner admissible, in an action by the partner against another partner, to prove the partnership, because such declarations are merely self-serving.

The old rule was that the declaration of one joint obligor was admissible against his co-obligor, but this rule has now been abrogated on the ground that the joint liability does not create the relationship of principal and agent. Hence if one obligor makes a part payment on the obligation this does not set the statute of limitations running anew against his co-obligors.

A declaration by one conspirator, made in furtherance of the common object, is admissible against the others; but not a declaration made after the common design has been accomplished or abandoned. Such a declaration cannot, of course, be used, as against the other supposed conspirators, to prove the conspiracy.

§ 49. Admissions by former owners of property—miscellaneous.[9] A declaration made by the owner of real property, while such owner, is admissible against those who claim under him, whether heirs, devisees or grantees. A declaration made by the owner of personal property is admissible against his executor, administrator, legatee, distributee, or assignee in bankruptcy but as to whether it is admissible against an ordinary transferee *inter vivos* there is conflict of authority.

A declaration made by a sole executor while acting in his official capacity is admissible against the estate but a declaration made by one executor or administrator is not admissible against his co-executor or co-administrator. A declaration made by the guardian *ad litem* of a party under disability is not admissible against such party. The mere fact that A and B are joined as co-plaintiffs or co-defendants does not make the declaration of one admissible against the other.

8 20 **Am Jur**, Evidence, §§ 596–603. 42 **Harv. L. R.** 461, The Rationale of Vicarious Admissions.

9 20 **Am Jur**, Evidence, §§ 604–607.

B. Confessions

§ 50. In general—confession obtained by deception—corroboration.[10] An admission may be either express or implied, and is used both in civil and criminal cases not only for the purpose of discrediting a party's case but as substantive proof of the facts stated or implied in the admission. A confession is an acknowledgment of guilt; it may be informal but it must be in express words, and is used only in criminal cases.

The fact that a confession is obtained by a deception does not make it inadmissible.

In most jurisdictions a confession must be corroborated in order to sustain a verdict of guilty.

A confession by a third person that he committed the crime charged against the defendant is inadmissible as mere hearsay not under oath, without opportunity of cross examination.

Where a confession has been introduced in evidence the defendant may impeach it by any evidence showing it to be false.

Where defendant pleads guilty to an indictment such a plea when entered of record becomes conclusive and the court must then pronounce sentence unless the plea is withdrawn by leave of court in which case the confession is receivable in evidence as if it were a confession made outside of court.

§ 51. Confessions obtained by force or by threats or by promise of favor.[1] In order to be admissible a confession must be voluntary; that is, it must not have been obtained by force or by threats or by promise of immunity or other favor, the theory being that such a confession is necessarily untrustworthy.

The threat need not be that of an officer; it may be made by a private individual or by a mob, but it must actually put the accused in fear. The mere fact that the confession was obtained by questioning does not make it involuntary, but it is otherwise if it is obtained by persistent questioning over such a long period of time as to overcome the will of the accused. It is not objectionable that the confession was made while under arrest; but unreasonable delay in taking the accused before a magistrate may tend to make the confession involuntary.

Promises of immunity or other favor by persons of such standing that the accused might reasonably believe them to be able to give him aid render any confession obtained thereby inadmissible. But by the better view, telling the accused he "had better tell the truth" does not render the confession inadmissible.

If in making a confession which is inadmissible the accused makes any admission, such admission is receivable in evidence against him.

Though the trial court passes upon the admissibility of the confession before allowing it to be presented to the jury, yet if the facts are in dispute the question of whether the confession was or was not voluntary is

10 20 **Am Jur**, Evidence, §§ 477–541.
Proof of entire conversation containing alleged confession. 2 **ALR** 1017–1041; s. in 26 **ALR** 541, 542.
Corroboration of confession. 127 **ALR** 1130–1142.

1 20 **Am Jur**, Evidence, §§ 482, 483, 506–519.
Voluntariness of confession admitted by court as question for jury. 85 **ALR** 870–908.
Duty of court to institute preliminary investigation as to voluntary or involuntary character of confession. 102 **ALR** 605–634.
Confession by one who has been subjected to or threatened with physial suffering. 24 **ALR** 703–715.
Whose promises are contemplated by rule excluding confession made under promise of immunity. 7 **ALR** 419–439.

ultimately for the jury under instructions by the court, the burden of establishing that the confession was voluntary being upon the prosecution.

Where the defendant, not having been accused of the crime, testifies at the coroner's inquest, without claiming his privilege against self-incrimination, such evidence may be used against him.

The exclusion of involuntary confessions merely because they are involuntary has been criticised as an unnecessary obstruction of justice, the contention being that the facts surrounding the obtaining the confession should merely go to the credibility of the confession, to be weighed by the jury.

CHAPTER VII

THE BEST EVIDENCE RULE

§ 52. Scope of and reason for the rule.[2] It was formerly said that the best evidence that the nature of the thing will afford is always required, but the best evidence rule today is limited to writings, and may be briefly stated as follows: Whenever it is necessary to establish the terms or contents of a writing, the writing itself must be produced unless some good reason is shown for not producing it. The chief purpose of the rule is to avoid errors due to a faulty memory or to mistakes in copying.

The rule embraces all kinds of writings, including deeds, public records, contracts, assignments, letters, telegrams, checks, or mere memoranda, but does not apply where the terms of the writing are not in issue, but are merely collateral. Where the writing is inscribed on a chattel the trial court may, in its discretion, take the case out of the best evidence rule where it would be difficult to produce the chattel in court. Where the removal of public records would inconvenience the public, they may be proved by certified copies. And where other records are voluminous, the court may allow an expert accountant to state the results of such records to the jury.

§ 53. What are documentary originals?[3] Where a writing already in existence has been copied, either by letter press or photograph or otherwise, such copy is not a documentary original. But if the writing is not already in existence and several copies are made at the same time by the same mechanical operation—for example, by a printing press or typewriter—each one is regarded as an original. If a typewriter is used to make one original and several carbon copies and only the one is signed that one is apparently the only documentary original.

Where contracts or other writings are executed in duplicate, each party retaining a copy each is regarded as a duplicate original.

[2] 20 **Am Jur,** Evidence, §§ 403–425.
3 **Wash. and Lee L. R.** 185, The Parol Evidence Rule in Virginia.

[3] 20 **Am Jur,** Evidence, §§ 405–432.
Carbon copies of letters or other written instruments as evidence. 51 **ALR** 1498–1502.
Proof of authenticity or genuineness of letter other than by proof of handwriting or typewriting. 9 **ALR** 984–993.
Review on appeal of evidence as to genuineness of disputed documents. 6 **ALR** 507–527; s. in 12 **ALR** 212–215; 27 **ALR** 319–322.
Admissibility of hospital chart or other hospital record. 75 **ALR** 378–394; s. in 120 **ALR** 1124–1144.
Photographic representation of writing as primary or secondary evidence. 142 **ALR** 1270–1279.
Admissibility of secondary evidence of incriminating document in possession of defendant. 67 **ALR** 77–92.
Financial statement or report to stockholders as admissible in evidence on issue between seller and purchaser as to value of stock sold. 147 **ALR** 1150–1154.

§ 54. Lost or destroyed writings—notice to opponent to produce.[4] If a party who had possession of a documentary original wishes to introduce secondary evidence of its contents he must first convince the court that it has been destroyed or that he is unable, after diligent search, to find it; what amounts to a diligent search depends upon the circumstances of each case. That the original was intentionally destroyed is not objectionable provided that it was not done fraudulently. If the document is merely outside the state, the party must show a diligent effort to procure its production or the deposition of the party who has custody of it.

If the writing is in the possession or control of one's opponent, reasonable notice to produce it must first be served upon him before secondary evidence of its contents is admissible. Notice to produce is unnecessary if the pleadings give him notice. If the opponent fails to produce or if opponent's lawyer has it in court and secondary evidence is then received it is too late for the opponent to offer the original in evidence; but this rule has been criticized as preferring punishment to getting the truth. Since the defendant in a criminal case is not bound to produce writings which would tend to incriminate him, a notice to produce such writings is, of course, of no legal effect.

The mere fact that there is a copy of the original available does not shut out oral evidence of contents; there are no degrees of secondary evidence.

CHAPTER VIII

THE PAROL EVIDENCE RULE

§ 55. In general.[5] Where parties to a transaction—either a conveyance or a contract—integrate that transaction by reducing it to a single memorial, that memorial is the transaction. This is usually said to be based upon the presumed intention of the parties to exclude all prior and contemporaneous agreements or understandings. Though the rule is one of substantive law as to what constitutes a transaction, it is usually stated in terms of evidence because the question is usually raised at the trial by offers to introduce evidence of the prior or contemporaneous agreements. The most common form of statement is that parol evidence is not admissible to vary or contradict a written instru-

4 20 **Am Jur**, Evidence, §§ 434–449.

5 20 **Am Jur**, Evidence, §§ 1091–1176.

Parol-evidence rule: tests for determining whether entire agreement is embodied in the writing (rule of integration). 70 **ALR** 752–771.

Applicability of parol-evidence rule in favor of or against one not a party to contract of release. 80 **ALR** 477–488.

Parol-evidence rule as applied to lease. 25 **ALR** 787–876; s. in 88 **ALR** 1380–1416.

Trade custom or usage to explain or supply essential terms in writing required by Statute of Frauds (or Sales Act) in sale of goods. 29 **ALR** 1218–1227.

Parol-evidence rule as applicable to agreement for improvements or alterations by vendor of real property. 68 **ALR** 245–254.

Parol-evidence rule as applied to letters or other informal writings not purporting to be the agreement itself. 68 **ALR** 1251–1257.

Parol-evidence rule: evidence of agreements as to manner or medium of payment of bill or note, or as to credit, setoff, or counterclaim with respect to the same. 71 **ALR** 548–577.

Admissibility of parol or extrinsic evidence to show promise of employment or other consideration not embodied in written release of claim for bodily injury or death. 92 **ALR** 248–264.

Admissibility in favor of beneficiary of life or accident insurance of statements or declarations made by insured outside of his application. 93 **ALR** 414–432.

Admissibility of parol or extrinsic evidence to alter or supplement written records of local legislative bodies. 98 **ALR** 1229–1256.

"Contractual" consideration as regards parol-evidence rule. 100 **ALR** 17–45.

Legal effect of parol evidence inadmissible under parol-evidence rule but admitted without objection. 92 **ALR** 810–827.

Admissibility of oral or extrinsic evidence on question of liability on bill of exchange, promissory note, or other contract where signature is followed by word or abbreviation which may be either descriptive or indicative of contracting character 113 **ALR** 1364–1385.

ment, the term "parol evidence" including not only oral evidence but any evidence extrinsic to the instrument. The rule does not prevent the parties from entering into a subsequent oral agreement modifying the integrated transaction, unless the contract was within the statute of frauds.

If by mistake of the scrivener the written instrument does not express the real agreement of the parties the remedy is a bill in equity to have the instrument reformed or corrected; there can be no reformation at law.

Where only a part of a transaction has been integrated, the other part may be proved by extrinsic—usually oral—evidence.

The rule cannot be invoked in favor of or against a stranger to the instrument.

§ 56. Evidence to aid interpretation.[6] The rule does not prevent the introduction of extrinsic evidence of all the facts and circumstances surrounding the execution of the written instrument in order to aid in the interpretation of the instrument where the language is ambiguous—for example, for the purpose of identifying the persons or property mentioned in the instrument; but this does not permit declarations of a testator to be received, except to clear up an ambiguity. But if the language is not ambiguous such evidence is usually held to be inadmissible to show that the parties used the language with another than the ordinary meaning.

The rule does not prevent the introduction of a business custom which was known or should have been known to both parties because the parties are supposed to have entered into their transaction with reference to such custom. It is frequently said that the custom "must not contravene fixed rules of law" but the meaning of such a limitation is not clear.

§ 57. Evidence to show lack of consideration—illegality—alteration—date.[7] Where the transaction would be invalid without consideration the rule does not prevent the introduction of extrinsic evidence to show that there was no consideration and therefore no valid transaction; but where the consideration is expressed in the written instrument as a substantive part of the contract the rule prevents the introduction of extrinsic evidence to show that the real consideration was different from that expressed. Where, however, as in a bargain and sale deed, the validity of the instrument depends, not upon the existence of consideration but upon the mere recital of consideration, and there is such a recital, it is not relevant evidence to show that there was in fact no consideration.

The rule does not prevent the introduction of extrinsic evidence to show that the transaction was illegal; or that there has been a material alteration in the written instrument; or the date upon which the writing was executed even though a different date appears on the instrument.

§ 58. Evidence to show fraud, duress, mistake or undue influence.[8] The rule does not prevent the introduction of extrinsic evidence to show that the execution of the written instrument has been procured by fraud in the induce-

[6] 20 **Am Jur**, Evidence, §§ 1142–1158.
Admissibility of parol evidence to explain ambiguity in description of land in deed or mortgage. 68 **ALR** 4–105.
Admissibility of extrinsic evidence of custom or usage to show that words employed in a contract unambiguous on their face have a special trade significance. 89 **ALR** 1228–1253.
Admissibility of extrinsic evidence to aid interpretation of will. 94 **ALR** 26–293.

[7] 20 **Am Jur**, Evidence, §§ 1111–1118.

[8] 24 **Am Jur**, Fraud and Deceit, § 267.
36 **Am Jur**, Mistake, § 1.
Parol-evidence rule; right to show fraud in inducement or execution of written contract. 56 **ALR** 13–152.

ment, by duress, by mistake or by undue influence, and that it is therefore voidable.

Where there has been fraud in the execution the instrument is not merely voidable but a nullity; that there was fraud in the execution may be proved by extrinsic evidence.

§ 59. Evidence to show conditional delivery of contract.[9] The rule does not prevent the introduction of extrinsic evidence to show that a written contract—but not a conveyance—was delivered only upon a condition which has not been satisfied, and therefore never became operative. But if the contract did become operative, but to be cancelled upon the happening of a condition subsequent, this reasoning does not apply.

Where the written contract is a negotiable instrument, however, the failure of performance of the condition will not affect the rights of a holder in due course.

§ 60. Evidence to show relationship of parties to a transaction.[10] The rule does not prevent the introduction of extrinsic evidence to show the relationship between the parties in a written contract. It may be shown that a comaker or the indorser of a negotiable instrument was an accommodation party—that is, a surety. Or that a party whose name is signed to a written contract was in fact the agent of an undisclosed principal who is suing or being sued on the contract.

§ 61. Evidence to show independent collateral agreement—warranties.[1] The rule does not prevent the introduction of extrinsic evidence to show that at the time the written agreement was executed, an independent collateral agreement with regard to the same subject matter but founded upon a separate consideration, was entered into.

The rule does not prevent the introduction of extrinsic evidence to show, in a sale of a chattel, a warranty as to the future condition or capacity of the chattel sold; but it does apply to an oral warranty of the present condition of the chattel.

CHAPTER IX

BURDEN OF PROOF—PRESUMPTIONS—COURT AND JURY

§ 62. In general as to burden of proof.[2] The phrase "burden of proof" is unfortunate because it is sometimes applied to the burden of establishing

9 8 **Am Jur,** Bills and Notes, §§ 1050-1116.
20 **Am Jur,** Evidence, §§ 1095, 1096.

10 50 **Am Jur,** Suretyship, § 235.
20 **Am Jur,** Evidence, § 1125.
Admissibility of parol evidence to vary or explain the contract implied from the regular indorsement of a bill or note. 4 **ALR** 764-804; s. in 11 **ALR** 637-639; 22 **ALR** 527-529; 35 **ALR** 1120, 1121; 54 **ALR** 999-1001; 92 **ALR** 721-726.
Admissibility of parol evidence to show that a bill or note was conditional, or given for a special purpose. 20 **ALR** 421-502; s. in 54 **ALR** 702-719; 105 **ALR** 1346-1360.
Parol evidence in relation to assumption of mortgage debt by grantee of mortgaged property. 50 **ALR** 1220-1232; s. in 143 **ALR** 548-575.

1 20 **Am Jur,** Evidence, §§ 131-156.

2 20 **Am Jur,** Evidence, §§ 131-156.
Burden of proof as regards payment or nonpayment of renewal premiums or assessments on policy of life or accident insurance. 95 **ALR** 745-760.
Burden of allegation and proof in civil cases as regards exception in statute. 130 **ALR** 440-486.
Rule of reasonable doubt as applicable to reasonable doubt on part of individual juror. 137 **ALR** 394-408.
Burden of proof, in action upon an accident policy or accident feature of life policy, as regards conditions which, by the terms of the policy, limit or exclude coverage. 142 **ALR** 742-768.
Weight of oral testimony as to law of another state or country. 6 **ALR** 1344-1349.
Disregarding uncontradicted testimony in civil actions. 8 **ALR** 796-830.
Propriety of instructions as to the sig-

which usually does not shift and sometimes to the burden of going forward with the evidence which may shift one or more times during a trial. In order to avoid confusion the term "burden of proof" will not be used in the following pages.

The burden of establishing lies generally upon the party who has the affirmative of an issue and that question is usually, but not always, dependent upon the pleadings. If A sues X for assault and battery and X pleads in denial the burden of establishing that X committed the assault and battery lies upon A; but if X pleads self defense the use of force by X is admitted and X has the burden of establishing that he did it in reasonable self defense. So as to pleas generally in confession and avoidance.

Where facts are peculiarly within the knowledge of the adverse party the burden of going forward with the evidence and explaining shifts to such party. For example, if one is charged with selling liquor without a license, the burden of going forward shifts—as a matter of convenience—to the defendant because it is easy for him to produce the license if he has it. The same reasoning is the basis of the doctrine in the law of negligence of *res ipsa loquitur.* But the reasoning is not applied where fraud or other serious misconduct is charged against a defendant.

In criminal cases the state has the burden of establishing its entire case beyond a reasonable doubt; in civil cases the party having the burden of establishing need to do so only by a fair preponderance of the evidence; if the evidence on such side is of equal weight he loses. As an offset to this, the one who has the burden of establishing has the right to open and close to the jury.

§ 63. In general as to presumptions.[3] The party who has the burden of establishing or the burden of going forward with the evidence is sometimes

nificance of evidence concerning the defendant's good character as an element bearing upon the question of reasonable doubt. 10 **ALR** 8–120; s. in 68 **ALR** 1068–1102.

Error in instructions as to the effect of res ipsa loquitur on the burden of proof as prejudicial. 42 **ALR** 865–872.

Degree of proof necessary in contempt proceedings. 49 **ALR** 975–989.

Instructions defining term "preponderance or weight of evidence." 93 **ALR** 155–173.

Burden and degree of proof as to alibi. 29 **ALR** 1127–1202; s. in 67 **ALR** 138–150; 124 **ALR** 471–496.

Degree or quantum of evidence necessary to establish a lost instrument and its contents. 148 **ALR** 400–408.

47 **Harv. L. R.** 59, Instructing the Jury upon Presumptions and Burden of Proof.

3 20 **Am Jur**, Evidence. §§ 157–166.

Presumption of payment from lapse of time. 1 **ALR** 779–831.

Presumption and burden of proof where subject of bailment is destroyed or damaged by fire. 9 **ALR** 559–577; s. in 71 **ALR** 767–779.

Conclusiveness of account stated. 11 **ALR** 586–611; s. in 75 **ALR** 1283–1292.

Presumption and burden of proof in actions for injury to or loss of boat during bailment. 11 **ALR** 690–698.

Production of paper purporting to be indorsed in blank by payee or by a special indorsee, as prima facie evidence of plaintiff's title to the paper. 11 **ALR** 952–962; s. in 85 **ALR** 304–306.

Validity of by-law of mutual benefit association preventing recovery upon presumption of death from seven years' absence. 17 **ALR** 418–430; s. in 21 **ALR** 1346; 36 **ALR** 982, 983; 40 **ALR** 1274.

Presumption and burden of proof in agistment cases. 23 **ALR** 276–286.

Character and sufficiency of evidence to show that letter was mailed. 25 **ALR** 9–22; s. in 86 **ALR** 541–546.

Flight as evidence of guilt. 25 **ALR** 886–909.

Presumptions flowing from marriage. 34 **ALR** 464–500; s. in 77 **ALR** 729–743.

Presumption of innocence as evidence. 34 **ALR** 938–952; s. in 94 **ALR** 1042–1046.

Presumption as evidence. 95 **ALR** 878–894.

Rebuttal of presumption of receipt of letter properly mailed and addressed. 91 **ALR** 161–173.

Inference on inference; presumption on presumption. 95 **ALR** 162–196.

Presumption against suicide as evidence. 103 **ALR** 185–195.

Circumstances justifying inference of death of insured before the lapse of seven years from his disappearance. 34 **ALR** 1389–1399; s. in 61 **ALR** 1327–1333.

Ownership of automobile as prima facie evidence of responsibility for negligence of person operating it. 42 **ALR** 898–922; s. in 74 **ALR** 951–968; 96 **ALR** 634–645.

Presumption and burden of proof as to

aided by rebuttable presumptions which are usually based upon probability; for example, the presumption that if a person has been absent and not heard from for seven years he is dead, and the presumption that a child between seven and fourteen years of age is incapable of committing a crime. These rebuttable or true presumptions or presumptions of fact are to be carefully distinguished from the so-called irrebuttable or conclusive presumptions or presumptions of law which are merely hard and fast rules of law stated in terms of presumption. When it is said that a child under seven is conclusively presumed to be incapable of committing a crime what is meant is that the criminal law does not hold responsible children under seven. When it is said that every one is presumed to know the law this is an inaccurate way of saying that ignorance of the law is usually no excuse to one who has committed a wrong such as a crime or tort or breach of contract; it should not be applied to one who has committed no wrong. When it is said that a seal imports consideration the meaning is that no consideration is necessary. When it is said that in an action for libel or slander malice is presumed the meaning is that it is not necessary to show an improper motive unless the defendant sets up conditional privilege in defense.

§ **64. Some specific burdens and presumptions.**[4] Where a will is presented for probate the presumption is that the testator was sane and the burden is upon the contestant to establish insanity. Similarly, in an action upon an insurance policy where the insured committed suicide the burden of showing insanity of the insured is upon the beneficiary of the policy. But in criminal cases, though the presumption is that the defendant was sane, yet if the defense offers evidence of insanity most courts require the state to prove sanity beyond a reasonable doubt, as a part of its case.

The presumption is that a child born in wedlock is legitimate and hence that if a marriage ceremony between the parents was performed, that there was a valid marriage; or, if no marriage ceremony be shown, but the parents hold themselves out as man and wife, that there was a valid marriage. But if the question is not one of legitimacy but whether one of the parties was guilty of bigamy the presumption of marriage yields to the presumption of innocence and direct proof of the marriage is required.

voluntariness of nonjudicial confession. 38 **ALR** 116–131; s. in 102 **ALR** 641–648.

Presumption of negligence from foreign substance in food. 4 **ALR** 1559–1561; s. in 47 **ALR** 148–156; 105 **ALR** 1039–1044.

Constitutionality of statutes or ordinances making one fact presumptive or prima facie evidence of another. 51 **ALR** 1139–1186; s. in 86 **ALR** 179–190.

Presumption as to payment or discharge of obligation from obligor's possession of paper evidencing it. 70 **ALR** 859–886.

Conclusiveness of uncontradicted testimony of interested witness where opposed to presumption. 72 **ALR** 94–102.

Presumption and burden of proof as regards good faith and consideration on part of purchaser or one taking encumbrance subsequent to unrecorded conveyance or encumbrance. 107 **ALR** 502–531.

Presumption of ownership of personal property as between husband and wife. 111 **ALR** 1374–1393.

Presumption of gift, advancement, or settlement where husband takes title from third person to property paid for by or with funds of wife. 113 **ALR** 339–350

Presumption and burden of proof as to consignee's title to or interest in respect of goods comprising shipment, in consignee's action against carrier for loss, damage, delay, nondelivery or conversion. 135 **ALR** 456–474.

Presumption or inference from party's failure to produce witnesses within his control, as affected by his introduction of some evidence on the matter in question. 135 **ALR** 1375–1387.

Presumption that public officers have properly performed their duty, as evidence. 141 **ALR** 1037–1041.

Succession to property as affected by death in common disaster in absence of presumption or proof of survivorship. 43 **ALR** 1348–1352.

19 **Harv. L. R.** 401, Presumption of the Foreign Law.

44 **Harv. L. R.** 906, Some Observations Concerning Presumptions.

16 **So. Calif. L. R.** 244, Further Observations on Presumptions.

26 **Marq. L. R.** 115, Effect of Presumptions

[4] 20 **Am Jur,** Evidence, §§ 194–244.

While disappearance unheard from for seven years raises a presumption of death, there is no presumption as to when during the seven years that death occurred; and if two persons die in a common disaster there is no presumption that either one survived the other.

It is sometimes said that possession of property raises a presumption of ownership and that possession of the fruits of a crime raises a presumption of some guilt in connection with the crime, but the weight of such presumptions vary considerably with the circumstances of the particular case.

Where a party withholds or intentionally destroys material evidence it is a fair inference that such evidence was unfavorable and this is sometimes stated in terms of presumption.

There is a presumption that the common law of a sister state or of any country having the common law system is the same as the common law of the forum; but this does not apply to statute law.

In the case of negotiable instruments there is a presumption of consideration, but not in the case of non-negotiable instruments or other simple contracts.

In criminal cases the rule that the state must establish its case by proof beyond a reasonable doubt is sometimes stated as a presumption of innocence.

Where presumptions conflict it is usually said that the stronger prevails; perhaps it would be more accurate to say that the one resting upon the sounder and more important public policy prevails.

§ 65. Court and jury.[5] It is usually said that questions of law are for the court and questions of fact are for the jury. A more accurate statement is that the jury decides doubtful questions of issuable fact and in a few states questions of law in criminal prosecutions, while the court decides all other questions except the credibility of witnesses which is usually for the jury. But where the evidence on a question of fact is such that twelve reasonable men could decide only one way the court will usually decide the question itself either by setting aside a verdict as against the weight of the evidence and ordering a new trial or, in a clear case, by directing a verdict; such questions are often called erroneously questions of law because the court decides them.

Since in earlier days members of the jury could not read or write the court interpreted writings even though such interpretation involved only pure matters of fact as to the meaning of the language, and that is still the usual practice.

The court also passes upon all preliminary matters of fact, such as those involved in the question of the competency of witnesses and the general admissibility of evidence. Although the law of a foreign state must be proved

[5] 53 **Am Jur**, Trial, §§ 156-161.

Construction and effect of foreign statutes or judicial decisions as question for court or for jury. 68 **ALR** 809-820.

Province of court and jury respectively as to construction of written contract where extrinsic evidence as to intention has been introduced. 65 **ALR** 648-663.

Question whether express contract was made as one for court or jury when not evidenced by formal instrument but in whole or part by informal writings. 100 **ALR** 969-991.

Direction of verdict: effect of explanatory or qualifying testimony to nullify prima facie case made by plaintiff. 66 **ALR** 1532-1553.

Right or duty of court to instruct jury as to presumptions. 103 **ALR** 126-130.

Coercive effect of verdict—urging by judge in civil case. 109 **ALR** 72-105.

40 **Harv. L. R.** 392, Preliminary Questions of Fact in Determining the Admissibility of Evidence.

43 **Harv. L. R.** 165, Functions of Judge and Jury in the Determination of Preliminary Questions of Fact.

55 **Harv. L. R.** 1303, Law and Fact.

56 **Harv. L. R.** 899, Fact and Law in Judicial Review.

and made a part of the record the better view is that it is for the court to say what the foreign law is on the matter.

The original and better practice was that the court should give to the jury the aid of its own opinion of the evidence and this practice still prevails in the common law countries of the British Empire, in the federal courts and in the courts of a few states but in the great majority of the states it is regarded as reversible error for the court to do so.

[illegible] upon a part of the record the better view is that it is for the court to [illegible] on the matter.

The original English practice was that the court should give to the jury the aid of its own opinion of the evidence, and this practice still prevails in the common law countries of the British Empire, in the federal courts and in the courts of a few states, but in the great majority of the states it is regarded as reversible error for the court to do so.

INDEX

INDEX

BILLS OF INTERPLEADER

BILLS OF LADING

BILLS OF PEACE

BILLS QUIA TIMET

DOMICILE

DOUBLE JEOPARDY

DOUBTFUL CLAIMS

DOWER

DRAINAGE

DRAINAGE DISTRICTS

DRUGS

DRUNKENNESS

DUE PROCESS

DUKE OF NORFOLK'S CASE

DUPLICATE COPIES

FRANCHISES

FRAUD AND DECEIT

MONOPOLIES

MONTH

MOON

MORAL CONSIDERATION

MORAL INCAPACITY

MORALITY

MORALS

MORTGAGES

MORTGAGES—continued

MOTIONS

MOTIVE

MULES

MUNICIPAL CORPORATIONS

PUBLIC UTILITY HOLDING ACT

PUNITIVE DAMAGES

PURCHASE MONEY

PURCHASE MONEY MORTGAGES

PURE FOOD AND DRUG ACT

PURSUIT

QUALIFIED PRIVILEGE

QUARANTINE

QUARE EJECIT INFRA TERMINUM

QUASI CONTRACTS

QUASI-MUNICIPAL CORPORATIONS

TRUST RECEIPTS

TRUSTS

END OF VOLUME

APPENDIX—LAW QUIZZER

Clark's Summary of American Law

By

GEORGE L. CLARK

AUTHOR OF CLARK'S SUMMARY OF AMERICAN LAW

THE LAWYERS CO-OPERATIVE PUBLISHING COMPANY
ROCHESTER 3, NEW YORK

1956 Reprint

LAW QUIZZER

SUMMARY OF AMERICAN LAW

PART I—ELEMENTARY

PART II—EQUITY AND COMMERCIAL

PART III—PUBLIC LAW

PART IV—PROCEDURE

SUMMARY OF
AMERICAN LAW

APPENDIX—LAW QUIZZER

FORMS OF ACTION

1. A, while quarreling with B, struck at B and accidentally hit X, who happened to be standing near. *What action, if any, may X maintain against A?* (FORMS OF ACTION § 1, p. 2.)

2. A, while driving his car negligently, drove so close to X and Y that both were frightened and Y, because of the nervous shock, was confined to her bed for two weeks. *What remedy, if any, does X have against A?* (FORMS OF ACTION § 2, p. 2.) *What remedy, if any, does Y have against A?* (TORTS § 118, p. 91.)

3. A shot at X, intending to kill him but X did not know about it till later. *May X recover against A in an action of trespass for an assault?* (By the better view, yes. FORMS OF ACTION § 2, p. 2.)

4. While X was in a room asleep, A locked all the doors so that X could not have gotten out of the room, but before X awakened, A unlocked the doors. *Has X any remedy against A?* (FORMS OF ACTION § 3, p. 3.)

5. A, having a warrant for the arrest of B, telephoned to B, read the warrant to him over the telephone and asked B if he submitted; B said that he did; A said "Wait for me ten minutes and I will come and get you"; B replied that he would. At the end of five minutes B changed his mind and left. *Is that an escape from imprisonment?* (FORMS OF ACTION § 3, p. 3.)

6. B wished to attend a ball game which was to be played at 3 P. M. On his way to the ball park in his car, A wrongfully obstructed the highway so that he was unable to see the game. *What remedy, if any, has B against A?* (FORMS OF ACTION § 3, p. 3.)

7. Because of a heavy windstorm, levelling A's fences, A's horses and cows and pigs escaped from his field and damaged B's crops in the adjoining field. *What remedy, if any, has B against A?* (FORMS OF ACTION § 5, p. 4; TORTS, § 40, p. 50.)

8. Because of a mistake in the boundary line between A's farm and B's farm, B sprinkled fertilizer on a strip of land belonging to A. A sues B in an action of trespass. *Is he entitled to recover?* (FORMS OF ACTION § 5, p. 4.)

9. A entered upon B's land and took possession of it. *What remedy or remedies does B have?* (FORMS OF ACTION § 5, p. 4; § 43, p. 24.)

10. A built a house on his land with the eaves projecting over B's land adjoin-

ing. *What remedy or remedies does B have?* (FORMS OF ACTION § 5, p. 4; § 43, p. 24; EQUITY § 51, p. 256.)

11. A leased his farm to B for three years and while B was in possession he cut down some valuable trees and C drove frequently across the land creating a deep gully in it. *What remedy or remedies does A have against B?* (FORMS OF ACTION § 5, p. 4; § 11, p. 8; EQUITY § 46, p. 254.) *Against C?* (FORMS OF ACTION § 13, p. 8.)

12. B, a sheriff, with a writ of execution issued on a judgment against X, levied the execution by mistake against Y's goods but merely took possession of them, not removing the goods because he discovered the mistake. Y sues B in trespass. *Is he entitled to recover?* (FORMS OF ACTION § 7, p. 5; TORTS § 2, p. 29.)

13. B wrongfully took a chattel out of A's possession and then C wrongfully took it from B's possession. *How advise A as to his rights and remedies? Is it important that A himself did not own the chattel?* (FORMS OF ACTION § 7, p. 5.) Suppose that B delivers the chattel peaceably to C. *Is C liable in trespass?*

14. A hired his automobile to B for two months at $20 a month; while B was in possession of the automobile, X damaged it. *What action, if any, may be maintained against X by A? By B?* (FORMS OF ACTION § 7, p. 5.)

15. Facts similar to 14 ante, except that the lending to B was gratuitous. *What change in your answer?* (FORMS OF ACTION § 7, p. 5.)

16. A sent his servant B to town in his (A's) automobile; X thereupon took possession of the automobile, claiming it as his own. *What remedies does A have? B?* (FORMS OF ACTION § 7, p. 5, § 9, p. 6.)

17. A seduced B's female servant X. *What remedy or remedies does B have against A?* (FORMS OF ACTION, § 7, p. 5.) *What remedy or remedies does X have against A?* (TORTS § 3, p. 29.)

18. A loaned a chattel to B for a month for hire; during the month X took the chattel from B's possession intending to keep it. *May B maintain trover against X? May A?* (FORMS OF ACTION § 9, p. 6.)

19. Facts same as 18 ante, except that the loan was a gratuitous one; same questions. (FORMS OF ACTION § 9, p. 6.)

20. B, by fraud, persuaded A to sell a chattel to him, giving him a worthless check in payment therefor. *May A maintain trover against B?* (FORMS OF ACTION § 9, p. 6.) Suppose that B sold and delivered the chattel to X who paid B for the chattel in good faith without notice of B's fraud. *Is X liable to A?*

21. A for hire loaned a chattel to B for a month; B wrongfully sold and delivered the chattel to X, who paid value to B, thinking B owned it. *Is B liable to A in trover? Is X?* (FORMS OF ACTION § 9, p. 6.)

22. Same facts as 21 ante, except that the chattel was not delivered to X; same questions. (FORMS OF ACTION § 9, p. 7.)

23. B wrongfully took A's chattel out of A's possession but with no intent to deprive A of the chattel permanently. *Is B liable to A in trover?* (FORMS OF ACTION § 9, p. 6.)

24. A loaned a chattel to B who later, by mistake, delivered the chattel to X thinking he was delivering it back to A. *Is B liable to A in trover?* (FORMS OF ACTION § 9, p. 7.)

25. A wrongfully entered on B's land and harvested a crop of wheat, claiming that he had a right to do so. *What remedy or remedies does B have against A?* (FORMS OF ACTION § 5, p. 3; § 9, p. 7.)

26. A while in wrongful possession of B's land, harvested a crop of wheat belonging to B. *What remedy or remedies to B?* (FORMS OF ACTION § 9, p. 7; § 12, p. 8; § 43, p. 25.)

27. A contracted in writing to sell a chattel to B for $200, delivery to be made ten days later; at the end of the ten days A refused to let B have the chattel; B brings trover. *What decision?* (FORMS OF ACTION § 9, p. 7.)

28. B borrowed an automobile from A and while using it he had a collision with a truck driven by X and the automobile was destroyed. A sued B in trover. *What decision?* (FORMS OF ACTION § 9, p. 7.)

29. B borrowed an automobile from A to make a trip to town X; in violation of the bailment, he drove beyond town X to town Y and there the automobile was accidentally destroyed. *Is B liable to A and, if so, in what action?* (FORMS OF ACTION § 9, p. 7.)

30. A devised land to B for life, then to C for life, then to D in fee. While B was in possession he cut down valuable timber trees. *What remedy or remedies to C? To D?* (FORMS OF ACTION § 11, p. 8; EQUITY, § 46, p. 255.)

31. A while in wrongful possession of B's land negligently destroyed B's barn. *What remedy to B?* (FORMS OF ACTION § 12, p. 8.)

32. A leased his farm and his farm machinery to B for a year; during the year X entered upon the land and caused damage to the land and to the machinery. *What remedy has A against X? What remedy has B against X?* (FORMS OF ACTION § 13, p. 8; § 5, p. 3; § 7, p. 5.)

33. A induced B to invest $10,000 in stock of the A Manufacturing Co. by negligently making a false representation to B as to the financial condition of the company. *What is B's remedy?* (FORMS OF ACTION § 14, p. 9.)

34. A wished to sell his horse to B; the horse was a crib biter not worth more than $50; if he had not been a crib biter he would have been worth $150. In order to prevent B from finding out that the horse was a crib biter, A hitched him so close to the crib that he could not bite it. After buying the horse for $150 B learned the truth. *What remedy?* (FORMS OF ACTION § 14, p. 9; EQUITY § 40, p. 251.)

35. A sold and delivered to B an automobile with a defective wheel; while driving the automobile the wheel broke and B was injured. *What remedy to B if A knew the wheel was defective?* (FORMS OF ACTION § 14, p. 9.) *If A did not know?* (TORTS § 39, p. 49.)

36. For over twenty years A dumped sewage into a stream running through his land; during that time this did not cause any damage to B, who owned land down the stream but now B wishes to use the water for domestic purposes and upon A refusing to quit dumping sewage into the stream, B asks

you as to his rights. *How advise?* (FORMS OF ACTION § 15, p. 9; EQUITY § 54, p. 257.)

37. A so obstructed the road running through his farm that B, driving an automobile truck was compelled to detour two miles to reach his destination with a load of coal. *How advise B as to his rights and remedies, if any, against A?* (FORMS OF ACTION § 16, p. 10.)

38. The X Railroad Co. wrongfully refused to serve A. *What remedies, if any, are available to A?* (FORMS OF ACTION § 17, p. 10.)

39. B, driving an automobile truck, negligently collided with A's automobile, damaging the automobile and injuring A. *What remedies, if any, are available to A?* (FORMS OF ACTION § 1, p. 2; § 17, p. 10.)

40. B while driving an auto truck, negligently ran over X and killed him. *Discuss B's liability.* (FORMS OF ACTION § 17, p. 10; TORTS § 117, p. 91.)

41. In the X newspaper was a news item stating that one Charles H. Hanson had been convicted of accepting a bribe; the statement was true of Charles P. Hanson but not true of Charles H. Hanson, a business man of integrity and good reputation, and he sues the X newspaper company for libel. *What decision?* (FORMS OF ACTION § 19, p. 12.)

42. In the X newspaper was an item stating that John Sutton had discontinued his engineering business. The statement was not true. *Under what circumstances, if any, may Sutton recover against the X Company?* (FORMS OF ACTION § 19, p. 12.)

43. A wrote a libellous statement in regard to Y and locked it up in his office desk. That night A's secretary opened the desk and read the statement to Z another employee of A. *What remedy, if any, has Y against A?* (FORMS OF ACTION § 19, p. 12.)

44. A was arrested by B for larceny on a void warrant; A was guilty of the larceny. *What remedy, if any, has A against B?* (FORMS OF ACTION § 21, p. 12.)

45. A was arrested by B for larceny on a valid warrant. A was innocent of the larceny. *Under what circumstances, if at all, may A recover against B?* (FORMS OF ACTION § 21, p. 12.)

46. A contracted with B to erect a building for him. By fraudulently misrepresenting to A that B was insolvent, X persuaded A not to erect the building for B but to erect one for himself. *What remedy, if any, has B against X?* (FORMS OF ACTION § 22, p. 13.)

47. B, a butler in A's employ, was injured by the negligent conduct of X in driving his auto truck, so that B was unable to work for four weeks. *What action, if any, may A maintain against X?* (FORMS OF ACTION § 23, p. 13.)

48. A leased land to B for three years the lease containing a promise not to assign the lease. *What remedy does A have against B for breach if B also executed the lease? If B did not execute the lease?* (FORMS OF ACTION § 24, p. 14.)

49. A leased land to B for three years at $1,200 a year rental; B is in default to the extent of $600. *What remedies are available to A?* (FORMS OF ACTION § 24, p. 14.)

50. A leased land to B for three years at $1,200 a year rental; at the end of a year B transferred his interest to X. *What is A's remedy against X for non-payment of rent?* (FORMS OF ACTION § 24, p. 14.)

51. A leased to B for three years at a rental of $1,200 a year, B agreeing not to use the land for business purposes. B is behind in his rent and is using the premises for business purposes. *How advise A as to his remedies against B?* (FORMS OF ACTION § 27, p. 15; EQUITY § 16, p. 241.)

52. A statute imposed upon farmers the duty to cut all Canada thistles upon their farms or in default to pay a penalty of $50 to be collected by the prosecuting attorney. *What is the appropriate form of action?* (FORMS OF ACTION § 29, p. 15.)

53. A sued B in an action on the case for negligently causing A personal injuries and recovered a judgment for $2,000. *What is the appropriate form of action to collect the judgment?* (FORMS OF ACTION § 30, p. 16.)

54. A insured his building against fire with the X Company, for $4,000 and there was a total loss. *In what form of action may A recover the* $4,000 *due?* (FORMS OF ACTION § 31, p. 17.)

55. A and B had a dispute and finally referred the matter to arbitrators who made an award to A of $4,500. *How may A enforce the award?* (FORMS OF ACTION § 31, p. 17.)

56. A sold and delivered to B some goods on 60 days credit for $1,800; at the end of the 60 days B failed to pay. *What different actions may A use to get a judgment for the* $1,800 *due?* (FORMS OF ACTION § 31, p. 16; § 33, p. 18; § 35, p. 19.)

57. A contracted to sell a chattel to B for $250 but B later refused to accept it and pay the price. *What is A's remedy?* (FORMS OF ACTION § 33, p. 18.)

58. A contracted to sell his farming implements to B for $900, title to pass on October 1; B paid $200 toward the price. On October 1, A refused to let B have the implements. *What remedies does B have against A?* (FORMS OF ACTION § 33, p. 18; QUASI-CONTRACTS § 13, p. 295.)

59. The X Telephone Co. wrongfully refused to put in a telephone for A. *What remedies has A for such refusal?* (FORMS OF ACTION § 33, p. 18.)

60. A bought goods from X for $800 on credit, Y guaranteeing in writing that A would pay when due. A completely defaulted. *In what form of action may X recover from Y on the guaranty?* (FORMS OF ACTION § 33, p. 18; § 35, p. 20.)

61. A loaned his automobile to B for a week, B to turn over the possession to X at the end of that period. *If B defaults, what is X's remedy?* (FORMS OF ACTION § 37, p. 21.)

62. B wrongfully took A's chattel out of his possession and C wrongfully took it from B. *May B maintain replevin against C?* (FORMS OF ACTION § 39, p. 22.)

63. B brings replevin against C. *Who is entitled to the possession of the chattel during the litigation?* (FORMS OF ACTION § 39, p. 22.)

64. *When did the common law action of account lie and what remedy or remedies superseded it?* (FORMS OF ACTION § 41, p. 23.)

65. A claims that he is entitled to the minerals under B's land. *What is the appropriate action?* (FORMS OF ACTION § 43, p. 24.)

66. A has an easement of way over B's land; X has obstructed it so that A cannot use it. *What remedies are available to A?* (FORMS OF ACTION § 16, p. 10; § 43, p. 24; EQUITY § 56, p. 258.)

67. A wrongfully occupied B's land for three years at the end of which period B succeeded in getting back into possession by winning in an action of ejectment. The value of the three years' use and occupation was $3,000. *What is B's remedy therefor?* (FORMS OF ACTION § 43, p. 25.)

TORTS

1. While driving his automobile, A ran into B and caused him personal injuries; A contends that it was an accident; B contends that A was negligent. *Which one has the burden of proof?* (TORTS § 1, p. 29.)

2. A, an officer, had a warrant for the arrest of John Smith; A reasonably and in good faith arrested the wrong John Smith, who brought suit against A for false imprisonment. *Is A liable?* (TORTS § 2, p. 29.)

3. A and B owned and occupied adjoining farms; there was a dispute over the boundary line and A sued B in trespass for walking across a strip two rods wide; A proved that the strip was part of his land; B acted reasonably and in good faith and caused no damage to the land. *What decision?* (TORTS § 2, p. 29.)

4. A and B had a dispute and finally tried to settle it in a fist fight in which both A and B were injured. A sues B in trespass for battery. *Is B liable?* (TORTS § 3, p. 30.)

5. By fraudulent representations as to the condition of A's teeth, B, a dentist, persuaded A to let B pull his teeth. *What action should A bring against B?* (TORTS § 3, p. 30.)

6. In the presence of several persons B called A "a dirty bastard", whereupon A struck B and knocked him down. *What is B's remedy, if any, against A? Of A against B?* (TORTS § 4, p. 30; § 76, p. 72.)

7. A and B had had several quarrels; they met on a sidewalk; A threatened to strike B if B would not get off the sidewalk; B refused to get off, whereupon A struck him. B sues A for battery; A contends that B should have stepped off the sidewalk. *What decision?* (TORTS § 4, p. 30.)

8. A came on B's land and refused to leave. *What may B do about it?* (TORTS § 5, p. 31.)

9. A set a spring gun in order to kill a would-be burglar; X, a mere trespasser, was seriously injured by the gun. *Is A liable to X?* (TORTS § 5, p. 31.)

10. A, an outgoing tenant of B, left chattels on the land when he moved out. *What should B do with them?* (TORTS § 5, p. 31.)

11. A and B own and occupy adjoining farms; A has several fruit trees on his land the branches of which, with fruit thereon, overhang B's land. *What advice to B as to his rights and remedies?* (TORTS § 5, p. 31.)

12. A and B own and occupy adjoining farms; B's dog, worth $200, came on A's land and was about to kill one of A's chickens, worth $1.50, when A shot and killed the dog. *Is A liable to B?* (TORTS § 5, p. 31.)

13. A heavy storm and flood carried several logs from A's land down on B's land. *How advise A as to getting back his logs?* (TORTS § 6, p. 31.)

14. A owed B $12; he handed B a $20 bill, expecting to receive back $8 in change. B insisted upon keeping the $20. A thereupon took the $20 bill back by force. *Is A liable to B?* (TORTS § 6, p. 31.)

15. A rented B's farm for a year and upon moving out he forgot to remove a mowing machine. When he went back to get it, B would not let him enter to get it. *How advise A?* (TORTS § 6, p. 31.)

16. A rented a house from B for a year and at the end of the year he refused to move out. *How advise B?* (TORTS § 6, p. 31.)

17. A arrested B for larceny (a felony); B sues A for false imprisonment, A not acting under a warrant. *What must A show in defense if he was an officer? If he was not an officer?* (TORTS § 8, p. 32.)

18. A discovered X and Y engaged in a mutual affray; upon being discovered they apparently stopped the affray, but A suspects that they merely suspended their activity till he should leave. *May A arrest them without a warrant?* (TORTS § 8, p. 32.)

19. A burglary was committed at A's residence and A recognized the burglar; there was plenty of time to get a warrant because a magistrate lived next door, but A arrested the burglar without a warrant. *Was such action legal?* (TORTS § 8, p. 32.)

20. A, an officer, levied an attachment upon B's property, the attachment having been issued under a statute which has later been declared unconstitutional. *Is A liable to B?* (TORTS § 9, p. 33.)

21. A arrested B upon a John Doe warrant. *Is A liable to B if the crime was a misdemeanor? If it was a felony?* (TORTS § 8, p. 31; § 9, p. 32.)

22. A, an officer, levied an execution upon the goods of X thinking that the goods belonged to the judgment debtor Y. *Is A liable to X?* (TORTS § 9, p. 33.)

23. A, an officer, was directed by a replevin writ to take possession of an automobile supposed to be in the possession of X but which was in the possession of Y. *Is A liable for seizing the automobile?* (TORTS § 9, p. 33.)

24. A had a warrant for the arrest of B; reasonably thinking that X was B. he attempted to arrest X, whereupon X resisted the arrest and killed A. *What is X's liability?* (TORTS § 10, p. 34.)

25. A had an execution writ for the seizure of X's goods; thinking that Y's goods belonged to X, he attempted to levy upon them, whereupon Y resisted and A committed an assault and battery upon Y in order to make the levy. *Is A liable to Y?* (TORTS § 10, p. 34.)

26. A had a warrant for the arrest of X; reasonably thinking that Y was X, he attempted to arrest Y and called upon B to assist him; B did assist him and they arrested Y. *Is A liable? Is B liable?* (TORTS § 10, p. 34.)

27. A in punishing his child X used unnecessary force, causing serious injuries to X. *What is A's liability?* (TORTS § 11, p. 34; § 114, p. 90.)

28. *Under what circumstances may the captain of a ship discipline the passengers?* (TORTS § 11, p. 34.)

29. A was seriously injured and rendered unconscious in an automobile collision: a surgeon amputated one of his legs in order to save his life. *Is the surgeon liable to A?* (TORTS § 12, p. 34.)

30. A, a railroad switchman, turned a switch so that a runaway engine crashed into an accommodation train in which there were 20 passengers instead of into an express train in which there were 160 passengers. X, a passenger on the accommodation train was hurt and sues A for battery. *Is A liable?* (TORTS § 13, p. 34.)

31. Because of a great conflagration, Z's residence was dynamited by the city of Y and destroyed in order to stop the fire. *How advise Z as to his rights and remedies?* (TORTS § 13, p. 35; CONSTITUTIONAL LAW § 30, p. 479.)

32. A, having a private right of way over B's land, deviated from the way onto B's land because a storm had blown a tree down and obstructed his way. *Is A liable to B?* (TORTS § 13, p. 36.)

33. A, a judge presiding over a trial of B for the commission of a crime, misdirected the jury as to the law, with the result that B, though innocent, was found guilty and served several months in prison before a higher court reversed the conviction. *Is A liable to B?* (TORTS § 14, p. 35.)

34. A, a sheriff, entered upon B's land to levy a valid execution upon B's goods. Having made the levy he quarreled with B and committed a battery upon him. B thereupon sued him for the battery and for levying upon his goods. *Is A liable?* (TORTS § 15, p. 35.)

35. A, a sheriff, levied a writ of execution upon the goods of X instead of on the goods of Y the judgment debtor; as soon as he discovered his mistake he tendered the goods back to X but X refused to receive them and brought trover against A. *Is A liable?* (TORTS § 16, p. 36.)

36. A sold his farm to B representing that he had paid $200 an acre for the farm five years earlier, whereas he had paid only $110 an acre for it. The farm is worth very much less than the $225 an acre which B paid. B sues A in deceit. *Is A liable?* (TORTS § 17, p. 36.)

37. A induced B of Missouri by false representations as to the law of Texas, to buy from A some Texas land at a price much above its real value. B sues A in deceit. *Is A liable?* (*Yes, because B is not bound to know the law of any other state than his own*; TORTS § 18, p. 37.)

38. A, about to form a corporation, issued a prospectus to persuade prospective investors to buy stock in the corporation and B, relying thereon, bought some of the stock; the prospectus contained statements which A thought were

true but which he would have known were untrue if he had exercised ordinary care. *What is A's liability to B?* (TORTS § 18, p. 37.)

39. A, wishing to sell his farm to B, made false representations to B about the fertility of the soil, the location of the farm, etc., inducing B to buy the farm at more than its real value; B sued A in deceit and A set up in defense that B could have easily found out the truth. *Is this a good defense?* (TORTS § 19, p. 37.)

40. A sold to B for $400 a chattel worth $600, warranting and representing that it was worth $850. *How would you advise B as to his rights and remedies against A?* (TORTS § 20, p. 37.)

41. While A was in Florida for the winter X dumped some garbage on his land and A's neighbors sued A in an action on the case for a nuisance; A set up in defense that X acted without his assent. *Is the defense good?* (TORTS § 21, p. 38.)

42. A and B, owning and occupying adjoining residences, quarreled, and A erected on his lot near the boundary line between his lot and B's a board fence 10 feet high and painted it yellow. *How advise B?* (TORTS § 22, p. 39; CONSTITUTIONAL LAW § 19, p. 474.)

43. A had a valuable spring on his land; B, in order to damage the spring, bored a deep well on his land adjoining, thus ruining the spring. *How advise A?* (TORTS § 22, p. 39.)

44. A, B, C and D each conducted a summer hotel near the X River, and each one dumped sewage from the hotel into the river thus making the water unfit for any domestic use. *How advise X, who owns and occupies land down stream and who can no longer allow his cattle to drink the contaminated water?* (TORTS § 23, p. 39; EQUITY § 54, p. 257.)

45. A owns a very large building next to a low building owned by B. A fears that B will tear down his low building and erect one as high as his own, thus shutting out light and air from the upper stories. *How advise A?* (TORTS § 24, p. 39.)

46. X wrongfully obstructed the street in front of A's land. *What action may A maintain against X if A owns the fee to the middle of the street? If the city owns the fee?* (TORTS § 25, p. 39.)

47. A sued B for running against him (A) with his (B's) auto truck. B contended that he was not liable because (1) he was using the same amount of care that he ordinarily used and because (2) he was using the same amount of care that other truck drivers in that locality ordinarily used. *What decision?* (TORTS § 26, p. 40.)

48. A, a child ten years old, was negligently injured by X, who now sets up in defense that he should not be held liable because of the contributory negligence of A. *How should the jury be instructed as to the care which A was bound to use?* (TORTS § 26, p. 41.)

49. A, a blind man, crossing a street, was negligently injured by X, who sets up the defense of contributory negligence of A. *How should the jury be instructed as to the care which A was bound to use?* (TORTS § 26, p. 41.)

50. A, a Christian Science healer, undertook to treat X for appendicitis. *How should the jury be instructed as to the care which A was bound to use?* (TORTS § 26, p. 41.)

51. A ran into X with an auto truck and injured him. A was intoxicated. *Under what circumstances, if at all, is his intoxication a defense?* (TORTS § 26, p. 41.)

52. A statute provided that there should be liability toward one who was wrongfully on a highway only if the defendant was guilty of gross negligence. *What is the significance here of the word "gross"?* (TORTS § 27, p. 42.)

53. A loaned a chattel to B gratuitously and B damaged the chattel. *How should the jury be instructed as to the care which B was bound to use?* (TORTS § 27, p. 41; PERSONAL PROPERTY § 10, p. 166.)

54. A railroad engineer was about to run over X, a child on the track, negligently; Y, seeing the danger, rescued the child but was himself injured. *May Y recover against the railroad company?* (TORTS § 28, p. 42; § 56, p. 60.)

55. A street car company was negligent as to X and this negligent conduct caused serious injury to Y, a bystander. *Is the company liable to Y?* (TORTS § 28, p. 42.)

56. Pedestrians were accustomed to cross over the defendant's railroad tracks in order to make a short cut to and from a nearby village. *Is the defendant under a duty, in running its trains, to keep a lookout for such trespassers?* (TORTS § 29, p. 44; § 31, p. 45.)

57. A's horses were afflicted with a contagious disease; he turned them out to pasture in a field next to B's field where B's horses were and B's horses contracted the disease. *Is A liable to B for the loss?* (TORTS § 29, p. 44.)

58. A in erecting a building on his land, dug an excavation close to the sidewalk. *How advise A as to his duty toward those using the sidewalk?* (TORTS § 30, p. 45.)

59. A in erecting a building on his own land, dug an excavation close to B's building. *How advise A as to his duty to B?* (TORTS § 30, p. 45.)

60. A so cultivated his hillside that soil was washed down by the rains and filled up B's pond at the bottom of the hill. *Is A liable?* (TORTS § 30, p. 45.)

61. On A's farm remote from the highway there is an old well covered by rotten boards; A sees B, a trespasser, approaching the well. *Is A under a duty to warn him?* (TORTS § 31, p. 45.)

62. B is a trespasser on A's farm; A is driving a truck thereon. *May he drive just as if B were not there?* (TORTS § 31, p. 45.)

63. A kept a swimming pool on his land for the use of his own children; children in the neighborhood were attracted by it and use it without A's consent and one of them was drowned while thus using it. *Is A liable?* (TORTS § 32, p. 46.)

64. On a dark night B asked A for permission to cross over his land; that afternoon A had made a deep excavation where B was likely to walk. *Is A under a duty to warn B thereof?* (TORTS § 33, p. 46.)

65. A invited B to dinner at his home; the floors had just been waxed and polished and B slipped and fell and was injured. *Is A liable?* (TORTS § 34, p. 46.)

66. B went into A's store taking with her two of her small children whom she took into the children's room. While B was shopping one of the children fell through an unguarded window and was injured. *How advise A as to his liability?* (TORTS § 34, p. 47.)

67. *What is the doctrine of Fletcher v. Rylands? Is it often followed in this country?* (TORTS § 35, p. 47.)

68. The X county allowed its roads to be out of repair and A, a traveler on the road, suffered personal injuries thereby. *Is the X county liable to A?* (TORTS § 36, p. 47.)

69. X, who was building a house for A, allowed a pile of sand and lime to be in the street after the house had been completed; Y drove his automobile into the sand and lime and damaged his automobile. *Is the city liable to Y?* (TORTS § 36, p. 47.)

70. A rented to B for the summer his premises on which there was a toboggan slide which was for the use of the public. X used the slide and was injured because of a defect therein. *What is X's right against A?* (TORTS § 37, p. 48.)

71. A rented an apartment to B; the ceiling of the hall was unsafe and fell upon B's wife as she was going through the hall to the street. *What is A's liability to her?* (TORTS § 37, p. 48.)

72. A rented a house to B for a year; he was under no liability to keep the house in repair but he undertook to do so and left it in an unsafe condition, so that B's son was injured. *Is A liable?* (TORTS § 37, p. 48.)

73. A gratuitously loaned a stepladder to his neighbor B; it was defective and B in using it fell and was injured. *Is A liable to B?* (TORTS § 38, p. 48.)

74. A sent his automobile to B to be repaired without notifying B that the gasoline tank had a leak in it; while repairing the car the gasoline tank exploded and injured B. *Is A liable to B?* (TORTS § 38, p. 49.)

75. A bought from B, a retailer of pies and cakes manufactured by X, a cake in which there was a nail. A's daughter, Y, injured her mouth because of the nail while eating the cake. *Is X liable to Y?* (TORTS § 39, p. 49.)

76. A's chickens went over upon the adjoining farm of B and ate grain worth $70. *Is A liable to B?* (TORTS § 40, p. 50.)

77. A's dog while on the highway bit X, a neighbor. *Is A liable to X?* (TORTS § 40, p. 50.)

78. A loaned his horse to B to drive to town. B drove the horse to town and then used the horse in plowing where the horse was injured without B's fault. *Is B liable to A?* (TORTS § 40, p. 50.)

79. While A was watching a circus parade, his horse became frightened because of the smell of the circus animals and ran away and injured himself and A. *What are A's rights, if any?* (TORTS § 40, p. 50.)

80. A used explosives on his land to blow out old stumps; a piece of wood was blown over into the highway and injured X, a traveler. *Is A liable to X?* (TORTS § 41, p. 51.)

81. A municipal ordinance required the blowing of a whistle and the ringing of a bell whenever a locomotive engine approached a crossing. A was injured due to the failure of the locomotive engineer to perform the duty imposed on him. *Is A entitled to recover against the railroad?* (TORTS § 42, p. 52.)

82. A railroad company, though under no legal duty to do so, kept a flagman at one of its crossings for two years; it then discontinued the service and A, who supposed the flagman was still there, drove onto the track and was injured. *May A recover from the railroad company?* (TORTS § 43, p. 53.)

83. *What is the doctrine of res ipsa loquitur and what is its effect?* (TORTS § 44, p. 54.)

84. A sued B for injuries occasioned by an automobile collision, alleging negligence on the part of B. B's defense is that A was also negligent. *Must A allege and prove that he himself was in the exercise of ordinary care?* (TORTS § 44, p. 54.)

85. *What is meant by the statement that negligence and legal cause are mixed questions of law and fact?* (TORTS § 45, p. 54.)

86. *What is meant by remote consequences?* (TORTS § 46, p. 55.)

87. *What is the probable consequence rule? Do courts which lay down this rule allow recovery for improbable consequences which follow immediately?* (TORTS § 47, p. 55.)

88. *For what further consequences will an application of the proximate consequence rule allow recovery?* (TORTS § 48, p. 55.)

89. A and B had an automobile collision; both were driving negligently; X, a pedestrian, was injured. *Are A and B each liable to X for the full amount of X's damage?* (TORTS § 49, p. 56.)

90. *What is the difference between a case of an intervening human cause and a case of concurrent human causes?* (TORTS § 50, p. 57.)

91. *Under what circumstances is A liable in spite of the fact that another person's negligence has intervened between A's negligent conduct and the damage to X?* (TORTS § 50, p. 57.)

92. A was seriously injured in an automobile collision; a few weeks later he became insane and killed himself. *Are the negligent automobile drivers liable for the death?* (TORTS § 51, p. 58.)

93. A shipped some whisky by auto truck; because of the delay in shipping, the whisky was exposed to unexpected very severe cold weather and was damaged. *Under what circumstances is A entitled to recover against the carrier?* (TORTS § 51, p. 58.)

94. A sued B for negligently running into him on the public highway. The jury by special verdict found that B was negligent and that A was also negligent but that A's negligent conduct was no part of the cause of A's injuries. *Is A entitled to recover?* (TORTS § 52, p. 59.)

95. *What logical objection is there to allowing contributory negligence merely to reduce plaintiff's recovery instead of barring him entirely?* (TORTS § 52, p. 59.)

96. *Under what circumstances is the conscious last chance rule explainable on the basis of legal cause? When not?* (TORTS § 53, p. 59.)

97. *Under what circumstances would a negligent plaintiff be allowed to recover under the unconscious last chance rule but not under the conscious last chance rule?* (TORTS § 54, p. 60.)

98. *Under what circumstances would a negligent plaintiff be allowed to recover under the humanitarian rule but not under the unconscious last chance rule?* (TORTS § 54, p. 60.)

99. *Distinguish between contributory negligence and unjustifiable assumption of risk.* (TORTS § 55, p. 60.)

100. A's horse strayed onto X railroad company's track because the company had failed to maintain a fence as required by statute. A saw that the horse was about to be run over by the train, so he tried to save it and was himself injured. *May he recover from the company?* (TORTS § 56, p. 61; § 42, p. 52.)

101. The X Railroad Company negligently failed to maintain a good fence between its right of way and A's pasture. A turned out his horses and they jumped the fence, got on the track and were injured. *Is the company liable to X?* (TORTS § 56, p. 61.)

102. A physician called to attend a patient took the risk of the defective condition of the highway and was injured. *Does such conduct bar his recovery?* (TORTS § 56, p. 61.)

103. A, riding in an automobile which had not been registered as required by statute, was injured because of the negligence of X. *Is A barred from recovery?* (TORTS § 57, p. 61.)

104. A loaned his automobile to B, and while using it, X negligently collided with it; A sued X who set up in defense the contributory negligence of B. *Is it a good defense?* (TORTS § 58, p. 62.)

105. A drove an auto delivery truck for his employer B; while making a delivery he intentionally ran the truck against the automobile of X with whom he had quarreled. *Is B liable to X?* (TORTS § 59, p. 63.)

106. For a day B loaned his servant A to his friend X; while A was working for X, he negligently injured Y. *Is B liable to Y?* (TORTS § 59, p. 63.)

107. X, who was being treated at a charity hospital, was injured because of the negligence of a nurse. *Does X have any rights against the hospital?* (TORTS § 59, p. 64; TRUSTS § 13, p. 271.)

108. A employed X, a contractor, to erect a residence for him according to certain specifications; while engaged in the work Y, an employee, was injured because of X's negligence. *Is A liable to Y?* (TORTS § 60, p. 64.)

109. A while repairing the sidewalk in front of his property, left some sand and cement in the street; later he employed X to remove the sand and cement and while doing so X negligently injured Y. *Is A liable to Y?* (TORTS § 60, p. 64.)

110. *What is meant by the fellow servant rule? When was it first decided in this country?* (TORTS § 61, p. 64.)

111. A, owner of a factory, instructed his servant B to provide a safe place for his employees to work; because of B's negligence in doing so, X, a fellow employee, was injured. *Is A liable to X?* (TORTS § 62, p. 65.)

112. A, owner of a factory, negligently failed to provide a safe place for his employees to work, but X continued to work there without protest because of fear of dismissal and was injured. *Is A liable to X?* (TORTS § 63, p. 65.)

113. Facts similar to 112 ante, except that X did protest against the danger and A thereupon assured him that the danger would be eliminated and because of this X continued and suffered injury because of the dangerous situation. *Is A liable to X?* (TORTS § 63, p. 66.)

114. *What were the main provisions of the Federal Employers' Liability Act? Does it take precedence over the Workmen's Compensation Act?* (TORTS § 64, p. 66.)

115. *What is the distinguishing feature of the Workmen's Compensation Acts?* (TORTS § 65, p. 67.)

116. A was employed as a teacher in X's private school for boys; one of A's pupils committed a battery upon him causing him serious injuries. *Is A entitled to workmen's compensation?* (TORTS § 66, p. 67.)

117. A is employed by B as a travelling salesman. *For the purpose of the Workmen's Compensation Acts, when does his employment begin and end?* (TORTS § 67, p. 68.)

118. *What is meant by the requirement of the Workmen's Compensation Acts that the injury must "arise out of the employment"?* (TORTS § 68, p. 68.)

119. A, an employee, became insane as the result of an industrial accident and then committed suicide. *Is there liability under the Workmen's Compensation Acts?* (TORTS § 69, p. 68.)

120. A had an industrial accident which caused the loss of an eye; later he had another industrial accident causing the loss of the other eye. *To how much compensation is he entitled for the loss of the second eye?* (TORTS § 69, p. 69.)

121. *What is meant by the Workmen's Compensation Act phrase "serious and wilful misconduct"?* (TORTS § 70, p. 69.)

122. A, the president and manager and majority stockholder of a small corporation, suffered an industrial accident. *Is he entitled to compensation as an employee under Workmen's Compensation Acts?* (TORTS § 71, p. 69.)

123. A, a plumber, volunteered in an emergency to help the city marshal and was accidentally hurt. *What right, if any, does he have against the city under Workmen's Compensation Acts?* (TORTS § 71, p. 69; § 75, p. 71.)

124. A was employed in State X to work in State Y; while so working he was injured. *Does the Workmen's Compensation Act of State X govern his rights?* (TORTS § 72, p. 70.)

125. A while employed by the B company was negligently injured by X; the

company paid the Workmen's Compensation Act compensation to B. *Does it have any rights against X? Does A?* (TORTS § 73, p. 70.)

126. A, a waitress at B's restaurant, had an industrial accident; her wages were $20 a week but she received an average of $10 a week in tips. *How should her compensation be figured?* (TORTS § 75, p. 71.)

127. A called B a thief but no one heard the accusation except B. *Is A liable to B in an action for slander?* (TORTS § 76, p. 72; § 81, p. 74.)

128. A told B that X had had syphilis some two years before. *What is X's right against A if the statement was not true?* (TORTS § 77, p. 73.)

129. A was a public school teacher; B told X that A was insolvent. *What is A's right against B if the statement was not true?* (TORTS § 78, p. 73.)

130. A was a physician; B told X that A had had illicit sexual relations with one of his patients. *What is A's right against B if the statement was not true?* (TORTS § 78, p. 73.)

131. A made a defamatory statement about B to X; X repeated the statement to Y thereby causing B to lose his employment with Y. *Is A liable to B for such loss?* (TORTS § 79, p. 74.)

132. *What is the difference between the law of libel and the law of slander in England? In some states in this country?* (TORTS § 80, p. 74; FORMS OF ACTION § 19, p. 12.)

133. A sent to B a letter making a defamatory charge against B; the letter was opened by B's clerk. *Is A liable to B?* (TORTS § 81, p. 74.)

134. A wrote a letter to X containing a defamatory statement against B; A did not mail the letter but read it to Y. *Is A liable to B, and, if so, for what?* (TORTS § 81, p. 75.)

135. A newspaper innocently put into its column of birth notices that a son had just been born to X and his wife Y. They had been married only two months. *Is the newspaper publisher liable to them if the statement was untrue?* (TORTS § 81, p. 75.)

136. A sent to B a post card containing a statement defamatory of B; the charge was false. *Is A liable to B?* (TORTS § 81, p. 75.)

137. In making his will, A included a statement defamatory of B; the statement was false. *What remedy, if any, has B?* (TORTS § 82, p. 75.)

138. A, while a youth of eighteen, was sent to a reform school because of theft. After he was released, he emigrated to a distant state, and became a successful business man. Becoming a candidate for a public office the fact of his having been guilty of theft was brought out in the campaign by his rival X. *Has A any right against X?* (TORTS § 83, p. 74.)

139. A brought action against B for libel; B proved that he honestly believed that the charge was true. *Of what significance is such proof?* (TORTS § 83, p. 76.)

140. A brought action against B for slander; B proved that he was merely repeating a statement that he had heard from X. *What liability, if any, of B to A?* (TORTS § 84, p. 76.)

141. A brought action against the X newspaper for publishing a defamatory charge against him. The X newspaper proved that it was innocent in making the statement and that as soon as its attention was called to the falsity of the statement it published a complete retraction. *Is it liable to A?* (TORTS § 85, p. 76.)

142. *What is the extent of judicial immunity for the making of defamatory charges and what is the reason for it?* (TORTS § 86, p. 77.)

143. *What is the extent of legislative immunity?* (TORTS § 87, p. 77.)

144. *Under what circumstances may a seller of goods on credit be privileged to make a charge that his vendee had committed an act of bankruptcy?* (TORTS § 88, p. 78.)

145. *Under what circumstances may a corporation send a report to its stockholders charging that its manager is short in his accounts?* (TORTS § 89, p. 78.)

146. A sought employment of B, and gave as a reference his former employer X; B asked X about A and X said he discharged A because he stole money from him; because of this A did not get employment from B. *Is X liable to A?* (TORTS § 90, p. 79.)

147. A, a friend of B's family, warned B against her proposed marriage to X and made a defamatory statement about X. *Is A liable to X?* (TORTS § 90, p. 79.)

148. *Why is a newspaper not liable for a defamatory statement contained in the report of a trial?* (TORTS § 91, p. 79.)

149. A has been asked to state his opinion of X by a prospective employer of X; A dictates his answer, containing a defamatory statement about X, to his stenographer. *What liability, if any, of A to X?* (TORTS § 92, p. 80.)

150. Upon being asked by B, a prospective employer of X, A, her present employer, made a defamatory statement about X, charging theft, and then promised X that he would not say anything more about it if she would continue to work for him. *What liability, if any, of A to X?* (TORTS § 93, p. 80.)

151. In the midst of a political campaign the X newspaper severely criticised B, a candidate for public office and made a defamatory charge against him of embezzlement. *Is X liable to B?* (TORTS § 94, p. 81.)

152. *What are the four essentials of an action for the malicious prosecution of a criminal charge?* (TORTS § 95, p. 82.)

153. A sued B for malicious prosecution and succeeded in proving the four essentials, but B proved that although the prosecution of A had failed A was really guilty of the crime charged. *Is B liable to A?* (TORTS § 95, p. 82; § 98, p. 84.)

154. A was prosecuted on a criminal charge and was convicted; the arrest of A was, however, on an invalid warrant. *What liability, if any, of B to A?* (TORTS § 96, p. 82.)

155. A was arrested under a valid warrant and B had the prosecution begun but later voluntarily abandoned it. *What liability, if any, of B to A?* (TORTS § 97, p. 83.)

156. *Under what circumstances may A recover against B for malicious prosecution where the sole activity of B was having A's house searched?* (Torts § 94, p. 82.)

157. A sued B for malicious prosecution and proved that B was actuated by an improper motive in instituting the prosecution; he now contends that the jury may properly infer therefrom that B had not reasonable and probable cause for instituting the prosecution. *Is the contention valid?* (Torts § 98, p. 83; § 99, p. 84.)

158. A sued B for malicious prosecution and proved that B did not have reasonable and probable cause for instituting the prosecution; A now contends that from this the jury may infer the existence of an improper motive. *Is the contention valid?* (Torts § 98, p. 83; § 99, p. 84.)

159. B had A arrested and prosecuted upon a criminal charge but A was acquitted. *Does this show that B had no reasonable and probable cause for instituting the prosecution?* (Torts § 98, p. 83.)

160. *Under what circumstances, if at all, may A recover from B for the malicious institution of a civil action?* (Torts § 100, p. 84.)

161. *What is meant by malicious abuse of process?* (Torts § 101, p. 84.)

162. A entered into a contract to erect a building for B; X by fraud persuaded A that B was insolvent and induced A to break his contract with B and to erect a building for X instead. *Is X liable to B?* (Torts § 102, p. 85.)

163. Facts similar to 162 ante, except that X did not act fraudulently. *What answer?* (Torts § 102, p. 85.)

164. *Why are not all strikes held to be unlawful conspiracies?* (Torts § 103, p. 86.)

165. *What is meant by a boycott? When is picketing permitted?* (Torts § 104, p. 86.)

166. *What has been the judicial attitude toward the blacklist?* (Torts § 105, p. 86.)

167. There were four competitors in a particular field of business; A, B and C combined to drive out D and succeeded. *Does D have any common law rights against them?* (Torts § 106, p. 87.)

168. A, a man of considerable wealth, conceived a deep dislike for B, a small business man; in order to drive B out of business he established C in the same business in the same neighborhood and directed C to lower prices so much that B was compelled to quit his business. *Has B any right of action at common law against A?* (Torts § 106, p. 87.)

169. B seduced X, the daughter of A. *What is the nature and extent of A's right against B? Of X's right?* (Torts § 107, p. 87; § 3, p. 29.)

170. A negligently injured X who was the sole support of his minor child, B. *What are B's rights against A?* (Torts § 107, p. 87.)

171. A negligently injured X, who was the sole support of his wife, C. *What are C's rights against A?* (Torts § 108, p. 88.)

172. A, a lifelong Democrat, was not permitted by the Democratic party leaders, to vote at a Democratic primary. *What legal rights, if any, has A?* (TORTS § 109, p. 88.)

173. *What is meant by common law copyright?* (TORTS § 110, p. 88.)

174. *What is the factual and legal difference between a trade mark and a trade name?* (TORTS § 111, p. 88.)

175. *What is meant by disparagement of property? By slander of title?* (TORTS § 112, p. 89.)

176. A newspaper published the false statement that X had discontinued his insurance business, thus causing X considerable damage. *What right, if any, has X?* (TORTS § 112, p. 89.)

177. A and B, partners in the grocery business, employed X to deliver groceries; in doing so X negligently injured Y who sued A and collected a judgment of $1,200. *What is A's right, if any, against B? Against Y?* (TORTS § 113, p. 90.)

178. A negligently injured X who later gave birth to a child Y who was also injured. *What right, if any, of Y against A?* (TORTS § 114, p. 90.)

179. B, a ten year old boy, seriously injured A, a nine year old boy, at school. *What is A's right against B? Against X, B's father?* (TORTS § 114, p. 90.)

180. A committed rape upon his fourteen year old daughter X. *What right, if any, has X against A?* (TORTS § 114, p. 90.)

181. A drove his car so negligently that he caused serious injuries to his wife B. *What, if any, are B's common law rights against A?* (TORTS § 115, p. 90.)

182. A committed an assault and battery upon X; X brought action to which there was a plea that A was insane. *Is this a good defense?* (TORTS § 116, p. 91.)

183. A negligently caused the death of B. *What is A's liability (a) at common law, (b) under Lord Campbell's Act, (c) under a survival statute?* (TORTS § 117, p. 91.)

184. *Under what circumstances may there be recovery for mental pain or nervous shock? When no recovery?* (TORTS § 118, p. 91.)

CONTRACTS

1. *What is the difference between a quasi contractual obligation and a public service obligation?* (CONTRACTS § 1, p. 93.)

2. *What are the different meanings of parol contract? Of an executed contract?* (CONTRACTS § 2, p. 94.)

3. *What is the meaning of unilateral contract? What are the different meanings of implied contract?* (CONTRACTS § 2, p. 94.)

4. *Under what circumstances is it not necessary that there be a meeting of the minds in order to form a contract? When is it necessary?* (CONTRACTS § 3, p. 94.)

5. A wrote to B offering to sell to B all the goods of a certain kind which he might need in his business during the ensuing year. B replied, "I accept." *Is there a contract?* (Contracts § 4, p. 95.)

6. A wrote to C offering to sell to B all the goods of a certain kind which he might want during the next year. C replied, "I accept." *Is there a contract?* (Contracts § 4, p. 95.)

7. A advertised certain goods at a very low price in the newspaper. There was such a heavy demand for the goods at that price that he raised the price 25 per cent. *May he do so and escape liability to those persons who wish to buy at the advertised price?* (Contracts § 5, p. 95.)

8. *Under what circumstances, if at all, may an auctioneer refuse to sell to the highest bidder?* (Contracts § 5, p. 95.)

9. A, candidate for governor, made certain definite promises as to what he would do if elected. He was elected but failed to carry out his promises. *What legal liability, if any, to the voters who elected him?* (Contracts § 6, p. 95.)

10. A, who had just learned that some one had stolen his gold watch worth only $40 but an heirloom, exclaimed that he would give $100 to any one who would give information leading to the arrest of the thief. X gave the information asked for and claims the promised $100. *Is he entitled?* (Contracts § 6, p. 95.)

11. A had been trying to buy B's farm but they had been unable to agree upon a price. Finally A mailed a letter to B offering to buy the farm for $12,000 and at about the same time B mailed a letter to A offering to sell the farm for $12,000. *Is there a contract?* (Contracts § 7, p. 95.)

12. A's residence was burned and he offered $500 to any one who would furnish information leading to the arrest of the criminal. The information was furnished to A by X who had not learned of the offer. *May X recover against A?* (Contracts § 7, p. 95.)

13. A mailed a letter to B offering to sell to B his farm for $8,000. Immediately thereafter X offered A $8,500 for the same farm and A sent a letter to B revoking his offer, but before B received the letter B had mailed to A a letter of acceptance. *Is there a contract?* (Contracts § 7, p. 96; § 8, p. 96; § 9, p. 97.)

14. A mailed a letter to B offering to sell his Ford truck for $1,100 and giving B five days within which to accept. The next day, however, A sold the truck to X for $1,150 and at once revoked his offer to B. *How advise B?* (Contracts § 8, p. 96.)

15. A sent to B an offer to sell his farm for $10,000; B wired to him, "Will you accept $9,500?" A wired back, "No." Thereupon B mailed an acceptance at the $10,000 price. *Is there a contract?* (Contracts § 8, p. 96.)

16. A mailed B a letter containing an offer to sell his farm for $9,000. B sent a wire accepting but the telegram was not delivered. *Was there a contract?* (Contracts § 9, p. 97.)

17. A mailed B a letter containing an offer to sell his farm for $9,000. B mailed a letter of acceptance but then changed his mind and got the letter back from the post office. *Is there a contract?* (Contracts § 9, p. 97.)

18. A, living in Joliet, Illinois, sent to B in Chicago, a letter agreeing to guarantee the payment by X for goods which X expected to buy from B up to $15,000. B furnished the goods but did not notify A that he had furnished them. X did not pay for the goods. *Is A liable to B?* (CONTRACTS § 10, p. 97.)

19. A wrote to B: "If you will promise to make the repairs on my office which are listed below, you may begin at once." B did not reply but began making the repairs. *Is there a contract?* (CONTRACTS § 10, p. 97.)

20. A offered to pay B $50 to harvest for him a field of wheat. After B was about half done A notified him not to do any more. *What liability, if any, of A to B?* (CONTRACTS § 10, p. 97.)

21. *Under what circumstances, if at all, will silence by an offeree operate as an acceptance?* (CONTRACTS § 11, p. 98.)

22. *Under what circumstances, if at all, may A recover from B for services performed where they are members of the same household?* (CONTRACTS § 11, p. 98; QUASI CONTRACTS § 19, p. 297.)

23. *At common law what gives validity to a contract under seal? To a simple debt?* (CONTRACTS § 12, p. 98.)

24. *What is the modern concept of consideration and how was it developed from an action on the case for deceit?* (CONTRACTS § 12, p. 98.)

25. A fell overboard on a yachting trip and B rescued him; A thereupon promised to pay B $500 for the services rendered. *What liability, if any, of A to B?* (CONTRACTS § 13, p. 99.)

26. A was running a factory and used a great deal of coal; B offered to supply him with whatever amount of coal he should wish at a certain price; A assented but later bought his coal from X at a lower price. *What liability, if any, of A to B?* (CONTRACTS § 14, p. 99.)

27. *What is the effect of the recital in a conveyance of land "In consideration of $1"? In a contract?* (CONTRACTS § 15, p. 99; REAL PROPERTY § 36, p. 191.)

28. *What is meant by the doctrine of promissory estoppel?* (CONTRACTS § 16, p. 100.)

29. *Under what circumstances is the so-called doctrine of moral consideration valid?* (CONTRACTS § 17, p. 100.)

30. A had some dental work done by B, a dentist. When B sent him a bill for $27, A sent B a check for $20 with the words written thereon, "Payment in full." B cashed the check but now insists upon being paid the other $7. *Is he entitled?* (CONTRACTS § 18, p. 100; § 19, p. 101.)

31. B owed A $275 and A was pressing him for payment; B thereupon promised that at the end of the month he would turn over to A his Ford truck in payment. At the end of the month B failed to turn over the truck. *How advise A?* (CONTRACTS § 20, p. 101.)

32. B owed A $275; A promised that if B would turn over to him his Ford truck, he (A) would never sue B for the money. B thereupon turned over the truck; A later sued for the $275. *How advise B?* (CONTRACTS § 21, p. 101; EQUITY § 10, p. 237.)

33. A owed B $275; B promised that if A would not sue him for six months he would turn over to him a pair of boxing gloves. The boxing gloves were thereupon turned over, but B sued him the next week. *How advise A?* (CONTRACTS § 21, p. 102.)

34. A claimed that B owed him $500 and threatened to bring suit on it though he knew it to be groundless. B thereupon gave A his note for $150 to compromise the claim. *May A enforce the $150 note?* (CONTRACTS § 22, p. 102.)

35. A entered into a contract with B to build a residence for B for $12,500. The next week Y offered to A a very much more desirable and profitable contract, whereupon B promised A $1,000 additional to complete the contract. After completing the contract A seeks to enforce the promise to pay the additional $1,000. *Is he entitled?* (CONTRACTS § 23, p. 102.)

36. A entered into a contract with B to build a residence for him; A met unexpected difficulties in digging the foundation and was about to quit when X, who owned several vacant lots in the neighborhood and would be benefited by the building of the residence for B, promised A $1,000 if he would complete the contract. A thereupon did so and sues X on his promise. *Is X liable?* (CONTRACTS § 24, p. 103.)

37. A's store was robbed and A offered a reward of $1,000 for the capture and conviction of the robber. The city marshal, X, captured and brought about the conviction of the robber. *Is he entitled to recover against A?* (CONTRACTS § 25, p. 103.)

38. *What was the historical explanation of the origin of the phrase, "a seal presumes consideration"?* (CONTRACTS § 27, p. 104.)

39. *What was the effect upon conveyances of land of the statutes abolishing seals? The effect upon contracts?* (CONTRACTS § 27, p. 104.)

40. A sold his automobile to B for $800 to be paid at the end of thirty days, B agreeing to pay $500 to A's creditor X and $300 to A's daughter Y. At the end of the thirty days B defaulted. *What liability, if any, to A? To X? To Y?* (CONTRACTS § 28, p. 104; § 29, p. 105; § 30, p. 105.)

41. A borrowed $5,000 from X and gave X a note therefor and a mortgage on his farm; A transferred the land to B who does not undertake to pay the debt; B transfers the land to C who does undertake to pay the debt. *Is C liable to X?* (CONTRACTS § 31, p. 106.)

42. *Upon what theory is the assignee of a non-negotiable chose in action able to recover at common law against the obligor?* (CONTRACTS § 32, p. 107.)

43. *What was the effect of the real party in interest statutes upon the substantive rights of the assignee?* (CONTRACTS § 32, p. 107.)

44. A has a claim against X for $500; A owes Y $200 and having no cash wherewith to pay Y, he assigns to Y two-fifths of his claim against X. *What remedy, if any, has Y?* (CONTRACTS § 32, p. 107.)

45. A has a claim against X for $1,000; he wishes to make a valid gift of this claim to his son B. *Under what circumstances and how can such a gift be made?* (CONTRACTS § 32, p. 107.)

46. X agrees with A to work on A's farm for six months; the next week A sells the farm to B and assigns his right to X's labor. *Is such transfer effectual?* (CONTRACTS § 33, p. 108.)

47. X, wholesaler, agrees to sell goods to A, retailer, on 90 days credit; A sells out his retail business to B and B asks X to supply goods on the same credit terms. *Is he entitled?* (CONTRACTS § 33, p. 108.)

48. *When and why was the English statute of frauds passed?* (CONTRACTS § 34, p. 108.)

49. *When, if ever, must a promise to marry be in writing?* (CONTRACTS § 35, p. 108; § 36, p. 109.)

50. A contracted orally to support X during X's natural life; after supporting X for five years A defaulted. *Is A liable to X?* (CONTRACTS § 36, p. 109.)

51. A contracted orally to support Y for three years; at the end of six months A defaulted. *Is A liable to X?* (CONTRACTS § 36, p. 109.)

52. A contracted orally to support Z for two years; at the end of three months Z refused to go on with the contract. *What right, if any, has A?* (CONTRACTS § 36, p. 109.)

53. *What is the difference between an express condition precedent and an express condition concurrent?* (CONTRACTS § 37, p. 109.)

54. *What is a condition subsequent and how does it operate?* (CONTRACTS § 38, p. 109.)

55. A was elected county treasurer and gave a bond to pay $200,000, "but if A shall well and truly perform his duties as county treasurer of Warren County for the years 1942 to 1944 inclusive, then this bond is to be of no effect." *What is the effect of this condition upon the liability of A and his fellow bondsmen?* (CONTRACTS § 38, p. 109.)

56. A engaged B to paint a portrait of A's wife C "to the satisfaction of A." When the picture was finished A declared himself not satisfied with it. *Is he liable to B?* (CONTRACTS § 39, p. 110.)

57. A and B make a bilateral contract; A sues for breach of contract; B denies liability because A is himself in default. *Why was this worked out as an implied condition instead of an excuse for non-performance?* (CONTRACTS §§ 40, 41, 42, pp. 110, 111.)

58. *What is the difference between an implied condition precedent and an implied condition concurrent?* (CONTRACTS § 42, p. 111.)

59. A contracted to sell his automobile to B for $750, delivery to be made and price paid on the first of the following month. The next day B sent word to A that he had decided that he did not want the automobile. *What is the legal effect of such a message?* (CONTRACTS § 42, p. 111.)

60. A and B on March 1 contracted to marry the following June 1. On March 23 A broke off the engagement. *What may B do?* (CONTRACTS § 43, p. 111.)

61. *What is the doctrine of Hochster v. De La Tour and what is the most serious criticism of the doctrine?* (CONTRACTS § 43, p. 111.)

62. *What is the difference in legal effect between a contract which the court construes to be divisible and one which is construed to be indivisible?* (CONTRACTS § 44, p. 112.)

63. A contracted to work for B for a year at $200 a month; at the end of three months, A became too ill to work. *How advise B?* (CONTRACTS § 45, p. 112.)

64. A contracted with B to do an act which the legislature the next month declared to be illegal. *What is the effect of such a statute upon the contract?* (CONTRACTS § 46, p. 113.)

65. A contracted to build a residence for B on B's lot; when it was about two thirds completed the partly erected building burned. *What right, if any, has B?* (CONTRACTS § 47, p. 113.)

66. A contracted to build a porch on X's house; when it was half completed the house with the partly completed porch, was entirely destroyed by fire. *How advise A?* (CONTRACTS § 47, p. 113; QUASI-CONTRACTS § 11, p. 293.)

67. A sold to B his practice as a physician and agreed never to engage in the practice of medicine in that county. *Is such contract valid.* (CONTRACTS § 48, p. 113; EQUITY § 10, p. 238.)

68. *Why are some wagers valid and some invalid?* (CONTRACTS § 49, p. 113.)

69. *Under what circumstances is it valid for a lawyer to take a case on a contingent fee? What was the English common law?* (CONTRACTS § 50, p. 113.)

70. *What is meant by usury and what is its legal effect?* (CONTRACTS § 50, p. 114.)

71. *Under what circumstances is an agreement not to marry valid?* (CONTRACTS § 51, p. 114.)

72. A, on Sunday, in violation of the Sunday statute, sold and delivered his horse to B for $150 on thirty days' credit. *At the end of thirty days what rights, if any, has A?* (CONTRACTS § 51, p. 114.)

73. A paid B $100 to procure a husband for her; not being satisfied with B's performance A sued to get back the $100. *Is she entitled?* (CONTRACTS § 51, p. 114.)

74. A contracted with B to erect for B a large business block for $300,000, both parties agreeing to submit to arbitration any points of dispute that might arise. *What is the modern judicial attitude toward such contracts?* (CONTRACTS § 52, p. 114.)

75. A, not having passed the bar examination, undertook to conduct some litigation for B. He was successful in the litigation and now sues to collect the $100 promised him by B in case of success. *Is A entitled?* (CONTRACTS § 52, p. 115.)

76. A, in Nebraska, sold liquor on credit to B, knowing that B intended to sell the liquor in Kansas in violation of the Kansas dry law. *Is A entitled to recover from B?* (CONTRACTS § 52, p. 115.)

CRIMINAL LAW

1. *In states which have abolished common law crimes, does the common law of crimes have any significance?* (CRIMINAL LAW § 1, p. 117.)

2. *What was a felony at English common law? Under modern law in this country?* (CRIMINAL LAW § 2, p. 117.)

3. *What are some of the interests protected by the law of crimes?* (CRIMINAL LAW § 3, p. 117.)

4. *Does the law of crimes ever punish the omission to act?* (CRIMINAL LAW § 4, p. 118.)

5. *What constitutes the crime of conspiracy? Of solicitation?* (CRIMINAL LAW § 4, p. 118.)

6. A was informed that a burglary was likely to be attempted on his house the following night, but he took no precautions against it. *What is the significance, if any, of his conduct?* (CRIMINAL LAW § 5, p. 118.)

7. *What is meant by statutory rape?* (CRIMINAL LAW § 5, p. 118; § 11, p. 122.)

8. *What specific intent is necessary in the crime of burglary? Arson? Larceny?* (CRIMINAL LAW § 6, p. 118.)

9. *What is the meaning of felony murder?* (CRIMINAL LAW § 6, p. 119; § 8, p. 120).

10. *Is a public nuisance or the obstruction of a public easement such as a public highway properly classified as a crime or as a public tort?* (CRIMINAL LAW § 6, p. 119.)

11. *From what angle is the motive for the alleged commission of a crime important? When not important?* (CRIMINAL LAW § 6, p. 119.)

12. A sold liquor to X, a minor, reasonably and in good faith thinking that X was an adult; X was a minor. *Is A punishable for such an act?* (CRIMINAL LAW § 6, p. 119.)

13. *Under what circumstances may one be guilty of murder by failure to act?* (CRIMINAL LAW § 7, p. 119.)

14. A inflicted upon B a mortal wound which would have caused his death within twenty-four hours; then X shot B and killed him instantly. *Is A guilty of homicide?* (CRIMINAL LAW § 7, p. 120.)

15. *How is the meaning of the phrase "with malice aforethought" determined?* (CRIMINAL LAW § 8, p. 120.)

16. A attempted to commit suicide; he failed in the attempt but in doing so accidentally killed B. *Is A guilty of any crime?* (CRIMINAL LAW § 8, p. 120.)

17. *What is usually the statutory difference between murder in the first degree and murder in the second degree?* (CRIMINAL LAW § 8, p. 121.)

18. *What are the elements of voluntary manslaughter? Of involuntary manslaughter?* (CRIMINAL LAW § 9, p. 121.)

19. *At common law what was the test of the crime of mayhem?* (CRIMINAL LAW § 10, p. 121.)

20. *What was the crime of kidnapping at common law? Under modern statute?* (CRIMINAL LAW § 10, p. 121.)

21. A obtained X's consent to sexual intercourse through fraud. *May he be guilty of rape?* (CRIMINAL LAW § 11, p. 122.)

22. *What was the importance at common law of the quickening of an unborn child that was then destroyed?* (CRIMINAL LAW § 11, p. 122.)

23. *Distinguish between a battery in the law of torts and in the law of crimes.* (CRIMINAL LAW § 12, p. 122.)

24. *In what different ways may a battery be committed?* (CRIMINAL LAW § 12, p. 122.)

25. *What kind of batteries have been made felonies by modern statutes?* (CRIMINAL LAW § 12, p. 122.)

26. *What were the five essential elements of common law burglary?* (CRIMINAL LAW § 13, p. 123.)

27. A window was left raised two inches for ventilation; A raised the window and entered the room intending to have illicit sexual intercourse with X. *Is that burglary?* (CRIMINAL LAW § 13, p. 123.)

28. In order to constitute an entry, *may it be enough if there is an entry of a finger?* (CRIMINAL LAW § 13, p. 123.)

29. *What is meant by a dwelling house?* (CRIMINAL LAW § 13, p. 123.)

30. *What legislative changes of common law burglary have been made?* (CRIMINAL LAW § 13, p. 123.)

31. A insured an old building for $6,000, much more than it was worth, and then burned it in order to collect the insurance money. *Is that arson?* (CRIMINAL LAW § 14, p. 123.)

32. A walked through B's orchard and picked a peck of apples off a tree and put them in his overcoat pockets. *Was that larceny?* (CRIMINAL LAW § 15, p. 124.)

33. B stole goods from A and then C stole the same goods from B. *Is that larceny in C?* (CRIMINAL LAW § 15, p. 124.)

34. *What changes have been made by modern statutes as to the taking of a piece of paper on which is written or printed a chose in action?* (CRIMINAL LAW § 15, p. 124.)

35. A took B's automobile merely for a ride, intending to return it. *Is that larceny?* (CRIMINAL LAW § 15, p. 124; § 19, p. 125.)

36. A hired B's horse for two days intending at the time never to return it. *Is that larceny?* (CRIMINAL LAW § 16, p. 124.)

37. A delivered a chattel to B by mistake; at the time of the delivery B knew of the mistake and decided to keep the chattel. *Is that larceny?* (CRIMINAL LAW § 17, p. 125.)

38. *What is meant by larceny by breaking bulk?* (CRIMINAL LAW § 17, p. 125.)

39. A sent his servant B to town with his (A's) horse and buggy; B sold the chattels to X and absconded with the money. *Did B commit larceny?* (CRIMINAL LAW § 17, p. 125.)

40. A bought some coal from X and sent his servant B with his (A's) wagon to get it; instead of putting the coal into A's wagon B sold the coal to Y and ran off with the money. *Is that larceny by B?* (CRIMINAL LAW § 17, p. 125).

41. A tapped a gas main beyond the meter so that he did not need to pay for the gas. *Is that larceny?* (CRIMINAL LAW § 18, p. 125.)

42. On a dark night A took B's automobile by mistake for his own. *Is that larceny? Suppose he had intended to take B's automobile but by mistake took his own?* (CRIMINAL LAW § 19, p. 125).

43. In order to prevent a horse from being used as evidence against his friend in a prosecution for larceny, A took and destroyed the horse. *Is that larceny in A?* (CRIMINAL LAW § 19, p. 126.)

44. *What is the difference between grand larceny and petit larceny? Between simple larceny and compound larceny?* (CRIMINAL LAW § 20, p. 126.)

45. A bought goods with intent not to pay for them. *Is he liable in tort for deceit? Has he committed any crime?* (CRIMINAL LAW § 21, p. 127.)

46. *Who may be guilty of embezzlement?* (CRIMINAL LAW § 22, p. 127.)

47. *What are the essentials of common law robbery?* (CRIMINAL LAW § 23, p. 127.)

48. A's goods were stolen by B and later recovered by A, but X did not know this and thought the goods were still in B's possession when he received them. *Is he guilty of a crime?* (CRIMINAL LAW § 24, p. 127.)

49. A painted a picture and in the corner thereof he painted in the name of a well known artist and sold the picture for $1,000; A was comparatively unknown. *What crime, if any, did A commit?* (CRIMINAL LAW § 25, p. 128.)

50. A bought goods from X and gave X a check for $100 in payment thereof; X raised the amount to $200 and cashed the check. *Was he guilty of forgery?* (CRIMINAL LAW § 25, p. 128.)

51. *Of what did the common law crime of uttering consist?* (CRIMINAL LAW § 25, p. 128.)

52. *In what important respect does the law of criminal libel differ from the law of tort libel?* (CRIMINAL LAW § 26, p. 128; TORTS § 83, p. 76.)

53. *Under what circumstances is a trespass upon land a crime?* (CRIMINAL LAW § 26, p. 129.)

54. *What is subornation of perjury?* (CRIMINAL LAW § 27, p. 129.)

55. *What is meant by compounding a felony?* (CRIMINAL LAW § 27, p. 129.)

56. *What is maintenance? Champerty?* (CRIMINAL LAW § 27, p. 129; CONTRACTS § 50, p. 119.)

57. A, having a slaughterhouse close to a stream, polluted the stream. *For what crime or public tort may he be prosecuted?* (CRIMINAL LAW § 28, p. 129; § 6, p. 119.)

58. *What is the crime of bigamy and where did it originate?* (CRIMINAL LAW § 29, p. 130.)

59. *What is incest?* (CRIMINAL LAW § 29, p. 130.)

60. *What constitutes insanity in the criminal law?* (CRIMINAL LAW § 30, p. 131.)

61. *What is the effect of insanity in the law of crimes? In the law of torts?* (CRIMINAL LAW § 30, p. 131; TORTS § 116, p. 91.)

62. *Under what circumstances, if at all, is voluntary drunkenness a defense to a criminal prosecution?* (CRIMINAL LAW § 30, p. 131.)

63. *As to the effect of infancy, contrast the law of crimes with the law of torts.* (CRIMINAL LAW § 31, p. 131; TORTS § 114, p. 90.)

64. *Under what circumstances, at common law, was coverture a defense to a criminal prosecution?* (CRIMINAL LAW § 31, p. 131.)

65. *Under what circumstances may mistake of law be a defense?* (CRIMINAL LAW § 32, p. 131.)

66. *Under what circumstances may mistake of fact be a defense?* (CRIMINAL LAW § 32, p. 131.)

67. A had sexual intercourse with X, a girl of fifteen who looked to be eighteen and whom A thought to be eighteen. *Is this a defense to a prosecution for statutory rape?* (CRIMINAL LAW § 32, p. 131.)

68. A took food from B in order to preserve his life. *Is this a defense to a prosecution for larceny?* (CRIMINAL LAW § 32, p. 132.)

69. *What is meant by a principal in the second degree?* (CRIMINAL LAW § 33, p. 132.)

70. *Who is an accessory before the fact? An accessory after the fact?* (CRIMINAL LAW § 33, p. 132.)

71. *May State X punish one of its own citizens for an act done in State Y?* (CRIMINAL LAW § 34, p. 132.)

72. A shoots across the state line and kills X. *In which state has A committed the crime of murder?* (CRIMINAL LAW § 34, p. 132.)

73. A stole goods in State X and carried them into State Y. *May the latter State punish A for larceny?* (CRIMINAL LAW § 34, p. 132.)

74. A killed B in State X and fled to State Y to escape prosecution. *Must the governor of State Y surrender A to the peace authorities of State X?* (CRIMINAL LAW § 35, p. 133.)

75. A shot across the line between State X and State Y and killed B; the governor of State X undertook to extradite A to State Y. *May he do so?* (CRIMINAL LAW § 35, p. 133.)

76. *What is the purpose of a preliminary examination of a person arrested for crime?* (CRIMINAL LAW § 36, p. 133.)

77. Where A had been arrested on a charge of larceny of $100 the court fixed the bail at $1,000; A claims that this is excessive. *What is his remedy?* (CRIMINAL LAW § 36, p. 133.)

78. *What is an indictment? An information?* (CRIMINAL LAW § 37, p. 134.)

79. *Need the indictment state the name of the person indicted? Need it describe the crime charged? Why?* (CRIMINAL LAW § 37, p. 134.)

80. In an indictment for larceny, *must the value of the property alleged to have been stolen be set forth? Why?* (CRIMINAL LAW § 37, p. 134.)

81. *Must the indictment allege a day upon which the crime charged was committed? Must it prove it?* (CRIMINAL LAW § 37, p. 139.)

82. *Must the indictment allege the place where the crime charged was committed? Under what circumstances must it be proved?* (CRIMINAL LAW § 37, p. 135.)

83. *What is meant by counts in an indictment and why are they used?* (CRIMINAL LAW § 38, p. 135.)

84. *When may several persons be joined in one indictment?* (CRIMINAL LAW § 38, p. 135.)

85. *When is a motion to quash sustained?* (CRIMINAL LAW § 39, p. 135.)

86. *What is meant by an arraignment? By a plea of nolo contendere?* (CRIMINAL LAW § 39, p. 135.)

87. *What is the function of a demurrer?* (CRIMINAL LAW § 39, p. 135.)

88. *What defenses may defendant prove under a plea of not guilty?* (CRIMINAL LAW § 39, p. 136.)

89. *What is meant by double jeopardy, and where does jeopardy begin?* (CRIMINAL LAW § 39, p. 136.)

90. A negligently ran over and killed X and Y; he was prosecuted for involuntary manslaughter for the killing of X and was acquitted. *May he later be prosecuted for involuntary manslaughter for the killing of Y?* (CRIMINAL LAW § 39, p. 136.)

91. *May a defendant charged with crime validly consent to being tried by less than twelve jurors?* (CRIMINAL LAW § 40, p. 137.)

92. *Is it important that the judge be present throughout the trial? The defendant?* (CRIMINAL LAW § 40, p. 137.)

93. *When will a motion in arrest of judgment be sustained?* (CRIMINAL LAW § 40, p. 137.)

94. *Does the court or jury determine the amount of the punishment?* (CRIMINAL LAW § 41, p. 138.)

95. *What is the purpose of an indeterminate sentence?* (CRIMINAL LAW § 41, p. 138.)

96. *What are the grounds for a motion for a new trial?* (CRIMINAL LAW § 41, p. 138.)

97. *What is meant by a writ of error?* (CRIMINAL LAW § 41, p. 138.)

98. *May the state take an appeal?* (CRIMINAL LAW § 41, p. 138.)

DOMESTIC RELATIONS AND PERSONS

1. A who was separated from his wife X, promised B that if X should die or procure a divorce from A then A would marry B. The following month X died. *May B recover from A for breach of contract if A refuses to marry her?* (DOMESTIC RELATIONS § 1, p. 140.)

2. A, being married to X, concealed this fact from B upon A's engagement to marry B. A refused later to marry B because he was already married to X. *Is it a good defense to an action for breach of contract to marry?* (DOMESTIC RELATIONS § 1, p. 140.)

3. *In what two respects is a breach of contract to marry similar to a tort?* (DOMESTIC RELATIONS § 1, p. 140.)

4. A orally agreed, on March 10, 1947, to marry B in June, 1948. *Is the contract enforcible?* (DOMESTIC RELATIONS § 1, p. 140.)

5. *In what respect, if at all, is marriage a civil contract?* (DOMESTIC RELATIONS § 2, p. 140.)

6. *What is meant by a common law marriage?* (DOMESTIC RELATIONS § 2, p. 141.)

7. A, while living apart from his wife X, married B and continued to live with her after X died. A then died and B claims a widow's right in A's property. *Under what circumstances, if at all, is B entitled?* (DOMESTIC RELATIONS § 2, p. 141.)

8. A, while living apart from his wife X, married B; later A wished to have the marriage to B declared void on the ground that he was already married. *Is he entitled?* (DOMESTIC RELATIONS § 3, p. 141.)

9. A and X married before either reached the age required by statute; after both reached the required age they lived together for a year and then X asked for a decree of annulment. *Is she entitled?* (DOMESTIC RELATIONS § 4, p. 141.)

10. *In what state may a decree of annulment be rendered?* (DOMESTIC RELATIONS § 4, p. 142.)

11. *If one of the parties to a marriage is feeble minded or insane which one may maintain a suit for annulment?* (DOMESTIC RELATIONS § 5, p. 142.)

12. *Under what circumstances, if at all, is impotency or sterility a basis for an annulment?* (DOMESTIC RELATIONS § 5, p. 142.)

13. *What fraudulent representations furnish sufficient basis for an annulment?* (DOMESTIC RELATIONS § 6, p. 142.)

14. A was forced by bastardy proceedings to marry X; later A sued for annulment on the ground of duress. *Is he entitled?* (DOMESTIC RELATIONS § 6, p. 142.)

15. *Where a marriage is annulled what effect does this have upon the legitimacy of the children?* (DOMESTIC RELATIONS § 7, p. 142.)

16. *How is divorce different from annulment?* (DOMESTIC RELATIONS § 8, p. 143.)

17. *What is the modern meaning of adultery?* (DOMESTIC RELATIONS § 9, p. 143.)

18. *How is adultery usually proved?* (DOMESTIC RELATIONS § 9, p. 143.)

19. *What is meant by mental cruelty?* (DOMESTIC RELATIONS § 10, p. 143.)

20. *Does inexcusable refusal of sexual intercourse amount to cruelty? To desertion?* (DOMESTIC RELATIONS §§ 10, 11, pp. 143, 144.)

21. *Is divorce sometimes granted for grounds existing at the time of marraige? What practical advantage is this?* (DOMESTIC RELATIONS § 12, p. 144.)

22. *What is meant by collusion? Is it frequently set up as a defense to a suit for divorce?* (DOMESTIC RELATIONS § 13, p. 144.)

23. *What is meant by connivance?* (DOMESTIC RELATIONS § 13, p. 144.)

24. *What is the effect of condonation upon a later suit for divorce?* (DOMESTIC RELATIONS § 13, p. 145.)

25. A brought suit for divorce against X on the ground of adultery and proved it; X set up in defense and proved that A had also been guilty of adultery. *What decision?* (DOMESTIC RELATIONS § 13, p. 145.)

26. *Does bankruptcy of the husband put an end to his obigation to pay alimony? His death?* (DOMESTIC RELATIONS § 14, p. 146.)

27. A of New York brought suit for divorce in Nevada against X after A had been in Nevada for the six weeks required by Nevada law; X entered appearance in the suit. *Is the divorce valid in other states?* (DOMESTIC RELATIONS § 15, p. 146; CONFLICT OF LAWS § 16, p. 420.)

28. Facts same as 27 ante, except that X did not enter appearance and was not served with process in Nevada. *Is the divorce valid in other states?* (DOMESTIC RELATIONS § 15, p. 146.)

29. *What is the usual reason for bringing a suit for judicial separation? What is the effect of a judicial separation decree?* (DOMESTIC RELATIONS § 16, p. 146.)

30. *At common law what was the right of the husband to the wife's property? In equity? Under modern statutes?* (DOMESTIC RELATIONS § 17, p. 147.)

31. *At common law how could a married woman convey her land? Her inchoate right of dower in her husband's land?* (DOMESTIC RELATIONS § 18, p. 147.)

32. *Under modern statutes what is the liability of the husband for torts committed by the wife?* (DOMESTIC RELATIONS § 19, p. 147.)

33. *Why were marriage settlements desirable a hundred years ago?* (DOMESTIC RELATIONS § 20, p. 148.)

34. *At common law was the husband entitled to the wife's earnings? Under modern statutes?* (DOMESTIC RELATIONS § 21, p. 148.)

35. *Under what circumstances, if at all, is a husband liable for torts committed by him upon his wife? What effect, if any, is the fact that the husband carries insurance and the loss would ultimately fall upon the insurance company?* (DOMESTIC RELATIONS § 22, p. 148.)

36. *What is the present status of actions by the husband for alienation of affections, criminal conversation and seduction?* (DOMESTIC RELATIONS § 23, p. 149.)

37. *Under what circumstances, and to what extent are separation agreements valid and enforcible?* (DOMESTIC RELATIONS § 24, p. 149.)

38. A decides that his wife X has been buying too heavily upon his credit and he wishes to stop any further buying by her on his credit. *How should he proceed?* (DOMESTIC RELATIONS § 25, p. 149; AGENCY § 13, p. 161.)

39. A abandoned his wife X, and she was compelled to borrow $100 from B and use $200 of her own money with which to buy necessaries. *How advise A?* (DOMESTIC RELATIONS § 25, p. 149.)

40. A abandoned his wife X, and notified B not to supply goods to her on his (A's) credit. *What is the effect of such notice?* (DOMESTIC RELATIONS § 25, p. 149.)

41. Facts same as 40 ante except that A supplied X with enough money with which to buy necessaries. *Would you change your answer?* (DOMESTIC RELATIONS § 25, p. 149.)

42. *What is the modern attitude of courts in awarding the custody of minor children in divorce and separation cases?* (DOMESTIC RELATIONS § 26, p. 150.)

43. *What is the origin and extent of the father's duty to support his minor children?* (DOMESTIC RELATIONS § 27, p. 150.)

44. *What is the effect of emancipation upon the right of the father to the earnings of his minor child? To his duty to support?* (DOMESTIC RELATIONS § 28, p. 151.)

45. A's sixteen year old son B was employed by the month on the farm of A's neighbor C; X negligently injured B. *What is A's right against X?* (DOMESTIC RELATIONS § 29, p. 151.)

46. A, seventeen years old, negligently drove his father's car, damaging the car, and causing personal injuries to his father. *Is A liable?* (DOMESTIC RELATIONS § 30, p. 151.)

47. A, eighteen years old, employed a chauffeur X, who, as such chauffeur, negligently drove against Y and injured Y and his automobile. *Is A liable?* (DOMESTIC RELATIONS § 30, p. 151.)

48. A, twenty years old, made a contract with B to buy B's car for $700, and after getting the car refused to pay for it; A had falsely represented to B that he was of age. *How advise B?* (DOMESTIC RELATIONS § 30, p. 152.)

49. A, twenty years old, bought food from B, a grocer, and clothing from C and now refuses to pay. *What is his liability?* (DOMESTIC RELATIONS § 31, p. 152.)

50. A, twenty years old, was employed by X to work for six months at $100 a month, but inexcusably quit after working for a month. *What are A's rights and liabilities?* (DOMESTIC RELATIONS § 31, p. 152.)

51. A, an infant, entered into a partnership with B, contributing $1,000 to the partnership capital. After the partnership had bought goods on credit from X to the amount of $600, A put an end to the partnership. *What are his rights and liabilities?* (DOMESTIC RELATIONS § 31, p. 152.)

52. A, an infant of nineteen years of age, bought a tract of land from X for $1,000 which he paid and an automobile from Y for which he paid $700. At the end of a year A consults you. *How advise him?* (DOMESTIC RELATIONS § 32, p. 152.)

53. While A was absent from the country his wife gave birth to a child. A feels sure that the child is illegitimate. *How will he prove the fact?* (DOMESTIC RELATIONS § 33, p. 153.)

54. *What is the modern rule as to inheritance by or from an illegitimate child?* (DOMESTIC RELATIONS § 33, p. 154.)

55. A, an unmarried woman, gave birth to a child; she insists that X is the child's father. *To what extent may blood grouping tests be used in deciding the question of paternity?* (DOMESTIC RELATIONS § 33, p. 154.)

AGENCY

1. The X Insurance Company employed A to solicit insurance. While so engaged and operating his own car A negligently collided with B and damaged B's automobile. *Is the X Insurance Company liable to B?* (AGENCY § 1, p. 155.)

2. A was purchasing agent for the Y Company. B, salesman for the Z Manufacturing Company, paid A $1,000 for A's entering into a contract for supplies furnished to the Y Company. *Upon learning of this, what are the rights of the Y Company against A?* (AGENCY § 2, p. 155.)
What effect, if any, did such conduct of A have upon A's right to compensation for his services?

3. T, trustee for C, contracted to sell the trust property to X but later refused to convey the property to X. *What remedy does X have against T? Against C?* (AGENCY § 2, p. 156.)

4. B sends goods to A upon consignment; A sells only half the goods, and goes into bankruptcy. B claims the unsold goods as against A's general creditors. *Is he entitled?* (AGENCY § 3, p. 156.)

5. B sells goods to X, retaining title to the goods by way of security. X becomes bankrupt; B claims the goods as against X's general creditors. *Is he entitled?* (AGENCY § 3, p. 156.)

6. A, desiring some selling experience, undertook to act gratuitously as X's

agent; in thus acting he exceeded his authority in making a contract with Y; Y sued A for breach of implied warranty of authority (AGENCY § 7, p. 158) and A sets up in defense that there was no contract of agency. *Is it a good defense?* (AGENCY § 4, p. 156.)

7. T is suing P for breach of a contract made by A who purported to act for P; P denies that A had any authority to act for him. *Is A a competent witness to prove the agency? Is a declaration made by A out of court competent evidence against P to prove the agency?* (AGENCY § 4, p. 156).

8. T is suing P, an infant, for breach of a contract made by A. *Of what importance is the fact that P acted through an agent?* (AGENCY § 4, p. 156.)

9. T is suing P for breach of a contract made by A. *Of what importance is the fact that A was an infant?* (AGENCY § 4, p. 156.)

10. A was authorized by P to receive payment of a note against T; T paid A the note before it was due and A absconded with the money. *May P recover from T?* (AGENCY § 5, p. 157.)

11. T, an employee of the X. R. R. Co. was seriously injured due to the negligence of another employee; in settling with T, the president of the railroad company agreed that T should have a job for the rest of his life as watchman at a crossing. *Is the railroad company bound by the agreement?* (AGENCY § 5, p. 157.)

12. P authorized A to buy supplies on credit, but not to exceed $ 12,000. After buying $12,000 worth of supplies he contracted with T to buy $3,000 worth more on credit. *Is P bound on the contract? What remedy has T?* (AGENCY § 5, p. 157; § 7, p. 158.)

13. P entrusted a bill of lading to A with instructions that A should not sell the goods represented by the bill of lading until the following month. The same day, however, A indorsed the bill of lading to T who advanced to A $3,000 toward the purchase price of the goods and A absconded with the money. *Is T entitled to the goods upon paying the rest of the price?* (AGENCY § 6, p. 158.)

14. A, on behalf of P, purported to make a contract with T. P defaulted on the contract and T sued him for breach of contract; P escaped liability by setting up and proving that he was an infant. T now seeks to hold A liable for not telling T that P was an infant. *May he do so?* (AGENCY § 7, p. 158.)

15. A deliberately exceeded his authority in purporting to enter into a contract with T on behalf of P. When P refused to ratify the purported contract T asks you whether he may recover in tort against A. *What answer?* (AGENCY § 7, p. 158.)

16. A on behalf of P, entered into a contract with T a trustee for the purchase of trust property, knowing that the trustee was acting in violation of his trust. After the trustee conveyed the trust property to P, the beneficiary of the trust claimed the property on the ground that P was not a bona fide purchaser for value without notice. *What answer?* (AGENCY § 8, p. 159.)

17. P wished to buy a piece of land from T but feared that T would either not sell it to him at all or would demand an exorbitant price for it; thereupon P employed A to buy it from T, purporting to act for himself. After the written

contract was made T learned that A was acting for P. *May P enforce the contract against T?* (AGENCY § 8, p. 159.)

18. A contracted in writing to sell land to T purporting to act for himself; the land really belonged to P who now seeks specific performance of the contract. *Is P entitled?* (AGENCY § 8, p. 159.)

19. A, purporting to act for himself but really acting for P, contracted to buy goods from T; the market value of the goods increased rapidly and T refused to perform; A sues T for breach of contract. *May he recover?* (AGENCY § 9, p. 159.)

20. A purporting to act for himself but really acting for P, contracted to buy goods from T; the market value of the goods decreased rapidly and P refused to perform; T sues P for breach of contract. *May he recover?* (AGENCY § 10, p. 159.)

21. Facts similar to 20 ante; T sues A for breach of contract. *May he recover?* (AGENCY § 10, p. 160.)

22. Facts similar to 20 ante; T sues A and gets judgment and finds that A is execution proof; he then sues P. *May he recover?* (AGENCY § 10, p. 160.)

23. Facts similar to 20 ante, except that A gives to T a negotiable note for part of the purchase price of the goods. *May T recover from P on the note?* (AGENCY § 10, p. 160.)

24. In excess of his authority, A undertook to make a contract between P and T. When P learned of the contract he was pleased with it and ratified it, but when T learned that A had acted in excess of his authority, he repudiated the transaction. *How advise P?* (AGENCY § 11, p. 160.)

25. *What effect does P's later ratification have upon A's liability to T? His failure to ratify?* (AGENCY § 11, p. 160.)

26. *Under what circumstances must P act promptly in ratifying?* (AGENCY § 12, p. 160.)

27. P contracted to employ A as his agent for a year but at the end of a month wrongfully discharged him. *What effect does this have upon the continued existence of the agency?* (AGENCY § 13, p. 161.)

28. P employed A for a year; after P's death but before A learned of his death he entered into a contract with T. *Is P's executor liable on this contract?* (AGENCY § 13, p. 161.)

29. When it is said that a particular power to act as agent is irrevocable because it was coupled with an interest, *what is the meaning of the word "interest"?* (AGENCY § 14, p. 161.)

30. P employed A for a year and agreed that A's authority should be irrevocable. In spite of this stipulation P later revokes A's authority. *What effect does this have upon P's rights and liabilities to A and to a third party?* (AGENCY § 14, p. 161.)

PERSONAL PROPERTY

1. *What is the technical difference between personal property and chattels? Between real property and land?* (PERSONAL PROPERTY § 1, p. 162.)

2. A, while hunting, shot and killed a silver fox and he sold the pelt to X for $75. The fox had escaped from B's land where B was engaged in breeding and selling silver foxes. *How advise B?* (PERSONAL PROPERTY § 2, p. 163.)

3. A employed B as a farm laborer; B while working for A found a pocket book containing a hundred dollars. *As between A and B who is better entitled?* (PERSONAL PROPERTY § 3, p. 163.)

4. A while riding on the subway, left a parcel on the seat when he arrived at his destination. *Who is better entitled, A or the subway company?* (PERSONAL PROPERTY § 3, p. 163.)

5. A wrongfully took B's chattel and concealed it until the statute of limitations had run. *How advise B?* (PERSONAL PROPERTY § 4, p. 163.)

6. A wrongfully took B's chattel and B sued A in trover and recovered judgment for the value of the chattel; then B found out that A, being married, was execution proof. *How advise B?* (PERSONAL PROPERTY § 5, p. 164.)

7. A wrongfully took a pine log from B and made it into tooth picks. The log was worth $10, the toothpicks $200. *How advise B?* (PERSONAL PROPERTY § 6, p. 164.)

8. A wrongfully took 4,000 bricks from B and used them in making a chimney in a house he was erecting. *How advise B?* (PERSONAL PROPERTY § 6, p. 164.)

9. A mixed 1000 bushels of B's wheat with 2,000 bushels of his own and became insolvent. *How advise B?* (PERSONAL PROPERTY § 7, p. 164.)

10. A wrongfully took several head of B's cattle and put them in his own herd of somewhat similar cattle. *How advise B?* (PERSONAL PROPERTY § 7, p. 164.)

11. A and X were engaged to be married and A gave X an engagement ring. X later wrongfully broke off the engagement. *How advise A?* (PERSONAL PROPERTY § 8, p. 165.)

12. A wishes to transfer to B who lives in Australia, the legal title to all his office furniture by way of gift. *How may he do it? How may he transfer the equitable interest in the furniture to B?* (PERSONAL PROPERTY § 8, p. 165; TRUSTS § 11, p. 270.)

13. A wishes to transfer to B by way of gift a life insurance policy on A's own life, payable to A's estate. *How may he do this effectually?* (PERSONAL PROPERTY § 8, p. 165.)

14. *In what respects is a bailee like a trustee? How unlike?* (PERSONAL PROPERTY § 9, p. 165.)

15. *In what respects is a bailee different from a servant?* (PERSONAL PROPERTY § 9, p. 165.)

16. *How does a bailee differ from an ordinary vendee? From a conditional vendee?* (PERSONAL PROPERTY § 9, p. 165.)

17. *What is the duty of a bailee to a bailor with respect to the goods bailed?* (PERSONAL PROPERTY § 10, p. 166.)

18. A gratuitously loaned his automobile truck to B; while in B's possession X took it from B. *How advise X at to his liability to A? To B?* (PERSONAL PROPERTY § 11, p. 166.)

19. A rented his automobile truck to B for two months at $30 a month; while thus in B's possession X took it from B. *How advise X as to his liability to A? To B?* (PERSONAL PROPERTY § 11, p. 166.)

20. *At common law who was entitled to a retaining lien and how did he enforce it?* (PERSONAL PROPERTY § 12, p. 167.)

21. *How is the holder of a common law retaining lien different from a pledgee? From a chattel mortgagee?* (PERSONAL PROPERTY § 12, p. 167.)

22. *Is an agister of animals entitled to a common law retaining lien? Why?* (PERSONAL PROPERTY § 13, p. 167.)

23. A took a pair of shoes to a shoe cobbler to be half-soled but failed to pay for the services. Later A took another pair to him and now the cobbler wishes to hold the second pair for the value of his services on the first pair. *Is he entitled?* (PERSONAL PROPERTY § 13, p. 167.)

24. *What is the basis of the lien of the common carrier and that of the innkeeper?* (PERSONAL PROPERTY § 14, p. 167.)

25. *What is the basis of the warehouseman's lien?* (PERSONAL PROPERTY § 14, p. 167.)

26. *Under what circumstances is an innkeeper's lien good against some one other than a guest?* (PERSONAL PROPERTY § 14, p. 107.)

27. B stole A's goods and sent the goods by motor truck from St. Louis to Kansas City. *Is the motor truck company's lien for carriage good against A?* (PERSONAL PROPERTY § 14, p. 167.)

28. *What is the basis and extent of the lien of a commission merchant?* (PERSONAL PROPERTY § 15, p. 167.)

29. *What is the extent of an attorney's retaining lien?* (PERSONAL PROPERTY § 15, p. 168.)

30. *What were some of the difficulties of the lien holder?* (PERSONAL PROPERTY § 16, p. 168; "Pigs is Pigs" by Ellis Parker Butler.)

31. *In what ways may a lien be lost?* (PERSONAL PROPERTY § 16, p. 168.)

32. *What is the effect of a surrender to the owner of a part of the goods on which there is a lien?* (PERSONAL PROPERTY § 16, p. 168.)

REAL PROPERTY

1. *How was an estate in fee simple created at common law? Under modern statutes?* (REAL PROPERTY § 1, p. 170.)

2. *How was an estate tail created and what was its purpose? What is the present status of estates tail in this country?* (REAL PROPERTY § 2, p. 170.)

3. A, having a life estate in some land, conveyed it to B who died before A. *Who is entitled to the unexpired portion of the estate?* (REAL PROPERTY § 3, p. 170.)

4. As between a life tenant and the reversioner or remainderman, *who pays ordinary taxes? Special assessments? A mortgage on both interests?* (REAL PROPERTY § 3, p. 171.)

5. *Is an estate for years personal property or real property?* (REAL PROPERTY § 4, p. 171.)

6. *What is the difference between a tenant for years and a licensee? Is a share-cropper a licensee?* (REAL PROPERTY § 5, p. 171.)

7. A entered into a written contract to sell his farm to B for $7,000 and turned over possession to B. *What is B's right at law? In equity?* (REAL PROPERTY § 6, p. 171; EQUITY § 5, p. 234.)

8. A entered into possession of land under an oral lease for four years at $1,200 a year; the lease was invalid by a local statute but A stayed in possession and paid rent after the expiration of the first year. *What is his status?* (REAL PROPERTY § 6, p. 171.)

9. A entered into possession of farm land without any stipulation as to the length of his tenancy. B, the landlord, consults you as to putting an end to the tenancy. *How advise him?* (REAL PROPERTY § 6, p. 171.)

10. A entered into possession of land under a year's lease; at the end of that period he refused to give up possession. *How advise B, the landlord?* (REAL PROPERTY § 7, p. 172.)

11. A entered into possession of land under a year's lease. *Must he give notice that he expects to move out at the end of the year? If he stays another year?* (REAL PROPERTY § 8, p. 172.)

12. *Is it necessary that a landlord turn over the premises in a tenantable condition? Must he keep the premises in repair?* (REAL PROPERTY § 9, p. 172.)

13. *Who pays the taxes on leased land?* (REAL PROPERTY § 9, p. 172.)

14. A leases to B for a year at $100 a month rent; at the end of a month X notifies B that he (X) is the owner, and not A. *How advise B?* (REAL PROPERTY § 10, p. 173.)

15. A leases to B for the year a piece of land upon which there is a building, at $80 a month rent. At the end of two months the building burns. *What advice to B as to his liability to pay rent?* (REAL PROPERTY § 10, p. 173.)

16. A leases to C for two years an apartment at $100 a month rent. After six months the apartment house burns. *Must C continue to pay rent?* (REAL PROPERTY § 10, p. 173.)

17. A leases to B for two years; the premises become uninhabitable because of A's default. *How advise B?* (REAL PROPERTY § 10, p. 174.)

18. A leased to B for a year at $75 a month rent; B defaults. *What remedies has A?* (REAL PROPERTY § 10, p. 174.)

19. *What is the difference between an assignment by the lessee of his interest and a sub-lease? What difference does it make to the landlord?* (REAL PROPERTY § 11, p. 174.)

20. A leases to B for three years at $120 a month rent and two months later A transfers his interest in the land to X. *To whom should B pay rent?* (REAL PROPERTY § 11, p. 174.)

21. Same facts as 20 ante. *What effect does this have upon A's liability to B as to other covenants?* (REAL PROPERTY § 11, p. 174.)

22. A leases to B for two years at $110 a month; at the end of six months B moves out. *How advise A?* (REAL PROPERTY § 12, p. 175.)

23. *What constitutes a joint tenancy and how may it be destroyed?* (REAL PROPERTY § 13, p. 176.)

24. *What is the chief practical difference between a joint tenancy and a tenancy in common?* (REAL PROPERTY § 13, p. 175.)

25. A conveyed land to "X and Y". *Do they take as joint tenants or tenants in common?* (REAL PROPERTY § 13, p. 175.)

26. *How is a tenancy by the entirety created?* (REAL PROPERTY § 14, p. 176.)

27. *What is the effect of a divorce upon a tenancy by the entirety?* (REAL PROPERTY § 14, p. 176.)

28. *At common law what was the husband's rights in the wife's property during the marriage? Under modern statutes?* (REAL PROPERTY § 15, p. 177.)

29. *When was a surviving husband entitled to curtesy? Of what did it consist?* (REAL PROPERTY § 16, p. 177.)

30. *Of what did dower consist? In what way could a wife release her inchoate dower right?* (REAL PROPERTY § 17, p. 177.)

31. *If the husband makes a provision for his wife in his will, may she have that in addition to dower?* (REAL PROPERTY § 17, p. 177.)

32. *Was a widow entitled to dower in land in which her deceased husband held only the equitable interest?* (REAL PROPERTY § 17, p. 177.)

33. *What is the difference between the effect of a condition precedent and a condition subsequent?* (REAL PROPERTY § 18, p. 178.)

34. *When will a court tend to construe language as creating a condition subsequent rather than a condition precedent?* (REAL PROPERTY § 18, p. 178.)

35. *When will a court tend to construe language as creating a covenant rather than a condition subsequent?* (REAL PROPERTY § 18, p. 178.)

36. A leased to B with a condition against assigning the lease and B does assign it to C and A accepts rent from C. *What is the effect of such acceptance?* (REAL PROPERTY § 18, p. 178.)

37. *What is a base or determinable fee and how does it differ from an estate subject to a condition subsequent?* (REAL PROPERTY § 19, p. 179.)

38. By will A devised land to X in fee but if X should die without issue, then to Y in fee. *What does Y get and what is it usually called?* (REAL PROPERTY § 19, p. 179.)

39. A conveys to B for life, then to C for ninety-nine years. *What does A have left?* (REAL PROPERTY § 20, p. 180.)

40. A conveys to B for life then to the heirs of C who was still alive at the time of the conveyance. *What estate do C's heirs take and why?* (REAL PROPERTY § 20, p. 180.)

41. A devises to X for life and then to executors to divide the property in fee between Y and Z. *Are the remainders to Y and Z vested or contingent?* (REAL PROPERTY § 20, p. 180.)

42. *What was the rule in Shelley's Case?* (REAL PROPERTY § 20, p. 180.)

43. A by bargain and sale deed conveyed to X one estate in fee to begin five years after A's death. *What estate, if any, does X get?* (REAL PROPERTY § 21, p. 181.)

44. A conveyed land to X for life with remainder in fee as X shall appoint. X is insolvent. *How advise his creditors?* (REAL PROPERTY § 22, p. 181.)

45. A conveyed land to X for life with power to appoint the remainder among the children of Y. X died without exercising the power. *How advise Y's children?* (REAL PROPERTY § 23, p. 182.)

46. A conveyed land to X for life with remainder in fee as X should appoint by will. X undertook to appoint to the children of B but the will was not valid. *How advise B's children?* (REAL PROPERTY § 24, p. 182.)

47. *What caused the development of the so-called rule against perpetuities?* (REAL PROPERTY § 25, p. 182.)

48. *What is a more accurate name for the rule?* (REAL PROPERTY § 25, p. 182.)

49. *What is the usual statement of the rule?* (REAL PROPERTY § 25, p. 183.)

50. *In order that a contingent devise or bequest shall be valid is it sufficient that it may vest within the period or is it necessary that it must vest within the period?* (REAL PROPERTY § 26, p. 183.)

51. A devised property to X "from and after the date of the probate of this will". *Is the devise valid?* (REAL PROPERTY § 26, p. 184.)

52. A in 1947 devised property to X for life with remainder in fee to those children, grandchildren and great grandchildren of A who might be living at

the death of all the members of the present United States Supreme Court. *Is the devise in fee good?* (REAL PROPERTY § 26, p. 184.)

53. A, having large real estate holdings, devised forty acres of land to each son of X who shall reach twenty one years of age. *Is the devise valid?* (REAL PROPERTY § 27, p. 185.)

54. Same as 53 ante except that twenty-five years is substituted for twenty-one. *Is the devise valid?* (REAL PROPERTY § 27, p. 185.)

55. *Which of the following interests are within the rule: (a) springing and shifting uses; (b) executory devises; (c) contingent remainders; (d) vested interests; (e) possibility of reverter after a determinable fee; (f) right of entry after breaking of a condition subsequent?* (REAL PROPERTY § 28, p. 186.)

56. A leased to X for forty years with an option to buy the fee for $40,000 at any time before the expiration of the lease. *Is the option valid?* (REAL PROPERTY § 28, p. 186.)

57. *Is an option to buy chattels within the rule?* (REAL PROPERTY § 28, p. 186; EQUITY § 6, p. 235.)

58. A devised property upon trust to B for life, but if B should die without issue then to C for thirty years, then to the D hospital. *Is the gift to the hospital valid?* (REAL PROPERTY § 29, p. 183.)

59. *What is the expressed basis of the New York rule against perpetuities?* (REAL PROPERTY § 30, p. 187.)

60. Same facts as 54 ante. *Is the devise valid under the New York rule?* (REAL PROPERTY § 31, p. 187.)

61. *In what five ways may an easement be acquired?* (REAL PROPERTY § 32, p. 188.)

62. A owned a tract of land which he divided into two tracts; one, X was on the highway; the other, Y had no outlet to any highway; he sold tract X to B. A consults you as to his right to reach a highway. *What is your advice?* (REAL PROPERTY § 32, p. 188.)

63. A owned two adjoining lots upon each of which he built a residence with a party wall. He sold one of the lots to B and later decided to tear down the house on the lot retained. *How advise B?* (REAL PROPERTY § 32, p. 188.)

64. A is driving across B's land, claiming a right to do so; B denies any such right. *How advise B?* (REAL PROPERTY § 32, p. 189.)

65. A owned a tract of land to which he had access over B's land to the highway. He divided the tract into three lots and sold a lot each to X, Y and Z. *How advise X, Y and Z?* (REAL PROPERTY § 33, p. 189.)

66. A had a right of way over B's land; he discontinued using it for several years and B claims that A has lost his right of way. *How advise B?* (REAL PROPERTY § 33, p. 189.)

67. A had a right to take firewood from B's land for use on his own tract of land; he divides his tract into three lots and conveys a lot each to X, Y and Z. *How advise X, Y and Z?* (REAL PROPERTY § 34, p. 189.)

68. A leased to B for two years at a rental of $100 a month and then sold his interest in the land to X. *Is X entitled to collect the rent from B?* (REAL PROPERTY § 35, p. 189.)

69. A leased to B for two years agreeing that at the end of that period he would renew the lease for another two years at the same rental; at the end of one year B assigned his lease to Y. *Is Y entitled to have the lease renewed?* (REAL PROPERTY § 35, p. 189.)

70. *How was a conveyance by livery of seisin made? To what kind of estates was it applicable? Is it still possible to use it?* (REAL PROPERTY § 36, p. 190.)

71. *At common law what interests in land were conveyed by a simple deed?* (REAL PROPERTY § 36, p. 190.)

72. *What is the distinguishing feature of a bargain and sale deed?* (REAL PROPERTY § 36, p. 191.)

73. *When may a conveyance be made by a covenant to stand seised?* (REAL PROPERTY § 36, p. 191.)

74. *What six covenants are usually contained in the modern warranty deed?* (REAL PROPERTY § 36, p. 191.)

75. *Under modern law which of these covenants run with the land? Under the earlier rule?* (REAL PROPERTY § 37, p. 191.)

76. *What is the usual rule of construction where there is an inconsistency between metes and bounds on the one hand and courses and distances on the other?* (REAL PROPERTY § 38, p. 192.)

77. *When the phrase "along the highway" is used in a deed what is the presumption as to its meaning? Why?* (REAL PROPERTY § 38, p. 192.)

78. *What is meant by a ceremonial delivery of a deed? By a delivery in escrow?* (REAL PROPERTY § 39, p. 193; WILLS § 1, p. 200.)

79. A executed a deed to B and delivered it to X to be delivered to B upon A's death; X made the delivery after A's death. *When did title pass to B?* (REAL PROPERTY § 39, p. 193.)

80. A executed a deed to B and delivered it to X to be delivered to B upon B's paying the purchase money of $10,000. Before this happened A sold and conveyed the land to Y for $11,000, Y not knowing of the previous conveyance. *How advise B?* (REAL PROPERTY § 39, p. 193.)

81. A executed a deed to B and delivered it to X to be delivered to B upon A's death; X, however, delivered the deed to B before A's death and B sold and conveyed the land to Y who did not know of the escrow condition. *How advise Y?* (REAL PROPERTY § 39, p. 193.)

82. A entered into possession of B's land and occupied it adversely for 20 years. Then he moved off and B then sold and conveyed the land to X who did not know of A's adverse possession. *How advise A?* (REAL PROPERTY § 40, p. 194.)

83. A conveyed a tract of land to B who did not record his deed; A then in fraud of B, sold and conveyed the same land to C who did not know of B's deed

but who also did not record his deed. *How advise C?* (REAL PROPERTY § 40, p. 194.)

84. A purported to convey to B land to which he had no title, and B put the deed on record; then A obtained title to the land and conveyed it to X who recorded his deed not knowing of the deed to B. *Who is entitled to the land, B or X?* (REAL PROPERTY § 40, p. 194.)

85. A conveyed to B who did not record his deed. Later A conveyed to X who knew of B's deed. X placed his deed on record. *How advise B?* (REAL PROPERTY § 40, p. 194.)

86. A devised land to B for life with remainder in fee to X; B occupied the land for twenty years and then the will of A was declared invalid. *How advise X?* (REAL PROPERTY § 41, p. 195.)

87. *What is the doctrine of constructive adverse possession?* (REAL PROPERTY § 41, p. 195.)

88. A took possession of B's land and held it adversely for five years and then sold his rights to the land to X who entered and stayed in possession for fifteen years. *How advise B?* (REAL PROPERTY § 42, p. 195.)

89. A took possession of B's land and held it adversely for twenty years but at the end of eight years B died and left as his heir a child X three years old. *How advise A?* (REAL PROPERTY § 42, p. 195.)

90. *In what three different situations may the law of fixtures become important?* (REAL PROPERTY § 43, p. 196.)

91. *What is meant by the intent of the party placing the chattel on the land?* (REAL PROPERTY § 43, p. 196.)

92. *Of what importance is the character of the chattel which was placed on the land?* (REAL PROPERTY § 44, p. 196.)

93. *Are gas and electric light fixtures regarded as fixtures legally? Why?* (REAL PROPERTY § 44, p. 196.)

94. A sells and delivers to B an engine to be used in running B's mill, reserving title by way of security for the unpaid purchase price. B becomes insolvent, and X, who has a mortgage on B's land, forecloses and there is not enough proceeds to pay both A and X. *Which one is entitled to priority?* (REAL PROPERTY § 45, p. 196.)

95. A leases a farm to B for three years and B during that time puts in a power plant to operate his electrical apparatus; at the end of the three years B renews the lease for two more years. *At the end of that time how advise B as to his right to remove the power plant?* (REAL PROPERTY § 46, p. 197.)

96. A and B own and occupy adjoining lots; on the boundary line is an elm tree; B wishes to cut it down; A objects. *How advise A?* (REAL PROPERTY § 47, p. 197.)

97. A contracts to sell to X for $125 some cordwood to be cut from A's land. *Which section of the statute of frauds must be complied with to make the contract enforcible?* (REAL PROPERTY § 47, p. 197.)

98. A died in May; on his farm was a crop of alfalfa and a crop of wheat which would be ready to be cut about July 1. *How advise A's executor as to his right to the two crops?* (REAL PROPERTY § 47, p. 197.)

99. A leased his farm to B for a year; at the end of that time B bought a farm and planned to move to it all the manure which had been produced on A's farm during the year. *May he do so?* (REAL PROPERTY § 47, p. 197.)

100. *What are emblements, who is entitled to them and why?* (REAL PROPERTY § 48, p. 198.)

WILLS, INTESTACY AND ADMINISTRATION

1. *In what ways does a will differ from a deed of conveyance?* (WILLS § 1, p. 200.)

2. A conveys property to B upon trust for A for life and then to A's nephews. *Is it necessary that the instrument be attested?* (WILLS § 2, p. 200.)

3. *How is a will different from a gift causa mortis?* (WILLS § 3, p. 200.)

4. A makes a contract to bequeath to B $1,000 and dies without doing so. *How advise B?* (WILLS § 4, p. 200.)

5. A contracts to devise land to his nephew X and later quarrels with X and is about to sell the land. *How advise X?* (WILLS § 4, p. 201.)

6. *What was the English law as to the age necessary to make a valid will?* (WILLS § 5, p. 201.)

7. *What effect does conviction for crime have upon testamentary capacity?* (WILLS § 5, p. 201.)

8. *Under what circumstances will an insane delusion render a will invalid?* (WILLS § 6, p. 201.)

9. A was seventy years old; he had accumulated considerable property and had several children and grandchildren some of them being almost destitute; he was at that time converted to an unusual religious sect; he devised and bequeathed to it all his property and died at the age of seventy-one. *Do the above facts make the will invalid?* (WILLS § 6, p. 201.)

10. *What is meant by fraud in the execution?* (WILLS § 7, p. 202.)

11. A was about to make a will leaving the bulk of his property to his grandson X; B falsely represented to A that X had become a person of dissolute habits and persuaded A to leave his property to B's daughter Y, who was innocent of the fraud. *How advise X?* (WILLS § 7, p. 202.)

12. *What is the evidence usually relied upon to prove undue influence?* (WILLS § 8, p. 202.)

13. By mistake of the draftsman a legacy to B was omitted from A's will. *How advise B?* (WILLS § 9, p. 202.)

14. *Under what circumstances will a court strike words out of a will?* (WILLS § 10, p. 203.)

15. If there is an equivocal expression in a will, *how will the court likely deal with the matter?* (WILLS § 11, p. 203.)

16. A was too ill and weak to sign a will that had been drawn up according to his directions. *How advise him?* (WILLS § 12, p. 203.)

17. A's will contained a legacy to X who was one of the attesting witnesses. *How advise X?* (WILLS § 13, p. 204.)

18. A statute required that the attesting witnesses sign as such in the presence of the testator. *What is meant by the word "presence"?* (WILLS § 13, p. 204.)

19. *What is meant by the doctrine of incorporation by reference?* (WILLS § 14, p. 204; § 20, p. 208.)

20. *What is a holographic will?* (WILLS § 15, p. 205.)

21. *When is an oral will valid?* (WILLS § 15, p. 205.)

22. A and B orally agreed to make mutual wills each in favor of the other with remainders to the relatives of each equally; A executed his will and died; B then devised all his land to his own relatives. *How advise A's relatives?* (WILLS § 15, p. 205.)

23. *What various physical acts are usually provided for by statutes on the subject of revocation of wills? Is an intent to revoke always necessary?* (WILLS § 16, p. 206.)

24. *If a man makes a will and then marries, does this revoke the will? Does the birth of a child to the marriage?* (WILLS § 17, p. 206.)

25. *What is the effect of a divorce upon wills made by the spouses?* (WILLS § 17, p. 206.)

26. A made a will in 1946 and a later will in 1947. *To what extent, if at all, does the second will revoke the first?* (WILLS § 18, p. 207.)

27. A made a will in 1944 and then he made a will in 1945. Thinking that the second will was valid A then canceled the earlier will, but the later will was invalid. *Is the earlier will valid?* (WILLS § 19, p. 207.)

28. A destroyed his will, expecting to make a new will but that expectation was never realized. *Did he die intestate?* (WILLS § 19, p. 207.)

29. A revoked his will by merely cancelling it; later he decides that he wishes that will to be his will. *How advise him?* (WILLS § 20, p. 207.)

30. A executes a will in 1946 and then another will in 1947, expressly revoking the earlier will; then he revokes the second will by destroying it. *Does this revive the earlier will?* (WILLS § 21, p. 208.)

31. *Under modern law in this country who are the heirs of a decedent? Who are his next of kin?* (WILLS § 22, p. 209.)

32. *Is the old distinction between real property and personal property of any importance today?* (WILLS § 22, p. 208.)

33. *What is the modern legislative attitude as to the widow or widower of an intestate decedent?* (WILLS § 23, p. 209.)

34. *What is meant by ancestral property?* (WILLS § 24, p. 209.)

35. *What is the purpose and value of probating a will?* (WILLS § 25, p. 210.)

36. *Where should a will be first probated?* (WILLS § 25, p. 210.)

37. A contracted to devise his farm to his nephew X but in breach of that contract devised it to his brother Y. *Is this a valid objection to probating the will?* (WILLS § 25, p. 210.)

38. A died leaving a will in favor of his nephews X and Y; A's niece Z, obtained possession of the will and destroyed it. *How advise X and Y?* (WILLS §§ 25, 26, p. 210.)

39. *What are the usual grounds for contesting a will?* (WILLS § 26, p. 211.)

40. *What is the purpose of administering a decedent's estate? Is such administration always necessary?* (WILLS § 27, p. 211.)

41. *What is the meaning of an administrator with the will annexed? Of an administrator de bonis non? Of an executor de son tort?* (WILLS § 28, p. 212.)

42. *When is an ancillary administration necessary?* (WILLS § 29, p. 212.)

43. *What is the usual order of preference in appointing an administrator?* (WILLS § 30, p. 212.)

44. A died having some real estate worth $20,000, personal property, including leaseholds, worth $5,000 and debts amounting to $7,500. *How advise the administrator of A's estate?* (WILLS § 31, p. 213.)

45. *What choses in action held by A survive his death? What ones do not survive?* (WILLS § 31, p. 213.)

46. A died July 15, 1947; on July 16, X took a horse which had belonged to A, claiming it as his own. B was appointed administrator July 20 and qualified July 22. *Is he entitled to recover against X in trover?* (WILLS § 31, p. 213.)

47. A died and B, his executor, employed X undertaker to conduct the funeral. *How advise B as to his rights and liabilities in respect thereto?* (WILLS § 32, p. 214.)

48. A contracted with B to build a residence for B on B's land according to certain specifications, for $12,000. After it was about one third completed B died. *How advise his executor?* (WILLS § 33, p. 214.)

49. Upon A's death, X was appointed the administrator of his estate. Thinking that the estate was fully solvent he paid Y and Z, creditors of A, the full amount of their claims. It now appears that there are only enough assets to pay creditors 60%. *How advise X?* (WILLS § 34, p. 214.)

50. A had three children, X, Y and Z. He advanced $15,000 to X to set him up in business and died soon after, leaving an estate of $25,000. *How advise X?* (WILLS § 35, p. 215.)

51. *What is meant by the ademption of legacies or devises?* (WILLS § 36, p. 215.)

52. A made a will bequeathing $6,000 to X; later he made a gift to X of

$7,500 and then died. *What was the effect of the gift upon the legacy?* (WILLS § 36, p. 215.)

53. *Where there are enough assets to pay debts but not enough to pay all the legacies what is the order of preferment?* (WILLS § 37, p. 217.)

54. The executor, thinking that there are enough assets to pay legacies in full, pays X the full amount of his legacy; it now appears that there is only enough to pay general legatees 60 cents on the dollar. *How advise X?* (WILLS § 37, p. 217.)

DAMAGES

1. *What is the meaning of damage? Of damages?* (DAMAGES § 1, p. 217.)

2. *What are the two different meanings of the phrase "special damage"?* (DAMAGES § 1, p. 217.)

3. *When is special damage a part of the law of torts? When a part of the law of damages?* (DAMAGES § 2, p. 218.)

4. *What is the result if the uncertainty of the damage has been caused by defendant's wrong?* (DAMAGES § 2, p. 218.)

5. *How will a plaintiff prove the amount of the loss of commercial profits due to defendant's wrongful act?* (DAMAGES § 2, p. 218.)

6. *What is the doctrine of avoidable consequences?* (DAMAGES § 3, p. 219.)

7. A negligently injured B; in a suit by B, A contends that B should reduce the damage by undergoing a surgical operation. *How advise B?* (DAMAGES § 3, p. 219.)

8. A negligently set fire to B's house and nearly all of B's furniture was destroyed. The furniture had cost B $2,000; its market value at the time of the fire was $400. *How advise B?* (DAMAGES § 4, p. 220.)

9. A sued B for the conversion of certain stock; at the time of conversion the stock was worth $12,000; three months later it was worth $14,000; at the time of the trial it was worth $9,000. *How advise A?* (DAMAGES § 4, p. 220.)

10. A, in 1946, sued B for slander uttered in June, 1945; the trial was held in 1947. A contends that he is entitled to interest on the amount of the verdict and judgment from June 1945. *Is he so entitled?* (DAMAGES § 5, p. 221.)

11. A sold a bill of goods to B in August, 1944, on sixty days' credit; B defaulted and A finally sued and recovered judgment in June 1948. A contends that he is entitled to interest on the amount due from October, 1944. *Is he entitled?* (DAMAGES § 5, p. 221.)

12. *What is the common law rule as to liability for costs of the litigation?* (DAMAGES § 6, p. 221.)

13. A sold and conveyed a farm to B by warranty deed; B in turn conveyed and warranted to C. Then X ousted C with a paramount title and C sued B for breach of warranty and got judgment for $8,000; B now sues A for breach of warranty and contends that he is entitled to judgment for $8,000 plus the

amount of his attorney's fees spent in defending himself in C's action against him. *Is he entitled?* (DAMAGES § 6, p. 221.)

14. A negligently injured B and B brought action claiming damages for the loss of his time, for medical expenses and for nursing; it appeared, however, that B's daughter, being a skillful nurse, rendered her services gratuitously. *How advise B?* (DAMAGES § 7, p. 222.)

15. A negligently injured B so that he was no longer able to work. *How arrive at the value of his probable future earnings?* (DAMAGES § 7, p. 223.)

16. A negligently injured Y, the fifteen-year-old son of X. *How measure the recovery due to X? To Y?* (DAMAGES § 7, p. 223.)

17. A negligently injured B, the wife of C. *How measure the recovery due to B? To C?* (DAMAGES § 7, p. 223.)

18. A negligently injured X and three months later X died of the injuries. *How advise A as to his liability to X's administrator? To X's widow?* (DAMAGES § 8, p. 223.)

19. A negligently damaged B's automobile truck. *What is the measure of B's recovery if the truck can be satisfactorily repaired? If it cannot?* (DAMAGES § 9, p. 224.)

20. A sued B in replevin and gave a counter bond for the delivery up of the chattel if he lost. A lost. *Is he liable in damages for the detention?* (DAMAGES § 9, p. 224.)

21. A wrongfully cut B's shade trees. *How advise B as to his right against A?* (DAMAGES § 10, p. 225.)

22. A negligently damaged an old, dilapidated building of B's on B's land. *How advise B?* (DAMAGES § 10, p. 225.)

23. A wrongfully erected a permanent structure on B's land. *How advise B on the question of damages?* (DAMAGES § 10, p. 225.)

24. *Under what circumstances, in this country, must a plaintiff in a libel case allege and prove special damage?* (DAMAGES § 11, p. 225.)

25. *What is necessary to prove as special damage in defamation cases?* (DAMAGES § 11, p. 226.)

26. *When may mental pain and humiliation be recovered for in defamation cases?* (DAMAGES § 11, p. 226.)

27. *What is meant by punitive, exemplary or vindictive damages and when may there be recovery therefor?* (DAMAGES § 12, p. 226.)

28. *May exemplary damages be recovered against an employer for the tort of his employee?* (DAMAGES § 12, p. 226.)

29. *When property is taken under eminent domain proceedings, what is the measure of compensation?* (DAMAGES § 13, p. 226.)

30. *May there be recovery for the "strategic value" of such property?* (DAMAGES § 13, p. 227.)

31. *What is the general rule of damages in contract cases? What modification of this rule was made by the rule laid down in Hadley v. Baxendale?* (DAMAGES § 14, p. 227.)

32. *In what contract cases may there be recovery for mental pain?* (DAMAGES § 14, p. 227.)

33. *Where the plaintiff has lost profits but the amount is impossible to prove, what is the measure of recovery?* (DAMAGES § 14, p. 228.)

34. *What is meant by liquidated damages and when are they recoverable?* (DAMAGES § 14, p. 228.)

35. A contracts to erect a building for X and then, after part performance, X wrongfully refuses to let A finish the building. *How advise A?* (DAMAGES § 15, p. 228.)

36. A contracts to erect a building for X and then, after part performance A refuses to complete it. *How advise X?* (DAMAGES § 15, p. 229.)

37. A contracted to employ B for a year at $300 a month; at the end of a month A wrongfully discharged him. *What is the measure of B's recovery?* (DAMAGES § 16, p. 229.)

38. A contracted to sell land to X for $10,000 but X wrongfully refused to perform the contract; thereupon A sold the land to Y for $9,000. *What is the measure of A's recovery against X?* (DAMAGES § 17, p. 230.)

39. A contracted to sell land to X for $10,000, but was unable to convey a marketable title. *What is the measure of X's recovery against A?* (DAMAGES § 17, p. 231.)

40. A sold and conveyed his farm by warranty deed to B for $7,000. A's title failed completely and B was evicted by C. *What is the measure of B's recovery against A?* (DAMAGES § 17, p. 231.)

EQUITY

1. *What two limitations on equity jurisdiction did the early English chancellors adopt and why?* (EQUITY § 1, p. 223.)

2. *Is there any logical reason today why equity courts should still refrain from exercising in rem jurisdiction?* (EQUITY § 1, p. 223.)

3. A sued B in Illinois to compel B to convey to A land in Missouri and to compel B to abate a nuisance to A's own land in Missouri. *Is A entitled to recover?* (EQUITY § 2, p. 223.)

4. A sued B for specific performance of a contract to convey land to B; B's argument was that the contract merely bound B either to convey the land or pay damages. *How answer the argument?* (EQUITY § 3, p. 234.)

5. *Which of the following is a bar to the granting of specific performance of a contract: (1) a provision for a penalty in case the defendant refused to perform; (2) a provision for liquidated damages if defendant refused to perform?* (EQUITY § 4, p. 234.)

6. *What is the hard and fast rule as to the adequacy of damages in contracts to sell land?* (EQUITY § 5, p. 235.)

7. *What is the positive rule of mutuality and what is its practical justification?* (EQUITY § 5, p. 235.)

8. A contracted to sell his farm and his farm machinery and livestock to B for $8,300. Later A refused to perform. *How advise B?* (EQUITY § 6, p. 235.)

9. A contracted to sell stock in a private corporation to B, but later, A refused to let him have it. *How advise B?* (EQUITY § 6, p. 235.)

10. A contracted to sell all his farm machinery to B for $2,300, to be delivered at the end of the summer. B paid $1,200 cash. Before the end of the summer, A became insolvent. *How advise B?* (EQUITY § 6, p. 235.)

11. *What is the reason for giving specific performance of a contract to sell an annuity?* (EQUITY § 7, p. 235.)

12. A borrowed $1,000 from B for a year and agreed that the next week he would give B a mortgage on his household goods. The mortgage was not given and A is now insolvent. *How advise B?* (EQUITY § 7, p. 236.)

13. *Under what circumstances will equity give specific performance of contracts to sell and deliver chattels in installments?* (EQUITY § 7, p. 236.)

14. A sold a building lot to B who agreed as a part of the consideration that he would erect on the lot within one year a residence to cost at least $12,000. B defaulted. *How advise A?* (EQUITY § 8, p. 236.)

15. A contracted with B, a famous portrait painter, to have his portrait painted; B defaulted. *How advise A?* (EQUITY § 8, p. 236.)

16. A contracted to lend $10,000 to B upon first mortgage security on real estate. *How advise B if A refuses to perform?* (EQUITY § 9, p. 237.)

17. *What has been the attitude of equity courts toward contracts to arbitrate? What is the attitude of modern legislatures?* (EQUITY § 9, p. 237.)

18. *Why is a contract to enter into a partnership not specifically enforcible?* (EQUITY § 9, p. 237.)

19. *What is the equitable remedy where the defendant has broken his contract never to sue the plaintiff? Not to sue for a limited time?* (EQUITY § 10, p. 237.)

20. A sold out his hardware business to X and agreed that he would not for five years enter into the hardware business in the same city. *What remedy to X in case of breach?* (EQUITY § 10, p. 238.)

21. *What was the decision of the court in the famous case of Lumley v. Wagner?* (EQUITY § 11, p. 238.)

22. *What was the most important criticism of that decision and the answer thereto?* (EQUITY § 11, p. 238.)

23. *In drawing up such a contract today would it be desirable, from the employer's standpoint, to provide part compensation for breach of the negative promise?* (EQUITY § 11, p. 238.)

24. *Was it important, in Lumley v. Wagner, that there was an express negative promise?* (EQUITY § 11, p. 239.)

25. *Was it important that the breach of Miss Wagner's negative promise caused separate damage to Lumley?* (EQUITY § 11, p. 239.)

26. *Was it important that Miss Wagner's services were unique?* (EQUITY § 11, p. 239.)

27. *Does the doctrine of Lumley v. Wagner operate also in favor of an employee against an employer?* (EQUITY § 11, p. 239.)

28. A contracts in writing to sell his farm to B for $11,000, title to be transferred and purchase money paid two months later. *When does B's equitable property right come into existence? Why?* (EQUITY § 12, p. 239.)

29. It is sometimes said that from the moment when a specifically enforcible contract is entered into, V becomes trustee for the land for P and P becomes trustee of the purchase money for V. *Criticise.* (EQUITY § 12, p. 240; TRUSTS § 8, p. 269.)

30. V contracted to convey to P and later V became bankrupt. *What effect did this have upon P's equitable right to get the land?* (EQUITY § 13, p. 240.)

31. Suppose P became bankrupt instead of V. *What effect did this have upon V's right to get the purchase money? Why?* (EQUITY § 13, p. 240.)

32. P assigns his right under the contract to X who does not undertake to perform it. *What is X's right against V? V against X?* (EQUITY § 13, p. 240.)

33. A contracts to devise land to B. *At what time, if at all, does B get an equitable property right in the land?* (EQUITY § 14, p. 240.)

34. *What new important equity doctrine began with Tulk v. Moxhay?* (EQUITY § 15, p. 241.)

35. *Why did the doctrine of that case become a part of the law of technical property rights?* (EQUITY § 15, p. 241.)

36. A owned land bound by an equitable servitude in favor of X; B took possession of the land and occupied it adversely for twenty years and thereby obtained title. *How advise X.* (EQUITY § 16, p. 241.)

37. *May an equitable servitude last indefinitely? May it be so limited that only the covenantee may enforce?* (EQUITY § 16, p. 242.)

38. *Is an equitable servitude within the statute of frauds? Why?* (EQUITY § 17, p. 242.)

39. *What effect may a change in the character of a neighborhood have upon the enforcibility of an equitable servitude?* (EQUITY § 17, p. 242.)

40. *May equitable servitudes be imposed upon chattels?* (EQUITY § 17, p. 242.)

41. P dies intestate. *What happens to his equitable property right in the land? To his right to recover damages against V if V defaults?* (EQUITY § 18, p. 243.)

42. V dies intestate. *What happens to his equitable right to compel P to take*

the land and pay the full purchase price? To his right to recover damages against P if P defaults? (EQUITY § 18, p. 243.)

43. A leases to B for seven years with an option to B to buy the land at any time before the expiration of the lease, for $15,000. At the end of six years B dies. *How advise B's heir X?* (EQUITY § 19, p. 243.)

44. Same facts as 43 ante except that it is A, not B, who dies at the end of six years; B decides to accept the option. *Who is entitled to the purchase money, A's heir or A's executor?* (EQUITY § 19, p. 243.)

45. V transferred to B his right to the purchase money but P is insolvent. *Is B entitled to hold the land as security?* (EQUITY § 20, p. 243.)

46. V wrongfully sold and transferred to Y, a bona fide purchaser for value without notice of P's rights. *How advise P?* (EQUITY § 20, p. 243.)

47. V contracted to convey his house and lot to P, conveyance to be made and price paid two months later. At the end of a week the house was destroyed by fire. *How advise V?* (EQUITY § 21, p. 244.)

48. V contracted to sell his farm which he represented to contain 160 acres, to P for $16,000. After the contract was made the farm was surveyed and found to contain only 140 acres. *How advise P?* (EQUITY § 22, p. 244.)

49. In a state where it is still possible to have contracts under seal, A gave to B an option to buy his farm at any time within 60 days, for $15,000. B decided to accept the option; A contends that B cannot get specific performance because he paid nothing for the option. *What decision?* (EQUITY § 23, p. 245.)

50. *What is the doctrine of marketable title?* (EQUITY § 24, p. 245.)

51. A orally contracted to sell and convey his farm to B for $6,000 and put B in possession. B changed his mind and moved off the farm. *How advise A?* (EQUITY § 25, p. 246.)

52. A orally contracted to sell and convey his farm to Y for $9,000 and Y paid all the purchase money expecting to get the conveyance the following day. A refuses to convey. *How advise Y?* (EQUITY § 25, p. 246.)

53. A orally promised to make a gift of a forty-acre tract to his son John; John took possession and made valuable improvements; A was killed in an automobile accident, leaving seven children surviving him. *How advise John?* (EQUITY § 25, p. 246.)

54. After making the contract with V, P became insolvent. *Of what importance is this fact?* (EQUITY § 26, p. 246.)

55. A leased to B for three years with an option to buy for $20,000 up to 60 days before the end of the lease. B decided to accept, but, because of sudden illness in his family his acceptance was actually made one day late. *How advise B?* (EQUITY § 26, p. 246.)

56. V contracted to sell to P, the title to pass and purchase money paid on the following March 1, with a stipulation that "time shall be of the essence of the contract". *What is the effect of such a stipulation?* (EQUITY § 26, p. 246.)

57. P has delayed a long time in completing the contract in spite of repeated prodding by V. *How advise V?* (EQUITY § 26, p. 247.)

58. *Under what circumstances may non-disclosure of important facts to the other party be a bar to specific performance?* (EQUITY § 27, p. 247.)

59. *That giving specific performance of a contract would result in great hardship to the defendant is of what significance?* (EQUITY § 28, p. 247.)

60. V represented to P that he was twenty-one years old whereas he was only nineteen. *Of what significance is this fact if V sues for specific performance while still under age? If he sues after becoming of age?* (EQUITY § 29, p. 247.)

61. *What is the usual statement of Fry's supposed rule of lack of mutuality of remedy? Of Ames' rule of lack of mutuality of performance?* (EQUITY § 29, p. 248.)

62. *Why were written instruments invulnerable at common law?* (EQUITY § 30, p. 248.)

63. *What is the meaning of "reformation"?* (EQUITY § 30, p. 248.)

64. A sold and conveyed a farm to B supposed to contain 300 acres, at $200 an acre; B had the farm surveyed and found that it contained only 276 acres. B has paid the entire purchase money. *How advise B?* (EQUITY § 31, p. 248.)

65. A contracted to sell his farm to B for $7,800; both A and B thought there was no incumbrance on the land but there was a valid equitable mortgage of $1,400 held by X; A persuaded B to accept a quitclaim deed. *How advise B?* (EQUITY § 32, p. 248.)

66. A sold and conveyed his farm to B for $15,000, B mistakenly thinking there was oil under the land; the value of the land merely for farming purposes was not over $9,000. *How advise B?* (EQUITY § 32, p. 249.)

67. A by way of gift conveyed 20 building lots to B though intending to convey only 15, the mistake being that of the draftsman. *How advise A?* (EQUITY § 33, p. 249.)

68. A by way of gift conveyed 15 building lots to B though intending to convey 20, the mistake being that of the draftsman. A died shortly thereafter without discovering the mistake. *How advise B?* (EQUITY § 33, p. 249.)

69. *What is the modern attitude of equity courts toward granting reformation for mistakes of law?* (EQUITY § 34, p. 249.)

70. *Why do equity courts require clear and convincing evidence of mistake in reformation cases?* (EQUITY § 34, p. 249.)

71. A orally sold to B an eighty acre tract; by mistake of the draftsman only sixty of the eighty acres were described in the conveyance. *How advise B?* (EQUITY § 35, p. 249.)

72. A orally sold to B his 160 acre farm and B went into possession of it and also, by mistake, of another 20 acre tract of A's which both parties thought was included in the farm. After being in possession for ten years and discovering the mistake B consults you. *How advise him?* (EQUITY § 36, p. 250.)

73. *Apart from a special statute of limitations applying to equity suits, what length of delay will bar a plaintiff from getting reformation?* (EQUITY § 36, p. 250.)

74. *How is rescission to be distinguished from reformation?* (EQUITY § 37, p. 250.)

75. *When can rescission be had at law?* (EQUITY § 37, p. 250.)

76. *What three possible bases are there for granting rescission in equity for mistake? What is a misunderstanding?* (EQUITY § 38, p. 250.)

77. A bought from B a note on X which he mistakenly thought was secured by mortgage. *How advise B?* (EQUITY § 38, p. 250.)

78. The reverse of 77 ante. *Is A entitled to enforce the mortgage?* (MORTGAGES § 6, p. 368.)

79. A released B from a debt due to A, mistakenly thinking that B was insolvent; there was no fraud. *How advise B?* (EQUITY § 38, p. 250.)

80. *What is the present tendency toward giving rescission for mistake of law?* (EQUITY § 39, p. 251.)

81. Upon the basis of a decision of the Supreme Court of the state in the case of A v. B, X and Y entered into a transaction; later, in the case of C v. D, the earlier decision of A v. B was overruled. X now asks that the transaction with Y be rescinded. *What answer?* (EQUITY § 39, p. 251.)

82. A bought a chattel from B for $100, inducing the sale by fraud. *Upon discovery of the fraud, what different remedies may B choose from?* (EQUITY § 40, p. 251; FORMS OF ACTION § 14, p. 8; QUASI-CONTRACTS § 15, p. 296.)

83. *When is there a presumption of fraud?* (EQUITY § 40, p. 251.)

84. By fraudulently misrepresenting the quality of the soil A induced B to buy his farm for $10,000; the fair value was not over $8,000; B wishes recission. *How advise him?* (EQUITY § 41, p. 251.)

85. *What is the modern test of what constitutes such duress as will furnish a valid basis for rescission?* (EQUITY § 42, p. 252.)

86. Shortly after she became of age A, who had inherited considerable property from her uncle, made a gift of a large part of it to her mother who had also been her guardian. A now wishes she had not made the gift. *How advise her?* (EQUITY § 42, p. 252.)

87. A and B played poker and A lost; A gave B a check for the amount that he lost; B has not yet received payment on the check. *How advise A?* (EQUITY § 43, p. 252.)

88. A at the age of eighty conveyed his home farm to his son B upon the latter promising to take care of A for the rest of his life. After six months A found it impossible to continue to live there because of the attitude of B's wife X. *How advise A?* (EQUITY § 43, p. 253.)

89. The phrase quia timet means, because he fears. *Fears what?* (EQUITY § 44, p. 253.)

90. *Why is not a bill to perpetuate testimony an adequate substitute for a bill to cancel a written instrument on quia timet grounds? For a bill to remove a cloud on title?* (EQUITY §§ 44, 45, pp. 253, 254.)

91. *What is the proper test of what amounts to a cloud on title?* (EQUITY § 45, p. 254.)

92. Suppose that the defendant's claim to plaintiff's land is merely oral. *What effect does this have upon giving relief against a cloud on title?* (EQUITY § 45, p. 234.)

93. A claims a right to B's land based upon an instrument which has been recorded though the registry act did not provide for such recording. *How advise B?* (EQUITY § 45, p. 254.)

94. *How does the Torrens system of registering land titles operate?* (EQUITY § 45, p. 254.)

95. *Of what did common law waste consist? What action was allowed at common law? Under what circumstances will an equity court give relief?* (EQUITY § 46, p. 254.)

96. *What is the doctrine of equitable waste and how did it originate?* (EQUITY § 47, p. 255.)

97. *What is its real basis?* (EQUITY § 47, p. 255.)

98. A mortgagor in possession is about to cut down valuable timber. *Under what circumstances may the mortgagee get an injunction?* (EQUITY § 47, p. 255; MORTGAGES § 8, p. 369.)

99. Land was left to A for life, to B for life without impeachment of waste, to C in fee. Some timber which was deteriorating was cut by order of court while A was in possession. *How advise A, B and C?* (EQUITY § 48, p. 255.)

100. *What is the meaning of trespass to land at common law? In equity?* (FORMS OF ACTION § 5, p. 3; EQUITY § 49, p. 255.)

101. *What was the reason for an English equity court requiring a plaintiff to establish his right at law before getting an injunction against a trespass?* (EQUITY § 50, p. 258.)

102. *What is the present attitude of courts about requiring a plaintiff to first establish his right at law?* (EQUITY § 50, p. 256.)

103. A has been crossing over B's land claiming a right thereto. *Is B entitled to an injunction? Why?* (EQUITY § 51, p. 256.)

104. A wrongfully strings a telephone wire across B's land. *What are B's possible remedies?* (EQUITY § 51, p. 256; FORMS OF ACTION § 5, p. 4.)

105. A is in possession of land which B contends belongs to B; A is cutting down valuable timber. *Under what circumstances may B enjoin such activity?* (EQUITY § 52, p. 256.)

106. A borrowed from B a chattel which is an heirloom in B's family and A refuses to return it. *How advise B as to his common law and equitable remedies?* (EQUITY § 53, p. 257; FORMS OF ACTION § 39, p. 22.)

107. *In case of a private nuisance, in what respect is an injunction preferable to an action at law? To private abatement?* (EQUITY § 54, p. 257.)

108. The X Company built a smelting plant remote from human habitations; later, however, a large number of persons built residences near it and now seek to have it enjoined, but the X Company contends that no injunction should issue because of the plant's great value to the community in furnishing labor to several hundred persons. *How decide?* (EQUITY § 55, p. 257.)

109. X wrongfully obstructed the street in front of A's place of business. *How advise A?* (EQUITY § 56, p. 258.)

110. Y wrongfully runs a slaughterhouse close to a small village; Z, one of the residents of the village, asks your advice as to his remedy and the remedy of the village. *How answer?* (EQUITY § 56, p. 258.)

111. *What is meant by a common law copyright? What protection does equity give?* (EQUITY § 57, p. 258.)

112. B infringed A's patent, causing A $10,000 damage to his business, but profiting from the infringement only $1,500. *How advise A?* (EQUITY § 57, p. 258.)

113. A employed B for a year and disclosed to B a valuable trade secret which B sold to X, a bona fide purchaser for the value without notice. *How advise A as to his remedy against B? Against X?* (EQUITY § 58, p. 259.)

114. *What two objections have been raised against giving injunctions against libel and slander? What objection to giving an injunction against disparagement of property?* (EQUITY § 60, p. 259.)

115. *What is the usual attitude of equity courts toward giving relief against interference with domestic relations?* (EQUITY § 61, p. 259.)

116. *What it the present day attitude of equity courts toward giving relief against crimes?* (EQUITY § 62, p. 260.)

117. *When will an equity court enjoin a criminal proceeding?* (EQUITY § 63, p. 260.)

118. *What is the purpose of a bill of interpleader? What is necessary in order to get relief?* (EQUITY § 64, p. 260.)

119. *Is it necessary that the claimants claim the same amounts?* (EQUITY § 64, p. 261.)

120. *Is it necessary that one of the claimants be entitled?* (EQUITY § 64, p. 260.)

121. *Is it necessary that all the claimants bring the same action against the applicant?* (EQUITY § 65, p. 261.)

122. *Is it fatal to interpleader relief that the applicant is a tort feasor?* (EQUITY § 66, p. 261.)

123. *May a claimant interplead?* (EQUITY § 66, p. 261.)

124. *What is meant by a bill in the nature of a bill of interpleader? When does it lie and what is its advantage over a bill of interpleader?* (EQUITY § 66, p. 261.)

125. *What is the purpose of a bill of peace?* (EQUITY § 67, p. 261.)

126. *How distinguish such a bill from a bill of interpleader?* (EQUITY § 67, p. 262.)

127. *Is it necessary that there be a claim of an exclusive property right or is it enough that there be a community of interest in common questions of law and fact?* (EQUITY § 68, p. 262.)

128. *What is the difference between a bill to remove a cloud from title and a bill to quiet title?* (EQUITY § 45, p. 253; § 69, p. 262.)

129. *If A sues B in ejectment and recovers judgment, why does not that become res judicata without the necessity of a bill to quiet title?* (EQUITY § 69, p. 262; FORMS OF ACTION § 42, p. 23.)

130. *Under what circumstances is a bill to quiet title necessary to put an end to repeated actions of trespass?* (EQUITY § 70, p. 262.)

131. A devised land to X in trust to sell and distribute the proceeds to his two nephews, Y and Z. Before X made the sale Y died, leaving B his heir and C his next of kin. *How advise C?* (EQUITY § 72, p. 263.)

132. *What is the doctrine of equitable reconversion?* (EQUITY § 72, p. 264.)

133. *What has been the attitude of equity courts towards the enforcement of penalties?* (EQUITY § 73, p. 264.)

134. *Will a court of equity ever enforce a forfeiture?* (EQUITY § 73, p. 264.)

135. A contracts to sell his farm to B for $3,000, title to be transferred and the rest of the purchase money paid six months later, on September 1, 1948; B paid $2,000 down. There was a provision in the contract that time should be of the essence. On September 1, B is unable to raise the other $1,000. *How advise B?* (EQUITY § 73, p. 264; § 26, p. 246.)

TRUSTS

1. *At what date and how did uses originate as an enforcible right in land?* (TRUSTS § 1, p. 266.)

2. *For what purposes were uses frequently employed before the statute of uses?* (TRUSTS § 1, p. 266.)

3. *When was the statute of uses passed and what was its main provision?* (TRUSTS § 2, p. 266.)

4. *What was the most important result of the statute?* (TRUSTS § 2, p. 266.)

5. *What three uses were not affected by the statute?* (TRUSTS § 2, p. 266.)

6. *How did the modern passive trust arise?* (TRUSTS § 2, p. 266.)

7. *How are trusts classified according to form? According to substance?* (TRUSTS § 3, p. 267; § 19, p. 275.)

8. *How is a trust similar to a debt? How dissimilar?* (TRUSTS § 4, p. 267.)

9. If it is doubtful whether a particular transaction is a debt or a trust, *what is the significance of the payment of interest?* (TRUSTS § 4, p. 267.)

10. *In what way may a trust be changed into a debt? In what way may a debt be changed into a trust?* (TRUSTS § 4, p. 268.)

11. *Under what circumstances may the beneficiary of a trust maintain an action at law against the trustee?* (TRUSTS § 4, p. 268.)

12. A sold a horse to B for $300 to be paid for in thirty days, $180 to A's creditor X and $120 to A's daughter Y. *How advise X and Y?* (TRUSTS § 5, p. 268.)

13. A devised land to his nephew X subject to the payment of $1,200 a year to A's wife Y. *What is the nature of Y's right against X?* (TRUSTS § 6, p. 268.)

14. A had two non-negotiable choses in action, one against X, the other against Y. A assigned the first one to B and declared himself trustee of the second one for C. *How advise B and C?* (TRUSTS § 7, p. 268.)

15. *Is the vendor of land under a specifically enforcible contract a trustee of the land? Is he a constructive trustee? Is the purchaser a trustee of the purchase money?* (TRUSTS § 8, p. 269; EQUITY § 12, p. 240.)

16. *In order to create a trust, is it necessary to use the word trust? What is the doctrine of precatory trusts?* (TRUSTS § 9, p. 269.)

17. *Was consideration necessary to create a use before the statute of uses? After the statute of uses?* (TRUSTS § 10, p. 269.)

18. *What is meant by the doctrine of "good consideration"?* (TRUSTS § 10, p. 270.)

19. *Is consideration necessary today to create a trust? What is necessary to pass the legal title to a chattel by way of gift? The equitable interests?* (TRUSTS § 11, p. 270.)

20. *Who is the proper party to make the memorandum required by the statute of frauds as to trusts in land?* (TRUSTS § 12, p. 270.)

21. *What is a charity? In what four important respects does a charitable trust differ from a private trust?* (TRUSTS § 13, p. 271.)

22. *Who is the proper party to enforce a charitable trust?* (TRUSTS § 13, p. 271.)

23. A left $500 to X upon trust to provide flowers to be laid on the grave of A's wife each year on the anniversary of her death. *Is the trust valid?* (TRUSTS § 14, p. 271.)

24. A left $50,000 to X upon trust the income of which was to be used for the care of A's twelve dogs. *Is the provision valid? Is it enforceable?* (TRUSTS § 14, p. 272.)

25. A devised land to X upon trust to manage and turn over the income each year to Y for life and then to sell and divide the proceeds among A's children. X has become insane. *How advise Y?* (TRUSTS § 15, p. 272.)

26. Suppose a conveyance to Y upon trust for C but Y refuses to accept the trust. *What effect does this have upon C's rights?* (TRUSTS § 15, p. 272.)

27. *May C maintain an action of special assumpsit against T? Indebitatus assumpsit?* (TRUSTS § 16, p. 273; § 4, p. 268.)

28. T, of Georgia, trustee of land in Tennessee, is guilty of a breach of trust. *How advise C, a resident of Alabama, as to the proper court in which to sue?* (TRUSTS § 16, p. 273.)

29. A devised a large amount of real and personal property to T upon trust for C; a part of the property consisted of a claim against X which C thinks T should collect. *How advise C as to his remedy?* (TRUSTS § 17, p. 273.)

30. Facts same as 29 ante except that the statute of limitations has run in favor of X. *How decide?* (TRUSTS § 17, p. 274.)

31. T wrongfully conveys the trust property to X. *May T recover it back from X? Suppose the statute of limitations has run against T, how advise C?* (TRUSTS § 17, p. 274.)

32. T rightfully conveyed trust property to P. *Is P under obligation to see to it that T applies the purchase money properly in performance of the trust?* (TRUSTS § 17, p. 274.)

33. In making a contract with X in performance of his trust, T stipulated that he was not to be personally liable on the contract. *How advise X?* (TRUSTS § 18, p. 274.)

34. As a part of the trust property, T holds a claim against Y; he brings action against Y; Y has a claim against T. *Under what circumstances, if at all, may Y use this as a setoff to his own obligation?* (TRUSTS § 18, p. 274.)

35. Same facts as 34 ante except that Y's claim is against C, not T. *How decide?* (TRUSTS § 18, p. 274.)

36. *Under what circumstances does it become important to distinguish between resulting trusts and constructive trusts?* (TRUSTS § 19, p. 275.)

37. *What was the origin of the present day doctrine of purchase money resulting trusts?* (TRUSTS § 20, p. 275.)

38. A buys land from B for $8,000 and directs that the title be transferred to X from whom A has borrowed $3,500 of the purchase money. *How advise A?* (TRUSTS § 21, p. 275.)

39. A buys land from B and directs that the title be transferred to Y; this was done in order to defraud A's creditors. *How advise the creditors? How advise A?* (TRUSTS § 21, p. 275.)

40. A buys land from B and directs that the title be transferred to Z. Z wishes to show that A meant the transfer to him to be by way of gift. *May he do so?* (TRUSTS § 21, p. 276.)

41. A buys land from B and directs that the title be transferred to X, A's wife. *What is the presumption? May it be rebutted?* (TRUSTS § 21, p. 276.)

42. *What legislation with regard to purchase money trusts is desirable? What undesirable?* (TRUSTS § 21, p. 276.)

43. A devised property to T upon trust for certain purposes which did not exhaust all the trust property. *Who is entitled to the beneficial interest in the residue?* (TRUSTS § 22, p. 276.)

44. A conveyed property by deed to X upon an oral trust for A. *How advise A?* (TRUSTS § 23, p. 276.)

45. A devised property to X upon an oral trust for Y. *How advise Y?* (TRUSTS § 24, p. 277.)

46. A made his will devising most of his property to B. A and B then quarreled and B, fearing that A would revoke his will, murdered him and before the fact of the murder was discovered B sold and conveyed part of the devised property to D. *How advise B and D?* (TRUSTS § 25, p. 277.)

47. A quarreled with his son and prospective heir, X, and threatened to make a will leaving his property to his nephew Y; in order to prevent this X murdered A. *How advise Y?* (TRUSTS § 25, p. 277.)

48. X took trust property from T claiming it as his own. *How advise C?* (TRUSTS § 26, p. 278.)

49. T took $1,000 of his own money and $1,500 of trust money and invested the money in land. *How advise C if the land is now worth $5,000? If the land is now worth $2,000?* (TRUSTS § 27, p. 278.)

50. T deposited $2,000 of trust money and $1,600 of his own in his personal bank account. He then checked out $1,800 which he used for his own purposes. *How advise C?* (TRUSTS § 27, p. 278.)

51. T deposited $2,000 of trust money and $1,600 of his own money in his personal bank account. He then checked out $2,200 which he invested in property, taking title to himself; later he checked out the other $1,400 and used for his personal expenses. *How advise C?* (TRUSTS § 27, p. 278.)

52. As part of the trust property, T had a lease upon some property for three years. At the end of that time, T tried to get a renewal of the lease but the lessor refused because C, the beneficiary of the trust, was a minor. Thereupon T took a lease for himself. *How advise C?* (TRUSTS § 28, p. 278.)

53. T was authorized by the instrument creating the trust to sell some trust land at public sale. T wishes to buy the land for himself. *How advise him?* (TRUSTS § 29, p. 279.)

54. T wishes to buy trust land from C at private sale. *May he do so?* (TRUSTS § 29, p. 279.)

55. P turned over $10,000 to his agent A and authorized him to buy certain land from X at a public sale. For lack of bidders the land was auctioned off for $8,000. Since it was a bargain at that price, A paid his own money for the land and took title to himself. *How advise P?* (TRUSTS § 29, p. 279.)

56. *How did the doctrine of constructive trust originate?* (TRUSTS § 30, p. 279.)

57. *What are the three requirements of the doctrine of bona fide purchaser for value without notice?* (TRUSTS § 30, p. 280.)

58. *Is giving up a pre-existing claim against T value?* (TRUSTS § 30, p. 280.)

59. *Under what circumstances, if at all, may a judgment creditor become a bona fide purchaser for value without notice?* (TRUSTS § 30, p. 280.)

60. T wrongfully contracted to sell trust property to X for $6,000 and X paid the entire purchase price; then X found out about the trust. *How advise X?* (TRUSTS § 31, p. 280.)

61. T borrowed $3,800 from Y and for security gave him a mortgage on the trust property. *How advise Y?* (TRUSTS § 31, p. 280.)

62. As part of the trust property T holds a non-negotiable chose in action against X for $2,700. T wrongfully sells this to Y for $2,630, Y not knowing that it was trust property. *How advise Y?* (TRUSTS § 32, p. 280.)

63. C declares himself trustee of his equitable interest for X and then in fraud of this he transfers his equitable interest to Y who acts in good faith. *How advise Y?* (TRUSTS § 32, p. 281.)

64. In violation of his trust T transfers the trust property to X, a bona fide purchaser for value without notice. Then X transfers the property to Y, who has notice of T's breach of trust. *How advise Y?* (TRUSTS § 33, p. 281.)

65. T held land in trust for C; C sells and conveys his interest to X and then later, in fraud of that conveyance he purports to convey his interest to Y who pays C therefor without notice of the transaction with X; Y notifies T but X does not. *How advise Y?* (TRUSTS § 34, p. 282.)

66. Same facts as 65 ante except that the trust property is personal property. *How advise?* (TRUSTS § 34, p. 282.)

67. T and X were co-trustees of property devised to them by A. X later died and then T. *What happened to the title to the trust property?* (TRUSTS § 35, p. 282.)

68. *Upon C's death without heirs or next of kin, who is entitled to his equitable interest?* (TRUSTS § 35, p. 282.)

69. *If C dies leaving a widow, is she entitled to a dower interest?* (TRUSTS § 36, p. 283.)

70. *If T becomes bankrupt, does the trust property pass to his assignees in bankruptcy?* (TRUSTS § 37, p. 283.)

71. A devised property to T upon trust for C for life free from any right of C's creditors. *Is such a provision valid? Why?* (TRUSTS § 37, p. 284.)

72. *In what way can A reach practically the same result as if he had created a spendthrift trust?* (TRUSTS § 37, p. 284.)

73. A, having a prosperous business, by will left the business to T upon trust to carry it on for the benefit of A's wife and children. In thus carrying on the business, T bought supplies from X on credit. *How advise X as to his remedy?* (TRUSTS § 38, p. 284.)

74. *In what four ways may a trust be extinguished?* (TRUSTS § 39, p. 285.)

75. A having a very large estate left it by will to trustees for the benefit of

A's grandson X, then 18 years old, with a proviso that X should not receive the title to the estate until he should become thirty years old. *Is such a proviso valid?* (TRUSTS § 40, p. 285.)

76. *When, if at all, may a cestui for life be entitled to possession of the trust property?* (TRUSTS § 41, p. 286.)

77. T kept his own personal account in the X Bank; he kept trust money in the Y Bank in his own name; the Y Bank became insolvent. *How advise C?* (TRUSTS § 41, p. 286.)

78. T, a county treasurer, placed county funds in the Z Bank in his name as trustee. The Z Bank failed. *How advise the county?* (TRUSTS § 41, p. 286.)

79. *Apart from statute, what investments are proper for a trustee to make? What are improper?* (TRUSTS § 42, p. 287.)

80. As part of the trust property turned over to T there was a claim against X; T did not press for payment and later X became wholly insolvent. C seeks to hold T liable for the loss; T's defense is that X was an old friend of the creator of the trust and the latter would not have pressed for payment. *What decision?* (TRUSTS § 43, p. 287.)

81. *If T is guilty of a breach of trust causing loss, must he pay interest on the amount of the loss?* (TRUSTS § 43, p. 288.)

82. *Under what circumstances, if at all, may a majority of the trustees administer a trust over the protest of a minority?* (TRUSTS § 44, p. 288.)

83. *To what extent, if at all, may T delegate his duties as trustee?* (TRUSTS § 44, p. 288.)

QUASI CONTRACTS

1. *In what respect is quasi contract like constructive trust? In what respect is it different?* (QUASI CONTRACTS § 1, p. 289.)

2. *What are the two special difficulties with the subject of quasi contracts?* (QUASI CONTRACTS § 1, p. 290.)

3. A owed X $90 but mistakenly thought he owed him $190; he turned over to X in payment a chattel worth approximately $190. He has now found out his mistake. *How advise him?* (QUASI CONTRACTS § 2, p. 290.)

4. *What is the difference between an intrinsic fact and an extrinsic or collateral fact?* (QUASI CONTRACTS §§ 2, 3, pp. 290, 291.)

5. A owed B $500 but, because of a mistake of law, he paid B $1,500. *How advise A?* (QUASI CONTRACTS § 4, p. 291.)

6. *Under what circumstances, if at all, is a plaintiff barred from recovery in quasi contracts because he was negligent in making the mistake?* (QUASI CONTRACTS § 5, p. 291.)

7. *When, if at all, must plaintiff give notice to the defendant before bringing suit in quasi contracts based upon mistake?* (QUASI CONTRACTS § 6, p. 291.)

8. *From what date does the statute of limitations begin to run against a plaintiff in mistake cases?* (QUASI CONTRACTS § 6, p. 291.)

9. *If a plaintiff suing in quasi contract has received a benefit from the transaction, what must he do in regard thereto?* (QUASI CONTRACTS § 7, p. 292.)

10. *Under what circumstances, if at all, is compromise not a good defense to an action based upon mistake?* (QUASI CONTRACTS § 8, p. 292.)

11. A, for $250, bought from X a chattel which both thought belonged to Y who now claims and takes the chattel from A. *How advise A as to his rights and remedies of the chattel was reasonably worth $300. If it was reasonably worth $200?* (QUASI CONTRACTS § 9, p. 292.)

12. T, trustee for C, sold and conveyed trust property to X for $8,000, and, being a trustee, gave a quitclaim deed, instead of a warranty deed. The title to the property failed; $8,000 was the approximate value of the property. *How advise X?* (QUASI CONTRACTS § 9, p. 292.)

13. A and B attempted to enter into a contract but failed because the language used was equivocal; A sues B for the reasonable value of the benefit conferred by him upon B under the supposed contract. *Is A entitled?* (QUASI CONTRACTS § 10, p. 293.)

14. A contracted to work for B for a year at $200 per month; after working four and one half months and having been paid for four months, A was unable to work longer, because of illness. *How advise A?* (QUASI CONTRACTS § 11, p. 293.)

15. A contracted to erect a residence for B on B's lot; after the house was about half done B's lot and the incomplete house were washed away by the river. *How advise A?* (QUASI CONTRACTS § 11, p. 293.)

16. X turned over to his agent A $ 1,200 to be used in buying liquor in violation of the state's prohibition law. After A had bought $800 worth, X revoked his authority. *How advise X as to his right to recover the other $400?* (QUASI CONTRACTS § 12, p. 294.)

17. X persuaded A to bet $50 on a foot race, assuring A that he was betting on a sure thing; it was a sure thing in that the race was fixed so that the runner on whom A bet lost the race. *How advise A?* (QUASI CONTRACTS § 12, p. 294.)

18. X paid A $100 to find her a husband; she was not satisfied with any of A's clients and now wants her money back. *Is she entitled?* (QUASI CONTRACTS § 12, p. 294.)

19. A contracts with X to work for X for a year at $300 a month; after two and a half months, X wrongfully discharges A. *How advise A as to his rights and remedies?* (QUASI CONTRACTS § 13, p. 295.)

20. A contracted to sell a chattel to B for $1,000 and B made a part payment of $200. Then B wrongfully refused to accept the chattel in pursuance of the contract, but wishes to get back his $200; A is willing to go on. *How advise A?* (QUASI CONTRACTS § 14, p. 295.)

21. A orally contracted to work for B for two years at $1,500 per year. After working four and a half months and having been paid for four months, A unjustifiably quit. *How advise B?* (QUASI CONTRACTS § 14, p. 295.)

22. X kidnapped A and forced A to work for him for three months. *How advise A as to his rights and remedies against X?* (QUASI CONTRACTS § 15, p. 295.)

23. X bought goods from A for $350 upon six months' credit, not intending at the time to pay for them. *How advise A at the end of the six months' period?* (QUASI CONTRACTS § 15, p. 296.)

24. B took A's chattel from A, claiming it to be his own, and sold it to X for $90. The chattel was reasonably worth about $100. *How advise A as to his rights and remedies against B? Against X?* (QUASI CONTRACTS § 16, p. 296.)

25. B wrongfully took possession of A's land and is still in possession after six months of occupancy, worth $ 75 per month. *How advise A as to his rights and remedies against B?* (QUASI CONTRACTS § 16, p. 296.)

26. X threatened to prosecute A's son B for theft, whereupon A paid X $700. *How advise A?* (QUASI CONTRACTS § 17, p. 296.)

27. The X Gas Co. wrongfully contended that A owed them $30 for gas and refused to give him service until the $30 was paid. *How advise A?* (QUASI CONTRACTS § 18, p. 296.)

28. The Y Hospital rendered services gratuitously to A, erroneously thinking that A was without funds. *How advise the Y Hospital?* (QUASI CONTRACTS § 19, p. 297.)

29. In a railroad accident, A was rendered unconscious; X, a bystander asked Y a physician present to render services to A and Y did so. *How advise Y as to his rights against A? Against X?* (QUASI CONTRACTS § 19, p. 297.)

30. *Under what circumstances, if at all, may a member of a family recover in quasi contract against another member of the family?* (QUASI CONTRACTS § 19, p. 297.)

31. A, knowing that he has paid a debt to B, pays it again because he has lost the receipt. *How advise A?* (QUASI CONTRACTS § 19, p. 297.)

32. For his own purposes A drained his quarry and because B's quarry was connected with it, he thereby drained B's quarry also. *How advise A.* (QUASI CONTRACTS § 19, p. 297.)

33. A farmer living alone died suddenly and until an administrator was appointed to take charge of A's property, a neighbor, X, fed the live stock and milked the cows. *How advise X?* (QUASI CONTRACTS § 19, p. 297.)

34. A, an agent of P, being in default to P, obtained money by fraud from X in order to cover his default and deposited it to P's credit in the bank; later he checked out the money and absconded. *How advise X?* (QUASI CONTRACTS § 20, p. 298.)

SALES

1. *In what respect is a sale to be distinguished from a gift? From a bailment? From a barter? A contract to sell?* (SALES § 1, p. 299.)

2. A contracts to sell B his automobile for $600; but at that moment the auto-

mobile had already been burned in A's garage. *Is there a sale? A contract to sell?* (SALES § 2, p. 300.)

3. A, about to go hunting deer, purports to sell to B the game he expects to kill. A unexpectedly kills a large moose which he transfers at once to X; B brings replevin against X for the moose. *What decision?* (SALES § 2, p. 300.)

4. A, a farmer, planted forty acres of corn and purported to sell to B the corn which he expected to harvest. When the corn was husked he sold it to Y. B brings replevin against Y. *What decision?* (SALES § 2, p. 300.)

5. A sold and delivered to B a chattel expecting to receive cash immediately. The cash was not paid. *How advise A?* (SALES § 3, p. 300.)

6. *Under what circumstances, if at all, does title to goods pass when the contract to sell is made?* (SALES § 3, p. 300.)

7. A had a thousand bushels of wheat in his granary. *Is it possible for him to transfer to B a property right in three hundred bushels of it without separating it?* (SALES § 3, p. 301.)

8. A sold three barge loads of oil to B and B sent his own barges for the oil to be put into them. *When did title pass to B?* (SALES § 4, p. 301.)

9. *Where the seller of goods is authorized to send the goods to the buyer by carrier, when does title usually pass?* (SALES § 5, p. 301.)

10. *What is the effect of C. O. D. upon the passing of title?* (SALES § 5, p. 301.)

11. X ordered goods to be sent by Y in Chicago to X in Cincinnati; Y shipped the goods, taking out the bill of lading in his own name and sent it with draft attached to a bank in Cincinnati. *What is the effect of such a transaction upon the title to the goods?* (SALES § 6, p. 302.)

12. Facts like 11 ante but X is unable to pay for the goods until he resells them at retail. *How can he accomplish his purpose by use of a trust receipt?* (SALES § 6, p. 302.)

13. *What is the purpose and effect of factors' acts?* (SALES § 7, p. 303.)

14. *What is usually required of a retailer where he sells at one time his entire stock of goods?* (SALES § 7, p. 303.)

15. *What is meant by a conditional sale and how does it operate to protect the seller?* (SALES § 8, p. 303.)

16. *What is the effect, as to creditors, of a seller retaining possession after selling the goods?* (SALES § 8, p. 303.)

17. A sells a chattel to B, but retains possession; then in fraud of B, A sells and delivers the chattel to X who pays value without notice of the transaction with B. *How advise X?* (SALES § 8, p. 303.)

18. A makes a conditional sale of goods to B who pays the purchase price by installments, A retaining title by way of security. The goods are accidentally destroyed. *Must B continue to pay the installments?* (SALES § 9, p. 304.)

19. *When, by modern law, is an affirmation construed to be a warranty?* (SALES § 10, p. 304.)

20. *What is the obligation of one who sells by description or by sample?* (SALES § 10, p. 304.)

21. *When is there no implied warranty of title?* (SALES § 11, p. 304.)

22. *When is there an implied warranty of merchantability? Of fitness for purpose?* (SALES § 12, p. 305.)

23. X, a retailer, sells food in the original package to A, a consumer; the goods are not fit for human consumption. *How advise A as to his rights and remedies against X? Against the manufacturer or wholesaler?* (SALES § 12, p. 305.)

24. A contracts to sell goods to B. *Where must A deliver them?* (SALES § 13, p. 305.)

25. A contracts to sell goods to B but delivers an amount in excess of the amount contracted for. *What may B do?* (SALES § 13, p. 305.)

26. A contracts to deliver goods in 10 installments, each installment to be paid for on delivery. B pays for the first two but defaults as to the third. *What may A do?* (SALES § 13, p. 305.)

27. *Under what circumstances is a buyer entitled to inspect the goods he has contracted to buy?* (SALES § 14, p. 306.)

28. *Under what circumstances may the buyer reject the goods delivered to him and resell them on account of the seller?* (SALES § 15, p. 306.)

29. A sells goods to B on thirty days credit; at the end of the thirty days A is still in possession. *How advise B?* (SALES § 16, p. 306.)

30. A orders goods from B to be sent to him by carrier; after the goods have been shipped but before they have been delivered to A, B learns that A is insolvent. *What may B do?* (SALES § 17, p. 307.)

31. *Does reservation of the title by way of security prevent the seller from recovering the price?* (SALES § 18, p. 307.)

32. *If the buyer refuses to accept and pay for the goods and the seller sues for such non-acceptance, what is the measure of his damages?* (SALES § 19, p. 307.)

33. A sells goods to B for $200, payable in twenty installments, title being reserved by way of security. After paying $120, B defaults. *How advise A as to his rights and remedies?* (SALES § 20, p. 307.)

34. *Where the seller wrongfully refuses to transfer title to the goods, what is the remedy of the buyer at common law? In equity? Under the Sales Act?* (SALES § 21, p. 308.)

35. A sold and delivered a chattel to B with a warranty, B being given credit of 90 days for half the purchase price of $500. There is a breach of warranty. *How advise B at the end of thirty days?* (SALES § 22, p. 308.)

36. *Is a contract for the sale of trees within the section of the statute of frauds dealing with interests in land or within the section dealing with goods, wares and merchandise?* (SALES § 23, p. 309.)

37. *Under what circumstances, by the Uniform Sales Act, may the seller recover the contract price of goods manufactured to the buyer's order in spite of the buyer's refusal to accept the goods?* (SALES § 23, p. 309.)

38. *What is meant by the phrase in the statute of frauds, "accept part of the goods . . . and actually receive the same"?* (SALES § 24, p. 309.)

39. *What is meant by "give something in earnest"?* (SALES § 25, p. 310.)

40. *May part payment consist of the buyer's note or check?* (SALES § 25, p. 310.)

41. *At what time must the memorandum be given?* (SALES § 26, p. 310.)

42. A made an oral contract to sell goods to B for $300. Later A sent to B a written memorandum of the contract and asked "Do you assent?" B replied in a letter saying: "I do not assent, I rely on the statute." *Is the contract binding?* (SALES § 26, p. 310.)

43. *What points must be covered by the memorandum?* (SALES § 26, p. 310.)

44. *In a sale by auction, who may sign the memorandum?* (SALES § 26, p. 310.)

BILLS AND NOTES

1. *What are the usual words of negotiability?* (BILLS & NOTES § 1, p. 311.)

2. *Must the words "promise" or "order" be used?* (BILLS & NOTES § 2, p. 312.)

3. A note contained a statement that it was secured by a mortgage on a certain piece of land. *Did this render the note non-negotiable?* (BILLS & NOTES § 2, p. 312.)

4. *What is the significance of consideration as between the original parties to a note? To a bona fide purchaser from the payee?* (BILLS & NOTES § 2, p. 312.)

5. *What is the requirement as to time of payment of a negotiable instrument?* (BILLS & NOTES § 3, p. 312.)

6. *At what time is a demand note payable?* (BILLS & NOTES § 3, p. 312.)

7. *What is the effect, if any, of a provision for the payment of attorney's fees?* (BILLS & NOTES § 4, p. 313.)

8. A executed a note to B and delivered it to B upon condition that title was not to pass until B obtained a loan for A; B did not obtain the loan but transferred the note to X, who paid value without notice of the condition. *How advise X?* (BILLS & NOTES § 5, p. 313.)

9. *When is an indorsement necessary? When not necessary? What is an allonge?* (BILLS & NOTES § 6, p. 313.)

10. A executed a note to the order of B and delivered it to him; B then indorsed it in blank to C who indorsed it specially to D. *May D transfer title to it to E by mere delivery?* (BILLS & NOTES § 6, p. 313.)

11. *What is the effect of the payee or other holder indorsing "without recourse"?* (BILLS & NOTES § 6, p. 314.)

12. *Does the possession of an indorsed negotiable instrument raise a presumption that the possessor has title?* (BILLS & NOTES § 6, p. 314.)

13. A of Indianapolis has a negotiable note made by B of Denver; he deposits it in his own bank in Indianapolis for collection; that bank sends it to its correspondent bank in Denver for collection; because of the negligence of the Denver bank the note is not collected and B is now insolvent. *How advise A?* (BILLS & NOTES § 7, p. 314.)

14. Facts like 13 ante except that the Denver bank before collection becomes bankrupt. *How advise A?* (BILLS & NOTES § 7, p. 314.)

15. Facts like 13 ante except that the Denver bank becomes bankrupt after collection and before remittance to the Indianapolis bank. *How advise A?* (BILLS & NOTES § 7, p. 314.)

16. X, the holder of a note against Y, indorses it to his agent A for collection. *Does this authorize A to sue Y on the note?* (BILLS & NOTES § 7, p. 314.)

17. X, the holder of a negotiable note made by Y payable to order, transfers it for value to A and delivers it to A without indorsing it. *How advise A?* (BILLS & NOTES § 8, p. 315.)

18. X, the holder of a negotiable note payable to order and indorsed in blank, lost it; Y found it and transferred it before maturity for value to Z who did not know how Y had acquired it. *How advise Z?* (BILLS & NOTES § 9, p. 316.)

19. A executed a note to B but did not deliver it; B, however, wrongfully obtained possession of it and indorsed it before maturity for value to X, who had no notice of the lack of delivery to B. *How advise X under the Negotiable Instruments Law? Before the Negotiable Instruments Law?* (BILLS & NOTES § 9, p. 316.)

20. A executed a note and left blank the name of the payee; he entrusted the note to X to negotiate and turn the proceeds over to A; X negotiated the note to Y whose name is inserted as payee and absconded with the proceeds. *How advise Y?* (BILLS & NOTES § 9, p. 316.)

21. B owed A $2,000 and A was pressing him for payment; B thereupon transferred to A a note against X for $100 upon A's promise not to sue B for six months. The note had been procured from X by fraud. *How advise A as to his rights against X?* (BILLS & NOTES § 10, p. 316.)

22. A, having a negotiable instrument subject to an equitable defense, deposits it in Bank X to his account. *Under what circumstances, if at all, does the X Bank become a holder for value?* (BILLS & NOTES § 10, p. 316.)

23. *If one buys a note from an utter stranger, is he regarded as buying in good faith?* (BILLS & NOTES § 11, p. 316.)

24. *What is the effect of buying a negotiable instrument before its date?* (BILLS & NOTES § 11, p. 316.)

25. *What is the effect of buying an instrument from a known trustee?* (BILLS & NOTES § 11, p. 316.)

26. If a trustee deposits trust money in a bank in his name as trustee and

later checks out the money and absconds with it, *under what circumstances is the bank liable?* (BILLS & NOTES § 11, p. 317.)

27. From the standpoint of negotiation, *when does a demand note become due?* (BILLS & NOTES § 12, p. 317.)

28. *What is the effect of a stipulation in a note that upon default in the payment of interest the holder may declare the note due at once?* (BILLS & NOTES § 12, p. 317.)

29. A, having a note to which there was an equitable defense, transferred it for value before maturity to B who had no notice of the equity; B made a gift of the note to his son C. *How advise C?* (BILLS & NOTES § 13, p. 317.)

30. *To what extent, if at all, are the following defenses real defenses:* (a) *forgery;* (b) *lack of authority of an agent;* (c) *duress;* (d) *infancy;* (e) *illegality;* (f) *insanity;* (g) *fraud in the inducement;* (h) *fraud in the execution;* (i) *fraudulent alteration by holder?* (BILLS & NOTES § 14, p. 318.)

31. *What is the difference between lack of consideration and failure of consideration? Are they real or equitable defenses?* (BILLS & NOTES § 15, p. 319.)

32. *What is the effect of altering a negotiable instrument?* (BILLS & NOTES § 15, p. 319.)

33. *What is the position of an accommodation maker of a note?* (BILLS & NOTES § 16, p. 319.)

34. *What is the position of the drawee of a bill of exchange who refuses to accept it?* (BILLS & NOTES § 17, p. 319.)

35. *What is the position of an accommodation acceptor of a bill of exchange?* (BILLS & NOTES § 18, p. 320.)

36. A presented to the X Bank a check purporting to be the check of one of the bank's depositors; the check had been forged. The X Bank paid the check to A and later, finding out that the check had been forged, sued to recover back from A. *Is it entitled?* (BILLS & NOTES § 18, p. 320.)

37. *What is the liability of an indorser? His right?* (BILLS & NOTES § 19, p. 320.)

38. *What is an anomalous indorser and what is his position under the Negotiable Instruments Law?* (BILLS & NOTES § 20, p. 320.)

39. *If an agent executes a negotiable instrument for his principal, how may he escape personal liability?* (BILLS & NOTES § 20, p. 321.)

40. *When is presentment necessary and why? When not necessary?* (BILLS & NOTES § 21, p. 321.)

41. *What is meant by dishonor of a negotiable instrument and what is its significance to the holder?* (BILLS & NOTES § 22, p. 321.)

42. *When is a protest necessary and how is it made?* (BILLS & NOTES § 22, p. 321.)

43. *What is an acceptance for honor and how is it made?* (BILLS & NOTES § 22, p. 322.)

44. *What are the rights of an acceptor for honor?* (BILLS & NOTES § 22, p. 322.)

45. *What is the effect of payment by the principal debtor or the one primarily liable on the instrument?* (BILLS & NOTES § 23, p. 322.)

46. *What is the effect of payment by one who is secondarily liable on the instrument and who is not the principal debtor?* (BILLS & NOTES § 23, p. 322.)

47. *What is the right of a payor for honor?* (BILLS & NOTES § 23, p. 322.)

48. A, having a note made by B, received from B a new instrument covering the same liability. *What is the effect of this?* (BILLS & NOTES § 24, p. 323.)

49. *What are the four differences between a check and a bill of exchange?* (BILLS & NOTES § 25, p. 323.)

50. *At what time must a check be presented for payment? What is the effect of failure to present it within that time?* (BILLS & NOTES § 25, p. 323.)

51. A buys goods from B and gives in payment a check on the X Bank. A dies before B presents the check for payment. *How advise B?* (BILLS & NOTES § 25, p. 323.)

52. A gives B a check on the X Bank; B gets it certified. *What is the effect of this?* (BILLS & NOTES § 26, p. 323.)

53. A gives B a check on the X Bank; the X Bank refuses to pay the check. *How advise B and A as to their rights against the X Bank?* (BILLS & NOTES § 26, p. 323.)

54. *When, if at all, does a check operate as absolute payment?* (BILLS & NOTES § 26, p. 323.)

CORPORATIONS

1. *What are the usual statutory requirements for the formation of a corporation? How does the corporation usually accept the certificate of incorporation?* (CORPORATIONS § 1, p. 326.)

2. *What are the essentials of a corporation de facto? How does such a corporation differ from a corporation de jure?* (CORPORATIONS § 2, p. 326.)

3. *What is the doctrine of corporation by estoppel? Is it necessary that the usual requirements of estoppel be present?* (CORPORATIONS § 3, p. 327.)

4. A, as director of the X association, represents to the public that it is a corporation and Y acts thereon. *May Y hold the X association liable as a corporation?* (CORPORATIONS § 3, p. 327.)

5. X contracts with the Y association on the basis that such association was a corporation; the Y association sues X for breach of contract. *May X set up in defense that he supposed the Y association was a corporation? Why?* (CORPORATIONS § 3, p. 327.)

6. X contracts with Y and Z as if they were a corporation. Later X seeks to hold Y and Z liable individually. *May he do so?* (CORPORATIONS § 3, p. 327.)

7. *In what two important respects is a corporation different from a partnership?* (CORPORATIONS § 4, p. 327.)

8. *Is a joint stock company a corporation or a partnership?* (CORPORATIONS § 4, p. 328.)

9. *In what two respects is a corporation different from a business trust?* (CORPORATIONS § 4, p. 328.)

10. A bought all the shares in the X Corporation. *Did this put an end to the existence of the corporation?* (CORPORATIONS § 5, p. 328.)

11. *What are the rights of a corporate shareholder?* (CORPORATIONS § 6, p. 328.)

12. *Under what circumstances, if at all, may an individual who buys all the stock in a corporation become individually liable for corporation debts?* (CORPORATIONS § 7, p. 329.)

13. *Under what circumstances, if at all, may the X Corporation, which owns all the stock of the Y Corporation, become responsible for the liabilities of the Y Corporation?* (CORPORATIONS § 7, p. 329.)

14. *What is the doctrine of the implied powers of a corporation?* (CORPORATIONS § 8, p. 329.)

15. *What was the early view as to ultra vires?* (CORPORATIONS § 9, p. 329.)

16. *What is the modern trend as to ultra vires?* (CORPORATIONS § 10, p. 329.)

17. A enters into an ultra vires contract with the X Corporation and it is performed on both sides. *What result? Suppose it is not performed on either side?* (CORPORATIONS § 11, p. 330.)

18. *Suppose the contract is fully performed by one of the parties? Partially performed?* (CORPORATIONS § 11, p. 330.)

19. *Under what circumstances may a corporation be unable to set up ultra vires against a bona fide purchaser of negotiable paper to which it is a party?* (CORPORATIONS § 11, p. 330.)

20. *What argument is sometimes made, based upon the fact that the corporate charter is a matter of public record? How answer it?* (CORPORATIONS § 11, p. 330.)

21. *How far may stockholders bind the corporation to an ultra vires contract by ratification?* (CORPORATIONS § 11, p. 330.)

22. *What is the effect of a conveyance inter vivos of land or chattels to a corporation where the conveyance is ultra vires? Of a conveyance by will?* (CORPORATIONS § 12, p. 331.)

23. *Is a corporation liable for exemplary or punitive damages?* (CORPORATIONS § 13, p. 331; DAMAGES § 12, p. 226.)

24. *To what extent and how, if at all, is a corporation punishable for a crime?* (CORPORATIONS § 14, p. 331.)

25. *Upon what theory, if any, does a corporation become liable on a contract made on its behalf by the promoter of the corporation?* (CORPORATIONS § 15, p. 332.)

26. *What is the liability of a corporation promoter and to whom? Is he properly classified as a fiduciary?* (CORPORATIONS § 16, p. 332.)

27. *May the directors act separately or must they act as a board? What may they and what may they not do?* (CORPORATIONS § 17, p. 333.)

28. *What may be delegated by a board of directors?* (CORPORATIONS § 17, p. 333.)

29. *Is a director an agent of the corporation?* (CORPORATIONS § 17, p. 333.)

30. *When is notice to a director not notice to the corporation?* (CORPORATIONS § 17, p. 333.)

31. *When, if at all, is it not necessary to send notice of directors' meetings to the directors?* (CORPORATIONS § 17, p. 333.)

32. *What is the extent of the liability of directors?* (CORPORATIONS § 18, p. 334.)

33. *Under what circumstances does a director become personally liable though acting for the corporation?* (CORPORATIONS § 18, p. 334.)

34. *Under what circumstances may a director make a valid contract with the corporation? When not?* (CORPORATIONS § 19, p. 335.)

35. A director buys stock from X, a stockholder. *Is he under a duty to disclose to X knowledge of corporate affairs obtained by him as such director?* (CORPORATIONS § 19, p. 335.)

36. *What is the effect of a subscription for shares if the corporation is already in existence? If it is not yet in existence?* (CORPORATIONS § 20, p. 335.)

37. *What is the effect of a contract to subscribe for shares in the future?* (CORPORATIONS § 20, p. 335.)

38. *Under what circumstances will a subscriber for shares be released from his contract? When not?* (CORPORATIONS § 20, p. 336.)

39. *Under what circumstances is a shareholder entitled to inspect the corporate books? When not?* (CORPORATIONS § 21, p. 336.)

40. *What shares are not entitled to vote?* (CORPORATIONS § 22, p. 336.)

41. *What is a proxy? May it be made irrevocable?* (CORPORATIONS § 22, p. 336.)

42. *Is there any obligation on the part of the majority stockholders toward the minority?* (CORPORATIONS § 22, p. 336.)

43. *May stockholders ever compel the directors to declare a dividend?* (CORPORATIONS § 23, p. 337.)

44. *What is the effect of a declaration of a dividend out of profits? Out of capital?* (CORPORATIONS § 23, p. 337.)

45. *What is a stock dividend and what is its effect?* (CORPORATIONS § 23, p. 337.)

46. *To what are holders of non-cumulative preferred shares entitled? Holders of cumulative preferred shares?* (CORPORATIONS § 23, p. 337.)

47. The X Corporation issued stock to A as fully paid up, but it was only partially paid up. A transferred the stock to B who paid value in good faith. The X corporation is now insolvent. *How advise A and B?* (CORPORATIONS § 24, p. 338.)

48. *When may par value stock be validly issued for less than par?* (CORPORATIONS § 24, p. 338.)

49. Where stock certificates are indorsed in blank by A to B and B does not have a transfer made on the books of the corporation, *what is the effect of such a transfer?* (CORPORATIONS § 25, p. 338.)

50. X, a shareholder, indorsed his stock certificate in blank and entrusted it to his agent A who fraudulently sold it to B and absconded with the money. *How advise B, aside from the Uniform Stock Transfer Act? Under the Uniform Stock Transfer Act?* (CORPORATIONS § 25, p. 339.)

51. Facts like 50 ante except that A procures the corporation to issue a new certificate to B who pays value in good faith. *How advise X? The corporation?* (CORPORATIONS § 25, p. 339.)

52. X transfers his shares to Y but the corporation wrongfully refuses to register the transfer on its books. *How advise Y?* (CORPORATIONS § 25, p. 339.)

53. *When may a shareholder maintain an action against the corporation?* (CORPORATIONS § 26, p. 339.)

54. If the corporation has a cause of action against X, *in what way can a shareholder bring about the collection thereof?* (CORPORATIONS § 26, p. 340.)

55. *What is the effect of Blue Sky Laws?* (CORPORATIONS § 27, p. 340.)

56. *What is meant by saying that the corporate assets are a trust fund for the benefit of creditors?* (CORPORATIONS § 28, p. 340.)

57. *When may a creditor obtain an injunction against the corporation?* (CORPORATIONS § 29, p. 341.)

58. *What remedies are available to a judgment creditor?* (CORPORATIONS § 29, p. 341.)

59. *May a corporation prefer some creditors over others?* (CORPORATIONS § 29, p. 341.)

60. *When will the court appoint a receiver for the corporation?* (CORPORATIONS § 29, p. 341.)

61. Without legislative authority, a corporation issued new stock and some of it was transferred to X who paid value in good faith. *How advise X?* (CORPORATIONS § 30, p. 342.)

62. *What is meant by a right of pre-emption, and what is the reason for it?* (CORPORATIONS § 30, p. 342.)

63. *When may a corporation validly buy back its own stock? Is this a reduction of capital stock?* (CORPORATIONS § 30, p. 342.)

64. Corporation Y buys all the assets of Corporation X. *How advise A, an unpaid creditor of X?* (CORPORATIONS § 31, p. 342.)

65. Corporation A wishes to do business in State X. *May State X exclude it entirely? Why?* (CORPORATIONS § 32, p. 343.)

66. State X allows Corporation A to do business within the State. *What may State X insist upon? What may it not do?* (CORPORATIONS § 32, p. 343.)

67. *What is meant by "doing business"?* (CORPORATIONS § 32, p. 343.)

68. *What does a state usually require of a foreign corporation as a condition precedent to its doing business within the state?* (CORPORATIONS § 32, p. 343.)

PARTNERSHIP

1. *What is the entity or mercantile theory of a partnership? The aggregate theory? Which one is followed by the courts? By the legislatures?* (PARTNERSHIP § 1, p. 345.)

2. *What is the effect today of sharing profits? What formerly?* (PARTNERSHIP § 2, p. 346.)

3. *In a limited partnership, what is the position of a limited partner?* (PARTNERSHIP § 3, p. 347.)

4. *In what way is a joint stock company different from an ordinary partnership?* (PARTNERSHIP § 3, p. 347.)

5. *In what respect is a joint adventure different from a partnership?* (PARTNERSHIP § 3, p. 347.)

6. *What is meant by a sub-partnership?* (PARTNERSHIP § 3, p. 347.)

7. A wished B to enter into partnership with him. B was willing to put up the necessary capital but persuaded X to become a partner with A in his place. *How advise B as to his liability to creditors of the partnership of A and X?* (PARTNERSHIP § 3, p. 347.)

8. A falsely represented to X that he was a member of the partnership of Y, Z and Co., whereupon X extended credit to the partnership. *How advise X?* (PARTNERSHIP § 3, p. 347.)

9. X, Y and Z attempted to organize a corporation but did not succeed in organizing even a de facto corporation. *What is the measure of liability of X, Y and Z toward creditors of the attempted corporation?* (PARTNERSHIP § 3, p. 347.)

10. A conveys land to the partnership of X and Y. *What was the effect of this at common law? Under the Uniform Partnership Act?* (PARTNERSHIP § 4, p. 348.)

11. *Why does each partner have the right to have partnership assets applied first to pay partnership debts?* (PARTNERSHIP § 5, p. 348.)

12. *Why do separate creditors have a right to priority in the individual property of the partners?* (PARTNERSHIP § 5, p. 348.)

13. *May the separate creditor of a partner levy upon his interest in the partnership assets under the Uniform Partnership Act? Apart from the Uniform Partnership Act?* (PARTNERSHIP § 5, p. 348.)

14. *What happens to the title to specific personal property of the partnership upon the death of a partner under the Uniform Partnership Act? Apart from the Uniform Partnership Act?* (PARTNERSHIP § 5, p. 348.)

15. *How determine whether a partnership is insolvent?* (PARTNERSHIP § 6, p. 349; § 20, p. 355.)

16. Suppose an insolvent partnership conveys partnership property for less than its fair value. *What is the right of partnership creditors under the Uniform Partnership Act? Apart from the Uniform Partnership Act?* (PARTNERSHIP § 6, p. 349.)

17. *To what extent may a partner bind the partnership? What may he not do?* (PARTNERSHIP § 7, p. 349.)

18. There are three partners; one dissents from the proposed action of the other two. *How advise him?* (PARTNERSHIP § 7, p. 349.)

19. *Under the Uniform Partnership Act, what acts are valid only by unanimous consent of the partners?* (PARTNERSHIP § 7, p. 349.)

20. *To what extent is a partnership liable for the torts of a partner?* (PARTNERSHIP § 8, p. 350.)

21. A, member of the firm A & B, while acting within the scope of the partnership business, negligently injured A's wife X. *How advise X as to her rights against the firm?* (PARTNERSHIP § 8, p. 350.)

22. Y committed a tort to property owned by A and B, a partnership. *How advise A and B as to the remedy?* (PARTNERSHIP § 9, p. 350.)

23. Facts like 22 ante, except that the firm was composed of A, B and Z, a dormant partner. *How advise?* (PARTNERSHIP § 9, p. 350.)

24. A, B and C, a partnership, entered into a contract with X. *How advise X as to his remedy for breach of contract?* (PARTNERSHIP § 10, p. 350.)

25. Same facts as 24 ante except that C dies. *May X reach C's estate?* (PARTNERSHIP § 10, p. 350.)

26. Same facts as 24 ante except that C is a non-resident. *How advise X?* (PARTNERSHIP § 10, p. 351.)

27. A advanced money to the firm of A, B & C. *Upon dissolution of the firm, how advise A?* (PARTNERSHIP § 11, p. 351.)

28. A, B & C contribute unequal amounts to the firm capital, but there is a provision in the partnership agreement that they are to be equal partners. *What is the effect of the provision?* (PARTNERSHIP § 11, p. 351.)

29. *When, if at all, is a partner entitled to be paid for his services?* (PARTNERSHIP § 11, p. 351.)

30. *What is the rule as to secret profits? As to the right of inspection of partnership books?* (PARTNERSHIP § 12, p. 352.)

31. A, in business for himself, contracts to take in B as his partner for three years, but later refuses to form the partnership. *How advise B?* (PARTNERSHIP § 13, p. 352.)

32. X and Y form a partnership, each agreeing to contribute $10,000 capital. X made his contribution, but Y did not. *How advise X?* (PARTNERSHIP § 13, p. 352.)

33. The firm of X and Y enters into a contract with X; X defaults. *How advise Y?* (PARTNERSHIP § 14, p. 352.)

34. *What is the effect of the death of a partner? Of his bankruptcy?* (PARTNERSHIP § 15, p. 353.)

35. *What is the effect of a partner becoming insane? Of his assigning his interest?* (PARTNERSHIP § 15, p. 353.)

36. X, Y and Z were a partnership, Z retired from the firm and the business was continued by X and Y who assumed the obligations of the partnership. *How advise A, a creditor of the firm of X, Y and Z?* (PARTNERSHIP § 16, p. 353.)

37. *In winding up a partnership, what is the power of the partners?* (PARTNERSHIP § 17, p. 354.)

38. A makes a contract with the firm of X, Y and Z without notice that Z's bankruptcy had caused dissolution of the firm. *How advise A as to his rights against the partnership assets? As to his rights against Z's estate?* (PARTNERSHIP § 17, p. 354.)

39. X, a member of the partnership of X, Y and Z, is planning to retire from the firm. *How advise him as to protecting himself against further undertakings by the firm?* (PARTNERSHIP § 18, p. 354.)

40. D is admitted to the partnership of A, B and C. *To what extent does he become responsible for the existing liabilities of the firm?* (PARTNERSHIP § 18, p. 354.)

41. The firm of X, Y and Z sells all its assets to the A corporation, formed by X, Y and Z. *How advise B, a creditor of the firm?* (PARTNERSHIP § 18, p. 354.)

42. *What is the order of distribution of partnership assets upon a winding up?* (PARTNERSHIP § 19, p. 355.)

43. The firm of X, Y and Z is insolvent and has committed an act of bankruptcy; A, a creditor, wishes to put them into bankruptcy, but Z is a farmer. *How advise A?* (PARTNERSHIP § 20, p. 355.)

44. *When is an act of bankruptcy of the partnership committed?* (PARTNERSHIP § 20, p. 355.)

45. *May the trustee in bankruptcy of a partnership reach the individual assets of the different partners?* (PARTNERSHIP § 20, p. 355.)

46. A is selling goods on credit to the firm of X, Y and Z. *How can he avoid the rule that separate creditors are entitled to priority out of the separate property of the partners?* (PARTNERSHIP § 20, p. 355.)

47. The partnership of X, Y and Z goes through bankruptcy and gets a discharge. *What is the effect of this upon the liabilities of each partner?* (PARTNERSHIP § 20, p. 355.)

48. *What is the effect of a discharge in bankruptcy of a partner upon his obligation to the partnership creditors?* (PARTNERSHIP § 20, p. 355.)

SURETYSHIP

1. *What does the word surety mean in the broader sense. In the narrower sense?* (SURETYSHIP § 1, p. 356.)

2. *What is the rule of construction as to the undertaking of an uncompensated surety?* (SURETYSHIP § 1, p. 356.)

3. X wished to buy goods at various times on credit from A; B offered to guarantee the payment for such goods; A thereupon sold goods to X on credit. *What is the effect of B's death?* (SURETYSHIP § 2, p. 357.)

4. The statute of frauds requires a written memorandum to charge a defendant upon "any special promise to answer for the debt, default or miscarriage of another person". *To what two kinds of transactions does this apply?* (SURETYSHIP § 3, p. 357.)

5. A held a note against X for $300; he assigned it to B for $270 orally guaranteeing that X would pay the note at maturity. *Is A liable on the oral guaranty?* (SURETYSHIP § 3, p. 358.)

6. Facts like 5 ante except that A's promise is to pay B out of assets of X in A's hands. *How advise B?* (SURETYSHIP § 3, p. 358.)

7. X borrowed money from Y and A undertook to be X's surety but Y insisted upon two sureties so A persuaded B to become co-surety with him for X by orally agreeing to indemnify him against loss. *Is A bound on his oral promise?* (SURETYSHIP § 3, p. 358.)

8. A sent goods from Kansas City to B in Chicago on a del credere commission. B sold the goods to X who defaulted. *Is B's obligation to A within the statute of frauds?* (SURETYSHIP § 3, p. 358.)

9. *In order to satisfy the statute is it necessary that the memorandum state the consideration for the guaranty?* (SURETYSHIP § 3, p. 359.)

10. A borrows money from X and B signs the note as co-obligor. *What is the legal effect upon B's obligation to X that A was insane or an infant?* (SURETYSHIP § 4, p. 359.)

11. *May a surety co-obligor set up that his principal has become bankrupt?* (SURETYSHIP § 4, p. 359.)

12. A induced B by fraud to enter into a contract with him and X became B's surety. X later finds out the fraud. *How advise X?* (SURETYSHIP § 4, p. 359.)

13. A, holding a note to which he had forged B's name, persuades X to become a surety on the note. X later finds out about the forgery. *How advise X?* (SURETYSHIP § 4, p. 359.)

14. A borrowed money from X and A and B sign the note as co-obligors. Later X releases A. *What effect, if any, does this have upon B's obligation to X?* (SURETYSHIP § 5, p. 359.)

15. A borrowed money from X and A and B signed the note as co-obligors.

A pays the note but within four months X becomes bankrupt and his assignee in bankruptcy compelled A to return the money paid. *How advise B?* (SURETYSHIP § 5, p. 360.)

16. A borrowed money from X and A and B signed the note as co-obligors; later A tendered payment to X but X refused it. *How advise A and B?* (SURETYSHIP § 5, p. 360.)

17. A borrowed money from X and A and B signed the note as co-obligors. A asks X to extend the time of payment. *How advise X?* (SURETYSHIP § 5, p. 360.)

18. Same facts as 17 ante except that B is a compensated surety. *How advise X?* (SURETYSHIP § 5, p. 360.)

19. A borrowed money from X and A and B sign the note as co-obligors. Both default and X sues A and gets judgment but finds A execution proof. He then sues B. *Of what effect, if any, is his judgment against A?* (SURETYSHIP § 5, p. 360.)

20. A borrowed money from X and A and B sign the note as co-obligors. B is out of the state for two years; the statute of limitations has run in favor of A. *How advise B?* (SURETYSHIP § 5, p. 360; § 10, p. 364.)

21. A borrowed money from X and A and B sign the note as co-obligors. A also, without B's knowledge, turns over property to X by way of security. Later X releases the property. *How advise B?* (SURETYSHIP § 6, p. 360.)

22. A contracted to erect a building for X, the contract providing that ten per cent of the amount due to A should be retained by X as security for further performance. X does not retain the full ten per cent. *What effect does this have upon the obligation of A's sureties?* (SURETYSHIP § 6, p. 360.)

23. A borrows money from X and A and B sign the note as co-obligors. Upon default X sues B and B wishes to set off a claim which A has against X. *May he do so?* (SURETYSHIP § 7, p. 361.)

24. A borrows $1,000 from X Bank and A and B sign the note as co-obligors. When the note becomes due A has $700 on deposit at the X Bank. Later A withdraws the $700 and is hopelessly insolvent. *How advise B?* (SURETYSHIP § 8, p. 361.)

25. A is employed by X for a year and B guarantees to X that A will faithfully perform his contract. Later X sues B because of A's default and B sets up in defense that X had discovered that A was dishonest but did not notify B. *Is the defense good?* (SURETYSHIP § 8, p. 361.)

26. A borrows $1,000 from X and A and B sign the note as co-obligors. At maturity A has plenty of liquid assets but refuses to pay; B demands that X sue A before bringing suit against B. *How advise X?* (SURETYSHIP § 8, p. 362; § 12, p. 365.)

27. *What is the right of subrogation and when does it arise?* (SURETYSHIP § 9, p. 362.)

28. A borrows $1,000 from X and A and B sign the note as co-obligors. Without B's knowledge A also gives X a mortgage on two building lots. At

maturity B pays and asks X to assign to him the mortgage. *How advise X?* (SURETYSHIP § 9, p. 363.)

29. A's house was negligently set on fire by the X Railroad Company which paid A $4,000 in satisfaction of his claim. A had his house insured for $3,500. *How advise the X Railroad Company?* (SURETYSHIP § 8, p. 363; INSURANCE § 9, p. 380.)

30. *After the surety pays the creditor how long does he have within which to take advantage of his right of subrogation?* (SURETYSHIP § 9, p. 363.)

31. *When does the surety's right of reimbursement arise?* (SURETYSHIP § 10, p. 363.)

32. *Where did the right originate? Is it today equitable, contractual or quasi-contractual?* (SURETYSHIP § 10, p. 363.)

33. The surety gives the creditor his note in full satisfaction of the debt and at once, before the note is paid, sues the principal for reimbursement. *May he recover?* (SURETYSHIP § 10, p. 364.)

34. A borrowed money from X and A and B signed the note as co-obligors; A is out the state for two years; the statute of limitations has run in favor of B; B pays. *Is he entitled to reimbursement from A?* (SURETYSHIP § 10, p. 364.)

35. Facts like 34 ante except that the statute of limitations has run also in favor of A. *How advise?* (SURETYSHIP § 10, p. 364.)

36. *What was the origin of the surety's right of contribution? Is it today regarded as contractual or quasi contractual?* (SURETYSHIP § 11, p. 364.)

37. *When does the right to contribution arise?* (SURETYSHIP § 11, p. 364.)

38. *May the surety still enforce contribution in equity? When is it advantageous to do so?* (SURETYSHIP § 11, p. 364.)

39. *In order that there be a right to contribution, is it necessary that the sureties sign the same instrument?* (SURETYSHIP § 11, p. 364.)

40. *What is a sub-surety and what are his rights?* (SURETYSHIP § 11, p. 364.)

41. A surety makes a partial payment to the creditor. *Does this set the statute of limitations to running again as to the creditor's right against a co-surety?* (SURETYSHIP § 11, p. 364.)

42. *What is meant by a surety's right of exoneration and under what circumstances is such a right important?* (SURETYSHIP § 12, p. 365.)

43. *When does the right of exoneration arise?* (SURETYSHIP § 12, p. 365.)

44. *What effect does it have upon the rights of the creditor?* (SURETYSHIP § 12, p. 365.)

45. A borrowed money from X and A and B signed the note as co-obligors; in order to induce B to sign as co-obligor, A placed securities in his hands. X now wishes to reach those securities. *Is he entitled?* (SURETYSHIP § 13, p. 365.)

MORTGAGES

1. *At common law, of what did the mortgage consist? What change was brought about by equity?* (MORTGAGES § 1, p. 366.)

2. *What is the lien theory of the mortgage?* (MORTGAGES § 2, p. 366.)

3. *What change was wrought by the lien theory on the mortgagee's right to possession?* (MORTGAGES § 2, p. 367.)

4. *What is the effect of tender after the day in lien theory states?* (MORTGAGES § 2, p. 367.)

5. A borrowed $10,000 from B and conveyed to B the title to his farm upon B's oral assurance that if at the end of two years A should repay the $10,000 with interest B would reconvey the farm to him. *How advise A?* (MORTGAGES § 3, p. 367.)

6. A borrowed $200 from B and mortgaged to B his crop of corn already planted on forty acres of land. When the crop matured, A harvested it and sold it to X. *How advise B?* (MORTGAGES § 4, p. 367.)

7. A borrowed $5,000 from B and agreed to give to B a mortgage on land which he expected to inherit from his father X. Shortly thereafter X died and A, inheriting the land, sold it to Y. *How advise B?* (MORTGAGES § 4, p. 368.)

8. A borrowed $3,000 from B and gave him a mortgage on his farm, B agreeing that he would, if A desired it, advance a further sum of $2,000 on the same security. Later that advance was made. *Upon A's insolvency, is B entitled to enforce the mortgage as to the full $5,000?* (MORTGAGES § 4, p. 368.)

9. A borrowed $5,000 from B for 3 years and gave B a note secured by a mortgage on his farm. Action on the note was barred by the ten year statute of limitations applicable thereto; the statute of limitations applicable to foreclosure of a mortgage is twenty years. *How advise B?* (MORTGAGES § 5, p. 368.)

10. B the mortgagee assigned his mortgage to X without transferring the note which was secured by the mortgage. *How advise X?* (MORTGAGES § 6, p. 368.)

11. A borrows $7,000 from B and gives him a mortgage on his farm; A later transfers his interest in the farm to X subject to the mortgage. *How advise B?* (MORTGAGES § 7, p. 369.)

12. Same facts as 11 ante except that X assumes the payment of the mortgage debt. *How advise?* (MORTGAGES § 7, p. 369.)

13. Same facts as 11 ante, except that A transfers only half of his farm to X. *How advise?* (MORTGAGES § 7, p. 369.)

14. Same facts as 12 ante except that X assumes payment of only part of the mortgage debt. *How advise?* (MORTGAGES § 7, p. 369.)

15. *What are the rights and liabilities of a mortgagee in possession?* (MORTGAGES § 8, p. 369.)

16. *What are the rights and liabilities of a mortgagor in possession?* (MORTGAGES § 8, p. 369.)

17. *If the mortgagor fails to pay taxes, how advise the mortgagee?* (MORTGAGES § 8, p. 369.)

18. *What is the extent of the insurable interest of the mortgagor? Of the mortgagee?* (MORTGAGES § 8, p. 369.)

19. *What is meant by clogging the equity of redemption?* (MORTGAGES § 8, p. 370.)

20. A mortgagor is in financial straits and wishes to sell his interest in the mortgaged property to the mortgagee. *How advise the mortgagee?* (MORTGAGES § 8, p. 370.)

21. A borrows $3,000 from B and contracts to give B a mortgage on his household goods; later A sells his household goods to Y. *How advise B if his contract was not covered by the registry act and Y knew of the contract?* (MORTGAGES § 9, p. 371.)

22. A borrows $4,000 from B and gives him a mortgage on his farm; B fails to record the mortgage; A then borrows $2,000 from C who does not know of B's mortgage. *How advise C?* (MORTGAGES § 9, p. 371.)

23. *In what respect is a purchase money mortgage different from other mortgages?* (MORTGAGES § 9, p. 371.)

24. *What is strict foreclosure and in what situation is it appropriate?* (MORTGAGES § 10, p. 371.)

25. A borrowed $5,000 from B and gave him a mortgage on his farm; later he borrowed $2,000 from C and gave him a second mortgage; still later he borrowed $1,000 from D and gave him a third mortgage. *In bringing suit to foreclose, whom should C make parties?* (MORTGAGES § 10, p. 372.)

26. Same facts as 25 ante except that D did not record his mortgage. *How advise?* (MORTGAGES § 10, p. 372.)

27. A borrows $6,000 from B for five years at 6 per cent interest, and gives him a mortgage on some land, the mortgage stipulating that upon default in the payment of interest the entire debt should become due. At the end of a year A defaults in the payment of interest. *How advise B?* (MORTGAGES § 10, p. 373.)

28. *Under what circumstances is it proper for the court to appoint a receiver to take charge of the rents and profits of the mortgaged property?* (MORTGAGES § 10, p. 373.)

29. *When may the mortgagee get a deficiency judgment?* (MORTGAGES § 10, p. 373.)

30. *What is the advantage of the mortgage providing that the mortgagee may sell the mortgaged property?* (MORTGAGES § 10, p. 373.)

INSURANCE

1. *What is the function of insurance?* (INSURANCE § 1, p. 374.)

2. *When does the insured make a real promise?* (INSURANCE § 1, p. 374.)

3. *Why is a high degree of good faith required of the insured? Of the insurer?* (INSURANCE § 1, p. 375.)

4. *May an insurance contract be oral?* (INSURANCE § 1, p. 375.)

5. A takes out a policy on his own life in favor of X. *Is it necessary that X have an insurable interest in A's life?* (INSURANCE § 2, p. 375.)

6. *What insurable interest does a husband have in his wife's life? A wife in her husband's life?* (INSURANCE § 2, p. 375.)

7. *To what amount, if any, may a parent insure the life of his minor child?* (INSURANCE § 2, p. 376.)

8. A borrowed $1,000 from B. *To what amount, if any, may B insure A's life?* (INSURANCE § 2, p. 376.)

9. A contracted to sell his house and lot to B for $10,000; only B signed the memorandum so that he could not enforce the contract. *Does he have an insurable interest in the property? Why?* (INSURANCE § 3, p. 376.)

10. *Where a real estate mortgage is given, what is the usual provision in the mortgage as to insurance?* (INSURANCE § 3, p. 376.)

11. A contracted to buy 100 head of mules to be delivered to him at the end of 10 days. *Does he have an insurable interest in the mules?* (INSURANCE § 3, p. 376.)

12. A loaned $1,000 to B without security. *Has A an insurable interest in B's property?* (INSURANCE § 3, p. 377.)

13. *Must the insurable interest exist at the time the policy was issued?* (INSURANCE § 3, p. 377.)

14. *Under what circumstances, if at all, will concealment by the insured invalidate a policy?* (INSURANCE § 4, p. 377.)

15. *What is the effect of a misrepresentation of a material fact made by the insured innocently?* (INSURANCE § 5, p. 377.)

16. *What is the effect of a misrepresentation as to his opinion made by the insured?* (INSURANCE § 5, p. 378.)

17. *In what respect does a warranty by the insured differ from a representation?* (INSURANCE § 6, p. 378.)

18. *What is the effect of a policy excepting certain risks?* (INSURANCE § 6, p. 379.)

19. *What is the difference in effect between a condition precedent and a condition subsequent in a policy?* (INSURANCE § 6, p. 379.)

20. X took out a policy on his life with the Y Company; at the time he was in military service and the agent knew it but assured X that the stipulation in the policy would not be enforced against him. X was killed while in military service. *How advise the Y Company?* (INSURANCE § 7, p. 379.)

21. *What is the difference between the doctrine of waiver and the doctrine of estoppel?* (INSURANCE § 8, p. 380.)

22. X took out a policy with the Y Company and gave his note at 60 days to pay the premium, the insurance company stipulating that it might cancel the policy if X defaulted. X did default and the Y Company sued to collect the note. *How advise X?* (INSURANCE § 8, p. 380.)

23. *Is an agreement to waive a condition valid and enforcible if based upon consideration?* (INSURANCE § 8, p. 380.)

24. A took out an accident policy on his own life with the X Company; later A was negligently killed by B; the X Company paid the amount of the policy to A's executor and asked to be subrogated to the executor's right against B. *Is it entitled?* (INSURANCE § 9, p. 381.)

25. *What is the effect of a stipulation in a life insurance policy against suicide by the insured "sane or insane"?* (INSURANCE § 10, p. 381.)

26. *What is the purpose of a stipulation in a policy making it incontestable? What bases for contest are not covered by such a stipulation?* (INSURANCE § 10, p. 381.)

27. X takes out a policy on his own life in favor of Y; later he announces his determination to quit paying the premiums. *How advise Y?* (INSURANCE § 10, p. 382.)

28. Same facts as 27 ante except that Y murders X while the policy is still in force in order to collect the insurance. *How advise the insurance company?* (INSURANCE § 10, p. 382.)

29. *What is the attitude of courts in construing insurance policies and why?* (INSURANCE § 11, p. 382.)

30. *What is a binder and what is its purpose?* (INSURANCE § 11, p. 383.)

31. *What is the difference between hostile fires and friendly fires as to the liability of a fire insurance company?* (INSURANCE § 12, p. 383.)

32. *May the insured recover for damage caused by water used to extinguish a fire?* (INSURANCE § 12, p. 383.)

33. Fire policies usually require satisfactory proof of loss within sixty days after the fire. *What is the effect of a default in meeting this stipulation?* (INSURANCE § 12, p. 383.)

CREDITORS' RIGHTS AND BANKRUPTCY

Part I Creditors' Rights

1. *How does the sheriff execute a judgment for a plaintiff in ejectment? In replevin? In trover or indebitatus assumpsit?* (CREDITORS' RIGHTS § 1, p. 386.)

2. *What is the effect of the rendering of a judgment for money damages upon the judgment debtor's land? Upon his chattels?* (CREDITORS' RIGHTS § 1, pp. 386, 387.)

3. Money judgments are rendered against X in favor of A, B and C. A month later X's father dies and X inherits a piece of land. *How advise A, B and C?* (CREDITORS' RIGHTS § 1, p. 386.)

4. A gets a money judgment against X in New Jersey but finds that X has no property in New Jersey, but does have some in Delaware. *How advise A?* (CREDITORS' RIGHTS § 1, p. 386.)

5. *What two kinds of exemption statutes have been passed in most states?* (CREDITORS' RIGHTS § 1, p. 387.)

6. *Upon what kinds of property may a sheriff levy execution?* (CREDITORS' RIGHTS § 1, p. 387.)

7. *When may a judgment creditor maintain a creditor's bill for equitable execution? What is the basis of equity jurisdiction here?* (CREDITORS' RIGHTS § 2, p. 387.)

8. *What is meant by proceedings supplementary to judgment?* (CREDITORS' RIGHTS § 2, p. 388.)

9. *What is the relation of garnishment statutes to a creditor's bill for equitable execution?* (CREDITORS' RIGHTS § 3, p. 388.)

10. *How does a creditor proceed under a garnishment statute?* (CREDITORS' RIGHTS § 3, p. 388.)

11. *When may a creditor proceed under a foreign attachment statute?* (CREDITORS' RIGHTS § 3, p. 388.)

12. *When may the creditor have his debtor imprisoned for debt?* (CREDITORS' RIGHTS § 3, p. 389.)

13. X, in failing circumstances, transferred his property to his friend Y in order to defraud his creditors. A, a creditor of X, asks your advise. *How advise him?* (CREDITORS' RIGHTS § 4, p. 389.)

14. *What did the Statute of Elizabeth provide? What advantage do proceedings under that statute have as compared to a bill for equitable execution? What disadvantages?* (CREDITORS' RIGHTS § 5, p. 390.)

15. *What are the important provisions of the Uniform Fraudulent Conveyance Act? Does that Act apply to choses in action?* (CREDITORS' RIGHTS § 5, p. 390.)

16. Suppose A sells a chattel to X but retains possession of the chattel and

later sells it to Y, who pays value without notice of the sale to X. *How advise Y?* (CREDITORS' RIGHTS § 6, p. 390.)

17. *What is the purpose and the usual provisions of the various bulk sales statutes?* (CREDITORS' RIGHTS § 6, p. 390.)

18. A, a wholesaler, sends goods on consignment to X; later X becomes insolvent. *How advise X's creditors as to their right to reach the consigned goods?* (CREDITORS' RIGHTS § 7, p. 391.)

19. A, a wholesaler, sells a chattel to X for $400 payable each month in twenty installments of $20 each, title being reserved to A by way of security for the complete payment of the price. X becomes insolvent. *How advise X's creditors as to their right to reach the chattel?* (CREDITORS' RIGHTS § 7, p. 391.)

20. X, insolvent, borrowed $500 from Y and conveyed to him $3,000 worth of property, Y agreeing to reconvey the property upon repayment of the loan. *How advise Z, a creditor of X?* (CREDITORS' RIGHTS § 8, p. 391.)

21. *Under what circumstances, if at all, is a general assignment by a debtor of all his property valid?* (CREDITORS' RIGHTS § 9, p. 391.)

22. *At common law may a debtor making a general assignment prefer some creditors rather than others?* (CREDITORS' RIGHTS § 9, p. 391.)

23. *What is meant by a creditors' agreement and what is its purpose?* (CREDITORS' RIGHTS § 10, p. 391.)

24. *Do the creditors under such an agreement become liable for new debts incurred by those chosen by the creditors to manage the business?* (CREDITORS' RIGHTS § 10, p. 391.)

25. *Are the new creditors entitled to priority over the old creditors?* (CREDITORS' RIGHTS § 10, p. 391.)

26. *What is the purpose and effect of a creditors' composition agreement?* (CREDITORS' RIGHTS § 10, p. 391.)

27. *What is the purpose of appointing a receiver of a debtor's property?* (CREDITORS' RIGHTS § 11, p. 391.)

28. *Who is entitled to have a receiver appointed?* (CREDITORS' RIGHTS § 11, p. 392.)

29. *What is a consent receivership and what is its purpose?* (CREDITORS' RIGHTS § 11, p. 393.)

30. *What is the purpose of an ancillary or auxiliary receiver?* (CREDITORS' RIGHTS § 12, p. 393.)

31. *What is the privilege and duty of a receiver as to a lease held by the debtor?* (CREDITORS' RIGHTS § 13, p. 394.)

32. *What is the personal liability of a receiver?* (CREDITORS' RIGHTS § 12, p. 394.)

33. *Under what circumstances, if at all, may a receiver borrow money?* (CREDITORS' RIGHTS § 14, p. 394.)

34. *In what kind of receiverships are receivers' certificates given priority?* (CREDITORS' RIGHTS § 14, p. 394.)

Part II Bankruptcy

35. *What was the date and occasion of passing the present bankruptcy statute?* (BANKRUPTCY § 15, p. 396.)

36. *What is the justification for the statute's giving effect to the exemption laws of the various states?* (BANKRUPTCY § 16, p. 396.)

37. *What is the justification for extending the Act to cases where there is no insolvency?* (BANKRUPTCY § 16, p. 397.)

38. *How was the three year stay given to a mortgagor by the Frazier-Lemcke Act justified?* (BANKRUPTCY § 16, p. 397.)

39. *What was the defect of the old state insolvency laws?* (BANKRUPTCY § 17, p. 397.)

40. *What was the effect of the National Bankruptcy Act upon the state insolvency statutes? Upon general assignments for the benefit of creditors?* (BANKRUPTCY § 17, p. 397.)

41. *In which district court may bankruptcy proceedings be held?* (BANKRUPTCY § 18, p. 397.)

42. *When may summary proceeding be used by the trustee in bankruptcy to get control of the bankrupt's property? When is a plenary proceeding necessary?* (BANKRUPTCY § 19, p. 398.)

43. *Can there be an appeal from the decision of the lower court where there has been a jury trial on the question of insolvency?* (BANKRUPTCY § 19, p. 398.)

44. A files suit against X on a note; the next week X files a petition in bankruptcy. *What happens to A's suit?* (BANKRUPTCY § 20, p. 398.)

45. *Who selects the trustees in bankruptcy?* (BANKRUPTCY § 20, p. 398.)

46. *When may the court appoint a receiver?* (BANKRUPTCY § 20, p. 398.)

47. *Who may file a petition in involuntary bankruptcy?* (BANKRUPTCY § 21, p. 399.)

48. *Who may become a voluntary bankrupt? An involuntary bankrupt?* (BANKRUPTCY § 21, p. 399.)

49. *Does the discharge of a partnership discharge each partner? Does the discharge of each partner discharge the partnership.* (BANKRUPTCY § 21, p. 399.)

50. *Who may oppose the granting of a discharge and upon what grounds?* (BANKRUPTCY § 22, p. 400.)

51. *What provable debts are not dischargeable?* (BANKRUPTCY § 22, p. 400.)

52. *What are the six possible acts of bankruptcy?* (BANKRUPTCY § 23, p. 400.)

53. *What was the earlier test of insolvency? The more usual test today? Which test is used in bankruptcy proceedings?* (BANKRUPTCY § 23, p. 400.)

54. *In determining assets, in the assets and liabilities test, are exempt assets included?* (BANKRUPTCY § 23, p. 400.)

55. *When is the stopping payment test likely to be too harsh?* (BANKRUPTCY § 23, p. 400.)

56. A borrows $2,000 from X for two years and B becomes his surety. At the end of a year A conveys all his property to his son in fraud of creditors. *May B take advantage of this as an act of bankruptcy on the part of A?* (BANKRUPTCY § 24, p. 400.)

57. *What is the test of intent in the doctrine of conveyances with intent to defraud creditors?* (BANKRUPTCY § 24, p. 400.)

58. *What is the effect of filing a petition in bankruptcy upon a general assignment for benefit of creditors?* (BANKRUPTCY § 24, p. 401.)

59. *To what extent, if at all, do assets include contingent interests?* (BANKRUPTCY § 25, p. 401; § 26, p. 402.)

60 *What fraudulent transfers may be avoided by the trustee in bankruptcy?* (BANKRUPTCY § 25, p. 401.)

61. *When is a preference or a fraudulent transfer deemed to be made?* (BANKRUPTCY § 25, p. 401.)

62. A makes a contract with B and becomes bankrupt before the contract has been performed. *How advise the trustee in bankruptcy?* (BANKRUPTCY § 26, p. 402.)

63. *What tort actions of the debtor pass to his trustee in bankruptcy?* (BANKRUPTCY § 26, p. 402.)

64. A borrows $1,000 from B and gives a note to B, waiving his exemption; before the note is paid A becomes bankrupt. *How advise B?* (BANKRUPTCY § 27, p. 402.)

65. A becomes bankrupt and conceals assets from his trustee in bankruptcy. *What effect does that have upon his exemption?* (BANKRUPTCY § 27, p. 402.)

66. A took out a $5,000 policy on his life naming his wife as beneficiary, but reserving the right to change the beneficiary. A becomes bankrupt; the cash surrender value of the policy is $600. *How advise A?* (BANKRUPTCY § 27, p. 402.)

67. A devised land to B as trustee for B, C and D. B became bankrupt. *How advise the trustee in bankruptcy?* (BANKRUPTCY § 28, p. 402.)

68. *To what extent, if at all, does a trustee in bankruptcy take subject to liens?* (BANKRUPTCY § 28, p. 402.)

69. *May a bankruptcy court order the sale of land outside the district in which the bankruptcy proceedings are being held?* (BANKRUPTCY § 29, p. 403.)

70. A conveyed property in fraud of creditors and X brought suit in a state court to have the conveyance set aside. Then A became bankrupt. *How advise the trustee in bankruptcy?* (BANKRUPTCY § 29, p. 403.)

71. A conveyed property to B in fraud of creditors and the conveyance was

recorded; then Y, a creditor of B, attached the property in good faith. A is now bankrupt. *How advise his trustee in bankruptcy?* (BANKRUPTCY § 29, p. 403.)

72. Within four months before bankruptcy of A, he gave B security for a loan which B had made to him. *How advise the trustee in bankruptcy?* (BANKRUPTCY § 30, p. 404.)

73. A borrowed $2,000 from X and gave him a note therefor. X indorsed the note to Y who indorsed to Z. A paid the note to Z, but within four months A became bankrupt, and the trustee in bankruptcy compelled Z to pay the amount to him. *How advise Z as to his rights against X and Y?* (BANKRUPTCY § 30, p. 404.)

74. A, insolvent, borrowed $3,000 from X and later gave X a mortgage as security. X then persuaded A not to file a petition in bankruptcy until after four months from the date of giving the mortgage. *How advise the trustee in bankruptcy?* (BANKRUPTCY § 30, p. 404.)

75. A borrowed $10,000 from B and X signed the note as co-maker. Before the note was due A became bankrupt and later received his discharge and X was compelled by the trustee in bankruptcy to pay $8,000. *How advise X as to his rights against A?* (BANKRUPTCY § 31, p. 405.)

76. A contracted to buy personal property from B but defaulted and then became bankrupt. *How advise B as to his right against A?* (BANKRUPTCY § 31, p. 405.)

77. A negligently damaged B's property and B became bankrupt. *How advise B's trustee in bankruptcy?* (BANKRUPTCY § 31, p. 405.)

78. A leased property to B, the lease providing that if B should become bankrupt A should be entitled to the difference between the rent reserved and the rental value. B became bankrupt. *How advise A?* (BANKRUPTCY § 31, p. 405.)

79. Knowing that he was insolvent, A bought goods from X on six months' credit; within the six months A became bankrupt. *How advise X?* (BANKRUPTCY § 32, p. 406.)

80. A borrows $1,000 from X and B gives X a mortgage to secure the loan. A becomes bankrupt. *For what amount may X prove?* (BANKRUPTCY § 32, p. 406.)

81. *What six claims have priority in bankruptcy proceedings?* (BANKRUPTCY § 33, p. 406.)

82. A made a preference to B and within four months filed a petition in bankruptcy. The trustee in bankruptcy had the preference set aside. *How advise B?* (BANKRUPTCY § 34, p. 406.)

83. A borrowed $1,000 from the X Bank; before it was paid A became bankrupt with a deposit of $100 in the X Bank. *How advise the X Bank?* (BANKRUPTCY § 34, p. 406.)

84. A had been buying goods on credit from X; X, knowing that A had become insolvent, insisted upon being paid cash on the next order; after getting

the cash X did not deliver the goods. A is bankrupt. *How advise his trustee in bankruptcy?* (BANKRUPTCY § 34, p. 406.)

85. *What is the consideration for a common law composition of creditors?* (BANKRUPTCY § 35, p. 407.)

86. *What is the effect of the bankruptcy court confirming a composition of creditors?* (BANKRUPTCY § 35, p. 407.)

87. *What was the purpose of Section 75 of the Act and to whom does it apply?* (BANKRUPTCY § 36, p. 407.)

88. *What is the function and application of an arrangement under Chapter XI?* (BANKRUPTCY § 37, p. 407.)

89. *What is the purpose and effect of corporate reorganization under Chapter X and what corporations could take advantage of it?* (BANKRUPTCY § 38, p. 408.)

90. *What is the basis of an involuntary proceeding for corporate reorganization?* (BANKRUPTCY § 39, p. 408.)

91. A was in difficulty with his business, so he organized a corporation which took over the business. Then the corporation asked for a reorganization under Chapter X. *Is it entitled?* (BANKRUPTCY § 39, p. 409.)

92. *Is the prospect of a beneficial and orderly liquidation enough to invoke the aid of Chapter X?* (BANKRUPTCY § 39, p. 409.)

93. *What right does a trustee in reorganization proceedings have as against a receiver appointed by a state court?* (BANKRUPTCY § 40, p. 409.)

94. The A Corporation, which is a subsidiary of the X Corporation, is taking advantage of Chapter X. *Is the X Corporation entitled to share with other creditors of the A Corporation?* (BANKRUPTCY § 41, p. 410.)

95. By state law A, a mortgagee in possession after default of B, the corporation mortgagor, was regarded as owner. *What are his rights if B reorganizes under Chapter X?* (BANKRUPTCY § 42, p. 410.)

96. *In the reorganization proceedings who determines how the various security holders shall be classified?* (BANKRUPTCY § 43, p. 410.)

97. The A Corporation, covered by liability insurance, is being sued by X for a negligent tort. *How should such an action be dealt with in a reorganization of the A corporation under Chapter X?* (BANKRUPTCY § 44, p. 411.)

98. The A Corporation has such heavy liabilities that it has no equity in the assets. *Does this prevent reorganization under Chapter X?* (BANKRUPTCY § 46, p. 411.)

99. *What reasons may induce a court to reject a plan of reorganization submitted to it?* (BANKRUPTCY § 46, p. 411.)

CONFLICT OF LAWS

1. *With what two important questions does the subject of Conflict of Laws deal?* (CONFLICT OF LAWS § 1, p. 412.)

2. *What is the objection to the term "Conflict of Laws"? To the term "Private International Law"?* (CONFLICT OF LAWS § 1, p. 413.)

3. *What is the relation between tribal law and territorial law?* (CONFLICT OF LAWS § 2, p. 413.)

4. *How is law introduced into a previously uninhabited territory?* (CONFLICT OF LAWS § 3, p. 413.)

5. *In what three different ways may law be changed? What is the effect of a change of political sovereignty?* (CONFLICT OF LAWS § 3, p. 413.)

6. *What is the significance of the phrases "general common law" and "weight of authority"?* (CONFLICT OF LAWS § 4, p. 414.)

7. *What is the objection to the use of the word "comity" in the subject of Conflict of Laws?* (CONFLICT OF LAWS § 5, p. 414.)

8. *What is the renvoi doctrine and what has been urged in objection to it?* (CONFLICT OF LAWS § 6, p. 415.)

9. *What is the relation between the law of conflict of laws and the due process clause of the Fourteenth Amendment?* (CONFLICT OF LAWS § 7, p. 415.)

10. *To what extent, if at all, will State X act in regard to a crime committed by A in State Y?* (CONFLICT OF LAWS § 8, p. 415.)

11. *To what extent, if at all, will State X act in regard to penalties imposed by State Y?* (CONFLICT OF LAWS § 8, p. 415.)

12. *On what theory does a state get jurisdiction over a foreign corporation doing business within the state? Over a non-resident driver of a motor vehicle for a tort committed on the highways of the state?* (CONFLICT OF LAWS § 9, p. 416.)

13. *Where is it proper to serve process upon one domiciled within the state?* (CONFLICT OF LAWS § 9, p. 416.)

14. A wishes to get possession of land or of chattels located in Vermont. *In the courts of what state must the action be brought?* (CONFLICT OF LAWS § 10, p. 417.)

15. *How far into the Pacific Ocean does the jurisdiction of the California courts extend?* (CONFLICT OF LAWS § 10, p. 417.)

16. *Who are bound by a judgment in ejectment or replevin? By a libel in admiralty against a ship? By proceedings under statutes modeled on the Torrens Act?* (CONFLICT OF LAWS § 11, p. 417.)

17. A of Iowa has a $1200 claim against B of Nebraska on a note. B has land and chattels in Iowa. A does not wish to go to the trouble of bringing action

against B in the Nebraska courts. *How may he proceed?* (CONFLICT OF LAWS § 12, p. 418.)

18. Facts same as in 17 ante except that the land and chattels which A thought belonged to B really belonged to X. *How advise X?* (CONFLICT OF LAWS § 12, p. 418.)

19. *What proceedings are sometimes called proceedings quasi in rem?* (CONFLICT OF LAWS § 12, p. 418.)

20. Facts same as 17 ante; A is able to realize only $900 on the land and chattels of B in Iowa. *How advise A?* (CONFLICT OF LAWS § 12, p. 418.)

21. Facts same as 17 ante, except that B has merely a chose in action against X of Iowa for $1,000. *How advise A?* (CONFLICT OF LAWS § 13, p. 418.)

22. *How is a foreign garnishment proceeding started? A foreign attachment proceeding?* (CONFLICT OF LAWS § 13, p. 418; § 12, p. 418.)

23. Facts same as 21 ante, except that A's claim against B is not a valid one but X pays A the $1,000 by decree of the Iowa court. *How advise B?* (CONFLICT OF LAWS § 13, p. 418.)

24. *What is the older theory of situs of movables for purpose of taxation? The modern theory?* (CONFLICT OF LAWS § 14, p. 419.)

25. A railroad company had an average of 75 cars in the state of Kansas all the time. *What is the right of Kansas to tax?* (CONFLICT OF LAWS § 14, p. 419.)

26. A of Wisconsin has a claim against B of Minnesota for $15,000. *Is this taxable by Wisconsin? By Minnesota?* (CONFLICT OF LAWS § 15, p. 419.)

27. Facts same as 26 ante except that the claim is evidenced by a negotiable note which is in the possession of C in Chicago. *May Illinois tax it?* (CONFLICT OF LAWS § 15, p. 419.)

28. A of Massachusetts lends a large amount of money in Michigan the money being handled by A's agent X in Detroit who makes remittances regularly to A and reinvests money for him in Michigan. *May Michigan tax such choses in action?* (CONFLICT OF LAWS § 15, p. 420.)

29. *In what state is it proper to bring a suit for divorce? A suit for annulment?* (CONFLICT OF LAWS § 16, p. 420.)

30. *What four important questions are dependent upon domicile?* (CONFLICT OF LAWS § 17, p. 421.)

31. *What is necessary in England in order to change one's domicile? In this country?* (CONFLICT OF LAWS § 17, p. 421.)

32. *May one have a domicile in Pennsylvania without having a domicile in a particular city or county of Pennsylvania?* (CONFLICT OF LAWS § 17, p. 421.)

33. A was born in Ohio, moved to Indiana and then to Illinois. Then he abandoned his home in Illinois and started west to settle in California and died on the way. *Where was his domicile at death?* (CONFLICT OF LAWS § 17, p. 421.)

34. A is a prosperous merchant who has a fine city residence in Connecticut but has a country place in the Adirondacks in New York where he spends about half the year. *Where is his domicile?* (CONFLICT OF LAWS § 18, p. 422.)

35. A is a farmer whose residence is on the line between Warren County and Green County. *In which county is his domicile?* (CONFLICT OF LAWS § 18, p. 422.)

36. A married X; they had a child Y and then A died; X married Z. *Where is Y's domicile?* (CONFLICT OF LAWS § 19, p. 422.)

37. *Whether a particular act gives rise to a tort action depends upon the law of what state?* (CONFLICT OF LAWS § 20, p. 423.)

38. A in Kentucky wrote a letter to B in Tennessee offering to contract with him. B in Tennessee wrote a letter of acceptance and mailed it in Tennessee. *The law of which state determines the measure of damages for a breach of the contract?* (CONFLICT OF LAWS §§ 20, 21, p. 423.)

39. A statute of Rhode Island provided that no contract should be admitted in evidence unless it had a stamp. *Does this statute apply to a contract made in Rhode Island and sued upon in New Hampshire?* (CONFLICT OF LAWS § 21, p. 424.)

40. X and Y make a contract in Nebraska to be entirely performed in Kansas. By the local law of Nebraska the contract is not valid; by the local law of Kansas it is valid. Action is brought for breach of contract in Colorado. *Should the contract be regarded as valid?* (CONFLICT OF LAWS § 22, p. 424.)

41. *What is the rule as to contracts which are usurious by the law of the state of performance but not usurious by the law of the state of making, and vice versa?* (CONFLICT OF LAWS § 22, p. 424.)

42. Courts frequently say that the law governing the validity of a contract is that law which the parties intended should govern it. *Criticise.* (CONFLICT OF LAWS § 22, p. 425.)

43. In interpreting contracts where there is a difference in the usage prevailing at the domiciles of the respective parties, *which usage should govern?* (CONFLICT OF LAWS § 23, p. 425.)

44. *What creditors are affected by state insolvency proceedings? By the federal bankruptcy act?* (CONFLICT OF LAWS § 23, p. 425.)

45. *What law governs capacity to marry?* (CONFLICT OF LAWS § 24, p. 425.)

46. A New York divorce decree forbids the guilty party from remarrying without leave of court for three years. *Does this prevent A from entering into a valid marriage in New Jersey?* (CONFLICT OF LAWS § 24, p. 426.)

47. *Under what circumstances is a marriage valid where celebrated on the high seas?* (CONFLICT OF LAWS § 24, p. 426.)

48. A and X have an illegitimate child; they now live in different states. *Which state may by legislation legitimate the child?* (CONFLICT OF LAWS § 24, p. 426.)

49. A contracted with B in Arkansas to convey land in Oklahoma. *Which law determines whether the contract gives to B a property right in the land?* (CONFLICT OF LAWS § 25, p. 426.)

50. A loaned B $600 and took a mortgage on B's automobile located in Texas;

A recorded the mortgage. Then B took the automobile into Mississippi and sold it to X who did not know of A's mortgage. *How advise A?* (CONFLICT OF LAWS § 25, p. 427.)

51. *Which law governs the transfer of corporation stock? The assignment of an ordinary chose in action? The creation of a trust right in property? The imposition of a constructive trust upon property?* (CONFLICT OF LAWS § 26, p. 427.)

52. *What law governs the succession to immovable property? To movable property?* (CONFLICT OF LAWS § 27, p. 427.)

53. A lived most of his life in Delaware and, without changing his domicile, went to California for the winter. He died there having made a will in California which complied with the requirements of California law but not with the requirements of Delaware law. *How advise his executor?* (CONFLICT OF LAWS § 27, p. 428.)

54. A trespassed upon X's land in Utah and took away from it several hundred bushels of wheat. A then moved to Idaho. *How advise X?* (CONFLICT OF LAWS § 28, p. 428.)

55. *The law of what state governs procedure?* (CONFLICT OF LAWS § 29, p. 428.)

56. *The law of what state governs presumptions? Why?* (CONFLICT OF LAWS § 29, p. 429.)

57. *What is the effect of the legitimation by statute of an illegitimate child?* (CONFLICT OF LAWS § 30, p. 429.)

58. After the death of A some of the chattels belonging to A's estate were moved into another state by X. *How advise A's administrator?* (CONFLICT OF LAWS § 31, p. 429.)

59. A dies having a contract claim against X who lives in another state. *How advise A's administrator?* (CONFLICT OF LAWS § 31, p. 430.)

60. *What is an ancillary administrator?* (CONFLICT OF LAWS § 32, p. 430.)

61. A dies owning a negotiable instrument against X who lives in another state. *How advise A's administrator?* (CONFLICT OF LAWS § 33, p. 430.)

62. *May a creditor prove his claim in more than one state?* (CONFLICT OF LAWS § 34, p. 431.)

63. *After all the creditors have been paid, what may the court direct the ancillary administrator to do?* (CONFLICT OF LAWS § 34, p. 431.)

64. *What should the court direct if some of the creditors of the estate have not been paid?* (CONFLICT OF LAWS § 34, p. 431.)

65. *When is it necessary to appoint an ancillary receiver?* (CONFLICT OF LAWS § 35, p. 431.)

66. *Under what circumstances, if at all, may a receiver sue in a state other than the one in which he has been appointed?* (CONFLICT OF LAWS § 35, p. 431.)

67. *Under what circumstances, if at all, may a receiver be sued in a state other than the one in which he has been appointed?* (CONFLICT OF LAWS § 35, p. 431.)

68. *What are the five requirements of a judgment to entitle it to be enforced in another state?* (CONFLICT OF LAWS § 36, p. 432.)

69. A gets an equitable decree in a Georgia court against X for the payment of money; X has no assets in Georgia but he has assets and lives in Florida. *How advise A?* (CONFLICT OF LAWS § 36, p. 432.)

70. A sues X in an Oklahoma court for the specific performance of a contract to convey Oklahoma land and gets a decree after X has removed from Oklahoma to Arizona. *How advise A?* (CONFLICT OF LAWS § 37, p. 432.)

71. A has a judgment against X in Ohio for the payment of money. *Under what circumstances, if at all, may A sue on that judgment in Ohio? In Indiana? What is the effect on the Ohio judgment of getting a judgment in Indiana?* (CONFLICT OF LAWS § 37, p. 432.)

72. *When, if at all, may A sue in Virginia upon a judgment which he obtained in France?* (CONFLICT OF LAWS § 37, p. 433.)

PUBLIC UTILITIES

1. *What public utilities have existed from early days? What ones are modern—within the past century?* (PUBLIC UTILITIES § 1, p. 434.)

2. *What was the reason for imposing a strict liability upon common carriers and innkeepers?* (PUBLIC UTILITIES § 2, p. 435.)

3. *What was the theology back of the "act of God" exception? Why the public enemy exception?* (PUBLIC UTILITIES § 2, p. 435.)

4. *What partial compensation do some public utilities enjoy to offset their peculiar liability?* (PUBLIC UTILITIES § 2, p. 436.)

5. *Which of the public utilities have a monopoly? Which do not?* (PUBLIC UTILITIES § 3, p. 436.)

6. *What characteristic is common to all public utilities?* (PUBLIC UTILITIES § 3, p. 436.)

7. *Of what importance is the undertaking to serve the public indiscriminately?* (PUBLIC UTILITIES § 3, p. 436.)

8. *What was formerly required to make an inn? What today?* (PUBLIC UTILITIES § 3, p. 436.)

9. *How did grain elevators become public utilities?* (PUBLIC UTILITIES § 4, p. 437.)

10. *What other modern public utilities are the creatures of statutes?* (PUBLIC UTILITIES § 4, p. 437.)

11. *Under what circumstances may a common carrier of goods refuse service?* (PUBLIC UTILITIES § 5, p. 437.)

12. *A common carrier of passengers? An innkeeper?* (PUBLIC UTILITIES § 5, p. 437.)

13. *What determines whether the service furnished is adequate?* (PUBLIC UTILITIES § 6, p. 438.)

14. *To what extent, if at all, may a public utility discriminate between its customers?* (PUBLIC UTILITIES § 7, p. 438.)

15. *What other excuses does a common carrier of goods have except act of God and of the public enemy?* (PUBLIC UTILITIES § 8, p. 439.)

16. *What is the liability of a common carrier for accidental loss of goods during an unlawful deviation from the route prescribed by the shipper?* (PUBLIC UTILITIES § 8, p. 439.)

17. *What is the measure of liability of a common carrier of passengers for their safety?* (PUBLIC UTILITIES § 9, p. 440.)

18. *To what extent may an innkeeper by regulation reduce its liability for the guest's goods?* (PUBLIC UTILITIES § 10, p. 441.)

19. *When does the extraordinary liability of a common carrier of goods begin? When does it end?* (PUBLIC UTILITIES § 11, p. 441.)

20. *A common carrier of passengers?* (PUBLIC UTILITIES § 11, p. 441.)

21. *An innkeeper?* (PUBLIC UTILITIES § 11, p. 441.)

22. *In what way, if at all, may a common carrier of goods limit its liability?* (PUBLIC UTILITIES § 12, p. 441.)

23. *A telegraph company?* (PUBLIC UTILITIES § 12, p. 442.)

24. *May a common carrier of passengers limit its liability to those carried gratuitously?* (PUBLIC UTILITIES § 12, p. 442.)

25. *What is the liability of an initial common carrier of goods for loss or damage to the goods beyond its own lines?* (PUBLIC UTILITIES § 13, p. 442.)

26. *What may be decided by an ordinary court about the fairness of rates?* (PUBLIC UTILITIES § 14, p. 442.)

27. *How are rates usually fixed today?* (PUBLIC UTILITIES § 14, p. 443.)

28. *What was the objection to holding that fair value as the basis of rate making meant fair exchange value?* (PUBLIC UTILITIES § 15, p. 443.)

29. *What is the objection to the reproduction cost test of fair value?* (PUBLIC UTILITIES § 15, p. 443.)

30. *What is regarded today as the best single test of fair value?* (PUBLIC UTILITIES § 15, p. 443.)

31. *What items must be considered in determining a fair return?* (PUBLIC UTILITIES § 16, p. 444.)

32. *Is a railroad having both interstate and intrastate business entitled to a fair return on each one?* (PUBLIC UTILITIES § 16, p. 444.)

33. *In fixing a fair return, should business cycles be considered?* (PUBLIC UTILITIES § 16, p. 445.)

34. *Should effect upon competitors ever be considered?* (PUBLIC UTILITIES § 16, p. 444.)

MUNICIPAL CORPORATIONS

1. *What are the three meanings of the term municipal corporation?* (MUNICIPAL CORPORATIONS § 1, p. 445.)

2. *How are municipal corporations usually created today?* (MUNICIPAL CORPORATIONS § 1, p. 445.)

3. *Must there be consent by the inhabitants?* (MUNICIPAL CORPORATIONS § 1, p. 446.)

4. *What is the effect of acting as a municipal corporation for several years? Of legislative recognition? Of acquiescence by the state?* (MUNICIPAL CORPORATIONS § 2, p. 446.)

5. *What is necessary for a de facto municipal corporation?* (MUNICIPAL CORPORATIONS § 2, p. 446.)

6. *How may the boundaries of a municipal corporation be changed?* (MUNICIPAL CORPORATIONS § 3, p. 446.)

7. *In what way, if at all, may a state validly discriminate between municipal corporations?* (MUNICIPAL CORPORATIONS § 3, p. 446.)

8. *What is the effect of failure to elect corporate officers upon the existence of a municipal corporation?* (MUNICIPAL CORPORATIONS § 3, p. 447.)

9. When a legislature creates new counties out of the territory of an existing county, *what is the effect upon the rights and obligations of the latter?* (MUNICIPAL CORPORATIONS § 4, p. 447.)

10. *What is the effect of the legislature dissolving a municipal corporation and then creating a new one with practically the same territory as the old?* (MUNICIPAL CORPORATIONS § 4, p. 447.)

11. *How is valid action taken by a New England town? By a corporation with a mayor and common council?* (MUNICIPAL CORPORATIONS § 5, p. 447.)

12. *Who binds the corporation which has a commission form of government? A city manager?* (MUNICIPAL CORPORATIONS § 5, p. 447.)

13. *What power does the state legislature have over municipal corporations?* (MUNICIPAL CORPORATIONS § 5, p. 448.)

14. *What is the difference between judicial and ministerial functions? For the exercise of which kind is the corporation liable?* (MUNICIPAL CORPORATIONS § 6, p. 448.)

15. *How far, without express legislative authorization, may a municipal corporation celebrate public holidays? Build a public hospital? Offer a reward for*

the arrest and conviction of incendiaries? (MUNICIPAL CORPORATIONS § 7, p. 449.)

16. *May the legislature authorize a city to own, maintain and operate public utilities? To erect houses to replace slums? To engage in the business of selling gasoline to its inhabitants?* (MUNICIPAL CORPORATIONS § 7, p. 449.)

17. *May a city fix fire limits? May it regulate amusements?* (MUNICIPAL CORPORATIONS § 8, p. 450.)

18. *May a city prohibit billboards on aesthetic grounds?* (MUNICIPAL CORPORATIONS § 8, p. 450.)

19. *What has been the effect of city zoning upon equitable servitudes on land?* (MUNICIPAL CORPORATIONS § 9, p. 450; EQUITY § 16, p. 241.)

20. *Under what circumstances will a court refuse to enforce a zoning ordinance?* (MUNICIPAL CORPORATIONS § 9, p. 450.)

21. *To what extent may a municipality enter into contracts?* (MUNICIPAL CORPORATIONS § 10, p. 451.)

22. *What is the effect of a municipality's violation of statutory provisions as to advertising for offers and letting the contract to the lowest bidder?* (MUNICIPAL CORPORATIONS § 10, p. 451.)

23. *What is the right of a city official who contracts to sell goods to the city?* (MUNICIPAL CORPORATIONS § 10, p. 452.)

24. *To what extent and for what reasons can there be recovery in quasi contract against a city?* (MUNICIPAL CORPORATIONS § 10, p. 452.)

25. *To what extent, if at all, may a municipality borrow money?* (MUNICIPAL CORPORATIONS § 10, p. 452.)

26. *To which of their obligations does a constitutional provision limiting the amount of indebtedness not apply:* (a) *tort;* (b) *warrants issued for ordinary expenses;* (c) *long term contract for supply of gas and water;* (d) *money borrowed to construct waterworks to be paid out of waterworks receipts;* (e) *money borrowed to erect a public building to be repaid out of a special tax levy?* (MUNICIPAL CORPORATIONS § 11, p. 453.)

27. *Is a debt incurred by a city board of education considered a debt of the city?* (MUNICIPAL CORPORATIONS § 11, p. 453.)

28. *May a city acquire land outside the city limits?* (MUNICIPAL CORPORATIONS § 12, p. 454.)

29. *May a city accept property upon a charitable trust?* (MUNICIPAL CORPORATIONS § 12, p. 454.)

30. *To what extent may a statute authorize a city to exercise the power of eminent domain?* (MUNICIPAL CORPORATIONS § 12, p. 454.)

31. *To what extent may a city sell city property?* (MUNICIPAL CORPORATIONS § 13, p. 454.)

32. *What is the advantage of a city's owning the fee of the streets?* (MUNICIPAL CORPORATIONS § 14, p. 455.)

33. *May a city authorize the construction of a bridge over a highway?* (MUNICIPAL CORPORATIONS § 14, p. 455.)

34. *May a city reimburse a defeated mayoralty candidate for expenses of election contest? May it levy a tax for group insurance for teachers?* (MUNICIPAL CORPORATIONS § 15, p. 455.)

35. *May a city impose upon an abutting owner the burden of removing snow from the sidewalk?* (MUNICIPAL CORPORATIONS § 15, p. 455.)

36. A city paves a street and then passes an ordinance and assesses the abutting property owners for the cost. *Is such assessment valid?* (MUNICIPAL CORPORATIONS § 16, p. 456.)

37. *If an assessment is proved to be unfair, what is the effect?* (MUNICIPAL CORPORATIONS § 16, p. 456.)

38. *To what extent may a city impose a personal liability to pay an assessment?* (MUNICIPAL CORPORATIONS § 16, p. 456.)

39. *What is the present trend toward imposing liability upon a city for the torts of its employees?* (MUNICIPAL CORPORATIONS § 17, p. 457.)

40. *In what class of cases is a city clearly not liable in tort?* (MUNICIPAL CORPORATIONS § 17, p. 457.)

41. *Is a city liable for damage caused by failure to keep highways in repair? A county?* (MUNICIPAL CORPORATIONS § 18, p. 458.)

42. *What is the practical argument in favor of holding a city liable to a bona fide purchaser of its bonds though the bonds were not properly issued?* (MUNICIPAL CORPORATIONS § 19, p. 459.)

43. *May a city impose license fees upon a public utility which has a franchise to use the city streets?* (MUNICIPAL CORPORATIONS § 20, p. 459.)

44. *May a city be authorized to regulate the sale of goods outside the city limits?* (MUNICIPAL CORPORATIONS § 21, p. 459.)

CONSTITUTIONAL LAW

1. *Upon what basis did the United States Constitution take effect upon ratification by only nine states when the Articles of Confederation provided that they should be amended only by unanimous consent?* (CONSTITUTIONAL LAW § 1, p. 462.)

2. *May a state legislature grant a new trial? Why?* (CONSTITUTIONAL LAW § 2, p. 462.)

3. *May a state legislature confer upon a court the legislative power of fixing public utility rates?* (CONSTITUTIONAL LAW § 2, p. 462.)

4. *When does an executive exercise legislative power? When does the legislative department exercise executive power? Judicial power?* (CONSTITUTIONAL LAW § 2, p. 462.)

5. *What was the holding in the famous Schechter case and why?* (CONSTITUTIONAL LAW § 3, p. 463.)

6. *Why may legislatures delegate legislative powers to municipal corporations?* (CONSTITUTIONAL LAW § 3, p. 463.)

7. *What is the legal status of referendums?* (CONSTITUTIONAL LAW § 3, p. 463.)

8. *What is the practical argument behind the courts declaring legislation unconstitutional?* (CONSTITUTIONAL LAW § 4, p. 463.)

9. *What are the usually accepted limitations upon the courts' power to declare statutes unconstitutional?* (CONSTITUTIONAL LAW § 4, p. 463.)

10. *Is a decision that a particular statute is unconstitutional retroactive?* (CONSTITUTIONAL LAW § 4, p. 464.)

11. The Fourteenth Amendment is limited to persons "subject to the jurisdiction" of the United States. *What five classes of persons are excluded thereby?* (CONSTITUTIONAL LAW § 5, p. 464.)

12. *May one be a citizen of a state but not of the United States?* (CONSTITUTIONAL LAW § 5, p. 465.)

13. *May one who is not a citizen be given the right to vote?* (CONSTITUTIONAL LAW § 6, p. 465.)

14. *What was the purpose and effect of the "grandfather clause" in statutes passed in some southern states?* (CONSTITUTIONAL LAW § 6, p. 466.)

15. *What was the purpose of the fifteenth amendment? Of the nineteenth? What was the form of the two amendments?* (CONSTITUTIONAL LAW § 6, p. 466.)

16. *What is the effect of the thirteenth amendment upon peonage?* (CONSTITUTIONAL LAW § 7, p. 466.)

17. *Upon what basis may a state forbid the practice of polygamy by a religious sect? Or require the calling of a physician to treat minor children, against the tenets of a religious sect?* (CONSTITUTIONAL LAW § 7, p. 466.)

18. *Which amendment prohibits Congress from abridging freedom of speech or of the press? Which one prohibits the states from doing so?* (CONSTITUTIONAL LAW § 8, p. 467.)

19. *Upon what basis may Congress interfere with the publication of libels?* (CONSTITUTIONAL LAW § 8, p. 407.)

20. *Why were "Jehovah's Witnesses" not permitted to parade upon a public street in furtherance of their religious propaganda?* (CONSTITUTIONAL LAW § 8, p. 467.)

21. *What is a bill of attainder and what West Virginia statute was held to be one?* (CONSTITUTIONAL LAW § 9, p. 467.)

22. *To what does the term ex post facto apply?* (CONSTITUTIONAL LAW § 10, p. 468.)

23. A state statute reduced the penalty for murder from death to life imprisonment. *Does this validly apply to an offense committed before the statute was passed?* (CONSTITUTIONAL LAW § 10, p. 468.)

24. A state statute imposed a heavier penalty for a second offense. *Does this validly apply to one whose first offense was committed before the statute?* (CONSTITUTIONAL LAW § 10, p. 468.)

25. *In what respect are the fifth and fourteenth amendments similar? In what respect dissimilar?* (CONSTITUTIONAL LAW § 11, p. 468; § 12, p. 469.)

26. *What are the usual requirements for due process of law?* (CONSTITUTIONAL LAW § 12, p. 469.)

27. *May a state validly require a defendant in a criminal case to be a witness against himself?* (CONSTITUTIONAL LAW § 12, p. 469.)

28. Suppose that a judge in a criminal case makes a mistake of law in instructing the jury, and because of this the defendant suffers imprisonment. *Is this a violation of the due process clause?* (CONSTITUTIONAL LAW § 12, p. 470.)

29. Recall an instance of a violation of the equal protection clause; an instance which was held not a violation. *What were they?* (CONSTITUTIONAL LAW § 13, p. 470.)

30. *What social interests are protected by the police power?* (CONSTITUTIONAL LAW § 14, p. 470.)

31. *Upon what basis has legislation discriminating against oleomargarine been upheld?* (CONSTITUTIONAL LAW § 15, p. 471.)

32. *Under the police power what does the subject of gambling include?* (CONSTITUTIONAL LAW § 16, p. 472.)

33. *Upon what bases may a statute authorizing the sterilization of criminals be upheld?* (CONSTITUTIONAL LAW § 16, p. 472.)

34. *Upon what basis is the regulation of liquor traffic usually upheld?* (CONSTITUTIONAL LAW § 16, p. 472.)

35. A state statute made injuries inflicted by the running of locomotives or automobiles prima facie evidence of negligence. *Is such a statute valid? Why?* (CONSTITUTIONAL LAW § 17, p. 472.)

36. *What is the basis for upholding state statutes providing for the segregation of races in schools and public conveyances?* (CONSTITUTIONAL LAW § 18, p. 473.)

37. *In what way can a city validly get rid of unsightly billboards?* (CONSTITUTIONAL LAW § 18, p. 473.)

38. *Upon what basis may a state require licenses of liquor sellers? Of physicians?* (CONSTITUTIONAL LAW § 19, p. 473.)

39. *Upon what basis may a state pass a statute imposing a penalty upon land owners and land occupiers for letting noxious plants go to seed on their land?* (CONSTITUTIONAL LAW § 19, p. 474.)

40. *Upon what basis may a state statute require that employees be paid in cash, at stated intervals?* (CONSTITUTIONAL LAW § 20, p. 474.)

41. *Upon what basis may the state forbid the owners of natural gas from wasting it?* (CONSTITUTIONAL LAW § 21, p. 474.)

42. *Upon what basis may a state regulate banking and insurance?* (CONSTITUTIONAL LAW § 22, p. 475.)

43. *May a state place upon railroads the cost of maintaining a railroad commission?* (CONSTITUTIONAL LAW § 22, p. 475.)

44. *May a state impose upon a railroad the burden of elevating or depressing its tracks to avoid grade crossings?* (CONSTITUTIONAL LAW § 22, p. 475.)

45. *What are the general limits of the taxing power?* (CONSTITUTIONAL LAW § 23, p. 475.)

46. *How may a state tax the intangible assets of a corporation?* (CONSTITUTIONAL LAW § 24, p. 475.)

47. *What is meant by a commercial domicile of a corporation and what is its significance?* (CONSTITUTIONAL LAW § 24, p. 476.)

48. *Where X of Kentucky has a pecuniary claim against Y of Virginia, which state ordinarily has the right to tax? Under what circumstances may a third state levy a tax?* (CONSTITUTIONAL LAW § 25, p. 476.)

49. *May a state tax both corporate assets and shares of stock?* (CONSTITUTIONAL LAW § 26, p. 476.)

50. *May shares of stock be taxed at the domicile of the corporation and also at the domicile of the share owner?* (CONSTITUTIONAL LAW § 26, p. 476.)

51. *May corporate franchises be taxed separately from the tangible corporate assets?* (CONSTITUTIONAL LAW § 26, p. 477.)

52. *Where may the devolution of land be taxed? The devolution of tangible chattels, where the owner lives in one state and the chattels are located in another?* (CONSTITUTIONAL LAW § 27, p. 477.)

53. A dies domiciled in New York; X, a distributee, lives in Indiana. *May both states tax the transmission of A's personal property? Why?* (CONSTITUTIONAL LAW § 27, p. 477.)

54. A of Delaware owns shares of stock in the X corporation of New Jersey; he transfers the shares in New York. *May New York tax such a transfer?* (CONSTITUTIONAL LAW § 27, p. 477.)

55. *May the question of whether a particular purpose is public be affected by local conditions?* (CONSTITUTIONAL LAW § 28, p. 478.)

56. *Must tax exemptions always be made for a public purpose?* (CONSTITUTIONAL LAW § 28, p. 478.)

57. *May a state, having licensed a foreign corporation to do business within the state levy an additional tax therefor?* (CONSTITUTIONAL LAW § 29, p. 478.)

58. *May a succession tax be levied only upon collateral heirs, devisees, distributees and legatees?* (CONSTITUTIONAL LAW § 29, p. 478.)

59. *In order that a special assessment be valid as to a particular piece of land is it necessary to make definite proof of value?* (CONSTITUTIONAL LAW § 29, p. 478.)

60. *Would a progressive direct tax on land or chattels probably be upheld?* (CONSTITUTIONAL LAW § 29, p. 479.)

61. "The power to tax is the power to destroy". *To what extent, if at all, is this statement true?* (CONSTITUTIONAL LAW § 29, p. 479.)

62. *Under what power may the state take private property even without giving compensation therefor?* (CONSTITUTIONAL LAW § 30, p. 479.)

63. *From what source is derived the power of eminent domain? The police power? The power to tax?* (CONSTITUTIONAL LAW § 30, p. 479.)

64. *May the power of eminent domain be delegated?* (CONSTITUTIONAL LAW § 30, p. 479.)

65. *Are telephone poles and wires in the highway a public purpose? Why?* (CONSTITUTIONAL LAW § 31, p. 480.)

66. *May the right to exercise the power of eminent domain be affected by local conditions?* (CONSTITUTIONAL LAW § 31, p. 480.)

67. The X Water Co. was given a franchise for twenty years. Five years later the state took the franchise for the purpose of supplying a large city with water. *Was such taking valid?* (CONSTITUTIONAL LAW § 31, p. 480.)

68. *Under what circumstances, if at all, may an owner of land be entitled to compensation for annoyance from smoke, noise, dirt and cinders of a steam railroad?* (CONSTITUTIONAL LAW § 32, p. 481.)

69. An acre of land belonging to A was taken by the X Railroad Company. The land taken was worth $300; the rest of A's land was benefited $200 by the proximity of the railroad. *To how much is A entitled?* (CONSTITUTIONAL LAW § 33, p. 482.)

70. *Must the eminent domain proceedings be before a court? Is there a right to a jury trial?* (CONSTITUTIONAL LAW § 33, p. 482.)

71. *Does the provision in the United States Constitution in regard to impairing the obligation of contracts apply to decisions in state courts?* (CONSTITUTIONAL LAW § 34, p. 482.)

72. *Does the term "contract" include a judgment? A deed of conveyance? Why? Does it include marriage? Why?* (CONSTITUTIONAL LAW § 35, p. 482.)

73. *Is the charter of a corporation a contract? Of a municipal corporation?* (CONSTITUTIONAL LAW § 35, p. 483.)

74. *May the public interest sometimes justify the impairment of the obligation of contracts?* (CONSTITUTIONAL LAW § 36, p. 483.)

75. *How are mortgage moratorium laws justified?* (CONSTITUTIONAL LAW § 36, p. 484.)

76. *Are there any provisions in state constitutions as to retroactive laws?* (CONSTITUTIONAL LAW § 37, p. 484.)

77. *What is the usual judicial attitude toward validating or curative statutes?* (CONSTITUTIONAL LAW § 38, p. 484.)

78. *To what extent, if at all, may a tax be laid upon exports?* (CONSTITUTIONAL LAW § 39, p. 485.)

79. *To what extent may a state levy a tax upon goods which have been imported into the state?* (CONSTITUTIONAL LAW § 39, p. 485.)

80. *What expenses may a state include as being necessary to the execution of its inspection laws?* (CONSTITUTIONAL LAW § 39, p. 485.)

81. *What is meant by the phrase in the Constitution, "duty of tonnage"?* (CONSTITUTIONAL LAW § 39, p. 486.)

82. *Is the power of Congress over interstate commerce exclusive or only paramount?* (CONSTITUTIONAL LAW § 40, p. 486.)

83. *Is the business of correspondence schools commerce? Insurance? Manufacturing articles to be shipped to another state?* (CONSTITUTIONAL LAW § 40, p. 486.)

84. A state statute required animals to be slaughtered for sale to be inspected within twenty-four hours before being slaughtered. *Why was this held unconstitutional?* (CONSTITUTIONAL LAW § 41, p. 486.)

85. A state imposed a tax upon a telegraph company on its total authorized capital. *Is the tax valid? Why?* (CONSTITUTIONAL LAW § 42, p. 487.)

86. The X Company of Illinois kept merely a selling office in Wisconsin, its salesman there merely soliciting orders. *May Wisconsin tax the company?* (CONSTITUTIONAL LAW § 42, p. 487.)

87. New Jersey has a statute regulating ferries operating between New Jersey and New York. *To what extent, if at all, is such a statute valid?* (CONSTITUTIONAL LAW § 43, p. 488.)

88. A Kansas statute required all foreign corporations to file reports. *Is such a statute valid?* (CONSTITUTIONAL LAW § 43, p. 488.)

89. A Michigan statute imposed a license fee upon ferries operating between Michigan and Canada. *Is it valid?* (CONSTITUTIONAL LAW § 43, p. 488.)

90. *What are the limitations of the power of Congress over interstate commerce?* (CONSTITUTIONAL LAW § 44, p. 488.)

91. *Does the fact that an act of Congress incidentally affects intrastate commerce necessarily make a statute regulating interstate rates invalid?* (CONSTITUTIONAL LAW § 44, p. 489.)

92. *To what extent, if at all, is a state statute regulating intrastate traffic on a navigable river valid?* (CONSTITUTIONAL LAW § 45, p. 489.)

93. *What are the two bases of jurisdiction of the federal courts?* (CONSTITUTIONAL LAW § 46, p. 489.)

94. A of Baltimore sued B of Washington, D. C. upon a contract involving more than $3,000, suit being brought in the Maryland court. B wishes to have the case removed to the federal court. *Is he so entitled?* (CONSTITUTIONAL LAW § 47, p. 490.)

95. *Is a federal court sitting in Maryland bound to follow the decisions of the Maryland courts?* (CONSTITUTIONAL LAW § 47, p. 490.)

96. *To what extent, if at all, may the Eleventh Amendment be evaded by a citizen of State Y, having a claim against State X, assigning his claim to State Y?* (CONSTITUTIONAL LAW § 48, p. 490.)

97. A, a citizen of Minnesota, brought suit against the State of Minnesota in the federal court sitting in that state. *Is the suit maintainable?* (CONSTITUTIONAL LAW § 48, p. 490.)

98. *May State X maintain a suit in a federal court against a citizen of State Y?* (CONSTITUTIONAL LAW § 48, p. 490.)

99. *May the United States maintain an action in a federal court against a state? May a state maintain an action in a federal court against the United States?* (CONSTITUTIONAL LAW § 49, p. 491.)

100. *Upon what basis was the Civil Rights Act of 1875, providing that all persons in the United States should be entitled to equal privileges in inns, public conveyances and places of amusement without discrimination on account of race, held valid?* (CONSTITUTIONAL LAW § 50, p. 491.)

101. *Is a corporation organized in Montana entitled to do business in North Dakota?* (CONSTITUTIONAL LAW § 50, p. 491.)

ADMINISTRATIVE LAW

1. *What is the advantage of an administrative tribunal over an ordinary court? Over a legislature?* (ADMINISTRATIVE LAW § 1, p. 493.)

2. *What objections to such tribunals have been urged?* (ADMINISTRATIVE LAW § 1, p. 493.)

3. *What is the basis for the doctrine of separation of powers?* (ADMINISTRATIVE LAW § 2, p. 493.)

4. *What is the basis of the doctrine forbidding the delegation of legislative power?* (ADMINISTRATIVE LAW § 3, p. 494.)

5. *To what extent, if at all, may Congress authorize the President to exercise legislative power?* (ADMINISTRATIVE LAW § 3, p. 494.)

6. *Why may a legislature delegate legislative power to municipal corporations?* (ADMINISTRATIVE LAW § 3, p. 495.)

7. *What five possible safeguards against arbitrary action of administrative tribunals have been suggested?* (ADMINISTRATIVE LAW § 4, p. 495.)

8. *Must a legislature give notice to parties of contemplated action? Must a court? Must an administrative tribunal?* (ADMINISTRATIVE LAW § 5, p. 495.)

9. *What reasons have been given for sometimes advising an administrative tribunal to act without giving notice subject to being held liable for damages later if its action was not justified?* (ADMINISTRATIVE LAW § 5, p. 495.)

10. *If notice is necessary, what notice should be given and to whom?* (ADMINISTRATIVE LAW § 6, p. 495.)

11. *What may be done if there is a large number of persons to be affected by the proceedings?* (ADMINISTRATIVE LAW § 6, p. 496.)

12. *To what extent, if at all, must the standard of fair hearing required in court action be applied to proceedings before administrative tribunals?* (ADMINISTRATIVE LAW § 7, p. 497.)

13. *May a party to proceedings before an administrative tribunal always insist upon being represented by counsel?* (ADMINISTRATIVE LAW § 7, p. 497.)

14. *Must the witnesses be put under oath? Must there be opportunity to cross examine?* (ADMINISTRATIVE LAW § 7, p. 497.)

15. *May an administrative tribunal take judicial notice of its own specialized knowledge?* (ADMINISTRATIVE LAW § 8, p. 498.)

16. *To what extent may such a tribunal not take judicial notice of a financial depression?* (ADMINISTRATIVE LAW § 8, p. 498.)

17. *What is the usual attitude of administrative tribunals toward admitting hearsay evidence in their proceedings?* (ADMINISTRATIVE LAW § 9, p. 498.)

18. *To what extent must such tribunals be unbiased?* (ADMINISTRATIVE LAW § 10, p. 498.)

19. *Is it always necessary in common law courts that "the one who decides must hear"? In equity courts? In proceedings before administrative tribunals?* (ADMINISTRATIVE LAW § 10, p. 499.)

20. *What is the argument against requiring an administrative tribunal to make a statement of its findings and to give an opportunity of examination thereof to the parties before it, before making its final decision?* (ADMINISTRATIVE LAW § 11, p. 499.)

21. *Must such a tribunal give findings of fact with its final decision? Why?* (ADMINISTRATIVE LAW § 12, p. 499.)

22. *What kind of facts must be stated?* (ADMINISTRATIVE LAW § 12, p. 500.)

23. *To what extent will an ordinary court feel bound by the findings of fact made by an administrative tribunal?* (ADMINISTRATIVE LAW § 13, p. 501.)

24. *In what kind of cases may a party aggrieved by the decision of an administrative tribunal resort to* (a) *a writ of habeas corpus;* (b) *suit in equity for an injunction;* (c) *taxpayers' suit;* (d) *action for a declaratory judgment;* (e) *writ of quo warranto?* (ADMINISTRATIVE LAW § 14, p. 501.)

25. *In what kinds of cases may a writ of mandamus be maintained?* (ADMINISTRATIVE LAW § 15, p. 501.)

26. *In what kind of cases will a writ of certiorari lie? In what refused?* (ADMINISTRATIVE LAW § 16, p. 502.)

TAXATION

1. *What is the older theory of taxation? The later theory?* (TAXATION § 1, p. 503.)

2. *Whence is the power of the states to tax? The United States?* (TAXATION § 1, p. 503.)

3. *Why may a state tax anthracite but not bituminous coal?* (TAXATION § 2, p. 504.)

4. *Why may a state impose a heavier tax on chain stores than upon those individually owned?* (TAXATION § 2, p. 504.)

5. *Why may not a state impose a graduated gross sales tax?* (TAXATION § 2, p. 504.)

6. *May a state tax a legacy to the United States?* (TAXATION § 3, p. 504.)

7. *May the United States tax the salary of a state official?* (TAXATION § 3, p. 505.)

8. *Why was the Sixteenth Amendment necessary?* (TAXATION § 4, p. 505.)

9. *What is the constitutional requirement as to excise taxes? Why was this not violated by a graduated succession tax?* (TAXATION § 4, p. 505.)

10. *May a state levy a tax both on the mortgagor and mortgagee of land? Why?* (TAXATION § 5, p. 506.)

11. *Who pays taxes on agricultural land, the lessor or lessee? On mineral land? On tide lands?* (TAXATION § 5, p. 506.)

12. *Why are state taxes sometimes levied upon the taxpayer's average monthly bank deposits instead of upon the amount he has on deposit on taxing day?* (TAXATION § 5, p. 506.)

13. *What is the usual method of assessing land in agricultural districts and in the towns and smaller cities? In the larger cities? Should the assessor modify his assessment because of a business depression?* (TAXATION § 6, p. 507.)

14. *What is the usual method of assessing large public utilities? Why?* (TAXATION § 6, p. 507.)

15. *What is the usual remedy of an aggrieved taxpayer? Is he entitled to notice?* (TAXATION § 7, p. 507.)

16. *If the assessment is unequal, how is this usually remedied?* (TAXATION § 7, p. 508.)

17. *When, if at all, is notice necessary in case of a local assessment?* (TAXATION § 7, p. 508.)

18. *Where is the difference between an estate tax and an inheritance tax?* (TAXATION § 8, p. 508.)

19. *Is a widow's interest subject to an inheritance or succession tax? Why?* (TAXATION § 9, p. 509.)

20. ***Is a succession tax necessarily limited to amounts left by will gratuitously?*** **(TAXATION § 9, p. 509.)**

21. A statute provided that all gratuitous transfers made within two years before the death of the donor were presumed to be made in contemplation of death. *Is such statute valid?* (TAXATION § 10, p. 509.)

22. A transferred property to X, Y and Z upon trust for B, C and D, subject to its being revoked with the consent of the trustees or the beneficiaries or a majority thereof. *Is such property taxable to A?* (TAXATION § 10, p. 509.)

23. X conveyed property to A and B jointly: A died. *Must B pay a succession tax? Why?* (TAXATION § 11, p. 510.)

24. X bought land and had it conveyed to himself and wife Y; X died. *Must Y pay a gift tax?* (TAXATION § 11, p. 510.)

25. X conveys property to Y for life with remainder to such persons as Y shall appoint by deed or will and in default of appointment to A; Y does not appoint. *For tax purposes, does A receive the property from Y or from X?* (TAXATION § 11, p. 510.)

26. X insured his life for the benefit of A and died. *Must A pay a gift tax upon the money received from the insurance company? Why?* (TAXATION § 12, p. 510.)

27. X insured his life, the policy being a single premium policy payable to his estate. Later he made a gift of the policy to A. *Must A pay a gift tax?* (TAXATION § 12, p. 511.)

28. A bequeathed a large block of corporation stock to X and died. *How determine the value of the shares?* (TAXATION § 13, p. 511.)

29. X devised land to A for life, with a contingent remainder to Y in fee. *How is the value of Y's estate determined?* (TAXATION § 13, p. 511.)

30. *Is compensation to be paid to a trustee to manage for several years a business left by the testator deductible as an administration expense?* (TAXATION § 14, p. 512.)

31. *What is the objection to regarding increase of net worth each year as income?* (TAXATION § 15, p. 513.)

32. *Can a net loss of one year be used to offset a net gain the following year?* (TAXATION § 15, p. 513.)

33. *Why was not a subsidy received from a foreign government for building a railroad regarded as income?* (TAXATION § 15, p. 513.)

34. *What is included in gross income? What must be deducted from gross income to arrive at net income?* (TAXATION § 15, p. 513.)

35. A donee of shares worth $10,000 when the donor bought them and $12,000 when the gift was made, later sold them for $15,000. *On what amount must the donee pay income tax?* (TAXATION § 16, p. 514.)

36. *Is a stock dividend ever taxable as income to the shareholder?* (TAXATION § 17, p. 514.)

37. A corporation issues bonds at par and later buys them back at less than par. *Is the difference taxable income?* (TAXATION § 17, p. 515.)

38. *Why are capital gains taxable as income?* (TAXATION § 17, p. 515.)

39. *What expenses of the taxpayer are not deductible?* (TAXATION § 18, p. 515.)

40. *At what time must a business loss be deducted?* (TAXATION § 18, p. 516.)

41. *May one claim as dependents persons who are not related to the taxpayer and do not live with him as a member of his family?* (TAXATION § 18, p. 516.)

42. *When is it preferable to keep accounts on an accrual rather than on a cash basis?* (TAXATION § 19, p. 516.)

43. A conveys property to T upon an irrevocable trust but with T having absolute discretion as to paying the income to C, the beneficiary of the trust. *Who is liable to pay tax on the trust income?* (TAXATION § 20, p. 517.)

44. *Under what circumstances, if at all, may an accountant with a large income, take his wife and two sons into partnership with him in order to avoid the large surtaxes?* (TAXATION § 20, p. 517.)

LABOR LAW

1. *What was the purpose and scope of the National Labor Relations Act of 1935?* (LABOR LAW § 1, p. 518.)

2. The N. L. R. A. imposes upon the employer the duty to bargain collectively. *Can you compare this with the attitude of equity courts in refusing to give specific performance of contracts for continuous performance?* (LABOR LAW § 2, p. 519; EQUITY § 8, p. 236.)

3. *What does the phrase "appropriate bargaining unit" include?* (LABOR LAW § 2, p. 519.)

4. *To what extent must the employees be willing to negotiate with the employer?* (LABOR LAW § 3, p. 519.)

5. *What various practices have employers resorted to in order to evade the statutory requirement of sincere bargaining?* (LABOR LAW § 4, p. 520.)

6. *What is the effect upon the laborer's right to reinstatement of a lawful strike? Of an unlawful strike?* (LABOR LAW § 5, p. 520.)

7. *Under the N. L. R. A. what is the duty of the employer toward unions in the matter of employing and discharging employees?* (LABOR LAW § 5, p. 521.)

8. *What was the effect of the Clayton Act of 1914 as to the issuance of injunctions in labor dispute cases? The Norris-LaGuardia Act?* (LABOR LAW § 6, p. 521.)

9. *What is the effect of the use of deliberate violence and intimidation upon the issuance of an injunction?* (LABOR LAW § 6, p. 522.)

10. *Does the Sherman Anti-Trust Act apply to combinations of labor?* (LABOR LAW § 7, p. 524.)

11. *Is increased cost of production making a business unprofitable to the employer an excuse for violating a trade agreement as to wages and hours?* (LABOR LAW § 8, p. 525.)

12. *If a trade agreement is violated by a labor union, what remedy, if any, has the employer?* (LABOR LAW § 9, p. 526.)

13. *If a local union changes its affiliation from the American Federation of Labor to the Congress of Industrial Organizations does this forfeit their rights under a trade agreement?* (LABOR LAW § 10, p. 526.)

14. *What remedy, if any, has an employee who is refused membership in a union?* (LABOR LAW § 11, p. 526.)

15. *What is a "yellow dog" contract, and how were such contracts affected by the Norris-LaGuardia Act of 1932?* (LABOR LAW § 12, p. 527.)

16. *If a laborer becomes in arrears in his dues to the union what is the union's remedy, if any?* (LABOR LAW § 13, p. 527.)

17. *If a laborer contends that he has been unfairly expelled from a union, what remedy, if any, does he have?* (LABOR LAW § 14, p. 527.)

COMMON LAW PLEADING

1. *What was the chief purpose of original writs in England?* (COMMON LAW PLEADING § 1, p. 530.)

2. *What was the purpose of the provision in regard to original writs contained in the Statute of Westminster II?* (COMMON LAW PLEADING § 1, p. 530.)

3. *What was the chief result of that statute?* (COMMON LAW PLEADING § 1, p. 531.)

4. *What were the chief reasons for the development of the English court of chancery or equity?* (COMMON LAW PLEADING § 2, p. 531.)

5. *What was the fundamental aim of common law pleading?* (COMMON LAW PLEADING § 2, p. 531.)

6. *What were the chief reasons for the adoption of code pleading?* (COMMON LAW PLEADING § 2, p. 531.)

7. *What are the three reasons, in code pleading states, for the law student to become familiar with common law pleading?* (COMMON LAW PLEADING § 2, p. 532.)

8. *How did English common law courts acquire jurisdiction of the subject matter of the action?* (COMMON LAW PLEADING § 3, p. 532.)

9. *How do courts acquire jurisdiction of a defendant?* (COMMON LAW PLEADING § 3, p. 532.)

10. *How may a plaintiff proceed today if the defendant is outside the state but has property within the state?* (COMMON LAW PLEADING § 3, p. 533.)

11. *In what three ways may a defendant meet the case stated by the plaintiff in his declaration?* (COMMON LAW PLEADING § 4, p. 533.)

12. *What are the names of the first four possible pleadings by a plaintiff? Of the first three possible pleadings by a defendant?* (COMMON LAW PLEADING § 4, p. 533.)

13. *What were the eleven important common law actions? What are the most important actions which grew out of the Statute of Westminster II?* (COMMON LAW PLEADING § 1, p. 531; § 4, p. 533.)

14. *Why were dilatory pleas so called? What has been the usual judicial attitude toward them?* (COMMON LAW PLEADING § 5, p. 534.)

15. *When may a defendant use **a plea to the jurisdiction**?* (COMMON LAW PLEADING § 5, p. 534.)

16. *When may a defendant enter a plea in suspension of the action?* (COMMON LAW PLEADING § 6, p. 535.)

17. *What is the prayer of a defendant in a plea in abatement?* (COMMON LAW PLEADING § 7, p. 536.)

18. *If a plea in abatement is held bad on plaintiff's demurrer, what judgment does the court give?* (COMMON LAW PLEADING § 7, p. 536.)

19. *If a plaintiff puts in a replication to a plea in abatement and wins a verdict, what is the effect of such a verdict?* (COMMON LAW PLEADING § 7, p. 536.)

20. *Suppose the verdict is for the defendant, what is the effect of such a verdict?* (COMMON LAW PLEADING § 7, p. 536.)

21. *To what extent, if at all, may a defendant by a plea in abatement raise an issue of disability of parties to sue?* (COMMON LAW PLEADING § 8, p. 536.)

22. A brings action against X for breach of contract. X contends that Y should also have been made a party. *How may he raise the issue if the defect of parties appears on the face of the declaration? If it does not?* (COMMON LAW PLEADING § 9, p. 537.)

23. A and B bring action against X; X contends that action should have been brought only by A. *How may X raise that issue if the defect appears on the face of the record? If it does not?* (COMMON LAW PLEADING § 10, p. 537.)

24. A brings a contract action against X and Y and Y contends that he should not have been joined. *How may Y raise the issue if the defect appears on the face of the record? If it does not?* (COMMON LAW PLEADING § 10, p. 538.)

25. A brings a tort action against X and Y and Y claims that he should not have been joined. *What is the effect of such misjoinder?* (COMMON LAW PLEADING § 10, p. 538.)

26. A brings an action against X; X wishes to show that there is another action by A against him in the same jurisdiction still pending. *How must he plead?* (COMMON LAW PLEADING § 11, p. 538.)

27. *What is the nature and purpose of a demurrer?* (COMMON LAW PLEADING § 12, p. 538.)

28. *When was a special demurrer necessary at common law? Under the Statute of Elizabeth of 1585?* (COMMON LAW PLEADING § 4, p. 533; § 12, p. 539.)

29. *What is the effect of a special demurrer under the Statute of Elizabeth?* (COMMON LAW PLEADING § 12, p. 539.)

30. *Which of the following defects are defects of substance which may be reached by a general demurrer?* (a)*Misjoinder of counts;* (b) *pleading in confession and avoidance instead of in denial;* (c) *departure;* (d) *duplicity;* (e) *wrong form of action;* (f) *one or more of the essential allegations missing from the declaration?* (COMMON LAW PLEADING § 13, p. 539.)

31. *Where a declaration has two or more counts, how should defendant demur if he wishes to attack each count?* (COMMON LAW PLEADING § 13, p. 540.)

32. *What is meant by a court searching the record for defects of substance and where does the rule apply? Where does it not apply?* (COMMON LAW PLEADING § 14, p. 540.)

33. Suppose a defendant demurs to a declaration and the demurrer is overruled; then the defendant puts in a plea to which the plaintiff demurs. *Does this demurrer search the record?* (COMMON LAW PLEADING § 14, p. 540.)

34. A sues B; B puts in two pleas; A puts in a replication in denial to one plea and demurs to the other. *Does such a demurrer reach the declaration?* (COMMON LAW PLEADING § 14, p. 540.)

35. *What is meant by the statement that a demurring party admits the truth of facts well pleaded?* (COMMON LAW PLEADING § 15, p. 541.)

36. *What allegations in a pleading are not admitted by a demurrer?* (COMMON LAW PLEADING § 15, p. 541.)

37. A sues B; B demurs to the declaration; the demurrer is overruled; B then pleads in denial. *May A then introduce the declaration as evidence?* (COMMON LAW PLEADING § 15, p. 541.)

38. A sues B; B demurs to the declaration; the demurrer is overruled. B then fails to plead. *How advise A?* (COMMON LAW PLEADING § 15, p. 541.)

39. *What was the scope of the traverse in the early days of common law pleading? What was the later development into the general issue?* (COMMON LAW PLEADING § 16, p. 542.)

40. *What is the effect of a plea in confession and avoidance?* (COMMON LAW PLEADING § 16, p. 542.)

41. *What are the two kinds of pleas in confession and avoidance?* (COMMON LAW PLEADING § 16, p. 542.)

42. *What were the two distinct uses of pleading several counts in one declaration?* (COMMON LAW PLEADING § 17, p. 542.)

43. *What did the Statute of Anne provide and why was it passed?* (COMMON LAW PLEADING § 17, p. 543.)

44. *Is a plea in denial logically consistent with one in confession and avoidance? What is the practical reason for permitting joinder?* (COMMON LAW PLEADING § 17, p. 543.)

45. *What was the purpose and effect of the English Hilary Rules which were in force from 1834 until 1873 in England?* (COMMON LAW PLEADING § 18, p. 543.)

46. *What was the scope of the general issue in trespass? When was it necessary to plead in confession and avoidance?* (COMMON LAW PLEADING § 19, p. 544.)

47. *What was the scope of the general issue in trover? When was it necessary to plead in confession and avoidance?* (COMMON LAW PLEADING § 20, p. 544.)

48. *What was the scope of the general issue in case? When was it necessary to plead in confession and avoidance?* (COMMON LAW PLEADING § 21, p. 544.)

49. *What was the scope of the plea of* non est factum *in covenant? When was it necessary to use a specific traverse? When a plea in confession and avoidance?* (COMMON LAW PLEADING § 22, p. 544.)

50. *What was the scope of* non est factum *in debt on a specialty? When must defendant plead affirmatively?* (COMMON LAW PLEADING § 23, p. 545.)

51. *What was the scope of* nil debet *in debt on a statute?* (COMMON LAW PLEADING § 24, p. 545.)

52. *What was the scope of* nul tiel record *in debt on a record? How must the defendant set up lack of jurisdiction where action is on a judgment of a court of record of another state?* (COMMON LAW PLEADING § 25, p. 545.)

53. *What was the scope of* nil debet *in debt on simple contract?* (COMMON LAW PLEADING § 26, p. 545.)

54. *What was the scope of* non assumpsit *in special assumpsit? When might the defendant plead affirmatively?* (COMMON LAW PLEADING § 27, p. 545.)

55. *What was the scope of* non assumpsit *in general assumpsit?* (COMMON LAW PLEADING § 28, p. 545.)

56. *What was the scope of* non detinet *in detinue?* (COMMON LAW PLEADING § 29, p. 546.)

57. *What was the scope of* non cepit *in replevin? When was a specific traverse necessary?* (COMMON LAW PLEADING § 30, p. 546.)

58. *What was the nature of an avowry? Of a cognizance? If the defendant succeeds in either one, to what did this entitle him?* (COMMON LAW PLEADING § 30, p. 546.)

59. *What was the scope of a specific traverse in account? Of a plea in confession and avoidance?* (COMMON LAW PLEADING § 31, p. 546.)

60. *What was the scope of the general issue in ejectment?* (COMMON LAW PLEADING § 32, p. 546.)

61. *In what respect was a motion in arrest of judgment like a demurrer? In what respect different?* (COMMON LAW PLEADING § 33, p. 547.)

62. *What was the effect of sustaining a motion in arrest of judgment?* (COMMON LAW PLEADING § 33, p. 547.)

63. *In what respects was a motion for judgment* non obstante veredicto *like a motion in arrest of judgment? In what respects different?* (COMMON LAW PLEADING § 34, p. 547.)

64. *When was a defendant entitled to a judgment notwithstanding the verdict?* (COMMON LAW PLEADING § 34, p. 547.)

65. *When was a repleader awarded?* (COMMON LAW PLEADING § 35, p. 548.)

66. *What was a special or absque hoc traverse and when was it considered necessary or at least desirable?* (COMMON LAW PLEADING § 36, p. 548.)

67. *When may the other party ignore the denial part and plead to the inducement?* (COMMON LAW PLEADING § 36, p. 549.)

68. *When was a declaration bad for duplicity? A plea? A replication? Was duplicity a defect of substance?* (COMMON LAW PLEADING § 37, p. 549.)

69. *What was a replication de injuria and how did it come to be developed?* (COMMON LAW PLEADING § 38, p. 549.)

70. *What was its scope?* (COMMON LAW PLEADING § 38, p. 550.)

71. *What was a departure and why was it considered objectionable? How could it be reached by the other party?* (COMMON LAW PLEADING § 39, p. 550.)

72. A sues B to collect a debt; B pleads the statute of limitations; A replies that B made a new promise to pay the debt. *Is that a departure by B?* (COMMON LAW PLEADING § 39, p. 550.)

73. *What was the nature of a new assignment? Why was it necessary? In what action was it most commonly used?* (COMMON LAW PLEADING § 40, p. 550.)

74. *What was a bill of particulars? How did it come to be developed?* (COMMON LAW PLEADING § 41, p. 551.)

75. *What is the effect of a bill of particulars as far as pleading is concerned? As far as proof is concerned?* (COMMON LAW PLEADING § 41, p. 551.)

76. *When is it necessary for a plaintiff to prove the exact date alleged in his declaration? When not?* (COMMON LAW PLEADING § 42, p. 551.)

77. *When is it still necessary to prove the exact place alleged in the declaration?* (COMMON LAW PLEADING § 42, p. 551.)

78. *In which actions is it necessary for a plaintiff to allege and prove matters of description and value? Why?* (COMMON LAW PLEADING § 42, p. 552.)

79. *What was the purpose and the effect, in English practice, of a plea since the last continuance? Why was it not necessary in an action on the case?* (COMMON LAW PLEADING § 43, p. 552.)

80. A sold goods to B for $1,200 to be paid for in twelve monthly installments. After paying two installments, B defaulted on the next three. *How advise A?* (COMMON LAW PLEADING § 44, p. 552.)

81. In an automobile collision X negligently damaged Y's automobile and caused Y serious personal injuries. *How advise Y?* (COMMON LAW PLEADING § 44, p. 552.)

82. *May counts in trover be joined with counts in case? Why?* (COMMON LAW PLEADING § 45, p. 553.)

83. *May counts in debt be joined with counts in detinue? Special assumpsit with general assumpsit?* (COMMON LAW PLEADING § 45, p. 553.)

84. A brought an action against B joining a count in trespass with a count in trover. *How advise B?* (COMMON LAW PLEADING § 45, p. 553.)

85. *How did setoff originate and what is its scope?* (COMMON LAW PLEADING § 46, p. 553.)

86. *How did recoupment of damages originate and what is its scope?* (COMMON LAW PLEADING § 46, p. 553.)

CODE PLEADING

1. *What were the two main characteristics of common law pleading?* (CODE PLEADING § 1, p. 555.)

2. *What were the two main characteristics of code pleading?* (CODE PLEADING § 2, p. 556.)

3. *What was the main advantage expected of providing for "one form of action"?* (CODE PLEADING § 3, p. 556.)

4. *Was this expectation always realized?* (CODE PLEADING § 3, p. 556.)

5. *Why is it necessary in code pleading states to have a jury docket and an equity docket?* (CODE PLEADING § 3, p. 556.)

6. *What was the chief reason for the real party in interest provision in the codes?* (CODE PLEADING § 4, p. 557.)

7. *Did the real party in interest provision change the substantive law as to assignments of choses in action?* (CODE PLEADING § 4, p. 557.)

8. A borrows $1,000 from X and B becomes A's surety. B pays X. *Is it necessary, under the codes, for B to get an assignment from X of X's claim against A?* (CODE PLEADING § 4, p. 557.)

9. *What was the effect of the code provision upon the remedy of a contract beneficiary?* (CODE PLEADING § 4, p. 557.)

10. *What effect, if any, did the code provision have upon the trustee of an express trust?* (CODE PLEADING § 4, p. 557.)

11. *What effect, if any, did the code provision have upon executors and administrators?* (CODE PLEADING § 4, p. 557.)

12. *What effect, if any, did the code provision have upon agents?* (CODE PLEADING § 4, p. 557.)

13. *What was the common law rule as to joinder of parties plaintiff? Was there any merely permissive joinder?* (CODE PLEADING § 5, p. 558.)

14. *What was the equity rule as to joinder of parties plaintiff?* (CODE PLEADING § 5, p. 558.)

15. *Are the code provisions as to joinder similar to the common law rule or to the equity rule?* (CODE PLEADING § 5, p. 558.)

16. *What is the code rule as to parties jointly interested? As to tenants in common of property?* (CODE PLEADING § 5, p. 558.)

17. *Is community of interest in questions of law or fact enough to permit joinder?* (CODE PLEADING § 5, p. 558.)

18. *What was the common law rule as to joinder of parties defendant?* (CODE PLEADING § 6, p. 559.)

19. *What was the equity rule?* (CODE PLEADING § 6, p. 559.)

20. *What is the rule under the codes as to compulsory joinder in the ordinary case? Where the question is one of common interest or where the parties defendant are very numerous?* (CODE PLEADING § 6, p. 559.)

21. *What is the code rule as to permissive joinder?* (CODE PLEADING § 6. p. 560.)

22. *What is meant by joinder in the alternative?* (CODE PLEADING § 6, p. 560.)

23. *What is the code practice of allowing new parties to be brought in at the instance of the plaintiff, the defendant or the court?* (CODE PLEADING § 6, p. 560.)

24. *What is meant by intervention?* (CODE PLEADING § 6, p. 560.)

25. *In the case of a partial assignment of a chose in action, what change was effected by the codes?* (CODE PLEADING § 7, p. 560.)

26. *What was the effect of the codes upon the common law rules as to joinder of actions?* (CODE PLEADING § 8, p. 561.)

27. *What was the new basis of joinder of actions under the codes?* (CODE PLEADING § 8, p. 561.)

28. By his negligent act, A caused damage to X's person and property. *May X, under the codes, join the two actions?* (CODE PLEADING § 8, p. 561.)

29. *If causes of action are misjoined under the code, what may the defendant do?* (CODE PLEADING § 8, p. 562.)

30. *What has been done recently as to joinder in some of the codes?* (CODE PLEADING § 8, p. 562.)

31. *What is the effect of the separate statement requirement of the codes?* (CODE PLEADING § 9, p. 562.)

32. *Is the use of different counts to state a single cause of action permitted under the codes?* (CODE PLEADING § 9, p. 562.)

33. *If a complaint would have been good under common law pleading, is it likely to be good under the codes?* (CODE PLEADING § 10, p. 563.)

34. *What was the meaning of a verification at common law? Under the codes?* (CODE PLEADING § 10, p. 563.)

35. *What is required by way of verification under the codes?* (CODE PLEADING § 10, p. 563.)

36. *Do the codes permit pleading in the alternative?* (CODE PLEADING § 10, p. 563.)

37. *If a plaintiff brings the wrong form of action, what was his remedy at common law? Under the codes?* (CODE PLEADING § 10, p. 563.)

38. *Is the use of the common counts permitted under the codes?* (CODE PLEADING § 10, p. 563; FORMS OF ACTION § 35, p. 20.)

39. *What change, if any, was made by the codes where it was necessary at common law to bring special assumpsit?* (CODE PLEADING § 11, p. 563.)

40. *What change, if any, was made in alleging performance of conditions? In alleging consideration?* (CODE PLEADING § 11, p. 563.)

41. *What changes, if any, were made by the codes in the bringing of tort actions?* (CODE PLEADING § 12, p. 564.)

42. *If A in Indiana sues upon a cause of action based upon the common law of Ohio, which is different from the common law of Indiana, what must he allege?* (CODE PLEADING § 13, p. 564.)

43. *In construing a pleading, what was the judicial attitude under common law pleading? Under the codes?* (CODE PLEADING § 13, p. 564.)

44. *In what respects is a demurrer under the codes like the demurrer in common law pleading? In what respects different?* (CODE PLEADING § 14, p. 565.)

45. *By what has the demurrer been superseded in some code states, and for what purpose?* (CODE PLEADING § 14, p. 565.)

46. *What is the difference between the common law general issue and the code general denial?* (CODE PLEADING § 15, p. 565.)

47. *If a defendant wishes to deny some but not all of the allegations in a code complaint, how may he do it?* (CODE PLEADING § 15, p. 565.)

48. *If a defendant wishes to deny the allegations in the code complaint but does not have enough knowledge to verify his denial, what may he do?* (CODE PLEADING § 15, p. 565.)

49. *Under the codes, may a defendant plead both in denial and affirmatively at the same time?* (CODE PLEADING § 16, p. 565.)

50. *What is meant by allowing a defendant to plead equitable defenses at law?* (CODE PLEADING § 16, p. 566.)

51. *Under what circumstances may a defendant use a counterclaim? May he counterclaim in tort actions? May he thus take advantage of contingent claims?* (CODE PLEADING § 17, p. 565.)

52. *If a particular code provides for a reply and plaintiff does not file one, what is the effect of such failure upon an affirmative defense? If the code does not provide for a reply?* (CODE PLEADING § 18, p. 566.)

53. *What is the code pleading attitude toward a departure? A new assignment?* (CODE PLEADING § 18, p. 567.)

54. *What is the code substitute for the special demurrer?* (CODE PLEADING § 19, p. 567.)

55. *What is the code attitude toward motions in arrest of judgment? Toward*

motions for judgment notwithstanding the verdict? (CODE PLEADING § 19, p. 567.)

56. *When is a motion for a summary judgment on the pleadings proper if provided for by the code?* (CODE PLEADING § 19, p. 568.)

57. *What other uses are there for motions under the codes?* (CODE PLEADING § 19, p. 567.)

58. *What is the usual code provision for amendments?* (CODE PLEADING § 20, p. 568.)

59. *Are amendments ever allowed after the trial?* (CODE PLEADING § 20, p. 568.)

60. *What is the purpose and scope of supplemental pleadings? For what common law device are they a substitute?* (CODE PLEADING § 21, p. 568.)

EVIDENCE

1. *Will a court take judicial notice of what the court actually knows but is not a matter of common knowledge?* (EVIDENCE § 1, p. 571.)

2. *Upon what basis will a court take judicial notice of the time of the rising of the sun on a certain day?* (EVIDENCE § 1, p. 571.)

3. *Of what facts may a jury take notice without proof?* (EVIDENCE § 1, p. 571.)

4. *Is taking judicial notice of a fact conclusive?* (EVIDENCE § 1, p. 571.)

5. *Of what law will the United States Supreme Court take judicial notice upon appeal from a state court upon a question of constitutional law?* (EVIDENCE § 2, p. 571.)

6. *Of what law will the United States Supreme Court take judicial notice upon appeal from a federal court whose jurisdiction is based upon diverse citizenship of the parties?* (EVIDENCE § 2, p. 571.)

7. *Will a state court take judicial notice of the common law of a sister state?* (EVIDENCE § 2, p. 572.)

8. *In a litigation in a Maine court, what will be its attitude toward proving the law of New Hampshire? Of New Brunswick?* (EVIDENCE § 2, p. 572.)

9. *To what extent, if at all, is a statement by a witness as to his belief admissible in evidence?* (EVIDENCE § 3, p. 572.)

10. *If a witness cannot speak English, how may he testify?* (EVIDENCE § 3, p. 572.)

11. *What is the difference between a witness's present recollection revived and his past recollection recorded?* (EVIDENCE § 4, p. 572.)

12. *Under what circumstances, if at all, may a witness read to the jury a prepared statement?* (EVIDENCE § 5, p. 573.)

13. *What is the advantage of a witness giving his testimony in narrative form? The disadvantage?* (EVIDENCE § 5, p. 573.)

14. *Under what circumstances, if at all, may leading questions be put to a witness?* (EVIDENCE § 5, p. 573.)

15. *If in a witness's answer he makes statements which are hearsay, what is the remedy? Is it always entirely effective?* (EVIDENCE § 5, p. 573.)

16. *If a witness dies after giving his testimony without being cross examined, what is the duty of the court? Why?* (EVIDENCE § 6, p. 573.)

17. *May a witness be cross examined upon any matters covered by the issues of the litigation but only upon the matters covered by the direct examination?* (EVIDENCE § 6, p. 573.)

18. *Which is the better view? Why?* (EVIDENCE § 6, p. 574.)

19. *May you impeach your opponent's witness by showing that his general reputation for veracity is bad? That his general character is bad?* (EVIDENCE § 7, p. 574.)

20. *How may such evidence be met? What is the literal meaning of character? Of reputation?* (EVIDENCE § 7, p. 574.)

21. *If a defendant in a criminal prosecution takes the witness stand, is he subject to being impeached as a witness?* (EVIDENCE § 7, p. 574.)

22. *In order to impeach a witness by showing conviction of a crime, just what is necessary to be shown? What is the effect of a suspended sentence or of a pardon?* (EVIDENCE § 8, p. 574.)

23. *If a witness is asked whether he has committed specific criminal or merely disgraceful acts and he denies it, what may the cross examiner do? What should he not be permitted to do?* (EVIDENCE § 9, p. 575.)

24. *If a witness is asked whether he had not made a statement inconsistent with his present testimony, what foundation must first be laid if such statement was oral? If it was in writing?* (EVIDENCE § 10, p. 575.)

25. *If the witness denies making such statement, may such previous statement then be proved? Of what value is such proof?* (EVIDENCE § 10, p. 575.)

26. *If the witness is a party to the action, what difference does this make?* (EVIDENCE § 10, p. 575; § 45, p. 594.)

27. *What may be done by the party calling the witness in re-examining him?* (EVIDENCE § 10, p. 575.)

28. *May bias or interest of a witness be shown without laying a basis therefor in his cross examination?* (EVIDENCE § 10, p. 576.)

29. *May a witness be impeached by evidence that he was suffering from mental derangement?* (EVIDENCE § 11, p. 576.)

30. *What is the historical explanation of the rule forbidding one to impeach his own witness?* (EVIDENCE § 12, p. 576.)

31. *What logical reason has been suggested for the rule? What illogical reason?* (EVIDENCE § 12, p. 576.)

32. *What two things may not be done under the rule?* (EVIDENCE § 13, p. 576.)

33. *Does the rule apply where the law requires the calling of a witness?* (EVIDENCE § 13, p. 576.)

34. *To what extent may a judge testify? To what extent should he testify?* (EVIDENCE § 14, p. 577.)

35. *To what extent may counsel testify? To what extent should he testify?* (EVIDENCE § 14, p. 577.)

36. *To what extent, if at all, should mental derangement be a bar to giving testimony?* (EVIDENCE § 15, p. 577.)

37. *To what extent, if at all, should young children be allowed to testify?* (EVIDENCE § 15, p. 577.)

38. *Of what import is it today that a proposed witness has been convicted of crime?* (EVIDENCE § 15, p. 578.)

39. *What is the present status of the theological belief of a proposed witness?* (EVIDENCE § 15, p. 578.)

40. *In what instance does interest in the outcome of the litigation still disqualify in civil cases?* (EVIDENCE § 16, p. 578.)

41. *What is the present tendency in regard to this rule of exclusion?* (EVIDENCE § 16, p. 578.)

42. *May the accused in a criminal prosecution testify in his own behalf? What is the usual effect on the jury if he may testify but does not do so?* (EVIDENCE § 17, p. 579.)

43. *May a husband or wife testify for each other?* (EVIDENCE § 18, p. 579.)

44. *What is the effect, if any, of A telling B expressly in confidence and of B assenting thereto?* (EVIDENCE § 19, p. 579.)

45. *What was the former basis of the attorney and client privilege? The present basis?* (EVIDENCE § 20, p. 579.)

46. A consults X as attorney but later decides not to employ him. A's opponent offers to prove communications made by A to X. *May he do so?* (EVIDENCE § 20, p. 579.)

47. *Who may waive the attorney and client privilege?* (EVIDENCE § 20, p. 580.)

48. A consults X, an attorney, as to an illegal act which he is contemplating. *Is the communication privileged?* (EVIDENCE § 20, p. 580.)

49. *Who may waive the privilege of communications between husband and wife?* (EVIDENCE § 21, p. 580.)

50. *Is it necessary that such communications be expressly confidential?* (EVIDENCE § 21, p. 580.)

51. *In what cases does the privilege not exist?* (EVIDENCE § 21, p. 580.)

52. *What is meant by the statement that a juror is incompetent to impeach his own verdict?* (EVIDENCE § 22, p. 581.)

53. *How long does the privilege of a complainant or a witness before a grand jury last?* (EVIDENCE, § 22, p. 581.)

54. *To what extent, if at all, is the relationship of clergyman and penitent privileged?* (EVIDENCE § 23, p. 581.)

55. *What is the origin and extent of the physician-patient privilege?* (EVIDENCE § 24, p. 581.)

56. *In what three classes of cases does the question of privilege usually arise?* (EVIDENCE § 24, p. 582.)

57. *What criticisms have been urged against the privilege?* (EVIDENCE § 24, p. 582.)

58. *How may the privilege be waived?* (EVIDENCE § 24, p. 582.)

59. *What are the two reasons for not requiring a wife or husband to testify against the other?* (EVIDENCE § 25, p. 582.)

60. *Who may waive the privilege and how long does the privilege last?* (EVIDENCE § 25, p. 582.)

61. *What is the present legislative tendency in regard to the privilege?* (EVIDENCE § 25, p. 582.)

62. *What was the origin of the privilege against self-incrimination?* (EVIDENCE § 26, p. 583.)

63. *May a witness be compelled to testify about a criminal act for which he has received a pardon?* (EVIDENCE § 26, p. 583.)

64. *May a witness be compelled to produce documents which might incriminate him?* (EVIDENCE § 26, p. 583.)

65. *Who may claim the privilege and when?* (EVIDENCE § 27, p. 583.)

66. *Who decides whether an answer to a question put to the witness might incriminate him?* (EVIDENCE § 27, p. 583.)

67. *If an accused in a criminal prosecution goes on the witness stand in his own behalf, does he waive the privilege against self incrimination?* (EVIDENCE § 27, p. 584.)

68. *What is the effect upon the privilege of modern statutes granting immunity from prosecution to certain classes of persons?* (EVIDENCE § 27, p. 584.)

69. *What is the argument made against the existence of the privilege? The answer thereto?* (EVIDENCE § 27, p. 584.)

70. *What is meant by the term real evidence? What is the objection to the phrase "autoptic proference"?* (EVIDENCE § 28, p. 584.)

71. *In what cases and upon what basis is real evidence sometimes excluded?* (EVIDENCE § 28, p. 584.)

72. *What objection has been raised to admitting real evidence and what is the answer thereto?* (EVIDENCE § 28, p. 584.)

73. *Does the fact that evidence was illegally obtained make it inadmissible?* (EVIDENCE § 29, p. 585.)

74. *What is the basis and extent of the rule of the United States Supreme Court on this point?* (EVIDENCE § 29, p. 585.)

75. *What is the attitude of the United States Supreme Court toward evidence obtained by illegal wire tapping?* (EVIDENCE § 29, p. 585.)

76. *What is meant by circumstantial evidence? Is it more or less reliable than testimonial evidence?* (EVIDENCE § 30, p. 585.)

77. *Is evidence that a defendant in a criminal prosecution for murder had a reputation for being a peaceable, law abiding citizen properly classified as circumstantial evidence? How may the state meet such evidence?* (EVIDENCE § 30, p. 585.)

78. *What is meant by saying that remote evidence is inadmissible? What is the test, if any, of remoteness?* (EVIDENCE § 31, p. 586.)

79. A sued B for negligently damaging A's property. B offered in evidence that he was an habitually careful person. *Is this admissible?* (EVIDENCE § 31, p. 587.)

80. A sued B for so negligently keeping his premises that A, a business visitor thereon, suffered personal injuries. In order to help prove B's negligence, A offered to show that after the alleged negligence occurred B made repairs on the premises. *Is this admissible? Why?* (EVIDENCE § 31, p. 587.)

81. *To what extent, if at all, may the state in a criminal prosecution introduce evidence to show that the defendant had committed other crimes?* (EVIDENCE § 31, p. 587.)

82. *What was the earlier attitude toward a witness giving his opinion? The later attitude? Why?* (EVIDENCE § 32, p. 587.)

83. *What is the current objection to allowing a witness to state his opinion? What is the answer thereto?* (EVIDENCE § 32, p. 587.)

84. *What is the basis of the exception allowing opinion evidence in certain classes of cases?* (EVIDENCE § 33, p. 588.)

85. *In what classes of cases is opinion evidence of experts admissible and why?* (EVIDENCE § 34, p. 588.)

86. *To what extent is expert testimony admissible in sanity cases? In personal injury cases?* (EVIDENCE § 34, p. 589.)

87. *To what extent is expert evidence based upon finger prints admissible? Upon blood group tests? Upon a lie detector?* (EVIDENCE § 34, p. 589.)

88. *May opinion evidence be based upon "all of the evidence in the case"? Why?* (EVIDENCE § 35, p. 589.)

89. *What is the usual scope of the hypothetical question?* (EVIDENCE § 35, p. 589.)

90. *Who may qualify as a handwriting expert? Upon what is his testimony based?* (EVIDENCE § 35, p. 590.)

91. *How may such an expert be cross examined?* (EVIDENCE § 35, p. 590.)

92. *What is the modern basis of the rule excluding hearsay?* (EVIDENCE § 36, p. 590.)

93. A brought action against X for slander and offered to prove by Y that he heard X make certain defamatory statements about A. *Is Y's testimony admissible? Why?* (EVIDENCE § 36, p. 590.)

94. *Why are declarations in matters of pedigree admissible? Under what circumstances are they admissible?* (EVIDENCE § 37, p. 590.)

95. *Upon what basis may a witness testify as to his own age?* (EVIDENCE § 37, p. 591.)

96. *What are the three requirements for the admission of dying declarations and why are they admissible? What was the former basis of admissibility?* (EVIDENCE § 38, p. 591.)

97. *What was the original reason for allowing a party's shop or account book to be introduced in evidence?* (EVIDENCE § 39, p. 591.)

98. *What is the New York rule as to shop books?* (EVIDENCE § 39, p. 591.)

99. *What is the New England rule?* (EVIDENCE § 39, p. 592.)

100. *When are entries made in the regular course of business admissible?* (EVIDENCE § 40, p. 592.)

101. *How are such entries verified?* (EVIDENCE § 40, p. 592.)

102. *What is the basis of the res gestae doctrine and what is its scope?* (EVIDENCE § 41, p. 592.)

103. *What is the reason for allowing in evidence declarations as to pain then being suffered?* (EVIDENCE § 41, p. 593.)

104. *When may a declarant's statement as to his intent be admitted in evidence?* (EVIDENCE § 41, p. 593.)

105. *Are such declarations admissible to show that the act intended was actually done?* (EVIDENCE § 41, p. 593.)

106. *Under what circumstances, if at all, are declarations by a testator that he has done a particular act admissible to show that he did it?* (EVIDENCE § 41, p. 593.)

107. *Under what circumstances are declarations as to matters of public interest admissible?* (EVIDENCE § 42, p. 593.)

108. *What is the basis for the rule permitting the introduction of ancient documents into evidence?* (EVIDENCE § 42, p. 593.)

109. *When may testimony at a former trial be admitted, and who may prove it?* (EVIDENCE § 43, p. 593.)

110. *Why is a declaration against interest admissible?* (EVIDENCE § 44, p. 594.)

111. *When is such a declaration admissible?* (EVIDENCE § 44, p. 594.)

112. *For what two purposes are admissions by a party made out of court admissible?* (EVIDENCE § 45, p. 594.)

113. *Are such admissions an exception to the hearsay rule?* (EVIDENCE § 45, p. 594.)

114. *Is it necessary to lay a foundation by first asking him if he had made such statements?* (EVIDENCE § 45, p. 595.)

115. *May an admission be based upon hearsay?* (EVIDENCE § 45, p. 595.)

116. *Are judicial admissions evidence in the case in which they are made?* (EVIDENCE § 46, p. 595.)

117. *May they be evidence in other cases?* (EVIDENCE § 46, p. 595.)

118. *May an admission sometimes be implied from silence?* (EVIDENCE § 47, p. 595.)

119. *Is an offer to compromise an admission? An offer of help by an employer to an injured employee?* (EVIDENCE § 47, p. 595.)

120. *Is the discharge of an employee after an accident admissible as an implied admission that he was negligent?* (EVIDENCE § 47, p. 595.)

121. *Under what circumstances is an admission made by an agent or servant admissible against his principal or employer?* (EVIDENCE § 48, p. 596.)

122. *An admission by a partner as against his co-partners?* (EVIDENCE § 48, p. 596.)

123. *What is the present rule as to an admission by a joint obligor?* (EVIDENCE § 48, p. 596.)

124. *Under what circumstances is an admission made by one conspirator admissible against the others?* (EVIDENCE § 48, p. 596.)

125. *Under what circumstances is a declaration made by a former owner of property admissible against the present owner?* (EVIDENCE § 49, p. 596.)

126. *Is a declaration made by an executor admissible against his co-executor?* (EVIDENCE § 49, p. 596.)

127. *What is the difference between a confession and an admission?* (EVIDENCE § 50, p. 597.)

128. X is being tried for the murder of A; Y confesses that he, not X, committed the murder. *Is this admissible at X's trial?* (EVIDENCE § 50, p. 597.)

129. *Under what circumstances, if at all, is a withdrawn plea of guilty receivable in evidence?* (EVIDENCE § 50, p. 597.)

130. *What is the effect of a confession being made under threats of force or promises of favor?* (EVIDENCE § 51, p. 597.)

131. *Under what circumstances does the jury pass upon the question as to whether an admission was voluntary?* (EVIDENCE § 51, p. 597.)

132. *What criticism has been urged against excluding involuntary confessions?* (EVIDENCE § 51, p. 598.)

133. *What is the best evidence rule and the reason for it?* (EVIDENCE § 52. p. 598.)

134. *What is the scope of the rule? What may be done where it is very difficult to produce the writing in court?* (EVIDENCE § 52, p. 598.)

135. *When may there be more than one documentary original?* (EVIDENCE § 53, p. 598.)

136. *When may secondary evidence of a documentary original be introduced?* (EVIDENCE § 54, p. 599.)

137. *What must be done if the documentary original is in the possession of one's opponent?* (EVIDENCE § 54, p. 599.)

138. *What is the parol evidence rule? Is it a rule of evidence?* (EVIDENCE § 55, p. 599.)

139. *What is the real meaning of the word "parol" in this connection?* (EVIDENCE § 55, p. 599.)

140. *What is the supposed basis of the rule?* (EVIDENCE § 55, p. 599.)

141. *What is the remedy if there is a mistake in an integrated instrument?* (EQUITY § 30, p. 248; EVIDENCE § 55, p. 600.)

142. *Under what circumstances are the declarations of a testator admissible?* (EVIDENCE § 56, p. 600; WILLS § 11, p. 203.)

143. *When may evidence of custom be admitted?* (EVIDENCE § 56, p. 600.)

144. *When does the parol evidence rule prevent the introduction of evidence with regard to the consideration of a contract?* (EVIDENCE § 57, p. 600.)

145. *Does the parol evidence rule prevent the introduction of evidence of fraud or mistake?* (EVIDENCE § 58, p. 600.)

146. *May extrinsic evidence be admitted to show that a written contract was delivered upon a condition which had not been satisfied?* (EVIDENCE § 59, p. 601.)

147. *May it be shown that a co-maker of a negotiable instrument was a surety?* (EVIDENCE § 60, p. 601.)

148. *In the sale of a chattel, may a warranty as to the future condition of the chattel be shown?* (EVIDENCE § 61, p. 601.)

149. *What are the two possible meanings of the phrase "burden of proof"?* (EVIDENCE § 62, p. 601.)

150. *Upon whom does the burden of establishing usually rest?* (EVIDENCE § 62, p. 602.)

151. *When does the burden of going forward with evidence sometimes shift?* (EVIDENCE § 62, p. 602.)

152. *How does the burden of establishing in criminal cases differ from the burden of establishing in civil cases?* (EVIDENCE § 62, p. 602.)

153. *What is the basis of rebuttable or true presumptions?* (EVIDENCE § 63, p 603.)

154. *What is meant by irrebuttable presumptions or conclusive presumptions of law?* (EVIDENCE § 63, p. 603.)

155. *What is meant by the phrase: "a seal imports consideration"?* (CONTRACTS § 27, p. 104; EVIDENCE § 63, p. 603.)

156. *What is the effect of the presumption of sanity in civil cases? In criminal cases?* (EVIDENCE § 64, p. 603.)

157. *What is the effect of a presumption of marriage in legitimacy cases? In bigamy cases?* (EVIDENCE § 64, p. 603.)

158. *When and to what extent is there a presumption of survivorship?* (EVIDENCE § 64, p. 604.)

159. *When is there a presumption of consideration?* (EVIDENCE § 64, p. 604.)

160. *What questions are decided by the jury? What ones by the court?* (EVIDENCE § 65, p. 604.)

161. *When will a court set aside a verdict?* (EVIDENCE § 65, p. 604.)

162. *Why does the court interpret written documents?* (EVIDENCE § 65, p. 604.)

163. *Who decides questions of the competency of witnesses to testify?* (EVIDENCE § 65, p. 604.)

164. *May a trial judge express to a jury his opinion of the evidence?* (EVIDENCE § 65, p. 605.)

END OF VOLUME